Roosevelt and Hopkins

An Intimate History

Louise Dahl-Wolfe

Harry L. Hopkins

10-8

ROOSEVELT AND HOPKINS, AN INTIMATE HISTORY

COPYRIGHT, 1948, BY ROBERT E. SHERWOOD

PRINTED IN THE UNITED STATES OF AMERICA

FIRST EDITION

I-X

ROOSEVELT
AND
HOPKINS

An Intimate History

BY

ROBERT E. SHERWOOD

ILLUSTRATED

HARPER & BROTHERS
Publishers: New York

Table of Contents

v

List of Illustrations

DOCUMENTARY ILLUSTRATIONS

Introduction

IMMEDIATELY after Franklin D. Roosevelt's death, virtually everyone who was in any way associated with him received offers from editors and publishers to write memoirs—and it is by now a matter of record that most of these offers were accepted. I doubt that there have ever been so many books written so soon about the life and times of any one man.

I myself had no intention of adding to the burden on the library shelves. I had some wonderful, ineradicable memories and an unorganized assortment of notes from the years 1940-1945, and I intended to put these down in more or less haphazard form to be contributed to the Roosevelt Library at Hyde Park and filed there for whatever use future biographers might be able to make of them, for I knew how much of our knowledge of Abraham Lincoln has depended on chance bits of recollection written down by comparatively unimportant contemporaries.

I knew that Harry Hopkins was planning to write a book—indeed, he had talked to me about it some months before Roosevelt's death and had begun at that time to make arrangements with publishers. When I saw him occasionally during the summer and fall of 1945 he talked as if he were making progress with the book and I eagerly awaited its publication. I did not know at that time, but have learned subsequently, that he hoped to have the benefit of aid in the writing from his friend, Raymond Swing. In November I saw Hopkins for the last time and went to Hollywood to work for Samuel Goldwyn on a movie, "The Best Years of Our Lives." (This title referred hopefully to the future as opposed to the past.) I was there in the Goldwyn studio when David Hopkins telephoned me the news of his father's death, and a week or so thereafter Louise Hopkins telephoned from New York to ask me if I would consider finishing the work on the book. I said I would do anything I could for Harry's memory, but I had no conception of what the task would involve. I knew that this book was to be limited to the war years— and that was the one period when I had close associations with Roosevelt and Hopkins—but I did not know what form the book was taking, nor how far Hopkins had got with it, nor how much of his writing was based on memory and how much on documentation. It was obvious that I could not attempt to perpetrate a fake by carrying on the book as though it had all been done by Hopkins; but it occurred to me that I might have to start off with the lame admission: "At this point Hopkins died, so the rest of his story can be no more than a series of fragments." When I finished the Hollywood job and returned to New York some weeks later I discovered that Hopkins had not written so much as the words "Chapter One," but that the documentation was enormous. There were some forty filing cabinets packed with papers in the Hopkins house, and a great many more in a warehouse, the latter being records of the New Deal years which I have never seen. Fortunately Hopkins had engaged an assistant, Sidney Hyman, who had been working for eight months putting the papers into order in folders marked "Casablanca Conference," "Aid for Russia—1943," etc., so that, in the months that it took me merely to read them, I could proceed chronologically and begin to get a sense of narrative. I could also begin to see where the holes were in the record and what parts of it were obscure or confusing to me, and I decided that I must do some interviewing in an effort to gain fuller information and clarification. This led to a considerable amount of traveling and correspondence, and the work, which I at first estimated might take as much as a year to complete, has gone on for two and a half years with very little respite, morning, noon or night.

The first reading of the papers was an exciting experience for me, and I must confess that this sense of excitement has continued through all the labor involved. For I found here so many answers to so many questions that had been piling up in my mind when I was near to high authority; I found solution of much that I had wondered about in my observation of the moods as well as the words and deeds of Roosevelt and Hopkins. I meant at first to try to write the book completely impersonally, but more and more I came to realize that I could not keep out of it my own recollections—those that I had intended to put down some day in haphazard form—and many more that were revived by the reading of these papers; and, of course, the recollections of others to whom I talked began to merge with my own.

It seemed that I should write the book as a biography of Hopkins in the war years, preceding it with a prefatory sketch of his career, including the New Deal, before he became directly involved in major world events. I could not write with any intimate personal knowledge of the years before 1940, but I went much more deeply into his career than I had intended mainly through my own curiosity to know how any man so obscure in origin and so untrained for great responsibility could have come to the extraordinary position that he held. One thing that impressed me deeply was the realization of the extent to which the New Deal conditioned Roosevelt and Hopkins and indeed the American people as a whole for the gigantic efforts demanded of them in global war. Spiritual preparedness for coping with powerful evil was required before it began to occur to people that some tanks and bombers and aircraft carriers might also be helpful. For Hopkins in particular the New Deal provided ideal training in combat conditions, for his life then was a series of ferocious battles against widespread misery, natural disasters, local politicians, other government agencies and the innumerable critics in the Congress and the press who kept his free-spending program constantly under fire. Fortunately for me, he kept voluminous scrapbooks—or his various secretaries kept them for him—of press clippings about himself, starting with the day of his first arrival in Washington. Those volumes certainly teem with vilification which was maintained steadily for twelve years, and some of it hit Hopkins much harder and hurt him much more than he cared to admit. But it can be said that he never lost his conviction that freedom to make such attacks on him or anyone else provides the red corpuscles which carry the oxygen through the life blood of democracy; he indicated the depth of this conviction in words that he wrote (on the subject of future relations with Russia) which appear in the final chapter of this book.

Looking backward, as I have been compelled to do so constantly throughout this work, it seems to me that the hostility of so large a part of the press to his Administration was essential to Roosevelt—as an inspiration even more than as a deterrent—and that he would not have been the President he was without it. He would never have thrived in an atmosphere of cloying unanimity.

Of all the attacks upon Hopkins, the one that probably angered and amazed him most was the fantastic charge that, in the fall of 1943, he had plotted behind the scenes in the White House to have General Marshall removed from his position as Chief of Staff and "kicked upstairs" to some sinecure command in Europe. (This is in Chapter XXX.) I became very interested in this, for the Hopkins papers provided considerable evidences of the influences brought to bear on the President, but no indication as to why, at the second Cairo Conference, Roosevelt suddenly announced that Eisenhower instead of Marshall would be the supreme commander of OVERLORD (the major invasion of Europe—and no sinecure). I attempted to find out what was the determining factor in this tremendous decision. I went to Washington and talked to Admiral King. He gave me his recollection in very precise terms (he gave me a great deal more invaluable information and guidance in the preparation of this book). I talked to Laurence Steinhardt, John J. McCloy and Lewis Douglas, all of whom had been present at Cairo, and to Averell Harriman and Charles E. Bohlen who had been at the immediately preceding Teheran Conference. I received General "Hap" Arnold's version by letter. I went to London and saw Winston Churchill, who sent me fourteen typewritten pages of answers to a questionnaire I submitted to him, and whom I interviewed on three subsequent occasions. I talked to Churchill's Chief of Staff, General Sir Hastings Ismay (later Lord Ismay) and to Anthony Eden, Lord Beaverbrook, Brendan Bracken and many other associates of Churchill's. I talked a great deal about this and many more subjects with John G. Winant. Later I asked Henry L. Stimson, Admiral Leahy and General Eisenhower for their versions of the background of the OVERLORD command decision, and I finally obtained General Marshall's after he returned from China early in 1947 to render further distinguished service to his country as Secretary of State.

The versions of this one story that I obtained all varied from each other, although they were by no means mutually exclusive, and I came out of this investigation as I came out of others with the knowledge that no one will ever know just what finally went on in Roosevelt's complex mind to determine his decision.

Shortly after I had started work on this book, President Truman most kindly wrote me a letter expressing his satisfaction that "the papers of that valiant servant of the public, the late Harry L. Hopkins," were to be prepared for publication. The President added, "If I can be of assistance please do not hesitate to call upon me. I hope also you will receive the fullest co-operation of all whom you approach in the performance of this great trust." Later, I had a talk with the President about his own associations with Hopkins which had gone back to the very beginnings of the Relief Program in 1933. Neither the President nor any other official of the government ever told me either directly or indirectly what I should say or not say nor made any requests or suggestions for the suppression or soft-pedaling of any of the material included herein. I voluntarily submitted the complete manuscript to the Department of Defense for clearance solely on the ground of military security, and I must express my appreciation to Secretary Forrestal and his Aide, Captain Robert W. Berry, USN, for the co-operation I received. No requests for omissions were made, but I was asked to paraphrase a considerable number of the cables since publication of the literal text might compromise codes. I also sent the manuscript to the Historical Section of the Joint Chiefs of Staff and I am most grateful to Captain T. B. Kittredge, USN, and his associates for many helpful suggestions and corrections on points of fact and of interpretation. I have also had the benefit of great aid from Miss Grace Tully, Frank C. Walker, Samuel I. Rosenman, Aubrey Williams and Commander C. R. Thompson in reading and checking the manuscript, or parts thereof, but this certainly does not involve any of them in responsibility for the whole.

One afternoon and evening in Washington Leon Henderson was good enough to arrange a meeting for me at his house which lasted for some eight hours. Present were: Robert Kerr, who had been a very close friend of Hopkins since their days together at Grinnell College; Miss Jane Hoey and Mrs. Frances Kelley, who had been associated with Hopkins when he first went into social welfare work in New York City and continued with him throughout the New Deal years; Aubrey Williams, Isador Lubin, Miss Ellen Woodward, Howard Hunter, Colonel Lawrence Westbrook, Mr. and Mrs. Arthur E. Goldschmidt and Henderson, all of whom were associated with the Relief Program. Copious notes were taken at this meeting by Sidney Hyman and my secretary, Miss Grace Murphy, both of whom have worked with me steadily from the beginning to the end of this book. As a result of this session I was guided in the exploration of many channels of Hopkins' career of which I had previously known little or nothing. Later, I had a long talk and correspondence with Hopkins' sister, Mrs. Adah Aime, and correspondence with his first wife, Mrs. Ethel Gross Hopkins, and their surviving sons, David and Robert; also with Dr. Lewis Hopkins (Harry's brother), with Dr. John Nollen (formerly President of Grinnell College) and with Dr. Edward A. Steiner, one of the most distinguished of Grinnell professors. I had an extremely pleasant and enlightening session at lunch with Hopkins' stalwart opponent and comrade in arms, Harold L. Ickes.

The list is very large of those whom I have interviewed one or more times, or with whom I have corresponded. Some of the interviews were conducted by Hyman alone. I should give here a personal word of appreciation to every one of those who have helped me—not, of course, because of any particular interest in my own work but because of a desire to have this story told as accurately and as fully as possible—but I must apologetically lump a large number of names together in alphabetical order:

Herbert Agar; Joseph Alsop; Paul Appleby; Frank Bane; Bernard M. Baruch; Lord Beaverbrook; Mrs. Anna Boettiger; Louis Brownlow; General J. H. Burns; Dr. Vannevar Bush; Lord Cherwell; Marquis Childs; Grenville Clark; Benjamin V. Cohen; Dr. James B. Conant; Captain Granville Conway, USN; Oscar Cox; Wayne Coy; Dr. Samuel H. Cross; Joseph E. Davies; Chester Davis; Clarence Dykstra; Stephen Early; Morris Ernst; Dr. Herbert Evatt; Colonel Philip R. Faymonville; Herbert Feis; Judge Jerome Frank; Justice Felix Frankfurter; Dr. James R. Fulton; Richard V. Gilbert; Dr. Jacob Goldberg; Philip Graham; Lord Halifax; Robert Hannegan; William D. Hassett; Frances Head; General Sir Leslie Hollis; Herschel Johnson; John Kingsbury; Fiorello La Guardia; Thomas W. Lamont; Dr. William Langer; Lord Layton; Lord Leathers; Walter Lippmann; Sir Robert Bruce Lockhart; Oliver Lyttelton; Archibald MacLeish; General Robert McClure; Dr. Ross T. McIntire; Wing Commander D. C. McKinley;

Admiral John McCrea; John E. Masten; Charles E. Merriam; Dr. James Alexander Miller; Jean Monnet; Henry Morgenthau, Jr.; Edward R. Murrow; Robert Nathan; David K. Niles; Robert P. Patterson; Frederick Polangin; Quentin Reynolds; Franklin D. Roosevelt, Jr.; Elmo Roper; Beardsley Ruml; Bishop Bernard Sheil; Admiral Forrest Sherman; Victor Sholis; Harold Smith; Admiral Harold R. Stark; Sir William Stephenson; Edward Stettinius; Robert Stevens; Raymond Swing; Herbert Bayard Swope; Myron C. Taylor; Dorothy Thompson; Rexford Tugwell; Mrs. Edwin M. Watson; Sumner Welles; Mrs. Wendell Willkie; General Arthur Wilson; Ira Wolfert.

I also had a brief talk with Andrei Gromyko. When I told him that I had undertaken to write a book based on the papers of the late Harry Hopkins and that I should like to consult authorities of the Soviet Union in connection with it, he said that such a book might be helpful—and, again, it might not.

One name that is conspicuously absent from the list of those that I interviewed is that of Eleanor Roosevelt. I have seen her on a number of occasions while I have been working on this book, and I know that if I had asked her for help she would have given it with her own incomparable generosity, but I simply could not bring myself to put any questions to her, because her memories are her own, and I felt reluctant to intrude upon any part of them.

I have received aid and guidance from a great many others with whom I have talked casually, and from persons unknown to me who, having heard that this book was in process of preparation, have kindly written me about contacts that they had with Harry Hopkins. Of course I have attempted to read all of the books about the Roosevelt era and the Second World War, and this has not been the least part of the labor involved for it has seemed, at times, that the books were coming out at the rate of one a day. Unquestionably the best of these books, in my opinion—and pending the publication of Eisenhower's memoirs and the completion of Churchill's—have been *The Roosevelt I Knew*, by Frances Perkins, and *On Active Service in Peace and War*, by Henry L. Stimson and McGeorge Bundy. There have been some other publications which, I hope, posterity will view with extreme suspicion.

I must express my appreciation to Miss Phyllis Moir and Mrs. Eva Marks, who worked for a time with Miss Murphy and Hyman and me in New York, and also to Alex. A. Whelan, who worked with me on the final stages of this book in England, and to Sam Simone and the admirable staff of the Hart Stenographic Bureau in New York. I also want to express my gratitude to Miss Lucy Mitchell, Victor Samrock, William Fields and others of the Playwrights' Company who gave me great help and also a long leave of absence from my usual professional activities.

When I started writing this book, I spent some time considering whether to use the proper courtesy titles in referring to living persons. But I felt it would be both cumbersome and absurd to write, for instance, "Roosevelt then cabled to Mr. Churchill, etc." Similarly, I have avoided to the greatest possible extent the complexities of changing military titles—for example, "Lieutenant-Colonel (later Colonel, later Brigadier General, later Major General, later Lieutenant General, later General, later General of the Army) Dwight D. Eisenhower."

As to the problem of footnotes—as an inveterate reader of history and biography, I have long been plagued and angered and aged prematurely by contemplation of pages of type which were pock-marked with asterisks, daggers and other nasty little symbols which pulled my eye down to small type at the bottom of the page and sometimes forced me to read on through the bottoms of subsequent pages before I could get back to the middle of the sentence from which I had been diverted and resume the narrative. Therefore, in this book, I have indulged myself in the luxury of no interruptions by footnotes, all of which are put in the back of the book. I have, however, interrupted some of the documentary material with parenthetical notes, largely for explanatory purposes.

I determined when I started this work that I must attempt to immerse myself so completely in the period of which I was writing that I would not permit myself to be influenced by subsequent events; I felt that I must not let my judgment of something that I was considering in the Hopkins papers—concerning, for instance, the desperate need to get aid to Russia during the Battle of Stalingrad—be colored in any way by what I had read in that morning's newspaper. This was a great deal easier than I had expected. It was a privilege to escape from the appalling and inexplicable present into the days when, as Herbert Agar has written, "Good men dared to trust each other," when "the good and the bad, the terror and the splendor, were too big for most of us," when "our spirits and our brains were splitting at the seams, which may be why so many are today denying that life was ever like that." This book tells a part of the story of those days, and I can assure the reader that I have withheld no important part of the record as it was known to me or made available to me in the papers of my friend Harry Hopkins. I hope that all the rest of the record will now be made public, and the sooner the better, for there are lessons in it which the people of the world need most urgently to learn.

ROBERT E. SHERWOOD

Roosevelt and Hopkins

An Intimate History

PART I: *BEFORE 1941—THE EDUCATION OF HARRY HOPKINS*

CHAPTER I

Foreword

DURING the years when Harry Hopkins lived as a guest in the White House, he was generally regarded as a sinister figure, a backstairs intriguer, an Iowan combination of Machiavelli, Svengali and Rasputin. Hostility toward him was by no means limited to those who hated Franklin Delano Roosevelt. There were many of Roosevelt's most loyal friends and associates, in and out of the Cabinet, who disliked Hopkins intensely and resented the extraordinary position of influence and authority which he held. He was unquestionably a political liability to Roosevelt, a convenient target for all manner of attacks directed at the President himself, and many people wondered why Roosevelt kept him around.

But the Presidential aide who developed in the war years—and of whom General (later Secretary of State) George C. Marshall said, "He rendered a service to his country which will never even vaguely be appreciated"—was in large measure Roosevelt's own creation. Roosevelt deliberately educated Hopkins in the arts and sciences of politics and of war and then gave him immense powers of decision for no reason other than that he liked him, trusted him and needed him. A welfare worker from the Cornbelt, who tended to regard money (his own as well as other people's) as something to be spent as quickly as possible, a studiously unsuave and often intolerant and tactless reformer, Hopkins was widely different from Roosevelt in birth, breeding and manners. But there were qualities in him, including some of the regrettable ones, which Roosevelt admired and enjoyed, perhaps partly because they were so different. One of the best statements of this relationship was written by the perceptive Raymond Clapper in 1938:

I

Many New Dealers have bored Roosevelt with their solemn earnestness. Hopkins never does. He knows instinctively when to ask, when
to keep still, when to press, when to hold back; when to approach
Roosevelt direct, when to go at him roundabout . . . Quick, alert,
shrewd, bold, and carrying it off with a bright Hell's bells air, Hopkins
is in all respects the inevitable Roosevelt favorite.

Clapper wrote that description in the New Deal years when Hopkins
had lofty political ambitions of his own. His position was drastically
changed during the war years, when all personal ambition had been
knocked out of him by near-fatal illness. Yet I heard from a distinguished European, who came into contact with both men for the first
time in these years, a description of the relationship that almost exactly
tallied with Clapper's; this observer said: "Hopkins has an almost
'feminine' sensitivity to Roosevelt's moods. He seems to know precisely
when Roosevelt wants to consider affairs of State and when he wants to
escape from the awful consciousness of the Presidency." (While agreeing
with that statement, I must add that I don't understand quite why this
kind of sensitivity should be described as "feminine"; I have heard of
women who could bring up disagreeable subjects at inopportune moments
just as well as any man.)

A revealing story of Roosevelt's regard for Hopkins was told by
Wendell Willkie, who was not one of the more fervent admirers of
either man. It will be remembered that, after his defeat at the polls in
November, 1940, Willkie provided a fine example of good citizenship and
good sportsmanship in accepting the verdict. Supporting Roosevelt's
foreign policy, he felt it would be useful for him to visit Britain which
was then fighting alone against Hitler's seemingly all-conquering German
war machine and was being bombed night after night with all the power
and all the fury that the Nazi world conquerors could project by air.
Roosevelt readily agreed to Willkie's proposal and invited him to come
to the White House on January 19, 1941, the day before the first Third
Term Inaugural in American history.

At that time, Hopkins was in England, having gone there to explore
the prodigious character of Winston Churchill and to report thereon to
Roosevelt (which reports will be recorded in later chapters of this
book); so Roosevelt suggested to Willkie that he must be sure to see
Hopkins when he arrived in London. Willkie did not greet this suggestion with much enthusiasm. He probably had more cordial dislike and
contempt for Hopkins than for anyone else in the Administration against
which he had fought so recently and so bitterly. Indeed, he asked Roosevelt a pointed question: "Why do you keep Hopkins so close to you?
You surely must realize that people distrust him and they resent his
influence." Willkie quoted Roosevelt as replying: "I can understand
that you wonder why I need that half-man around me." (The "half-man"

was an allusion to Hopkins' extreme physical frailty.) "But—someday you may well be sitting here where I am now as President of the United States. And when you are, you'll be looking at that door over there and knowing that practically everybody who walks through it wants something out of you. You'll learn what a lonely job this is, and you'll discover the need for somebody like Harry Hopkins who asks for nothing except to serve you."

Roosevelt did not talk much about the loneliness of high office. Indeed, in his letters, he was forever saying that he was having a "grand," "fine" or "bully" time. But that loneliness was a reality. Roosevelt was naturally a gregarious man who preferred talking to reading or writing. Like anybody else, he wanted to get away from his job now and then, but people wouldn't let him do it. Even in a poker game, while the cards were being shuffled, some member of the Cabinet was apt to interject, "By the way, Mr. President, the boys over at the Bureau of the Budget are taking what I consider a dangerously narrow-minded point of view toward our program—and I'm sure if you study the details you'll agree that—" etc. Roosevelt became more and more suspicious of the people associated with him and kept more and more to himself. When he could choose his own company, he preferred to be with old friends and relatives who had nothing to do with government and with whom he could talk about the old days in Hyde Park and about his innumerable, varied plans for his own future when he would retire to private life. It was characteristic of him that, when he went on his last journey to Warm Springs in a belated attempt to get some rest, his only companions apart from his personal staff were two gentle cousins of his own generation, Margaret Suckley and Laura Delano—and also his dog, Fala.

It is true that, in their final years, a special bond developed between Roosevelt and Hopkins, due to the fact that both men had fought with death at close range, both were living on borrowed time. But Hopkins achieved his favored position long before he had his own first encounter with death—and long before he could be described as one who crossed the Presidential threshold wanting nothing. In the F.E.R.A. and W.P.A. days, he was not reluctant to use his close friendship with the President for the advancement of his own interests and those of the agencies with which he was personally concerned.

I first met Hopkins on a week end on Long Island early in September, 1938, under the hospitable roof of Herbert and Margaret Swope. At the time I was keeping a diary (I stopped doing so regularly in June, 1940, which is just when I should have started) and I noted at the time: "Long talk at breakfast with Harry Hopkins, the W.P.A. Administrator, a profoundly shrewd and faintly ominous man." That was all I put down, but I remember that on that occasion Hopkins talked to me very agreeably, revealing a considerable knowledge of and enthusiasm for the theater. He took obvious pride in the achievements of W.P.A. in the Federal Theater and Arts Projects, and I believed he had every right to be proud. But I did not quite like him. He used such phrases as, "We've got to crack down on the bastards." I could not disagree with his estimate of the targets in question but I did not like the idea of cracking down. I had the characteristically American suspicion of anyone who appeared to be getting "too big for his breeches." A year or so later, when he was beaten down and chastened by terrible illness, I came to know him much better and to form a friendship which must color everything I write about him and for which no apologies are offered.

When, after Roosevelt's death, President Truman conferred the Distinguished Service Medal on Hopkins, the War Department citation spoke of the "piercing understanding" which he had displayed in attacking the manifold problems of the war. That is a wonderful phrase for Hopkins—"piercing understanding"—indicating the penetrating sharpness of his mind and the relentless, tireless drive that was behind it. In the year before Pearl Harbor, and the years of war that followed, Hopkins made it his job, he made it his religion, to find out just what it was that Roosevelt really wanted and then to see to it that neither hell nor high water, nor even possible vacillations by Roosevelt himself, blocked its achievement. Hopkins never made the mistake of Colonel Edward M. House, which caused the fatal breach with Wilson, of assuming he knew the President's mind better than the President did. Roosevelt could send him on any mission, to the Pentagon Building or to Downing Street, with absolute confidence that Hopkins would not utter one decisive word based on guesswork as to his Chief's policies or purposes. Hopkins ventured on no ground that Roosevelt had not charted. When Hopkins first journeyed to Moscow, in July, 1941, within a month after Hitler's assault on the Soviet Union, Roosevelt sent a message to Joseph Stalin: "I ask you to treat him with the identical confidence you would feel if you were talking directly to me." At that time, Roosevelt had never had any personal contact with Stalin, but Stalin took him at his word and talked to Hopkins with a degree of candor that he had displayed to no previous wartime emissary from the democratic world. What was remarkable about this first contact with Stalin—which will be recorded verbatim in a later section of this book—is that Hopkins carried with him no written instructions whatsoever from Roosevelt as to what he should say or do. The President could and did trust him fully.

Roosevelt used to say, "Harry is the perfect Ambassador for my purposes. He doesn't even know the meaning of the word 'protocol.' When he sees a piece of red tape, he just pulls out those old garden shears of his and snips it. And when he's talking to some foreign dignitary, he knows how to slump back in his chair and put his feet up on the conference table and say, 'Oh, yeah?'" It was this same ability to break all speed records in getting down to brass tacks that endeared Hopkins to the heart of Winston Churchill, who has said:

> I have been present at several great conferences where twenty or more of the most important executive personages were gathered together. When the discussion flagged and all seemed baffled, it was on these occasions Harry Hopkins would rap out a deadly question: "Surely, Mr. President, here is the point we have got to settle. Are we going to face it or not?" Faced it always was and being faced, was conquered.

One time Churchill, Roosevelt and Hopkins were having lunch together upstairs in the Oval Study in the White House. They were thrashing out in advance major problems which were coming up for discussion at a full dress conference to be held later that afternoon. As usual, both Roosevelt and Churchill were wandering far afield. (Churchill might have been refighting the Battle of Blenheim and Roosevelt recalling the tactics employed by John Paul Jones when the *Bonhomme Richard* defeated the *Serapis*.) It was for Hopkins to bring these soaring imaginations down to earth, to contemplation of the topic immediately at hand.

When he did so, with his usual brusqueness, Churchill turned on him and said:

"Harry! When this war is over His Majesty's Government is going to reward you by conferring upon you a noble title."

Hopkins remarked sourly that membership in the House of Lords was one reward that he did not covet. But Churchill went right ahead:

"We have already selected the title. You are to be named 'Lord Root of the Matter.' "

Hopkins had very little of Roosevelt's or Churchill's powers of vision and almost none of their historical sense. He looked to the immediate rather than the long-term result. He was an implementer rather than a planner. He was accustomed to divide people he knew into two groups, the "talkers" and the "doers," and he placed himself proudly in the second category. When Roosevelt contemplated a subject, his mind roamed all around it; he considered it in its relation to past, present and future. Hopkins, contemplating the same subject, was interested only in thrusting straight through to its heart and then acting on it without further palaver. In that respect, Hopkins was remarkably useful to Roosevelt— but Roosevelt was essential to Hopkins.

Despite his furious devotion to duty, and despite his persistent ill health, Hopkins had a zest for living which caused him often to revert to the role of a Grinnell (Iowa) College freshman when turned loose in the Big Town. He loved the race tracks ($2 window), the theaters and night clubs, he loved the society of the fashionable, the beautiful, the talented, the gay and of such taverners as Sherman Billingsley, Jack and Charlie, and Toots Shor. He was pleased and rather proud whenever the hostile press denounced him as a "playboy." That made him feel glamorous. The President's physician, Admiral Ross T. McIntire, once said: "Our biggest job is to keep Harry from ever feeling completely well. When he thinks he's restored to health he goes out on the town—and from there to the Mayo Clinic." Hopkins was not a hard drinker—he was physically incapable of being one—but almost any drink that he did take was more than was good for him.

Roosevelt regarded the mild frivolities of his wayward friend with amusement not unmixed with considerable concern. His attitude was that of an indulgent parent toward an errant son whose wild oats, while forgivable, must be strictly rationed.

Following is a handwritten letter, dated May 21, 1939, during one of the many periods when Hopkins was bedridden with wasting sickness:

DEAR HARRY—

   Good Boy! Teacher says you have gained 2 pounds.
$$2 \text{ Lbs.} = 2\$$$
   Keep on gaining and put the reward into your little Savings Bank. But you must not gain more than 50 lbs. because Popper has not got more than 50$.

As ever

F.D.R.

Clipped to that letter were two one-dollar bills. They are still clipped to it as this is written, eight years later. There was not a great deal more money left in the Hopkins estate.

Another letter of May 18, 1944, when Hopkins was in the Ashford General Hospital:

DEAR HARRY :—

   It is grand to get the reports of how well you are getting on at White Sulphur Springs, and I have had a mighty nice letter from [Dr. Andrew B.] Rivers—couched mostly in medical terms—which, however, I have had translated!

   The main things I get from it are two. First, that it is a good thing to connect up the plumbing and put your sewerage system into operating condition. The second is (and this comes from others in authority) that you have got to lead not the life of an invalid but the life of common or garden sense.

   I, too, over one hundred years older than you are, have come to the same realization and I have cut my drinks down to one and a half cocktails per evening and nothing else—not one complimentary highball or night cap. Also, I have cut my cigarettes down from twenty or thirty a day to five or six a day. Luckily they still taste rotten but it can be done.

   The main gist of this is to plead with you to stay away until the middle of June at the earliest. I don't want you back until then. If you do come back before then you will be extremely unpopular in

THE WHITE HOUSE
WASHINGTON

From 26
'39

Dear Harry –

Good Boy! Teacher says you
have gained 2 pounds.

2 lbs = 2 $

Keep on gaining & put the reward
into your little Savings Bank.
But you must not gain more
than 50 lbs, because Poppy
has not got more than 50 $

As ever

F.D.R.

Washington, with the exception of Cissy Patterson who wants to kill you off as soon as possible—just as she does me.

My plans—my medical laboratory work not being finished—are to be here about three days a week and to spend the other four days a week at Hyde Park, Shangri-la or on the Potomac. For later in the Summer I have various hens sitting but I don't know when they will hatch out.

I had a really grand time down at Bernie's [Baruch]—slept twelve hours out of the twenty-four, sat in the sun, never lost my temper, and decided to let the world go hang. The interesting thing is the world didn't hang.

I have a terrible pile in my basket but most of the stuff has answered itself anyway.

I am off to Hyde Park to stay until Tuesday or Wednesday next.

Lots of love to you both. Tell Louise to use the old-fashioned hat-pin if you don't behave!

Affectionately,

F.D.R.

It is of incidental interest to note that the foregoing letter was written two weeks before the Allied Forces were due to land in Normandy, a time when Roosevelt was bearing a formidable weight of responsibility and anxiety. Roosevelt was all too well aware that the attempt at invasion of Hitler's "Fortress of Europe" was incalculably hazardous and might fail; the English Channel might become, in the oft-reiterated words of Winston Churchill, a "river of blood." But Roosevelt simply could not be obsessed by fears and apprehensions. To say that he took the most terrible moments of the war with apparently insouciant lightness would seem to suggest that he was callous and heartless. He was neither of these things. He had a faculty—and it was always incomprehensible to me—for sloughing off care and worry, no matter how grave the emergency. In the words of his friend, Morris Ernst, "He had humor and gaiety arising out of a deviation from the ordinary pattern of man, which is fear of death." That was most evident at the time of Pearl Harbor. It was this quality which enabled him to survive until victory was in sight.

One time when Hopkins, Samuel I. Rosenman and I were working with him, Roosevelt dictated a paragraph for insertion in a speech. He said something to indicate that the current problems were giving him "sleepless nights." One of us protested: "You may get away with that at the moment, Mr. President, but future historians are bound to find out that every night you go to sleep practically at the moment your head touches the pillow and you don't wake up until at least eight hours later." Roosevelt laughed and eliminated the reference to sleepless nights.

Despite all the differences between their characters and experience, Roosevelt and Hopkins were alike in one important way: they were thoroughly and gloriously unpompous. The predominant qualities in both were unconquerable confidence, courage and good humor.

Frances Perkins has written of Roosevelt that he was "the most complicated human being I ever knew." Henry Morgenthau, Jr., has written, "Roosevelt is an extraordinarily difficult person to describe . . . weary as well as buoyant, frivolous as well as grave, evasive as well as frank . . . a man of bewildering complexity of moods and motives." Miss Perkins and Morgenthau were members of Roosevelt's Cabinet and knew him far longer and better than I did. But I saw enough of him, particularly in hours when he was off parade and relaxed, to be able to say "Amen!" to their statements on his complexity. Being a writer by trade, I tried continually to study him, to try to look beyond his charming and amusing and warmly affectionate surface into his heavily forested interior. But I could never really understand what was going on in there. His character was not only multiplex, it was contradictory to a bewildering degree. He was hard and he was soft. At times he displayed a capacity for vindictiveness which could be described as petty, and at other times he demonstrated the Christian spirit of forgiveness and charity in its purest form. He could be a ruthless politician but he was the champion of friends and associates who for him were political liabilities, conspicuously Harry Hopkins, and of causes which apparently competent advisers assured him would constitute political suicide. He could appear to be utterly cynical, worldly, illusionless, and yet his religious faith was the strongest and most mysterious force that was in him. Although he was progressive enough and liberal enough to be condemned as a "Traitor to his class" and "That Red in the White House," he was in truth a profoundly old-fashioned person with an incurable nostalgia for the very "horse and buggy era" on which he publicly heaped so much scorn. He loved peace and harmony in his surroundings and (like many others) greatly preferred to be agreed with, and yet most of his major appointments to the Cabinet and to the various New Deal and War Agencies were peculiarly violent, quarrelsome, recalcitrant men. He liked to fancy himself as a practical, down-to-earth, horse-sense realist—he often used to say "Winston and Uncle Joe and I get along well together because we're all *realists*"—and yet his idealism was actually no less empyrean than Woodrow Wilson's. Probably the supreme contradiction in Roosevelt's character was the fact that, with all his complexity, he achieved a grand simplicity which will make him, I believe, much less of a mystery to biographers than Lincoln was and must forever remain. Roosevelt wrote himself by word and deed in large plain letters which all can read and in terms which all can understand. Whatever the complexity of forces which impelled him, the end result was easily understandable to his countrymen and to the world at large. In his first Inaugural Address as Governor of New

York he spoke of the program of social legislation which had been instituted by his predecessor, Alfred E. Smith, and said:

I object to having this spirit of personal civil responsibility to the State and to the individual which has placed New York in the lead as a progressive commonwealth, described as "humanitarian." It is far more than that. It is the recognition that our civilization cannot endure unless we, as individuals, realize our personal responsibility to and dependence on the rest of the world. For it is literally true that the "self-supporting" man or woman has become as extinct as the man of the stone age. Without the help of thousands of others, any one of us would die, naked and starved. Consider the bread upon our table, the clothes upon our backs, the luxuries that make life pleasant; how many men worked in sunlit fields, in dark mines, in the fierce heat of molten metal, and among the looms and wheels of countless factories, in order to create them for our use and enjoyment.

In reading those words, it must be remembered that they were spoken in January, 1929, almost a year before the beginnings of economic collapse—four years before the rise of Hitler to power—more than ten years before the start of the Second World War—twelve years before Lend Lease. Yet, those who heard them might have anticipated precisely the principles and policies of the man who was to be Governor for four years and President for twelve. Those words when spoken were extremely radical; it was considered downright Bolshevism to talk of interdependence in those days of the Coolidge boom, rugged individualism and "every man for himself," when the American attitude toward the rest of the world was summed up in that magnificently unanswerable question, "They hired the money, didn't they?"

When you consider the words of Roosevelt's first Albany Inaugural together with those of his first Washington Inaugural you wonder that anyone was ever surprised at what he did when he became President of the United States—which is hindsight prescience, to be sure, but so is all of history.

When Roosevelt took Hopkins into the White House to live on May 10, 1940, Hopkins was still nominally Secretary of Commerce and such direction as he could give to the affairs of that Department was given largely by telephone. He was to all intents and purposes physically a finished man who might drag out his life for a few years of relative inactivity or who might collapse and die at any time. And it was not only the perilous state of his health that made him seem unlikely to be of any real use to the President in meeting the unprecedented demands of the Second World War: for Hopkins knew nothing about military matters. He had never fixed a bayonet in basic infantry drill; he had never answered general quarters as an able seaman. In the First World War, he had been rejected by the Army and Navy on physical grounds and his war experience was limited to welfare work with the Red Cross in the deep South. Furthermore, his New Dealer pacifism inclined him emotionally toward a kind of isolationism. However, the fact is that by 1940 Roosevelt valued the peculiar kind of service rendered and the companionship provided by Hopkins to such an extent that he converted his friend to war purposes just as surely and as completely as, in the general upheaval of that same year, a Chicago industrialist named Albert J. Browning converted his wallpaper factory into a plant for the production of incendiary bombs.

Hopkins was one of the many Americans who believed that National Defense meant just that. If an enemy fleet approached our shores, we would merely line up our own Navy (which was always "second to none") like a football team defending its goal line in the days before the invention of the forward pass; any hostile ships that might break through the Navy would be handled by our coast defenses. Hopkins did have a considerable conception of the importance of air power but again it was on a purely defensive basis so far as the United States was concerned: we needed masses of fighting planes to keep invaders and marauders away from our own skies and bombers to sink enemy ships when they ventured within range. But Roosevelt educated him in the military facts of life and so did General Marshall for whom Hopkins had profound respect and whose appointment as Chief of Staff he had strongly recommended. It was consistent with Roosevelt's whole character that he should believe in attack as the best means of defense. That was evidenced by his championship of the airplane carrier as a weapon and his advocacy of all measures which permitted the fleet to operate far from home bases for ever-increasing periods of time. (Long before the end of the war our ships could remain in the remote Pacific indefinitely, being able to distill their own fresh water and to take on all necessary fuel, munitions and supplies at sea, an improvement which was not popular with the crews.)

One evening—it was August 15, 1940, when the Battle of Britain was beginning—Roosevelt and Hopkins were talking in the Study at the White House and Roosevelt, who was particularly interested in the possibilities of amphibious warfare, drew a map of the East Coast of the United States, locating the coastal defenses and explaining that they actually could defend less than one and one-half per cent of our coastline. Roosevelt pointed out that an enemy could land an expeditionary force at any one of innumerable points on our shores and therefore, if we were involved in war, it would be highly desirable for us to land on the enemy shores first—as for instance, the northwest coast of Africa.

There were many military men, and General Dwight D. Eisenhower was one of them, who came into contact with Hopkins for the first time in 1941, and all of those to whom I have talked have said substantially

the same thing: knowing him only as one of those New Deal "vision-
aries" (i.e., crackpots) they had been rather dubious of his ability to
understand purely military problems but, when they talked with him,
were amazed at his grasp of the essentials of grand strategy. That was
the result of Roosevelt's teaching and of Hopkins' ready ability to learn.
He needed plenty of that ability as the years went by and the problems

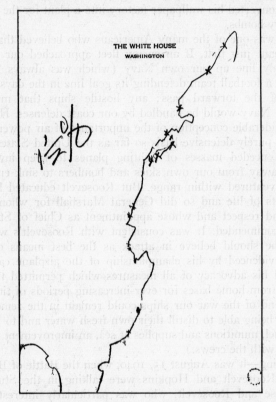

THE WHITE HOUSE

WASHINGTON

*Roosevelt's sketch illustrating inadequacy
of fixed coastal defenses.*

multiplied in a war that touched every continent and every ocean and the
skies above them and ended in the dread birth of the Atomic Age.

At the start of this first chapter I said that there were members of
Roosevelt's Cabinet who resented the close relationship of Hopkins and
the President. An exception was the Secretary of War, Henry L. Stimson, a lifelong Republican who must have been vigorously opposed to the
whole philosophy of W.P.A. and, as a stickler for form, must have

been disturbed by the irregularity of Hopkins' extraofficial position of authority. Yet, in his diary, Stimson wrote: "The more I think of it, the more I think it is a Godsend that he [Hopkins] should be at the White House."

The date of that entry was March 5, 1941, when the great Lend-Lease debate was coming to an end, when Hopkins was coming into a position in the world that no man had ever occupied before.

Other officers of the government who did not consider Hopkins' presence in the White House a "Godsend" credited him with the power to exert a baneful influence over Roosevelt, to compel Roosevelt to take actions against his own better judgment and personal inclinations. Indeed, that overworked scholar, the historian of the future, reading various memoirs of this era, may come to the perplexed conclusion that Roosevelt never did anything on his own—that everything good that he accomplished was done at the instigation of the authors of the memoirs, and everything bad was due to "other influences," which usually meant Hopkins. Hopkins always laughed at the suggestion that he was a Svengali, for this implied that Roosevelt must be a sweetly submissive Trilby. Roosevelt was many things, but he was not that.

CHAPTER II

Sioux City to Washington

HOPKINS was born on August 17, 1890, in Sioux City, Iowa, a seemingly immeasurable distance from Hyde Park, New York. On his fifty-first birthday, he returned to Washington with President Roosevelt after the Atlantic Conference, previous to which he had flown to Moscow via London. A friend asked him about his first encounter with Stalin, and he said, "I couldn't believe it. There I was, walking up the staircase of the Kremlin, going to talk to the man who ruled 180 million people. And I kept asking myself—what are *you* doing here, Hopkins, you—the son of a harness maker from Sioux City—?" Whereupon the friend, who was a somewhat outspoken type, interrupted: "Now, for God's sake, Harry—don't give me that old line again. You told me when you first set foot in the White House that there you were, the son of a harness maker—and you said the same thing about your first visit to No. 10 Downing Street. Can't you ever stop boasting about your humble origin? It's the only sign of pretentiousness I've ever seen in you. And, anyway, there have probably been plenty of other harness makers' sons in the Kremlin. When you go in there, or anyplace else— all you ought to think about is that you're the personal representative of the President and, by God, you have a *right* to be there!"

Hopkins was impressed by this point. In 1945 when he returned from his final trip to Moscow, which was also his last mission in the public service, he answered a congratulatory message by saying, "It isn't so difficult to do a job like this reasonably well when you have the whole force of the United States Government behind you."

He was the fourth of five children born to David Aldona and Anna Pickett Hopkins. His brothers were Lewis, John Emory and Rome, and his sister Adah (who became Mrs. Frank Aime). An old friend of the family, Robert Kerr, has said, "To anyone interested in genetics,

Harry presented a wonderful study as a combination of the characters of his father and mother."

David Hopkins—known as "Al" and "Dad"—was evidently a charming, salty, easygoing but erratic and somewhat shiftless man who was always among the most popular citizens of any town where he happened to be living but who did not stay for long in any one place. He had been, at various times, a newspaper "carrier," prospector, harness maker, traveling salesman and storekeeper, but his main interest in life was bowling, at which he was expert and from which he derived a good income in side bets. Harry told a story of his father's prowess on the bowling alleys: "One night Dad came home after a big match against someone who thought himself a champion. Dad took me down to the cellar on some pretext, like fixing the furnace, then reached in his pocket and pulled out $500 for me to look at. He had won it all that evening, but of course I wasn't supposed to tell my mother there was that amount of money in the house; she would have made Dad give it away to church missions."

At the top of all of David A. Hopkins' letterheads in his various ventures were the words, "Business is Good," which suggested a quality of defiant optimism some part of which was imparted to his son Harry, who could slip now and then into skepticism but who always returned to a state of passionate hopefulness.

Dad Hopkins was born in Bangor, Maine, but his family moved west after the Civil War. He was prospecting for gold in South Dakota when he met and married Anna Pickett, a school teacher. She had been born in Hamilton, Ontario, and her family had moved from there to Vermillion, South Dakota, as homesteaders. She was strong in mind and body and in religious faith. As her husband found both diversion and the exercise of his greatest skill in the bowling alleys, she found her supreme interest in the Methodist Church. She was active and dominant in church functions and achieved prominence as a devoted worker in the Methodist Missionary Society of Iowa. She was determined to bring up and educate her children strictly in the faith. There is no doubt that Harry inherited his missionary zeal, as he did his sharp features and penetrating eyes, from his mother; the sporting side of his nature was his father's contribution. Shortly after his birth the family moved from Sioux City to various new homes in Council Bluffs, Kearney and Hastings in Nebraska and then, for two years, Chicago—the location of the home being selected as close as possible to the center of the area in which Dad was traveling at the time as salesman for a wholesale harness concern. A bad accident brought a happy change in the family fortunes and produced a period of stability: Dad was run down by a horse-drawn truck and suffered a broken leg. He sued the truck's owners who settled, out of court, for $10,000. Half of this prize went to Hopkins' lawyer, and with the remaining $5,000 he bought a harness store of his own in Grinnell, Iowa. As the demand for harness declined, he added newspapers, magazines and candy to his stock and sold cigarettes under the counter. He was extremely popular with Grinnell College students and, it was said, knew more of them by their first names than did anyone else in town, including the college president. Grinnell was selected by Mrs. Hopkins as a good place in which to settle down because of the exceptional educational opportunities that it provided for the children; it remained the family home for many years.

While his family lived in Chicago, Harry had a severe siege of typhoid which was the start of his long record of ill health. His nickname in school thereafter was, of course, "Skinny." Later, at college, he was addressed as "Hi." While in high school in Grinnell, he engaged in his first politicking, but it was then inspired more by a hell-raising impulse than by any lust for power. *Fortune* magazine has recorded that "he didn't like the way the teachers fixed the class elections in favor of the best students so he organized a ballot stuffing for a boy named Sam O'Brien who was none too academic. The teachers threw out the vote but Harry kept on electioneering and on the next supervised ballot O'Brien was elected just the same—by a bigger vote than he had got the first time."

An ardent baseball player and fan, Hopkins used to crash the gate at the big games at Grinnell. He and his friend, Dwight Bradley, got into Ward Field as armor bearers for the star catcher, B. M. Benson —one of the boys would carry his mask, the other his glove—but Hopkins himself was only a mediocre right fielder. Grinnell was a great town for basketball and it was at this sport, both in school and college, that Harry excelled. He was on a team which had the distinction of winning the Missouri Valley Championship. His team-mates described his style of play as "rough"; his opponents described it as "dirty."

He entered Grinnell College with the class of 1912. Spurred by his success as campaign manager for Sam O'Brien, he engaged in a great deal of electioneering (now usually for himself) and was a consistent vote getter all through college, ending up his senior year with election as permanent president of the class. (That was probably the last time in his life that he ever actually ran for electoral office; his subsequent ascents were all by appointment.) During one summer at college he worked in a nearby brickyard and during another on a farm without, apparently, learning much about agriculture. He remained a persistent practical joker—a generally uninhibited extrovert with acute powers of calculation and a penchant for extracurricular activities. As a senior at Grinnell he was approached by sophomore leaders for advice on strategy and tactics in the annual sophomore-freshman class battle. He gave it, freely. Then he was approached, quite independently, by freshman leaders for advice. He gave that, freely, too—telling the freshmen how to counter the "possible" sophomore strategy (which he had suggested). Neither side knew that Hopkins had masterminded both sides. The battle ended as Hopkins had planned it, with the sophomores taking up defensive positions in a barn and the freshmen dropping stink bombs through a hole in the roof. These tactics were regarded by the college authorities as unworthy of Grinnell's traditions of sportsmanship and fair play and various culprits were punished; but Hopkins' guilt was never exposed. Also in his senior year he organized the Woodrow Wilson League in Grinnell and, learning that the Princeton president was to make a pre-Convention trip west, he wrote Wilson urging him to stop in Grinnell. Wilson did so for all of two minutes, appearing on the back platform of his train. Hopkins had the college band out for the occasion at a cost to himself of $1.50 which, I believe, he never paid.

Curiously mixed with this prankish tendency was a deeply puritanical sense, the result of his elaborate religious training, and although he was outspoken on most subjects he was secretive about his emotions. His sister, Adah Aime, has told me that in undergraduate days he had a girl, a Grinnell coed, with whom he "went steady" for a long time. Suddenly he broke it off, which precipitated an embarrassing crisis in Grinnell social circles. According to Mrs. Aime, "The girl was quite serious and later took up social work herself. But she did not practice religion in the same narrow way as Harry had been brought up to do and he felt that was a bar to their happiness." And that, presumably, was why he sanctimoniously ended the relationship. But he would not talk about it to his family. His good mother, distressed by this development said, "I can't ever make Harry out. He never tells me anything about what he's *really* thinking." He remained secretive, but not always so priggishly censorious of lack of religious regularity in girls to whom he was attracted.

In the early years of the twentieth century Grinnell College had established a high reputation for scholarship which Hopkins neither increased nor appreciably lowered. He appears to have been about average or maybe a little below that as a student. He certainly did not reveal much of the ability to learn with speed and accuracy which was to be his most remarkable attribute in later years. His favorite professor was Jesse Macy, who was, I believe, the originator of the first college course in political science in the United States. Macy, a Quaker farmer by birth, had been at Grinnell since before the Civil War, during which he served in Sherman's army in the march from Atlanta to the sea. He was one of the first converts to the Darwinian theory and believed it "his duty to use every endeavor toward the attainment of a more righteous order in the state and in society, regardless of the prospects of success." He expressed the belief that the democratic nations would "learn to cooperate through a United States of the World." It would be difficult to exaggerate the influence of this pioneer teacher upon an alert, receptive young student who had within him the makings of an aggressive New Dealer and internationalist. Macy was an exponent of the Socratic method, which Hopkins used with penetrating effect in later years. Furthermore, Macy could tell his pupil a great deal about the differences between the British and American constitutional systems, for he had spent considerable time in England and had formed a close friendship with James Bryce and the members of the London Economic Club and the Fabian Society at the time when the Sidney Webbs and Bernard Shaw were first forming what Beatrice Webb called "this union of pity, hope and faith." Indeed, when Bryce was revising his classic work, *The American Commonwealth*, he went to spend several weeks of collaboration in Grinnell with Professor Macy. The great British Ambassador and scholar lived at the Macy house, which was a modest one, with no servants except for a part-time cook. On his first night, Bryce put his shoes outside the door, in the traditional British country house fashion. Professor Macy took the shoes to the kitchen and shined them himself—and this process was repeated through every night of Bryce's stay in Grinnell; indeed, this distinguished British statesman died without ever knowing that his collaborator and host in Grinnell, Iowa, had worked overtime every night to shine his shoes. But the scholarly associations established between Macy and Bryce were transmitted to Harry Hopkins and were of vital importance at the time (in 1941) when Britain faced death at the hands of Hitlerism.

There was another great teacher at Grinnell, Dr. Edward A. Steiner, and from him Hopkins gained his first knowledge of the social sciences and of the strange, remote, gigantic mass that was Russia. Steiner, a Jew, had been born in Czechoslovakia and graduated from Heidelberg, then emigrated to the United States where he became ordained as a Congregationalist minister. He went to Russia in 1903 and stayed with Tolstoy at Yasnaya Polyana, gathering material for his book on "Tolstoy, the Man" (he described the Countess Tolstoy as "my reluctant hostess"). His course at Grinnell was called Applied Christianity and was, in fact, sociology. Hopkins was permanently influenced by what he learned from Steiner on the Christian ethic and the teachings of Tolstoy. He had *War and Peace* in mind when, in July, 1941, he flew over the vast Russian forests on the way to Moscow when it came the turn of the Soviet Union to face death at the hands of Nazi Germany.

In the Steiner course, Hopkins had an "A." In Macy's courses he averaged "B." But in English composition he was usually a low "D"— and once an "E" (total failure)—which is no surprise to those who have read any of his writings. When he talked, his language was extraordinarily vivid and original and to the point. When he wrote for publication, he was apt to become self-conscious, sententious and awkward.

The influence of Grinnell—the college and the town itself—was always with Hopkins. He became something of an expatriate in the gaudy atmosphere of Jimmy Walker's New York and then he became in effect a citizen of the world, but he never became urbane. All of the Hopkins family left Grinnell, scattering over the continent. Dad Hopkins spent his last years happily combining business with pleasure in Spokane, Washington, where he was proprietor of the bowling alleys in the Davenport Hotel. The old man had an enduring grudge against Grinnell. There had been a drive for funds to build a hospital there and Dad Hopkins pledged a handsome contribution but, when it came time to pay it, he was in one of his recurrent phases of extreme financial embarrassment. This led him into a violent argument with the hospital board members and there was even a threat of legal proceedings which was averted when friends quietly chipped in enough money to meet the pledge. Dad Hopkins eventually paid this off but he never forgot nor forgave the authorities. Years later, he told Harry quite calmly that he was dying of cancer of the stomach and then he exploded, "And you can bury me any Goddamned place except Grinnell!" When he did die, in 1930, Harry was notified by his brother Lewis that burial would be in the family plot at Grinnell. He did not obey his father and raise any protest for he knew that his mother wanted the burial to be there and she was the one who was living. This good woman died in 1932, just when her son Harry was on the threshold of fame and, in some quarters, notoriety.

In 1939, after his appointment as Secretary of Commerce, Harry Hopkins revisited his native State—a visit which, as will be seen, was charged with political implications—and he stopped off at Grinnell to visit his old friends the Kerrs and to speak to the student body at the college. Most of this speech is given herewith because, being largely unprepared, it sounds like Hopkins when he talked without benefit of ghost writers:

When I hear people talking about what a College is for—its curriculum—I know the plural of that too, I know that one of the best things in College is to have fun. You have plenty of time later in life to get banged around or to get solemn about it, but here you have great fun, and I think that is good, of and by itself. . . .

I was around this town for many years, and I found that this town had a government, had wards, and I learned that there were townships in the counties, and that there was a State Legislature. I did not know much about it. I heard they collected taxes. I used to hear rumors that the railroads owned the Legislature in the State of Iowa. I learned later it was true. I had the vaguest knowledge about government. The less government interfered with me around this town, the better I liked it. I didn't even like to have the College authorities interfere with me too much. . . .

Since then, and for the last 27 or 28 years, I have lived around various parts of the country, and, in more recent years of my life, have come in intimate contact with government. I have seen government wage wars; I have seen government baffled and unable to meet economic problems; I have seen and lived with a government which has struck out boldly attempting to meet our economic problems. I have lived to see the time when the Government of the United States worries about how much a farmer gets for his corn, wheat, or cotton. I have lived to see the time when a farmer gets a check signed by the Treasurer of the United States for doing something. I see old people getting pensions; see unemployed people getting checks from the United States Government; College students getting checks signed by the United States Government.

I have seen people battling for control of the United States Government, and many years ago, when I first saw this struggle, I wondered why they made such an effort to control it, and I saw great and powerful interests spend a lot of money in an attempt to control government. I saw them do that, and you don't have to go very far away to see them still doing it. Make no mistake about it, there are many interests in this country who want to control government whether it be local, State, or Federal. I have no quarrel with that theory. I think it's perfectly proper for any group of people in a Democracy to do anything they can to influence government. As long as the farmers out here talked it out by holding a lot of meetings and writing articles, nobody paid any attention to them, but when they formed a political bloc and went to the State Legislature, the Congressmen, and the Senators, and said, "Either you do what we want you to do or we won't send you back," Congressmen and everyone who ran for office in this great farm belt, then began to make political speeches saying what they would do for the farmers. Each candidate wanted to do more than the other. I think that is good. . . .

In this last Congress, 83 Democratic Congressmen were pitched out and 83 Republican Congressmen went in because they promised bigger and better old age pensions. I think, politically, they were very smart and intelligent. I don't see anything wrong about that. I do not see anything wrong in these pressure groups of one kind or another trying to influence government. They have simply taken a lesson out of the public utilities and railroads. They ran most of the State governments 25 and 50 years ago. You don't have to go back more than 50 years, and you will find that members of the State Legislature were on the payroll of the railroads. You don't have to go back very far, and you will find a great many of the lawyers were working for the utilities. I could make a speech about the lawyers, but I will just skip it.

I have seen this government at close range working with the American people, and I have seen them do these things, and I have a firm conviction, they are going to keep on doing them. It does not make any difference what Party is in power, the government is going to treat the people in ways we have never dreamed of before, and, therefore, government should be good.

With the world situation the way it is today, almost a mad house, with hate and fear sweeping the world; with this nation almost the last stronghold of Democracy; with the American people determined to maintain that Democracy, the kind of government that we have is extremely important, and it is the one thing in America that is important.

This government is ours whether it be local, county, State, or Federal. It doesn't belong to anybody but the people of America. Don't treat it as an impersonal thing; don't treat it as something to sneer at; treat it as something that belongs to you. I don't care how much you criticize it, or to what Party you belong, just remember that this government belongs to you, and needs you, and it is going to take brains and skill to run it in the future because this country cannot continue to exist as a democracy with 10,000,000 or 12,000,000 people unemployed. It just can't be done. We have got to find a way of living in America in which every person in it shares in the national income, in such a way, that poverty in America is abolished. There is no reason why the people of America should dwell in poverty. A way must be found, and a way will be found.

And, finally, let me say this. Growing up in this town, moving to the East, and having been almost every place in this Union, I have grown to have a tremendous affection and love for this country—the fields—the land—and the people. Nothing must happen to it, and those of us who get a chance, and many of us will because of the things this nation has done for us, should and will be motivated when the time comes to serve it well.

That Grinnell speech, incidentally, contained one of the few public references that Hopkins ever made to the prospect or the actuality of another World War until 1941 when he himself was so heavily involved in it.

When Hopkins was about to graduate from Grinnell College, he went around to see Dr. Steiner to say good-by. He had not made up his mind as to his future career: he had talked of going into the newspaper business in Bozeman, Montana, in partnership with Chester Davis who also was to serve with Franklin Roosevelt as War Food Administrator. But Hopkins avoided journalism by a narrow margin. Dr. Steiner showed Hopkins a telegram he had received from Christadora House, a charitable institution on Avenue B in the New York slums. The telegram asked if Steiner could suggest a Grinnell student to act as counselor that summer at the Christadora camp for poor children near Bound Brook, New Jersey, and Steiner asked Hopkins if he might be interested in this temporary job. Despite his mother's influence, Hopkins had never been much interested in missionary or social work; he had been identified with the Y.M.C.A. in college but this was merely a part of regular undergraduate activities. Nevertheless, he jumped at the opportunity offered through Dr. Steiner, not because he had any intention of making a career as a welfare worker but because this was a chance to get to New York. The newspaper in Bozeman could wait until he had had a good look at the Big Town. Chester Davis, President of the Federal Reserve Bank of St. Louis, has written me:

> The correspondence with a view to getting Harry out to Montana never got out of the pipe dream stage. Harry had done some work for the Scarlet and Black, the Grinnell College newspaper, as I had done, and he would have made a good newspaper man. . . . It was Paul Appleby whom we did bring out to Montana for that job. [Appleby, a member of the Grinnell Class of 1913, was Under Secretary of Agriculture in the Second World War.]

On the way east, Hopkins stopped off at Chicago for the Republican Convention, worming his way into it by posing as Elihu Root's "secretary" (again he was carrying the catcher's mask). He heard Theodore Roosevelt shout that thieves were running the Republican party—that the renomination of William Howard Taft was "naked theft." That was the year T.R. bolted and formed the Bull Moose party. Hopkins also attended the Democratic Convention in Baltimore and saw some of the battle of William Jennings Bryan to nominate Woodrow Wilson, but I do not know what guise he assumed to get into this one. The sight and sound of the political giants excited him and for the next twenty years he nourished a desire to become a combatant in that bloody arena.

On arrival at the Christadora Summer Camp at Bound Brook, he confessed that he was bewildered by his first contacts with the products of the East Coast slums. He had certainly known poverty in his own family and friendly neighborhood in the Middle West, but that kind of poverty involved the maintenance of a kind of dignity and self-respect and independence; it did not involve hunger, or squalor, or degradation. The poverty of the city slums was, to him, something alien, shocking and enraging. At Bound Brook, he said later, he was brought sharply to the realization that, "I'd never seen a Jewish boy before in my life." This was his real birth as a crusader for reform. The missionary impulse that he had inherited from his mother became the most powerful force within him. As with other changes in the circumstances of his life, he adjusted himself to his new environment with remarkable rapidity. After two months in the camp at Bound Brook he was the zealous champion of the underprivileged which he would always remain. He went to work for Christadora House and began to learn of life as it was lived on the lower East Side of New York, which was as complete a sociological laboratory as one could find anywhere on earth. He worked for his board and lodging and, I believe, $5.00 a month pocket money. In 1912 New York was still the fabulous "Bagdad on The Subway" of O. Henry, whose stories were just beginning to achieve posthumous success. It was still the city of Diamond Jim Brady and the Tenderloin and Millionaire's Row and the Five Points, where young Al Capone was learning his trade. And it was still the city of Tammany which had enjoyed a half century of corruption and free enterprise on the loose under Boss Tweed, "Honest John" Kelly and Richard Croker. But the forces of reform were finding a glamorous champion in John Purroy Mitchel, "the Young Torquemada," and were mobilizing to drive the rascals out (temporarily). This cause was aided greatly by the results of an event which occurred in that summer of 1912: the murder of Herman Rosenthal, proprietor of one of the town's many gambling houses. This appalling story, broken by another young Middle Westerner, Herbert Swope, helped to elect Mitchel Mayor, and Charles S. Whitman, who prosecuted the case, became Governor of the State.

The day after the execution of the "Four Gunmen"—who bore the unforgettable names of Gyp the Blood, Dago Frank, Lefty Louie and Whitey Lewis—Hopkins was attending a meeting of a boy's club in one of the East Side settlement houses where he was giving inspirational talks on civic betterment. He was horrified and profoundly puzzled when the boy who was the leader of this group arose and said very seriously to the meeting, "I move that the whole club stand up for two minutes in honor of the four gunmen who died today." The motion was carried unanimously. Hopkins mentioned this discouraging incident in an article he wrote for the *Survey Graphic* and asked but did not attempt to answer the question: "What is responsible for the fact that thirty-five boys, all under sixteen, should wish to rise to their feet to pay homage to four men whose crimes their keen sense of right and wrong would naturally condemn under normal circumstances?"

Hopkins worked very hard then as always and had neither time nor money for exploration in the more enjoyable institutions of New York but he did find a way to get into the Metropolitan Opera House free by enlisting in the organized claques for such stars of the period as Enrico Caruso and Geraldine Farrar.

During his first winter in New York, Hopkins went to see Dr. John A. Kingsbury, a scholarly, humane and humorous man who was General Director of the Association for Improving the Condition of the Poor (A.I.C.P.), a powerful and well-supported charitable organization. Hopkins asked for a job that would pay slightly more than his present $5.00 a month. Kingsbury took a liking to the gangling, open-faced Iowa youth and, although he had no regular job to offer, put him on the payroll at $40 a month on a "training" basis, thus giving him a chance to learn something under expert guidance about social work and the conditions which made it necessary. Hopkins continued to live at Christadora House on Avenue B and work there during the day, and at night he went out on assignments for A.I.C.P. in the tougher districts, particularly along the waterfront, where it was considered unsafe for the women workers to venture after dark. When Hopkins had been at this interesting occupation for a few months, he went to Kingsbury and asked for a raise in pay. Kingsbury laughed and asked, "On what possible grounds would I be justified in giving you a raise?" In great embarrassment Hopkins confessed that he had fallen in love with Miss Ethel Gross, a co-worker at Christadora House, and they wanted to get married. Kingsbury was so impressed and amused by the sheer bravado of this that he agreed to increase Hopkins' allowance—it was not a wage or salary— to $60 a month, and the wedding took place. This marriage, which ended in divorce seventeen years later, was productive of three sons, David (named after Dad Hopkins), Robert (named after Robert Kerr), and Stephen (named after a possible ancestor who had been a signer of the Declaration of Independence). In the Second World War these sons served in the Navy, Army and Marine Corps, respectively. Stephen, the youngest, was killed in action when the Marines attacked Kwajalein Atoll in February, 1944.

In 1913-14, preceding the outbreak of the First World War, times were bad—they were always bad on the lower East Side, but now they were worse—and Kingsbury asked Hopkins to make a study of unemployment in the city. In those days if a man was out of work it was his own responsibility; it was probably his own fault and certainly his own tough luck. If he knew the right people, he could get some help at his local Tammany Club House. Or he could get food in a breadline and perhaps shelter in a flophouse and he could seek relief for his family from one of the numerous private charitable organizations which overlapped one another and competed with one another, often with bitter jealousy, for prestige and funds. However, there were distinct signs of change in the old, anachronistic order, and the spokesmen of change were such as Kingsbury, the great Lillian Wald, Henry Bruere and William H. Mathews. Hopkins' report on unemployment was one of the most searching that had ever been made and showed remarkable understanding for one only twenty-three years old and fresh from the Cornbelt where such conditions were unheard of. His period of apprenticeship ended and he was given a regular job with A.I.C.P.

He was put in charge of an emergency employment bureau which took care of—or, at least, did its best to care for—destitute transients in New York. There were many of these: some were hopeless derelicts who had drifted to the panhandler's paradise, but most were bewildered people who had come to the Big City full of hope and determination and the conviction that fabulous fortune awaited them expectantly around every corner (this was still the age of Horatio Alger). On rare occasions, Hopkins was able to guide them to jobs. The vast majority, however, could only be directed to a Salvation Army soup kitchen or a mission where floor space was available for sleeping. Hopkins advised many of the younger ones to swallow their pride and write to their families for the price of a ticket back to the home town, and doubtless some of them resented these words of wisdom from one who was himself so freshly out of Iowa. If they had doubts about his right to advise them, he was developing more doubts of his own; he was beginning to wonder what kind of country this really was which vaunted its lofty principles of freedom and equality and yet allowed such miserable conditions of injustice to persist.

When Mayor Mitchel took office in January, 1914, it seemed that the chance had come to do something about these conditions. The new Mayor appointed Kingsbury Commissioner of Public Charities. Within this Department was the Board of Child Welfare. On the recommendation of Kingsbury and Mathews, Chairman of this Board, Hopkins became its Executive Secretary at a salary of $3,000 a year, which must have seemed a fortune. This was Hopkins' first job in public service and his last until 1931.

The outbreak of war in Europe in August, 1914, caused worse unemployment conditions in New York and the progressive minds of the Mitchel reform Administration—a sort of intimation of the New Deal—began to experiment with new measures, among which were the first free employment agency and the institution of "made" work by the city government in connection with the municipal park system. Here then was the beginning of rehearsals for Hopkins in the spectacular role he was to play in support of Franklin D. Roosevelt twenty years later. He enjoyed this work greatly and was beginning to raise a family and to establish a new identity for himself as an up-and-coming New Yorker; but there was no future for him in the city Administration. Mitchel was a young man of considerable personal charm, courage and talent, but he demonstrated a gift for antagonizing all kinds of people. Tammany Hall, of course, hated him and so did William Randolph Hearst. His predilection for the companionship of High Society made him unpopular with the masses who charged there was "Too much Fifth Avenue, too little First Avenue." The Republicans, High Society included, considered him too radical. To make the opposition virtually unanimous, he incurred the wrath of Catholic and Protestant Churches by investigations of gross mismanagement in State charities which had ecclesiastical patronage. He was defeated for re-election by the Hearst protégé, John F. ("Red Mike") Hylan, after which he entered the Army Air Corps and was killed in an accident while training.

In the city elections of 1917, Hopkins was disgusted with both the Democratic and Republican parties, the latter having also rejected Mitchel, and he supported Morris Hillquit, the Socialist candidate—a fact which returned to plague him in later years when he came up before the United States Senate for approval as Secretary of Commerce. After the entry of the United States into the First World War in 1917, Hopkins attempted to enlist in the Army, Navy and Marine Corps, but was kept out by defective vision—a "detached retina" in his left eye. He finally joined the Red Cross and was sent to New Orleans to direct the Gulf Division. Later, he was promoted to direct all Red Cross activities in the Southeastern States with headquarters in Atlanta. In 1921 he returned to New York to look for a job and immediately got one through his old friend and benefactor, John Kingsbury, who had served with the Red Cross in France and then, after the war, had become Director of the Milbank Fund and therefore a highly influential figure in the whole field of organized charities in New York. This fund had been established by Albert G. Milbank, Chairman of the Borden (Milk) Company, largely for the promotion of public health, and Kingsbury set up a new division within the structure of A.I.C.P. for the study of health conditions throughout New York and the formulation of a program to meet them. Hopkins was offered and quickly accepted the post of Director of this division at a salary of $8,000. He remained there for three years. There was a certain amount of friction between him and Bailey B. Burritt, Director of A.I.C.P., because the Health Division was separately financed by the Milbank Fund and Hopkins felt he should be independent of Burritt's authority. He was one who always chafed at ordinary, orderly administrative procedure, which is one of the reasons why he found himself so completely at home in the unconventional Roosevelt scheme of things. Much of his experience at this time gave him valuable preparation for problems which he was to encounter later in Washington, for there was a distinct resemblance between the point of view of the welfare worker and that of the voluntary civil servant. Both were commercially unselfish, animated by public spirit and reconciled to careers uncomplicated by the profit motive. It was therefore not unnatural that both should strive to be paid off in the currency of increased authority and opportunity to extend influence. This ambition led to competitive struggle which inevitably produced endless jurisdictional disputes—and the border warfare between one charity organization and another was much the same as between one government agency and another.

Hopkins discovered that the study of health conditions in New York City presented many difficulties—indeed, that it was virtually impossible to do it thoroughly on a purely local basis. The shifting of population was too great. One could select any given section for a study of case histories in any given disease over a period of ten years, only to find that in this time most of the old cases had moved away to parts unknown and entirely new cases had moved in. This led Hopkins to think in larger and larger terms; he began to feel cramped by the city limits or even by the State lines. Moreover, he began now, under the influence of his wise friend, Kingsbury, to extend his intellectual explorations into the humanities in which he had previously taken little interest.

Both Kingsbury and his wife had a paternal feeling for Hopkins and this continued through the years and through various drastic changes in Hopkins' professional and domestic life until Mrs. Kingsbury ventured the opinion to her husband, "Maybe you'd have more influence with Harry if you stopped treating him as your own boy." But Kingsbury, even when he became Hopkins' assistant in W.P.A., could not detach the New Deal Administrator from the callow youth who had come into his office looking for a job. During the 1920's, the Hopkins family lived first in Yonkers and then in Scarborough because the Kingsburys lived there—and Kingsbury got them a cottage near his own summer place in Woodstock, New York. Kingsbury had a large library, from which Hopkins borrowed constantly, the while he attempted to build up a library of his own; on payday he would go out and spend a large part of his ready cash on books before starting to worry about the pressing needs of his growing family. He developed a passion for the life and works of John Keats, and would read Keats and Shelley and Amy Lowell on the commuter trains when all his neighbors were engrossed in the financial or sports pages. He also developed an improbable interest in fungi—this being a hobby of Kingsbury's—and the two men would spend hours on week ends tramping through woods with their children in quest of specimens, Kingsbury explaining to Hopkins, "This one is edible—but that one is deadly poison." Hopkins also played some tennis and bridge, at both of which he was fairly good, and some golf, at which he was not. When he took friends or relatives to dinner in New York he generally went to some expensive speakeasy and they were appalled at the insouciance with which he would pay a $20 check and $5 in tips as if he could afford it.

In 1924 he moved from A.I.C.P. to the Executive Directorship of the New York Tuberculosis Association with the agreement and endorsement of Burritt and Kingsbury. The President and moving spirit of the Association was Dr. James Alexander Miller, the distinguished specialist who had long been a national leader in the fight against tuberculosis. A careful, conservative man, Miller had managed to make the Association solvent and solid, with a surplus of some $90,000. Hopkins managed to convert this surplus eventually into a deficit of some $40,000, but at the end of his seven years with the Association, when he entered government service, the Directors adopted a statement including the following expressions of appreciation:

> During the period of his directorship, the Association has grown enormously. Largely due to Mr. Hopkins' efforts, the New York Heart Committee was amalgamated with the Tuberculosis Associa-

tion and the name of the Association was changed from the New York Tuberculosis Association to the New York Tuberculosis and Health Association. . . .

It was due to Mr. Hopkins' leadership that the Committee on Social Hygiene was organized and its work inaugurated. The work of the Heart Committee was enlarged, strengthened and placed upon a sound, scientific basis.

A closer affiliation was arranged with the Children's Welfare Federation which became a committee of the Association on all children's activities.

Through his efforts, contacts were made with the Department of Health and Hospitals and his influence brought about many minor changes in policy and improvements in methods of work in both of these departments. . . .

The Board of Directors of the New York Tuberculosis and Health Association hereby records its deep appreciation of the services rendered by Mr. Hopkins and extends to him an expression of its most hearty gratitude for all that he has done for the development of the Association, and heartfelt good wishes for the successful use of the federal relief funds and of the great opportunities for leadership in public relief throughout the United States.

Hopkins had greatly increased the Association's income—principally through the stimulation of the sale of Christmas seals—and he had also greatly increased its expenditures. Dr. Miller and his successor as President, Dr. Linsley R. Williams, were unable to devote much attention to the business affairs of the Association and Hopkins was consequently pretty much on his own, which was what he liked to be. He had visions of an expanding empire—his intense ambition, be it said, being animated not by greed but by incurable restlessness and discontentment. Tuberculosis would have seemed a big enough evil for any one organization to tackle, but Hopkins pushed the Association into new fields until it had absorbed the New York Heart Association, the Children's Welfare Federation, the Associated Out-Patient Clinic and the Allied Dental Clinic. He wrote an article for the *Nation's Health* (January, 1927) indicating that he contemplated adding cancer control and mental hygiene to the already numerous activities. He wanted to drop the word "Tuberculosis" from the Association name and have it the New York— and even ultimately the National—Health Association. One day, early in 1928, Dr. Haven Emerson, former Health Commissioner of New York, told Hopkins of having watched men drilling in the rocks under 42nd Street and said that it was outrageous that these men were being subjected to the dread occupational disease known as silicosis. Emerson felt that something should be done about it, so Hopkins immediately promised to do something. After Emerson had left him, he went to Dr. Jacob A. Goldberg, Secretary of the Tuberculosis Association, and asked, "Say, Jack—what *is* silicosis?" Hopkins thereupon organized and financed an exhaustive study of the subject under a committee which included Dr. Emerson, Goldberg and himself. The report of this committee, published in February, 1929, resulted in the development of an elaborate vacuum device to eliminate silica dust and this was used successfully in the work on Rockefeller Center and other excavations and tunneling in New York City since then. That is typical of the way in which Hopkins worked: he was never deterred from attacking a problem by total ignorance of it for he had an exceptional ability to cure his own ignorance and gain a "piercing understanding."

Dr. Goldberg has described Hopkins at this time: "You could mark him down as an ulcerous type. He was intense, seeming to be in a perpetual nervous ferment—a chain smoker and black coffee drinker. He was always careless in his appearance. Most of the time he would show up in the office looking as though he had spent the previous night sleeping in a hayloft. He would wear the same shirt three or four days at a time. He managed to shave almost every day—usually at the office. While other executives that have run the Association would say, 'We have this amount of money available—and this is how much we can spend,' Hopkins, by contrast, never worried about the cost until later, when the Association had been committed to the program, and then he would scramble around to get the money."

Dr. Miller has said, "Harry never had the faintest conception of the value of money. But then, that is true of most social workers I have known. Although in no sense personally dishonest, they can become unscrupulous in the handling of funds. They can convince themselves that the worthy end justified the means."

When, after the 1929 crash, Herbert Hoover's "chicken in every pot" was replaced by a discharge slip in every other pay envelope, Hopkins' friend, William Mathews of the A.I.C.P., was struggling with the problem of workless, homeless men and managed to obtain $75,000 from the Harvey Gibson Emergency Committee of the American Red Cross. Mathews, who had been one of the pioneers in work relief back in 1914, conferred with Hopkins as to the best way of administering this fund. Together with Dr. Goldberg, they made an arrangement with the Park Commission whereby jobs for unemployed men would be provided on park projects, the cost of the labor to be defrayed from Mathews' fund. Hopkins and Dr. and Mrs. Goldberg went to A.I.C.P. every evening after their day's work at the Tuberculosis Association and remained until late at night assigning jobs to applicants for work relief. There was no planning board for these assignments. No questions were asked—no investigations were conducted—there being no staff to conduct them. Any man who asked for a job was given one. "Some of the men," Goldberg has recalled, "came in to us carrying violin cases. We could see they were not fit for heavy work, so they were assigned to projects like sawing off dead limbs from trees, grading walks, leaf raking, etc." Leaf raking! That term appeared many more times in Hopkins' career.

Of course, the $75,000 ran out quickly but more funds were raised and the volunteer employment bureau continued its hand-to-mouth operations until the Governor of New York, Franklin D. Roosevelt, proclaimed unemployment relief to be a State responsibility. Hopkins was harshly criticized for these irregular activities by the established welfare agencies, which claimed it was "unprofessional conduct" to hand out work tickets without thorough investigation into the background of each applicant, his own or his family's financial resources and probably his religious affiliations. "Harry told the agencies to go to hell," said Goldberg.

Hopkins met Roosevelt for the first time during the campaign of 1928, when Alfred E. Smith was running for President and Roosevelt for Governor. Hopkins was impressed by this meeting, for he had been thrilled to hear the radio broadcast of Roosevelt's "Happy Warrior" nominating speech for Smith, who was then Hopkins' idol and for whom he campaigned ardently; but for Roosevelt the meeting with the sallow social worker was just another handshake. However, Hopkins was coming more and more to the attention of various of Roosevelt's friends and of Mrs. Roosevelt who was perpetually interested in welfare work.

To anyone with a mystical sense—and Hopkins, being his mother's son, had one which was strong though well concealed—that election of 1928 eventually gave cause for wonderment. It could have been attributed to all manner of occult forces—to the hand of God or to the grim resolution of fate or to the inexorable turning of the tides of history— or merely to an inexplicable freak of luck. But there was something strange and tremendous in the fact that, although Al Smith was badly beaten throughout the nation and lost his own New York by over a hundred thousand votes, Roosevelt carried the State by the exceedingly narrow margin of twenty-five thousand. There were thus a relative handful of people in New York who failed to vote the straight Republican ticket and thereby enabled Franklin Roosevelt to become a logical candidate for the Presidency in 1932 and to run again in 1936, 1940 and 1944 and to receive more than a hundred million votes from the American people in times of terrible crisis.

Roosevelt's narrow victory in 1928 was due partly to public recognition of his cheerful gallantry in fighting a fearful disease and partly to the fact that the people of New York approved of Al Smith's policies as Governor even though they did not wish to promote the author of them to the White House. There was no reason whatsoever to interpret the results as any indication that the formidable power of the Republican party was threatened. The Republicans had ruled the country for nearly seventy years except for two interludes produced by schisms within their own ranks and it seemed as Herbert Hoover assumed the Presidency that nothing less than economic calamity or another World War could upset the political balance of power within the foreseeable future. The American people could see not the slightest sign of either misfortune coming to pass, but less than a year had passed after Hoover's triumphant election before the boom burst, starting the creation of the enormous vacuum which was to be filled by the New Deal. On August 28, 1931, Governor Roosevelt made a speech to an extraordinary session of the State Legislature which sounded the very keynote of his social philosophy:

What is the State? It is the duly constituted representative of an organized society of human beings, created by them for their mutual protection and well-being. "The State" or "The Government" is but the machinery through which such mutual aid and protection are achieved. The cave man fought for existence unaided or even opposed by his fellow man, but today the humblest citizen of our State stands protected by all the power and strength of his Government. Our Government is not the master but the creature of the people. The duty of the State toward the citizens is the duty of the servant to its master. The people have created it; the people, by common consent, permit its continual existence.

One of these duties of the State is that of caring for those of its citizens who find themselves the victims of such adverse circumstance as makes them unable to obtain even the necessities for mere existence without the aid of others. That responsibility is recognized by every civilized Nation. . . .

To these unfortunate citizens aid must be extended by Government, not as a matter of charity, but as a matter of social duty.

I do not know what was the immediate effect of these words on Hopkins. He may have been inclined to dismiss them as mere pious rhetoric from a politician. But, syllable for syllable, they were to form the directive which guided him throughout the next seven years of extraordinary adventure.

As a first means of implementing these words, Roosevelt set up the Temporary Emergency Relief Administration in New York State. The headline writers referred to this as T.E.R.A. and thereby designated the first of the many "alphabetical agencies." Furthermore, in forming this new agency, Roosevelt was setting a precedent for himself which he was to follow again and again in the New Deal and in the organization of the national effort to meet the demands of the Second World War: he was devising a new agency to meet a new problem rather than relying on the established department or bureau (in this case, the State Department of Public Welfare).

As Chairman of the T.E.R.A., Roosevelt named his old friend, Jesse Isador Straus, president of the great department store, R. H. Macy & Co., and a distinguished philanthropist. Straus did not want the job but yielded to Roosevelt's incomparable blandishments; the Governor of New York was already a master in the art of giving a radical development a conservative mantle, not for the purpose of fooling the public but rather to persuade himself that it was a perfectly reasonable and moderate evolution. Straus, being a good businessman, wanted first to find a shrewd, competent executive to be his deputy. He sought the counsel of various leaders in welfare work, such as Henry Bruere, John Kingsbury and Homer Folks. They all agreed that William Hodson, of the Russell Sage Foundation, was the best possible selection and Straus offered him the job. Hodson consulted friends and colleagues and they advised him to refuse the invitation; many of them believed that Roosevelt's radical experiment in forming this new agency was doomed to failure and that Hodson would inevitably take the blame for it. Hodson thereupon suggested Harry Hopkins for the job and telephoned him to ask if he would take it. Hopkins instantly replied, "I would love it." So he started to work on the largest and most daring program for the relief of unemployment that had ever been undertaken by any State in the Union. After a year, Straus resigned and recommended that his efficient and energetic deputy be appointed Chairman, to which the Governor readily agreed. During his two years' service with T.E.R.A., Hopkins did his work in the manner that Roosevelt liked best: imaginatively, speedily, and giving the least possible amount of trouble to Roosevelt himself. Of course, in the latter part of 1931 and in 1932, Roosevelt was looking beyond New York State toward his own candidacy for the Democratic nomination and he and his principal political advisors, Louis MacHenry Howe, James A. Farley and Frank Walker, would have been concerned with Hopkins only if he had been a conspicuous failure and, therefore, an embarrassment.

In those uncertain days, when the return of prosperity was always "just around the corner," it was difficult for anyone to accept the fact that the emergency would eventually be measured in terms of years rather than months; so when Hopkins undertook the T.E.R.A. he continued his position with the Tuberculosis and Health Association, but as he worked he became less sure that the new job was merely "temporary." On September 8, 1932, he wrote to his brother, Lewis:

> For the past eight or ten months I have been trying to carry two jobs. The Governor asked me to be Chairman of the Temporary Emergency Relief Administration of New York State, which has al-

ready administered a fund of about $30,000,000, and if a bond issue
of another $30,000,000 passes on election day, we will have that to
administer too. We have now taken care of about a million people in
the State. The situation here is very bad, and in spite of the "polly-
annish" announcements that are coming out from Washington, and
the rise in the stock market, there is a steady decline in employment
and an increase in the number of those in need of relief.

I have no confidence whatever that the R.F.C. [the Reconstruction
Finance Corporation, established by President Herbert Hoover] will
help the situation much this winter, other than bolster up the railroads
and the banks. I very naturally am earnestly hoping that Roosevelt
will be elected. I think he would make a far better president than
Hoover—chiefly because he is not afraid of a new idea, and furthermore, is not identified with big business after the fashion of "the
great engineer." I am convinced that Roosevelt is not only fearless,
but a very able executive. All this business about his health is utter
nonsense. I have seen a great deal of him within the past few months,
and the amount of work that he can carry out is perfectly amazing.
To be sure, I don't believe that the election of either of them is going
to increase our respective salaries a bit.

That last statement proved to be a very good guess by Hopkins in so
far as he himself was concerned. Although his man, Roosevelt, was
elected, and Hopkins was thus catapulted into a position of world importance, he worked for the next twelve years at a salary lower than
that of 1932 and he was broke when he died; but he was empowered to
spend in those years of government service nine billion dollars for the
relief of others and to direct the expenditure of many billions more in
Lend Lease. This reference in this letter to Roosevelt's health was due
to the whispering campaign which had started even in 1928 to the effect
that Roosevelt's disease was not infantile paralysis but syphilis.

A month after Roosevelt's election to the Presidency, and with repeal
of prohibition apparently assured, Hopkins wrote again to his brother:

It seems to me that the principal idea of the public administrators
for the past several years has been to protect big business and I have
a great deal more confidence in the "hoi polloi" that are going into
office on the fourth of March than I ever had in Andy Mellon and his
crowd of highbinders. For my part I would abolish the whole federal
[prohibition] enforcement crowd as well as the local crowd, at once,
and not spend another dime on enforcing a law that could not be enforced for ten times that amount of money. The "noble experiment"
is on the way out.

I agree with you entirely on the fact that we are not going to get
nearly as much from taxes as some of the people think. For my part I
do not believe in a high tax on liquor, especially on beer, and as you indicate, if they try to tax it too much the bootleggers and those of us
who have learned how to make homemade gin will keep right at it.

I look to see some pretty drastic changes made in Washington after the fourth of March. Certainly the unemployment situation is no better, and I can see no earthly reason for an upturn of business. It is going to be quite impossible, in my judgment, to get these ten or twelve million men back to work unless we have a universal five-day week, and I am not too sure about it even then. I have no sympathy with the "share the work" movement that the big boys are advocating. Nor do I approve of the sales tax or other methods of taxation which have a horizontal base because that means that the people pay the taxes who can least afford it. I would shove the income taxes, inheritance, gift taxes, etc., higher than they now are. Certainly that should be done before we begin to tax every working man for each pair of shoes that he buys. . . .

When Hopkins wrote that, he was bursting with ambition to expand on a national scale. He could not bear to go back to the Tuberculosis and Health Association where he had already achieved about as much advancement as he could hope for. His experience with T.E.R.A. in New York State had given him a taste of and for public life and the service of millions of people and the expenditure of millions of dollars. I believe that when Jesse Straus was appointed Ambassador to France he asked Hopkins to go along with him as an aide, but Hopkins could not see himself in the role of a "cookie pusher" (a term that both he and Roosevelt later loved to use to describe routine diplomats). Hopkins wanted to get into the Roosevelt Administration. Particularly in the weeks following the Inauguration, when the New Deal was bursting out in a series of bewildering pyrotechnical explosions, he felt that he must be part of this historic show. When he finally got the call, more than two months after Roosevelt took office, he answered it with alacrity and with no qualms.

When Hopkins went to Washington he had broken sharply with his previous life. He had been divorced by his first wife and had married again. He was at odds with his old friends, even John Kingsbury, and was virtually estranged from his sister, Adah Aime, to whom he had been particularly close in childhood and who was the only member of his family living in the East. There can be little doubt that Hopkins was ashamed of himself and therefore on the defensive, for the home that he broke up involved not only his wife but their three small sons with no means of support other than his own uncertain earnings. I have had no intention of going into the intricacies of Hopkins' private, emotional life; for one thing, they appear far too complicated for me to cope with, and for another thing he had shaken them out of his system by the time he was called upon to take his place in the Second World War. But the developments of these final years before he entered public service cannot be glossed over without a word. As his old Professor, Dr. Edward A. Steiner, said in a letter to me, they were "not to his credit."

About 1927—I do not know the exact date—he fell in love with Barbara Duncan, an attractive, well-educated, well-bred girl who had come from her native Michigan to New York for training as a nurse at Bellevue Hospital. She developed tubercular symptoms and was given employment as a secretary at the Tuberculosis Association. Under the unhappy circumstances, it could hardly be called a glamorously romantic attachment which Hopkins had formed and both he and Miss Duncan attempted to resist it. He went to a psychoanalyst, Dr. Frankwood E. Williams, and started to read voluminously in the works of Freud, Jung and Adler. Both his sister, Mrs. Aime, and John Kingsbury have told me that, if he had been secretive about himself in his youth, he was the exact opposite now: he talked endlessly and boringly to his close friends about his personal troubles, trying to rationalize his behavior through exercises in self-psychoanalysis. In the summer of 1928, under the benevolent influence of Dr. Williams, Hopkins was firmly resolved that his home must not be destroyed and he and Miss Duncan agreed that their romance must develop no further. Kingsbury was going to Europe with a group to study social conditions and suggested that Hopkins go along as a member of the delegation which was financed by the Milbank Fund. This seemed a good opportunity for Hopkins to get away from all domestic problems and pull himself together and he accordingly went on his first trip to France and England. I am indebted to Mrs. Ethel Gross Hopkins for providing me with excerpts from letters that he wrote to her during that summer when he was struggling miserably to renew the bonds of their married life. He wrote from the Royal Palace Hotel in Kensington:

I have just had the most exalting experience. Having had a real English dinner with a delightful physician in his very English home, he took me for a tramp over Hampstead Heath—a great park on the outskirts of London. We were discussing the Mental Deficiency Act of England or some equally uplifting subject when we suddenly came on a lovely path upon which was a very impersonal sign which read "Keats Walk."

Upon enquiry it developed that here Keats walked with Fanny Brawne and over this very Hampstead Heath—Keats had roamed for hours and it is just the same now as then. Imagine my feeling! The doctor not knowing Keats could not share my enthusiasm but that didn't restrain mine for at last I was in Keats' country and every memory of the years I have known him (—how long has it been—I think it dates from the time I was ill in New Hospital about eight years ago—) swelled to my imagination and I saw his red head and proud step sauntering thru the green. It was as tho I could reach out and touch him—quite like a dream. But it was not—for not two blocks away was his home where he lived for three years and where the *Ode to the Nightingale* was written and other heavenly music. I saw his very house—and his garden that he sat in for hours on end. It is now state property and of course was closed but it is open during the day and I am going back soon. . . .

I know you will be glad to hear of this and are the only one that will fully understand what this incident is to me. That it was quite accidental made it all the more delightful. I fairly walk on air and wanted you to know. . . .

Following are more comments that he wrote at that time from London which he was to visit again in the terror of the Blitz:

Today I spent in the heart of London's East End—the poorest dock workers—miserable poverty—dirty rotten slums but magnificent school health work under the direction of skilled and devoted doctors and nurses. It was thrilling. We are amateurs indeed! I am spending the week looking at the school work, the administration of which is complicated and extensive.

Next week the T.B. health service and then the district health service—it would take six months instead of weeks to do this adequately. I am being royally received and the whole works is open.

I had dinner with Harry Day last night at his very sporty club— a heavenly swim first. We sat on the veranda talking over a stein of beer and cigarettes and then for a long walk through Hyde Park where dozens of speakers harangued a friendly and intelligent crowd. . . .

I have had no time for sight-seeing and am going to put that off until I learn the town better. . . .

London is big, old and stolid and no stranger can ever get on the inside. . . .

I had an interesting day at East Stepney a poverty borough of London. I saw the finest school work I ever hope to see—was entertained at lunch by the social workers of the neighborhood—visited some miserable tenements and arrived here thoroughly tired out. . . .

I finished the school work Friday and am beginning on the T.B. stuff tomorrow. Sight-seeing is no fun alone and apart from visiting all of Keats' haunts I shall not do much. . . .

I am going to try to do some writing this summer and will let you know later how that works out. My job is altogether interesting and I am seeing and learning many things. . . . I tramped all over London today. . . .

Hopkins at this time wrote fragments of poetry. Here is one:

> See the snow—see it
> Come on and see
> White like my bed.
> The snow is a white bed
> Sleep in its coolness
> Crawl under its clean covers and sleep.

Best sleep under the still white snow.
Than go to sleep standing up.
See the snow—see it
Come on and see
White like my bed.

Here is another, an expression of his persistent love for his homeland
and of his attitude toward the money changers:

In long straight rows the corn's laid by in hot June days.
Almost tenderly Iowa's corn is nourished
Its yellow mellowness is soft—its yellowness is precious
Iowa tends its corn like a slick banker watches a ticker tape
Too wet—too dry—early frost—late frost.
An Iowa farmer always looks in the dark.

The psychoanalytic experiment did not work. Hopkins never succeeded in reassembling the pieces of his shattered marriage. Two years
later his wife divorced him and he and Barbara Duncan were married.
One daughter, Diana, was born in 1932 of this marriage, which was a
brief but very happy one. The second Mrs. Hopkins died of cancer
in 1937.

CHAPTER III

The Relief Program

ADOLF HITLER became Chancellor of Germany on January 30, 1933, and some Americans who had read *Mein Kampf* and had taken seriously its implications were frightened as they tried to peer into the heavily clouded future. It was not that there was any immediate prospect of war, for Germany still seemed to be prostrate militarily and faith in the precautionary measures of the Treaty of Versailles still persisted. Far more immediate as a threat was the deeply disquieting suspicion that *it could happen here*. The dragon's teeth of Fascism and Communism were being sown throughout the world and in that winter of closing banks, of "scrip" currency and interminable breadlines, it was all too possible to fear that these destructive seeds might take root in American soil. The people as a whole knew very little of the true character of the new man who was coming into the White House on March 4. What if he should prove to be another Man on Horseback? Under the existing circumstances, it might not have been difficult for him to seize dictatorial power.

The American people were literally starved for leadership. Herbert Hoover, who had appeared to possess exceptional qualifications for the Presidency, had failed lamentably under the stress of major emergency. Although he had been honored as "a Great Humanitarian," his performance as President of a depressed nation was that of one who was pathetically inept in the exercise of common, human understanding. He first coldly assured the people that the depression was an illusion which it was their patriotic duty to ignore; then, when economic collapse occurred in Europe, he angrily denounced the depression as something un-American from which we should isolate and insulate ourselves; and, finally, he truculently scolded the people for blaming the depression on his own Republican party which had taken full credit for the preceding boom. (As a noble Republican, Dwight Morrow, said at the time, "Those who took credit for the rainfall should not complain when they are blamed for the drought.") The unfortunate fact was that Herbert Hoover was, in a word—and the word was applied by that sage Hoosier, George Ade—"clammy." Under his hapless Administration the prestige of the Presidency had dropped to an alarmingly low level and so had popular faith in our whole constitutional system and particularly in what Hoover himself stoutly maintained to be "the American way of life." The temper of the people was fearful and bitterly resentful and ominous.

There is a persistent theory held by those who prate most steadily about "the American way of life" that the average American is a rugged individualist to whom the whole conception of "leadership" is something foreign and distasteful—and this theory would certainly seem to be in accord with our national tradition of lawlessness and disrespect for authority. But it is not entirely consistent with the facts. We Americans are inveterate hero worshipers, to a far greater extent than are the British or the French. We like to personalize our loyalties, our causes. In our political or business or labor organizations, we are comforted by the knowledge that at the top is a Big Boss whom we are free to revere or to hate and upon whom we can depend for quick decisions when the going gets tough. The same is true of our Boy Scout troops and our criminal gangs. It is most conspicuously true of our passion for competitive sport. We are trained from childhood to look to the coach for authority in emergencies. The masterminding coach who can send in substitutes with instructions whenever he feels like it—or even send in an entirely new team—is a purely American phenomenon. In British football the team must play through the game with the same eleven men with which it started and with no orders from the sidelines; if a man is injured and forced to leave the field the team goes on playing with only ten men. In British sport, there are no Knute Rocknes or Connie Macks, whereas in American sport the mastermind is considered as an essential in the relentless pursuit of superiority.

In times of peace and prosperity, it is true, when the American people feel they are doing all right for themselves, they do not give much thought to the character of the man in the White House; they are satisfied to have a President who merely "fits into the picture frame," as Warren G. Harding did, and who will eventually look sufficiently austere on the less frequently used postage stamps. But when adversity sets in and problems become too big for individual solution then the average citizen becomes conscious of the old "team spirit" and he starts looking anxiously toward the sidelines for instructions from the coach. That is when the President of the United States must step out of the picture frame and assert himself as a vital, human need. American faith in the recurrence of that miracle is unlimited. There is deep rooted in our consciousness the conviction that a great President will appear "whenever we really need him," and in the years 1929-33 the question was being asked, constantly and apprehensively, "Where is he *now*?"

No cosmic dramatist could possibly devise a better entrance for a new President—or a new Dictator, or a new Messiah—than that accorded to Franklin Delano Roosevelt. The eternally ironic fact is that the stage was so gloriously set for him not by his own friends and supporters, who were then relatively obscure people, but by those who were to become his bitterest enemies. Herbert Hoover was, in the parlance of vaudeville, "a good act to follow." Roosevelt rode in on a wheel chair instead of a white horse, but the roll of drums and the thunderclaps which attended him were positively Wagnerian as emotional stimuli and also as ugly warnings of what might happen to American democracy if the new President should turn out to possess any of the qualities of a Hitler or even of a Huey Long. The people did not have to wait long for him to reveal himself, clearly and irrevocably. As the occasion of his entrance was tremendous, so was the manner of his rising to it. Harry Hopkins, who was to participate in the preparation of so many of the President's later speeches, wrote after Roosevelt's death, "For myself I think his first inaugural address was the best speech he ever made." It was certainly most thoroughly representative of the character of the man himself. In something under two thousand words he made it abundantly clear that there was going to be action on a wide variety of fronts— "and action now." The most famous phrase, and deservedly so, was "the only thing we have to fear is fear itself"—and one thinks of these words over and over again when considering Roosevelt's career and the wellsprings of his philosophy. But there were other memorable words which gained weight as they gained implementation:

The money changers have fled from their high seats in the temple of our civilization. We may now restore that temple to the ancient truths. . . .

There will be an end to speculation with other people's money. . . .

I favor as a practical policy the putting of first things first. . . .

Our greatest primary task is to put people to work. . . .

In every dark hour of our national life a leadership of frankness and vigor has met with that understanding and support of the people themselves which is essential to victory. . . .

We do not distrust the future of essential democracy. The people of the United States have not failed. . . .

In the event that the national emergency is still critical . . . I shall ask the Congress for the one remaining instrument to meet the crisis —broad Executive power to wage a war against the emergency, as great as the power that would be given to me if we were in fact invaded by a foreign foe. . . .

In the field of world policy I would dedicate this nation to the policy of the good neighbor. . . .

Our Constitution is so simple and practical that it is possible always to meet extraordinary needs by changes in emphasis and arrangement without loss of essential form. . . .

The last quotation in particular became recognized—and with acute pain in the more conservative and, later, isolationist circles—as expressive of the very core of Roosevelt's political doctrine. No President since Lincoln had tested the elasticity of the Constitution as he did—but I do not think that Roosevelt equaled Lincoln's record in circumventing the Constitution nor did he ever declare, as did William H. Seward, "There is a higher law than the Constitution which regulates our authority." Roosevelt never saw the need for a higher temporal law; he considered the Constitution broad enough to cover all foreseeable eventualities.

The records of Roosevelt's early career indicate an inclination toward Jeffersonian principles of democratic decentralization of power as opposed to the Hamiltonian concept of concentration of power in the Federal Government—and especially to John Jay's dictum that, "This country should be governed by the people who own it." Roosevelt's experience in elective office had all been on the State level. As President, he sometimes irritated his progressive advisers by his tendency to resolve every problem in terms of the exceptional circumstances of Hyde Park Township in the venerable Hudson River Valley, and yet he had been profoundly influenced by the belligerent progressivism of his cousin, Theodore Roosevelt. While F.D.R. was serving his first term in the New York State Senate, in 1910, T.R. gave a speech at Osawatomie, Kansas —the battleground of John Brown. In the crowd that day were many Civil War veterans and T.R. addressed himself primarily to them, emphasizing their struggle to establish human rights above property rights and to do so within the framework of a united nation. Because that Osawatomie speech was of such great importance in shaping the structure of the New Deal, I venture to quote from it at some length:

I stand for the square deal. But when I say I am for the square deal, I mean not merely that I stand for fair play under the present rules of the game, but that I stand for having those rules changed so as to work for a more substantial equality of opportunity and of reward for equally good service. . . .

The true conservative is the one who insists that property shall be the servant and not the master of the commonwealth; who insists that the creature of man's making shall be the servant and not the master of the man who made it. The citizens of the United States must effectively control the mighty commercial forces which they have themselves called into being. . . .

The absence of effective State, and especially national, restraint upon unfair money getting has tended to create a small class of enormously wealthy and economically powerful men whose chief object is to hold and increase their power. The prime need is to change the conditions which enable these men to accumulate power which it is not for the general welfare that they should hold or exercise. We grudge no man a fortune which represents his own power and sagacity when exercised with entire regard to the welfare of his fellows. . . . We grudge no man a fortune in civil life if it is honorably obtained and well used. It is not enough that it should have been gained without doing damage to the country. We should permit it to be gained only so long as the gaining represents benefits to the community. This, I know, implies a policy of far more active government interference with social and economic conditions in this country than we have yet had, but I think we have got to face the fact that such an increase in governmental control is now necessary. . . .

The National Government belongs to the whole American people, and where the whole American people are interested, that interest can be guarded only by the National Government. The betterment which we seek must be accomplished, I believe, mainly through the National Government. The American people are right in demanding that New Nationalism without which we cannot cope with new problems. The New Nationalism puts national need before sectional or personal advantage. It is impatient of the utter confusion that results from local legislatures attempting to treat national issues as local issues. It is still more impatient of the impotence which springs from over-division of governmental powers, the impotence which makes it possible for local selfishness or legal cunning, hired by wealthy special interest, to bring national activities to a deadlock. This New Nationalism regards the executive power as the steward of the public welfare. It demands of the judiciary that it shall be interested primarily in human welfare rather than in property, just as it demands that the representative body shall represent all the people rather than any one class or section of the people. I believe in shaping the ends of government to protect property as well as human welfare. Normally, and in the long run, the ends are the same; but whenever the alternative must be faced, I am for men and not for property, as you were in the Civil War.

Theodore Roosevelt died before his fifth cousin achieved any degree of prominence on the national scene and, during the years of the New Deal, the "Oyster Bay Roosevelts" were implacably opposed to the Hyde Park "maverick." However, the words of the great and gallant T.R. and the actions of F.D.R. were curiously in harmony with one another.

Eight days after the spectacular inauguration of the New Deal—eight days during which all the banks in the country had been closed—Franklin Roosevelt gave his first Fireside Chat. "It has been wonderful to me to catch the note of confidence from all over the country. . . . Confidence and courage are the essentials of success in carrying out our plan . . . Together we cannot fail." Here was the first real demonstration of Roosevelt's superb ability to use the first person plural and bring the people right into the White House with him. The very fact of a "chat" was in itself surprising and immeasurably stimulating: traditionally, when a President spoke to the people, it was an "Address," which might be intended as an exhortation, or an elaborate apologia, or a stern lecture. But Roosevelt spoke simply, casually, as a friend or relative, who had figured out a way to prevent foreclosure of the mortgage, and those of us who heard that speech will never forget the surge of confidence that his buoyant spirit evoked. It was all the more thrilling after the hair-shirted carping and petulance that we had been hearing from Hoover. During the three days following this Fireside Chat, 4,507 national banks and 567 state member banks reopened and Roosevelt sent a Message to the Congress asking for modification of the Volstead Act to permit the manufacture and sale of beer, thus writing the beginning of the end of fourteen years of prohibition and attendant crime. This long-overdue reform was tossed in as a sort of bonus and it was hailed joyfully by the people as proof that the new Administration was not only progressive and dynamic but also essentially cheerful. Happy days were here again! More than eleven years later, when Roosevelt was running for President for the fourth time, he evoked roars of agreement from a crowd in Fenway Park in Boston when he said:

> If there ever was a time in which the spiritual strength of our people was put to the test, that time was in the terrible depression of 1929 to 1933.
> Then our people might have turned to alien ideologies—like communism or fascism.
> But—our democratic faith was too sturdy. What the American people demanded in 1933 was not less democracy—but more democracy—and that is what they got.

The difference of opinion (to use the mildest of expressions) that existed between Roosevelt and his domestic foes was based on the definition of that word "democracy." Indeed, they came to hate the word so vehemently that they claimed it had never been applied to our form of government until Woodrow Wilson dreamed it up. They said that our government, as conceived and established by the Founding Fathers, was a *republic*, not a *democracy*, but they were reluctant to explain just what was the difference; they didn't dare. (It might be noted in this connection that, in his first Message to Congress, more than two years before he spoke at Gettysburg, Abraham Lincoln defined the United States as "a constitutional republic or democracy—a government of the people by the same people.") The political attacks on Roosevelt and the New Deal always resolved themselves into a plea, "Let us get back to the Constitution," but Roosevelt successfully persuaded a majority of the people that what this really meant was, "Let us get back to special privilege," or "Let us get back into the temple from which That Man ejected us."

In *The Roosevelt Revolution,* the authoritative Ernest K. Lindley covered the first six months of the New Deal and it is interesting to note that in this book he considered Hopkins as worth no more than a paragraph of mention as among those present in Washington. The conspicuous figures of that first year of the New Deal were Raymond Moley, Rexford G. Tugwell and Adolf Berle, of the "Brains Trust"; Louis MacHenry Howe, Roosevelt's close friend and most intimate adviser; Henry Morgenthau, Jr., another old friend who was at first Governor of the Farm Credit Administration; Lewis Douglas, Director of the Budget; Hugh S. Johnson, of N.R.A.; and, in the Cabinet, William H. Woodin, Harold L. Ickes, Frances Perkins and Henry Wallace. However, well within Roosevelt's first term, Hopkins came to be regarded as the Chief Apostle of the New Deal and the most cordially hated by its enemies. I think it may fairly be said that he earned this distinction. He was brought into the government on May 22 when seventy-nine of Roosevelt's "First Hundred Days" had already passed. He was made Federal Emergency Relief Administrator and it is my understanding that, as in the case of his Albany appointment two years previously, he was not the first choice for the job. Roosevelt later wrote of him:

> The task he faced was stupendous. Little was known at Washington about the efficiency of the various State and local relief organizations throughout the country. There were no such organizations in some of the States and in many of the counties. There were no immediately available reliable statistics either about relief needs or relief expenditures.
>
> Action had to be immediate. It was immediate. The day after he [Hopkins] took office he telegraphed his first communication to the Governors of the respective States; and before nightfall he had made grants of money to Colorado, Illinois, Iowa, Michigan, Mississippi, Ohio and Texas.
>
> From the very beginning two important points of policy were evident: (1) The operations of the program, aside from certain basic standards and stipulations, were to be decentralized and local in character, and (2) work, rather than idleness on a dole, was preferred.
>
> The original grant of money, in accordance with the statute, was on the basis of $1.00 of Federal funds for every $3.00 of local, State and Federal funds spent during the preceding quarter year. The statute also provided that part of the fund could be used in states without such matching where the amount available by matching would be insufficient to meet the needs for relief in any State.

The day after Hopkins went to work for the Federal Government the *Washington Post* printed a somewhat mournful headline, "Money Flies," and stated, "The half-billion dollars for direct relief of States won't last a month if Harry L. Hopkins, new relief administrator, maintains the pace he set yesterday in disbursing more than $5,000,000 during his first two hours in office."

Hopkins was off. He sat down at his desk and started flashing out telegrams even before the men had arrived to move the desk out of the hallway into his office. He said, "I'm not going to last six months here, so I'll do as I please." He had been told by Roosevelt that his job was to get relief to people who needed it and to have no truck with politicians. Of course, the Relief Program offered more juicy plums in the way of political patronage than had ever before been known in peacetime. But at first, while Hopkins was still an amateur in Washington politics, he was scornful of these sordid considerations. In the early days of the New Deal he worked, as he was to work later in war, with regard for nothing but the interests of the American people and of Franklin D. Roosevelt, which to him meant one and the same thing. In appointing men and women to positions of authority he was concerned only with consideration of their competence and zeal; he did not give a damn whether they were Methodists, Baptists, Catholics or Jews—and he was specifically instructed by the President never to "ask whether a person needing relief is a Republican, Democrat, Socialist or anything else." Hopkins said, "I don't like it when people finagle around the back door." He thus soon found himself involved in controversy with James A. Farley and with various members of Congress and State Governors whose duty it was to look out for the interests of "deserving Democrats." Confident of Roosevelt's support, Hopkins continued for a long time on the principle that relief was entirely nonpartisan. For that was a period of soaring altruism. In the first, triumphant sweep of the New Deal, it was possible to afford the luxury of being nonpolitical—but Hopkins learned better (or perhaps one should say "worse") later on when the opposition began to recover its dissipated strength and elections became less easy to win.

There had been a pretense of a relief program before F.E.R.A. Confronted with the obvious, overwhelming need for some kind of Federal Government aid for the idle and hungry victims of economic collapse, Hoover had found himself in one of the many impossible dilemmas that beset him: the "dole" system was naturally repugnant to him, but the only logical alternative appeared to be a form of government subsidy of public works projects which smacked of State Socialism. Since the dole was traditional, and had been since the institution of the "Old Poor Law" in the reign of Queen Elizabeth, Hoover favored that, however much he hated it, simply because it was traditional. Thus, American citizens who had so recently been given the assurance of two cars in every garage and a chicken in every pot were now given basically the same kind of treatment that was accorded to paupers in sixteenth-century England. Hoover tried to meet this problem, as he tried to meet so many others, by appointing commissions to "study" it. (His principal committee was headed by Walter S. Gifford, of the American Telephone and Telegraph Company.) But this was an emergency which demanded action first and study later. Finally, in the summer of 1932, with an election imminent, Hoover supported legislation which provided for loans, at three per cent interest, of $200 millions from the Reconstruction Finance Corporation to the various States for relief—the Federal Government to assume responsibility for the bookkeeping but not for the actual application of these funds. This was known as the Emergency Relief and Construction Act and it provided a nuclear regional organization which Hopkins took over when he started work; but it provided him with no funds, for the money had run out when he started to minister to the needs of some seventeen million people who were subsisting on the relief rolls. Under the new dispensation of F.E.R.A., the funds appropriated—$500 millions—were in the form of outright grants rather than loans to the States; but, otherwise, there was no essential departure from the principle of the dole. The main burden of cost and of administration was still on the local authorities to whom the needy must go, cap in hand, to accept charity. This is precisely where Hopkins came in and produced a profound change in the whole conception of governmental responsibility and function.

Hopkins inherited from the previous relief organization several key men who were predominantly social workers, like himself, trained to think that local problems should be handled with funds locally raised and administered by local and, to the greatest possible extent, *private* charitable organizations. In other words, the fact of Federal relief must be disguised in all possible ways. This was in deference to the creed that private enterprise must always provide the cure for any and every ill and that anyone who said that it might be unable to do so was a declared enemy of the American way of life. But Roosevelt as Governor had proclaimed the principle of State responsibility to "the humblest citizen" and Hopkins took those words literally. This was the great tenet of the New Deal, which became the number one item in Roosevelt's Economic Bill of Rights of eleven years later: the right to work.

One of the first men that Hopkins brought into F.E.R.A. to advise him was Frank Bane, whom he had met in the First World War when he was working for the Red Cross in the South. In 1931 Bane had organized the American Public Welfare Association and had consulted with Roosevelt and Hopkins on relief problems in New York State and with the Gifford Committee on the problems in the nation as a whole. The Gifford Committee was interested in developing the activities of private charitable agencies, whereas Bane insisted that all levels of government—Federal, State and community—should be directly and openly responsible for the administration of public relief. The Bane slogan was, "Public funds expended by public agencies," which did not find favor under the Hoover Administration but was right in line with Hopkins' thinking.

Bane agreed to work for Hopkins without pay on a temporary basis. He named, as his permanent successor, another social worker, Aubrey Williams, of Alabama, whom Hopkins did not then know but who was to become one of his ablest, most loyal and most smeared aides in the whole New Deal achievement. Williams had been a field representative of the American Public Welfare Association, of which Bane was Director. The long-scorned social workers were coming into their own as figures of national importance.

On June 17—three and a half weeks after he had entered government service—Hopkins went to Detroit to speak at the National Conference of Social Work. Bane and Williams were already there when he arrived. They begged him to take a stand in favor of direct Federal relief—as opposed to relief administered through private agencies. He was in grave doubt as to the practicability of this; but it was the way his natural inclinations tended, and he followed his natural inclinations. He spoke out in favor of relief as an obligation of the Federal Government to the citizens—without any pretense of private agencies interposed—thereby putting into effect the Roosevelt doctrine that this relief was a sacred right rather than an act of charity, an obligation of government to its citizens rather than a mere emergency alleviation of suffering in the form of alms. Hopkins' Detroit speech was given scant notice in the press and such attention as it received overlooked utterly its main import. I do not know if Roosevelt himself or any of his then advisers knew at the time just what it was that Hopkins had said; but the principle had been stated, and it was followed religiously in the administration of F.E.R.A., and Roosevelt supported it and came to admire Hopkins and to give him more and more opportunities to exert his influence in the official family.

There were two other important principles that Hopkins advocated successfully in the beginnings of F.E.R.A. One was the payment of cash instead of grocery slips to those on relief rolls. The other, considered revolutionary and wildly impractical by the more conservative social workers, was the extension of relief to the provision not only of food but of clothing, shelter and medical care to the needy. These principles have continued and have affected the whole concept of social work, particularly in the field of public health.

It may be interposed at this point that I have often wondered about the accuracy of the famous statement, attributed to Thomas Corcoran, that "we planned it that way." Roosevelt had contemplated, in broad outline, the Tennessee Valley power project, the Agricultural Adjustment, Conservation and Public Works programs, the Securities and

Exchanges Control and something like the National Industrial Recovery Act, more than a year before he became President, and they were all quickly put into effect. But the vast Relief Program, as Hopkins administered it, certainly did not work out according to any plan. It was a series of remarkable improvisations impelled by the character of the myriad problems that were discovered from day to day. By enforced research and a great deal of shrewd guesswork Hopkins found out what was really going on in the country as a whole and brought the facts home to Roosevelt. He personalized the problems for the President, and also most importantly for Mrs. Roosevelt who made the concerns of helpless individuals her own. Any appraisal of the Roosevelt Administration must begin with the fact that the government in Washington in the years following 1933 achieved an incomparable knowledge of the aspirations and the fears and the needs of the American people and that knowledge became of supreme importance when those same people had to be called upon for unprecedented efforts in the waging of the Second World War. The research needed to get the program started was multiplied by the various, extensive research projects carried out subsequently under the program itself.

Although Hopkins will never be celebrated as a "sound money" man or a champion of the sanctity of the taxpayer's dollar, he was exceptionally economy minded in one respect: he liked to run his own organization on the smallest possible budget. Unlike most bureaucrats, he hated to have a lot of civil servants around. What he wanted and what he obtained was a small staff composed of people of such passionate zeal that they would work killing hours. At the end of the first year Hopkins' relief organization had handled on its rolls the vital problems of some seventeen million people and had spent a billion and a half dollars, but the organization itself consisted of only 121 people with a total payroll of only $22,000 a month. To anyone in any way familiar with the normal workings of government, the lowness of those figures is well nigh incredible. But Hopkins managed to obtain people to whom a sixty-hour work week would be a holiday. Hopkins' own salary was under $8,000 as opposed to $15,000 he had earned before entering the government. He and his wife and baby lived for a considerable time on $250 a month, the remainder of his salary going for the support of the three sons by his first marriage. He told a reporter, "I'd like to be able to forget this $500,-000,000 business long enough to make some money for clothes and food. Mrs. Hopkins is yelling for a winter coat. I don't blame her." Hopkins was by no means frugal in his personal tastes. He would like to have had a great deal of money and if he had he would have spent it lavishly, but he never did have it to the end of his days. Now and then he would supplement his income by writing a magazine article and would feel very flush for a while. In 1944, in his last year in government service, his salary was raised to $15,000; so he ended up just where he had been before he started.

In his perpetual haste, Hopkins was contemptuous of bureaucratic procedure. When inspectors from the Bureau of the Budget came around asking to see the "organizational chart" they were told there wasn't any, as Hopkins would not permit one to be made. He said, "I don't want anybody around here to waste any time drawing boxes. You'll always find that the person who drew the chart has his own name in the middle box." He was also contemptuous of the formality—or "dignity"—with which a high government official feels it necessary to surround himself: the wainscoted office with thick carpets and two flags on standards behind the huge mahogany desk. Hopkins owned no morning coat and striped pants, but he rented this diplomatic uniform for the visit of King George VI and Queen Elizabeth to Washington in later years when he was a member of the Cabinet.

There was a kind of fanaticism in Hopkins' drive toward the objectives that he had to a large extent established for himself. This fanaticism was communicated to his co-workers who felt that they were fighting a holy war against want. But—lest this analogy be misinterpreted—it is necessary to add that no fighter in this war who served under Hopkins was compelled to wear the sackcloth uniform of asceticism. Despite the rigid Methodism of Hopkins' early training, many of his most important staff conferences during the New Deal years were held in automobiles en route to or returning from the Maryland racetracks around Washington. The organization which became W.P.A. was first outlined by Hopkins in a suite in the aristocratic Hotel St. Regis in New York. As Joseph E. Davies has said of Hopkins, "He had the purity of St. Francis of Assisi combined with the sharp shrewdness of a race track tout."

Hopkins, in his first few months in office, sloughed off some of the tradition-bound social workers whom he had inherited from the previous, halfhearted regime and brought in men and women who agreed with his own unrestricted conception of governmental responsibilities. This did not mean that his staff was composed of yes men and yes women; they were on the contrary tireless and inveterate needlers, as he was, who would not hesitate to prod and goad anyone, including their own boss, who seemed at any instant to show signs of slacking on the job. Hopkins always thrived in an atmosphere of protest.

Years later, when I came to know Hopkins, I was given a demonstration of the exasperating way in which he stimulated those who worked with him. It was the summer of 1940 and I was engaged in frenzied work for the William Allen White Committee to promote aid to Britain. I encountered Hopkins on a Sunday on Long Island when he was staying at Mrs. Harvey Cushing's house and he drew me aside to ask, "What are you warmongers up to now?" I assumed he was using that noun face-tiously, and I told him that we were working on a campaign to transfer fifty American over-age destroyers to the British Navy.

Hopkins assumed a look of disgust. "You mean you're going to come right out publicly and ask the President to give fifty of our fighting ships to a belligerent?"

I said these destroyers were of no immediate use to us, they were lying idle and had been for years.

"But," he asked, "don't you realize that a public demand like that would be a big embarrassment to the President—especially now, with an election coming up?"

I said that some of us were working privately to get Wendell Willkie's agreement to the proposal which was in line with Roosevelt's whole policy.

Hopkins snapped at me, "What do *you* know about the President's policy? Don't you know that this country is neutral?"

I was getting angrier by the minute and also depressed at the thought that this man, so close to Roosevelt, was revealing himself as a narrow-minded isolationist. I expressed this thought.

"The whole country's isolationist," said Hopkins, "except for a few pro-British fanatics like you. How do you imagine that the President could possibly justify himself with the people if he gave up fifty of our destroyers?"

I answered this with a tirade of much more vehemence and eloquence than I can usually summon. I said that the people were a lot less neutral than Hopkins seemed to think—that they hated Nazism—that if Roosevelt would speak to them with his own great courage and clarity they would support him, etc., etc. When I had concluded my impassioned oration, Hopkins grinned and said, "All right then—why do you waste your breath shouting all this at *me*? Why don't you get out and say these things to the people?" He had just wanted to find out if I had any real arguments to support my emotional bias.

The direct result of this interview was that Hopkins brought me into the White House to work with Sam Rosenman and himself in helping President Roosevelt to prepare his next speech.

Hopkins pulled that same goading tactic on a great many people to find out just how sound their arguments were and how sincere was their advocacy of them; but one could never be entirely sure if it were a trick for sometimes this was his method of telling an overzealous proponent to pipe down.

In October, 1933, Hopkins knew that with winter coming on the unemployment problem was bound to become more desperate and he believed that the only decent solution was a huge work program. Aubrey Williams and other aides were urging him to propose such a program to the President but Hopkins felt sure that it would be turned down. He knew that Roosevelt would be under fire on this not only from the conservatives: organized labor was strongly opposed to a program of governmentally "made" jobs. This was one of the times when Hopkins was impatient and irascible with those who were prodding him to do the very thing that he himself most wanted to do.

On Saturday, October 28, Hopkins arrived in Chicago to have lunch with Robert Hutchins, President of the University of Chicago, and to attend a football game. He was met at the station by Frank Bane and Louis Brownlow, Director of the Public Administration Clearing House, who had been talking to Williams about the work program and who now joined in hammering at Hopkins to bring it to the President. Both men, experts in public administration, were able to give Hopkins an abundance of facts and figures and he was able to absorb them; but he still did not know how to sell the idea to Roosevelt who was concerned about the attitude of organized labor. He went from Chicago to Kansas City to make a speech; among the people with whom he conferred on relief problems while there was the Federal Unemployment Director for Missouri, Judge Harry S. Truman. Williams reached Hopkins in Kansas City by telephone to announce that he had just seen Dr. John R. Commons in Madison, Wisconsin. Dr. Commons was one of the country's greatest authorities on all matters pertaining to labor and, when he heard what was on Williams' mind, he dug into his voluminous files and came up with a clipping dating from 1898 of a statement by Samuel Gompers in which the father of American organized labor advocated precisely the form of work program then suggested. Gompers called it "The Day Labor Plan." That was just what Hopkins had hoped for. It was his convenient conviction that a precedent can almost always be found for a new idea, however revolutionary it may seem, if you really search for it; the precedent for Lend Lease was found in an unimportant law passed by Congress in 1892, during the Benjamin Harrison Administration. Thus, when Hopkins learned what Gompers had said, he knew he had the persuasive argument that Roosevelt needed to overcome the labor leaders' objections to the work relief program. He telephoned to the White House and was given an appointment for lunch on the day of his return to Washington.

During that lunch, Roosevelt asked how many jobs would have to be provided and Hopkins said about four million.

"Let's see," said Roosevelt, "Four million people—that means roughly four hundred million dollars." He thought this could be provided from the Public Works fund which was under the guardianship of Harold Ickes, who was neither then nor subsequently extravagant in his admiration for Harry Hopkins or for his methods. When Hopkins left the White House after this lunch he "fairly walked on air," as he had when he saw the house in which Keats wrote "Ode to a Nightingale." He put through a telephone call to Williams, who was by then in New Orleans making a speech for the Community Chest Fund, and insisted that Williams interrupt the speech and get to the telephone to hear the news that the work program was going to start with $400 millions. Williams, Brownlow and Bane were summoned immediately to Washington where they assembled Saturday night, one week after the football game in Chicago, together with Hopkins, Howard Hunter, Jacob Baker, Julius F. Stone, Clarence M. Bookman, Ellen Woodward, Robert S. McClure, Corrington Gill, Pierce Williams and T. S. Edmonds. They worked most of Saturday night and Sunday in the Hotel Powhatan (later named the Roger Smith) and drew the plans for the Civil Works Administration which put the four million people to work in the first thirty days of its existence and, in less than four months, inaugurated 180,000 work projects and spent over $933 millions. It was the parent of W.P.A. and marked the real establishment of the principle of the right to work from which there could be no retreat.

Of the formation of C.W.A. Roosevelt wrote:

The Public Works Administration (P.W.A.) had not been able by that time to commence a very extensive program of large public works because of the unavoidable time consuming process of planning designing and reviewing projects, clearing up legal matters, advertising for bids and letting contracts.

This was Roosevelt's tactful means of explaining why he took nearly a billion dollars away from Ickes and entrusted the spending of it to Hopkins at that time (he eventually did the same with many times that sum). Ickes was a very careful, deliberate administrator, who took pains to examine personally every detail of every project and the disposition of every nickel that it cost, whether it be a village post office or a Triborough Bridge. This is hardly to his discredit for it was the approach to each problem of a hardheaded businessman as well as a conscientious public servant. Ickes was concerned about the return on the taxpayers' investment. Hopkins did not give a damn about the return; his approach was that of a social worker who was interested only in getting relief to the miserable and getting it there quickly. His ultimate argument was, "Hunger is not debatable." Ickes thought primarily of the finished job —Hopkins of the numbers of unemployed who could be put on the job immediately. As an instance of Hopkins' impatience: someone came to him with an idea for a project which would take a lot of time to prepare in detail but which, Hopkins was assured, "will work out in the long run," and his exasperated comment on this was, "People don't eat in the long run—they eat every day."

To quote further from Roosevelt's review of C.W.A.:

Its organization and operation were essentially different from that of the F.E.R.A. [which was] mostly a State and local program loosely supervised and in part financed by the Federal Government but actually administered and exercised locally. The C.W.A. was, however, completely operated and 90 per cent financed by the Federal Government.

It was, actually, one of the broadest programs ever instituted by the United States Government. It sought to provide for individuals work as near as possible to their previous employment and to pay the prevailing wage in each category and region with a minimum of thirty cents an hour. It abolished the "Means Test" whereby a man who sought government relief was denied it if a member of his family was already employed; Hopkins felt that the Means Test was an insult to the dignity of the individual who, able and anxious to work, was forced into the status of an idle dependent. The organization of C.W.A. was a clean sweep for the Hopkins theories of work relief, and keen were the fears and violent the trembling of those who did not trust him, who suspected him of being an apostle of State Socialism rather than Jeffersonian Democracy. But Roosevelt had confidence in Hopkins' imagination and ingenuity and both those qualities were required in abundance on this program.

The charge has often been made that Roosevelt was "so intoxicated with the pomp and privilege of power that he could not bear to delegate authority." Much of that came in later years when the defense effort was mounting and Roosevelt for some eighteen months stubbornly refused to appoint one man to be head of the huge production program; but, when he did finally appoint Donald Nelson, he delegated to him more authority than Nelson was able to handle. The record in general seems to prove that Roosevelt delegated authority with a lavish hand when he could find a man willing to take it—and he certainly found one in Hopkins. When he told Hopkins to invent jobs for four million men and women in thirty days he expected him to do it in his own way and without continually coming back to the White House for advice on details. The President also told Hopkins to talk the whole thing over with Harold Ickes and "straighten it out" with him; but that proved a much more difficult task than the four million jobs.

Roosevelt was greatly comforted by the fact that he had his old friend Frank Walker on hand to keep an eye on Hopkins' activities. Walker, as President of the National Emergency Council, exercised a supervisory control over all the sudden New Deal agencies. Montana born, a graduate of Notre Dame, he was a quiet, gentle, trustworthy, unquenchably friendly man who was invaluable to Roosevelt through the years as spreader of oil on troubled administrative waters. He later became Chairman of the Democratic National Committee and Postmaster General after Farley "took a walk." Roosevelt knew he could trust Walker to report if Hopkins were showing signs of going crazy and producing dangerous political repercussions throughout the country. Indeed, in the early days of C.W.A., such reports did come into the headquarters of the National Emergency Council from its State Directors. Some of them were almost hysterical with alarm at the intimations of wholesale waste and even corruption in the program. Walker decided to take a trip through the country and see for himself. He returned to Washington with the assurance that C.W.A. was doing more than all the other New Deal measures to boost morale. He said that in his own home State of Montana, "I saw old friends of mine—men I had been to school with—digging ditches and laying sewer pipe. They were wearing their regular business suits as they worked because they couldn't afford overalls and rubber boots. If I ever thought, 'There, but for the grace of God—' it was right then." The sight of these old friends made him feel sick at heart, but when he talked to individuals he felt very differently, for they were happy to be working and proud of what they were doing. One of them pulled some silver coins out of his pocket and showed them to Walker. "Do you know, Frank," he said, "this is the first money I've had in my pockets in a year and a half? Up to now, I've had nothing but tickets that you exchange for groceries." Another said, "I hate to think what would have happened if this work hadn't come along. The last of my savings had run out. I'd sold or hocked everything I could. And my kids were hungry. I stood in front of the window of the bake-shop down the street and I wondered just how long it would be before I got desperate enough to pick up a rock and heave it through that window and grab some bread to take home." It was not only hunger from which these men suffered; it was the deep sense of indignity and of grave injury to their national pride. The analogy used by President Roosevelt in his Inaugural Address was far from inappropriate: Americans felt as if, at a time when their country was being invaded and ravaged by alien enemies, their government had failed to provide them with any weapons for defense. Now, armed with a shovel, or even a rake, they felt able to fight back. "Leaf raking" became the term of supreme opprobrium for the New Deal, but great numbers of people who did the raking preferred it to breadlines or grocery tickets.

Walker said to Roosevelt: "I'd pay little attention to those who criticize the creation of C.W.A. or its administration. Hopkins and his associates are doing their work well. They've done a magnificent job. It is amazing when you consider that within the short time since C.W.A. was established four million idle have been put to work. During Christmas week many of them were standing in a payroll line for the first time in eighteen months. You have every reason to be proud of C.W.A. and its administra-

tion. It is my considered opinion that this has averted one of the most
serious crises in our history. Revolution is an ugly word to use, but I
think we were dangerously close at least to the threat of it."

Walker was not always so cordial in his approval of Hopkins' administrative methods, but in his reports to the President throughout the
New Deal years, he was stanch in supporting Hopkins against the
numerous and violent critics. A large part of Hopkins' original prestige
with Roosevelt was undoubtedly attributable to Walker. The direct and
unmistakable benefits to the jobless and their families were augmented
by many evidences of business revival. Within the first weeks of C.W.A.
shoe stores all over the country began to report that they were sold out
and shoe factories began to reopen to meet the enormously increased
demand.

C.W.A. came none too soon. That winter of 1933-34 was a terrible
one. The temperature went to 56° below zero in parts of New England
and to 6° below even in Washington, D.C., where the legislators could
feel it. This was the first of a series of natural calamities—including
droughts, floods and hurricanes—which occurred during these years as
if to test the Roosevelt Administration in its program for national
recovery. Hopkins had to increase his efforts to meet widespread suffering. By mid-January nearly twenty million people were dependent on
Federal relief for the essentials of life and the $400 millions granted to
C.W.A. was almost gone. Hopkins, with White House approval, went
to the Congress for $950 millions more.

The Republican National Committee denounced him and C.W.A.
for "gross waste" and "downright corruption" and one Democrat,
Congressman George B. Terrell of Texas, arose to say, "The Constitution is being violated here every day because there isn't a line in the
Constitution that authorizes the expenditure of Federal money for other
than Federal purposes. . . . I think [C.W.A.] is going to start civil war
and revolution when we do stop it anyway. . . . The others [in Congress]
can go through on these things like dumb driven cattle if they want to,
but . . . I won't sacrifice my independence for any office I ever heard of."

But Terrell's was a lone voice on Capitol Hill. The members of Congress were hearing from their constituencies the same kind of reports
that Frank Walker had brought back to Washington, and there was an
election coming up in 1934. So Hopkins got the money. One lamentably
profane Senator was quoted by *Time* magazine as saying, "If Roosevelt
ever becomes Jesus Christ, he should have Harry Hopkins as his
prophet."

Time ran Hopkins' picture on its cover and, in a long article about
him, paid tribute to him for having done "a thoroughly professional
job" as administrator. *Time* reported:

Of the $950,000,000 given him by the new law, Mr. Hopkins said he intended to use $450,000,000 to taper off C.W.A. gradually and $500,000,000 for direct relief. Congress would like him to use more for C.W.A. but he came out strongly against it, declaring that C.W.A. was an emergency measure, should not be permanent, should be gradually demobilized.

Hopkins was not then speaking from the heart. He was, with utmost reluctance and deep disappointment, obeying orders. For, even while he was scoring triumphs on Capitol Hill, C.W.A. was being torpedoed at the other end of Pennsylvania Avenue and this was done not by Republican enemies of the New Deal but by conservative elements within the Democratic party itself. The first crack in it came when Southern influence caused the abandonment of the thirty cents an hour wage minimum—causing wages in some parts of the South to drop to ten cents an hour or worse. Then Roosevelt was persuaded by Lewis Douglas and other economic advisers that there was something in what Terrell of Texas had said. They felt that there was serious potential danger in the work relief program, their argument being that if you got large numbers of people settled in government-made jobs, with guarantees of security that they would not readily obtain from private industry, *you might never be able to get them off the public pay roll.* That argument carried weight with Roosevelt and he told Hopkins that C.W.A. must be liquidated before spring and the former F.E.R.A. program of direct relief resumed.

Although this was a bitter blow to Hopkins, it provided him with his first opportunity to demonstrate his utter loyalty to Roosevelt. He did not afflict the President with a threat to resign. He was harsh in compelling his shocked associates to take this setback without complaint and to get on with the job of relief. Roosevelt was keenly sensitive to this and his personal fondness for as well as confidence in Hopkins increased more than ever at this time. The more he contemplated the C.W.A. record, the less he thought of the advice given him by Douglas, who soon came to the breaking point with his Chief and left the government. (He returned after Pearl Harbor and worked very closely and amicably with Hopkins during the war years.)

The ending of C.W.A. produced protests throughout the country which could not possibly be ignored. In one week upwards of 50,000 letters and 7,000 telegrams came into the White House. There were riots in various parts of the country. The people on the relief rolls made it clear that they agreed with Hopkins in his theory that direct relief had a demoralizing effect: they did not want tickets for baskets of groceries—they wanted *work.* In a review of the whole Relief Program and problem, *Fortune* magazine made the following rather supercilious statement:

Direct relief is—purely and simply—the Dole. Almost as purely and simply, work relief is the Dole, too, except that it does provide a little more self respect for its recipients: at least it creates for them the fiction that they are still useful citizens and that there is work for them to do.

Yet, in this same article, *Fortune* presented many illuminating instances of work relief which belied the cynical use of the word "fiction." For example: Hopkins took over 250,000 bales of surplus cotton from the A.A.A. for the dual purpose of supplying work relief for women who made the cotton into mattresses and then distributing the mattresses to people who could not otherwise afford them. (This evoked howls of protest from mattress manufacturers but it was pointed out to them that they were not being subjected to unfair competition since the purchasing power of the recipients of the work relief mattresses was zero.)

For another example, as cited by *Fortune*:

In Bay City, Michigan, an underwear manufacturing concern went bankrupt, and the closing of its plant threw some 250 workers on relief. Whereupon the State Relief Administration rented the plant, reopened it, and put the 250 workers back at their jobs on a subsistence level to make enough underwear to give every relief family in the state two sets for the winter.

The C.W.A. was unquestionably an expensive program and could not have been continued for long on its original scale. But its achievement in three and a half months was a memorable one. It included: 40,000 schools built or improved; 12,000,000 feet of sewer pipe laid; 469 airports built, 529 more improved; 255,000 miles of road built or improved; 50,000 teachers employed to teach adults or to keep open rural schools which must otherwise have been closed; 3,700 playgrounds and athletic fields built or improved.

Among the 4,264,000 for whom work was found were 3,000 writers and artists, the inception of the Federal Arts Program, to the numerous criticisms of which Hopkins replied, "Hell! They've got to eat just like other people."

In the generally thankless task of government service—and in other fields of endeavor as well—a few words of encouragement from a respectworthy source can wipe out the effects of thousands of words of vituperation from the hostile press or the Congress. Shortly after the start of C.W.A., Aubrey Williams received a letter from Gutzon Borglum, the American sculptor of heroic mold. Williams turned this letter over to Hopkins who treasured it all the rest of his life. Borglum wrote:

You have the only department that is free to help the creative impulses of the Nation, all other aids take on the character of hard business. The Government continues the hard banker-broker business man we have become.

Mr. Hopkins—the C.W.A.—almost immediately shifted public aid from cold business to human helpfulness and that to usefulness, converting mass employment into an army of workers whose goal must be to better, to make more livable our towns and cities, our schools more cheerful, our playgrounds and parks a pride and a delight. . . .

It is not a long step from this to one of organizing the latent talent whose belly has been longer empty and who carries a double hunger, unexpressed, creative longing, fitted and anxious to be a part in the great comeback.

Mr. Hopkins' department has opened the door, a crack, but opened to this great field of human interest and thought. The world of creative impulse, without which people perish. Frankly, a people have as much right to be saved as the trees, the birds, the whole animal kingdom, and no more, but their civilization must be saved.

I am not orthodox religiously, but all there is of God in creation is what man has in lonely martyrdom wrung from nowhere and everywhere, and it has been his consciousness of that that makes him master of the world, and not business or money, we must save that, civilization contains all that is precious in what we think we are. Will a basket of bread save that, a full belly and a dry back? Is there nothing about this fine young—still young, still virgin continent—that civilization needs, in which civilization can spread a greater wing? Have we in gold—the worship of Aaron's calf—made our final bow in the hall of world fame, to be remembered with Rome for our abuse of wealth?

We are the heirs, if not the children, of Washington, Jefferson, Franklin, Tom Paine, Pat Henry. Have we reached the life line's end of the little Republic they shaped for us, have we wholly forgotten that what we are is something quite outside business and our bellies, and that something in our minds and what there is in our hearts is of real importance? Mr. Hopkins, you and his aides, have it in your hands to give to young America a chance for heart and soul growth which she has never had. I don't mind telling you I hammered T.R. for years to throw some small part of our vast official power behind the civil life into the soul and heart of human endeavor. I awakened interest, Root was for it, but little happened. Taft laughed all such plans out of court, and Wilson, who gave me a degree, said "the creative impulse must submit to business competition."

I knew Harding almost intimately, and he was a kind, fine soul, destroyed by his friends. He could see a "welfare department," but the creative impulse does not want or need a welfare department! . . .

I answered a call to go to the West and carve Mount Rushmore. Coolidge . . . was interested; he knew as much about art as I do about the late Llama of Thibet; but he knew history; he knew the story of peoples; he knew the eternal fight civilization had to make to master its own physical mass. . . .

Hoover was indifferent and dead from the top down. His heart seemed to have ceased beating to the call of laughter, to music, the charm of letters, the color and mystery of Innis and Millet—the power of Angelo or the burning words of Tom Paine. Everything seemed to die in his hands; I believe if a rose was put into his hand it would wilt. . . .

I want to suggest to you that you make your thought of aid to the creative ones among us greater, more effective in its scope, make it a feature, make your aid more than ½ of one percent; make it at least five percent; concentrate on the schools, the poor schools, the little schools, the public schools, put our educators to work; start with the children; make their classrooms, studyrooms and halls pleasant, with color and design, fairytales and history, home life. You are not after masterpieces, and you should not be discouraged if you have many failures; the real success will be in the interest, the human interest, which you will awaken; and what that does to the Nation's mind. There are twenty-odd million children that will be affected; some millions of teachers and mothers, and an occasional father! I wish you would think of this very studiously; I believe that's the door through which Hopkins, you and his aides can coax the soul of America back to interest in life.

Gutzon Borglum to the contrary notwithstanding, the Federal Arts Projects were subjected to more derision and more charges of "un-American activities" than almost any other part of the huge relief program. And, they were the first to be lopped off by Congress when the revolt against the program set in. The word "boondoggle" came into the language to describe the more fantastic projects dreamed up by Hopkins and other "wild-eyed radicals" for the purpose of wasting the taxpayers' money. For years the anti-New Deal press had a great deal of fun digging up new work relief projects which sounded very comical, particularly those involving jobless white collar workers who could not build bridges across San Francisco Bay, or dams in the Columbia or Tennessee Valleys. One of these projects, discovered in New York City, involved the study of ancient safety pins. This led to an exchange between Hopkins and reporters at a press conference, the literal transcript of which provides an excellent example of his explosive method of speech:

Question. Are you contemplating any Federal investigation of any kind of the general situation in New York City?

Answer (Hopkins). No. You mean apropos of this stuff in the paper a day or two ago?

Q. Apropos of the project for safety pins.

A. Sure, I have something to say about that.

Q. I asked first, have you contemplated making an investigation?

A. Why should I? There is nothing the matter with that. They are damn good projects—excellent projects. That goes for all the projects up there. You know some people make fun of people who speak a foreign language, and dumb people criticize something they do not understand, and that is what is going on up there—God damn it! Here are a lot of people broke and we are putting them to work making researches of one kind or another, running big recreational projects where the whole material costs 3%, and practically all the money goes for relief. As soon as you begin doing anything for white collar people, there is a certain group of people who begin to throw bricks. I have no apologies to make. As a matter of fact, we have not done enough. The plain fact of the matter is that there are people writing and talking about these things in New York who know nothing about research projects. They haven't taken the trouble to really look into it. I have a pile of letters from businessmen, if that is important, saying that these projects are damn good projects. These fellows can make fun and shoot at white collar people, if they want to. I notice somebody says facetiously, "repair all streets." That is all they think about—money to repair streets. I think there are things in life besides that. We have projects up there to make Jewish dictionaries. There are rabbis who are broke and on the relief rolls. One hundred and fifty projects up there deal with pure science. What of it? I think those things are good in life. They are important in life. We are not backing down on any of those projects. They can make fun of these white collar and professional people if they want to. I am not going to do it. They can say, let them use a pick and shovel to repair streets, when the city ought to be doing that. I believe every one of these research projects are good projects. We don't need any apologies!

Q. In that connection, I am not trying to argue with you.

A. I am not really mad. . . .

Q. About this white collar—there are 300 million for white collar relief. Would it be your idea in administering 300 million, that you might just as well continue?

A. The best of them will be continued, sure. Those are research projects they are jumping on.

Q. As a matter of fact, don't you think there are a lot of research projects that would be more valuable to mankind in general than the classic example of ancient safety pins?

A. That is a matter of opinion. You may be interested in washing machines—somebody else in safety pins. Every one of those projects are worked out by technical people. In the field of medical science, we have doctors; in physical, we have physicists; in the social, social economists. Every one of those is under the direction of competent research people. You can make fun of anything; that is easy to do. A lot of people are opposed to the whole business. Let these white collar professional fellows sit home and get a basket of groceries, that is what a lot of people want.

Q. You say that people don't want to work?

A. No, these fellows want to work, but there are a lot of people who don't believe in the work program and want people to go back to direct relief. These people who want direct relief will always kick about these technical projects. Anything that from their point of view isn't utilitarian.

The reports of this conference quoted Hopkins as saying that "people are too damned dumb," and this phrase was given plenty of circulation in the press. Even ten years later in the midst of war, Hopkins was assailed in scathing editorials as the man who believed that "the American people are too damned dumb." The *Washington Post* published a poem by a Virginia lady ending with the verse:

> Though we still pay up our tax,
>   Mr. Hopkins!
> We are sharpening the ax,
>   (Mr. Hopkins)
> Testing it with cautious thumb—
> And we're telling you, by gum,
> We are not quite too damned dumb,
>   Mr. Hopkins!

Nevertheless, Hopkins generally got on very well with working newspapermen (not including publishers). They appreciated the quickness and directness of his answers and the quotability of his cracks. A description of him at a press conference was written by the immortal Ernie Pyle in the *Washington News*:

And you, Mr. Hopkins, I liked you because you look like common people. I don't mean any slur by that either, because they don't come any commoner than I am, but you sit there so easy swinging back and forth in your swivel chair, in your blue suit and blue shirt, and your neck is sort of skinny, like poor people's necks, and you act honest, too.

And you answer the reporters' questions as tho you were talking to them personally, instead of being a big official. It tickled me the way you would say, "I can't answer that," in a tone that almost says out loud, "Now you knew damn well when you asked me that I couldn't answer that. . . ."

And that old office of yours, Mr. Hopkins, good Lord, it's terrible. It's so little in the first place, and the walls are faded and water pipes run up the walls and your desk doesn't even shine. But I guess you don't care. Maybe it wouldn't look right for you to have a nice office anyway, when you're dealing in misery all the time.

One nice thing about your office being so little, tho, the reporters all have to pack close up around your desk, and they can see and hear you well, and it's sort of like talking to you in your home, except there they'd be sitting down, I hope.

The reporters tell me, Mr. Hopkins, that you're about the fastest thinker of any of the big men who hold press conferences. Ickes is fast, too, and so is Farley, they say, but you always come back right now with something pretty good. And you've got a pleasant, clean-cut voice, too, and they say you never try to lie out of anything.

Hopkins' office, as described by Ernie Pyle, was in the Walker-Johnson Building, on New York Avenue, between the Corcoran Gallery and the Girl Scouts' Little House. It was a shabby, old building, with a blind newsdealer by its front steps. When you went into it you were assailed by an odor of antiseptic which suggested the smell of a combination of hospital, locker room and stable. As *Fortune* described it, "This, you might also say, is the very odor of Relief. It is at once prophylactic and unclean." Hopkins' first office had been in the Federal Security Building, but he fought his way out of that and continued for five years to resist all attempts to move his headquarters into new government buildings which were marbled and air conditioned. In addition to his natural aversion to pomp and circumstance he had for a long time the feeling that he was only a temporary figure on the Washington scene. His position seemed insecure in the extreme; he had arisen suddenly to this prominence and he might as suddenly be blown back into obscurity. Although he attempted to give the impression of being lighthearted and carefree, it was obvious to those closest to him that he was forever fearful that the critics of the Relief Program might one day achieve vindication—that someone would be proved guilty of graft for which Hopkins himself would inevitably assume responsibility, however spotless his personal record or that of his immediate staff. He knew all too well how powerful were the interests which were continually trying to detect and expose evidences of graft and corruption, and he knew also that it was humanly impossible to keep completely clean a program that was administered to such a large extent by local politicians. It was understandable that the result of his constant worrying should be severe digestive disorders. Actually, there were amazingly few instances of actual embezzlement of public funds, and in each of these the blame was very clearly fixed on local officials (some of them Republicans) and not on the Federal Government.

During his years in Washington, Hopkins wrote very few personal letters—and in those managed to tell very little of interest—but at the end of June, 1934, he revealed something of his state of mind in a letter to his brother, Lewis:

> I am planning to sail for Europe on Wednesday the 4th unless something interferes at the last moment. This, of course, is always possible around here. I can scarcely realize that I have been with the Government now for a year. I had no intention of remaining longer than that but I seem to be well on my way to stay through next winter anyway. I think you know, one of the great difficulties about this place

is what to use for money. When I decided to come it looked fairly simple from that point of view because the Board of Directors of the N.Y.T.B. Association decided to give me a year's salary for my ten years work there. The finances of the organization, however, went sour and the President died. Recently one of the Board told me that they are anxious to at least fill part of that agreement and I have some substantial hope now that I can get enough money at least to keep me from getting head over heels in debt.

The other side of the picture is that this has been a fascinating experience. It is worth any amount of money to have a ringside seat at this show. I have learned enough about it to know that one should not bank too heavily on anything here for more than a few months at a time. While the work is fascinating and the President is a grand person to work for I have no desire to stay here indefinitely.

Hopkins at this time was showing definite signs of physical strain and the European trip was taken largely at Roosevelt's urging. Indeed, it was more than urging—it was an order. Always a master at the art of relaxing himself, Roosevelt could enforce relaxation on an overworked subordinate by sending him off on some comparatively meaningless mission, preferably one which involved a sea change. He wrote to Hopkins:

It is my desire that you make a trip abroad as soon as you can possibly get away and look over the housing and social insurance schemes in England, Germany, Austria and Italy, because I think you might pick up some ideas useful to us in developing our own American plan for security.

Incidentally, in view of the steady grind you have had, I think that the sea trip will do you a lot of good.

Hopkins told a friend that the President also asked him to have a look at the personnel in American embassies and legations and to report to him confidentially thereon. Roosevelt felt then that there were individuals in the Foreign Service who were not entirely sympathetic to the policies of his Administration and as the years went by and he received reports from Hopkins and many others who traveled abroad he became increasingly sure of it.

Hopkins and his wife sailed on the *S.S. Washington* on July 4, returning August 23. During this summer there occurred the Nazi blood purge, followed by Hitler's statement to the quivering Reichstag, "The Supreme Court of the German people during these 24 hours consisted of myself!" Which should have been enough to inform anyone of just what to expect from the Nazi regime. During that same summer the Nazis murdered Chancellor Dollfuss in Vienna, and Hindenburg died, thereby removing the last formal obstacle to Hitler's seizure of total power. However, I can find no record of the effect on Hopkins of these revealing events or of anything that he saw and heard in the police states. In his only published comments on his trip to Europe he expressed enthusiasm for the social security and public housing programs in Britain, saying that even the Conservatives there were well ahead of the New Deal in social progress. The day of his return to Washington he lunched with the President and then spent the week end with him at Hyde Park but he left no notes on these conversations. It is quite possible that, since Roosevelt himself had lately returned from a 10,000-mile cruise on the *U.S.S. Houston* through the Caribbean and the Panama Canal to Cocos Island and Hawaii, and back to Portland, Oregon, Hopkins was not called upon to do much of the talking.

A Congressional election was then coming up and this was to be the first real test of the New Deal with the voters. Roosevelt's political opponents, who had been rendered relatively speechless during the "honeymoon" period of 1933, were now regaining the powers of public protest, and violent criticisms of the "spending orgy" and the conversion to "State Socialism" were being heard throughout the land. The Republicans knew that they had no hope of regaining any real power in 1934 but they were energetically starting the counterrevolution which might come to triumph in 1936. A minor amusement in the course of this campaign was provided when Hopkins learned that his brother, Lewis, was running for the post of coroner of Tacoma on the Republican ticket. When Hopkins was informed of this he said, "I thought that party was buried two years ago. Why do they need a coroner now?" A few days before the election, Hopkins sent the following affectionate telegram to his brother:

Well, Lew, Tuesday is the bad news. I hear your campaign for a lost cause was magnificent but that you confused the voters so that they are not sure which ticket you are running on so that they will all vote for your opponent, which is as it should be. Now, Lew, the telegraph companies have form messages for defeated candidates. Don't fail to observe this old-time custom. The least your supporters if any can do is provide a respectable autopsy. The nation is going to lose a great coroner.

The Democrats won that election by an overwhelming margin and the Republicans found themselves feebler as a minority in the new Congress than they had been at any time since before the Civil War. This was an emphatic vote of confidence for the New Deal and particularly for the Work Relief Program. Roosevelt immediately started to discuss a formidable expansion of that program along the lines that had been established under C.W.A. The Hopkins star was now definitely in the ascendant.

One afternoon, while driving with Aubrey Williams and others of his staff to a racetrack near Washington, Hopkins suddenly said "Boys —this is our hour. We've got to get everything we want—a works program, social security, wages and hours, everything—now or never. Get your minds to work on developing a complete ticket to provide security for all the folks of this country up and down and across the board."

They went to work in the Walker-Johnson Building and in the St. Regis Hotel. The day before Thanksgiving, Hopkins headed south with the program in his pocket—a program based on one that he and Harold Ickes had jointly drawn up. He conferred first with Senator Byrnes in South Carolina and then went on to Warm Springs to see the President and Rexford Tugwell and Donald Richberg, who had succeeded Frank Walker as Executive Director of the National Emergency Council. They played around for a while in the swimming pool, tossing a water polo ball back and forth—leading a reporter watching from the crest of a nearby hill to remark, "They seem to be practicing passing the buck"; then they got down to work on the 1935 development of the New Deal. The next day the *New York Times* published an article by Delbert Clark, saying:

> The fire-eating Administrator of Federal Emergency Relief, Harry L. Hopkins, may safely be credited with spoiling the Thanksgiving Day dinners of many conservatives who had been led to believe that President Roosevelt's recent zig to the right would not be followed by a zag to the left.
>
> Not that Mr. Hopkins had any idea that his EPIA (End Poverty in America) plan would leak out unauthorized, but now that it has leaked out it will bear examination.
>
> From the fragmentary advices in Washington, what Mr. Hopkins proposes to the President is about as follows:
>
> An expansion of the subsistence homesteads and rural rehabilitation programs to include as many families as need such accommodations or are in a position to accept them.
>
> A large-scale removal of families from submarginal (unprofitable) land to home sites where they can live on a more civilized scale.
>
> Federal advances of funds to both categories to equip their homesteads with tools, live stock, etc.
>
> An expansion of the program already in progress on an experimental scale to give factory work to the idle, through what the FERA softly calls "canning centres," "needlecraft centres," or the like.
>
> A large-scale, low-cost housing program to shelter those unable for one reason or another to move to subsistence homesteads, since it appears there is no purpose entirely to depopulate the large cities.
>
> A social insurance program to give security in the future.

When the 74th Congress convened a month later, Roosevelt announced the new Relief Program. He said:

The Federal Government must and shall quit this business of relief. . . .

Work must be found for able-bodied but destitute workers. . . .

I am not willing that the vitality of our people be further sapped by the giving of cash, of market baskets, of a few hours of weekly work cutting grass, raking leaves or picking up papers in the public parks. We must preserve not only the bodies of the unemployed from destruction but also their self-respect, their self-reliance and courage and determination. This decision brings me to the problem of what the Government should do about approximately five million unemployed now on the relief rolls.

It is my thought that with the exception of certain of the normal public building operations of the Government, all emergency public works shall be united in a single new and greatly enlarged plan.

With the establishment of this new system we can supersede the Federal Emergency Relief Administration with a coordinated authority which will be charged with the orderly liquidation of our present relief activities and the substitution of a national chart for the giving of work.

I do not know whether Hopkins helped with the preparation of that message, but it certainly showed his influence. The President laid down six fundamental principles for work relief:

(1) The projects should be useful.

(2) Projects shall be of a nature that a considerable proportion of the money spent will go into wages for labor.

(3) Projects which promise ultimate return to the Federal Treasury of a considerable proportion of the costs will be sought.

(4) Funds allotted for each project should be actually and promptly spent and not held over until later years.

(5) In all cases projects must be of a character to give employment to those on the relief rolls.

(6) Projects will be allocated to localities or relief areas in relation to the number of workers on relief rolls in those areas.

When the Work Relief Bill of nearly five billion dollars was presented to the Congress there were wails of protest from the Republican minority and some signs of revolt by Southern Democrats, but the Bill passed the House of Representatives quickly and overwhelmingly. In the Senate, however, it encountered rough going. The days of legislation by the "rubber stamp" method were unquestionably over. There was much pious talk in the Senate and the Republican press about the Legislative branch maintaining its integrity vis-à-vis the Executive—and the words Fascist and Communist dictatorship were hurled about recklessly then, as later. But the argument had nothing to do with ideology. There was no real dispute over the propriety of spending the taxpayers' money on such a vast scale for work relief. It boiled down simply to the question: why should Capitol Hill yield to the White House absolute control over the spending of these billions which could yield such rich returns in pork barrel patronage? The leading proponents of this question were Democrats rather than Republicans, the latter being glad to go along on anything that was opposed to Roosevelt. The opposition to the Bill was strengthened enormously by the unrefuted claim that Roosevelt was asking for a blank check. As Walter Lippmann wrote:

> The Senators were not told who was going to administer the program. They were not given definite information about the scope or character of the program. They were not even furnished a thorough, cogent, and considered argument in favor of the Bill. . . .
> The Senate was confronted not with a policy but a mystery. This aroused the opposition of Senators who do not believe in work relief, of Senators who conscientiously object to voting money and powers blindly. It was the opportunity of Senators who for partisan reasons were glad to frustrate the President, of Senators who wished to get at the pork barrel.

Hopkins was called before the Senate Appropriations Committee but he evidently did not help much to clarify matters, for the Associated Press subsequently reported so much dissension and confusion in the Committee that one member who did not wish his name used predicted the Bill would be completely redrafted from beginning to end. The truth was that Hopkins himself did not know what was really in Roosevelt's mind. He noted, after a private talk with the President, "We went over the organization of the work program—more charts in pencil—he loves charts—no two of them are ever the same which makes it a bit baffling at times."

The two men most frequently mentioned as Administrators of the Relief Program were, obviously, Hopkins and Ickes. But it was part of Roosevelt's technique not to let anyone know—including the two men themselves—which one he favored. Thus, neither of them was really in a position to go before the Senate and fight for the Bill. Neither of them knew just exactly where he stood or with what authority he might speak either to the Congress or to the press. There was no definite spearhead of opposition to various amendments proposed and the Administration leaders on the Senate floor could only compromise here and there to safeguard the main interests of the Bill. It was finally passed, after two months, with restrictions which were highly disappointing to Hopkins. One of these restrictions, sponsored primarily by Senator William E. Borah, had a melancholy ring in view of subsequent developments: "No part of the appropriations . . . shall be used for munitions, warships, or military or naval matériel." (Roosevelt had already used P.W.A. funds for naval construction, including the aircraft carriers

Enterprise and *Yorktown*, but the isolationists were already cherishing
the belief that the way to keep out of war was not to prepare for it.)
The most important amendment of all in its political implications was
one providing that "any Administrator receiving a salary of $5,000 or
more per annum in this Program shall be appointed by the President
by and with the advice and consent of the Senate."

This, of course, spelled just one word: patronage. It provided some
new education for Hopkins in the political facts of life. In his early
dealings with the Congress, particularly on the sore subject of the
minimum wage, he had encountered vehement assertion of States' rights
by the conservative Democrats. But it was a very different matter when
it came to patronage privileges in connection with the disbursement of
Federal funds. The Senators wanted to keep control of these privileges
in their own hands rather than let the States' Governors get first licks
at the enormous gravy spoon. Hopkins had been able to cope with the
political demands of the Governors and Mayors, sometimes by resorting
to the primitive tactics of telling them to go to hell. But he could not
do that to the Congress. He knew that from here on out he must clear
each appointment in each State with the appropriate Senators, and he
must pay heed to the recommendations of James A. Farley and the
Democratic National Committee as to who should be "taken care of."
This was the real basis of the political coloration of the Works Progress
Administration. I believe that this was the nearest that Hopkins ever came
to quitting the job in Washington and that Roosevelt talked him out of
it, persuading him that he could square his conscience with the realities
of the two-party system of government. Hopkins said later, "I thought
at first I could be completely non-political. Then they told me I had
to be part non-political and part political. I found that was impossible,
at least for me. I finally realized there was nothing for it but to be all-
political." So, the altruistic welfare worker—the lover of Keats—developed into one of the toughest of politicians.

With the passage of the Work Relief Bill, Roosevelt was brought
face to face with some difficult political problems of his own. He left
for a Caribbean vacation just as the Bill was assured of passage, at the
end of March, and, when it became known that Hopkins was on the
Presidential train headed south, the press jumped to the conclusion that
the F.E.R.A. Administrator had stolen the inside track. The controversies between Hopkins and Ickes had by that time been widely advertised, and Roosevelt knew that whichever of these men he appointed
to the top job would be a prime target for the snipers' fire. Whereas, if
he passed over them both and named a new man, it would imply repudiation of the whole Relief Program up to date. He settled the problem in
a superbly characteristic manner: he called back to Washington the
moderate, reliable Frank Walker—who was everybody's friend and no-

body's target—and formed a triumvirate of Walker, Ickes and Hopkins to run the gigantic show.

I have neither the knowledge nor the physical strength to set down in detail the whole, intricate details of the workings of the new triheaded organization. I can only attempt to describe, in a general way, what was the division of responsibility.

Walker directed the *Division of Applications and Information*, which "received all suggested plans for the useful expenditure of public funds, no matter what the source of these suggestions may be," and sorted, checked, studied and tabulated these plans, then passed them on to

The Advisory Committee on Allotments, of which Ickes was named Chairman, and which was to recommend projects to the President for approval. This Committee was directed "to meet in round table conference at least once a week." It was composed of the Secretaries of the Interior, Agriculture and Labor; the Directors of the National Emergency Council, the Progress Division, Procurement, the Bureau of the Budget, Soil Erosion, Emergency Conservation Work, Rural Resettlement, Relief and Rural Electrification; the Chief of Engineers, U.S. Army; the Commissioner of Reclamation; the Chiefs of the Forest Service, Bureau of Public Roads, Division of Grade Crossing Elimination and the Urban Housing Division; together with representatives of the Business Advisory Council, organized labor, farm organizations, the National Resources Board, American Bankers' Association and the U.S. Conference of Mayors. When this Committee—which must have required quite a large round table—made their recommendations, the projects went to the President's desk for final approval.

The third division of the organization—the Hopkins part—was given the name *Works Progress Administration.* Its original terms of reference, as one reads them, are not entirely clear. It was assigned various co-ordinating, investigating, recommending, regulating and reporting functions, and Roosevelt suggested that it would be mainly a "bookkeeping" organization. Only as a sort of afterthought in the Executive Order establishing W.P.A. did the President give it authority also to "recommend and carry on small useful projects designed to assure a maximum of employment in all localities." That was a loophole for Hopkins—and Roosevelt was well aware of it—which assumed continental proportions. Those "small projects" represented an expenditure eventually of over ten billion dollars.

Such was the cumbersome high command of the Relief Program: Ickes at the head of an enormous committee and with P.W.A. as an operating agency in his Department; Hopkins with responsibility for the millions of individuals on the relief rolls and with W.P.A. as the major operating agency; and Frank Walker squarely in the middle as Chief Accountant, custodian of facts and figures and keeper of the peace between the two jarring New Dealers. Thus, with this apparently overelaborate and diffuse set of controls, Roosevelt enforced at least the semblance of harmony in operations but, more importantly, established a kind of political insurance for the relief projects. He certainly did this the hard way for himself, for he imposed upon himself apparently staggering obligations in the maintenance of personal relations with all the diverse elements involved, including organized labor and the American Bankers' Association; but he was supernally confident of his ability to do this, and events proved that his confidence was not misplaced. In the first three years of this program something like a quarter of a million individual projects —ranging from suspension bridges to sewing circles—passed through Walker's office to Ickes' committee and thence across the President's overcrowded desk from which the vast majority of the projects approved were passed to Hopkins who converted them into actual man hours of work. The operation of relief was not all directed by Hopkins; there were sixty different agencies involved, including of course P.W.A. and the important Farm Resettlement Administration which, to Hopkins' regret, was moved from his area of authority and placed in the Department of Agriculture under the direction of Rexford Tugwell. But Hopkins was the guardian of the entire relief rolls and it was thus his responsibility to see to it that the millions of destitute, unemployed individuals were given work by some agency—and his W.P.A. was by all odds the biggest of the· Federal employers and spenders.

At this point, it may be well for me to confess that I was one of the large number of Roosevelt supporters who, during the New Deal years, could not understand what was the difference between W.P.A. and P.W.A. and why there should have been two of them with the same three initials. Actually, the difference between the two organizations was fundamental: it was the difference between two opposed philosophies; it was essentially the difference between Hopkins and Ickes. The former had the point of view of a welfare worker—that the main object was to get the greatest possible number of people to work in the shortest possible space of time and that the productivity of the work that they performed was a matter of only secondary importance. Ickes had the point of view of a businessman (albeit an exceptionally liberal one); he believed that the best way to relieve unemployment on a long-range basis was to "prime the pump" by subsidizing private enterprise for the construction of massive, self-liquidating projects. Ickes was proud of the amount of heavy, durable materials that went into the P.W.A. projects, such as Bonneville Dam; whereas Hopkins boasted of the small percentage of the W.P.A. dollar that went for materials and the consequently large percentage that went directly into the pockets of the workers on relief. Since the Hopkins point of view was the one that prevailed with Roosevelt, it would have seemed logical to have merged

P.W.A. into W.P.A. and thereby end the confusion; but if this had been done, Ickes would undoubtedly have resigned in a cloud of sulphur, and Roosevelt was always ready to go to almost any lengths to forestall a resignation in his own official family.

It was (and, as this is written, still is) Ickes' conviction that the confusion of initials was deliberate, that Hopkins picked W.P.A. for his new organization, instead of reviving the former C.W.A., so that the public would in its alphabetic bewilderment give him credit for the achievements of P.W.A. Be that as it may, there can be no doubt that the interminable criticisms of Hopkins' "leaf-raking" projects had got under his skin and he sought to develop projects which could be pointed to with pride as of lasting value to the nation. This led to a new form of cutthroat competition between Hopkins and Ickes: when the possibility of an important new project appeared—for example, the reconstruction and modernization of the sewage system in Atlanta, Georgia—there would be warfare between P.W.A. and W.P.A. for possession of it. There would be political maneuvering, propaganda campaigns, lobbying among the Georgia delegation in the Congress, etc., until the dispute had to be referred to the harassed umpire, Frank Walker, who would usually render what Ickes has described as a "Solomonian verdict," giving half of the project to each agency. Since this decision usually satisfied neither contestant, the dispute would end with both Ickes and Hopkins executing sweeps around Walker's flanks to the President himself, and he would be forced to decide which of them would enjoy the prestige to be derived from laying the sewer pipes. (In the case of the Atlanta project, it was Ickes who won out; but Hopkins was not often thus defeated.)

In this connection, I intrude a personal recollection of Roosevelt which fixed itself in my memory as a revelation of one of the facets of his incomprehensible character. Early in the war I had been on a long airplane flight to visit one of the remote outposts of the Office of War Information Overseas Branch of which I was director. The return trip was very rough and I got the sensation in my ears that one sometimes has after swimming. After my return, I spent the week end at Shangri-la, Roosevelt's retreat in the Maryland hills. I was still inclining my head and shaking it, as though to pour the water out of my ears. The President asked what was the matter with me. I told him about the long, bumpy trip.

"I didn't know you'd been away," he said. "What did you go there for?"

I explained that there had been trouble in our outpost office and I had gone to fire the man in charge of it. I hastened to add, to the President of the United States, that the man in question was not in any way disloyal or corrupt—merely not the right personality for the particular

job. Roosevelt looked at me with that expression of wide-eyed innocence
that he could always assume and asked, "And did you fire him?"

"Yes, sir," I said.

His face now expressed wondering incredulity.

"How did you do it?" he asked.

My answer was pretty lame: "Well, sir—I just asked the man up to my
hotel room, and then I said to him, 'Jack—I—I'm terribly sorry, but
—I've got to ask for your resignation.' Fortunately, he was very decent
about the whole thing and resigned."

Roosevelt now had an expression of open amazement and said, "I
can't believe it. I can't believe you had the courage to fire anybody. I
thought you were a complete softy—like me."

That scrap of highly unimportant conversation can indicate why those
who knew Roosevelt well could never imagine him assuming the role of
dictator. He could be and was ruthless and implacable with those whom
he considered guilty of disloyalty; but with those in his Administration
who were inefficient or even recalcitrant or hopelessly inept, but loyal, he
was "a complete softy." He wasted precious hours of time and incalculable quantities of energy and ingenuity trying to find face-saving jobs
—or "kicking upstairs" methods—for incompetents who should have
been thrown out unceremoniously.

Roosevelt's methods of administration—typified in his handling of
the work relief organization—were, to say the least, unorthodox. They
filled some practical-minded observers with apprehension and dismay,
and some with disgust; they filled others with awe and wonder. I am
sure that no final appraisal of them can be made for a long time to come;
but there is one thing that can be said about these methods—whether
they were good or bad, sensible or insane, they *worked*.

While preparing this book I interviewed Harold Smith, who was
Director of the Budget from 1939 to 1946. Smith was a modest, method-
ical, precise man, temperamentally far removed from Roosevelt and
Hopkins. But I know of no one whose judgment and integrity and
downright common sense the President trusted more completely. In
the course of a long conversation, Smith said to me, "A few months
ago, on the first anniversary of Roosevelt's death, a magazine asked me
to write an article on Roosevelt as an administrator. I thought it over
and decided I was not ready to make such an appraisal. I've been thinking about it ever since. When I worked with Roosevelt—for six years
—I thought as did many others that he was a very erratic administrator.
But now, when I look back, I can really begin to see the size of his
programs. They were by far the largest and most complex programs that
any President ever put through. People like me who had the responsibility of watching the pennies could only see the five or six or seven per
cent of the programs that went wrong, through inefficient organization

or direction. But now I can see in perspective the ninety-three or -four or -five per cent that went right—including the winning of the biggest war in history—because of unbelievably skillful organization and direction. And if I were to write that article now, I think I'd say that Roosevelt must have been one of the greatest geniuses as an administrator that ever lived. What we couldn't appreciate at the time was the fact that he was a real *artist* in government."

That word "artist" was happily chosen, for it suggests the quality of Roosevelt's extraordinary creative imagination. I think that he would have resented the application of the word as implying that he was an impractical dreamer; he loved to represent himself as a prestidigitator who could amaze and amuse the audience by "pulling another rabbit out of a hat." But he was an artist and no canvas was too big for him.

He was also, of course, a master politician, and most artists are certainly not that; but, by the same token, you rarely find a professional politician who would make the mistake of being caught in the act of creating an original idea. The combination of the two qualities in Roosevelt can be demonstrated by the fact that it required a soaring imagination to conceive Lend Lease and it required the shrewdest kind of manipulation to get it passed by the Congress.

It was often said by businessmen during the Roosevelt Administration that "What we need in the White House is a good businessman." But in the years of the Second World War there were a great many patriotic, public-spirited businessmen who went to Washington to render important service to their country and they learned that government is a weird world bearing little resemblance to anything they had previously known—a world in which the only competitive struggle was for authority and prestige instead of for profits. The more analytical of these businessmen came to the conclusion that it was no accident that not one of the great or even above-average Presidents in American history had been trained in business. (Abraham Lincoln once tried to run a grocery store and failed dismally. Thereafter, he never tried commerce again but went where he belonged—into politics.)

There were even some businessmen who observed that the New Deal was not what they had feared it to be: the prologue to Communism in America. It was, in fact, as Roosevelt conceived it and conducted it, a revolution of the Right, rising up to fight in its own defense. Although, in one election after another during his Administration, his bitter opponents raised the charge, "If That Man wins—this will be the last free election ever held in this country," free elections somehow managed to continue and more voters than ever went to the polls, giving no evidence whatsoever that they were forced there by bayonet points compelling them to vote in strict obedience to the Democratic (or Communist) party line. I think that the best statement on this subject was written by

Gerald W. Johnson in *Roosevelt: Dictator or Democrat?* Speaking of Roosevelt as a traditional American, he wrote:

No man has shattered more precedents. No man has torn down more ancient structures. No man has altered more rapidly and radically the whole American scheme of things. Yet no man believes more implicitly that the building of America was, on the whole, a pretty good job.

People to whom this seems doubtful should ponder the fact that nobody has been more bitterly disappointed in Mr. Roosevelt than the extreme radicals. No Republican has denounced him with such invective as Huey Long used to pour out for hours in the Senate. The crustiest member of the Union League Club has never hurled at him such objurgations as the Communist press used constantly until suddenly it became apparent that whereas he needed them not at all, they needed him desperately. The reason for this radical hatred is not far to seek. It arises from the fact that he who they had hoped would be the executioner of capitalism, because he applied the knife to it ruthlessly, may be, in fact, a surgeon, from whose operations capitalism may emerge, not dead, but stronger than ever and possessed of a renewed lease of life. The radicals may not be certain of this, but they certainly fear it, and their fears are patently well-founded. . . .

Call it what you will, call it patriotism, or call it merely an intelligent interest in the perpetuation and betterment of the nation, *a desire to improve upon the existing system is the very antithesis of a desire to demolish it.* Pride in it, pride that goes to the point of condoning even those villainies through which great things were done, is certainly not likely to be fruitful of a desire to demolish it. The political extremist may be the most honest of men, but he is always a despairing man. No matter how bright his vision of the ideal social order may be, his view of the existing order is hopeless; and that gives rise to his wish to demolish it.

Now Franklin D. Roosevelt has been called many things in the course of a long political career, but it is not on record that anyone has called him a despairing man.

The nondespairing quality—this quality of effulgent faith in the people—illuminated the New Deal. The critics of the New Deal, in the face of Roosevelt's tremendous electoral triumphs, could justify themselves only by concluding that the masses of the American people were lazy, shiftless, ne'er-do-well panhandlers who would vote for any demagogue who promised them a handout. The standard cartoon in the conservative press pictured the man on W.P.A. relief as a hopeless derelict leaning on a shovel, and the young man or woman who received aid from the National Youth Administration as a cynical Red and the farmer who benefited from Rural Resettlement as a piece of contemptible white trash; but more than twenty millions of American citizens

were at times directly dependent on relief and immeasurably many more
—contractors, manufacturers, wholesalers, shopkeepers, landlords, etc.
—were indirectly dependent. Thus, Roosevelt's opponents were, in effect,
giving mortal insult to a large section of the American people and were
thereby helping to identify him as the champion of the people's dignity.
As it turned out, this became a great asset to our national security:
when war came, the extraordinary prestige and popularity of Franklin
D. Roosevelt was the most powerful weapon in our arsenal.

There is no evidence that Harry Hopkins had any idea, certainly not
before the Munich crisis of September, 1938, that he was helping to
prepare and condition the country for war. But, despite the prohibitions
against any military activities which had been written into the Work Relief Bill, W.P.A. accomplished a great deal of construction—airports,
highways, bridges, etc.—that had deliberately strategic importance. In
the beginnings of the works program, Hopkins encountered great difficulty in meeting engineering problems. He and his enthusiastic staff
were long on understanding of human needs but short on technical knowledge, and it was difficult to employ competent civilian engineers at the
civil service wage scale. One of the principal executives in W.P.A.,
Colonel Lawrence Westbrook, a reserve officer, urged Hopkins to bor-
row personnel from the corps of engineers of the Army. Hopkins was at
first cool to this suggestion; he knew nothing of the Army and was inclined to be suspicious of all brass hats, feeling that they would have no
sympathy with the sociological purposes of relief. But, as criticism of
W.P.A. multiplied, and after one especially glaring example of bad engineering had made the headlines, Hopkins told Westbrook to go ahead
and see what he could do about getting an Army officer to serve as Chief
Engineer of W.P.A. Roosevelt approved of this and the War Department, with some reluctance, agreed to lend Hopkins the services of
Colonel Francis C. Harrington, who was then studying at the École de
Guerre in France. Harrington remained with W.P.A. until his death in
1940 and did a memorable job. Westbrook has written:

For the first two months after Harrington reported, Hopkins saw
very little of him. He was not even invited to some of the most important staff meetings. Harrington pitched into his work, however,
with great zeal and began to get real results. I took every opportunity
to bring Hopkins and Harrington together, and finally Hopkins began
to realize the latter's great worth and potentialities.

The rest of the story is well known. Within six months after Harrington reported for duty, he had Army engineers in every region
and many assigned to important specific projects. Their work was
excellent and Hopkins gave them full credit.

There is no doubt that the experience gained by engineer officers
in W.P.A. played a large part in qualifying them for the outstanding

parts that so many of them played in World War II. Furthermore, the experience of Hopkins with these officers gave him a knowledge of the Army that he could not have otherwise possessed, and, I think, prepared the way for the close cooperation that was so effective during World War II.

When General George C. Marshall became Deputy Chief of Staff in 1938 he made a considerable study of the Relief Program as it had affected the Army. He discovered that W.P.A. and P.W.A. between them had spent about $250 millions on War Department projects. This figure may seem diminutive, but it looked tremendous at the time. (It was not far from the average annual expenditure for the War Department for the preceding fifteen years; which indicates the awful aptness of the statement that, in peacetime, "we Americans treat our Army like a mangy old dog.") When he saw what opportunities the Relief Program had offered—and particularly when he talked to officers who had been associated with W.P.A.—General Marshall deplored the extent to which the War Department had failed to take full advantage of these opportunities; but it seemed that some of the aging generals had been too afraid of the Congressional criticism they might incur if they became involved in dealings with such vulgar, radical fellows as Hopkins. Marshall himself never had any such qualms.

Among the Army engineers who came into W.P.A. were Brehon B. Somervell, who was Commanding General of the Army Service Forces in the Second World War, and there were many others whom Marshall marked for advancement.

In its issue of May 16, 1942, the *Army and Navy Register* said:

> In the years 1935 to 1939, when regular appropriations for the armed forces were so meager, it was the W.P.A. worker who saved many Army posts and Naval stations from literal obsolescence.

But more important than that to our national security—more important than the vast works of strategic importance built by W.P.A. under the direction of Army engineers—were the things that were saved from obsolescence within the relief workers themselves, including their self-respect and their essential patriotism and, most importantly, their skills.

CHAPTER IV

The Presidential Bees

SOME of Hopkins' associates recall that it was early in 1935 that he first began to consider the possibility that he might become a candidate for the Presidency—not, of course, in 1936, when Roosevelt would surely run for a second term, but in 1940, when Roosevelt would retire. It was taken for granted by everyone in the Administration, the President included, that the second term would be the last one. Few if any were those who could conceive that the pressure of world events might become strong enough to break the third term tradition, although some of Roosevelt's opponents charged repeatedly that he was plotting to make himself permanent dictator. So far as I know, there is no actual proof that Hopkins had the Presidential bee in his bonnet before 1936 but, as has been seen, he was an extremely ambitious man and once he had established a position for himself he started restlessly to look toward the next step upward.

He was becoming increasingly prominent as a front-page figure and increasingly close to the President and to Mrs. Roosevelt, who was undoubtedly more deeply interested in the Relief Program than in any other phase of government activities. In her constant, tireless trips about the country (the subject of so many repetitious jokes at that time) her principal concern was with the "ill-housed, ill-clad, ill-nourished," the beneficiaries of the work that Hopkins was doing, and it was this work that she brought repeatedly to her husband's attention. Most appealing to Roosevelt were Hopkins' repeated, widely publicized fights with various dignitaries in the States—Huey Long of Louisiana, Gene Talmadge of Georgia, William Langer of North Dakota, Martin Davey of Ohio—for in these the Federal Government appeared as the champion of probity and the State authorities as players of politics.

On March 15, Hopkins noted:

77

The Ohio politicians have been raising campaign funds thru our office which pleases me not at all.

And the next day:

The evidence is complete on Ohio—the political boys went too far this trip and I shall take great delight in giving them the "works." Took the evidence to the President this morning—he wanted to get into the scrap and asked me to prepare a letter for him to sign to me —instructing me to take over the state. He later signed it and approved one of my own which was pretty hot. The President doesn't take a week to decide things like this nor does he need the advice of the politicians—in fact no one was consulted about an action which will throw into the ash can a Democratic Governor and his political machine. In fact I think the boss liked the idea of their being Democrats.

Davey blasted Hopkins as one "who could be expected to tear down the Democratic Party." But Hopkins said, "Politics has no business in relief and wherever it gets in, we intend to get rid of it damned fast." Of course, Roosevelt was well aware that such publicity was extremely helpful to the Democratic party—or, at any rate, to his own Administration which would face the electorate the next year—and it was doing no harm to Hopkins, either.

Far less pleasing to the President were the increasing reports of bickerings between Hopkins and Ickes. He liked fights, but not within his own official family. After the triumvirate commanding the Work Relief Program was formed in the spring, and despite the pacifying influence of Frank Walker, the Hopkins-Ickes "feud" received more and more attention. On July 3 Roosevelt issued a statement spelling out in detail the division of responsibility between the two: roughly, Ickes was to handle the projects costing individually more than $25,000, Hopkins those costing less than that. With the result that when W.P.A. undertook to build a million-dollar highway, or airport, the job would be divided on paper into forty separate projects.

At the end of September, Roosevelt went on a trip which took him across the country and then, again aboard the cruiser *Houston*, to Cocos Island and back through the Panama Canal. On this trip he took along both Ickes and Hopkins, to compel the quarrelsome boys to learn to fish and to love each other.

In the ship's paper, *The Blue Bonnet*, during this cruise, appeared the following news item under the heading "Buried at Sea":

The feud between Hopkins and Ickes was given a decent burial today. With flags at half mast . . . the President officiated at the solemn ceremony which we trust will take these two babies off the front page for all time.

Hopkins, as usual, was dressed in his immaculate blues, browns and whites, his fine figure making a pretty sight with the moon-drifted sea in the foreground.

Ickes wore his conventional faded grays, Mona Lisa smile and carried his stamp collection. . . .

Hopkins expressed regret at the unkind things Ickes had said about him and Ickes on his part promised to make it stronger—only more so—as soon as he could get a stenographer who would take it down hot.

The President gave them a hearty slap on the back—pushing them both into the sea. "Full steam ahead," the President ordered.

Of course, that particular bit of shipboard badinage could have been written by no one but the President himself. It provides pretty good evidence of the kind of joshing humor that prevailed in the Roosevelt entourage—humor suggestive of the atmosphere of the Elks' Club rather than of a potential Berchtesgaden or Kremlin.

During this gay cruise, on a ship that was to go to its death in the Java Sea six years later, Roosevelt received news of Mussolini's attack on Ethiopia, the beginning of the series of European Fascist aggressions. Hopkins noted:

No luck at fishing tho it was a gorgeous day. I think we were out too far for the rest of the party did fairly well. Back at six.

This evening cocktails as usual—Pa Watson doing the honors with what appeared to be powerful Martinis. The President was irritated because the State Department wanted to hold up his Neutrality proclamation and during dinner wrote the note at the table instructing its release at once. The Department had wanted to await the League's action but F.D.R. would have none of it. He wanted to act first. "They are dropping bombs on Ethiopia—and that is war. Why wait for Mussolini to say so." The President said that world sympathy was clearly with Ethiopia. His certainly are. He scanned the news dispatches and everything favorable to Ethiopia brought a loud "Good." He went over the large war maps with great care—places every important town—the railroads and the mountains and rivers. To bed early.

On returning to Washington, Hopkins wrote to his brother Lewis:

I am just back from the trip and am in no mood to do any work. I am terribly sorry that the trip out west did not materialize, but the President at the last moment asked me to go with him, and, of course, there was nothing to do but go. I had a perfectly grand time, saw a part of the country that I had never visited before, and am really rested.

If it would please you any to know it, this letter will also advise you that we are going to get our full quota of men to work sometime in November. It has been a tough job loaded down with government red tape of an almost unbelievable variety. They have tied pink ribbons on everything but the telephone poles and may have to do that yet!

The President got a great reception everywhere he went and unless the Republicans can trot out somebody better than any I have seen suggested, I think there is no question but that he will be re-elected. For my own part, however, I have no desire to remain in Government service forever. Don't be surprised if you hear of my getting out sometime before another year is out. . . .

Just what he meant by this last hint, I do not know. His political activities were constantly increasing and they were not those of a man who still considered himself a transient in government. However, he was also suffering more and more ill health; he had developed a duodenal ulcer which resulted in the imposition for awhile of rigid diet and total abstinence and he probably had despairing moods. He was certainly becoming less tolerant of the mounting attacks against W.P.A. and himself personally and the wisecracks with which he retaliated were sharp and well aimed but not always politic. Hopkins lacked the gift for picturesque invective possessed by Harold Ickes and General Hugh Johnson. He had neither the ability nor the inclination to find gaudy words to express his meaning. He was addicted to the naked insult. Hugh Johnson once wrote of him that "he has a mind like a razor, a tongue like a skinning knife, a temper like a Tartar and a sufficient vocabulary of parlor profanity—words kosher enough to get by the censor but acid enough to make a mule-skinner jealous. . . . He's just a high-minded Holy Roller in a semi-religious frenzy." One of the many States' Governors against whom Hopkins directed his skinning knife was Alfred M. Landon of Kansas; when a reporter mentioned that Landon had balanced the State budget, Hopkins said, "Oh, yeah—and he is taking it out of the hides of the people!" This remark was given wide circulation and undoubtedly was of some help to Landon in winning the Republican nomination for President in 1936, a development which proved to be no misfortune for Roosevelt.

That year of 1936 was one in which an inestimable amount of breath was expended and conservative blood pressure raised—and all of it, as it turned out, added up to the winning of eight electoral votes. Seldom has there been more political passion to less avail. An organization known as the Liberty League was formed to mobilize a popular crusade against the New Deal, but this League assumed the aspect of a veritable caricature of capitalism at its most reactionary. Its principal spokesman, sadly enough, was the embittered Alfred E. Smith who had been Hopkins' (and Roosevelt's) hero in liberal politics. A Talburt cartoon of the time showed how the "Topeka Tornado" (Landon) had blown Al Smith, Herbert Hoover and William Randolph Hearst into the same stewpan.

The forces of reaction were making desperate attempts to re-form their lines behind the respectable but unexciting Landon and their principal hope was to identify the New Deal with Moscow in the public mind. The epithets "Communist" and "Bolshevik" were hurled at the Roose-velt Administration and most of all at Hopkins, who was granted the dubious satisfaction of seeing himself and his work program become a violent issue in the campaign. The Washington correspondent of the *Daily Oklahoman* wrote:

> No. 2 man in the United States Government just now is salty Harry Hopkins, czar of all he surveys in the relief world and confidante of President Roosevelt.
>
> Although he holds no cabinet post, despite the fact that his job is "temporary" and not overlooking the classification of his department as "emergency"—the scrappy Hopkins holds more power in his hands than almost any other man beside the President.

In a Senate debate over a new $1½ billion appropriation for work relief, Senator Dickinson, a Republican of Hopkins' native state of Iowa, exploded:

> If Congress passes this bill giving Hopkins this huge amount, we will be raising an American Caesar in our midst. This bill is simply a starter for Hopkins. . . . He has his eye on the presidency. This is a laudable ambition, but I am against his using the taxpayers' money to build a political machine. The use of public money in politics is a national scandal.

The *Chicago Tribune* used a masthead and published a lead editorial which Hopkins had enlarged and framed. Under the bold-faced heading, "Turn the Rascals Out," it said:

> Mr. Hopkins is a bull-headed man whose high place in the New Deal was won by his ability to waste more money in quicker time on more absurd undertakings than any other mischievous wit in Washington could think of.

In the *Akron Times Press* and many other newspapers throughout the country appeared a political advertisement featuring a photograph of an anonymous "W.P.A. worker," who bore a striking resemblance to one of those advertising photographer's models who appear over and over again as genial railroad engineers (proudly displaying their split-second accuracy watches) or as genial foremen (pointing to man hours saved). The heading of this "statement" by a "W.P.A. worker" was, "IF YOU KNEW WHAT I KNOW ABOUT WPA! YOU'D VOTE REPUBLICAN TOO!" And it continued:

> I had to register democratic, and get my friends and relations to register democratic. On top of that, we have to subscribe to a New

Chicago Daily Tribune
THE WORLD'S GREATEST NEWSPAPER

FRIDAY, APRIL 17, 1936.

THE TRIBUNE'S PLATFORM FOR 1936

Turn the Rascals Out.

Only 201 days remain in which to save your country.
What are you doing to save it?

HUMAN NEEDS AND WASHINGTON POLITICIANS.

Mr. Hopkins is a bullheaded man whose high place in the New Deal was won by his ability to waste more money in quicker time on more absurd undertakings than any other mischievous wit in Washington could think of. The scandal of the political manipulation of funds under his control is growing and to it may be added the scandal of the uncared for destitute.

Deal political paper, and kick in every time someone wants to sell a ticket to a political shindig. And we do it *or else*. . . . The whole trouble is with the bosses put in by the New Deal, not one in a hundred knows what he is doing *or why*. But you can't blame them. They weren't put on the job to lay sewers or fix highways. Their real trade is politics, and believe me, they work it all the time.

The Detroit priest, Father Charles E. Coughlin, who was later to become one of the arch isolationists, denounced Roosevelt as "a scab President" leading "a great scab army."

Various newspapers printed each day the fearsome warning, "Only 27 (or 13, or 3) more days to save the American Way of Life."

Hopkins sent repeated, elaborate instructions to all W.P.A. units informing all workers on the rolls that they were not to be intimidated in any way, shape or manner by politicians, nor compelled to indicate support of any political party or candidate, or to contribute to any campaign funds—and that, on election day, they were to vote as they pleased. These notifications had some pathetically humorous consequences, particularly in the Southern States, when W.P.A. workers who could not afford to pay the poll tax went to the polls and displayed letters from the Honorable Harry L. Hopkins which, they felt, gave them full authority to vote.

Hopkins spent a large part of 1936 on the road, beating the drum for W.P.A. and for Roosevelt. His innumerable speeches were not prepared —so that there were no reading copies—and were considered insufficiently important to be reported at length in the oratory-crowded press. But at one of them, in Los Angeles, a transcript was made by stenographers from the local W.P.A. office then under the direction of Colonel Donald H. Connolly of the Army engineers. Hopkins started off with one of those jokes that are calculated to get an audience into a warmly amiable mood:

> I gained six pounds this summer and am looking pretty well after all the things people have called me, and the reason is I don't worry any more. A fellow told me the story about the eighteen-year-old girl that had her first date. Her father sent for her and told her there were certain things she should know. "This young fellow is very apt to hold your hand, and daughter, that is all right. Then he will want to put his arm around you, and that is all right. Then he will want you to put your head on his shoulder—you must not do that because your mother will worry." So the young girl went out and the next morning her father asked her how the evening had gone. She replied, "Well, Dad, everything happened just as you said it would, he held my hand, then he put his arm around me, then he wanted me to put my head on his shoulder, but I said, 'Hell, no!—you put your head on my shoulder and let your mother worry.'" . . .
> I am getting sick and tired of these people on the W.P.A. and local

relief rolls being called chiselers and cheats. It doesn't do any good to call these people names, because they are just like the rest of us. They don't drink any more than the rest of us, they don't lie any more, they're no lazier than the rest of us—they're pretty much a cross section of the American people. . . .

I want to finish by saying two things. I have never liked poverty. I have never believed that with our capitalistic system people have to be poor. I think it is an outrage that we should permit hundreds and hundreds of thousands of people to be ill clad, to live in miserable homes, not to have enough to eat; not to be able to send their children to school for the only reason that they are poor. I don't believe ever again in America are we going to permit the things to happen that have happened in the past to people. We are never going back again, in my opinion, to the days of putting the old people in the alms houses, when a decent dignified pension at home will keep them there. We are coming to the day when we are going to have decent houses for the poor, when there is genuine and real security for everybody. I have gone all over the moral hurdles that people are poor because they are bad. I don't believe it. A system of government on that basis is fallacious. I think further than that, that this economic system of ours is an ideal instrument to increase this national income of ours, not back to 80 billion where it was, but up to 100 billion or 120 billion. The capitalistic system lends itself to providing a national income that will give real security for all.

Now I want to say this, I have been at this thing for three and a half years. I have never been a public official before. I was brought up in that school of thought that believed that no one went on the public payroll except for political purposes or because he was incompetent or unless he had a job that he didn't work at. One of the most insidious things is the propaganda that something is wrong about one that works for the people. I have learned something in these three and a half years. I have taken a look at a lot of these public servants. I have seen these technical fellows working for three or four thousand a year—not working seven hours a day but working fifteen hours a day. I have seen these fellows in the Army engineer corps. The motivation can't be money—they don't get very much. I have seen them work just as hard as any engineers in America and just as qualified and just as competent, and I have come to resent an attitude on the part of some people in America that you should never be part of this business of public service. I am proud of having worked for the Government. It has been a great experience for me. I have signed my name to about $6,000,000,000 in the last three and a half years. None of it has stuck to the fingers of our administrators. You might think some of it has been wasted. If it has been wasted it was in the interest of the unemployed. You might say we have made mistakes. I haven't a thing to apologize for about our so-called mistakes. If we have made mistakes we have made them in the interests of the people that were broke.

When this thing is all over and I am out of the Government the things I am going to regret are the things I have failed to do for the unemployed. I don't know whether you would have liked the job. Every night when you went home and after you got home and remembered there was a telegram you didn't answer, the fact that you failed to answer the telegram and the telephone call may have resulted in somebody not eating. That is the kind of a job I have had for the last three and a half years, and still have. When it is all over, the thing I am going to be proudest of are the people all over America, public officials, volunteers, paid workers, thousands of people of all political and religious faiths who joined in this enterprise of taking care of people in need. It has been a great thing. I am not ashamed of one of them and I hope when I am through they are not going to be ashamed of me, and as I go around this country and see the unemployment and see the people who are running this show of ours, I am tremendously proud of this country of ours and I am tremendously proud that I am a citizen of it. Thank you very much.

Colonel Connolly wrote to Hopkins telling him what a profound impression this speech had made, saying that some who had heard it were advising Jim Farley that the same speech should be repeated all over the country. It is evident that Farley was not greatly impressed by these reports for, in the final stages of the campaign, Hopkins was not encouraged to make speeches; in fact, he was muzzled. Farley himself was a target for criticism at this time—the word "Farleyism" being used by the Republicans to suggest the corruption of political machines. Thus, Farley and Hopkins were linked together in editorials and cartoons as twin conspirators in the heinous plot to "buy" Roosevelt's re-election with relief funds. Of course, Farley was no New Dealer at heart and eventually gained the same degree of respectability as Al Smith in conservative circles. It was therefore particularly galling to him to be confused in any way with Hopkins whom he considered a radical and who, he was convinced, was a major political embarrassment to the President.

Hopkins made a savage reply on the radio to Landon's charges against the Relief Program. He said that Roosevelt's Administration had given the country "peace and rapid recovery" instead of "riots and tear gas," the latter a crack at the Hoover Administration. He said the W.P.A. workers should be given a "vote of thanks" by the nation "instead of being lambasted and caricatured as a bunch of slow-motion leaf rakers."

Shortly thereafter, he was condemned to silence and he suffered mutely during the last weeks before election as the attacks against him personally and the Relief Program in general increased steadily in sound and in fury.

At this time, Hopkins' one and only book, *Spending to Save*, was published. It appears to have been largely the work of ghost writers. Although the reviews of it in the press were, naturally, somewhat colored by the political bias of each paper, they seem to have been in the main fair and calculated to help the book's sale. For example, Lewis Gannett said, in the Republican *New York Herald Tribune*, "The Works Progress Administrator tells his story proudly. I think he has a right to his passion and his pride." The pro-Landon *Kansas City Times* said, "The chapters on the work of the relief administration are important in revealing the imagination and the vast efforts that went into the various forms of relief. In many respects, it is an inspiring record." But, the *Times* added, "There is no admission of mistakes—and mistakes are inevitable in such a huge enterprise; no reply to the charges of political administration." However, the comments on his literary output were of scant interest to Hopkins. He wanted to get out and talk—and shout—and that he was not permitted to do. It seems ridiculous that anyone as well informed as Hopkins was about sentiment throughout the country should have believed for an instant that Landon had a chance to win. But people in Washington are bound to become jittery as the day of solemn verdict approaches, for then they are judged and there is no hope of appeal. Hopkins was particularly sensitive because this was his first experience as an issue in an election: if the opposition could convict him of malfeasance in the public's eye, he might be responsible for the defeat of Roosevelt, and it would never do him any good to know that he had actually been not guilty.

In its poll of public opinion, the *Literary Digest* announced that Landon would win the election easily, carrying 32 States with 370 electoral votes, while Roosevelt would carry only 16 States with 161 electoral votes. The *Literary Digest*, it may be remembered, had never previously been wrong in predicting the outcome of a national election. The Gallup and the Roper Polls, then relatively unknown quantities, disagreed violently with their well-established competitor; Gallup gave Roosevelt a minimum of 315 and a maximum of even "more than the 472 he polled in 1932"; Roper figured the percentages: Roosevelt— 61.7, Landon—38.3. The final score of 523 for Roosevelt and 8 for Landon marked the end of the *Literary Digest* and the start of successful careers for Gallup and Roper.

Election night Hopkins and his wife, together with Dorothy Thompson, Mrs. Howard Wilson (Miss Thompson's sister), and Lawrence Westbrook were in the Iridium Room of the Hotel St. Regis as the returns were coming in. Miss Thompson, who was then a columnist on the *Herald Tribune*, was wearing a Landon sunflower. So was practically everybody else in the room, with the obvious exception of the Hopkinses and Westbrook. Miss Thompson has described this scene in a letter to me:

> The room was filled with much dressed up supper guests who were dancing in dim lights to a Russian balalaika orchestra. Every soul

in the room was obviously for Landon. The screen that had been set up flashed, however, only landslides for FDR except for one New Jersey county which had gone overwhelmingly for Landon. The returns from this county were reported over and over again, every time to applause, and Harry started to chuckle in his throat at the idiotic way in which the management was trying to keep up his guests' morale. Finally, however, the returns were all for FDR and the dancing Republicans simply ceased looking at the screen. When, somewhere around midnight Landon conceded the election and his telegram was flashed on the screen, no one even stopped dancing to look. Harry whispered, "My God, they don't know what's going to hit them," and laughed outright. I didn't awfully like this. But I did think the behavior of the crowd was preposterous, and said to Harry and Lawrence, "Get up and propose a toast to the President of the United States." Harry said, "Here? Are you crazy? We'd probably be lynched." I was obstinate and insisted. I wasn't for Roosevelt (nor against him) in that campaign, and Harry said, slyly, "Why don't you do it yourself?" I said, "If you won't drink a toast to your own candidate, why should I?" He said, "Because you are the stickler for the proprieties." I said, "All right; if you think I'm afraid, I will." So I got up, rapped on my champagne glass, and said: "Ladies and Gentlemen," in as full a voice as I could command. A few people stopped and looked around, and I said, lifting my glass, "I should like to propose a toast to the President of the United States, Franklin D. Roosevelt." Harry, Lawrence, and my sister had meanwhile, of course, stood up and we all raised our glasses. At that moment the orchestra which had paused for a moment started to play again and everybody started to dance, not an eye looking in our direction. We drank our toasts and Harry choked on his, he was so amused, and spurted champagne just past my nose.

I think that was the first time I was ever really for Roosevelt and, as ever after, it was not so much he as his opponents who made me so. I thought I had never seen such rotten sportsmanship. After all, the decision was made, the people in the room would have to accept it, so why not with better grace?

Still, I thought Harry's own feeling a little hilariously vindictive. Whereas I was perturbed by the attitude of the crowd, he was delighted with imagining the further chagrins they would feel before the next administration was over.

I did not see Harry for a long time after that. I thought he became progressively more mellow and—tolerant.

Westbrook has told me that after Miss Thompson sat down, she "publicly cast off her sunflower—forever." In 1940, she supported Roosevelt against her old friend, Wendell Willkie, and in 1944 she gave a speech for Roosevelt against Dewey which many people consider one of the most powerful and effective campaign speeches they ever heard over the radio.

The following day Hopkins returned to Washington. On the train with him and Mrs. Hopkins and "Pa" Watson was Helen Essary, who reported in the *Washington Times* that he said, among other things: "What a day this is! What a day! I tell you I'm the happiest man in the world. I was supposed to be the millstone around the President's neck. Am I rejoicing? Am I!" But, in this expansive moment, he was far from ready to forgive and forget, to let bygones be bygones. During the next three years, he had one purpose in mind: to make the New Deal permanent—and he believed that he was the chosen instrument for the accomplishment of this mission. He continued to pursue that objective until the world's and his own grave illness compelled him to change.

During the winter of 1936-37, there were many rumors about Washington that he was going to leave the government service and accept one of several "attractive offers" from private industry. It is quite probable that there were some industrialists who would have paid Hopkins plenty to get him out of the government, but he denied the reports as "cockeyed." More reasonable sounding was the persistent report that the President planned to establish a new Cabinet post—a Secretary of Public Welfare, or something like that—and give the job to Hopkins.

On January 15, 1937, while Roosevelt was preparing his Second Inaugural Address—"I see one third of a nation ill-housed, ill-clad, ill-nourished"—two thousand marchers, marshaled by the Workers' Alliance of America, circled the White House, chanting, "We don't want promises; we want jobs. . . . President Roosevelt, keep your promises. . . . President Roosevelt, we've just begun to fight. . . . Give the bankers home relief; we want jobs!" But the protests and rumors were washed away by another of the natural calamities which were sent periodically to test and strengthen the New Deal. The great waters rose in the valleys of the Ohio and the Mississippi and overflowed their banks. A vast program of emergency relief and rehabilitation had to be organized and put into effect within a few days. Less than two weeks after the floods started, Hugh S. Johnson wrote, in his column: "Never in our history have one-tenth so many people been affected by a great disaster and certainly never before have affected people been so skilfully relieved." He gave the credit for this to General Malin Craig, Chief of Staff, General Edward Markham, Chief of the Engineer Corps, Admiral Cary T. Grayson, of the Red Cross, and Harry Hopkins, whom he described as "a doer of good deeds, executor of orders, go-getter, Santa Claus incomparable, and privy-builder without peer, but . . . not so hot as a reorienter of economic universes."

Largely as a result of the shock occasioned by the floods, the Congress appropriated nearly a billion dollars for relief during the next five months, and there were no more protest marchers around the White House for a long time. However, as the waters receded, Roosevelt provided another spectacular front-page story, and this without any aid whatsoever from Divine Providence. On February 5, he presented to the Congress a "Plan for the Reorganization of the Judicial Branch of the Government," which came instantly to be known as the "Supreme Court Packing Scheme." This was the most startling—and, to many, the most alarming—development of Roosevelt's adventurous Administration, and it was the first major battle that he lost. Evidently Hopkins knew nothing about this sudden move, and had no part in preparing it—he was away from Washington on a flood survey trip during the week preceding the Message—but as soon as it became a hot controversial issue (as it did, almost immediately) he was called upon to defend it over the radio. In his broadcast on March 1, Hopkins said:

> It is a plain fact at the present time that unless the complexion of the Supreme Court can be changed, two or three elderly judges living in cloistered seclusion and thinking in terms of a bygone day can block nearly all the efforts of a popularly elected President and a popularly elected Congress to correct these ills. . . . Those who oppose this plan are not afraid *for* democracy. They are afraid *of* democracy.

However, Hopkins' defense of the Supreme Court plan was made merely in the line of duty and of unquestioning loyalty. Two years later, on a visit to Warm Springs, he wrote a memorandum in longhand, describing a conversation he had with Thomas J. Corcoran in which he learned of the background of the Supreme Court fight. Hopkins quoted Corcoran as saying that, after his famous "Horse and buggy" press conference, the President was thoroughly aroused "and determined to prevent" the Court from blocking what he believed to be the very fundamentals of our democracy. The Court, in his opinion, was "prejudiced and delivering opinions based on their outmoded political philosophies." Hopkins continued his quotation of Corcoran:

> Cummings [Homer S. Cummings, then Attorney General] discovered that McReynolds, our bitterest opponent on the Court, had while Attorney General in the Wilson Administration proposed a scheme to provide substitutes for judges who were disabled. Cummings brought this to the White House—received the President's approval and was told to work very confidentially with Richberg on a message to Congress. Cummings prepared the first draft—but Richberg added the venom. No one saw the draft or the rewriting so far as I know but Cummings—Richberg and Sam Rosenman. The latter acquainted me with some of the statements which I was sure

were wrong—notably the one about the crowding of the Court calendar—I tried to see the President to caution him . . . but Rosenman said the President was determined to send the message at once. I did get in to see him the morning the message went to the hill—I urged him to tell Brandeis in advance, hoping to soften the blow on him—the President told me to see him at once—I crashed the sacred robing room—he walked with me in the hall while the balance of the Court filed by—not knowing of the bombshell that was awaiting them. Brandeis asked me to thank the President for letting him know but said he was unalterably opposed to the President's action and that he was making a great mistake.

The fight in the Senate was bungled from the beginning—the message itself was weak—we had no adequate line of communication with the leaders—the President's messengers were incompetent and perhaps disloyal. I tried to keep Senator Wheeler in line but he hated Cummings and walked out on us. We missed a compromise when that could have been accomplished—Cummings and Richberg were advising the President to stand pat altho neither of them had any influence in the Senate and in fact completely misjudged the sentiment of that body. Cummings went for a holiday right in the middle of the fight. I don't believe we would have won the compromise even tho Joe Robinson had lived. A grand idea was lost by . . . bad political strategy.

To which Hopkins added a footnote:

Neither Tommy Corcoran or Ben Cohen had anything much to do with the Court fight. Tommy believed the Court should have simply been enlarged by three members. Once the President moved Tommy and Ben did what they could but Cummings and Richberg were jealous of all other legal advice and kept Tommy at arm's length.

In the spring of 1937, in the rancorous atmosphere produced by the Court fight, Hopkins went before the Congress with a request for another appropriation. He received a slap from the House of Representatives, which inserted a clause in the Bill cutting his salary from twelve to ten thousand dollars a year. The *Baltimore Sun* commented on this:

It was a remarkable outburst in the House yesterday that cut Harry Hopkins' salary from $12,000 to $10,000. This was pure spite, for what is a saving of $2,000 a year in a job like that?

But while the business has no monetary significance, it is highly significant as revealing the emotional state of members. They must hate Hopkins with a frantic hatred when they are driven to do as childish a thing as cutting $2,000 off his salary to express their anger and resentment.

No member voiced on the floor the real reason for this feeling toward Hopkins, but there is no mystery about it. They hate Hopkins because they are afraid of him; and they are afraid of him because

they think he is capable of building up an organization in their
individual districts to fight them, if they do not vote according to
his orders.

There is a widespread belief among members that Hopkins is a
vindictive man. Whether this is true or false makes little difference;
for as long as members believe it they will act on the belief. Unquestionably this feeling had something to do with the "ear-marking"
that turned the relief bill into a pork-barrel, and it is likely to
influence legislation in many ways. It is one factor that must be kept
in mind by anyone who hopes to understand the course of the House
during the remainder of the session.

Less objective in comment on this salary slash was columnist Franklyn
Waltman of the *Washington Post*. He said:

> Nothing that has happened around here in a long time has given
> us so much pleasure . . . it was a pleasant sight to see someone slap
> the smartalecky Harry Hopkins down.

In 1937, a vote hostile to Hopkins in the Congress could have been
achieved only by a coalition of the minority Republicans with the conservative (mostly Southern) Democrats. The opposition of the latter to
him was, of course, based on his espousal of the minimum wage. It was
also based on the fear that he might be a candidate for the Democratic
nomination in 1940. That was a possibility which was beginning to receive considerable attention in the press. General Johnson wrote:

> Harry Hopkins who, up to recently, was just a loyal, modest and
> highly efficient go-getter, is changing in several respects. In the first
> place, he has become No. 1 boy in the inner circle of the New Deal
> economists. . . . In the second, his personal staff of adulating water-
> boys has filled his head with the ineffable nonsense that he has political
> possibilities—heir apparent No. 42.

But the *Aberdeen* (South Dakota) *News* was not so sure that this
was "ineffable nonsense." It said, editorially, that Hopkins

> undoubtedly is closer to Roosevelt than any of his Cabinet members or
> unofficial advisers. Hopkins is the only prominent New Dealer who
> came to Washington in 1933 who has done a good enough job of his
> difficult assignment to keep from embarrassing his superior. . . . Who
> then, at this early stage, has any better right for consideration as a
> [Presidential] candidate than Mr. Roosevelt's right-hand man—
> Harry Hopkins?

His own home-town paper, the *Sioux City Journal*—for which his
father, Al Hopkins, had worked—viewed his candidacy with restrained
local pride:

> Mr. Hopkins' first qualification for the job is the fact that he is
> extremely liberal, even charitable. He can hand out money from the

United States Treasury in a way to gladden the hearts of voters in city, in town, in country. He is most generous, having given away billions already and being willing to dispense more billions as the need arises.

In the December, 1937, issue of *Forum* magazine there appeared an article on Hopkins by Raymond Clapper, one of the ablest and fairest American columnists, who was killed in action at Eniwetok in the Pacific in 1943. Clapper wrote, "Some of his friends have talked of him as a presidential possibility. Mr. Hopkins is too realistic about himself to take this seriously." For once, Raymond Clapper was wrong—or maybe not wrong, merely friendly. Hopkins did take himself seriously as a candidate at that time, and one of the last requests that he made before his death was that, if anything should be written about him, there should be no attempt to disguise the fact that he once had ambitions for the highest office and that he worked and schemed to further them.

It is impossible to tell whether his ambitions were impelled primarily by the normal politician's hunger for power and glory or by a natural desire for revenge. My guess is that the latter goad was the stronger. Although he liked to picture himself as thick skinned and impervious, he was actually extremely sensitive. His pride had been hurt by the frequent statements that he was a liability to Roosevelt, but of far more importance in his will to hit back was the injury done to his idealistic, Iowan concept of the purity of the democratic process. Some men, when confronted with the discovery that various Congressmen were more interested in feeding themselves out of the pork barrel than in feeding the hungry people, would have elected to quit in disgust, and some did just that. But Hopkins did the opposite: he developed the fierce determination to possess himself of the Big Stick with which to smite the venal politicians hip and thigh.

I cannot pretend to know just when Roosevelt first considered Hopkins as a possible successor, but it is quite clear that after 1936 he began to toy with the idea, to say the very least. (To say the very most, the President eventually acted as an unofficial but extremely competent campaign manager for Hopkins.)

The summer of 1937 produced a tragic interruption in Hopkins' career and almost put an end to it. He knew that his wife was dying of cancer and he suspected that he too was suffering from this disease which had killed his father. He took Mrs. Hopkins to Saratoga Springs for a final holiday. They were entertained there by the Swopes and other friends and each pretended to the other that it was all very carefree and gay; but awareness of death was in both of them. A few weeks later Mrs. Hopkins died, and a few weeks after that Hopkins went to the Mayo Clinic where a large part of his stomach was removed. The analysis showed that he did have cancer. It never recurred, but the operation produced nutritional maladjustments which made him prey to various weird diseases that afflicted him over and over again during the following years and ultimately proved fatal.

After the death of Barbara Hopkins, and before Hopkins himself caved in and went to the Mayo Clinic, he had a telephone call from his implacable antagonist, Harold Ickes, who had lost his own wife by death two years previously. Ickes told Hopkins that he was alone at his farm in Maryland and invited him to come out and stay for awhile if he wanted to get away from Washington and from all associations which involved harrowing memories. Hopkins accepted this invitation—and this was one isolated occasion when the feud was suspended. Describing this to me, Ickes said, with a sort of reluctant wistfulness, "Harry was an agreeable scoundrel, when he wanted to be."

Hopkins left the Mayo Clinic about New Year's, 1938, and went to Florida to stay at the house of Joseph P. Kennedy. The President then wrote him:

> Missy has told me that you telephoned on Saturday night. I am sorry I had not returned from the speech, as it would have been grand to have talked with you.
>
> I hope so much that you are not trying to hurry things up. It seems to me almost incredible that you should be walking around so soon. However, it is, of course, grand news.
>
> Joe Kennedy's sounds like an ideal spot for peace and quiet and recuperation.
>
> We all had great fun with Diana at Christmas time. She is a lovely youngster and stole the show that day. As you know, of course, she is now at Jimmy's "political" farm in Massachusetts where Jimmy and Bets say they are all having a grand time.
>
> The figurehead picture is bully and I am really awfully glad to have it. Thank you ever so much.
>
> Do keep us in touch with where you are and how you are, and take good care of yourself.

While in Florida, Hopkins was able to do some work with Aubrey Williams and Corrington Gill and was accused of politicking in connection with the primary campaign of Senator Claude E. Pepper. He returned to Washington in April after an absence of some six months and was invited to spend ten days in the White House, where his daughter, Diana, had been living since her mother died. Roosevelt took over the supervision of Hopkins' health and attempted to control his habits. He started to build him up in more ways than one. If Hopkins had not previously been told that he was Roosevelt's candidate for 1940, he was unquestionably told so now. There are notes of an extraordinary private conversation in the spring of 1938.

Roosevelt started off on the subject of the Supreme Court. He said that it had been the custom each year when the Court convened, early in October, for the secretary to the Chief Justice (then Charles Evans Hughes) to telephone the White House and announce that the Court is in session, whereupon the President would send a message inviting the Justices to call upon him. When they arrived, he would greet them in the Blue Room, whence they all proceeded into the Red Room where the President and Chief Justice would sit on a couch and take turns conducting the general conversation. Always on these occasions, Roosevelt said, Justice McReynolds would tell a story about the hot temper of Woodrow Wilson and of the mistakes in his Mexican policy.

Roosevelt said that in October, 1936, he was away campaigning but returned to Washington to be present for the annual Supreme Court visit. He knew the Court convened on Monday; he read it in the newspapers; but there was no telephone call to the White House. After waiting three days, he had Marvin McIntyre get in touch with Justice Stone's secretary to find out what was going on. McIntyre was informed that "There will be no visit to the White House this year." This was interpreted as a deliberate snub. "And remember," said Roosevelt to Hopkins, "this was six months before the Court fight started." (It was, however, more than a year after Roosevelt had started to assail the "Nine Old Men" for thinking in terms of the horse and buggy era.)

Roosevelt then discussed his next appointment to the Supreme Court in the event that Justice Brandeis resigned. An obvious selection would be Felix Frankfurter, to whom the President said he was both friendly and grateful, but the need was for a man from west of the Mississippi since that entire area was then unrepresented on the Court. (As it turned out, Frankfurter was appointed.) After which, the conversation settled down to the subject in which Hopkins was most interested: the identity of the Democratic nominee in 1940.

I gather from Hopkins' notes that Roosevelt did not entirely rule out the possibility that he might seek a third term. He seems to have left a very slight margin of doubt about it in the event of war. But he spoke of his own "personal disinclination" and the strong opposition of Mrs. Roosevelt to a third term. He told Hopkins that there were financial reasons for his wish to return to private life—that his mother was digging into capital to keep the place at Hyde Park going. (I cannot decipher the financial figures that Hopkins jotted down in this connection.)

Coming down to individuals, Roosevelt stated his opposition to these men as candidates: Cordell Hull, Henry Wallace, Harold Ickes, Paul McNutt, Frank Murphy (then Governor of Michigan) and George Earle (then Governor of Pennsylvania). The only apparent reasons noted were that Ickes was too combative and Hull too old. There were also some comments on Hull's direction of the State Department but the notes are not clear as to just what Roosevelt said.

Roosevelt mentioned Robert M. La Follette. The note on this was "fine—later—Secretary of State soon"—which is particularly interesting in view of the fact that La Follette subsequently became identified with the extreme isolationist group and therefore violently opposed to Roosevelt's foreign policy.

There appears to have been more discussion of Jim Farley than of any of the others. Roosevelt considered him "clearly the most dangerous" of the candidates. He knew that Farley was actively campaigning for the nomination, that he might run that year for Governor of New York State and, if he won, he might well be nominated and elected President in 1940. Roosevelt was against Farley on two main counts: his opposition to the New Deal and his attitude toward foreign affairs.

Then the President came to Hopkins himself, dwelling first on the liabilities. There was the circumstance of his divorce, but Grover Cleveland had survived a much more damaging scandal on his record and the second Hopkins marriage, tragically ended, had been a conspicuously happy one. On the question of Hopkins' health, Roosevelt was aware that the Mayo Clinic doctors had said the odds were two to one against a recurrence of cancer, but he also was aware that the Presidency is a killing job and that Hopkins had better get himself completely recovered by 1940. He recalled that he himself would have been able to shed the brace from his left leg if he had not been persuaded by Al Smith to leave his cure and return prematurely to public life in 1928.

Having considered these liabilities, Roosevelt expressed the belief that Hopkins would be elected and would do the best job as President of any of those then in the running. He then discussed strategy, saying that he would appoint Hopkins Secretary of Commerce and Louis Johnson Secretary of War. He felt that Hopkins should "keep back a little," stating that although his own aspirations for the 1932 nomination had started in 1930, he had not begun to work actively for it until the autumn of 1931.

This conversation ended, Hopkins notes, with an expression by Roosevelt of "assurances and hopes."

Some months after this conversation Jim Farley wrote in a private memorandum that "Roosevelt is a very strong character, and he might insist on naming his successor." It seems strange that, knowing Roosevelt, Farley should have used the word "might." It was Farley's guess that the President favored "Harry Hopkins, Robert Jackson or Frank Murphy, in the order named." Farley listed as his own selections, John Nance Garner (then Vice President), Hull and Farley—also "in the order named." In the Hopkins notes on his intensely confidential talk with Roosevelt there is no mention of either Jackson or Garner; in the case of the latter, it seems evident that the President had ruled him out as a possibility long before.

Hopkins told a few friends, all under oaths of strictest secrecy, that

Two pages from Hopkins' notes of a private conversation with Roosevelt,

6 . Machiavellian who of
Job for Farley - would
take it + "out of the way"

Me
Handicaps
  Divorce - Barbara helps -
  our divorced + Clevelands
  bastard
  Health - Mayo told him
  2 - 1 against recurrence
  but important - like
  his own - left leg
  would have shed
  brace had he not
  gone back

recording Roosevelt's promise to back him for the Presidency in 1940.

Roosevelt had definitely given him the green light and the campaign was on.

Bernard M. Baruch advised Hopkins that he should go into the Cabinet as Secretary of War rather than Commerce. Baruch, acutely conscious of the storm warnings heard from abroad in that year of the Sino-Japanese War, the Spanish Civil War, the Anschluss and Munich, believed that the War Department was to become the most important of all agencies and that Hopkins, at the head of it, would have immeasurable opportunities to gain distinction. I do not know whether Hopkins was given any choice in the matter; some of his friends believe that he was, but the only notes I have seen suggest otherwise. It is probable that Roosevelt himself believed that Hopkins would be better off in the Commerce Department as it would help him to establish some respectability for himself among the more conservative elements, and particularly the business community, where he needed it most.

Actually, the inclusion of Hopkins in the regular Cabinet seemed to be no promotion whatsoever. As Relief Administrator he received far more publicity than did Daniel C. Roper, then Secretary of Commerce, and had far more contact with masses of voters. But, too much prominence at this time might be detrimental. There was a Congressional election coming up in 1938 and it seemed possible that, in view of the Supreme Court fight and the unpopular purge attempt, the Administration might suffer serious reverses at the polls. A hostile Congress—even with the Democrats still in control—would be bound to concentrate its fire on W.P.A. and on Hopkins personally. Ammunition had been provided by a series of articles in the Scripps-Howard papers by Thomas L. Stokes "exposing" the political activities of W.P.A. in behalf of Senator Alben W. Barkley in Kentucky. Stokes later won the Pulitzer Prize for this series. There were a great many Senators and Representatives who piously approved the Stokes articles, as slams at the hated Harry Hopkins, and who secretly thanked heaven that this investigation had been conducted in Kentucky and not in their own States. I can say with assurance that there were not many members of Congress at that time who had never used W.P.A. in one way or another to shore up their own political fortunes. Just as post-office employees have been used from time immemorial to beat the bushes in behalf of the "right" candidates, so it was inevitable that local politicians all over the country would find ways and means of taking advantage of the vast W.P.A. organization. Hopkins hated these activities, but he most certainly knew about them and he made only occasional attempts to stop them, and to that extent he was culpable. Had Hopkins been hauled before a Congressional investigation of W.P.A., he could have done enormous damage to the reputations of many of his inquisitors but, in the process of doing so, he would have ruined himself politically. Thus, it was important

to get him out of that particular beam of limelight. But he must not be
relegated to dignified obscurity. The "build-up" must go on. A Presidential aspirant like a movie star must keep in the public eye, otherwise
people will not recognize his name when they see it on the ballot. That
is why Roosevelt never mentioned the name of his opponent in a speech.
"There are a great many people who never heard of him," the President would say. "Why should I advertise him?" You may call that
cynicism, if you will, or you can call it the plain truth. To one who
observed Roosevelt in political action it seemed that he had a better
grasp of the fundamental realities and the ultimate finesse of this art,
or science or trade, than did all of his enemies and all of his friends put
together. Although the astute but limited Jim Farley has promulgated
the doctrine—which I am sure he himself believes with all his heart—
that he "made" Roosevelt and was rewarded only with base ingratitude,
there would seem to be some reason for placing this particular shoe on the
other foot. Nor was Farley the only one whose name will be mentioned
in the indexes of the history books solely because he managed to hitch
his wagon to the ascendant Roosevelt star.

There is no question that in 1938 Roosevelt did all he could—and that
was a very great deal—to aid the Hopkins build-up. When the President was photographed at a baseball park or on the back platform of a
train, or on a fishing cruise, he had Hopkins at his elbow. This was not
by accident. There were many people who went along with the President when he appeared in public who did not feature prominently in
the news photographs. Indeed, it was a matter of discretion as well as
courtesy to make oneself inconspicuous when the flashbulbs were
popping unless the President distinctly asked one to be with him. It
was plain to see that while Hopkins was receiving this preferred treatment other potential candidates were not.

Mrs. Roosevelt, who often reflected her husband's views in her
column, "My Day," wrote the following significant reference:

It was good to see Mr. Harry Hopkins yesterday and to have him
spend the night with us. He is one of the few people in the world who
gives me the feeling of being entirely absorbed in doing his job well.
. . . He seems to work because he has an inner conviction that his job
needs to be done and that he must do it. I think he would be that way
about *any job he undertook*. He would not undertake it unless he felt
that he could really accomplish something which needed to be done.
[The italics therein are mine.]

On September 12, 1938, Hopkins and Howard Hunter were with
Roosevelt on his railroad car at Rochester, Minnesota, when the President listened to Adolf Hitler's Nuremberg speech of that date, two weeks
before the betrayal of Czechoslovakia. (Roosevelt was in Rochester because his son James was undergoing an operation at the Mayo Clinic.)

Also listening to that Hitler speech, in Prague itself, was William L. Shirer who wrote, in his *Berlin Diary*: "I have never heard Adolf so full of hate, his audience quite so on the borders of bedlam. What poison in his voice. . . ." Thereafter Roosevelt, who could understand the German language, among other things, told Hopkins to go out to the Pacific Coast and take a look at the aircraft industry with a view to its expansion for war production.

Shortly after Pearl Harbor, Hopkins wrote the following note:

> This letter which Colonel Wilson gave me was the result of a secret survey I made in 1938 for the President on the capacity of airplane factories to build military airplanes.
> The President was sure then that we were going to get into war and he believed that air power would win it.
> About this time the President made his startling statement that we should have 8000 planes and everybody in the Army and Navy and all the newspapers in the country jumped on him.

The letter referred to by Hopkins was a report that Colonel Arthur R. Wilson sent to the War Department from the West Coast where he and Colonel Connolly, the local W.P.A. Director, had been with Hopkins on his visits to airplane factories. (Five years later, Wilson was Commander in Casablanca when the Conference was held there and Connolly was Commander in the Persian Gulf area at the time of the Teheran Conference.) Wilson acted as liaison officer between the Army General Staff and W.P.A. during the prewar years when the armed forces were being starved to death by the pacifist-minded Congress and he was understandably excited when he wrote:

> Mr. Hopkins sang the same tune he did in Washington—that the Army and the Navy are sitting pretty to get a lot of money in the next relief bill for the national defense *if* they can sell the idea to the President. . . .
> Mr. Hopkins thinks that the War Department should present a big program which will include the manufacture of modern armament, airplanes, perhaps the employment of men in all arsenals so they can go at top speed—all this without regard to the present rules of relief labor and material. . . .
> The point is that Mr. Hopkins has the ear of the President as no other man, probably—rates higher than a great many of the Cabinet. And as we have talked about before, the way, or rather the entry to the President is through Mr. Hopkins. . . . The Chief of Staff or the Deputy [should] get an appointment with him . . . This question is not a matter of weeks and general staff studies but a matter of fast action and days.

As a direct result of this, after Hopkins returned to Washington he was visited by the new Deputy Chief of Staff, Brigadier General George

C. Marshall; this was the beginning of a friendship that was deep and enduring and important. In May, 1945, a few days after the German surrender, Hopkins wrote Marshall that he was leaving the government and Marshall replied:

> You have literally given of your physical strength during the past three years to a degree that has been, in my opinion, heroic and will never be appreciated except by your intimates.
>
> For myself I wish to tell you this, that you personally have been of invaluable service to me in the discharge of my duties in this war. Time after time you have done for me things I was finding it exceedingly difficult to do for myself and always in matters of the gravest import. You have been utterly selfless as well as courageous and purely objective in your contribution to the war effort.

After he became Secretary of State, Marshall told me that he believed that his appointment as Chief of Staff in 1939 had been primarily due to Harry Hopkins. It was Marshall's impression that Roosevelt did not develop complete confidence in him until after the war had actually started. For three years before Pearl Harbor, and for at least a year thereafter, Hopkins was Marshall's principal channel of communication with the White House.

General Wilson has written me of his contacts with Hopkins in 1938:

> I remember well the events leading up to my memorandum as a member of the General Staff when it was evident that a sleepy War Department plus an overzealous attitude on the part of many WPA officials backed by a local, rather than a national minded Congress, was spending millions in useless projects and letting the national defense starve. After several personal talks with Harry Hopkins, who shared my views and was very critical of the lack of plans of the War Department for sharing in the "relief money" (they were going after it with pitchforks when they should have been using shovels), I wrote a memorandum to General Marshall who had just recently been made Deputy Chief of Staff and who was in a mood and in a position to change some of the thinking of the War Department urging that more use be made of relief funds to further the national defense. You may know that after his meeting with Harry Hopkins several millions of dollars of WPA funds were transferred (secretly) to start making machine tools for the manufacture of small arms ammunition. This was before Hitler declared war in Europe; and this one move put the production of small arms ammunition at least a year ahead when England went into the war and started to place orders in this country for the manufacture of small arms ammunition.

Thus, there was at least one tangible, immediate result of the Wilson memorandum. But the total efforts at rearmament at that time were pitifully small; it is evident from the dismal record of unpreparedness in 1938, 1939 and well into 1940 that neither Roosevelt, Hopkins, Marshall nor anyone else got very far with the plan to rearm a nation which believed that the way to avoid war was to deny by legislative action the possibility of it. The ominous events in Europe and Asia were only serving to make the Congress more isolationist in temper and more truculent in its relationship with the White House. Congress wanted no relief funds spent for armaments. It must be added that Hopkins himself, with his ambition focused on new goals, did little to advance the interests of national security at this time. He was working for the election of a Democratic Congress in November and for the ultimate promotion of his own candidacy. In a speech at Chautauqua, he made further attempts to ingratiate himself with the business community:

> I can say from personal knowledge that the Government is not, and never has been opposed to business. It has no desire whatever to harass or punish business. It fully realizes that business must succeed, and must be able to work with Government, if our economic system is to be preserved. It seeks an understanding and a meeting of minds, not only as to present points of conflict but as to methods which will assure for the future, on the one hand, justice and fair dealing to all the people, and on the other, the confidence, success and legitimate profits of legitimate business enterprise.

Those worthy sentiments received far less publicity than did a remark, attributed to Hopkins: "We shall tax and tax, and spend and spend, and elect and elect."

This was published first by Frank R. Kent and then by Joseph Alsop and Robert Kintner in their syndicated columns and by Arthur Krock in the *New York Times*. (Alsop and Kintner, be it said, described the quotation as "probably apocryphal.") Hopkins stated categorically that he had said no such thing: "I deny the whole works and the whole implication of it." But the phrase was too juicy to be canceled. It was given national circulation and enjoyed a very long run; indeed, as this is written, nearly ten years later, it is still quoted by Roosevelt's domestic enemies when their hatred of the New Deal regurgitates. It was the subject of intense investigation when Hopkins appeared before the Senate Commerce Committee. Kent, Alsop, and Krock were called upon to testify. All of them wrapped themselves in the cloak of journalistic immunity and refused to reveal the "source" of this remarkable quotation. Kent, the only one who had actually talked to the "source," did not even appear in person before the Committee, but wrote a letter explaining, "I was first told of the remark in New York by a friend of Mr. Hopkins who is also a friend of mine. It was repeated with a good deal of emphasis as part of a conversation that occurred between Mr. Hopkins and this mutual friend in August (1938) at one of the New York racetracks. This friend is a man of reputation and standing." But, wrote Kent, after the remark had been published and Hopkins had denied it, "I called up the friend who had told me and asked if he would let his name be used to substantiate the truth. Somewhat alarmed at the prospect of a controversy, he was much averse to this. He gave several personal reasons why it would only embarrass him and asked me not to use his name. I told him that if that was the way he felt, of course I would protect him—and I have."

When Krock was on the stand he admitted that he had not interviewed any of the eyewitnesses to the conversation in question, including Hopkins, but said that the phrase "seemed to me a concentrated gem of Mr. Hopkins' philosophy." The Krock testimony, as set forth in the record of the hearings, provides a fairly good example of the sanctimoniousness with which the American press can seek to justify its occasional venality. A bit of dialogue:

> *Mr. Krock.* I have not thought of perjury. As I say, I made what seemed to me serious efforts to discover whether it was a chance remark, in which event I would not have printed it. It was a most logical statement, it seemed to me, of what Mr. Hopkins might have said.
>
> *Senator Clark of Missouri.* Do you not think the balance of credibility would be very strongly on the side of a prominent, responsible officer of the Government, when he comes into a hearing of this sort and makes an explicit, categorical denial, as against an anonymous, clandestine, and mysterious witness, who has not manhood to come forward with a confirmation of the statement which it has been said he made, and which has been printed by you and Mr. Kent?
>
> *Mr. Krock.* Senator, I think that is a tenable position for you to take.

The "anonymous, clandestine, mysterious witness" in the case was Max Gordon, a successful New York theatrical producer. He met Hopkins at the Empire City Race Track one summer's afternoon. Also present were Heywood Broun and Daniel Arnstein, the transportation specialist who, in 1941, made a prodigious but futile attempt to straighten out traffic on the Burma Road. Both of them reported their versions of the momentous conversation, which was extremely offhand and perhaps somewhat bored on Hopkins' part, and neither recalled that he had made the famous "tax and tax" statement or any other statement worthy of quotation. According to Gordon's recollection of the racetrack conversation, even though Hopkins didn't actually say those precise words, "That's what he meant!"

Thus are the eggs of canards laid. They are happily hatched out by presumably reputable journalists and, when they have taken wing, the denials seldom catch up with them. This particular one created a great deal of trouble for Hopkins and produced considerable wear and tear on his frazzled nervous system, but it did not greatly affect the course of events. It was too late for the elections of 1938 and by 1940 much larger circumstances had supervened. But the unscrupulous malice which impelled it is of much more enduring importance than the incident itself. (Years later, Krock came to the defense of General Eisenhower who was the intended victim of another canard. Krock wrote that the discussion in which the general made the imputed remarks was "of the private and informal character that important public men should be able to engage in without distortion through 'leaks.' ")

Just before the 1938 elections, Hopkins went to Hyde Park with the President and issued predictions which proved to be grotesquely overoptimistic. For one thing, he predicted that Frank Murphy, running for re-election as Governor of Michigan, would win by half a million votes. The election was close and Murphy lost. Furthermore, the fabulous Democratic majorities in the House of Representatives were reduced from 244 to 93 and, in the Senate, from 58 to 46. Of course, these majorities were still formidable but the coalition of conservative (mostly Southern) Democrats and Republicans was forming with sufficient strength to serve notice on Roosevelt that Capitol Hill was capable of revolt; the hostility that had been generated was to be a severe handicap to him in his attempts to get increased appropriations for the Army and Navy as war approached. The expected Congressional demands for investigations of the Relief Program were immediately raised. The swashbuckling headline hunter Martin Dies, Chairman of the Committee for the Investigation of Un-American Activities, announced that he would ask the new Congress for one million dollars to finance a full-dress investigation of W.P.A. and P.W.A. He stated his determination to rid the government of such subverters as Harry Hopkins, Harold Ickes, Frances Perkins and other "Communists and fellow-travellers."

There were two polls of public opinion on Hopkins taken in December, 1938, just before his appointment as Secretary of Commerce. The Gallup question and results as published were:

Hopkins has been mentioned for the post of Secretary of Commerce. Would you approve of his appointment?

Yes   —   34%
No   —   66%

These figures were followed by the inconspicuous, parenthetical admission that "Approximately 4 voters in every 10, however, said they had formed no opinion." Thus, the figures for those in favor should have been approximately 20 per cent and those opposed 40 per cent, with 40 per cent saying "Don't know."

The Roper poll taken at the same time was more detailed:

What is your opinion of W.P.A. Administrator Harry Hopkins,—do you feel that:

		Sex			Economic Level	
	Total	Male	Female		Highest	Lowest
	%	%	%		%	%
He has done a fine job and should be kept in mind for higher office.	9.4	11.2	7.6		3.7	13.0
He has made mistakes but on the whole has handled a difficult job well.	31.5	33.8	29.2		29.5	32.9
He has done a fairly good job but not good enough.	15.0	16.5	13.5		20.0	11.0
He has done a bad job and should retire to private life.	12.5	16.1	8.9		24.2	8.3
Don't know	31.6	22.4	40.8		22.6	34.8

Here it will be seen that those generally in favor represented 40.9 per cent, those opposed 27.5 per cent, with fewer confessing ignorance. It is understandable that Hopkins—and Roosevelt as well—always preferred the Roper to the Gallup polls, and fortunately Roper proved to be phenomenally accurate in his forecasts of votes. (In 1936 his margin of error was nine tenths of one per cent, in 1940, one half of one per cent and in 1944, three tenths of one per cent.) Roosevelt was always keenly aware of the importance of the "Don't Know" percentage, which was larger on the lower economic levels and therefore more inclined to be his supporters. He believed that, in national elections, there were many who had every intention of voting for him but who answered "Don't Know" for fear of provoking controversy and even jeopardizing their jobs. In the case of an appointment such as that of Harry Hopkins, he presumed that the thirty or forty per cent who did not know how they felt about it also did not greatly care and there would be neither dancing nor riotous mobs in the streets when he made known his choice.

On the day that the Gallup poll on Hopkins was published, newspapermen asked him whether, if he were named Secretary of Commerce, he would accept the post. He emitted his characteristic short, sharp laugh— a laugh that seemed to have an exclamation point at the end of it—and said, "Don't kid me, boys. This is the Christmas season and I'm accepting anything." Later that same day Roosevelt announced the appointment and the following day, Christmas Eve, Hopkins went to the White House to be sworn in by Justice Stanley Reed of the Supreme Court in the presence of President Roosevelt. Six of Hopkins' close associates were there—Aubrey Williams, Colonel Harrington, David Niles, Ellen Woodward, Corrington Gill and Malcolm Miller—and his secretary, Mary Van Meter, who went on with him to the Commerce Department. There was pride over this promotion in the W.P.A. staff and there was also lamentation. Hopkins commanded a degree of loyalty and devotion in his staff that approached the Jesuitical. Many of them believed him to be the only man in Washington who was really whole souled in his concern for human welfare; they loved him for the slings and arrows that he had withstood; they loved him for the very eccentricity of his administrative methods. They hoped that his successor in W.P.A. would be Aubrey Williams, for Hopkins and Williams had been an unusual team in that they paralleled rather than complemented one another; Williams was also taut and sharp, intolerant of cant, contemptuous of red tape and "channels." Roosevelt did not appoint him for he believed that Williams would provide the same kind of target as Hopkins for Congressional criticism—and this proved to be the case for, in the position of National Youth Administrator, which he now assumed, he was subjected to continuous, savage attack.

As Administrator of W.P.A. the President named Colonel Harrington, and it was a politic choice. For one thing, Harrington was serving for his Army pay, and therefore his appointment did not have to be confirmed by the Senate as would have been the case with a civilian appointee; for another thing, as a regular officer he was less likely to be confused with Communism.

Hopkins and his six-year-old daughter, Diana, were guests in the White House over the holidays, and he had a conversation with Mrs. Roosevelt for which he was forever grateful. Solicitous about Hopkins' health, Mrs. Roosevelt asked him what provision he had made for Diana if he were to die. It appeared that he had done nothing about making a new will since the death of his second wife a year previous; so Mrs. Roosevelt told him he must attend to this immediately and said that she would like to be named guardian of Diana. Hopkins described this conversation in a letter to his daughter years later. He wrote:

At that time I discussed with her the amount of my insurance and financial affairs and she said she would undertake to see that you got a good education and have a little money when you were through your schooling.

Mrs. Roosevelt has always believed that the main business of a modern education is to teach people not only to live in this world with other people, but for girls to have the kind of education which would enable them to earn their own living.

Mrs. Roosevelt was quite right about my being disturbed about your care in the event that anything happened to me and, naturally, I was greatly relieved at her offer which was made with great sincerity. She had become very fond of you during the time you had lived at the White House. I was, naturally, quite overcome by her suggestion, not only because it was an offer that would relieve my mind, but because I was sure was one that would be very good for you.

Hopkins made out a new will in accordance with Mrs. Roosevelt's warmhearted suggestion and she took care of his small daughter until his marriage to Louise Macy in July, 1942.

News of the appointment of Hopkins as Secretary of Commerce received what is known as a "mixed reception" in the press—and it was George S. Kaufman who once defined the term "mixed reception" as meaning "good and rotten." The *Chicago Daily News* said, "Surely, this is the most incomprehensible, as well as one of the least defensible, appointments the President has made in his six and one-half years in the White House." Said the *Los Angeles Times*, "By neither training nor experience is Hopkins acquainted with the problems which arise in the Commerce Department, nor is it likely he has much sympathy for them." The *Cincinnati Times Star* was more philosophical: "We fail to see ground for excitement in the appointment. . . . Obviously Hopkins isn't up to Cabinet size. But how many members of Mr. Roosevelt's official family are?" Raymond Clapper called this a "well-earned promotion" and added, "Hopkins may prove a notable success in Commerce—but if he does, he will have to change roles in a way that will stamp him as the most versatile character actor of these times."

The *Lansing* (Michigan) *State Journal* summed up its views with the words, "The nomination offends common sense." Perhaps the shrewdest comment of all was made by Senator Davis (Republican) of Pennsylvania who said, "I think that the President saw that the Department of Commerce had been a pretty good route to the Presidency (i.e., for Herbert Hoover) and he was training Harry."

Since most of the editorial blasts against Hopkins appeared on Christmas Day, it is improbable that any great numbers of people paid any attention to them; it is also not entirely impossible that Roosevelt timed it that way. By the time the holiday season had passed, and the new Congress had convened, Hopkins was established in the grandeur of the Commerce Building, far from the raffish atmosphere of Relief Headquarters where he had spent the past five happy and fruitful if costly years. He was now dignified. When photographed at his massive and relatively clean desk, in his enormous paneled and vaulted office, he did not appear lounging in shirt sleeves: he sat erect, wearing not only a coat but a waistcoat. He had, however, another hurdle to cross: his appointment must be confirmed by the United States Senate. "God bless you, Harry; may we always be friends," was the cordial greeting of Senator

Arthur H. Vandenberg when Hopkins appeared for hearings as to his fitness before the Senate Commerce Committee. It is likely that Vandenberg meant just what he said, even though he ultimately voted against Hopkins. There were, however, several men of Hopkins' own party, notably Senators Guy M. Gillette and Millard Tydings—intended victims of the unsuccessful purge—who did not disguise their opinion of Hopkins as a "White House termite," even though eventually they voted for Hopkins or abstained from voting at all.

At the outset of his hearings before the Senate Committee he surprised his chop-licking inquisitors by a display of disarming candor. Senator Josiah Bailey, the Committee Chairman, questioned him at great length about political speeches he had made in his supposedly nonpolitical role as an administrator of relief. Hopkins replied, "I do not want to duck that question. I do not want to imply I withdraw the contents of those speeches, but if I had the road to go over again I would not have made them as Relief Administrator."

During the hearings there were long hours of nagging, hairsplitting questioning by Senator Hiram Johnson of California—under which Hopkins appears to have displayed commendable patience and self-control—but the passages between him and other Republican Senators, Vandenberg and Wallace White, were characterized by a degree of courtesy and good humor that is not always evident in such Congressional investigations. (Vandenberg, by the way, was like Hopkins the son of a harness maker.) Here is one passage from the record:

> *Senator Vandenberg.* I think, perhaps, before going into any W.P.A. phase, I would like to ask you about one other matter, which is of personal interest to me. Mr. Hopkins, in the New York Times of May 18, 1938, after you had appeared as a witness before the Senate subcommittee which was considering testimony on the W.P.A. appropriation, you were quoted as follows:
>
> Asked if he had studied Senator Vandenberg's plan of returning relief distribution to the States, and requiring the States to provide 25 per cent of relief funds, Mr. Hopkins answered: "He had not seen it but that he was opposed to it anyway, which is a Republican measure, and I naturally assume it is no good. That is a pretty good assumption to go on in relief matters. Of course I am opposed to anything Senator Vandenberg would introduce."
>
> (Laughter, followed by applause from the audience.)
> *Senator Vandenberg.* Is that a fair quotation? Do not disappoint your friends out here in the audience who are clapping their hands.
> *Mr. Hopkins.* Senator, I really do not recall it.
> *Senator Vandenberg.* Well, I think it is rather interesting if you did say it, because—well, I would not quarrel with you about—
> *Mr. Hopkins* (interposing). I might have said it, Senator. I do not deny having said it.

Senator Vandenberg. Well, it is going to be somewhat important to find out what you did say on some of these occasions, and I am wondering how close that comes to your statement.

Mr. Hopkins. I think that was pretty close, Senator. (Laughter.) Very close; yes. (Applause on the part of the audience.)

Senator Vandenberg. Therefore it becomes important, in the first place, if that is your state of mind, and we will eliminate what you think about Senator Vandenberg—

Mr. Hopkins (interposing). I think very well of Senator Vandenberg.

Senator Vandenberg. Well, that is not of any importance. But if it is a good assumption to go on, that anything that emanates from a Republican source is worth condemning before you have heard it, I wonder how you are going to deal as Secretary of Commerce with the business of America, which is still occasionally in the hands of Republicans. . . .

Mr. Hopkins (referring to the quoted statement). That was a political aside, Senator.

Senator Vandenberg. Well, now, let me come to another political aside. I am very much interested in the statement made June 27, 1938, by your deputy, Mr. Aubrey Williams, who was addressing a relief conference in Washington. In the course of his address Mr. Williams said, in part:

"We have got to stick together. We have got to keep our friends in power."

Do you remember the reports of that statement?

Mr. Hopkins. Yes; very well.

Senator Vandenberg. Did you approve it?

Mr. Hopkins. No; I did not approve it. I think it was an indiscreet remark on Mr. Williams' part.

Senator Vandenberg. Did you censure Mr. Williams for it in any way or suggest to the public that you did not approve of it?

Mr. Hopkins. Well, I think Mr. Williams happens to be a very great man and a very good public servant, to whom this country is greatly obligated; but I think, perhaps, that all of us doing jobs around here are entitled to some indiscretions. And I think Williams was entitled to one.

Senator Vandenberg. Do you reserve a few for yourself, as we all do, I assume, in the same connection? (Laughter.)

Hopkins was ill at ease and somewhat evasive at one point in the hearings when Vandenberg asked if he had ever registered as a member of the Socialist party. Hopkins said he had voted for Wilson in 1916, for Cox in 1920, for La Follette (Progressive) in 1924, for Smith in 1928 and thereafter for Roosevelt. He eventually admitted that he might have registered as a Socialist in a New York municipal election many years before as "I was then profoundly moved by a desire to see reforms in New York City and to see the United States keep out of war."

(This last was undoubtedly a shrewdly chosen point, for Vandenberg at the time was a leading isolationist.)

Except for that one bit of uncertainty, Hopkins made an excellent showing and impressed the Committee with his downright honesty. At the end of the first day's hearings, Senator White said to him: "After listening for twenty-one years to witnesses at Congressional hearings, I am about to award you first place as a witness." Hugh Johnson wrote, "It was Harry Hopkins whom this Committee saw and heard. It was all of him—the best and worst of him without any false whiskers of bluff, pretense, alibi or excuse. It was as his friends have heard him either in 'moments of relaxation' or on some other hot spot—able, brilliant, candid, intense, impulsive, in some things impractical and above all things, personally loyal."

At the same time that Hopkins' appointment was being considered, the Senate was also considering Roosevelt's appointments of Frank Murphy as Attorney General and Felix Frankfurter to the Supreme Court. Both of them got through the Senate more easily than Hopkins, the latter being confirmed, after three days of hearings and a week of some truculent debate, by a vote of 58 to 27. Five Democrats voted with the Republicans against him and at least three others deliberately abstained. The next day the *New York Herald Tribune* said editorially and despondently, "If the President sits unrepentant in the White House, splashing the nation's money . . . demanding more and higher taxes and displaying not the faintest evidence of any fundamental change of heart or mind or outlook, how can the most willing of businessmen see any salvation in the shouting of one repentant sinner in the Commerce Department?"

Hopkins went faithfully to work to prove that the process of transmogrification had really set in. His old haunts and cronies knew him not. His good friend, Heywood Broun, attempted to give him a helping hand on the road to respectability. Broun wrote, "Not by any stretch of the imagination could Hopkins be called a radical. He is not dedicated to revolutionary changes in the political and economic structure of America. . . . His devotion to American democracy is complete and uncompromised by any reservations. To sum it all up, a strong, able and progressive person comes into the President's official family." This, particularly as coming from Broun, failed to convey much reassurance to the business community, but Hopkins tried hard to make new friends in Chamber of Commerce circles. The names that began to appear with increasing frequency in his daily engagement book tell the story: Averell Harriman, of the Union Pacific; Howard Coonley, President of the N.A.M.; General Robert E. Wood and Donald Nelson, of Sears Roebuck; E. A. Cudahy, Cudahy Packing Co.; Franklin W. Hobbs, Arlington Mills; James D. Mooney, General Motors; Clarence Francis, General

Foods; William L. Batt, S.K.F.; Edward R. Stettinius, U. S. Steel; M. B. Folsom, Eastman Kodak; Sidney J. Weinberg, Goldman, Sachs; Carle C. Conway, Continental Can; John D. Biggers, Libbey-Owens-Ford; and, of course, Bernard Baruch and Jesse Jones. Significantly, one old associate who moved with Hopkins into his new world was David K. Niles who had been his chief political adviser and campaign strategist. In the Commerce Department, Niles was flanked by two energetic young men, Victor Sholis and Fred Polangin, in promoting Hopkins as an ascendant statesman. It was their purpose to "play up" Hopkins' grass-roots background and his experience as a hardheaded, two-fisted executive and to "play down" his career as a social worker, this last being suggestive of starry-eyed idealism if not of sinister radicalism. Their greatest publicity asset was the Business Advisory Council of the Department of Commerce. This included many of the men whose names have already been mentioned. Some of them—notably Harriman, Stettinius and Batt—were close friends of Hopkins' and associated with him throughout the war; they came to be known, among less friendly businessmen and also among inveterate New Dealers, as "Hopkins' tame millionaires."

Because of his desire to identify himself as an Iowan, Hopkins selected Des Moines as the scene of his first major speech as Secretary of Commerce. When he appeared there, at the Des Moines Economic Club, he was accompanied by Harriman who acted as a sort of chaperon or guarantor of economic stability. The Hopkins speech, broadcast nationally, was a persuasive document, and generally reassuring to businessmen, but it was too carefully prepared, too meticulously conciliatory to all groups, to be a characteristic expression of Hopkins himself. It was the kind of speech which appeared to have been written by a large committee rather than by the individual speaker; it was synthetic, characterless. The political overtones and undertones of this Des Moines speech were so obvious to any trained observer that Farley referred to it as "Hopkins' Acceptance Speech." Near the end of this lengthy oration, Hopkins took some cognizance of the perilous state of the human race as of February, 1939. He said:

> We find ourselves in a world which seems to have gone almost crazy in a welter of hates and fears, and in which a new and competitive philosophy has suddenly emerged. A world in which dictatorships —both red and black—have swept aside with ruthless decision almost all of the liberties and freedoms that have made life beautiful and wholesome. It is said that in respect to some of the harsh brutalities of life, these dictatorships are vastly more efficient than the democratic government with which we are familiar. I suppose that it is true that they can raise armies and manufacture guns and mobilize military power more quickly and more destructively than a democratic nation.

But he had no solution to offer other than the obvious, isolationist one that the United States must be sure to put and keep its own house in order.

While in Iowa, Hopkins visited his old friends, Robert and Florence Kerr. He told them that he was anxious to buy a farm in Iowa, and they worked in his behalf on the investigation of properties around Grinnell and they also looked into the legal aspects of the proposal that he re-establish his voting residence in his native State. Kerr reported discouragingly that the mere purchase of property would not be enough. Iowans were inclined to be suspicious of such measures. Hopkins would have to prove the sincerity of his intentions by moving all his household goods and his daughter to Iowa and visiting there himself just as often and for as long as his official duties would permit; it would help further if he were to rejoin the local Methodist Church and also to join some local clubs and emphasize repeatedly through publicity that Iowa was his home and that he intended to return and live there permanently as soon as his term as Secretary of Commerce should come to an end. "I know," said Kerr, with authority, "you don't want to do these things."

This situation amused Roosevelt who said, "We've got to pass the hat to raise the money to buy that farm for Harry."

Hopkins finally took a two-year lease on a farm near Grinnell, Iowa, and then rented it in turn to the tenant farmer who had been operating it. As a strictly absentee landlord, Hopkins derived a profit of two or three hundred dollars a year from his farm, but he never lived on it and visited it only once.

After his return to Washington following the Des Moines speech, he wrote to his brother, Lewis:

I had a very delightful trip to Iowa although I was feeling pretty miserable all the time I was there since I had a touch of the flu before I started. I met some of our old friends and all of them asked about you. I am greatly tempted to get a house out there so that I will have some place to call my own. I can't think of any place in the country in which I would rather spend my declining years than that little college town, and now that I am approaching fifty I might as well get ready for it.

Hopkins could be excused from the charge of arrant hypocrisy in those remarks only on the ground that he was a sick man. The "touch of the flu" developed into a complexity of nutritional diseases which laid him low and, a few months later, nearly killed him. During the next year and a half before his resignation as Secretary of Commerce he spent no more than thirty days off and on at his office. He did conduct a certain amount of business from his house, largely through Edward J. Noble who had taken leave of absence as Chairman of the Board of Life-Savers (Candy) Corporation to serve first with the

Civil Aeronautics Authority and then with Hopkins as Under Secretary of Commerce. The public relations men in the Department worked overtime to keep Hopkins in the news, issuing statements to suggest that he was still a dynamo of activity. But it was a masquerade and it provided, in my opinion, the one serious blot on Hopkins' public record. To begin with, the fact that he had cancer in 1937 was completely hushed up. Hopkins might possibly have been able to justify this concealment on the ground that his operation had been successful. However, on his own admission, the Mayo Clinic specialists had told him the odds were two to one against recurrence of the disease, and those odds seem hardly long enough in the case of one who aspired to be President of the United States. Fortunately, the question of Hopkins' health became an academic one in so far as the people's interest was concerned. Near-fatal illness drained him of all personal ambition and converted him into the selfless individual who rendered such great service to the President during the war years.

Early in March, 1939, Hopkins was still feeling worn out and spent from that "touch of flu" and he was glad to accept an invitation from Bernard Baruch to spend a few days at Hobcaw Barony near Georgetown, South Carolina. Baruch's huge plantation was near the coast, at the confluence of the Pee Dee and Waccamaw Rivers, a beautiful and largely wild place, full of live oaks, Spanish moss, magnolias, camellias, azaleas, many kinds of game and fish—and the serene wisdom, the overwhelming prestige and the unshakable self-confidence of its owner. In the cultivation of his own political garden, Hopkins could do no better than seek out the advice and counsel (and, above all, the support) of Bernard Baruch, who held the title of Elder Statesman Number One longer than any man had since Thomas Jefferson.

But when Hopkins visited Hobcaw, Baruch was not inclined to give much attention to political prospects or business conditions at home. His concern was with the gathering calamity abroad. He scoffed at a statement made on March 10 by Neville Chamberlain that "the outlook in international affairs is tranquil." Baruch agreed passionately with his friend, Winston Churchill, who had told him, "War is coming very soon. We will be in it and you [the United States] will be in it. You [Baruch] will be running the show over there, but I will be on the sidelines over here." (That last prophecy was proved inaccurate.) Baruch talked to Hopkins of the realities of the situation as he had seen them in Europe and reported them privately to Roosevelt the previous year; he talked of the amount of misinformation that was being collected and transmitted by our official representatives in Europe; he talked of the woeful state of our unpreparedness and of the measures that had been taken to meet production problems in the First World War. Years later, Baruch said: "I think it took Harry a long time to realize how greatly we were involved in Europe and Asia—but once he did realize it, he was all-out for total effort." And he added, "Harry didn't want much to listen to me, but I kept at him."

Chamberlain's assurance of tranquillity held good for just about as long as his later proclamation that Hitler had "missed the bus." On March 14 Czechoslovakia was broken in two by the Nazi fifth column and the following day Hitler and his army marched from the surrendered Sudeten bastion to Prague, in contemptuous violation even of the humiliating assurances he had given at Munich. Europe and the world were again plunged into a state of crisis which might mean war at any moment. Churchill gave a speech to his constituents, some of whom were complaining that he was disloyal to the Prime Minister and to the cause of peace in his attacks on the Munich agreement. He said:

> To suppose that we are not involved in what is happening is a profound illusion. Although we can do nothing to stop it, we shall be sufferers on a very great scale. We shall have to make all kinds of sacrifices for our own defense that would have been unnecessary if a firm resolve had been taken at an earlier stage. We shall have to make sacrifices not only of money, but of personal service in order to make up for what we have lost. This is even more true of the French than of ourselves.

After the visit to Hobcaw, Hopkins underwent exhaustive tests and X rays to make sure that there was no recurrence of cancer; there apparently was none. Dr. George B. Eusterman wrote from the Mayo Clinic to Dr. Kenneth Johnson, "If we can get our distinguished patient to give us a little more cooperation with respect to a more hygienic mode of living this would pay big future dividends." But Hopkins himself was then too discouraged about his health to take much interest in café society or in the situation in Europe.

At the end of March he went to Warm Springs with the President. He wrote a description of this visit:

> We left Washington early in the afternoon of Wednesday, March 29—Mrs. Roosevelt had invited Diana to stay at the White House while I was in Warm Springs—so promising real live ducks for Easter—I kissed my adorable one good-by and for the first time in two weeks stepped out of doors on my all too wobbly legs. I had a room in the President's car and slept the afternoon through—and now more than a week has passed and I am feeling ever so much better.
> There is no one here but Missy—the President and me—so life is simple—ever so informal and altogether pleasant. And why not—I like Missy—the President is the grandest of companions—I read for hours—and sleep ever so well. The food as ever around the W. H. menage is medium to downright bad.

The President wakes up about eight thirty—breakfasts in bed—
reads the morning papers and if left alone will spend a half hour or
so reading a detective story. I would go in about nine thirty—usually
much talk of European affairs—Kennedy and Bullitt our ambassadors
in London and Paris would telephone—Hull and Welles from the
State Department so we had the latest news of Hitler's moves in the
international checkerboard. His secretaries and aides would come in
at ten thirty with mail, schedule of appointments—gossip of the
Foundation—light chit-chat for half an hour when the President
dressed before going to the pool for his daily treatment at eleven. He
may keep an appointment before eleven—gets in his little car—drives
by the press cottage for an interview—this takes about twenty
minutes—after the pool he will drive by the golf links—home for
lunch at one.

Lunch has usually been F.D.R. with Missy and me—these are the
pleasantest because he is under no restraint and personal and public
business is discussed with the utmost frankness. The service incidentally is as bad as the food. There are thousands of men in America
who get infinitely better care than the President—this in spite of the
fact that he is crippled. I would fire them all.

He will sleep a bit after lunch—and at three drive over the countryside with a guest—visit his farm—look at the new tree plantings—
back around four thirty for an hour's dictation. Then relax till
dinner at seven. The ceremonial cocktail with the President doing
the honors—gin and grapefruit juice is his current favorite—and a
vile drink it is! He makes a first rate "old fashioned" and a fair
martini—which he should stick to—but his low and uncultivated taste
in liquors leads him woefully astray. Missy and I will not be bullied
into drinking his concoction which leads him to take three instead of
his usual quota of two.

Dinner therefore is gay—as it should be—and the President
reminisces long over the personal experiences of his life—he tells
incidents well—tho he has a bad habit of repeating them every year
or so. I fancy Missy has heard them all many times but she never
flickers an eyebrow.

After dinner the President retreats to his stamps—magazines and
the evening paper. Missy and I will play Chinese checkers—occasionally the three of us played but more often we read—a little conversation—important or not—depending on the mood. George Fox comes
in to give him a rub down and the President is in bed by ten.

The above is interesting—aside from Hopkins' random style and his
peculiar addiction to the embellishment "ever so"—in that it shows
that he was still after five years something of a stranger in the Roosevelt
entourage. It also shows how quickly Roosevelt could pass from a
state of utter relaxation to one of historic action. On April 14, a few
days after his return from Warm Springs, the President addressed a
message to Adolf Hitler, in which he said:

You have repeatedly asserted that you and the German people have no desire for war. If this is true there need be no war.

Nothing can persuade the peoples of the earth that any governing power has any right or need to inflict the consequences of war on its own or any other people save in the cause of self-evident home defense.

In making this statement we as Americans speak not through selfishness or fear or weakness. If we speak now it is with the voice of strength and with friendship for mankind. It is still clear to me that international problems can be solved at the council table.

Hitler's reply to that, two weeks later, was a derisive speech to the Reichstag which led Senator William E. Borah to suggest with some satisfaction that, in the German Fuehrer, Roosevelt had met his match. At the same time the War Department received a long report from the Acting Military Attaché in the American Embassy in Berlin expressing the expectation that if Germany could not coerce Poland through negotiations she would attack within the next thirty days. He added:

> The present situation when viewed in the light of an active war which Germany is now in the process of waging becomes clear. It is an economic war in which Germany is fighting for her very existence. Germany must have markets for her goods or die and Germany will not die.

From which it is evident that the Military Attaché was not only attending to his job of observing the Wehrmacht and the Luftwaffe; he was also listening faithfully to Goebbels' propaganda and reflecting it in his official reports.

The extent to which Roosevelt suspected the accuracy of his official sources of information—as well as the extent to which he was interested in odd details—is revealed by a bit of highly unimportant correspondence that passed between him and Hopkins during that same critical period. Roosevelt sent Hopkins the following memorandum:

> Will you get for me a memorandum on the relative cost of living in Caracas, Venezuela, as compared with Washington, D.C.—in terms of American dollars? The State Department tells me that for a given income of say $2,000 in Washington, the same person would have to be paid about $5,000 in American money in order to live in the same way in Caracas. I don't believe it.
>
> In having this looked up, don't let the State Department know about this query.

The reply to the President came not from Hopkins but from Willard L. Thorp, and proved that the State Department's information was correct. This report covered more than five typewritten pages of details on the cost of living in Venezuela, such as: "bottle of catsup (14 oz.) . . . 98c." I feel sure that Roosevelt read all of this with utmost interest and perhaps with some disappointment that he had not caught the Foreign Service off base.

After returning from Warm Springs with the President, Hopkins was again too ill to go to his office and a few days later he left Washington for another rest, this time at the home of his friend, Roy Carruthers, in Versailles, Kentucky. There, with Mr. and Mrs. John Hertz, he attended the Keeneland Race Track and paid a visit of homage to the great horse, Man O'War. Thereafter, for awhile, he was able to do some work in Washington and to give some replies in person rather than through press agents to the increasing criticisms of his absences from his desk in the Commerce Department. (All of the camouflage in the world could not fool the Washington newspapermen who knew that, when Hopkins was really working, he was accessible to them and unfailingly talkative.)

It was at this time—June, 1939—that Hopkins first spoke publicly of his advocacy of a third term for President Roosevelt. When he told a United Press reporter that he was determined to urge Roosevelt to seek the Democratic nomination in 1940, the reporter asked, "How is President Roosevelt going to get around the third term bugaboo?" Hopkins answered, "You have got the answer when you say 'President Roosevelt.' " Some of those who were close to Hopkins at this time have told me that by now Hopkins was hoping to get the Vice Presidential nomination and thus be Roosevelt's running mate on the Democratic ticket. His attempts to re-establish himself as an Iowan would seem to support that. However, I have no record of that nor of the President's possible attitude toward such a suggestion. There is a private memorandum written by Hopkins on May 28, 1939, which gives an indication of Mrs. Roosevelt's attitude—as follows:

I had luncheon today with Mrs. Roosevelt at the White House. She asked Diana to come with me, and together with two or three of her friends we lunched out on the porch. After luncheon we went out in the gardens—Mrs. Roosevelt had her knitting—and discussed for three hours the State of the Nation.

Mrs. Roosevelt was greatly disturbed about 1940. She is personally anxious not to have the President run again, but I gathered the distinct impression that she has no more information on that point than the rest of us. She feels the President has done his part entirely. That he has not the same zest for administrative detail that he had and is probably quite frankly bored. She thinks that the causes for which he fought are far greater than any individual person, but that if the New Deal is entirely dependent upon him, it indicates that it hasn't as strong a foundation as she believes it has with the great masses of people. Mrs. Roosevelt is convinced that a great majority of the voters are not only with the President, but with the things he stands for, and that every effort should be made to control the Democratic

Convention in 1940, nominate a liberal candidate and elect him. She has great confidence in his ability to do this, if, and it seems to be a pretty big "if" in her mind, he is willing to take his coat off and go to work at it.

Early in June, Hopkins had to rent his one and only cutaway coat and striped pants for the ceremonies attendant upon the visit to Washington of King George VI and Queen Elizabeth, whom he was to meet again during the Blitz in London in January, 1941. (He had no cutaway or striped pants on that occasion.) Since James A. Farley has made something of a point of the fact that the President and Mrs. Roosevelt did not invite him to Hyde Park when the King and Queen visited there after their trip to Washington, it might be added that Hopkins was not invited either, nor, so far as I know, was any other Cabinet member except Henry Morgenthau who was a near neighbor.

During the royal visit, Mrs. Roosevelt wrote in her column, "My Day," of an encounter with Queen Elizabeth and Diana Hopkins and, with characteristic considerateness, she had this passage typed out on White House stationery and signed it so that Diana might have it as a souvenir of this experience. The description follows:

> The young people in the Cabinet group have been given the opportunity to meet Their Majesties. Only one very young member, Diana Hopkins, has not as yet had this opportunity, and I told the Queen that I thought Diana envisioned her with a crown and sceptre.
>
> With true understanding, she responded that perhaps the child would be more satisfied if she saw her dressed for dinner, as that might be more like her dream, so this has been arranged.
>
> At 7:45 little Diana Hopkins and I were waiting in the hall for Their Majesties to come out of their rooms on their way to the British Embassy for dinner. Diana is a solemn little girl and she was speechless when the King and Queen came down the hall. She made her little curtsy to each one and when they asked her questions she managed to answer, but her eyes never left the Queen. After it was over I said: "Diana, did she look as much like a fairy queen as you expected?" With a little gasp she said: "Oh, yes." And she did, for the Queen's spangled tulle dress with her lovely jewels and her tiara in her hair, made her seem like someone out of a story book.

During the tense summer of 1939, at the suggestion of Ross McIntire, Hopkins spent most of his time at Delabrooke, a beautiful, old, pre-Revolution house on the Patuxent River in Maryland some fifty miles southeast of Washington. His sons Robert and Stephen spent part of their holidays with him there. Robert has written me:

> We were both amazed at how sick he was. His letters never indicated this. When we first arrived, he was quite active. He went out fishing in the motor launch almost every morning. He took a nap each

afternoon. Then he began having trouble with his legs. The muscles in his calves seemed to tighten up. Soon he didn't have the strength to step into the rowboat. He spent more and more time in bed.

On about July 5th, the President came up the river on the "Potomac." He was due to arrive at six in the evening. Dad sent Stephen and me up on the roof of Delabrooke so that we could let him know as soon as we sighted the "Potomac." This would give him time to dress. I remember, at this point, that Dad was furious when Lottie dressed Diana up in a little starched white dress. He made her change into a playsuit. The President's ship arrived exactly on schedule. We went aboard and the "Potomac" headed out for the Chesapeake Bay where we were to fish. . . .

Apparently Ross McIntire put Dad on a pretty rugged diet. This was a source of frustration for Dad. He constantly talked about the rich and wonderful foods that he couldn't have. He talked about delicious ways of preparing steaks and seafood, and then would sit down to a dinner of strained vegetables. Still he maintained his sense of humour. On more than one occasion I can remember him saying, "Well, it's time for me to have my spinach"—whereupon he would whip out a hypodermic and give himself a shot in the leg.

On August 22, Hopkins went again to the Mayo Clinic. On August 25, Roosevelt wrote to him:

Your birthday has come and gone and although I had it very much on my mind to send you a ribald radio, things began to pop in Europe and I let the day pass by. This is to send you my congratulations and every kind of good wish for many happy returns of the day.

I am delighted that you are at Mayo's. It was the only wise thing to do.

Why don't you stop off at Hyde Park on your way back if I am there—which means if there is no war in Europe. Things are looking a little brighter today.

Do telephone me to let me know how you are.

As ever yours,

/s/ F.D.R.

P.S. I am counting on you to help entertain the ———— who will be back this Fall if there is no war. However, don't pray for a war! [The name deleted was of two friends of Roosevelt's whom Hopkins found boring.]

While the crisis developed and finally burst in Europe, Roosevelt kept in touch with Hopkins and with his doctors by telephone. His condition was very grave. On August 31, Hopkins wrote to the President:

It was so good to talk to you the other night. You sounded so cheerful and encouraging in spite of the fact that the world seems to be tumbling around our heads. I think your letter to Hitler was grand and I am sure it is having a very real effect on the present delays.

The thing I am disturbed about more than anything else is the danger of another Munich which I think would be fatal to the democracies.

They are not through with my tests here yet and I doubt if they will be for another two or three days but I don't imagine I will be out of here until after Labor Day at least. It looks more and more like a dietary problem. I am sure there is nothing wrong with my stomach.

I will be in touch with you during the next few days and will surely accept your cordial invitation to come to Hyde Park if the doctors here will prescribe it. The place is full of your acquaintances, all of whom ask about you.

It is a matter of tragic record that whatever the "delays" produced by Roosevelt's message to Hitler, they did not last more than a few hours after Hopkins' letter was written. The Germans attacked Poland that night and thereby started the Second World War.

Hopkins' brother, Emory, of Portland, Oregon, wrote him a letter which contained the following prescient paragraph:

The war will, of course, change all our lives more than we can now anticipate. You may be called upon for a still bigger job of organizing and administrating than the W.P.A. was. I hope your health will permit you to carry on any job that may come your way.

However, Hopkins was not then concerned with any thoughts of changes in his life which the war might bring about; he was concerned only with the increasingly slim chance that his life could be saved. On September 8, he sent a letter to his brother, Lewis, which caused the doctor to travel east with all possible haste. This letter, indicative of near-despair, was as follows:

I am sorry I haven't written you before but I have been undergoing some pretty heroic treatments here and have no conclusive news to give you. On the positive side, I think this can be said—I am not absorbing proteins and fats in any adequate manner. My protein count, or whatever you call it, is one-third normal. This is in spite of a very well-regulated diet. In other words, nothing that I can take by mouth seems to make any difference so they are pushing a variety of things intravenously and intra-muscularly, including some material which they are using experimentally here.

I have had a very serious edema in my feet which is fairly well cleared up. My eyesight is going back on me, and I have lost about thirty pounds from my top weight a year ago. I weigh about 130 pounds now. Of course, if they can find the technique to assure the absorption of proteins and fats, my weight naturally will go back up.

They have found no evidence of a recurrence of my old difficulty although there are one or two suspicious signs but in the main the doctors tell me that they believe a recurrence is not in the picture. They simply haven't ruled it out as yet.

I have no idea how long I am to be here, but I am going to stay until the doctors either can or cannot get absorption of protein and fats.

If they can't, then of course there is nothing more that can be done about it here or, for that matter, anywhere else. I assume they will make a deduction from that that I have other difficulties not directly associated with malnutrition. I am quite confident however that they are going to break through this and find a treatment that will substantially clear up the whole business.

This thing began about nearly a year ago and has grown progressively worse through the months until I finally quit work entirely on the 4th of July. I have been in bed most of the time since then. I have a general feeling of well being, excellent appetite, no nausea or headaches, and have had no diarrhea since I have been here.

Doctor Eusterman told me he was writing you today and I will let you know later about my progress. I wouldn't be surprised if I stayed here another two or three weeks, but at times I get pretty discouraged about it, particularly about the doctor's ability to find an adequate treatment for my difficulties. The best I can tell you is that I have a very severe malnutrition. But I am relaxed and altogether comfortable and, as you know, getting the best possible care. Needless to say I have the greatest confidence in the physicians here.

A letter which Hopkins wrote from the Mayo Clinic to his daughter, Diana, suggested that he thought this might be the last communication he would ever have with her:

I had hoped that I would be back home with you long before this but I am going to stay here for a few days more visiting with old friends of mine. Some day when you are older you will learn of what a fine place this is.

I hope you are swimming every day and have given up the use of water wings because no little girl ever learned to swim with water wings. I haven't forgotten that you want to go to the Fair and somehow, some way we will get up there before school begins. I wish ever so much you were here with me and see this lovely farming country. Here are endless numbers of real cows and herds of cattle.

I presume you have finished "Hittie" by this time. I do hope the poor doll finally landed in the museum without too much damage.

Do take care of yourself and Mr. and Mrs. Hunter and Lottie and Mary at the same time and remember me to all of them.

As for yourself, ever remember that I love you very much.

Hopkins' son, David, was informed at this time that his father had about four weeks more to live. And Roosevelt told friends, "The doctors have given Harry up for dead." Hopkins himself believed he could not live more than a few weeks. However, Roosevelt proceeded to assume charge of the case himself. Ever intolerant of the defeatist attitude, he indignantly rejected the possibility that Hopkins' life could not be saved.

He turned the problem over to the U.S. Navy, and Dr. McIntire called
in Admiral Edward R. Stitt, Surgeon General of the Navy and one of
the greatest authorities on tropical diseases. Hopkins was moved from
Rochester to Washington to become a guinea pig for all manner of
biochemical experiments; it was a tremendous ordeal, but it was ultimately successful in prolonging a few weeks' margin of life into six years
of memorable accomplishment.

Hopkins offered the President his resignation as Secretary of Commerce but Roosevelt wouldn't hear of it, saying, "Why you'll be back
in your office in a couple of weeks and going great guns!" It was eight
months before Hopkins could emerge from his Georgetown house and
the records indicate that he did not put in a full day's work in his office
at the Commerce Department until nearly a year later when he went
there to clean out his desk preparatory to retirement. His life had been
saved, for the time being, but his career as a political aspirant had ended
forever—a development which produced a great improvement in his
character and which makes the task of a friendly biographer considerably more agreeable from here on out.

I would add that, during the five years that I spent as a transient with
a temporary visa in the realm of politics, I came to the conclusion that
Lord Acton's oft-quoted statement, "Power corrupts. Absolute power
corrupts absolutely," is one of those pontifical pronouncements which do
not bear analysis. In a democratic society, the desire for power and the
ruthless pursuit of it may have a corruptive influence; that was true of
Pericles and it was true even of Abraham Lincoln; but the realization
of power and of the responsibility that it entails can and often does
produce an ennobling effect. (In such obvious modern instances as Hitler
and Mussolini, Boss Tweed and Al Capone, and various businessmen
and labor leaders whom one might name, it is not unreasonable to assume
that they were sufficiently corrupt to begin with. Certainly, the man who
aspires to absolute power is corrupt, per se.) The rise of Franklin
Roosevelt to power was due more to the extraordinary circumstances
of the times than to any clever conspiracy; but Harry Hopkins, in the
promotion of his own slender chances, was impelled to connive, plot and
even to misrepresent, and this was undoubtedly the least creditable phase
of his public career. In the war years when, with no more authority than
Roosevelt's personal confidence in him, he achieved tremendous power
in the shaping of historic events, he became and remained one of the
most incorruptible of men.

CHAPTER V

The Phony War

WHEN the Second World War started the defenses of the United States consisted primarily of a scrap of paper called the Neutrality Law, which the Congress had passed and which President Roosevelt had signed "with reluctance." That piece of legislation, passed originally in 1936, was carefully designed to prevent us from getting into war in 1917. It was purely retroactive, as though its framers believed that it would restore life to the brave men who had died at Chateau Thierry and in the Argonne. It was born of the belief that we could legislate ourselves out of war, as we had once legislated ourselves out of the saloons (and into the speakeasies). Like Prohibition, it was an experiment "noble in motive" but disastrous in result.

The Second World War started with Hitler's brutal invasion of Poland from the West, followed by the Soviet Union's march into Poland from the East. Britain and France declared war on Germany, in fulfillment of their pledge to Poland, but for nearly eight months there was no fighting by the Western Allies except for isolated naval engagements. The Soviet Union attacked Finland and gained certain territorial advantages thereby, but Hitler remained quiescent and allowed his neighbors to continue in a state of quivering suspense during the autumn and winter of 1939-40. This became known as the period of "the Phony War" and it was the heyday of isolationism in the United States. It was one crisis in Roosevelt's career when he was completely at a loss as to what action to take—a period of terrible, stultifying vacuum.

In October, 1939, Hopkins wrote from his sickbed to his brother Emory in Portland, Oregon. He said:

The only interest here, as everywhere, is the war and I believe that we really can keep out of it. Fortunately there is no great sentiment in this country for getting into it although I think almost everyone wants to see England and France win.

In those two sentences Hopkins unconsciously stated the greatest problem that Roosevelt had to face in his entire Administration, the greatest problem any President had faced at least since Lincoln made the determination against the urgent advice of almost all of his Cabinet to send relief to Fort Sumter. I believe that Hopkins' tendency was naturally isolationist, he was certainly a pacifist, as were so many other liberals; he had only the vaguest concept of the deadly peril to American security that Roosevelt saw in the world situation.

In his speech to a Canadian audience at Queens University in Kingston, Ontario, a year previously, Roosevelt had said:

We in the Americas are no longer a far away continent to which the eddies of controversies beyond the seas could bring no interest or no harm. Instead, we in the Americas have become a consideration to every propaganda office and to every general staff beyond the seas. The vast amount of our resources, the vigor of our commerce and the strength of our men have made us vital factors in world peace whether we choose it or not.

When Roosevelt said that, as when he made the Quarantine Speech, he was accused by the isolationists of exaggerating dangerously for the purpose of creating undue alarm. "What European general staff," they asked, "could possibly be concerned with the Western Hemisphere?" But Roosevelt in his own mind was not exaggerating in any of his prewar speeches: he was erring on the side of understatement. Although he was no great authority on military strategy, and gave almost unqualified freedom of decision during the war to his Chiefs of Staff, the knowledge that he did possess was basic. The first point in his military credo was that an ocean is not necessarily a barrier—it is a broad highway. His considerable knowledge of geography and of navigation gave him understanding of the importance of the bases from which traffic on that highway could be controlled. His thinking was, of course, essentially naval, which meant that he did not look very far beyond the bridgeheads secured by Marines; however, he knew what the essential bridgeheads were—the British Isles, France, the Iberian Peninsula, the North and West Coasts of Africa and, in the Pacific, the Netherlands East Indies, the Philippines and the Marianas. Early in 1939, some unidentified Senator told the press that, in the course of a secret White House conference on the European situation, the President had said, "Our American frontier is on the Rhine." That quotation was hailed joyously in Britain and in France, and with threatening indignation in Nazi Germany and Fascist Italy. The isolationists at home set up angry howls of protest. When questioned about it at a subsequent press conference, Roosevelt denounced the quotation as a "deliberate lie" and referred to the anonymous informant as "some boob." Nevertheless, whether or not Roosevelt actually made the statement, he most certainly did believe that America's eastern frontier was on the Rhine and it was on this belief that he acted when he risked political suicide in his efforts to break through the Neutrality Law and to get aid to those who fought against Axis aggression. He was unable to get such aid through effectively in time to keep the frontier on the Rhine; but he was able to help incalculably in keeping it on the English Channel and the Straits of Gibraltar.

When war actually broke out in Europe, Roosevelt was tame enough in his first public statements to satisfy the most timid. He said:

> This nation will remain a neutral nation, but I cannot ask that every American remain neutral in thought as well. Even a neutral has a right to take account of facts. Even a neutral cannot be asked to close his mind or his conscience. . . .
> I hope the United States will keep out of this war. I believe that it will. And I give you assurance and reassurance that every effort of your Government will be directed toward that end.

This last may be denounced as, at worst, deliberately misleading or, at best, as wishful thinking. The inescapable fact is that this was what Roosevelt felt compelled to say in order to maintain any influence over public opinion and over Congressional action. Two weeks after the war started he called Congress into extraordinary session to repeal the arms embargo provisions of the Neutrality Law and thus permit the sale of war matériel to England and France on a "cash and carry" basis. Even this meager concession had to be asked for on the grounds that the embargo provisions were, "in my opinion, most vitally dangerous to American neutrality, American security and, above all, American peace." It is my belief—and this is pure speculation—that at this time and up to the fall of France Roosevelt was wishfully hoping that Britain and France would prove indomitable in the West, that the Soviet Union would keep Germany contained in the East, that this stalemate would last until the German people would become fed up with "guns before butter" and revolt, thereby bursting the Nazi bubble so that peace would be restored without the need for American armed intervention. It seems quite evident that Roosevelt did not have full comprehension of the real, paralyzing force of the Nazi fury, nor of the imminence of the danger to the United States, until the Blitzkrieg was hurled into France in the spring of 1940. At that point, I am sure, he became convinced—and this is not speculation—that if Britain fell disastrous war for the United States would be inevitable, that Germany would attack the Western Hemisphere, probably at first in Latin America, as soon as she had assembled a sufficient naval force and transport and cargo fleet (not too long a process, with all the shipbuilding facilities of Europe at Germany's disposal) and that Japan would concurrently go on the rampage in the Pacific.

One major factor in Roosevelt's thinking as the war began is a matter of certainty: his greatest fear then and subsequently was of a negotiated peace, another Munich. Here again was demonstration of the fear of fear itself. He communicated his concern to the British Government through extra-official channels (specifically, Lord Beaverbrook) and he started his historic correspondence with Winston Churchill—whom he addressed as the "Naval Person"—recognizing in him his foremost British ally in awareness of the folly of any attempt to do business with Hitler. (Churchill's cables to Roosevelt were usually addressed to "POTUS," the initials of "President of the United States.") Roosevelt's fear of a negotiated peace was based on the conviction that it would be dictated by the same craven considerations that dictated the surrender at Munich—fear of Nazi might and fear that, if Nazi might were eliminated, Germany would no longer be a buffer state between Russia and the West. It was obvious to Roosevelt as it should have been to any other informed observer that Hitler wanted a negotiated peace because it would work in so many ways to his advantage:

(1) It would further strengthen his position in Germany, providing conclusive proof to the German people that he could hoodwink Britain and France into selling another small country into slavery (in this case, Poland) rather than to risk actual war.

(2) It would give Germany time to consolidate her gains in Czechoslovakia and Poland and further to increase her rearmament, particularly in the building of submarines, airplanes and the Siegfried Line.

(3) It would tend to push public sentiment in Britain and France—and most of all in the United States—back into the peacetime isolationist ruts, and thereby retard if not nullify all efforts in the democracies to prepare for war.

(4) It would convince the Russians—and the Japanese—that the Western democracies were completely spineless and decadent, as Hitler and Mussolini had so long and so loudly proclaimed them to be.

Thus, Roosevelt was on sure ground when he urged that a negotiated peace would give Hitler the one or two years' respite that he needed to prepare for conquest of Europe, Africa, the Middle East and the major part of the Atlantic world; but, when the European Allies asked Roosevelt, as France in effect did, "What will *you* do to back us up?"— he could only reply that he had virtually nothing to offer more tangible than his personal good will. He could utter brave words but, when deeds were called for, he was hogtied by the prevailing isolationist sentiment.

Since I use the word "isolationists" frequently in these pages, perhaps it would be well to clarify it. Actually, in the first year or more of war, the ranks of the isolationists included the overwhelming majority of the American people who would have been glad to see the European war end on almost any inconclusive terms merely as a guarantee that the United States would not be drawn into it. Public opinion on this score was much more nearly unanimous and more clearly expressed than it had been in 1914-17. It is true that in the First World War there was substantially more pro-German sentiment in the United States: large numbers of German-Americans then still held close cultural and emotional ties with the Fatherland, for the Hohenzollern brand of imperialism, while objectionable to the average American, did not inspire the same horror and loathing as Nazism. The American people were, in a way, more truly neutral in 1914 than they were twenty-five years later. However, Americans in 1939 were fortified with the experience that the previous generation had conspicuously lacked, the experience of involvement in European war, and they wanted no more of it. The impulse to let "Europe stew in its own juice" was a very powerful one and an entirely understandable one, for there were too many Americans who considered that their country's only reward for coming to the aid of Britain and France in 1918 was to be given the name of "Uncle Shylock." (As Roosevelt remarked many times, "We fortunately never had a chance to find out what our 'reward' would have been if Germany had won that war.") Thus, isolationist sentiment in 1939 was not limited to Americans of German birth or descent, or to those who loved German music and admired German science and industry, or to those who were pure pacifists: it was representative of the entire American people save for a diminutive minority of those who believed that a victory for Hitler would put the security of our own country and our own constitutional democracy in deadly peril. The first wartime Roper poll taken in September, 1939 (see p. 128), gave eloquent testimony to the state of the nation's thinking.

It will be seen that the extreme interventionist sentiment was limited to 2.5 per cent of the population. Isolationist sentiment was, of course, much stronger among women than among men. The sectional breakdown of this analysis showed very little difference between the New England and Middle Atlantic States and those in the Middle West but far more interventionist sentiment below the Mason-Dixon Line and, somewhat surprisingly, in the Rocky Mountain and Pacific Coast States. (It should be remembered that this public opinion poll did not contemplate the possibility of war with Japan, the Rome-Berlin-Tokyo Axis not having been formed at that time.)

Which of these comes closest to describing what you think America should do about the present European war?

	Total %	Sex Male %	Female %	Age Under 40 %	Over 40 %
Enter the war at once on the side of England, France and Poland.	2.5	3.6	1.3	2.1	2.8
Find some way of supporting Germany.	.2	.2	.1	.1	.3
Take no sides and stay out of the war entirely, but offer to sell to anyone on a cash-and-carry basis.	37.5	43.0	32.2	37.8	37.2
Do not enter the war but supply England, France and Poland with materials and food, and refuse to ship anything to Germany.	8.9	9.0	8.7	8.8	9.0
Stay out for now and for as long as we can, but go into war on the side of England and France if they are in real danger of losing, and in the meantime help that side with food and materials.	14.7	16.1	13.3	15.4	14.0
Have nothing to do with any warring country—don't even trade with them on a cash-and-carry basis.	29.9	23.6	36.1	29.9	29.9
Other—Pro-Ally	.6	.8	.6	.7	.6
Other—Pro-Germany					
Other—Favoring neither side	1.8	1.8	1.9	1.5	2.2
Don't know	3.9	1.9	5.8	3.7	4.0

The all-out isolationist faction which would have "nothing to do with any warring country" was close to thirty per cent and this remained a pretty constant figure through all of the opinion tests that were made over such issues as Selective Service, the destroyers-for-bases deal, Lend Lease, etc. This thirty per cent represented the hard core of isolationists and included in it were such strange bedfellows as all the native Fascist organizations, which hailed Hitler as the champion against Bolshevism, and all the members of the Communist party and their fellow travelers; for this was the age of that colossal anomaly, the Nazi-Soviet mutual nonaggression pact. The Fascist groups and individuals were unimportant numerically but they had an altogether disproportionate capacity for noisemaking (like the Communists) and they were by no means a negligible force in spreading the propaganda line as dictated by Goebbels from Berlin.

Immeasurably stronger were the racial and religious groups who favored extreme isolationism. I do not believe that the German-Americans should be included among these for the great majority of them were appalled by what Hitler had done to the land of their forefathers and those who joined or even tolerated the German-American Bund were fortunately few in number. The Scandinavians, particularly in the North Middle West, were considerably more emphatic than the Germans in championing strict neutrality but this sentiment was later affected by the invasions of Denmark and Norway. The Italian-Americans as a group were not necessarily in favor of Fascism but they admired the seeming accomplishments of Mussolini in restoring Italy to the dignity of a great power and there were many of them who were mortally offended by Roosevelt's reference to the "stab in the back." The more rabid Irish-Americans who constituted a potent political force in some of the larger metropolitan areas were, as always, inclined to cheer for anyone who was fighting against England and they were at this time given effective leadership by the violent pamphleteer and radio star, Father Charles E. Coughlin. Because of Father Coughlin and the activities of such subversive organizations as the Christian Front, as well as the sentiments of so many Irish- and Italian-Americans, the Catholic Church became identified to a certain extent in the public mind with the cause of extreme isolationism. However, the Polish-Americans, who formed an important part of the Catholic community, were of course bitterly anti-Nazi as well as anti-Communist.

Organized labor, the greatest unit of support for Roosevelt, was now an uncertain quantity. The unions under Communist domination dutifully followed the party line of all-out isolationism and so did those under the control of John L. Lewis, the bitterest Roosevelt-hater of them all. The great bulk of labor while unquestionably anti-Nazi was also anti-war, fearing that United States involvement would retard or even destroy the gains made by labor under the New Deal. I believe that much the same sentiment had prevailed in the Labor party in Great Britain before the war; it had certainly prevailed in the C.G.T. in France.

The chief leadership and the essential financing of isolationism as a political faction were provided by men and women who belonged to no particular group: there were a number of businessmen, like General Robert E. Wood, Jay Hormel, and James D. Mooney, who simply believed that Hitler was going to win and that the United States had better plan to "do business" with him; and there were technicians, of whom the arch example was Colonel Charles A. Lindbergh, who were so impressed with the technological achievements of Hitler's regimented state, as contrasted with the hopeless inefficiency of democracy, that they believed Fascism constituted "the wave of the future." It was such as these, together with assorted sufferers from the virulent xenophobia of the Hearst-Patterson-McCormick press, who formed the America First Committee, the ultimate spearhead of isolationism.

There were, in addition, considerable numbers of liberals, and many of them in the Roosevelt Administration itself, who opposed the President's unneutral policy because of a pacifistic fear that involvement in war, or even preparation therefor, would produce an interruption in social progress and an assault upon civil liberties such as that which occurred under A. Mitchell Palmer, Alien Property Custodian and Attorney General in the Wilson Administration. As I have indicated, Harry Hopkins would undoubtedly have been included with his friends Senator Robert M. La Follette and Robert M. Hutchins in this category of liberal isolationists had it not been for his fervent conviction that Roosevelt could not possibly be wrong on any major issue. It was the liberal group—and, to a much lesser extent, the Communists—who made the greatest appeal to youth in the country and inspired so many "Keep Us Out of War" demonstrations on so many campuses.

There was another and extremely important element in the thinking of liberals and of countless middle-of-the-road Americans whose political affiliations were hazy but whose impulses were essentially decent: that was profound distrust of the reactionary leaders in Britain and France who had gone to Munich once and might well go there again. Here was an honest and intelligent sentiment which dishonest and dangerously stupid men could exploit. The records of calculated British propaganda in America in the First World War as they had been set down by such thoughtful and reasonable writers as Walter Millis and Quincy Howe evoked too many malodorous memories. Before the advent of calamity in Western Europe and of Winston Churchill, the Allied cause did not have a good smell even in the nostrils of those who hated Fascism and all its evil works. The same general sentiment applied—although to a far lesser extent, because of public ignorance of the area—to the Kuomintang regime in China. It was not easy to answer the question: should American boys die fighting Fascism in Europe and Asia in order to defend neo-Fascism? The unworthy Frenchmen who raised the cry, "Why should we die for Danzig?" raised more echoes in American hearts than Goebbels or Gayda ever did. Early in 1939 that understanding, objective, sharp-witted Scot, Robert Bruce Lockhart, author of *British Agent* and many other books, went on a lecture tour of the United States. In a later book, *Comes the Reckoning*, he wrote:

The effect of my lectures, like that of most British lecturers, was insignificant, if not indeed harmful, and the only benefit of my tour was self-education.

Lockhart summarized the average American's attitude toward Britain's problems in these words:

"We Americans went into the last war to save democracy. We pulled you out of a hole and we received very grudging thanks. At Versailles and after Versailles you trampled on democratic ideals. Now, largely through your own fault, you are in trouble again and you want our help. Well, we've learnt our lesson."

Lockhart later became Director General of the Political Warfare Executive, which was attached to the Foreign Office and the Ministry of Information. Perhaps because of his own experience and his remarkably realistic appraisal thereof, the British sent no lecturers to the United States during the entire war, except when specifically requested to do so by the American authorities. The mistakes of the First World War were not repeated.

What Lockhart encountered may be described as the essential "grass roots" sentiment, which was strongly represented in the Congress together with all the various prejudices and fears that always beset little men. There was another powerful influence in the Congress: this was the kind of crossroads chauvinism which afflicts minor politicians who know they can always get applause by indulging in eagle-screaming—the kind of picayune parochialism which contends that all "furriners," particularly Englishmen and Frenchmen, are slick deceivers who are out to pull the wool over the eyes of poor, innocent, gullible Uncle Sam the while they deftly extract the gold from his teeth. I am not suggesting that Congress was dominated by this spirit, nor that the Republicans had any more of it than the Democrats; but it was always there and always highly vocal and such forceful isolationist leaders as Senator Burton K. Wheeler (Democrat, of Montana), and Representative Joseph W. Martin, Jr. (Republican, of Massachusetts), knew well how to mobilize it.

When I speak of the "isolationists," from now on, I shall refer particularly to those in the Congress who were in a position to block the Roosevelt measures and, from their rostrum on Capitol Hill, to publicize what they considered his attempts to dupe the American people into a war which they believed was none of our business. It was a curious fact that these extreme isolationists were not pacifists in the sense that they opposed war, as such; indeed, their attitude toward the Soviet Union—and also, in some cases, toward Japan—was one of extreme belligerency. They seemed to be in favor of fighting under two essential conditions: (1) that all battles be staged on our own home grounds, in the Western

Hemisphere (otherwise, it would be a "foreign" war) ; and (2) that in
the war we keep ourselves pure, and therefore "100 per cent American,"
by having no allies whatsoever. Evidently it was felt that we had made
a terrible mistake in 1918 by fighting in France together with Allies who
had turned out to be ingrates, and so we must be careful never to do
that again. The Roosevelt doctrine was that if we were to get into a war
we should fight it as far from our own shores as possible and with the
greatest number of allies, regardless of ideology, that we could enlist,
accepting whatever risks there might be of potential ingratitude after
the common enemies had been disposed of.

The myopic form of Congressional isolationism can best be expressed
by two quotations of the period. The first was from Representative John
G. Alexander, a Minnesota Republican. In a letter to the President on
Selective Service, he wrote:

> Why take our youth from their homes and out of the wholesome
> environment in which most of them are living, and transplant them
> into the lonely inhospitable and disturbing and discouraging arena of
> a training camp? Their mental, moral and physical well-being is too
> important to be disregarded in that way. . . . Mr. President, we want
> no foreign wars, we want none of our American boys to fight in
> foreign lands or seas, we want only to prepare to protect and defend
> our own shores and border.

The other quotation was from Senator Robert A. Taft:

> I do not know what the Germans may do, and no one knows what
> they may do until they are freed from the present war and have an
> opportunity to show. When they do, we can adopt the same methods.
> We can take the same steps that may be necessary to meet the partic-
> ular kind of German "blitzkrieg," if there is such a blitzkrieg, at the
> time we find out what it is.

In other words, we were to fight only (1) when the enemy, having
previously disposed of all of our potential allies, had arrived at our
shores or "border" and (2) after he had revealed to us all of the new
weapons and tactics that he proposed to employ for our destruction.
These two quotations might well be printed at the start of the most
elementary textbook used at West Point and Annapolis in order to teach
student officers what they must first contend with in their careers of
service to the United States.

In his constantly delicate and difficult relations with the Congress in
matters of foreign policy, Roosevelt was constantly careful to avoid what
Tolstoy called "the irrevocable act." He now carried a heavy share
of responsibility for the future history of the world. If he were to go
before the Congress with a request for action on an issue of international
importance and were defeated, it would involve more than gleeful

editorials in the *Chicago Tribune* and possible losses for the Democratic party at the next elections; it could well involve utter, world-wide disaster. The melancholy story has been told of the meeting in the President's study one evening a few weeks before war broke out in Europe at which Roosevelt and Cordell Hull told Vice President Garner, Senator William E. Borah and other Senators of their conviction that war might be averted by immediate amendment of the Neutrality Act. Hull argued the point with tears in his eyes, but Borah brushed him off with the statement that his private sources of information assured him there would be no war ("Germany isn't ready for it"); and Garner ended the meeting by saying, cheerfully, to Roosevelt: "Well, Captain, we may as well face the facts. You haven't got the votes, and that's all there is to it." Roosevelt did not forget that experience and neither did Hull, who had more respect than Roosevelt did for the dignity and authority of the Congress. Before Roosevelt asked for anything else in the next two years, he was extremely careful to make sure that he had "the votes." He hesitated to take a chance which might result in an adverse vote—or even a fairly close vote—in the Congress and thereby render aid and comfort to the Germans and Japanese and discouragement and demoralization to those who fought them. It is not easy for the average citizen to appreciate the extent to which every word, every implication, uttered by the President of the United States, as well as every action committed by him, may bolster the courage or deepen the despair of hundreds of millions of people in lands overseas. But Roosevelt appreciated it. His cautious policy of one step at a time often infuriated the extreme interventionists who often asked, "Why doesn't he go to Congress and demand a declaration of war *now*?" Had he done so in the summer of 1940, for example, when Britain was fighting alone, he would undoubtedly have been repudiated by the Congress and that might well have been the signal to the British people that their cause was hopeless and that they had no choice but surrender. I think that the criticism aimed at Roosevelt by the interventionists caused him more temporary irritation than that hurled at him day after day by the isolationists. Shortly before Christmas, 1939, someone sent him a copy of a poem written by Joseph Warren in 1775, the first verse of which was as follows:

> Lift up your hands, ye heroes,
> And swear with proud disdain;
> The wretch that would ensnare you
> Shall lay his snares in vain.
> Should Europe empty all her force
> We'll meet her in array
> And fight and shout and fight for free Amerikay.

The correspondent—name unknown to me—who sent that to the
President explained that "according to Carl Sandburg, the pronunciation
'Amerikay' was customary with both Lincoln and Jeff Davis."

Roosevelt sent a copy of this verse to Hopkins with the following
letter:

> Those verses by Joseph Warren, written in 1775, are interesting as
> showing that a matter of four million people with few resources
> thought even in those days that they could lick the world. I fear that
> today altogether too many people in Amerikay want, as they did then,
> to "fight and shout and fight." Some of us believe there would be
> more shouting than fighting.

Roosevelt, normally one who interpreted his constitutional powers in
the broadest possible terms, might have used the immediate impact of
European war to assume authority far beyond that of the normal peacetime President. But he did just the opposite. In a press conference following his Proclamation of Limited Emergency, on September 8, 1939,
he clarified his intentions by saying:

> There is no intention and no need of doing all those things that
> could be done. . . . There is no thought in any shape, manner or form,
> of putting the Nation, either in its defenses or in its internal economy,
> on a war basis. That is one thing we want to avoid. We are going to
> keep the Nation on a peace basis, in accordance with peacetime
> authorizations.

Those were probably the weakest words that Roosevelt ever uttered.
He was outdoing even Warren G. Harding by getting the country "back
to normalcy" before the war had really started. He was revealing the
woeful weakness of his own Administration, especially in the three
Departments that mattered most in a time of international crisis—the
State Department, War Department and Navy Department.

It is always easy to poke fun at the State Department—indeed, it
ranks second only to the Congress as a target for those who like to
indulge in the inexpensive pastime of ridiculing our government—but it
is considerably less easy to understand the peculiar difficulties which
afflicted the Department in 1940 and thereafter. Cordell Hull had set as
his worthy goal the prevention of a Second World War. He was deeply
injured when Borah contemptuously dismissed the Department's information as inferior to his own; for Hull, any reflection on his Department constituted an affront to his personal honor and pride—and, as
an old soldier of Tennessee, he had plenty of both. Hull's admirable
crusade for reciprocal trade was frustrated by the war, and he found
himself largely restricted to the maintenance of hemispheric solidarity—
in itself a form of isolationism, according to the Roosevelt concept—as
a means of keeping the State Department a factor of importance in the

Federal Government. While the British Foreign Office was organized on a basis that contemplated the constant possibility of war as "continuation of policy by other means," the State Department was compelled by twenty years of isolationism to operate on the principle that the Alpha and Omega of American foreign policy is to *keep out of war*. When this became impossible, the functions of the State Department, except in regard to neutral countries, became atrophied. This was a bitter pill for Hull to swallow, and he never did fully digest it. He was extremely jealous of his reputation as one officer of the Administration who had been guilty of no conspicuous blunders and who had been spared the criticism lavished on all the others, including the President himself. However, in times of desperate emergency when drastic, daring action had to be taken quickly, Roosevelt was bound to become impatient with anyone whose primary concern was the maintenance of a personal record of "no runs—no hits—no errors." To an ever greater extent, Roosevelt bypassed Hull to deal directly with Sumner Welles, or to assign what should have been State Department functions to the Treasury Department, the War Department, or to any other agency or individual who might get things done, including eventually Harry Hopkins, the archetype of what Hull called "the extreme left fringe" surrounding the President. Hull believed that he had been selected by Roosevelt as the man to succeed him at the end of the second term, and this belief was assiduously cultivated and encouraged by James A. Farley— as is discussed elsewhere in these pages. Although Hull had conducted no campaign in his own behalf (Farley was doing that for him) he felt that he had been betrayed, if not by Roosevelt, then by Hopkins and the "extreme left fringe." However, unlike Farley, he finally stood by Roosevelt in the campaign of 1940 and was a powerful force in his re-election; and Roosevelt did not forget this.

Unquestionably, the most lasting and most deplorable element in the distant relations between the White House and its next-door neighbor to the west was the President's close association with Sumner Welles— an association based on long friendship and genuine admiration. I cannot pretend to give the reasons for the animosity that existed between the Secretary and Under Secretary of State. But there is no question of doubt that their conflict became so ugly and so extremely dangerous that it eventually compelled the resignation of Welles, which was a serious loss to Roosevelt, for he placed great dependence on Welles's judgment particularly in all matters relating to the framing of the ultimate peace. These are circumstances of which it is not agreeable to write, and impossible for a contemporary to write without evidence of bias in one form or another. However, history will achieve no complete understanding of Franklin Roosevelt's Administration without knowledge of the intramural feuds which so frequently beset it. (I do not believe that even

history will ever be able to understand why he tolerated them to the
extent that he did.)

The War Department was weakened by a more obvious and even
more impolite running battle between the Secretary, Harry H. Woodring, and Louis A. Johnson, Assistant Secretary. Woodring was isolationist at heart while Johnson believed in all-out armament. Their
severe clashes were hardly helpful to the Army at a time when its needs
were most desperate.

The Navy Department was in much better shape although its Secretary, Charles Edison, was frail in health and insufficiently enthusiastic
about his job. Furthermore, Edison appears to have been singularly
complacent about the world situation. On June 21, 1940—the very day
when Hitler dictated his armistice terms to Pétain's stunned representatives in the forest of Compiègne—Edison wrote to Hopkins urging the
use of airships (dirigibles) for the increase of trade with South America.
The following words in this letter were underscored by Hopkins:

*We may safely assume, I feel, that as soon as the present situation clears
in Europe, Germany will immediately resume her South American air-
ship service, even despite her lack of helium or possibly with Russian
helium.*

The Navy, like the War Department, was to a lamentable extent cowed
by the force of isolationist sentiment on Capitol Hill and was trained to
be timid in requests for appropriations. The officers most successful
in the Department in peacetime were those whom Congress identified as
the most economy minded—and sailors or soldiers who are economy
minded rarely win wars.

The officer personnel in both services were anything but blind in devotion to the policies of their Commander in Chief. In the Army, there was
a tendency among officers of both ground and air forces to admire Germany for her achievements in building up these arms. This led in some
extreme cases to the hope that Germany would conquer England thereby
providing historic demonstration of the superiority of land and air
power over sea power. Obviously, these sentiments were not shared by
Navy officers but, for many of them, the main interest was in the Far
East, rather than Europe, and it was their hope that if the United States
must go to war the main battleground would be the Pacific.

There was another reason for the weakness of Roosevelt's position
during the period of the Phony War, and it was probably the most important reason of all: he was in the last year of his second term as President,
and it is one of the classical weaknesses of our American constitutional
system that a President who is approaching the end of his tenure of office
can exercise little authority in the conduct of foreign affairs. The old
theory that politics "ends at the waterline" is nonsense. In times of partisan struggle for power there is no point at which politics ends and this

was particularly true in 1939-40 when all domestic issues became indistinct and insignificant in the shadow of war. If Roosevelt had indicated in 1939 or early 1940 that he *would* run for a third term, then he would have become a candidate rather than a President; his own party would have been divided into pros and cons and the Republicans would have been united in attacking his every policy, foreign and domestic. If he had indicated he would not run again, then his authority would have become negligible at home and nonexistent abroad. His only solution was to shroud his intentions in mystery; in addition to which, it is apparent that for a long time he himself did not know just what these intentions were. This was a period of impotence when, with all of civilization in peril, the leader of the most powerful nation on earth had to wait, day after anxious day, for his own course of action to be shaped by events over which he had no control. It was particularly agonizing for one of his venturesome spirit to be unable to act boldly or even cautiously to plan action in face of impending calamity, of which the Blitzkrieg in Poland had given a suggestion. The world now knew how the Nazis could strike —how their Air Force could paralyze communications—that their tanks were not, as had hopefully been reported, made of ersatz steel. But the French could only crouch behind the Maginot Line, and the British behind the Royal Navy, and the Americans behind the Neutrality Law. And Roosevelt was, for once in his life, deedless and, so far as he was able to say anything of any consequence, speechless. Early in January, 1940, he sent for Sumner Welles, who has written, "He admitted frankly that the chances seemed to him about one in a thousand that anything at all could be done to change the course of events." The one chance as Roosevelt then saw it was to send Welles to Europe to talk to the heads of government in Germany, Italy, France and Britain to determine "the possibilities of concluding any just and permanent peace" but not any "temporary or tentative armed truce." If Roosevelt believed there was any possibility that Hitler would agree to disarm—or even to give up one acre that Germany had seized—he most certainly was thinking wishfully. Welles returned from his mission with discouraging reports about everything except the temper of the British, but with much useful information on the personalities of the men he had met, and Roosevelt was one who knew how to use such information. It was always of tremendous importance to him to be able to size up the characters of the leaders of both enemy and friendly states.

One may wonder why Welles did not also go to the Soviet Union at the time, but Roosevelt "did not feel that a visit to Moscow would serve any useful purpose." Indeed, then, the prestige of the Soviet Union was so low that it was counted as only a potential victim of Germany and not as a valid aggressive factor. Russia was then involved to the discredit of its arms in the Winter War with little Finland and was making a woefully unimpressive showing. There was no hint revealed of the eventual magnificence of the Red Army in action. Many people have assumed that this was an act of deliberate deception on Russia's part—simulating weakness in order to mask her real strength—but a remark made by Joseph Stalin, printed later in this book, indicated that the weakness then was real.

The war in Finland caused intensification of the isolationist activities of the Communist party in the United States and led to a singular episode at the White House: An American Youth Congress held a convention in Washington in February, 1940, and the delegates assembled on the south lawn of the White House on a raw, rainy day to hear a speech by the President. It was one of the few occasions in his life when Roosevelt was booed and hissed to his face by an audience of Americans. He referred to a resolution, passed by one of the councils of this Youth Congress, against the granting of American aid to Finland on the ground that such action was "an attempt to force America into the imperialistic war." Roosevelt said:

> More than twenty years ago, while most of you were very young children, I had the utmost sympathy for the Russian people. In the early days of Communism, I recognized that many leaders in Russia were bringing education and better health and, above all, better opportunity to millions who had been kept in ignorance and serfdom under the imperial regime. I disliked the regimentation under Communism. I abhorred the indiscriminate killings of thousands of innocent victims. I heartily deprecated the banishment of religion—though I knew that some day Russia would return to religion for the simple reason that four or five thousand years of recorded history have proven that mankind has always believed in God in spite of many abortive attempts to exile God.
>
> I, with many of you, hoped that Russia would work out its own problems, and that its government would eventually become a peace-loving, popular government with a free ballot, which would not interfere with the integrity of its neighbors.
>
> That hope is today either shattered or put away in storage against some better day. The Soviet Union, as everybody who has the courage to face the fact knows, is run by a dictatorship as absolute as any other dictatorship in the world. It has allied itself with another dictatorship, and it has invaded a neighbor so infinitesimally small that it could do no conceivable possible harm to the Soviet Union, a neighbor which seeks only to live at peace as a democracy, and a liberal, forward-looking democracy at that.
>
> It has been said that some of you are Communists. That is a very unpopular term these days. As Americans you have a legal and constitutional right to call yourselves Communists, those of you who do. You have a right peacefully and openly to advocate certain ideals of theoretical Communism; but as Americans you have not only a right

but a sacred duty to confine your advocacy of changes in law to the methods prescribed by the Constitution of the United States—and you have no American right, by act or deed of any kind, to subvert the Government and the Constitution of this Nation.

Those words, which appear to have been very carefully chosen, and the boos that greeted them, provide eloquent testimony to the weirdness of the atmosphere that prevailed during the Phony War. For Roosevelt was the President who had first established friendly relations with the Soviet Union, after sixteen years of attempts by the U.S. Government to ignore its existence, and who subsequently rendered decisive aid to the Russians when they became victims of the savage forces they had sought to appease.

During this winter of the Phony War, Churchill paid his respects to the neutral nations of Europe who sought to buy immunity from German aggression by appeasement. He said, "Each one hopes that if he feeds the crocodile enough, the crocodile will eat him last." Churchill evidently liked to use the crocodile as the symbol of Nazi voracity. Years later, when he was explaining the North African operation to Stalin, he drew a picture of a crocodile on a sheet of Kremlin paper and said, "We shall strike him here, in the soft underbelly [the Mediterranean] while at the same time we hit him here, in the snout" [Northern France].

In March, 1940, Hopkins was sufficiently recovered to get out of bed for a few hours each day and go downstairs and even, when the weather was sunny and warm, go out for an occasional drive. But he was still very weak. He wrote to Henry Wallace, Secretary of Agriculture, asking for help in obtaining some seeds for his garden. Among them were petunias, begonias, ageratums, candy tufts, sweet alyssum, pansies, forget-me-nots, calliopsis, bachelor buttons and white and yellow rose bushes. He told Wallace, "This is to be the extent of the kind of thing I am going to be able to do this spring." (In the years that I knew Hopkins I never saw him take any interest in a flower.)

CHAPTER VI

The Former Naval Person

IN THEIR swift invasion of Norway, the German ground troops were transported secretly to many points on that long and complicated coastline under the very eyes and guns of the British Home Fleet. This was the contemptuous answer to Neville Chamberlain's stupendously unfortunate remark about Hitler having "missed the bus." When the British attempt to intervene in Norway proved a fiasco, an elder Prime Minister, David Lloyd George, described it as "another tragedy of too little—and too late." Those last words formed the epitaph on the grave of wishful thinking in the democracies. They were burned into the very soul of Franklin Roosevelt. They had a continuing effect through the years on all those who were involved in the direction of the Allied war effort. They created the sense of desperate urgency which the desperate times demanded. As crisis after crisis burst it was repeated that, "Never again must we be *too little and too late*!" But we almost were. The margin between victory and defeat proved to be very narrow indeed: it was no wider than the English Channel—no wider than one street in Stalingrad—no wider than the Solomons' "Slot." The invasions of Norway and Denmark on April 9, 1940, marked the beginning of the end of the Phony War and, with the invasions of Holland, Belgium, Luxembourg and France on May 10, the period of impotence at last came to its overdue conclusion. In the course of the next six months, Roosevelt made by all odds the most momentous decisions of his career —and he made them, it must be remembered, without previous authorization by Congress and against the earnest advice of many of his most influential associates and friends.

On the day that the Germans marched—or, rather, hurtled—into the Low Countries, Chamberlain resigned and Winston Churchill was at last called to Buckingham Palace to accept the post of the King's First

Minister. (He thereupon became, in his correspondence with Roosevelt, the "Former Naval Person.") He told the House of Commons, "I have nothing to offer but blood, toil, tears and sweat." Anthony Eden, who had been out of the Cabinet for a year before the war started because of his opposition to Chamberlain's policies, was brought back to prominence as Secretary of State for War in the new coalition government. The British people now had leaders worthy of them.

On May 14, the Dutch Army surrendered and the German Blitzkrieg began to turn westward toward the classic battlefields of Northern France. The Ardennes again became the scene of massive German victory. The hapless French Commander in Chief, General Gamelin, was replaced by General Weygand, and Churchill broadcast to the world, "We may look with confidence to the stabilization of the front in France." But the world looked in vain. The famous "sickle" movement was in full stride and within two days of Churchill's reassurance the mobile columns had cut through north of the Somme to the English Channel at Abbeville, had then swung northeastward along the coast to Boulogne and Calais and were within sight of England. The Germans under Hitler had accomplished in eleven days what they had failed to do in the four years of bitter fighting in the First World War. It was a brilliant campaign of calculated panic which led to fierce demoralization. On May 28, King Leopold of Belgium surrendered. Weygand attempted to form a line of defense on the Somme. For a time there was great question in the public mind whether Hitler would attack this line and strike southward to Paris or would direct his catapulting force across the Channel for the invasion of England.

When the Blitzkrieg in the West was in its fifth day, Churchill sent Roosevelt a cable which was full of dark forebodings for the German conquest of Europe with "astonishing swiftness." He contemplated the possibility of heavy bombing of Britain and of paratroop attacks. He predicted that Mussolini would burst into the war to collect his share of the "loot of civilization." (This was twenty-five days before Mussolini did so.) He asked the President to proclaim a state of "nonbelligerency" for the United States, which would mean supplying all kinds of aid but no armed action. The aid that Churchill wanted immediately included the lease of forty or fifty destroyers, several hundred war planes, antiaircraft guns and steel. He asked for American diplomatic co-operation to persuade the Irish Free State to take measures to prevent German invasion. He asked for co-operation in preventing further Japanese aggression in Southeast Asia. In connection with the latter, Churchill suggested the U.S. Navy use Singapore as a base. Most important of all in this cable, Churchill said that, if necessary, Britain would fight on alone. In a cable sent five days later (May 20) Churchill said that, if Britain went down, he and his government would perish with it, and he could not be responsible for the terms that might be imposed on whatever form of British "authority" the Germans might decide to recognize. Roosevelt did not discount these and subsequent cabled reports from Churchill as exaggerations. During these weeks when horror was piled upon horror, Roosevelt believed that if Churchill erred at all in his estimates he erred on the side of optimism; but Roosevelt rarely objected to that kind of error.

British troops in Boulogne and Calais managed by determined if ultimately hopeless resistance to delay the German advance just long enough to permit the flooding of the water lines at Gravelines, which in turn could be defended by French troops for a few days. Those few days were of historic importance, for within ten miles of Gravelines was the final objective of the sickle movement, Dunkirk, the last remaining port of evacuation. Had the Germans managed to reach it, at the rate they had maintained since the Blitzkrieg started, they would have completed the destruction of the French forces of the north as well as the entire British and Belgian armies—while the bulk of the French Army sat, helpless and innocuous, in the unmolested Maginot Line. But in this one, last stage of their timetable the Germans failed, and they thereupon turned their main attention away from the English Channel to the Rivers Somme and Aisne and the drive on Paris.

A sense of terror swept through the civilized world as a result of these bewildering events, these incredible achievements of mechanized barbarism. The horrible confusion and hysteria of the civilians of the Low Countries—driven to panicked flight along narrow roads by the fifth column and machine-gunned and bombed as they fled by the screaming Stuka dive bombers—communicated itself to peoples far from the scene of combat. It was the supreme triumph of what Edmond Taylor has correctly called the "Strategy of Terror." It seeemed to many that the boasts of Nazi propaganda were not mere bombast, after all; the Germans *were* supermen, and nothing would ever be able to stop them. There was a perceptible lifting of hearts when announcement was made of the evacuation at Dunkirk—but those with any knowledge of military reality could derive little immediate satisfaction from this remarkable achievement, for the 335,585 men taken off the beaches had been forced to leave all of their heavy equipment behind them and there were pitifully inadequate replacements in Great Britain. It was at that point that the United States became the decisive strategic factor in the war.

There could be no further doubt in the minds of Roosevelt or his Chiefs of Staff that, with virtually all of the British Army's equipment lost and with metropolitan France doomed, the survival of the United Kingdom and of any remnants of French power would depend on the extent of the supplies produced in and delivered from the United States.

These supplies could be financed for the time being, a matter of a few months, on the "cash and carry basis"; but when the last dollar of Britain's dwindling reserve had been spent Roosevelt would be faced with the choice of finding some other basis for furnishing aid (undoubtedly at the American taxpayers' expense) or of conceding victory to Germany.

On June 4, William Bullitt, the American Ambassador in Paris, had lunch with Pétain and reported to Roosevelt that the old Marshal had said that the British would permit the French to fight without help until the last available drop of French blood should have been shed and that then, with quantities of troops on British soil and plenty of planes and a dominant fleet, the British after a very brief resistance, or even without resistance, would make a peace of compromise with Hitler, which might even involve a British Government under a British Fascist leader.

However, on that same day, Churchill electrified the British people and most of the world with one of the greatest of all his great speeches. He seldom imposed upon his listeners the burden of having to read between his lines and one could hardly misinterpret the exact meaning of these thundering words:

> We shall defend our Island, whatever the cost may be, we shall fight on the beaches, we shall fight on the landing grounds, we shall fight in the fields and in the streets, we shall fight in the hills; we shall never surrender, and even if, which I do not for a moment believe, this Island or a large part of it were subjugated and starving, then our Empire beyond the seas, armed and guarded by the British Fleet, would carry on the struggle, until, in God's good time, the New World, with all its power and might, steps forth to the rescue and the liberation of the old.

This was the great rallying cry for the slowly awakened people of Britain—who themselves had been afflicted with isolationism and complacency—and it was the first call for help from America. Roosevelt made an attempt to answer it in his Charlottesville speech on June 10, the day that Italy entered the war. Timid souls in the State Department blanched with horror when, on his own initiative and without consultation with anyone, he inserted the words, "the hand that held the dagger has plunged it into the back of its neighbor." They felt that he was going much too far. But he was all too well aware that he could not possibly go far enough. In that same speech, he gave to the world a tremendous assurance, for which he had no Congressional authority but on which he eventually made good:

> In our American unity, we will pursue two obvious and simultaneous courses; we will extend to the opponents of force the material resources of this nation; and, at the same time, we will harness and speed up

the use of those resources in order that we ourselves in the Americas may have equipment and training equal to the task of any emergency and every defense.

This was the first pledge of aid to the "opponents of force"—the first proclamation of the policy which led to Lend Lease and to the all-out production "without which," as Stalin said at Teheran, "this war would have been lost."

When news of Roosevelt's speech was broadcast to France, Premier Reynaud cabled his desperate appeal for "aid and material support by all means short of an expeditionary force." But Roosevelt ultimately could offer in reply only assurances of "my utmost sympathy" and promise that the United States Government would not "recognize the results of conquest of territory acquired through military aggression." By means of some subtle and possibly questionable legal shenanigans worked out by Henry Morgenthau's lawyers in the Treasury Department, about a hundred and fifty American war planes were flown to Canada and there loaded aboard the French aircraft carrier *Béarn*, but they never reached their destination; they and the carrier were at sea when France surrendered and they and a lot of useless French gold spent the war idly in the Caribbean island of Martinique.

The day after the Charlottesville speech Churchill and Eden made a sudden trip to France to confer with Reynaud and others near Tours. Weygand told Churchill very bluntly that France could no longer conduct what he called "co-ordinated war." Reynaud was determined to continue the fight under any and all circumstances and was supported vigorously by his new Under Secretary for War, General Charles de Gaulle. Admiral Darlan was in favor of sending the French Fleet to Canada.

Years later, after the European war had ended, Édouard Herriot was interviewed by the *New York Times* and he said that on this occasion, June 11, 1940, Churchill had broken down and wept like a child, but clenched his fists in fierce determination and said that he almost hoped that Hitler would now turn to attempt an attack on Britain and thus give Weygand an opportunity to stabilize the front on the Somme. Churchill promised that he would make more attempts to induce the Cabinet to send squadrons of R.A.F. fighter planes to France. He said:

> Great Britain refuses to abandon the contest unless utterly crushed. If the French army is obliged to stop fighting, England will carry on in the hope that Hitler will be ruined by his very victories. With its airforce and its fleet, the British Empire can last out for years, and can impose upon Europe the most stringent of blockades.

Churchill sent a full report of this meeting to Roosevelt. He said that the aged Marshal Pétain, who had been "none too good" even in 1918, appeared to be now ready to negotiate an armistice with Hitler. On June 13, Roosevelt sent the following cable to Reynaud:

I have been deeply moved by your message of June 10th. This government, as I have already stated to you and Mr. Churchill, is doing everything in its power to make available the material to the Allied Governments which they require so urgently and we are redoubling our efforts to do still more. This is an expression of our support of and our faith in the ideals for which the Allied Governments are fighting. The American people have been profoundly impressed by the magnificent resistance of the French and British armies. I am impressed particularly by your declaration that France will fight on in behalf of democracy even though it means deliberate withdrawal, even to the Atlantic and North Africa. It is of utmost importance to remember that the French and British Navies shall continue their mastery of the Atlantic and other oceans, and also to remember that all armies can be maintained only through supplies of vital materials from the outside world. I have been greatly heartened also by what Mr. Churchill said a few days ago pledging continued resistance by the British Empire and I am sure this determination applies equally to the great French Empire throughout the world. As Admiral Darlan well knows, we can learn from history the importance of naval power in world affairs.

Churchill cabled the President expressing his enthusiasm for this "magnificent" message and begged that it be made public so that the French and British people, and also the Germans, would fully appreciate the uncompromising position taken by the United States of America. Roosevelt quickly replied through Kennedy that the Prime Minister had evidently misinterpreted his message. He emphasized the fact that, under the Constitution, he could make no commitments beyond the material aid already announced.

That same day, June 13, the day before the fall of Paris, Churchill again flew to France in a final effort to beg the French Government to fight it out on any and every line that could be established and, in the event of bitter necessity, to evacuate itself to North Africa and continue the war from there while the French Fleet merged with the Royal Navy.

Reynaud informed Churchill that it was hopeless to continue fighting unless the British gave him more squadrons of R.A.F. fighter planes.

According to General Sir Hastings Ismay, Personal Chief of Staff to the Prime Minister, "Before we left for the meeting at Briare, Air Marshal Dowding, Commander-in-Chief, Fighter Command, had given the Cabinet the most solemn warning that if any more fighter squadrons were sent to France, he could not guarantee the security of the British Isles." Some of Churchill's associates feared that he would not heed this warning because of his emotional attachment to France as well as his sense of obligation to an Ally; but he refused Reynaud's request. When he was told of Weygand's prediction, "In three weeks England will have her neck wrung like a chicken," Churchill filed those words in the back of his mind for possible future reference. Reynaud was thereupon compelled to yield to Marshal Pétain who immediately started to sue for a separate peace. When Churchill and his party had returned to London (flying, incidentally, over German-held territory) he sent a cable to Roosevelt saying that France might still be saved by a Presidential announcement that the United States would, if necessary, enter the war. Roosevelt replied again that he could make no such commitment, only Congress could make such a commitment. Churchill was well aware of that but, in the moment of desperation, he was ready to try anything. He now knew that Britain must fight alone and that the first phase of the coming decisive campaign would be an all-out battle for control of the air over England itself; the second phase would be fought on the waters of the Channel, and Churchill repeated several times in cables his hope that the President could arrange for the lease of American destroyers to the British.

In the days while the venerable defeatist, Pétain, was negotiating with Hitler, the cables between the White House and Downing Street continued, but now it was Roosevelt who was asking most of the anxious questions. First, the President wanted to know when Churchill expected that the German attack against Britain would start. The answer was: in all probability immediately. Then Roosevelt asked what would be done with the British Home Fleet in the event of successful German invasion. He expressed the hope that the fleet would be disposed among bases such as Newfoundland, Aden, Capetown and Singapore, stating that the American fleet would assume responsibility for the defense of the Western Hemisphere, including Canada. Roosevelt said, "As naval people, you and I fully appreciate that the vital strength of the Fleet and command of the seas mean, in the long run, the saving of democracy and the recovery of those suffering temporary reverses."

The reply from London contained ugly truths dressed up in immaculate terminology. Roosevelt was informed that of course the Royal Navy or any part of it would never be surrendered to Hitler, and that all surviving units of the Home Fleet would be disposed in overseas bases as the President suggested; however, it was pointed out, every available British armed ship would be violently engaged in the defense of the British Isles and, therefore, the very fact of successful German invasion would presuppose the total destruction of the Home Fleet.

That was precisely what Roosevelt wanted to hear. He knew now that the Former Naval Person was determined that, if Britain were to go down, she would go with colors flying and guns blazing, and with no servile requests for terms. Being a naval person himself, he now began to feel confident that with such determined spirit and with such a fleet she would not go down. He further asked what were the intentions as to the transfer of the seat of government from London to Canada or some other point in the Commonwealth in the event of successful invasion. He wanted to be assured that the British would do what the Dutch, Belgians, Norwegians, Czechs and Poles had done and set up a Government in Exile—which Pétain had failed to do. He received only an equivocal reply on this point. But when Harry Hopkins went to London, seven months later, he learned the truth: *the British Government did not have even a skeleton plan for evacuation to Canada or anywhere else overseas.* Churchill believed that if the United Kingdom fell, the Empire would be ended—at least temporarily—and the leadership of the remaining units of the British Commonwealth would pass to Washington.

The Dominion Governments were sending messages to London at that time urging that the royal family, or at least the two young princesses, be sent to a place of safety at once so that the institution of the Crown be continued regardless of the fate of the home islands. This request was not accepted. Queen Elizabeth said, "The Princesses could not leave without me—and I could not leave without the King—and, of course, the King will never leave."

There was a plan for the evacuation of London, worked out in utmost detail, according to which most of the government would move to Malvern, in the west of England. I do not know whether Churchill has ever committed himself as to his own personal opinion of this plan, but members of his staff at that time have expressed the conviction that he never had any intention of quitting London under any circumstances whatsoever. If the Nazis succeeded in taking London—which he was pleased to call "this Imperial City"—they would take him with it, or anything that might be left of him.

I cannot quote in full the cables that passed between Downing Street and the White House at this time because, although I have read them, they are not part of the Hopkins papers. Those from the British end made the following further points:

The only British hope of defeating Germany was in the retention of the United Kingdom itself as a base, and to that end every resource and every life would be directed. If the United Kingdom were conquered, and the fleet destroyed, then North and West Africa as well as Europe would inevitably fall under German domination. All that the British could do in the Mediterranean would be to deny the Germans use of the Suez Canal, not by defending but by destroying it. Germany would have a formidable naval striking force with the Italian Fleet and substantial units of the French Navy joined to her own. Furthermore, with all the shipyards of Western Europe at her disposal, Germany would have enormous naval productive power. Hitler's triumphs in Europe would undoubtedly stimulate the Japanese to acts of aggression against French Indo-China and the Netherlands East Indies, thereby gaining for themselves bases for attacks on other points, including British and American territory. Churchill expressed the belief that the whole world situation could be greatly helped if the United States Government would proclaim that any violent attempt to alter the status quo in the Far East would "produce a state of belligerence" or (toning it down a little) would "not be tolerated."

Roosevelt repeated (not once but several times) that, for constitutional reasons, he could not give any assurance that the United States would declare war no matter what the provocation, short of direct attack upon the United States itself. But he made it quite clear that if Britain fell his own purpose would be to do all that he possibly could—"more than mere words but short of war"; for he knew that with Britain and her Navy gone all of our traditional concepts of security in the Atlantic Ocean— the Monroe Doctrine, the principle of freedom of the seas, the solidarity of the Western Hemisphere—would become mere memories, and the American people would be living constantly "at the point of a Nazi gun."

In the notes that he made for a speech at a secret session of the House of Commons on June 20, Churchill stated that if Britain could get through the next three months she could get through the next three years. He placed great stress upon superiority in air power and said that the issue depended primarily upon the outcome of the impending air Battle of Britain. He expressed the opinion that nothing would so stir the people of the United States as fighting in or over England. He felt that the best provocation to the American people to enter the war would be furnished by the heroic struggle of the British people. He paid tribute to Franklin Roosevelt and said that all depended upon the British people's maintaining a resolute bearing and holding out until the election issues were settled in America. (Although Churchill constantly warned his associates and the people in general against wishful thinking, he was humanly incapable of resisting the temptation to indulge himself in that agreeable vice now and then; neither, as I have said, was Roosevelt.)

With the signing of the Armistice in the forest of Compiègne, the British Government faced the problem of the French Navy. The decision was taken, "with aching hearts," to destroy all possible ships of this Navy which would not voluntarily join with the British or consent to move out of German reach and be demilitarized for the duration of the war. Various alternatives were presented to the ships at Oran, in Algeria, among them the possibility that they might be "entrusted to the United States and remain safe until the end of the war, the crews being repatriated." The proposals made at Oran were refused by the French Admiral Gensoul and the British Navy attacked with guns and naval aircraft. The damage done and the loss of life were heavy—although one valuable cruiser escaped to Toulon. This action provided powerful ammunition for Nazi anti-British propaganda in France throughout the next four years, but it had a tremendous effect on world opinion, particularly in the United States. It served forcibly to underscore Churchill's defiant assurance that "we will fight them in the streets" and "never surrender." It exerted a particular effect on Roosevelt who, it is reasonable to assume, knew of the action well in advance.

The President had scraped the bottom of the barrel in American arsenals for half a million rifles, eighty thousand machine guns, a hundred and thirty million rounds of ammunition, nine hundred 75 mm. guns and a million shells, as well as some bombs, TNT and smokeless powder, all to be shipped to Britain. This was done by means of more legal manipulation in a "damn the torpedoes" spirit. It was done at a moment when many men close to the White House were shouting almost hysterically that this represented suicide for Roosevelt and quite possibly for the nation— that Britain was finished and that all this material would merely fall into the hands of Hitler who would turn it against us in our own relatively defenseless state. But—it was done, and it was of inestimable value to Britain in her hour of greatest need. These shipments were of such vital and immediate importance that Churchill gave instructions that their delivery be treated as a "military evolution." Trucks and vans were awaiting them at the dockside so that, at the instant of unloading, they could be rushed to various strategic points exactly as though they were arms delivered to sorely beset troops fighting to hold a precarious beach-head. The British Home Guardsman, who had been preparing to meet German invasion with a pitchfork or a flail, now had a rifle in his hands and ammunition in his belt. He felt much better. He felt, in fact, unbeatable.

When the Blitz was at its height, Churchill said in a secret-session speech:

> The deployment of the enemy's invasion preparations and the assembly of his ships and barges are steadily proceeding, and at any moment a major assault may be launched on this island. . . . Upwards of seventeen hundred self-propelled barges and more than two hundred seagoing ships . . . are already gathered at the many invasion ports. . . . I am confident that we shall succeed in defeating and largely destroying this most tremendous onslaught by which we are now threatened, and anyhow, whatever happens, we will all go down fighting to the end.

It is perhaps a bit of unnecessarily grim speculation, but I believe there were some in England—and I should not be surprised if Churchill were one of them—who later regretted rather wistfully that Hitler never tried that invasion. As a member of the staff remarked later to Hopkins, "It would have been a hell of a fight." The British were deficient in modern weapons, but they had millions of antitank grenades, made with beer bottles containing TNT and sulphur, and they were literally spoiling for a chance to hurl them. They knew that the President of the United States, however limited his and their means, was with them, at least in spirit. This consideration was worth far more to their morale than the paper that it was not written on.

This, then, was Roosevelt's first tremendous wartime decision: to back the seemingly hopeless cause of Britain with everything that he could possibly offer in the way of material and moral encouragement. This decision was entirely on his own. There was no time in his Presidential career when he met with so much opposition in his own official family or when his position in the country was less secure. His two principal ambassadorial advisers, Bullitt in France and Kennedy in Britain, were bleakly defeatist about Britain's chances. Bullitt, passionately pro-French, felt that the British had betrayed their allies because of Churchill's refusal to send the final R.A.F. fighter strength to France. Kennedy vehemently advised the President against "holding the bag in a war in which the Allies expect to be beaten." But Roosevelt made his decision and proclaimed it—let it be remembered—on the brink of a Presidential political campaign and even before he had announced that he would run for a third term or before he knew that the Republican nominee would be Wendell Willkie instead of Robert A. Taft, Thomas E. Dewey or Arthur H. Vandenberg, all of whom were then avowed isolationists. In this decision, Roosevelt was influenced undoubtedly by strategic considerations: he well knew the importance of the United Kingdom as a base and of the Royal Navy as a weapon for the defense of the Western Hemisphere. But there were considerations of morality which were even more important to him. His inability to offer any kind of satisfactory reply to the desperate calls for help from France had given him, I believe, the bitterest sense of defeat that he had ever experienced. He was determined not to repeat that national humiliation. He was now asserting leadership of the American people—and most of the people, be it said, were glad of it for they had been shocked and stunned by the impact of events.

The vast mail that came into the White House in those days was full of fear, not of any known peril, but of the awful uncertainty and confusion that afflicted the people. Many letters carried pitiful appeals from mothers and wives to the President to "Tell the country that you won't send our boys into any foreign wars. Promise us they won't be sent out of the Western Hemisphere." (As though it were preferable to have the war in this part of the world and the boys to perish in the Brazilian jungles or the Alaskan wastes.) There were letters that expressed fear for our national honor and the future of our freedom. One such was from Hopkins' old friend, William Hodson, Commissioner of Welfare in New

York City, who had been so largely responsible for bringing Hopkins to the attention of Franklin D. Roosevelt. Hodson wrote:

> There can be no doubt that America is on the brink of disaster, and I am conscious of the appalling responsibility which the President and all his advisers are assuming in this dark hour. I hope that the President will speak out and tell America the worst, as Churchill has done in Great Britain, so that we may steel ourselves for the trials ahead which the American people do not fully understand.
>
> What can be done at this point by the citizens to bring about immediate American help to the Allies in every possible way? What can the citizens do to support and sustain the President's effort to reorganize and enlarge the armaments of the country without delay?
>
> It seems to me that there is still a lethargy and inertia, which may confuse and deaden our efforts, unless we hear quickly the clarion call, which only the President can give. God grant that we are not already too late!

Hodson was killed two and a half years later in the crash of an Army airplane en route to North Africa where he was to organize the first program of the United Nations Relief and Rehabilitation Administration. He had lived to see the war reach its turning point at Midway, El Alamein and Stalingrad. But Roosevelt never clearly sounded "the clarion call" which Hodson and many others demanded; he waited until the Japanese war lords sounded it for him. He has been criticized for this by many thoughtful people, including his most loyal "lieutenant," Henry L. Stimson. Perhaps history will find him at fault for not having laid his cards on the table in 1940 or 1941 and demanded a showdown with Congress as to whether or not the United States should enter the war and fight. I do not know about that. I can only express the belief that had he done so he would have been badly defeated and Germany and Japan between them would have conquered all of Europe and Asia, including the Soviet Union, by 1942. I hesitate even to guess what the results of this would have been in the Western Hemisphere. Not that it matters. For better or for worse, history never needs to be seriously concerned with what *might* have happened. Whatever Franklin Roosevelt might have done that he did not do, the fact remains that the decisions he made in 1940, on his own authority and without clarion calls, involved commitment of the United States to the assumption of responsibility for nothing less than the leadership of the world. It was a coincidence but an appropriate development of the pattern of history that Roosevelt should have proclaimed his decision at Charlottesville, Virginia, in the presence of the genius of Thomas Jefferson, who had boldly and without Congressional authority set the young United States on the way to continental dominance and thereby, he hoped, had given it strength to avoid the entanglements of the Old World.

CHAPTER VII

The Chain Reaction

IT IS generally assumed that propaganda is nothing but a maze of words dreamed up by fiendish minds for the purpose of deceiving and cajoling, lulling or frightening. But the only war propaganda that really matters is that which proclaims action or which threatens it, and in the latter case the action must always follow or the propaganda boomerangs. The devastating Nazi propaganda campaign, the strategy of terror, was not the mere creation of Goebbels' phrase factory; it was the sequence of events—the blood purges, the pogroms, the rearmament, the annual Black Mass of force worship at Nuremberg, the concentration camps, the reality of the fifth columns operating with brazen, contemptuous candor behind the frontiers of intended victims all over Europe and the Western Hemisphere; finally, it was the sudden application of overwhelming force itself and the proof that "resistance is futile." Hitler dancing a jig on the grave of the 1918 Armistice— Hitler paying magnanimous tribute at the tomb of his late colleague, Napoleon Bonaparte—these illustrated events provided the supreme peak in the course of Nazi propaganda. If the strategy of terror were enough in itself to conquer the world, Hitler need fear no future battles. But there are some peoples whom it is dangerous to alarm, and the first of these was the British, and the second the Russians and the third the Americans.

One of the most forcible and persuasive although unwitting purveyors of Nazi propaganda was the famous American hero, Colonel Charles A. Lindbergh. Largely because of personal tragedy, and the refusal of the more sensational press (which was also the most vehemently isolationist section of the press) to allow him and his family to lead anything resembling a normal life, Lindbergh had lived for several years in Europe before the war. He had seen the flabby weakness of the England of Stanley Baldwin and Neville Chamberlain, and the chaotic disunity of France, and the apparent deficiency of Russian industry, as contrasted with the superb organization and regimentation of Hitler's and Goering's Germany which presented a model of efficiency to his technological mind. He was given every opportunity by Goering to study the building of the mighty Luftwaffe. Because he had an exceptional understanding of the power of machines—as opposed to the principles which animate free men—he came to the seemingly logical conclusion that Nazi Germany was invincible and that Britain, France, the United States and everybody else should wake up and, facing the facts of modern life, yield to "the wave of the future." A retiring and taciturn man by nature as well as by force of cruel circumstance, Lindbergh became a violent and extremely eloquent crusader for the cause of isolationism. He was undoubtedly Roosevelt's most formidable competitor on the radio.

When the Blitzkrieg in the West was at its height, Roosevelt asked the Congress for a program which would involve, among other things, the production of 50,000 war planes for the Army and Navy. He said:

> The brutal force of modern offensive war has been loosed in all its horror. New powers of destruction, incredibly swift and deadly, have been developed; and those who wield them are ruthless and daring. No old defense is so strong that it requires no further strengthening and no attack is so unlikely or impossible that it may be ignored.

Lindbergh denounced this as "hysterical chatter," adding:

> We are in danger of war today, not because Europeans attempted to interfere in our internal affairs, but because Americans attempted to interfere in the internal affairs of Europe.
> Our dangers are internal. We need not fear invasion unless Americans bring it through their own quarreling and meddling with affairs abroad. If we desire peace, we need only stop asking for war. Nobody wishes to attack us, and nobody is in a position to do so.

Lindbergh did not say much publicly at this time of what he had seen of German might and of British, French and Russian weakness. But when he recited facts and figures at private meetings he could generally scare the living daylights out of his listeners and some of them were impelled to write to Roosevelt urging him to command Churchill to surrender at once to prevent the impending carnage. But one of Lindbergh's listeners had a somewhat different reaction. This was Dr. Vannevar Bush, formerly Dean of Engineering at the Massachusetts Institute of Technology, now President of the Carnegie Institute in Washington. The effect upon Dr. Bush of the scaring process was not at all what Lindbergh had intended. He was impelled to action by the very threat which Lindbergh so forcefully presented. Bush was in consultation and correspondence with various like-minded men of science, among them Presidents James B. Conant of Harvard, Karl T. Compton of the Massachusetts Institute of Technology and Frank B. Jewett of the Bell Telephone Laboratories. They had discussed a plan for the mobilization of American scientists to work on new weapons to meet and overcome the awful challenge that Nazi technology had presented to the free and civilized world. Bush had been named spokesman for this group principally because he was the one who happened to be in Washington, but he proved to be (in the words of Conant) "an ideal leader of American scientists in time of war . . . his analysis of a tangled situation and his forceful presentation of a course of action produced results far removed from his official sphere of influence."

Bush had no quick access to anyone on the higher levels of government, but he knew that the man to see en route to Roosevelt was Harry Hopkins and he accordingly went to him with his plan for a National Defense Research Council. Hopkins was already interested in the subject, for the Bureau of Standards of the Commerce Department was engaged in research, and through the Bureau of Patents he had received a suggestion along somewhat similar lines offered by Lawrence Langner, a public-spirited New Yorker who divided his time between the practice of patent law and directing the Theatre Guild (Langner's proposal was for a National Inventor's Council to stimulate development of new weapons and equipment, and this was established).

Always receptive to new ideas that were both daring and big, Hopkins was immediately impressed with Bush's proposal and with Bush himself. There were certain points of resemblance between the two men. Bush was also thin, quick, sharp and untrammeled in his thinking. He knew what he was talking about and he stated it with brevity and, like Hopkins, with a good sprinkling of salt. He had prepared a succinct memorandum outlining his proposals. Hopkins read it with approval and then arranged an appointment for Bush to talk with the President about it. When Bush went to the White House he was prepared to answer all kinds of questions and meet probable objections, but he found that Roosevelt had already studied the memorandum with Hopkins: after uttering a pleasantry or two, he wrote on it, "O.K.—F.D.R."—and Bush was out of the President's office a few moments after he had entered it.

Subsequently Bush, in consultation with Hopkins, drafted a letter to himself for the President's signature. That letter, with a few additions which provided for close co-operation between N.D.R.C. and the military authorities, was signed by Roosevelt on June 15, the day after the fall of Paris, when it seemed that Christian civilization was coming to an end. It was the day when Churchill sent his most desperate cable, asking the President to announce that the United States would, if necessary, enter the war, and when Roosevelt made his discouraging reply to Reynaud. Included in that letter to Dr. Bush were these words:

Recently I appointed a special committee, with Dr. Briggs of the Bureau of Standards as Chairman, to study into the possible relationship to national defense of recent discoveries in the field of atomistics, notably the fission of uranium. I will now request that this committee report directly to you, as the function of your Committee includes this special matter, and your Committee may consider it advisable to support special studies on this subject.

The function of your Committee is of great importance in these times of national stress. The methods and mechanisms of warfare have altered radically in recent times, and they will alter still further in the future. This country is singularly fitted, by reason of the ingenuity of its people, the knowledge and skill of its scientists, the flexibility of its industrial structure, to excel in the arts of peace, and to excel in the arts of war if that be necessary. The scientists and engineers of the country, under the guidance of your Committee, and in close collaboration with the armed services, can be of substantial aid in the task which lies before us. I assure you, as you proceed, that you will have my continuing interest in your undertakings.

Such was the authorization to Vannevar Bush to go ahead with his plans—which he did without delay and without ceremony. And such is the story of how Hitler's strategy of terror, relayed through Lindbergh, influenced the establishment of the organization which was responsible for the invention of the atomic bomb.

As a footnote on Lindbergh, who had derided Roosevelt's call for 50,000 war planes as "hysterical chatter": he eventually proved himself highly useful in experimental work for the Air Force; his precise recording mind retained all the intelligence material that had been so hospitably offered to him in Germany and he applied it effectively; he rendered valuable service as a civilian flyer testing some of the more than 300,000 war planes that this nation actually did produce before victory in 1945. Incidentally, Lindbergh of all people should have known this much about his own countrymen: you may say to the average American (if there is one) that some other country has a better form of government than ours, or a superior culture, or a purer religious faith, and he is apt to reply, without much interest, "Maybe you've got something there, brother"; but try to tell him that some other country can outdo us in the manufacture and use of any kind of gadget and he will be up in arms.

Another object of the chain reaction to the strategy of terror was a group of men in New York City who had been officers in the First World War and who had formed the Military Training Camps Association to keep alive the "Plattsburg idea." One of them was Grenville Clark, a distinguished lawyer, Chairman of the Board on the Bill of

JUN 15 1940

-2-

industry. Rather it is to be hoped that you will supplement this
activity by extending the research base and enlisting the aid of
scientists who can effectively contribute to the more rapid improvement of important devices, and by study determine where new effort on
new instrumentalities may be usefully employed. In order to facilitate
your contact with the needs and opportunities of the armed services, I
will request that an officer be detailed from the Army and from the
Navy to your office.

You are authorized to appoint subcommittees on special fields,
composed of scientists and engineers of distinction, together with
officers designated by the services. It is understood that all members
of the main Committee, and of the subcommittees, will serve as such
without remuneration. It will be proper, however, to charge the
reasonable travel expenses of such members to the funds of the Committee.

The National Academy of Sciences, and the National Research Council,
were formed primarily to advise the agencies of government on scientific
matters, when called upon for such service. They will, I feel sure,
respond cordially to requests from your Committee for advice on such
broad scientific problems as may arise. The members of the Academy and
Council, when thus engaged, devote their services to government without
remuneration, but it will be proper for your Committee to provide, by
suitable agreement, for defraying the incidental expenses of such groups
when they are thus engaged.

The National Bureau of Standards, and other government laboratories,
may well be able to carry on effectively some of the research which your
Committee deems necessary.

The National Advisory Committee for Aeronautics carries on research
on the problems of flight. It is not expected, therefore, that your
Committee will be directly concerned with problems in the special field
already covered by the activities of the NACA. I trust that you will
maintain close relationship with their affairs.

Recently I appointed a special committee, with Dr. Briggs of the
Bureau of Standards as Chairman, to study into the possible relationship
to national defense of recent discoveries in the field of atomistics,
notably the fission of uranium. I will now request that this committee
report directly to you, as the function of your Committee includes this
special matter, and your Committee may consider it advisable to support
special studies on this subject.

The Commissioner of Patents is considering plans for effectively
evaluating, in cooperation with the Army and Navy, new ideas which may

*Roosevelt's letter to Vannevar Bush, signed the day after the fall of
Paris, in which he set up the organization leading to the development of
the atomic bomb.*

Rights of the American Bar Association, a Republican and an old friend of Franklin Roosevelt's. At a private meeting during the days of Dunkirk, Clark came forth with the startling proposal that the nation must conscript its manpower. It was a supremely daring suggestion and a seemingly hopeless one at a time when young men all over the country were demonstrating against increased armament. Never before had the United States enacted a draft law until it was in a war and actually fighting. But Clark and his associates prepared the first draft of the Selective Service Bill and persuaded Senator Edward R. Burke, of Nebraska (one of the most isolationist of the States) and Representative James W. Wadsworth, a Republican from upstate New York, to sponsor the Bill in Congress. It was of course highly desirable to give it a bipartisan appearance, and the words "Selective Service" provided an effective euphemism. Clark made an appointment to see the President on May 31 to urge him to come out in favor of Selective Service and also to name Henry L. Stimson as Secretary of War and Judge Robert P. Patterson as Under Secretary. This appointment did not come off. General Watson called Clark and told him that it was inconvenient for the President to see him at that time and that his appointment had been shifted to Harry Hopkins, who would be glad to talk with him. Clark, however, was afraid that Hopkins would merely advise him to call off the whole dangerous Selective Service project, at least until after the November election. Since Clark had no intention of retreating under any circumstances, he concluded it was best not to talk to Hopkins. Some three weeks later, Clark and Hopkins did meet and talked for two hours. Hopkins made no commitments on behalf of the President in support of Selective Service—this being an "irrevocable act" which Roosevelt wished to avoid until he was sure he could win the vote in the Congress —but Hopkins gave Clark his own personal encouragement and at least the intimation that Roosevelt would support the Bill when he felt that the time was right for him to do so. Indeed, Roosevelt by then had already decided on the appointments of Stimson and Patterson, two of the foremost champions of Selective Service.

This was one of Hopkins' first appearances in a role that was to become of major importance—the confidential contact man between Roosevelt and private citizens who were advocating some policy of which the President approved but which he did not want to advocate publicly for political reasons at the time. There was more than one occasion when Roosevelt wanted to be "attacked" for inactivity and thus "goaded" into action by public demand.

In these same grim days at the end of May, Hopkins participated in the formation of the National Defense Advisory Commission, the parent of all the war production, food production, priorities and price control organizations. This was the beginning of the mobilization of manpower for civilian purposes as was Selective Service for the military. The N.D.A.C. was composed of the following:

William S. Knudsen, Industrial Production.
Sidney Hillman, Labor.
Edward R. Stettinius, Industrial Materials.
Leon Henderson, Price Stabilization.
Ralph Budd, Transportation.
Chester C. Davis (Grinnell '11), Farm Products.
Dr. Harriet Elliott, Consumer Protection.
William H. McReynolds, Secretary.

Later, Donald M. Nelson became associated as Co-ordinator of National Defense Purchases.

It will be seen that there was no chairman. For the next year and a half Roosevelt was criticized bitterly for his failure to appoint any one man head of the production effort. He steadfastly and perhaps stubbornly refused to do so until a month after Pearl Harbor. I have never known what his real reasons were for this delay.

There was some preliminary dispute as to just where the N.D.A.C. would be placed in the government structure. The Under Secretary of Commerce, Edward J. Noble, believed that it belonged logically in the Commerce Department, and I imagine that Hopkins was not opposed to having it under his own direction. But the President decided that the new agency should be kept independent, placed in that limboesque area known as the Office of Emergency Management. Roosevelt thereby established the pattern for his war administration: the special war agencies were for the most part set up by themselves, apart from the permanent structure, with their Directors reporting to the President rather than to any Cabinet officer. Thus, the war agencies—or "defense agencies," as they were known in the euphemistic days before Pearl Harbor—formed a kind of government within a government. Roosevelt was criticized also for this, particularly by members of his own Cabinet who saw all that power and all those funds going to the new mushroom agencies. But Roosevelt's two main reasons for this policy are quite clear:

(1) The Congress was inclined to view with suspicion any increases in the authority, personnel and money of the permanent Departments—for it is traditional that once a new function gets into a permanent agency it is extremely difficult to get it out. Temporary agencies can simply be abolished when the emergency ends. For instance, there were logical arguments that the administration of price control be put in the permanent Securities Exchange Commission or war manpower in the Department of Labor; but Roosevelt knew that the Congress would be much more likely to support these highly unpopular measures if they were so segregated that they could be canceled at any time.

(2) Of greater importance was Roosevelt's conviction that the regular Departments were not geared to meet the extraordinary demands of war. Bound by convention, tradition, red tape and bureaucratic fear of irregularity, they moved at glacial pace—when the times demanded jet propulsion. The "career man" in government is inclined to consider the interests of his career above the immediate problems of any given moment, his cardinal principle being, "Never stick your neck out." In peacetime, patience is a requirement as well as a virtue in a civil servant who knows that haste makes waste and waste makes you liable to Congressional investigation; whereas, in wartime, impatience is essential. Impatience was rife in the temporary agencies which were run and staffed to a large extent by men and women whose main concern was to do all they possibly could to help win the war in the shortest possible time and then "get the hell out of government service forever." Such temporary people, Republicans and Democrats alike, started swarming toward Washington as the German Panzers swarmed into France—and it must be admitted that some of them showed remarkable aptitude for picking up the petty jealousies and wranglings and wanglings that sometimes beset bureaucracy. Harold Smith, wartime Director of the Bureau of the Budget, talked to me years later of Roosevelt's method of handling these emergency problems in administration, and said:

> The President was the only one who really understood the meaning of the term *total war* and the necessity for it. The others believed you could fight a war with one hand and carry on domestic business pretty much as usual with the other. Roosevelt saw the Cabinet officers not as members of his own staff but as theater commanders, each with his own special area, interests, problems and demands. You couldn't expect any one of them to see the picture whole, as the President had to do. That is where Hopkins became so valuable after he left the Department of Commerce. Hopkins' sole job was to see everything from the President's point of view. He was bound by no preconceived notions, no legal inhibitions and he certainly had absolutely no respect for tradition.

Smith expressed the belief that if Roosevelt had had ample time to prepare for war—and the authority to do so—he might have reorganized the Departments to meet the emergency, which would certainly have involved some drastic changes in personnel. But there was not ample time and Roosevelt had to improvise as best he could.

In *Arsenal of Democracy*, Donald Nelson wrote:

> But let's think back to that June of 1940: Who among us, except the President of the United States, really saw the magnitude of the job ahead, the awful mission of the United States in a world running berserk? I can testify that all the people I met and talked to, including

members of the General Staff, the Army and Navy's highest ranking officers, distinguished statesmen and legislators, thought of the defense program as only a means for equipping ourselves to keep the enemy away from the shores of the United States. None of us—not one that I know of, except the President—saw that we might be fighting Germany and Japan all over the world. He took his stand against the advice of some of this country's best minds, but his foresight was superior to theirs, and this foresight saved us all.

Hopkins was certainly one of the many who had no comprehension of total war, but he was beginning to learn from Roosevelt, as he indicated in a press conference near the end of May. Asked by Nicholas Gregory of the *New York Herald Tribune*, what he thought of the war situation in general, as it affected the United States, he replied:

We cannot go on sitting here and saying that the war is so many miles away and we do not need to worry about it because we are a rich country and it will not affect us or our economic life. We cannot get ourselves into an economic vacuum here. We must get realistic, and put our minds on it, and decide what we are going to do and then make every move necessary to carry out that decision.

Mr. Hermann, of *The American Banker*, asked, "Just how far can we project that?"
Hopkins replied, "To any point you want to put it—just as far as you want to go."
Mr. Hermann then started to ask, "Even if—"
Hopkins did not permit him to finish saying, "—if it means our getting into the war?" He interposed:

Hell, I mean the tough implications! Suppose that Germany wins the war in the next two months and does on the economic fronts what they have done on the military fronts. What will they do in South America presuming they win, and then, what are we going to do about it? Or—suppose this war lasts two or three years. What effect is that going to have on the economy of this country? This is not a matter of sitting down at the dinner table and talking about it . . . I belong to the school that does not talk about things—you *do* them.

Hopkins now began to acquire experience in war production and allocation, subjects with which he was to gain so much familiarity in so little time. He became closely associated with Major General James H. Burns, of the Army Ordnance Department, and this association remained throughout Lend Lease, the Victory production program, the program of aid for the Soviet Union and the work of the Munitions Assignment Board. John J. McCloy, Assistant Secretary of War under Stimson, has written of Burns, "He gave inspiration and impetus to the program in a manner for which he forever deserves well of his country." Burns was what Hopkins liked most—a "doer"—and he worked fast. Early in June there was a conference between Knudsen, Louis Johnson and Burns at which Knudsen—the able, genial automotive production man, with no experience in weapons—kept asking, "How many pieces do you want?" The word "pieces" referred to such items as heavy bombers, bullets, paratroop boots, tanks, etc. The Army's estimates on everything had been so deliberately timid and modest, because of the fear of ever asking for more than a minimum, that the sudden rush of Congressional appropriations caught its officers unprepared. They did not know how many "pieces." But Hopkins advised Burns to ask for everything. Working with his staff incessantly for twenty-four hours, Burns produced a new program which included provision for, among other things, construction of the 50,000 war planes for which the President had asked. This program was rushed through the General Staff and presented to Knudsen within two days after he had requested it.

It is difficult to exaggerate the bewilderment and frenzied uncertainty that prevailed in Washington in those days. It was ridiculous, in a way, and in a way it was intensely inspiring; it presented the concentrated picture of a great people groping, without direction, for the opportunity of service. Among the many patriotic industrialists called to Washington was Robert T. Stevens, one of the country's leading textile manufacturers. When he arrived he had only the vaguest idea of his duties, but Donald Nelson told him, "Look around in the War and Navy Departments and find out what their requirements are in textiles and figure out a way to meet them." Stevens found out about the needs for uniforms, blankets, blackout curtains, etc., which required no special talents, and then he began to think that perhaps he was called upon for the exercise of his own imagination. Trying to consider every phase of war activity that might involve the use of textiles he thought of parachutes. It then occurred to him that with French and Italian manufacturers of silk closed to us, our only source was Japan and, while he knew next to nothing about the international situation, it seemed conceivable to him that this source might be shut off, also. He therefore felt that perhaps we should start stockpiling silk. He learned that the average requirement was four parachutes per war plane—figuring the heavy bombers (eleven men) plus the pursuit planes (one man) plus the essential reserves. He consulted the procurement officers in the Army and Navy and was told that they estimated they would need a total of 9,000 parachutes for the coming year, 1940-41—6,500 for the Army Air Corps, 2,500 for the Navy. Stevens did some multiplication of his own and told the officers that he figured they would need 200,000 parachutes instead of the 9,000 for which they were asking. They asked him how he had arrived at this fantastic figure. He replied, "The President has asked for 50,000 war planes. I just multiplied that by four."

So, the number of parachutes on the production program was boosted from 9,000 to 200,000 and, later, this figure was increased into the millions. This may have been an extreme case, but in 1940 the extreme case was the typical one. I do not cite this in any sense of discredit to the procurement officers involved but simply as an instance of the extent to which the normal peacetime, indoctrinated concern for the sanctity of the taxpayers' money can in time of peril endanger the taxpayers' lives, not to mention the security of the Republic itself.

It is important to remember that Roosevelt established the parent agencies for war production, war manpower, price control, food production, transportation, etc., without the need for any legislation by the Congress. In this, he reverted to a law passed in the First World War, just as in the creation of the Vannevar Bush organization, N.D.R.C., he reverted to authorizations dating from the Civil War. In both ultramodern instances he used antiquated and generally inadequate legislation as his authority for action because he did not want to risk possible conflict with the Congress on any issue other than what he considered the main one—which was Selective Service. As Commander in Chief in a time when the national security was imperiled, he had to put first things first: he may have been wrong in his judgment of what were the first things, but—right or wrong—he had to take action, in the national interest, and he took it. His personal position was far weaker than at any other time in the New Deal or war years. Whatever unity and harmony and even loyalty there had been in his Administration was to a serious degree disrupted by the third term issue and the selection of the Vice-Presidential nominee. During the most critical weeks of May and June, it was not known whether Roosevelt would run again or, if he did, whether he would be able to overcome the obstacles of isolationist sentiment and of popular respect for the tradition established by George Washington and solidified by Thomas Jefferson.

Outside of the Service Departments—which, as has been said, were at the time in enfeebled condition—the Treasury was the only one that was functioning on an emergency basis. Indeed, in his prolonged dealings with the French and British Purchasing Commissions, and in his promotion of aid for China, Henry Morgenthau had been exercising some of the most vital functions of the War Department and even of the State Department, not by a process of usurpation, but by default.

In mid-June, Roosevelt was bitterly attacked from both sides of the political fence when he appointed Stimson and Frank Knox, both distinguished Republicans, to serve as Secretaries of War and Navy. Both men had expressed themselves very vigorously in favor of Roosevelt's foreign policy and in opposition to the isolationist tendencies of their own party. Indeed Stimson, as Secretary of State under Hoover, had laid the foundation for that policy when he advocated collective resistance to the first act of Fascist aggression, the Japanese invasion of Manchuria in 1931. Stimson had been much too far ahead of his time in a timorous, shortsighted world, and Roosevelt admired him all the more for that. Knox, publisher of the *Chicago Daily News,* had run as Vice-Presidential nominee with Landon against Roosevelt four years previously and had been one of the hardest-hitting critics of the New Deal, but he had also been a fellow Rough Rider and lifelong friend of Theodore Roosevelt and, as such, capable of unorthodoxy. Both Stimson and Knox had held the rank of colonel in the First World War and both could recognize national peril when they saw it.

When Roosevelt called Knox on the long distance telephone and invited him to take over the Navy Department, Knox accepted but expressed the conviction that it would be unwise to make announcement of it until after the Republican Convention, which was then about to assemble in Philadelphia. He said that he wanted to attend this convention and fight for a nonisolationist policy and a nonisolationist candidate, Wendell Willkie, which would obviously be in the national interest for it would remove this highly dangerous issue from the campaign. Roosevelt replied that it was all important that the announcement be made *before* the Convention, for the following reasons:

The entry of Knox into the Cabinet must be publicly recognized for what it was—an act of pure patriotism, animated by the belief that the conduct of the whole defense effort and of foreign policy in general should be placed above all partisan considerations. This would be difficult if not impossible if Knox waited until after the Convention when the issue was joined. If the Republican party espoused an isolationist policy and nominated an isolationist candidate, then his entry into the Democratic Administration would be interpreted as an act of disgruntlement and bad sportsmanship. If, on the other hand, Willkie and the nonisolationists won out at Philadelphia, Knox could hardly desert with good grace the candidate and principles he had fought for, and thus his services would be denied to the President at this critical time.

Stimson, also notified by telephone, indicated his acceptance under certain stringent conditions, the chief of which was that all traces of the warring factions in the War Department be eliminated and that Grenville Clark's proposal of Robert P. Patterson be approved. Roosevelt agreed.

Announcement of the appointment of these two public-spirited men was made on the eve of the Philadelphia Convention and it brought roars of protest from leading Republican politicians, who charged a "double cross" and demanded that Stimson and Knox be "read out of the party." Farley and other leading Democratic politicians decried the appointments as a betrayal of party regularity. Ickes was angry because he wanted to be Secretary of War himself.

It is impossible to exaggerate the extent to which Stimson and Knox strengthened Roosevelt's hand in dealing with the immediate problems of 1940 and the longer-range problems of aid to Britain and the building up of our armed forces, as well as in the eventual fighting of the war. Of the two men, Stimson bore appreciably heavier responsibilities because of the President's predilection for the Navy. Stimson, with General Marshall at his side, had to start very close to scratch in the creation of a gigantic Army and Air Force establishment. He surrounded himself with civilian aides of remarkable ability—the Under Secretary, Judge Patterson, and Assistant Secretaries, John J. McCloy and Robert A. Lovett. Knox was similarly wise and fortunate in the selection of his Under Secretary and (in 1944) successor, James Forrestal. None of these men was naturally sympathetic with the New Deal philosophy. Undoubtedly most of them never changed in their antipathy to Roosevelt's domestic policies; even so, they provided a memorable example of devotion and of superb capability in the service of the Roosevelt Administration in wartime.

The Chief of Staff of the Army, General Marshall, and the Chief of Naval Operations, Harold R. Stark, had been appointed by Roosevelt shortly before the outbreak of the European war in 1939, and had been his advisers on all matters relating to world strategy. Both of them were military philosophers, possessed of the long view on major problems, and both had the sense of statesmanship that enabled them to consider the political as well as purely military aspects of the global situation. Stark had been on duty in the Navy Department most of the time during the prewar years, particularly as Chief of the Bureau of Ordnance. He had exceptional qualities as a staff officer, but lacked the quickness and the ruthlessness of decision required in wartime and, after Pearl Harbor, he was relieved by Admiral Ernest J. King, who lacked neither. Stark served out the war most faithfully and usefully in London, as Commander of U.S. Naval Forces in Europe; his contribution to the formation of grand strategy was immeasurable as will be seen in later chapters.

As a result of his years in the Bureau of Ordnance, Stark had made many friends on Capitol Hill and had the confidence of Congressmen who regarded him as a man modest in his demands. Marshall gained confidence by his quiet assurance, mastery of facts and exceptional courtesy, although he was suspect when he talked in terms of armored divisions and long-range bombers, for this seemed to suggest that he might have in mind taking the offensive, instead of concentrating on the work of building and manning coast defense fortifications. Faced with stupidity and shortsightedness which would have driven a weaker man to despair, Marshall maintained at least the semblance of calmness and patience;

but it can never be doubted that he endured intense inward suffering, not from frustration for himself but for the integrity and security of the Republic. There can be few people of any Allied nation who came in contact with Marshall during the war who would question the statement made to him by Secretary Stimson on the day of Germany's unconditional surrender: "I have seen a great many soldiers in my day and you, sir, are the finest soldier I have ever known."

If public opinion had been indicative of indifference and lethargy in the days of the Phony War, giving way to confusion and fear approaching hysteria during the Blitzkrieg, it began rapidly to assume a more intelligent and respectworthy appearance once Churchill in Britain and Roosevelt in the U.S. had made evident the pattern of policy for the immediate future. The knowledge that Britain would fight alone and America would extend all possible aid as a noncombatant clarified the situation in the public mind, at least until the next crisis should arise; and that represented far more clarification of issues than the people had had at any time since Munich. Roosevelt now discovered that he was gaining popular support for his policies to a gratifying and surprising extent. He was given unprecedented support by the press, the great majority of which had opposed him with mounting fury throughout the New Deal. Most of the widely syndicated columnists were with him, although there were exceptions, notably the increasingly intemperate General Hugh S. Johnson. Leading Republican newspapers, such as the *New York Herald Tribune*, the *Boston Herald*, the *Chicago Daily News*, the *Des Moines Register*, and the *San Francisco Chronicle*, which had been among his severest critics on domestic issues, now gave wholehearted approval to his measures of aid for Britain. The great American foreign correspondents had for years been warning of the menace of German and Japanese imperialism. There was no group in or out of government who had been so consistently accurate in their estimates. Now it was possible to broadcast their warnings all over the country and the voices of Edward R. Murrow and Fred Bate from London, William L. Shirer from Berlin, Elmer Davis from New York, Raymond Gram Swing from Washington, among many others, did much to strengthen Roosevelt's position.

Organizations of private citizens began to become active in the mobilization of public opinion. The largest of these had started on a small scale in September, 1939, when various members of the League of Nations Association got together to form a committee to support Roosevelt's request for repeal of the arms embargo provisions. The Chairman of this "Non-Partisan Committee for Peace through Revision of the Neutrality Law" (what a title) was the distinguished and widely beloved Kansan, William Allen White, whom no one could accuse of being a tool of British Imperialism or of the New Deal. A stanch Republican and admiring biographer of Calvin Coolidge, White was also one of the great friends and private counselors of Franklin D. Roosevelt. After Congress had repealed the arms embargo, the first White Committee was dissolved, its object having been achieved; but it was revived in May, 1940, and was called the "Committee to Defend America by Aiding the Allies." It was the first organization to combat isolationism on a national scale. White certainly was no interventionist and it is significant of the spirit of the times that he stipulated that the Committee should accept "no munition-makers' money, no international bankers' money, and no money from the steel interests"—these being the interests which were popularly supposed to impel nations to war. White had written when the Phony War was in its last stages:

> What an avalanche of blunders Great Britain has let loose upon the democracies of the world! The old British lion looks mangy, sore-eyed. He needs worming and should have a lot of dental work. He can't even roar. Unless a new government takes the helm in Britain, the British empire is done. These are sad words to say, but the truth is the truth.

Early in May, White was urging aid for Britain because, with the British Fleet intact, "we could have two years in which to prepare for the inevitable attack of the totalitarian powers upon our democracy, which must come unless Great Britain wins this war." When a new government did take the helm in Britain, White came forth as one of its firmest and most valuable friends.

Father Coughlin wrote of the White Committee in his journal, *Social Justice*:

> Like thieves who operate under the cover of night, there are in our midst those who operate beneath the cloak of protected auspices to steal our liberty, our peace and our autonomy. . . . "The Committee to Defend America by Aiding the Allies" is a high-sounding name composed of high-handed gentlemen who are leaving no stone unturned to throw everything precious to an American to the dogs of war. . . . Sneakingly, subversively and un-Americanly hiding behind a sanctimonious stuffed shirt named William Allen White, these men form the most dangerous fifth column that ever set foot upon neutral soil. They are the Quislings of America. They are the Judas Iscariots within the apostolic college of our nation.
> They are the gold-protected, Government-protected, foreign-protected snakes in the grass who dare not stand upright and speak like men face to face.

With such tributes as that, the White Committee soon had chapters operating vigorously in all the States and was putting on coast-to-coast radio broadcasts by such public figures as President James B. Conant, of Harvard, Henry R. Luce,. the publisher, and Mrs. Dwight W. Morrow, the mother-in-law of Colonel Lindbergh. My own first contribution to the campaign was a full-page advertisement, under the headline "STOP HITLER NOW," which was published in newspapers throughout the country on June 10, the day Italy entered the war. This advertisement was given public endorsement by President Roosevelt (whom I did not then know) and evoked the sneering question "Stop Hitler? With what?" from Dr. Joseph Goebbels in Berlin. I made the somewhat strong statement in this advertisement that "Anyone who argues that the Nazis will considerately wait until we are ready [to go to war] is either an imbecile or a traitor." This subjected William Allen White to many protests including one from his friend, Oswald Garrison Villard, who wrote that he and millions like him felt there was no danger to the United States and "we are just as loyal, just as sincere, and just as earnest Americans as Sherwood or anybody else." White was impressed with these protests and ticked me off for having gone too far. But it was not long before such epithets as mine were commonplace. The great debate was on and it surged and seethed and was brought to an end only by the Japanese bombs on Pearl Harbor.

In the more violent isolationist arguments was the ugly undercurrent of accusation that what the country faced was a Jewish plot to get us into war. Lindbergh eventually brought this out into the open with his statement that the only people who favored American intervention were the Roosevelt family, the British and the Jews. Obviously, the Jewish community had ample reason to be anti-Nazi, but it was by no means unanimous in opposition to isolationism. There were Jews, particularly on the upper economic levels, who supported the America First Committee because their fear of anti-Semitism in America far transcended their resentment of Nazi barbarism in Europe; and there were some Jews who were just as ready as anyone else to "do business" with a victorious Hitler.

The strength of the White Committee was that it could not be successfully attacked as "un-American" although there were many like Father Coughlin who tried to do so. It could be identified with no group or faction or partisan interest; in fact, most of its founders were like White himself Republicans. It was bitterly assailed by the Communists from the left as well as by the Fascist "lunatic fringe" organizations on the extreme right. Thus, it enjoyed a certain respectability in the eyes of the mass of the American people in the middle.

The White Committee and its numerous offshoots—notably the Fight For Freedom Committee—never dented the hard core of American isolationism, but they did exert an effect on the thinking of millions who were neither isolationist nor interventionist and they helped immeasurably to promote popular acceptance of Selective Service, the destroyers-for-bases deal and Lend Lease. Most importantly, this Committee, because of its bipartisan nature, acted as an unofficial liaison channel between the rival political camps of Roosevelt and Willkie for the achievement of agreement on the development of foreign policy.

Here indeed, in the field of American politics, were some of the most important consequences of the German Blitzkrieg; it brought about the nomination of Wendell Willkie, instead of a Republican isolationist; it provided the final push that was needed to impel Roosevelt to run for a third term; it was by all odds the most important factor in Roosevelt's re-election.

CHAPTER VIII

The Third Term Campaign

THE question has often been asked: just when did Roosevelt finally and definitely decide to seek a third term? So far as I know, that question will never be answered authoritatively. One may speculate endlessly and fruitlessly as to what went on in that mysterious mind. It is safe to say that, if there had been no international crises, he would not have run; but one might as well say that, if there had been no flood, Noah would never have elected to land on the top of Mount Ararat. Anyone who watched Roosevelt closely would know that in all matters relating to politics he had most acute powers of calculation and he used them with utmost care and finesse. It is true that he burned his fingers badly on the Supreme Court packing issue when, following his smashing victory in the 1936 election, he suffered from an access of overconfidence, and his exasperation resulting from defeat on this issue led him to burn his fingers again in the attempted purge. These experiences had a very sobering effect and led him to be if anything overcautious in his handling of issues arising from the calamitous world situation. The third term was such an issue and he studied it from every conceivable angle, and most of all in relation to his own position in history, a subject of supreme importance to him and one of which he was rarely forgetful. It seemed in the spring and early summer of 1940 that he would have little to gain in the way of glory from four more years in the White House, whereas he might have a vast amount to lose. He had already been by any standards one might apply a memorable President. He firmly believed that the New Deal achievement would stand out on the record as a remarkable one; but, now, the New Deal was no longer new or exciting or urgent and all the signs indicated that it must yield at least temporarily to a phase of reaction. Indeed, from 1938 on, it became evident that if Roosevelt should run again on purely domestic issues he would be none too sure of winning the election and, if he did win, he would face the reasonable certainty of a Congress determined to block him at every turn and at last possessed of the power to do so. It was a bleak prospect and, although Roosevelt never revealed his innermost thinking on this to any man, I feel sure that for a long time he was determined to avoid it. In this, I am speaking of a third *consecutive* term. There was another possibility that, I believe, was not absent from Roosevelt's mind. From chance remarks that he made to various friends, it would seem that he contemplated the possibility that, after four years of retirement, and of conceivably blundering mismanagement of the public interests by a reactionary Congress and a reactionary Administration in Washington, he might be called back to run for a third term in 1944. But he was in no hurry to cross that remote bridge until and if he should come to it.

All of this thinking, I repeat, was based solely on domestic considerations, and these became of less and less importance, especially to Roosevelt himself, after Munich. It was then that the third term issue began to come out into the open, and the Cabinet officer who brought it out first was Harold Ickes. Having gone to Europe during the summer of 1938—he was on his honeymoon there following his second marriage, which took place in Dublin—Ickes had talked with Chamberlain, Churchill and Attlee in England and then gone on to France. He has told me:

> Everywhere I went, I heard the same thing: "war is inevitable" —"war is imminent." It was Mrs. Ickes' first visit to France and she was enchanted with it, and when we sailed away and looked back at that lovely coastline she said sadly that we might never see it again —or, if we did, it might not still be France, it might be a province of Germany. During the voyage home, I thought hard about this war prospect and about the Presidential election in 1940. I considered in my mind the whole field of candidates and I came to the conclusion there was only one man big enough to handle the world situation: Roosevelt. When I got home, I came out for a third term and I went right on urging it at every opportunity. The President did not give me one word of encouragement on this. But he also did not tell me to stop. I was then the only one in the Cabinet for Roosevelt. Most of the others were candidates themselves—Hopkins, Hull, Farley, Wallace, Garner—you couldn't throw a brick in any direction without hitting a candidate.

As I have said in a previous chapter, Hopkins was publicly urging a third term in June, 1939, despite the determined opposition to it of Mrs. Roosevelt. Farley has recorded his own vigorous opposition to it —and Hull's and Garner's—and has stated that the President told him in the summer of 1939, *"Of course I will not run for a third term."* (The italics are Farley's.) I cannot question Farley's accuracy or Roosevelt's sincerity. However, Roosevelt's intention (at that time) not to run himself certainly did not imply any lack of interest in the selection of his successor. Farley quotes Garner as having said at about the same time, "Jim, the two of us can pull together to stop Roosevelt," and there can be no doubt that Roosevelt was determined to stop the two of them from gaining control of the Democratic party for he believed they represented the forces of reaction and isolationism. Farley has often protested that his antipathy to a third term was based on his respect for the sanctity of tradition, and no doubt this is true—but he may have had other reasons in mind and one of them may have been the fact that both he and Roosevelt were natives of New York State. The Constitution provides that candidates for the Presidency and Vice Presidency should not come from the same State. Since Farley, on his own admission, was not entirely indifferent to his chances of winning the nomination as candidate for President or, failing that, for Vice President, it is obvious that he was personally concerned in preventing Roosevelt from becoming again the Democratic candidate.

Any politician as knowledgeable as Farley must have been fully aware that there was no real possibility that Garner could be nominated and elected; but Garner, with the Texas delegation solid for him, would be an important factor in the Democratic Convention and it is quite plain that, with Roosevelt out of the picture, Farley planned to swing the Garner strength to the support of Hull for President and himself for Vice President. The great question was: how to get Roosevelt out of the picture? That proved to be a problem that neither Farley nor anyone else could solve.

The outbreak of the European War gave Roosevelt a legitimate reason to declare a moratorium on all political discussions involving himself for the time being. Impenetrable silence on this subject then settled down about the White House and, at press conferences, whenever a reporter asked the President about his third term intentions, Roosevelt would tell him, in effect, or in so many words, to go stand in the corner. I do not know to what extent these matters may have been discussed between Roosevelt and Hopkins, who was bedridden throughout this period. It is doubtful that Roosevelt ever went to see Hopkins, for the Hopkins house in Georgetown was tiny and the stairs very narrow and steep. But Hopkins was in touch with Roosevelt's state of mind through frequent telephone calls and visits from Mrs. Roosevelt and Marguerite LeHand, "Missy," who had been Roosevelt's trusted secretary for many years. I know that Roosevelt was then teeming with plans for his retirement in 1941: he was going back to Hyde Park to work on his papers, among other things, and Hopkins was to go with him to collaborate on the history of the New Deal. The Franklin D. Roosevelt Library, Inc., had already been set up and Roosevelt had arranged with Frank Walker, treasurer of the Library Committee, that

Hopkins be given a job there. Incidentally, when Walker heard of these plans from Roosevelt, he knew that the Hopkins for President in 1940 boom had ended—Walker having been one of the very few of Roosevelt's confidants who knew of the part the President was playing in promoting this boom.

On January 22, 1940, Hopkins told me he was virtually certain that Roosevelt would decide to run for a third term, but three months later, April 23, he expressed grave doubts about it. He said then that the President seemed disinclined to do anything about the nomination or to permit any of his friends to do anything, which would have meant that it would go to the Farley faction by default. (Hopkins himself was, of course, completely out of the running by this time.) Hopkins asked me if I really believed Roosevelt should run. I answered that I considered it was his duty to run. He then asked me what were my reasons for this conviction, and I made the obvious answers: the United States was the only power that could prevent the world from going to hell, and Roosevelt was the only man with the personal strength and prestige as well as intelligence to lead the United States in the way it should go. Hopkins then said to me, "I wish you'd sit down and write all of that to the President, emphasizing the 'duty' part of it."

"But," I said, "he'd pay no attention to a letter from me. He wouldn't even read it."

"You'd be surprised," said Hopkins, "how many letters from private citizens he does read and how seriously he takes some of them."

Hopkins urged me to persuade the greatest possible number of my friends who felt as I did to write similar letters to the President, and I did so. Those letters were not acknowledged, even by the customary note from a secretary saying, "The President has directed me to express his appreciation . . ." etc. I doubt that any or all of them exerted the slightest influence on Roosevelt's final decision. Farley has written that it was sometime after May 17 that he began to believe that Roosevelt had made up his mind; Edward J. Flynn, another professional Democratic politician, has said much the same thing. Pending the appearance of further evidence (which is always possible but, I should judge, highly unlikely) it may be assumed that it was Hitler and Mussolini—and also Churchill—who made up Roosevelt's mind for him. Had the Phony War still continued, with no sign of a break—or, after it did break, had the British Government advised the White House that it must sue for peace in the event of the fall of France—then nothing but overinflated personal vanity could have induced Roosevelt to seek a third term. Granted that Roosevelt had his full share of personal vanity —no man would run for President of the United States in the first place without it—he also had the ability to form a highly realistic estimate of the odds against him and, taking the most cynical view of the prospect, and leaving all questions of patriotic duty out of it, he would best serve the interests of his own present prestige and his ultimate place in history by retiring gracefully before the storm broke and thereby leaving the reaping of the whirlwind to his successor. However, as long as Britain held out, and as long as there remained a chance that German victory might be prevented, Roosevelt wanted to stay in the fight and sincerely believed that there was none among all the available candidates as well qualified to aid in the prevention as he.

On May 10, the day of the attack on the Low Countries, Hopkins went to his office in the Commerce Department—and, as nearly as I can make out, this was the second time he had appeared there in ten months. That evening he went to dinner at the White House. He was feeling miserable and Roosevelt prevailed on him to stay there overnight. He remained, living in what had been Lincoln's study, for three and a half years. Later, Missy LeHand remarked, "It was Harry Hopkins who gave George S. Kaufman and Moss Hart the idea for that play of theirs, 'The Man Who Came To Dinner.' " From then on, his work was done in his room at the White House. After breakfast in the morning and after dinner in the evening and at odd times during the day he talked with the President about the shocking cables that were coming in from Europe; Hopkins undoubtedly had little real understanding of the full import of this news, but Roosevelt was teaching him. On Sundays they usually went cruising on the yacht, *Potomac*. On June 20, Hopkins went with the President for a four days' stay at Hyde Park, during which the news arrived of France's surrender together with some of the cables from Churchill which have been mentioned in a previous chapter. A week after the return to Washington, Hopkins went to Chicago to discuss arrangements for the Convention with Mayor Edward J. Kelly. Acting without express instructions from Roosevelt, but also without prohibition, Hopkins was now moving to take charge of the third term nomination himself.

Willkie's nomination at the Republican Convention had represented an extraordinary triumph by a group of suddenly organized amateur zealots over the steam-rolling political bosses of the Republican party. These bosses distrusted Willkie, despite the fact that, as President of the Commonwealth and Southern Corporation, he was one of the few businessmen who had ever fought against a New Deal agency (the Tennessee Valley Authority) and won at least a moral victory in his fight. For one thing, he was deeply suspect because he had formerly been a Democrat. For another thing, the isolationist fetish was so strong in the Republican hierarchy that anyone who opposed it must, they felt, be tainted in some sinister way with the poison of Rooseveltism. Furthermore, they did not know whether Willkie would prove to be the kind of amenable, controllable time-server that they preferred to have in public office. (They found out later!) On the eve of the Republican Convention, Walter Lippmann shocked many conservative readers of the *New York Herald Tribune* and other dignified papers by putting the case thus strongly:

> For eighteen months the Republican party has been walking in its sleep. At no one of the critical junctures of this period has the party understood the situation or proposed measures to deal with it or offered the country positive leadership. There have been many individual Republicans, of course, who were aware of what was going on. But they have been in a helpless minority and, as an organized party, the Republicans have had no policy at all. A year and a half ago when they were told that war was coming, the politicians said that this warning was "ballyhoo" and "war-mongering." . . . One can, I think, search the speeches of Mr. Taft and Mr. Dewey, and search them in vain, for any evidence of foresight as to what has happened, for a single proposal which was sought, in advance of the Administration, to strengthen the national defense. The speeches of Messrs. Taft and Dewey during these critical months make Mr. Neville Chamberlain seem like a far-sighted and strong statesman.

This was precisely the kind of support from sober authority that Willkie needed. Luckily, the old Republican steam roller proved to be a rusty, rattletrap vehicle, directed by "sleepwalkers," and the Willkie forces prevailed, backed as they were by the unmistakably spontaneous enthusiasm of the more independent Republican voters for the rugged, untrammeled and picturesque candidate.

Roosevelt considered Willkie the most formidable opponent for himself that the Republicans could have named. Willkie had the glamor which previous Republican opponents had so conspicuously lacked. What is more, Willkie had no previous political record to attack as did those who, for isolationist reasons, had opposed every move toward national defense. Nevertheless, despite Roosevelt's respect for Willkie as a dangerous competitor, he considered this nomination a "Godsend to the country," for it tended to remove the isolationist-interventionist issue from the campaign (at least, until the final days) and thereby prevented the splitting of the people into two embittered factions. It guaranteed to the rest of the world—and particularly to the warring nations—a continuity of American foreign policy regardless of the outcome of the election. The importance of this consideration could hardly be overestimated. To begin with, Willkie came out in favor of Selective Service, thereby eliminating that extremely controversial issue.

Another important issue came up—the destroyers deal. As we have seen, Churchill had first told Roosevelt of Britain's desperate need for destroyers in a cable written five days after he became Prime Minister. After the fall of France, Joseph Alsop, the Washington columnist, urged Benjamin Cohen to use all his influence in support of the transfer of

fifty or sixty U.S. destroyers of First World War vintage to the
British, saying that without such naval reinforcement Britain might
not be able to hold the Channel against invasion. Cohen conveyed this
to his chief, Harold Ickes, who took it up with the President. Ickes
noted: "I spent a lot of time arguing with the President that, by hook
or by crook, we ought to accede to England's request. He said that,
considering the amendment that was put into the last Naval Appropriations Bill [June 28, 1940] we could not send these destroyers to
England unless the Navy could certify that they were useless to us for
defense purposes." The amendment referred to was an expression of
Congress' profound distrust of Roosevelt: it provided that no item of
military matériel could be turned over to a foreign government without
the certification by the Chief of Staff (Marshall) or the Chief of Naval
Operations (Stark) that it was useless for the defense of the United
States. This put Marshall and Stark in the embarrassing position of
being able to countermand orders of their Commander in Chief. In the
case of the destroyers, Stark could not certify them useless, for he had
lately testified to their potential value before Congressional Committees
which had asked him, "Why should we go on, year after year, wasting
the taxpayers' money keeping these old 'boats' in cold storage?" Thus
was created one of the vacuums that abounded in Washington in those
days and Roosevelt welcomed anyone, in the government or out of it,
who would rush in to fill them. Many of these vacuums were filled by
the Secretary of the Treasury, ranging far outside his own province,
and, although the destroyers deal represented a purely naval and diplomatic matter, it was the Secretary of the Interior, of all unlikely people,
who was among the first to rush in.

Various suggestions were made to the President for new legislation
to be asked of Congress to free his hands—but he was having none of
that. He was determined to find a way to circumvent Congress on this
problem, and he found it. There were concurrent negotiations for the
granting of leases for American bases on eight British possessions in
the Western Atlantic. Roosevelt decided that these could be used as a
quid pro quo for the destroyers, thereby enabling Stark to certify that the
total measure would strengthen rather than weaken America's defense,
which was of course the truth. Churchill at first resisted this. He wanted
the transfer of the bases to be a spontaneous gesture by His Majesty's
Government—an expression of Britain's gratitude for American aid—
and not merely part of a sordid "deal." He had to yield on this, but
he insisted that the two most important bases, Bermuda and Newfoundland, should remain free gifts, apart from the deal, "generously
given and gladly received"—an academic point, as it turned out.

The progress of these secret negotiations—announced to the Congress
as an accomplished fact on September 3—was known to Wendell

Willkie, who had privately approved of it (through William Allen White) and agreed not to make a campaign issue of Roosevelt's action. Indeed, Willkie's main criticism was on the ground that the transfer of fifty over-age destroyers was not nearly enough aid for Britain, which was very different from the criticisms which might have been heard had the Republican nominee been, for instance, Senator Taft. As it was, isolationists accused Roosevelt of having taken the first, long, treasonous step toward delivering the United States back into the British Empire, but the American people as a whole were not greatly interested, for by the time the deal was announced, the air Battle of Britain had started and the swapping of a few old destroyers for a few dots on the map seemed a relatively trivial matter.

The agreements between Roosevelt and Willkie on foreign affairs were strictly circumscribed and even those went by the board before the campaign ended. Otherwise, Willkie was loudly and vigorously out for the kill. Even before his nomination, he had challenged Roosevelt to run for a third term, saying that he wanted the privilege of meeting and beating the toughest opponent the Democrats could name. His cry was, "Bring on The Champ!" A shrewder politician would not have said that. The people interpreted Willkie literally as saying, "The hell with the third term tradition. Let's make this a *real* fight!" That dramatized the contest—made it an exciting sporting event—and the more popular excitement there was in a campaign, the better it always was for Roosevelt. When Roosevelt agreed to run, people took it not so much as violation of a tradition as acceptance of a challenge to an old-fashioned, bare-knuckled slugfest.

The Democratic Convention opened in Chicago on July 15. Previous to it, there were meetings at the White House of pro-Roosevelt (which meant anti-Farley) Cabinet officers and Congressional and party leaders to discuss ways and means. Roosevelt was urged to put in an appearance at the Convention himself, but refused. When asked about strategy and organization of his supporters as opposed to the Farley faction, he seemed rather vague, saying only that the Convention should have its own way and he would accept its verdict. Everyone knew of course that if the Roosevelt forces did not control the Convention, Farley would. At one of the meetings Roosevelt was asked, "Suppose at some point we want to know your directions on strategy—whom do we ask?" Roosevelt thought for a moment and then replied, "In that event, if I were you, I'd consult Jimmy Byrnes." However, when Secretaries Frances Perkins, Ickes, Wallace and the rest arrived in Chicago they found, to the dismay of some of them, that Roosevelt headquarters had already been firmly established in a Blackstone Hotel suite by Harry Hopkins. Here was the Chicago end of the private line to the White House. (This telephone was in the bathroom, the only place where privacy could be assured.) The Farley offices—which would normally have been Democratic National Headquarters—were across the street in the Stevens Hotel, which made it convenient for the bewildered leaders of the State delegations, reducing the distance that they had to walk going from one rival headquarters to the other to receive their conflicting instructions. Be it said that most if not all of these local leaders greatly preferred Farley to Hopkins, whom they considered the kingpin of the left-wing New Dealers and therefore the avowed enemy of the regular Democratic organization. Their chief complaint against the New Dealers was that they were political amateurs with no knowledge of or respect for the sacred traditions of party regularity. As Edward J. Flynn has written, "many of the appointments in Washington went to men who were supporters of the President and believed in what he was trying to do, but who were not Democrats in many instances, and in all instances were not organization Democrats." (e.g.—Stimson, Knox, Fiorello La Guardia, William S. Knudsen, Felix Frankfurter, John G. Winant, etc.)

Hopkins carried in his pocket three penciled paragraphs in Roosevelt's handwriting on a sheet of yellow, ruled paper. It was addressed to the Speaker of the House of Representatives, William B. Bankhead, Temporary Chairman of the Convention. It read:

DEAR WILL—

When you speak to the Convention on Monday evening will you say something for me which I believe ought to be made utterly clear?

You and my other close friends have known and understood that I have not today and have never had any wish or purpose to remain in the office of President, or indeed anywhere in public office after next January.

You know and all my friends know that this is a simple and sincere fact. I want you to repeat this simple and sincere fact to the Convention.

To the best of my knowledge, that is the only instruction that Roosevelt put in writing before the Convention. There was a change of plan on this; the message was not delivered by Bankhead on the first day, Monday, but by Senator Alben W. Barkley, the Permanent Chairman, on the evening of the second day. This was the signal for the fifty-three-minute "demonstration" led by Mayor Kelly's notorious "voice from the sewers." The machine Democrats obediently climbed aboard the band wagon. The vote on the first ballot was Roosevelt 946, Farley 72, Garner 61, Tydings 9, Hull 5 (fractions omitted). This was on Wednesday, the third day of the Convention. Again quoting Flynn: "They did not support Roosevelt out of any motive of affection or because of any political issues involved"—or, it might be added, any sympathy with or even understanding of his objectives—"but rather they knew that opposing him would be harmful to their local organizations. The Roosevelt name would help more than it could hurt, and for that reason these city leaders went along on the third-term candidacy." They were given an even more bitter pill to swallow when Hopkins announced that the President's choice for his Vice Presidential running mate was Henry Wallace, and for some time they gave rebellious evidence of refusing

Roosevelt's letter to William Bankhead, Temporary Chairman of the Democratic National Convention stating his position on the Third Term.

to choke this one down. Even some of the President's most loyal adherents were shocked at this selection; Ickes, who might well have accepted the Vice Presidential nomination himself, threatened to bolt the party and it later took all of Roosevelt's powers of persuasion to hold him in the fold. In the White House, on the evening of the fourth and last day, Roosevelt had become so angered by the sordid shambles in Chicago that he was actually preparing a draft of a speech refusing the nomination. (He had not yet publicly stated that he would run if nominated.) Hopkins, who was not even a delegate to the Convention and got in only by courtesy of a badge from Mayor Kelly designating him a Deputy Sergeant at Arms, was feverishly telephoning the White House almost from minute to minute while the radio in the President's study blared forth the raucous expressions of discord. One impassioned delegate shouted into the microphone: "Just because the Republicans have nominated an apostate Democrat [Willkie], let us not for God's sake nominate an apostate Republican [Wallace]." However, the insurrection was not quite strong enough to stop Wallace's nomination on the first ballot, and Roosevelt relaxed and started to dictate his acceptance speech with the aid of Sam Rosenman, for whom this was one of the worst nights of his life. At the Convention, Wallace wanted to give an acceptance speech of his own, but Hopkins harshly advised him not to show himself—there had been enough hostile demonstrations broadcast already. The Convention closed with numerous resolutions of thanks to various dignitaries who had participated, not including Harry Hopkins.

The job that Hopkins had to do at this dreadful display of democracy at its tawdriest was disagreeable and thankless. He was under fire from all sides, friend and foe alike. But he had assumed this job on his own initiative because it had to be done and there was no one else who had the courage or perhaps the effrontery to do it without written instructions from the President. He handled it only by dint of supreme toughness and a demonstration of political ruthlessness which must have caused some of the professional politicians to reconsider their estimate of him as an amateur. Hopkins knew, however, that his dilemma in Chicago was only a minor projection of Roosevelt's. In ordinary times, Roosevelt would probably have enjoyed a knock-down drag-out political Donnybrook against such opponents as Farley and Garner and legions of ward heelers and he would have handled it without much perceptible difficulty. But this Convention was staged against a background of world catastrophe, of which the delegates had scant conception, and Roosevelt, in his distaste for the whole vulgar proceeding, displayed none of his customary adroitness in controlling the unruly situation. It was a lucky thing for him and for the country that he had Hopkins there to absorb so much of the hatred that was generated.

After Chicago, it became all too clear to Hopkins that he must resign as Secretary of Commerce and, if he had not had the idea himself, there were plenty of Roosevelt's friends ready to convey it to him. He was more of a political liability than ever: he was no longer in the conspicuous role of champion of the underprivileged—unemployment was beginning to go down as the defense effort increased—and, because of his long illness, he had little to show for himself in the way of accomplishment as a Cabinet officer. On August 22 he submitted his resignation in a letter which stated his physical inability to perform his duties under the rigorous demands of war—which seems an odd excuse in the light of his subsequent activities:

MY DEAR MR. PRESIDENT:

The tenth of May, 1940 was an important and fateful date.

It seemed to me then that our situation was similar to that of the British before the outbreak of war. In the months preceding that event many Englishmen believed the conflict could be avoided by concession. Others thought there was no immediate threat from Germany; that defense preparation could be delayed with safety. Still others maintained that anyone who wished to strengthen the defenses of Britain was a "war mongerer."

The experience of Britain has shown that where the national interest and security are at stake, we are justified in making only the most pessimistic assumptions. To do otherwise is to be too late at every stage, to invite attack when it suits the aggressor, to face conflict half prepared.

The only questions at this time are with regard to the character, pace and magnitude of our defense effort. We must build armaments, and because of your own foresight and determination, this is being done. We must marshal our complete economic strength for the task of defense. This means that instead of retreating from our social and economic objectives, we should push forward vigorously with a program to abolish poverty from the land. To do less would be to undermine our security.

That you have resolved these fundamental questions in your own mind; that you are now leading the nation in its gigantic effort to defend itself,—is the surest guarantee of peace for America.

I wanted to resign last May because it seemed to me that you and the country needed the services of cabinet officers whose strength permitted vigorous and continuous assumption of the duties required of them. You indicated then that I should remain throughout the Summer in the hope that I would completely recover my strength. This recovery I have not fully accomplished, therefore, I feel that I must resign as Secretary of Commerce, the resignation to become effective in the immediate future.

An expression of good-will and appreciation from me to you at this time is unnecessary. My abiding devotion and affection for you and Mrs. Roosevelt cannot be authenticated in any exchange of letters.

Roosevelt replied as follows:

I have your letter of August twenty-second and I fully understand all that you say and much that you have left unsaid.

In giving me this letter of resignation it is possible only for you to break the official ties that exist between us—not the ties of friendship that have endured so happily through the years. I am accepting your resignation, therefore, to take effect at a date to be determined later and, I repeat, that this resignation is accepted only in its official sense.

In other words, you may resign the office—only the office—and nothing else. Our friendship will and must go on as always.

There was a cordial exchange between the old feudists, Ickes and Hopkins. Ickes wrote:

I can understand your reasons [for resigning] but I shall miss you. We haven't always seen eye to eye on every matter, but I hope that you have never doubted my personal feeling toward you. Even when we have differed you have added zest to my life.

Hopkins replied:

Your nice note to me need not have been sent. True, our relations from time to time have been strained and difficult, but now that the time has come for me to leave the Government I think I could sum up my feeling this way. No one has battled as consistently for the New Deal and for the President, week in and week out, as have you. You have never failed the President and liberals of this country in a single instance that I can recall and I think that is important and nothing can ever take that away from you. There must go with such a record a personal intellectual integrity that few people possess.

The truth of the matter is that this morning the things I think about you are the many pleasant associations we have had—the trip to Cocos Island, that little holiday we took together in Florida, dinner with you and Jane, and the warm cordiality of our informal evenings with the President. I have completely washed up in my mind as I leave the Government many of the unpleasant rivalries or clash of personalities which made our relations at times unsatisfactory. Those are over for me just as I am sure they are for you.

(*Note.* They were not over for either of them.)

Vannevar Bush, whom Hopkins had helped to get started with the N.D.R.C., wrote "I was very sorry to hear that the change is to be made, for the very selfish reason that I sincerely regret that our pleasant associations are soon to cease in a formal manner." Hopkins thanked him and added, "I will be seeing you soon." This association certainly did not end, for Hopkins never lost interest in the fission of uranium.

In addition to his formal letter, Hopkins wrote one in longhand to the President which represented one of his rare outpourings of the heart:

A public letter of resignation is almost a vulgar institution. Why don't you abolish it? At any rate I have told you little that is in my mind and heart as I leave the government's service.

I think of the things that have made my years with you the happiest time of my life. The first exciting days—the exaltation of being part of government—our first formal dinner at the White House when I met Cardozo and another [when] Bob Jackson tried to sell me some old underwear—and Cocos Island—did you ever see anything so green? Then there were those cigarettes in my pocket—it seems to me in all decency you should forget that one.

And one day you went to church with me when the going wasn't so good—and life seemed ever so dark.

Those nine old men—a better fight none of us ever took in—

And there was always New Year's Eve—and the warm glow of Auld Lang Syne—with champagne. That's about the only time we get champagne around your house. Or am I wrong?

I've always been getting on and off trains—and I saw America and learned to know its people. I like them. Whenever I was with you there were the everlasting Secret Service men—they seemed to be always at a dog trot—how many miles do you suppose they have dog trotted beside your car?

You remember the day we got you up a blind road in Nevada and Mc [Marvin McIntyre] wanted to give up his life if the car rolled over the hill? And people at trains with nice faces that smiled. All of them work hard for a living and are devoted to you.

And one day two nice people came to visit you—he was a king—and I hope will be for a long time and she was a Scotch girl who got to be a Queen. And after dinner that night you and Missy and I talked it all over till 2 A.M.

Then there were picnics! I suppose the Roosevelts have always had picnics—cold weather and nothing to drink.

I never knew there were so many mayors and governors and congressmen and senators and county auditors and school boards and irrigation districts in the world. I have met them all. One of them had me arrested and you thought it was funny and promised to visit me in jail.

I presume Henry Morgenthau will ever go to the bathroom when he gets ahead—and "Dollar Watson" will talk about the Powder River.

The cheese store on 42nd St.—and fresh fish in Iowa—and maps and rivers and forests and Admirals and dams and power plants—funny things that no President ever talked about before.

All these things I think of—and Mac and Steve and Tommy and Ben and Rex and Felix and Sam and Missy—I know they are important because I remember them—and they are good.

This letter is simply to say that I have had an awfully good time—and to thank you very much. And by the way—my weather bureau tells me that it will be fair tomorrow.

The "blind road in Nevada" referred to an occasion when the President and Hopkins were inspecting a W.P.A. project. When the President's car teetered on the brink of a steep hill, the frail Marvin McIntyre rushed to hold it up singlehanded. The allusions to Morgenthau and

Watson refer to poker game habits. The "cheese store on 42nd St." was neither a cheese store nor on 42nd Street; it was the delicatessen of Barney Greengrass, known as "The Sturgeon King," patronized by Sam Rosenman who often brought special food to augment the President's Spartan White House diet; it came to be a standing joke that when Roosevelt had some special delicacy put before him he would say, "I suppose this came from that cheese store on 42nd Street." The final reference to the weather meant that Hopkins had information from the Middle West expressing confidence that Roosevelt was going to win the 1940 election.

There was no doubt that Hopkins hated to leave the government for he was well aware that, despite the sincerity of Roosevelt's assurance that he could not resign from their friendship, the President was dependent for advice and counsel upon those who are deeply and continuously involved in high-level activities and associations, and one who is on the outside can quickly lose touch with the rapidly changing course of events and of policy. Although his standing invitation to stay at the White House remained, Hopkins went to New York and took a suite, bedroom and sitting room, at the Essex House. He was planning then to take the job at the Hyde Park Library and, vaguely, "to do some writing on the side." But he was soon back in the fray. Early in October I went to see him at his hotel and he said, "The President has to give a speech on Columbus Day. It's supposed to be one of those routine State Department speeches about Western Hemisphere solidarity, directed primarily to South America. But the President wants to talk to the American people about Hitler. So far as he is concerned, there is absolutely nothing important in the world today but to beat Hitler." Hopkins looked at me sharply as though he might be expecting me to dispute this point, which I did not. Then he asked me, "What do you think the President ought to say?"

Somewhat flabbergasted, I expressed some views and we talked about them for awhile and then Hopkins said, "Come on— Let's go and see Sam Rosenman." I had never met Rosenman, but had heard of him as one of those vague figures in the background of the Roosevelt palace guard. Although there was always criticism of these extraofficial people —the term "Brains Trust" persisted long after its original members had melted away—I could never understand why the President of the United States should not have the same right as anyone else to choose his own personal friends and even, on occasion to listen to their advice; but the very suggestion of a palace guard has an eternally sinister connotation.

Born in San Antonio, Texas, Rosenman had been graduated from Columbia Law School, entered New York politics and served in the State Legislature and, in 1929, became Counsel to the new Governor. In 1932 he was appointed and later elected Justice of the New York State Supreme Court but, in his spare time, he worked for the President in all sorts of helpful capacities, receiving for this work neither glory nor pay. From 1940 on he was a constant commuter between New York and Washington until finally, in 1943, he retired from the bench at Roosevelt's request and became Counsel to the President working full time in the White House. Roosevelt loved him, and with good cause.

When Hopkins and I went to see him he was living on Central Park West, a few blocks from the Essex House. We found him in his dining room, the table littered with papers including notes from the White House and material that Roosevelt had dictated. At first, I did not know why I was there but I soon found out that I had been pressed into service as a "ghost writer" (another sinister term). I also found out what an unsubstantial wraith a ghost writer really is; when working for Franklin D. Roosevelt, his one purpose was to haunt the White House, day and night, until a speech by Franklin D. Roosevelt (and nobody else) had been produced. Hopkins and Rosenman were practiced hands at this work and I became so interested in their talk that I forgot to be impressed and even started arguing. After a considerable amount of discussion Rosenman suddenly slapped a pencil on the dining room table and said, "Well, gentlemen—there comes a time in the life of every speech when it's got to be written." So this was my induction. From that moment on, for the next five years, Hopkins, Rosenman and I worked closely together on all the major Roosevelt speeches until the President's death. (There were a few exceptions when one or another of us was out of the country or ill and therefore unavailable; but at least one of the trio was always there.)

At this time Willkie was barnstorming up and down the country, giving several speeches a day, shouting himself hoarse, conducting a vigorous, aggressive but largely aimless campaign. The public opinion polls showed him trailing by a substantial margin. He made an appealing, gallant appearance to the crowds who heard him—but, as always, these crowds were largely composed of Republicans who would vote for him anyway; over the radio, which had become the supreme test for a Presidential candidate, his speeches sounded harsh, hurried and diffuse —short-range blasts of birdshot rather than pinpointed high explosive shells. The trouble was that he had no precise issues to emphasize: he attacked Roosevelt's domestic and foreign policies in general terms but did not promise to repeal any of the New Deal reforms or to stop aid to Britain or to advocate appeasement of Germany or of Japan, which had by now become formally a partner in the Axis. It seemed that the one real target for attack was the arrogance of Roosevelt in considering himself worthy of a third term—and, as an incidental but popular target, the appointment of the President's son, Elliott, to be a Captain in the Army Air Corps. It was strictly *ad hominem* attack, and it extended to the personalities of the Administration. What Willkie was saying, in effect, was, "You can trust me to do the same thing, only better"—or as the more embittered members of the Republican Old Guard put it, "Me too." Willkie was extremely effective in one way: by giving the Republicans the kind of dynamic leadership they had lacked for twenty years, he aroused many long-dormant voters and impelled them to the polls instead of to the Country Club or the Great North Woods on election day; thus, he swelled his own party's strength, but he could make no appreciable dent in Roosevelt's on any issue other than that of American involvement in war. In his zestful lambastings of Roosevelt, Wallace, Madame Perkins, Ickes, Morgenthau, Hopkins and the rest—Hopkins was out of the government but back in the White House—Willkie was most careful to avoid any attacks on Cordell Hull. Indeed, Hull's prestige was so great at the time that Willkie made it clear that, in the event of his election, he would urge Hull to continue in office as Secretary of State. This inevitably weakened the Republicans' position, for while their orators could hammer away at the Administration with charges of boondoggling, leaf raking, willful waste, strangling of free enterprise— points which had been belabored in 1936 with negligible success—they could not prosecute the attack directly against the conduct of foreign affairs, which was the most overwhelmingly important factor of all.

During the first weeks of the campaign Roosevelt gave Willkie what is known as "the silent treatment." In his acceptance speech (the speech to the Chicago Convention that he almost did not deliver) Roosevelt had said: "I shall not have the time or the inclination to engage in purely political debate. But I shall never be loath to call the attention of the nation to deliberate or unwitting falsifications of fact."

This, of course, left the door wide open for Roosevelt to start campaigning whenever he felt the moment was propitious. In the meantime, Willkie was compelled to roar across the land, conducting a unilateral debate, without reply. In the Columbus Day speech, October 12, Roosevelt never even alluded to the existence of a political campaign. This, of course, was all carefully calculated. Willkie repeatedly challenged "The Champ" to get up on the same hustings with him and fight it out in the old-fashioned Lincoln-Douglas manner. But Roosevelt appeared to be too preoccupied with world events to be paying attention—and he had ample reason for this, in view of the manifold perils suggested by the formation of the Berlin-Rome-Tokyo Axis, the Blitz on England, the increase in U-boat warfare in the Atlantic and the indications of new explosions in Southeastern Europe. The strain on Willkie's temper and natural good humor thus deliberately imposed was becoming intolerable.

Early in October, four weeks before election day (which, that year, was November 5) the Democrats were becoming more and more worried. The impact of the vast sums spent by the Republicans was being felt. The press was overwhelmingly pro-Willkie—such newspapers as the *New York Times, Daily News* and the Scripps-Howard chain, which had supported Roosevelt previously, having now turned violently against him. The White House mail was full of letters protesting the tendency of the press to minimize or even to suppress news favorable to Roosevelt while devoting headlines, columns, editorials and cartoons to the deification of Willkie. These letters begged the President to expose these partisan malpractices in his broadcasts, the radio being considered his only means of full and free access to the people.

The Democratic party itself, however, was no devoted band of loyalists, united against the forces of entrenched greed. The Democratic machine, such as it was, had been seriously weakened by the dissensions at Chicago. After the Convention, Farley had "taken a walk," as Al Smith had done before him, and the National Chairmanship had been taken over by Ed Flynn, a most agreeable man and a successful leader in a highly specialized district (The Bronx, New York City), but hardly at that time a national figure. The most spirited element in the Democratic campaign was the newly formed Independent Committee, headed by Senator George W. Norris and Mayor Fiorello La Guardia, but this Committee—more "amateurs," according to the professionals—was working for the election of Roosevelt without regard for the regular Democratic organization. The local politicians were not much worried about Roosevelt's election; they felt that this problem could be left to the "Great White Father" himself. They were concerned about the Congressmen, the Governors, Mayors, County Supervisors, etc., and they were loudly demanding that the President come down from his high horse of world statesmanship and start fighting and save the party. Roosevelt, however, stuck to his plan to limit himself to five frankly political speeches in the final two weeks of the campaign. In the first of these speeches in Philadelphia on October 23, he said: "I consider it a public duty to answer falsifications with facts. I will not pretend that I find this an unpleasant duty. I am an old campaigner, and I love a good fight."

This was the signal that was needed to proclaim that "The Champ" had gone into action. This Philadelphia speech, reread after seven years, does not appear to qualify as one of Roosevelt's better efforts. But it was effective at the time, and the gleeful roars of the partisan crowd in Convention Hall that greeted each precision punch were as important when broadcast as anything specific that he said. Roosevelt did not once mention Willkie's name in this speech, nor at any other time during the campaign, nor did he ever mention Dewey four years later. Shortly after this speech, Willkie broadcast from the *New York Herald Tribune* Forum and listeners noted that he sounded shaken. Willkie's confidence in the triumph of his cause had been almost fanatical, but by now the

politicans, supported by newspaper publishers for whose opinions he had
more respect, were beginning to bring home to him the possibility that
defeat stared him in the face. Aside from his own personal ambition which
had led him to seek the nomination and to drive himself unsparingly in the
campaign, he would have been less than human if he had not come to
believe his own words and those of other Republican orators to the effect
that the re-election of Roosevelt would be an unutterable calamity, to be
prevented by any and all means, fair or foul. His principal advisers in the
first part of the campaign were the same "amateurs" who had backed
him for the nomination and helped him to win it—honorable, intelligent
men like Russell Davenport who despised the Old Guard reactionaries
and isolationists as they despised the "cynical men" (like Hopkins of
the free-spending New Deal). The Republican National Chairman, Congressman Joseph W. Martin, and other hard-boiled veterans of innumerable "smoke-filled rooms," scorned these amateurs and told Willkie
vehemently that his high-minded advisers were making him an easy
mark for Roosevelt. The Republican professionals begged Willkie to
abandon this nonsense about a bipartisan foreign policy—to attack
Roosevelt as a warmonger—to scare the American people with warnings
that votes for Roosevelt meant wooden crosses for their sons and brothers and sweethearts. Willkie succumbed to these heated urgings from men
who loved him no more than the professional Democrats loved Roosevelt
but who knew they must win with him or suffer another four years in
the political wastelands where no flowers of patronage could bloom.
When Willkie started to shout charges that American boys were already
on the transports—that we should be involved in a foreign war within
five months if Roosevelt won—the campaign really descended to the lower
depths and became, for two impassioned weeks, pretty much of a national
disgrace. Willkie knew that these charges were contemptible, and when
some of them were repeated to him by the isolationist Senator Bennett
Champ Clark, during Willkie's testimony in favor of Lend Lease a few
months later, he dismissed them with disarming candor by saying, "In
moments of oratory in campaigns we all expand a little bit."

However, there was no doubt about the immediate efficacy of Willkie's
discreditable attacks on the war issue. The advice of the Republican professionals that the only way to get votes was to terrify people proved
unhappily sound. The effects of this were felt powerfully in the White
House during the last week of October. I had to read the letters and
telegrams and reports that flooded in and, being a neophyte in such matters, I was amazed and horrified at the evidences of hysteria. Of all the
communications, the most disturbing were those from newspapermen
who, even though most of them worked for Republican papers, were
personally devoted to Roosevelt and were doing all they could privately
to help him. They reported mounting waves of fear throughout the coun-

try which might easily merge into tidal proportions by election day and sweep Willkie into office. There were all sorts of other reports from all over: notices from insurance companies to policyholders that Roosevelt's election would make their policies relatively worthless; telegrams to doctors warning that Roosevelt's election would mean the socialization of medicine; an extremely solvent bank advertised in the *Chicago Tribune*: "In a last stand for democracy, every director and officer of this bank will vote for Wendell Willkie"—a warning to depositors that they had better do likewise if they wanted to protect their money. There were various other scarecrows designed to frighten workers, farmers, housewives. Some of these, however, had been set up by the Republicans in 1936 and had fooled practically no one. The fear of war was another matter; it was something new and unreasoning and tending toward a sense of panic. Or, at any rate, so the reports indicated. Reading them, it was difficult to avoid the dismaying thought that perhaps the American people were ready to stampede along the road which led to Bordeaux and so to Vichy even before the Panzers arrived on our home soil; it seemed possible that the strategy of terror had won its greatest victory here, that the Nazis had made good their boast that the conquest of the Western Hemisphere would be an "inside job." Even more alarming reports were coming into Democratic National Headquarters in New York and were relayed, perhaps in somewhat magnified form, from there to the White House. All the messages said much the same thing: "Please, for God's sake, Mr. President, give solemn promise to the mothers of America that you will not send their sons into any foreign wars. If you fail to do this, we lose the election!"

Strangely enough, the previous Willkie arguments which had most effectively bruised Roosevelt had tended to charge him with a kind of isolationism. Willkie likened Roosevelt to Léon Blum, who had attempted to steer France toward social progress rather than preparedness; he identified himself with Winston Churchill, whom he quoted often, Churchill having made some remarks a few years before in disparagement of the American New Deal. Willkie tried to assign to Roosevelt a share of the guilt for the Munich surrender and the fall of France, and full guilt for the torpedoing of the London Economic Conference seven years earlier. Most of all, Willkie blamed Roosevelt and his "Socialistic" Administration for the present military weakness of the United States—and those accusations stung Roosevelt worse than any others because he knew all too well just how frighteningly weak we were. Roosevelt spent a great deal of time answering these earlier accusations even though they hardly tallied with the later charges that American troops were already on the transports headed for Europe or Asia or both. The diversity of Willkie's attack and its fine disregard for consistency were bewildering even to Roosevelt and he was forced for a time to take a defensive position, where he was at his worst.

On October 28, Roosevelt went to New York City and made a regular campaign tour of four boroughs, speaking at two ceremonies, the ground-breaking for one tunnel and the dedication of another, both timed conveniently for this occasion by La Guardia. There were short speeches also at Hunter College and Fordham University, at the Queensbridge Housing Project and Roosevelt Park, and the grand windup with a rally at Madison Square Garden that evening. The night before, Mussolini had contributed to the drama of the moment and, although this was certainly not his intention, had thereby helped Roosevelt, by launching his shameful and ultimately (for Italy) disastrous invasion of Greece. But Roosevelt did not denounce this; he made no further reference to a "stab in the back," for by now the Italian-American vote was of substantial importance, particularly in New York and other large cities. He said, "I am quite sure that all of you will feel the same sorrow in your hearts that I feel—sorrow for the Italian people and the Grecian people, that they should have been involved together in conflict—" an unassailably safe statement. Ironically enough, two paragraphs later in the same speech, he quoted Theodore Roosevelt's famous term, "weasel words."

That Madison Square Garden speech was one of the most equivocal of Roosevelt's career. The first two thirds of it was a reply to Willkie's charge that the Administration had neglected our national defense, Roosevelt reading the record of Republican opposition to all attempts to increase the armed force and to give aid to embattled Britain. The last third of the speech was a reply to the charge of warmongering. Here, Roosevelt went to the length or depth of taking credit for the Neutrality Law and other measures which he had thoroughly disapproved and had fought to repel and had contrived by all possible means to circumvent. While boasting of the Neutrality Law as part of the Administration record, he deliberately neglected to make any mention of his own Quarantine Speech; in a campaign as irrational as this one, he felt it necessary to soft-pedal the fact that he had been ahead of other world statesmen in telling the world the truth.

This speech was brightened by one fortuitous catch phrase. In citing the voting records of such prominent Republicans as Congressmen Joe Martin, Hamilton Fish and Bruce Barton, the three names fell into such a euphonious pattern—Martin, Barton and Fish—that Roosevelt repeated the phrase later in the speech, and when he did so, the crowd roared the names with him. Two days later, in his Boston speech, Roosevelt mentioned Martin, and immediately someone in the gallery shouted "What about Barton and Fish?" and the crowd thereupon took up the chant. American crowds love to indulge in organized exercises of derision. Willkie said later, "When I heard the President hang the isolationist votes of Martin, Barton and Fish on me, and get away with it, I knew I was licked." (I must say that I doubt that statement; it was a virtue of Wendell Willkie's that he never knew when he was licked.)

The day after the New York appearance, Roosevelt was back in Washington for a momentous ceremony: the drawing of the first numbers under the Selective Service Act. This lottery would determine the names of the first 800,000 men—roughly, five per cent of the total registrants—to be drafted into the Army. This would have been a tense, nervous occasion at any time; with the current state of the world, and with the word "warmonger" being thrown about so recklessly it was all the more harrowing. Roosevelt had to choose his words with extraordinary care. This was no moment for trick phrases. The nation was listening breathlessly for the broadcast announcement of the fateful numbers as they were drawn. With his marvelous gift for finding homely, old-fashioned words to fit new circumstances, Roosevelt did not refer to Selective Service as a "draft"—certainly not "conscription"—he called it a "muster," thereby evoking race memories of the rugged farmers of Lexington and Concord taking their flintlock muskets down from above the fireplace. Roosevelt had prepared himself with letters from leaders of the Protestant, Catholic and Jewish faiths, supporting Selective Service as a democratic procedure, and he quoted from these in his broadcast. The best of these—and, in view of the uncertainty of the Catholic attitude, the most important—was from Archbishop (later Cardinal) Francis J. Spellman, who wrote:

It is better to have protection and not need it than to need protection and not have it. . . . We really cannot longer afford to be moles, who cannot see, or ostriches who will not see. . . . We Americans want peace and we shall prepare for a peace, but not for a peace whose definition is slavery or death.

Those were stronger words of justification of Roosevelt's position than any he himself uttered in this campaign.

It seemed as though the fear-of-war hysteria, as expressed in the messages to Washington, reached its peak on this day. The Gallup poll indicated that Willkie was steadily gaining in strength. Roosevelt himself was inclined to shrug this off on the theory that Gallup's conclusions could be colored by wishful thinking as well as those of anyone else. But the Democratic leaders were becoming more and more jittery and attributing everything to the peace mania. It seemed that Roosevelt had gone about as far in the New York speech as one could go in the provision of reassurance, but the frightened politicians protested that he had not gone far enough: they demanded that he provide absolute guarantee to the mothers of America that their sons would not fight.

On October 30, we were on the Presidential train going up into New

England, with stops for short speeches at New Haven, Meriden, Hartford, and Worcester, and the final speech at the Boston Arena. That Boston speech was a terrible one to prepare and also to remember. Every time the train stopped more and more telegrams were delivered stating almost tearfully that, if the President did not give that solemn promise to the mothers, he might as well start packing his belongings at the White House.

Roosevelt as always worked hard on the speech between stops. He sat in a low-backed armchair in his private car, the latest draft of the speech on his lap, with Missy LeHand, Grace Tully, Hopkins, Rosenman and me, all working with carbon copies. We came to a passage which gave assurance to the mothers and fathers that their "boys" would be well fed and well housed in the Army and their health well guarded. Hopkins handed the President a telegram from Ed Flynn containing the usual urgent request.

"But how often do they expect me to say that?" Roosevelt asked. "It's in the Democratic platform and I've repeated it a hundred times."

Whereupon I remarked, "I know it, Mr. President, but they don't seem to have heard you the first time. Evidently you've got to say it again—and again—and again."

So it was put in, as follows:

And while I am talking to you mothers and fathers, I give you one more assurance.

I have said this before, but I shall say it again and again and again: Your boys are not going to be sent into any foreign wars.

That passage has been given almost as much quotation (in the isolationist press) as Roosevelt's somewhat complementary observation that "The only thing we have to fear is fear itself."

Rosenman, whose duty it was to remember everything, mentioned the fact that the Democratic platform had added the words, "except in case of attack." Roosevelt said he could see no need to tack that on now. "Of course we'll fight if we're attacked. If somebody attacks us, then it isn't a foreign war, is it? Or do they want me to guarantee that our troops will be sent into battle only in the event of another Civil War?" He was plainly sick and tired of these jugglings of euphemisms, as well he might be.

The Boston speech provoked a political issue over the use of a personal pronoun. As a gesture to the Boston Irish, Roosevelt paid tribute to one of them, Joseph P. Kennedy, who had just returned from his post at the Court of St. James. Roosevelt described him as "my Ambassador." Both Hopkins and Rosenman protested this, asking if it would not be better to say "our Ambassador." But Roosevelt insisted that "my" was correct and he was technically right, for an Ambassador is the personal

representative of the head of one state to the head of another. That ex-
planation did no good whatever once the fatal pronoun was out. Every
Republican orator from then on pointed to the word "my" as proof of
Roosevelt's colossal egotism and dictatorial ambitions.

Before the Boston speech, Roosevelt went for a rest and quiet dinner
at the apartment of his son John on the Charles River. An adjoining
building was some sort of club for undergraduates of the Massachusetts
Institute of Technology. They had displayed a huge banner inscribed
with the words WE WANT WILLKIE!—and when the President was
pushed out in his wheelchair, the students chanted, "Poppa—I wanna
be a captain!" which was the popular, taunting reference to the commission given to John Roosevelt's brother, Elliott. While waiting for the
President to come out at that time I was collared by Boston police because I could not give a satisfactory explanation of my presence there.
While being led away, I was fortunately spotted by General Watson and
Captain Callaghan, the Naval Aide, and rescued. They turned me over
to Colonel Starling, of the Secret Service, and I rode to the Arena in the
open Secret Service car which, bristling with submachine guns, followed
the President's car through the Boston streets. Passing through Back
Bay, the crowds seemed none too friendly and there were occasional
catcalls and boos for Roosevelt. But, after the turn from Boylston into
Tremont Street, and thence through Scollay Square, the crowds increased tremendously in numbers and enthusiasm.

After this Boston speech—which, I think, ranks below even the one
at Madison Square Garden—the President seemed to return to form.
On October 31, he was able to give some attention to the war, having
only one nonpolitical speech to make, at the dedication of the National
Health Center in Bethesda, Maryland. The following morning the Presidential train left for Brooklyn. We all felt cheerful on that trip—it was
an undefined feeling that the worst was over—and the speech that night
was a vast improvement over its unworthy predecessors in this strange
campaign. Roosevelt had abandoned the defensive, he had stopped listening to the party prophets of calamity, he was going into the attack with
the confident buoyancy and vitality that were his.

The fearsome labor leader, John L. Lewis, in one of the ugliest
speeches on record, had proclaimed that he and the millions of workers
who presumably did his bidding would vote for Willkie; moreover, he
promised that, if Roosevelt were to win the election, he would quit the
Congress of Industrial Organizations of which he was then President
and go sulk in his tent. So now it became a personal issue between Lewis
and Roosevelt. This was more like it! It is my opinion that Roosevelt
had not really been able to put his heart into the contest against Willkie,
who presented so indistinct a target; but a battle to discredit John L.
Lewis loomed as a real pleasure. Willkie had no more in common with

Lewis politically, ideologically or sociologically, than he had with such implacable Tory die-hards as Tom M. Girdler or Ernest T. Weir, but he was stuck with this discordant support and could not disown it. The Republican dilemma was illustrated by a story told ruefully (after the election) by Albert Lasker, a highly successful advertising man and a vigorous force in the Republican National Committee. With the campaign in its final, frantic stages, Lasker went to Chicago to gather a group of prominent businessmen about the dinner table and extract from them some hundreds of thousands of dollars for the Republican fund. It was no easy job, for all present had undoubtedly contributed heavily already and some of them were none too enthusiastic about Willkie's tendencies to say "Me Too" on the New Deal reforms and aid for Britain. During the evening the radio was turned on and the assembled company listened to John L. Lewis broadcast his Hymn of Hate against Roosevelt. At the end of it, there were a few moments of pained silence, broken by Lasker, who said, "Now, gentlemen—having heard that speech in our support, you will understand why the need of the Republican Party is truly desperate." He was given the funds for which he asked.

In the Brooklyn speech, Roosevelt said:

There is something very ominous in this combination that has been forming within the Republican Party between the extreme reactionary and the extreme radical elements of this country.

There is no common ground upon which they can unite—we know that—unless it be their common will to power, and their impatience with the normal democratic processes to produce overnight the inconsistent dictatorial ends that they, each of them, seek.

No elements in American life have made such vicious attacks upon each other in recent years as have the members of this new unholy alliance against each other.

I do not think that some of the men, even some of the leaders, who have been drawn into this unholy alliance realize what a threat that sort of an alliance may bring to the future of democracy in this country.

I am certain that the rank and file of patriotic Republicans do not realize the nature of this threat.

They should remember, and we must remember, what the collaborative understanding between Communism and Naziism has done to the processes of democracy abroad.

Something evil is happening in this country when a full page advertisement against this Administration, paid for by Republican supporters, appears—where, of all places?—in the *Daily Worker*, the newspaper of the Communist Party.

Something evil is happening in this country when vast quantities of Republican campaign literature are distributed by organizations that make no secret of their admiration for the dictatorship form of government.

Those forces hate democracy and Christianity as two phases of the same civilization. They oppose democracy because it is Christian. They oppose Christianity because it preaches democracy.

Their objective is to prevent democracy from becoming strong and purposeful. We are strong and purposeful now and intend to remain so.

These were strong words and one may perhaps call them unfair ones considering that their hapless victim was a man of the character of Wendell Willkie. But they were at the time unanswerable, and this was the kind of fighting talk that the people wanted to hear from the President rather than arrays of statistics summoned for purposes of defense.

One relatively minor item which greatly enlivened the preparation of the Brooklyn speech was a clipping from Arthur Krock's column in the *New York Times*. Krock, writing in the tone of a benevolent uncle, was warning the Republican party that some of its orators were indulging in excesses which did more harm than good to the cause. He recommended that such well-intentioned zealots should be discreetly curbed. He cited, for example, this statement made by a Philadelphia judge in the course of a campaign speech:

The President's only supporters are paupers, those who earn less than $1,200 a year and aren't worth *that,* and the Roosevelt family.

When this incredibly ill-advised remark was read aloud on the train to Brooklyn, the chortling was unbridled, for it was hastily estimated that this definition of "pauper" applied to approximately half of the total population of the United States. What made the blunder even more welcome was the fact that, had Krock not printed it in a friendly admonition to the Republicans, no one in the Roosevelt entourage would ever have heard of it. The President used this quotation as the keynote of his peroration. He said:

"Paupers" who are not worth their salt—there speaks the true sentiment of the Republican leadership in this year of grace.

Can the Republican leaders deny that all this all-too-prevailing Republican sentiment is a direct, vicious, unpatriotic appeal to class hatred and class contempt?

That, my friends, is just what I am fighting against with all my heart and soul.

I am only fighting for a free America—for a country in which *all* men and women have equal rights to liberty and justice.

I am fighting against the revival of Government by special privilege —Government by lobbyists—Government vested in the hands of those who favor and who would have us imitate the foreign dictatorships. . . .

And I will not stop fighting.

After the Brooklyn speech we left for Cleveland where on the following night Roosevelt was to wind up his campaign. Hopkins, Rosenman
and I had adjoining compartments in the car next to the President's and
these formed the main workshop. There were four secretaries on duty—
Grace Tully, Dorothy Brady, Roberta Barrows and Ruthjane Rumelt.
In other cars forward were other members of the White House staff,
the press and radio representatives, the communications car and, of
course, masses of Secret Service men. There was a dining car in the
middle of the train which was a sort of press club and it was a fine place
to go to get ideas for the speech then in progress. The White House
correspondents provided extremely pleasant and stimulating company
and some of those who worked for the most stanchly Republican papers
were most helpful in suggesting what points Roosevelt should make.
Many of these correspondents were tired of Roosevelt and annoyed by
him, but, when it came to a choice between him and Willkie or (especially) Dewey, they were for him.

The Cleveland speech was considered to be of decisive importance, it
being the last Saturday night of the campaign and the occasion for a
résumé of all the points at issue, but there had been no time for any real
preparation until we boarded the sleeping cars after the Brooklyn speech.
Fortunately, the President's train always traveled slowly. There were
three reasons for this: (1) security, to reduce chances of serious accident; (2) to give people along the right of way a good chance to watch
the train go by; and (3) Roosevelt's repugnance for speed in any vehicle
in which he was traveling (he liked to look at every detail of the scenery; when passing through a small town, he could often tell you what
were its principal local problems and how it voted in the last election).

Hopkins, Rosenman and I went through all the speech material that
had been brought from the White House: passages dictated by the
President at random moments, drafts written and submitted by various
people in the government, innumerable suggestions in letters and telegrams from Roosevelt's supporters all over the country. (It might be
added that in this week of intensive campaigning not one of us read or
listened to any of Willkie's speeches. We merely looked at the headlines
and talked to the newspapermen to learn if he was making any new,
important points.) The best suggestions in the assembled material came
from Dorothy Thompson, who was still with the *New York Herald
Tribune*, and Dean Acheson, who had walked out of the New Deal in its
first year but was now giving strong support to the President.

Hopkins was too ill to continue work and went to bed about 2 A.M.,
but Rosenman and I worked the rest of Friday night, having a series of
sandwiches brought in from the dining car, then slept for about an hour
in beds littered with toast crusts and gobs of cottage cheese. On Saturday, the President gave short speeches at Batavia, Buffalo, Rochester,
Dunkirk, New York, and Erie, Pennsylvania. He inspected airplane

plants. When we gathered for lunch in his car, he looked gray and worn and sagging. I was shocked at his appearance and thought, "This is too much punishment to expect any man to take." I almost hoped he would lose the election for it seemed that flesh and blood could not survive another six months—let alone four years—in this terrible job. During lunch he started reminiscing about his old sailing days along the New Brunswick and New England coasts and told long, rather dull stories about Maine lobstermen that everybody else present had heard many times before, and I saw for the first time his powers of recuperation in action. The grayness of his face gave way to healthy color, the circles vanished from under his eyes, the sagging jowls seemed to tighten up into muscles about his jawbone. By the end of a brief, light lunch he was in wonderful shape and was demanding, "Now! What have you three cutthroats been doing to my speech?" He worked with us for the next six hours, pausing every so often when warned that the train was about to slow down; then he would put on his leg braces and walk out to the back platform on the arm of General Watson to greet the crowd that had gathered at some small station to see him. It was always the factory workers and their womenfolk who were most emotional in their enthusiasm. They surged out on the tracks and ran after the train shouting "God bless you!" The faith these people had in this man was wonderful to behold, and I felt ashamed of myself for having misinterpreted the hysteria of the past days in Washington as representing the voice of America.

The crowd in Cleveland was the most vociferous of the campaign, and with reason, for this was far and away the best speech. Indeed, Sam Rosenman, who worked with Roosevelt on speeches over a course of seventeen years, believes this was the second-best campaign speech he ever made—first place being held by the speech at the Teamsters' Union dinner in September, 1944. Because there has been so much talk about the ghost writing of Roosevelt's speeches (and there will be more on that subject throughout these pages) it may be wondered why the speeches were not more uniform in quality. The answer to that is that the speeches as finally delivered were always the expression of Roosevelt himself: if he were in a confident, exuberant, affirmative state of mind, the speech was good and sometimes great; if he were tired, and defensive, and petulant, all the ghost writers on earth couldn't equip him with impressive words.

In the Cleveland speech, he made his first and last reference to the third term issue. It was a glancing reference and produced a surprising reaction from the crowd. Roosevelt said that, when the next four years are over, "there will be another President"—at which point the crowd started to shout "No! No!" Thinking remarkably quickly, Roosevelt thrust his mouth close to the microphone and went right on talking so that the shouts which suggested that he might be elected permanently should not be heard over the radio.

After Cleveland, there was not much more to do except to close up the President's final speech to be delivered from Hyde Park at 11:00 P.M. on election eve. That final speech was pretty much the same in three campaigns for re-election—in 1936, 1940 and 1944. It was short and nonpartisan, a moving reaffirmation of faith in the democratic process, expressing assurance that regardless of the outcome of tomorrow's balloting, "the United States will still be united." These speeches were pure Roosevelt. No mere politician, and certainly no mere ghost writer, could put into them the same degree of conviction and the same deep spiritual quality that he conveyed. It was natural for Roosevelt's enemies to assume that his professions of religious faith must be hypocritical; but those who knew him best—including some irretrievable agnostics—knew that one could joke with him on almost any and every subject, but not this one (another one was his family). He could be called extremely irreverent in regard to many temporal sacred cows, but not in regard to his own religion or that of any other formally religious man. I really believe, extreme as it may seem to say it, that he regarded these nonpartisan speeches at the end of a rowdy campaign as a form of expiation for any excesses of which he might previously have been guilty. He regarded them literally as "last words" by which he would prefer to be remembered in the event of his defeat.

For this 1940 speech, even before the intensive campaign started, he had said that he wanted to close with a prayer for the nation which he remembered had been in an Episcopalian Book of Common Prayer in use when he was at Groton School. The Library of Congress was put to work to locate this and had dug up all sorts of old prayer books with various prayers for the nation. Each had been submitted to the President and he had examined it and said, "No—that's not the one I want." He would recite parts of the prayer from a memory that went back more than forty years.

When we returned to the White House, from Cleveland, we found that several more prayer books had been sent over from the energetic Library and one of them—published, as I recall, in the 1880's—proved to be the one he wanted. It was a beautiful prayer, containing these words:

> Bless our land with honourable industry, sound learning, and pure manners. Save us from violence, discord, and confusion; from pride and arrogancy, and from every evil way. Defend our liberties, and fashion into one united people the multitudes brought hither out of many kindreds and tongues.

Hopkins made one negative contribution to this speech which revealed an old sore. The President had included a quotation from the Cleveland speech that "freedom of speech is of no use to the man who has nothing to say and freedom of religion is of no use to the man who has lost his God" and added "a free election is of no use to the man who is too indifferent *or too lazy* to vote." Hopkins urged that the italicized words be stricken out. He said, "I don't think you ought to insult the people in this speech." After some argument, Roosevelt agreed. Later I said to Rosenman that I couldn't understand why Hopkins had made such an issue of this, since there undoubtedly were far too many people who were too lazy to vote. Rosenman said, "I guess that word gets under Harry's skin. It reminds him of the accusations that most of the people who went on W.P.A. did so only because they were too lazy to work." I am sure this was correct; Hopkins was one who never forgot nor forgave such slurs.

On Sunday evening, the President and Hopkins were to go by train to Hyde Park and Rosenman and I were flying back to New York. Before we left, we offered somewhat self-conscious best wishes. "It has been grand fun, hasn't it!" said Roosevelt, with more warmth than accuracy. "And, don't forget—the Missus is expecting you and Dorothy and Madeline for supper Tuesday evening." As if anyone could forget an invitation to Hyde Park to listen to the returns on election night! (Dorothy was Mrs. Rosenman and Madeline my own wife, whom the President had met once but who was, of course, known to him immediately by her first name.)

The final Gallup poll showed Willkie so close to Roosevelt that, if the "trend" continued, the challenger might well have overtaken "The Champ" by dawn on election day. The Roper poll showed Roosevelt—55.2 per cent, Willkie—44.8 per cent, which was ½ of 1 per cent away from the final result.

I suppose that, on the day before every Presidential election in American history, each rival camp has been nerve racked with rumors that, at the fifty-ninth minute of the eleventh hour, the opposition would come out with some unspeakable charges of corruption or personal scandal which could not possibly be answered and exposed until too late. I do not know whether this has ever actually happened, but it will probably always be expected, making for that much extra tension. I know I sat constantly at the radio that election eve. I heard a transcribed Republican broadcast that was bloodcurdling. It was addressed to that overworked audience, the Mothers of America, and delivered in the ominous, insidious tones of a murder mystery program: "When your boy is dying on some battlefield in Europe—or maybe in *Martinique*—and he's crying out, 'Mother! Mother!'—don't blame Franklin D. Roosevelt because he sent your boy to war—blame YOURSELF, because YOU sent Franklin D. Roosevelt back to the White House!" There was nothing new in that, however; that sort of threat had been uttered many times. (Martinique was mentioned because it was then the strongest Vichy outpost in the Western Hemisphere and there were rumors, not entirely baseless, that American troops might be sent to seize it.)

The Democrats had possession of the election eve airwaves from 10:00 P.M. to midnight and devoted these two hours to short speeches by Roosevelt, Hull, Carl Sandburg, Alexander Woollcott and Dorothy Thompson mixed in with a great deal of entertainment from Broadway and Hollywood. The Republicans had the radio from midnight to 2:00 A.M. There were no shocking last-minute surprises, and the next day 49,815,312 people went to the polls and voted—most of them, in all probability, having made up their minds before a single word of oratory had been uttered by either candidate. To one who had never before known anything from personal observation of the inner workings of politics it was overwhelming to think of this vast mass moving into the privacy of the balloting booth; they had been given every opportunity to listen to all the charges and countercharges, all the *ad hominem* thrusts and ripostes, all the promises and all the threats, all the formulae for a better future and the warnings that this was the "last stand for democracy"; and now they could rest their eardrums and go on their own to render the verdict on which there could be no appeal short of armed rebellion.

On election night, after a stand-up supper at Mrs. Roosevelt's cottage, we drove through the Hyde Park woods, beloved by Franklin Roosevelt, to the big house to listen to the election returns. In a little room to the left off the front hall sat the President's mother with several old lady friends. They were sewing or knitting and chatting. A radio was on, softly, but they seemed to be paying little attention to it. In the big living room there was another radio going and a large gathering of weirdly assorted guests. The President was in the dining room in his shirtsleeves, with his sons and his Uncle Fred Delano and members of his staff. Large charts were littered on the dining table and news tickers were clattering in the pantry. The Roosevelt boys were excited, but not their father. Mrs. Eleanor Roosevelt moved about from one room to another, seeing to the wants of the guests, apparently never pausing to listen to the returns. If you asked her how she thought things were going she would reply, impersonally, "I heard someone say that Willkie was doing quite well in Michigan," in exactly the tone of one saying, "The gardener tells me the marigolds are apt to be a bit late this year."

My wife and George Backer and I joined Hopkins in his bedroom. He had a small, $15 radio, similar to the one he later gave Churchill. He had a chart and had been noting down a few returns, but most of it was covered with doodles. The first returns early in the evening indicated that Willkie was showing unexpected strength and Hopkins for a time seemed really worried; I have been told that early in the evening even Roosevelt himself was doubtful of the outcome, but I saw no signs of that. After ten o'clock, the sweep of Roosevelt's victory was so complete that there was no point in trying to keep the exact score. Later, the President and all the guests went out on the front porch to greet a parade of Hyde Park townspeople, one of whom carried a hastily improvised placard bearing the legend, "SAFE ON 3RD." Roosevelt was particularly elated because he had carried his own home district, normally solidly Republican, by a vote of 376 to 302. That was the best he ever did on election day in Hyde Park.

Of all the political battles in which he had been involved, this campaign of 1940 is, I believe, the one that Roosevelt liked least to remember. It was no clean-cut issue between two philosophies or ideologies, nor even between two contrasted personalities. It had the atmosphere of a dreadful masquerade, in which the principal contestants felt compelled to wear false faces, and thereby disguised the fact that, in their hearts, they agreed with one another on all the basic issues. I have said that Willkie presented an indistinct target. This was not because he was evasive, an artful dodger; he was in fact the exact reverse—a toe-to-toe slugger; but, as a candidate, he presented two images which seemed to move farther and farther apart. One image was Willkie as a symbol of reactionary opposition to the New Deal—the Wall Street lawyer, the public utilities holding companies tycoon—whereas, the other image was Willkie himself. He was then a relatively unknown quantity—to Roosevelt, at any rate—but he was beginning to establish the identity which later became so clear: a fighting liberal—even something of a freethinker of the old-fashioned, Robert G. Ingersoll school—possessed of a fierce, bull-in-a-china-shop hostility toward the icons of Toryism which caused him to become more cordially hated by the extreme reactionaries even than Roosevelt himself.

Although Roosevelt had obvious advantages in this campaign, the chief of them being his long experience in public life as compared with Willkie's total lack of experience in elective or even appointive office, Willkie had one substantial advantage of his own—freedom from responsibility. The challenger could later dismiss his statements as "campaign oratory"; the President of the United States, in the midst of an unprecedented world crisis, knew that he could not. Willkie could say that, if Roosevelt were elected, we might well be in a war by April; Roosevelt could not truthfully say that we would not, no matter who was elected. Day by day, Roosevelt had to read the intelligence from Tokyo, Madrid, Athens, Moscow, Chungking and everywhere else— he had to confront the somber facts of Britain's position which, in a matter of months or even weeks, would become utterly hopeless without some new form of aid as drastic as Lend Lease—and he could not step up on the rostrum at Madison Square Garden and recite these facts to the people. Perhaps he might have done a better and more candid job of presenting his case. For my own part, I think it was a mistake for him to go so far in yielding to the hysterical demands for sweeping reassurance; but, unfortunately for my own conscience, I happened at the time to be one of those who urged him to go the limit on this, feeling as I did that any risk of future embarrassment was negligible as compared with the risk of losing the election. I burn inwardly whenever I think of those words "again—and again—and again."

Roosevelt probably meant it when, in the Philadelphia speech, he said, "I am an old campaigner and I love a good fight." But he certainly was not enjoying himself when, a few days later, he was impelled to make those lame, equivocal speeches in Boston and New York. By then, this was a fight that he despised. It left a smear on his record which only the accomplishments of the next five years could remove.

CHAPTER IX

The White House

ONCE during the early New Deal years, Hopkins said: "If you want to get ahead in Washington, don't waste your time trying to cultivate the favor of the men with high-sounding titles. Make friends with their office boys. They're the real Big Shots. If you want to get something done in some Department, concentrate on the office boy. If he likes you, he will put you through straight to the one man who can do what you want. If he doesn't like you, he will shunt you off onto somebody who will give you a note to somebody else and so on down the line until you're so worn out and confused you've forgotten what it was you were asking for in the first place."

During the war years, when Hopkins lived in the White House, he said impatiently to a persistent petitioner: "Why do you keep pestering *me* about this? I'm only the office boy around here!"

I am sure that he was unconscious of any connection between these widely separated statements; but it was certainly there. One might say that Hopkins became, by his own earlier definition, the supreme office boy of them all. He was of course a channel of communication between the President and various agencies of the Administration, notably the War Department, and the ready means of informal contact with foreign dignitaries. (A British official once said to me, "We came to think of Hopkins as Roosevelt's own, personal Foreign Office.") He also acted in the capacity of a buffer state. He kept problem-laden officials away from Roosevelt; one of his most frequent statements was, "The President isn't going to be bothered with anything as nonsensical and unimportant as that if I can help it!" It was this function that made many of Roosevelt's most loyal friends agree with his worst enemies that Hopkins was an unmitigated menace. For instance: when, for a period of some ten months, Harold Ickes did not have one private appointment with the President, he blamed it all on the vindictiveness of Hopkins.

Whether this was just or unjust, it was certainly a comfort to Roosevelt to have someone around to take the blame. It cannot be said that Hopkins suffered unduly in the performance of this unsympathetic role. His loyalty to Roosevelt in the war years was the supreme justification of his continued existence and he enjoyed every opportunity to exercise it. As Marquis Childs wrote:

Should the President on a dull day suggest casually to his friend and confidant, Harry L. Hopkins, that the national welfare would be served if Mr. Hopkins were to jump off the Washington Monument, the appointed hour would find Mr. Hopkins poised for the plunge. Whether with or without parachute would depend on what the President seemed to have in mind.

Mr. Hopkins would know about that, for he has made a career of understanding, sensing, divining, often guessing—and usually guessing right—what is in Franklin Roosevelt's mind. It is a career that has taken him from the dull routine of social-service work to the upper reaches of diplomacy, where he has had a thrilling preview of the shape of things to come. And, what is more, history may show that he was one of the shapers.

Hopkins did not have to do so much sensing, divining or guessing while he lived in the White House. He could traipse down the upstairs hall in his old dressing gown to the President's room and ask what his chief wanted done or not done about any given problem, and then act accordingly, without having to reveal to anyone that he was guided not by his own prejudices or hunches but by Roosevelt's express instructions.

The quarters occupied by Hopkins for so long in the White House was a suite on the second floor, in the southeast corner. It consisted of one large bedroom, with a huge four-poster double bed, a small bedroom (used at first as office for Hopkins' secretary) and a bath. The whole suite had originally been one room, with three high windows looking across the long lawn toward the Washington Monument, the Jefferson Memorial and the Virginia hills. This had been Abraham Lincoln's study, and there was a plaque over the fireplace stating that the Emancipation Proclamation was signed here. It was considered the best guest room and had been assigned to King George VI during his visit in 1939.

There was a similar arrangement of rooms in each corner of the second floor. In the southwest corner, the large room was Mrs. Roosevelt's sitting room and the small one was her bedroom. The northwest suite was for guests and contained the massive furniture used in Lincoln's bedroom. The northeast suite was also for guests. It had been used by Queen Elizabeth and especially decorated for that occasion with beautiful prints of the court of Queen Victoria. This was Winston Churchill's bedroom during his visits in the war years. It was conveniently located for Churchill, being right across the hall from Hopkins.

The second floor was bisected from east to west by a long, dark, dismal hall. The eastern end was, for some reason, higher than the rest and approached by a short flight of steps, on which a rubber-matted ramp had been constructed for the President's wheelchair. This hall was furnished in a haphazard manner. There were low bookcases, containing some hundreds of modern books presented during the Roosevelt Administration by the American Booksellers Association; otherwise, the White House possessed no library of its own. On top of the bookcases were silver-framed, autographed photographs of crowned heads, most of them throneless. The hall could be equipped with a projection booth and screen for the showing of motion pictures during the evening. Later, a regular projection room was built along the colonnade leading to the new East Wing outside the House itself. The west end of the hall, partially shut off by a screen and some potted palms, was used by Mrs. Roosevelt for small tea parties and sometimes the President had dinner here with his family or members of his staff.

On the south side of the second floor, next to Hopkins' room, was a stuffy sitting room, called the Monroe Room because here the great Doctrine was written. Next to that was the President's Oval Study and off that his bedroom and bath. Across from the study, on the north side, were two smaller bedrooms, each with bath, which were usually allotted to Sam Rosenman and me when we were there. On the wall of the room that I sometimes occupied was an original of a colored cartoon. It was signed by "McKay" and came, I think, from *Esquire* magazine. It showed the exterior of a suburban house. The mother was on the porch in the background. A little girl on the garden path was calling mother's attention to a nasty little boy who, with fiendish malice, was chalking an inscription on the sidewalk.

The caption was, "Look, Mother—Wilfred wrote a bad word!"— and the word was ROOSEVELT.

Before I ever went upstairs in the White House I had imagined it was permanently furnished like the ground floor and that living in it would be something like living in a museum. Such was certainly not the case. It seems that each new family that moves in can shift things around at will, convert bedrooms into offices or vice versa, and change not only the appearance but the very atmosphere of the place to suit its own tastes. President Roosevelt's Oval Study—which was the focal point of the nation and, in a sense, of the whole world—had, I believe, been used hardly at all except as a formal reception room during the preceding Hoover Administration. On the walls were a great many of Roosevelt's old naval prints and portraits of his mother, his wife and John Paul Jones; there was also a dreadful-looking mechanical pipe-organ device which someone had presented to him but which he never learned how to operate.

The progressivism of Franklin and Eleanor Roosevelt certainly did not extend to interior decoration. They did not hold with the modern American theory that furniture, curtains, etc., should be ornamental first and utilitarian second, nor that a certain uniformity of décor should be observed, with due regard for period and style as well as color scheme. To them, a chair was something to sit down on—and all that one asked of it was comfort; a table was something to put things on and a wall was something to be covered with the greatest possible number of pictures of sentimental value. Thus, the rooms occupied by the President and Mrs. Roosevelt in the White House came to be as nearly as possible duplications of the rooms at Hyde Park, which seemed to have changed hardly at all in fifty years except as more enlarged snapshots of new children and ponies and sailboats were tacked up here and there. The other upstairs bedrooms in the White House contained some furnishings that might have come out of an old and ultrarespectable summer resort hotel and some that appeared to have emerged from a W.P.A. Arts and Crafts Project. Although the appearance of these rooms must have given shudders of revulsion to any professional interior decorators who may have happened in—whether they were addicted to the Petit Trianon, Adam, early American, Rococo or Modern Functional schools—there was a general sense of unstudied comfort and also of literal democracy. Most of the rooms were dingy with the darkness of southern mansions from which the sunlight is excluded by surrounding colonnades and big trees, but what the White House lacked in light it more than made up in warmth of hospitality. There was a remarkable air of small-town friendliness about the place which extended through all the varied members of the large staff, including the necessarily grim and suspicious Secret Service men and uniformed armed guards. You were made to feel really welcome.

On the third and top floor there were more guest rooms, used largely for the overflow of grandchildren at Christmas time and other family reunions, and there was a small bedroom and sitting room occupied by Missy LeHand which provided a pleasant retreat for those of us who were working in the White House. Missy was a lovely person and an extraordinarily level-headed one; the crippling illness which came upon her suddenly in 1941 and her subsequent death were severe blows for the President. In 1920, she had been in the stenographic pool of the Fleet Emergency Corporation and was called from that to work for Charles H. McCarthy, a friend of Franklin Roosevelt's and his manager in the unsuccessful Vice Presidential campaign of that year. After the election of Warren G. Harding, and the retreat to normalcy and isolationism, Missy was invited by Mrs. Roosevelt to come to Hyde Park to help clean up a huge accumulation of correspondence. Subsequently, Roosevelt became Vice President of the Fidelity and Deposit Company of Maryland; Missy LeHand went with him as his secretary and continued in that capacity through his battle with infantile paralysis, his return to the practice of law and his service as Governor of New York. In 1933, she went with him to the White House, Grace Tully going along as her assistant and eventual successor. Grace also had worked at first for Mrs. Roosevelt, starting during the campaign of 1928. When the Roosevelts moved into the Executive Mansion in Albany, she went with them and remained with them. She was at the President's side in Warm Springs when he died and later became Executive Secretary of the Franklin D. Roosevelt Memorial Foundation.

The friendly atmosphere that prevailed in the White House was the creation of the people who were in it. When I looked at the faces of some of the past Presidents who glared down from the walls, I could imagine that there had been times when the atmosphere was painfully austere. (There were doubtless other times when it was deplorably rowdy.) In the years of Franklin Roosevelt the whole place was obviously filled with the fierce loyalty and warm affection that he inspired. If you could prove possession of these sentiments in abundance, you were accepted as a member of the family and treated accordingly.

Roosevelt started his day with breakfast in bed—generally wearing an old blue sweater over his pajama top or a blue cape with a red F.D.R. monogram on it. He wore the cape because a bathrobe was too difficult for him to put on; for the same reason, he wore a cape out of doors in cold weather instead of an overcoat. The usher on duty—Mr. Krim, Mr. Searles or Mr. Claunch—brought him the morning's dispatches and the social schedule which, in peacetime, is formidable enough to ruin the stoutest digestion and to disrupt the most even temper but which was gratefully abandoned in wartime. During breakfast he looked through the dispatches and read the newspapers with great speed but with remarkable care, seldom missing anything of importance to himself. In addition to the Washington papers, he read the *Chicago Tribune*, the *New York Times* and *Herald Tribune* and the *Baltimore Sun*. For years friends tried to talk him out of reading the *Chicago Tribune* but he evidently wanted to know the worst about himself. As he was finishing breakfast, his personal staff came in—usually General Edwin M. Watson, Stephen T. Early, Marvin H. McIntyre, William D. Hassett, Rosenman and Hopkins to discuss the work program for the day—appointments, press conferences, etc. The President's physician, Admiral Ross T. McIntire, would also be present to watch him closely for any indications of ill health. These morning sessions covered a great deal of ground in a very short time, for all the aides participating knew Roosevelt so well, and he trusted them so fully, that beatings about the bush were unnecessary. They could gauge his state of mind and its probable results during the day. As they left the bedroom, they could be heard muttering, "God help anybody who asks him for any favors today," or, "He feels so good he'll be telling Cotton Ed Smith that it's perfectly all right for the South to go ahead and secede."

General Watson, always known as "Pa," was a big, florid, jovial Virginian who was described by everybody as "lovable" and by a few as somewhat simple minded. The latter appraisal, sometimes carefully encouraged by Pa himself, was highly inaccurate. His soldierly bluffness and his personal sweetness masked a devastating astuteness in penetrating the disguises of others; few if any were the phonies who succeeded in fooling him. He had been the President's Military Aide from the beginnings of the Administration and, in the ordinary course of events, would have been transferred long since to other duty in the Army; but he had become indispensable to Roosevelt as a tower of strength in every sense of the term. He had the highly responsible position of Presidential Secretary in charge of appointments. It was a difficult and delicate job and the measure of his success in it was the respect in which he was held by innumerable importunate people who hammered at him continually for a share of the President's time.

Steve Early was the ranking veteran in point of service—he had been a close friend of Roosevelt's since the Democratic Convention of 1912—and he was the only one of the original staff still alive when Roosevelt died. When he finally retired in June, 1945, he was awarded the Distinguished Service Medal by President Truman and the White House correspondents were unanimous for once in agreeing that he had earned it. Early was, like Watson, a Virginian and passionately loyal to his Chief, but otherwise there was no resemblance between the two men; Early was quick tempered and, being intolerant of the arts of diplomacy, felt no great urge to hide his emotions. (That may be the main reason for his survival.) A fine newspaperman himself, he was superlatively skillful in handling the President's frequently strained relations with the press. In this, his unassailable candor was his greatest asset. He was rigorously uninquisitive about White House secrets; he wanted to be told no military plans, he wanted to avoid reading speeches in advance lest they contain some important announcement on policy, so that he could truthfully tell the Correspondents who were always on his doorstep, "You know as much about that as I do." He had sense enough to know that anyone working for Franklin D. Roosevelt did not need to indulge in the press agent's practice of fabricating news, or minting slogans, but when he did have a story to release (and few were the days in the twelve years when he didn't) he knew how to "play" it for the last ounce of front-page headline value. He suffered acutely from his Chief's tendency to snap back at the hostile press but there was nothing he could do about that. Early's assistant, Bill Hassett, was a man of great gentleness; he was scholarly and devoted and a good, quiet companion for Roosevelt when he wanted to get away from the hurly-burly of Washington.

Marvin McIntyre was another Washington newspaperman. An old friend of Josephus Daniels, he had served during the First World War as Chief of the Press Offices of the Navy Department and it was then that he came into contact with Franklin Roosevelt. In 1932, he traveled about the country with Roosevelt as Press Officer and then became Secretary in charge of appointments in the White House. During the second term, illness made it impossible for him to continue in this exacting job, and it was taken over by Pa Watson, but McIntyre continued to work for the President until his death in 1943. He was particularly valuable as a contact man between the White House and Capitol Hill, two points on the same avenue in the same city which sometimes seemed to be located on different planets.

Ross McIntire was well known in his capacity as White House physician but received insufficient recognition for his achievements as Chief of the Navy's Bureau of Medicine and Surgery throughout the Second World War. Because of the enormous demands of this job in the war years, McIntire left a large part of the daily clinical routine in the White House to his assistant, the highly competent Lieutenant Commander George Fox, who had earned his way upward from the ranks in the Navy.

Aside from the Secretaries, there were a number of Administrative Assistants to the President, an anonymous and shifting group which included from time to time James Forrestal, James Rowe, David K. Niles, Lauchlin Currie and Jonathan Daniels. Their function was "to get information and to condense and summarize it for his [the President's] use." They had "no authority over anyone in any department or agency" and were expressly prohibited from "interposing themselves" between the President and any other officer of the government. The best description of the activities of these Assistants—known for their "passion for anonymity"—has been written by one of them, Daniels, in his *Frontier On The Potomac.*

The most important permanent White House official was the Executive Clerk, Rudolph Forster, who, with his Assistant and successor, Maurice Latta, was responsible for "the orderly handling of documents and correspondence" and the supervision of the large clerical staff. Both Forster and Latta had been in the White House since the McKinley Administration. For them, individual Presidents came and went, but the office went on forever, and so did the dozens and hundreds of state papers—laws, orders, commissions, etc.—which had to be properly signed and recorded and distributed every working day. It was a proud moment in Franklin Roosevelt's life when, in October 1944, as he was about to leave on a campaign trip, Forster came to him and, with the air of one who was willfully breaking all of the Ten Commandments but prepared to take the consequences, warmly shook his hand and wished him good luck. Forster stood outside the Executive Offices and waved as the President's car pulled away and Roosevelt said, with real emotion in his voice, "That's practically the first time in all these years that Rudolph has ever stepped out of character and spoken to me as if I were a human being instead of just another President."

All of the aides on the White House staff were, in effect, officials of the President's "household" and not officers in any chain of administrative command. Thus, the President before 1939 had no real executive organization of his own. There was no one between him and the Cabinet officers through whom he could exercise authority. One might presume that the Vice President would perform the function of Deputy President or Chief of Staff; the Constitution, however, provides that the Vice President shall serve as President of the Senate and that the powers and duties of the Presidency shall devolve on him only in the event of the President's "Death, Resignation, or Inability to discharge" said powers and duties. Thus, the innumerable lines of authority which converged in the White House ran not to the President's staff but to the President's solitary person, and he had no constitutional means of "interposing" anyone between himself and the ten Cabinet members and the dozens of heads of agencies and missions who reported directly to him and who were often reluctant to make an important move without his authorization in writing. When one Department came into conflict with another, the President must resolve it according to his own judgment based on the information which came to him officially only through the contestants themselves—although, of course, he might be informed unofficially through the press or through friends in contact with the omnipresent Washington "grapevine." It was a system which could not have existed in any well-ordered big business organization. When Department "A" asked for an appropriation of three hundred million dollars, and Department "B" protested that this request was so out of proportion that it would tend to influence the Congress to make cuts in "B's" request for six hundred millions, the President could fairly appraise the merits of the case only by going through all the books of both Departments and figuring their legitimate needs down to the last penny. Of course, he could assign this figuring to the Treasury Department, but that itself might have been either Department "A" or "B" in the argument; if it were neither, and made its decision in favor of "A," then "B" could and often would bring the matter right back to the President for review.

In 1938 Roosevelt proposed a sweeping reorganization of the government, the purpose of which was "to make the business end, i.e., the Executive Branch, of the Federal Government, more businesslike and more efficient" and also to "eliminate overlapping and duplication of effort" of the kind which produced the endless and often virulent juris- dictional disputes between Cabinet officers as well as lesser officials. This request for reorganization, however, came most unfortunately at a time when Roosevelt's prestige was low, following the Supreme Court fight and during the attempted purge. The cries of "would-be Dictator" were raised and it did Roosevelt no good to protest, "I have too much his- torical background and too much knowledge of existing dictatorships to make me desire any form of dictatorship for a democracy like the United States of America." He was defeated in the Congress, but a year later he managed to have a part of the Reorganization Bill enacted into law.

On September 8, 1939, the day when Roosevelt issued his "Limited National Emergency" Proclamation after the outbreak of war in Europe, he also issued an Executive Order which received scant attention in the press and the vital importance of which has never been even remotely apparent to the American people. It provided for reorganization of the Executive Office of the President and involved the transfer of the Bureau of the Budget to that office from the Treasury Department. I have heard this action compared to the invention of the radio as an asset to Roosevelt in his exercise of authority, and that is not so much of an exaggeration as one might think. In the Director of the Budget he acquired an oper- ational officer, with a large and potent organization, who was responsible solely to himself in carrying out his over-all policies. The duties of this Director, Harold Smith, comprised far more than the mere keeping of books: he was enjoined, among other things, "to keep the President informed of the progress of activities by agencies of the Government with respect to work proposed, work actually initiated, and work com- pleted." The Bureau of the Budget could and must send its agents into every Department of the government—into every American Mission abroad and every theater of war—to find out for the President himself exactly how the money was being spent, and by whom, and with what results. Thus, the Bureau was actually the President's personal intelli- gence service—or, as some disgruntled officers called it, "his own private Gestapo."

Harold Smith has said, "Before the Bureau was moved over, I often thought of the Presidency as a stately colonial mansion, in which lived and worked the most powerful individual in the most powerful nation on earth. Attached to that stately mansion was an old, rickety shanty or 'lean-to,' which was the Executive Office, the only work-shop available to that most powerful individual. When the Bureau was moved over, we at least added one new wing with modern equipment and an adequate staff for one part of the work. But another wing should be added, and

I believe it would have been added if Roosevelt had been given time enough to finish his job."

The stately mansion in Smith's metaphor was the expression of the Presidential power as granted by the Constitution, and the shanty the expression of the manner in which the exercise of that power had been restricted by the Congress, ever jealous of its own prerogatives. The cries of "dictatorship" raised against Roosevelt's reorganization proposals were much the same as those raised by the enemies of ratification of the Constitution, except that then the scare word used was "monarchy." The Federalists certainly fostered the principle of the strong Executive, restrained from excess but not hobbled from action by the system of checks and balances. After the Administration of Jefferson, a strong President himself, but an apostle of decentralization, the original conception waned, being revived only when such strong individuals as Jackson, Lincoln, Theodore Roosevelt and Wilson—aided by the exceptional circumstances of their times—chose to assert the power which had always been there from the beginning. Franklin Roosevelt came into office, as did Lincoln, amid such conditions of domestic crisis that power to act in a rapid and even arbitrary manner was thrust upon him while a frightened Congress representing a frightened people meekly rubber-stamped his drastic proposals for recovery. His ultimate measures of reorganization, which came fortuitously as the war emergency was mounting, did not add an iota to his constitutional powers but greatly facilitated his ability to exercise them.

Harold Smith died, from sheer exhaustion, in January, 1947, and I never did learn from him just what he had in mind for that unbuilt wing of the Executive Offices, but it involved the regularization by law of the function that had been improvised for Hopkins by Roosevelt. No great amount of love was lost between Smith and Hopkins, who was indifferent to the problems of dollars and cents for which Smith was responsible. To one like Smith, who liked to have everything tidy, Hopkins' harum-scarum methods were naturally disturbing, and Hopkins was impatient with Smith's determination to count the cost. But there was a considerable amount of respect between the two men and the disputes they may have had were never permitted to trouble the President. As Smith saw the function that Hopkins should have performed—and which should have been duly provided for by Act of Congress—it was, roughly, that of a Cabinet Officer without Portfolio—a civilian Chief of Staff without much of a staff of his own but with constant access to the President's mind and to all the official intelligence available to that mind—an adviser on policy freed of the special interests and prejudices imposed on any officer who had special responsibility for any one phase of the total government effort. Hopkins came as close to filling that post as was possible in view of the fact that he had no legal authority whatever for it. Roosevelt could delegate all sorts of authority to him, but any Cabinet member who wanted to ignore this could do so, on firm legal grounds, and most of them did. The extraordinary fact was that the second most important individual in the United States Government during the most critical period of the world's greatest war had no legitimate official position nor even any desk of his own except a card table in his bedroom. However, the bedroom was in the White House.

As I have said, Hopkins did not originate policy and then convince Roosevelt it was right. He had too much intelligence as well as respect for his Chief to attempt the role of mastermind. He made it his job to provide a sounding board for discussions of the best means of attaining the goals that the President set for himself. Roosevelt liked to think out loud, but his greatest difficulty was finding a listener who was both understanding and entirely trustworthy. That was Hopkins—and this was the process that Rosenman and I watched over and over again in the preparation of the speeches and messages in which Roosevelt made known his policies to the nation and to the world. The work that was put in on these speeches was prodigious, for Roosevelt with his acute sense of history knew that all of those words would constitute the bulk of the estate that he would leave to posterity and that his ultimate measurement would depend on the reconciliation of what he said with what he did. Therefore, utmost importance was attached to his public utterances and utmost care exercised in their preparation. In the previous chapter I have mentioned the Cleveland speech which took a night and a day to prepare, but such speed in preparation was unusual, even for a campaign speech, which was necessarily a creature of the moment. The important speeches sometimes required a week or more of hard labor, with a considerable amount of planning before the intensive work started. I don't know what was the record number of distinct drafts of a single speech but it must have been well over twelve, and in the final draft there might not be one sentence that had survived from the first draft. There were of course numerous routine speeches of a ceremonial nature which were not considered of major significance—but, in wartime, even in these Roosevelt was aware that he had a world audience and that everything he said might be material for the propaganda which flooded the air waves. If such a speech were opening a Bond Drive, a first draft would be prepared in the Treasury Department; if it were launching a new campaign for funds for the Red Cross, the Community Chest, National Brotherhood Week, etc., the organization concerned would send in suggestions as to what it wanted the President to say. This submitted material was almost always so rhetorical, so studiously literary, that it did not sound at all like Roosevelt's normal style and it had to be subjected to the process of simplification or even oversimplification that he demanded. He was happiest when he could express himself in the homeliest, even tritest phrases, such as "common or garden," "clear as crystal," "rule of thumb," "neither here nor there," "armchair strategists," or "simple as ABC."

When he wanted to give a speech for some important purpose, whether it was connected with a special occasion or not, he would discuss it first at length with Hopkins, Rosenman and me, telling us what particular points he wanted to make, what sort of audience he wished primarily to reach and what the maximum word limit was to be (he generally put it far too low). He would dictate pages and pages, approaching his main topic, sometimes hitting it squarely on the nose with terrific impact, sometimes rambling so far away from it that he couldn't get back, in which case he would say, "Well—something along those lines—you boys can fix it up." I think he greatly enjoyed these sessions, when he felt free to say anything he pleased, uttering all kinds of personal insults, with the knowledge that none of it need appear in the final version. When he stopped dictating, because another appointment was due or it was time to go to bed, we would go to the Cabinet Room in the West Wing and start reading through all the assembled material. The President kept a special "Speech Folder" into which he put newspaper clippings that he had marked, indicating either his approval of some sentiment expressed or indignation that such falsehood should get into print (he could not always remember what the marking signified). There were also all sorts of letters from all sorts of people, known and unknown, containing suggestions as to what he should say, and there were random bits of his own dictation, thoughts that had suddenly occurred to him during preceding days and weeks which might be useful sometime. All of this material was sifted, and added to the newly dictated material with the aid of scissors and paste and a few connecting clauses, until something resembling a coherent speech was put together and fair copies of it made. It was generally two or three times too long. When the President was free to see us again, we handed him this draft and he looked immediately at the last page to see its number, whereupon he announced that at least ninety-two per cent of it must be cut. He then started to read through it, pausing frequently to dictate "Insert A," "Insert G," etc. Each time he decided to dictate something he said, "Grace—take a law," a line he gladly borrowed from the Kaufman-Hart-Rodgers musical show, "I'd Rather Be Right," in which George M. Cohan played the part of Franklin D. Roosevelt. The President himself had never seen this show but he enjoyed what he heard about it.

When he had finished dictating inserts, the speech was far longer than it had been and farther from any coherent form. We then returned to the Cabinet Room and started a second draft. This process went on day and night. Sometimes, while the work was in progress, events would intervene—for instance: on a Sunday evening in July, 1943, we were at Shangri-la finishing up a speech devoted primarily to home-front problems—price stabilization, rationing, manpower, etc.—when news came of the fall of Benito Mussolini, and the speech had to be started all over again; this, however, was a pleasure for all.

Most of Roosevelt's work on speeches was done during the evening. We would gather for the standard cocktail ceremony in the Oval Study at 7:15. The President sat behind his desk, the tray before him. He mixed the ingredients with the deliberation of an alchemist but with what appeared to be a certain lack of precision since he carried on a steady conversation while doing it. His bourbon old-fashioneds were excellent, but I did not care for his Martinis, in which he used two kinds of vermouth (when he had them) and sometimes a dash of absinthe. Hopkins occasionally talked him into making Scotch whisky sours, although he didn't really like them. The usual canapés of cream cheese or fish paste on small circles of toast were served, also popcorn. Roosevelt was an extremely mild drinker—he did not have wine with meals except at large, formal dinners, and I don't recall ever having seen him drink brandy or other liqueurs or a highball; but he certainly loved the cocktail period and the stream of small talk that went with it.

Dinner was generally served in the study about 7:45. It ill becomes a guest to say so, but the White House cuisine did not enjoy a very high reputation. The food was plentiful and, when simple, good—but the chef had a tendency to run amuck on fancy salads. There was one favorite in particular which resembled the productions one finds in the flossier type of tea shoppe: it was a mountain of mayonnaise, slices of canned pineapple, carved radishes, etc. It was served frequently and each time the President merely looked at it and shook his head and murmured sadly, "No, thank you." Once when this happened, Sam Rosenman laughed and said, "Mr. President, you've been in this House for eight years, and for all I know you'll be here eight years more—but they'll never give up trying to persuade you to find out what that salad really tastes like." Roosevelt was always grateful for delicacies, particularly game, which friends sent in to enliven his diet. I never heard him complain about food or anything else in the way of service, but he did complain bitterly about the security supervision of every article of food sent to him. Once he said, "I happen to be very fond of roasted peanuts. But if somebody wanted to send me a bag of peanuts, the Secret Service would have to X-ray it and the Department of Agriculture would have to open every shell and test every kernel for poison or high explosives. So, to save trouble, they would just throw the bag away and never tell me about it." Deeply moved by this, Rosenman and I went to the corner of Pennsylvania Avenue and 15th Street and

bought a large bag of peanuts and sneaked it in to the President. He
put it under his coat and ate the whole contents.

After dinner he sat on the couch to the left of the fireplace, his feet
up on the stool specially built for him, and started reading the latest
speech draft. Grace Tully sat next to him, taking more dictation until
Dorothy Brady or Toinette Bachelder came in to relieve her. Sometimes Roosevelt read the speech out loud, to see how it sounded, for
every word was judged not by its appearance in print but by its effectiveness over the radio. About 10 o'clock, a tray with drinks was brought
in. The President sometimes had a glass of beer but more often a
horse's neck (ginger ale and lemon peel). He was by now yawning and
losing interest in the speech and he usually went to bed before eleven.
During these evening sessions, the telephone almost never rang. Now
and then a dispatch might be brought in, which Roosevelt would read
and pass on to Hopkins without a word or a change of expression, but
otherwise one would have thought this house the most peaceful, remote
retreat in a war-wracked world.

After leaving the Study, we would spend most of the night in the
Cabinet Room producing another draft which would go to the President
with his breakfast in the morning. Sometimes we would send a call for
help to Archibald MacLeish, Librarian of Congress, who would come in
late at night to help bring a diffuse speech into focus. More than once,
before the White House windows were blacked out after Pearl Harbor,
Mrs. Roosevelt saw the lights burning in the Cabinet Room at 3:00 A.M.
and telephoned down to tell us we were working too hard and should go
to bed. Of course, the fact was that she herself was sitting up working
at that hour.

We had to get up early in the morning to be ready for summons in
case the President wanted to work on the speech before his first appointment. We generally had breakfast on trays in Hopkins' room and it was
rarely a cheerful gathering. The draft that had been completed a few
hours previously looked awful in the morning light and the judgment
on it that we most often expressed was, "I only hope that the reputation
of Franklin Delano Roosevelt does not depend on this terrible speech."

After the session in the President's bedroom, Rosenman and I went
over to the Cabinet Room to await the summons. The signal bells announced the President's approach to his office and we stood by the
French windows leading out to the colonnade and watched him go by
in his armless, cushionless, uncomfortable wheelchair, pushed by his
Negro valet, Chief Petty Officer Arthur Prettyman. Accompanying him
was the detail of Secret Service men, some of them carrying the large,
overflowing wire baskets of papers on which he had been working the
night before and the dispatches that had come in that morning. When
Fala came abreast of the wheelchair as it rolled along, Roosevelt would

reach down and scratch his neck. This progress to the day's work by a crippled man was a sight to stir the most torpid imagination; for here was a clear glimpse of the Roosevelt that the people believed him to be —the chin up, the cigarette holder tilted at what was always described as "a jaunty angle" and the air of irrepressible confidence that whatever problems the day might bring, he would find a way to handle them. The fact that this confidence was not always justified made it none the less authentic and reassuring.

When I saw the President go by on these mornings, I felt that nobody who worked for him had a right to feel tired. That was not an unusual feeling: it went all through the wartime Administration in Washington, extending to all sorts of people, some of whom disagreed with him politically and most of whom never laid eyes on him. It was, I think, Henry Pringle who, when working in a government agency shortly after Pearl Harbor, suggested as a wall slogan for bureaucrats' offices: EXHAUSTION IS NOT ENOUGH!

The speeches had to be checked and counterchecked with various departments and agencies, most of all with the Army and Navy; many speeches that were sent over to the War Department came back with corrections and suggestions penciled in the handwriting of General Marshall. The work of the so-called "ghost writers" consisted largely of the painstaking, arduous verification of facts and figures. We felt, "The *New York Times* can make mistakes—the *World Almanac* can make mistakes—but the President of the United States must not make mistakes." This constant thought imposed a harrowing responsibility. After 1940, the White House had its resident statistician—Isador Lubin, the Commissioner of Labor Statistics, who was constantly available and incalculably valuable to Roosevelt and to Hopkins in checking every decimal point.

Although the speeches were usually seen in advance by the War and Navy Departments and sometimes (though not always) by the State Department, they were kept otherwise under close wraps of secrecy. There were always various eminent officials who wanted to know what the President was going to say. They were particularly anxious to make sure that he was going to include the several pages of material that they had submitted on their own particular departments. They knew they could get nowhere with Hopkins in their quest of inside information; so they concentrated on Rosenman, who would fob them off with the misstatement that, "The President is weighing that in his mind right now." We used to derive enjoyment from the thought of various important personages around Washington listening to the Presidential broadcasts and then, as the strains of "The Star Spangled Banner" broke out at the finish, cursing, "He didn't use a *word* of that stuff that I sent him." It was even more enjoyable to picture the amazed expression of some anonymous citizen in Council Bluffs who had written a letter to the President and then heard something from that letter incorporated in a Fireside Chat.

On the final two days of preparation of a speech Roosevelt would really buckle down to serious work and then what had seemed a formless, aimless mess of words would begin to assume tautness and sharpness. He studied every implication for its effect on various groups in the nation and on allies and enemies and neutrals. He paid a great deal of attention to the punctuation, not for its correctness but for its aid or hindrance to him in reading the speech aloud. Grace Tully liked to insert a great many commas, and the President loved to strike them out. He once said to her, "Grace! How many times do I have to tell you not to waste the taxpayers' commas?" He liked dashes, which were visual aids, and hated semicolons and parentheses. I don't think he ever used the sonorous phrase, "And I quote—." If he had to have quotation marks, he did not refer to them, knowing they would appear in the printed version.

In the final draft of a speech, every word was counted and Roosevelt finally decided the precise number that he would be able to crowd into thirty minutes. His sense of timing was phenomenal. His normal rate was 100 words a minute, but he would say, "There are some paragraphs in this speech that I can take quickly so I can handle a total of 3,150 words"—and that did not mean 3,162. At other times, he would feel that he had to be deliberate in his delivery and the words would have to be cut to 2,800. This cutting was the most difficult work of all because, by the time we had come to the ninth or tenth draft, we felt sure the speech had been boiled down to the ultimate monosyllable. Roosevelt's estimates were rarely off more than a split second on his broadcasts. Speeches before audiences were difficult to estimate, of course, because crowd responses are unpredictable, but he was generally accurate even on these. In the Teamsters' speech, the roars of laughter and applause were so frequent and prolonged that the speech ran some fifteen minutes overtime, but that did not upset Roosevelt at all despite the fact that, since it was a campaign speech, the Democratic National Committee had to pay the heavy excess charges.

When a speech was finally closed up, about six o'clock in the evening, the President was wheeled over to Dr. McIntire's office for the sinus treatments that were a regular part of his day. Then he went upstairs for cocktails and dinner, after which he chatted or worked on his correspondence or his stamp albums, without seeming to give much attention to the final reading copy of his speech which was typed on special limp paper, to avoid rustling noises as he turned the pages, and bound in a black leather loose-leaf folder. But when he started to broadcast he seemed to know it by heart. When he looked down at his manuscript, he was usually not looking at the words he was then speaking but at the next paragraph to determine where he would put his pauses and which of his large assortment of inflections he would employ. As one who has had considerable experience in the theater, I marveled at the unfailing precision with which he made his points, his grace in reconciling the sublime with the ridiculous, as though he had been rehearsing these lines for weeks and delivering them before audiences for months. Those who worked with him on speeches were all too well aware that he was no slave to his prepared text. He could and did ad-lib at will, and that was something which always amused him greatly. During the days of preparation, Hopkins, Rosenman and I would sometimes unite in opposition to some line, usually of a jocose nature, which the President wanted to include. It was our duty to make every effort to avoid being yes men and so we kept at him until we had persuaded him that the line should be cut out; but, if he really liked it well enough, he would keep it in mind and then ad-lib it, and later would be full of apologies to us for his "unfortunate slip of the tongue." He was almost always immensely good humored about the arguments we offered him —he liked to appear persecuted and complain that "They won't let me say anything of my own in my own speech." There were times, however, when he was worn out and angered by something else and then he would be cantankerous with us because we were the only convenient targets; we learned that on such occasions it was best to shut up and to revive our arguments later after he had had some rest and felt more amiable. Referring again to my experience in the theater, I can testify that he was normally the most untemperamental genius I have ever encountered. That is one of the reasons why he was able to sleep so well at night.

During the campaign of 1940, Carl Sandburg came to call at the White House and had a long talk with the President who said to him, "Why don't you go down to Missy LeHand's office and dictate some of the things you've just been saying to me?" Sandburg did so and said, among other things:

The Gettysburg speech of Abraham Lincoln or the farewell address of Robert E. Lee to his Army, would be, in our American street talk, "just a lot of words," unless we look behind the words, unless we see words throwing long shadows—and out of the shadows arises the mystery of man consecrated to mystic causes. . . .

If we go back across American history we find that as a nation among the other nations of the world this country has never kept silence as to what it stands for. For a hundred and fifty years and more we have told the world that the American Republic stands for a certain way of life. No matter what happened to the map of Europe, no matter what changes of government and systems went on there, no matter what old thrones and dynasties crashed to make way for something else, no matter what new philosophies and orbits of influence were proclaimed, America never kept silence.

Despite his strenuous avoidance of solemnity, and the frivolousness and irrelevance of his small talk when he was off the record, Roosevelt knew that he was the voice of America to the rest of the world. In the darkest days before and after Pearl Harbor he expressed the hopes of civilized humanity. Churchill's was the gallant voice of the unconquerable warrior, but Roosevelt's was the voice of liberation, the reassurance of the dignity of man. His buoyancy, his courage, his confidence renewed hope in those who feared that they had forever lost it. Roosevelt seemed to take his speeches lightly, but no one knew better than he that, once he had the microphone before him, he was speaking for the eternal record—his words were, as Sandburg said, "throwing long shadows."

In a foreword to an anthology of Roosevelt speeches, Harry Hopkins wrote:

> Roosevelt made many great speeches. But some were not so good. He occasionally did not try, because he was frankly bored. A President of the United States has to speak many times on subjects which do not interest him. He would prefer to read a book or go to bed.

This was particularly true of the last two years of Roosevelt's life, when he made just as few speeches as possible and rarely appeared to take a great deal of interest in those that he did make. The time of challenge when words were the only weapons had at last passed and great and terrible events were speaking for themselves. He seemed to relax to save himself for the time when events would cease and words would again become the instruments of international politics.

CHAPTER X

The Garden Hose

IMMEDIATELY after election day, the major problem confronting Roosevelt was one that had not been mentioned either by him or by Willkie during the campaigns: Great Britain was on the verge of bankruptcy in terms of dollar credits. Her balances which had amounted to four and a half billion dollars before the war were gone, including the holdings in America of British individuals which had been expropriated by His Majesty's Government and liquidated. It was obvious that Britain could not survive much longer without supplies from the United States and, under the "Cash and Carry" law, she could not obtain these supplies without dollars. In the endless discussions of this problem Roosevelt began to say, "We must find some way to lease or even lend these goods to the British," and from this came the vast concept which Churchill later described as "a new Magna Carta . . . the most unselfish and unsordid financial act of any country in all history."

In mid-November the German Air Force, defeated in the Battle of Britain, gave a shocking demonstration of its power in the intense raid on Coventry in which more than a thousand people were killed or wounded. This saturation bombing was extended to one British town after another, the propagandists in Berlin boasting that the whole island was to be systematically "Coventryized," while the Blitz on London continued with deadly monotony. Toward the end of November, the British Ambassador, Lord Lothian, returned to Washington from a trip to London and saw the President. At a press conference (on November 26) Roosevelt was asked:

> *Question.* Mr. President, did the British Ambassador present any specific requests for additional help?
> *The President.* I am sorry, I shall have to disappoint quite a number

of papers; nothing was mentioned in that regard at all, not one single thing—ships or sealing wax or anything else.

(Laughter)

It is doubtful that Lord Lothian was greatly amused at the time, for his country's stock was very low and Roosevelt did not appear to be in any hurry in coming to the rescue. There had been a notable British victory in the Mediterranean when dive bombers of the Royal Navy Air Arm inflicted heavy damage on Italian ships lying in apparent security at their Taranto base. (This action, by the way, might have provided an intimation of what could happen at Pearl Harbor.) It was well known in British Government circles that General Sir Archibald Wavell, commanding the British forces in Egypt, had been so strongly reinforced with troops and tanks and aircraft from the United Kingdom that he was ready to take the offensive against the Italians and drive into Libya. However, it was impossible to be greatly impressed by victories over Mussolini's reluctant legions, who were then being subjected to a severe and humiliating mauling by the surprising Greek Army. The German monster remained, relatively quiet on land for the moment, but always absorbing new strength while preparing for the delivery of the next devastating attack. Any and all local victories that might be gained in the Mediterranean would be inconsequential unless the United States were to provide formidable aid before the "invasion season" should be reopened on the English Channel in the spring.

It seemed to some alarmed British officials that Roosevelt, following his victory at the polls, had lost interest in the war situation—or, at any rate, was blithely wasting the time that was running so short. On December 2, the President left Washington as carefree as you please for a Caribbean cruise on *U.S.S. Tuscaloosa,* taking with him only his immediate staff—Pa Watson, Dr. McIntire and Captain Callaghan— with Harry Hopkins as the only guest, and it was noted that the party included no one qualified to advise or even consult on the grievous problems of Europe and the Far East. The White House announced that the main purpose of the cruise would be to inspect some of the new base sites recently acquired in the West Indies, but those most familiar with Roosevelt's vacation habits suspected that such inspections might be somewhat desultory and superficial and that the main business of each day would be fishing, basking in the sun and spoofing with cronies. This impression was borne out by the scraps of news sent back by the three press association representatives on the trip—Thomas F. Reynolds, Douglas B. Cornell and George E. Durno. It seemed that this cruise was about the same as all others when Roosevelt had nothing graver to worry about than the Hopkins-Ickes feud.

At Guantanamo Bay, a large stock of Cuban cigars was purchased.

At Jamaica, St. Lucia and Antigua, the President entertained British colonial officials and their ladies at lunch. Off Eleuthera Island he was visited by the Duke of Windsor, Governor General of the Bahamas; he told the Duke that what the British needed most in their West Indian colonies was something along the lines of the Civilian Conservation Corps.

There was one serious meeting when the *Tuscaloosa* lay to just outside the territorial waters of Martinique and the U.S. Naval Observer there and the Consul came aboard to give the President a firsthand report on conditions on that potentially dangerous French island. During this brief conference many on board the *Tuscaloosa* were focusing their binoculars on the aircraft carrier *Béarn*, lying in the harbor of Fort-de-France, an ominous symbol of the French "fleet in being" which was still under the flimsy control of the Vichy Government.

According to custom, evenings on board ship were devoted either to poker games or to movies, the latter including "Northwest Mounted Police," starring Gary Cooper, Paulette Goddard and Madeleine Carroll; "I Love You Again," with William Powell and Myrna Loy; "They Knew What They Wanted," with Carole Lombard and Charles Laughton; "Arizona," with Jean Arthur and William Holden; and "Tin Pan Alley," with Alice Faye and Betty Grable—the last quite naturally being the favorite with the crew.

The records of the fishing on this cruise were pretty unimpressive. The largest catch by far was a twenty-pound grouper which was hooked by Hopkins, but he did not have the strength to reel it in and turned the rod over to Dr. McIntire. A radio message was received from Ernest Hemingway saying that many big fish had been caught on a stretch of Mona Passage between the Dominican Republic and Puerto Rico; the President trawled here for an hour or more, using a feathered hook baited with a piece of pork rind as directed by Hemingway, but he failed to get a strike.

At stated points along the route Navy seaplanes landed alongside the *Tuscaloosa* and delivered the White House mail, including the quantities of State papers for the President's signature. One of these deliveries, on the morning of December 9, brought a long letter from Winston Churchill.

In upwards of 4,000 words, Churchill covered the broad picture and most minute details of the war situation from the North Sea to Gibraltar to Suez to Singapore. He dealt at great length with the critical problems of production and shipping and explained the dangers to both from the persistent attacks by bombers and U-boats. He stated Britain's present financial position in a few, blunt words. He asked for more destroyers either by a process of gift or loan. He concluded this memorable document with an expression of confidence that the American nation would support Britain's cause and meet her urgent needs, but he offered no suggestions as to how the President was to go about accomplishing all this with the Congress and the people.

This message from the Prime Minister had a profound effect on Roosevelt, and it filled Hopkins with a desire to get to know Churchill and to find out how much of him was mere grandiloquence and how much of him was hard fact.

Three days after Roosevelt read that letter, he received a radio message from Secretary Hull informing him of the sudden death of Lord Lothian. Roosevelt immediately sent a message through the State Department to King George VI in which he said that he was shocked beyond measure to hear of the death of his old friend, and that he was certain that the last message that Lord Lothian would wish to give to the world was that victory must and will come in this war.

This was no perfunctory expression of routine regret. Lord Lothian had been a notably successful Ambassador. A Liberal and a close associate of Lloyd George in the First World War, he was well qualified to talk Roosevelt's language and, in turn, to interpret Roosevelt to Churchill. He had been able to understand, as a less flexible Briton might have failed to do, the manifold domestic obstacles that beset Roosevelt's path and he most scrupulously avoided adding to the President's embarrassments by making excessive, impatient demands. His loss at this particular moment was a severe one, for he seemed almost irreplaceable.

The following day, when homeward bound, Roosevelt held a press conference with the three correspondents, and talked affably about some of the advantages and disadvantages that he had noted in the various base sites visited, but he gave them nothing in the way of news calculated to cause the slightest excitement in their home offices. It still seemed that he had spent two weeks in a state of total relaxation and utter indifference toward the prospects of world calamity.

That, however, was only as it seemed.

Hopkins said later, "I didn't know for quite awhile what he was thinking about, if anything. But then—I began to get the idea that he was refueling, the way he so often does when he seems to be resting and carefree. So I didn't ask him any questions. Then, one evening, he suddenly came out with it—the whole program. He didn't seem to have any clear idea how it could be done legally. But there wasn't a doubt in his mind that he'd find a way to do it."

That "refueling" process was a vital function for Roosevelt. Nobody that I know of has been able to give any convincing explanation of how it operated. He did not seem to talk much about the subject in hand, or to consult the advice of others, or to "read up" on it. On this occasion he had Churchill's remarkable letter to provide food for thought; but this—though it was a masterly statement of the problems involved, of

which Roosevelt was already quite well aware—presented no key to the
solution other than an expression of confidence that "ways and means
will be found."

One can only say that Roosevelt, a creative artist in politics, had put
in his time on this cruise evolving the pattern of a masterpiece, and once
he could see it clearly in his own mind's eye, he made it quickly and very
simply clear to all.

On December 16, he returned to Washington, tanned and exuberant
and jaunty. The next day, he held a press conference, starting off with
his usual statement that, "I don't think there is any particular news. . . ."
Having thus paved the way, he said, "There is absolutely no doubt in
the mind of a very overwhelming number of Americans that the best
immediate defense of the United States is the success of Britain in
defending itself." Then he jumped back to the outbreak of the First
World War and told an anecdote at the expense of bankers on the
Bar Harbor Express. "In all history," he said, "no major war has
ever been lost through lack of money." He went on to say that some
people thought we should lend money to Britain for the purchase of
American matériel, while other people thought we should deliver it as
an outright gift. Roosevelt described this kind of thinking as "banal."
(Actually, there were very few people who seriously made such ridiculous
suggestions, neither one of which would have stood a chance in Congress;
but Roosevelt brought them into his introduction to show what a
reasonable middle-of-the-roader he really was.) He said,

> Now, what I am trying to do is eliminate the dollar sign. That
> is something brand new in the thoughts of everybody in this room,
> I think—get rid of the silly, foolish, old dollar sign.
> Well, let me give you an illustration. Suppose my neighbor's home
> catches fire, and I have a length of garden hose . . .

I believe it may accurately be said that with that neighborly analogy,
Roosevelt won the fight for Lend Lease. There were to be two months
of some of the bitterest debates in American history, but through it all
the American people as a whole maintained the conviction that there
couldn't be anything very radical or very dangerous in the President's
proposal to lend our garden hose to the British who were fighting so
heroically against such fearful odds. There were probably very few who
had any expectation that we would ever get the hose back; there was
indeed a devout popular hope that this new measure would eliminate the
possibility of another twenty years of fruitless bickering and niggling
over war debts.

Following the press conference, Roosevelt determined to go on the air
with a Fireside Chat to explain the seriousness of the war situation. He
could not give much attention to the speech until after Christmas, which

was always a real, old-fashioned family festival in the White House, with aunts and uncles, children and grandchildren, stockings and packages galore, and invariably a highly dramatic reading by the President of *A Christmas Carol*. In his message to the American people he said, "Let us make this Christmas a merry one for the little children in our midst. For us of maturer years it cannot be merry." This well-meant statement was not really true in Roosevelt's own case; for him, with his superhuman resilience, any occasion under almost any circumstances could be merry; I am sure his Christmas was merry when first he was felled by disease and had not yet regained the power to move.

In the preparation of the Fireside Chat (delivered December 29) Hopkins provided the key phrase which had already been used in some newspaper editorial: "We must be the great arsenal of democracy." I have been told that the phrase was originated by William S. Knudsen and also by Jean Monnet, but whoever originated it, Roosevelt was the one who proclaimed it. There was some debate at first over its use by the President, since it might seem to preclude the eventual extension of aid to the Soviet Union or to certain Latin American "republics," but the phrase was too good to be stopped by any quibbles. Roosevelt really enjoyed working on this speech for, with the political campaign over, it was the first chance he had had in months and even years to speak his mind with comparative freedom. He had indulged himself once, six months previously, in the "stab in the back" reference, but the political consequences of that were so awkward that he had felt compelled subsequently to confine himself to the most namby-pamby euphemisms in all references to the international situation. Now, for the first time, he could mention the Nazis by name. He could lash out against the apostles of appeasement. He could say, "We cannot escape danger, or the fear of danger, by crawling into bed and pulling the covers over our heads." He could speak plainly on the subject which was always in his mind—the disastrous folly of any attempt at a negotiated peace. He said:

> A nation can have peace with the Nazis only at the price of total surrender. . . .
> Such a dictated peace would be no peace at all. It would be only another armistice, leading to the most gigantic armament race and the most devastating trade wars in history. . . .
> All of us, in all the Americas, would be living at the point of a Nazi gun—a gun loaded with explosive bullets, economic as well as military.

That was Roosevelt's profound belief. It was an essential essence in the formulation of all his wartime policies. He repeated it over and over again, but there were more than a few in the United States and in other countries who remained permanently convinced that Britain would have done better to come to terms with the Nazis, and China with the warlords of Japan.

As Roosevelt sat at the end of the long table in the Cabinet Room working on that speech and other speeches during the war years, he would look up at the portrait of Woodrow Wilson, over the mantelpiece. The tragedy of Wilson was always somewhere within the rim of his consciousness. Roosevelt could never forget Wilson's mistakes, which had been made with the noblest will in the world, impelled by the purest concept of the Christian ethic. Wilson had advocated "peace without victory," he had produced the Fourteen Points as a basis on which Germany could surrender honorably. The violation of these principles had plagued the postwar world, had led to the rise of Hitler and a Second World War, and there was no motivating force in all of Roosevelt's wartime political policy stronger than the determination to prevent repetition of the same mistakes.

The "arsenal of democracy" speech was one of the most tightly packed of all the Fireside Chats. It had to cover the map of the world. There were innumerable points for inclusion, including the danger to Ireland and the Azores, the aid to Germany rendered by the Soviet Union and Sweden, the presence of our Fleet in the Pacific, bottlenecks in production, the Monroe Doctrine and B-29s (which were not mentioned by name). When, after days and nights of hard labor, the speech was in something like its final form, it was sent over to the State Department for comment—of which plenty was forthcoming. The Department's suggested insertions and deletions were marked on the draft with a red pencil.

At one point in the speech, Roosevelt spoke of the agents of the fifth column operating throughout the United States and Latin America. Then followed the sentence, "There are also American citizens, *many of them in high places,* who, unwittingly in most cases, are aiding and abetting the work of these agents."

The words that I have italicized came back from the State Department circled in red to indicate they should be cut out. When Roosevelt read this draft and saw that mark, he asked, "Who put this red line in here?" We explained that the State Department suggested it would be well to delete these dangerous words.

"Oh, *do* they!" he said. "Very well. We'll change it to read—'There are also American citizens, many of them in high places—*especially in the State Department*—and so forth.'"

During the very last session on the speech late in the afternoon of the day it was to be delivered, Hopkins said, "Mr. President—do you feel that you could include in this speech some kind of optimistic statement that will hearten the people who are doing the fighting—the British, the Greeks and the Chinese?" Roosevelt thought that over for a long time, tilting his head back, puffing out his cheeks as was his habit. At length he dictated: "I believe that the Axis powers are not going to win this war. I base that belief on the latest and best information." Rosenman and I wondered at the time what that "latest and best information" could be. We learned later from Hopkins that it was no more than Roosevelt's own, private confidence that Lend Lease would go through and his certainty that this measure would make Axis victory impossible. Otherwise, his secret sources of information were not a great deal better than were those of the *New York Times* or the *Chicago Daily News* and were in some important respects shockingly inaccurate.

On the night when Roosevelt gave his Fireside Chat, the Germans subjected London to one of the heaviest bombings of the war; this was the raid in which so large a part of the city was destroyed by fire, St. Paul's Cathedral escaping miraculously. The Germans used this psychological warfare tactic frequently on Roosevelt speeches, and so later did the Japanese. They timed the creation of some major disturbance in the hope that it would blanket the speech in the morning's news and mitigate the effect that Roosevelt's words might produce on American and British morale. But they needed far more bombs and bombers than they possessed to nullify the lasting effect of those words, "the arsenal of democracy."

The Lend-Lease Bill was drafted largely in the Treasury Department by Edward H. Foley, General Counsel, and his assistant, Oscar Cox, who subsequently became General Counsel for Lend Lease and one of Hopkins' most brilliant aides. Important spadework on the whole British financial problem had previously been done by another Treasury lawyer, Herman Oliphant, who had literally killed himself in the process. The War Department had been working along similar lines, for both Stimson and Marshall had been determined to break through the legal restrictions preventing aid for Britain, not because of any sentimental attachment to the land of Shakespeare, Keats and leafy lanes, but because it was their duty to promote the interests of our national security. An old statute of 1892 had been dug out of the files, whereby Congress authorized the Secretary of War to lease Army property "when in his discretion it will be for the public good." I do not know how it was arranged to give the Lend-Lease Bill the significant designation, "HR-1776," but it sounds like a Rooseveltian conception, for it was the veritable declaration of interdependence.

This was one of the few "irrevocable acts" to which Roosevelt committed himself before Pearl Harbor. In asking the Congress to pass this revolutionary law, granting to him such tremendous powers over the lives and fortunes of his countrymen, he was running what then appeared to be by all odds the greatest risk of his career. The isolationists had not been set back by the election, for they considered that the American people had been compelled to choose between two interventionists. Indeed, with the formation of the powerful America First Committee, the isolationists became for the first time well organized, and also very well financed, and they were mobilized for the battle against Lend Lease. Certainly, the Congress provided favorable ground on which Roosevelt's opponents could fight him. Roosevelt knew this and he knew the consequences if he should lose this battle. But he was confident that he would not lose it. His Administration was now far stronger than it had been during the terrible events of the preceding summer: Stimson and Knox were in, and Farley and Garner were out. Whatever Hull's previous feelings about the third term and his own prospects of being Roosevelt's successor, he had been active in the President's behalf in the campaign against Willkie and he put his weight behind Lend Lease. Some of the New Dealers, such as Henry Wallace, who had been hesitant about supporting the President's foreign policy, were now realizing that this involved something more than a mere surrender to "British imperialism." So, for the first time in years, the Administration presented a united front to the Congress. Furthermore, Roosevelt had been given over twenty-seven million votes by the American people, and those votes were the kind of facts that Congressmen ignore at their peril.

There was still plenty of venom. Senator Burton K. Wheeler, who had himself just been re-elected and was therefore safe from the voters for another six years (they defeated him in 1946), coined a slogan to the effect that Lend Lease would mean "ploughing under every fourth American boy." Roosevelt described this as "the most untruthful, the most dastardly, unpatriotic thing that has been said in public life in my generation." He added, "Quote me on that."

What Lend Lease meant primarily was the end of the period of sham in which the United States sought to protect its own security by bootlegging methods. The concept of where the interests of our national security began was determined not by Roosevelt alone, but with the emphatic concurrence of his constitutional advisers, the Secretaries of War and Navy, and the Chief of Staff of the Army and the Chief of Naval Operations. It was their decision that since the British were holding positions vital to American defense, it was our duty either to strengthen the British by all possible means or to send our own armed forces to occupy these positions and defend them ourselves.

Lend Lease kept the Allied cause alive and fighting on all fronts for the two years needed for the United States to become a decisive force in actual combat. It further provided an historic precedent for meeting a comparable crisis abroad by methods short of immediate armed intervention.

CHAPTER XI

No. 10 Downing Street

AROUND Christmas, 1940, Roosevelt was mulling over the numerous implications of the letter he had received from Churchill, particularly in relation to the strategic importance of Ireland and the part that the United States might play in negotiations with De Valera. The names of such eminent Irish-Americans as Joseph P. Kennedy and William J. Donovan were mentioned as possible emissaries. Roosevelt said,

"You know—a lot of this could be settled if Churchill and I could just sit down together for awhile."

"What's stopping you?" Hopkins asked.

"Well—it couldn't be arranged right now. They have no Ambassador here—we have none over there."

The gleam of high adventure came into Hopkins' sharp eyes. "How about me going over, Mr. President?"

Roosevelt turned that suggestion down cold. He pointed to all the work he had ahead of him—a State of the Union Message, a gigantic budget, the Third Inaugural, the Lend-Lease fight.

"I'll be of no use to you in that fight," said Hopkins. "They'd never pay any attention to my views, except to vote the other way. But—if I had been in England and seen it with my own eyes, then I might be of some help."

Still Roosevelt refused to hear of such a proposal. However, Hopkins now had an idea that seemed to him eminently sound, and certainly intensely exciting, and he would not let go of it. He enlisted the aid of Missy LeHand and of Justice Felix Frankfurter who seldom offered any advice to Roosevelt after his elevation to the Supreme Court, but who was listened to when he did speak.

Roosevelt remained obdurate and, after days of intensive effort, Hopkins was about ready to give up. We were working at the time on the Message to Congress. It was the one which proclaimed the Four Freedoms. Nobody ghost-wrote those. Roosevelt had mentioned them somewhat casually at a press conference six months previously when asked a question about his long-term peace objective. There were then five freedoms—two of them coming under the heading of "Freedom of Speech." Roosevelt had no name in mind for the Third Freedom, though he was clear about its social import, and Richard L. Harkness of the *Philadelphia Inquirer* suggested it be called, "Freedom From Want." After that conference the Freedoms were forgotten until Roosevelt suddenly recalled them to us on New Year's, 1941.

On the morning of January 5, Hopkins was in his room when Steve Early telephoned from the West Wing to say, "Congratulations!"

"On what?" said Hopkins.

"Your trip!"

"What trip?" Hopkins suspected some ill-timed joke inspired, no doubt, by Roosevelt himself.

"Your trip to England," said Early. "The President just announced it at his press conference."

Two days later, Hopkins was off.

Roosevelt had told the press that Hopkins would go "as my personal representative for a very short trip—a couple of weeks—just to maintain —I suppose that is the word for it—personal relations between me and the British Government."

The questions followed:

Q. Does Mr. Hopkins have any special mission, Mr. President?
The President. No, no, no!
Q. Any title?
The President. No, no! . . .
Q. Mr. President, is it safe to say Mr. Hopkins will not be the next Ambassador?
The President. You know Harry isn't strong enough for that job.
Q. Will he be on the government pay roll?
The President. I suppose they will pay his expenses—probably on a per diem, not very large—either for you or Hopkins!
(Laughter) . . .
Q. Will anyone accompany Mr. Hopkins?
The President. No. And he will have no powers.
Q. Will he have any mission to perform?
The President. No; you can't get anything exciting. (Laughter) He's just going over to say "How do you do?" to a lot of my friends! (Laughter)

(The boys seemed to have laughed easily in those days.)

Before Hopkins left Washington he was persuaded to have a long talk with Jean Monnet, whom he had never met but with whom he was to become closely associated later on in the problems of production and eventually in the diplomatic mess which followed the Allied landings in North Africa. Monnet was one of the least obtrusive men in Washington during the early years of the war, but one of the most determined and most useful. A French businessman, member of the famous cognac family, he had been in America in 1938 and 1939 stimulating the production of fighting aircraft for France. He was in London as a member of the Allied Economic Coordinating Committee when France fell and he then offered his services to the British Government. He was sent to Washington to work with Arthur Purvis on the British Purchasing Commission. He had the kind of calm, cool reasoning and self-disciplined mind which is supposed to be typically French but which is all too seldom found in Frenchmen; he was positively puritanical in his refusal to deviate from the straight line which led to his objectives. His advice to Hopkins was to waste no time with the Minister of This or That in the British Cabinet but to concentrate on Churchill, for "Churchill *is* the British War Cabinet, and no one else matters." Hopkins became a bit fed up with hearing about the almighty Churchill and exclaimed, "I suppose Churchill is convinced that he's the greatest man in the world!"

A friend who was present said, "Harry—if you're going to London with that chip on your shoulder, like a damned little small-town chauvinist, you may as well cancel your passage right now." Hopkins, however, maintained his reservations about Churchill as he set off on the Pan-American Clipper to Lisbon. He also maintained the gnawing fear of air travel which had once caused him to refuse an invitation to make an inspection flight over Boulder Dam—saying, in explanation of his refusal, "No, God-damn it, I'm scared!" Several people tried to thumb a ride with him on the Clipper, including Averell Harriman and the present biographer, but he preferred to travel alone.

He carried with him his official letter of authorization:

Reposing special faith and confidence in you, I am asking you to proceed at your early convenience to Great Britain, there to act as my personal representative. I am also asking you to convey a communication in this sense to His Majesty King George VI.

You will, of course, communicate to this Government any matters which may come to your attention in the performance of your mission which you may feel will serve the best interests of the United States.

With all best wishes for the success of your mission, I am,

Very sincerely yours,
/s/ Franklin D. Roosevelt

Enclosed with this was a letter from the President to King George VI:

Your Majesty:

I have designated the Honorable Harry L. Hopkins as my personal representative on a special mission to Great Britain. Mr. Hopkins is a very good friend of mine in whom I repose the utmost confidence. I am asking him to convey to you and to Her Majesty the Queen my cordial greetings and my sincere hope that his mission may advance the common ideals of our two nations.

Cordially your friend,
/s/ FRANKLIN D. ROOSEVELT

The Hopkins mission received a largely unfavorable press with many references to the travels of Colonel House twenty-five years before and to Hopkins' record as a free and easy squanderer of the taxpayers' money. Raymond Clapper, always more friendly than most of his colleagues, assumed that Hopkins was going in his capacity as a veteran welfare worker to make a study of the new democracy that was arising from the ruins in Britain and to make charts of social progress; in this guess, Clapper was uncharacteristically wide of the mark. At the other extreme was the Communist *Daily Worker* which likened Hopkins to Colonel House saying in its editorial that House had pledged "American entrance into the first imperialistic war on the side of the Allies while Woodrow Wilson was assuring the American people that he would keep the country out of the war. . . . The secret diplomacy involved in the Hopkins appointment can put the American people on the alert—in insisting that no further aid be given British imperialism, since such aid brings the shadow of war closer and closer to our homes." The *Daily Worker* urged the American people to shout loudly, "The Yanks are *not* coming."

(Less than seven months later, Hopkins arrived in Moscow to talk to Joseph Stalin and the same *Daily Worker* said, editorially,

The sending of Mr. Hopkins on this mission, his statements and pledges will meet the approval of the entire American people. . . . The time is long overdue for the people to inform their Representatives and Senators to establish unity to defend the country and to defeat the common enemy of mankind. The fact that concrete steps have been taken in this direction, through Mr. Hopkins' visits to London and Moscow, makes this unity imperative. Any voices raised to prevent these steps from being taken are helping Hitler, or are agents of Hitler and Fifth Columnists in the country.)

Shortly after Hopkins' departure, the suggestion was made that Wendell Willkie also make a trip to London. It was obvious that Roosevelt would heartily approve of this. There was far more news value in Willkie than in Hopkins; and, as the Lend-Lease debate started, this evidence of solidification of bipartisan foreign policy was all important. When Willkie went to the White House on the eve of his departure, Roosevelt was working on his Third Inaugural Address with Rosenman and me. We were in the Cabinet Room when it was announced that Willkie had arrived in General Watson's office. Roosevelt shifted into his wheel-

chair and was going through Missy LeHand's office into his own to
greet the man who had been his opponent in the recent, bitter campaign.
He looked into his office and saw that his desk was clean of papers.
Then he stopped his wheelchair, and turned to us, and asked us to give
him a handful of papers from the litter on the Cabinet table. We asked,
"Which particular papers do you want, Mr. President?"

"Oh, it doesn't matter," said Roosevelt, "just give me a handful to
strew around on my desk so that I will look very busy when Willkie
comes in."

Sometime later, when I came to know Wendell Willkie, I told him of
that episode, and he was considerably amused. His comment was,
"That's typical!" It was during this brief meeting of the two men that
Roosevelt took a sheet of his personal stationery and, without apparent
premeditation, wrote the famous message to Churchill in Longfellow's
words:

> Sail on, O Ship of State!
> Sail on, O Union, strong and great!
> Humanity with all its fears,
> With all the hopes of future years,
> Is hanging breathless on thy fate!

Roosevelt never made a more graceful or effective gesture than that,
and none of us who were with him in the White House at the time had
any idea how he happened to think of it.

When Churchill was informed that Harry Hopkins was coming to
visit him his first question was, *"Who?"* He was quickly informed by
his Parliamentary Private Secretary, Brendan Bracken, who had met
Hopkins at the Swopes' house some years before and had watched his
career with interest ever since. As the close friend and confidant of the
Prime Minister, Bracken occupied a position that corresponded in one
or two respects (but not more) to Hopkins'. When Churchill heard
who his curious guest really was, he ordered the unrolling of any red
carpets that might have survived the Blitz.

Hopkins was five days en route, traveling the last leg, Lisbon to
Poole on the South Coast of England, in a British Overseas Airways
Clipper. In those days of the Neutrality Law, the Pan American Clippers, rating as merchant vessels, could not go into the ports of belligerent
countries. Churchill sent Bracken to Poole to meet the airplane, but
when the passengers debarked Hopkins was not among them. Bracken
got aboard and found Hopkins still sitting, looking sick and shrunken
and too tired even to unfasten his safety belt. He had to rest for a long
time before he felt well enough to take the train journey to London. But
then he began to perk up. He looked with great interest at the bomb
damage on the South Coast and felt, like every other American who

reached England in those bleak days, that he had arrived on the other side of the moon. As the train moved through the countryside, which seemed as tranquil and untroubled as ever, Hopkins said to Bracken, "Are you going to let Hitler take these fields away from you?" That was his first leading question about British intentions. Bracken answered with authority, and with unaccustomed brevity, "No."

The Hopkins entry into London on Thursday, January 9, was described years later in a letter to the *Sunday Times* from Sir Eustace Missenden, General Manager of the Southern Railway:

> Mr. Churchill had given instructions that the best was to be done, and arrangements were made for the most modern Pullman cars to be formed in the train. The conductors wore white gloves; a good meal, with liquid refreshment, was available, together with papers, periodicals, etc. Mr. Harry Hopkins was obviously impressed.
>
> It was late afternoon and the engine driver put up a grand performance, but when nearing Clapham Junction the siren was heard, and during that period Clapham Junction was particularly favoured by the Luftwaffe. However, on we went, and within one minute of the train's arrival at Waterloo, just after 7 p.m., hundreds of incendiaries showered down on the line between Clapham Junction and Waterloo, blocking all tracks for several hours. The intense relief on the faces of the train crews will always be remembered as they watched the waiting car spring into life carrying our distinguished visitor on his way to Downing Street.

He was met at the station by Herschel V. Johnson, Chargé d'Affaires at the American Embassy. Although Hopkins was invited to dinner at No. 10 Downing Street that first evening, he felt too tired to face Churchill and had dinner with Johnson in his room at Claridge's Hotel where he could hear the antiaircraft batteries blazing away in Hyde Park. Johnson, who was ranking American diplomat in London during the interval between Ambassadors Kennedy and Winant—and later Minister to Sweden and Representative on the United Nations Security Council—has told me that before Hopkins' arrival he had been in a state of deep pessimism as to American ability to appreciate the serious urgency of Britain's plight. About all that he received officially from home was a series of admonitions to maintain strict observance of the Neutrality Law and to do or say nothing that might bring down isolationist criticism on the State Department. Having been through almost six months of intensive Blitz, and having himself narrowly escaped death more than once when bombs landed in and around Grosvenor Square, he had begun to feel a certain sense of frustration and impotence as of one who is a guest in an upstairs room of a burning building and is told to be careful to take no sides as between the fire department and the flames.

"I was immediately heartened," Johnson has said, "by the sincerity and the intensity of Harry Hopkins' determination to gain firsthand knowledge of Britain's needs and of finding a way to fill them. Some other Americans who had come to London devoted themselves to investigations to determine if the British really needed the things they were asking for. Harry wanted to find out if they were asking for *enough* to see them through. He made it perfectly clear that he did not know how or where he was going to begin, or what his methods would be, but he knew precisely what he was there for. He made me feel that the first real assurance of hope had at last come—and he acted on the British like a galvanic needle."

Another American whom Hopkins wanted to see and did see at the beginning of his London visit was Edward R. Murrow, of the Columbia Broadcasting System. From the outbreak of war, when he had lain in the Mayo Clinic believing that he was soon to die, Hopkins had listened to Murrow's grim voice announcing, "This—is London," in a tone which seemed to suggest the thuds of the German bombs. When Murrow was summoned to Claridge's to see Hopkins he thought he was being granted an interview, which proved to be the case except that he, Murrow, was the one interviewed. Hopkins plied him with searching questions, most of them concerned with personalities and with public morale rather than with physical conditions. All that Hopkins told him of his own mission was, "I suppose you could say that I've come here to try to find a way to be a catalytic agent between two prima donnas," which was not for quotation. Hopkins then believed that the formidable egos of Roosevelt and Churchill were bound to clash, and, in anticipation of that, he said, "I want to try to get an understanding of Churchill and of the men he sees after midnight."

Churchill had been informed of Hopkins' devotion to Roosevelt and of his possible suspicion of anyone who might presume to challenge Roosevelt's position of pre-eminence among world statesmen. On the day of Hopkins' arrival, the Prime Minister made a speech at a luncheon in honor of Lord Halifax, the new British Ambassador to the United States, and in the course of his remarks on the long belabored subject of Anglo-American amity he said,

I hail it as a most fortunate occurrence that at this awe-striking climax in world affairs there should stand at the head of the American Republic a famous statesman, long versed and experienced in the work of government and administration, in whose heart there burns the fire of resistance to aggression and oppression, and whose sympathies and nature make him the sincere and undoubted champion of justice and of freedom, and of the victims of wrongdoing wherever they may dwell.

And not less—for I may say it now that the party struggle in the United States is over—do I rejoice that this pre-eminent figure should newly have received the unprecedented honor of being called for the third time to lead the American democracies in days of stress and storm.

When Hopkins learned of this speech from Johnson, who had been present at the luncheon, he began to believe that he and the British Prime Minister might be able to get along with one another.

The next morning, Johnson brought the Military Attaché, General Raymond E. Lee, and the Naval Attaché, Admiral Robert Lee Ghormley, to Claridge's to give Hopkins the American estimate of the war situation—and it was not an optimistic one—and then Johnson took Hopkins to the Foreign Office for the inevitable courtesy call. Hopkins was not at first favorably impressed with Anthony Eden, though they later became very good friends. Other Americans on first acquaintance with Eden have made the mistake of writing him off as a charming, ornamental, casual young gentleman of Mayfair. Those who jumped to this conclusion had forgotten that Eden had the strength and courage to risk political extinction by refusing to go along with Neville Chamberlain on appeasement.

Hopkins wrote his first reports to Roosevelt in longhand on Claridge's stationery and they were dispatched by courier. He said:

> He (Eden) thought Hitler would have a "go" at England and un-successfully—that Turkey would fight if the German moved through Bulgaria—that therefore, Hitler would more likely move through Italy to attack the Greeks—that Russia was frightened and would keep out —that there was a real chance of Abyssinia kicking up a rumpus soon —that the British Army in Egypt were using successfully some big tanks over the desert.

That was about all that emerged from that brief meeting, after which Johnson took Hopkins to see Lord Halifax, whom he described as,

> A tall stoop-shouldered aristocrat greeted me in an old office taken over by the ministers of Churchill's government. I did the talking—or most of it—telling him the people that I thot were important for him to see and know in Washington. When I got beyond the President and Hull I was in deep water and quit. I liked him. I think and hope the President will like him. He has no side—has been about—I presume is a hopeless Tory—that isn't too important now if we can but get on with our business of licking Hitler. I would not like to see him have much to say about a later peace—I should like to have Eden say less. I understand he is off to America on Tuesday next aboard a British cruiser.

Hopkins then returned to Claridge's, made an unsuccessful attempt to neaten up, and then drove down through Berkeley Square and Trafalgar Square to Downing Street for the big moment. He wrote Roosevelt:

Number 10 Downing St. is a bit down at the heels because the Treasury next door has been bombed more than a bit. The Prime Minister is no longer permitted to sleep here and I understand sleeps across the street. He told me they are building a real shelter for him so that he can sleep in peace near by. Everyone tells me that he works fifteen hours a day and I can well believe it. His man Friday—Brendan Bracken—met me at the door—showed me about the old and delightful house that has been home of prime ministers of the Empire for two hundred years. Most of the windows are out—workmen over the place repairing the damage—Churchill told me it wouldn't stand a healthy bomb.

Bracken led me to a little dining room in the basement—poured me some Sherry and left me to wait for the Prime Minister. A rotund —smiling—red faced, gentleman appeared—extended a fat but none the less convincing hand and wished me welcome to England. A short black coat—striped trousers—a clear eye and a mushy voice was the impression of England's leader as he showed me with obvious pride the photograph of his beautiful daughter-in-law and grandchild.

The lunch was simple but good—served by a very plain woman who seemed to be an old family servant. Soup—cold beef—(I didn't take enough jelly to suit the P.M. and he gave me some more)—green salad—cheese and coffee—a light wine and port. He took snuff from a little silver box—he liked it.

I told him the President was anxious to see him in April—he expressed regret that Bermuda would not be the place—the climate was nice—he would bring a small staff—go on a cruiser and by accident meet the President at the appointed place—and discuss our problems at leisure. He talked of remaining as long as two weeks and seemed very anxious to meet the President face to face. We discussed the difficulty of communication with the President at long range—there is no question but that he wants to meet the President—the sooner the better.

I told him there was a feeling in some quarters that he, Churchill, did not like America, Americans or Roosevelt. This set him off on a bitter tho fairly constrained attack on Ambassador Kennedy who he believes is responsible for this impression. He denied it vigorously— sent for a Secretary to show me a telegram which he had sent to the President immediately after his election in which he expressed his warm delight at the President's re-election.

I told of my mission—he seemed pleased—and several times assured me that he would make every detail of information and opinion available to me and hoped that I would not leave England until I was fully satisfied of the exact state of England's need and the urgent necessity of the exact material assistance Britain requires to win the war.

He reviewed with obvious pride his own part in the war to date— he didn't *know* that England could withstand the onslaught after France fell—but he felt sure that it could—it did—and it will withstand the next one—he thinks the invasion will not come but if they gain a foothold in England with 100,000 men "we shall drive them out"—beside its excellent coast defenses Britain has twenty five well trained and equipped divisions—trained only in offensive warfare which will drive Germany's army into the sea. Germany cannot invade Britain successfully. He thinks Hitler may use poison gas but if they do England will reply in kind killing man for man—"for we too have the deadliest gases in the world"—but under no circumstances will they be used unless the Germans release gas first. He said he believed Hitler would not strike at Spain now because the population is starving and Hitler does not want sullen people around his armies—he has enough of that already—but the spring might tell a different story—and left me the impression that Spain would be over-run in the spring.

He thinks Greece is lost—altho he is now reinforcing the Greeks—and weakening his African Army—he believes Hitler will permit Mussolini to go only so far down hill—and is now preparing for the attack which must bring its inevitable result. He knows this will be a blow to British prestige and is obviously considering ways and means of preparing the British public for it. He realizes it will have a profound and disappointing effect in America as well. Churchill too, thinks Turkey will stay put and probably be in the war when Germany moves thru Bulgaria. This Churchill thinks will be the route.

This debacle in Greece will be over-come in part by what he considers to be the sure defeat of the Italians in Africa. He feels England can bring great military pressure on Italy—and fully intends to—Britain will control the Mediterranean and the Suez against Germany. He has offered Weygand six divisions—if the former strikes—he is in close touch with Pétain on this point—he spoke with no great assurance about it—but it is clear Churchill intends to hold Africa—clean out the Italians and cooperate with Weygand if the opportunity permits. He expressed the hope that we would not go too far in feeding any of the dominated countries. He feels that tough as it is that one of Hitler's great weaknesses is to be in control of territory inhabited by a dejected and despairing people.

Churchill said that while Germany's bombers were at the ratio of 2-½ to 1 at the present time—that would be soon reduced to 1-½ to 1—and then he felt they could hold their own in the air—indeed he looks forward with our help to mastery in the air and then Germany with all her armies will be finished. He believes that this war will never see great forces massed against one another.

He took me up to the Cabinet Room where there was "a better fire" and showed me on the map where the convoys are coming thru to Liverpool and Glasgow—and of the route the German bombers are taking from France to Norway to intercept the ships.

The sentence in the foregoing, *"He believes that this war will never see great forces massed against one another,"* should be noted as a suggestion of the strategic thinking which later led Churchill into so many arguments over the Second Front.

After that luncheon, Hopkins held two press conferences, one with the British press and one with American correspondents, and managed in both of them to say nothing. But his presence in London was used to a considerable extent in Britain's propaganda barrage to the continent of Europe, via BBC broadcasts and leaflets dropped by the R.A.F. The gigantic Goebbels machine did not ignore it, either, the principal line being that Hopkins had come for the purpose of taking over the rest of the British Empire (following Bermuda, Trinidad, etc.) in return for some more rusty and obsolete American matériel.

The following day was Saturday and, war or no war, many of the high officials of His Majesty's Government went off for the week end. Churchill normally went to Chequers but the security authorities would not let him use this official and well-known house when there was a full moon. So he went instead to Dytchley which is near Woodstock, north of Oxford, and one of the most beautiful of all the stately homes of England. Built in the latter part of the seventeenth century, the greatest period of English architecture, it had become the property of Ronald Tree, whose mother was the daughter of the original Marshall Field of Chicago. Tree was Parliamentary Secretary to Brendan Bracken, and he was skillful enough as a host to meet the exacting requirements of Winston Churchill. Three of the handsome rooms on the ground floor were set aside as offices for the Prime Minister and equipped with all the devices by which he could keep in touch with every development of the war at every instant day or night. Week ends were anything but restful, because of the incessant concern of Churchill with everything that was going on everywhere (Roosevelt could get away from it all now and then, but Churchill never even wanted to try) and also because of the habits of the Axis powers; indeed, Churchill was week-ending when he received the news of the war's most important events in the years when the enemy was making the news—including the attacks on the Soviet Union and Pearl Harbor.

During Hopkins' two days at Dytchley the only news was of the appearance for the first time of German dive bombers in the Mediterranean; they attacked British naval units and inflicted serious losses. Hopkins was amazed at the calmness with which Churchill and his staff took this bad news. Having had no direct experience of the realities of warfare, he was shocked by the stark immediacy of the information that ships had been sunk and that British sailors had been killed and maimed. But he had to learn that those who make the great decisions in this brutal business can take no time out for mourning or for penitence; and Winston Churchill, no respecter of his own safety, was a good man from whom to learn it. As it turned out, the presence of the Stuka bombers in the Mediterranean had a significance which was not apparent at the time;

the German records eventually showed that this was the week end selected by Hitler for the capture of Gibraltar.

Hopkins was particularly struck by the extreme difference between Churchill's ménage and Roosevelt's. Although hell might be popping all about Roosevelt, it was rarely audible in his immediate presence, where tranquillity prevailed. Churchill, on the other hand, always seemed to be at his Command Post on the precarious beachhead and the guns were continually blazing in his conversation; wherever he was, there was the battlefront—and he was involved in the battles not only of the current war but of the whole past, from Cannae to Gallipoli. While it took a Pearl Harbor or a national election or a particularly tense poker game to keep Roosevelt up as late as midnight, Churchill was getting full steam up along about ten o'clock in the evening; often after his harassed staff had struggled to bed at 2:00 or 3:00 A.M. they would be routed out an hour or more later with an entirely new project for which a plan must be drawn up immediately. Churchill needed little sleep at night but took a nap after lunch, whereas it was Roosevelt's custom to work hard all day and sleep soundly all night. Churchill's consumption of alcohol has been widely advertised: it could be described as unique, for it continued at quite regular intervals through most of his waking hours without visible effect on his health or on his mental processes. Anyone who suggests that he became befuddled with drink obviously never had to become involved in an argument with him on some factual problem late at night when everyone else present was drooping with fatigue. He was really Olympian in capacity. His principal aides—General Sir Hastings Ismay, Professor F. A. Lindemann, Commander Charles Thompson, Sir Desmond Morton, J. M. Martin and Bracken—made no attempt to keep up with him in consumption of champagne, Scotch whisky and brandy (he detested cocktails and his whiskies were weak by American standards), and they had to summon reserves of energy to be able to keep up with him in work.

Roosevelt engaged in social life no more than was absolutely necessary, and he eliminated it almost entirely when the circumstances of war gave him a good excuse for doing so. Churchill, however, loved to have gay and amusing company at the dinner table. He had little opportunity for it, of course, during the Blitz in London, when he was largely confined during the hours of darkness to the elaborate system of offices and small living quarters in the air-raid shelters under the Cabinet office building in Great George Street, a few steps from Downing Street. But on week ends there was usually a peacetime house-party atmosphere surrounding Churchill whenever he wanted some relaxation. In Hopkins' opinion, there was no doubt that the most charming and entertaining of all the people that he met on these week ends was Mrs. Churchill.

On Saturday night, in the beautiful library at Dytchley, he heard

Churchill for the first time launch forth into one of the after-dinner war summaries for which, among other things, he was famous. Churchill could talk for an hour or more and hold any audience spellbound, including those who had heard him many times and to whom nothing that he said was news. It might be misleading to say that these Churchill talks were "impromptu"— for it is doubtful that he was ever unprepared for a speech—but they were always exercises in incredible virtuosity. For Hopkins, this was the opening of new horizons. Churchill's eloquence came as no surprise, but his remarkable, encyclopedic knowledge of the situation in all of its intricate involutions convinced Hopkins that here was one who certainly knew his stuff, who could recite fact and figure and chapter and verse, and in superb English prose.

There is a story which has been often told and sometimes printed, to the effect that Churchill, having been advised of Hopkins' background as a social worker and rabid New Dealer, attempted to woo him by talking at the outset of all that the British Government was doing for the underprivileged and the forgotten man, and of how his dearest dream for the postwar world was the more abundant life for all . . . whereupon Hopkins rudely interrupted him by saying, "The President didn't send me here to listen to any of that stuff. All he wants to know is: how do you propose to beat that son of a bitch in Berlin?"

That is a fine story, all right, but in so far as I know it is not true. Churchill subsequently stated that, within a few minutes after their first meeting in Downing Street, he felt sure that he had at last established "a definite, heart-to-heart contact with the President." It may be added that the members of Churchill's entourage were mostly men of superior wit—that may have been an important qualification in their selection for these highly confidential posts—and they were adroit in developing anecdotes about their gusty chief. Thus there exists a whole library of Churchill jokes almost as extensive as that fabricated about the legendary figure of Samuel Goldwyn. Some of these stories, of course, are true.

After his return to London, Hopkins paid his respects at Buckingham Palace; this was only a brief meeting but subsequently Hopkins had a longer visit with the King and Queen, his description of which appears later in this chapter. On January 14, Hopkins cabled Roosevelt:

I saw the King yesterday after spending the week end with Churchill. The King is well and confident and sends his warm regards to you. Today I am leaving for a tour of naval bases with Churchill. Your message to Congress has been well received here. I am urging the British Government not to advertise or accentuate any differences that may exist between us pending passage of the Lend Lease Bill. What is your best judgment as to when this Bill will pass? I hope no major amendments will be made. Please keep us informed as to the Bill's progress. The going here is pretty rough but all is well. I am seeing everything here from German bombs to some of your cousins. A courier is delivering a letter to you from me.

The President also received a cable from the Former Naval Person saying, "I am most grateful to you for sending so remarkable an envoy who enjoys so high a measure of your intimacy and confidence."

The letter to which Hopkins referred in his cable was written, like the previously quoted report, in longhand on small Claridge stationery and never passed through any diplomatic channels whatsoever:

DEAR MR. PRESIDENT:—

These notes are sent by Col. Lee who is returning with Halifax. Will you save them for me until I get back when I shall try to put them into readable form.

The people here are amazing from Churchill down and if courage alone can win—the result will be inevitable. But they need our help desperately and I am sure you will permit nothing to stand in the way. Some of the ministers and underlings are a bit trying but no more than some I have seen.

Churchill is the gov't in every sense of the word—he controls the grand strategy and often the details—labor trusts him—the army, navy, air force are behind him to a man. The politicians and upper crust pretend to like him. I cannot emphasize too strongly that he is the one and only person over here with whom you need to have a full meeting of minds.

Churchill wants to see you—the sooner the better—but I have told him of your problem until the bill is passed. I am convinced this meeting between you and Churchill is essential—and soon—for the battering continues and Hitler does not wait for Congress.

I was with Churchill at 2 A.M. Sunday night when he got word of the loss of the *Southampton*—the serious damage to the new aircraft carrier [*Illustrious*]—a second cruiser knocked about—but he never falters or displays the least despondence—till four o'clock he paced the floor telling me of his offensive and defensive plans.

I cannot believe that it is true that Churchill dislikes either you or America—it just doesn't make sense.

Churchill is prepared for a set back in Greece—the African campaign will proceed favorably—German bombers in the Mediterranean make the fleet's operation more difficult—convoys must all go around the Cape. An invasion they feel sure can be repelled—Churchill thinks it will not come soon but Beaverbrook and others think it will come and soon.

This island needs our help now Mr. President with everything we can give them.

There is no time to be out of London so I am staying here—the bombs aren't nice and seem to be quite impersonal. I have been offered a so called bomb proof apartment by Churchill—a tin hat and gas mask have been delivered—the best I can say for the hat is that it looks

MAYFAIR 8860

TELEGRAMS: CLARIDGES, LONDON.

Claridge's
Brook Street, W.1

Dear Mr. President:-

These notes are sent by Col. Lee who is returning with Halifax – will you save them for me until I get back when I shall try to put them into readable form.

The people here are amazing from Churchill down and if courage alone can win – the result will be inevitable. But they need our help desperately and I am sure you will permit

Two pages of a letter from Hopkins to Roosevelt, written during his

nothing to stand in the way. Some
of the ministers and underlings are
a bit trying but no more than
some I have seen.

Churchill is the gov't in
every sense of the word — he
controls the grand strategy and
often the details — labor trusts
him — the army, navy, air force
are behind him to a man.
The politicians and upper crust
pretend to like him. I cannot
emphasize too strongly that he is
the one and only person over here
with whom you need to have
a full meeting of minds

*first visit to England, in which Hopkins by-passed diplomatic channels
to state England's urgent need.*

worse than my own and doesn't fit—the gas mask I can't get on—so I am alright.

There is much to tell but it will have to wait—for I must be off to Charing Cross.

HARRY

The reference to being out of London referred to a suggestion that he stay at a house in the country to avoid the bombing, but that naturally was the last thing he wanted to miss. The train he was to take left from King's Cross, not Charing Cross, but luckily he was guided by an Embassy representative so he went to the right station.

He traveled with Churchill in his private train to Scotland where Lord Halifax was about to embark on the new battleship, *King George V*, for his journey to the United States. The final stage of the trip to Scapa Flow had to be made on a destroyer which was boarded under utmost difficulties, while pitching badly. Churchill was talking rapidly at the time about the African campaign. He scrambled aboard the destroyer easily, but Hopkins, being no old salt (nor even a young one), missed his footing and was narrowly saved from falling into the sea. He was dragged aboard by the scruff of his neck while Churchill went right on talking. On board the destroyer, off the North Coast of Scotland in January, Hopkins was horribly cold, tired and generally miserable. He borrowed General Ismay's flying boots to keep his feet warm and sat down to rest on some object on the deck, but was promptly hauled off it by a chief petty officer who said, apologetically, "Excuse me, sir—but I don't think you should sit just there, sir—that, sir, is a depth charge."

When the destroyer came in view of the Home Fleet, riding at anchor in Scapa Flow, Churchill or someone else (I do not know who) waved to the impressive sight and said to Hopkins, "There is our shield! If that should go, we'd be for it. The Germans have attempted some bombing here. If they should intensify it, and had some luck with their hits, our shield would be gone and we should be defenseless." (Eleven months later Hopkins thought that it was a lucky thing for civilization that the Germans never developed the carrier-based air power nor the peculiar tactical skill that the Japanese concentrated on Pearl Harbor.)

Hopkins wished good-by and good luck to Lord Halifax, with whom he was to have close and cordial association during the next four years. When Halifax arrived off Annapolis, Maryland, President Roosevelt did him the signal honor of sailing out to meet him. There was considerable quiet mirth in the White House over that episode. We all knew that of course the President was glad of the opportunity to welcome the new British Ambassador and thereby to advertise again his support for the British cause; but we all suspected that, as a naval enthusiast, he was also impelled by an irrepressible desire to have a good look at the new battleship.

The career of Lord Halifax as Ambassador was a remarkable one. He started out under many handicaps, being branded as one of the men of Munich. He was photographed indulging in his favorite sport of fox hunting in Virginia while his countrymen were absorbing fearful punishment, thereby evoking a diatribe from Carl Sandburg, among many others. Some months after his arrival in Washington, an acidulous and irreverent representative of the British Government in the United States returned to London and, when asked how Lord Halifax was getting along, replied, "Oh, he's doing famously! His popularity has risen from zero to freezing point." And yet, when five years later Halifax completed his mission and left the United States, he took with him a wealth of respect and affection such as could have been given to very few Ambassadors anywhere at any time. The size and character of the obstacles that he had been forced to face in the beginning made his ultimate accomplishment all the more admirable.

On the return journey from Scotland, Churchill stopped at various points, always keeping Hopkins with him and always being at pains to explain that this odd-looking, unkempt individual was "the personal representative of the President of the United States of America," an assurance well calculated to bolster local morale. At Glasgow there was a large inspection by the Prime Minister of anti-air-raid personnel. They were formed up in rank after rank. Churchill wanted Hopkins to walk with him the entire distance and to be introduced over and over again. Churchill was tireless but Hopkins was exhausted and tried several times to duck out and hide behind the spectators. But every time Churchill noted his absence and summoned him forth.

That night Churchill and Hopkins attended a dinner given by the Lord Provost of Glasgow. Churchill spoke, making graceful references to President Roosevelt, to Hopkins and to "the Democracy of the great American Republic" (a phrase calculated to please both sides of the political fence). Hopkins also was called upon for a few words. He quoted the Book of Ruth—"Whither thou goest, I will go . . . even to the end." Publication of this unprepared speech was censored, but word of it spread all over Britain and it had an effect far greater than Hopkins had dared to intend: it was interpreted as assurance that "the Americans are with us." Lord Beaverbrook told me years later that Hopkins' warmhearted sympathy at this time and his confidence and the conviction that went with it provided more tangible aid for Britain than had all the destroyers and guns and rifles and ammunition that had been sent previously.

It was on this trip, and other trips to Dover, Southampton and Portsmouth, that Hopkins noted the absolute reverence in which Churchill was held by the British people. They literally wanted to touch the hem of his garments. He had been a famous man in these islands for thirty years before the war, but they did not entrust him with the job of King's First Minister until they were *in extremis*. And as soon as they were out of it they voted overwhelmingly for his opponents. But this was their "finest hour" and Churchill was their acknowledged leader and spokesman and the living symbol of their will to survive as a free people. The Prime Minister and the President, as Hopkins saw them, were widely different characters, but they both possessed to a superlative degree the ability to provoke loyalty, enthusiasm, devotion, even a kind of adoration —and also the ability merely to provoke.

Returning to London, Hopkins plunged into a schedule of appointments with British and American officials, and those of various governments in exile. One official with whom he established a lasting friendship —after an unpropitious start—was Lord Beaverbrook, the press baron and Minister of Aircraft Production. (They first met at luncheon with Herschel Johnson and disliked each other automatically.) Hopkins attended a session of the House of Commons at which Churchill made one of his historic reports on the war situation. In this one he described the composition and functions of his War Cabinet. Coming to Beaverbrook, he said, "The Minister of Aircraft Production, who was described as an 'old sea raider,' which is a euphemistic method of describing a pirate, is a man of altogether exceptional force and genius who is at his very best when things are at their very worst." The relationship of Churchill and Beaverbrook was a matter of considerable interest and often amusement to Hopkins. Here were two determined and inherently powerful men whose very similarities clashed: both were supreme patriots on an imperial scale, both were tireless and tenacious, both extremely worldly, with great zest and capacity for good living, both were superb showmen with an alert ability for spotting and appreciating the main chance; and each of the many disagreements between them seemed utterly irreconcilable until a common contempt for the purely transient issue brought them together again.

Beaverbrook gave a dinner for Hopkins at Claridge's, inviting his colleagues and competitors of the London press. This dinner was off the record but an account of it has been written by one of the editors present:

> We were all tired men, suffering from a succession of long nights during which London had been bombed by explosives and incendiaries, and during which the difficulties of newspaper production had been extreme. But on that midwinter evening in the peak period of the first series of London blitzes we were also intensely curious men—which is the happiest and healthiest state for a journalist in any clime or circumstance. All of us were wondering as our cars advanced cautiously through the blackout toward Claridge's (and they miraculously found it, though its patrician and once-brilliant entrance was as subtly con-

cealed as that of any dubious dive) what Hopkins would have to say to us.

He had said so little since he arrived in London, to the tune of an anti-aircraft bombardment, on January 9. Our reporters, when they met him on arrival, were obliged to record that he "smiled quizzically" in answer to their questions; and even a full-dress Press Conference at the American Embassy two days later had produced nothing more definite from the President's envoy than that he was here "to discuss matters of mutual interest to our two countries." Though it must be admitted that he rewarded the zeal of one particularly determined questioner by agreeing, "Yes, I think you can say *urgent* matters."

The gathering at Claridge's was one of the biggest of the Beaverbrook war-time occasions. Not only were the editors and some of the leading writers present. Proprietors and managers were there, and the provincial Press, as well as that of London, was represented.

When the waiters had cleared the tables the doors were closed, and Beaverbrook stood up, smiling. He addressed himself not to us, but to Harry Hopkins. For days, he said, Hopkins had been talking to members of the Government. But tonight was a yet more important occasion, for those present were "the masters of the Government"— the leaders of the British Press. And so he invited Mr. Hopkins to speak to us.

Hopkins rose, looking lean, shy and untidy, grasping the back of his chair, and he continued to look shy throughout his speech.

His words were private, so no notes were taken. But if it had been possible to record the sentences that came quietly and diffidently from the lips of Harry Hopkins they would have compared well for nobility of expression with the splendid oration which Mr. Roosevelt had delivered two days earlier when he was sworn in for the third time as President of the United States.

Not that Hopkins repeated or even echoed the President's speech. He talked in more intimate terms. Where the President had spoken of America's duty to the world, Hopkins told us how the President and those around him were convinced that America's world duty could be successfully performed only in partnership with Britain. He told us of the anxiety and admiration with which every phase of Britain's lonely struggle was watched from the White House, and of his own emotions as he travelled through our blitzed land. His speech left us with the feeling that although America was not yet in the war, she was marching beside us, and that should we stumble she would see we did not fall. Above all he convinced us that the President and the men about him blazed with faith in the future of Democracy.

In addition to addressing us as a whole, Hopkins, encouraged by Beaverbrook, went on a slow journey around the table, pulling up a chair alongside the editors and managers of various newspapers and talking to them individually. He astonished us all, Right, Left and Centre, by his grasp of our newspapers' separate policies and problems.

We went away content—Hopkins to bed; Beaverbrook to his desk at the Ministry of Aircraft Production to read the night's reports and prepare orders for his factory managers on the morrow; the rest of us to our offices, to find that production had gone forward well in the evening blessedly free from the crash of bombs or the smell of burning buildings.

Many a tragic and terrible chapter was to be added to our country's history before our prayers were answered and our efforts rewarded. None of us British journalists who had been listening to the man from the White House was in any illusion about the peril which encompassed our island. But we were happy men all; our confidence and our courage had been stimulated by a contact for which Shakespeare, in "Henry V," had a phrase: "A little touch of Harry in the night."

A footnote to this is provided in a letter from J. Edgar Hoover to General Watson for the President's information. It seemed there were F.B.I. men in Claridge's that evening. Hoover wrote:

At the conclusion of the dinner it appeared from facial expressions that all the guests were quite happy as the result of the dinner and discussions. Small groups of them stopped in the coffee room, where representatives of this Bureau were seated at the moment, and the gist of the conversations related to the very charming manner of Mr. Hopkins, his keen insight into current problems and the very remarkable fact that he combined a very charming but almost shy personality with a very vigorous and dynamic mentality. In no instance was any unfavorable comment made and the entire gist of their conversations relative to Mr. Hopkins was positive and commendatory.

It delighted Roosevelt to know that the G-men were checking up on his personal representative.

Although Hopkins had paid his respects at Buckingham Palace shortly after his arrival he did not have an opportunity for a real talk with the King and Queen until two weeks later. His description of this meeting follows:

January 30, 1941
I had lunch today with Their Majesties The King and Queen at Buckingham Palace today. Sir Alan Lascelles and the Equerry in Waiting greeted me at the door and took me through the long, cold, narrow, windowless passages to the King's office, where apparently he meets all his visitors.

First the King and then the Queen came in. We chatted a moment about inconsequential things and the King then asked me about my trip to Scapa Flow with Halifax, and I told him details of the amusing incidents including the firing of the U.P. gun, and about the bomb landing five feet from me instead of on the enemy. He told me that the Prime Minister had failed to tell him of this incident. I told the King the reason for that was that the Prime Minister didn't think it was funny and I did!

The three of us had lunch together in the next room. We discussed at great length their visit to America a year ago last May, and it was perfectly clear that the President made a great impression on both of them.

I told the King how much the President enjoyed meeting them, how dear his friendship was to him personally, and how great his pleasure was in receiving personal mesages from the King. I urged the King, whenever he was of a mind, to send the President appropriate personal notes because I believed that that was one of the ways to keep our two countries closely related during these trying times.

The Queen told me that she found it extremely difficult to find words to express her feeling towards the people of Britain in these days. She thought their actions were magnificent and that victory in the long run was sure, but that the one thing that counted was the morale and determination of the great mass of the British people.

The King discussed the navy and the fleet at some length and showed an intimate knowledge of all the high ranking officers of the navy, and for that matter, of the army and air force. It was perfectly clear from his remarks that he reads very carefully all the important dispatches and, among other things, was quite familiar with a dispatch which I had sent Sunday night through the Foreign Office.

He thinks very highly of the Commander-in-Chief of the military forces and, as with everybody else, has great confidence in Churchill. He discussed quite freely with me the great difficulties this country would have if anything should happen to Churchill.

If ever two people realized that Britain is fighting for its life it is these two. They realize fully that this conflict is different from the other conflicts in Britain's history and that if Hitler wins they and the British people will be enslaved for years to come.

The Queen told an amusing story about going to Church with Mrs. Roosevelt senior and the President. It appears that the old lady dropped her Prayer Book over and over again and the Queen had to pick it up. This was no sooner done than she would drop her handkerchief. Eventually the Prayer Book went over the bench and there was nothing further that could be done. The Queen had been amused at the fact that the Rector of the Church had urged the parishioners to come to Church even when such distinguished visitors were not present.

The King talked at great length about the President and his obvious deep interest in the defeat of Hitler.

The air raid alarm had gone off just as we sat down to lunch, and as we reached coffee and port the bell rang in the Palace and the King said, "That means we have got to go to the air raid shelter," so we immediately walked down two or three flights of stairs, through a dark hallway, led by a guard, through several doors and finally landed in a small lighted room with a table and chairs.

We talked in the shelter for an hour longer about Washington and America's relationship to the war. The Queen urged the King to take the time to write to the President as frequently as he could, and said on her part she was going to continue to write to Mrs. Roosevelt.

He asked about Mr. Willkie and his visit, and seemed greatly pleased that I was sure Mr. Willkie and the President would see eye to eye in regard to the President's foreign policy.

He told me the story of Queen Wilhelmina's escape from Holland. It seems she had, after some urging, asked for fighter planes, which could not be sent, but the British Government instead sent a destroyer. She was refusing to leave Holland and took the destroyer in order to get to Flushing. The commander of the destroyer could not get into Flushing and told the Queen there was nothing to do but go to a British port, which she did. She got to Buckingham Palace at 5:00 o'clock in the afternoon wearing a tin hat given her by the commander of the destroyer. The Queen said she was a fine courageous woman, and it was perfectly clear from this conversation that she arrived in England entirely by accident and not by intent on her own part.

I told the King the story about the Belgian King, and of Queen Wilhelmina's desire that the President send a message to him. He expressed a good deal of sympathy with the King of the Belgians. It was perfectly clear that he felt that the King had had two responsibilities—one as Commander-in-Chief of the Belgian Army and the other his job as King, and that he had got the two jobs mixed up. He apparently had little or no criticism of him as Commander-in-Chief of the Army, but as King he thought he should have left the country and established his government elsewhere.

The Queen said she felt Hitler and the German people were a pretty cruel lot and realized they would have no mercy on them; that she liked the fact that the British people did not seem to have much hatred in their hearts but rather determination to resist to the end. She seemed to have a wide acquaintance with British politics and affairs and showed great interest in all I had to tell her about my trips throughout the country, particularly my visit to Glasgow. . . .

The King expressed the great hope that somehow the President and Churchill could get together personally in the near future. He believed that it might be arranged.

When I emphasized the President's great determination to defeat Hitler, his deep conviction that Britain and America had a mutuality of interest in this respect, and that they could depend upon aid from America, they were both very deeply moved.

The Queen asked particularly about Diana and told me to be sure to give her her love. She too wished to be remembered warmly to Mr. and Mrs. Roosevelt. The King on his part told me how greatly he appreciated the President's speeches and said he was sure from the last visit that he knew what was deeply embedded in the President's mind. He told me to tell the President how much beloved he was by the people of Britain and asked that I give to the President his warmest expressions of thanks and appreciation and a personal word of friendship.

I have made some deliberate deletions in the foregoing document relating largely to the British political scene. None of the material deleted was concerned with President Roosevelt or U.S. Government policy or problems. The same applies to the following document in which I have made one deletion of a passage concerned solely with Norwegian matters:

January 30, 1941

I saw the King of Norway this morning at his house, the Norwegian Embassy, 10 Palace Green, Kensington, W.8. Dr. Beneš, the former President of Czechoslovakia, was just coming out. I just had a chance to shake hands with him.

The King told me something of his flight from Norway and mentioned the fact that it was impossible for women and children to follow him, and that is why he ordered the Crown Princess and her two children to leave and go into Sweden. The same thing applied to Mrs. Harriman, who he was sure could not stand the arduousness of the retreat and he asked that she too leave for Sweden. He seemed to have a very warm feeling in his heart for Mrs. Harriman. ·

The King was a tall man and spoke very vigorously and in perfect English. He deprecated his own part in the whole affair and said that Norway could not have resisted unless the Norwegian people had wished to resist and without their support he could never be carrying on a government here. He said he tried to impress on the 30,000 sailors of the merchant marine that they were not working for their employers but really working for the rehabilitation of Norway.

He expressed great appreciation of the kindness of the British Government and his very high regard for the spirit of the British people.

He asked me to give the President his warmest thanks not only for his kindness to his family, but for the warm sympathy which America had for Norway.

When Roosevelt had first announced the Hopkins mission at a press conference he said that the trip would last no more than two weeks. It lasted nearly six weeks. Hopkins wanted to stay on and the President cabled him permission to do so, adding, "Do get some sleep!" Roosevelt told Hopkins to inform the Former Naval Person that he hoped for action on the Lend-Lease Bill some time between February 20 and March 1 but that he had made arrangements to enable nearly all the British orders to go through in the meantime. He said that the general situation in the United States was very encouraging, and wished Hopkins the best of luck. January 30 was Roosevelt's fifty-ninth birthday and Hopkins cabled that he wished he could be with him for the annual dinner of the Cuff Links Gang but that, even though absent, he could be counted on at the proper moment to raise his glass and drink to the long life and good health of the President of the United States.

Hopkins spent three week ends with Churchill at Chequers and one with Beaverbrook at his place, Cherkley, near Leatherhead. Churchill invited Hopkins for this one, too, but Willkie was also to be there and Hopkins felt (probably correctly) that Willkie would prefer not to have him present when he was engaging in intimate talks with Churchill. There is record of only one meeting of Hopkins and Willkie in London, reported in a cable to the President:

Last night I saw Wendell Willkie. He told me that he believes the opposition to Lend Lease is going to be vehemently expressed and it should not be underrated under any circumstances. It is his belief that the main campaign against the Bill will be directed from Chicago and heavily financed. As perhaps he told you it is his opinion that Herbert Hoover is the real brains behind this opposition. Willkie said he hoped that you would make a radio speech, preferably from Chicago, and thereby take your case right to the people. He said that he himself might make some speeches after he returns home in about two weeks. He said that he approved the Bill with some amendments but did not specify what they were. He is receiving all the attentions which the British know so well how to provide for distinguished guests. I shall have further observations to make on Willkie's visit here when I see you.

Hopkins had imagined that life in England was fraught with hardship as well as danger during the Blitz and he was surprised at the amount of comfort which he at least enjoyed. He discovered, as did thousands of other Americans who were to come to London in the next five years, that living conditions in Claridge's could hardly be described as "rugged." Most of the other London hotels had, of necessity, deteriorated in service and conspicuously in the quality of food. But Claridge's had some sort of official status. Being just around the corner from the American Embassy and Grosvenor Square (later known as "Eisenhowerplatz") it was usually housing one or more American missions as well as all varieties of royalty in exile and Allied military leaders and even, now and then, a few fortunate natives. Its service was of prewar standard and the meals served in the rooms were much more interesting though no more nourishing than the ordinary English fare. Hopkins questioned the waiters about this, asking them to tell him in detail what their families had to eat at home. They were glad to tell him, and they found the former W.P.A. Administrator quick to understand. One of the waiters, Wilfred Harold Hall, told me, "Mr. Hopkins was very genial—considerate—if I may say so, lovable—quite different from other Ambassadors we've had here." Hopkins awoke at 7:30 and his standard breakfast order was "Coffee, toast and whatever you've got in the way of fruit," which generally turned out to be a sour compote of plums. Hopkins received gifts of such rare items as eggs (ordinarily the ration of eggs was one or two a month) from friends who had country places, but he generally gave these away to the staff. He wanted to be scrupulous in avoiding special privileges, but that was obviously impossible.

His room was always a mess, with papers, some of them highly secret, littered about. He had not yet learned the meaning of that awesome word, Security, and he caused plenty of alarm in the staff of the Embassy and the F.B.I. men and, no doubt, among the British who made it a point to watch such things. The hotel valets, when they could persuade him to part with a wrinkled suit for pressing, often found the pockets stuffed with secret papers, as well as his wallet and passport, which he had forgotten. (There was a story in Washington during the war that Hopkins once kept an unopened cable from Stalin in the pocket of his old bathrobe for three weeks, but that unfortunately is apocryphal.) One Claridge valet, Albert Perry, told me that he always tried to be on hand when Mr. Hopkins was going out so that he could straighten his collar and tie. Hopkins accepted these ministrations meekly, saying, "Oh, yes— I've got to remember I'm in London now—I've got to look dignified." Another valet, James Denyer, learning early in the morning that Hopkins would not be leaving the hotel before lunch time, swiped his old felt hat and made an unsuccessful attempt to steam it and block it into some semblance of shape.

The only real hardship that Hopkins experienced in living conditions in England was at Chequers, the official country seat of Prime Ministers. Hopkins voted that the coldest house he had ever visited. Although Churchill seemed to thrive there in his siren suit, Hopkins seldom took his overcoat off. His favorite haunt was the downstairs bathroom, the only room where the "central heating" was detectable. He would go there and sit reading newspapers and dispatches; but he wore his overcoat even there. He was enormously popular with his British hosts who like Americans best when they are making the least effort to be anything else. Hopkins naturally and easily conformed to the essential Benjamin Franklin tradition of American diplomacy, acting on the conviction that when an American representative approaches his opposite numbers in friendly countries with the standard striped-pants frigidity, the strict observance of protocol and the amenities, and a studied air of lip-curling suspicion, he is not really representing America—not, at any rate, the America of which Franklin D. Roosevelt was President. Hopkins' approach to Britain in the Blitz was fundamentally the same as his approach to southern Illinois in the great flood or to the Connecticut coast in the hurricane: all he knew was that here were human beings, friends of ours, who were in trouble, and it was his job to find out what they needed and to get it for them. He had the same essential attitude when he went to Moscow in July, 1941.

He wrote this record of one week end at Chequers:

This morning I have awakened on a cold, dreary morning—and the formal garden of this lovely old place seems very unhappy under the onslaughts of wind and snow and cold. I have just finished my breakfast in bed—of kidney and bacon and prunes—the papers have been read telling of Halifax's arrival and the President's personal welcome. This will please the P.M. no end.

I have just read the amazing document given to me last night. It is a war cabinet document of 17 pages printed on light green paper—8x14—and contains the principal telegrams relating to operations in the Middle East exchanged between the Prime Minister of the Defense and the Commander in Chief—Middle East together with certain telegrams from Secretary of State for War and the Chiefs of Staff. It includes the general directives to Wavell written by the P.M.—laying the Middle East campaign out in detail. When you realize that this directive was written and indeed ordered in September 1940—whilst Britain was fighting for her life—it gives some indication of Churchill's boldness—daring and determination. Italy invades Greece—precious planes must be taken away to bolster the Greeks—and guns too—but the P.M. ever urging Wavell to press on—planes desperately needed in England rushed to Wavell's support by the P.M.'s insistent orders—the P.M. impatient—prodding Wavell—but ever giving him his confident support—but Greece must be supported for political reasons and Wavell grudgingly agrees for these are explicit orders from the Minister of Defense—but the "Compass" has been made and the personal tho authoritative telegrams show the ever increasing pressure on Italy.

Dec. 18 '40 P.M. to Wavell

"St. Matthew, Chapter 7, Verse 7—the verse reads 'Ask, and it shall be given to you; seek, and ye shall find, knock and it shall be opened unto you.'"

Dec. 19 Wavell to P.M.

"St. James, Chap. 1, Verse 17—first part. More aircraft our immediate need. The verse reads 'Every good gift and every perfect gift is from above, and cometh down from the Father of lights, with whom there is no variableness, neither shadow of turning.'"

A few days later Hopkins filed by cable his full report to the President. It took up some thirty pages of cable forms mostly devoted to details of British requirements. In the first section he said:

In the two weeks since my arrival in England I have spent twelve evenings with Mr. Churchill and I have explored every aspect of our mutual problems with him. I have also had extended conferences with all the Cabinet Ministers and most of the Undersecretaries. I have had long and detailed conferences with the Chief of the Imperial General Staff, Sir John Dill, and with the First Sea Lord, Admiral Pound, and with the Chief of the Air Staff, Sir Charles Portal, and with the Chiefs of the Fighter and Bomber Commands. I have visited Scapa

Flow and the Coast Defenses at Dover and various cities and towns and airfields. They have given me complete access to all confidential material which is concerned with my mission here. I believe that insofar as it is possible to get a picture of the situation here in a short time, I have got a reasonably clear perception not only of the physical defenses of Britain but of the opinions of the men who are directing the forces of this nation. Your "former Naval person" is not only the Prime Minister, he is the directing force behind the strategy and the conduct of the war in all its essentials. He has an amazing hold on the British people of all classes and groups. He has particular strength both with the military establishments and the working people. The most important single observation I have to make is most of the Cabinet and all of the military leaders here believe that invasion is imminent. They are straining every effort night and day to meet this. They believe that it may come at any moment, but not later than May 1st. They believe that it will certainly be an all out attack, including the use of poison gas and perhaps some other new weapons that Germany may have developed. The spirit of this people and their determination to resist invasion is beyond praise. No matter how fierce the attack may be you can be sure that they will resist it, and effectively. The Germans will have to do more than kill a few hundred thousand people here before they can defeat Britain. I therefore cannot urge too strongly that any action you may take to meet the immediate needs here must be based on the assumption that invasion will come before May 1st. If Germany fails to win this invasion then I believe her sun is set. I am convinced that if we act boldly and promptly on a few major fronts we can get enough material to Britain within the next few weeks to give her the additional strength she needs to turn back Hitler. . . . I read in the papers that you are sick in bed with flu. You can be sure there are many people here who hope as I do that you will take good care of yourself.

In the remaining cables Hopkins stated Britain's specific requirements and made his recommendations for meeting them. When Herschel Johnson read these cables as they passed over his desk in the Embassy, he was amazed by the accuracy of Hopkins' reports and even more by his disregard for the taboo of isolationism. Hopkins later drew up the following memorandum for the President, summarizing his recommendations for aid to Britain:

(1) 10 destroyers a month beginning April 1st. Destroyers to be reconditioned in the United States—reconditioning to begin immediately.
(2) The urgent need of more merchant shipping at once. British cannot wait until new ships are built.
(3) 50 PBY Planes in addition to the PBY which the British are receiving on their own account; fully equipped with radio, depth charges, bombs, guns and ammunition. Adequate operating spare supplies. Urgent need for crews.

(4) There are 29 engineless Lockheed planes in England. They need 58 Wright 1820 engines at once.

(5) There are 100 Curtiss Tomahawks without propellers in England. 764 fifty caliber and 1000 thirty caliber machine guns required to complete armament. Curtiss Tomahawks already in England.

(6) Consideration to be given immediately to the replacement of fifty caliber guns manufactured by Colt which are unsatisfactory with the same gun which has already been manufactured by our own arsenals.

(7) 20 million rounds of fifty caliber ammunition and as many extra fifty caliber gun barrels as are available urgently needed.

(8) The maximum number of B-17, BS C's or D's in addition to the 20 already agreed upon to be sent to England immediately. Planes should be sent completely ready for immediate operation, including spare parts, bombs and ammunition. Crews urgently needed.

(9) Transfer to the British 200 North American Harvards or Vultee Valiants trainers in excess of all present deliveries.

(10) At least 5 additional civilian flying training schools completely equipped.

(11) Work out plan to ferry bombers to England. This would release nearly 800 British R.A.F. personnel.

(12) 250,000 Enfield rifles and 50,000,000 rounds of ammunition have been sent.

(13) Give priority to tools for the manufacture of Point 303 rifles for the British. Same applies to 303 ammunition.

(14) Send 80 trained observers—half from the factories and half from the Army and Navy—to acquaint Britain with the use of our planes.

Hopkins had further talks with Eden concerning German infiltration in the Balkans which led to the attacks later on Yugoslavia and Greece. Eden reported that the appointment of John G. Winant as American Ambassador would be received very warmly in England and that Colonel William J. Donovan's confidential mission to the Balkans had been most helpful. After a meeting with Eden, Sir Alexander Cadogan, Sir Orme Sargent and Johnson, Hopkins cabled Roosevelt:

Eden told me that he had had a stiff conversation with the Japanese Ambassador here in London yesterday in which he took a very strong line, the main point being that he was asking the Japanese to state what were their real intentions. He informed the Ambassador that the British Government intended to stand for no nonsense in the Far East and British interests there would be protected to the limit if they were attacked. Eden has cabled Halifax about this. He and his colleagues from the foreign office reviewed at length all of the various moves major and minor which they think Japan is making. Eden believes that the Japanese consider the presence of our fleet at Pearl Harbor to be purely a routine matter. Eden is very anxious that we find a way to emphasize our determination to prevent Japan from making further encroachments. He believes that if we take a positive line towards Japan we might make them pause before attacking Hong Kong. I want to emphasize to you the British belief that Japan, under the influence of Germany, is considering making a positive move against British territory in the near future. Eden fears that Japan would be able at least for the time being to cut off the transport route around the Cape from their Thailand bases. From the same bases they could also cut off the route from the Eastern Mediterranean to Australia and New Zealand. Eden believes that a recent temporary blocking of the Suez Canal was a German move to impress the Japanese with their ability to close the Canal.

It seems strange that there was apparently little or no discussion of the Soviet Union as a potential factor during the first Hopkins visit to London, although by then the U.S. Government was in possession of intelligence (which it communicated to the British and Russians) indicating strongly that the direction of Hitler's next major drive would be eastward, and Churchill in a broadcast at the time said, "In order to win the war Hitler must destroy Great Britain. He may carry havoc into the Balkan states; he may tear great provinces out of Russia; he may march to the Caspian; he may march to the gates of India."

In a note written later, Hopkins revealed more of his conversation with Eden than he cared to put in a cable which must necessarily pass through various hands in the Embassy and the State Department before it reached the President:

Eden asked me repeatedly what our country would do if Japan attacked Singapore or the Dutch East Indies, saying it was essential to their policy to know. Of course, it was perfectly clear that neither the President nor Hull could give an adequate answer to the British on that point because the declaration of war is up to Congress, and the isolationists and, indeed, a great part of the American people, would not be interested in a war in the Far East merely because Japan attacked the Dutch.

These urgent questions by the British as to American intentions in the event of further Japanese aggression in the Far East were repeated many times during subsequent months but they remained unanswered until the day of Pearl Harbor.

At the conclusion of his extended series of cables to Roosevelt, Hopkins said, "I believe that I have in no way overstated Britain's need. In fact, the cable provides an altogether inadequate means of expressing the determination of the British to defend this island and finally to win this war. It has been emphasized more than ever in my mind that Churchill is leading this country magnificently in every respect and that the whole nation is behind him. I hesitate to urge you in matters about which I know you are already convinced, or to presume to advise you since you have seen the needs here far more clearly than anyone else in the United States. But I feel sure that there has been no time in your Administration when the actions that you have taken and the words that you have spoken have meant so much to the cause of freedom. Your decisive action now can mean the difference between defeat and victory in this country."

Because of the very nature of his assignment in England, Hopkins' associations were almost entirely on the higher official levels; he had little opportunity to move about freely, as it would have been his natural inclination to do, and talk to the people themselves. (Willkie was notably successful in doing that and received a great deal of publicity which was far more valuable to Britain than to himself.) On at least one occasion Hopkins managed to get out and walk the streets at night during an air raid and, when a German bomb was falling near at hand, he was pushed flat on his face in the gutter by an experienced companion.

However, if he did not get to meet the people face to face, he had a very large number of letters which must have reminded him of the type of mail that flowed into W.P.A. Headquarters. There were letters asking him whether he was related to the Hopkinses of Somersetshire; letters describing new weapons that would win the war between dawn and dusk; letters complaining that the Royal Society for the Prevention of Cruelty to Animals was not doing enough to protect dogs and cats during air raids; letters enclosing stamps for President Roosevelt's collection and appeals to Mrs. Roosevelt to send over some warm clothes for the children; there were invitations to visit "an average English home" and to address this or that local group on the subject of social progress; there was one letter which declared definitely that England would never be victimized by the bloodstained American dollar, and one from the ninety-three-year-old widow of an American Civil War veteran who complained that her pension checks were being lost at sea through U-boat action and would Mr. Hopkins please look the matter up on his return to Washington? Lady Astor sent him a brisk message, inviting him for a week end at Cliveden, informing him that he had been making great mistakes in the selection of people that he had seen and assuring him that she could provide much better company than he had picked up thus far. (He had to decline this invitation.)

On Saturday, February 8, Hopkins went to Chequers to say good-by to the Churchill family. They had received word that day that the House of Representatives had passed the Lend-Lease Bill by a vote of 260 to 165. The Prime Minister was working on a speech which he was to broadcast the following evening to the entire world, but with American public opinion the principal target. This was to be Churchill's contribution to the Lend-Lease debate in the Senate and he consulted Hopkins on many of its points. There was by now an intimacy between the two men which developed to such a degree that it is no exaggeration to say that Churchill reposed the same confidence in Hopkins that Roosevelt did. In the lengthy discussions of this important speech Hopkins was fascinated to observe Churchill's methods of speech preparation, which were very different from Roosevelt's. Trained to think on his feet by his forty years of give-and-take debate in the House of Commons, he usually dictated his speeches pacing up and down, acting out his points as though his audience were already there, sometimes keeping at it for hours, occasionally referring to notes that he had been making in preceding days or weeks, but most of the time carrying the material in his head. To Hopkins it was an astonishing performance.

When Hopkins left Chequers late Saturday night he took a special train to Bournemouth. He was accompanied again by Brendan Bracken and Commander Thompson, representing the Prime Minister, and by a British security officer, Lieutenant Anthony McComas, who traveled all the way to Washington with him to carry and safeguard his by now voluminous papers. Hopkins by now had learned enough about security to take no chances of leaving vital documents lying around a room in the Hotel Aziz in spy-infested Lisbon. For he was going back by no means empty handed; the British had turned over to him some of their most important technical secrets which were now made available to the U.S. Armed Forces.

In a cable to Roosevelt Churchill said that Hopkins had been "a great comfort and encouragement to everyone he has met. One can easily see why he is so close to you."

Arriving in Bournemouth Sunday morning Hopkins found that weather conditions prevented a flight to Lisbon that day. He made use of the extra time by visiting two government officials who lived in the neighborhood: Colonel J. I. Lewellin, who was Beaverbrook's Parliamentary Secretary and later his successor as Minister of Aircraft Production, and Lord Cranborne, Secretary of State for Dominion Affairs. The Cranbornes told Hopkins that their son, a lieutenant in the Grenadier Guards, was stationed nearby (waiting for the German invasion); so, early the next morning, before his airplane took off, Hopkins went to visit him and was called upon to make an after-breakfast speech to the Guardsmen.

Sunday evening, in the lounge of the Branksome Tower Hotel, Hopkins, Bracken and the rest listened to the broadcast of Churchill's famous "give us the tools and we'll finish the job" speech which Hopkins had seen in preparation the day before. In that speech Churchill said, "It seems now to be certain that the Government and people of the

United States intend to supply us with all that is necessary for victory. In the last war the United States sent two million men across the Atlantic. *But this is not a war of vast armies, firing immense masses of shells at one another.* We do not need the gallant armies which are forming throughout the American Union. We do not need them this year, nor next year; nor any year that I can foresee."

Some suspicious persons considered that statement the ultimate in insincerity. But the sentence which I have italicized represented another expression of Churchill's profound conviction and he stuck to it in the years that followed Pearl Harbor and in the protracted and sometimes bitter arguments over General Marshall's plan to end the war in Europe by a frontal attack against the German armies in the West. It was most certainly no fault of Churchill's that two American Expeditionary Forces went into France, north and south, in the summer of 1944.

Hopkins traveled back by way of the new Clipper route—from Lisbon to Bolama in Portuguese Guinea on the West Coast of Africa and thence to Brazil and north over the Caribbean. This was the first air route linking the four continents; its establishment was the first pioneering move toward exploitation of one of the most vital strategic lines of communication in the Second World War—the route across the South Atlantic at its narrowest, across Africa to the Persian Gulf and thence to the Soviet Union or to India and the Far East, with spur lines via North Africa to the United Kingdom or to points in the Mediterranean basin. This was the network of air lanes that Roosevelt was determined to control before Hitler could, for they were all two-way streets.

When he arrived in New York, Hopkins had a talk with John G. Winant who was about to fly to take up his post in London. Winant did not need to be told that he faced one of the most difficult jobs ever undertaken, involving dangers far worse than those presented incidentally by the German bombs. He approached that job with the eager enthusiasm and the altruism and the quiet courage which distinguished him to the tragic end of his life.

Back in the White House, Hopkins brought forth among his souvenirs a bottle of pills Churchill had given him with the assurance that he himself took them frequently and found them very bracing. Roosevelt asked what was in them and, when Hopkins said he hadn't the faintest idea, ordered that some of them be given to Dr. McIntire for analysis. The analysis was duly sent to Hopkins from the Naval Medical Center and he noted, "I am told by the Navy that the whole prescription is a conglomeration of everything that couldn't do anybody much harm. It couldn't possibly do them very much good, either."

Hopkins told Roosevelt that just about the most difficult problem he had to face in England was explaining our constitutional provision that only Congress can declare war. Churchill understood this—perhaps he had learned it at his mother's knee—but there were others of eminent rank in the British Government who couldn't seem to get it through their heads. "But surely," they would say, "your President understands the situation. He is the leader of Congress. Surely, they will loyally follow him if he says that the time has come for the United States to enter the war."

Despite all the explanations given by Hopkins—and, after him, by Winant, Harriman and other Americans—there persisted the belief in London that Roosevelt would have the United States in the war by May 1, 1941. This strange misapprehension may have been due in part to the prediction made by Willkie, as part of his "campaign oratory," that if Roosevelt were re-elected we would be at war in April. It may also have been due to the eternal conviction that history repeats itself: there was the vivid memory of the Democratic party's campaign slogan of 1916, "He kept us out of war," and of Woodrow Wilson's contradictory action the following April.

Had those who nourished their morale with this wishful thinking been familiar with Roosevelt's real character, they would have known that the last thing he wanted to do was repeat any of the history of the First World War or of the phony peace that followed it.

CHAPTER XII

The Common-Law Alliance

ALTHOUGH debate over the Lend-Lease Bill created considerable uproar for two months—and although so distinguished a citizen as President Robert M. Hutchins of the University of Chicago predicted that with its passage "the American people are about to commit suicide" —there was little serious argument over the essential principle of giving aid to Britain, Greece or China. The big sticking point was over the provision that Lend Lease could be extended to "any country whose defense the President deems vital to the defense of the United States." That put the decision entirely in the President's hands; it meant that, if he so decided (as he eventually did), aid could be rendered to the Soviet Union. That was what the isolationists feared most; even those who grudgingly conceded that perhaps Britain might be deserving of some charity were horrified at the thought that American taxpayers might be called upon to pay for supplies for the Red Army. There was a determined fight on this provision, and some of Roosevelt's more timid friends urged him to compromise on terms that would exclude the Soviet Union; but he was firm on this point, for it then seemed possible if not probable that Russia would be attacked by Germany or Japan or both and would be desperately in need of American help. The Administration leaders in the Senate, of whom James F. Byrnes was the most vigorous and the shrewdest strategist, waged the battle on the President's lines, and on Saturday night, March 8, the Bill finally passed the upper house by a vote of 60 to 31. This was a historic victory for Roosevelt. Churchill called it "The Third Climacteric" of the Second World War. (The first two were the fall of France and the Battle of Britain, the fourth was the attack on Russia and the fifth Pearl Harbor.) When word of the vote was sent from the Capitol to the White House, Hopkins immediately picked up the telephone and put through a call to Chequers. Because of the time difference, it was past even Churchill's bedtime. Hopkins spoke to one of the secretaries who said the Prime Minister was asleep and should he be awakened? Hopkins said never mind—to give him the report of the Senate vote in the morning. When he got it, Churchill immediately cabled Hopkins: "The strain has been serious so I thank God for your news."

A few days later, Hopkins wrote Churchill:

I seem to have had no opportunity to write letters since I returned, because of a multitude of things that have interfered. This note is just to tell you how greatly I appreciate the many courtesies which you and Mrs. Churchill showed me while in England. I shall ever be grateful to you for your many kindnesses to me.

I am going off with the President on a short trip in the South. I hope by the time we get back the appropriation bill will have been signed. In the meantime, I have worked out a scheme with Purvis last night which will keep your orders moving. I have agreed to take on, in behalf of the President, a responsibility here for the promotion of the whole of our aid to Britain program and I am trying to avoid getting my mind cluttered up with any other problems. I am sure the country is behind the President and I have great hopes of our ability to be of very genuine help to you.

It looks very much as though we are going to get four million tons of brand new shipping out of the Maritime Commission and I have high hopes on other fronts which are a bit premature to discuss now. The President is in good spirits and ever so determined.

I have seen Lord Halifax several times and I am in daily touch with your Purchasing Commission. Under my new responsibilities, all British purchasing requests are now routed through me.

Morgenthau, Stimson and Knox and Hull are a tower of strength and you and your country have innumerable friends here.

I find my thoughts constantly with you in the desperate struggle which I am sure is going to result, in the last analysis, in your victory.

Do remember me ever so cordially to Mrs. Churchill and Mary. I hope to send you some victrola records in a few days and am on the trail of a Stilton cheese.

The day after Roosevelt signed the Lend-Lease Bill, I had dinner with him and Hopkins and Missy LeHand off a card table in the Oval Study. As usual, the talk was wildly irrelevant. After dinner, Hopkins went to his room to work and Toie Bachelder came in to take dictation for the speech the President was to give at the dinner of the White House Correspondents' Association the following Saturday. He had his speech folder in his lap and he started going through it, searching for clippings that he had saved for this opportunity. He had been enormously cheerful at dinner, but now he seemed to have changed to one of his combative moods. He said to me, "I'm going to get really tough in this one. There have been so many lies going around about this Aid-for-the-Democracies bill" (that's what he called it then) "and so many deliberate attempts to scare the people that they have got the main issue all confused. I couldn't answer all these lies while the Bill was still being debated. But now I'm really going to hand it to them."

He then started to dictate, referring constantly to the clippings, dragging out one after another of the vicious charges that had been flung about so recklessly in the Congress and in the Press during the past months. It was one of the most scathing, most vindictive speeches I have ever heard. He never mentioned a newspaper or an individual by name—it was always "a certain columnist" or "a certain Senator" or "certain Republican orators." After an hour or so, he grew weary of it and I said good night and went to talk to Hopkins, to tell him the nature of the dictated material and to confess that it made me feel very depressed. I thought it was a terrible mistake for the President to take that petulant tone. Now, it seemed to me, in the hour of his great triumph, it would be in character for him to be magnanimous, and reassert his faith in the wisdom and the courage of the people who had accepted the revolutionary doctrine of Lend Lease. Hopkins listened to me and then said, sharply, "You ought to know that is precisely what he will do. He has no intention of using all that irritable stuff you say he dictated. He's just getting it off his chest. It has been rankling all this time and now he's rid of it. He probably feels a lot better for it and he'll have a fine sleep." Hopkins then spoke in a way that was very unusual for him: "You and I are for Roosevelt because he's a great spiritual figure, because he's an idealist, like Wilson, and he's got the guts to drive through against any opposition to realize those ideals. Oh—he sometimes tries to appear tough and cynical and flippant, but that's an act he likes to put on, especially at press conferences. He wants to make the boys think he's hard-boiled. Maybe he fools some of them, now and then—but don't ever let him fool you, or you won't be any use to him. You can see the real Roosevelt when he comes out with something like the Four Freedoms. And don't get the idea that those are any catch phrases. *He believes them!* He believes they can be practically attained. That's what you and I have got to remember in everything we may be able to do for him. Oh—there are a lot of small people in this town who are constantly trying to cut him down to their size, and sometimes they have some influence. But it's your job and it's mine—as long as we're around here —to keep reminding him that he's unlimited, and that's the way he's got to talk because that's the way he's going to act. Maybe we'll make ourselves unpopular now and then—but not in the long run, because he knows what he really is, even if he doesn't like to admit it to you or me or anybody."

I don't think that the President ever referred again to the draft he had dictated that evening. On the final day of preparation of the speech, we were having lunch off trays in the Cabinet Room—it was corned beef hash with poached egg, followed by chocolate pudding—and Hopkins suggested that, since Churchill had made so many respectful references to Roosevelt in his speeches, perhaps the President might care to mention him. So Roosevelt dictated, "In this historic crisis, Britain is blessed with a brilliant leader in Winston Churchill." He thought that over for a moment, then added, "Make that 'a brilliant and a *great* leader.'"

In the speech as finally delivered, Roosevelt spoke with an unusual amount of emotion in his voice. He was stirring because he himself seemed deeply stirred. There was no evidence of petty vindictiveness now. He started by praising the co-operation given him throughout his years in office by his hosts, the press correspondents. He spoke of the mistakes of the past and said, "That is water over the dam. Do not let us waste time reviewing the past, or fixing or dodging the blame for it. We, the American people, are writing new history today." He gave the British people the specific assurance for which they had been waiting, saying, "The British people and their Grecian allies need ships. From America, they will get ships. They need planes. From America they will get planes. They need food. From America they will get food. They need tanks and guns and ammunition and supplies of all kinds. From America they will get tanks and guns and ammunition and supplies of all kinds." (In the case of Greece, however, the Nazis got there before any of the American supplies did.)

Roosevelt designated Hopkins to "advise and assist" him on Lend Lease but never formally gave him the title of Administrator. However, Hopkins performed that function. This was the first official government post he had held since his resignation as Secretary of Commerce seven months previously. During that time he had actually been a private citizen with no title and no pay, except the per diem allowance on his trip to England. When Roosevelt announced that Hopkins was back on the public payroll he said that his role would be merely that of a "bookkeeper," recording the various transactions and watching the balances but exerting no authority over the allotment of funds. Roosevelt had said much the same thing about the nature of Hopkins' job when W.P.A. was started, and the analogy was even less accurate now than it had been then. The Lend-Lease appointment brought Hopkins out of the shadows in which he had dwelt as a mysterious confidant and made him, in one huge area of authority, the *de facto* Deputy President. The nine billion dollars expended on relief appeared trivial by comparison with the budget for the new and revolutionary program. Congress first appropriated seven billions for Lend Lease, and by the time Japan surrendered the appropriations had amounted to over sixty billions. Representative John W. Taber, the redoubtable Senior Minority Leader and

later Chairman of the House Appropriations Committee, roared in the
Congress that this appointment was "the worst blow the President has
struck at national defense." He said that Hopkins' record as Administrator of W.P.A. was, "the grossest record of incompetence of any of
the notorious incompetence that this Administration has produced."

Joseph Alsop and Robert Kintner had this to say in their column:

> Hopkins is a completely changed man. Before he went to London
> he was only just beginning to grasp the war picture, and was still an
> advocate of compromise and slow-motion action. As all major policy
> must be passed on at the White House, the White House is inevitably
> the major bottleneck in the Government. Hopkins, living in the White
> House, always telling the President to go slow, was a major obstruc-
> tion in the bottleneck. His only trouble was, however, that he had not
> come into sufficiently direct contact with the facts.
>
> His trip to Britain was widely represented as political in purpose,
> and part of a grand international plot between British and American
> left-wingers. Actually, of his less than a month on British soil, he
> passed nearly three weeks living in the same house with Winston
> Churchill, who is hardly a leading left-winger. On many days, he
> started with Churchill at breakfast, and stayed with him until it was
> time for a last Churchillian cigar, a nightcap and a final chat about the
> day's events. Thus he formed an intense admiration for Churchill, the
> man. Thus also, he acquired a grasp of the war picture far more
> direct and complete than that of any other man in the President's en-
> tourage. Since his return to this country, far from being an obstruction
> in the White House bottleneck, he has shown a fuller sense of urgency,
> and has pushed affairs forward faster than most of his coworkers.

Hopkins was not, as Alsop and Kintner stated, a "completely changed"
man. He had been drastically reoriented, to be sure, but his method
of attack on the manifold problems at hand was essentially that of the
New Deal days. Now, instead of breadlines, droughts, floods or hurricanes, he was confronting the greatest disaster that had ever befallen
the human race. Hopkins had to aid Roosevelt in promoting in the American people an entirely new conception of their responsibilities and their
capabilities, and this was a job entirely congenial to one of his peculiar
temperament. It was at this time that Secretary Stimson noted in his
diary his thought that it is "a Godsend that Harry Hopkins is at the
White House."

Hopkins' position became more violently controversial than ever, for
his activities cut across many lines of authority in Washington. Lend
Lease involved not only war weapons but merchant shipping, vehicles,
food, fuel, industrial equipment, innumerable services and, most importantly, much of the day-to-day business of diplomacy. This was when
Hopkins became identified as "Roosevelt's own personal Foreign Office."
It was obvious that Lend Lease should become the most vital element

in the relations between the United States and all the Allied combatant nations and many neutrals as well, with the result that more and more foreign missions in Washington were conducting, or attempting to conduct, their most important business directly with Hopkins, thus by-passing the State Department. This was a development which, quite understandably, did not set well with Cordell Hull. The predicament was best demonstrated by the appointment of W. Averell Harriman as "Expediter" of Lend Lease, with the rank of Minister, in London.

The Harriman Mission was housed in the Embassy in Grosvenor Square, but it was largely independent of Embassy authority and Harriman was able to report directly to Hopkins through Naval communications rather than through the usual State Department channels. Although Winant and Harriman were good friends, neither of whom had become infected with the bureaucrat's occupational disease of jurisdictional jealousy, the situation between them became uncomfortably embarrassing. For, although Winant had the superior rank and the dignity and prestige—as well as the enormous affection of the British people—it was Harriman who had the principal, personal contacts with No. 10 Downing Street on the one hand and the White House on the other. Churchill left relations with Ambassadors largely to the Foreign Office but Lend Lease was a matter of wartime life or death and came directly into his department as Minister of Defense. Furthermore, it was evident that Harriman was Hopkins' man and thus provided an easy, direct and secure pipeline of communication.

There was started at this time correspondence without precedent: an informal, off-the-record but none the less official correspondence between the heads of two governments through a third party, Hopkins, in whose discretion and judgment each had complete confidence. Time and again, when the Prime Minister wanted to sound out the President's views on some new move, he would address a private cable to Hopkins saying, in effect, "If you think well of it, perhaps you would ask our great friend for his opinion on the following proposal . . . etc." Hopkins, having consulted Roosevelt, might decide that he did not "think well of it" and would reply that this did not seem an opportune moment to submit the proposal. Or, if it were approved, Hopkins would reply, "It is felt here that you should go ahead with your proposal to . . . etc."

Since almost every message in this unique correspondence touched in some way on military estimates and plans, the security authorities required that it must pass through military channels, the State Department codes being considered vulnerable. This applied to many of Winant's messages as well as Harriman's, and the Ambassador himself communicated more and more with Hopkins through Navy or Army or even sometimes British channels. Here again the State Department was by-passed, and it provided inadequate balm to Hull's pride to receive occasional polite notes from Hopkins enclosing copies of cables "for your information." It was all irregular, but so was the fundamental situation in which the United States Government found itself at that time.

The Webster's Dictionary definition of "common-law marriage" is:

> An agreement between a man and a woman to enter into the marriage relation without ecclesiastical or civil ceremony, such agreement being provable by the writings, declarations, or conduct of the parties. In many jurisdictions, it is not recognized.

That definition would seem to apply perfectly to the alliance which existed between the United States and Great Britain following the passage of Lend Lease. It was certainly "not recognized" in such "jurisdictions" as the Congress, and if the isolationists had known the full extent of it their demands for the impeachment of President Roosevelt would have been a great deal louder. But it was a fact of incalculable importance in the whole process of American preparedness for war. By the spring of 1941, six months before the United States entered the war, the following developments, among others, were in progress:

1. The exchange of scientific information—on all manner of subjects, including atomic energy and radar—had started with Sir Henry Tizard's Mission (approved by Roosevelt) to Washington in September, 1940. During his London trip, Hopkins had urged much closer collaboration and fuller exchange in this field and, shortly after his return, President James B. Conant of Harvard went to England as representative of Vannevar Bush's Research Council.

2. The pooling of military intelligence had started, largely through the efforts of General Marshall and his Assistant Chief of Staff, General George V. Strong. (The U.S. Navy remained for a long time reluctant to pool its own intelligence with anyone, even with the U.S. Army.)

3. There was, by Roosevelt's order and despite State Department qualms, effectively close co-operation between J. Edgar Hoover and the F.B.I. and British security services under the direction of a quiet Canadian, William Stephenson. The purpose of this co-operation was the detection and frustration of espionage and sabotage activities in the Western Hemisphere by agents of Germany, Italy and Japan, and also of Vichy France, Franco's Spain and, before Hitler turned eastward, the Soviet Union. It produced some remarkable results which were incalculably valuable, including the thwarting of attempted Nazi Putsche in Bolivia, in the heart of South America, and in Panama. Hoover was later decorated by the British and Stephenson by the U.S. Government for exploits which could hardly be advertised at the time.

4. A steady stream of American military and civilian specialists, mostly technical, had started to England, to study British and instruct in American methods, and even to test the performance of American air-

planes and other weapons under actual combat conditions. (For instance: the armament of the B-17 Flying Fortress was substantially increased as a result of its first encounters in 1941 with the Luftwaffe.)

5. The U.S. Atlantic Fleet was constantly being strengthened, with some new ships and some transferred from the Pacific, for the purpose of guarding the sea lanes in the Western Atlantic and thereby relieving the British Navy of a large area of responsibility.

6. Plans were drawn up for the occupation by U.S. Forces of Greenland, Iceland, the Azores and Martinique. (There were other plans for operations all over creation, but these were the nearest to fruition; in the cases of Greenland and Iceland, of course, they were carried out.)

7. Damaged British warships were repaired in American shipyards.

8. R.A.F. pilots and air-crews were trained in the U.S.

9. Most important of all—the first American-British staff talks had been instituted for the formation of joint grand strategy in the event of American entry into the war. These talks started on a purely exploratory basis in mid-August, 1940, when Marshall and Stårk sent a mission headed by Admiral Ghormley, General Delos C. Emmons (of the Air Corps) and General Strong to London. They arrived in time to occupy front-row seats at the Battle of Britain and the Blitz. Their principal function was to gain the fullest possible information as to Britain's strength and prospects, as well as estimates of German strength and intentions, the main purpose being, as Samuel Eliot Morison has pointed out, to avoid the disastrous mistakes made by the King of the Belgians the previous winter and spring when, in consequence of an overscrupulous regard for neutrality, he refused to conduct any conversations with British and French authorities on plans in the event of a German invasion of Belgium. In the midst of these London talks, on September 27, came the announcement of the signing of the Tripartite Treaty in Berlin, whereby Japan recognized German and Italian leadership in creating the "New Order" in Europe and Germany and Italy recognized Japan's leadership in organizing the "Greater East Asia Co-Prosperity Sphere." That presented so obvious a challenge to the United States that many of Roosevelt's advisers, among them Cordell Hull, urged that the staff talks assume a more formal and constructive character; but an election was coming up, and charges were being made that Roosevelt was involving the nation in "secret treaties," and he would not agree to any extension of the nebulous authority granted to the Ghormley-Emmons-Strong mission. Indeed, Roosevelt at that time did not even want to discuss any of the long-range plans for possible operations. He was too busy denying the reports that "the boys are already on the transports."

In mid-November, Stark prepared a memorandum for Secretary Knox in which he stated, as our major national objectives, defense of the Western Hemisphere and "prevention of the disruption of the

British Empire, with all that such a consummation implies." He believed that it would ultimately be necessary for America "to send large air and land forces to Europe or Africa, or both, and to participate strongly in this land offensive." In these tremendous matters, Stark's thinking closely paralleled Marshall's, but it was by no means typical of the Pacific-minded Navy point of view. Admiral Harry E. Yarnell wrote in a memorandum:

> The following are considered the fundamentals of adequate national defense:—
> (a) A navy and air force equal to that of any nation or coalition that threatens our security.
> (b) An army adequate to garrison outlying bases and to provide a highly mobile, fully equipped force of about 600,000 men, thoroughly trained in modern warfare. *We should never send an army of millions abroad in any future war.*
> The navy and air force must be adequate to carry on offensive war in enemy waters. *The frontier must be the enemy coast.*

I have italicized two sentences in the above because they expressed a theory with which, I believe, Roosevelt agreed at that time—and so, in a way, did Churchill. Both of them thought in terms of the relentless application of superior sea power augmented by ever-increasing air power and both shied away from contemplation of great masses of land forces coming into competition beyond the "frontier" on the enemy coast.

Churchill's reasons for this were obvious: Britain could never hope to meet Germany on equal terms on land; therefore she must rely on (a) superior sea power, (b) comparable air power, (c) longer endurance due to superior moral strength, and (d) sharper wits. Roosevelt, representing a nation which could far outmatch Germany in manpower and resources, still thought in strictly Navy terms, his concept of logistics beginning at the home base and ending at the strip of hostile shore line secured by the Marines; it was a long time before he could adjust himself to the Army concept, which began at the beachhead base, maintained by a steady, sea-borne "supply train," and from there penetrated tens or hundreds or thousands of miles into enemy territory, ending only with attainment of the ultimate objectives (Berlin and Tokyo) which represented total victory.

The real American-British staff talks began in Washington the end of January, 1941. The chief American representatives were Admirals Ghormley and Richmond Kelly Turner and Captains A. G. Kirk, C. M. Cooke and DeWitt Ramsey, for the Navy, and Generals S. D. Embick, Sherman Miles and L. T. Gerow, and Colonel J. T. McNarney, for the Army. The British representatives were Admirals R. M. Bellairs and V. H. Danckwerts, General E. L. Morris and Air Commodore J. C. Slessor. The opening sessions were addressed by Marshall and Stark, who urged that utmost secrecy surround these conferences, since any publicity might provide ammunition for the opponents of Lend Lease and produce other consequences which "might well be disastrous."

The members of the British delegation wore civilian clothes and disguised themselves as "technical advisers to the British Purchasing Commission." It seemed virtually impossible to keep the conferences entirely hidden from the prying eyes of the press, especially in view of the fact that, where American reporters failed, Axis agents were glad to help out with tips dispatched by way of South America to the D.N.B. News Agency in Berlin, or to the Domeii News Agency in Tokyo, and thence broadcast to the world; however, there were no serious leaks.

The staff talks continued until March 29 and produced a plan, known as ABC—1, which suggested the grand strategy for the war. The basic point was that in the event of Anglo-American involvement in war with both Germany and Japan, the concentration of force should be on *Germany first*, while a containing war of attrition was to be waged against Japan pending Germany's defeat. (This was precisely in line with the conclusions reached by Marshall and Stark months previously.) The primary measures to be taken against Germany were:

1. Blockade.
2. Constantly intensified aerial bombing.
3. Subversive activities and propaganda. (No ground operations planned at this time.)

The conference in Washington also provided for continuing joint Anglo-American military missions as a focus for exchange of information and co-ordination of plans; the British Joint Staff Mission accordingly established in Washington provided the working basis for the Combined Chiefs of Staff organization which came into being a month after Pearl Harbor.

These staff talks, and the complete interchange of expert opinions as well as facts that they produced, provided the highest degree of *strategic preparedness* that the United States or probably any other nonaggressor nation has ever had before entry into war. This made for far greater efficiency in all planning of Army and Navy organization and training, of production and, most importantly, of administration of Lend Lease. Some system of priorities could now be established for the guidance of Hopkins in his constant negotiations with Robert Patterson and James Forrestal, the procurement authorities of the War and Navy Departments, and with the Office of Production Management and the Maritime Commission. Plenty of confusion remained, of course, because no civilian below the highest level could know on what the system of priorities was based; but, at least, it reduced misunderstanding and discord at the top.

Although the common-law alliance involved the United States in no undercover commitments, and no violations of the Constitution, the very existence of any American-British joint plans, however tentative, had to be kept utterly secret. It is an ironic fact that in all probability no great damage would have been done had the details of these plans fallen into the hands of the Germans and the Japanese; whereas, had they fallen into the hands of the Congress and the press, American preparation for war might have been well nigh wrecked and ruined as, indeed, it came perilously close to being when the House of Representatives voted on the extension of Selective Service.

The American historian, Charles A. Beard, who was at this time one of the more reputable proponents of the isolationist policy, has subsequently written a severe indictment of Roosevelt's dealings ("binding agreements") with Britain before Pearl Harbor and with the Soviet Union at Yalta. He has written, "If these precedents are to stand unimpeached and to provide sanctions for the continued conduct of American foreign affairs, the Constitution may be nullified by the President, officials, and officers who have taken the oath, and are under moral obligation to uphold it."

Roosevelt never overlooked the fact that his actions might lead to his immediate or eventual impeachment. Having taken the oath of office as President three times, he knew it by heart, and was well aware that he was sworn not only to "uphold" but to "*defend*" the Constitution of the United States. It was a matter of his own judgment—and the judgment of his advisers whom he was empowered to appoint—as to where that defense should begin. The same independent responsibility has devolved on every Chief Executive in the past—including Abraham Lincoln in 1861—and it will devolve on every Chief Executive in the future unless the Constitution is amended to restrict the present powers and duties of the President.

Roosevelt, before Pearl Harbor, made no "binding agreements" save those authorized under the Lend-Lease law and no secret treaties with Britain nor any other nation which should have been subject to confirmation by the Senate. The plans drawn up at the staff conferences bound nobody. They could have been altered or renounced at any time "in the light of subsequent events" and, in fact, the British expected that Roosevelt and the U.S. Chiefs of Staff would renounce them when extraordinary developments in the Pacific changed drastically the whole global picture.

Whether Roosevelt's judgment was good or bad is, of course, an entirely different question for historians to ponder in their own good time.

CHAPTER XIII

Unlimited Emergency

THE Roosevelt-Churchill meeting which Hopkins had discussed when he went to London in January did not take place as planned in the spring. There were far too many and too critical immediate problems to permit time for talks about long-range prospects and projects. The German Blitzkrieg, appearing more devastating and irresistible than ever, burst through the mountain passes of Yugoslavia and then turned into Greece, as Churchill had predicted it would. The British had to face the grim decision either of leaving the Greeks to their unavoidable fate, or of sending in reinforcements which could not possibly be strong enough to render more than token aid. Churchill chose the latter and more honorable but hopeless alternative, and took the consequences. Greece was overrun with terrifying speed, the remnants of the small British Expeditionary Force were evacuated in a minor Dunkirk, and then the Germans launched their remarkable attack by airborne troops on the strategic island of Crete. The defense of Crete meant far more to the British than the mere saving of prestige involved in the attempt to render aid to a brave Ally, and the defeat administered by the German paratroopers was one of the most decisive and humiliating of the whole war. Serious injury was done to British morale in general and, in particular, disagreeable disputes were provoked between the three British services, Navy, Army and Air Force. Following this disaster, General Rommel, who had taken over command in Africa from the hapless Italians, launched the first of his dashing campaigns and regained all the ground in Libya (except the fortress of Tobruk) that Wavell had captured the previous winter. The British were thrown back into Egypt and their ability to defend the Suez Canal was in considerable doubt.

In the midst of the Greek fighting, Roosevelt and Hopkins read a remarkably prescient memorandum prepared in the Navy Department. It was written by Admiral Richmond Kelly Turner, who was later to become one of the great masters of amphibious warfare in the Mediterranean and the Pacific. He foresaw the ominous possibility that, by June, the British might have been driven out of the Mediterranean and, if that happened, "The German Army will go by sea to Syria, and the end will then be in sight." The last two paragraphs of Turner's memorandum were as follows:

> Because of the present tragic situation of the British Government, I do not recommend troubling them further at this time by informing them as to our opinion on the seriousness of the situation. They realize it pretty well themselves, even though they are somewhat too optimistic. Warning them on this score could have only a bad influence on their morale, and could serve no useful purpose.
>
> On the contrary, I believe that a public statement by the President praising the courage and self-sacrificing stand taken by the British in sending troops to Greece would strengthen Mr. Churchill's position, might give some uplift to morale, and might influence neutrals, particularly if coupled with praise of the Greeks themselves. However, I suggest that any such statement not be made until we clearly see the end of the hostilities in Greece.

Harriman wrote from London in a personal letter to Hopkins:

> It has been as if living in a nightmare, with some calamity hanging constantly over one's head. I have not expected any war news that would make us happy. . . .
>
> I am with the P.M. at least one day a week and usually the weekend as well. He likes to take me on his trips to the devastated cities—so I can report to the President, but also, I am sure, so the people can see an American around, for the morale. At Portsmouth last week the destruction was fantastic (I think details had best be omitted), but the people are amazing—(5 all-night raids out of nine). People who had lost everything they possess and perhaps a member of the family, all seemed more determined than ever to carry on—and smiling about it. But how long can they last out unless there continues real confidence in victory?

Harriman's extreme despondency was a reflection of the atmosphere prevailing in the upper levels of the British Government at that time—not to mention the mounting anger of the British people as a whole at the new demonstrations of "too little and too late." This, it will be remembered, was the psychological moment that had been selected by the British, with no real authority but with reason-shattering hopefulness, for American entry into the war. Here it was April, the fateful month, and the British listening posts were tuned to beams from the West eager to pick up any shouts or even murmurs that "the Yanks are coming," but there were none; in fact, if the information coming through was accurate, it showed that the American people were farther

than ever from any inclination to intervene in Europe. This could hardly
be called unreasonable. From the American point of view, there was no
Europe left. After the conquest of Yugoslavia and Greece, there was no
part of the Continent that was not physically possessed by Hitler with
such dubious exceptions as Vichy France, Franco's Spain, Salazar's
Portugal, in addition to the satellite nations (Hungary, Bulgaria,
Rumania and Finland), and the Soviet Union. To the average American, Britain was now a last outpost seemingly as lonely and as exposed
as Guam. The public opinion polls showed that, while public sentiment
in favor of aid to Britain even at a risk of going to war took a marked
dip *downward* in the spring of 1941, the public conviction that we
would eventually get into the war against Germany zoomed *upward*,
being held by more than eighty per cent of the population. This seeming
contradiction was, again, not entirely unreasonable, for it suggested
that the American people were now sure that the Germans would eventually move against the Western Hemisphere and a defensive war
would have to be fought. Nobody with superior strategic knowledge or
authority explained to the people the extreme desirability of starting
this American defense from bases in the British Isles and Africa; for
such action, by the peculiar definition of that befuddled period, would
have involved advocacy of entry into a "foreign" war, against which so
many solemn pledges had been made.

On March 19, shortly after the passage of Lend Lease, Roosevelt
and Hopkins had gone on the yacht, *Potomac*, for a cruise in the
Bahamas. This, as it happened, was the last of the "carefree" fishing
trips for either of them. There was no pretense of inspecting bases this
time and the yacht never ventured more than a few hours' sail from the
Florida Coast. Also included in the ship's company on this cruise were
Robert H. Jackson, the Attorney General, Harold Ickes and Steve
Early; oddly enough, the presence of Jackson and Ickes among the
guests was cause for considerable satisfaction among the more rabid
New Dealers in Washington, who took it as evidence that the President
was again paying attention to his social objectives at home and not
concentrating on the alien war in Europe—although, be it said, neither
Jackson nor Ickes was any more likely than Hopkins was to underrate
the German menace.

Since, in an earlier chapter, some reflection has been cast on Hopkins'
prowess as a fisherman, it should be recorded in justice to him that on
this cruise he not only hooked but actually landed a twenty-five-pound
kingfish, four feet long. Otherwise, I do not think that he enjoyed this
cruise very much; his thoughts were elsewhere. On March 28, a radio
message to the *Potomac* informed the President of the coup d'état in
Yugoslavia by which the pro-German Regency had been overthrown
and a new government, under young King Peter, was put into power

to fulfill the people's determination to fight Hitler. The *Potomac* then returned to Port Everglades, Florida.

There was a German ship, the *Arauca*, tied up at Port Everglades. She had been chased in there by a British cruiser in December, 1939, and had remained ever since, flying one of the last Nazi flags visible from American soil. Early in the morning of the last day of Roosevelt's holiday, word came to the *Potomac* that the F.B.I. had uncovered a plan for the wholesale sabotage of Axis ships by their crews, so the President ordered them seized immediately. Later that day, Sunday, March 30, Coast Guardsmen boarded the *Arauca,* removed her crew "for safekeeping," and hauled down the Nazi flag. This episode gave Roosevelt and Hopkins considerable pleasure: at least, it was action of a sort.

On returning to Washington, Hopkins plunged into the organization of Lend Lease. It was believed at first that the huge new program would be under a Cabinet Committee consisting of the Secretaries of State, Treasury, War and Navy, with Hopkins as a sort of Executive Secretary. But the President fought shy of that. After several weeks' delay, he set up a new agency called Division of Defense Aid Reports of the Office of Emergency Management which, by its title, suggested a dusty, fusty bookkeeping agency at the end of some blind alley in the bureaucratic labyrinth. Thus, it was an inconvenient target for criticism. (It did not become formally designated as the Lend-Lease Administration until seven months later.) Harry Hopkins' name was not even on its rolls. His valued associate, General Burns, was appointed by the President to be Executive Officer of this Division, but there was no Director or Chairman, which meant that Roosevelt kept control in his own hands—or, rather, Hopkins'—and for this, as always, he was severely criticized. The State Department did not like the arrangement which separated an all-important instrument of foreign policy from its control except in so far as Hull or Welles could bring influence to bear on the President personally. Morgenthau did not like it for it took from his Treasury Department the function it had exercised so long of handling supplies for Britain and China. The Bureau of the Budget, however, supported the President. It stated the problems of Lend Lease in its record, "The United States at War":

What countries should receive lend-lease aid? On what terms should they receive it? In what quantities should goods be transferred to particular countries? What weight should be given to the immediate necessities of our own military services in comparison with the advantages to be gained by aiding other countries? Only the President could decide these kinds of questions; they were not delegable. Operating authority, however, was freely delegated.

Burns was in a dual capacity, remaining as a member of the staff of Undersecretary Patterson in the War Department and therefore in immediate touch with the huge procurement problem. Oscar Cox and Philip Young were brought into Lend Lease from the Treasury Department, the former as counsel and general improviser, and the latter as administrator. One General Spalding (Sidney P.) was in charge of the production division and another General Spalding (George R.) was in charge of storage and shipping. The Lend-Lease staff grew in the first few months to about a hundred people, a mere handful by Washington wartime standards. They were housed in the Federal Reserve Building.

Because Lend Lease involved matters of utmost secrecy, Hopkins for the first time in his life worried about the imposition of measures of strict security. He wrote sharply to Young:

> Be sure and organize a filing system over there that is absolutely secret with locks on all files and a guard who has been carefully investigated by the FBI or the Secret Service as to his reliability. We simply cannot take any chances on anything getting out of the files.
>
> Incidentally, I think all employees over there should be carefully investigated by the Secret Service. I particularly want an inquiry made as to their attitude about the war. I don't want anybody working anywhere about us who by any chance wants Germany to lick Britain.
>
> Be sure and spread the word around that no one in our crowd should give any interviews to newspapermen, privately or publicly. If anybody asks what you are doing simply say that any announcement about it must come from the White House and refer them to Mr. Early. It is very important that we don't get caught off base in regard to this matter.

Most of Hopkins' scanty, personal correspondence at this time revealed his extreme impatience. Having received several letters from a Deserving Democratic politician who wanted him to do a favor for another D.D., Hopkins wrote:

> I do not know why in the light of things I am doing today I should be burdened by handling a purely personal matter for ————. I have repeatedly sent word to ———— that I am not handling any political matters of any kind or description and I simply think I should not be asked to do it. I am refusing to see other people on similar missions and there is no more reason for my seeing ———— than there is for seeing a dozen others.

One former W.P.A. associate of whom Hopkins was particularly fond sent him a letter which he wished to have transmitted to the President. Hopkins returned the letter to him with this curt note:

I think you ought to keep your shirt on about the W.P.A. There is nothing you can do but let the President handle this and there is just no sense in precipitating any moves. I would not send the attached letter to the President. He would never read it anyway because it is far too long. Your poker-playing habits are much better than your letter-writing habits!

In a moment of extreme irritability at this time Hopkins said to me, "I'm getting sick and tired of having to listen to complaints from those goddam New Dealers!" I could hardly believe my ears.

Hopkins had plenty of excuse for impatience, for his responsibilities were far heavier than ever before and his health was miserably bad. He was forced to resume the rigorous treatments involving repeated transfusions and injections of various kinds to keep him alive. He rarely left the White House but managed to do an enormous amount of business in his bedroom, aided primarily by Isador Lubin who provided exceptionally acute and accurate pairs of eyes and ears.

Actually, Lend Lease in itself provided no overwhelming difficulties in the beginning. It was, in fact, merely an offshoot of the basic problems of production and transportation. There were seven billion dollars to spend but the weapons to buy were not coming off the assembly lines fast enough nor were there enough ships to carry them overseas even when they did. This was a time when one of the most important words in the American language was "bottleneck," and the most formidable bottleneck of all was created by the ancient principle that you cannot eat your cake and have it: the nation could not meet the reality of wartime demands for production while maintaining the illusion that it was still "at peace." There existed an Industrial Mobilization Plan which, in the words of Bernard M. Baruch, its principal author, was designed to enable the country "to pass from a peace to a war status with a minimum of confusion, waste and loss." But—the thinking behind this and all other plans before 1940 was based on the assumption that a nation passed from a peace status to a war status as quickly and as decisively as one passes from one room to another. No provision whatsoever had been made for the maze of corridors, blind alleys and series of antechambers—labeled "Phony War," "cash and carry," "more than mere words," "Lend Lease," etc.—which the United States was compelled for the first time in its own or any other nation's history to traverse between September 1, 1939, and December 7, 1941. This was particularly confusing for the Army officers charged with responsibility for the supply problem. Although Stimson, Patterson and Marshall were well aware of the urgency, the generals and colonels charged with the implementation of policy were men trained to adhere rigidly to the established Table of Organization and to base all calculations upon that. It was their job to take the number of American soldiers currently authorized by Congress and multiply that by the various items of equipment—rifles, blankets, C-rations, howitzers, toothbrushes, etc. They had been trained to believe that if they asked for more than the irreducible minimum they would find themselves detailed to instruction at some boys' military academy in South Dakota, where promotion is apt to be slow.

The thought that they should sponsor a program which within a given span of years would enable the United States to exceed the combined production of Germany, Italy, Japan and all their slave states was too outrageously ridiculous to be worth considering. This understandable hesitancy represented multiplication of the fears, previously described, which had limited Air Force officers to an estimate of only nine thousand parachutes as the production target for 1941. The fear was a mark of respect for isolationist suspicion that we were arming not for "defense," but for war—as though they were two entirely separate and distinct activities. Thus, although every calculation of the staff planners foresaw the vital importance of amphibious warfare, no military authority would dare to ask for heavy appropriations for landing craft, for this would surely suggest a nefarious intention to get into some "foreign" war. There was even a considerable ruckus among isolationists in Congress when, in 1941, a list of Army requirements from the textile industry included the item, *"overseas caps."* Although it would be hard to imagine a more innocuous implement of offensive warfare, to the isolationists that word "overseas" spelled another A.E.F.

A friend of General Marshall's told me at this time that he had been with the Chief of Staff after a grilling of several hours by some Congressional Committee which sought to trap him into admissions which would prove Roosevelt a warmonger. Driving away from Capitol Hill, Marshall closed his eyes and said, "If I can only keep all personal feelings out of my system, I may be able to get through with this job."

The reluctance of American industry to convert itself to war production on anything like the necessary scale was also understandable. Of course some of the industrial leaders, notably Henry Ford, were themselves violent isolationists and refused (as Ford did) to fill orders involving weapons for the British. But among others there was inevitable doubt that the war with its extraordinary demands would last much longer, particularly in view of the sweeping German victories at that time. Business was booming in consumer goods—indeed, in 1941, the automobile industry reached an all-time high in sales of cars for civilian purposes. The government could plead and cajole but it could not compel manufacturers to convert their plants nor could it fortify contracts with satisfactory long-term guarantees. No one could tell how long the present emergency would last, nor what form the next emergency might take. The wise manufacturer knows that if he expands his production too far beyond the probabilities—estimated on the basis of market analysis and consumer research as well as his own experience—he will end up in bankruptcy. Now he was being asked to provide for the needs of X million men of X nations in a potential war to be fought under every possible condition and circumstance that the great globe itself could present. Small wonder that he quailed at the prospect. His problems were further complicated by serious stoppages through strikes, largely the result of persistent Communist attempts to sabotage war production in every way possible; one of them, in the North American Aviation Plant at Inglewood, California, compelled Roosevelt for the first time in his career to order armed intervention by the U.S. Army, a decision that was deeply repugnant to him.

Hopkins moved into this situation as the recognized and designated representative of the President in all considerations of production, transportation, raw materials, priorities, allocation, etc. He had no experience whatsoever in handling such problems. He had none of the "know-how" of a Knudsen or a Batt. But then, he had known nothing of the disease silicosis when he undertook to combat it. He had the amazing ability to find out about things quickly—to talk to people who did know and to determine who was making sense and who wasn't.

Admiral Emory S. Land, head of the Maritime Commission, with whom Hopkins had many tough but friendly tussles, gave him the admiring title, "Generalissimo of the Needle Brigade." That was a precise description. Needling was one form of activity in which Hopkins did not lack experience. When some failure was brought to his attention, he would pick up the telephone and say "Get me General So-and-so." When the War Department reported that So-and-so was at the moment en route to Los Angeles, Hopkins would bark, "Get him wherever he is!" And the superefficient White House switchboard operators would have the General hauled off the train or plane at Dodge City, Kansas, and brought to the telephone and compelled to explain, "Why are there 280 P-39's waiting at the Bell Plant for those Pesco pumps? What the hell is going on here, anyway?" Hopkins was making these telephone calls even when undergoing the painful treatments without which he would have starved to death. Because of his addiction to word-of-mouth communication, there are not many copies of outgoing documents among his papers, but the number and variety of those that came to his card-table desk and that littered his four-poster bed on the problems of supply and shipping are staggering to contemplate.

Here are a few scraps of excerpts picked from a bale of documents of this spring of 1941:

(From the Greek Minister to Hopkins:) As you know, the needs of Greece in aircraft are mentioned in the consolidated list handed

to you by me last week, and I should be much obliged to you if you would. . . .

(From John D. Biggers to Hopkins:) You asked me about alloyed steels, such as nickel steel, chrome steel, etc. There are no exact figures available, but the following tabulation indicates the approximate percentages. . . .

(From Sumner Welles to Hopkins:) I am enclosing herewith a copy of a memorandum of my conversation with the Minister of Yugoslavia last night. I am attaching to it a list of the Yugoslav ships which he handed me. . . .

(From Bernard M. Baruch to Hopkins:) The questions you asked and which I told you I was in no position to answer, and which you asked me to revolve in my mind, have given me the gravest concern. . . . We are improperly organized. It has cost us 20% more in money (which is comparatively unimportant) but also $33\frac{1}{3}$% in time which cannot be measured. . . . I am sorry I cannot be more encouraging but if my opinion is wanted, no one knows better than you that we must look grim realities in the face. . . .

(From Hopkins to Mayor La Guardia:) I am enclosing photostats of a couple of communist documents which show the way they are operating on this. It just seems to me that we have got to find a way to beat these people. From my point of view they are just as much a potential enemy as the Germans. I realize that you are not responsible for prosecuting law breakers but. . . .

(From Major G. K. Heiss of the Army and Navy Munitions Board to Hopkins:) With reference to your telephonic inquiry relative to information concerning quartz crystals. . . .

(From Col. William J. Donovan to Hopkins:) You will remember that when we talked last we discussed the danger of Germany striking in through French North Africa and also of coming in through Spain and Portugal. If this should happen . . .

(From Arthur B. Purvis to Hopkins:) Regarding your note . . . on the new thermal process for producing aluminum. . . .

(From Robert A. Lovett to Hopkins:) I want to confirm the statement made to you on Sunday afternoon regarding the existence at this time of critical shortage of alloy steels. I have checked into the matter and find. . . .

(From James Forrestal to Hopkins:) Shortage of steel for propeller blades due to strikes at Universal Cyclops Steel Corporation has practically halted delivery of propellers for Navy Fighters. . . .

(From Admiral H. L. Vickery to Hopkins:) I just want to inform you that I have one shipbuilding way vacant at this time because I can't get steel delivery. . . .

(From Oscar Cox to Hopkins:) You asked me about locating a man who might advise you from time to time on steel. I asked one of my classmates at M.I.T. who is on the staff up there. . . .

(From General Burns to Hopkins:) In regard to your inquiry con-

cerning the amount of small arms ammunition being manufactured for private purposes. . . .

(From the President—penciled note:) H.H. to put Lauch Currie in as his asst. in China aid *& announce*? FDR

(From Lauchlin Currie to Hopkins:) As you may have noticed, the President made no specific commitment re aid to China at his Press conference today. You left me in a bit of a quandary today as to procedure and status. . . .

(From Russell W. Davenport to Hopkins:) This letter will probably turn out to be long. My head has been crowded with ideas ever since I saw you, and I find we never got around to discussing a lot of things I wanted to discuss. However, I'll stick to one point in this letter, namely, Political Warfare. . . .

(Again Lovett to Hopkins:) The President asked me whether or not our four-engine equipment (such as the B-24's) could carry a spare engine in the North Atlantic hop. I indicated that from the point of view of weight. . . .

(From the President to Hopkins:) Take this up with [Sol] Bloom and Walter George and see if you can get the law amended. The alternative to Congressional action is to send the oil in Government owned, undocumented ships.

(From Sir Arthur Salter to Hopkins:) I enclosed the best note I can do in answer to your question as to the rate of building needed in the U.S. in order (with British building) to off-set losses, on the hypothesis that. . . .

(From Admiral Land to the President and Hopkins:) Vickery and I dined with Sir Arthur Salter last evening. My primary reaction is as follows:—If we do not watch our step, we shall find the White House en route to England with the Washington Monument as a steering oar.

(From Secretary Frank Knox to the President:) I am becoming more and more convinced that the British face imminent defeat unless they are given immediate aid by the United States in the matter of getting an adequate amount of shipping into United Kingdom ports. . . .

(From James Norman Hall to Hopkins:) In the name of old time Grinnell friendship, I am going to ask a favor of you, and please don't curse me out until you learn what the favor is. The little island of Tahiti, in French Oceania . . . has, for more than three months, been deprived of the right to purchase any gasoline or kerosene from the U.S.A. . . .

(From Lt. Col. Rex Benson of the British Embassy to Hopkins:) The Ambassador has asked me to let you know that on the basis of confidential information that was conveyed to Mr. Casey regarding alleged dissatisfaction existing amongst Australian and New Zealand troops in the Middle East. . . .

(From Representative Albert J. Engel of Michigan to Hopkins:) Herewith is sent you a self-explanatory letter . . . with reference to shipment of quantities of tin plate to England. . . .

(From Isador Lubin to Hopkins:) I have had a check made of the situation at the Frankfort Arsenal and the report that I get is that the equipment is adequate for greater production on the second and third shifts. . . .

(From Edward Stettinius to Hopkins:) The Russian Ambassador cabled to Moscow two days ago again saying he had to have an estimate immediately of the raw copper Russia would need. . . .

(From Ward Canaday, Chairman of the Board of Willys-Overland Motors, Inc., to Hopkins and Biggers:) The following is in summary of our talk last week about Bauxite transfers in the Virgin Islands. . . .

(From Ambassador Anthony Biddle to Hopkins:) It would have done your heart good to see General Sikorski's face when I conveyed your message regarding the decision to include Poland on the "Lease-Lend" list. . . . He is profoundly grateful and asked me to tell you so immediately—and at the same time to send you his warmest respects. . . .

(From Oscar R. Ewing to Hopkins:) The deeper I get into this aluminum situation, the more obvious it is that the bottleneck is *power*. Something must be done. . . .

(Again from Stettinius to Hopkins:) You asked me on the phone Sunday how much magnesium was going into civilian use. You will find herewith a statement showing. . . .

(From Philip Young to Hopkins:) Attached is the summary of the Netherlands East Indies purchasing situation, which I promised you some time ago. . . .

(From Harriman to Hopkins:) Reference is made to your 2121. . . . The view that aircraft should have the first call on production of this material is shared by the British. . . .

(From Richard G. Casey, Australian Minister, to Hopkins:) Your American requirements of Australian wool, zinc, lead, chrome and probably zircon-bearing sands, and other not unimportant commodities —on the one hand—and our urgent Australian requirements of war materials and machine tools from the United States—these matters are undoubtedly in the minds of your advisers and we hope very much. . . .

(Again from Baruch to Hopkins:) Any trouble in the Pacific will change our whole defense production. Aluminum is the most outstanding example of incompetency and procrastination, but there are other situations almost as bad.

(From Secretary Hull to the President, who referred it to Hopkins:) In the attached papers Mr. Moffett states that unless King Ibn Saud receives financial assistance at once there is grave danger that this independent Arab Kingdom cannot survive the present emergency. . . .

(Again from Lovett to Hopkins:) You will observe that in spite of the agreement of the automotive industry to cut down by 20% it is practically meaningless in view of the substantial increase in automobile production. . . .

(From Admiral Land to Senator Vandenberg:) Between January 1

and April 30, 1941, 158 vessels, of 781,914 gross tons, were reported sunk in all parts of the world. . . .

(Again from Harriman to Hopkins:) It would be of real help if you could cable me today any background of why Land divulged British information given to him in confidence. . . .

(From Isador Lubin to Hopkins:) I thought you might be interested in the following statements which are the summary of the report of one of my men who attended the recent meeting of the American Management Association. . . .

(Again from Lovett to Hopkins:) British Ferry Service now used for the Blenheim Bombers, Hurricanes, P-40's, and DB-7's, normally uses the following airports for the run from Takoradi to Cairo. . . .

(Again from Cox to Hopkins:) General Arnold delegated to Lt. Col. Meyers the job of getting the planes delivered as soon as possible. Meyers ran into some Neutrality Act and other legal snarls yesterday and called for help. To avoid bothering you, I have arranged with. . . .

(Again from Currie to Hopkins:) I dropped in on Mr. Howe, Minister of Munitions and Supply in Ottawa on Tuesday on the off chance that the Canadians might be able to help out on some items for China on which we are having difficulty. I met with such encouraging response that. . . .

(From Mrs. Emil Hurja to Hopkins:) With wrath and moral indignation and proudly as an American of Scandinavian stock I denounce William Bullitt's insulting attack on Col. Charles Lindbergh last night also that of the President. I further am proud to be listed among thousands of [people] who believe in "America First." I would be grateful if you draw attention to this to the President.

(From Breckenridge Long to Hopkins:) I am responding to your note of yesterday about Jay Allen. We have done everything which could have been done and are still attentive to his case. He acted deliberately in the face of warning and was caught by the military authorities. In spite of our many representations he is still held. He also had a history of activity in connection with smuggling refugees across the military line (occupied France). His case is not an easy one. Attached is a memorandum of some length which indicates the action we have taken. . . .

(From Hopkins to Miss LeHand:) They tell me that a picture called "Citizen Kane," produced by RKO, is excellent. It apparently takes Hearst over the hoops. If you can get it, I think the President would like very much to see it.

(Again from Harriman to Hopkins:) Greatly expanded program for use of incendiary bomb is cause of increase over figures in paragraph three of my 1786. In fact . . . scheduled number of units. . . .

(Again from Vickery to Hopkins:) I am still having a great deal of trouble with steel. . . .

(From the Former Naval Person to the President and Hopkins:) The result which may follow from American and British tank design proceeding for the future on independent lines is something about

which I am greatly concerned. Three types of the M-3 American medium tank are already being produced. . . .

(From Lord Beaverbrook to Hopkins:) May I persuade you to lift up the M3 Medium Tank to the highest place priority. If you would take such a decision, you would help us with our pressing need. . . .

(From the President to the Former Naval Person:) We have had a thorough review of our whole tank situation here during the last few days and I can now give you the following results. We plan to increase our peak production of our medium tank from 600 to 1000 a month reaching that goal. . . .

(Again from Land to the President and Hopkins:) Our shipbuilding expansion program is now far enough along so that we can and should move swiftly to. . . .

(From Hopkins to James Rowe, Jr.:) I know nothing whatever about a row between Pan American and American Export Lines. I have no interest whatever how the decision is reached. I simply cannot be responsible for what Wayne Johnson tells someone else that Juan Trippe has said. If I spent my time running down things like this I would do nothing else, so will you tell anybody who asks you that I have no opinion about this on either side; that he is a damn liar and let it go at that. Incidentally, this might go for anything else you might hear anybody say about me on any such things as these. I trust you will do it effectively.

Hopkins believed that the best way to break bottlenecks was to expose them. Although it was the natural tendency of government officials to attempt to cover up sore spots and hide them from public view, Hopkins believed that in this case advertisement exerted a healthy effect. When, as indicated in a message from Forrestal, masses of new airplanes were grounded because of a bottleneck in propeller production, Hopkins asked that photographs of these impotent planes be displayed in the press and in plants responsible for the propeller shortage. He believed that manufacturers and workers could be stimulated by blows to their pride.

Despite Hopkins' annoyance at old friends of his who insisted that the social objectives of the New Deal were of greater importance than the future of the British Empire—and that Hopkins' concern for the latter was making him in effect a "traitor to his class"—he depended to a very large extent on men with the New Deal point of view in the performance of his job as Generalissimo of the Needle Brigade. Aside from his own aides, Cox, Young and Lubin, there were, conspicuously, Leon Henderson, Director of Price Administration and Civilian Supply, and Sidney Hillman, Robert Nathan and Stacy May, of O.P.M. They were all aggressive battlers for the principle of unlimited production, impatient with the tendency of the more cautious industrialists and Army and Navy officers who protested, "But you can't *do* that!" Which provides a commentary on the oft-repeated accusation that the typical New Dealer was one who believed in a "satiated economy," who lacked faith in the productive power of America, who was forever advocating the plowing under of little pigs and big businessmen. In the 1940 campaign, Wendell Willkie had said, "The only jobs the New Deal has made are Government jobs. . . . For eight years they have been telling us that America is a land without a future." But the industrialists who came into constant contact with Hopkins and the zealots of his entourage discovered that these men, far from despairing of American industry, had sublime confidence in its capacity to achieve the utterly impossible; of course this confidence may have been due largely to deficiency in practical, businesslike, hard common sense, but even so it was certainly not misplaced.

One adviser who remained in the background, but who exerted considerable influence, was the Frenchman, Jean Monnet. He was no New Dealer. He was, in fact, a coldly calculating businessman who had seen his own country suffer terrible defeat and Britain come close to it because of the refusal or the inability of industrialists and soldiers to face the facts of total war. Monnet was the great, single-minded apostle of all-out production, preaching the doctrine that ten thousand tanks too many are far preferable to one tank too few.

Be it said that the businessmen in government in Washington were not slow to respond when they realized that this was a game played according to no previous rules and for stakes no smaller than the life or death of the Republic. Production was their game and here was the greatest challenge ever offered. Many of them were ruthless in putting the fear of God (and of public opinion) into the hearts of their old buddies of the Detroit Athletic Club. It was not too easy for private manufacturers to get away with slacking or profiteering under the eyes of men who knew all the tricks of their trade.

Hopkins, who had once appeared to believe that the terms "big business" and "entrenched greed" were virtually synonymous, now found himself working on new but common ground with men who had once appeared to fear him as the avowed destroyer of "the American way of life." One of the distinguished industrialists who came into government service in 1941 was James S. Knowlson, a Chicagoan and Republican, President and Chairman of the Board of the Stewart-Warner Corporation. It was a proud day for Hopkins when years later he read an article in the *Atlantic Monthly* in which Knowlson described his Washington experience:

> I lost ten pounds and a lot of personal prejudices. I find to my rather shocked surprise that I once made a memorandum like this: "I have been talking with Hopkins and I can't escape the conviction that he has the clearest, coolest mind of anyone I have ever seen here. He

factors complicated problems into simple terms, and he has given direction to my thought." I don't know anything about Mr. Hopkins' social planning or his other ideas, but my one regret is that I did not see more of him in Washington.

The whole production imbroglio before Pearl Harbor and even after it was a story of endless tugging and hauling between the proponents of the total war effort and the protectors of the civilian economy. It was sometimes known as "The Battle of 7-Up" because of Robert Patterson's vehement complaint that valuable trucks were being used to deliver the soft drink of that name to bobby soxers when they ought to be delivering ammunition to troops. In this conflict, Hopkins was just about 100 per cent anti-civilian. He was enraged chiefly by the gross wastage, as he considered it, of invaluable transport planes in maintaining the schedules of the commercial airlines, and he put in a great deal of time figuring out ways to steal these planes for service across the Atlantic to Britain and Africa or over the Hump to China.

The first measure taken by Hopkins toward aid for China was an attempt to clear up the fearful congestion on the one land communication route, the Burma Road. In consultation with his friend, John M. Hertz, he considered various candidates for this Augean job and finally settled on Daniel Arnstein, a trucking and taxicab expert who had been with Hopkins that day at the races when Max Gordon engaged in the conversation which was parlayed into "tax and tax, and spend and spend, and elect and elect."

Arnstein has told of the beginnings of his remarkable adventure in high-pressure diplomacy in the following way:

> In the Spring of 1941 I was sunning myself in Florida when Harry called me up and said, "Dan, I got a tough job to be done and I need your advice. Can you come back to Washington?"
>
> I told him that I would and did. When I saw Harry in Washington he told me that not a god-damn thing was moving over the Burma Road. . . . I had just taken over the Terminal Cab Company of New York the year before and my business needed a lot of attention. I did not want to leave it, but the way Harry put it to me, I agreed to go to China and promised him that he would get some results. So I went to China.
>
> When I got to Rangoon I saw a lot of stuff piled up but nothing was moving. The reason for this was that the Burmese had put a tax on all goods that went over the Road leading into China. I was boiling mad, so I went to see the Governor General of Burma, Sir Reginald Dorman Smith, and told him, "The American people would give $70,000,000 away without a murmur if somebody asked for it, but they get sore as hell if someone tries to take ten cents away from them by a fast trick and I'm sore as hell now."

Arnstein did a good job in Burma and China, but it meant little in the long run. Lend Lease was not extended to China until two months after the Bill passed, and then it was pathetically inadequate because of the vast distances involved, the demands elsewhere and the policy prevailing at the time of attempting to appease Japan. Soon after Pearl Harbor, the Japanese cut the Burma Road.

In the spring of 1941, strategic attention was concentrated on the Atlantic and particularly on Iceland, the Azores, the Cape Verdes and Dakar. Of these, Iceland was of first importance because of its position on the flank of the direct life line from North America to the United Kingdom. Although a fiercely independent republic, Iceland had bonds of union with Denmark which gave Denmark's present master, Adolf Hitler, some claim to control of the island. British forces had therefore moved in there to defend it against sudden German occupation. In December, 1940, the American Consul in Reykjavik, Berbel E. Kuniholm, discussed with the Icelandic Prime Minister a proposal to include Iceland in the Monroe Doctrine area which would enable its defense to be undertaken by the United States. The following month Hull put a damper on further negotiations, but on April 14, 1941, Hopkins and Welles met with Thor Thors, the Icelandic Consul General in Washington, and opened the extremely secret negotiations which ended with the sending of an invitation by Iceland's Prime Minister and the sending of the First Marine Brigade "to supplement and eventually to replace the British forces . . . which were needed elsewhere." There were to be in the first months of the operation, before further American forces could be sent, 4,000 U.S. Marines and 20,000 British troops. Therefore, the British authorities suggested to Admiral Ghormley in London that the normal thing to do would be to have unity of command and that this command logically should be British, at least until such time as the American forces on the island outnumbered the British. Admiral Stark wrote to Hopkins, "I know the President has thought this all out, nevertheless he has been so interested in the details and there is so much potential dynamite in this order, that I feel it should have his okay before I sign it. Secretary Knox concurs so I am sending it over to you as I don't want it to get in the general mail." Even in this vital military-diplomatic matter, the Chief of Naval Operations was using Hopkins as a means of rapid access to Roosevelt. Stark enclosed with this letter his orders to the Commander in Chief, U.S. Atlantic Fleet (then Admiral King) and to the Commanding General, First Marine Brigade, for the transportation of the troops and for their organization in Iceland. He said, "I realize that this is practically an act of war." He felt it would be going too far to put the American troops under British command, for, in the event of attack on Iceland by the Germans, the British officer would have responsibility for sending Americans into action. Stark, therefore, specified in his orders to the Marine General "you will coordinate your operations for the defense of Iceland with the defense operations of British forces by the method of mutual cooperation." There was no doubt in anyone's mind that the Marines would fight in the event of German attack, and while the public announcement of their presence in Iceland provoked new storms of protest from the isolationists the American people in the main took it calmly, considering it as a perfectly reasonable precaution. Hitler and the Nazi Government were sensible enough not to interpret it as an act of war. The question now arose: if the Marines on Iceland were at battle stations ready to repel any German attack, should not the United States Navy be similarly ordered to take action against German raiders (including U-boats) along the sea lanes between the North American continent and Iceland? This was the most dangerous problem of the time for the President to decide. The chances were remote of a German attempt to seize Iceland. But the risk of naval action was so great that it could be called a virtual certainty. Those sea lanes were full of raiders, not only U-boats but also the battleships *Bismarck* and *Tirpitz* and the cruisers *Scharnhorst, Gneisenau* and *Prinz Eugen.*

On April 2, Roosevelt had talked about a plan for providing U.S. Naval escort for the Atlantic convoys. He gave orders for the Navy to draw up what was called Hemisphere Defense Plan No. 1; this made definite provision for aggressive action by American warships against German submarines and surface raiders in the Western Atlantic. On April 13, however, the news of the neutrality pact between Japan and the Soviet Union raised such alarms concerning the situation in the Pacific that Hemisphere Defense Plan No. 2 was drawn up and was made effective by Presidential directive on April 24. This revised plan provided that American ships were merely to *report* movements of German vessels west of Iceland as they observed or detected them. There was to be no shooting unless shot at.

The responsibility for the active protection of passing convoys was still entirely with the British. In a statement on the limits of this patrol which Roosevelt and Hopkins drafted in longhand, the President wrote, "All navigable waters in the North and South Atlantic lying west of longitude 25°. This line is determined by taking a point half way between the land mass of the American hemisphere and the land mass of Europe, Africa, in other words half way between Brazil and the West Coast of Africa." It may be noted that the 25th parallel runs just west of Iceland, but the line was later bent to include that island. Roosevelt and Hopkins drafted a cable to Churchill on this:

> Before taking unilateral action I want to tell you of steps that we propose to take in relation to the security of the Western Hemisphere and favorably to affect your shipping. The United States Government

proposes to extend the security zone and patrol area utilizing naval vessels and aircraft working from Newfoundland, Greenland, Nova Scotia, the West Indies, Bermuda and the United States with possible later extension to Brazil if this can be arranged. We will want to be notified by you in great secrecy of movements of convoys so that our patrol units can seek out the ship of an aggressor nation operating west of the new line of the security zone. We propose to have our ships refueled at sea when advisable. We suggest that your long shipping hauls move to the greatest possible extent west of the new line up to the latitude of the northwestern approaches. As soon as you clear out the Red Sea we propose to declare it no longer a zone of combat. We propose to send all types of goods in unarmed American flagships via the Red Sea or the Persian Gulf to Egypt or any other non-belligerent port. We think we can work out a plan for sending wheat and other transferable goods to Greenland and Iceland in American ships through the next six months. We expect very soon to make use of Danish ships and in about two months Italian ships. We hope to make available for the direct haul to England a large amount of our shipping which is now being utilized for other purposes.

In all these developments, Hopkins was continually urging bold action and Roosevelt was taking the more moderate, temperate, cautious course. One has only to read Henry Stimson's record of his own profound dissatisfaction in this spring of 1941 to know how sorely Roosevelt tried the tempers of those trusted advisers who were urging him that the time had passed when "all aid short of war" was enough.

A Roosevelt speech was scheduled for May 14, which was Pan-American Day, one of the State Department's favorite occasions, and the Department had prepared a draft, emphasizing hemispheric solidarity. The mere announcement of this speech provoked widespread speculation at home and abroad, for it was the President's first important address since the enactment of Lend Lease. Would this be the long-expected request for a Declaration of War? The Nazi and Communist anti-Roosevelt propaganda was greatly intensified and Lindbergh came alarmingly close to an outright demand for open revolt against the Administration. At the same time, the extreme interventionists, now led by the Fight for Freedom Committee, were matching the isolationists in the stridency of their demands. It was a period of loud noise in the nation.

Roosevelt was very disturbed by all the speculation about his speech, largely because he was so far from clear in his own mind as to just what he could say. It was obviously impossible for him to refer to his plans for Iceland and patrols—or to the possibility of an American occupation of the Azores—or to the fact that part of the Pacific Fleet was at that moment moving into the Atlantic. Speaking on behalf of the President, Steve Early had cautioned the newspapermen not to attach any special importance to the speech—an intended tip-off that it would be merely a routine performance. This suggestion from Early, who always chose his words carefully, in itself created reverberations in the anti-isolationist press, in England and other countries. The tension was heightened by a number of public utterances by high officers of the government, notably Stimson and Knox, which seemed to place the United States on the very brink of war. Roosevelt had read these speeches before they were delivered. It was generally assumed that he approved the position taken—as indeed he did. But that did not mean that he was willing or ready to go so far himself.

Then, suddenly, Roosevelt postponed his speech on the grounds of ill health. When it was later announced that the speech was to be given on May 27, newspapermen asked Early if he cared to repeat his admonition not to attach special importance to it, and he declined to do so. So the anticipation was intensified.

During those days in mid-May Roosevelt spent a great deal of time in bed and rarely went to his office. He said that this was one of the most persistent colds he had ever had. One day, after a long talk with him in his bedroom, I came out and said to Missy LeHand, "The President seems in fine shape to me. He didn't cough or sneeze or even blow his nose the whole time I was in there and he looked wonderfully well. What is really the matter with him?" Missy smiled and said, "What he's suffering from most of all is a case of sheer exasperation." Indeed, he seemed at the time to be exasperated with practically everyone—the isolationists, on one side, who were demanding in effect that he resign; and, on the other side, the extreme interventionists who were demanding that he immediately send expeditionary forces to England, the Azores, Dakar, the Netherlands East Indies, Singapore, the Aleutian Islands and other points of interest.

Very few people were allowed to see the President during those days. There were a lot of very nervous men in high places in Washington wondering what was the reason for this inaccessibility and, when the President should finally emerge from it, which way he would jump. Those of us who were in the White House at the time were subjected to an exceptionally large amount of flattering attention by officials who hoped that we could get some message through to him or call his attention to some memorandum that was presumably reposing in his baskets. I reported to Hopkins what seemed to me to be the most important of the requests that came even to me and in every case he told me to "forget it."

On May 10 came the amazing news of Rudolph Hess's sudden landing by parachute on the Duke of Hamilton's estate in Scotland. This happened on a Saturday evening, and Churchill was at Dytchley. He was, in fact, watching a Marx Brothers movie—at least, that was the story as Hopkins was told it. The Duke of Hamilton telephoned from Scotland. Churchill wouldn't leave the movie; he told a secretary to inform His Grace that the Prime Minister was otherwise engaged. But the Duke insisted that this was an urgent matter of Cabinet importance. So Churchill sent Bracken to take the message while he concentrated on Groucho, Harpo and Chico. Bracken returned to announce that Rudolph Hess had arrived in Britain.

Churchill snorted. "Will you kindly instruct the Duke of Hamilton," he growled, "to tell that to the Marx Brothers?"

Subsequently Ivone Kirkpatrick was dispatched to the Hamilton place to identify Hess. Kirkpatrick had been in the British Embassy in Berlin for years before the war and therefore knew Hess well and disliked him cordially. When he verified the identification, curt announcement was made and then the British Government covered the whole affair with a thick pall of secrecy. Practically everybody in the world who could read a newspaper or listen to a radio was in a fever of anxiety to know what was really behind this strange story. There was no limit to the rumors and speculations. Like everyone else, I was consumed with curiosity, but I knew I was not supposed to ask questions around the White House that were not directly connected with the performance of my own duties.

One evening about ten days after Hess landed I was at dinner with the President, Hopkins and Sumner Welles. Suddenly, in the midst of a conversation about something else, Roosevelt turned to Welles and said, "Sumner, you must have met Hess when you were in Europe last year." Welles said that he had. I was excited for I thought that now I was going to hear the inexplicable explained.

"What's he like?" Roosevelt asked.

Welles gave a thoughtful description of his impressions of Hess— fanatical, mystical devotion to his Fuehrer, apparently brutish stupidity, etc. Roosevelt was silent for a moment, then: "I wonder what is *really* behind this story?" Welles said he did not know.

So all I learned was that the President was asking precisely the same question that was being asked at thousands if not millions of other American supper tables. Months later, when Lord Beaverbrook was in Moscow, Stalin asked him what was the real truth about Hess, as will appear in a later chapter. *Everybody* was mystified.

On May 24, the monster German battleship *Bismarck*, which had emerged from its hide-out at Bergen, Norway, attended by the cruiser *Prinz Eugen*, was intercepted between Iceland and Greenland by the battleship *Prince of Wales* and the battle cruiser *Hood*. In an engagement that lasted only a few minutes the *Prince of Wales* was slightly damaged and the *Hood* was sunk. The German ships got away. When last seen, the *Bismarck* was on a southwesterly course, heading right into the convoy routes toward Newfoundland and the U.S. East Coast.

For nearly two days after that the whereabouts of the *Bismarck* was un-known. There was all sorts of speculation as to her intended destination. Among the guesses were:

She would shell Halifax, New York, Norfolk, and various other targets.

She would go to Rio de Janeiro to make a big propaganda display for South Americans.

She would go around Cape Horn and all the way across the Pacific to Japan. (There were several theories as to how she would refuel.)

Certainly, after the Hess episode, it seemed that no possibility was too absurd to be considered improbable.

Roosevelt thought it not unlikely that the *Bismarck* would go into the Caribbean to Martinique and perhaps take possession of that strategic outpost. He said, "Suppose she does show up in the Caribbean? We have some submarines down there. Suppose we order them to attack her and attempt to sink her? Do you think the people would demand to have me impeached?"

Roosevelt was speaking in such a detached, even casual manner that one might have thought he was playing with some time-machine fantasy, such as, "Suppose you suddenly found yourself living in the middle of the thirteenth century. . . ." Yet here was the reality of one murderous ship, off on some wild, unpredictable career, guided by the will of one man who might be a maniac or a genius or both, capable of converting one inexplicable impulse into a turning point of history. And here was the President of the United States, sitting in the White House in an atmosphere of oppressive calm, wondering what the next naval dispatch would tell him, wondering what he would be able to do about it. He was behind his desk in the Oval Study, and he had his coat off. It was a very hot day. He had air-conditioning apparatus in the Study and his bed-room and office, but he hated it and never, to my knowledge, turned it on. The windows were open. Outside the one to the southwest was a big magnolia tree which, they said, had been planted by Andrew Jackson. It was now covered with big white blooms and their lemony scent drifted into the Study. You could look from these windows across to Virginia which, when Lincoln lived in this house, was enemy territory. But Roosevelt was wondering whether he'd be impeached.

It was the opinion of those of us who were there, sitting about the desk, that if the U.S. Navy did a thorough job on the *Bismarck* off Martinique, or anywhere else in western waters, the American people would applaud the action vigorously. The demand for impeachment would come only if it appeared that the Navy had fired and missed.

However, the big German ship turned eastward, heading apparently for a French port. Two days later, on May 26, the flash came that she had been spotted by a Catalina PBY, one of the naval patrol bombers

which Hopkins had helped to turn over to the British R.A.F. Coastal
Command. The next day the Royal Navy closed in on the *Bismarck* and
sank her. This was the day of Roosevelt's speech, and Hitler had helped
greatly to give it a melodramatic background. I do not know just what
Hitler had in mind in sending the *Bismarck* toward the Western Hemisphere at this time, thereby risking the greatest ship in his Navy and
perhaps in the world. The only logical explanation at the time was that
he hoped to sink one or more entire convoys and thereby intimidate the
United States and discredit anything that Roosevelt might say in his
widely advertised speech. This seems likely for, this same week—although it was not known until later—the Germans for the first time in
the war sank an American merchant ship, the *Robin Moor*.

There were further alarming indications of the next probable trends of
German aggression. Following their fierce, quick conquests of Yugoslavia and Greece, it seemed logical for the Germans to attempt to complete the process of driving the British from the Mediterranean. Roosevelt had been advised by Admiral Leahy in Vichy that Marshal Pétain
"expects an early advance of German troops through Spain with the
purpose of either taking Gibraltar or occupying some place on the coast
from which the Straits can be controlled by gunfire and from which
troops can be sent to Spanish Morocco"—and there will undoubtedly
always be plenty of room for speculation (and for gratitude) as to why
Hitler failed to do just that.

Darlan went to Berchtesgaden for a conference with Hitler, and
Churchill sent intelligence from London confirming Leahy's reports of
the dangers to North Africa by way of Spain. Indeed, Churchill's messages at this time were grimly pessimistic and with lamentably ample
reason. Roosevelt, who was always interested in North Africa as a theater of operations, was deeply concerned with the effect of these possible
developments on the Portuguese and Spanish islands in the Atlantic and
ordered that plans be drawn for American occupation of the Azores.

On the day when the first news of the *Bismarck* reached the White
House, Hopkins said to Rosenman and me that he believed the President
had decided to end the speech with a proclamation of Unlimited National
Emergency (up to then, since September, 1939, the emergency had been
"limited") and told us to try drafting such a proclamation. Somewhat
awe-struck, we went down to the Cabinet Room and wrote a proclamation consisting of one sentence. Later, when the new draft of the speech
had been typed by Grace Tully (no one else was permitted to do it for
reasons of secrecy), Sumner Welles and Adolf Berle came over from
the State Department to go through it. When they came to the proclamation, Welles asked, "Who drafted this?" We confessed that we had.
Welles asked if the President had seen it. We had to confess, "Not yet."
Welles and Berle could hardly be blamed for feeling that these were

pretty strange goings on. The four of us then went upstairs to dinner with Roosevelt and Hopkins and afterward the President sat down at his desk to read through the latest draft. He read it aloud, as he often did, to see how it sounded and to detect any tongue-twisting phrases that would be difficult on the radio. Just before he came to the final crucial paragraph, Hopkins had to leave the room to take some medicine. Rosenman and I were appalled at being left to face it out alone. Roosevelt read, "I hereby proclaim that an unlimited national emergency exists . . . what's *this*?" He looked up from the typescript with the expression of artless innocence that he frequently put on, and asked very politely, "Hasn't somebody been taking some liberties?"

I managed to explain, in a strangled tone, that Harry had told us that the President wanted something along these general lines. I am sure that Welles and Berle expected that Rosenman's and my heads were about to come off. But there was not another word about the proclamation: it remained in the speech.

There were two important prohibitions in this speech. The President would not mention Japan and he would not mention the Soviet Union. He would not even use the word "dictatorships" which he had used often to describe all the Nazi-Fascist-Communist states. It was official policy then to avoid provoking Japan so as to keep her out of the war and to avoid provoking Russia in case Germany forced her into it. Thus, the only blanket term that could be used in a sense of opprobrium was "Axis." As an example of how this proposition worked: in the speech there was a review of the events of the war since September, 1939, with the line, "In the subsequent months the shadows deepened and lengthened. And the night spread over Poland, Finland, Denmark, Norway, Holland, Belgium, Luxembourg and France." But, before the speech was delivered and after careful consideration, the word "Finland" was omitted.

The occasion for the delivery of this speech was a curiously inappropriate one. It was still in observance of Pan-American Day, and the guests were the Ambassadors and Ministers from the twenty Latin-American republics with their families. Roosevelt insisted on including the Canadian Minister, his old friend, Leighton McCarthy, although Canada was not particularly enthusiastic about Pan-Americanism. It was a black-tie affair, the guests seated during the speech on the little gilded chairs in the East Room and then moving out on to the south lawn for a sort of garden party with refreshments and Japanese lanterns. (Sam Rosenman said to me, "We've got to be careful and call them Axis lanterns.")

It was oppressively hot in the East Room while the President was speaking. All around the edges of the room were the newsreel and still cameramen, but they didn't put their lights on during the speech. The movies were taken after the guests had gone out, Roosevelt repeating selected portions.

The speech evoked very few signs of enthusiasm from its audience and was followed by merely polite applause. Many of those who could understand English seemed disturbed and even alarmed by what he said. It was certainly not the standard Pan-American, hemisphere-solidarity oration. Indeed, after the opening paragraph of courteous reference to those present, Roosevelt seemed to forget that there *was* anyone present. He was talking to the radio audience all over the United States and the world. This was his strongest utterance:

> From the point of view of strict naval and military necessity, we shall give every possible assistance to Britain and to all who, with Britain, are resisting Hitlerism or its equivalent with force of arms. Our patrols are helping now to insure delivery of the needed supplies to Britain. *All additional measures necessary to deliver the goods will be taken. Any and all further methods or combination of methods, which can or should be utilized, are being devised.* . . .

Those italicized words could certainly be taken as a guarantee of American action in the North Atlantic against German attempts to break the supply line, but months passed before the orders for action were given.

Irving Berlin was with me at the speech, and afterward we went upstairs to Harry Hopkins' room. He was lying there in his old bathrobe. He always preferred to listen to speeches over the radio. After the diplomatic guests had departed, Mrs. Roosevelt came in to invite us into the Monroe Room where the President was sitting with a few friends and relatives. He was delighted to see Berlin and begged him to go to the piano and play and sing "Alexander's Ragtime Band" and many other songs.

Later I went into the President's bedroom to say good night. He was in bed surrounded with telegrams. There must have been a thousand or more of them. He had looked at them all.

"They're ninety-five per cent favorable!" he said. "And I figured I'd be lucky to get an even break on this speech."

The response of the press and, in so far as one could judge, of the people, was indeed overwhelmingly favorable. Roosevelt's words were taken as a solemn commitment; the entry of the United States into the war against Germany was now considered inevitable and even imminent. Yet, the very day after the speech, Roosevelt at a press conference vitiated most of his own effect. He dismissed airily any suggestion that he contemplated using the U.S. Navy for convoy duty or asking Congress for any changes in the Neutrality Law. Hopkins, who thought he knew Roosevelt's mind, was totally unable to account for this sudden reversal from a position of strength to one of apparently insouciant weakness. The fact of Roosevelt's unaccountability was a lesson to be learned over and over again. In the awful crisis produced by Blitzkrieg in the West, and Dunkirk, and the fall of France, he had been almost alone in his own Administration in making bold, even desperate decisions. Now, exactly a year later, with Britain's fortunes again at terribly low ebb, he was again almost alone—but now alone in reluctance to take decision and action. It can be said that the isolationists' long and savage campaign against the President—emphasizing such phrases as "plowing under every fourth American boy"—had failed to blind American public opinion to the huge accumulation of events, but it certainly had exerted an important effect on Roosevelt himself: whatever the peril, he was not going to lead the country into war—he was going to wait to be pushed in.

When news of the torpedoing of the *Robin Moor* reached the White House, Hopkins wrote the following memorandum for the President:

> The sinking of the *Robin Moor* violated international law at sea; it violates your policy of freedom of the seas.
>
> The present observation patrol of the Navy for observing and reporting the movement of ships that are potential aggressors could be changed to a security patrol charged with the duty of providing security for all American flag ships traveling on the seas outside of the danger zone.
>
> It occurred to me that your instructions to the Navy Department could be that the United States Atlantic patrol forces, to be specific are to, in effect, establish the freedom of the seas, leaving it to the judgment of the Navy as to what measures of security are required to achieve that objective.

But Roosevelt refused to issue any such instructions.

On June 2, Hitler and Mussolini staged one of their portentous conferences at the Brenner Pass and the world wondered what new terrors were being hatched. But there were no invasion signs on the Northern French or Belgian coasts, whereas there were indisguisable evidences of German concentrations on the Eastern front in conquered Poland. And Laurence Steinhardt, the American Ambassador in Moscow, was cabling that nearly all of the wives of the high German and Italian diplomats there were leaving for their homes, giving reasons for this exodus which sounded highly unconvincing, and the Counselor of the German Embassy had even sent his pet dog, from which he was inseparable, by special plane to Berlin.

These scraps of information were only the final bits of evidence which had been accumulating for months in the State Department and all of which had been passed on to the British, who added to it other evidence of their own, and also to the Soviet Government. I do not know just how much real credence the Russians attached to it; their expressed attitude was that it was merely Anglo-American propaganda fabricated to drive a wedge between Russia and Germany, to break up the Ribbentrop-Molotov mutual nonaggression pact.

Certainly, Roosevelt attached so much importance to it that he was determined to wait to see what these indications forebode. He soon found out.

CHAPTER XIV

The Drive to the East

EARLY in June, 1941, Ambassador Winant returned to Washington to report and Averell Harriman started off from London on a flight to the Middle East to study supply problems at first hand. It was a brief period of suspension between crises when these harassed men could leave their posts. Hopkins was interested in an appreciation of the situation, brought to him by Winant, written by an American Army observer in London:

> The Imperial situation, as a whole, seems to be deteriorating. The forces which Germany can exert are too enormous to be halted at once. At the same time, like lava, I am confident that as they spread further from the volcano's mouth, they will cool and slow down. It would be unfortunate if the Middle East fell, but if it absorbs the German effort all summer it will be worth while.
>
> I still believe the British can resist invasion. It will be a hard, bloody business, but what has occurred so far in Crete does not alter my opinion. By some error of judgment or lack of imagination, the R.A.F. withdrew all its planes. Even a few fighters would have wrought havoc amongst the German troop carriers at the outset and would have been well expended. There is likely to be serious criticism of this decision and technical reasons will not serve to quell it.
>
> At the same time I have never believed and cannot see how the British Empire can defeat Germany without the help of God or Uncle Sam. Perhaps it will take both. God has undoubtedly been on the side of the big battalions so far, but may change sides. The equation at present is too unbalanced: 80,000,000 Germans in one lump+the labor of n slaves+8 years of intense rearming and organization+ frenzied fanaticism *versus* 70,000,000 British in 4 continents+zero slaves+only 3 years of real rearmament and no industrial mobilization+dogged determination.
>
> It is another example of the old prize ring rule, "A good big man will beat a good little man every time."

What our position and policy is at home, it is difficult to discern at this range. From here our steps in aid of Britain appear to follow along well behind the development of events. The lag is great and may prove too much. It seems already to have had its effects in the slow and discouraged crumbling of France. There was some chance that this might have been much slower otherwise. As it is, there seems to be no more sense of resistance among the French than there is in a wet dishrag.

At any rate, should we find ourselves at war, I hope that it won't be a piecemeal affair. Total war requires throwing everything available at once, military, naval, air, economic, moral—including the kitchen stove, and following this up with everything else as soon as it can be got to working.

One may question now, a year later, whether the decision to try and defend the whole Empire was a practical one. Nevertheless, any other decision at that time (after the French collapse) would have been unthinkable militarily, as well as directly opposed to the British character and tradition.

Hopkins approved particularly the "lava" analogy, that being the one optimistic note in an otherwise dismal picture. Hopkins often appeared on the surface a sour skeptic who made a profession of looking on the dark side of everything; but, in his heart, he was an incorrigible optimist, as his father had been before him and as he himself proved by innumerable $2.00 bets on hopeless long shots. He was confirmed in this by close association with Roosevelt and with Churchill, two of the really Olympian optimists of all time. One could not be with either of them for long without seeing the glow and feeling the warmth of the fires of confidence that burned so strongly and so steadily in both of them. (A point for historians to consider is that had these Allied leaders not been optimists in the blackest hours the Germans and the Japanese would undoubtedly have won the war; it was the pessimists, like Pétain, Darlan and Weygand, who went down to quick defeat.)

During the week of June 16 Hopkins had many conferences with James Forrestal, Admiral Stark, Admiral Turner and others in connection with the Iceland expedition. He saw Arthur Purvis, Jean Monnet, Sir Clive Baillieu (Australian), Air Marshal Harris and Major Victor Cazalet, M.P., of the British Delegation. He saw Princess Juliana, of the Netherlands, and her husband, Prince Bernhardt. (In fact, at 8:30 one morning, he had as breakfast guests in his room in the White House Prince Bernhardt and Mayor La Guardia, which must have provided an entertaining mixture with the orange juice.) He saw the Secretary of War, the Secretary of the Navy, Postmaster General Frank C. Walker, Secretary of Commerce Jesse Jones, Marriner S. Eccles, William S. Paley, General S. D. Embick and a great many other people. On Saturday Hopkins took a happy day off and went to the races.

That night, June 21, a short-wave listening post picked up a report that Hitler had invaded the Soviet Union. Hopkins' first thought when he heard this news was, "The President's policy of support for Britain has really paid off! Hitler has turned to the left." But if Hopkins had a moment of relief it was no more than a moment; for he was compelled instantly to face the new and gigantic problems of aid for Russia.

The immediate response of the isolationists to this news was one of exultation. They had been profoundly embarrassed by the Communist alignment with the Nazis—and Roosevelt had been strengthened by it in the eyes of the American people—but now they were free to go berserk with the original Nazi party line that Hitler represented the only bulwark against Bolshevism.

There was a curious and revelatory episode in which I happened to be involved on the Sunday when Hitler invaded the Soviet Union. I was scheduled to attend a Fight for Freedom rally in the Golden Gate Ballroom in Harlem. It was an insufferably hot day and there was no pretense at air conditioning in the ballroom. When we went in there was a picket line outside (obviously a Communist one) with placards condemning the Fight for Freedom warmongers as tools of British and Wall Street Imperialism. Pamphlets were being handed out urging a Negro March on Washington to demand Equality and Peace! The Communists were very active among the Negro population in these days and since. We went through the picket line and conducted the meeting, the principal speakers being Herbert Agar and Dorothy Parker, and when we left the Golden Gate Ballroom, an hour and a half later, we found that the picket line had disappeared and the March on Washington had been canceled. Within that short space of time, the Communist party line had reached all the way from Moscow to Harlem and had completely reversed itself (or rather, had been completely reversed by Hitler). The next day, the *Daily Worker* was pro-British, pro-Lend Lease, pro-interventionist and, for the first time in two years, pro-Roosevelt.

Among the first high officers of the Administration to put himself on record about this startling new development was the Secretary of War, who wrote to the President:

> For the past thirty hours I have done little but reflect upon the German-Russian war and its effect upon our immediate policy. To clarify my own views I have spent today in conference with the Chief of Staff and the men in the War Plans Division of the General Staff. I am glad to say that I find substantial unanimity upon the fundamental policy which they think should be followed by us. I am even more relieved that their views coincide so entirely with my own.
> *First:* Here is their estimate of controlling facts:
> 1. Germany will be thoroughly occupied in beating Russia for a

minimum of one month and a possible maximum of three months.
  2. During this period Germany must give up or slack up on
      a. Any invasion of the British Isles.
      b. Any attempt to attack herself or prevent us from occupying
         Iceland.
      c. Her pressure on West Africa, Dakar and South America.
      d. Any attempt to envelop the British right flank in Egypt by
         way of Iraq, Syria or Persia.
      e. Probably her pressure in Libya and the Mediterranean.
  Second: They were unanimously of the belief that this precious
and unforeseen period of respite should be used to push with the
utmost vigor our movements in the Atlantic theater of operations.
They were unanimously of the feeling that such pressure on our part
was the right way to help Britain, to discourage Germany, and to
strengthen our own position of defense against our most imminent
danger.
  As you know, Marshall and I have been troubled by the fear lest
we be prematurely dragged into two major operations in the Atlantic,
one in the northeast and the other in Brazil, with an insufficiency
of Atlantic Naval and shipping strength and an insufficient demonstrated superiority of American seapower to hold politics steady in
South America. By getting into this war with Russia Germany has
much relieved our anxiety, provided we act promptly and get the
initial dangers over before Germany gets her legs disentangled from
the Russian mire. . . .
  Germany's action seems like an almost providential occurrence. By
this final demonstration of Nazi ambition and perfidy, the door is
opened wide for you to lead directly towards the winning of the battle
of the North Atlantic and the protection of our hemisphere in the
South Atlantic, while at the same time your leadership is assured of
success as fully as any future program can well be made.

In its estimate of "a minimum of one month and a possible maximum
of three months" for the Russian campaign the War Department thinking was not far removed from that of the British military authorities,
although the latter were careful to cover themselves in the event of
miracles. Their appreciation of the situation reached Hopkins a week
after the invasion started. They said, "It is possible that the first phase,
involving the occupation of Ukraine and Moscow, might take as little
as three, or as long as six weeks, *or more.*" (The italics are mine.) The
British authorities also stated:

  An attempted invasion of the United Kingdom may now be considered to be temporarily postponed, since so much of the German
  Air Force and so many essential German Army formations are
  engaged in the East. It cannot be over-emphasized, however, that
  this is only temporary. If the German campaign in Russia is a lightning
  one, say from three to four weeks duration, the re-grouping of the

German formations in the West might be expected to take from four to six weeks after the conclusion of the campaign in Russia. If the campaign were of longer duration, it might take from six to eight weeks.

(Ribbentrop's estimate, according to Ciano, was that *"the Russia of Stalin will be erased from the map within eight weeks."*)

Regardless of predictions, Churchill made instant response to Hitler's move into Russia. He received the news early Sunday morning and he was, of course, in the country. He conferred that day principally with Beaverbrook and with Sir Stafford Cripps, then British Ambassador to Moscow, who had come home to report the dismal failure of all his efforts to exert any influence on Russian policy. Although one would hardly have expected it of him, Beaverbrook was a vehement supporter of immediate and unstinted aid for the Soviet Union and was subsequently an ardent, persistent and sometimes (to Churchill) embarrassing proponent of the Second Front. At the urging of these two men as well as of his own inclinations, and after hasty consultation by telephone with other War Cabinet ministers, Churchill went on the air that same Sunday with one of his most powerful speeches.

He said, "No one has been a more consistent opponent of Communism than I have for the last twenty-five years. I will unsay no word that I have spoken about it. But all this fades away before the spectacle which is now unfolding." Referring in characteristic terms to Hitler, he said:

This bloodthirsty guttersnipe must launch his mechanized armies upon new fields of slaughter, pillage and devastation. Poor as are the Russian peasants, workmen and soldiers, he must steal from them their daily bread; he must devour their harvests; he must rob them of the oil which drives their ploughs; and thus produce a famine without example in human history. And even the carnage and ruin which his victory, should he gain it—he has not gained it yet—will bring upon the Russian people, will itself be only a stepping-stone to the attempt to plunge the four or five hundred millions who live in China, and the three hundred and fifty millions who live in India, into that bottomless pit of human degradation over which the diabolic emblem of the Swastika flaunts itself. It is not too much to say here this summer evening that the lives and happiness of a thousand million additional people are now menaced with brutal Nazi violence.

Churchill declared the decision of His Majesty's Government to give all possible help to Russia and the Russian people. I do not know for sure whether he communicated with Roosevelt by telephone or cable during the day before he made this speech, but it is my impression that he did. Following the speech, Roosevelt was urged to step up and do likewise. All manner of suggestions came into the White House as to what the President should say to the American people. The most intel-

ligent of these were summarized in a memorandum to Hopkins from
Herbert Bayard Swope:

> We are opposed to the Communists' formula and we are opposed
> to the Nazi formula.
>
> In the twenty-seven years since Russia became Communistic, our
> national interests and our way of life never have been seriously
> threatened by the Soviets. But in the two years of Hitler's mad drive
> for world enslavement, our very existence, as a free people, has been
> gravely endangered.
>
> Attempts to divide us have been made by would-be Quislings,
> acting within our borders. They have tried to create racial and
> religious differences; they have promised peace and quiet through
> Nazi appeasement.
>
> Now we see what a grim tragedy a Nazi peace treaty is. Now we
> see again the fate that has overtaken fifteen nations which, relying
> upon Nazi promises, were destroyed, one by one.
>
> We are not for Communism, but we are against all that Hitler
> stands for. He and his godless Nazis are the pressing threats to a
> world of peace and justice and security. In his defeat lies our safety.
>
> At this time, as ever, we must keep in mind that our greatest
> strength is in unity; our greatest danger in discord.

Joseph E. Davies wrote the following memorandum to Hopkins when
the war in Russia had been going for two weeks:

> The resistance of the Russian Army has been more effective than
> was generally expected. In all probability the result will depend upon
> air power. If Hitler dominates the air, it is likely that the same thing
> will occur in White Russia and in the Ukraine that occurred in Flan-
> ders and in France, namely, the inability of land forces, without air
> protection, to resist the combined attack by air, mechanized forces and
> infantry.
>
> In such an event, Hitler will take White Russia, Moscow and the
> Ukraine which will provide him with 60% of the agricultural resources
> and 60% of the industrial production of Russia. . . .
>
> If Hitler occupies White Russia and the Ukraine, as he may, and
> Stalin falls back into the interior, Hitler will be confronted with three
> major problems:
>
> 1. Guerrilla warfare and attack;
> 2. Sabotage by the population who resent that "Holy Mother
> Russia" has been attacked; and
> 3. The necessity of policing conquered territory and making it
> produce.
>
> In 1918 under similar circumstances in the Ukraine, the Germans
> found that they did not get but 80% of the agricultural and other
> products which they had reasonably believed they could get.
>
> Obviously, under such circumstances, it would be to Hitler's interest
> to put on a peace drive to induce Stalin to consent to an arrangement

based on the then status quo leaving Stalin to find his outlet to the South and East to China, possibly India.

Even though Hitler takes the Ukraine and White Russia, in all probability Stalin can maintain himself back of the Urals for a considerable time.

There are two contingencies which might prevent such resistance. They are:

1. An internal revolution which would overthrow Stalin and by a coup d'état put a Trotzkyite Pro-German in power, who would make a Hitler peace.

The possibility of that is lessened because of the tendency of the people to rally around the Government in power in the face of an attack on their homes and "Holy Mother Russia."

2. The possibility of Stalin himself making a Hitler peace.

Stalin is oriental, coldly realistic and getting along in years. It is not impossible that he might again even "fall" for Hitler's peace as the lesser of two evils. He believes that Russia is surrounded by capitalistic enemies. In '38 and '39 he had no confidence in the good faith of either Britain or France or the capacity of the democracies to be effective against Hitler. He hated and feared Hitler then just as he does now. He was induced to make a pact of non-aggression with Hitler as the best hope he had for preserving peace for Russia, not so much on ideological grounds as on practical grounds to save his own government.

It is, therefore, of vital importance that Stalin be impressed with the fact that he is not "pulling the chestnuts out of the fire" for allies who have no use for him or who will be hostile to him after the war and who will be no less enemies, in the event of an allied peace, than the Germans in the event of their victory. Churchill and Eden, profiting by their previous mistake, apparently recognized this and have promised "all out" support to Russia.

I do not overlook the fact that in this country there are large classes of people who abhor the Soviets to the extent that they hope for a Hitler victory in Russia. Hitler played on that string in Europe for the past six years to his enormous advantage and to the disruption of "collective security." He will play upon it again here if he can and will use it once again and to the utmost in any overtures for a new peace with Stalin. That should be offset, if possible. It could measurably be thwarted if Stalin could find some assurance that regardless of ideological differences the Administration is disinterestedly and without prejudice desirous of aiding them to defeat Hitler. . . .

Vis-à-vis with Japan, it is obviously to our advantage to have a friendly Russia at Japan's rear. It is my opinion that it is not their intent to seek to project communism in the United States, nor would it be within the realm of possibility after this war or for many years thereafter for the Soviets to project communism if they wished in the United States or even in Europe.

Specifically, I fear that if they get the impression that the United States is only using them, and if sentiment grows and finds expression that the United States is equally a capitalistic enemy, it would be playing directly into the hands of Hitler and he can be counted upon to use this in his efforts to project either an armistice or peace on the Russian front after he takes the Ukraine and White Russia. Word ought to be gotten to Stalin direct that our attitude is "all out" to beat Hitler and that our historic policy of friendliness to Russia still exists.

Roosevelt, at this point, believed in the policy of making haste slowly. Churchill had spoken and there can be no doubt that Roosevelt backed him up. But before he took public action on aid for Russia, he wanted to know, first, what were their needs and, second, how could the goods be delivered? (It will be remembered that, at that particular moment, American forces were en route to Iceland.)

The most serious aspect of the situation was that the supplying of Russia involved considerable extension of the convoy routes—and the route from Britain to Murmansk was by all odds the most terrible of the whole war, subject as it was to attack not only by U-boats but by surface raiders darting from Norwegian fiords and bombing planes from Norwegian air bases. The British Navy, stretched tenuously over all the lifelines of the North and South Atlantic and the Mediterranean and Indian Ocean, could not possibly take on this new and expensive assignment unless they were relieved of some of their responsibilities elsewhere.

On Friday evening, July 11, Hopkins had a long talk with Roosevelt in the Study and the President drew a line on a small map of the Atlantic Ocean, which he had torn from the *National Geographic* magazine. Roosevelt scribbled a cable instructing Winant to inform the Former Naval Person that Hopkins would be with him again soon. The next morning, Hopkins had an engagement for breakfast with Sidney Hillman on production problems and at 11:30 he was due to go for a week end with the President on the Potomac, but that was canceled. He had lunch with Sumner Welles and in the afternoon conferred with Admiral Vickery on shipping and with General Burns on supplies. He had dinner with Lord Halifax. Early Sunday morning he flew to Montreal, to Gander, Newfoundland, and from there in one of the Lend-Lease B-24 bombers to Prestwick, Scotland. He was very ill when he arrived but he went immediately to Churchill to discuss the entirely new situation which had developed since their last meeting.

Hopkins noted many changes in Britain: it was summer, and he did not have to wear his overcoat indoors in Chequers; there had been no substantial air raids for two months and Britain was no longer fighting

alone, which marked the faces of the people in the streets with an
expression of almost incredulous relief. Yet mixed with the relief was
a new kind of undefined anxiety. It was as though the British people
had become so adjusted to the bombing that they had come to depend
on it as a reliable morale builder. Now, without it, they seemed to be
puzzled as to just what was expected of them in the waging of the
war. They were thrilled by every scrap of news concerning Russian
resistance to the Germans, but they could not avoid the fear that this
development was no more than a temporary respite for themselves and
that once Hitler had mopped up in the East, their case would be worse
than ever. They were beginning to suspect that the long-sustained hope
of armed aid from America was a delusion.

They were not aware—nor were the American people—of the extent
to which the American invasion of the United Kingdom had really
started, but it was this phenomenon which interested Hopkins most,
for his previous visit had been responsible for so much of it. So
many military, naval and air attachés and aides were being attached
to the U.S. Embassy that it was becoming a sizable force in itself. These
were classified as "observers," which was no misnomer, for they were
certainly observing, and profiting thereby. For instance: the B-17 Flying Fortresses had already been used by the R.A.F. in bombing raids
and had belied their name, proving extremely vulnerable. Study of this
combat experience was enabling U.S. Air Force officers to recommend
the changes in armament which made the B-17 the tough, murderous
aircraft that it became when later it was flown in action by American
crews.

In addition to the American military representatives there were in
London all manner of missions dealing with Lend Lease, scientific
research, food, shipping, aircraft and ordnance production and every
other subject of wartime importance. The American Embassy was
bursting at the seams with personnel and overflowing into other buildings in Grosvenor Square and environs.

When Hopkins saw Churchill, the war in Russia was in its fourth
week. Thus it had already passed the minimum set by the British authorities and it was evident that it would pass the minimum set in Washington. There was beginning to be the faintest glimmering of hope that
perhaps the Russians might hold out until winter set in, and Churchill
was never one to overlook a glimmer. His principal concern was that
so many German infantry divisions were now getting combat experience
—or learning to be "battleworthy," in the term he loved to use—which
would make them all the harder to handle later on. Hopkins gathered
that Stalin had not been tremendously impressed by Britain's offer of
aid but had been concerned, from the very beginning, with the political
aspects of the enforced alliance. Even with its very life in peril the

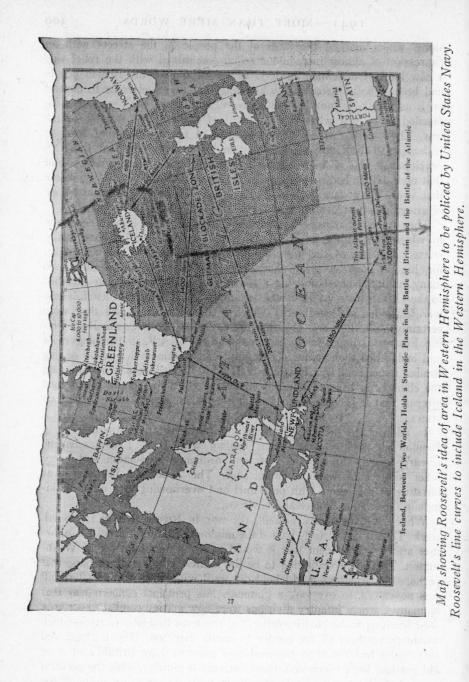

77

Map showing Roosevelt's idea of area in Western Hemisphere to be policed by United States Navy. Roosevelt's line curves to include Iceland in the Western Hemisphere.

Iceland, Between Two Worlds, Holds a Strategic Place in the Battle of Britain and the Battle of the Atlantic

Soviet Government appeared to be more anxious to discuss future frontiers and spheres of influence than to negotiate for military supplies. The British Government was reluctant to negotiate any purely political treaty at that time. But, a few days before Hopkins arrived in London, the two powers had signed an "agreement for joint action" which contained two provisions:

(1) An undertaking on the part of the two Governments to render each other assistance and support of all kinds in the war against Hitlerite Germany and (2) a mutual undertaking that during this war neither party would negotiate or conclude an armistice or treaty of peace except by mutual agreement. It was understood between the two Governments that this agreement might be supplemented by more detailed political and military agreements at a later date.

Hopkins showed Churchill the map from the *National Geographic* magazine which Roosevelt had marked. The penciled line followed Longitude 26° north from the South Atlantic, missing the Cape Verde Islands but cutting through the Azores. About two hundred miles southwest of Iceland it turned sharp right (eastward) and then curved around Iceland, at a radius of roughly two hundred miles, which was to be the area of U.S. air and sea patrol. The sea lanes west of this line would be—subject to further discussion—the area for the policing of which the U.S. Navy would assume responsibility, thereby freeing British escort ships for service elsewhere, particularly the Murmansk route.

In Hopkins' notes of his final talks with the President were three brief items:

Economic or territorial deals—*NO*.
Harriman not policy.
No talk about war.

The first of these speaks for itself; the last was an indication of Roosevelt's determination that, at his forthcoming meeting with Churchill, no questions were to be asked as to when the United States would enter the war. The reference to Harriman was the result of the awkward situation between him and Winant which has been mentioned previously. Hopkins was instructed to inform Churchill that Harriman, as expediter of Lend Lease, was an instrument not a maker of policy—that Winant was still Ambassador and, therefore, the President's personal representative to the King. (It is doubtful that this explanation had any appreciable effect on the situation.)

At the time of Hopkins' arrival in London, Harriman returned from his trip to the Middle East and over the new African air lanes, from the Gold Coast to the Persian Gulf. He had been given the same oppor-

Hopkins' notes of a conversation with Roosevelt on eve of his trip to London in July 1941.

tunities for inspection that he would have commanded if he were a member of the British War Cabinet. Indeed, he was accompanied by a Directive from Churchill to General Wavell which said, in part, "Mr. Harriman enjoys my complete confidence and is in the most intimate relations with the President and with Mr. Harry Hopkins. No one can do more for you. . . . I commend Mr. Harriman to your most attentive consideration. He will report both to his own Government and to me as Minister of Defense." Which provides an indication of the extent to which the common-law alliance was in actual operation.

Harriman's report was clear and candid but too long and detailed to reproduce here in full. He was not sparing in criticism of some of the organization in the Middle East—particularly the eternal problem of division of command as between the Army, Navy and Air Force.

In the Middle East, as in the United Kingdom, he had heard the persistent demand for American technicians—radio mechanics, ordnance artificers, boilermakers, coppersmiths, welders, machine tool setters, even carpenters and bricklayers. Hopkins conferred on this endless subject with Lord Hankey, the Paymaster General, with Ernest Bevin, then Minister of Labor, with generals, admirals, air marshals. His records show that he was still trying to find ways to meet Britain's need for technicians right up to the day before Pearl Harbor. He also discussed innumerable problems of production and supply with which he had familiarized himself despite his total lack of military and industrial experience. He surveyed the tank and ordnance situation with Beaverbrook, now Minister of Supply, the aircraft situation with Sir Archibald Sinclair, the food situation with Lord Woolton.

Hopkins and Winant had the disagreeable task of going into most careful investigation of the disposition of certain Lend-Lease items. The ugly charge had been made in the United States, and taken up joyfully by isolationists who were fighting Lend-Lease appropriations in Congress, that the British were using Lend-Lease raw materials and even some finished products not for war purposes but to revive their export trade, particularly in South America. This was a recurrent accusation, which came to plague Winant time and again, and files of the State Department must be filled with the detailed explanations that the harassed Ambassador obtained from Sir John Anderson, President of the Privy Council, Sir Kingsley Wood, Chancellor of the Exchequer, and other dignitaries of His Majesty's Government. There was hardly a time in the whole war when there wasn't some dangerous rumor to be investigated and refuted.

Most of Hopkins' conversations with Churchill on the forthcoming Atlantic Conference and the proposed American naval activities between the U.S. and Iceland were conducted in private and Hopkins kept no record of them. The results of them, however, are a matter of historic record. He did keep a full account of an interesting meeting at No. 10 Downing Street in which he participated with the Prime Minister, Harriman, the British Chiefs of Staff (Admiral Sir Dudley Pound, General Sir John Dill, Air Marshal Sir Charles Portal, General Sir Hastings Ismay) and the three ranking American officers in London, Admiral Ghormley, General James E. Chaney and General Raymond E. Lee.

In the background of this meeting was serious disagreement, albeit at long range, between the American and British Chiefs of Staff as to the defensibility of Britain itself and the wisdom of continuing to attempt to hold the Middle East. Although the R.A.F. was much stronger than it had been in 1940 when it won the Battle of Britain and thereby made German invasion at the time impossible, it was the American opinion that the Germans had profited by the lessons learned and had demonstrated in the battle of Crete that they now knew how to immobilize the R.A.F. It was felt that the British air fields were particularly vulnerable to attack by airborne forces and Hitler now had 60,000 trained parachutists which he evidently did not plan to use on the Russian Front. Therefore, it was questionable whether the British should be diverting substantial numbers of men and quantities of supplies to the Middle East when all of them might be needed for the desperate defense of the United Kingdom. Similarly, naval forces and merchant shipping now traversing the long sea lanes to Suez would be better employed in the Battle of the Atlantic and the carrying of supplies to Britain.

After the Prime Minister had opened the meeting at No. 10 Downing Street with his customary parliamentary courtesy and grace, Hopkins immediately got down to the root of the matter. He stated the American attitude bluntly, saying,

> Insofar as I am concerned, I am absolutely convinced that if it is decided to continue the campaign in the Middle East, the United States has got to send supplies there. Up to now, this supply problem has been handled on a day-to-day hit-or-miss basis. If it is to be continued, it will have to be done systematically and on a regular schedule, using maybe 100 ships or even more to carry regular, carefully planned cargoes of airplanes, tanks, ammunition, etc.
>
> Our Chiefs of Staff—the men who make the big decisions on all matters relating to defense—believe that the British Empire is making too many sacrifices in trying to maintain an indefensible position in the Middle East. At any moment the Germans might take Gibraltar and seal up the Western Mediterranean. They might block the Suez Canal. They might concentrate enough air and armored forces to overwhelm the British Armies in the Middle East. Our Chiefs of Staff believe that the Battle of the Atlantic is the final, decisive battle of the war and everything has got to be concentrated on winning it. Now, the President has a somewhat different attitude. He shares the

belief that British chances in the Middle East are not too good. But he realizes that the British have got to fight the enemy wherever they find him. He is, therefore, more inclined to support continuing the campaign in the Middle East.

I know perfectly well that all of you here in Britain are determined to go on fighting to hold the Middle East at all costs and that it's difficult for you to understand the American attitude. But—you have got to remember that we in the United States just simply do not understand your problems in the Middle East, and the interests of the Moslem world, and the interrelationship of your problems in Egypt and India. That is largely due to the fact that we have insufficient information on these subjects. The President himself has never been given a comprehensive explanation of the broad strategy of the Middle East campaign. The whole thing has been dealt with on a piecemeal basis, with attention being focussed on Ethiopia, or Libya, or Syria or whatever happened to be the scene of local operations at the moment. I think that everyone in the United States appreciated why you had to go in and try to help Greece, and why you had to try to defend Crete. But there are now grave doubts as to whether it is wise for you to go any further in that region. I don't want to overstate the case but it is vitally important that we come to an understanding on this whole matter so that the people in authority in Washington will really know why we must get supplies to the Middle East and then develop and carry through a program to that end.

The next speaker was General Chaney who stated that, in the American military view, the order of priority was as follows:

(1) The defense of the United Kingdom and of the Atlantic sea lanes.

(2) The defense of Singapore and the sea lanes to Australia and New Zealand.

(3) The defense of the ocean trade routes in general.

(4) The defense of the Middle East.

Chaney dwelt on the difficulties that the Germans would face in conducting successful land operations in the Middle East and also in the invasion of Britain. He said that their ability to overcome these difficulties would depend upon how soon the Russians collapsed. (Every calculation seemed to be based on the assumption that the Russians would collapse.) He said that if the Russians could hold out until the end of September, then the invasion peril would recede until the following spring which would give time for the building up of defenses both in the United Kingdom and the Middle East. But he urged that the British divert to the Middle East only the minimum necessary for defense and that they should not send any armored forces for offensive purposes.

General Lee echoed these sentiments and said that the American authorities were anxious to know whether the British would contemplate offensive operations in the Middle East and, if so, where would the necessary troops come from and what would be the general strategy?

Churchill then said that the British Chiefs of Staff would comment on all of these interesting questions in detail but that he would like first to comment on general aspects. He felt that conditions were improving in the Battle of the Atlantic and would improve still further in view of the increased activities of the U.S. Navy as they had been outlined to him by Hopkins. In so far as invasion of Britain was concerned, he was confident that they had this situation well in hand. However, the Prime Minister was much less sure of his ground when he talked of possibilities in the Far East. He was convinced that the Japanese would not enter the war until they were certain that the British Empire was beaten. He was convinced that the Japanese did not want to fight the United States and the British Empire together. (This conviction, shared by Roosevelt, was of enormous importance in the formulation of policy prior to Pearl Harbor.) Churchill said that, in the event of a Japanese attack on British possessions in the Far East, Singapore of course would hold out but the Japanese Navy would constitute a very grave threat to the whole traffic along the eastern trade routes and might well offer serious threats to Australia and New Zealand. In that case, it would obviously be necessary to send naval forces, including battleships, from the Mediterranean to the Far East. Needless to say, the situation would be entirely different if the United States were to enter the war in the Pacific after Japan had attacked Britain . . . and, since it was needless to say it, Churchill did not pursue that dynamite-laden subject any further. He summed up by saying that, in the meantime, and awaiting all contingencies—and in spite of all objections from transatlantic friends—it would be British policy to go ahead with the reinforcement of the Middle East. The Prime Minister revealed that during the past eight months nearly half of Britain's war production had been sent to that theater.

Admiral Pound, Air Marshal Portal and General Dill then spoke for the Navy, Air Force and Army. It was obvious that the German production of tank-carrying barges pointed to plans for an invasion but it was believed that the British would be able to tell three weeks in advance if any trans-Channel operation by the Germans was imminent. Churchill said that all the lessons of Crete had been taken to heart. He confronted the possibility that the Germans would use gas but, if they did so, the British were ready for retaliation on a large scale. Dill emphasized the disastrous moral effect of withdrawal from the Middle East particularly in its effect on the Moslem world all the way from West Africa through North Africa and the Arab States on into India.

Churchill then brought up a point which impressed Hopkins and which he duly communicated to Roosevelt when they met again at the Atlantic Conference. It was the ever-present possibility of the Germans' smashing down through Spain and past Gibraltar into North and West Africa to Dakar. He said that, in the event that the United States were drawn into the war against Germany and Italy, North and West Africa might well prove to be areas favorable for the operations of American forces. Churchill also mentioned the possibilities of operations in Norway —a country he said, "where there was a great people burning to be liberated"—and this was a project that he never dropped until the war in Europe was nearly over.

As a result of this meeting Hopkins decided to urge the President to bring Marshall and Arnold along with him to the Conference. Presumably, before then, the only military matters that were contemplated for discussion had to do with the Battle of the Atlantic, but Hopkins felt it would be useful for Marshall to learn something of the British Army point of view. He also suggested that Harriman fly back immediately to Washington to give Roosevelt a report on all the matters that had been discussed.

Hopkins realized all too clearly that, in one vitally important respect, the discussions at the Atlantic Conference would be held in a vacuum without some real knowledge of the situation and the prospects on the Russian Front. It was obvious that all the prevailing estimates, both British and American, were based on inadequate information and speculation. There was a British military mission in Moscow but it was gathering no more information than was vouchsafed by Molotov's Foreign Office to the Embassies, which was to say none at all. Since all deliberation on all phases of the war at that time, including American production and Lend Lease, depended on the question of how long Russia could hold out, Hopkins decided that he should make a quick trip to Moscow and try to get an answer to that question from Stalin himself. He asked Churchill whether it would be possible to fly to Moscow and return within a week. Churchill informed him that the R.A.F. Coastal Command had recently opened up a new air route for PBY (Catalina) flying boats from Invergordon in Scotland around the North Cape of Norway to Archangel; a few flights had already been made on this extremely difficult route. Churchill agreed that it would be valuable to learn the truth about the Eastern Front and he felt that Stalin might agree to disclose some part of it to the personal representative of the President of the United States, but he was not enthusiastic about the idea of Hopkins taking so long and hazardous a trip. However, Hopkins was excited at the thought of it and on Friday evening, July 25, he and Winant drafted the following cable to Roosevelt:

FOR THE PRESIDENT ONLY:
When I was in Canada the Government officials stated they hoped that you could go to Ottawa on the seventh of August. I wanted to

phone you from Gander but there were no communications there. I am going to remain here a day or two longer for conference with Commander Middle East. His visit here very secret. I am wondering whether you would think it important and useful for me to go to Moscow. Air transportation good and can reach there in twenty four hours. I have a feeling that everything possible should be done to make certain the Russians maintain a permanent front even though they be defeated in this immediate battle. If Stalin could in any way be influenced at a critical time I think it would be worth doing by a direct communication from you through a personal envoy. I think the stakes are so great that it should be done. Stalin would then know in an unmistakable way that we mean business on a long term supply job. I of course have made no moves in regard to this and will await your advice. If you think Moscow trip inadvisable I will leave here not later than Wednesday. Am spending weekend with Prime Minister but message through Navy will reach me quickly. There is no news here about Russia or Japan that you do not already have.

Prime Minister does not believe Japan wants war. Russian ambassador told me this morning he did not believe Japan would attack Russia immediately. Long conference last night with military chiefs and our military representatives on the strategic position of the British in the Middle East. They are determined to fight it out in that sector and it seems to me they gave very convincing reasons to all of us for that determination. I do hope you are well and am sorry my mission has taken longer than I anticipated. We had news this morning that the Scharnhorst is out. British making very powerful air attacks but bomber losses substantial. Everybody here in good spirits but realize that the Russian business gives them only a temporary breather. Everyone here asks about you and are delighted to know that you are in good health.

HARRY

It is remotely possible though unlikely that Roosevelt had discussed the possibility of a trip to Moscow before Hopkins left Washington. If so, there is no mention of it in any of the notes that Hopkins took with him to London and it is the recollection of Churchill, Winant and Harriman that Hopkins himself conceived the idea for the trip very suddenly and acted on it immediately. Hopkins was at Chequers, late Saturday evening, when he received Roosevelt's reply:

Welles and I highly approve Moscow trip and assume you would go in a few days. Possibly you could get back to North America by August eighth. I will send you tonight a message for Stalin.

All well here. Tell Former Naval Person our concurrent action in regard to Japan is, I think, bearing fruit. I hear their Government much upset and no conclusive future policy has been determined on. Tell him also in great confidence that I have suggested to Nomura that Indo-China be neutralized by Britain, Dutch, Chinese, Japan and ourselves, placing Indo-China somewhat in status of Switzerland.

Japan to get rice and fertilizer but all on condition that Japan withdraw armed forces from Indo-China in toto. I have had no answer yet. When it comes it will probably be unfavorable but we have at least made one more effort to avoid Japanese expansion to South Pacific.

The first, short paragraph in that cable provided Presidential authorization for one of the most extraordinarily important and valuable missions of the whole war. Early Sunday morning Hopkins went into Churchill's bedroom. The Prime Minister always did a great deal of his business while still in bed and often carried it on while he was in his bath (he bathed in very hot water twice a day with inexorable regularity). On this occasion, Churchill picked up the telephone and put through the orders for transporting his guest to Archangel on the White Sea. Hopkins would have to leave by train that night for Invergordon on the East Coast of Scotland where the PBY Catalina would be ready for him. In the meantime, Winant was busily engaged locating the Russian Ambassador, M. Maisky, in order to get a Soviet visa on Hopkins' passport. This was no easy matter as Maisky had gone sufficiently native in England to be away in the country himself for the week end, but Winant finally tracked him down.

That Sunday at Chequers must have been an interesting one with few evidences of peace or quiet. Quentin Reynolds was there Saturday working with Hopkins on a speech which he was to broadcast Sunday from Churchill's personal microphone. Churchill himself was preparing an enormous speech, which would last more than two hours, reporting to the House of Commons on the whole, intricate production situation. Professor Lindemann, now Lord Cherwell, was helping in the marshaling of facts, some of which represented proud boasts and some apologies. Winant came out on Sunday for a hurried conference. In the late afternoon, Averell Harriman and his daughter Kathleen arrived. There was the usual complement of week-end guests who were supposed to provide relaxation for the harried Prime Minister. In addition to all this, that indefatigable fighter for freedom, Dorothy Thompson, came to Chequers for Sunday lunch in the course of a whirlwind tour of embattled Britain. Of course, none of those present except Churchill and his personal staff and Winant and Harriman knew that Hopkins was leaving that night for a visit to Stalin.

Miss Thompson recalls that at lunch that day there was some discussion of the Russian situation and it was largely expressions of pessimism, which Churchill and Hopkins seemed to share. "In fact," she has said, "from what I recall of my London visit in the summer of 1941 the only person I met who was confident about the power of the Russians to hold the Germans was Eduard Beneš," the exiled President of Czechoslovakia.

Reynolds has provided me with the following description of his participation in that week end at Chequers:

> I was invited by Mrs. Churchill, but at the instigation of Hopkins
> who wanted me to help him write the BBC speech. Harry felt I'd
> know how to word things so that the British people would know what
> he was trying to say. He had been working very long hours—attend-
> ing British Cabinet meetings—and he showed it. He was dog-tired
> and had a touch of "grippe." At least, that is what he told Mrs.
> Churchill. I am sure it was his old ailment bothering him, but he
> always sloughed that off by saying a casual, "Got a little cold during
> the trip over."
> Mrs. Churchill was very concerned over Harry's health. She knew
> Harry so well that she could tell when he was in pain by looking at
> him I think. Around 11 o'clock in the evening she would start trying
> to persuade him to go to bed, saying, "You have a long day tomorrow
> and you can have a nice talk with Winston in the morning. I've fixed
> your bed and put a hot water bottle in it." I am sure Harry never
> got such a mothering in his life, except maybe from Mrs. Roosevelt.
> When Harry talked to me about his speech, he said he wanted to
> give the British public hope that big things were on the way; that
> substantial help was coming under Lend Lease. But he couldn't be
> too specific. Security was involved (submarines were very active;
> at home the isolationists were screaming bloody murder). Harry said,
> "Anything I say will be construed as a direct message from FDR.
> People know I'm only the President's messenger boy." (I heard
> Harry say that quite often.) "Funny thing, but a lot of politicians at
> home who hate the administration credit me with a Svengali-like
> influence over the Prez." Harry always laughed at that. "If they only
> knew I just deliver messages." (I don't know if Harry actually felt
> that way. But that's the line he always took with me when I'd meet
> him in London.)

After they had talked out the speech at length—while Hopkins played
with the Churchills' cat which was named Nelson and was very ill
natured—Reynolds sat down at a typewriter that had been provided in
Hopkins' bedroom, and Hopkins lay down on the bed and slept. When
the speech was finished, Hopkins read it through and exclaimed, "Hell,
Quent, you've got me declaring war on Germany." Said Reynolds: "We
should have done that long ago." Hopkins then proceeded to tone it
down.

Hopkins broadcast the speech from Chequers at 9:15 on Sunday
evening, July 27. From the point of view of the BBC audience in
Britain and on the Continent, far and away the most important statement that he made was: "I did not come from America alone. I came
in a bomber plane, and with me were twenty other bombers made in
America." That statement, accurate in itself, gave people who were hun-

gry for hope a highly inaccurate picture of a steady swarm of bombers flying from the United States to Britain and, from British bases, to their devastating missions over Europe.

After the speech, Hopkins and Churchill walked out on the lawn at Chequers. It was still daylight. Churchill told Hopkins in minutest detail of the efforts that Britain was making and planned to make to bring aid to Russia. He talked with his usual vigor and eloquence of the importance of Russia in the battle against Hitler. Hopkins asked if he could repeat any of this to Stalin.

"Tell him, tell him," Churchill said. "Tell him that Britain has but one ambition today, but one desire—to crush Hitler. Tell him that he can depend upon us. . . . Good-by—God bless you, Harry."

Hopkins then drove with Harriman and his daughter, Kathleen, to Euston Station, where he was to take the train for Invergordon. He had no time to go back to Claridge's. Dorsey Fisher, of the U.S. Embassy, had been there to collect Hopkins' sparse luggage which he delivered at the station. (Hopkins did not pay his hotel bill until six weeks later.) As the train was pulling out, Winant ran up and, through the car window, handed Hopkins his passport, containing Maisky's handwritten visa—which proved to be a total waste of time and effort since no one in Russia ever looked at the passport.

As the special train left the gloomy, smoky, faintly lit station, Winant and Harriman felt that they had said good-by to someone who was about to step into a rocket bound for interstellar space, for Russia then seemed immeasurably far away.

The only authority that Hopkins carried with him on this strange, sudden journey, aside from the passport, was a cable which had arrived that day from Sumner Welles, acting Secretary of State:

> The President asks that when you first see Mr. Stalin you will give him the following message in the President's name: "Mr. Hopkins is in Moscow at my request for discussions with you personally and with such other officials as you may designate on the vitally important question of how we can most expeditiously and effectively make available the assistance which the United States can render to your country in its magnificent resistance to the treacherous aggression by Hitlerite Germany. I have already informed your Ambassador, Mr. Oumansky, that all possible aid will be given by the United States Government in obtaining munitions, armaments and other supplies needed to meet your most urgent requirements and which can be made available for actual use in the coming two months in your country. We shall promptly settle the details of these questions with the mission headed by General Golikov which is now in Washington. The visit now being made by Mr. Hopkins to Moscow will, I feel, be invaluable by clarifying for us here in the United States your most urgent requirements so that we can reach the most practicable decisions to simplify

the mechanics of delivery and speed them up. We shall be able to complete during the next winter a great amount of matériel which your Government wishes to obtain in this country. I therefore think that the immediate concern of both governments should be to concentrate on the matériel which can reach Russia within the next three months.

"I ask you to treat Mr. Hopkins with the identical confidence you would feel if you were talking directly to me. He will communicate directly to me the views that you express to him and will tell me what you consider are the most pressing individual problems on which we could be of aid.

"May I express, in conclusion, the great admiration all of us in the United States feel for the superb bravery displayed by the Russian people in the defense of their liberty and in their fight for the independence of Russia. The success of your people and all other peoples in opposing Hitler's aggression and his plans for world conquest has been heartening to the American people."

Hopkins at this time again became an important figure in the psychological warfare which, apart from the endless Battle of the Atlantic, was about the only form of combat between the British and the Germans. The BBC European services advertised Hopkins' peregrinations constantly in broadcasts to all of the occupied countries of Europe as well as to Germany and Italy. His own radio speech was translated and broadcast in many different languages and printed in leaflets distributed by the thousands and millions by the R.A.F. Bomber Command. It took a good deal of ingenuity on the part of the British propaganda experts to explain just who Hopkins was but they managed to convey the implication that he represented the vanguard of an enormous American Expeditionary Force. The Germans used Hopkins plentifully in their propaganda to the United States, announcing that he was committing his country to intervention in the war to defend British Imperialism and Russian Communism—and this charge was, of course, loudly echoed by the isolationists. However, Dr. Goebbels could not use this same line in his propaganda to Britain—or to France, Norway, Poland or other occupied countries—since American intervention was the one development for which they were praying. In his propaganda to these countries, about the best that Goebbels could do was represent Hopkins as the instrument of Western barbarism, intent upon the enslavement of Europe by Wall Street and the reduction of Europe's ancient culture to the levels of Hollywood. The amount of attention that the Nazi propagandists gave to Hopkins served greatly to increase the warmth of his welcome in Moscow.

CHAPTER XV

The Kremlin

O N SUNDAY, July 26, the PBY Catalina W. 6416 of the R.A.F.
Coastal Command was resting on the calm waters of Loch
Lomond after weeks of rough work patrolling the northwest approaches
between Scotland and Iceland. The members of its crew were enjoying
swimming, picnicking and the Highland scenery in the summer sun-
shine. It was the general practice to fly these planes periodically from
their salt-water base to a lake to wash them down in fresh water, and
the crews always converted these trips into little holidays. On this day,
however, the relaxation was cut short. At four o'clock in the afternoon
a reconnaissance plane came over and flashed light signals to the Catalina's captain, Flight Lieutenant D. C. McKinley, D.F.C. He was ordered to return immediately to base, which was at Oban on the West
Coast of Scotland.

When he had reported there, McKinley was informed that he was to
proceed next day to Invergordon, on the East Coast, for a highly
important mission ; he had a good idea what this meant, for Invergordon
was the base from which other Catalinas had been opening up the new
air route to northern Russia. The next day, Monday, they flew to
Invergordon and there McKinley was briefed on his flight and told that
his passengers were Americans—Mr. Harry Hopkins, General Joseph
T. McNarney and Lieutenant John R. Alison of the U.S. Army Air
Corps. Weather conditions were bad and the flight was delayed. Hopkins
was taken for a drive over the Scottish moors and then to a cocktail
party at a small hotel and was going on from there to dinner with R.A.F.
officers and a group of Americans who were secretly in training, but a
message came from London that the aircraft was ordered to ignore the
weather and take off at once. When Hopkins came down to the waterfront and saw the PBY out in the harbor, he felt a sort of pride of

possession in it; he had put in a good deal of time persuading the U.S. Navy to agree to the transfer of any of these valuable patrol bombers to the British.

In a report on this mission, McKinley wrote:

The names of [passengers] or broad nature of the mission were not transmitted to the remainder of the crew prior to departure, on the wishes of the Station Commander. Owing to the shortage of time following the arrival of Mr. Hopkins' party at Invergordon and the intended time of departure for Archangel, little time was available for properly kitting the party with flying clothing. This factor was doubtless a contributory one in the subsequent discomfort of the party. Although each person was finally issued with a full list of items the fact that many were illfitting detracted from their usefulness. An additional factor that was seriously overlooked was that of briefing the crew as to Mr. Hopkins' state of health. Twenty-four-hour flights in the very stern austerity furnishings of a warplane and living on hard tack rations are not ideal conditions for a man in a critical state of health.

In view of the general crowding and the forecasted length of flight, with the resulting increase in fuel load, we were forced to reduce the crew to five. This in turn was to place an additional strain on the passengers since we could not spare flight personnel from flight duties to prepare meals and attend to the needs of our passengers.

About an hour after the take-off, McKinley told Pilot Officer C. M. Owen to go aft and "see how Mr. Hopkins is—he's the very thin one in a gray hat."

"And who is Mr. Hopkins?" asked Owen.

"He's a very important person. That's all we need to know."

The hat that Hopkins was now wearing was a dignified, well-blocked gray Homburg which bore inside the initials W.S.C. He had lost his old, misshapen "benny" on a trip out of London (or, perhaps, someone had deliberately mislaid it for him) and the Prime Minister had given him one of his own. Hopkins sat most of the time on this flight on a machine gunner's pivoted stool in the "blister" near the tail watching for signs of the enemy. The plane followed a course about a hundred miles from the Norwegian coast but it flew at comparatively low altitude and slow speed and, if a scouting German plane or destroyer had spotted it, it could have been shot down easily. Furthermore, visibility was uncomfortably good, for on the entire flight out and back through those far northern latitudes there was virtually no night. In the event of attack by enemy aircraft, Hopkins might have been called on to man a machine gun, and this possibility naturally interested him very much. But, fortunately, he was not subjected to this test; he served occasionally as cook and steward in the absence of the sixth crew member.

Because of the secrecy as well as the haste which surrounded the preparations for this trip there was no opportunity to provide anything in the way of comfort for the passengers. The aircraft was in its ordinary operational status and anyone who has flown a long distance in a PBY knows that is "very stern austerity" indeed. Since these planes sometimes were out as long as thirty hours at a stretch on patrol, there were canvas stretchers to be used as bunks for crew members to snatch intervals of rest. Hopkins tried to get some sleep on one of these but in the last third of the flight he suffered severely from the arctic cold.

The PBY was to make its first landfall at Kanin Point at the northeast tip of the White Sea. But here the only error was made by the navigator, Pilot Officer G. J. D. Bryand (who was later killed in action). The plane was somewhat to the north of its intended course and, missing Kanin Point, they continued on until they sighted Kolzuev Island, some 150 miles eastward. They then turned south into Cheshskaya Bay, thinking it was the White Sea. Lacking adequate charts of that remote coast, they might have become completely lost had they not picked up the faint signal of the Archangel radio and they "homed" on that beam. McKinley's report described the arrival:

> On arrival at Archangel the Mission was met by representatives of the Soviet Armed Forces and a very cordial welcome extended to all including the flight crew. Mr. Hopkins and his staff were hurriedly transferred to a waiting aircraft for the onward flight to Moscow. At this stage, Mr. Hopkins was looking very tired although he was most convincing that he had passed a pleasant journey. Such a statement was in itself mildly untrue because little could be further from an accurate description . . . This was an early indication of his determination to totally disregard personal comfort.

Owen, the first pilot, added to this that during the days they remained at Archangel, waiting for Hopkins to return from Moscow, they were confined to their quarters on a houseboat on the Dvina River. A woman interpreter was assigned to them and they continually asked her if they couldn't go ashore and see something of the people and the town but the reply was always flatly negative. However, there was another R.A.F. Catalina crew there which had landed a few days previously and, said Owen, "We were treated with so much more deference than they were and got such better food that we finally realized Mr. Hopkins must be very important indeed."

At Archangel, Hopkins was met by representatives of the American and British Embassies, Russian Army, Navy and Air Force officers, local commissars and the inevitable secret police. He noted later that "The latter looked neither more nor less obvious than the American plain-clothes man." He was introduced to his interpreter, an attractive-.

looking Russian woman, and informed through her that unfortunately
it would be impossible to fly him to Moscow that night but that they
hoped to be able to get him off at 4:00 A.M. the following morning. He
made no objection to this, for he was glad of a chance to get some sleep
after his long flight, but the admiral who was in command there invited
him and the American officers to dinner aboard his yacht. This was
Hopkins' first experience with the hospitality shown by Soviet officials
to visiting dignitaries. He later wrote a description of this dinner:

> It was monumental.
> It lasted almost four hours. There was an Iowa flavor to it, what
> with the fresh vegetables, the butter, cream, greens. For some reason
> the cucumbers and radishes surprised me. They were grown on the
> farms that hem in the city. Anyway the dinner was enormous, course
> after course. There was the inescapable cold fish, caviar and vodka.
> Vodka has authority. It is nothing for the amateur to trifle with.
> Drink it as an American or an Englishman takes whiskey neat and
> it will tear you apart. The thing to do is to spread a chunk of bread
> (and good bread it was) with caviar, and, while you are swallowing
> that bolt your vodka. Don't play with the stuff. Eat while you're
> drinking it—something that will act as a shock absorber for it.

Because of the length of this dinner, Hopkins had only two hours to
sleep before being taken to the airport. The plane, flown by Russians,
was an American Douglas Transport with very comfortable appointments.

On the take-off, Hopkins was given his first taste of the "special
salutes" which the Russians give to distinguished visitors: the plane
buzzes the field, dips first one wing then the other, and then, as he
wrote, "seems to spring vertically upward, then bounce." This is a mark
of signal honor but it tends to scare the hell out of the recipient.

The flight to Moscow took four hours and during it Hopkins began
to be reassured as to the future of the Soviet Union. He looked down
upon the hundreds of miles of solid forest and he thought that Hitler
with all the Panzer divisions in the Wehrmacht could never hope to
break through country like this.

At the airport in Moscow, Hopkins was met by the American Ambassador, Laurence A. Steinhardt, and another large reception committee.
He wrote, "In Russia I shook hands as I have never shaken hands
before. Several times I grinned at myself asking myself whether I were
running for office. However, I kissed no babies." Steinhardt took him
to the American Embassy, Spasso House, and put him to bed, but he
was too excited at being in Moscow to be able to sleep very long. He
did not want to waste a moment during his brief stay in the Soviet
capital—he wanted to spend all the time that he possibly could observing, listening, absorbing. He was now at the other end of the cables

upon which the United States and British Governments had depended
for information about the great unknown quantity of Russia.

He had a long talk with Steinhardt in which he said that the main
purpose of his visit was to determine whether the situation was as disastrous as it was pictured in the War Department—and particularly
as indicated in the cables from the Military Attaché, Major Ivan Yeaton.

Steinhardt said that anyone who knew anything of Russian history
could hardly jump to the conclusion that the Germans would achieve
easy conquest. Russian soldiers might appear inept when engaged in
offensive operations—they had done so in the Napoleonic wars and again
in Finland. But when they were called upon to defend their homeland
they were superb fighters—and there were certainly a great many of
them. But, Steinhardt emphasized, it was supremely difficult for any
outsider in Moscow to get a clear picture of what was really going on.
He and other diplomats in Moscow had been continually frustrated in
their attempted dealings with the Soviet authorities because of the
prevailing attitude of suspicion toward all foreigners and consequent
secretiveness. Hopkins said he was determined somehow or other to
break through this wall of suspicion.

He had a long rest that night and the next day drove about Moscow
with Steinhardt on a sight-seeing tour. At 6:30 P.M., Steinhardt
took him to the Kremlin to meet Stalin. Hopkins' report to the President of that meeting follows, in full:

> I told Mr. Stalin that I came as personal representative of the
> President. The President considered Hitler the enemy of mankind
> and that he therefore wished to aid the Soviet Union in its fight
> against Germany.
>
> I told him that my mission was not a diplomatic one in the sense
> that I did not propose any formal understanding of any kind or
> character.
>
> I expressed to him the President's belief that the most important
> thing to be done in the world today was to defeat Hitler and Hitlerism.
> I impressed upon him the determination of the President and our
> Government to extend all possible aid to the Soviet Union at the
> earliest possible time.
>
> I told Mr. Stalin that I had certain personal messages from the
> President and explained my relationship to the Administration in
> Washington. I told him further that I just left Mr. Churchill in
> London who wished me to convey to him the sentiments which I had
> already expressed from the President.
>
> Mr. Stalin said he welcomed me to the Soviet Union; that he had
> already been informed of my visit.
>
> Describing Hitler and Germany, Mr. Stalin spoke of the necessity
> of there being a minimum moral standard between all nations and
> without such a minimum moral standard nations could not co-exist.

He stated that the present leaders of Germany·knew no such minimum moral standard and that, therefore, they represented an anti-social force in the present world. The Germans were a people, he said, who without a second's thought would sign a treaty today, break it tomorrow and sign a second one the following day. Nations must fulfill their treaty obligations, he said, or international society could not exist.

When he completed his general summary of the Soviet Union's attitude toward Germany he said "therefore our views coincide."

I told Mr. Stalin that the question of aid to the Soviet Union was divided into two parts. First, what would Russia most require that the United States could deliver immediately and, second, what would be Russia's requirements on the basis of a long war?

Stalin listed in the first category the immediate need of, first, anti-aircraft guns of medium calibre, of from 20 to 37 mm., together with ammunition. He stated that he needed such medium calibre guns because of the rapidity of their fire and their mobility. He stated that all together he needed approximately 20,000 pieces of anti-aircraft artillery, large and small. He believed that if he could acquire such a quantity it would immediately release nearly 2,000 pursuit ships which are today required for the protection of military objectives behind the Soviet lines and such planes, if released, could be used as attacking forces against the enemy.

Second, he asked for large size machine guns for the defense of his cities.

Third, he said he heard there were many rifles available in the United States and he believed their calibre corresponded to the calibre used in his Army. He stated that he needed one million or more such rifles. I asked Mr. Stalin if he needed ammunition for these rifles and he replied that if the calibre was the same as the one used by the Red Army "we have plenty."

In the second category, namely, the supplies needed for a long range war, he mentioned first high octane aviation gasoline, second, aluminum for the construction of airplanes and, third, the other items already mentioned in the list presented to our Government in Washington.

At this point in the conversation Mr. Stalin suddenly made the remark, "Give us anti-aircraft guns and the aluminum and we can fight for three or four years."

I referred to the 200 Curtiss P-40's which are being delivered to the Soviet Union and, in reply to a question from Mr. Stalin, I confirmed the fact that 140 were being delivered by way of England and 60 from the United States.

In connection with the delivery of these planes I referred to Lt. Alison's presence in Moscow and said he was an outstanding expert in the operation of this type of plane. I asked if he would care to have Lt. Alison stationed in Archangel in an advisory capacity, to which Mr. Stalin replied affirmatively.

Mr. Stalin stated that he would be glad if we would send any technicians that we could to the Soviet Union to help train his own airmen in the use of these planes. He stated that his own airmen would show us everything about the Russian equipment, which he stated we would find very interesting.

He described at some length, but not in great detail as he did in the conference the next day, the planes which he had available. Mr. Stalin said the plane he needed particularly was the short-range bomber, capable of operating in a radius of 600 to 1100 kilometres, or with a total range of 1200 to 2200 kilometres.

I asked Mr. Stalin what he thought was the best route to ship supplies from the United States to the Soviet Union. Mr. Stalin stated that the Persian Gulf-Iranian route was not good because of the limited capacity of the Iranian railways and highways. He stated, "furthermore we do not yet know the view of the Iranian Government on this subject."

Mr. Stalin stated that the Vladivostok route was not a favorable one. I emphasized the danger of its being cut off by the Japanese and Mr. Stalin in turn emphasized the great distance from the scene of battle.

Mr. Stalin believed that the Archangel route was probably the most practicable. Both Mr. Stalin and Mr. Molotov stated that the Archangel harbor could be kept open in the winter by the aid of ice breakers. Mr. Stalin pointed out that the only two absolutely ice free ports in the north were Murmansk and Kaldalaksha.

I told Mr. Stalin that my stay in Moscow must be brief. I wished to accomplish as much as possible in the short time which I had at my disposal. I asked Mr. Stalin whether he wished to carry on the conversations personally or would prefer that I would discuss some of the details with other representatives of the Soviet Government. I said that, of course, I would prefer to confer directly with him but I realized he had a great many responsibilities at the moment. I told him that I had some personal messages from the President which I wanted to deliver at an appropriate time.

Mr. Stalin replied, "You are our guest; you have but to command." He told me he would be at my disposal every day from six to seven. It was then agreed that I confer with representatives of the Red Army at ten o'clock that night.

I reiterated to Mr. Stalin the appreciation of the people of the United States of the splendid resistance of the Soviet Army and of the President's determination to do everything to assist the Soviet Union in its valiant struggle against the German invader.

Mr. Stalin replied with an expression of gratitude of the Soviet Government.

I told Mr. Stalin that I expected to interview the representatives of the Anglo-American press following my meeting and asked whether Mr. Stalin had any wishes in connection with what I should say or whether he would prefer that no interview be held at all. I told him that under any circumstances the correspondents' stories would be subject to the control of his censorship.

To this Mr. Stalin replied that anything I might have to say would require no censorship by his Government.

I expressed to Mr. Molotov my desire to call upon him and it was arranged that I should see Mr. Molotov at three the next day.

Later that evening Hopkins engaged in technical discussions with General Yakovlev, an artilleryman of the Red Army, General McNarney and Major Yeaton. Most of the discussion was of the items previously mentioned by Stalin—antiaircraft guns, aluminum, rifles, etc. When that list was exhausted, Hopkins went on to suggest that a Russian technical mission be sent to Washington and kept there permanently to discuss new problems as they came up day by day. Yakovlev refused to comment on this suggestion saying it should be taken up with Stalin. This was Hopkins' first real encounter with the limitations imposed on the lower levels (which meant any level below the very top) of the Soviet system; they did not dare to utter a word on any topic beyond the prescribed agenda. Hopkins asked Yakovlev if he couldn't think of other items that the Army might need and Yakovlev—doubtless with the utmost reluctance—said that he could think of nothing else, that the most important items had been covered. In the minutes of this meeting appears the following revealing passage:

> Mr. Hopkins stated that he was surprised that General Yakovlev did not mention tanks and anti-tank guns. General Yakovlev replied, I think we have enough. Mr. Hopkins remarked that many tanks were necessary when fighting this particular enemy. General Yakovlev agreed. When asked the weight of Russia's heaviest tank, General Yakovlev replied, it is a good tank.
>
> General Yakovlev was asked if Russian artillery had been able to stop the German tanks. He replied, our artillery shoots any tank—conditions vary. After further discussion of the tank question General Yakovlev stated that the Russians could use extra tanks and anti-tank guns and said America could provide Russia with them. He went on further to say, "I am not empowered to say whether we do or do not need tanks or anti-tank guns."

Hopkins was greatly impressed with the black-out in Moscow which was even more impenetrable than London's. He was also impressed by the tremendous concentration of antiaircraft fire when German bombers came over on a raid. A bomb shelter had been placed at his disposal and he and Steinhardt went there. Hopkins was amazed at the champagne, caviar, chocolates, cigarettes with which the bomb shelter had been equipped and, according to Steinhardt, "He laughed heartily when I told him that no bomb shelter had ever been placed at *my* disposal and I owed this night's protection to his presence."

On Hopkins' second day in Moscow, July 31, he met with Stafford Cripps, who had returned in haste from England after Hitler's attack on the Soviet Union. They discussed principally the forthcoming Roosevelt-Churchill conference in its relation to Russia. They agreed that the President and Prime Minister should send a joint message to Stalin at the end of the conference and discussed the wording of this message. Cripps wrote a draft of the message based on their discussion and Hopkins took this draft with him to the Atlantic Conference. Although some of this was cut out, the wording was essentially the same in the cable that was sent to Stalin from Argentia two weeks later—including the opening sentence, "We have taken the opportunity afforded by the consideration of the report of Mr. Harry Hopkins on his return from Moscow to consult together as to how best our two countries can help your country in the splendid defence that you are putting up against the Nazi attack." (The only change there was that "making" was substituted for "putting up.")

That afternoon Hopkins and Steinhardt called upon Molotov in the Kremlin as arranged. The main topic was the situation in the Far East and the growing menace of Japan. In his report to the President on this conversation Hopkins did not record what he himself said in introducing the subject since this would have no news value for Roosevelt. However, Steinhardt summarized it in a cable to the State Department, the first part of which follows:

I was present this afternoon at an interview at which Harry Hopkins presented to Molotov the point of view of the President and the American people with respect to Japan and China in their relations with the United States and the Soviet Union. He made it clear that in the event of continued Japanese aggression the temper of the American public and the disposition of the President is to make no threat which would not be followed by action if necessary. He stressed the fact that the long-standing amicable relations between the United States and Russia, which the American public has come to accept as assuring stability in the north Pacific, would be jeopardized by a Japanese venture in Siberia and said that the United States could not look with complacency on the occupation of any part of that area by Japan. In this connection he stated that he had reason to believe that the Japanese Government is awaiting the outcome of the great battle now in progress on the Soviet western frontier and that it might take action against the Soviet Union should the outcome of this battle be unfavorable to the Soviet Union. Molotov stated that he understood and appreciated the point of view of President Roosevelt.

At this point Steinhardt's message joins up with Hopkins' report:

Mr. Molotov stated that while the Soviet-Japanese relations presumably had been fixed by, first, the conversations with Matsuoka and, secondly, the neutrality pact signed between the two countries, nevertheless, the attitude of the new Japanese Government toward the Soviet Union is uncertain and, since the Soviet Government is by no means clear as to the policy which the Japanese Government intends to pursue, it is watching the situation with the utmost care.

He stated that the one thing he thought would keep Japan from making an aggressive move would be for the President to find some appropriate means of giving Japan what Mr. Molotov described as a "warning."

While Mr. Molotov did not use the exact words, it was perfectly clear that the implication of his statement was that the warning would include a statement that the United States would come to the assistance of the Soviet Union in the event of its being attacked by Japan.

Mr. Molotov did not express any immediate concern that Japan was going to attack Russia and on Russia's part Mr. Molotov stated repeatedly that Russia did not wish any difficulties with Japan.

He left me with the impression, however, that it was a matter of very considerable concern to him and that he felt the Japanese would not hesitate to strike if a propitious time occurred. Hence his great interest in the attitude of the United States toward Japan.

I told Mr. Molotov that the Government of the United States was disturbed at the encroachments which Japan was making in the Far East and I was sure the American people would not look with any favor on Japan gaining a further hold in Siberia; that our long period of friendly relations between Russia and the United States, with our two countries only fifty miles apart, should be some indication of our interest in seeing stability in the Far East, including Siberia.

I told him that our Government was watching developments in the Far Eastern situation with great care and looked with misgivings and concern at the threatening attitude of Japan, both to the South and to the North. I told him, however, that our attitude towards Japan was a reasonable one and that we had no desire to be provocative in our relations with Japan.

I told him I would give the President his message regarding his, Molotov's, anxiety about Siberia and his desire to have the President indicate to Japan that further encroachments would not be tolerated.

I asked Mr. Molotov what their relationships with China were in the light of new developments and whether or not they could continue rendering the substantial material assistance they had been giving to Chiang Kai-shek or whether the Soviet Union's requirements in its own war with Germany would preclude their continuing to supply China.

Mr. Molotov replied that, of course, the Soviet Union's requirements for war material must of necessity adversely affect delivery to China; that while they do not wish to cut them off entirely and would continue to give everything they could, the necessities of their own situation required them to divert the Chinese supplies to their own battle line. Molotov expressed the hope that the United States would increase its own deliveries to make good the deficiency caused by Germany's attack on the Soviet Union.

I told Mr. Molotov that the American people were impressed by the gallant defense of the Soviet Army and assured him of the desire of the President to render every possible aid in the terms of materials to the Soviet Union as speedily as possible.

Mr. Molotov asked me to convey the Soviet Government's thanks to the President for sending his personal representative on this mission to Moscow.

It is interesting to note that Molotov expressed much the same point of view that Churchill had expressed previously and expressed again at the Atlantic Conference: that the United States should adopt a tough attitude toward Japan as a means of preventing further extension of the war in Asia.

When Hopkins returned to the Kremlin at 6:30 that evening for a three-hour meeting with Stalin he was unaccompanied by Steinhardt or anyone else. The interpreter was Maxim Litvinov who had been the Soviet Foreign Commissar in the days of Geneva and "collective security" and then had disappeared into the vast silences after the Nazi-Soviet pact in August, 1939. Now, Hopkins said later, he seemed like a morning coat which had been laid away in mothballs when Russia retreated into isolation from the West but which had now been brought out, dusted off and aired as a symbol of completely changed conditions.

Hopkins divided his report of this long meeting with Stalin into three parts. The first two, in full, were as follows:

PART I

I told Mr. Stalin that the President was anxious to have his—Stalin's—appreciation and analysis of the war between Germany and Russia. Mr. Stalin outlined the situation as follows:

He stated that in his opinion the German Army had 175 divisions on Russia's western front at the outbreak of the war, and that since the outbreak of the war, this has been increased to 232 divisions; he believes that Germany can mobilize 300 divisions.

He stated that Russia had 180 divisions at the outbreak of the war, but many of these were well back of the line of combat, and could not be quickly mobilized, so that when the Germans struck it was impossible to offer adequate resistance. The line which is now held is a far more propitious one than the more advanced line which they might have taken up had their divisions been prepared. Since war began, however, divisions have been placed in their appropriate positions, and at the present time he believes that Russia has a few more divisions than Germany, and places the number of Russian divisions at 240 in the front, with 20 in reserve. Stalin said that about one third of these divisions had not as yet been under fire.

Mr. Stalin stated that he can mobilize 350 divisions and will have that many divisions under arms by the time the spring campaign begins in May 1942.

He is anxious to have as many of his divisions as possible in contact with the enemy, because then the troops learn that Germans can be killed and are not supermen. This gives his divisions the same kind of confidence that a pilot gets after his first combat in the air. Stalin said that "nothing in warfare can take the place of actual combat," and he wants to have as many seasoned troops as possible for the great campaign which will come next Spring. He stated that the German troops seemed to be tired, and the officers and men that they had captured had indicated they are "sick of war."

The German reserves are as much as 400 kilometres back of the front, and the communications between the reserves and the front line are extremely difficult. These supply lines require many thousands of German troops to guard and protect them from Russian raids.

He said that in the battle now in progress, very many Russian and German troops are fighting far forward from their respective lines because of the advances made by both sides with their mechanized forces. Stalin said that his soldiers did not consider the battle lost merely because the Germans at one point and another broke through with their mechanized forces. The Russian mechanized forces would attack at another point often moving many miles behind the German line. Merely because German forces pierce the Russian line does not mean the Russians are lost. They fight behind the Germans, are adept at the use of cover and fight their way out in the night. He said, "Even the German tanks run out of petrol." This is merely a phase of modern warfare, and accounts for the fact that there have been no mass surrenders of troops on either side. The Russians therefore have many "insurgent" troops which operate behind Germany's so-called front line. They constantly attack German aerodromes and lines of communications. The Russians are more familiar with the terrain and know how to use the natural cover which nature has provided better than the Germans. These "insurgent" troops are proving a great menace to the German offensive.

He believes that Germany underestimated the strength of the Russian Army, and have not now enough troops on the whole front to carry on a successful offensive war and at the same time guard their extended lines of communications. He repeatedly emphasized the large number of men Germany was forced to use for this purpose, and believes that the Germans will have to go on the defensive themselves. There is considerable evidence that they are already doing this. They are burying many of their large tanks in the ground for defensive purposes. The Russians have already found 50 such defensive positions.

Mr. Stalin stated that in his opinion Hitler fears that he has too many men on the Russian front, which may account for their preparing some defensive positions so that some of their divisions might be returned to the German western areas of actual or potential operation.

He thinks the Germans have now on his front about 70 tank and motorized divisions. He also states that the Russo-German war has already changed the character of divisional organization; that the Germans had broken up their large armoured divisions and dispersed this equipment through what Stalin called their tank and motorized divisions. Stalin stated that the war has already shown that infantry divisions must include a larger number of mechanized units. While Russia had a large number of tank and motorized divisions—none of them were a match for the German "Panzer" division, but were far stronger than other German divisions. Hence the great pressure on the German infantry divisions which caused the diversion of German armoured equipment all along the line.

Stalin believes that Germany had 30,000 tanks at the outbreak of the Russian war. Russia herself had 24,000 tanks and 60 tank divisions with about 350 to 400 tanks in each division. They have always had about 50 tanks in each infantry division. Stalin believes that the large divisions are being broken up by the German Staff and as the war progresses the number of men in the divisions will be decreased in both armies.

He stated that the pressure on his army in the last ten days had become considerably less, and the only reason he could give for it was that he thought Germany had been unable to supply their mechanized divisions and air forces with adequate fuel. He stressed the great difficulty the German armies had encountered in moving vast quantities of fuel to the front, and believes these difficulties are going to increase. He does not think this is because Germany has any lack of fuel, but rather because of transportation difficulties, the lack of good roads and more particularly the effective interference of the Russians with the German communications.

Stalin says that even though the war has been going on only six weeks, his troops are meeting brand new divisions at the front, and some of the original divisions seem to have been withdrawn. He believes that the morale of his own troops is extremely high, and realizes that this is partly due to the fact that they are fighting for their homes and in familiar territory. He said that Germany has already found that "moving mechanized forces through Russia was very different than moving them over the boulevards of Belgium and France."

Stalin said that the Russian Army had been confronted with a surprise attack; he himself believed that Hitler would not strike but he took all precautions possible to mobilize his army. Hitler made no demands on Russia, hence they were forced to organize a defensive line of battle. Now the Russians were counter-attacking at many points.

He said the Russian Army had met few of the 70-ton German tanks but that this was probably due to the inability of the Russian bridges to hold the tanks. He believes the terrain too difficult to manœuvre these giant tanks. Where the 70-ton tanks were encountered, they were pierced by the Russian 75 mm. guns. He does not think that the very large German tank will play an important part in the war in Russia, although there are parts of the southern front where these tanks can manœuvre. The roads are very bad for the big tanks to operate over.

He believes that his largest tanks are better than the other German tanks, and that they have repeatedly shown their superiority in the war to date. He stated that the two largest Russian tanks were of 48 to 52 tons respectively, with 75 mm. armour and 85 mm. guns. They have approximately 4,000 of these tanks at present. The Russian medium tank of just over 30 tons has 45 mm. armour and 75 mm. guns. The infantry tank is 13 tons and has 37 mm. armour and 45 mm. guns. They have approximately 8,000 medium (30-ton) tanks at present and 12,000 light (13-ton) tanks. He stated their present production of tanks was 1,000 per month. He stated that his production was equally divided between medium and heavy tanks on the one hand, and light tanks on the other. He stated they would be short of steel for tank manufacture and urged that orders for this steel be placed at once. He later said it would be much better if his tanks could be manufactured in the United States. He also wished to purchase as many of our tanks as possible to be ready for the Spring campaign. Stalin said the all-important thing was the production of tanks during the winter—the tank losses on both sides were very great but that Germany could produce more tanks per month this winter than Russia. Hence the aid of the United States in supplying steel and tanks is essential. He would like to send a tank expert to the United States. He stated that he would give the United States his tank designs.

He emphasized the fact that Germany has a strong and powerful air force, and that their present production of planes was probably 2,500 fighters and bombers per month, but not more than 3,000 a month. Germany has more planes than the Russians at the front at this time but the quality of many of the German planes is not first-class—they are rough, plain machines, in which pilots fly without a long training. Some pilots they have captured indicated that their training was short and consisted of only a "practical course." He realizes that Germany moved to the Russian front a great many aircraft which types are no longer being built in German factories. He thinks that Germany under-rated the ability of the Russian Air Force and thought that these second-rate planes could operate successfully against them. The Russians have experienced no trouble in destroying these planes. The Henkel plane was faster than the new Messerschmitt. On the whole the most useful plane the Germans have against the Russians is the Junkers 88, which is as good or better than anything of that type that the Russians have.

He stated that the Germans are putting 20 mm. cannon in their fighters; some have 12 mm. machine guns. Stalin said that all fighters must have cannon in modern warfare. He has equipped all his fighters with cannon or heavy calibre machine guns, and he stated the Russians proposed to have no fighters without cannon or the heaviest calibre machine guns.

The Russians put their old fighter planes on the front, and these have a speed of only 440 kilometres per hour, but they have been very useful and successful against many of the planes that the Germans put on Russia's western front. They have seven to eight thousand of these older type fighters.

The new fighters are of three types. They have approximately 2,000 of these at the front, and are producing 1,200 a month. The speediest of these newer one-motor fighters is the M.I.G. 3, with heavy armour and cannon, and a speed of 650 kilometres per hour. The second fighter is the L.A.G. 3, which carries a cannon, has heavy machine guns and a speed of 590 k.p.h. The third is the J.K. 1; this carries a cannon, and has a speed of 590 k.p.h.

Stalin said the Russians have three new medium bomber types. First a single-motor bomber, flying at 510 k.p.h., for close range bombing. Second, the 2-motor dive bomber, flying at 540 k.p.h. with a flying range of 800 kilometres. The third bomber, which is only just being produced in quantity, is a 2-motor dive bomber with a range of 2,200 kilometres and a speed of 610 k.p.h., and carries one ton of bombs on its full flight range, but double that amount of bombs on more than half range. It has 7 heavy machine guns. Stalin spoke of it as "a very good bomber."

He said he has three types of long-range bomber. One, a 2-motor bomber which is quite slow, doing 440 k.p.h. with a range of 3,000 kilometres. Second, a 2-motor bomber, just in production, with a Diesel engine; range 5,000 kilometres, carrying one ton bomb load, 2 tons at 4,000 kilometres range; speed 500 k.p.h. Third, a 4-engine bomber, just now getting into production; range 3,500 kilometres, carrying 3 tons of bombs. He said they had at present about 600 heavy long range bombers.

He said that his total production of planes at present was 1,800 per month; by January 1st, this would increase to 2,500 per month. 60% of these would be fighter planes, and 40% bombers. This was exclusive of training planes, now being produced at 15 per day. The Russians have approximately 3,500 training planes. Stalin said the training course for pilots was 8 months.

He expressed considerable interest in training pilots in America and left me the impression there would soon be a shortage of pilots. Stalin said the German claims of Russian air losses were absurd. The Russians lost more planes than the Germans at first, but he thinks the advantage is the other way now. He would not indicate the number of losses other than there were a "good many on both sides."

He stated there had been some damage to aircraft factories but that there had been considerable disbursal of the machinery before the destruction took place. (I saw two factories, which I was told by our Ambassador were aircraft factories, just outside Moscow completely destroyed.)

I asked Mr. Stalin about the location of his munitions plants. He did not reply to this in detail but indicated that about 75% of the sum total of his munitions plants, the percentage varying depending on the type of plant, were in the general areas of which Leningrad, Moscow and Kiev were the centers.

I gained the impression from him that if the German army could move some 150 miles east of each of these centers, they would destroy almost 75% of Russia's industrial capacity.

Stalin said they had dispersed a good many of their larger factories and were moving many machine tools eastward to escape the bombing attacks.

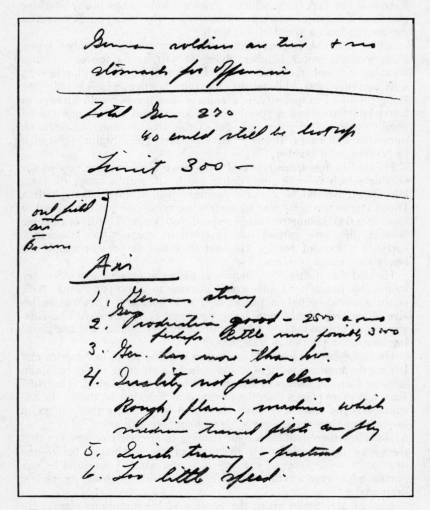

Page of original notes taken by Hopkins on July 31, 1941, during a conversation with Stalin.

Stalin repeatedly stated that he did not under-rate the German Army. He stated that their organization was of the very best and that he believed that they had large reserves of food, men, supplies and fuel. He thinks that we may be underestimating Germany's oil supplies, and he bases this on the fact that under the two-year agreement they had with Germany, the Germans asked for less fuel than the agreement provided for during the year 1940-41. He thought one weakness the British had was under-rating their enemy; he did not propose to do this. He, therefore, thinks that so far as men, supplies, food and fuel are concerned, the German Army is capable of taking part in a winter campaign in Russia. He thinks, however, that it would be difficult for the Germans to operate offensively much after the first of September, when the heavy rains will begin, and after October 1st the ground would be so bad that they would have to go on the defensive. He expressed great confidence that the line during the winter months would be in front of Moscow, Kiev and Leningrad—probably not more than 100 kilometres away from where it is now. He thinks that one of the great advantages the Russian Army has at the moment is that the Germans "are tired" and have no stomach for an offensive. He realizes that Germany can still bring up about 40 divisions, making 275 divisions in all at the Russian front, but these divisions probably cannot get there before the hard weather sets in.

He told me that the first need of the Russian Army was light anti-aircraft guns, 20 mm., 25 mm., 37 mm., and 50 mm., and that they need vast quantities of these guns to give protection to their lines of communications against low flying planes.

His second great need was aluminum needed in the construction of airplanes.

The third was machine guns of approximately 50 calibre, and the fourth rifles of approximately 30 calibre. He stated that he needed large anti-aircraft guns for the defense of cities. In his opinion the Russian supply of ammunition was satisfactory. He stated the outcome of the war in Russia would largely depend on the ability to enter the spring campaign with adequate equipment, particularly in aircraft, tanks and anti-aircraft guns.

He expressed an urgent desire that the British send large planes as soon as possible to bomb the Rumanian oil fields, and made a point of urging that pilots and crews be sent with the planes.

He told me one of the great problems was to determine the ports of entry which were to be used for supplies; and that Archangel was difficult but not impossible; he was sure his ice-breakers could keep the port free all winter. He stated that Vladivostok was dangerous because it could be cut off by Japan at any time, and he feared the railroads and roads in Persia were inadequate. But all would have to be used for the present.

Mr. Stalin expressed repeatedly his confidence that the Russian lines would hold within 100 kilometres of their present position.

No information given above was confirmed by any other source.

Memorandum in Stalin's handwriting, given to Hopkins in the Kremlin July 31, 1941, indicating order of importance of supplies Stalin wanted from America. 1) light anti-aircraft guns; 2) aluminum (which he said he wanted for airplanes); 3) 50 calibre machine guns; 4) 30 calibre rifles.

It was during this conversation that Stalin wrote down in pencil on a small pad the four basic Russian requirements and handed the sheet to Hopkins. There was another passage, not recorded in the above report, which Hopkins noted later:

I asked Mr. Stalin whether he had seen any of the Italian divisions on his front, or Franco's volunteers, which had been announced in the papers.

Stalin laughed at this, and said there was nothing his men would like better than to see either the Italians or the Spaniards on their front.

He said that the Soviet Army discounted all divisions other than the Germans. Neither the Finns, Rumanians, Italians nor Spaniards count, and he was quite sure that neither the Italians nor the Franco troops would ever appear on his front. He stated that he thought Hitler had even more contempt for them than he had.

The Hopkins report continued:

PART II

I told Mr. Stalin at this conference that our Government and the British Government (Churchill having authorized me to say this) were willing to do everything that they possibly could during the succeeding weeks to send matériel to Russia. This matériel, however, must obviously be already manufactured and that he—Stalin—must understand that even this matériel could in all probability not reach his battle lines before the bad weather closes in.

I told him that we believed that plans should be made for a long war; that so far as the United States was concerned we had large supply commitments in relation to our own Army, Navy and Merchant Marine, as well as very substantial responsibilities for supplies to England, China and the Republics of South America.

I told him that the decisions relating to the long range supply problem could only be resolved if our Government had complete knowledge, not only of the military situation in Russia, but of type, number and quality of their military weapons, as well as full knowledge of raw materials and factory capacity.

I told him that I knew that our Government, and I believed the British Government, would be unwilling to send any heavy munitions, such as tanks, aircraft and anti-aircraft guns, to the Russian front unless and until a conference had been held between our three Governments, at which the relative strategic interests of each front, as well as the interests of our several countries, was fully and jointly explored.

I suggested that, in as much as he was so fully engaged with the immediate prosecution of the battle now in hand, he could not give the time and attention to such a conference until after this battle is over.

Stalin had previously indicated that the front would be solidified not later than October 1.

I was mindful of the importance that no conference be held in Moscow until we knew the outcome of the battle now in progress. I felt it very unwise to hold a conference while this battle was in the balance. Hence my suggestion to him to hold a conference at as late a date as was possible. Then we would know whether or not there was to be a front and approximately the location of the front during the coming winter months.

Stalin said he would welcome such a conference and said that of course it would be impossible for him to go to a conference anywhere other than in Moscow; that he would be glad to make available to our Government all information which was required and he offered to give us the Soviet designs of their airplanes, tanks and guns.

I told him that I was not authorized to make this suggestion of a conference to him officially.

Stalin then stated that in case our Government wished to have such a conference he would receive such a proposal sympathetically and would give the conference his personal attention.

Stalin has not given hitherto any information of any kind to any of the Embassies or to any of the Military Attaches of foreign governments. The British Naval Attache has been given information confined to the Russian Navy because of certain joint operations.

There is literally no one in the whole Government who is willing to give any important information other than Mr. Stalin himself. Therefore, it is essential that such a conference be held with Mr. Stalin personally.

I believe he would give this conference his personal attention.

My suggestion is that the conference be not held prior to October 1, but not later than October 15.

Copies of these Parts I and II of the Hopkins report of his meeting with Stalin were sent to the Secretaries of State, War and Navy. There followed a Part III which Hopkins marked "FOR THE PRESIDENT ONLY." He made only one copy of this part and recommended to the President that it should not be let out of his office but suggested that its contents might be communicated verbally to Secretary Hull. The reason for this secrecy was that Stalin spoke bluntly of the desirability of U.S. entry into the war against Germany. The full text of Part III follows:

After Stalin had completed his review of the military situation, he expressed to me his great thanks to the President for the interest he was showing in their fight against Hitler. He stated that he wanted to give the President the following personal message; that he had considered putting the message in writing but believed it would be more desirable to have the message delivered to the President by me.

Stalin said Hitler's greatest weakness was found in the vast numbers of oppressed people who hated Hitler and the immoral ways of his Government. He believed these people and countless other millions in nations still unconquered could receive the kind of encouragement and moral strength they needed to resist Hitler from only one source, and that was the United States. He stated that the world influence of the President and the Government of the United States was enormous.

Contrary wise, he believed that the morale of the German army and the German people, which he thinks is already pretty low, would be demoralized by an announcement that the United States is going to join in the war against Hitler.

Stalin said that he believed it was inevitable that we should finally come to grips with Hitler on some battlefield. The might of Germany was so great that, even though Russia might defend herself, it would be very difficult for Britain and Russia combined to crush the German military machine. He said that the one thing that could defeat Hitler, and perhaps without ever firing a shot, would be the announcement that the United States was going to war with Germany.

Stalin said that he believed, however, that the war would be bitter and perhaps long; that if we did get in the war he believed the American people would insist on their armies coming to grips with German

soldiers; and he wanted me to tell the President that he would welcome the American troops on any part of the Russian front under the
complete command of the American Army.

I told Stalin that my mission related entirely to matters of supply
and that the matter of our joining in the war would be decided largely
by Hitler himself and his encroachment upon our fundamental interests. I told him that I doubted that our Government, in event of war
would want an American army in Russia but that I would give his
message to the President.

He repeatedly said that the President and the United States had
more influence with the common people of the world today than any
other force.

Finally, he asked me to tell the President that, while he was confident that the Russian Army could withstand the German army, the
problem of supply by next spring would be a serious one and that he
needed our help.

This was Hopkins' last meeting with Stalin on that brief trip. In two
days he had gained far more information about Russia's strength and
prospects than had ever been vouchsafed to any outsider. Stalin had
certainly taken Roosevelt's request to heart and had reposed complete
confidence in Hopkins, and Hopkins for his part left the Kremlin with
the profound conviction that Stalin was not talking through his or
anyone else's hat. This was indeed the turning point in the wartime
relations of Britain and the United States with the Soviet Union. No
longer would all Anglo-American calculations be based on the probability of early Russian collapse—after this, the whole approach to the problem was changed. Hopkins later wrote of Stalin in the *American*
magazine:

Not once did he repeat himself. He talked as he knew his troops
were shooting—straight and hard. He welcomed me with a few, swift
Russian words. He shook my hand briefly, firmly, courteously. He
smiled warmly. There was no waste of word, gesture, nor mannerism.
It was like talking to a perfectly co-ordinated machine, an intelligent
machine. Joseph Stalin knew what he wanted, knew what Russia
wanted, and he assumed that you knew. We talked for almost four
hours on this second visit. The questions he asked were clear, concise,
direct. Tired as I was, I found myself replying as tersely. His answers
were ready, unequivocal, spoken as if the man had had them on his
tongue for years.

Only once while we talked did his telephone ring. He apologized
for the interruption, telling me he was making plans for his supper at
12:30 that night. Not once did a secretary enter with dispatches or
memoranda. And when we said good-by we shook hands again with
the same finality. He said good-by once, just as only once he said
hello. And that was that. Perhaps I merely imagined that his smile
was more friendly, a bit warmer. Perhaps it was so because, to his

word of farewell, he had added his respects to the President of the United States.

No man could forget the picture of the dictator of Russia as he stood watching me leave—an austere, rugged, determined figure in boots that shone like mirrors, stout baggy trousers, and snug-fitting blouse. He wore no ornament, military or civilian. He's built close to the ground, like a football coach's dream of a tackle. He's about five feet six, about a hundred and ninety pounds. His hands are huge, as hard as his mind. His voice is harsh but ever under control. What he says is all the accent and inflection his words need. . . .

If he is always as I heard him, he never wastes a syllable. If he wants to soften an abrupt answer or a sudden question he does it with that quick, managed smile—a smile that can be cold but friendly, austere but warm. He curries no favor with you. He seems to have no doubts. He assures you that Russia will stand against the on-slaughts of the German army. He takes it for granted that you have no doubts, either. . . .

He offered me one of his cigarettes and he took one of mine. He's a chain smoker, probably accounting for the harshness of his care-fully controlled voice. He laughs often enough, but it's a short laugh, somewhat sardonic, perhaps. There is no small talk in him. His humor is keen, penetrating. He speaks no English, but as he shot rapid Russian at me he ignored the interpreter, looking straight into my eyes as though I understood every word that he uttered.

I said there were no interruptions in our interview. There were —two or three. But not by the telephone nor an unbidden secretary. Two or three times I asked him questions which, after a split second of consideration, he couldn't answer to his own satisfaction. He touched a button. Instantly, as if he'd been standing alertly at the door, a secretary appeared, stood at attention. Stalin repeated my question. The answer came like a shot. The secretary disappeared just like that.

In the States and in London such missions as mine might be stretched out into what the State Department and Foreign Office call conversations. I had no conversations in Moscow—just six hours of conversation. After that there was no more to be said. It was all cleaned up at two sittings.

Of course, Hopkins saw nothing of the actual battlefront in Russia. Even if he had, he would hardly have been able to understand what was going on. He gained his confidence in Russian powers of resistance mainly from the very nature of Stalin's requests, which proved that he was viewing the war on a long-range basis. A man who feared immediate defeat would not have put aluminum so high on the list of priorities. As a result of this, Hopkins later expressed extreme irritation with the military observers in Moscow when they cabled pessimistic reports that could be based on nothing but mere guesswork colored by prejudice.

Hopkins was elated by his meetings with Stalin, but he was also depressed—for he had been given a glimpse of something that he had never seen before, the true nature of the totalitarian state. He wrote, "Before my three days in Moscow ended, the difference between democracy and dictatorship were clearer to me than any words a philosopher, historian or journalist could make it." He had seen the awful fear which was a part of the respect with which any subordinate, even a high-ranking officer, like General Yakovlev, regarded his superiors. Through the years that followed, Hopkins was a sincere and even aggressive friend of Russia and an intense admirer of Russia's gigantic contribution to the winning of the war. He had nothing but contempt for those jittery Americans who were forever looking for Communists under the bed. But he could never reconcile himself to a system which seemingly concentrated such absolute power in one mortal man. His whole concept of government was based on the American system of checks and balances, and he had seen at firsthand the continuous and direct responsibility of the British Prime Minister to Parliament. Later on, as the record will show, when evidences of discrepancy began to appear in the application of Soviet policy, Hopkins suspected that if he had ever been permitted to attend meetings of the Politburo, as he had attended Cabinet meetings in Washington and London, he might have learned that Stalin's power was not so absolute as he had at first imagined. But he never gained any clear idea as to how the Politburo really operated, and neither did Roosevelt. As time went on, and as the tide of battle turned, they became more and more aware of it as an unseen, incomprehensible and unpredictable but potent influence on Stalin and thus on all Allied long-term policy.

There was not much excitement in the U.S. press over the Hopkins trip to Moscow because, despite Stalin's assurance that nothing he said would be censored, Hopkins in a press conference in Moscow played it safe by saying little of any particular interest. Editorial comment was largely favorable but tepid. The *Wall Street Journal* disapproved of the trip, saying that to render aid to Russia was "to fly in the face of morals." The Knoxville, Tennessee, *Journal* disapproved of Hopkins, saying,

He has always been such a generous man with other people's money. The great heart of him has always been so easily touched. Sometimes we think it might have been better if Mr. Roosevelt could have chosen a less free-hearted ambassador to send to Europe. Because a man as susceptible to leaf-raking projects as Harry always was, is likely, in the face of real need in Britain and Russia, to give away more than we've got. . . . We shall be glad when Harry comes home!

The Jacksonville, Florida, *Times-Union* was similarly worried that Hopkins would promise too much because "he told the Britons that the

United States would, in 1942, put in service 6 million tons of new merchant shipping. That figure, everyone must admit who keeps at all in touch with what is going on in American shipping, is way off. . . . Mr. Hopkins has just about doubled the figures that can be expected." (*Note.* American merchant ship production in 1942 was over eight million tons.) But the Sioux City, Iowa, *Journal* said,

> Isolationists will attempt to make capital of the Hopkins flight to Moscow . . . there no doubt will be revived the 'crawling into bed with Stalin' cry . . . but majority public opinion in the United States may be depended upon to express its outright approval of what has been done. The thing to keep forever in mind is that Hitlerism must and shall be destroyed.

Hopkins was particularly grateful for this broad-minded expression from the supposedly isolationist Cornbelt, for Sioux City was his birthplace and the *Journal* was the paper for which his father had worked as delivery boy.

His plane left Moscow on August 1. After his departure, the Chinese Ambassador called at the American Embassy and delivered the following message which had been cabled from Chungking: "To Mr. Harry Hopkins. On behalf of the Chinese Government we send you hearty greetings and a cordial invitation to visit Chungking on your way back to the United States. We hope that you may find it possible to do so. Chiang Kai-shek, H. H. Kung." Hopkins never did get to Chungking but throughout the war he had close association with the Generalissimo's and Kung's brother-in-law, T. V. Soong. He and the President met Chiang Kai-shek only once—at Cairo in November, 1943—but Hopkins formed a warm friendship with Mme. Chiang during her visit to the United States in 1942.

Steinhardt cabled the State Department his résumé of the Hopkins visit:

> The reception accorded Harry Hopkins by the Soviet Government and the unusual attention which has been devoted to him by the Soviet press clearly indicate that extreme importance has been attached to his visit by this Government. He was met at the port of entry by a number of high ranking Army and Navy officials and by the Acting Chief of Protocol, who flew with him to Moscow, where an unusually large delegation headed by Lozovski had been assembled to await his arrival. He was received promptly by Stalin, who granted him very extended interviews and discussed with a frankness unparalleled in my knowledge in recent Soviet history the subject of his mission and the Soviet position. All Soviet newspapers have put photographs and items concerning his visit on their front pages—a position of much greater significance here than in any other country.
> I am certain that the visit has been extremely gratifying to the

Soviet Government and that it will prove to have exercised a most beneficial effect upon Soviet American relations in general and in particular to have greatly encouraged the Soviet war effort.

When the plane carrying Hopkins from Moscow arrived at Archangel, McKinley and his crew watching from their houseboat could see its peculiar maneuvers as it buzzed the air strip. They thought it must be in serious trouble and that Hopkins was probably a goner, but this was only the final special salute. When Hopkins got aboard the PBY, which was now loaded with a cargo of platinum (Russia's most concentrated export), McKinley informed him that they had been unable to get adequate information on the weather prospects ahead but, from what he had observed on the flight out, they were pretty sure to encounter severe head winds and it might be rather rough going. Hopkins said, "Whatever it is, it will seem easy after what I've been doing the last couple of days." McKinley said further that from what they had been able to learn "landing conditions in the northern reaches of the U.K. were most unfavorable." He considered it prudent to delay the flight until they could be surer of their chances of completing it. But Hopkins was urgent. He knew, although he could not say so, that if they delayed another day he might miss the battleship *Prince of Wales* which was to carry Churchill to the Atlantic Conference.

Hopkins carried his essential medicines—without which he could not live—in a small satchel. Through some unaccountable error, this had been left behind in Moscow. He was desperately ill on the return flight which, as McKinley had predicted, was very rough because of head winds and, for the same reason, the plane's speed was so reduced that it took twenty-four hours to reach Scapa Flow. Hopkins was so exhausted that, despite the discomfort, he slept for seven of these hours. At one time he was awakened and told that the aircraft was being fired on by an unidentified destroyer off the Murman Coast. McKinley flashed the Russian call signal repeatedly but the only response was more flak. Hopkins did not see any of the bursts but was told that some were close enough to shake the aircraft.

McKinley's instructions for landing at Scapa Flow were so indefinite that he did not know where he was supposed to come down for delivery of Hopkins. He therefore picked the spot which looked most sheltered and least cluttered with ships. On landing, he managed to establish contact by blinker signal with an armed trawler and was told this was the wrong place. The sea was too rough to taxi several miles to the right place, so he took off again and finally spotted the admiral's launch which was to take Hopkins off. When they landed in a narrow and turbulent lane between ships, the tail of the PBY was slapped up and down by the waves and Hopkins was being slapped with it. The plane and the launch maneuvered about until the launch got her bow close enough to the blister for Hopkins to jump. A sailor with a boathook hauled him, sprawling, across the slippery deck to safety. His luggage was then tossed after him, including the priceless papers which set forth the Soviet position in detail.

McKinley's report of this mission concluded:

> As he waved us farewell we could not help feeling that very few persons could have taken what he had endured since we met at Invergordon on July 28th. Circling overhead prior to our return flight to Oban we saw a launch wallowing heavily across the harbour and we wondered if there was to be any rest for a man so obviously ill and yet showing unbelievable courage, determination and appreciation for the services of others. His was a noteworthy example of unparalleled devotion to duty.

This was August 2, just a week after Hopkins had asked for permission to go to Moscow and a week before he rejoined President Roosevelt at the Atlantic Conference.

CHAPTER XVI

The Atlantic Conference

WHEN the launch delivered Hopkins to Admiral Sir John Tovey, Commander in Chief of the Home Fleet, at Scapa Flow, it was feared that President Roosevelt's personal representative might not live long enough to make his report from the Kremlin. Hopkins seemed to be not only at the end of his rope but at the end of the last filament of the spider's web by which he was hanging on to life. Winant had come from London to Scapa Flow and Hopkins managed to stay up for dinner with the Ambassador and the Admiral, but then he started to wilt and Tovey ordered him to bed, having summoned all the medical skill that was available to drug him into the sleep that he so desperately needed. Hopkins asked Winant to "wait until I've had a little rest." Winant went to Hopkins' cabin in the morning and sat by his bed for an hour, but when Hopkins awakened the following afternoon Winant had gone back to London. (Harriman had already arrived in Washington, having left England the day Hopkins took off for Moscow.)

Churchill arrived aboard the *Prince of Wales,* bringing with him his Chiefs of Staff, Admiral Pound and General Dill. Air Marshal Portal could not go along, for some reason, so the R.A.F. was represented by the Vice-Chief of the Air Staff, Air Marshal Sir Wilfrid Freeman. Churchill left General Ismay behind "to keep the shop open," but brought with him Sir Alexander Cadogan, Permanent Under Secretary of State for Foreign Affairs, Lord Cherwell (the "Prof"), Colonel L. C. Hollis (Assistant Secretary of the War Cabinet), Commander Thompson and J. M. Martin, Principal Private Secretary, as well as various staff officers of the three services.

Hopkins was given the Admiral's cabin on the *Prince of Wales,* but later asked to be moved from it, saying that "the ship's propellers are a bit too close to my eardrums." During the trip across the North

Atlantic through the U-boat's happy hunting ground Hopkins worked on the preparation of the reports from Moscow which are published in the previous chapter. He told Churchill all the points from his talks with Stalin which touched on Russia's military situation and her needs, and the Prime Minister, as he listened, understood all the better why Hopkins was of such value to the President, for he had never before heard harshly objective and salty reporting quite like this. They discussed the phraseology of the Atlantic Charter which the Prime Minister was to present to the President, and Churchill again emphasized the necessity of a firm warning to Japan. There was also a considerable amount of relaxation. Hopkins noted:

> During the trip back on the *Prince of Wales* I played backgammon with the Prime Minister several times for a shilling a game. The enclosed Canadian money was handed me by the Prime Minister on the last day of the Conference, August 11, 1941.
> The Prime Minister's backgammon game is not of the best. He likes to play what is known to all backgammon addicts as a "back game." As a matter of fact he won two or three very exciting games from me by these tactics. He approaches the game with great zest, doubling and redoubling freely.

Attached to this memorandum was $32 in Canadian bills and about a dollar's worth of small change—all of which was saved to go into the Hopkins estate along with the $2.00 from President Roosevelt mentioned in the first chapter of this book.

Hopkins wanted to teach Churchill the insidious, two-handed game of gin rummy, which was then a mounting mania in the United States, but the Prime Minister would have none of it—although, on a visit to Miami Beach years later, he succumbed to the game and became a demon at it.

Before leaving the U.K., Churchill had notified all the Dominion Prime Ministers that he was going to meet the President of the United States who had extended an invitation to him through Harry Hopkins. This notification was not only a matter of routine courtesy. Churchill hoped that from the meeting some momentous agreement might be reached which would require ratification by the Dominions, and it was therefore a matter of prudence as well as respect to make them privy to the secret in advance. The agreement that Churchill hoped for was definitely not the Atlantic Charter: it was the establishment of a common policy of resistance to further Japanese aggression. Churchill informed the Prime Ministers that through the war years he had had intimate correspondence with Roosevelt and had talked to him on the telephone but had never met him. This, by the way, was a somewhat sore point with Roosevelt; when he was Assistant Secretary of the Navy in the

First World War, he had gone to London and had met Churchill at a banquet. Churchill, already an eminent statesman, had apparently failed to take much notice of the young American official and had promptly forgotten this encounter, but Roosevelt remembered it clearly.

There was no question about Churchill's attitude toward Roosevelt now. Hopkins later told friends, "You'd have thought Winston was being carried up into the heavens to meet God!" Roosevelt had become an almost legendary figure in Britain. He was known simply but warmly to the man in the rubble-strewn street as "The best friend we ever had." Churchill, who knew and undersood America far better than most of his compatriots, was all the more impressed by Roosevelt's achievements in overcoming isolationism and in breaking the sacred third term tradition. In the many meetings that were to follow, from Argentia to Yalta, Churchill's respect for Roosevelt may have wavered at times but it never ceased. Nor did Churchill ever lose sight of the fact that Roosevelt was his superior in rank—the President being the Head of State, on the level with the King, whereas the Prime Minister is Head of Government. To the average American this may seem a rather academic distinction, but it was of great importance in the relationship of the two men.

As the *Prince of Wales* approached the Western Hemisphere, Hopkins managed to write a few letters in which, as usual, he said little:

To Herbert Morrison, then Home Secretary and Minister of Home Security:
I have your tin hat for LaGuardia and shall give it to him with your warmest greetings. I much regretted not seeing you and having a discussion over a highball. We shall do that yet.

To Ambassador Winant:
I ran off without paying my bill at Claridge's. . . . Won't you also arrange to tip the valet and my waiter a couple of pounds apiece because I forgot to do that. . . . I do hope you take care of yourself. It seems to me you all work too hard. That is very absurd advice coming from me; hence, I withdraw it.

To General Ismay:
I should so much have liked to tell you about the trip to Moscow. At least I was not air sick, although the caviar and smoked salmon were almost too much. . . . The Prime Minister failed to work yesterday for the first time in his life. The trip will be a great rest for him. So far, we have seen nothing worse than fog. Pound, Dill and Freeman get on as gentlemen should, and there is never a cross word between any of the Services. They knew better than to discuss Crete in mixed company.

To Air Chief Marshal Portal:
I want particularly to thank you for the arrangements for my flight to Archangel. It could not have been better. If you get a chance, will

you tell Captain McKinley and his crew how fine and patient I thought they were. There wasn't a hitch in the whole performance.

To Admiral Tovey:

Our trip has been uneventful so far, although we have moved out of our way a bit to miss a submarine. The bad weather for the first day out washed away the destroyers, but Canadian ones are alongside now.

To Brendan Bracken:

I would have liked so much to tell you about my visit to Uncle Joe which I think went off fairly well, but only events can tell.

To his daughter, Diana:

I presume by this time you are as brown as a berry, and that is as it should be when one is 8 years old. It is nearly 4 weeks ago now that I telephoned you at Betsy's [Mrs. James Roosevelt]. Since then I have been far away, to what is said to be one of the coldest countries in the world, Russia. Strange to say I found little boys and girls swimming in the White Sea.

In another far off country I have been to there is war, and bombs and guns going off in the night. Some day that will all be over and Mr. Hitler will be defeated. Then I shall bring you to England, and we will roam over the green hills and eat in what you will think to be very queer little restaurants. The strange part of it is, little English boys and girls think that our houses and hotels and beaches are just as queer.

I shall see you very soon now, and want you to know that I love you very much.

P.S. Tell Betsy I will call up as soon as I get back, but I am afraid my telephone call will come before this letter reaches you.

On Saturday, August 9, the great British battleship (which was to perish in Malayan waters four months later) arrived at the Newfoundland rendezvous. There had been endless rehearsals of the expected ceremonials on board and a sort of eve-of-battle tension prevailed. Hopkins went out on the bridge in his bathrobe for a look at Newfoundland, from which he had flown in a bomber less than four weeks before, but visibility was obliterated by the white summer mist. The sun was struggling to get through to the surface of the sea. Then out of the mist appeared the shapes of impressive new American destroyers—not at all like the old four-stackers that had been turned over in return for this and other bases—and then the cruiser *Augusta* herself. When Hopkins saw that he rushed to his cabin and started to pack. The orderly, or batman, or whatever the term is in the Royal Navy, who had been assigned to him, wanted to do this packing for him, but Hopkins figured that if he didn't throw the things in himself (including his papers) he'd never know where to find them.

Hopkins was transferred from the *Prince of Wales* to the *Augusta*. Captain John R. Beardall, the President's Naval Aide, went aboard the

Prince of Wales to communicate the President's wishes as regards arrangements for formal meetings, social engagements, etc. The President was to entertain the Prime Minister and his party at dinner that evening, and Hopkins wrote to Churchill:

> I have just talked to the President and he is very anxious, after dinner tonight, to invite in the balance of the staff and wants to ask you to talk very informally to them about your general appreciation of the war, and indeed to say anything that you would be disposed to say to a group as large as will be present. I imagine there will be twenty-five people altogether. The President, of course, does not want anything formal about it.

Hopkins had suggested this, for he wanted the President and his party to hear one of Churchill's after-dinner analyses of the war situation. Present at that dinner were, on the American side, Roosevelt, Welles, Stark, Marshall, King, Arnold, Hopkins and Harriman. On the British side, Churchill, Cadogan, Pound, Dill, Freeman and Cherwell. The menu: vegetable soup, broiled chicken, spinach omelet, lettuce and tomato salad, chocolate ice cream and a lot of side dishes. During dinner, Roosevelt, Churchill, Hopkins, Welles and Cadogan got down to business. There were two main topics of conversation: the growing menace of Japanese aggression, about which the British were primarily concerned, and the five-point proposed joint declaration which was to become the eight-point Atlantic Charter. Of course there was a great deal of interest in what Hopkins had to say about Russia, but even this brought the subject back to the Far East. For, although Hitler's attack on the Soviet Union had so far been an authentic blessing in the war against Germany, it had tended to decrease the threats to Japan's flank in Manchuria and thus increased the danger of further Japanese moves in other directions.

The next morning, Sunday, Roosevelt went across to the *Prince of Wales* for the church service under the big guns. The lesson was from the first chapter of Joshua: "There shall not any man be able to stand before thee all the days of thy life: as I was with Moses, so will I be with thee: I will not fail thee, nor forsake thee. Be strong and of good courage. . . ." The prayers were, first for the President of the United States, then for the King and his Ministers and his Admirals, Generals and Air Marshals, then prayers for the invaded countries, the sick and wounded, the prisoners, the exiled and homeless, the anxious and bereaved—and a prayer that "we may be preserved from hatred, bitterness and all spirit of revenge."

After the service, Roosevelt was introduced to members of the *Prince of Wales* crew and saw as much of the ship as was possible from his wheelchair. He was having a fine time and so was the Former

Naval Person. Here, on the decks of a mighty battleship, these two old-fashioned seafaring men were on common ground. However, in another part of the ship, Welles and Cadogan were in conference over documents which the British Government had drafted, "Parallel Communications to the Japanese Government." One message to Tokyo was to come from Washington:

Declaration by the United States Government that:

1. Any further encroachment by Japan in the Southwestern Pacific would produce a situation in which the United States Government would be compelled to take counter measures even though these might lead to war between the United States and Japan.

2. If any third Power becomes the object of aggression by Japan in consequence of such counter measures or of their support of them, the President would have the intention to seek authority from Congress to give aid to such Power.

The proposed communication to Tokyo from London was to read:

Declaration by His Majesty's Government that:

1. Any further encroachment by Japan in the Southwestern Pacific would produce a situation in which His Majesty's Government would be compelled to take counter measures even though these might lead to war between Great Britain and Japan.

2. If any third Power becomes the object of aggression by Japan in consequence of such counter measures or of their support of them, His Majesty's Government would give all possible aid to such Power.

There was a third proposed Declaration from the Netherlands Government. This was the same as the British except that it referred to "Her" instead of "His" Majesty.

In the official records of the Conference, Welles wrote:

As I was leaving the ship to accompany the President back to his flagship, Mr. Churchill said to me that he had likewise given the President copies of these documents. He impressed upon me his belief that some declaration of the kind he had drafted with respect to Japan was in his opinion in the highest degree important, and that he did not think that there was much hope left unless the United States made such a clear-cut declaration of preventing Japan from expanding further to the south, in which event the prevention of war between Great Britain and Japan appeared to be hopeless. He said in the most emphatic manner that if war did break out between Great Britain and Japan, Japan immediately would be in a position through the use of her large number of cruisers to seize or to destroy all of the British merchant shipping in the Indian Ocean and in the Pacific, and to cut the life-lines between the British Dominions and the British Isles unless the United States herself entered the war. He pled with me that a declaration of this character participated in by the United

States, Great Britain, the Dominions, the Netherlands and possibly the Soviet Union would definitely restrain Japan. If this were not done, the blow to the British Government might be almost decisive.

This is as clear a statement as could be made of the British point of view which, as has been shown in the previous chapter, was essentially the same as the Russian. Both Churchill and Stalin, engaged as they were in a veritable death grapple with Germany in Europe, considered it would be calamitous for their countries to become involved in war with Japan in the Far East.

It was this Asiatic phase of the discussions at the Atlantic Conference which occupied a vast amount of attention during the exhaustive Pearl Harbor investigation, because of the repeated isolationist charges that there had been "secret commitments." (As one of the British officials present at this meeting said to me, "We wished to God there *had* been!") All American records of the conference were brought forth and the testimony of living American participants were added to the voluminous testimony. In the preparation of this book, I have been given access to the British records of the Conference. I have found that all of the records put together not only fail to provide evidence of skullduggery but, in so far as discussion of military matters is concerned, fail even to provide much of interest. The agreements for which the British had hoped did not come near to realization, either in the Roosevelt-Churchill talks or in the Chiefs of Staff conferences which went on concurrently. Therefore, only a general summary of the military discussions need be given:

Churchill talked, as he had to Hopkins in London, of the prospect of a German eruption into Spain and Portugal—and North Africa—which would mean the end of Gibraltar as a British base. He said that "the situation in Spain is going from bad to worse" and that the British were prepared to launch, in a month's time (about September 15), a powerful expedition for the seizure of the Canary Islands to provide an alternate base to Gibraltar for operations in the South Atlantic, although nothing of course could replace Gibraltar in the Mediterranean. Roosevelt said that he had been putting out feelers with a view to obtaining an invitation from the Portuguese Government, similar to that extended by the Icelandic Government, for the dispatch of American forces to the Azores for the defense of these crucial islands. He was hopeful that something might come of this. Churchill said that if the United States should send troops to the Azores, the British would cover the approaches between these vital islands and the European mainland to forestall any German attempt to send an expeditionary force to prevent an American occupation with Portuguese consent.

All of these arrangements came to nothing as Hitler never did move forcibly into the Iberian Peninsula and the Portuguese Government extended no invitation to the Azores until two years later, when the tide of the war had unmistakably turned.

Following this discussion, Churchill took up the question of the "Parallel Communications" to Tokyo. Roosevelt showed him copies of the statements handed to Secretary Hull by Ambassador Nomura five days previously. These presented the Japanese occupation of Indo-China as a *fait accompli* which, the Japanese said, "was of entirely peaceful character and for self-defense," and offered proposals looking toward "a speedy settlement of the China Incident." There was no doubt, as Roosevelt and Churchill agreed, that the Japanese proposals could be acceptable only if the United States were prepared to sell China down the river. Roosevelt said that he felt "very strongly that every effort should be made to prevent the outbreak of war with Japan." But—the question eternally was: would a tough line, a medium line, or a soft line best suit that purpose? Roosevelt was well aware of the importance of "face" to the Japanese. Therefore, the adoption of a line which would not give them some kind of "face-saving out" would be practically a guarantee of war. On the other hand, the only kind of appeasement which the Japanese would consider satisfactory would seal the doom of China and would be humiliating and mortifying to the American people and calculated to depress the morale of all who were opposed to the Axis powers everywhere in the world. Roosevelt believed that any warnings to Japan should not be limited to the Southwestern Pacific area, but should be broad enough to encompass the possibility of new Japanese aggression against any friendly power in Asia—specifically, the Soviet Union, this being the result of Hopkins' talk with Molotov. As Sumner Welles expressed it, "the real issue which was involved was the continuation by Japan of its present policy of conquest by force in the entire Pacific region and regardless whether such policy was directed against China, against the Soviet Union or against the British Dominions or British colonies, or the colonies of the Netherlands." The only definite promise that Roosevelt gave was that he would see the Japanese Ambassador, Nomura, on his return to Washington, and he sent a radio to Hull to arrange this meeting. Following was the conclusion and crux of the warning given to Nomura on August 17, while Churchill was still at sea on the way home:

This Government now finds it necessary to say to the Government of Japan that if the Japanese Government takes any further steps in pursuance of a policy or program of military domination by force or threat of force of neighboring countries, the Government of the United States will be compelled to take immediately any and all steps which it may deem necessary toward safeguarding the legitimate rights and interests of the United States and American nationals and toward insuring the safety and security of the United States.

Which meant absolutely nothing except that the United States was electing to reassert its status as a sovereign power which would look out for its own interests. Churchill undoubtedly hoped for something much stronger than that, and Sumner Welles's notes indicate that for a time Roosevelt considered taking a firmer position; but the fact remains that he quickly compromised on what seemed to be a safe middle course between the tough line and the soft one. The proposed Anglo-American-Dutch parallel warnings to Japan were never made and from then on Churchill took the position that Britain would follow America's lead when and if Japan took further violent action and Roosevelt made known his policy.

There was plenty of backing for the tough policy in the American press and among Roosevelt's official family. After the first Cabinet meeting following Roosevelt's return to Washington, Vice President Wallace wrote him:

> When you mentioned Japan at Cabinet meeting this afternoon, I had a strong desire to express myself but reached the conclusion it might be better to do so to you privately.
>
> I do so hope that in the current conversations you take an exceedingly firm stand. It seems to me that the appeasing stand or partially appeasing stand is certain to bring bad results not only with regard to Japan, in the long run, but with regard also to the situation in Europe. If we take a strong stand, the entire Axis will be impressed and the psychology of the American people will be strengthened.
>
> I do hope, Mr. President, you will go to the absolute limit in your firmness in dealing with Japan. I am as confident as anyone can be in a matter of this sort that such a policy will bear rich dividends, and that any sign of weakness, concession or appeasement will be misunderstood by Japan and the Axis and will cost us, directly or indirectly, many millions of hours of man labor and much suffering.

However, all of the considerations of policy which seemed so momentous at the time proved of no avail in the light of subsequent developments and revelations. Matsuoka had told Hitler four months previously that "sooner or later a war with the United States would be unavoidable . . . in his opinion this conflict would happen sooner rather than later." And Hitler had promised the Japanese that "Germany would conduct a most energetic fight against America with her U-boats and her Luftwaffe . . . that no American could land in Europe . . . that the German soldier naturally ranks high above the American." It may be argued that if a really tough line had been taken the Pearl Harbor attack would have occurred a month or so earlier; in that case—it could also be argued—so would the ultimate victory.

The Chiefs of Staff discussions at the Atlantic Conference produced little of importance. No agenda had been prepared; there had been no previous cabled exchange of views. The British chiefs sat down at the conference table hoping that major problems of strategy would be discussed. The Americans, however, had no authority from the President to go beyond the tentative agreements already made; their main interest was in the subject of Lend-Lease priorities and production schedules as affected by the developments on the Russian Front.

The Navy men settled various details of the patrol and convoy problem, as a result of which more than fifty British destroyers and corvettes were released from service in the Western Atlantic; but the major decisions in respect to this had already been taken. On the Army and Air Force side, Generals Marshall and Arnold were more concerned with the debate then raging in the Congress over extension of the Selective Service Law than in the reinforcing of the Middle East or the bombing of Germany. The U.S. chiefs placed repeated emphasis on the fact that their job was the defense of the Western Hemisphere and they were reluctant to discuss anything farther away from that than the Azores, Canaries and Cape Verde Islands, Dakar, French Morocco and Spanish Morocco (in the last of which Roosevelt was particularly interested). So far as the records show, there was little discussion of strategic considerations in the Pacific, although there was some contemplation of the possible extension of Japanese naval power into the Indian Ocean and even of a Japanese attempt to seize Madagascar.

The British chiefs proposed that American-British-Dutch-Australian staff talks be held in Singapore to plan joint defense of the Southwest Pacific area. No agreement was reached on this. The British did, however, acquaint the Americans with their own plans for the immediate and far distant future, and among the latter was an extremely tentative one for an operation to be known as ROUNDUP, an invasion of the Continent of Europe. For this, "there would not be needed vast armies on the continent such as were required in World War I. Small forces, chiefly armored, with their power of hard hitting, would be able quickly to win a decisive victory." It is interesting to note that the chief planner of ROUNDUP was General Sir Frederick Morgan, who later became the chief planner of its fulfillment, OVERLORD.

The only development of really lasting importance in these military talks at Argentia was the beginning of the friendship between Marshall and Dill which was to be a vital element in the functioning of the Combined Chiefs of Staff.

At one point in the Roosevelt-Churchill talks, the Prime Minister pointed out that there were 150,000 men now guarding Britain's vital air fields who were armed only with "pikes, maces and grenades." Roosevelt promised to furnish rifles for these men. In a memorandum to Hopkins, delivered from the *Prince of Wales* to the *Augusta,* Churchill wrote:

> We hope . . . that the most rapid delivery possible of 150,000 rifles will be made, as the invasion season is fully operative after September 15th. In the event of our reporting to the President that great and active preparations are being made by the enemy in the Dutch, Belgian and French ports for invasion, of which there is no sign at present, we would ask as a matter of emergency that a further consignment of .300 ammunition could be rushed across, this being recovered later from our monthly quotas of production.

In this memorandum, Churchill also urged strongly that a conference be held in Moscow, for the re-equipment of the Russian Armies, along the lines that Hopkins had discussed with Stalin. He said that he would name Lord Beaverbrook as the British representative at this conference "with power to act for all British departments." It was then assumed that Hopkins would be the American representative, but Roosevelt later decided that Hopkins could not stand another long journey so soon and Harriman was named in his stead.

Beaverbrook arrived at Argentia on Monday, August 11. His principal concern was aid for Russia, a topic on which there was now virtually no argument as a result of Hopkins' encouraging reports. But when Beaverbrook learned of the proposal to issue a document known as the Atlantic Charter, and read the text of it, his deep-banked devotion to the economic solidarity of the British Empire flared up, and he became difficult.

Welles has told of the drafting of the Atlantic Charter in his admirable survey of Roosevelt's foreign policy, *Where Are We Heading?* and his description agrees with the British records in point of fact if not precisely in terms of interpretation. But there are one or two points to be added, chiefly in relation to the establishment of an international organization, which was the first planted seed for the United Nations. In the original draft of the Joint Statement which Churchill presented at Argentia and in the second draft prepared by Welles were the words, "They [the U.S. and Britain] seek a peace which will not only cast down forever the Nazi tyranny but *by effective international organization* will afford to all States and peoples the means of dwelling in security, etc." The italicized words were struck out by Roosevelt. Churchill pleaded that they be restored, but, as Welles has written,

> The President replied that he did not feel that he could agree to this because of the suspicions and opposition that such a statement on his part would create in the United States. He said that he himself would not be in favor of the creation of a new Assembly of the League of Nations, at least until after a period of time had passed and during which an international police force composed of the United States

and Great Britain had had an opportunity of functioning. Mr. Churchill said that he did not feel that he would be candid if he did not express to the President his feeling that point seven would create a great deal of opposition from the extreme internationalists. The President replied that he realized that, but that he felt that the time had come to be realistic and that in his judgment the main factor in the seventh point was complete realism. Mr. Churchill then remarked that of course he was wholeheartedly in favor of it and shared the President's view.

From which it was seen that Roosevelt was again being haunted by the ghost of Woodrow Wilson. The extreme internationalists, he felt, were lacking in "realism," which meant they did not take into account the power of isolationist sentiment. He was afraid that even an implication of another League of Nations would fill the American people with memories of the First World War—another A.E.F., another false "peace," another age of disillusionment, of boom and bust, another opportunity for another Hitler. However, if Churchill expressed himself as sharing "wholeheartedly" the President's point of view as this meeting broke up, within an hour or two thereafter he had not only reversed himself but persuaded Roosevelt in a large measure to do likewise. In this he was aided materially by Hopkins who urged upon Roosevelt his belief that the American people would be in favor of a strong organization for world peace—indeed, that they would settle for nothing less. He said that they would consider it idle to talk of disarmament, as in Point Seven, until there was an international organization strongly functioning. Roosevelt would not yield so far as to include the term "international organization" but he agreed to include the phrase "the establishment of a wider and permanent system of general security," which was generally accepted as meaning exactly the same thing.

On another point, Hopkins felt compelled to oppose Welles for reasons of expediency. That was the inclusion of the niggling qualification, demanded by the British, "with due respect for their existing obligations," which was widely and justifiably criticized in the United States at the time. This was where Beaverbrook came in. He assumed that Point Four—"to further the enjoyment of all peoples of access, without discrimination and on equal terms, to the markets and to the raw materials of the world"—meant the cancellation of the Ottawa Agreements for "Imperial Preference," and Welles conceded that indeed it did. Beaverbrook had fought for those agreements in the first place and he was now prepared to wade in and fight for them again. It was he who insisted that the qualifying line be included. Churchill made it clear that he "had always been, as was well known, emphatically opposed to the Ottawa Agreements," but Beaverbrook convinced him that he had no authority to approve Point Four of the Declaration as then drafted.

without consulting all the Dominion Governments and gaining their consent to this abrogation of the Ottawa Agreements. This complicated process would require too much time, and Hopkins felt strongly that publication of the Charter must coincide with announcement of the meeting itself. He did not like the hedging phrase any better than Welles did, but he was less aware of its consequences, and he so persuaded the President. Of course Welles was right on principle, and Hopkins was wrong.

There was also loud criticism of the Atlantic Charter among the isolationists on the ground that while it provided for three of the Four Freedoms, it made no mention of Freedom of Religion; this, it was said, provided proof of the subservience of the cynical Roosevelt and Churchill to the godless Soviet Union. Actually, this omission was an oversight. I have seen no record, either British or American, indicating that the inclusion of Freedom of Religion was ever in any way considered. So severe was the criticism, however, that when the Atlantic Charter was incorporated in the first Proclamation of the United Nations on January 1, 1942, Roosevelt was careful to see to it that Freedom of Religion was included (and with Russian agreement).

The Atlantic Conference gave Hopkins an opportunity to observe more clearly than ever the differences between the American and British systems of democracy. This was the first time he had seen both the President and Prime Minister in operation away from their own home bases. He remarked on the fact that whereas Roosevelt was completely on his own, subject only to the advice of his immediate and self-selected entourage, which advice he could accept or reject, Churchill was constantly reporting to and consulting the War Cabinet in London, addressing his communications to the Lord Privy Seal, who was then Clement Attlee. During three days more than thirty communications passed between the *Prince of Wales* and Whitehall, and the speed of communication and of action thereon was astonishing to the Americans. For example: on Monday, August 11, at 1:50 P.M. (Argentia time) Churchill filed a cable to London containing the agreed text of the Atlantic Charter which was then seven points, and describing in detail all the changes suggested and the reasons therefor. Because of the time necessary for coding and decoding, and the difference in time between Newfoundland and the U.K., this message did not reach Attlee until shortly after midnight. However, the War Cabinet was ready to go into session at that late hour. At 4:10 A.M. (London time) it cabled its approval of the document word by word and suggested the addition of an eighth point, which Roosevelt heartily approved (it was in line with Freedom from Want) and which was incorporated as Number Five in the Charter.

Churchill's final report to his government stated that, whatever the failures of the Atlantic Conference to achieve some hoped-for objective

—specifically, the mailed-fist threat to Japan—the big news was that he had established "warm and deep personal relations with our great friend."

The public announcement of the Atlantic Conference, made simultaneously from London and Washington, came as little surprise to anyone who had been reading the newspapers or listening to radio commentators. A Churchill-Roosevelt meeting had long been considered an obvious development—so much so that, even while the President was en route to Argentia, the Japanese were suggesting that he meet Prince Konoye somewhere in the Pacific. When the press started to discuss the mystery of the whereabouts of both the President and Prime Minister, as well as of the Chiefs of Staff, there could be little doubt that the cigarette-in-holder and the long cigar were at last being lit from the same match.

When the story was released unsupported or embellished by any reports from on-the-spot press correspondents, it proved to be something of an anticlimax, particularly in Britain. The isolationists in the U.S. managed to make the Conference seem more interesting than it actually was with their charges that there was far more in this meeting than met the eye—that, when the truth were finally known, Roosevelt would be proven a blacker traitor than Benedict Arnold. Thus, for Americans, there was created about the event a certain atmosphere of fascinating intrigue leading to the provocative "If we only knew what *really* went on. . . ." In Britain, however, there had been the expectancy of tremendous action resulting from the meeting—of vast American armadas sweeping across the seas—and all that came out of it was a grouping of pious words. The British people were of course glad to know that Roosevelt and Churchill were determined to see to it that in the postwar world there would be liberty, justice, prosperity and security for all, but they were far more concerned with the question of when the black-out and rationing would end.

The Atlantic Charter, however, turned out to be incalculably more powerful an instrument than the officers of the British Government intended it to be when they first proposed it. They never regarded it as a formal State Paper; it was, to them, not much more than a publicity handout. Roosevelt, who took it much more seriously, was compelled to foster this belief by insisting that it could not be considered as in any way a "Treaty"; if it had been, he should have had to submit it to the Senate for ratification, and he was taking no chances on that. Therefore, it was never inscribed on parchment and signed, sealed and taped. It was merely mimeographed and released. Nevertheless, its effect was cosmic and historic. The British learned that when you state a moral principle, you are stuck with it, no matter how many fingers you may have kept crossed at the moment. It was not long before the people of India, Burma, Malaya, Indonesia were beginning to ask if the Atlantic

Charter extended also to the Pacific and to Asia in general. So acute and embarrassing did the questions become that Churchill was later compelled to take cognizance of them in the House of Commons. He said:

> At the Atlantic meeting we had in mind, primarily, the restoration of the sovereignty, self-government and national life of the States and nations of Europe now under the Nazi yoke, and the principles governing any alterations in their territorial boundaries which may have to be made. So that is quite a separate problem from the progressive evolution of self-governing institutions in the regions, and people which owe allegiance to the British Crown.

However, the Atlantic Charter stated, in Point Three, "They respect the right of all peoples to choose the form of Government under which they will live" (that clause, incidentally, was taken intact from the first draft prepared by Churchill himself). Point Four referred to "all States, great or small," Point Five to "all nations," Point Six to "all nations" and also to "all the men in all the lands," Point Seven to "all men," Point Eight to "all of the nations of the world." Indeed, it may be said that one small word, "all," came to be regarded as the veritable cornerstone of the whole structure of the United Nations. Even the qualifying phrase about "existing obligations" became inconsequential under the superior weight of the new responsibilities firmly if not formally assumed.

On the last day of the Atlantic Conference, with all points of the Charter and the joint cable to Stalin straightened out, the President had the Prime Minister, Beaverbrook and Hopkins to lunch, and this, from Hopkins' point of view, was the most satisfactory session of all. There was no business to be transacted. Both Roosevelt and Churchill were relaxed and amusing and amused. This was Hopkins' ambition as a "catalyst" or "marriage broker": to prove to Roosevelt that it was possible to be utterly at ease with Churchill, and vice versa. Beaverbrook, whom Roosevelt had known of old, helped considerably in this process.

It would be an exaggeration to say that Roosevelt and Churchill became chums at this Conference or at any subsequent time. They established an easy intimacy, a joking informality and a moratorium on pomposity and cant—and also a degree of frankness in intercourse which, if not quite complete, was remarkably close to it. But neither of them ever forgot for one instant what he was and represented or what the other was and represented. Actually, their relationship was maintained to the end on the highest professional level. They were two men in the same line of business—politico-military leadership on a global scale —and theirs was a very limited field and the few who achieve it seldom have opportunities for getting together with fellow craftsmen in the same trade to compare notes and talk shop. They appraised each other through the practiced eyes of professionals and from this appraisal resulted a degree of admiration and sympathetic understanding of each other's professional problems that lesser craftsmen could not have achieved. Thus, when Churchill was being particularly unyielding on some point during the Yalta Conference, Roosevelt could say to Hopkins, "We've got to remember that Winston has an election coming up." And, as the record proves, there were many occasions when the Prime Minister yielded on major points in deference to the domestic political problems which were forever besetting the President.

It is a matter of sacred tradition that, when an American statesman and a British statesman meet, the former will be plain, blunt, down to earth, ingenuous to a fault, while the latter will be sly, subtle, devious and eventually triumphant. In the cases of Roosevelt and Churchill, this formula became somewhat confused. If either of them could be called a student of Machiavelli, it was Roosevelt; if either was a bull in a china shop, it was Churchill. The Prime Minister quickly learned that he confronted in the President a man of infinite subtlety and obscurity—an artful dodger who could not readily be pinned down on specific points, nor hustled or wheedled into definite commitments against his judgment or his will or his instinct. And Roosevelt soon learned how pertinacious the Prime Minister could be in pursuance of a purpose. Churchill's admirers could call him "tenacious, indomitable," and his detractors could describe him as "obstinate, obdurate, dogged, mulish, pigheaded." Probably both factions could agree on the word "stubborn," which may be flattering or derogatory. In any case, it was this quality which, at times, made him extremely tiresome to deal with and, at other times—and especially times of most awful adversity—made him great.

Roosevelt and Churchill certainly had the capacity to annoy each other, but the record of their tremendous association with one another contains a minimum of evidences of waspishness or indeed of anything less than the most amiable and most courteous consideration. For they had a large and wonderful capacity to stimulate and refresh each other. In one of the darkest hours of the war, Roosevelt concluded a long, serious cable to Churchill with the words, "It is fun to be in the same decade with you."

When Churchill left Argentia on the *Prince of Wales*, his ship was escorted as far as Iceland—where he stopped for a brief inspection tour —by American destroyers, on one of which Franklin D. Roosevelt, Jr., was serving as an ensign. Churchill later broadcast a speech in which he said,

And so we came back across the ocean waves, uplifted in spirit, fortified in resolve. Some American destroyers which were carrying mail to the United States Marines in Iceland happened to be going the same way too, so we made a goodly company at sea together.

That jocose little glimpse that Churchill gave of U.S. destroyers "going our way" meant a lot more than it seemed: it meant that our Atlantic Fleet under that grim realist, Admiral King, was operating and training twenty-four hours a day under battle conditions, no lights at night, the responsible officers watching with suspicion every uncharted speck on the radar screen, the crews constantly ready for the sounding of GQ; whereas, in the Pacific, the Fleet, relatively paralyzed with the obsession of neutrality, was being meticulously careful to avoid all semblance of awareness of tension, its officers trying to act and even to think in terms of peacetime routine as usual, movies on the hangar deck as usual, Saturday nights as usual at the Royal Hawaiian, the Officers Clubs, the Manila Hotel.

Back in England, Churchill seemed so bursting with confidence—he gave the new "V for Victory" sign with such exuberant assurance— the British people delightedly assumed, like the American isolationists, that perhaps there *had* been some secret agreements at the Conference, the results of which would become apparent in due course. It is improbable that Churchill did much to discourage this hopeful assumption.

CHAPTER XVII

Shoot on Sight

THE battle in Congress over extension of Selective Service was dis-agreeably synchronized with the Atlantic Conference. It proved to be one of the narrowest escapes of Roosevelt's wartime career. He had almost let it go by default. The Selective Service Law provided that the Army could draft no more than 900,000 men in any one year and only "for training and service unless Congress declares that the national security is imperilled, when such service may then be extended by the President to such time as may be necessary in the interest of national defense." The President's proclamation of a state of unlimited national emergency did not in any way bind Congress to concede that the national security was imperiled. Indeed, leaders in Congress had informed Roosevelt that they could never muster votes enough to extend Selective Service. The emotional appeal of families who wanted their "boys" back was over-whelming. Even more important was the shocking morale of the men themselves: they didn't know why they were in the Army, they were muttering and shouting about promises made to them of only one year of this useless subjection to the brass hats; and, worst of all, great numbers of them were training with broomsticks for guns and with trucks masquerading as tanks, which made the whole process seem a ridiculous waste of time. The war seemed more remote than ever from American soil, with the Japanese apparently bogged down in China and Hitler getting himself more and more involved in Russia. The initials "O.H.I.O." gained alarming currency, being scrawled on walls in training camps all over the country; these stood not for the State but for "over the hill in October" which meant that, when the first year of Selective Service had ended, if the drafted men were not released and sent home according to the letter of the law under which they had registered, they would desert. (Many of the same men who had once

truculently chalked up "O.H.I.O." later marked walls all over the world
with the prideful "Kilroy was here.") The situation in this summer of
1941 was so ugly that Roosevelt concluded it would be better not to
bring the issue up in Congress. He was again afraid of fear itself. But
Secretary Stimson and General Marshall felt otherwise. They knew
that this would mean, in Marshall's words, "disintegration of the Army."
It would mean starting all over again—and, in the light of subsequent
developments, it is appalling to contemplate the probable results. Hopkins
saw eye to eye with Stimson and Marshall on this but was of little help
to them in the most critical days because of his extended journeys overseas. Marshall, by dint of five days of concentrated work, produced his
first Biennial Report in which he courageously recommended the removal of "legal restrictions" which tended to "hamstring the development of the Army into a force immediately available for whatever defensive measures may be necessary." Marshall's presentation of the case
was so dignified, so statesmanlike and so incontrovertible that, while
the isolationists as usual railed at it and tried to damn its author as a
militaristic warmonger, the reputable press and the less timid elements
on Capitol Hill supported it. Roosevelt himself was persuaded to agree
to risk the fight, and it is no exaggeration to describe this as one of the
decisive battles of the war; it was certainly one that Americans, for
their own good, should never forget. The fight was won, in the House
of Representatives, by the perilous margin of one vote. This was on
August 12, the day when the Atlantic Conference ended. The news of it
dropped like enemy bombs on the decks of the *Augusta* and the *Prince of
Wales*.

A few days later, an American radio commentator in London quoted a
typical reaction of the British man in the street: "The Americans are
curious people. I can't make them out. One day they're announcing they'll
guarantee freedom and fair play for everybody everywhere in the world.
The next day they're deciding by only one vote that they'll go on having
an Army."

Senator Burton K. Wheeler made a statement which carried considerable weight in foreign countries, both friendly and hostile:

This vote clearly indicates that the Administration could not get
a resolution through the Congress for a declaration of war. It is
notice to the War Department that the Congress does not approve of
their breaking faith with the draftees. It is also notice that the Congress
does not take seriously the cry of the Administration that the so-
called emergency is greater now than it was a year ago.

The *New York Times* said editorially:

The record shows that every one of these four measures (indicated
below) was adopted solely because the President received the support

of a large majority of his own party. Not one of them would be law today if the decision had been left to the Republicans in Congress. The tally of Republican votes runs as follows:

On repeal of the Arms Embargo:
Senate: 8 in favor, 15 against
House: 21 in favor, 143 against

On the passage of the Lend Lease Bill:
Senate: 10 in favor, 17 against
House: 24 in favor, 135 against

On the adoption of Selective Service:
Senate: 7 in favor, 10 against
House: 46 in favor, 88 against

On the extension of the period of training:
Senate: 7 in favor, 13 against
House: 21 in favor, 133 against

The Republicans in Congress have achieved, in short, a perfect record of opposition to the measures recommended by the President, the Secretary of State, and by the Army's Chief of Staff. . . . It is impossible to dismiss the element of plain party politics from the votes so heavily one-sided as these.

Crisis or no crisis, the Republicans in Congress are still "fighting Roosevelt," still jockeying for position, still trying to write a record which they can turn to profit if and when there occurs that long-delayed "reaction" on which they have built their political hopes.

To the British, with their Parliamentary way of thinking, the ominous thing was not the Republican vote in Congress, but the extent to which members of Roosevelt's own majority party went against him in so critical a test. A division like this in the House of Commons would have been indicative of "No Confidence" and could well have resulted in the fall of a Cabinet.

When Beaverbrook left Argentia he traveled with Harriman to Washington to arrange for the Moscow Conference and Churchill instructed him to make some soundings of American public opinion on the side. Beaverbrook did so and his reports were discouraging to his colleagues in London. He stated, and truthfully, that there wasn't the slightest chance of the U.S. entering the war until compelled to do so by a direct attack on its own territory, and it seemed that this could not happen until Britain and Russia had been defeated. The words of Senator Wheeler were given ominous weight, and Roosevelt's enormous prestige with the combatant Allies began to ebb. There was increasing shrillness in the demands to know when the United States would abandon the role of sideline cheerleader and get into the game. Churchill, taking cognizance of this temper, said in an international broadcast:

> The question has been asked: how near is the United States to war? There is certainly one man who knows the answer to that question. If Hitler has not yet declared war upon the United States, it is surely not out of his love for American institutions; it is certainly not because he could not find a pretext. He has murdered half-a-dozen countries for far less.

There again Churchill, like virtually everyone else in authority at the time, assumed that it was the powerful Hitler who would decide when the time had come to attack the United States. The possibility that this act of incredible folly would be committed by the Japanese, the saving of whose "face" had been the object of so much solicitude in Washington, was hardly worth considering.

It happened that at that time, near the end of August, I had to go to England to study the British political warfare (i.e., propaganda) organization. Before I left, I had dinner with the President and Hopkins and was told, "You couldn't have picked a better time for getting a cool reception." While I was there, Churchill sent a lengthy cable to Hopkins about various matters and toward the end he said, "Today I saw Mr. Sherwood," which was my one and only appearance in that historic correspondence. This meeting was purely a courtesy one on Churchill's part—he had received a cable from the White House asking him to give me a few minutes (I was given fifteen, to be exact). He told me that he did not believe the Germans would get to Moscow before the Russian winter set in. He paid glowing tribute to Harry Hopkins, speaking of "the great heart that is within that frail frame." His eyes welled over with tears when he said this. Churchill, who was so completely English and who, therefore, according to the rules, should have been coldly phlegmatic in demeanor, was one of the most unashamedly emotional of men. Whereas Roosevelt, a sentimental American, always kept his emotions so far from the surface that one could only guess as to their nature or even their very existence.

On Labor Day Roosevelt made a short but vigorous speech, of which the *New York Times* said, editorially,

> We have not yet declared or taken a direct part in a shooting war. But we have taken a position which must force us ultimately to take such a direct part if our present policy does not prove sufficient to defeat Hitler. It is a position from which we cannot now retreat. It is a position from which the overwhelming majority of Americans have no wish to retreat.

Hopkins wrote of the preparation of the Labor Day speech:

The President indicated that he wanted to make a very straight forward speech about Hitler. It seemed to me that the drafts prepared were not taking the line which the President had in mind.

The President himself developed the paragraph on page 2 relative to the Navy but he toned down a similar paragraph which he had written about the Army. The President believes very strongly that as far as naval strength is concerned, that as long as the British fleet is afloat that fleet joined with ours can command the seas, but if the British fleet were defeated our fleet alone could not handle the job.

The President also worked considerably on the paragraph beginning "I give solemn warning."

The paragraph referred to read:

I give solemn warning to those who think that Hitler has been blocked and halted, that they are making a very dangerous assumption. When in any war your enemy seems to be making slower progress than he did the year before, that is the very moment to strike with redoubled force—to throw more energy into the job of defeating him—to end for all time the menace of world conquest and thereby end all talk or thought of any peace founded on a compromise with evil itself.

Here again was evidence of Roosevelt's perpetual concern about agitation for a negotiated peace. Three days after this speech, a German submarine attacked with two torpedoes, but did not hit, the U.S. destroyer, *Greer*, southeast of Greenland, and a week later Roosevelt made another broadcast, announcing the orders to the Navy to "shoot on sight." Hopkins wrote a description of the preparation of this speech as follows:

The genesis of this speech began as far back as the first of July after the President had initiated his first patrol of the North Atlantic which was merely a patrol of notification in event a submarine or raider were discovered in the waters between North America and Iceland.

The President determined upon a far more important patrol before I went to England late in July, namely one in which all ships flying all flags would be protected. At that time Secretary Stimson was urging the President to tell the people about the nature of the new patrol. The President agreed that this should be done.

At the Roosevelt-Churchill conference in August, the President reiterated that he was going to speak early in September on the implications of his new policy. He felt that the speech, however, should not be made until the patrol was fully effective and all merchant ships were in the protective custody of our naval ships and the permanent plan for the patrol worked out.

He had not set a date for the speech, although he had discussed it with me from time to time after our return from the conference. But with the attack on the *Greer*, he determined to make his speech at once.

He had Cordell Hull and me to lunch on September 5 and outlined his proposal and planned the speech for the following Monday night.

Hull then elaborated at some length on our general position and in very aggressive and stern language laid out the policy of the United States Government and the reason for this patrol. The President liked the statement Hull was making verbally and asked him to dictate what he had just said and send it to the White House late that afternoon. Because the President was then preparing to go to Hyde Park, he asked Hull to send him a copy of the memorandum by telegraph and to give me the other copy.

I was ill and tired and decided to remain in Washington. The draft from Hull arrived and instead of being the vigorous, determined memorandum that had been represented in his verbal talk with the President, it was a pretty weak document, although it built up a fairly strong case for the necessity for some action. But there was no recommendation of any action.

Judge Rosenman and I worked on the speech and I dictated the paragraphs which were proposed to the President for the end of the speech, which put the action that the circumstances required into the speech.

Beginning on page 5 of the mimeographed copy of the speech, with the paragraph "When you see a rattlesnake" was the substance of the language that I prepared for the President.

The President wrote the paragraphs specifically referred to "Do not let us split hairs" and all the historical references and the paragraph about "But let this warning be clear" on the last page.

I talked to the President about this on the phone during the weekend. (This was the weekend the President's mother died.) The President, of course, said at once that Hull's draft was totally inadequate and left the speech entirely in thin air.

I told him that Sam and I were working on an end for the speech with a wallop to it and he asked us to meet him in New York after the funeral and to ride down with him Wednesday afternoon, when the speech would be put in final form. He himself had dictated a few memoranda which had been sent down but which would not include an end for the speech.

I went to New York and met the train at 138th Street and worked all that afternoon on the speech.

Judge Rosenman and I had a draft of our own which we presented to the President and he dictated a few new paragraphs. We made another draft on the train and that night at 8:45 the President called in Hull, Stimson and Knox and myself and read us a draft of the speech.

All of them liked it very much. Knox urged that there be nothing facetious in the speech and that it have a very serious tone. Each of them made some very minor corrections but it was clear that all of them approved of it heartily.

The speech was to be given the next day. That night I told Judge Rosenman of the amendments which had been suggested, the most important of which was the clarification of the fact that we were going to protect foreign ships.

Judge Rosenman then worked up a new draft of the speech on the basis of the conference.

The next morning the Judge and I took it in the President's bedroom and he corrected a new draft in order to read it to the Congressional leaders at ten o'clock.

He later told me that the Congressional leaders had little comment to make on it and all of them thought it was good except Joe Martin, a Republican isolationist.

I had an appointment Thursday morning with the President, with Hull and the Soviet Ambassador on another matter and after that conference was over Hull remained behind, he having just before the conference with the Ambassador told me that the speech was too strong and that all reference to shooting first, or shooting of any kind, should be taken out of the speech.

This was a great surprise to me because Hull had fully agreed before.

On many previous occasions, however, in the last six months Hull has talked pretty strong in private conversation but when it comes down to putting it in writing he has tended to want to dilute everything. He has in recent months given me the impression that he isn't prepared for the implications of a tough row with Hitler.

I later learned from the President that Hull made a very strong argument urging the President to take out of the speech the real guts of it. The speech itself indicates that this was not done.

I have said in a previous section that Hopkins knew nothing of what went on in the mysteries of the Politburo in Moscow. It may be added that he was often almost as ignorant of and puzzled by the processes of policy interpretation in the innermost recesses of the State Department.

Early in September, Hopkins wrote to Brendan Bracken, who had been appointed Minister of Information in the British Cabinet, complaining about "the concerted attack in the British press on two fronts, one, that we won't fight and the other that our supplies are very slow. These editorials don't sit well over here but I presume there is some good reason for the outburst." Hopkins had learned enough about the procedures in wartime London to know that, when the British press was "concerted" on any angle, it generally had been given some sort of off-the-record "guidance" from the government. He went on to say,

We are having some difficulty with our public opinion with regard to Russia. The American people don't take aid to Russia easily. The whole Catholic population is opposed to it, all the Nazis, all the Italians and a lot of people who sincerely believe that Stalin is a great menace to the world. Still I think it will come out all right in the end. . . . The exhibition of the Russian Army has certainly made all of our military people look a little ill. Anglo-Saxons have a hard time believing that anyone can fight except themselves.

A very serious blow to Anglo-American negotiations, and particularly to Hopkins' large share of them, was the death of Arthur Purvis in a tragically unnecessary airplane accident on the R.A.F. Ferry Command run between Scotland and Newfoundland. As representative in Washington of the British Supply Council, Purvis, a Canadian, had gained such a thorough grasp of the complex situation, and so much experience in Hopkins' abrupt methods of doing business, that he and Hopkins could in a few words settle problems which would ordinarily have required hours of tiresome, diplomatic dickering. Hopkins recommended to British friends that Purvis be given some high decoration posthumously but I do not know whether this was ever done.

Only a few days after Churchill made his broadcast saying that only Hitler knew the date of U.S. entry into the war, Hopkins received one of the gloomiest messages that ever came to the White House from the normally confident, ebullient Prime Minister. He mentioned the concern of the British Cabinet over Roosevelt's repeated assurances (in answer to isolationist charges) that the Atlantic Conference had brought the U.S. "no closer to war," that there were no "secret commitments," etc. Each of these statements provided deflation of the confidence that Churchill had inspired on his return from Argentia. The propaganda effect of the Atlantic Conference was beginning to fizzle out. Churchill said that the Cabinet's concern would inevitably extend itself to Parliament and then to the people as a whole, and he added, "I don't know what will happen if England is fighting alone when 1942 comes." He pointed out that there were at that moment thirty U-boats on the line from Northern Ireland to Iceland and that the British had lost 50,000 tons of shipping in the past two days. He said that Hitler was keeping clear of the twenty-sixth meridian which constituted Roosevelt's frontier of the Western Hemisphere (this was before the attacks on the destroyers), so that there was little prospect of an "incident" serious enough to bring the United States into the war. He asked Hopkins if he felt inclined to express any hope for the future. If Hopkins replied directly to this, I can find no copy of it in his papers. But he made the following note which he attached to the Churchill message:

I talked to the President about this cablegram and the only thing we can make out of it is that Churchill is pretty depressed and takes it out on us in this fashion.

I told the President, however, that not only Churchill but all the members of the Cabinet and all the British people I talked to believed that ultimately we will get into the war on some basis or other and if they ever reached the conclusion that this was not to be the case, that would be a very critical moment in the war and the British appeasers might have some influence on Churchill.

Both Roosevelt and Hopkins well knew that, despite Churchill's enormous popularity and hold on the emotions of the British people, the sentiment for appeasement which had existed in Baldwin's time and Chamberlain's was still alive in a small but potentially powerful minority. The appeals to "reason" that had been made and were still being made by Rudolph Hess might well have found sympathetic listeners, particularly in the House of Lords. What Hess was continually offering, and with confidence that he spoke for Hitler, was a peace which would recognize and guarantee the power and prestige of the British Empire in toto while giving Germany control of the Continent of Europe and a free hand against the "Bolsheviks." Hess repeated over and over again that the hopes for effective American intervention were illusory, that Russia was doomed, that England's case was hopeless, and that, therefore, the British Government was insane if it failed to accept Hitler's proffer of friendship while there was yet time to save the aging lion's skin. Here are a few quotations from Hess's interminable monologue: "I am convinced that in any event—whether an Eastern Front persists or not—Germany and her allies are in a position to carry on the war until England collapses from lack of tonnage. . . . The convoy system, which, in the world war— but at the last minute—settled the U-boat war in favor of England, has in this war misfired. It could not prevent the big-scale sinking figures which must finally be fatal. . . . [If Germany must reluctantly conquer Britain] an occupation of the whole island does not come into question —for Germany would be burdened with the feeding of the population. In the long run, only the most important airfields would be kept in occupation. All these would be hermetically sealed over a wide area from the population, so that the troops of occupation would not be affected by the misery of their starvation. . . . I am conscious that in the above I have partly given away military secrets. But I believe I can answer to my conscience and to my people, for I believe that frankness makes possible the ending of a senseless war."

There was nothing that Roosevelt could do in response to Churchill's plea for more tangible evidences of American determination except to attempt to increase the rendering of aid "by all means short of war" (and, when one looks back on those days, one cannot escape the conclusion that never was the word "short" given a more liberal interpretation). Churchill's depression, as it turned out, was short lived, for within two days of the foregoing cable to Hopkins came one from the Former Naval Person to the President giving glowing reports of favorable developments in Persia, which provided opportunities for increased contacts with Russia in that part of the world, and asking for help in transporting two more British divisions aggregating 40,000 men to the Middle East. This involved the loan of the largest transports then in the U.S. service including such converted liners as the *Manhattan, Washington* and *America* (renamed, in wartime, U.S.S. *Wakefield, Mount Vernon* and *West Point*). Churchill said in his cable, "It is quite true that the loan of these liners would hamper any large dispatch of United States forces to Europe or Africa, but as you know I have never asked for this in any period we can reasonably foresee in the near future." Hopkins went to work on this immediately, referring Churchill's message to Admirals Stark and Land. On September 6, Hopkins noted:

> The President had a conference yesterday afternoon at 4 o'clock between Admiral Stark; Admiral King, Commander of the Atlantic Fleet; Admiral Ingersoll, Admiral Land and me.
>
> It was agreed at this conference that we should provide troop transports for 20,000 men and that Admiral Stark was to consult with Admiral Little and Admiral Land with Sir Arthur Salter about the details.
>
> The Admirals seemed quite willing to acquiesce in this program.
>
> One of the important decisions made was that these troop ships were to fly the American flag and be manned by the Navy crews which are now on them.
>
> It was decided it was unwise, however, for American destroyers to accompany these ships, which would be filled with British troops.

The arrangements went forward but, in early October, Roosevelt was again involved with Congress for legislation which would further amend the Neutrality Act to permit the arming of American merchant ships. Roosevelt thereupon cabled Churchill that, to his deep regret, he felt compelled to reopen the question of using American ships to transport British troops to the Middle East. He said, "I have utmost confidence that you will sympathetically consider the problem and my frank statement of it." He said that he had discussed with Congressional leaders his request for new legislation which would permit the arming of American merchant ships and the entry of these ships into British ports, and had reached the conclusion that no chances must be taken of any incidents occurring in the Atlantic while this legislation was being considered. Therefore, the President suggested two alternatives to the Prime Minister:

First—that the British Navy furnish enough officers and men to man the six American transports, which could then be loaned (under the Lend-Lease law) and sail from Canadian ports under the British flag.

The second alternative—that the British troops be sent to Halifax where the six transports (manned by American crews) would pick them up and then sail through Western Hemisphere waters to the South

Atlantic and thence around the Cape, keeping out of the main zones of danger from U-boats.

Roosevelt said that he preferred the first of these alternatives.

Churchill replied that he fully understood the President's position but that he definitely preferred the second alternative, whereby the British troops would be delivered to Halifax and then transshipped to the American transports—and this was done. After Pearl Harbor, these transports were diverted from the Middle East to the carrying of troops across the Indian Ocean for the reinforcement of Singapore. The ships themselves got away from that doomed stronghold in time, but the troops they carried were delivered into the hands of the Japanese.

Hopkins' health was failing again in the autumn of 1941. There was now a vast increase in the details of Lend-Lease administration details. The two-headed (Knudsen-Hillman) Office of Production Management had come to an unlamented end and been replaced by the Supply Priorities Allocation Board, a stopgap organization under the chairmanship of Vice President Wallace, with Donald Nelson as Executive Director and Hopkins one of the members of the Board. He determined to turn the job of Lend-Lease Administrator over to someone else and Edward R. Stettinius, Jr., was selected. Stettinius has described how he was summoned to the White House and found Hopkins in bed with the usual mess of papers littered over the blankets and stuffed under the pillows. The conversation was brief:

Hopkins. Ed, the President wants you to take over administration of the Lend-Lease Program. He thinks there is nothing more important now for the country than getting this Lend-Lease show moving at top speed. We stayed up late last night talking over the whole situation, and he feels you are the man to do it.

Stettinius. I'm here in Washington to serve wherever the President feels I can be most useful and if he wants me to run the Lend-Lease show, I'll take it on and do my best.

There was then some discussion of organization problems and policies and finally Stettinius asked: "Is there anything more to consider about this thing? Does the President want to talk it over with me first?"

Hopkins. Not unless you have something you particularly want to talk over with him. So far as the President is concerned you're elected, Ed.

That bit of the record provides a pretty good example of the unique nature of Hopkins' position in the annals of the government. Here he was calmly relinquishing an imposing title and a job of vast importance —and this in the city of Washington where men in top positions not only fought and bled to hold on to their own jobs but sat up nights figuring ways to take powers and functions away from others of equal eminence. However, Hopkins knew that the policy governing Lend

Lease would still be made in the White House and that the President would continue to delegate most of the responsibility for this to him. Stettinius was his friend and they could work well together—and that was that.

Even when relieved of the major part of the work of Lend Lease, he still was overburdened with responsibilities and worries and his temper became shorter and shorter. He read a public statement by a general on the unpreparedness of the Army and sent it to the President with a note:

> I think statements like this are beginning to do us a good deal of harm. I think many people hesitate to go all the way with you because they feel the Army is not ready to fight.
>
> I can't see any useful purpose in Army officers continuing to make statements like this.

To prove his impartiality as between the services he sent the President the following note attached to a clipping concerning a statement made by an admiral:

> I am not so sick but that reading a speech like this doesn't make me a little sicker.
>
> As a matter of fact I think Yarnell has made serious misstatements of fact in relation to Crete and has done a great injustice to the Royal Air Force.
>
> It seems to me that if our naval officers would spend more time getting our own Navy ready to do its job and less on criticizing the British we would be better off.

Roosevelt did not take either of these squawks very seriously. His temper was far evener than Hopkins'. If it had not been, he could not possibly have lived as long as he did.

Roosevelt could find apparently complete relaxation in talking about the past or the future—particularly, in both cases, his own. He could engage in hours of reminiscence about his Hyde Park and Campobello days before the First World War; or he could go into endless detail about his plans for retirement, which covered a wide range of activities —such as, starting an entirely new kind of country newspaper, a new kind of college and even a new kind of roadside hot-dog stand. In the midst of the uncertainty and hair-trigger danger of the months before Pearl Harbor, Roosevelt expended a great deal of time on a project for a fishing retreat for Hopkins and himself. He had the place all picked out. He wrote a note for Hopkins to obtain a "Large Scale Chart of Long Key, Fla., and Channel Key about 3 miles S.W. of it and just off North Side of Viaduct. This is about half way from Key West to the mainland along the Trestle." Hopkins noted that "we had been talking a good deal about getting a fishing camp in the deep South for use after the President leaves the White House. He has had his eye on Channel Key for a good many years. It was offered to him back in 1924 for

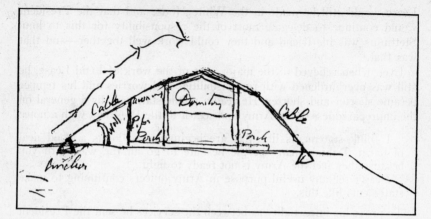

Roosevelt's sketch of a hurricaneproof house which he wanted to build on a Florida key.

$15,000 and the President thinks since the hurricane it probably could be bought very cheaply." Roosevelt designed a hurricaneproof house, which was to be lashed by cables to concrete anchors in the ground.

Hopkins got in touch with a friend, Julius F. Stone, Jr., a lawyer in Key West who had been a W.P.A. official in Florida specializing in hurricane relief. Stone investigated Channel Key and found it could be bought for $3,500 but that the island had been so beaten by a hurricane that most of it was underwater at high tide. The approximate cost of bulkheading and filling the island would be $18,000. Stone recommended that property on the mainland would be preferable. He wrote:

> As you know, there are some windy periods down in this part of the country quite aside from hurricanes, during which one is likely to get good and wet in any small boat going between the island and the mainland. The cost of building a small home on the mainland would be less than transporting everything on an island and likewise the cost and nuisance of maintenance would be considerably less.

However, Roosevelt was not to be talked out of it that easily. After reading Stone's letter, he wrote to Hopkins:

> This is another interesting letter. I still think that property directly off the main highway on a large Key would be a mistake and the Channel Key is the best bet. Unless the storm washed a lot of it away, I would not think of bulkheading or filling the whole of the Island.
> The real answer to it is that somebody has to look at the thing personally. The price of Channel Key is not out of the way. The chief question is whether, since the hurricane, there is enough water for a fishing launch to get to the Island from the highway and from the Island out to the fishing grounds.

Perhaps if we can go to Warm Springs within a week, you could run down and stay with Stone in Key West for a week and look it over. That we can decide later.

Roosevelt and Hopkins went on talking about Channel Key right up to the Japanese attack, nor was it forgotten thereafter. I feel sure that to the moment of his death Roosevelt was determined to build that house and then pray for a hurricane to come along and prove it practicable.

In a previous chapter I have mentioned the astonishment I always felt that there were so few interruptions, dispatches or telephone calls when the President was in his Study either working or relaxed. This was due to the superlatively good staff work in the White House by Grace Tully and other secretaries, by Louise Hackmeister and Russell McMullin who ran the telephone switchboard day and night, and by the three ushers. There were always during the war years plenty of triple priority, superurgent messages or calls coming into the White House from important officials who considered that the continued existence of the Republic and of freedom itself depended on immediate action by the President on whatever it was they were worrying about at the moment. Yet, somehow or other, the staff knew how to sort these out and divert the ninety-nine per cent that were not so crucial as the senders imagined, so that the President would not be disturbed when he wanted to sit around quietly telling lengthy anecdotes or pasting stamps in albums.

I do not believe there was ever a time when he was being more steadily assailed morning, noon and night than in those tense weeks in the autumn of 1941. He was constantly being goaded in one direction by those who favored bold action, of which Stimson and Morgenthau were the most vigorous proponents; and he was being hauled in another direction by others who were convinced that our only salvation lay in a policy of extreme caution; in addition, Churchill was augmenting his voluminous cables with telephone calls from the little booth in the bombproof quarters to which he had been consigned under Great George Street. (In that telephone booth were two clocks, one set at London time and the other at Washington time.)

At the end of September, Roosevelt had to make up his mind as to whether or not he should again put an issue up to Congress and run the risk of an unfavorable verdict. He was besieged with advice as to the dreadful perils that he faced in taking either one course or the other. The attitude of the War Department was obviously in favor of the frontal attack against the isolationists. The attitude of the Navy was less clear. Hull asked Admiral Stark to state his opinions on this matter, and the resultant memorandum from the Chief of Naval Operations was highly refreshing to the President. It was a complete statement of Stark's estimate of the possible advantages and disadvantages and need not be quoted in full. The most important parts of it were as follows:

A declaration of war by the United States against Germany, unless Germany had previously declared war against the United States, might bring Japan into the war as an active belligerent. This would be without question a decided disadvantage because the United States would then be engaged in actual hostilities on two fronts; something we may have to accept, but every effort should be made to avoid this situation. I might add that I believe efforts in this behalf will best be served by our continued strong stand against Japanese aggression. . . .

It has long been my opinion that Germany cannot be defeated unless the United States is wholeheartedly in the war and makes a strong military and naval effort wherever strategy dictates. It would be very desirable to enter the war under circumstances in which Germany were the aggressor and in which case Japan might then be able to remain neutral. However, on the whole, it is my opinion that the United States should enter the war against Germany as soon as possible, even if hostilities with Japan must be accepted. . . .

I might finally add that I have assumed for the past two years that our country would not let Great Britain fall; that ultimately in order to prevent this we would have to enter the war and as noted above I have long felt and often stated that the sooner we get in the better. . . .

P.S. I did not set down in the attached notes what I have mentioned to you before, namely, that I do not believe Germany will declare war on us until she is good and ready; that it will be a cold-blooded decision on Hitler's part if and when he thinks it will pay, and not until then.

He has every excuse in the world to declare war on us now, if he were of a mind to.

He had no legitimate excuse in the world (except to serve his own ends) to invade the countries he has.

When he is ready, he will strike, and not before.

On October 9, Roosevelt sent to the Congress his request for further amendments to the Neutrality Law which would permit the arming of American merchant ships and restoration of the right of these ships to carry trade into the war zones. This provoked another bitter debate on Capitol Hill; indeed, the President's position there was actually weaker than it had been when the Lend-Lease Bill was introduced the previous January. During this debate, the Germans were driving against Moscow along a 375-mile front and, in Tokyo, the so-called "moderate" Konoye Cabinet resigned to be replaced by the undisguisedly militaristic Cabinet of General Tojo. In addition to these portentous developments, the Germans drew the first American blood in the Battle of the Atlantic: on October 17, about 350 miles southwest of Iceland, a U-boat torpedo hit the U.S. destroyer *Kearny* and eleven of her crew were killed. The ship herself managed to limp into the harbor of Reykjavik.

Even this "incident" was taken pretty much as a matter of course by the American people who always have considered the men in their regular armed forces—Navy, Army and, most of all, Marine Corps—as rugged mercenaries who signed up voluntarily, as do policemen and firemen, for hazardous service; it was, of course, tough luck when any of them were killed in line of duty in a Central American revolution, or on an accidentally sunk submarine or on a deliberately sunk gunboat, like the *Panay*, but it was still all in the day's work. There was little or no self-identification of the normal American civilian with the professional American soldier or sailor. In the case of the drafted men, however, the attitude was entirely different. They were "our boys" who must be kept out of harm's way at all costs. Since there were no drafted men in the Navy at that time, there was no great popular indignation against Hitler for the attacks on the destroyers; but what is most important is that neither was there any serious popular indignation against Roosevelt for his responsibility in thus exposing our ships. The American people were merely waiting, in a seemingly apathetic state, comparable to that of the British people during the "Phony War" period—waiting for the Dunkirk which would impel them to positive action. The very fact that the British people remembered how dangerously complacent they themselves had been before the fall of France made it all the more difficult for them to understand the American confidence that "the war can never touch *us*."

Following is a quotation of a news story in the *Washington Times-Herald* which gives some suggestion of the depths touched in those days:

> Government officials were at a loss last night for a legal means of combatting a unique form of antiwar propaganda which has come to light since the torpedoing of the destroyer Kearny, with the loss of most of her officers and crew.
>
> This new method of assailing the Administration's foreign policy has taken the form of taunting messages to the families and relatives of the men who died when the Kearny went down in the Atlantic.
>
> A cartoon depicting Uncle Sam being crucified on "The Cross of Gold" with Justice and Liberty hanging from crosses on either side and penciled messages were received by the family of George Alexander Calvert jr., a fireman on the Kearny, who was reported missing.
>
> The taunting messages, which included the statement that "your dear son was sent to his death by the murdering imbecile head of our Government," were received by the Calvert family shortly after the newspapers reported the collapse of the mother when she learned that her son was lost.
>
> Among the messages was an engraved dodger depicting the hanging of Uncle Sam, with figures labeled "F.D.R." and "Me, too, W.W.", pulling on the rope. Other figures in the cartoon were labeled Carter Glass, Bernard Baruch, Dotty Tom Tom, Frank Knox, Harry Hopkins, La Guardia, Pepper, Henry L. Stimson and others.
>
> The Calvert family, living near Gillespie, Ill., sent the messages to

officials here asking that the persons who sent them be hunted down so "they will not torture any more families whose boys are lost."

A few days after the attack on the *Kearny*, General Robert E. Wood of the America First Committee issued a public appeal to the President to go before the Congress and ask for a definitive vote as to whether the United States should or should not enter the war. This was precisely the demand for bold, decisive action that had been urged on Roosevelt by Stimson and many other advisers in and out of the government for the past six months. The very fact that such a demand now came from an important spokesman for isolationism provided Roosevelt with sufficient confirmation of his conviction that, were he to do this, he would meet with certain and disastrous defeat.

On October 27, Roosevelt gave his annual Navy Day speech in the Grand Ballroom of the Mayflower Hotel in Washington. It was by far the strongest speech he had yet given. He said:

> The shooting has started. And history has recorded who fired the first shot. In the long run, however, all that will matter is who fired the last shot. . . .
> I say that we do not propose to take this lying down. . . .
> Today, in the face of this newest and greatest challenge of them all, we Americans have cleared our decks and taken our battle stations. We stand ready in the defense of our nation and the faith of our fathers to do what God has given us the power to see as our full duty.

Brave words—but they did not change the situation in the slightest degree. They may well have been greeted with derisive laughter by the war lords in Berlin and Tokyo. Three days after Roosevelt spoke, another U.S. destroyer, the *Reuben James*, was torpedoed and sunk. One hundred fifteen members of the ship's company, including all the officers, were lost. The bereaved families mourned, but among the general public there seemed to be more interest in the Army-Notre Dame football game. There was a sort of tacit understanding among Americans that nobody was to get excited if ships were sunk by U-boats, because that's what got us into war the other time. It has been said that in 1914 the French were prepared for the war of 1870, and in 1939 they were prepared for the war of 1914. It could be said with equal truth that in 1941 the Americans were fully prepared to keep out of the war of 1917.

On November 7, the Senate agreed to amend the Neutrality Act by the close vote of 50 to 37 and a week later the House passed the amendments by the much closer vote of 212 to 194.

The truth was that, as the world situation became more desperately critical, and as the limitless peril came closer and closer to the United States, isolationist sentiment became ever more strident in expression and aggressive in action, and Roosevelt was relatively powerless to combat it. He had said everything "short of war" that could be said. He had no more tricks left. The hat from which he had pulled so many rabbits was empty. The President of the United States was now the creature of circumstance which must be shaped not by his own will or his own ingenuity but by the unpredictable determination of his enemies. It is small wonder that he attempted in his spare time to find surcease by figuring out means of anchoring a holiday cottage against West Indian hurricanes.

On October 31, Roosevelt and Hopkins went to Hyde Park for five days, after which Hopkins went to the Navy Hospital where he remained for four weeks. The hospital was then on 24th and E Streets, only a short distance from the White House, and Hopkins drove over occasionally for dinner with the President. He was always in touch with Stettinius and General Burns at Lend Lease and was kept constantly informed on the general situation.

He always took more interest in his family affairs when he was ill and, while in the hospital, he made elaborate preparations for a birthday party for his daughter Diana at the White House on November 15. On November 24, he wrote to his son Stephen at Hill School:

> I didn't hear how the football team came out in its last game but I hope you managed to get into it.
>
> I have your report card indicating that you are failing in two of your four subjects. Some way, some how it seems to me you have to buckle down to your school work and forget about athletics for the balance of this year. Surely you are not so backward that you can't do reasonably good work, but you have got to learn really to study.
>
> It is far more important that you make good marks than that you make the football team. There is little chance of your ever getting to college with these kind of marks.
>
> I don't want you to think I underrate having a good time, but the world being the way it is these days each one of us has got to learn to take care of himself, and you are getting, it seems to me, a very special opportunity now that hardly one boy in a thousand in the United States has and I want you to take full advantage of it.

Stephen was his youngest son who was killed in action with the Marines two years later.

Hopkins left the hospital four days before Pearl Harbor and returned to his bedroom-office in the White House. He never managed to follow the advice that he gave his son—"each of us has got to learn to take care of himself."

CHAPTER XVIII

Aid for Russia

A S A measure for coping with the serious Catholic opposition to aid for the Soviet Union, Roosevelt decided to send Myron C. Taylor, his special Ambassador to Pope Pius XII, on another mission to Rome. Even this move raised difficult religious issues for there were many Protestants, including some important church leaders, who were deeply alarmed by any signs of collusion between the White House and the Vatican, as they had proved when Alfred E. Smith was a candidate for the Presidency in 1928. But Taylor was an ideal choice for this delicate mission. He was an eminent Protestant. He was also a former chairman of the board and continuing director of the U. S. Steel Corporation, and director of the American Telephone & Telegraph Company, the First National Bank of New York, the New York Central Railroad, etc.,—so that he could hardly be accused of subservience to Stalin.

In the handling of the supremely delicate problem presented by the antipathy of the Church toward Communism, Roosevelt received invaluable aid from such eminent Catholic laymen as Associate Justice Frank Murphy of the Supreme Court, Postmaster General Frank Walker and Philip Murray, who had succeeded John L. Lewis as president of the C.I.O. There were some impatient people who thought that the President exaggerated the strength of Catholic sentiment, but it was his way to tread with extreme wariness wherever religious sensibilities were involved; he knew a lot more than his advisers did about these sensibilities.

The preparations for the departure of the Harriman Mission to Moscow were immensely complicated, involving exhaustive negotiations and some heated arguments with the Army and Navy, the production and shipping authorities, and British representatives in Washington, over the long lists of items which might be pledged to the Soviet Union.

Both Churchill and Beaverbrook telephoned Hopkins from London begging that these preparations be concluded with all possible haste as the Russians, so hard pressed themselves, were pressing the British Government to advance the date of the Moscow talks.

In the midst of this, the elder Mrs. James Roosevelt died, and the President had to leave the final work on the schedule entirely in Hopkins' hands.

Those who were closest to Franklin Roosevelt could not presume to guess at the quality of sorrow caused him by his mother's death; one needed only a small realization of the tenacity with which he clung to every surviving link with the lovely world of his childhood—a world fantastically different from the one in which he now lived and fought— to know that his sorrow was very deep indeed. He kept it to himself. He permitted no sign of it to appear on the surface. He wanted no evidences of awareness of it from anyone else.

On September 9, before leaving for New York to attend Mrs. Roosevelt's funeral, Hopkins sent a long cable to Churchill saying that the President had requested the Secretaries of War and Navy to draw up immediately (in fact, by the following day) a program to cover allocation of matériel to Great Britain and the Soviet Union up to June 30, 1942. "With this information available," Hopkins wrote, "the President proposes that there be a conference about September 15th in London between high British and American officials"—this to be followed at the earliest possible date by a conference with the Russians in Moscow. Churchill replied that he and Beaverbrook were in complete agreement with the proposals and were making all necessary preparations for the conferences. He said that the entire American and British delegations would be transported to Russia in ships of the Royal Navy. As it happened, Harriman traveled with Beaverbrook and his Mission in a British cruiser, but the rest of the American Mission traveled from London to Moscow in the same B-24's which had brought them from Washington. These two bombers, piloted by Major A. L. Harvey and Lieutenant L. T. Reichers, made a remarkable flight at very high altitude over much the same route that Hopkins had flown in a PBY, this being the first mission of the U.S. Army Air Corps over areas controlled by the Luftwaffe. Quentin Reynolds, a close friend of Harriman's, managed to hitchhike a ride on one of these bombers and later cabled Hopkins recommending that Harvey and Reichers be awarded Distinguished Flying Crosses for an "amazing flight under terrific conditions." He added that the "Russian Air Force thinks it greatest flight ever made."

The American Mission included: William L. Batt, Admiral William H. Standley, General Burns, General Chaney and Colonel Philip R. Faymonville; and the British Mission: Harold Balfour, Sir Archibald

Rowlands, Sir Charles Wilson, General G. N. Macready and General Ismay.

As he sailed from the U.K., Beaverbrook cabled Hopkins:

We finished our work this evening in the big room of the War Cabinet and now with gratitude and affection I send you my personal thanks for your efforts in making this conference possible. The faith that you have had in our people has sustained our courage through dark hours and terrible attacks. We all recognize the influence you have exerted in our country and we shall continue to look to you for guidance and leadership.

Which sounds a little as if Beaverbrook contemplated the possibility that these might be his last words. Neither he nor any other senior members of the Mission could forget, as they started their journey aboard *H.M.S. London*, that Lord Kitchener had met his death on a torpedoed British cruiser en route to Archangel in the first year of the First World War.

Roosevelt wrote a letter of introduction for dispatch to Harriman in London, as follows:

My Dear Mr. Stalin:

This note will be presented to you by my friend Averell Harriman, whom I have asked to be head of our delegation to Moscow.

Mr. Harriman is well aware of the strategic importance of your front and will, I know, do everything that he can to bring the negotiations in Moscow to a successful conclusion.

Harry Hopkins has told me in great detail of his encouraging and satisfactory visits with you. I can't tell you how thrilled all of us are because of the gallant defense of the Soviet armies.

I am confident that ways will be found to provide the material and supplies necessary to fight Hitler on all fronts, including your own.

I want particularly to take this occasion to express my great confidence that your armies will ultimately prevail over Hitler and to assure you of our great determination to be of every possible material assistance.

> Yours very sincerely,
> FRANKLIN D. ROOSEVELT

This letter arrived after Harriman had left London and the extra-careful intelligence officers burned it rather than forward it in an airplane which might be shot down over territory held by the Germans. Roosevelt therefore transmitted its text by cable through the State Department to the American Embassy in Moscow and Steinhardt duly delivered it to Stalin. Evidently the Germans intercepted this cable for they released a version of Roosevelt's letter, deliberately garbled, through the DNB News Service to North and South America. This German version quoted the President as starting the letter with the salutation,

"My Dear Friend Stalin," and ending it, "In cordial friendship," instead of "Yours very sincerely."

Hopkins sent a memorandum to Stettinius shortly before the Moscow Conferences started:

> I would like to be in direct touch with Harriman and the Mission in Moscow and any replies to Harriman's telegrams I would like to have sent through me and signed by me.
>
> Will you please notify everybody over there about this so there will be no possible hitch about it.

Harriman and Beaverbrook had three evening meetings with Stalin—Sunday, September 28, Monday the 29th, and Tuesday the 30th, for a total of some nine hours. During the same days there were repeated meetings of the subcommittees on Army, Navy, Air Force, raw materials, transportation and medical supplies. These committee meetings were described at first as "protracted exercises in utter frustration," for the British and American officials and officers could seem to get little or no comment from their Russian opposite numbers on the various proposals for a program of supplies. As usual, nothing of any real importance could be accomplished below the topmost level.

At the first meeting with Stalin, cordiality prevailed. Stalin gave a candid review of the military situation, as he had done with Hopkins, saying that Germany's superiority to Russia was, in air power, in a ratio of three to two—in tanks, a ratio of three or four to one—in divisions, 320 to 280. However, Stalin said the preponderance in tanks was absolutely essential to the Germans for, without it, the German infantry was weak as compared with the Russian infantry. He said that, of Germany's satellites, the best fighters were the Finns, next the Italians, third the Rumanians and, last of all, the Hungarians. He estimated that there were at the time ten Italian divisions in the Eastern theater of operations. (This indicates a certain change of opinion since his talks with Hopkins two months previously.) Stalin went into considerable detail as to required items, ending up with the statement that his greatest need was tanks and, after that, antitank guns, medium bombers, antiaircraft guns, armor plate, fighter and reconnaissance planes and, high on the list, barbed wire.

Stalin had a great deal to say to Beaverbrook about the question of active British military co-operation with Russia. Even at that early stage of Russia's participation in the war, the desirability of opening a second front in the West had already become a lively issue and was providing the persistent theme song of Russian propaganda in Britain and the United States. However, Stalin does not appear to have pressed particularly for the second front at this conference. He did feel that the British might send forces to join the Russians in the Ukraine. Beaverbrook pointed out that British divisions were being built up in Persia and that these might be moved into the Caucasus. (The British obviously were interested in reinforcing the Caucasus to prevent a possible German breakthrough into the Middle East.) Stalin dismissed this with the brusque statement that, "There is no war in the Caucasus but there is in the Ukraine." Beaverbrook suggested that the Soviet and British staffs might engage in strategic discussions but this suggestion met with no welcome whatsoever.

Harriman took up the matter of the Siberian airports and the possibility of the delivery of American aircraft to the Soviet Union by the Alaskan route. Stalin agreed that information about the airports in Siberia should be made available, but when Harriman suggested that delivery of the planes might be made by American crews Stalin demurred that it was "too dangerous a route." Harriman gathered that Stalin did not wish to take any chances of provoking Japan.

Stalin asked about peace objectives. When Beaverbrook mentioned the eight points of the Atlantic Charter, Stalin asked, "What about getting the Germans to pay for the damage?" Beaverbrook evaded that question with some generality about, "We must win the war first." Harriman mentioned President Roosevelt's concern about the state of American public opinion, particularly on the religious issue. Stalin said that he did not know much about American public opinion toward Russia and did not seem to attach much importance to it. As it was getting late, Harriman did not press the matter but promised to give Stalin a memorandum on it.

At the end of this first session, Harriman noted, "Beaverbrook and I considered the meeting had been extremely friendly and were more than pleased with our reception. The meeting lasted over three hours."

At the second meeting, the following evening, the atmosphere was entirely different. In his report, Harriman noted,

The evening was very hard sledding. Stalin seemed discourteous and at times not interested, and rode us pretty hard. For example, he turned to me once and said, "Why is it that the United States can only give me 1,000 tons of armor plate steel for tanks—a country with a production of over 50,000,000 tons?" When I tried to explain the length of time required in increasing capacity of this type of steel he brushed it aside by saying, "One only has to add alloys."

At this meeting which lasted two hours, Lord Beaverbrook noted that, "Stalin was very restless, walking about and smoking continuously, and appeared to both of us to be under an intense strain." Beaverbrook handed him a letter from Churchill which Stalin opened and merely glanced at, then left lying on the table unread throughout the meeting. As Beaverbrook and Harriman were preparing to leave, Molotov reminded Stalin of the Churchill letter. Stalin thrust it back in the envelope and handed it to a clerk.

During the meeting Stalin made three telephone calls, each time dialing the number himself. Neither Beaverbrook nor Harriman could account for Stalin's mood at this meeting, but their likeliest guess was that he had just received some alarming news about the imminent German drive on Moscow. In all the lengthy review of all the items of arms, munitions, raw materials, etc., that was painstakingly made, Stalin betrayed evidence of enthusiasm only once and that was when Harriman mentioned an American offer of 5,000 jeeps to Russia. Stalin asked if he could have some more. But, when Harriman asked if he would like to have some ordinary armored cars for his troops, Stalin said that armored cars were death traps and he did not want any.

Beaverbrook and Harriman had hoped to conclude their business with Stalin at this meeting but when it broke up they were still so far from settlement on so many points that they asked for a third meeting the following evening. Stalin readily agreed to this—the only real agreement achieved at this session, except on the question of the merit of the jeep.

The next day the German propagandists were blasting to the world the news that the conferences in Moscow had bogged down—that bitter quarrels had developed—that the British and Americans could never find common ground with the "Bolshevists." It seemed to the members of the British and American Missions that this time, for once, Goebbels might be uncomfortably close to the truth. But, when Beaverbrook and Harriman met Stalin in the Kremlin at six o'clock that evening, they found that the atmosphere had again changed completely. Stalin mentioned the Nazi propaganda with some amusement and indicated that it was for the three of them to prove Goebbels a liar.

Beaverbrook went through a memorandum listing everything that the Russians had asked for, stating those items on which the Americans and British could not meet the demands immediately, and then a long list of items which could be met in full with even some extras thrown in. Beaverbrook asked Stalin if he was pleased with this list. Stalin replied that he had received the list with enthusiasm. Then, Beaverbrook noted:

> The interpreter, Litvinov, bounded out of his seat and cried with passion, "Now we shall win the war."
> When we had completed the recital of the list the atmosphere developed to the highest degree of satisfaction and pleasure on both sides. The assembly took on the form of closer and even intimate relations. . . . It was sunshine after rain.

In his records of this conference, Beaverbrook has given an interesting glimpse of Stalin's "doodling" habits: While Litvinov was translating the Russian words into English, "Stalin occupied himself by drawing numberless pictures of wolves on paper and filling in the background with red pencil."

During this meeting Stalin again emphasized the need for the greatest possible number of jeeps and also for American three-ton trucks. He said that the war depended on the gasoline engine—that the country with the biggest output in engines would be the ultimate victor. He also talked again about postwar aims and politics in general. Beaverbrook notes that at one point in the meeting Stalin "sent for tea and food. This was the first time food had been produced at our conferences. It was obviously the result of his pleased excitement."

In Harriman's notes is the following:

> Stalin asked about Hess and seemed much interested in Beaverbrook's amusing description of his talk with Hess and his size-up of the situation. Stalin indicated that he thought Hess had gone not at the request of Hitler but with the knowledge of Hitler, to which Beaverbrook agreed.
>
> The net of Beaverbrook's statement was that Hess had come thinking that with a small group of British aristocrats a counter-Churchill government could be set up to make peace with Germany which would be welcomed by the majority of the British. Germany with British aid would then attack Russia. Stalin relished the amusing and detailed comments by Beaverbrook who was in his best form as a raconteur.

In his notes on this part of the conversation, Beaverbrook wrote that Stalin said the German Ambassador (who was still in Moscow at the time of the Hess flight) had told him that Hess was crazy—but Beaverbrook expressed the view that Hess was not.

Harriman expressed to Stalin the hope that he would feel free to cable President Roosevelt directly on any matters that he considered of importance. Harriman assured him that Roosevelt would welcome such messages—as he did similar messages from Churchill. Stalin said he was glad to hear this as he had previously felt he should not presume to address the President directly. Beaverbrook suggested to Stalin that it would be highly desirable for him to meet with Churchill face to face. According to Harriman's notes, Stalin expressed to Beaverbrook his belief that the present military alliance and agreement of no separate peace should be extended to a treaty, an alliance not only for war but for postwar as well. Beaverbrook answered that he personally favored it and believed that it was an opportune time to take it up.

Harriman made repeated attempts to break through the continued discussion of European matters in order to obtain Stalin's views on the Far East. Stalin expressed the belief that Japan might be split from its Axis alliance with Germany. He said it was his impression "that Japan was not Italy and is not willing to be a serf to Germany and therefore could be won away."

Beaverbrook noted of Stalin, "We had got to like him; a kindly man, with a habit, when agitated, of walking about the floor with his hands behind his back. He smoked a great deal and practically never shows any impatience at all." Beaverbrook was somewhat disturbed because, during the second and third meetings, the door leading from the conference room to the outer office was left open, which indicated the possibility that somebody was checking on Litvinov's translations. Harriman did not feel that the open door had any significance whatever.

At the conclusion of this final meeting, Molotov exchanged a few sentences with Stalin, who then expressed the hope that Lord Beaverbrook and Mr. Harriman would have dinner with him the next evening. The invitation was accepted. Harriman wrote:

The meeting broke up in the most friendly fashion possible. Stalin made no effort to conceal his enthusiasm. It was my impression that he was completely satisfied that Great Britain and America meant business. In spite of my lack of knowledge of the language he had indicated by his manner throughout the three nights of conferences (totaling about nine hours) very clearly his reactions to everything we said, either favorable or unfavorable or that he was not interested.

I left feeling that he had been frank with us and if we came through as had been promised and if personal relations were retained with Stalin, the suspicion that has existed between the Soviet Government and our two governments might well be eradicated.

There can be no doubt that Stalin is the only man to deal with in foreign affairs. Dealing with others without previous instruction from Stalin about the matters under discussion was almost a waste of time.

Beaverbrook has been a great salesman. His personal sincerity was convincing. His genius never worked more effectively.

Harriman later wrote a memorandum on religion in the U.S.S.R.:

Throughout the week in Russia I took every occasion (and I believe covered most of the members of the Soviet delegation, including of course Stalin and Molotov) of explaining the American political situation and public opinion regarding Russia, particularly in relation to the religious subject, and urged that both statements and action be taken to indicate to America that the Soviets were willing to allow freedom of worship not only in letter but in fact.

Everyone at least nodded "Yes." In explaining the subject to Stalin, he nodded his head and indicated what I understood to mean a willingness to see that something was done.

Oumansky was the most expansive and assured me that the Soviets did allow religious worship and would reduce restrictions and would have the necessary publicity. He promised the last time I saw him, at the American Embassy Friday, October 3, categorically without qualification that the President's public statement on religion would be responded to by a high Soviet official in a manner to obtain maximum publicity in the United States.

In spite of all comments and assurances I leave with the impression that all the Soviets intend to do is to give lip service and to create certain instances which would give an impression of relaxation without really changing their present practices. At the dinner given for the Delegates in the Kremlin (October 1) Molotov expressed to me with great sincerity the high regard that he and the others had for the President, both in his motives and the fundamental wisdom of his conceptions. At one point in discussing the President, he asked me whether the President being such an intelligent man really was as religious as he appeared, or whether his professions were for political purposes. They look upon a man who believes in a religious doctrine or faith as we do a fundamentalist.

They do appear, however, to be much less afraid of religion than they were some years ago. For example Stalin's remarks in toasting the President's aims for the creation of a proper peace (as translated by Oumansky) ended with the old Russian colloquial phrase "May God help him." (I questioned Oumansky about this and he assured me that his translation was exact, but as one of the Embassy men said he had not heard Stalin say it I checked later with another member of the Embassy staff who told me Stalin had used the phrase. There is no doubt that Oumansky did not translate all the toasts accurately. Stalin even commented on this to Litvinov in Beaverbrook's hearing.)

The Polish refugees and army are going to be allowed some priests. Two have been released from confinement so far—more to follow. I discussed this subject with Sikorski in London before leaving for Moscow. I asked him to advise Washington what had been done, explaining why it was of interest. I understand subsequently this was done and the information released by the State Department.

I got conflicting reports regarding the amount of worship, the percentage of churches in the villages that were open, and the attendance. All, however, agreed on the following:

(1) That worship was engaged in by older people, practically nobody under thirty.

(2) That they were chiefly women.

(3) That there were, of course, no Communists.

Religion to the Communists is superstition and against the Communist philosophy, and in its organized form dangerous in developing anti-Communist political groups. It is of course a grave offense for anyone to teach the youth under sixteen religious philosophy.

Unless Stalin is ready to compromise the entire political philosophy of the Party, namely allowing no minority political parties to develop, freedom (including free balloting, etc.), religious worship will be tolerated only under closest G.P.U. scrutiny with a view to keeping it under careful control like a fire which can be stamped out at any time rather

than allowed to burn freely with the dangers of uncontrolled con-
flagration..

The Communists will unquestionably continue anti-religious education of the youth up to sixteen years without allowing religious education. Religious worshippers will be restricted in economic or political
advancement even if they are no longer persecuted. Priests or clergy-
men will be closely watched as will everybody with whom they have
intimate contact.

The type of concession that will be made is indicated by the following statements on religion, which are considered revolutionary, that
appeared in the official Communist Party paper, *"Pravda."*

(1) "We hold sacred the religious sentiments of our women."
(So translated to me by Oumansky.)

(2) The phrase "independently of race, wealth, creed or political
opinion."

Aside from the members of the American and British Embassies
the only foreigner I talked to was Father Braun, the only American
Catholic priest in Russia, whose sentiments are described in the
attached letter to Myron Taylor.

In the letter referred to, Father Braun reviewed at length the improvements that he had observed in the Russian tolerance of religion. He
attributed this largely to the influence of President Roosevelt.

Harriman also made note of certain evidences of friction between
Beaverbrook and the military members of the British Mission. Beaverbrook had by then become, as he was to continue, a vociferous advocate
of the second front in the West. He was forever opposing any diversions
from this fixed purpose. Following is his own original statement of
the matter, a copy of which he sent to Hopkins:

On my return from Russia in about the middle of October 1941
I stated a case for a second front to help the Russians.

I claimed that our military leaders had shown themselves consistently averse to taking any offensive action.

Our advance into Persia was a purely minor and preventive operation in which we employed less than one quarter of the troops used by
the Russians. And the only other operations we have undertaken have
been the bombing of Western Germany and Fighter sweeps over France
which have done nothing to help Russia or hinder Germany in the
present crisis and in which we have lost many of our finest airmen.

Our strategy is still based on a long-term view of the War which
is blind to the urgencies and opportunities of the moment. There has
been no attempt to take into account the new factor introduced by
Russian resistance.

There is today only one military problem—how to help Russia.
Yet on that issue the Chiefs of Staff content themselves with saying
that nothing can be done. They point out the difficulties but make
no suggestions for overcoming them.

It is nonsense to say that we can do nothing for Russia. We can, as soon as we decide to sacrifice long-term projects and a general view of the war which, though still cherished, became completely obsolete on the day when Russia was attacked.

Russian resistance has given us new opportunities. It has probably denuded Western Europe of German troops and prevented for the time being offensive action by the Axis in other theaters of possible operations. It has created a quasi-revolutionary situation in every occupied country and opened 2,000 miles of coastline to a descent by British forces.

But the Germans can move their Divisions with impunity to the East. For the Continent is still considered by our generals to be out of bounds to British troops. And Rebellion is regarded as premature and even deplored when it occurs, because we are not ready for it.

The Chiefs of Staff would have us wait until the last button has been sewn on the last gaiter before we launch an attack. They ignore the present opportunity.

But they forget that the attack on Russia has brought us a new peril as well as a new opportunity. If we do not help them now the Russians may collapse. And, freed at last from anxiety about the East, Hitler will concentrate all his forces against us in the West.

The Germans will not wait then till we are ready. And it is folly for us to wait now. We must strike before it is too late.

On Wednesday afternoon, October 1, the first "Confidential Protocol" between the U.S.A., and the U.S.S.R. and the U.K. was signed and sealed by Harriman, Beaverbrook and Molotov. It contained over seventy main items and more than eighty items of medical supplies—from tanks, planes and destroyers down to Army boots (of which the Russians asked for 400,000 pairs monthly) and shellac (300 tons monthly).

Hopkins wrote to Churchill:

I think the all-important thing now is to increase our monthly production during the coming months. We are bending every effort in that direction here and, as the President wired you the other day, we are going to very substantially increase our sights on the total output on all weapons.

At times I get terribly discouraged about getting the matériel fast enough but then I think of your own overwhelming problems and I am tempted to try again.

I have heard from Averell in Moscow and as long as that Mission is there I am spending all my time on their interests in Washington. There is still an amazing number of people here who do not want to help Russia and who don't seem to be able to pound into their thick heads the strategic importance of that front.

Roosevelt cabled Harriman, "I want to express to you and your associates the great satisfaction I have with the successful culmination of your mission in Moscow. I think that you all did a magnificent job."

Harriman did not realize it at the time but he was to learn on several later occasions that this first experience of a major conference in Moscow set a pattern which was to be followed time and again: extreme cordiality at the start of the conference, changing to disagreeable and even surly hostility at the second meeting—and then harmonious agreement and a jubilantly triumphant banquet with innumerable toasts to Allied co-operation at the finish.

Before Harriman left Moscow the military situation on the Eastern Front was becoming exceedingly grave. It was then that Hitler called in his press chief, Dr. Otto Dietrich, and ordered him to inform the universe that the Red Army had been crushed and the war in Russia was over.

At Hopkins' request, Harriman left Colonel Faymonville in Moscow to act as representative there for Lend Lease. This appointment led to a great deal of controversy between Hopkins and the War Department, for Faymonville was one Regular Army officer who was sympathetic to the Russians and confident of their ability to hold out against the powerful German forces. The protests against Faymonville began to be heard in Washington as soon as it was known that Hopkins was reposing so much confidence in him. General Marshall received a comment from an undisclosed source and referred it to Hopkins:

> I don't know him [Faymonville] well, but I do know that competent men who have served with him, such as ex-Ambassador Bullitt and Mr. Henderson of the Russian Division of the State Department, have serious doubts as to his judgment and his impartiality wherever the Soviets are concerned.

The remarkable disparity between the points of view of Faymonville and Major Yeaton, still the Military Attaché in Moscow, and the conflicting nature of the intelligence that they provided, can be demonstrated by two cables sent on successive days. On October 10, Yeaton reported that he considered it possible that the "end of Russian resistance is not far away." He reported that "commuters reaching Moscow from the suburbs today are speaking of being misled by their government and are saying that the Red Army's defense is not as effective as it should be." Yeaton added the grim thought that American shipments via Archangel might be destroyed or lost or seized by the Germans. On October 11, Faymonville reported the view of the Soviet General Staff that adequate reserves could prevent the encirclement of Moscow, that the military situation in the extreme south was serious but not hopeless, and that planned shipments of ammunition, small arms, machine guns, airplanes and tanks be exceeded wherever possible.

When, as so often happens, intelligence reports on the same subject come from observers who disagree with one another, the superiors in the home office to whom the reports are addressed are inclined to believe the one that fits in best with their own previously formed conceptions. That is why governments with even the most extensive intelligence organizations in foreign countries so often make such incomprehensible mistakes—and that, as will be seen, was particularly true of the Soviet Union itself.

When Hopkins read the Yeaton cable, he wrote the following letter to Secretary Stimson:

> There has been sent to us a copy of a report by our Military Attache in Moscow dated October 10. This report in my opinion should be accepted with the greatest reserve.
>
> When I was in Moscow, Yeaton was outspoken in his criticism of the Russians and was insisting at that time—over ten to twelve weeks ago—that Moscow was going to fall at any time.
>
> From my short observation in Moscow I can not see how any Military Attache could get any reasonable expression of opinion from commuters or the general public which would be worthwhile.

On October 30, Roosevelt cabled Stalin that he had approved all the items of matériel agreed to in the Protocol of the Moscow Conference and had ordered that deliveries be expedited. He had directed that shipments up to the value of one billion dollars be financed under Lend Lease, that "no interest be charged on the indebtedness resulting from these shipments" and that payments by the Soviet Government should "begin five years after the war and continue over a period of ten years thereafter"—these arrangements, of course, being subject to agreement with the Russians. Roosevelt said he hoped that Stalin would make special efforts to facilitate the purchase in the U.S.S.R. of such raw materials and commodities as were available and of which the United States might be in desperate need. He closed with an expression of appreciation for the manner in which the conference in Moscow was handled, and said he hoped Stalin would "not hesitate to communicate directly with me" whenever he felt that circumstances demanded it.

Hopkins wrote the following note on this cable:

> It seemed to me after my conference in Russia with Stalin that the President should personally deal with Stalin. . . .
>
> This telegram is the second wire the President has sent Stalin since I returned. The first one was on October 13 when the President wanted to let him know about some supply items.
>
> This telegram represents the President's decision to put the Russians under Lend-Lease. There has been an endless amount of discussion about that for some weeks and it has become more and more clear that this is the only technique to finance their purchases. Yesterday

I consulted both Morgenthau and Hull about it and they were agreeable to the contents of the wire, which I drafted this morning, and the President has since cabled it.

The President met with the Russian Mission and went over their work in some detail this morning.

I lunched with General Burns and spent the afternoon with Stimson and Marshall in the former's office.

Stimson is obviously unhappy because he is not consulted about the strategy of the war and I think he feels that I could be more helpful in relating him and Marshall to the President.

Stimson wanted me to be sure that I knew the War Department's full strategic plans and he and Marshall delivered them at great length, including the techniques to keep Japan out of the war and the various theaters in which we might operate in the event of our getting into the war.

Both Stimson and Marshall feel that we can't win without getting into the war but they have no idea how that is going to be accomplished.

Following is Stalin's reply, dated November 4, to Roosevelt's cable:

The American Ambassador, Mr. Steinhardt, through Mr. Vishinski, presented to me on November 2, 1941, an aide memoire containing the contents of your message, the exact text of which I have not yet received.

First of all I would like to express my sincere thanks for your appreciative remarks regarding the expeditious manner in which the conference was handled. Your assurances that the decisions of the conference will be carried out to the limit are deeply appreciated by the Soviet Government.

Your decision, Mr. President, to grant to the Soviet Union a loan in the amount of one billion dollars subject to no interest charges and for the purpose of paying for armaments and raw materials for the Soviet Union is accepted with sincere gratitude by the Soviet Government as unusually substantial aid in its difficult and great struggle against our common enemy, bloodthirsty Hitlerism.

I agree completely, on behalf of the Government of the Soviet Union, with the conditions which you outlined for this loan to the Soviet Union, namely that payments on the loan shall begin five years after the end of the war and shall be completed during the following ten-year period.

The Government of the U.S.S.R. stands ready to expedite in every possible way the supplying of available raw materials and goods required by the United States.

I am heartily in accord with your proposal, Mr. President, that we establish direct personal contact whenever circumstances warrant.

It is an indication of Roosevelt's concern for public opinion that he did not formally include the Soviet Union among the recipients of Lend

Lease until November 7. At that time, the Germans were some thirty miles from Moscow and it seemed that they must soon take the ancient capital; but the heroic fight that the Russian armies had put up had gone far toward convincing the world that the occupation of Moscow would do Hitler no more good than it had done Napoleon, and the over-whelming sentiment in the United States was that the Russians richly deserved and would know how to use every scrap of help that we could give them.

Shortly thereafter, with Moscow in a state of siege, Roosevelt and Hopkins discussed the possibility of expediting the delivery of fighter planes to Russia by sending an aircraft carrier to the Persian Gulf, thereby delivering the planes in a state of readiness for immediate action. Roosevelt was in favor of this and instructed Hopkins to investigate the matter with the Navy Department. The suggestion did not receive a cordial response. Hopkins thereupon wrote a memorandum to the President:

> I gather that what is really behind this is that in the light of the whole strategic situation as it is in the world today the Navy feels it would be unwise to send a carrier. Hence, unless you decide other-wise, we are going to move these planes at once by merchant ship, although as I have told you, the Maritime Commission is having a good deal of difficulty getting enough ships.

Roosevelt returned this to Hopkins with the following penciled no-tation:

H.L.H.:
OK but say to them from me: Hurry, hurry, hurry!
                                                    F.D.R.

In view of the date of this memorandum it can be seen that the Navy had some reason for feeling that "the whole strategic situation made it unwise to send a carrier" all the way around Africa to the Persian Gulf. The date was November 25, 1941, twelve days before Pearl Harbor.

Myron Taylor's mission to Rome was completed at the time when Harriman's to Moscow was starting. Taylor was one who really de-served the somewhat archaic title of "Ambassador Extraordinary." (The same might well be said of Hopkins, although both of them were designated only "Personal Representative of the President.") He made a supremely tactful and legitimate presentation of the President's case at the Vatican, where he met with a most sympathetic reception. While the results of this mission were given no great amount of publicity, they were reflected in the attitude of the Catholic hierarchy in the United States and no serious issue was raised over the more than eleven billion dollars of Lend-Lease materials which went to the Soviet Union.

THE WHITE HOUSE

WASHINGTON

November 25, 1941

MEMORANDUM FOR THE PRESIDENT:

I gather that what is really behind this
is that in the light of the whole strategic
situation as it is in the world today the Navy
feels it would be unwise to send a carrier.
Hence, unless you decide otherwise, we are
going to move these planes at once by merchant
ship, although, as I have told you, the
Maritime Commission is having a good deal of
difficulty getting enough ships.

HARRY L. HOPKINS

H.L.H.

OK but say to
them from me:
Hurry, Hurry,
Hurry!

FDR

Roosevelt urges Hopkins to expedite shipment of aircraft to Russia.

While on the way back from Rome, Taylor stopped off in Lisbon for an interview with Dr. Salazar, the "benevolent dictator" of Portugal. Roosevelt was naturally intensely interested to hear Taylor's report of this interview because of his preoccupation with the strategic importance of the Azores. The report was not encouraging. Salazar apparently hoped that the United States would not enter the war, as this would prolong it indefinitely; he seemed to believe that Britain and America together might destroy Hitler personally, although even that would be no easy task, but that they could not destroy Nazism which was the new social, political and economic evolution in Europe. Indeed, Roosevelt gained the impression that, in Salazar's opinion, the best interests of European evolution would be served by Britain's agreeing to the incorporation of the Ukraine into Germany as part of her vital "living space," and that, without the Ukraine, Russia could not continue to provide much of a military threat. It must be added that Roosevelt could not find it in his heart to blame Salazar for playing an extremely cautious game, for this was the time when German invasion of the Iberian Peninsula appeared to competent observers as an almost day-to-day probability, and Salazar was fully aware that the British were powerless to stop it, even with such aid as the Americans could give them.

It must also be added that it was not only the Catholics in the United States who made difficult the problem of aid for the Soviet Union. There was always a faction, and it was strongly represented in the State Department, which was sure that the Russians would make a separate peace with Germany as they had done at Brest-Litovsk in 1917, and again in the Ribbentrop-Molotov Mutual Non-Aggression Pact of August, 1939. The repeated warnings of possible Russian perfidy that Roosevelt received in 1941 and throughout the years that followed served only to make him increase his efforts to convince the Russians of America's incontestable good faith. A year after the United States entered the war, Hopkins attended a meeting of the President's Soviet Protocol Committee. The point was raised that, before we extended further aid to the Russians, we should demand that they provide us with full information concerning their military situation as the British had consistently done. According to the minutes of this meeting:

> On the whole, Mr. Hopkins felt that there were certain unsatisfactory aspects to the program. The Russians are at times difficult and hard to understand. The United States is doing things which it would not do for other United Nations without full information from them. This decision to act without full information was made with some misgivings but after due deliberation. Mr. Hopkins said that there was no reservation about the policy at the present time but that the policy was constantly being brought up by various persons for

rediscussion. He proposed that no further consideration be given to these requests for rediscussion.

Although Hopkins attempted thus summarily to dismiss the question, it remained to plague the relations between the two countries.

Indeed, evidence of strain had begun to appear even before the United States entered the war. As the ferocious German drive against Moscow spent itself, and Hitler's supermen began to confront the awful realities of the Russian winter for which they were so ill prepared, the Red Army demonstrated a reserve strength and resilience that few in the outside world had dared to hope for and even fewer had expected; counterattacks were launched and the Russians recaptured Rostov— the first point of importance that anyone had taken back from the Germans since Nazi expansion had started. With this reversal of fortune —which still seemed merely a temporary one, however heartening—the Soviet Government immediately started pressing for agreements looking toward political settlements in the postwar world. Stalin was not content to drop the embarrassing subjects that he had raised with Beaverbrook. He apparently felt that the time had come to fix the borders between the Soviet Union and Finland, Poland and Rumania, and the status of the Baltic states of Estonia, Latvia and Lithuania, and even to reach agreement on such far-flung subjects as the future of the Rhineland, Bavaria and East Prussia, the restoration of the Sudetenland to Czechoslovakia, and numerous territorial adjustments affecting Greece and Turkey. All of these were matters for negotiation primarily between Moscow and London, but the British were careful to keep Washington constantly informed. With the recapture of Rostov, the situation became so tense that it was decided that Anthony Eden should travel to Moscow in an attempt "to smooth out relations in general, to explore the possibility of some kind of political agreement, and to discuss certain postwar problems." Eden was to leave the United Kingdom on December 7.

On December 5, a vitally important cable was dispatched to Winant; it was signed by Hull and okayed by Roosevelt. Winant was instructed to read the cable to Eden but not to hand a copy of it formally to the British authorities. This cable stated that "the test of our good faith with regard to the Soviet Union is the measure to which we fulfill the commitments our representatives made in Moscow"—referring, of course, to the commitments for material aid made by the Beaverbrook-Harriman Missions. The cable then went on to say that the postwar policies of the United States Government had been "delineated in the Atlantic Charter which today represents the attitude of Great Britain and the Soviet Union as well. . . . In our considered opinion it would be unfortunate for any of the three governments . . . to enter into commitments regarding specific terms of the postwar settlement. . . . *Above all, there must be no secret accords . . . the constitutional limitations to which this Government is bound must be kept in mind.*" (The italics are mine.)

Winant communicated the contents of that cable to Eden on Saturday morning, December 6, and that night the British Foreign Secretary left London for Invergordon and embattled Russia; at that moment, the United States was still a nonbelligerent.

CHAPTER XIX

War in the Pacific

O N JULY 7, 1941, Sumner Welles wrote the following prescient
letter to Hopkins:

I know that you are keenly interested in seeing that the assistance
we are rendering China under authorization of the Lease and Lend
Act of March 11, 1941, shall be as prompt and effective as possible.
It is also clear that numerous causes over which you can have no
control, including imperative needs in other parts of the world, are
constantly operating to obstruct the shipment of supplies to China.

Nevertheless, the situation in the Far East is causing us anxiety,
and I venture to suggest that if anything further can be done to increase the speed and the volume of munitions and supplies going to
China it would appear highly advisable to make additional effort to
that end.

The fact is that the German invasion of Russia may very possibly
serve to cause Japan to take some further aggressive action. Among
the obvious possibilities are: (1) invasion of Siberia; (2) expansion
to the southward; and (3) intensification of Japanese military operations in China.

It seems to me that German successes against Russia and the opportunity which Japan may consider is afforded her by those successes
to take further aggressive action constitute a factor which increases
the importance of this country's rendering effective aid to China in
the shortest possible time. It is essential that this country take all
practicable steps to avert a possible serious weakening of the morale
of the Chinese Government. The surest means of averting such a
possible development is to do all we can to make available to China
urgently needed supplies and to see that those supplies reach China
promptly.

I am sending copies of this letter to General Marshall and to Admiral
Stark and I am sure that all of you will do your utmost in reference
to this very important aspect of our self-defensive effort.

(It will be noted that Welles's list of "obvious possibilities" of further Japanese aggressive action did not include an attack on the United States.)

The Japanese soon started to prove Welles correct in assuming that they might capitalize on the German invasion of Russia by making new moves of their own: on July 23 they compelled the feeble Vichy Government to yield them bases in Indo-China from which they could launch attacks against the Philippines, the Netherlands East Indies or Malaya. Thus, the situation in the Far East became acutely serious. Roosevelt placed General MacArthur and the Philippine armed forces under U.S. Army command.

Welles's concern for China was certainly shared by Hopkins but there was little he could do about it at the time because of his journeys to London, Moscow and Argentia. When he returned to Washington he read a cable which Owen Lattimore had sent to Lauchlin Currie, the Presidential assistant who was especially concerned with Far Eastern affairs. Lattimore, one of the wisest of Americans in matters relating to Asia, was serving at the time in Chungking as political adviser to Chiang Kai-shek. He reported:

> Recent propaganda by the Japanese and their puppets has been insinuating that China is being used by the Western democracies not as an ally but as a tool and will be victimized in the peace terms. This is exploiting a situation about which the Generalissimo is gravely concerned, for the Chinese feel politically isolated and there is growing apprehension that after the war they will not be given equal status and fair treatment. The Generalissimo feels that only President Roosevelt is in a position now to take the initiative and suggest to Britain and Russia that either they should form an alliance with China, or at least include China in their Pacific defense conferences. . . . Either of these measures, if initiated by the President, would serve to safeguard China's equal status among the anti-Axis powers and remove the stigma of discrimination . . . and thereby strengthen Chinese morale.

Shortly thereafter, Hopkins received the first detailed report from Daniel Arnstein, whom he had recommended for the Burma Road job. It was a long report, and a candid one. The first two paragraphs will convey the general idea:

> The main reason that practically no tonnage is moving the full length of the Burma Road, is due to an entire lack of knowledge of the fundamentals of motor transportation by the men now in charge at the various headquarters along the road. The present Governmental agencies that are trying to operate trucks on the road are overloaded with executives and office personnel. No one gets right down into the actual operating end of the business. No effort is made to see that the trucks are maintained, despatched early in the morning so as to

get a full day's run, properly loaded or many other things that require the personal attention and observations of the operating head at each station. Each and every executive has three or four assistants and several secretaries, and actually does not observe what is going on from the transportation standpoint.

At the moment, there are 16 Governmental agencies operating over the Burma Road, each and every one of them overstaffed with incompetent executives, and none moving anywhere near the tonnage that could be moved with co-ordinated effort. Naturally, each one of these agencies tries to move only the particular requirements of their respective departments. This situation will not improve until motor transportation is taken out of the hands of all these Government departments and coordinated, and placed in the hands of someone competent, with authority to correct this impossible situation. It will be necessary for whomever this person may be, that he have full and complete authority to select his own operating personnel, and be able to employ or discharge without fear or favour anyone in the organization who does not function. No employee's position in this organization should be determined by his connections, but must be based solely on his knowledge, ability and desire to work himself, and not through a number of assistants. All motor transportation facilities now being maintained by these various organizations should be placed under his direction.

This, so far as I know, was the first of a long series of depressing documents which brought home to Hopkins some plain truths about the situation in China. Both Roosevelt and Hopkins, like so many other Americans, were naturally and strongly pro-Chinese. On this they were often at variance with Churchill, who felt that any policy based on confidence in China was a "great illusion." As will be seen in later pages of this book, there were bitter and dangerously confusing differences of opinion between responsible Americans on the same subject; indeed, General Marshall told me that the Stilwell-Chennault controversy over our Chinese policy provoked the only serious disagreement he ever had with Hopkins. There were ardent friends of China in the U.S. who did not help to promote realistic thinking about a situation massive in its obscurity. Their wholehearted devotion to the cause of the Chinese people impelled them to paint pictures of Kuomintang China which were misleading, to say the least, and which resulted in angry disillusionment for many Americans who went to China on wartime missions as soldiers or civilians.

Major McHugh, a Marine Corps Attaché at the American Embassy in Chungking, informed Currie that the Generalissimo was pleased with the Arnstein report.

It provides him with a reference work which is almost a dictionary of the various ills of motor transportation. I believe it has the added value in his eyes of being a completely unbiased document. He has heard of many of these things before, but never from anyone in whom he had real confidence. The fact that Arnstein & Co. came without pay, gave their opinions without reservation and are going home gives the report a status which cannot be attacked. The record is there; it remains for the Chinese to correct the defects which it points out.

Madame Chiang Kai-shek wrote to Currie, "When you next meet Mr. Harry Hopkins please thank him for us for his assistance to China under the Lend-Lease Act. I understand that through you he has been taking great interest in supplies to China and is eager to see that China gets her quota." However, the measure of this "assistance" is indicated in a letter sent by T. V. Soong to Colonel William J. Donovan:

This is to summarize the conversation I had with you yesterday afternoon.

The concurrence of certain events has made it desperately necessary that help of aircraft to China be immediate, so immediate that the delivery will have to be effected by diversion from the nearest available sources of supply, such as the Philippines, Singapore or the Dutch East Indies.

A. The first of the events is a new type of continuous all-day bombing—twenty-two hours out of twenty-four—by relays of bombers in units varying from large squadrons to flights of a few planes to which Chungking has been continuously subjected since the Anglo-American protest about Japanese moves to the south. Without planes to fight off the bombers over the city and to bomb back at the bases from which the raiders come, there is no possibility of defense or retribution.

It is perfectly clear that the purpose of this bombing is to finish the "China Incident" before Japan moves in other directions—by demonstrating to the people of China the difference between reality and the hopes of the last fourteen months that American assistance would be effective.

This awful demonstration of the difference between reality and promises is underlined for the Chinese by two other events.

B. The second event is the swiftness with which it is announced that deliveries of aircraft are being made to the Soviet Union, after repeated earlier promises of delivery to the Chinese have been excused as non-performable because the aircraft simply does not exist.

C. The third event *and you must understand this not in the light of true justification but in the light in which it appears to the Chinese under bombardment of twenty-two hours a day—is the recent frank disclosure* of the American policy of appeasing Japan with materials of war—the very material and gasoline that are presently bombing Chungking—in order to keep Japan from attacking certain American supply routes to the south.

Adding these three events and their implication together, Chinese who are weary of Chiang Kai-shek's policy of resistance in the general democratic cause are saying, "Our resistance is just a pawn in the calculations of other democratic powers. Japan is being furnished the materials with which to destroy us in order to relieve the British from attack in the south and maybe even the Russians from attack in the north. Although we are being given polite non-offensive aid like road materials and trucks, nothing which would really offend Japan or give us striking power of retribution against Japan is being allowed to actually get here—even though this supposedly non-existent offensive material is available immediately for our friends the Russians." . . .

If planes are delivered to Russia *now*—even though the Russians are still our friends and allies—you must get planes to Chungking *now* or the Chinese will never understand.

I have now been in the United States over fourteen months pleading for the help of planes.

In response, the President, after pointing out the dangers of nonresistance to aggression, promised to call upon his advisors to give all practical assistance to us.

I then and there stressed the urgent necessity of providing us with aircraft to defend the main routes of supply, the key urban areas, and to enable strategic operations on the part of our land forces.

In the fourteen months which have followed not a single plane sufficiently supplied with armament and ammunition so that it could actually be used to fire has reached China.

Through the exertions of the President 100 Curtiss P-40's were released by the British last fall and eventually reached China, but the necessary spare parts and ammunition without which these craft are not fighting ships but only training ships, are just being arranged for now.

Last fall and winter we were offered a few bombers capable of raiding Japan. The offer was accepted but it did not materialize.

A special American air mission under General Claggett visited China following Mr. Currie's visit and after an intensive study of our airfields, air force, and facilities on the spot, favorably reported on our plans for an air force of 350 pursuits and 150 bombers. No action has materialized.

At the end of July an allotment of 66 bombers and 269 fighters was definitely ratified by the Joint Strategy Board on the President's authority and Chiang Kai-shek was assured of immediate delivery of 24 bombers. General Chiang was never happier than when Lauchlin Currie cabled back that assurance to Chungking.

Today I am told that deliveries cannot start before October and then on a scale that will extend into Spring, 1942.

Meanwhile Chungking is bombed incessantly day and night and China goes on the second month of her fifth year of war while the promises I cabled over for encouragement one by one fail. . . .

You will excuse me for having been so frank. But the Russian situation and the failure to mention China in all the new joint stra-

tegic plans that are being publicized has really precipitated a problem of Chinese morale about the immediacy of aircraft help to China. . . .
We have stuck for five years. Please help us stick now.

Of the sixty-six medium bombers mentioned by Soong as having been promised on Presidential authority in July, not one had been delivered by the end of October. This appears in a memorandum from Soong to Roosevelt on which the latter wrote in pencil, "H.H.—Speed up! F.D.R." After this, Hopkins and Soong started to work together and continued to do so, becoming very warm friends.

Shortly thereafter, when Hopkins was in the Navy Hospital, he had a letter from Soong:

I am indeed sorry to learn that you are indisposed, and I feel reluctant to disturb your convalescence. You will recall that I saw the President and yourself on the 31st of October, conveying General Chiang Kai-shek's urgent request for acceleration of delivery of planes and ordnance materials in view of imminent Japanese attacks on the Burma Road through Burma and Yunnan. The President was good enough to direct that the deliveries should be "hurried up," and you very kindly took steps immediately to implement his wishes. However, I wish to report that so far I have not been able to get any concrete results.

You were kind enough to promise to see me again after you returned from Hyde Park, which your illness no doubt prevented. In the meantime I am hard put to reply to General Chiang, and I shall appreciate it if you will advise me what I should tell him in answer to his repeated anxious enquiries.

One of Hopkins' first acts on the day of Pearl Harbor was to request a check on all the ships and airplanes in the Pacific that were carrying supplies to China. There were pitifully few of them. The aid was only a trickle and stopped altogether for a time when the Japanese cut off access to China by land and sea.

There was, indeed, a shocking shortage of most weapons and matériel when one considered the mounting demands of Britain, Russia, China as well as our own armed forces. For one instance: during the month of July, when Hopkins was visiting London and Moscow and learning so much of the importance of bombing Germany, the production of four-engined bombers in the U.S. achieved a total of two. The total hopefully scheduled for the final five months of 1941 was only 213. In view of the needs of the U.S. Army Air Corps for aircraft for training bomber crews, as well as the incessant and always urgent requirements of the British and Russians, the number left for the far-away Chinese was a minus quantity.

On November 13, Hopkins wrote his friend James Norman Hall, co-author of *Mutiny On The Bounty*, who was living in Tahiti:

HH — Speed up!

FDR

MEMORANDUM FOR THE PRESIDENT

To enable China to contribute its part in the common struggle against Japan and Germany as outlined to you, China needs immediate delivery of part of the modest allotment of airplanes and ordnance already made to it.

A. AIRCRAFT	Pursuits	Bombers
General Chiang Kai-shek's request	350	150
Delivered	100 P-40's	0
Present allocation	269	66
Promised '41 shipments	83	24
Needed immediate diversion	186	126

B. ORDNANCE	37 mm A.T.	75 mm Hows.	M3 Light Tanks	3" A.A.	Cal. 50 A.A.
Requested	720	600	120	96	1360
Delivered	0	44	0	0	100
Allocated	240	598	0	0	185
To be shipped '41	60	178	0	0	185
Additional needed immediately	300	300	120	24	750

Powder   800 tons needed immediately for small arms now in use.

C. CONCLUSION

If you think it wise, would it be possible for you to ask the Secretary of War for the immediate diversion of the needed aircraft, requisite crews, and ordnance?

T. V. Soong

October 24, 1941

Roosevelt's order to Hopkins to expedite shipment of material to China.

We are really getting on with our production program here, now. Airplanes, tanks, ammunition and guns are moving rapidly and I think they are going to play an important part in the next few months. I, however, don't believe we can ever lick Hitler with a Lend Lease program. It, unfortunately, is going to take, I believe, much more than that.

That was obviously not a complete statement of Hopkins' feelings. For he knew that we could not have even an adequate production program until the automobile and other industries could be converted from a peacetime basis to meet the requirements of total war—until the American people as a whole realized that production was not merely a matter of "aid" to foreigners, however deserving they might be, but a matter of life or death for their own sons.

It will be noted in the Hopkins letter to Hall that he again spoke of beating Hitler, with no reference to Japan. His advocacy of all possible aid for China (which meant very little) was based on moral rather than on practical grounds. It was a mere token payment—or one might call it "conscience money"—which could be of value in the distant future but not of primary importance in the winning of the present war.

One of the most important documents of the pre-Pearl Harbor period is called the "Joint Board Estimate of United States Over-all Production Requirements." This was a purely military estimate of the situation, requested by the President as a basis for the production program. It is, in my opinion, one of the most remarkable documents of American history, for it set down the basic strategy of a global war before this country was involved in it. It was dated September 11, 1941, and signed by the Chiefs of Staff, General Marshall and Admiral Stark. Its first section, of three paragraphs, cited the reasons for the estimate. Section II, starting with paragraph 4, was headed "Major Military Policy":

4. Germany, and all German-occupied countries whose military forces cooperate with Germany; Japan and Manchukuo; Italy; Vichy France; and possibly Spain and Portugal, are assumed potential enemies. Countries considered as friends or potential associates in war are the British Commonwealth, the Netherlands East Indies, China, Russia, Free France, peoples in German-occupied territory who may oppose Germany, and the countries of the Western Hemisphere.

5. Those major national objectives of the United States which are related to military policy may broadly be stated as: preservation of the territorial, economic and ideological integrity of the United States and of the remainder of the Western Hemisphere; prevention of the disruption of the British Empire; prevention of the further extension of Japanese territorial dominion; eventual establishment in Europe and Asia of balances of power which will most nearly ensure political stability in those regions and the future security of the United

States; and, so far as practicable, the establishment of regimes favorable to economic freedom and individual liberty.

6. Since the paramount territorial interests of the United States are in the Western Hemisphere, it is fundamental that the United States must provide armed forces appropriately disposed, which in all eventualities, and operating in cooperation with the forces of other American Powers, can successfully prevent the extension in the Western Hemisphere of European or Asiatic political or military power, even though the British Commonwealth had collapsed.

7. Attainment of this objective alone will not lead to the success of all of the national policies mentioned in paragraph 6. *These national policies can be effectuated in their entirety only through military victories outside this hemisphere, either by the armed forces of the United States, by the armed forces of friendly Powers, or by both.*

The italics in that last paragraph are mine. They underline one of the most vital points in our approach to the entire strategy of the Second World War—that the decisive battles must be fought outside of the Western Hemisphere and not as the isolationists persisted in believing, on our own one-yard line. The Estimate continues:

8. Should Germany be successful in conquering all of Europe, she might then wish to establish peace with the United States for several years, for the purpose of organizing her gains, restoring her economic situation, and increasing her military establishment, with a view to the eventual conquest of South America and the military defeat of the United States. During such a period of "peace," it seems likely that Germany would seek to undermine the economic and political stability of the countries of South America, and to set up puppet regimes favorable to the establishment on that continent of German military power. In such circumstances, Germany would have better chances to defeat the United States. This concept can not be accepted as certain, because it is conceivable that Germany might at once seek to gain footholds in the Western Hemisphere.

9. Were Japan to defeat China and Russia, and obtain control of Siam, Malaya and the Netherlands East Indies, it is probable that she likewise would endeavor to establish peace for the purpose of organizing the "East Asia Co-Prosperity Sphere." Almost inevitably the Philippine Islands would ultimately pass under Japanese hegemony.

Here again is the assumption that Japan will attack northward into Russia, westward into China and southward into Malaya and the Netherlands East Indies, leaving the Philippines (with the mandated islands to the eastward) completely surrounded. Following are the next five paragraphs on "Major Military Policy":

10. It is believed that the overthrow of the Nazi regime by action of the people of Germany is unlikely in the near future, and will not

occur until Germany is upon the point of military defeat. Even were a new regime to be established, it is not at all certain that such a regime would agree to peace terms acceptable to the United States.

11. Assuming the truth of the views expressed in the preceding paragraph, it is the opinion of the Joint Board that Germany and her European satellites can not be defeated by the European Powers now fighting against her. Therefore, if our European enemies are to be defeated, it will be necessary for the United States to enter the war, and to employ a part of its armed forces offensively in the Eastern Atlantic and in Europe or Africa.

12. The Joint Board also holds the view that, if, under present circumstances, Japan should advance against the British in Malaya and against the Dutch in the Netherlands East Indies, British and Dutch forces probably could not successfully withstand such an advance in the absence of active military assistance by the United States. The result of an attack by Japan on the Eastern Siberian Soviet Republic cannot now be predicted.

13. In view of the preceding considerations, the Joint Board recommends that the over-all production and material objective of the United States be designed to meet United States needs while engaged simultaneously in war against Germany and Japan, under either of the following sets of circumstances:

a. While associated as a belligerent with the British Commonwealth, the Netherlands East Indies, Russia, and China.

b. While associated as a belligerent with Canada and some of the Latin American countries, other belligerent Powers having been defeated by Germany and Japan.

14. Due to inadequate industrial capacity and material resources, friendly Powers must look to the United States for a large part of the munitions and other materials which they will require for success. The munitions and other materials which may be produced or controlled by the United States should be divided between itself and friendly Powers in such a manner as to effectuate the success of the military strategy adopted by the United States as best calculated to defeat our common enemies.

The next Section III is headed "Probable Character of the Enemy's Major Strategy: (A) German Strategy":

15. For Germany, the objective of the current phase of the war is the complete military and political domination of Europe, and probably of North and West Africa. If Germany is successful she may then seek a period of peaceful refreshment, during which she can reorganize Europe and prepare for further adventures. However, the possibility can not be dismissed that Germany might seek at once to continue into India, South Africa, or South America.

16. Germany's present major strategic objectives, and the means by which she seeks to attain them, seem to be some or all of the following:

a. The conquest of European Russia, the destruction of the Russian Armies, and the overthrow of the Soviet regime. This is a task for the German army and air forces, and will doubtless absorb most of the energy available to these contingents for some months to come. Final success in this aim is still in the balance.

b. The destruction of the power of resistance of the United Kingdom, through accelerated attrition of shipping, and continued bombing of British facilities. The forces employed will be surface raiders, submarines, and aircraft in the northwestern approaches and down through the Middle Atlantic, operating from bases in Norway, France, Portugal, and French West Africa; and merchant-type raiders distributed throughout all oceans. Invasion of England may possibly not be attempted unless these other measures fail.

c. The conquest of Egypt, Syria, Irak, and Iran. This may be the region in which the next major German offensive will be undertaken. Large land and air forces must be employed, both German and Italian, aided by Italian naval forces in the Eastern Mediterranean and the Black Sea. Success may depend upon whether or not a large concentration of British and Russian defensive forces are available, and upon the continued military capacity of Italy, now an uncertain quantity.

d. The occupation of Spain, Portugal, Morocco, French West Africa, Senegal, and the Atlantic Islands, for the purpose of strengthening the German offensive against British shipping, and for denying these positions to Germany's enemies. Considerable land, air, and naval forces will be required for this offensive, though not so great as would be required for conquest of the lands to the eastward of the Mediterranean.

17. In and near her own home territory, Germany can exert her full effort. As her forces move away from the home base, the effort that can be exerted at the point of military contact becomes reduced in proportion to the length and security of the lines of communication, and to the difficulties of transportation. Germany is experiencing these difficulties in Russia; she would experience them in an even greater degree in an offensive in the regions in the east of the Mediterranean; while the problem of the support of strong forces in Morocco, French West Africa, Senegal, and the Azores would be very great indeed. In the eastern part of European Russia, in Egypt, Irak, Iran, and North and West Africa, the effort that German military forces can exert is only a fraction of what they have been able to put forth in France, the Balkans, and Poland. Severe German defeats in these regions might readily affect the stability of the Nazi regime. This significant possibility should be taken into account in the development of the strategy of the Associated Powers.

That final paragraph is particularly interesting in that it foresees the Allied strategy which a little more than a year later resulted in the battle of El Alamein and the landings in Algeria and French Morocco. The second part of Section III (B) discusses "Japanese Strategy."

18. The Japanese objective is the establishment of the "East Asia Co-Prosperity Sphere." It is Japan's ambition ultimately to include within this Sphere Eastern Siberia, Eastern China, Indo-China, Thai, Malaya, the Netherlands East Indies, the Philippines, and possibly Burma. The accomplishment of this objective is a heavy task for Japan's strength, a fact well realized by the Japanese.

19. Dependent upon results in Europe, Japan's strategic moves might be as follows:

a. Building up and maintaining an effective screen in the Japanese Mandated Islands by the employment of minor naval forces and considerable air forces, supported by the Combined Fleet. This activity would include submarine and raider action against United States naval forces and United States and British lines of communication in the Central and Eastern Pacific Ocean.

b. The conquest of Eastern Siberia by means of land and air operations covered by the Combined Fleet operating to the eastward of Japan.

c. The conquest of Thai, Malaya, the Netherlands East Indies, and the Philippines. Success will require strong air forces, a considerable strength of light naval forces, and rather large land forces. It is unlikely that Japan will simultaneously attempt a major effort to the Northward and to the Southward, because of her lack of equipment and raw materials.

d. An offensive from Northern Indo-China against Yunnan for the purpose of cutting the Burma Road and eliminating further resistance of the Chinese Nationalist Army. This move might be supplemented by an attack on Burma. Considerable land and air forces would be required, as well as a large amount of shipping to provide the necessary support.

20. All of these prospective Japanese moves would be made at great distances from Japan. If Japan encounters stubborn and protracted resistance, her ability to continue offensives at these distances is problematical, owing to a lack of adequate resources and industrial facilities. Marked weakness or lack of cohesion on the part of her opponents might permit Japan to accomplish any one of these objectives within the next few months.

Subhead (a.) of paragraph 19 might be said to have included the possibility of an attack on Pearl Harbor, but in speaking of "submarine and raider action against United States naval forces and United States and British lines of communication in the Central and Eastern Pacific Ocean" it indicated sniping action against ships in transit rather than concerted attacks against bases.

Section IV of the Estimate discussed "Major Strategy of the United States and its Associates":

21. The Joint Board is convinced that the first major objective of the United States and its Associates ought to be the complete military defeat of Germany. If Germany were defeated, her entire European system would collapse, and it is probable that Japan could be forced to give up much of her territorial gains, unless she had already firmly established herself in such strength that the United States and its Associates could not afford the energy to continue the war against her.

22. An inconclusive peace between Germany and her present active military enemies would be likely to give Germany an opportunity to reorganize continental Europe and to replenish her strength. Even though the British Commonwealth and Russia were completely defeated, there would be important reasons for the United States to continue the war against Germany, in spite of the greatly increased difficulty of attaining final victory. From this it follows that *the principal strategic method employed by the United States in the immediate future should be the material support of present military operations against Germany, and their reenforcement by active participation in the war by the United States while holding Japan in check pending future developments.* Necessarily, only small Army contingents are now sufficiently equipped and trained for immediate participation in offensive operations. [The italics in the foregoing are General Marshall's and Admiral Stark's.]

23. Except in the case of Russia, the principal strength of the Associated Powers is in naval and air categories. Naval and air power may prevent wars from being lost, and by weakening enemy strength may greatly contribute to victory. By themselves, however, naval and air forces seldom, if ever, win important wars. It should be recognized as an almost invariable rule that only land armies can finally win wars.

24. It is out of the question to expect the United States and its Associates to undertake in the near future a sustained and successful land offensive against the center of the German power. It being obvious that the Associated Powers can not defeat Germany by defensive operations, effective strategic offensive methods other than an early land offensive in Europe must be employed. These methods may be found in a continuation of the economic blockade; the prosecution of land offensives in distant regions where German troops can exert only a fraction of their total strength; air and sea offensives against German military, economic and industrial resources; and the support of subversive activities in the conquered territories. Strategic methods to be employed against Japan (assuming her in the war) should be a strong defense of Siberia and Malaysia; an economic offensive through blockade; a reduction of Japanese military power by raids; and Chinese offensives against the Japanese forces of occupation.

25. The major strategic objectives which it is believed the United States and the Associated Powers should adopt are indicated below, as well as the means for attaining them. The material assistance to be supplied friendly Powers (where mentioned in the succeeding paragraphs), should be consistent with the needs of the United States.

a. *The security of the Western Hemisphere* against the extension into it of European or Asiatic political or military power is an essential of United States strategy. To provide this security under all eventualities, the United States must have naval, land, and air forces in such positions that they can be made promptly available in both the Atlantic and the Pacific Oceans in strengths adequate for preventing invasion should the British Isles and Russia collapse. In this connection, an important question is whether or not Northwestern Africa and the Atlantic Islands are in German or friendly hands. Similarly, Alaska, Hawaii, and the Islands of the South Pacific Ocean have an important relation to the security of the Eastern Pacific. United States naval strength, built up in accordance with the approved program, should be adequate for defensive needs until 1944. However, if Germany is successful in Europe, and Japan is successful in the Far East, naval strength for defensive purposes must be increased, even in excess of the present approved naval program. United States land and air forces may be required for the defense of the Western Hemisphere within the next few years, and it is necessary for Latin American countries to be provided with munitions and manufactured articles.

b. *The security of the United Kingdom* is essential to the prosecution in the Eastern Hemisphere of military operations against Germany and Japan. Its safety is also highly important to the defense of the Western Hemisphere. The security of the United Kingdom depends on an effective defense by sea, land, and air forces. In turn, this defense depends upon the safety of sea communications. The sea communications can continue to support the United Kingdom only if the damage now being inflicted upon them is greatly reduced through increases in the strength of the protective sea and air forces based in the British Islands, Iceland, and positions in the central and eastern Atlantic. Unless the losses of British merchant ships are greatly reduced, or unless there is an internal collapse of Germany, it is the opinion of the Joint Board that the resistance of the United Kingdom can not continue indefinitely, no matter what industrial effort is put forth by the United States. Therefore, the immediate and strong reenforcement of British forces in the Atlantic by United States naval and air contingents, supplemented by a large additional shipping tonnage, will be required if the United Kingdom is to remain in the war. These contingents must be manned by Americans, since the reserves of British manpower for employment in Europe are practically exhausted. To maintain present British strength, the United States must also continue to supplement the British blockade, and the naval building and repair potential; and to provide considerable numbers of aircraft.

c. *Safety of the sea communications of the Associated Powers* throughout the world is essential to the continuance of their war effort. Naval and air forces employed in and near Europe should, so far as practicable, be strong enough to prevent the escape of surface raiders to the open sea, and to defeat submarine and air raiders. In addition, a widespread distribution of naval and air forces for direct protection of shipping foci and shipping routes will be required.

d. *The enforcement of economic blockade* is, for the time being, likely to be the most effective offensive method for use against Germany and Japan. Naval and air forces must be maintained to close all avenues of sea approach to Germany. The continued existence of hostile land fronts in Russia and in the Middle East is necessary if this blockade is to be maintained. In addition, diplomatic, economic, and financial measures should be employed for increasing the effectiveness of the military blockade.

e. *The retention by the British of the control of the Red Sea, Irak, and Iran* is necessary for preserving opportunities for decisive land action against Germany. Of great importance are effective land and air forces of all categories; large numbers of merchant vessels for their support; and adequate naval forces for the protection of communications leading to the Persian Gulf and the Red Sea. These forces can not be fully supported by the material means available to Britain. The United States should undertake to provide a part of the munitions and raw materials required by these troops, and should supply much of the merchant shipping for their transport.

f. *The maintenance of an active front in Russia* offers by far the best opportunity for a successful land offensive against Germany, because only Russia possesses adequate manpower, situated in favorable proximity to the center of German military power. For Russia, ground and aviation forces are most important. Predictions as to the result of the present conflict in Russia are premature. However, were the Soviet forces to be driven even beyond the Ural Mountains, and were they there to continue an organized resistance, there would always remain the hope of a final and complete defeat of Germany by land operations. The effective arming of Russian forces, both by the supply of munitions from the outside and by providing industrial capacity in the Volga Basin, or to the east of the Ural Mountains, would be one of the most important moves that could be made by the Associated Powers.

g. *Prevention of Axis penetration into Northwest Africa and the Atlantic Islands* is very important, not only as a contribution to the defense of the Western Hemisphere, but also as security to British sea communications and as a potential base for a future land offensive. In French North and West Africa, French troops exist which are potential enemies of Germany, provided they are re-equipped and satisfactory political conditions are established by the United States. Because the British Commonwealth has but few troops available and because of the unfriendly relations between the British and the Weygand regime, it seems clear that a large proportion of the troops of the Associated Powers employed in this region necessarily must be United States troops.

h. *Retention by the United States and its Associates of the Philippines, Malaya, the Netherlands East Indies, Australasia, Burma, and China* would have far-reaching effects. The armed forces of the United States can not be greatly increased in the Far East if they are to discharge their heavy tasks in other regions, but the operations of the

Pacific Fleet will have an important influence on events. The United States should undertake to provide a part of the munitions and aircraft to China and the Netherlands East Indies. A large part of this material must be transported in United States bottoms.

i. *Retention of Eastern Siberia by Russia* is necessary if Japan is to be checked. Only material assistance can be provided by the United States to Siberia. No materials can be sent to Siberia by water when Japan is at war with Russia, but deliveries of aircraft could continue by air.

26. The following principles have been taken into consideration in arriving at recommendations concerning the strengths of the armed forces which the United States should undertake to raise or support, in whole or in part:

a. The Navy considers that, since the principal strength of the Associated Powers is at present in naval and air categories, the strategy which they should adopt should be based on the effective employment of these forces, and the employment of land forces in regions where Germany can not exert the full power of her land armies. The Army believes that the foregoing strategy may not accomplish the defeat of Germany and that it may be necessary to come to grips with the German armies on the continent of Europe. Consequently, the Army feels that the equipment of land armies necessary to meet this contingency should be provided as a part of the over-all production requirements.

b. Past experience of the United States and other Powers should condition estimates of the capability of the United States to support a war effort, with due regard to differences in over-all industrial capacity; differences in availability of materials; and an appropriate balance between the man-power to be employed in the armed forces, and the man-power to be employed in industry and essential civilian services. Because of the present high degree of mechanization, a greater proportion of man-power must be allocated to industry for the manufacture of equipment and munitions than was the case in former wars.

c. The sound use of diplomatic, economic, financial, and propaganda weapons, will serve to reduce the magnitude of the direct military effort.

d. The burdens of the war effort, even though continued by the United States over a long period of time, should be so adjusted as to maintain the morale and the will to fight of the civilian population.

Thus, in this document, was charted the policy to be followed by the United States throughout the remaining years of a global war in which she was still legally "neutral." It must be remembered that this Joint Board Estimate was the result of two years of wartime deliberation by Marshall, Stark and their staffs, and of upwards of a year of exchanges of information and opinion by the British and American staffs working together in secret and unofficial but highly effective co-operation.

On October 17, General Tojo ousted Konoye as Premier and the militarist extremists in Tokyo came into power in name as well as in fact. On the same day, Captain R. E. Schuirmann of Admiral Stark's staff wrote a memorandum a copy of which was sent to Hopkins:

I believe we are inclined to overestimate the importance of changes in the Japanese Cabinet as indicative of great changes in Japanese political thought or action.

The plain fact is that Japanese politics has been ultimately controlled for years by the military. Whether or not a policy of peace or a policy of further military adventuring is pursued is determined by the military based on their estimate as to whether the time is opportune and what they are able to do, not by what cabinet is in power or on diplomatic maneuvering, diplomatic notes or diplomatic treaties.

Prince Konoye has been Premier and Konoye Cabinets in office for the most of the last five years. Time and again he and his Foreign Ministers have expressed disapproval of the acts committed by the Japanese Military, but remedial action has not been taken.

Konoye was Premier when the attack on China began, he declared Japan's policy was to beat China to her knees.

The most that can be claimed for the last Konoye Cabinet is that it may have restrained the *extremists* among the military not that it has opposed Japan's program of expansion by force. When opportunities arise, during the coming months, which seem favorable to the military for further advance, they will be seized.

At the present time the influence of the extremists goes up and down depending on the course of the war in Russia.

The same bill of goods, regarding the necessity of making some concession to the "moderates" in order to enable them to cope with the "extremists" has been offered to the United States since the days when Stimson was Secretary of State and Debuchi Ambassador.

Present reports are that the new cabinet to be formed will be no better and no worse than the one which has just fallen. Japan may attack Russia, or may move southward, but in the final analysis this will be determined by the military on the basis of opportunity, and what they can get away with, not by what cabinet is in power.

Captain Schuirmann's Appreciation was supported by Lieutenant Colonel Harry I. T. Creswell, Military Attaché in Tokyo, who reported, on October 20:

Since the make-up of the new Cabinet appears to be essentially conservative in character, the resignation of the old Cabinet is not regarded as indicating any drastic change in Japan's policy in the immediate future, at least. . . . While General Tojo is first of all a thoroughgoing Japanese, with the national ambitions and welfare inherent in his make-up, he is believed to have a breadth of vision which would seem to preclude the possibility of his taking extreme radical actions.

On November 9, General Lee cabled from London:

The British Ambassador in Tokyo has reported the opinion that the Netherlands East Indies provide the most likely spot at which the Japanese will strike next. Since Japan already has control of all that she needs of the resources of Indo-China and Thailand she is unlikely to strike in this area. Attacks against British Malaya or a drive toward the Burma Road are considered too difficult, involving too great effort. Secret attacks against the N.E.I. could be launched from the Mandated Islands and this would give Japan access to the needed oil. The source of this information reverses a view he held previously: he now doubts that Japan will be deterred by a desire to avoid war with the United States, but is now ready to present this contemplated operation as an accomplished fact to the British and Americans.

On the same day, Harold Balfour, the British Undersecretary of State for Air, wrote a memorandum and gave a copy of it to Harry Hopkins. Balfour at the time was pressing for more and more heavy bombers for the R.A.F. to use against Germany. His account of his interview with the President on this subject gives some indication of Roosevelt's attitude toward the Far Eastern situation four weeks to the day before Pearl Harbor. The memorandum in full, was as follows:

I saw President today on heavy bomber question. The Lord Privy Seal [Clement Attlee] was also present.

2. The President did not wish to speak in specific terms of numbers or dates when we might expect a better allocation than at present proposed.

3. President said that he felt that we should have a substantially greater allocation than the round hundred proposed in addition to current British orders but that until the Far Eastern position developed one way or the other he felt unable to take definite steps to this end.

4. His present Japanese policy is one of stalling and holding off. If during the next few weeks this policy looks likely to succeed for some months ahead, or alternatively, if the President can sign up for peace with Japan so as to ensure no sudden hostilities then he will feel able at once to direct a further diversion of heavy bombers to U.K.

5. On the other hand the Japanese situation may blow up in the very near future, in which case U.S.A. and U.K. Joint Staffs will have to get together and decide in the light of combined war strategy where such equipment as becomes available can best be used.

6. I asked the President for guidance as to how great can be our expectations in the event of no war with Japan and he said that he hoped before the end of March to be able to direct a diversion and that it might be more than half the available heavy bomber production.

7. The President was most sympathetic to our urgent need of more heavy bombers on the Western Front. He asked that we should continue to use all pressure. He remarked "Keep on pushing us—the more we are urged the better." The President said that as soon as he

feels the Far Eastern situation allows him to come to a decision in numbers and dates he will communicate with Prime Minister.

Incidentally, it should be noted that British officials, Churchill included, considered it their sacred duty always to make such notes, or
"minutes," of conversations as important as this one, not for their own
personal diaries, but for the official records. A few Americans, principally those who had rigorous training in the Foreign Service, also did
this. Hopkins made such notes whenever he could find time to do so
but Roosevelt hardly ever wrote or dictated any record of a conversation in which he had been involved.

On November 20 the Japanese delivered a note to the United States
Government and this was followed, on November 22, by a secret message
from Foreign Minister Togo to Nomura which was intercepted and
decoded by the special process known as "Magic." In this message Togo
described the note as a Japanese "ultimatum," their "absolutely final
proposal," and "a last effort to prevent something happening." The time
limit on the ultimatum was given as November 29, and Togo informed
Nomura, "This time we mean it, the deadline absolutely cannot be
changed. After that things are automatically going to happen." The
American reply to the November 20 note was handed by Secretary Hull
to the Japanese Ambassadors on November 26. This reply, entitled
"Outline of Proposed Agreement Between the United States and Japan,"
has been described as an "ultimatum" by a few American isolationists
who have seemed anxious to absolve the Japanese of all guilt for the war
in the Pacific and to fix the guilt on their own President and Secretaries
of State, War and Navy. In this connection it should be noted that the
Japanese task force sailed for Pearl Harbor on November 25, the day
before the Hull outline was delivered in Washington, and four days
before the absolute "deadline" designated in the Togo message to
Nomura. The dogs of war had been unleashed while the solemn and futile
diplomatic exchanges continued.

On November 21, Lieutenant Colonel S. A. Greenwell, dispatched
from London a copy of the "Report by Joint Intelligence Sub-Committee, War Cabinet on Probable Japanese Intentions." This was a lengthy
British estimate of the situation of which the conclusions were as follows:

(i) Japan will make a last effort to obtain a general agreement with
the U.S.A. If she fails she will be faced with the necessity of deciding
whether or not to take aggressive action involving risk of war with
one or more major Powers.

(ii) Such action would be likely in the first instance to be against
Thailand which Japan might think would involve the least risk of a
major conflict. Occupation of bases in Thailand including the Kra
Isthmus would be a sound strategic preliminary to subsequent operations against Malaya or the Netherlands East Indies. Recent military

moves tend to support the opinion that Thailand is the next objective.

(iii) Action against Russia is likely to be deferred until there is a serious weakening of Russia's position in the Far East.

(iv) In the absence of a general agreement with America operations against China will continue.

(v) In view of the latest evidence of diversion of forces southwards from Northern Indo-China and Canton, we do not believe that the former concentrations in those areas imply an early attack on the Burma Road.

On November 26, Nomura and Kurusu cabled to their government in Tokyo:

We suppose that the rupture of the present negotiations does not necessarily mean war between Japan and the United States, but after we break off, as we said, the military occupation of Netherlands India is to be expected of England and the United States. Then we would attack them and a clash with them would be inevitable.

Which indicates that the two Japanese Ambassadors—or, at least one of them—were also ignorant of the real war plans and were assuming that the first clash would come in the Southwest Pacific with the British and Americans taking the initiative.

On the following day, November 27, there was a conference in the White House of Roosevelt, Hull, Kurusu and Nomura. In Hull's memorandum of this meeting he states:

I made it clear that unless the opposition to the peace element in control of the Government should make up its mind definitely to act and talk and move in a peaceful direction, no conversations could or would get anywhere as has been so clearly demonstrated; that everyone knows that the Japanese slogans of co-prosperity, new order in East Asia and a controlling influence in certain areas, are all terms to express in a camouflaged manner the policy of force and conquest by Japan and the domination by military agencies of the political, economic, social and moral affairs of each of the populations conquered; and that so long as they move in that direction and continue to increase their cultural relations, military and otherwise with Hitler through such instruments as the Anti-Comintern Pact and the Tripartite Pact, et cetera, et cetera, there could not be any real progress made on a peaceful course.

Hull also quotes Roosevelt as having said in effect to the Ambassadors:

We remain convinced that Japan's own best interests will not be served by following Hitlerism and courses of aggression, and that Japan's own best interests lie along the courses which we have outlined in the current conversations. If, however, Japan should unfortunately decide to follow Hitlerism and courses of aggression we are convinced beyond any shadow of doubt that Japan will be the ultimate loser.

The report of the Commission which was headed by Justice Owen J. Roberts states that on November 27:

> The Chief of Naval Operations sent a message to the Commander-in-Chief of the Pacific Fleet, which stated in substance that the dispatch was to be considered a war warning; that the negotiations with Japan in an effort to stabilize conditions in the Pacific had ended; that Japan was expected to make an aggressive move within the next few days; that an amphibious expedition against the Philippines, Thai, or Kra Peninsula, or possibly Borneo, was indicated by the number and equipment of Japanese troops and the organization of their naval task forces. It directed the execution of a defensive deployment in preparation for carrying out war tasks.

The foregoing message from Stark was one of the few documents in those weeks that considered the likelihood that the first attacks might be against the Philippines. (Similar warnings were sent at the same time to all commanders in the Pacific and Far East.)

On December 6, the day before Pearl Harbor, the British reported heavy Japanese forces moving along the Indo-Chinese Coast toward objectives in Thailand or possibly in Malaya. Ambassador Winant in London sent a cable marked "Triple Priority" and "Most Urgent" and "Personal and Secret to the President and Secretary":

> British Admiralty reports that at 3 a.m. London time this morning two parties seen off Cambodia Point, sailing slowly west-ward toward Kra 14 hours distant in time. First party 25 transports, 6 cruisers, 10 destroyers. Second party 10 transports, 2 cruisers, 10 destroyers. . . .
> British feel pressed for time in relation to guaranteeing support Thailand fearing Japan might force them to invite invasion on pretext protection before British have opportunity to guarantee support but wanting to carry out President's wishes in message transmitted by Welles to Halifax.

That Saturday night Anthony Eden left London for Invergordon in Scotland from which he was to travel by sea to Archangel and thence to Moscow for his meetings with Stalin and Molotov. He bore with him, among other things, a summary of the cable from Roosevelt and Hull which is mentioned at the end of the preceding chapter—the cable setting forth the position of the United States in regard to postwar policies, particularly the desirability of avoiding any secret agreements. The very fact that it was felt safe for Eden to leave England at this time was itself a significant indication of the state of mind which prevailed in London as it did in Washington.

Eden would be at sea for several days in a warship subject to wartime radio silence. As Secretary of State for Foreign Affairs, responsible directly to the King, and also as member of the War Cabinet, he occupied a vital constitutional position in the conduct of the day-to-day affairs of government. Thus, had it been thought that there was any likelihood of Japanese action which would produce such an overwhelmingly important political development as the immediate entry of the United States into the war, it is inconceivable that Eden would have left the Foreign Office where he not only worked but lived (he had a small apartment at the top of the building in Whitehall).

There was certainly the prospect of Japanese action in the Southwest Pacific. But there was also an exaggerated—as is proved—amount of respect for Japanese caution and calculation of all possible consequences. It was felt that, wherever the wily Japanese moved next, plenty of time would be allowed for the taking of adequate defensive measures.

On the same Saturday, December 6, that Eden left London, Harriman cabled Hopkins as follows:

> The President should be informed of Churchill's belief that in the event of aggression by the Japanese it would be the policy of the British to postpone taking any action—even though this delay might involve some military sacrifice—until the President has taken such action as, under the circumstances, he considers best. Then Churchill will act "not within the hour, but within the minute." I am seeing him again tomorrow [Sunday, December 7th]. Let me know if there is anything special you want me to ask.

The reference in this to postponing "any action even at some military sacrifice" referred primarily to possible British naval or air action from Singapore against the Japanese landings. Churchill had recently sent substantial reinforcements to Singapore, particularly the battleship *Prince of Wales* and the battle cruiser *Repulse*. But it seemed that he was not going to use force until he had been advised of Roosevelt's intentions after the Japanese moves had actually been made. In London, as in Washington, on the eve of Pearl Harbor, the best-informed thinking was that further Japanese aggression was imminent and that it would come in the Southwest Pacific, its probable objective being the Kra Isthmus, which joined the mainland of Thailand and Burma with the Malay Peninsula, six thousand miles from Pearl Harbor. Nowhere, in any of the official military intelligence reports, appraisals or estimates that came into the White House during the weeks preceding December 7 have I found one mention of the possibility that the Hawaiian Islands were likely to be the first object of attack. And what of the best-informed thinking in Pearl Harbor itself?

Here are two paragraphs from the Roberts report:

> General Short held discussions with Admiral Kimmel on November 27, December 1, 2, and 3 concerning this matter in an effort to compose certain differences of view.
>
> At one of these conferences Admiral Kimmel inquired of his warplans officer, Captain McMorris, who was present, concerning the

probability of a surprise attack on Oahu. According to General Short, Captain McMorris replied there was no probability of such an attack; and, according to Captain McMorris, his reply was that the Japanese would never so attack. According to the testimony Admiral Kimmel and General Short did not discuss means or measures for Hawaiian defense to be adopted in the light of the messages.

On and after November 27, 1941, the commanding general, Hawaiian Department, and the commander in chief of the Pacific Fleet, independently took such action as each deemed appropriate to the existing situation. Neither informed the other specifically of the action he was taking, and neither inquired of the other whether or not any action had been taken, nor did they consult as to the appropriateness of the actions taken by them respectively.

(The war plans officer mentioned, Captain C. H. McMorris, later became one of the finest fighting admirals in the Pacific.)

On December 7, the Navy Department gave the location of all the major warships in the Pacific—U.S., British, Japanese, Dutch and Russian—and the Congressional Joint Committee stated, of this report:

> The bulk of the Japanese Navy was listed as in the two major Japanese naval stations at Kure and Sasebo on the main Japanese islands of Honshu and Kyushu. Included among the Japanese ships listed by name as in those two Japanese naval stations that morning were all of the ships which, it is now known, were at that very moment less than 300 miles north of the Hawaiian Islands.

On the afternoon of Saturday, December 6, the Australian Minister in Washington reported to his Government:

> 1. President has decided to send message to Emperor.
> 2. President's subsequent procedure is that if no answer is received by him from the Emperor by Monday evening,
> (a) he will issue his warning on Tuesday afternoon or evening;
> (b) warning or equivalent by British or others will not follow until Wednesday morning, i.e., after his own warning has been delivered repeatedly to Tokyo and Washington.

This, of course, indicated an expectation that nothing would happen for three days at least. The "warning" referred to was presumably one drafted by Churchill for issuance by the United Kingdom and the Dominions; the text of this was delivered to Roosevelt the following day, December 7 itself. It ended with the words, "If Japan attempts to establish her influence in Thailand by force or threat of force she will do so at her own peril and His Majesty's Governments will at once take all appropriate measures. Should hostilities unfortunately result the responsibility will rest with Japan." It is not known whether Roosevelt even had time to read this before the blow came. Nor is it known whether he would have joined Churchill in such a strong threat or whether, as after the Atlantic Conference, he would have sent another inconclusive warning.

Saturday evening a long cable from the Japanese Government to Nomura was intercepted and decoded by "Magic." It was delivered to the President at 9:30 P.M. by Commander L. R. Schulz, then assistant to Captain Beardall, the Naval Aide. This cable was in thirteen parts with a fourteenth part to follow. Hopkins was with Roosevelt in the Study when it was delivered. Schulz described this scene under cross-examination by Seth W. Richardson, the General Counsel for the Joint Committee on the Investigation. Following is his testimony:

Mr. Richardson. Now, what happened when you delivered these papers to the President? You remained there?

Commander Schulz. Yes, sir, I remained in the room.

Mr. Richardson. What happened?

Commander Schulz. The President read the papers, which took perhaps ten minutes. Then he handed them to Mr. Hopkins.

Mr. Richardson. How far away from the President was Mr. Hopkins sitting?

Commander Schulz. He was standing up pacing back and forth slowly not more than ten feet away.

Mr. Richardson. Did the President read out loud when he was reading the papers?

Commander Schulz. I do not recall that he did.

Mr. Richardson. All right. Now go ahead and give us in detail just what occurred there, if you please, Commander.

Commander Schulz. Mr. Hopkins then read the papers and handed them back to the President. The President then turned towards Mr. Hopkins and said in substance—I am not sure of the exact words, but in substance, "This means war." Mr. Hopkins agreed and they discussed then for perhaps five minutes the situation of the Japanese forces, that is, their deployment and—

Mr. Richardson. Can you recall what either of them said?

Commander Schulz. In substance I can. There are only a few words that I can definitely say I am sure of, but the substance of it was that—I believe Mr. Hopkins mentioned it first, that since war was imminent, that the Japanese intended to strike when they were ready, at a moment when all was most opportune for them—

The Chairman. When all was what?

Commander Schulz. When all was most opportune for that. That is, when their forces were most properly deployed for their advantage. Indo-China in particular was mentioned, because the Japanese forces had already landed there and there were implications of where they should move next.

The President mentioned a message that he had sent to the Japanese Emperor concerning the presence of Japanese troops in Indo-China, in effect requesting their withdrawal.

Mr. Hopkins then expressed a view that since war was undoubtedly

Harry Hopkins shown before the Senate Commerce Committee, January 13, 1939, during the hearings on his appointment to the Cabinet as Secretary of Commerce.

Harry Hopkins holds his first press conference, May 21, 1933.

International News Photo

*Harry Hopkins and Harold Ickes, with some souvenirs picked up at
Balboa, Panama, during their trip from California with President Roosevelt on the U.S.S. Houston, in October 1935.*

Kansas City Star

S. J. Ray

Washington Evening Star

Berryman

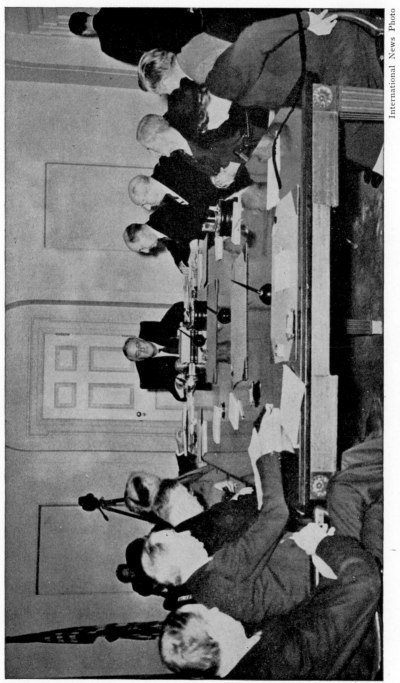

The President meets with his Cabinet to discuss the Czech-German crisis in September 1938. Harry Hopkins, who attended the meeting, is at the extreme left.

Vice Admiral Sir Gordon Ramsey, K.C.B., Prime Minister Churchill, and Harry Hopkins visit Scapa Flow during Hopkins' first visit to London in January 1941.

President Roosevelt, Prime Minister Churchill, Admiral Stark and Admiral King on board the U.S.S. Augusta at the Atlantic Conference in August 1941. Harry Hopkins in the background at the extreme left.

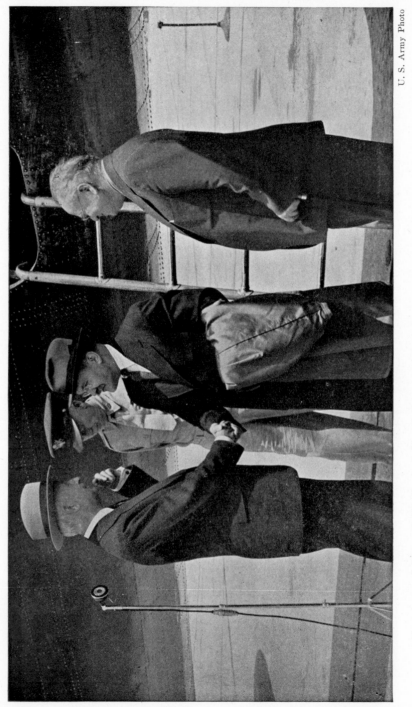

Secretary of State Hull, General Marshall and Ambassador Litvinov greeting Foreign Minister Molotov on his arrival in Washington in May 1942.

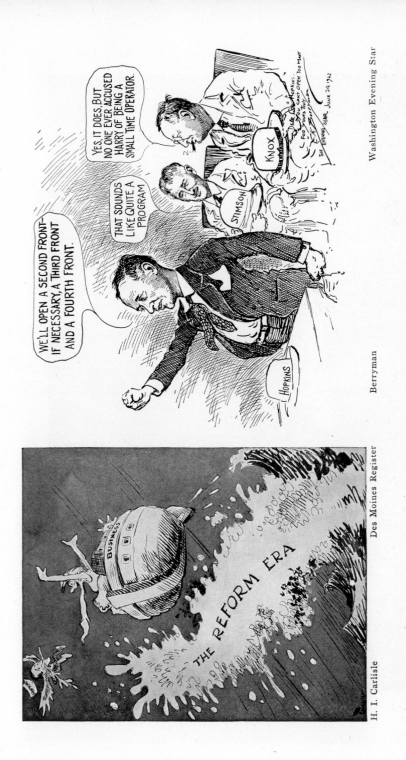

H. I. Carlisle · Des Moines Register

Berryman · Washington Evening Star

The Churchill-Roosevelt press conference at Casablanca in January, 1943, at which Roosevelt announced his famous "unconditional surrender" terms for Germany, Japan and Italy.

President Roosevelt studying dispatches aboard the plane flying him to Miami on the last leg of his return trip from the Casablanca Conference.

The Thanksgiving Day meeting in Cairo, Egypt, of the heads of government of China, Britain and the United States and their military and civilian staffs. Front row, left to right: Generalissimo Chiang Kai-shek, President Roosevelt, Prime Minister Winston Churchill and Madame Chiang Kai-shek. Among others in the picture are: (back row) Lord Cadogan (extreme left); Anthony Eden; John G. Winant (at Eden's left); Dr. Wang Chang-Hui (wearing glasses); R. C. Casey (at Dr. Wang's left); Lord Killearn (at Mr. Casey's left); Averell Harriman, Lewis Douglas, Alexander Kirk, Harry Hopkins is at the extreme right

President Roosevelt awarding the Legion of Merit to General Eisenhower at Cairo, in November 1943.

Captain Edwards, R.N., Captain of H.M.S. Sirius; Secretary of State Edward Stettinius, Jr., Anthony Eden and Harry Hopkins, watching the arrival of President Roosevelt on the U.S.S. Quincy at the harbor of Malta.

President Roosevelt and Foreign Minister Molotov at Yalta.

Prime Minister Churchill, President Roosevelt and Premier Stalin at Yalta. In the foreground is Pavlov, Stalin's interpreter. In the rear are (left to right): Admiral King, Admiral Leahy, General Marshall. The civilian in the background is Nikita Khrushchev, political boss of the Ukraine.

going to come at the convenience of the Japanese it was too bad that we could not strike the first blow and prevent any sort of surprise. The President nodded and then said, in effect, "No, we can't do that. We are a democracy and a peaceful people." Then he raised his voice, and this much I remember definitely. He said, "But we have a good record."

The impression that I got was that we would have to stand on that record, we could not make the first overt move. We would have to wait until it came.

During this discussion there was no mention of Pearl Harbor. The only geographic name I recall was Indo-China. The time at which war might begin was not discussed, but from the manner of the discussion there was no indication that tomorrow was necessarily the day. I carried that impression away because it contributed to my personal surprise when the news did come.

Mr. Richardson. Was there anything said, Commander, with reference to the subject of notice or notification as a result of the papers that were being read?

Commander Schulz. There was no mention made of sending any further warning or alert. However, having concluded this discussion about war going to begin at the Japanese convenience, then the President said that he believed he would talk to Admiral Stark. He started to get Admiral Stark on the telephone. It was then determined,—I do not recall exactly, but I believe the White House operator told the President that Admiral Stark could be reached at the National Theater.

Mr. Richardson. Now, that was from what was said there that you draw the conclusion that that was what the White House operator reported?

Commander Schulz. Yes, sir. I did not hear what the operator said, but the National Theater was mentioned in my presence and the President went on to state, in substance, that he would reach the Admiral later, that he did not want to cause public alarm by having the Admiral paged or otherwise when in the theater where I believe the fact that he had a box reserved was mentioned and that if he had left suddenly he would surely have been seen because of the position which he held and undue alarm might be caused and the President did not wish that to happen because he could get him within perhaps another half an hour in any case.

These statements by Schulz sound unassailably authentic, and when he made them many people regretted that he had not remained longer in the Oval Study to hear the rest of the Roosevelt-Hopkins conversation. I cannot pretend to guess what was said, and see no reason even to try. One thing is abundantly clear: Roosevelt at that moment faced the most grievous dilemma of his entire career.

After the Roberts report came out, some six weeks after Pearl Harbor, Hopkins wrote the following:

I dined with the President alone tonight and he discussed at some length the implications of the Roberts report on Pearl Harbor and the negotiations with Japan in the Far East prior to December 7.

The President told me about several talks with Hull relative to the loopholes in our foreign policy in the Far East in so far as that concerned the circumstances on which the United States would go to war with Japan in event of certain eventualities. All of Hull's negotiations, while in general terms indicating that we wished to protect our rights in the Far East, would never envisage the tough answer to the problem that would have to be faced if Japan attacked, for instance, either Singapore or the Netherlands East Indies. The President felt it was a weakness in our policy that we could not be specific on that point. The President told me that he felt that an attack on the Netherlands East Indies should result in war with Japan and he told me that Hull always ducked that question.

I remember when I was in England in February 1941, Eden, the Foreign Minister, asked me repeatedly what our country would do if Japan attacked Singapore or the Dutch, saying it was essential to their policy to know.

Of course, it was perfectly clear that neither the President nor Hull could give an adequate answer to the British on that point because the declaration of war is up to Congress and the isolationists and, indeed, a great part of the American people, would not be interested in a war in the Far East merely because Japan attacked the Dutch.

(*Note.* The two preceding paragraphs have already been quoted.)

I recall talking to the President many times in the past year and it always disturbed him because he really thought that the tactics of the Japanese would be to avoid a conflict with us; that they would not attack either the Philippines or Hawaii but would move on Thailand, French Indo-China, make further inroads on China itself and possibly attack the Malay Straits. He also thought they would attack Russia at an opportune moment. This would have left the President with the very difficult problem of protecting our interests.

He always realized that Japan would jump on us at an opportune moment and they would merely use the "one by one" technique of Germany. Hence his great relief at the method that Japan used. In spite of the disaster at Pearl Harbor and the blitz-warfare with the Japanese during the first few weeks, it completely solidified the American people and made the war upon Japan inevitable.

Apropos of the Roberts report, which indicates that the State Department had given up all hope of coming to an agreement with Japan, it seems to me that hardly squares with the facts. It is true that Hull told the Secretaries of War and Navy that he believed Japan might attack at any moment. On the other hand, up to the very last day, he undoubtedly had hopes that something could be worked out at the last moment. Hull had always been willing to work out a deal with Japan. To be sure, it was the kind of a deal that Japan probably would not have accepted but, on the other hand, it was also the type of a deal which would have made us very unpopular in the Far East.

Hull wanted peace above everything, because he had set his heart on making an adjustment with the Japanese and had worked on it night and day for weeks. There was no question that up until the last ten days prior to the outbreak of war he was in hopes that some adjustment could be worked out.

The ten days referred to in the last paragraph go back to November 27 when the Chief of Naval Operations sent to Admiral Kimmel the message directing "defensive deployment in preparation for carrying out war tasks." During these ten days a sort of paralysis set in, at Oahu and in the Philippines (where the unreadiness for attack at Clark Field still remains a mystery) and perhaps worst of all in Washington. Here was presented the awful picture of a great nation which had surrendered all powers of initiative and therefore must wait in a state of flabby impotence for its potential enemies to decide where, when and how action would be taken.

This, then, was Roosevelt's dilemma:

The Japanese were about to strike at British or Dutch possessions or both—and what could he do about it? The British and the Dutch were hopelessly unable to defend themselves and so were the exposed Dominions of Australia and New Zealand. Singapore might hold out for a while, but it and Manila would be rendered inoperative as bases with the Japanese in control of the air above them and the seas around them. Without formidable American intervention, the Japanese would be able to conquer and exploit an empire, rich in resources, stretching from the Aleutian Islands to India or even to the Middle East; and it was idle to assume, and Roosevelt knew it better than anyone else, that there could be any formidable American intervention without the full, final, irrevocable plunging of the entire nation into war. And what were the chances of that when the Japanese landed on the Kra Peninsula? What would the President have to say to the Congress in that event? It was the same Congress which only a month before had barely agreed to extend permission for the arming of American merchant ships. It was afflicted with the same myopia which had led the previous Congress to refuse to appropriate funds sufficient for the fortification of Guam.

In 1939, with a traditional enemy in armed force on the very frontier of France, the French isolationists—most of whom had later become collaborationists—had raised the scornful cry: "Why should we die for Danzig?" Why, then, should Americans die for Thailand, or for such outposts of British imperialism as Singapore or Hong Kong or of Dutch imperialism in the East Indies, or for Communism in Vladivostok?

Even if Roosevelt, through diligent use of the Democratic party whip, could compel the Congress to vote for war by a narrow margin after weeks or months of demoralizing debate (during which the Japanese would sweep ahead), what degree of unity or of fighting spirit could the American people achieve for the long and prodigious and bloody effort that must be demanded of them?

Roosevelt had been telling the people for a year and more that the real enemy was Hitler's Germany. His Administration had been rendering all possible aid to Hitler's enemies in Europe and, at the same time, often seeming to go out of its way to appease Japan. The people had supported his policy as long as it carried with it the assurance that this was the best way to keep out of war: Churchill had provided too convenient a slogan, and Americans felt too secure in the thought that "All we have to do is give the British (or Russians, or Chinese) the tools and let them finish the job." Even the killing of American sailors by Germans in the North Atlantic had apparently failed to set off any sparks of belligerence in the American soul. How much will to battle would be stimulated by the news that the Japanese were establishing a beachhead at Khota Baru on the Gulf of Siam?

And if the Congress and the people should refuse to go to war on this provocation, as it seemed inevitable that they would refuse, what would be the effect on the British, the Russians, the Chinese—as well as on the Germans, Italians and Japanese?

The plain fact was that the moment was imminent when the United States would be forced at gun point either to put up or forever shut up.

While Commander Schulz was still in the Oval Study with Roosevelt and Hopkins, there was some speculation as to where the Japanese blow would come; the only geographical point mentioned was Indo-China, that being the obvious base from which strong forces would be further deployed. After he left the room, the conversation may have turned to all sorts of eventualities—but they could not have included the inconceivable possibility that, before launching their major attacks against British and Dutch possessions, the Japanese would first take the precaution of forcing the United States into the war.

There was just one thing that they could do to get Roosevelt completely off the horns of the dilemma, and that is precisely what they did, at one stroke, in a manner so challenging, so insulting and enraging, that the divided and confused American people were instantly rendered unanimous and certain.

Before he went to bed on the night of December 7, Hopkins took the time to write down the events of that day in the White House:

> I lunched with the President today at his desk in the Oval Room. We were talking about things far removed from war when at about 1:40 Secretary Knox called and said that they had picked up a radio from Honolulu from the Commander-in-Chief of our forces there

advising all our stations that an air raid attack was on and that it was "no drill."

I expressed the belief that there must be some mistake and that surely Japan would not attack in Honolulu.

The President discussed at some length his efforts to keep the country out of the war and his earnest desire to complete his administration without war, but that if this action of Japan's were true it would take the matter entirely out of his own hands, because the Japanese had made the decision for him.

The President thought the report was probably true and thought it was just the kind of unexpected thing the Japanese would do, and that at the very time they were discussing peace in the Pacific they were plotting to overthrow it.

At five minutes after two he called Hull and told Hull of the report and advised Hull to receive Nomura and Kurusu, who had an appointment with him, and not to mention that he, Hull, had the news but to receive their reply formally and coolly and bow them out.

I heard Hull later report to the President about the interview and I gather he used some pretty strong Tennessee mountain language to the two Japanese emissaries. The burden of his remarks being that he didn't believe a word in the reply to his note and that it was false from beginning to end.

At 2:28 Admiral Stark called the President and confirmed the attack, stating that it was a very severe attack and that some damage had already been done to the fleet and that there was some loss of life. He discussed with the President briefly the next step and the President wanted him to execute the agreed orders to the Army and Navy in event of an outbreak of hostilities in the Pacific.

At 2:30 the President called Steve Early and dictated a news release which Steve was to release at once to the press. Steve came in half an hour later and the President dictated a further statement which the President promptly ordered Steve to release.

The President called a conference of Secretary Stimson, Secretary Hull, Secretary Knox, Admiral Stark and General Marshall at three o'clock.

The conference met in not too tense an atmosphere because I think that all of us believed that in the last analysis the enemy was Hitler and that he could never be defeated without force of arms; that sooner or later we were bound to be in the war and that Japan had given us an opportunity. Everybody, however, agreed on the seriousness of the war and that it would be a long, hard struggle. During the conference the news kept coming in, indicating more and more damage to the fleet. The President handled the calls personally on the telephone with whoever was giving the despatches. Most of them came through the Navy.

It was at this conference that Hull reviewed his interview with the Japanese.

It was agreed that some type of censorship had to be set up at once.

Churchill called from England. The President told him that we were all in the same boat now and that he was going to Congress tomorrow. Churchill apparently told him that the Malay Straits had been attacked and that he too was going to the House of Commons in the morning and would ask for declaration of war.

The President discussed at length with Marshall the disposition of the troops and particularly the air force, and with Hull the urgent necessity of keeping all of the South American Republics not only informed but to keep them in line with us. Marshall was clearly impatient to get away. He said he had ordered General MacArthur to execute "all the necessary movement required in event of an outbreak of hostilities with Japan."

The President ordered the Japanese Embassy and all the consulates in the United States to be protected and ordered all Japanese citizens to be picked up and placed under careful surveillance. It was agreed that this should be done by the Department of Justice.

The President also ordered Stimson and Knox to order that careful guards be placed not only on our own arsenals but on all private munitions factories and all bridges. Marshall announced that the military would guard the War Department from now on. The President refused to have a military guard around the White House.

Many of the moves required the President to sign an executive order. The President instructed the person to whom he talked to go ahead and execute the order and he would sign it later.

There was some discussion about the President's message to Congress, for by this time the President had decided to go to Congress Monday. The President expressed himself very strongly that he was going to submit a precise message and had in mind submitting a longer message later. Hull urged very strongly that the President review the whole history of the Japanese relations in a strong document that might take half an hour to read. The President objected. I thought at the time the President had in mind going on the radio to the American people and would at that time develop his case at length and that he proposed now to keep the case centered on the attack at Hawaii.

I told the President I thought he should have two conferences before the day was out, one with the Cabinet and he ordered Steve to call it for 8:30, and one with the legislative leaders. We discussed between us a list of the members and he finally decided to have only a few of the leaders. Later he added Hiram Johnson. He refused to have the chairman leaders because the ranking member of the House Committee is Ham Fish and the President will not have him in the White House.

It was finally agreed that the conference should include Vice President Wallace; Speaker Rayburn; John McCormack, Majority Floor Leader; Joseph Martin, Minority Floor Leader; Sol Bloom, Foreign Affairs Chairman; Tom Connally, Foreign Relations Committee; Charles Eaton, Foreign Affairs Committee; Warren Austin, Military Affairs Committee; and Charles McNary.

In the meantime various Cabinet members were calling the President and all of them out of the city were urged to take planes at once to return for the conference.

The conference adjourned about 4:30 and the President then dictated to Grace the first draft of his message to Congress. This was ready when the President, Grace and I had dinner together in the Oval Room.

Again the phone was ringing constantly. Jimmy [Roosevelt?] called up. The Attorney General, Secretary of the Treasury also called. Stark continued to get further and always more dismal news about the attack on Hawaii. We went over the speech again briefly and the President made a few corrections and decided to read it to the Cabinet.

The Cabinet met promptly at 8:30. All members were present. They formed a ring completely around the President, who sat at his desk. The President was in a very solemn mood and told the group this was the most serious Cabinet session since Lincoln met with the Cabinet at the outbreak of the Civil War.

The President reviewed the news with the Cabinet and they were all shocked by the damage wrought by the Japanese aircraft. He told them of his plan to go to Congress at noon tomorrow and read them the proposed message. Hull again argued strongly that the message was inadequate. The President, however, stuck to his guns, determined to make his statement to Congress what is in effect an understatement and nothing too explosive.

At this time we did not know whether or not Japan had actually declared war on us.

Even at this time the President had decided not to tell the Congressional leaders who were waiting outside precisely what was going to be in the message. They came in at approximately 9:30. Those present were Vice President Wallace, Senator Alben Barkley, Senator Charles McNary, Senator Connally, Senator Warren Austin, Senator Hiram Johnson, Speaker Rayburn, Congressman Sol Bloom and Congressman Charles Eaton.

The President outlined at some length the situation, reviewing the negotiations with Japan and giving them as much news as he could relative to the Japanese attack on Hawaii. Everybody realized that the implication of the conference was that a declaration of war would be made tomorrow.

The President asked the legislative leaders when they would be ready to receive him and it was agreed he would appear personally at 12:30 tomorrow. They asked him whether he wanted a declaration of war and what was going to be in the message and he said he had not as yet decided. As a matter of fact the President, of course, knew that he was going to ask for a declaration of war but he also knew that if he stated it to the conference that it would be all over town in five minutes, because it is perfectly footless ever to ask a large group of Congressmen to keep a secret. The legislative leaders left.

Welles had a draft of a war message which the President did not like, although Hull pressed very strongly that he use it. Hull's mes-

sage was a long-winded dissertation on the history of Japanese relations leading up to the blow this morning. The President was very
patient with them and I think in order to get them out of the room
perhaps led them to believe he would give serious consideration to
their draft.

Waiters brought in beer and sandwiches and at 12:30 the President
cleared everybody out and said he was going to bed.

The orders that the President told Admiral Stark to execute on confirmation of the news from Honolulu were based on every conceivable
eventuality listed in the Joint Staff Estimate quoted previously. I doubt
that any of them encompassed the circumstance of seven U.S. capital
ships being put out of commission within the first hour of hostilities.
Millions of words have been recorded by at least eight official investigating bodies and one may read through all of them without arriving at
an adequate explanation of why, with war so obviously ready to break
out *somewhere* in the Pacific, our principal Pacific base was in a condition of peacetime Sunday morning somnolence instead of in Condition Red.

When General Marshall appeared before the Joint Congressional
Committee, he was asked why he sent a telegram to alert General Short
in Honolulu on Sunday morning (the telegram arrived after the attack)
when he might have spoken to him instantly over the scrambler telephone
which was on his desk. The Committee report stated:

> General Marshall testified that among the possible factors which
> may have influenced him against using the scrambler telephone was the
> possibility that the Japanese could construe the fact that the Army
> was alerting its garrisons in Hawaii as a hostile act. [He said:]
> "The Japanese would have grasped at most any straw to bring to
> such portions of our public that doubted our integrity of action that
> we were committing an act that forced action on their part."

Marshall's hesitancy was precisely the same as that of Roosevelt when
he decided not to call Admiral Stark away from a performance of "The
Student Prince" because "undue alarm might be caused." Marshall and
Roosevelt were far more afraid of the isolationists at home—the "portions of our public that doubted our integrity"—than they were of the
enemies abroad. They were afraid of being called "alarmists," a word
which was then interchangeable with "warmongers." Therefore, neither
one of them, nor Stark, ever reached out to push the button which rang
the General Alarm, for that precautionary measure might have been
construed as the overt act.

Marshall could not forget the occasion, previously mentioned in these
pages, when in that same year of 1941 a Congressional Committee raised
a fearful rumpus because of its discovery that the Army was ordering
"overseas caps" for American troops!

"The only thing we have to fear is fear itself."

In addition to which is the equally inescapable fact that none of them believed it possible that Japan could commit an act of such seemingly suicidal folly as an attack on Pearl Harbor. Churchill referred to it repeatedly as "this irrational act"—it being particularly incomprehensible in view of the long-established reputation of the Japanese for diabolical cleverness.

It may well be said that those in high authority in both the United States and Britain made two original errors of calculation: they greatly underrated Japanese military strength and daring, and they greatly overrated Japanese political astuteness.

However, all possible explanations and recitals of extenuating circumstances cannot wipe out the responsibility of all concerned, including the Commander in Chief, for the appalling unreadiness. As an officer of the Japanese Naval Ministry said four years later, "We had expected a much greater defense at so important a base. We were amazed."

Hopkins made a valid comment on this question of responsibility, although not in relation to Pearl Harbor. Later, when the French liner *Normandie* burned and capsized at a pier in New York City while it was being converted for use as a troop transport, Secretary Knox produced a file of correspondence to prove that many months previously he had attempted to obtain funds from the Congress for the protection of naval vessels from sabotage while in port. Failing to obtain these funds, Knox had written the Chairman of the House Appropriations Committee:

> In reviewing the foregoing facts, I cannot but come to the conclusion that, as Secretary of the Navy responsible for the protection of its Shore Establishments from external and internal dangers, I have done all in my power to meet this grave responsibility. In my efforts to crystallize a measure to meet this serious problem, I have at all times considered and accepted the constructive objections of the Members of Congress. I cannot but feel that the responsibility for any catastrophe which might occur in a Shore Establishment of the Navy because of subversive activities no longer rests with me.

When Hopkins read this he wrote expressing the opinion that Knox should not have made such a statement because "no matter what Congress fails to do the Secretary of the Navy still has responsibility."

The news of the shocking extent of the casulties and the damage to capital ships spread rapidly throughout Washington. Many newspaper men knew the details but refrained from publishing them even before the government had time to put censorship into operation. The jittery conduct of some of the most eminent of our government officials was downright disgraceful. They were telephoning the White House shouting that the President must tell the people the full extent of this unmitigated disaster—that our nation had gone back to Valley Forge—that our West Coast was now indefensible and we must prepare to establish our battle lines in the Rocky Mountains or on the left bank of the Mississippi or God knows where. In going about Washington in those first days, it sometimes seemed that maybe the Nazi and Fascist propagandists were right, that maybe our democracy had become decadent and soft, that we could talk big but that there were too many of us who simply did not know how to stand up under punishment. But the atmosphere inside the White House was very different; here, one felt, was the United States of America. Telegrams and messages flowed by the hundreds and thousands from people all over the country. I read all of them that were received in the first few days and, if I had been misled by any doubts, these messages to the President put me right. The spirit that they expressed welled up in the press and over the radio and gave an inspiring and valid promise of the manner in which this country was to handle its gigantic job.

The same was true of Roosevelt himself. When he went before the Congress on the morning of December 8, he was taking his stand before the bar of history, and he knew it. As an evidence of his historical sense, he had asked that Mrs. Roosevelt be accompanied at this Joint Session by Mrs. Woodrow Wilson. The brief speech that he then gave represented Roosevelt at his simplest and most direct. Every word of this was Roosevelt's own except for the next to last sentence, which was largely suggested by Hopkins, and which is the most platitudinous line in the speech. Roosevelt's only literary flourish was his phrase, "a date which will live in infamy." Although he gave no details of the results of the attack—many of these details being still unknown—he certainly made no attempt to gloss over the essential, ugly truth or to put a good face on a bad situation. He listed the extraordinary events of the past twenty-four hours:

> The attack yesterday on the Hawaiian Islands has caused severe damage to American naval and military forces. Very many American lives have been lost. In addition American ships have been reported torpedoed on the high seas between San Francisco and Honolulu.
> Yesterday the Japanese Government also launched an attack against Malaya.
> Last night Japanese forces attacked Hong Kong.
> Last night Japanese forces attacked Guam.
> Last night Japanese forces attacked the Philippine Islands.
> Last night the Japanese attacked Wake Island.
> This morning the Japanese attacked Midway Island.
> Japan, has, therefore, undertaken a surprise offensive extending throughout the Pacific area. The facts of yesterday speak for themselves. The people of the United States have already formed their

opinions and well understand the implications to the very life and safety of our Nation. . . .

Hostilities exist. There is no blinking at the fact that our people, our territory, and our interests are in grave danger.

There was none of Churchill's eloquent defiance in this speech. There was certainly no trace of Hitler's hysterical bombast. And there was no doubt in the minds of the American people of Roosevelt's confidence. I do not think there was another occasion in his life when he was so completely representative of the whole people. If, as Hopkins wrote, Roosevelt felt a sense of relief that the Japanese had chosen this method of settling the issue of war or peace, so with remarkably few exceptions did the people themselves. They recognized Pearl Harbor as a tragedy and a disgrace—and that recognition provided a boost to national pride which expressed itself in tremendous accomplishment. On Tuesday night after Pearl Harbor Roosevelt spoke over the radio and said:

We may acknowledge that our enemies have performed a brilliant feat of deception, perfectly timed and executed with great skill. It was a thoroughly dishonorable deed, but we must face the fact that modern warfare as conducted in the Nazi manner is a dirty business. We don't like it—we didn't want to get in it—but we are in it, and we're going to fight it with everything we've got.

The American people, notoriously nondocile, accepted the unquestionable accuracy of that statement and acted accordingly. They cast off isolationism, readily, rapidly, even gratefully—though perhaps not permanently. The inveterate isolationists remained inveterate, ready to carry out guerrilla raids against the Administration whenever a line of communication to the rear appeared to be exposed. As Elmer Davis said, broadcasting for C.B.S. shortly after Pearl Harbor: "There are some patriotic citizens who sincerely hope that America will win the war—but they also hope that Russia will lose it; and there are some who hope that America will win the war, but that England will lose it; and there are some who hope that America will win the war, but that Roosevelt will lose it!"

Nevertheless, the historic fact remains that, throughout the forty-four months of war that followed, the American nation achieved its most massive effort: the fighting qualities of the individual men of the armed forces were at least equal to the most hallowed and possibly exaggerated traditions of our past, and so was the quality of military leadership; the mass production of arms, food, raw materials and everything else that was necessary was far beyond anything that had previously been imagined possible, and so was the expenditure of money; the scientific development was immeasurable. The over-all record could not have been approximated had the nation failed to attain and sustain an unprecedented degree of unity with its Allies and within itself. Strangely enough, insofar as the people as a whole were concerned, the element known as "morale" did not become a vital consideration. Morale was never particularly good nor alarmingly bad. There was a minimum of flag waving and parades. It was the first war in American history in which the general disillusionment preceded the firing of the first shot. It has been called, from the American point of view, "the most unpopular war in history"; but that could be taken as proof that the people for once were not misled as to the terrible nature and extent of the task that confronted them.

PART III: *1942—THE NARROW MARGIN*

CHAPTER XX

The Arcadia Conference

BOTH Winant and Harriman were at dinner with Churchill at Chequers on Sunday evening, December 7, 1941. The fifteen-dollar American radio that Hopkins had given the Prime Minister was on the dining table, and from it came the measured, emotionless tones of the B.B.C. newscaster announcing that the Japanese had attacked Pearl Harbor. Winant has told how Churchill was immediately on his feet, about to call the Foreign Office to give instructions that a declaration of war on Japan should be put through at once—"within the minute," as he had promised. He was talked out of this on the ground that one could not declare war on the strength of a news broadcast, even from the B.B.C. Winant suggested that perhaps the Prime Minister should telephone the White House for confirmation. (This was the call mentioned in the notes that Hopkins wrote on the night of December 7.) Roosevelt immediately agreed that Churchill should come to Washington with his Chiefs of Staff as soon as possible. Churchill then put through a call to Anthony Eden who was at Invergordon about to board a cruiser for his mission to Moscow.

When Eden heard of Pearl Harbor and Churchill's imminent trip to Washington, he felt that his own trip should be canceled: the Prime Minister and the Foreign Secretary should not be away from the United Kingdom at the same time. Actually, Churchill could not order Eden to go or stay, as a President could order a Secretary of State, for Eden had his own direct responsibility to the king; but Churchill convinced him that now that the United States was a belligerent his hand would be greatly strengthened in his talks with Stalin and Molotov, particularly in view of the cable from Hull which Winant had communicated the day before. So Eden went.

439

One of the immediate effects of United States entry into the war was an order by the War Department placing a stoppage on all Lend-Lease shipments then loaded at American ports. This meant that shipments of vital matériel allocated to the Middle East were tied up, presumably for diversion to the Pacific. The British were afraid that now there might be a drastic reorientation of American strategic thinking—that the formerly accepted strategy of "Germany first" might be abandoned and the whole weight of American power concentrated on Japan.

On December 11, Harriman cabled Hopkins that Beaverbrook would telephone him about five o'clock that afternoon to discuss the alarming fact that thirty ships which had been scheduled to sail shortly for the Middle East were now held up by this order. Harriman begged that Hopkins would be sympathetic to the plea that Beaverbrook was to make for the release of the ships.

The subsequent conversation is one of the few of Hopkins' many transatlantic telephone talks which were transcribed. It is not particularly important but it does show Hopkins' directness and the extent to which both Beaverbrook and Harriman accepted his terse assurances as absolute guarantees that their fears for the Lend-Lease shipments were baseless. Following is the complete dialogue:

Beaverbrook. Is that you, Harry?

Hopkins. Yes.

Beaverbrook. Did you get a telegram from Averell? Can you help us there?

Hopkins. I can assure you we can.

Beaverbrook. That is very fine.

Hopkins. And in very important ways. I will not mention details but it is encouraging and I am going to talk to Morris Wilson and Ed Taylor tonight.

Beaverbrook. That is very fine indeed. Thank you.

Hopkins. Don't worry.

Beaverbrook. That is grand.

Hopkins. In order to make it really tough for Hitler we will undoubtedly greatly increase our amounts.

Beaverbrook. I can't hear you.

Hopkins. We are going to do far better.

(Communication cut at this point and resumed later)

Hopkins. Hello, Max.

Beaverbrook. Yes, Harry.

Hopkins. I wanted to say that we are going to do far better than you or I ever thought. Much better.

Beaverbrook. That is very fine.

Hopkins. If Hitler thought he could start a war and do that he is going to be greatly mistaken.

Beaverbrook. Fine. I will put Averell on to you.

Hopkins. Hello, Ave. Things are going all right here.

Harriman. That is fine.

Hopkins. Don't worry.

Harriman. We're not at all.

Hopkins. Things are going to turn out far better for you over there in the long run and in the not distant future. They made another mistake, by God. Don't worry.

Harriman. I would like to hear from you once in awhile.

Hopkins. You can imagine what is going on here but you can count on it we are not going to let them down.

Harriman. All right. Good-bye.

Hopkins. Good-bye, Ave.

The telephone talks between the White House and London were frequently as uninteresting as this sample. No matter how secure the scrambler system might presumably be, the speakers were always inclined to be so extremely careful of what they said that they gave no really important information, saving that for the cables. One may wonder, therefore, why they used the telephone so much; the answer to that is easy—being strictly human, they enjoyed the thrill of talking to each other across three thousand miles of embattled ocean.

On that same day, December 11, while Harriman's first cable was en route, the news came that Germany and Italy had declared war on the United States. Ciano in his diary recorded that Ribbentrop was "joyful over the Japanese attack on the United States. He is so happy, in fact, that I can't but congratulate him, even though I am not so sure about the advantage." Ciano added that "Mussolini was happy" and that the king of Italy also "expressed his satisfaction." And Hitler told his staff at Berchtesgaden that American soldiers are "nothing but a bunch of rowdies. They can't stick in a crisis. They have absolutely no ideals."

On the day of Pearl Harbor Roosevelt had been urged to make mention of Germany and Italy in his Message to Congress asking for the declaration of war on Japan. He refused to do so. He wanted to wait for Hitler and Mussolini to declare war on the United States. He was aware that a cable from Berlin to Tokyo, on November 29, had been intercepted and decoded by "Magic"; this cable gave assurance to the Japanese that if they "became engaged in a war against the United States, Germany would of course join in the war immediately."

It seemed at the time that the German-Italian declaration of war was another "irrational act"; true, the Nazis and Fascists were in honor bound by their pledges to the Japanese, but they had not previously shown much inclination to let such bourgeois-democratic considerations interfere with their own conceptions of self-interest. Perhaps Hitler had completely taken leave of his senses and was now hysterically eager to fight all comers on all fronts; and perhaps he had been worn down by the psychological warfare that had been going on continuously for years between him and Roosevelt and he was at last glad of an excuse to abandon his sensible determination to avoid war with the United States until he had disposed of Britain and Russia. In any case, he seconded the Japanese in solving Roosevelt's sorest problems.

Churchill and the British people could of course make no secret of their exultation at these developments, but their celebration was short lived. The sinking of the *Prince of Wales* and *Repulse* off the Malayan coast and the quick capture of Hong Kong by the Japanese were the first of a series of irreparable blows to British imperial prestige in Asia.

Churchill arrived in Washington with his entourage on December 22 for the series of conferences which were known under the code name ARCADIA. He was installed in the big bedroom across the hall from Hopkins' room, and as the two of them walked back and forth to visit one another they had to pick their way through great piles of Christmas parcels. That upstairs hall in the White House underwent an extraordinary change. Ordinarily quiet and usually deserted, it was now the headquarters of the British Empire, and various dignitaries and staff officers and secretaries were continually hurrying through carrying the old, red leather dispatch cases which make British officials look really official. The White House staff were amazed and fascinated by these goings-on, and the British were even more amazed by the atmosphere of placidity and seeming detachment from events that surrounded the President and the incomprehensible fact that the total military staff on duty at the White House at some given moment might consist of one nervous Navy ensign. There was an even greater contrast, the other way around, between the size of Roosevelt's bodyguard and Churchill's; the British gave considerably less weight to the possibility of assassination.

The food in the White House was always better when Churchill was there and, of course, the wine flowed more freely. Since Churchill knew of Roosevelt's habits of going to bed early, he made a pretense of retiring himself at a fairly reasonable hour; but Roosevelt knew that his tireless guest and Hopkins would go on talking and he did not want to miss any of it so he stayed up much later than usual. The conversations that went on from early morning until late at night covered not only the entire world but a very large part of its history. Churchill was one of the few people to whom Roosevelt cared to listen, and vice versa.

Hopkins told many times a story of Roosevelt being wheeled to his guest's room, and, as he entered, Churchill emerged from the bathroom stark naked and gleaming pink from his bath. Roosevelt started to apologize and made as if to leave, but Churchill protested it was quite all right. "The Prime Minister of Great Britain," he said, "has nothing to conceal from the President of the United States."

I asked Churchill if this story was factual. He replied firmly that it was nonsense—that he never received the President without at least a bath towel wrapped around him. And, he said, "I could not possibly have made such a statement as that. The President himself would have been well aware that it was not strictly true."

Churchill was in the White House because he was the King's First Minister, but he could not forget that he was also a professional historian who was most sensitive to the radiations of the past. He looked questioningly at the portraits of the Presidents and undoubtedly had more than a nodding acquaintance with all of them that mattered. After his return to London, he cabled Roosevelt, "I was terribly sorry to have to leave you and, what is more than those can say whose pictures are on the walls, there is not a moment of it that I did not enjoy."

Ordinarily the White House surged with children at Christmas time, but this year Diana Hopkins was the only one; the President's sons were all in the service and their families scattered, and his daughter, Anna, was in Seattle. However, there could be no failure of Christmas spirit with the warmhearted and (despite all appearances to the contrary) tradition-loving Roosevelts. On Christmas Eve, Churchill joined Roosevelt in the ceremony of lighting the tree on the White House lawn. Both of them made short speeches, Roosevelt starting with the words, "Fellow workers for freedom" and introducing Churchill as "my associate, my old and good friend." The Prime Minister started off, "Fellow workers in the cause of freedom: I have the honor to add a pendant to the necklace of that Christmas good will and kindliness with which my illustrious friend, the President, has encircled the homes and families of the United States." Even in brief Christmas messages, which have tended throughout the centuries to become pretty well standardized, the two statesmen managed to emphasize the differences of their literary styles as well as the community of their interests. Their broadcasts gave a thrill to the American people, who needed it, for by that time the deadly seriousness of the war in the Pacific had become apparent: the gallant defense of Wake Island had ended in surrender and Manila seemed doomed.

On Christmas Day Roosevelt and Churchill attended an interdenominational service at the Foundry Methodist Church. The Reverend F. B. Harris gave prayers for the President and Prime Minister. Of the latter he said, "With Thy enabling help he continues to lead his valiant people even through blood and sweat and tears to a new world where men of good will may dwell together, none daring to molest or make afraid." The congregation sang "O Little Town of Bethlehem" with the lines:

> Yet in thy dark streets shineth
> The everlasting light;
> The hopes and fears of all the years
> Are met in thee tonight.

The day after Christmas, Churchill journeyed to Capitol Hill and addressed a joint session of the Congress. It was one of his greatest speeches and superbly attuned to the temper of as difficult an audience as he had ever faced. Hopkins had some worries as to the quality of the reception that Churchill might receive from the Senators and Representatives, but there was no further doubt about it when he heard the roars of laughter and the cheers from Republicans and Democrats alike which followed the Prime Minister's remark, "I cannot help reflecting that if my father had been American and my mother British, instead of the other way around, I might have got here on my own." A few days later Churchill went to Ottawa and gave another great speech before the Canadian Houses of Parliament, making his gloating reference to "Some chicken; some neck," which harked back to Weygand's grim prophecy when France was about to surrender.

Roosevelt was then preparing his 1942 State of the Union Message to Congress and some of his associates were becoming concerned at the quality of the oratorical competition being offered by Churchill. Steve Early was particularly exercised about this; fiercely loyal and jealous of his Chief's prestige, he kept charts showing the fluctuations of the size of the President's radio audiences and he did not welcome the appearance of a new star attraction in a field which Roosevelt had so long monopolized. It was as though the President's championship were at stake. However, Roosevelt was not troubled; he was greatly amused by his friends' concern. He had no desire to attempt to compete with Churchill as a master phrase maker. Indeed, he went more and more to the other extreme, striving to find the shortest and simplest and most obvious means of saying what he wanted to say. But he managed to make sure that his message to Congress of January 6, 1942, was one of his best efforts. It presented the whole program for the United States at war in terms that could not possibly be misunderstood by friend or foe. Before delivering it on Capitol Hill, he read it aloud in the Oval Study to Churchill and Beaverbrook, and he reported later that "it went over big."

Churchill had originally planned to stay only a week in the White House, then go on to Canada for two days and start home to England on January 1. This plan was revised after the intended week was more than half over and Churchill did not leave for England until the night of January 14. In the meantime, he had made the trip to Canada December 29 to January 1 and from January 5 to January 11 he was off on a trip to Florida, his first holiday in the sun since the war started in 1939. During the fourteen days that Churchill was in the White House he and Roosevelt and Hopkins had lunch and dinner together every day but one. It was at the lunches that most of the major problems were thrashed out, so that when the President and Prime Minister went into the full dress meetings they were often already in agreement. There were at least eight major White House meetings of the President, Prime Minister,

Secretaries of War and Navy, Beaverbrook, Hopkins and the British and American Chiefs of Staff, and twelve meetings of the two sets of Chiefs of Staff by themselves in the Federal Reserve Building. Christmas Day was perhaps the busiest of all. Unlike the Atlantic meeting, the Arcadia Conference had an agenda and it was followed through with remarkable precision and success. The first point on this agenda was a large one: "Fundamental basis of joint strategy." As the record shows, discussions of this had been started when Admiral Ghormley and Generals Emmons and Strong went to London during the Battle of Britain in August, 1940, and were continued in the secret staff conferences in Washington the following winter. Although joint strategy had then been determined, it was on a purely tentative, "if-as-and-when" basis; and, when the British gathered for the Arcadia Conference, they suspected that extraordinary events in the Pacific might well have produced a reversal in strategic thinking in Washington and that they would be met with plans for all-out American effort against Japan, leaving the British and Russians to handle the German enemy in Europe. Certainly, the isolationist press was clamoring at the time, and continued to do so, for just that policy. However, British apprehensions were quickly dispelled. When the Chiefs of Staff first sat down together, General Marshall and Admiral Stark immediately presented these two paragraphs as forming the basis for all plans:

1. At the A-B [abbreviation for American-British] Staff Conversations in February, 1941, it was agreed that Germany was the predominant member of the Axis Powers, and consequently the Atlantic and European area was considered to be the decisive theatre.
2. Much has happened since February last, but notwithstanding the entry of Japan into the War, our view remains that Germany is still the prime enemy and her defeat is the key to victory. Once Germany is defeated, the collapse of Italy and the defeat of Japan must follow.

Actually, on the day of Pearl Harbor, Marshall and Stark put into effect the war plans (RAINBOW Number 5, etc.) which had resulted from many months of Anglo-American staff conferences and which gave priority to the operations against Germany. The paragraphs quoted above represented an American redraft of British proposals radioed to Washington from the battleship which carried Churchill and the British Chiefs to the Arcadia Conference; they were included in the report of the Joint Army and Navy Board to Roosevelt on the day before Churchill's arrival at the White House.

The accusation has been made, particularly by officers who were attached to General MacArthur, that at the Arcadia Conference Churchill wheedled and cajoled Roosevelt into adopting the Germany-first policy when the President should have dedicated himself to the conquest of America's real enemy, Japan; but this assumption gives far too much credit to Churchill and too little to Marshall, Stark and the American staff planners, including Dwight D. Eisenhower who had only recently been promoted from temporary colonel to temporary brigadier general. The principle of Germany first was based on strictly military reasoning: it was assumed—and, it would seem from the results, correctly—that Germany had far greater potential than Japan in productive power and scientific genius and, if given time to develop this during years of stalemate in Europe, would prove all the more difficult if not impossible to defeat.

In point of fact, Churchill soon learned that if he wanted to influence American strategic thinking, as he often did, he must do his arguing with the generals and admirals. For Roosevelt respected the judgment of his Chiefs of Staff, and there were not more than two occasions in the entire war when he overruled them (it could be argued that there was only one such occasion—in Cairo, in December, 1943), although there were various times when the Chiefs of Staff were not in complete agreement among themselves and the President as Commander in Chief had to decide between one point of view and another. It was the American opinion that Churchill dominated his own Chiefs to a much greater extent.

The President and Prime Minister selected as their first, main business the formation of the grand coalition of the Allies. This was what Germany, Italy and Japan failed so signally to achieve for all their boasts about the solidarity of the Fascist states; they formed their Axis, but they could not work together and they could not hold together as did the Allied coalition until total victory was won.

By Christmas Eve, Roosevelt had prepared one draft of a Declaration of the "Associated Powers" and Churchill had prepared another. These were blended and the result cabled to London.

On Christmas Day, a cable was received from Attlee, the Lord Privy Seal, conveying the comments of the War Cabinet on the proposed draft. The War Cabinet was evidently surprised at this—for so vast a project had not been previously planned—and was not entirely clear as to whether the Declaration was to be signed by all the Allies, or only by the President and Prime Minister with provision for subsequent signatures in the future. In this cable, Attlee emphasized the War Cabinet's hope that all of the Allied governments would be given a chance to participate in this Declaration, even though this might mean a delay of a day or two in its publication. He said that such participation would provide proof "that this war is being waged for the freedom of the small nations as well as the great powers."

The War Cabinet suggested that the Declaration should contain a paragraph pledging each government not to conclude a separate peace, which had already been provided for in Roosevelt's draft but eliminated in the blend. It is interesting to note that the War Cabinet also suggested that the words "social security" should be included among the ideals for which the Allies were waging war. This was an indication of the fact that at that time Great Britain had a national government with members of the Labor as well as the Conservative party represented in the Cabinet. The Declaration as of December 25 was as follows:

The Governments of the United States of America, the United Kingdom of Great Britain and Northern Ireland, the Dominion of Canada, the Commonwealth of Australia, the Dominion of New Zealand, the Union of South Africa, Belgium, China, Czecho-Slovakia, Greece, Luxemburg, the Netherlands, Norway, Poland, the Union of Soviet Socialist Republics, and Yugo-Slavia,

Having subscribed to a common programme of purposes and principles embodied in the Joint Declaration of the President of the United States of America and the Prime Minister of Great Britain dated August 14th, 1941 and known as the Atlantic Charter,

Being convinced that the complete and world-wide victory of all the Governments is essential to defend and preserve life, liberty and independence as well as the righteous possibilities of human freedom, justice, and social security not only in their own lands but throughout the world, and that the struggle in which they are now engaged is the common defence of human decencies everywhere against savage and brutal force seeking to subjugate the world, declare:

1. Each Government pledges itself to employ its full resources against the Axis forces of conquest and to continue such employment until these forces have been finally defeated;

2. Each Government pledges itself to the other Governments associated in this Declaration to effect the full coordination of its military effort and the use of its resources against the common enemies;

3. Each Government pledges itself to continue war against, and not to make a separate peace with the common enemies or any of them.

Other Governments desirous of associating themselves with this Declaration are hereby privileged to accede to it.

It will be seen that in the opening paragraph of this draft, the United States was first, the United Kingdom second, then the Dominions, followed by other Allies in alphabetical order, which put the U.S.S.R. well down the list.

The War Cabinet definitely stated that India was not to be included among the signatory nations. Lord Halifax, who had been, in his time, Viceroy of India, wrote in a note to Churchill, "I think with all respect to the War Cabinet that this is a mistake, and I would hope it might be reconsidered."

Hopkins' comments on the above draft were communicated to Roosevelt in the following memorandum, written early in the morning of December 27:

I think, if possible, you should make every effort to get religious freedom in this document. I believe it will be necessary for you to talk to Litvinov this noon about this.

I think the wording in [paragraph] "1" on page 2 is a very difficult one for the U.S.S.R. to subscribe to. Paragraph 1 might read "Each Government pledges itself to employ its full resources against those Axis forces of conquest with which it is at war. Each government pledges itself to continue such employment until these forces have been finally defeated."

(*Note.* Hopkins suggested this change, of course, because the Soviet Union was not at war with Japan.)

As long as this list [in the opening paragraph] must include a great many names, I think we should include them all, including the South American Republics. I think there are distinct advantages having a long list of little countries joining with us.

I would lift the countries like China and the U.S.S.R. out of their alphabetical listing and place them with our own and the U.K., the distinction being those actively engaged in war in their own countries and those that have been over-run by the Axis.

I think this listing is extremely important and should be gone over with great care by the State Department.

I think it is up to the British to decide whether or not India should be included, although for the life of me I don't understand why they don't include it.

My own feeling is that at the moment the Free French should not be included.

At the end of the second paragraph of the Joint Declaration, another sentence should be added including a restatement of our aims for human freedom, justice, security, not only for the people in our own lands but for all people in the world. I think a good deal of care should be given to the exact words of this and I do not think the reference to the Atlantic Charter is adequate.

(*Note.* Hopkins' reference to the Free French in the foregoing was an indication of the storm that had broken over Washington following the St. Pierre-Miquelon incident, which is described in the next chapter.)

That day Litvinov lunched with the President, Churchill and Hopkins at the White House. Roosevelt urged on him the importance of including a reference to religious freedom. It will be remembered that the omission of this from the Atlantic Charter had brought down a great deal of criticism on that document and Roosevelt wanted to be sure to have it in this one. Litvinov felt that his government, to which he had already cabled the text of the Declaration, would not look with favor on this suggested change. He said that the Kremlin might possibly agree to the phrase "freedom of conscience" but Roosevelt assured him, and asked him to convey this assurance to the Kremlin, that it was precisely the same thing. He explained that he wanted to use the word "religion" because that had been in his oft-proclaimed Four Freedoms. He said that the traditional Jeffersonian principle of religious freedom was so broadly democratic that it included the right to have no religion at all—it gave to the individual the right to worship any God he chose or no god. I do not know how Litvinov managed to convey this to Stalin and the Politburo, but the fact remains that the words "religious freedom" appeared in the final Declaration.

Churchill asked that another change be made. After the word "governments," in the phrase "the governments signatory hereto," he wished to add the word "authorities." The purpose of this was to permit the inclusion either immediately or subsequently of the Free French. On this discussion Hopkins has written:

> The President and Churchill both tried to get Litvinov to accept the amendment which had been urged by the British Cabinet so that the Free French might subscribe to the document.
>
> Hull had been opposed to having the Free French in it and while he had not vigorously opposed the word "authorities," it was clear Hull wanted no part of the Free French. His antagonism to the Free French is very deep seated and he still believes there is some way we can get on with Vichy. Nevertheless the President overruled Hull and agreed to the word "authorities."
>
> Litvinov, however, told the President and Churchill that he had no power to agree to the inclusion of that word, that the approval of the Declaration was an approval by the Government in contradistinction to the Foreign Office and no ambassador of Russia has the power to agree to any textual change.
>
> Churchill tried to argue that the change was inconsequential but it was perfectly clear that Litvinov did not believe this and he insisted that he could not agree to a change and, because both the President and Churchill were anxious to have the text released at once, there was no time to cable to Russia.
>
> At this point Churchill became quite angry and told Litvinov in effect that he wasn't much of an ambassador if he didn't have the power to even add a word like this; that we were in a war and there was no time for long-winded negotiations. He said that we had agreed to every change in the text that the Russians wanted and it seemed to him they could agree to this.
>
> Litvinov stuck by his point, however, and the Declaration was issued without the word "authorities."
>
> Later I learned that Litvinov had cabled for approval to include the word "authorities" and his Government had given it to him.

JOINT DECLARATION BY THE UNITED STATES OF AMERICA,
CHINA, THE UNITED KINGDOM OF GREAT BRITAIN AND
NORTHERN IRELAND, THE UNION OF SOVIET SOCIALIST
REPUBLICS, AUSTRALIA, BELGIUM, CANADA, COSTA RICA,
CUBA, CZECHOSLOVAKIA, DOMINICAN REPUBLIC, EL SALVADOR,
GREECE, GUATEMALA, HAITI, HONDURAS, NETHERLANDS,
NEW ZEALAND, NICARAGUA, NORWAY, PANAMA, POLAND,
SOUTH AFRICA, AND YUGOSLAVIA.

The Governments signatory hereto,

Having subscribed to a common program of purposes
and principles embodied in the Joint Declaration of
the President of the United States of America and the
Prime Minister of Great Britain dated August 14, 1941,
known as the Atlantic Charter,

Being convinced that complete victory over their
enemies is essential to defend life, liberty,
independence and religious freedom, and to preserve
human rights and justice (not only in their own lands
but everywhere,) and that they are now engaged in a
common struggle against savage and brutal forces
seeking to subjugate the world, DECLARE:

(1) Each Government pledges itself to employ
its full resources, military or economic, against
those members of the Tripartite and its adherents
with which such government is at war.

(2) Each Government pledges itself to cooperate
with the other Governments signatory hereto; and to
continue war against, and not to make a separate
armistice or peace with the common enemies or any
of them.

-2-

The foregoing declaration may be adhered to

,by other nations which are, or which may be,

rendering material assistance and contributions
in the struggle for victory over Hitlerism ,
towards the defeat of members or adherents of

the Tripartite Pact.

****

Declaration of the United Nations, with Russian amendments indicated in ink in Roosevelt's handwriting.

However, this agreement must have come too late as the word "authorities" did not appear. The changes in the text requested by the Kremlin were actually negligible. They were all due to Russian reluctance to indicate any commitment to join the war against Japan. For instance, the Russians substituted the words "the struggle for victory over Hitlerism" for the words "the defeat of members or adherents of the Tripartite Pact." The Soviet Ambassador made it clear that in his country the word "Hitlerism" covers "Naziism, Fascism and Japanism." All of the Russian revisions were accepted and Roosevelt wrote them on the draft in his own hand.

By December 29, Anthony Eden had returned to London from Moscow. His mission had been largely fruitless. The Soviet Government had demanded that Great Britain, and presumably the United States as well, should recognize the frontiers held by the Russians on June 20, 1941, which included possession of the Baltic States and the portion of Poland seized in the first month of the Second World War. In refusing to agree to this recognition, Eden invoked the principles of the Atlantic Charter and the views of President Roosevelt, which had been definitely expressed by Winant to the British Government on the day before Pearl Harbor.

Roosevelt's regrouping of the order in which the signatories to the United Nations Declaration were to be listed.

Eden now cabled Churchill his plea for the inclusion of the Free French in the United Nations Declaration, saying that "They are in every sense an Ally," and pointing out that their forces were now collaborating with the Americans and the British in many places of the highest strategic importance, particularly in New Caledonia. Eden said quite frankly that he did not think that the U.S. Government had the right to veto the participation of the Free French in the proposed Declaration.

Eden also felt strongly that the Dominions should be kept together in the listing and not separated alphabetically from the United Kingdom and from each other. He stated that the Viceroy of India was in favor of India's inclusion and that the War Cabinet regretted that the words "social security" had been dropped out of the Declaration. I do not know why these words were omitted but it must have been at Roosevelt's insistence; probably he did not want to complicate matters by giving Congressional reactionaries the alarming idea that this was a Declaration of a permanent, global New Deal.

In the final listing of signatories, as written by Roosevelt in his own hand, it was U.S., U.K., U.S.S.R., China and then all the others (including those Latin American Republics which had already declared war) in alphabetical order.

When Churchill left for Canada on December 29, he and Roosevelt had agreed on the final language of the Declaration. There were twenty-four other nations involved, which meant that the representatives of all of them were cabling back and forth to their home governments all over the world, detailing every syllable and every suggested change. The last change was made by the President: for the words "Associated Powers" he substituted the name that he had conceived and of which he was very proud—"United Nations." All the governments, of course, had to send formal authorization to their representatives in Washington to sign the document. On December 30, Churchill telegraphed Roosevelt expressing the belief that if they could get the Declaration through on time it would represent "a pretty considerable achievement." It was all of that. Two days later, on New Year's Day, 1942, the representatives of twenty-six countries gathered in the White House and signed the document which gave birth to the United Nations and provided an uplifting message of hope for countless millions in all parts of the world who prayed for a restoration of freedom and the establishment of enduring peace.

It must be remembered that this prelude to a new world symphony was being composed against the reverberations of shocking defeats in the Pacific. The Japanese were sweeping through Malaya and the Philippines; they had made their first parachute landings in the East Indies; they had taken Guam, Wake and Hong Kong; they were advancing on Manila, leaving MacArthur and the last American Filipino force isolated beyond help on the southern tip of Bataan Peninsula and the rock of Corregidor.

It should also be remembered that American prestige was sinking rapidly at this time, particularly in the Far East. The Japanese propagandists were screaming in triumph: "Where is the U.S. Navy?" They were effectively and delightedly making capital of the inability of the arrogant, purse-proud Americans to bring aid to their Allies or even to their own beleaguered forces throughout the Western Pacific.

On December 28, General MacArthur sent an urgent cable to the War Department asking that Washington do something to offset this "crescendo of enemy propaganda" which was being used with "deadly effectiveness" in the Philippines. MacArthur added, with awful truth, "I am not in a position here to combat it." The best that Washington could do at the moment was a proclamation, hastily prepared, by the President to the people of the Philippines, which said in part, "I renew my solemn pledge to you that your freedom will be redeemed and your independence established and protected." Although this pledge could then have little meaning, the Filipino people will not forget that word "protected" if their independent Republic is ever imperiled again.

On December 30, Roosevelt sent the following memorandum to the Secretary of War:

> I wish that War Plans would explore every possible means of relieving the Philippines. I realize great risks are involved but the objective is important.

Unfortunately, that was a problem that could not be solved at the oddly named Arcadia Conference.

There was serious discussion in the White House of the possibility of Japanese attacks on the West Coast of North America by naval bombardment, minelaying in ports (Seattle or San Francisco), "attacks by human torpedoes" (such as those carried out by Italians in Alexandria)—or even carrier-borne air attacks or actual seaborne expeditions of troops. This last seemed improbable, to say the least, but the Japanese were demonstrating a will and a capacity for fantastic maneuvers. Churchill said he could see little likelihood that even the Japanese would attempt an invasion of the continent, but he did think that the West Coast might be "insulted" (that was his word) from time to time. (It was "insulted" once by a submarine a few weeks thereafter.) Roosevelt thought that the danger of carrier-borne bombing was great enough to warrant "dispersal" of aircraft factories on the West Coast, and Beaverbrook made available the British experience in working out this process. Far more serious than any spectacular demonstrations against Seattle, San Francisco or Los Angeles—or even Hollywood—was the possibility of a concerted attack on the Panama Canal. But even this vital point was considered as purely local and incidental. The main problem in the Japanese war was still on the other side of the Pacific. In his State of the Union Message, Roosevelt said:

We cannot wage this war in a defensive spirit. As our power and our resources are fully mobilized, we shall carry the attack against the enemy—we shall hit him and hit him again wherever and whenever we can reach him.

We must keep him far from our shores, for we intend to bring this war to him on his own home grounds.

This was reaffirmation of the tremendous principle stated in the Joint Board Estimate, quoted in an earlier chapter, that our "national policies can be effectuated in their entirety only through military victories outside this Hemisphere."

It had been assumed, when the grand strategy was laid down, that the Japanese could be contained within the line bounded by the Aleutian and Hawaiian Islands, Samoa, Fiji, the Solomon Islands, the East Indies, Singapore, Thailand, and the maritime provinces of Siberia. Now it was becoming evident that they could not be thus contained, that they might sweep southward over the East Indies to Australia and westward through Burma into India and even on to the Middle East.

A new theater of war was accordingly and hastily established, known as the A.B.D.A. Area, the initials standing for American, British, Dutch, Australian. This covered the huge, confused area from the Bay of Bengal to Australasia. It was during the first discussion of this problem, at a meeting of the British and American Chiefs of Staff on the afternoon of Christmas Day, that General Marshall made a proposal which was to assume utmost importance in the conduct of the Second World War. These are his words as directly quoted in the official minutes:

I express these as my personal views and not those as a result of consultation with the Navy or with my own War Plans Division. As a result of what I saw in France and from following our own experience, I feel very strongly that the most important consideration is the question of unity of command. The matters being settled here are mere details which will continuously reoccur unless settled in a broader way. With differences between groups and between services, the· situation is impossible unless we operate on a frank and direct basis. I am convinced that there must be one man in command of the entire theater— air, ground, and ships. We can not manage by cooperation. Human frailties are such that there would be emphatic unwillingness to place portions of troops under another service. If we make a plan for unified command now, it will solve nine-tenths of our troubles.

There are difficulties in arriving at a single command, but they are much less than the hazards that must be faced if we do not achieve this. We never think alike—there are the opinions of those on this side of the table and of the people on the other side; but as for myself, I am willing to go the limit to accomplish this. We must decide on a line of action here and not expect it to be done out there. I favor one man being in control, but operating under a controlled directive from here. We had to come to this in the first World War, but it was

THE WHITE HOUSE
WASHINGTON

You should
work on Churchill
He is being
advised
He is open
minded + needs
discussion.

Note passed by Beaverbrook to Hopkins during White House
meeting to discuss the question of unity of command.

not until 1918 that it was accomplished and much valuable time, blood, and treasure had been needlessly sacrificed. If we could decide on a unified command now, it would be a great advance over what was accomplished during the World War.

There was plenty of disagreement with that proposal. At a major meeting in the White House on December 26 Roosevelt expressed his approval of the Marshall suggestion but Churchill took issue with it. The Prime Minister said that unity of command was all very well when there was a continuous line of battle, such as the line from the Vosges to the Channel in the First World War, but that in the Far East some of the Allied forces were separated from each other by a thousand miles or more. He believed that these various forces, Army, Navy and Air, representing four different countries, should operate on their own with the individual commanders responsible only to the Supreme Command in Washington. At this point in the discussions, Beaverbrook jotted down a note on a White House memo pad and passed it to Hopkins. It read: "You should work on Churchill. He is being advised. He is open-minded and needs discussion." As a result of this, Hopkins arranged for a private meeting between Churchill and Marshall at which the latter was able to convince the Prime Minister of the soundness of his proposal and to gain his agreement to it. This was a demonstration of the peculiar role played by Hopkins at all the major conferences of the next three years. Because of the utter informality of his position as well as of his character he could act in an extraofficial capacity and thus bring about ready settlement of disputes which might have been greatly prolonged or completely stalled if left to the traditional, antiquated machinery of international negotiation. There were many more notes passed to Hopkins under conference tables and many more examples of his effective, off-the-record action. He was rarely confined by the customary "channels."

When the principle of unified command was accepted, Roosevelt suggested that General Sir Archibald Wavell be named for the unenviable post of Supreme Commander of the A.B.D.A. Area. Discussing this suggestion among themselves later, the British Chiefs of Staff were firm in their opposition to the appointment of Wavell or any other Briton to a command which seemed doomed to defeat and even disaster. Suspecting that this was a Roosevelt trick to shift the ugly responsibility, they felt that the British delegation should be unanimous in insisting that an American commander be given the post (and the blame). Lord Halifax agreed with them, but when they expressed their views to Churchill he exploded that this suspicious attitude implied doubt of the motives of the President of the United States and he would not stand for it. So far as he was concerned, Roosevelt's gesture was a friendly and a generous one, imposing high confidence in Wavell. So that settled that discussion, although there was an attempt to effect a compromise by having the naval command kept separate under the American Admiral T. C. Hart. General Marshall, however, insisted that Hart be placed under Wavell's command and Roosevelt instructed Marshall and Hopkins to draft the orders accordingly.

As it turned out, Wavell never had a real chance to exercise this command. The situation had gone to pieces before adequate forces could be assembled let alone deployed.

By December 29, four days after General Marshall had urged the principle of unity of command, Wavell's appointment had been cleared with the Dominion Prime Ministers and he himself had been notified. There remained the problem of what to do about China, for it was obvious that no part of the Chinese Republic could be put under any Anglo-American command. Marshall drafted a memorandum, which was approved informally by the Chiefs of Staff and dispatched to Hopkins for the President's approval. It contained the following recommendation:

> The advisability of a similar command of activities of the Associated Powers in the Chinese Theatre appears evident. This Theatre we suggest should include Northeast Burma and such portion of Thailand and Indo-China as may become accessible to troops of the Associated Powers.

Roosevelt inserted the word "initially" before "include" and he cut out the reference to Northeast Burma. Also, each time that the word "Associated" appeared, he changed it to "United"—for this was the day when the United Nations was given its name.

The announcement that Generalissimo Chiang Kai-shek had accepted Supreme Command of Allied land and air forces in the Chinese Theater was made coincidentally with that of Wavell's appointment. However, Roosevelt and Churchill, who had to think of so much in those and other days, overlooked the sensibilities of the Netherlands Government-in-Exile in London, who were naturally deeply concerned about any arrangements affecting command in the East Indies. Extensive apologies were made for this oversight.

There was no question of doubt that the attention of the American people at this time was directed almost entirely toward the Pacific. When Churchill spoke to the Congress, he was applauded many times but by far the greatest ovation greeted his challenge to the Japanese: "What kind of a people do they think we are? Is it possible they do not realize that we shall never cease to persevere against them until they have been taught a lesson which they and the world will never forget?" And when Roosevelt addressed the Congress, he paid tribute to our British allies and our Russian allies but the loudest and least punctilious applause was reserved for his tribute to the Chinese.

Most important of all, the country's heart was with the few Americans who were then fighting: the gallantry and efficiency of the little garrison at Wake had both stimulated and sobered the people, and now the tragic-heroic story of Bataan and Corregidor and of the hopeless sea fights off Java was beginning to be told. Nevertheless, the participants in the Arcadia Conference stuck to their purpose and devoted most of their planning to the war in Europe.

The agreed strategy involved the closing and the tightening of a ring around the territory under German control. This ring was defined roughly as running on a line from Archangel to the Black Sea, through Anatolia, along the northern seaboard of the Mediterranean and the western seaboard of the European continent. The main object was "to strengthen this ring, and close the gaps in it, by sustaining the Russian Front, by arming and supporting Turkey, by increasing their strength in the Middle East, and by gaining possession of the whole North African Coast, for the prevention of 'German eruptions' toward the Persian Gulf, or the West Coast of Africa, or elsewhere."

The basis for actual planning was provided in these three paragraphs:

15. In 1942 the main methods of wearing down Germany's resistance will be:—

a. Ever-increasing air bombardment by British and American Forces.

b. Assistance to Russia's offensive by all available means.

c. The blockade.

d. The maintenance of the spirit of revolt in the occupied countries, and the organization of subversive movements.

16. It does not seem likely that in 1942 any large scale land offensive against Germany except on the Russian front will be possible. We must, however, be ready to take advantage of any opening that may result from the wearing down process referred to in paragraph 15 to conduct limited land offensives.

17. In 1943 the way may be clear for a return to the Continent, across the Mediterranean, from Turkey into the Balkans, or by landings in Western Europe. Such operations will be the prelude to the final assault on Germany itself, and the scope of the victory program should be such as to provide means by which they can be carried out.

(In the British estimates, the final land offensives would be launched by the Russians from the east, the Americans from the south and the British from the west.)

The two obvious points of access to the European Continent were the United Kingdom, which was presently available, and Northwest Africa, which was not. Roosevelt therefore began to plan movements of American forces to both points as soon as possible. The first troops were en route to Northern Ireland before the conferences in Washington had ended. This expedition, known as MAGNET, was at the start largely a propaganda measure, designed to bolster the morale of the British people and to provide encouraging assurance to the Russians and the people of the German-occupied countries that the Americans were coming in force into the European theater. It also served notice on a few intransigent isolationists at home that Roosevelt was not heeding their demands that the war be fought on a defensive basis and solely against Japan.

The North African operation—first called GYMNAST, then SUPER-GYMNAST and finally TORCH—was planned for launching as early as March, 1942, provided an invitation were extended by the French, or if Hitler were to move into Spain. It was to consist of six divisions, three British and three American (one of them Marines). Roosevelt was always particularly favorable to this operation, which appealed to naval-minded men because it could result in the reopening of the Mediterranean route for shipping to the Middle East and Far East, thereby saving considerable tonnage employed in the long haul around the Cape of Good Hope. American Army men were less interested in it, for it involved no direct attack on German land power or production centers.

The records of the Arcadia Conference are too voluminous to be reproduced here but the minutes of one meeting, held on January 12, give an idea of the scope and complexity of the problems under discussion. Present at this meeting were: the President, the Prime Minister, Lord Beaverbrook, Mr. Harry Hopkins, Admiral Stark, Admiral King, General Marshall, General Arnold, General Watson, Admiral Pound, Field Marshal Dill, Air Chief Marshal Portal, Brigadier Hollis, Colonel Jacob, Colonel Sexton.

Hollis was substituting for General Ismay at this Conference, and Jacob (British) and Sexton (American) were the staff secretaries. I do not know why Secretaries Stimson and Knox who were usually present at the major meetings were absent from this one. The minutes follow:

The President suggested that the status of Super-Gymnast be discussed.

Mr. Churchill stated that he understood that the Staff had produced a time table which was approved in principle; that it looks as if Rommel might get away; that if defeated, his defeat would be preceded by a stern chase; that the British are getting a new armored brigade into the Near East and there will be a battle soon; that information had been received of a convoy arriving at Tripoli with additional German materiel; that the possible date at which the Germans will be pushed back to Tripoli will be delayed, and that more time exists for the completion of Super-Gymnast.

The President stated that politically there is more time available;

that there is a tendency on the part of Vichy to say No to German demands; that reports received indicate that a growing number of French Army officers have been making inquiries as to whether their overtures would be accepted if they did something. That Admiral Darlan had asked if he would be accepted into a conference; that the answer had been, not under present circumstances. That if he brought the French Fleet over to the Allies, the situation would change. However, more time exists for Super-Gymnast; it was desired to get a fairly well settled time table which could be fitted into the time of the negotiations. That as soon as the negotiations commence, the Germans are sure to know that a plan exists; that when the negotiations start, we should have the Army aboard ships ready to land in Casablanca in a week or ten days. [It had been figured that a period of three weeks grace could be obtained from the time the Germans commenced their movement into the Iberian Peninsula.]

The President then asked about transports.

General Marshall stated that both Staffs had engaged in negotiations last night and had reached a tentative agreement which involved a reduction of the schedule of troops to Ireland. Also, a reduction of the cargo ships available for the Magnet Expeditions, which brought up the question of quarters and supplies for troops involved in Magnet.

Mr. Churchill stated that there was no question about the quarters there; that one British Division was being moved out of Northern Ireland and the British will have quarters ready for the American troops.

General Marshall then explained briefly the substance of the plan agreed upon by the Joint Chiefs of Staff, in substance as follows:

21,800 American troops to sail from the East Coast on January 20th, to arrive in the ABDA Area approximately February 14th. This convoy to consist of 10,000 ground troops for New Caledonia, which with the artillery brigade now in Australia, would furnish approximately a division for New Caledonia. The remainder of the expedition would consist of engineers and other ground service troops for the bombers now arriving in the ABDA Area. Also moving out were 20 cargo ships, carrying 250 pursuit, 86 medium bombers, 57 light bombers, 220 ship tons of cargo, and four and one-half million gallons of gasoline. The airplanes involved were to replace those lost by attrition.

General Marshall further stated that in order to permit this expedition to depart, the following changes would have to be made in existing plans:

In the first convoy for Magnet, the 8,000 troops scheduled for Iceland on January 15th would be reduced to 2,500; the 16,000 scheduled for Ireland would be reduced to 4,000. The Queen Mary could carry 7,000 troops to Ireland February 1st; then transport the British troops desired to the Middle East. 9,000 troops would be carried to Ireland on the Andes, Oronzay, and Orion, to sail February 15–20.

Three Navy transports—the West Point, the Wakefield, and the Mount Vernon—now being used to transport troops from the Middle East to the Far East by Suez, would be available for another round trip to move British troops over the same route. In addition, 4,400 more troops could be moved to Ireland on the George Washington, February 24th. Under the plan, approximately 24,000 troops would be in or en route to Ireland by the 25th of February.

The involvements in this plan are as follows:

(1) It would cancel the present movements to Ireland and Iceland, which have already been arranged for.

(2) It would cause some confusion in the Port of New York, due to the necessity of unloading ships.

(3) It would require the utilization of the Kungsholm, which at present is being held for the State Department.

(4) Some difficulty would be incurred in crating the medium bombers scheduled for the ABDA convoy.

(5) It would be necessary to use two vessels now on the South American route, and would involve the loan of three British ships.

The President asked, with reference to the ABDA convoy, about the matter of refueling.

Admiral King stated that refueling would not be necessary en route.

General Marshall then stated that another serious consideration was the fact that the proposed ABDA convoy would result in a 30% reduction of lend-lease to Russia for a period of four months, and would also reduce the lend-lease materiel going to Basra.

The President stated that the plan sounded good.

Mr. Churchill asked what utilization was being made of the Queen Elizabeth and the Aquitania.

General Marshall stated that the Queen Elizabeth and the Aquitania were to be used for a third convoy to the Far East from the West Coast, which would involve the movement of three antiaircraft regiments. It was now understood, however, that the Aquitania would not be available until the end of February. Also, there are being moved from the West Coast, 7,000 troops on January 12th; 14,000 on January 30th; 11,000 early in February. With regard to the ABDA convoy from the East Coast, it would take three to four weeks to assemble the freight boats, and the American troops leaving on January 20th would arrive before their equipment. To split up the convoy would involve complications for the Navy. To delay added to the dangers of the voyage. It was therefore best to send a single troop convoy, even if some units arrived ahead of their materiel.

The President asked about troop accommodations in New Caledonia.

General Marshall stated that owing to the climate, little difficulty was anticipated in finding adequate shelter for the troops; that they could take tents.

Mr. Churchill observed that the plan as prepared would result in some confusion, that a fact to be given consideration was the delay of shipments to Russia; that the Russians would undoubtedly be disappointed.

He asked if the plan had been the subject of joint discussion between the Chiefs of Staff.

General Marshall stated that it had; and that this particular matter had been brought up but there was no use sending troops to the ABDA Area without their equipment. That if a cut becomes necessary, the New Caledonia increment should be eliminated. It is of urgent necessity that the air reinforcements be sent to the ABDA Area immediately.

Admiral Pound stated that the matter had been discussed in the Joint Chiefs of Staff Conference and that the people in London were working on a slightly different shipping schedule, particularly with respect to the use of American transports from the Middle East to the Far East, and the possible use of the Queen Mary from England to the Middle East; that an answer on this could be received by tomorrow noon.

The President asked, if the occupation of New Caledonia was eliminated, could we carry out our Russian promises?

General Marshall stated that he could not be sure, but if anything was to be pared, the New Caledonia portion should be the first reduction.

Mr. Hopkins observed that 30% of the shipping to Russia involves only seven ships, and that we should be able to find seven ships, even if it involved stopping the shipment of some reserve materials to England; that with the 1200 merchant ships we have available, locating seven should not be too difficult.

Admiral King observed that if Archangel is closed now, there is a question as to whether Russia could absorb the shipments.

The President stated that the Russians deny that Archangel is closed, and state that they can absorb the shipments.

Admiral Stark stated that the primary question was which was of the greater importance—the 30% reduction of lend-lease to Russia, or immediate reinforcements for the Far East.

Mr. Churchill observed that the fighting in the Far East and the fighting the Russians are doing should take priority over other things; that Magnet and the Iceland relief are secondary. That he was sorry about reducing Magnet, but he could understand the necessity therefor.

General Marshall observed that an early decision must be reached in order that the January 15th Magnet shipment may be altered.

General Arnold stated that there was no use sending planes to the Far East without their ground service crews.

Admiral Pound observed that the only immediate commitment was the matter of unloading the January 15th convoy for Magnet.

General Marshall stated that if we unload this convoy, we must immediately commence loading for the Australian convoy.

Mr. Churchill again asked whether this matter had been taken up with the British Chiefs of Staff.

General Marshall replied that the matter had been discussed jointly.

The President stated that he liked General Marshall's program, if only some means could be found to take care of the Russians.

Mr. Hopkins suggested that Admiral Land be directed to find 6 or 7 more ships a month for Russia; that he did not think General Marshall should be held up by the necessity for Russian lend-lease.

Lord Beaverbrook stated that he would be very sorry to see ships diverted from the Atlantic because of the increased strain on shipping which would result; also that it was important that certain items be continued to England in order to keep up production schedules, and he hated very much to stop shipments to Russia.

The President agreed that there might be unfortunate repercussions in Russia if at the very time they are pinched as at present we let them down. He then asked how important is the occupation of New Caledonia.

Admiral King replied that this is on the line of Naval communication and is a potential object for Japanese occupation.

The President asked if it would be easy to reconquer.

Admiral King replied that none will be easy to reconquer once they are occupied.

General Arnold stated that as far as flying routes are concerned, both New Caledonia and the Fiji Islands can be jumped if necessary.

Admiral King observed that the urgent question was assistance to the Far East.

Mr. Churchill agreed that it should come ahead of New Caledonia.

The President observed that the only thing holding up General Marshall's plan is the seven cargo ships.

Mr. Hopkins asked if Russia were not involved, would General Marshall's plan be approved?

It was agreed that it would be.

Mr. Hopkins then suggested that the President and the Prime Minister take the responsibility of getting lend-lease material to Russia, and not hold up General Marshall's plan on this account.

Mr. Churchill suggested that the present ships on the Russian run continue, and that we find other ships to make up the deficit. He then asked if the Chiefs of Staff agreed on the mechanics of the plan.

Admiral Pound stated that it must be approved in London, because they had been working on a slightly different arrangement.

The President asked Mr. Hopkins if he could get enough ships to take care of the Russians.

Mr. Hopkins stated that if the President would get Admiral Land and Sir Arthur Salter in and tell them the situation, he was sure it could be done.

General Marshall said that Admiral Land had told him earlier in the day that under our present protocol agreement with Russia, we were behind in furnishing material.

Mr. Churchill suggested that the plan be accepted and a search made for the seven ships, and asked if the British were behind in their deliveries to the Russians.

Lord Beaverbrook stated that the British are behind in some items, but that he anticipated they would catch up.

General Marshall added that what we are doing in the Far East would help the Russians anyway.

Mr. Churchill observed that there was a possibility, if Japan continued to succeed in the Far East, of a Pan-Asiatic movement all over the Far East, including all the brown and yellow race, which might complicate seriously our situation there; that a symbolic landing in Ireland would be satisfactory except that he hoped material for England would not be piled up on the docks in New York awaiting ships.

Lord Beaverbrook observed that additional shipping had been scraped up for convoy movements to the ABDA Area; and that more could be found if another search were made.

Mr. Churchill stated that the ABDA plan makes no provision for Super-Gymnast.

General Marshall stated that no ships arranged for combat loading are being used for the ABDA convoy.

The President asked, assuming that we go through with the ABDA plan, and enough shipping for Russia could be found, when would Super-Gymnast be possible?

Mr. Churchill stated that the Joint Staffs had already established that some days would be required for planning; and if January 7th was established as the beginning of planning, D-Day (the day loading would commence) would be February 4th; and the earliest arrival in Casablanca would be March 3rd.

General Marshall stated that the shortage was not in troop carriers, but in cargo carriers.

Mr. Churchill stated that the Staffs should get data as to the effect of this plan on Gymnast.

Admiral King stated that, for purposes of a round calculation, the date on which the ships could be available for Gymnast would be determined by the turn around between the East Coast and Australia, which would amount to approximately three months, which would set back the possible date of loading for Gymnast to about April 15th. Also Admiral King stated that 15,000 troops, combat loaded, can be embarked for Gymnast without delay at any time.

Mr. Churchill then observed that the whole problem is to get planes to the Far East.

General Arnold stated that this is the only way we can stop the Japanese advance to the south.

The President then stated, we approve General Marshall's plan. We will make Beaverbrook and Hopkins find ships and will work on Super-Gymnast at the earliest possible date.

Air Marshal Portal pointed out that one point of the agreement which the Chiefs of Staff had come to was that the ABDA movement would not interfere with the movement of pursuit ships to the Far East.

Mr. Churchill then stated that the Staff is to check up on the actual impact of the plan on Gymnast and establish the earliest date on which it would be possible; and also what would be available for the expedition if an invitation arrived suddenly.

Like all official minutes, the foregoing gives little suggestion of the quality of the dialogue. There may have been no heated exchanges at this particular session and no picturesque invective or thunderous oaths, but if there had been the recording secretaries would carefully have toned them down to a polite "exchange of views." Even so, one can hardly read these cold, dry minutes without sensing the Homeric awfulness of the responsibility imposed upon the few who were compelled to decide so much. These men represented the highest authority in nations which command gigantic resources; but, at this time, only fragments of the total of resources had been realized, and even when they were amply available there remained the incessant problem of where, when and how they should be applied. The seven ships that Hopkins argued should be kept on the supply routes to Russia seem like a negligible quantity in a war of such dimensions; yet, when this meeting was held, for all anyone could tell those seven ships and their cargoes might mean the difference to the Soviet Union between continuing the war or making a separate peace.

In the momentous determinations of strategy and priorities—where this ship or that division could best be employed—it was not a matter of dispute between Allies. The British did not invariably line up on one side and the Americans on the other. There could be conflict between the interests of an American commander in the Canal Zone, or in Africa, and another American in Alaska, or in China. There could be far more violent conflict between the three services in any one theater of war. For example: when it came to allotting the limited supply of Oerlikon antiaircraft guns, the British Navy and the U.S. Navy would stand together as stanch allies in favor of using these on ships—in joint opposition to demands that the guns be used for mobile batteries, or for the defense of London, Moscow, Rangoon, or various air bases, or even demands from Congressmen (this is not a joke) that they be used for the defense of Capitol Hill.

Such matters could be settled, quickly if not always correctly, when the President and Prime Minister and all the Chiefs of Staff were gathered conveniently together under the same roof. It was obvious, however, that the Arcadia Conference could not continue in session until V-E and V-J days. A means must be found to continue the application of this top authority on a day-to-day basis.

On December 28, during the hard-pressed discussions of the High Command in the A.B.D.A. Area, Churchill prepared a cable to the Lord Privy Seal reporting the decisions arrived at. He gave the draft of this cable to Hopkins, who subsequently noted, "I showed it to the President, who agreed there were certain things in it that shouldn't be there. General Marshall and Admiral King and I stepped in the next room and made the eliminations noted here. The Prime Minister's final draft represents these additions and deletions." (These changes were mostly to make sure that the American Admiral Hart should, as previously noted, be subject to General Wavell's command rather than independent.)

The cable as finally approved and transmitted to London said the intention was that Wavell should have a staff divided between British and Americans in about the same proportion as that of Foch's High Control in 1918. Wavell would receive his orders from "an appropriate joint body," which would be responsible to the President as Commander in Chief and to the Prime Minister as Minister of Defense. The Lord Privy Seal replied that the War Cabinet approved this proposal since the Prime Minister considered it "a war-winner," but the Cabinet was anxious to know just what would be the composition of the "appropriate joint body."

On December 29, the Chiefs of Staff drew up an outline of the system of command. This was sent to the White House in the evening and Roosevelt and Hopkins worked over it. The Chiefs of Staff had recommended as follows:

> It is suggested that no special body should be set up for this purpose because it would tend to clog the machine for the following reasons:
> (a) It would be necessary to have Dutch, Australian and New Zealand representatives on this body.
> (b) Each representative in (a) would probably wish for time to consult his Government before giving an opinion.
> It is proposed, therefore, that existing machinery should be used in the following manner:
> (a) The Supreme Commander would telegraph to the Chiefs of Staff Committee, both in London and in Washington, his proposal, whatever it might be.
> (b) The Chiefs of Staff Committee in London would immediately telegraph to the British Mission in Washington to say whether or not they would be telegraphing any opinions. . . .

Roosevelt's revision of this was drastic. Here are the same passages as he rendered them:

> It is suggested that a special body be set up for this purpose in Washington.
> (a) 3 Americans, 3 British
> (b) And 1 Australian, 1 New Zealander and 1 Dutch for consultation and advisory purposes.
> It is proposed, therefore, that above machinery should be used in the following manner:
> (a) The Supreme Commander would telegraph to the above Committee, in Washington, his proposal, whatever it might be.

Proposed method of handling matters concerning

the Southwest Pacific Theatre.

        It is assumed that the chief matters on which decisions
would have to be given would be:

(a) The provision of reinforcements.

(b) A major change in policy.

(c) Departure from the Supreme Commander's directive.

2.   It is suggested that ~~ae~~ a special body ~~should~~ be set up
for this purpose, *in Washington* ~~because it would tend to clog the machine~~
~~for the following reasons:~~

(a) ~~It would be necessary to have Dutch, Australian~~ *3 Americans 3 British*
~~and New Zealand representatives on this body.~~

(b) *And 1 Australian 1 New Zealander & 1 Dutch*
~~Each representative in (a) would probably wish to~~
~~time to consult his Government before giving an~~ *for consultation & advisory purposes*
~~opinion.~~

3.   It is proposed, therefore, that *above* ~~existing~~ machinery
should be used in the following manner:

(a) The Supreme Commander would telegraph to the ~~Chiefs of~~ *above*
~~Staff~~ Committee, ~~both in London and~~ in Washington,
his proposal, whatever it might be. *Washington*

(b) The ~~Chiefs of Staff~~ Committee in ~~London~~ would
immediately telegraph to ~~the British Mission in~~ *London to ask for any*
recommendations or opinions ~~Washington to say whether or not they would be~~
~~telegraphing any opinions.~~

(c) On receipt of these opinions, the ~~U.S. Chiefs of~~ *Committee*
~~Staff and the Representatives in~~ Washington ~~of the~~
~~British Chiefs of Staff~~ would ~~meet and consider the~~
~~problem and would~~ submit their recommendations to
the President and by telegraph to the Prime Minister
~~and Minister of Defence.~~ The Prime Minister would
then inform the President whether he was in agreement
with their recommendations. *He could of course*
consult with Australia New Zealand
and Netherland if advisable.

(b) The Committee in Washington would immediately telegraph to London to ask for any recommendations or opinions. . . .

The following day, December 30, Hopkins noted:

The suggestion of an "appropriate joint body" has kicked up a hell of a row.

As a matter of fact I suggested the words to the Prime Minister when I found he was getting all set to issue all the directions himself. It seemed to me so essential to get the unity of command through in the South West Pacific that rather than try to define what the "appropriate body" would be, I urged both the Prime Minister and the President to send it along and decide the make-up of the "appropriate joint body" later.

It now develops that everybody and his grandmother wants to be on the joint body and it now looks as if it would end by having the joint British and American staffs assist the President. At any rate they will run it.

The "appropriate joint body" was the organization which became known as the Combined Chiefs of Staff and the reference to "everybody and his grandmother" reflected the desire of other Allied nations to be represented on it—and not merely "for consultation and advisory purposes." As has been seen, the nucleus of the Combined Chiefs had been provided at the Staff talks in Washington a year before, but until the Arcadia Conference there was a general assumption that the permanent body when established would function as a sort of joint secretariat to pool records and intelligence and serve as liaison between the British Chiefs in London and their American opposite numbers. However, the traditional concept of liaison in Marshall's opinion—and in Roosevelt's —was simply not good enough to meet the new circumstances. The Navy's Kimmel and the Army's Short had maintained formal "liaison" within signaling distance of each other on Oahu, and the Japanese attackers had come and gone before the antiquated machinery could function. If the principle of unity of command was valid for each theater, it was all the more valid for the top command of the entire American-British effort. It was inconceivable that any one man could undertake such a job, and it was questionable whether any board, representing both nations and all the services, could ever come to agreement on major decisions. But there was little disagreement that the experiment should be tried—although, when it came to naming the location of supreme headquarters, it was obviously difficult for the British to accept the American contention that because the United States would contribute the bulk of the manpower and matériel, and because it was placed geographically between the two wars, Washington should be the seat of the Combined Chiefs of Staff. However, they did accept, and Field Marshal Sir John Dill was named ranking British officer on the new supreme body. There was some difficulty about this appointment at first, as Dill was designated personal representative of the Prime Minister. Marshall protested that this would give Dill a special, detached and therefore anomalous position, exercising political as well as military authority. Churchill agreed that this was a sound objection and the matter was quickly straightened out by cable after Churchill's return to London. Dill's American colleagues, Marshall, Arnold, and King, are the best witnesses to the extraordinary quality of his performance of high duty; long ill, he died in service in 1944 and his grave in Arlington National Cemetery is a memorial to an incalculably successful collaboration.

When the Combined Chiefs of Staff had been agreed on, it was logical to proceed to the establishment of combined boards for all war activities: Munitions Assignment, Shipping Adjustment, Raw Materials, Food, Production and Resources.

The first of these was by all odds the most important and controlled to a large extent the determinations of the others. Furthermore, it was obviously as vital to the carrying out of grand strategy as the deployment of men, ships and aircraft. I believe it can be said that the formation of the Munitions Assignment Board provoked more heated argument than any other topic considered at the Arcadia Conference; the only individual upon whom all elements could agree as bearer of final responsible authority was Harry Hopkins.

It was first intended that the Board would handle all problems of production and supply as well as ultimate allocation. On December 27, Beaverbrook wrote to the President:

It is my hope that you will permit Mr. Hopkins to take charge of a committee of production with full powers and entire authority.

Such a committee would not only dispose of the production requirements but would also be responsible for mobilising and distributing the necessary raw materials.

Beaverbrook sent a copy of this letter to Churchill, adding:

I support a Supreme Command in supplies as well as in strategy. Mr. Harry Hopkins is the proper authority and he should be asked to co-ordinate the production of the United States, Great Britain, and Canada, including raw materials.

However, Roosevelt was not likely to agree with this proposal; having refused for two years, and in the face of endless criticism, to name a supreme boss of American production, he would have provoked roars of protest from the Congress and the press had he appointed Hopkins czar of the entire Allied effort. One can readily imagine the charges that would have been made about putting the war on a "leaf-raking" basis. Furthermore, the War Department and Navy Department were actively hostile to civilian control of production of "end weapons";

actually, no Combined Production Board was formed until five months later, and even when set into operation it was unable to function successfully.

The arguments over Munitions Assignment had political roots, for it was obvious that decisions affecting the distribution of supplies as between one Ally and another, or one neutral and another, might assume considerable diplomatic significance. This was one of the few subjects on which a division appeared on nationalistic lines as between British and Americans, and it was never completely closed. For a time it seemed as if no agreement could be reached and the final resolution reached by Roosevelt was accepted by the British only on a temporary, trial basis.

General G. N. Macready, Assistant Chief of the British Imperial General Staff, had proposed a system of suballocation whereby the world would be divided in effect into two spheres of influence, with the U.S. and Britain "each caring for the needs of the Allies for whom it has accepted responsibility." The word "protégés" was used to describe these Allies, the U.S. protégés to include Latin American countries and China, and the British protégés to include France and other countries of continental Europe, and Turkey and the Arab states as well as all the British Dominions and colonies. I am not entirely clear as to the position of Russia in this proposed arrangement, but I believe it was to be treated as a separate problem jointly by the U.S. and Britain.

This proposal of General Macready's for a division of protégés, which was strongly backed by the British Chiefs of Staff, was not well received by the Americans, including Hopkins. It would mean that all allocation of American-produced matériel for Europe, Africa and the Middle East would be directed from London. When it was presented at the Combined Chiefs meeting on the next to last day of the Conference, the Americans struck it out; they stated that this was a matter for decision on the highest level.

Shortly before the final formal session of the Arcadia Conference in the White House at 5:30 P.M. on January 14, the President read to General Marshall the statement which he and presumably Churchill and Beaverbrook had prepared concerning the make-up of the Munitions Assignment Board. The Board was to be divided into two coequal parts, one in Washington, headed by Hopkins, and the other in London, headed by Beaverbrook. Hopkins and Beaverbrook were to report directly to the President and Prime Minister and thus be on a level with and independent of the Combined Chiefs of Staff. Roosevelt invited Marshall's comments on this—and he got them. Marshall made his position abundantly clear. He insisted that the Munitions Assignment Board must be under the authority of the Combined Chiefs of Staff. He "saw no objection whatever to having parallel Allocation Committees in Washington and London dealing with the allocation of American and British war matériel respectively," but "there could be no question of having any duplication of the Combined Chiefs of Staff organization in Washington and in London." (Which meant that the London "Allocation Committee" would be no more than a subordinate branch office, and this proved to be the case.)

Marshall felt so strongly on this subject that he informed the President that unless the conditions as he stated them were accepted he could not continue to assume the responsibilities of Chief of Staff. He advanced the unanswerable argument that neither he nor any other Chief of Staff could plan military operations and carry them through if some other authority, over which he had no control, could refuse to allocate the matériel required for such operations. When Marshall completed the brief but vigorous and clear statement of his views, Roosevelt turned to Hopkins and asked for his opinion. Marshall assumed that Hopkins had participated in the arrangement as Roosevelt had stated it and would therefore oppose him, but, to his surprise, Hopkins supported him vociferously, even stating that if the organization were not established as Marshall said it should be, he could not assume any responsibility for or in it, either. At this point Churchill, Beaverbrook, Stimson, Knox and the staffs arrived for the meeting, in the course of which Marshall again stated his positive opinions and Hopkins again supported them with vehemence. The formal records of this session give little indication of the tension and even embarrassment that prevailed; the historian must read a great deal between the lines to appreciate the fact that herein was the serving of notice on such proud men as Churchill and Beaverbrook that Roosevelt was the boss and Washington the headquarters of the joint war effort. Hopkins became the head of the Munitions Assignment Board, but he himself at this meeting described the M.A.B. as a "sub-committee" of the Combined Chiefs of Staff who, if they "do not like the sub-committee's recommendations, can alter them or throw them out." Both Churchill and Beaverbrook argued the point, but Roosevelt made it clear that he supported Marshall and Hopkins. The British then made their suggestion that "the system be set up and tried for one month." Roosevelt said, "We shall call it a preliminary agreement and try it out that way." It was accordingly tried out that way and continued that way throughout the war. All those involved in the Munitions Assignment Board seem to agree that whenever Hopkins was well enough to give it his personal attention it worked harmoniously; when he was too ill as he often was or too preoccupied with other matters to preside over its deliberations there was apt to be strife aplenty among the diverse, competitive factions involved. However, the fact remains that it worked: it handled the tremendous and bewildering job of allocating the supply of matériel to all of the services, all of the Allies, all of the various theaters of war. Needless to say, there was plenty of complaint from commanders in the field, particularly those operating in the Far East, who believed that they were being discriminated against and compelled to operate on a shoestring, but this complaint was directed against the essential grand strategy which gave priority to the conquest of Germany rather than to the manner in which this strategy was carried out by the Munitions Assignment Board.

The Roosevelt-Churchill memorandum creating the M.A.B. provided for the pooling of all munitions and for the fullest exchange of information. The Board was to confer with the Soviet Union, China and other United Nations whenever necessary. The memorandum stated that differences which could not be settled by the Board itself were to be resolved by the President and Prime Minister, both of whom, however, expressed confidence that such differences would be rare. Because this memorandum was insufficiently specific, the issue created by the Macready proposal of "suballocations" to "Allied protégés" persisted and created difficulties, especially when it came to furnishing Lend-Lease supplies to Turkey and to the French forces in North and West Africa. Each time the British contended that, since the benefiting nation was within their orbit, the allocations should be made by them, and each time the Americans went ahead on the assumption that no "orbits" existed. The disputes which resulted produced minor irritations but no serious discord. Hopkins usually moved in on these and his decision was accepted as final.

The production goals determined upon during the Arcadia Conference and announced in part by Roosevelt in his Message to Congress were so astronomic that they were greeted with derision and, in some cases, despair by military and civilian authorities alike. Some officers in the War Department were passing the remark, "The President has gone in for the 'numbers racket'!" Others could see nothing humorous in these impossible figures; believing that the goals could not possibly be realized, they foresaw grave criticism and probable injury to public morale when the failures became evident. Hopkins was freely blamed for deluding Roosevelt into propagating this dangerous fantasy. It was assumed that Hopkins, a notoriously free spender, had been misled by alien influences, particularly Beaverbrook, and by the reckless New Dealers, such as Leon Henderson and Robert Nathan. However, as Hopkins had once told Quentin Reynolds, he was no Svengali, and Roosevelt was in no trance when he proclaimed the Victory Program of production. It was in Roosevelt's nature to believe that the surest way to capture the imagination of the American people was to give them the greatest possible challenge. The total cost in money bothered him not at all; he always believed that it was far better to squander the taxpayers' dollars than to squander the taxpayers. As a matter of fact— and I can state it as such because I was one of those present when it happened—Roosevelt himself arbitrarily revised some of the figures upward on the eve of his speech to Congress. When Hopkins questioned him on this, Roosevelt said, "Oh—the production people can do it if they really try." He did the same thing years later en route to Chicago where he proclaimed a national, postwar goal of sixty million jobs. He was never afraid of big, round numbers.

Two sets of figures tell the story of the raising of the sights. The first set represents the estimates for 1942 arrived at after months of conferences by Stacy May in London, and by Harriman and Beaverbrook in Washington, London and Moscow, and by innumerable others:

Pre-Pearl Harbor Estimates for 1942

Operational Aircraft	28,600
Tanks	20,400
Anti-aircraft guns	6,300
Merchant ships (deadweight tons)	6,000,000
Anti-tank guns	7,000
Ground and tank machine guns	168,000
Airplane bombs (long tons)	84,000

Post-Pearl Harbor Directive (January 6, 1942)

	for 1942	for 1943
Operational Aircraft	45,000	100,000
Tanks	45,000	75,000
Anti-aircraft guns	20,000	35,000
Merchant ships (deadweight tons)	8,000,000	10,000,000
Anti-tank guns	14,900	(expansion not fixed)
Ground and tank machine guns	500,000	(expansion not fixed)
Airplane bombs (long tons)	720,000	(expansion not fixed)

When Churchill saw those final figures, he transmitted them to London in an exultant cable. He informed the War Cabinet that Beaverbrook had been "magnificent" and Hopkins a "godsend."

When Roosevelt announced a part of the Victory Program to Congress, he said, "These figures and similar figures for a multitude of other implements of war will give the Japanese and Nazis a little idea of just what they accomplished in the attack on Pearl Harbor." The Congress cheered that vociferously and proceeded to appropriate the necessary funds with few of the quivers that assailed those who were responsible for carrying out the incredible program. The two years set for its completion had not quite passed before Joseph Stalin raised his glass at Teheran and proposed a toast to American production "without which this war would have been lost."

At the conclusion of the Arcadia Conference, Roosevelt announced the formation of the War Production Board and the appointment of Donald Nelson as its chairman. This has been described at length in the official publication, "Industrial Mobilization For War," and by Nelson himself and James F. Byrnes. Here is Hopkins' story of it, written January 14, 1942:

For the past three months the President has been considering the appointment of a single person to direct war production but he never could find the right person. He discussed every conceivable possibility and played seriously with the idea of getting Bill Douglas off the Supreme Court and, in fact, talked to Douglas about it but Douglas never had much enthusiasm for it.

As recently as last week-end, which we spent in Hyde Park, the President talked of getting a three-man committee made up of Willkie, Douglas and Nelson to explore the matter for him and advise him about it. I urged very strongly that this not be done, primarily because neither Willkie nor Douglas knew anything about production and because Willkie was apt to use it as a political football.

He came back to the idea again later and I told him for the second time that I thought he was making a great mistake. I told him that if he were going to move in this manner, my suggestion was to appoint Don Nelson, who was the best of the lot.

He was sympathetic with the President, had had a good record under severe conditions; that furthermore he belonged to the school that wanted to increase production and believed that it could be done; that he was easy to get on with and that the President liked him. I told the President that the most important asset, apart from the man's ability, was that he had the President's confidence.

Upon our return to Washington, the President told me that he thought Nelson was the man. I then urged him to make the appointment at once because it would surely spread all over town and all the people who wanted the job would be bombarding him with reasons why Nelson should not be appointed.

On Tuesday morning (January 13), when I saw the President in his bedroom, I urged him to appoint Nelson that day. He told me to get Harold Smith and Jimmie Byrnes together and plan an announcement. They came to my room at the White House and we worked out a statement which the President later released.

It was necessary to ask Wallace to resign as Chairman of S.P.A.B. because the President had made up his mind to change the name of S.P.A.B. to the War Production Board and, hence, Wallace had to be seen prior to the announcement. The President decided to talk to none of the other interested parties.

At 5:30 that afternoon (January 13) he asked Wallace and Nelson to come to his office and wanted me present. He then reviewed the whole production business, including the short-comings and assets of Knudsen, and the fact that after examining carefully all the potential candidates he had made up his mind on this.

He then told Wallace that in order to give Nelson the kind of authority he must have, Nelson would have to be Chairman of the Board and the Chairman would have to have all the power. I had a few hours earlier seen Nelson to prepare him for the meeting. To the best of my knowledge the only people who knew the President was going to appoint Nelson were Justice Byrnes, Harold Smith and myself.

The amusing part of the whole business was that everybody was a candidate. Wallace, I am sure, hoped the President would ask him. Bernie Baruch was in a hotel room in Washington spreading propaganda for himself. A great many of my friends were pushing Bill Douglas, Morgenthau wanted it worse than anything in the world. So did Jesse Jones and, of course, Knudsen.

The hullabaloo in the press was in reality an attack on the President. The President's enemies wanted him to really give up being President and let somebody else exercise the power to which the people had elected him.

The truth of the matter is that production has gone pretty well, except in the conversion of plants and there the Government bumped head on into the selfish interests of big business, who refused to turn their hand unless they were forced to. The Army and Navy have been short-sighted and Congress has never seen the need of all-out production.

As far as I know the President is the only person in the whole crowd who, being sure we were going to get into the war sooner or later, was pushing the country, industry, the Army and the Navy harder and harder for all-out production.

As soon as Nelson and Wallace had left, the President told Steve Early to release the announcement, which appeared in the next morning's paper, (this morning, January 14).

Two days later, Hopkins added this:

In my conversation with Don Nelson immediately prior to his appointment (January 13) and, indeed, over a period of weeks when it became clear that Knudsen was not the man to run production during the war . . . it had occurred to me that the way to handle Knudsen, who had great standing with the American people and, indeed, great abilities, was to put him in the Army.

I suggested this once or twice to the President but at that time he was not disposed to make the change. The evening of Nelson's appointment I had dinner with the President and told him that I thought it would be very difficult for Knudsen to work directly under Nelson and that the simplest and best way out of the dilemma was to put Knudsen in charge of production in the Army and let him have nothing to do with procurement but to be an expediter in the great factories which had contracts with the War Department. Nelson had previously agreed to this.

I learned on the night of Nelson's appointment that Knudsen had taken it very badly, his feelings were hurt and he had told Jesse Jones he was going home. I urged Jones to do everything he could to induce Knudsen not to do this, for his own sake as well as for the President's. Nelson apparently saw Knudsen too that evening and I learned the next day that Knudsen had pretty much changed his mind and had indicated he was ready to do anything the President wanted him to do.

At the same time it was clear the President had asked him to come down here and only the President could ask him to make a change. It seemed necessary that the Knudsen matter be settled at once.

I called Robert Patterson, the Under Secretary of War, and asked him what he thought of putting Knudsen in the Army and he said he thought extremely well of it. I asked him to clear it with Stimson and Marshall, which he promptly did.

On Thursday, January 15th, I urged the President to handle the Knudsen matter promptly because I learned that Knudsen was expecting a call from the President and everybody in town was wondering what was going to happen to him. The President agreed to see Knudsen on Friday and later arranged that Knudsen have lunch with him. The President asked me to join them at luncheon. I had been planning to go into the hospital that morning but I postponed it until after luncheon.

I felt the President was not in his best form in dealing with Knudsen, although he was very kind and generous in his comments to Knudsen.

Knudsen was anxious to show the President what a good job he has done and gave him a lot of statistics showing the increase of production in a great many munitions of war between the time he came and the time he left.

It had been arranged that the President would offer him a job either as an officer or as a civilian. Knudsen had apparently been thinking about it because I told Jesse Jones what was in the wind and he had explored it with Knudsen. Knudsen said he thought he could work more effectively as an officer. There was a good deal of banter about Knudsen in a uniform but the luncheon ended with Knudsen saying he would do anything that the President wanted and accepting the appointment as Lieutenant General in the Army, in charge of production, to work under Patterson.

Churchill left for home on January 14 to face more criticism in the House of Commons than he had met at any previous time in the war. Serious defeats were multiplying not only in the Far East but also in the Libyan Desert where Rommel was now ready to push the British back for the second time over the line of advances made first by Wavell and then by General Sir Claude Auchinleck.

Hopkins wrote:

The last evening of Churchill's visit the President, Churchill and I had dinner together.

During dinner we wound up the last details of the agreements relative to shipping, raw materials and the allocation board. It was agreed that the text of these would not be given out but at the appropriate time the President would release a general statement governing all of them. The President and Churchill initialed the several documents.

The President and Churchill reviewed together the work of the past three weeks and Churchill expressed not only his warm appreciation of the way he and his associates had been treated but his confidence that great steps had been taken towards unification of the prosecution of the war.

Churchill had not decided even then whether to fly from Bermuda or to go in a battleship. The President did not know until later that Churchill had actually flown to England.

They were supposed to leave at 8:45 but it was a quarter of ten before we got up from dinner and the President and I drove with Churchill to his train to Norfolk, Virginia. A special train had been put on the siding at Sixth Street.

The President said goodbye to Churchill in the car and I walked with him and put him on the train and said goodbye to him, Pound and Portal.

On the way back, the President made it perfectly clear that he too was very pleased with the meetings. There was no question but that he grew genuinely to like Churchill and I am sure Churchill equally liked the President.

Hopkins sent with the Prime Minister's party some presents for his friend "Clemmie" (Mrs. Churchill) and a note in which he said:

You would have been quite proud of your husband on this trip. First because he was ever so good natured. I didn't see him take anybody's head off and he eats and drinks with his customary vigor, and still dislikes the same people. If he had half as good a time here as the President did having him about the White House he surely will carry pleasant memories of the past three weeks.

After which Hopkins went back to the Navy Hospital, understandably exhausted.

CHAPTER XXI

The Vichy Policy

THERE was another episode of the Arcadia Conference which must be treated separately because it could hardly be considered among the Conference's memorable achievements. Cordell Hull described it as "one of those footnotes of history that had dangerous possibilities of becoming whole chapters"; it did in fact become a chapter in Hull's memoirs, and it again becomes one herewith. The extraordinary resentment that it caused remained to affect other and far more important developments during the war years.

On December 24, while the President and Prime Minister were lighting the Christmas tree on the White House lawn, Admiral Emile Muselier led Free French naval forces (corvettes, escort craft, which had been aiding the Canadian Navy on the convoy routes) to the seizure of St. Pierre and Miquelon, two small fishing islands off Newfoundland. These were French possessions and under the command of Admiral Georges Robert, the Vichy Governor at Martinique some two thousand miles away. Unlike Martinique, these islands had little strategic importance but they had been objects of great interest to the U.S., Canadian and British Governments because there was on St. Pierre a powerful radio transmitter which might broadcast weather reports and other intelligence to German submarine and surface raiders. Therefore, it was obviously desirable that the islands be put under Allied control. A few weeks before Pearl Harbor, the Canadian Government suggested that it take the initiative in this matter and London and Washington agreed. However, this suggestion angered the redoubtable and incorrigible Free French leader, General Charles de Gaulle, who felt that such an action would be an insult to French sovereignty unless it were taken by French forces under his command. He accordingly sent Muselier to Canada to study the situation.

On December 16 the British Foreign Office cabled Washington saying they were "informing the Free French headquarters that we see no objection to undertaking this operation" but they had asked de Gaulle to postpone the issuance of orders for thirty-six hours to allow time to consult the view of the U.S. Government. Roosevelt was not favorable to the proposed action, for the United States Government had just concluded an agreement with Admiral Robert in Martinique involving maintenance of the status quo in French possessions in the Western Hemisphere.

On December 17 the Foreign Office cabled that the President's view had been communicated to de Gaulle "who agreed that the proposed action should *not* (repeat not) now be undertaken."

On December 19 the Foreign Office cabled that it was the opinion of the British Chiefs of Staff that nothing short of the occupation of the islands "would be satisfactory from the military point of view. This course, however, now seems to be ruled out by the American attitude."

There were continued discussions between the three governments up to December 22, the day of Churchill's arrival in Washington, when the Canadians indicated they did not want to go ahead with a State Department suggestion that they send representatives to St. Pierre in an attempt to gain control of the radio transmitter by persuading the Vichy Administrator there to be reasonable. At the same time, the Canadian Government gave assurance that any action by Free French forces had been called off. Presumably, the islands were to be discussed at the Arcadia Conference, during which the Canadian Prime Minister, Mackenzie King, was to meet with Roosevelt and Churchill. Nobody could foresee what a large and troublesome topic of conversation they were to provide.

For it turned out that on December 18, just one day after he had given the assurance previously noted, de Gaulle sent the following order to Muselier:

We know for certain that the Canadians intend to [destroy] radio station at St. Pierre. Therefore, I order you to carry out rallying of Miquelon Islands with means at your disposal and *without saying anything to the foreigners.* I assume complete responsibility for this operation, which has become indispensable in order to keep for France her possessions.

(The italics in the foregoing are mine.)

De Gaulle's action in this matter was plainly outrageous and inexcusable, even though it was in conformance with Allied military policy, and sound policy at that. It was an act calculated—and, it would seem, deliberately calculated—to cause acute embarrassment to three of France's

greatest and most powerful friends and Allies—Britain, Canada and the
U.S. It was a demonstration of the arrogance and recalcitrance as well as
the courage and fierce devotion to the cause of French sovereignty which
made him the strange character that he was. In the words of Admiral
Muselier, who was compelled to carry it out, "General de Gaulle's order
was that of a dictator." It was not "democratic enough to fit his [Muse-
lier's] ideal of France." (Muselier, whose conduct of the whole operation appears to have been blameless, was later disowned and even placed
under arrest by de Gaulle.)

The story broke in the morning papers on Christmas Day, the *New
York Times* carrying an eyewitness account by Ira Wolfert, a distinguished American war correspondent who was later to cover the landings at Guadalcanal and Normandy. He described the warm reception
accorded to the Free French forces, saying, "A little less than half an
hour after the first sailor had jumped ashore the islands had been secured
in the military sense. Not a shot was fired; the Admiral's Chief of Staff
was able to report with immense pride that not a drop of blood had been
shed." Muselier immediately announced that a plebiscite would be held
the following day. Wolfert, who watched the casting of every ballot,
wrote of this election:

> In the first free expression of opinion permitted Frenchmen who
> have been governed since the summer of 1940 by "we Henri Philippe
> Pétain," Chief of State of the Vichy regime, the male population of
> this island today voted better than 98 per cent for the policy of Free
> France, ally of the United States and Britain. So an extraordinary
> parable of the modern world at war comes on this obscure island on
> Christmas Day to the kind of climax for which the democratic world
> has been praying. A dictatorship that had been throttling the people
> was set aside temporarily by armed forces Wednesday until the people
> could speak and decide their fate. The people decided to do without
> the dictatorship.

The American people hailed this news joyfully. They had been absorbing terrible news for the past eighteen days and they were delighted to
cheer any evidence that anyone on the Allied side had actually done
something that was bold, adventurous and successful. The great majority of Americans had no idea who or what General de Gaulle was nor
had they been acutely aware of the existence of islands named St. Pierre
and Miquelon; all that mattered was that some French sailors and marines who had been fighting in the Allied navies had gone off on their
own to seize territory which belonged to their own country and had
thereby snatched from Hitler's grasp a radio station which might have
been used to help the Germans to kill Americans. As the *New York
Times* said in an editorial, "As an episode in a conflict sadly lacking in

the chivalrous gestures and romantic flourishes of old-fashioned wars, fought between soldiers according to set rules, it made a colorful story . . . as an exploit the incident was picturesque, but as an act of policy it seems to have been a blunder."

The news produced embarrassment and shock in official circles in Ottawa and London as well as in Washington. On Christmas Day Anthony Eden cabled to Lord Halifax, "This was a complete surprise to us since General de Gaulle had authorized an assurance to be given to us on December 17th that no orders for the operation had been issued and that it would not be carried out by the Free French naval forces." But no explanations or expressions of regret were sufficient to assuage the wrath of Secretary Hull who issued the following terse statement:

> Our preliminary reports show that the action taken by the so-called Free French ships at St. Pierre-Miquelon was an arbitrary action contrary to the agreement of all parties concerned and certainly without the prior knowledge or consent in any sense of the United States Government.
>
> This Government has inquired of the Canadian Government as to the steps that government is prepared to take to restore the status quo of these islands.

The Vichy Government issued a communiqué stating:

> French official circles have received with satisfaction the news that the Federal Government [in Washington] has publicly condemned the initiative taken against its knowledge and its sentiment by Former Admiral Muselier.

The Vichy Ambassador, Henry-Haye, emerged from a long conference with Hull to express confidence that Vichy sovereignty would be re-established over St. Pierre and Miquelon.

Then the protests began. American public opinion was outraged by the suggestion that the U.S. Government would support any demand that Allied fighting men—it made small difference to the average American whether they were French or Canadian or whatever—should restore the islands to the authority of the shabby government in Vichy. Hull was given plenty of cause to regret his singularly unfortunate choice of words in the reference to "the so-called Free French." There were numerous scornful remarks in the press about "the so-called State Department" and letters of protest were addressed to "the so-called Secretary of State." Hull did not accept this indignant outburst in a spirit of amused indifference. It should be remembered that in his eight years of distinguished service as Secretary of State he had been virtually exempt from the criticism which had been heaped on other members of the Cabinet—Morgenthau, Ickes, Hopkins, Frances Perkins and, certainly, on the President himself. As an elder statesman and a figure of great dignity, Hull had established for himself a position that was almost sacrosanct. It was bewildering as well as infuriating for him to find himself the target of the kind of insults and gibes to which many of his colleagues in the Administration had long since become accustomed.

On December 29 Hopkins passed on to the President memoranda from Eden and Halifax urging that the Free French be included in the United Nations Declaration. As we have seen, Hopkins opposed this, but he added in a note to the President:

> The Prime Minister just phoned me at 6:45, reading me a cable from the Foreign Office to him, in which they indicate the most strenuous objection to the ousting of the Free French from Miquelon.
> They claim de Gaulle will not issue the orders to throw his commander out.
> The burden of the message was that the whole business would kick up an unbelievable row, for which we could give no good public explanation. In spite of the fact that de Gaulle acted in bad faith, the British don't see how he can be forced out and think that the use of force would be very bad.

On December 30, in his speech at Ottawa, Churchill poured his full-flavored scorn upon Pétain, Darlan and company and also paid glowing tribute to the followers of de Gaulle. Although the Prime Minister had never made any secret of his feelings for the "men of Vichy," and although it seemed not out of order that he should refer to France in a Canadian speech, these words caused Hull's rage to mount to hurricane proportions. He and Churchill engaged in a "blunt conversation" and "indulged in some plain speaking."

An editorial comment on the Churchill speech in the *New York Herald Tribune* did not help matters:

> If there was any longer any question about it, the Prime Minister has certainly blown all question of St. Pierre-Miquelon and Washington's "so-called Free French" through the dusty windows of the State Department. To Mr. Churchill there is nothing "so-called" about the Free French, "who would not bow to their knees" and "whose names are being held in increasing respect by nine Frenchmen out of every ten"; there is no trucking to the Vichy politicians who "misled" France and who "fawned upon" the conqueror; there is no glossing over the "cat-and-mouse-game" which Hitler is now playing with the "tormented men" who live only by his "blows and favors." Here, as elsewhere, Mr. Churchill understands that in the grim psychology of war there are moments when the forthright and aggressive spirit, the boldness to demand as well as dicker, the capacity to grasp the emotional values of a situation, are more important than all the gains of deviousness and subtlety.

That is what the State Department has failed to realize in respect to the problem of France. Uninformed as to what the department is trying to do, most Americans will still hesitate to criticize its recent actions; few after this can do otherwise than criticize the befuddlement and want of courage in the manner of its utterances.

This comment by the *Herald Tribune* was representative of the criticism being expressed by newspapers all over the country and perhaps even more violently by various radio commentators. Hopkins noted in a private memorandum:

> Obviously Hull is so mad at Churchill because of his anti-Vichy speech in Canada, which he thinks made the settlement of this issue in the Islands so much more difficult for Hull.
>
> I think Hull also believes that the British have turned their press agents loose on him. He is obviously very sensitive of the criticism he is receiving and blames it on the British and particularly on Churchill..
>
> Hull really wanted to take the whole thing up through the normal diplomatic channels but the President insisted on handling it with Churchill.

The day after Churchill's Ottawa speech, Hull sent a memorandum to the President. This document has been quoted in part in the interesting book, *Our Vichy Gamble*, which was written by Professor William L. Langer at Secretary Hull's direction. But Langer failed to quote the most significant passages of this extraordinary memorandum and it is therefore given herewith in full:

DEPARTMENT OF STATE
THE SECRETARY
December 31, 1941

Memorandum for the President

Since our conversation this afternoon in regard to the St. Pierre-Miquelon seizure by the Free French and its possible consequence, I have carefully reviewed the record, including some despatches that came in during the afternoon. It is a mess beyond question and one for which this Government was in no remote sense responsible.

Hereto attached is a somewhat detailed memorandum covering the entire matter as prepared and agreed to by all of the appropriate members of the European Division. I think it very important that you read this so as to get an up-to-date perspective clearly set forth.

The repercussions, in my opinion, are going to be much greater than one would ordinarily suppose. For example, the following is a quotation from a cable giving the conversation between Darlan and the Marshal with Admiral Leahy:

"Darlan then referred to the St. Pierre-Miquelon incident and said that Germany has already used the seizure of those islands by de Gaulle as an argument for the entry of Axis troops into Africa in order that it may be protected against a similar invasion."

This is just the beginning of ominous and serious developments which, in my opinion, will occur. Our British friends seem to believe that the body of the entire people of France is strongly behind de Gaulle, whereas according to all of my information and that of my associates, some 95 per cent of the entire French people are anti-Hitler whereas more than 95 per cent of this latter number are not de Gaullists and would not follow him. This fact leads straight to our plans about North Africa and our omission of de Gaulle's cooperation in that connection. The developments revolving around the Vichy-North African situation and those revolving around the South American and Rio Conference situation are calculated to be very materially affected to our disadvantage if the fact goes out to the world that the British Government was really behind this movement and we abandon our own policies without serious protest, et cetera, et cetera. This may also seriously affect the question of the French naval units in Martinique by giving Robert a chance to pronounce our agreement null and void.

While, of course, I do not know yet just how agreeable the French [Vichy Government] will be in working this matter out in an amicable manner, provided Churchill would be disposed to talk with you, or rather to let you talk with him, about the necessity from our standpoint to work out the matter and announce to the general public that nobody is censurable and that the matter came up on account of confusions and misunderstanding as to the complications in this Hemisphere with respect to such action.

(signed) C.H.

The construction of that last paragraph, which Langer omitted, is a little difficult to follow, but the slur on both Churchill and Roosevelt is all too clear. The preceding statement that more than 95 per cent "are not de Gaullists and would not follow him" hardly agreed with the results achieved in the St. Pierre plebiscite. The people of St. Pierre, and of all other French regions when given a chance to express themselves in a free election, voted not necessarily for de Gaulle: they voted for freedom and against Vichy. The records proved there had long been public demands in St. Pierre and Miquelon that a plebiscite be held but it had been persistently barred by the Vichy Administrator because, he admitted, he knew it would result in an overwhelming vote in favor of the Free French. It was patently foolish to attempt to estimate what percentage of the French people were for or against de Gaulle at that time or any other time before liberation. Certainly, in 1941, there were large numbers of people in metropolitan France who knew little or nothing about de Gaulle as an individual, but they approved any force that

bore the name "Free France" and later "Fighting France." Such ruck-
uses as this one, however, served to give de Gaulle great advertisement
and contributed materially to the increase of his prestige with the French
people.

In Hull's memorandum he mentions the "fact" that "the British Government was really behind this movement" despite the mass of evidence
that de Gaulle had gone ahead completely on his own, ordering Muselier
to proceed "without saying anything to the foreigners."

Roosevelt refused at first to take all of this seriously. He could not
be deeply disturbed by an incident which seemed trivial to the point of
ridiculousness in comparison with all of his other problems. At a time
when he and Churchill were engaged in the planning of global war and
the formation of the greatest coalition in history, he could hardly consider entering into an open dispute with Great Britain in order to
assuage the injured feelings of Marshal Pétain, Admiral Darlan, Admiral Robert and Ambassador Henry-Haye. He refused to make any
reference to the St. Pierre-Miquelon incident in his Message to Congress
for he believed that the whole thing would quickly blow over and be
forgotten. He was wrong. Nothing could convince Hull that the British
had not double-crossed him. He has underscored the intensity of his
feelings about this in his memoirs:

> As for myself, the refusal of the President to bring more pressure
> on Mr. Churchill to clarify the relations between Great Britain and
> the United States with regard to de Gaulle and Vichy was one of
> several factors that almost caused me to resign as Secretary of State
> in January, 1942. I so seriously considered resigning that I penciled
> out a note to the President tendering my resignation.

I do not know what were the other "factors" referred to, but this
particular factor was so sudden in development and so insignificant in
origin that it could hardly have justified the resignation of a Secretary
of State in time of war. Before the St. Pierre and Miquelon episode,
the Vichy policy had not been subjected to any widespread criticism,
nor had it been considered a sacred cow in the State Department.

Professor Langer has written:

> [The Vichy] policy had been formulated long before and was ad-
> hered to unswervingly until the time of the invasion of North Africa.
> It never was and never became a policy that we thought we could rely
> on. Quite the contrary, it was a day-by-day, hand-to-mouth policy all
> the way through. No one in the State Department liked the Vichy
> regime or had any desire to appease it. We kept up the connection
> with Vichy simply because it provided us with valuable intelligence
> sources and because it was felt that American influence might prevail

to the extent of deterring Darlan and his associates from selling out completely to the Germans.

Churchill himself had been no more eloquent and vehement as a critic of the men of Vichy than had the American Ambassador, Admiral William D. Leahy. Only three weeks before Pearl Harbor, when Weygand was dismissed from his command in North Africa, Leahy wrote to Roosevelt describing Pétain as a "feeble, frightened old man, surrounded by self-seeking conspirators." He added, "This abject surrender to a Nazi threat at a time when Germany is completely occupied in Russia is the kind of jellyfish reaction that justifies the stoppage of all assistance to France."

At this same time, Leahy cabled recommendations that the time had come "to consider a complete revision of American policy in regard to the Vichy Government," since it seemed that the Vichy authorities were now beginning to collaborate with German moves to gain control of the French colonies. Leahy suggested that both he and Robert Murphy be recalled "for consultation," that all economic assistance to the French colonies be stopped for the time being, and that the U.S. Government should proclaim through all radiobroadcasting channels its attitude toward this latest surrender by the Vichy authorities to Axis demands.

Robert Murphy, who was then in Algiers, cabled urgent advice against any immediate change in policy. He said that his "contacts" had begged that the U.S. should not "slam the door in the French face now," that if economic assistance were now stopped, "France will surely and inevitably be thrown into the German camp." (This last was the unvarying argument in favor of continuance of the Vichy relationship.) Weygand himself managed to send a note to Murphy saying much the same thing. Therefore, the course recommended by Admiral Leahy was not then followed.

The British Government agreed with the State Department on that. When Churchill came to Washington for the Arcadia Conference the recommendations of the Foreign Office to the U.S. Government were summed up as follows:

1. Keep Admiral Leahy in Vichy.

2. Bring all possible pressure to bear on Pétain to use the strong cards that he still holds—the French Fleet and the African bases—to refuse excessive German demands.

3. Open negotiations with the French authorities in North Africa for the institution of an economic charter agreement.

On New Year's Day, 1942—which marked the birth of the United Nations—Eden cabled Churchill his view that it was impossible to reach any satisfactory settlement with the Vichy Government and that, in attempting to seek one, the State Department was merely courting a rebuff. However, he felt that the Vichy authorities must be very reluctant to break relations with the United States, this being "their sole remaining link with respectability," and he expressed his hope that the U.S. Government would not act too hastily in severing relations with Vichy.

Thus, there was no serious divergence between American and British thinking in regard to basic policy, nor even in awareness of the less appealing qualities of General de Gaulle. There seemed to be no good reason why the St. Pierre-Miquelon episode should be regarded as more than an isolated fleabite.

Langer has written,

> As the public clamor died down in the United States, Hull reluctantly concluded that the best thing would be to let the matter rest until the end of the war.
>
> Ostensibly de Gaulle had scored a resounding success, but he had forgotten the old diplomatic adage that it is dangerous to play little tricks on great powers.

One may comment that, in the first place, Hull never did "let the matter rest" and, in the second place, de Gaulle continued to forget the old adage and, three years later, was even more recalcitrant than ever.

A week after the end of the Arcadia Conference, Hopkins got out of bed at the Navy Hospital and went over to the White House to attend a Cabinet dinner, which he described as a "dull affair." He wrote:

> The only point to the whole business was a very moving toast by the President to the United States and victory and Hull's response, proposing a toast to the President.
>
> Hull was in excellent form and expressed the admiration and confidence that all of us have in the President's leadership.

Which indicates that, for the time being at least, Roosevelt had successfully talked the Secretary of State out of his determination to resign. But Hull retained possession of the threat of resignation which was for him a secret weapon that the President could seldom ignore.

There was no doubt that Roosevelt was at first amused by the St. Pierre-Miquelon "teapot tempest" as he called it. One might even be permitted the surmise that he derived a certain amount of mischievous pleasure from the spectacle of his esteemed old friend, the Secretary of State, learning at last how it felt to be the target of widespread criticism. However, this situation became less amusing for Roosevelt when it reached the point of a major rupture in his own Administration; this was a development that he always dreaded—and now, in such critical times, he was more than ever anxious to avoid it at almost any cost. Before the Arcadia Conference had ended, Roosevelt had become so irritated by the consequences of the teapot tempest that he was telling

Churchill he might send the battleship *Arkansas* to drive the Free French by force out of the tiny islands, or he might establish a blockade to starve them into submission. In the end, the semblance of Vichy sovereignty over St. Pierre and Miquelon was restored, with provisions for strict Allied supervision of the activities of the radio station so that no active aid and comfort could be given to the enemy. The United States Government protected this sovereignty throughout the Western Hemisphere for nearly two years after the Pétain Government itself had been obliterated by the German occupation of the remainder of France. It was not relaxed until after France had been liberated by the Allied forces under General Eisenhower and a new French Government formed under General de Gaulle.

The episode was, indeed, a fleabite but it developed into a persistent, festering sore. It was a source of infection before D-Day in Normandy and after it. As Henry Stimson has written, he "could not believe that it was wise for the State Department to have so long a memory for such annoyances."

CHAPTER XXII

Winter of Disaster

WITHIN a month after the announcement that the great coalition had been formed, there were alarming evidences that it was about to be knocked to pieces by the blows delivered by the reinforced Germans in Africa and the staggering procession of Japanese conquests southward and westward. The manifold accomplishments of the Arcadia Conference appeared to be so many melancholy scraps of paper and the relationship of Roosevelt and Churchill was subjected to strains which would have overtaxed to the breaking point the patience of smaller men. The accumulation of calamities provided a severe test in adversity for the American people—and, be it said, they met it admirably. For the British, the ordeal was far worse. This was their third wartime winter: in the first, they had been lulled by the illusions of the Phony War—in the second, they had been inspired to endure the Blitz by the glory of fighting alone—and now, with 750 million Russian, American and Chinese allies fighting on their side, they were compelled to confront some of the most humiliating and inexplicable disasters in their entire history. Similarly, the Chinese had been fighting alone against Japan for four and a half years—and now the sudden acquisition of powerful Allies put them in much worse peril than ever.

The underrated Japanese forces shattered all previous Allied appraisals and calculations, and did so with such bewildering speed that the pins on the walls of the map rooms in Washington and London were usually far out of date. Reinforcements would be rushed to some threatened point but even the radio messages to the isolated commanders announcing that reinforcements were on the way failed to arrive before the enemy did.

The area of Japanese conquest in the months following Pearl Harbor was an opened fan, with its handle in Tokyo, its radii more than three thousand miles in length, spreading eastward to the mid-Pacific, southward to the coast of Australia, and westward to the coast of India. It was probably the quickest conquest of a major empire that the world has ever seen.

Fortunately for the American people, they could be only dimly aware of the significance of this area which was so remote and unknown and full of unpronounceable names. But one did not need to be a military expert to see that the Japanese were possessing themselves of incalculably rich resources and of bases from which to make further advances in almost any direction that they might choose. The problem of preventing such further advances was bad enough by itself; but the problem of driving the Japanese out of the positions they had seized seemed too terrible to contemplate.

The most dreadful of all prospects, which came perilously close to realization, was that of a German breakthrough into the Middle East and a Japanese march through India, which would have enabled the two powerful Axis partners to join up and pool resources. This, of course, did not happen; but there were many moments in subsequent months when the "best informed sources" would not dare to bet against it.

During the two weeks while Hopkins was in the Navy Hospital following the Arcadia Conference, Rommel turned suddenly to the counterattack and the depressing story of reversal in Libya was beginning to be retold; the Japanese advanced to the tip of the Malay Peninsula from which they could start the siege of Singapore, they effectively bombed Rangoon, the port of entry for the Burma Road, they landed on Borneo, Celebes, New Guinea, New Britain and the Solomon Islands, from which they could threaten the life line between the United States and Australia.

Hopkins was very much worried about public morale. He was afraid that the flood of bad news would produce a resurgence of isolationist sentiment. He anticipated malicious cries of, "We told you so!" He favored the creation of a counterpart of the British Ministry of Information which would counteract attacks on the government at home and conduct the propaganda campaign abroad.

On January 24, he drove from the hospital to the White House for an evening with the President and subsequently noted:

> I dined with the President alone tonight and he gave me a despatch from Churchill covering the agreements on raw materials, shipping and the distribution of munitions of war and asked me to prepare an answer for him.
>
> This morning the various comments about the Justice Roberts Pearl Harbor report are coming out.
>
> One of the ironical and interesting things about these reports are the criticisms that come from the Senators who opposed every move to prepare for war and of all the people who shouldn't have anything

to say about Pearl Harbor these Senators like. . . . [*Note.* There followed some caustic remarks about personalities which I have felt, regretfully, should be deleted.]

It is perfectly clear that the President is going to have to go through just what Lincoln had to go through with this Senate Committee on the war and I fancy he is going to do it with the same imperturbability as did Lincoln.

He is going to have many of the same problems that Lincoln had with generals and admirals whose records look awfully good but who well may turn out to be the McClellans of this war. The only difference between Lincoln and Roosevelt is that I think Roosevelt will act much faster in replacing these fellows.

This war can't be won with . . . men who are thinking only about retiring to farms somewhere and who won't take great and bold risks and Roosevelt has got a whole hatful of them in the Army and Navy that will have to be liquidated before we really get on with our fighting.

Fortunately he has got in King, Marshall and Arnold three people who really like to fight.

The cables were coming in at great length from the A.B.D.A. Area and each one deepened the discouragement. Admiral Hart was making no secret to Wavell and to the Dutch authorities of his conviction that he was not the man for this job—despite the fact that he had been for a long time conspicuous among high-ranking American officers in warning against the tendency to underrate Japanese military strength.

Hopkins noted further:

The President is disturbed about Admiral Hart and has a feeling that he is too old adequately to carry out the responsibilities that were given him and I fancy before long there will be a change in our naval command in the Far West.

The President is amazingly calm about the war; pleased at the news of our destroyers having got into action in the Far East; talked at great length about a device he is working on to get tanks ashore and discussed ways and means of bombing Japan.

(The "ways and means" referred to here included the launching of Army medium bombers from Navy carriers, as was done three months later in the Doolittle raid.)

Roosevelt was not greatly worried about public morale. He was cool to the suggestion of a government information service. If he had been inclined to shilly-shally before Pearl Harbor, and to shirk leadership, he was now in time of disaster exercising the functions of Commander in Chief with all the confidence and courage and imagination that he possessed in such abundance. It may be said that the American people were following his leadership, or that he was merely reflecting the people's spirit; either way, he was right in refusing to become alarmed about public morale, and Hopkins was wrong. The people needed no hypodermic stimuli other than the daily doses of bad news that they were absorbing.

There was fortunately a minimum of crying over the milk spilled at Pearl Harbor. The swift destruction of the ultramodern *Prince of Wales* showed what would have happened had the antiquated battleships of the Pacific fleet attempted to operate in the enormous area controlled by Japanese air power west of the international date line and north of the equator. Roosevelt said in February, "The only way we could use those ships if we had them now would be for convoy duty in case the Japs ever started using capital ships to break the life line to Australia." This, however, never happened, because American and Australian air power was established and maintained over that life line and the Japanese were reluctant to risk their own battleships within its range. American weakness in these days could not be attributed to what happened at Pearl Harbor, where the enemy could have done far more serious damage had he attacked the vital installations of the base itself rather than the defensively huddled battleships: the weakness was the obvious result of years of puerile self-delusion which had manifested itself in such errors of calculation as the refusal to appropriate funds even for dredging the harbor at Guam.

General Marshall stated the case accurately and poignantly when he said: "The Army used to have all the time in the world and no money; now we've got all the money and no time."

The feeling of Americans was that the blame for the present situation was so widely distributed, from the top to the bottom of our national structure, that there wasn't much sense wasting any further time on recrimination. Much the same feeling had prevailed in Britain after Dunkirk and had produced the great rallying under Churchill. But Dunkirk was by now ancient history to the British people, who felt they had rendered full expiation for their previous sins of complacency. Now they were capable of angry protest against their government.

When Churchill arrived home in London he found to his surprise that he was being attacked in the press and Parliament for having overstayed his leave in Washington; he was being charged, in effect, with spending too much time surveying the great forest while paying insufficient attention to the toppling trees.

On January 27 the Prime Minister faced his critics in the House of Commons at the start of a three-day debate. In the course of a very long speech, he said:

> It is because things have gone badly and worse is to come that I demand a Vote of Confidence. . . . No one need be mealy-mouthed in debate, and no one should be chicken-hearted in voting. . . . Everyone in these rough times must do what he thinks is his duty.

His vote of confidence was 464 to 1. Beaverbrook cabled Hopkins that in all of Churchill's colorful life he had never achieved a triumph comparable to this one and that he was now "established in authority and power exceeding all that has gone before."

Hopkins cabled his hearty congratulations to Churchill, saying that the speech he had given and the magnificent victory that he had won in the House of Commons would prove to be tremendously heartening to all of the United Nations. Roosevelt also sent his congratulations, adding that "there was also one vote in opposition to us," a reference to the solitary vote cast by Jeannette Rankin in the House of Representatives against a declaration of war the day after Pearl Harbor. In this same cable Roosevelt told Churchill that he had been informed that Admiral Hart would like to be relieved of his combat command and he suggested the Dutch Admiral Helfrich as replacement. The President said that the combined organization which had been formed during the Arcadia Conference was working very smoothly and efficiently and, while there were many cases in which the Australian, New Zealand and Dutch authorities should be consulted, such discussions should not be permitted to delay the taking of decisions in critical matters by the Anglo-American combined staff. Roosevelt undertook to work out and maintain close and intimate relationships with the military missions representing the Australian, New Zealand and Netherlands Governments in Washington in regard to policies for the war in the Southwest Pacific.

This was the cable in which Roosevelt told Churchill, as previously quoted, "It is fun to be in the same decade with you."

Churchill replied immediately that these matters would be taken up with the War Cabinet. He added: "Thank you so much for all your kindness. . . . You can rest assured that you and I will have no disagreements."

When Hopkins returned to the White House from hospital he was on the following regimen:

Alutropin (Campbell Products Co.)—teaspoonful, ten (10) minutes before each meal (without water).

Amino-acid powder (Mead Johnson) and Hepavex Compound (Lilly) teaspoonful each in ounce of tomato juice five (5) minutes before meals.

Dry diet—no fluids with meals. (All fluids to be taken between meals. To rest fifteen minutes before meals and one hour after meals. Diet to be adjusted so that most calories given at breakfast and luncheon.)

V-caps (Abbott)—one capsule with each meal.

Haliver oil with Vitamin "D" (Abbott)—one capsule with breakfast.

Calcium bluconate (Abbott)—one tablet with each meal.

Liver extract (Lederle)—5 cc intramuscularly every other day for two weeks.

Appella powder, when required.

Roosevelt told Churchill at the end of another long cable: "Harry is much better but I am trying to confine him to barracks until he learns to take care of himself."

It seemed to me at the time that Hopkins was not particularly rigorous in following the regimen, but his health did improve considerably, and I felt that this was due more to the inspiring spectacle provided by Roosevelt in action under pressure than to any amino-acid powder or liver extract injections.

Aside from the thrills derived from the gallantry of the fight put up by the American-Filipino force on Bataan—and such thrills were always choked with the awareness that these brave men were doomed—the only source of good news was the Russian Front. The Red Army, continuing its amazing counterattacks, drove the snowbound, frost-bitten Germans out of many of their advance positions. Even these successes were considered only temporary, however, for the belief persisted that the Russians were dependent on their traditional ally, General Winter, and that with the coming of spring the dread march of German conquest would be resumed. An Anglo-American intelligence appraisal of the prospects stated elegantly but grimly:

The uncertainty which shrouds this facet of the general world situation causes the consideration of factors which are contradictory among themselves. The state of affairs most likely to produce a negotiated Russo-German settlement would be one where neither side envisioned a quick and sweeping victory. Such a situation might range from a true balance of forces to a definite German ascendancy.

More intelligence came from the British military mission in Moscow telling of talks with Stalin and a visit by General Mason Macfarlane to the Russian Front:

In reply to questions as to the prospects of a Second Front being opened in Europe, Stalin was told that although this could not be accomplished in the near future, one of the purposes of the present campaign in Libya was to obtain bases from which an attack on Italy could be launched. Stalin said that the Germans still possessed greatly superior strength in tanks and would undoubtedly resume their offensives against the Russians in the spring. He was asked for his views on the possibility of an attack by the Japanese on the Russians in the Far East and he said that he would "regard this without enthusiasm." He believed that the Japanese would attack the Soviet Union before the spring. If they did not, time would be given to reinforce the Russian armies in Siberia and bring them back to full

strength and Stalin would then consider resuming conversations on
the advisability of the Soviet Union joining the war against Japan.

This British report stated that "The Red Army was in a bad way in
the autumn but its tail is now up," and that there was a general feeling
of confidence in Moscow and high morale. In private conversations,
Stalin expressed a degree of confidence which "struck a more sober
note." He said that Russian strength might be so increased during the
rest of this year and the Germans might be so badly shaken that there
was a possibility of ending the war in 1942.

Laurence Steinhardt was appointed Ambassador to Turkey to conduct
the immensely important negotiations in that strategic though neutral
country and Admiral William H. Standley became the new American
Ambassador to the Soviet Union. An old friend of Roosevelt's, Standley
had been one of the President's most rugged supporters in the long battle
for aid for the Allies before Pearl Harbor.

Hopkins wrote to General Marshall asking that Colonel Faymonville be given the rank of general so that he might be able to operate
on a higher level when dealing with the Russians on questions of Lend
Lease. Hopkins added, "The Russian fighting front is undoubtedly
weakening Germany far more than all the theatres of war put together.
There is a real possibility that the Russians may smash them during
the next year." Marshall immediately complied with the request for
Faymonville's promotion.

In mid-January, Roosevelt wrote to Admiral Land saying:

> I am still terribly disturbed about the fact that an adequate
> number of ships are not available for Russia. . . . This Government
> has made a firm pledge to Russia and we simply cannot go back on it.
> . . . You simply must find some ships that can be diverted at once
> for this Russian business.

Roosevelt cabled Stalin a statement of the numbers of fighter planes,
bombers and medium and light tanks for shipment during January and
February and said, "although we are at present having our troubles
in the war with Japan, we are sending reinforcements to the Pacific
which I believe will be sufficient to stop the Japanese advance. We are
prepared for some more setbacks, however." He assured Stalin that
there would be no relaxation of efforts to keep the shipments going to
the Soviet Union.

To this Stalin replied:

> I have received your message informing me of consignments of
> armaments from the United States for January and February.
> I would like to emphasize the fact that at the present moment,
> when the peoples of the Soviet Union and its army are exerting all

their powers to thrust back, by their determined offensive, Hitler's troops, the fulfillment of American deliveries, including tanks and aeroplanes, is of the utmost importance for our common cause, for our further successes.

Stalin always gave evidence of very considerable respect for Roosevelt, but Soviet propaganda at that time was expressing scant admiration for the character of the American or British contribution to the total war effort. Indeed, the estimates of the fighting qualities of American troops as broadcast by Moscow did not seem to be very much higher than Hitler's, which have been quoted in a previous chapter. A marked change in the nature of this propaganda was brought about in a curious way. The twenty-fourth anniversary of the foundation of the Red Army was to be celebrated on February 23, and in preparation for that event the Tass News Agency was collecting expressions of tribute and salute from various eminent personages throughout the United Nations. It occurred to some workers in the embryonic psychological warfare agency in Washington that it would be a fine idea to include General MacArthur in this greeting to our Russian allies. MacArthur had by then become a tremendous figure as the only commander in the Pacific who had been able to stop the Japanese advance at any point. The idea was suggested to officers in the War Department, who scornfully refused to put through a cable from an obscure civilian agency to Corregidor requesting that General MacArthur take time from other duties to pay tribute to the Red Army. However, a short daily file of world news was then being sent through Navy communications to MacArthur's headquarters for the beleaguered men there and on Bataan and the enterprising psychological warriors, without authorization from anyone, tacked on to that a message to the general calling his attention to the forthcoming anniversary. MacArthur immediately replied with the following:

The world situation at the present time indicates that the hopes of civilization rest on the worthy banners of the courageous Russian Army. During my lifetime I have participated in a number of wars and have witnessed others, as well as studying in great detail the campaigns of outstanding leaders of the past. In none have I observed such effective resistance to the heaviest blows of a hitherto undefeated enemy, followed by a smashing counterattack which is driving the enemy back to his own land. The scale and grandeur of this effort marks it as the greatest military achievement in all history.

This message from MacArthur was turned over to the Tass Agency and transmitted to the Soviet authorities who broadcast it to the entire world as coming from the heroic and brilliant American general who commanded the valiant forces in the epic struggle for freedom in the

Philippines. From then on, the Russian propagandists were much more favorably disposed toward American fighting men.

The whole task of getting supplies to Russia—and to Britain, and for operations in Africa and the Middle East—was gravely complicated by new developments in the Battle of the Atlantic. In mid-January, Germany took the offensive against the United States. U-boats were the only weapons available for this purpose, but they were now weapons of terrible effectiveness and the defenses against them were inexcusably inadequate. The submarines came in within sight of the glow that arose from Broadway, sinking ships within a few hundred yards of the East Coast. The results are told in awful tables of losses during that winter of disaster. In two months, the U-boats sank 132 ships in the Western Atlantic. The meaning of these losses has been graphically demonstrated in a quotation by Professor Morison from a Navy Training Manual:

> The massacre enjoyed by the U-boats along our Atlantic Coast in 1942 was as much a national disaster as if saboteurs had destroyed half a dozen of our biggest war plants. . . . If a submarine sinks two 6000-ton ships and one 3000-ton tanker, here is a typical account of what we have totally lost: 42 tanks, 8 six-inch Howitzers, 88 twenty-five-pound guns, 40 two-pound guns, 24 armored cars, 50 Bren carriers, 5210 tons of ammunition, 600 rifles, 428 tons of tank supplies, 2000 tons of stores, and 1000 tanks of gasoline. Suppose the three ships had made port and the cargoes were dispersed. In order to knock out the same amount of equipment by air bombing, the enemy would have to make three thousand successful bombing sorties.

The ships moving along the Atlantic Coast at night, although showing no lights themselves, passed between the waiting submarines and the glare of lights from the shore and therefore presented easy targets. Morison has written,

> Miami and its luxurious suburbs threw up six miles of neon-light glow, against which the southbound shipping that hugged the reefs to avoid the Gulf Stream was silhouetted. Ships were sunk and seamen drowned in order that the citizenry might enjoy business and pleasure as usual.

After three months of this massacre, the military authorities ordered the lights dimmed in coastal areas—it was called "the brown-out"—and "squawks went up all the way from Atlantic City to southern Florida that *the tourist season would be ruined.*"

Since the defense of shipping in American coastal waters was obviously the responsibility of the U.S. Navy, Churchill was anxious to know what measures were being taken, aside from curtailment of neon signs. Roosevelt cabled on February 6: "This matter is being given urgent con-

sideration by Stark, King and me." But it took many months for this
urgent consideration to produce results.

Roosevelt was greatly annoyed with the Navy for paying insufficient
attention to the Battle of the Atlantic, and he remained so for a
considerable time. Incidentally, his extreme partiality for the Navy was
not always the advantage to that service that it was supposed to be;
he was continually asking the admirals embarrassing questions based
on his knowledge of naval matters, whereas he left the generals to shift
pretty much for themselves. More than once harassed officers in the
Navy Department were heard to mutter, "I wish to God he'd get absorbed in the *Army* for a change!"

In the February 6 cable referred to above Roosevelt confirmed the
substitution of Helfrich for Hart in the A.B.D.A. Area. Churchill replied
at length, expressing the belief that the Combined Chiefs of Staff
machinery, "ponderous and complicated though it was bound to be,
is functioning smoothly and well. I even think we may plume ourselves
a little having brought it all into action so soon." Churchill went on to
talk of Chinese troops in Burma and of the French situation, saying,
"The Vichy attitude described by you and manifesting itself in many
ways is rotten. They have certainly been helping Rommel with supplies.
. . . The Libyan set-back has been both a shock and a disappointment."
He mentioned British plans to occupy Vichy-controlled Madagascar
before the Japanese could get there. He commented on a new Lend-
Lease agreement—which will be discussed later in this chapter—and
concluded, "I trust Harry is improving. Please give him my regards.
You would like an American film I saw last night, 'The Remarkable
Andrew.' It stirs one's dander."

The reference to the "Vichy attitude" in Churchill's cable proves
that this sore subject was again a factor, but Roosevelt's reply indicated
that Hull was away from Washington and there was no disagreement
as to the desirability of taking a sharper tone toward Pétain.

Roosevelt cabled Churchill on February 10 that he had received information from many sources—and it had been confirmed by Pétain
and Darlan in admissions they had made to Leahy—that the French
had been shipping trucks and food supplies to Tunis for the use of the
German and Italian forces in North Africa. The President had therefore sent a message to Pétain which was, in substance, as follows:

> The American Government has information that the French
> Government has entered into some arrangement with the Axis Powers
> providing for the use of French ships for the transportation of sup-
> plies and possibly war material to Tunis for delivery to the enemy
> forces in Libya. There can be no possible justification under the
> terms of the Armistice for the shipment of war materials or other
> direct aid to the Axis Powers and without official assurances from

the Vichy Government that no military aid will go forward to the Axis in any theater of war and that French ships will not be used in the furtherance of their aggression, Admiral Leahy will be instructed to return immediately to the United States for consultation as to our future policy.

Shortly after that, Hopkins, Rosenman and I were having dinner with the President in the Study and there was talk of the forthcoming trials in Riom, France, where the Vichy Government was to charge Blum, Daladier and others of the Third Republic with failure to prepare France for war. It had been announced that the trials would be secret, with no representatives of the world press admitted. Rosenman said, "I certainly want to read the full records of those hearings after this war is over." Roosevelt thought about that for a moment, then asked that the telephone be brought to him; the telephone was on his desk with a cord so long it could be carried to him wherever he was sitting. He called Sumner Welles and said, "Send a cable to Bill Leahy asking him to tell Pétain that I want to get full transcripts of those Riom trials from day to day."

Roosevelt did not care to wait until the end of the war to read this interesting material.

I do not know whether or not it was a direct result of this message, but Pétain changed his mind about keeping the trials secret and the press was admitted. The courageous and eloquent statements of defendants were thus made known to the French people and the world and did more than anything that had happened since June, 1940, to stimulate the spirit of resistance in France and to discredit the Vichy Government. So effective was this defense of the Third Republic that the German masters of Vichy ordered that the proceedings at Riom be stopped.

The question of French aid to Rommel in Africa produced a considerable amount of bickering correspondence and Ambassador Leahy again became so disgusted with the Vichy attitude that he asked to be recalled. Two months later he was recalled to become Chief of Staff to the Commander in Chief.

Returning to Churchill's cable of February 7:

The Prime Minister said that seventy per cent of the British troops that had fought in Malaya had been evacuated successfully across the strait to Singapore. With the reinforcements that had arrived, there were the equivalent of four divisons for the defense of the great base. A hundred Hurricane fighter planes had also arrived to strengthen the air force, but the bombardment of the air fields reduced their operations materially. However, Churchill said, "the Japanese have to cross a broad moat before attacking a strong fortified and still mobile force. Tobruk was held for six months under these conditions, so I have good confidence. Every day that Singapore holds out gives Wavell time to get a strong grip on Sumatra and Java."

That was on February 7. It was the start of one of the worst weeks of the war.

On February 9 the Japanese began to stream across the "broad moat" of the Strait of Johore. On the same day, the huge liner *Normandie* burned at her dock in New York City, indicating that the long arm of the German saboteur had reached to West 49th Street.

On February 12, the German cruisers *Scharnhorst, Gneisenau* and *Prinz Eugen* escaped from Brest on the French Coast, passed through the English Channel and reached German ports, damaged but still navigable.

On February 15 Singapore surrendered with apparently no real battle having been fought in its defense.

For Churchill, the Naval Person, the escape of the cruisers was an "annoying incident" but no major misfortune, since these dangerous ships constituted less of a menace in German ports than they had in French ones; to Churchill, the imperialist, the fall of Singapore constituted, as he said, "the greatest disaster to British arms which our history records." The British people as a whole evidently did not agree with these relative estimates. They regarded Singapore with a certain detachment. The painfully sorry showing made by British colonial officials and officers in the Far East was a matter of rage and disgust to the London man in the street who had been taking punishment for going on two years; he now felt sure that Colonel Blimp, the flabby, bird-brained creature, who appeared in Low's cartoons, was no caricature. But when German warships, that were constantly under surveillance, managed to steam right under the guns of Dover and through everything that the Royal Navy and the R.A.F. could throw at them, then, it was assumed, there must be tragic incompetence right at home. Thus, the "annoying incident" had undoubtedly done more damage even than the "greatest disaster" to the confidence and to the pride of the average Englishman.

Churchill, who had won his greatest Parliamentary triumph a scant three weeks before, now faced the worst predicament of his career as Prime Minister. He made a broadcast speech in which he attributed the whole series of misfortunes in the Far East to the fact that America's shield of sea power had been "dashed to the ground" at Pearl Harbor. There were numerous expressions of irritation at this statement in Washington, as though Churchill were attempting to escape censure by blaming it all on the U.S. Navy, but it did not bother Roosevelt at all. He merely remarked, "Winston had to say *something*."

The day after the fall of Singapore, Hopkins noted:

Last evening the President and I had dinner and talked at great length about the immediate steps which should be taken by our Army and Navy.

This memorandum is the result of our talk. There were many implications in the conversation, of course, which are not in the memorandum. The memorandum itself is not inclusive.

LIST OF PRIORITIES—A

1. United States to take primary responsibility for reinforcing the Netherlands East Indies, Australia and New Zealand. The men, materiel and munitions to leave the United States prior to March 31. Supporting supplies of men and material to compensate for attrition rate to follow regularly. The force to include the men and materiel that the Joint Chiefs of Staff consider necessary.

2. In addition to convoy, the Navy to strike with every means available in that area the supply lines of concentration points of the Japs. The Navy to provide in Australia such naval base materiel as is required.

3. Every effort made to hold Java as well as defending with all means available all further advances of the Japanese. Hold the island of Timor. [*Note.* The Japanese landed on Timor, within striking distance of Australia, only four days later.]

4. The British to make such supplementary assistance as they have available in this area in ships and man power.

5. The British to take the primary responsibility for reinforcing Burma immediately and defending Rangoon. The United States to provide such supplementary aid as is available.

6. The United States to continue to take the primary responsibility for military assistance to China in terms of materiel, but confining that materiel for the present to the urgent munitions of war such as aircraft, ammunition, high octane gasoline and such other weapons of war as can be utilized when they reach the Chinese Army. The volunteer air force now in Rangoon to be considered part of American support of Chiang Kai-shek.

7. Intensification of the campaign against submarines in the Atlantic, including the great extension of the use of smaller ships.

8. The Russian Protocol, the supplies to the Middle East, the Persian Gulf, the United Kingdom and to selected South American countries.

9. The reinforcement of Hawaii. The increase in our attacking force on the Atlantic Seaboard to 100,000 men and the preparation of shipping for their purposes. The British to increase their special forces from 55,000 to 100,000 men.

10. Carry out the proposed plans for bomber squadrons in England.

11. The strengthening of the Atlantic Ferry Service.

12. Put up in the very top production priorities for the machine tools, the equipment and facilities required for the production of high-octane gasoline plants, of all combat aircraft of the Army and Navy and merchant ships.

LIST OF PRIORITIES—B

1. The complete occupation by American forces in Iceland and the reaching of our objective in the North of Ireland.

2. A complete plan for striking force in Alaska and the Aleutian Islands and pushing that plan as far as possible prior to July 1.

3. The induction and enlistment of ――― hundred thousand men for the Army and the Navy and the provision of training and equipment for these men.

Roosevelt then sent Churchill a cable which was so warmly friendly and sympathetic that I hesitate to attempt to make the paraphrase required by the security authorities. He said that the defeats suffered at Singapore and elsewhere had given the "back seat drivers a field day," but he knew that the Prime Minister would be of good heart, secure in the assurance that he was supported by the confidence of the great masses of the British people, and would never cease to look forward to the main task of fighting and winning the war. Churchill replied that he was deeply grateful for this "warmhearted message." He said that he had "found it difficult to keep my eye on the ball" during these days of personal stress. He said he had made some changes in the British Cabinet, including the appointment of Oliver Lyttelton to the newly created post of Minister of Production from which Beaverbrook had been compelled to resign because of ill health. Churchill said that he was grieved at the temporary loss of Beaverbrook from the British Government and added, "I know you will realise what friends we are and how helpful his driving power will be when he has recovered his health."

In Roosevelt's cable he had promised to talk about the escape of the German cruisers in his radio speech which had been announced for February 23. It was in celebration of Washington's Birthday, but February 22 fell on a Sunday that year and Roosevelt had recently departed from his long established practice of giving his speeches on Sunday evenings (when the radio audience was largest) because of complaints from church leaders that he was reducing attendance at Sunday evening services. Roosevelt did not fulfill his promise to Churchill. He dictated several lengthy explanations of why it was better for the German cruisers to have removed themselves from Brest, but they all sounded lame. For no matter how elaborate the explanations, he could not answer the really persistent question. "Why weren't those ships sunk in the Channel?" Instead, Roosevelt dwelt largely upon purely American misfortunes and promised that "soon we and not our enemies will have the offensive." Whenever criticism was being concentrated on the British, Roosevelt was wonderfully skillful, and graceful, in directing it elsewhere. In this speech, he even went back to Valley Forge:

For eight years General Washington and his Continental Army were faced continually with formidable odds and recurring defeats. Supplies and equipment were lacking. In a sense, every winter was a Valley Forge. Throughout the Thirteen States there existed Fifth Columnists—selfish men, jealous men, fearful men, who proclaimed that Washington's cause was hopeless, that he should ask for a negotiated peace.

And he ended with the famous words, "Tyranny, like hell, is not easily conquered," which Tom Paine had written on a drumhead in 1776.

Churchill cabled: "Warmest congratulations on your heartening declaration."

When Roosevelt finished his broadcast in the White House basement that night we went upstairs to the Oval Study for a drink and word came from California that, while the President was speaking, a Japanese submarine had surfaced off the coast near Santa Barbara and had fired some shells at a ranch. This was merely a demonstration—a minor "insult"—which resulted in no casualties and only negligible damage. It was one of the instances, previously alluded to, when the enemy attempted to nullify the propaganda effect of a Roosevelt speech by some spectacular, headline-gathering operation; but it taught Roosevelt a lesson never again to have speeches announced more than two or three days ahead of time.

Some twenty-four hours after the attack by submarine there was another disturbance in Southern California which provided the nation with some welcome comedy relief in the midst of all the far-flung tragedy. An air-raid alarm went off in the vicinity of Los Angeles which brought the Pursuit Interceptor Command into action and caused the antiaircraft artillery barrage to be opened up. Two versions of this episode were given out to the press, one by the Secretary of the Navy and the other by the Secretary of War. Knox said that wide reconnaissance indicated that no airplanes whatsoever had been over Los Angeles at the time of the alarm. Stimson stated that the available details indicated the presence of unidentified airplanes, perhaps as many as fifteen of them. He read a telegram from the West Coast which said that these planes "may be some from commercial sources operated by enemy agents for the purpose of spreading alarm, disclosing position of antiaircraft positions or effectiveness of black-outs." All that could be said for certain by either the War or Navy Department was that 1,430 rounds of ammunition had been fired by the antiaircraft batteries, no planes had been shot down, no bombs dropped, no casualties. In fact—this was precisely the kind of top-level snafu best calculated to delight the American people. As if the Army and Navy did not have trouble enough with this one, the very next night two air-raid alarms went off in Washington, which caused the President to write sharply to the War Department asking who had the responsibility for setting off air-raid alarms and who had the responsibility for explaining these occurrences to the press. From then on, the air menace to the continental United States diminished.

There was some hopeful news from MacArthur in this last week of February. On February 22 he reported that for the first time a surface vessel, the *Coast Farmer*, had run the blockade and got through to Mindanao in the Philippines with a cargo of balanced rations and ammunition. He said, "She had no difficulty getting through. The thinness of the enemy's coverage is such that it can readily be pierced along many routes including direct westward passage from Honolulu. I have secure bases for reception in Mindanao and the Visayas."

In another dispatch that day MacArthur reported indications that the Japanese had been so badly mauled during the Bataan fighting that there was the possibility that the American forces had gained the respite they so desperately needed. As MacArthur expressed it, "with his present forces, the enemy appears to be unable to make the attack required to destroy me." He requested that none of the encouraging material contained in this dispatch be given any publicity at this time.

Three days later the troops on Bataan even managed to launch a drive and advance five miles through the malarial jungle-choked hills.

Yet this was the time when Roosevelt had to make the indescribably difficult decision to order MacArthur to leave his men on Bataan and Corregidor and embark in a PT boat on the perilous attempt to reach Australia.

By February 23 it had become obviously impossible for Wavell to continue even the pretense of exercising command of the A.B.D.A. Area and he was ordered by the Combined Chiefs of Staff to dissolve his headquarters on Java and turn over responsibility for defense of that rich, populous and strategically vital island to the Dutch. On the same day that these fateful orders were dispatched to Wavell, Hopkins received a long and pitiful cable from H. J. Van Mook, Lieutenant Governor of the Netherlands East Indies. Van Mook had left Washington only three weeks previously to return to his post in Java, writing to Hopkins as he left, "I feel sure that the conduct of the war and the general policy towards the Far East are safe in your hands"; in words of desperation he now begged that there be no decision to abandon the fight in the A.B.D.A. Area. He gave details of means by which he believed that Java could be defended, particularly by the ferrying of fighter planes on the U.S. aircraft carrier, *Langley*. This cable ended with the words, "For God's sake take the strong and active decisions and don't stop sending materials and men pending deliberations as time factor more pressing than ever."

Hopkins replied that it was the determination of all the authorities in Washington to support the fighting in Java with all available means including any fighter aircraft that could possibly be dispatched. He said that there was no disposition to abandon the fight to hold Java—in fact, the very contrary was the case. These were wishful words but they were not, unfortunately, based on the dreadful realities of the situation.

Two days later the *Langley* was sunk in the Battle of the Java Sea. So were most of the ships of the Allied fleet in those waters, including the cruiser *Houston*, on which Roosevelt had cruised so often on saltwater holidays. There was now neither sea power nor air power available to stop the Japanese landings on Java, and the island surrendered a week later. Now, it seemed, the north coast of Australia was completely exposed to the enemy.

The day after the surrender of Java, the Japanese took Rangoon, and thus choked off access by sea to the Burma Road. The situation in the words of the Australian Foreign Minister, Dr. Herbert Evatt, was "practically desperate." The Rising Sun had indeed risen: the gigantic fan was now almost fully unfolded and it covered territory, land and sea, the security of which had previously depended largely upon the power of the British Empire. This traditional power was now frail indeed east of Suez, and none too sure of its chances of survival even in the Middle East. Roosevelt was consequently put in a position such as no previous President of the United States had ever occupied or dreamed of occupying. Hundreds of millions of people on the other side of the earth looked to him for deliverance or protection. He was considered, as the Chinese Foreign Minister said in a letter to Hopkins, "the Commander-in-Chief of the United Nations . . . the one hope of mankind." It was a position which imposed inconceivable responsibility—and it added many complications in his dealings with Winston Churchill, that proud and imperious man whom someone once described with rare accuracy as "half American and all English."

Even in the heat of battle, it was impossible to avoid arrangements affecting the postwar world, and here the President and Prime Minister were on most difficult common ground. I have mentioned the Lend-Lease Agreement which Churchill discussed in his long cable of February 7, just before the series of calamities culminating in the fall of Singapore. This Agreement had been under discussion for some time and was of very considerable importance in laying "the foundations upon which we may create after the war a system of enlarged production, exchange and consumption of goods for the satisfaction of human needs in our country, in the British Commonwealth, and in all other countries which are willing to join in this great effort."

Churchill reported that the majority of the British Cabinet felt that it would be a great mistake to consider any proposals for the abandonment after the war of imperial preference in return for Lend-Lease aid from the United States. (It will be recalled that, at the Atlantic Conference, Churchill himself had confessed to a lack of enthusiasm for the system of imperial preference set up under the Ottawa Agreements.) The Cabinet majority felt that any discussion of such a "barter" deal would provoke unpleasant debates in Parliament and throughout the Dominions; it would provide welcome material for the enemy propagandists who were constantly harping on the theme that the rich and greedy United States was using the war emergency as a means of seizing control of the entire British Empire. The negotiations relative to this Lend-Lease Agreement had been conducted by the State Department in communication with the Foreign Office, but Churchill expressed the hope that the President would take a personal hand in the matter and deal directly with him. The President did so.

A reply to the Prime Minister, drafted by the State Department, was couched in the usual formal terms, but Roosevelt rejected this and wrote a cable in his own intensely personal and considerate manner. He told Churchill, "I understand something of the nice relationships which are required by your constitution for dealings between your Home Government and the Dominions." He said that nothing could be further from his mind than an attempt to use Lend Lease as a trading weapon over the principle of imperial preference. He urged that there be "bold, forthright and comprehensive discussions looking forward to the construction of what you so aptly call 'a free, fertile economic policy for the post-war world.'" He expressed the belief that developments "which neither of us dreams of will be subjects of the most serious consideration in the not-too-far-distant future. So nothing should be excluded from the discussions." He did not want any agreements to be hedged with qualifications or footnotes which would give "to our enemies the impression that we are overly cautious." He said that it had been and remained the determination of the United States "to approach the whole subject of Lend Lease in a manner that will avoid the terrible pitfalls of the First World War."

In his Washington's Birthday speech Roosevelt gave clear statement of his own attitude toward the scope of the Atlantic Charter:

> We of the United Nations are agreed on certain broad principles in the kind of peace we seek. The Atlantic Charter applies not only to the parts of the world that border the Atlantic but to the whole world; disarmament of aggressors, self-determination of nations and peoples, and . . . freedom of speech, freedom of religion, freedom from want, and freedom from fear.

Every word of this, of course, was notice to the peoples of the far Pacific and East Asia that their interests and rights were of no less concern than those of the peoples of Europe or the Western Hemisphere. It was intended as an answer to the currently formidable Japanese propaganda, but it served to confirm Roosevelt's position as "the one hope."

The Australian Government demanded that their divisions in the Middle East be returned to their homeland for its defense. These troops could ill be spared nor could the shipping for their transport. Churchill begged that at least one Australian division be diverted to Burma. Prime Minister John Curtin, the head of Australia's Labor Government, refused this point blank.

Churchill appealed to Roosevelt to intervene and the President then cabled Curtin asking him, "in the interests of our whole war effort in the Far East," to reconsider the decision to move the First Australian Division to Australia. He pointed out that, in addition to all of the American troops and forces now en route, a further 27,000 men, fully equipped in every respect, were to be sent from the United States to Australia. He pointed out that the Americans were better able to reinforce the Allied right flank in the war against Japan—this right flank being represented now by Australia and New Caledonia—whereas the left flank in Burma and India must be the responsibility of Great Britain. It was on this left flank that the veteran Australian division was most sorely needed.

Curtin agreed to this, but events were moving so swiftly that before any troops could be sent from Suez, Rangoon had fallen and access to southern Burma was denied. Some Australian troops were consequently diverted to Ceylon, the last sea base that was left in the Indian Ocean.

However, more trouble flared up between the Dominion Government and London over Churchill's appointment of Richard G. Casey, Australian Minister in Washington, as member of the War Cabinet and Minister of State in the Middle East. The disputes over this led Roosevelt later to dispatch a cable in which he paid Churchill the compliment of speaking plainly:

The publicity from the Casey business disturbs me greatly. . . . It is particularly disturbing to learn from the newspapers that you, on the one hand, feel compelled to discuss this matter publicly in Parliament, while Curtin, on the other hand, may have decided to issue a detailed White Paper. It would be desirable all round if any way can be found to avoid all further public discussion of this which, it seems to me, plays right into the hands of our enemies. I realize that the Casey appointment is only an incident. The more important issue is the basic relationship of Australia to Great Britain. I sense in this country a growing feeling of impatience at what publicly appears to be a rather strained relationship at this critical time between the United Kingdom and Australia. . . . I say this to you because I myself feel greatly responsible for the turn of events. I still consider the decision to send Casey to the Middle East is a wise one and I told him quite frankly that I hoped he would take this job because of his knowledge of the American and Australian as well as the British angles in the Middle East area.

It was this "strained relationship," and the desperate predicament of Australia that caused it, which influenced the orders to MacArthur. Roosevelt knew full well that the departure of MacArthur from Corregidor would be a grievous blow to the heroic men of his command and thus to the whole United States. It was ordering the captain to be the first to leave the sinking ship. But Roosevelt had to weigh these considerations against the fact that no move he could make would be so well calculated to bolster the morale of the people of Australia and New Zealand. He made his serious decision at a conference with Hopkins, Marshall and King in the White House late in the afternoon of Sunday, February 22—which was the day before the orders went to Wavell to dissolve the A.B.D.A. command—but the news did not come out until MacArthur arrived in Australia three weeks later. During those three weeks a sense of panic was developing throughout the entire Southwest Pacific area, for it seemed that all the ambitious attempts to establish unified command, or any command at all, had collapsed. When the news of MacArthur did come out, Americans had to accept the chilling realization that the troops who were continuing resistance anywhere in the Philippine Islands had been written off. On April 9 the forces on Bataan surrendered and on May 5 General Jonathan M. Wainwright on Corregidor made the final surrender of all American-Filipino forces still in action.

While awaiting news of the passage of MacArthur to Australia, Roosevelt sent a long cable to Churchill setting forth the results of the current deliberations of the Chiefs of Staff. It stated, "The U. S. agrees that the Pacific situation is now very grave," and then went on to give in detail the effects of this in every quarter of the globe, from Iceland to Ceylon, and the measures to be taken to meet the crisis. (One of the most vitally important spots on earth was New Caledonia, on the life line to Australia, which was held by the Free French; there was no talk of restoring *that* to Vichy sovereignty.)

Following this long cable, which was obviously prepared by the Chiefs of Staff, Roosevelt sent another long one of his own giving his purely personal views of "the complexity of the present operational command set-up to which is added equal complexity in the political set-up." He said, "since our meetings in January the excellent arrangements established then have become largely obsolescent in relation to the whole

Southwest Pacific area," and he offered the following main suggestions for the Prime Minister's consideration:

1. The United States will assume responsibility for all operations in the Pacific area. Decisions governing this area will be made in Washington by the U.S. Joint Chiefs of Staff in consultation with an advisory council on operational matters composed of representatives of Australia, New Zealand, the Netherlands East Indies, China and possibly Canada. The supreme command will be American, and the main objective will be to regain the offensive. (Roosevelt cited as one example the offensive in a northwesterly direction from the main southern bases—and, as will be seen in a later chapter, this plan was developed as an actual alternative to the invasion of the continent of Europe.)

2. The area of British responsibility will extend from Singapore to the Persian Gulf and the Red Sea and include Libya and the Mediterranean area. But it is assumed that the Operation GYMNAST, the landings in Northwest Africa, has been temporarily shelved.

3. The North and South Atlantic, and the Western European continent, will form the area of joint British-American responsibility, with details of command to be worked out later as required. Roosevelt said that he was becoming "more and more interested in plans for the establishment of a new front on the European continent this summer." He said that such a front provided the shortest distance from the United States for supply lines of any possible front anywhere in the world and, while the development of it would undoubtedly involve heavy losses, he considered that these could be compensated by at least equal losses for the Germans and "by compelling Hitler to divert heavy forces of all kinds from the Russian front." He emphasized the necessity of maintaining the delivery of all possible aid to the Soviet Union.

Roosevelt added that the grand strategy governing operations in all areas would continue to be the subject of study and decisions by the Joint Chiefs of Staff and that the various Boards on munitions, raw materials and shipping would continue their functions subject to the joint approval of the President and the Prime Minister.

Churchill cabled general agreement to this, summing up, "I feel that your proposals as I have ventured to elaborate and interpret them will achieve the double purpose, namely (a) integrity of executive and operational action, and (b) opportunity of reasonable consultation for those whose fortunes are involved." He believed that division of responsibility should not extend to determination of naval strategy, saying, "Nothing must prevent the United States and British Navies from working to a common strategy from Alaska to Capetown." He suggested that a Pacific Council be set up in Washington as well as in London for "those whose fortunes are involved"—namely, China, Australia, New Zealand and the Netherlands.

It was impossible for the harassed Chiefs of Staff with all their charts and compasses to draw any enduring line of demarcation between one theater and another in the Far East, for the war was no respecter of man-made frontiers nor even of the natural obstacles imposed by Divine Providence. The Japanese surge on land through Burma, and a series of devastating blows to British naval units and shipping in the Bay of Bengal, brought India into the zone of war and, although this tremendous problem was one for which Roosevelt wanted to have no responsibility, it was deposited on him and remained with him for a long time.

On March 10, the day before Churchill announced the Cripps mission, Roosevelt wrote the Former Naval Person a long cable on the Indian problem. He said, "Of course this is a subject which all of you good people know far more about than I do and I have felt much diffidence in making any suggestions concerning it." He said that he had tried to consider it from the point of view of history and had gone back to the inception of the United States Government with the hope that this might provide "a new thought" for India.

Roosevelt then wrote that during the American Revolution the Thirteen Colonies had set themselves up as separate sovereignties under a temporary government with a Continental Congress, which he described as "a body of ill-defined powers and large inefficiencies." Following the war, a stopgap government was formed under the Articles of Confederation and this continued until real union was achieved under the Constitution in 1789. Roosevelt suggested a somewhat similar process for India: the setting-up of a government to be "headed by a small group representative of different religions and geographies, occupations and castes; it would be representative of the existing British Provinces and the Council of Princes and would be recognized as a temporary Dominion Government." This representative group would be charged with the duty of considering the structure of the permanent government of India, such consideration to extend "for a period of five or six years, or at least until a year after the end of the present war." In the meantime, it would exercise executive and administrative authority over public services, such as finances, railways, telegraphs, etc. Roosevelt wrote: "Perhaps some such method, with its analogy to the problems and travails of the United States from 1783 to 1789, might cause the people of India to forget past hard feelings, and to become more loyal to the British Empire, and to emphasize the danger of domination by the Japanese, and the advantages of peaceful evolution as contrasted with revolutionary chaos." Roosevelt added that this was, of course, "none of my business" and "for the love of Heaven do not bring me into this, though I do want to be of help." He expressed the hope that the move toward the achievement of self-government for India would originate in London and would be made in such a way that the people of India would have no grounds for criticism that it was "being made grudgingly or by compulsion."

It is probable that the only part of that cable with which Churchill agreed was Roosevelt's admission that it is "none of my business." Hopkins said a long time later that he did not think that any suggestions from the President to the Prime Minister in the entire war were so wrathfully received as those relating to solution of the Indian problem. As one of Churchill's closest and most affectionate associates has said to me, "The President might have known that India was one subject on which Winston would never move a yard." It was indeed one subject on which the normal, broad-minded, good-humored, give-and-take attitude which prevailed between the two statesmen was stopped cold. It may be said that Churchill would see the Empire in ruins and himself buried under them before he would concede the right of any American, however great and illustrious a friend, to make any suggestions as to what he should do about India. It may be added that, four years later, the Labor Government in Britain made a proposal to the Indian leaders which, Sumner Welles has written, was "almost identical in principle with the suggestions made by President Roosevelt in 1942."

After the fall of Singapore, Roosevelt had cabled Churchill his impression that the visit of Chiang Kai-shek to Burma and India "will be useful." It is doubtful that Churchill agreed with this, either, or that Roosevelt himself subsequently felt so confident of the results of the visit. The Generalissimo had gone presumably to put some anti-Japanese fighting spirit into the Burmese and Indian peoples, to tell them from the point of view of one who had been battling the Japanese for many years what a cruel mockery was their propaganda of "Asia for the Asiatics." This was a desperately urgent matter, for Gandhi was telling his people not to resist Japanese aggression if and when it came, and there seemed dreadful likelihood that the Japanese would be able to march through India at will and thus gain access to the Middle East and establish the dreaded link with the Germans.

Chiang Kai-shek met with Gandhi and evidently exerted no influence whatsoever on the Mahatma's determination to accord the Japanese the same treatment that he had for so long accorded the British. Indeed, it is possible that Gandhi was the one who exerted the greater influence. Chiang later quoted him as saying, "They [the British and Americans] never voluntarily treat us Indians as equals; why, they do not even admit your country to their staff talks." That was a home thrust for the Generalissimo, who was bound to resent the fact that China was considered as no more than a "consultant" by the Combined Chiefs of Staff.

The Chinese Foreign Minister, T. V. Soong, was working all this time in Washington with great persistence and tortured patience to secure and expedite aid to China. When it seemed evident that the

Burma Road might be cut off, he gave Averell Harriman a map showing an alternate land route by way of the Persian Gulf and Soviet territory. Harriman sent this map to the President with the following outline:

> The route marked in red follows the Iranian Railway for 840 miles from the Persian Gulf to the Caspian Sea—by boat about 200 miles on the Caspian Sea to the terminus of the Russian railroad—about 2,000 miles over the Russian-Turkestan Railway to Sargiopol near the Chinese border—and from this point over the motor road used by the Russians to get supplies to China, some 2,000 miles to Chungking. The total distance is upwards of 5,000 miles.

Soong felt that a life line by air from Assam, in Northeast India, into China, would be far more effective in meeting the emergency needs. He wrote to Roosevelt:

> Miraculously enough that new life line is conveniently at hand. From Sadiya, the terminus of the Indian Railways, to Kunming or Suifu [the center of land and water communications in Szechuan] is only 550 or 700 miles respectively, flying over comparatively level stretches.

This route covered some of the most terrible, murderous terrain to be found anywhere on earth; presumably the "comparatively level stretches" referred to the air strips at the start and the finish.

On February 9, General Joseph W. Stilwell paid a farewell visit to Hopkins before leaving to take command of the American and Chinese forces in Burma. Hopkins assured him that the President wished to do everything possible to further the success of his efforts. Stilwell agreed that the air route to China should be inaugurated regardless of the ability to keep open the Burma Road, but he was evidently not greatly worried about his own supply problem for the huge liner *Normandie*, on which more than two thousand men were then working for her quick conversion to war purposes, was to be used for the transport of troops and matériel to Stilwell's command. Hardly had the general left the White House before he heard that the *Normandie* was on fire, which was only the first of a long series of bitter discouragements for this rugged, fearless, tactless American soldier.

The same day Roosevelt sent a cable to Chiang Kai-shek telling him that the air ferry service by way of Africa and India to China was being increased rapidly and giving definite assurance that this supply route to China would be maintained even though there were further setbacks in Burma.

Thus was inaugurated the air service over "The Hump" into China, on which many thousands of missions were flown in the next three and a half years and thousands of brave young men gave their lives. It could not begin to supply, as General Marshall has written, "China's most critical needs [which] were in trucks and rolling stock, artillery, tanks, and other heavy equipment." But it was the only route there was. It represented far more in the expenditure of effort and courage than it could produce in tangible results.

The Generalissimo returned to Chungking after his trip through Burma and cabled the President a profoundly depressing report saying that "I have never seen anything in all my lifelong military experience to compare with the deplorable confusion, unpreparedness and degradation." In this message and in an accompanying cable to Soong, Chiang Kai-shek was bitterly critical of the British performance in Burma and of the attitude of both the British and the Russians toward the direction of the over-all strategy of the war. He urged Soong to have "a frank heart-to-heart talk with the President . . . who has consistently shown himself to be the one great friend of China."

The "heart-to-heart talks" were held with Hopkins, and after them Soong wrote him this letter:

I have given a great deal of thought to our talks of the last two days, and your desire to lift the plane of our efforts beyond the material difficulties of the day, to the necessity of close and lasting political and ideological associations between our two countries. After graduating from an American school and returning to China a quarter of a century ago to embark on the vicissitudes of politics, I have been a consistent advocate of this very idea. The Generalissimo's appointment of myself as Foreign Minister was directed to that end, and you can unhesitatingly count on me as your loyal collaborator.

Both you and I serve the President who is the one hope of mankind. You sustain him day by day. . . .

I am doing my utmost to keep the Generalissimo informed accurately of the situation at this end, with all its difficulties. On the other hand, I am doing my best to keep the President informed of the grim realities of our situation. . . .

I think your suggestion of associating the United States and China in periodic conversations with Great Britain and Russia holds great possibilities, and will be particularly conducive to better mutual understanding beyond our own narrow interests.

And I think if you could accept the invitation of the Generalissimo to visit Chungking, you will be opening a new chapter in Sino-American history. If you desire, I shall be glad to accompany you.

I feel I did not succeed in putting across to you our desperate need for planes and artillery as the mainspring of the Generalissimo's anxiety. We are in the 57th month of our war, embattled in Burma, and on us may soon be turned once again the full fury of the Japanese army, fresh from its recent laurels. This is not mere speculation on the part of London. On April 16th, a friend in Chungking in whose objective judgment I have great faith cabled me that the Japanese threaten to attack the most important strategic centers: "The situation looks ominous. I personally believe that in May or June the Japanese will attack Changsha and Hengyang (in Hunan Province) and at the same time attack Sian (in Honan Province)."

As you know we have but little artillery and planes left. Our economic situation is bad. It is true our request for planes and artillery is modest by British or Russian standards, but they will be the only essential weapons that stand between us and the enemy.

We have tried for a year to abide by the established procedure, but we have come to the conclusion that we need a simple and direct procedure of participation in the technical sub-committees which examine and determine the requirements and allocations.

None but we ourselves can explain properly our needs. It could not be done by American officers, not only because they do not have sufficient knowledge of our situation, but on political grounds such a procedure would be misunderstood by our people. I know you have real difficulties on your end, but certainly some workable method may be found.

With this participation in the procedure of allocation, and with the larger conversations envisaged by you, we may be filling some of the gaps in wholehearted collaboration at this crisis of the war and at this most critical moment for China.

The charge was sometimes made that Hopkins was "in Churchill's hip pocket" and was therefore constantly influencing the President to ignore the war against Japan and concentrate on Europe. Actually, the records prove that Hopkins was a tireless agitator for the interests of the Far Eastern theaters. When the Pacific War Council was organized, on April 1, Dr. Evatt of Australia (who was then in Washington) telegraphed:

After most careful consideration Australia has come to the conclusion that it is essential to success of Council scheme that chairman should be the President or his deputy and further that such deputy should be Harry Hopkins.

Of the organization of this Council, Hopkins wrote, on April 1:

The President and I have been discussing for some time the question of a Pacific War Council. The Army and Navy never had much enthusiasm for it because they were afraid it would require too much of the time of the military people and they fundamentally dislike any advice on strategic problems from political sources, a prejudice of theirs with which I have become sympathetic.

On the other hand, it was essential that there be an opportunity for the various countries in the Pacific to find a common meeting ground.

While in Hyde Park on this past week end, I told the President that I thought the matter must be decided affirmatively and he readily agreed and asked me to prepare a public statement to announce the formation of the Council, which I did in the notes that are attached.

Halifax yesterday urged the State Department to invite a representative of India, apparently feeling that it might help with the negotiations going on in India. However the President disagreed with this because, of course, India has nothing to do with our Pacific front. [*Note:* Australia was also originally opposed to the inclusion of India.]

The first meeting of the Council was held at 11:45 today and not much happened. The President outlined the problems in the whole Pacific Area but kept away from the tough tactics which are now in progress. It is perfectly clear, however, that this body wants to talk about military strategy and the distribution of munitions. How it is coming out I don't know.

The original Council consisted of the President, Hopkins, Lord Halifax, Dr. Soong, Dr. Evatt, Alexander Loudon (for the Netherlands), Hume Wrong (for Canada) and Walter Nash (for New Zealand). Both India and the Philippines were added to the Council later.

President Quezon had been evacuated from Corregidor at the same time as General MacArthur, and when he arrived in Washington as head of a Government in Exile he and Hopkins established a close relationship. Hopkins wrote to Roosevelt:

President Quezon of the Philippines came to see me yesterday morning to express the hope that he could become a member of the Pacific War Council.

He stated that the fact that he was a member would be known to every Filipino at an early date and would greatly hearten his people. He thinks that the Philippines have as much at stake as any of the commonwealths and, furthermore, guerrilla fighting is still going on in many parts of the Philippine Islands and will continue.

He told me that, while he had been advised by members of his Cabinet and by General MacArthur to come to the United States, he felt he was making no contribution here and told me that he was somewhat inclined to return to Australia at an early date.

He thought, however, that his membership on the Pacific War Council, together with some visits which he has in mind to American communities that have a substantial number of Filipinos and to South American countries, which he wants to visit on his own, would give him adequate reasons for remaining indefinitely.

Quezon subsequently wrote to Hopkins:

I shall never forget, as long as I live, the part that you have taken in securing for my government the recognition which the President of the United States has accorded us in making the Government of the Commonwealth of the Philippines a member of the United Nations and giving me a seat in the Pacific War Council.

With assurances of my heartfelt gratitude . . .

In view of Hopkins' unique position in relationship to Roosevelt, and his exceptional powers as chairman of the Munitions Assignment Board, he might well have become an object of abomination to all the leaders of the various contending national factions and the representatives of the various services—as he did with so many government officials and politicians who felt that he was always giving priority to the interests of somebody else, beginning with his own, and who poured on him the resentment that they did not dare to direct at the President. It is all the more remarkable that, among the various interests represented in the Pacific War Council, and in the Combined Chiefs of Staff, and with Churchill and Stalin and representatives of the European nations who dealt with him, including the Free French, Hopkins was respected and trusted and liked.

His position with the Congress and the press remained, however, unchanged. Along toward the end of March, he was ill again—he had to spend five days in the hospital—and he had time to catch up on his reading about himself. For instance—Hugh S. Johnson again raised the cry that "nobody ever elected Mr. Hopkins to any office"—as if a President were compelled by the Constitution to put the names of his friends and confidants on the ballot together with his own. Johnson added: "Many of the delays, false starts, bad selections of leaders and subsequent blunderings in getting our production machinery attuned for war over the past two and a half years are attributable directly to Mr. Hopkins and his palace janissariat of men of similar mind."

(It can be said that at this time the "janissariat" consisted primarily of Stimson, Knox, Marshall, King and Arnold—also Welles, Patterson, Forrestal, McCloy, Lovett and General Burns.)

Another news item: Representative John W. Taber addressed a meeting of the Women's National Republican Club on March 16, the day before MacArthur landed in Australia. According to the *New York Herald Tribune*, Taber told the ladies that "everyone in Washington with the exception of the President of the United States and a certain group that he has surrounded himself with is doing his best to put the defense program across." Taber put Hopkins at the head of the "certain group" and asked, "How much longer must he [Hopkins] with his proven incompetence have the major 'say' in our defense program and its operations? How much longer shall his incompetence interfere with our doing our part?" But the time had long passed when Hopkins could be bothered by such fulminations from Capitol Hill: there was a war on, and he was in it, and however dismaying the immediate circumstances might be he knew in his heart that he was doing a damned good job in his ultimate life's work, which was reducing the burden on President Roosevelt.

CHAPTER XXIII

The Decision to Attack

THE first meeting of the Pacific War Council was held on the morning of April 1, against the background of seemingly unmitigated disaster in the Far East. That was a Wednesday. After lunch that day, the President met with Secretaries Stimson and Knox, Generals Marshall and Arnold, Admiral King, and Hopkins. That night and the next night the President and Hopkins dined together, and the next day they lunched with General Marshall, then went for a drive to see how the construction on the new Naval Hospital (Roosevelt's pride) was getting along out in Bethesda, Maryland. That night they dined together alone again, and at 4:30 the next morning (Saturday, April 4) Hopkins and Marshall took off for London to propose the invasion of the Continent of Europe.

In his long cable to Churchill of March 9, Roosevelt had spoken of "plans for establishment of a new front on the European Continent," adding, "I am becoming more and more interested in the establishment of the new front this summer."

On March 14, Hopkins wrote the following memorandum to the President:

MATTERS OF IMMEDIATE MILITARY CONCERN

1. Australia. To be sure we have enough forces there to hold Australia, New Caledonia, Fiji and New Zealand. Believe Army should be pressed on this point, particularly as to air. We must not underrate the Japs' air strength.
2. China. We must keep that line to China open and get it going. Believe Army needs to be jogged on this regularly.
The second phase of the Chinese business is to get a springboard

from which to bomb Japan itself. For morale reasons this is extremely
important and the sooner it can be done the better.

3. England. I believe Arnold's plan in England should be pressed
home. There is nothing to lose. The bridgehead does not need to be
established unless air superiority is complete. I doubt if any single
thing is as important as getting some sort of a front this summer
against Germany. This will have to be worked out very carefully
between you and Marshall, in the first instance, and you and
Churchill, in the second. I don't think there is any time to be lost
because if we are going to do it plans need to be made at once.

4. Russia. Increase if possible our supplies to Russia. The Protocol
runs out in June. Believe it would be wise to have another conference
here as soon as possible to cover supplies after July 1st.

5. Real priorities for machine tools must be given merchant ships
and combat planes. Should reaffirm to people concerned, namely Land
and Stimson, that you want the planes and the ships in 1942.

At this time, a definite plan for invasion of Northern France was
being made by the War Plans Division, of which Eisenhower had recently become Chief. It involved direct assault across the Channel at its
narrowest point to the French Coast between Calais and Le Havre, east
of the Seine—as opposed to the Normandy area west of the Seine to the
Cotentin Peninsula where the landings were made two years later. The
beachheads were to be further extended to the eastward beyond Dunkirk to Ostend and Zeebrugge on the Belgian Coast.

The basic military argument for invasion of the Continent as stated
in a memorandum from Marshall to the President was as follows:

Western Europe has been selected as the theatre in which to stage
the first great offensive of the United Powers because:

It is the only place in which a powerful offensive can be prepared
and executed by the United Powers in the near future. In any other
locality the building up of the required forces would be much more
slowly accomplished due to sea distances. Moreover, in other localities
the enemy is protected against invasion by natural obstacles and poor
communications leading toward the seat of the hostile power, or by
elaborately organized and distant outposts. Time would be required to
reduce these and to make the attack effective.

It is the only place where the vital air superiority over the hostile
land areas preliminary to a major attack can be staged by the United
Powers. This is due to the existence of a network of landing fields in
England and to the fact that at no other place could massed British air
power be employed for such an operation.

It is the only place in which the bulk of the British ground forces
can be committed to a general offensive in cooperation with United
States forces. It is impossible, in view of the shipping situation, to
transfer the bulk of the British forces to any distant region, and the

protection of the British islands would hold the bulk of the divisions in
England.

The United States can concentrate and use larger forces in Western
Europe than in any other place, due to sea distances and the existence
in England of base facilities.

The bulk of the combat forces of the United States, United Kingdom
and Russia can be applied simultaneously only against Germany, and
then only if we attack in time. We cannot concentrate against Japan.

Successful attack in this area will afford the maximum of support
to the Russian front.

It will be seen that the desirability of meeting the Russian demands
for a Second Front was the last in the priority list of arguments in favor
of the proposal. However, this consideration weighed heavily with
Hopkins, as it did with Beaverbrook, who was in Washington at the
end of March and early April following his temporary retirement from
the British Government.

The invasion plan was originally known as ROUNDUP and eventually
OVERLORD. The main operation, involving thirty American and
eighteen British divisions, was planned to take place in the spring of
1943. The code name BOLERO was applied to the enormous preliminary process of building up the required forces and supplies in the
British Isles.

Provision was made for a more limited operation, known as SLEDGE-
HAMMER, to take place about September 15, 1942. Speaking of
SLEDGEHAMMER, the plan stated:

This Limited Operation Would Be Justified Only in Case
(1) *The Situation on the Russian Front Becomes Desperate,* i.e.,
the success of German arms becomes so complete as to threaten the
imminent collapse of Russian resistance unless the pressure is relieved
by an attack from the west by British and American troops. In this
case the attack should be considered as a sacrifice in the common good.
(2) *The German Situation in Western Europe Becomes Critically
Weakened.*

In the event that the operation was undertaken as a purely desperate,
emergency measure to relieve pressure on the Russian Front, it was
clearly foreseen that it might involve the loss of most of the troops
involved.

A further and more enduring justification for SLEDGEHAMMER
was later added: It might be employed to seize a bridgehead on the
Continent *and hold it* until such time as sufficient American forces were
available for the major drive through France into the heart of Germany.
The most favorable bridgehead would undoubtedly have been the
Cotentin Peninsula including the port of Cherbourg.

Roosevelt was inclined to be leary of a trans-Channel frontal attack.

He was still in favor of GYMNAST, the North African operation which had been planned at the Arcadia Conference and then shelved because of the need for diverting ships to the Pacific and the Indian Ocean plus the severe tonnage losses in the Western Atlantic. However, he was persuaded of the desirability of BOLERO-ROUNDUP by Stimson, Marshall and Hopkins. Roosevelt also attached great importance to the political importance of this in relation to Russia.

He approved it at the April 1 meeting in the White House and told Hopkins and Marshall to go at once to London and present it to the Prime Minister and his Chiefs of Staff. Hopkins sent a jubilant cable to Churchill: "Will be seeing you soon so please start the fire." (This was another of the frequent references to the temperature at Chequers.)

Roosevelt cabled Churchill:

Having completed a survey of the immediate as well as the long range military problems which face the United Nations, I have reached certain conclusions of such vital importance that I want the whole picture to be presented to you and to ask for your approval thereon. All of it is dependent on the complete co-operation of our two countries. Therefore, Harry and General Marshall will leave soon for London to inform you of the salient points. When I have heard from you after your talks with Harry and Marshall, I propose to ask Stalin to send immediately two special representatives. It is my hope that the Russians will greet these plans with enthusiasm. I want them to be identified as the plans of the United Nations and I think they can be worked out in full accord with the trends of British and American public opinion.

The Hopkins-Marshall mission which left from Baltimore in the early morning of April 4th was given the code name "Modicum" and the members of the party bore the following aliases: Mr. Harry Hopkins—Mr. A. H. Hones; General G. C. Marshall—Mr. C. G. Mell; Commander James R. Fulton—Mr. A. L. Foss; Colonel H. A Craig—Mr. J. H. Case; Lieutenant Colonel A. C. Wedemeyer—Mr. J. E. White.

Commander Fulton was a Navy doctor assigned by Ross McIntire to attempt to take care of Hopkins. Wedemeyer, who was then with Eisenhower on Marshall's brilliant planning staff, became Commander of American Forces in the Chinese theater two years later.

One odd feature of this mission was that Hopkins was given some editorial credit for it. The *Richmond* (Virginia) *News Leader* uttered these surprisingly kind words:

Harry Hopkins' record in administering relief during the depression years did not impress the nation, but Harry Hopkins' work during the war will be found of a different and higher level. The plain truth is that Hopkins is an ill man. He knows it. Frequently he has to slip away from the White House for a day or two and get blood trans-fusions. Then he comes back and, though he scarcely is able to keep on his feet, he is deep in his duties as chief of lease-lend. At that post, believe it or not, he is displaying much sagacity. Those who most deserve his support are getting it wholeheartedly.

Now Hopkins has gone once more to London—this time by bomber and doubtless on the "straight-away." That is a severe ordeal for a man in perfect health and with flesh enough to keep him from feeling the extreme cold of a flight at more than 20,000 feet. Often strong men have to take oxygen as they speed through the cold, thin air four or five miles above the sea. To Hopkins, thin and bloodless as he is, the flight must have been literally so many hours in hell. . . .

You may not like his former administration and you may not have forgotten the bitterness of his tongue during the days when he was dictator of relief expenditures; but you have to take off your hat to him now for as fine a display of persistent, day-by-day courage as this war has offered in America.

Although Hopkins had previously made the severe transatlantic flight by bomber (B-24) as well as the terrible round trip in a PBY to Arch-angel, on this trip he enjoyed comparative luxury. The Modicum party had an entire Pan American Clipper all to itself. The first stop was Bermuda, where they were delayed for two pleasant days over Easter Sunday. At the request of the Governor, Lord Knollys, Marshall read the lesson in church. Hopkins attended a children's party, admired the Easter lilies and slept a great deal. Both he and Marshall inspected the enormous work being done by the U.S. Army at one end of this lovely island and the Navy at the other end to convert it into a great land-plane, seaplane and submarine base.

Hopkins also asked a great many questions about the use of Pan-American Clippers for carrying civilian airmail. For more than a year he had been fussing and stewing almost constantly about civilian use of passenger and cargo space in commercial transport planes. A month before he had written the following angry note to Lovett in the War Department:

I noticed in the paper the other day that the New York Giants were flown to Havana and back in two or three transport planes.

Who authorizes such a trip as this, wearing out engines and burning high octane gasoline?

From now on he never stopped agitating to remove all civilian airmail from the Clippers. A month later he cabled to Harriman:

The President is issuing some new instructions with a view to removing the chit-chat mail from the commercial aircraft. Evidently there are some people who think that it is important that these commercial planes should be used to tell each other how Aunt Bessie is progressing with her lumbago. If you are feeling well enough I hope you will keep on raising hell about this at your end because it is all a lot of damned nonsense.

Marshall and Hopkins flew directly from Bermuda to Scotland and arrived in London on the morning of Wednesday, April 8.

Following are Hopkins' notes on their first sessions at No. 10 Downing Street:

Marshall and Hopkins with Prime Minister at 10 Downing Street, 4-6 p.m. Marshall presented in broad outlines our proposals to the Prime Minister. It was perfectly clear that the Prime Minister was well aware of the proposals which we were going to make because he stated they had them under careful consideration for many weeks and were prepared to go ahead, implying that they would go ahead without us. He made it, however, perfectly clear to me that he did not treat the proposals as seriously as either the facts warranted or as did the United States. On the other hand he indicated that he had told the Chiefs of Staff that, in spite of all the difficulties, he Churchill was prepared to go along. He repeated the several objections that had obviously been made to him by the Chiefs of Staff, all of which we had heard in Washington before coming to England. Marshall was more optimistic about the interview than I was. He thought that Churchill went a long way and (he, Marshall) expected far more resistance than he got. Churchill reviewed the whole military situation which was none too optimistic, particularly in the Indian Ocean. He also expressed a good deal of criticism of Auchinleck; said he had had pretty acrimonious correspondence with him by cable. Churchill as ever is pressing his commanders for action and they in turn indicate that they never have enough supplies. It is more of the old story. He told us that the Singapore business was a mess and he feels that the whole thing was very badly handled and that there is no explanation of the lack of resistance on the part of the British. He simply thinks they folded up and let him and the British Army down very badly.

At dinner at 10 Downing Street: Churchill, Marshall, Attlee, General Brooke and Hopkins. Eden came in after dinner. We dined at 10 Downing Street as the guests of the Prime Minister, but the conversation was in the main social. Churchill, displaying his talents as a military historian, spent most of the evening discussing the Civil War and the (First) World War and never really came to grips with our main business, although General Brooke got into it enough to indicate that he had a great many misgivings about our proposal. Brooke made an unfavorable impression on Marshall, who thinks that although he may be a good fighting man, he hasn't got Dill's brains. While at dinner, Churchill got word from the Bomber Command they were sending 350 bombers over Germany tonight.

The following day Hopkins cabled Roosevelt that he and Marshall had presented the proposals in full to Churchill whose response was sympathetic. It seemed that the outlook was hopeful for agreement right down the line. Hopkins added, "The Prime Minister has just sent for me for a discussion of India." He promised to telephone or cable the President further about this.

The discussions that day were described by Hopkins as follows:

In conference with the Prime Minister in the Cabinet Room at 10 Downing Street, 10:30 to 12. Prime Minister read me a despatch which he had just received from the Governor General of India indicating that Cripps had presented a new proposal to Nehru without consultation with the Governor General but presumably with the assistance of Louis Johnson. The gist of this proposal was that an Indian would on paper at any rate be given charge of the Defense Ministry. The Commander-in-Chief of the British Forces would have powers and duties substantially comparable to those in the original British proposal. The Governor General's despatch indicated that he and Cripps could have got Nehru's agreement to the original proposal had not Cripps and Johnson worked out this new arrangement. It was perfectly clear that the Governor General was irritated with the whole business and laid great stress on the fact that Johnson acts and talks as though he were sent to India as Roosevelt's personal representative to mediate in the Indian crisis. It is apparent that this new proposal, which is known as the Cripps-Johnson proposal, might well be turned down by the British Cabinet which is meeting at 12 today, in which case Roosevelt would be in the embarrassing position of having ostensibly made a proposal which the British Government rejected. I told the Prime Minister that Johnson's original mission to India had nothing whatever to do with the British proposals and that I was very sure that he was not acting as the representative of the President in mediating the Indian business. That I believed Cripps was using Johnson for his own ends, Cripps being very anxious to bring Roosevelt's name into the picture. That it was to Cripps' interest to get Roosevelt identified with his proposals. I told Mr. Churchill of the President's instructions to me, namely that he would not be drawn into the Indian business except at the personal request of the Prime Minister and then only if he had an assurance both from India and Britain that any plan that he worked out would be acceptable, and that he Roosevelt was unwilling to be put into a situation before the world in which he undertook to moderate between the conflicting forces and then have these forces turn down his proposals. Churchill at once wrote in longhand a cable to the Viceroy stating that he was sure Johnson was not acting as personal representative of the President in negotiations between the Indian Congress and Cripps.

It was clear that Churchill did not wish at this time to bring the United States into what he calls a constitutional question, and he is unhappy at the turn the press has taken, namely that public opinion in

America and Roosevelt in particular can handle this matter over the head of the British Government.

The Prime Minister also discussed at some length the Naval situation in the Indian Ocean. While he was there his secretary brought in a memorandum to say that the "Hermes," a small aircraft carrier, has just been sunk. He stated that the British Fleet in the Indian Ocean was badly out-gunned by the Japanese naval forces; that the Japanese had complete air superiority as evidenced by the sinking of two cruisers, which incidentally were attacked by 60 Japanese fighters each one carrying a 500-lb. bomb and in the attack the two cruisers both sank within fifteen minutes. He showed me the despatches received this morning from the Commander-in-Chief, Indian Fleet, stating that he was going to withdraw his major forces to East African ports; that he could not risk battle; and that he would leave behind a fast striking force to harass the enemy. He told me too that Ceylon has just been attacked by air a second time but that he has not learned as yet what the effect of this air attack is. The Commander-in-Chief's despatch this morning was quite discouraging and, while Ceylon can undoubtedly put up a good fight because of its heavy shore batteries and some aircraft, it was clear that the Prime Minister is not too hopeful about it.

This led to a discussion of the cooperation between our Fleet and the British Naval Forces in the Far East. Churchill feels, and I gather he expresses the point of view of the Admiralty, that there is no real joint planning of Naval strategy in the Far East and in the Pacific and Indian Oceans. He asserted that, while the Admiralty kept our Navy informed of everything, consultation ended here and that our Naval responses were that "we have the matter in hand." Churchill is obviously disturbed at this and would like to see the same kind of joint planning of Naval tactics and strategy as goes on between our two Armies. He was not critical of our various actions in the Pacific but rather expressed the belief that we were in the war together; that our two Fleets were acting as though they were two totally independent forces; and he thought this was not conducive to victory.

He showed me the maps of Rommel's advances in Libya where the patrol forces on both sides are in contact. He said that Auchinleck felt that he was not ready to conduct the major offensive until May but that Rommel's advance might force the fighting there sooner. He thinks Auchinleck is pretty well prepared, and that Rommel will have trouble in breaking through. I gather that he is quite impatient with Auchinleck but nevertheless considers Auchinleck a first-rate fighting man.

I then discussed again with the Prime Minister the purposes of General Marshall's and my visit to England and impressed upon him the serious weight which the President and Marshall gave to our proposals; and I made it very plain that our military leaders had, after canvassing the whole world situation, made up their minds that this plan was the one of all considered that was by far the most advantageous from a strategic point of view. I impressed as strongly as I could on Churchill that he should not agree to this proposal on any assumption that we do not mean business, nor should he assume that in all probability it will not require the use of ground forces. I told him that the President and Marshall were prepared to throw our ground forces in and that he did not wish an agreement on the basis that in all probability the ground forces would never be used. I said this to him because, in conversations the previous day, I sensed that his advisers had told him that the ground attack would never be made, at least for nearly a year. I particularly stressed the impossibility of immobilizing large numbers of our troops indefinitely, and that the disposition of the United States was to take great risks to relieve the Russian front. Churchill took this very seriously and led me to believe that he didn't fully take in before the seriousness of our proposals. He told me that he would send a message by Eden, with whom I am lunching, relative to the Indian business and asked me to return at 6 o'clock tonight to continue conversations.

Lunch at the Foreign Office with Eden, Lyttelton and Harriman. I outlined our proposal to Eden and Lyttelton today. Both of them responded very favorably and the only reservation was the timing. They think that as early in 1942 as possible is the time. It is their opinion that the Chiefs of Staff are going to come to a meeting of minds with Marshall. We discussed the Persian Gulf as a supply route to Russia but that does not seem too encouraging. I told Lyttelton I thought he ought to make a new effort to open that route up. Eden showed me a paper that had apparently been prepared by the soldiers about supplies to Russia after July 1. The memorandum clearly indicated that some of the military people here aren't too anxious to get supplies to Russia and that we have got to overcome a good deal of resistance. I also told Eden the President's position about signing the treaty with Russia, making it perfectly clear that the President did not approve of this action. I told Eden the President could not, of course, prevent them from signing it but in the last analysis it was a decision the British must make and that no useful purpose could be served by exploring it further with the Russians. I impressed on Eden as strongly as I could the President's belief that our main proposal here should take the heat off Russia's diplomatic demands upon England.

Marshall conferred at length with the British Chiefs of Staff, including Lord Louis Mountbatten, who had become Chief of Combined Operations, the mysterious organization which conducted the spectacular Commando raids and provided the laboratory for experiments in the techniques of amphibious warfare. Mountbatten, an adventurous and imaginative officer, was somewhat addicted to freakish schemes involving all manner of weird contraptions—one of them was a form of landing craft made out of shatterproof ice—but the work of Combined Operations produced much that proved valuable. In a war of this nature, no innovation seemed too fantastic to be unworthy of consideration.

Incidentally, as an item of extreme interest in the history of the Second Front, shortly after this Marshall-Hopkins visit, Churchill sent the following directive to Mountbatten:

PIERS FOR USE ON BEACHES

C.C.O. or DEPUTY.

They must float up and down with the tide. The anchor problem must be mastered. Let me have the best solution worked out. Don't argue the matter. The difficulties will argue for themselves.

W.S.C.
30.5.42

This was one of the first references to the artificial harbors—known as "Mulberries" and "Gooseberries"—which two years later were towed across the Channel to the Normandy beaches. American officers who knew the whole story of these amazing developments gave Churchill a very large share of the credit for their origination.

Hopkins also conferred with Attlee and Ernest Bevin on the immeasurably complex requirements of manpower, and with Lord Leathers, Minister of War Transport, on the shipping situation, particularly the calamitous losses of tankers on the U.S. Atlantic Coast. Harriman was involved in all of these discussions but Winant was in Washington at the time. The American Minister in London then was H. Freeman Matthews, later director of the State Department's Office of European Affairs.

On April 11 Hopkins cabled Roosevelt that the discussions with the Former Naval Person and the British Chiefs of Staff were progressing very satisfactorily and that he was about to meet with Lord Leathers to discuss the shipping problem in all its manifold implications. He said that all in the British Government were very much disappointed by the turn of events in India but they believed that they had made a fair offer and every effort to reach agreement. It seemed apparent that it would be futile for Cripps to conduct any further negotiations. Hopkins added, "Although I am not allowed to talk about the weather, I can tell you that my heavy underwear is itching like the devil. Please have a telephone message sent to Diana that General Marshall has got me well under control."

That same day Hopkins received a copy of the following cable which Roosevelt had sent to Stalin:

It is unfortunate that geographical distance makes it practically impossible for you and me to meet at this time. Such a meeting of minds in personal conversation would be greatly useful to the conduct of the war against Hitlerism. Perhaps if things go as well as we hope, you and I could spend a few days together next Summer near our common border off Alaska. But, in the meantime, I regard it as of the utmost military importance that we have the nearest possible approach to an exchange of views.

I have in mind very important military proposal involving the utilization of our armed forces in a manner to relieve your critical western front. This objective carries great weight with me.

Therefore, I wish you would consider sending Mr. Molotov and a General upon whom you rely to Washington in the immediate future. Time is of the essence if we are to help in an important way. We will furnish them with a good transport plane so that they should be able to make the round trip in two weeks.

I do not want by such a trip to go over the head of my friend, Mr. Litvinov, in any way, as he will understand, but we can gain time by the visit I propose.

I suggest this procedure not only because of the secrecy, which is so essential, but because I need your advice before we determine with finality the strategic course of our common military action.

I have sent Hopkins to London relative to this proposal.

The American people are thrilled by the magnificent fighting of your armed forces and we want to help you in the destruction of Hitler's armies and materiel more than we are doing now.

I send you my sincere regards.

This cable reflected what Hopkins had told Eden of "The President's belief that our main proposal here should take the heat off Russia's diplomatic demands upon England." The demands were substantially the same as those which had been made shortly before Pearl Harbor and had caused Eden's trip to Moscow in December. Roosevelt obviously saw the urgency of diverting the attention of the Soviet Government from such embarrassing postwar political considerations by emphasizing the British and American determination to establish the Second Front in the west for which Communist propaganda had been clamoring since the German invasion of Russia.

Hopkins cabled Roosevelt the main points of his discussions with Leathers on the shipping crisis:

In the period from 12th January to 12th April the shipping losses in the western part of the North Atlantic Ocean totaled 1,200,000 gross tons, more than half of this being tankers. The losses for the past week in the same area have been 150,000 tons, more than two thirds of which were tankers. The ships that we are losing, it seems to me, are far more important than their cargoes. Our need for ships during the next few months is going to be desperate.

Hopkins strongly recommended that none but the most vitally essential cargoes be shipped until adequate escorts could be provided for convoys. He said that he had intended to postpone discussions of these matters until his return to Washington but the situation seemed so urgent that immediate action must be taken to cut the losses.

Even during this visit to London when attention was concentrated on the English Channel and Hitler's "Fortress of Europe" that lay beyond it, Hopkins could not forget the endless plight of China and what General Marshall called its "unparalleled logistical problems." Word came that the Air Ferry Command had completed its first flight over the Hump. As Hopkins was leaving for a week end at Chequers on Saturday, he received a long cable from T. V. Soong which had been sent through the Chinese Ambassador in London, Dr. Wellington Koo. Soong suggested a new supply route by sea and land from the United States to China—and this must be rated the most fantastically difficult of all the various proposals. It involved, to begin with, extension of the shipping route around the North Cape of Norway, already as perilous as any of the life lines of the war, for a distance of nearly 2,000 miles beyond Murmansk. Shipping must go through the Arctic Ocean, past Nova Zembla, to the Yenesei River in northern Siberia; cargoes were to be transshipped to Soviet river vessels at Igarka, 500 miles up the Yenesei, and moved 1,100 miles south to Krasnoyarsk on the trans-Siberian Railway, from which point the transshipped material would travel 800 miles by rail to Sargiopol, and then another 2,000 miles by road to Chungking. Hopkins knew all too well that the mere fact that his friend, Dr. Soong, could seriously present such a proposal as this one was in itself sufficient proof of the desperateness of China's situation. He also knew that there was nothing now to be done about it except to make every effort to get more and more transport planes for the Ferry Command.

When Hopkins went out to Chequers on Saturday afternoon he had his first real look at the English countryside now that April was there. Experiencing something of the old lyrical impulse which had been so long suppressed within him, he later said, "It's only when you see that country in spring that you begin to understand why the English have written the best goddam poetry in the world." The usual gaiety and charm of a Chequers week end was lacking this time because Mrs. Churchill was ill with general exhaustion and Churchill himself was below normal in exuberance, the result of the fearful strain of the series of disasters which had by no means ended.

A cable arrived for Hopkins from Roosevelt saying that all possible efforts must be made to prevent a breakdown of the Cripps negotiations in India. The President asked that the following message be delivered immediately to Churchill:

I am unable regretfully to agree with the point of view you express in your message to me that American public opinion believes that negotiations have failed on general broad issues. The general impression here is quite the contrary. The almost universal feeling is that the deadlock has been due to the unwillingness of the British Government to concede the right of self-government to the Indian people notwithstanding the Indians' willingness to entrust technical military and naval defense control to the competent British authorities. American public opinion cannot understand why, if the British Government is willing to permit component parts of India to secede from the British Empire after the war, it is not willing to permit them during the war to enjoy what is tantamount to self-government.

I know you will understand my reasons for placing this issue before you very frankly. If the current negotiations are allowed to collapse and if India were subsequently to be invaded successfully by the Japanese with attendant serious military defeats for the Allies, it would be hard to overestimate the prejudicial effect of this on American public opinion. Therefore, is it not possible for you to postpone Cripps' departure on the ground that you have personally transmitted to him instructions to make final efforts to find some common ground of understanding? I gathered that last Thursday night agreement was almost reached. It appears to me that this agreement might yet be reached if you could authorize Cripps to say that he was empowered by you personally to resume negotiations as at that point with an understanding that minor concessions would be made by both sides.

It is still my feeling, as I have said before, that a solution can be found if the component groups in India could now be given an opportunity to set up a National Government similar in essence to our own form of government under the Articles of Confederation, with the understanding that after a period of trial and error the Indian people would then be enabled to decide upon their own form of constitution and their future relationship with the British Empire, as you have already promised them. If you should make such an effort, and if then Cripps was still unable to achieve agreement, then American public opinion would be satisfied that at least the British Government has made a fair and real offer to the Indian people upon whom the responsibility for failure of the negotiations would be clearly placed.

This cable reached Chequers at three o'clock Sunday morning when the Prime Minister and Hopkins—the latter disobeying all instructions —were still sitting up talking. Its contents undoubtedly postponed any plans for going to bed for some time to come. Churchill set forth to Hopkins in detail, and probably with some vehemence, his answers to the President's arguments. Hopkins' scribbled notes on this can be summarized as follows:

Churchill refused to be responsible for a policy which would throw the whole subcontinent of India into utter confusion while the Japanese invader was at its gates. A Nationalist Government such as indicated by Roosevelt, first, would almost certainly demand the recall of all Indian troops from the Middle East and, second, would in Churchill's belief make an armistice with Japan on the basis of free transit for Japanese forces and supplies across India to Karachi. In return, the Japanese would give the Hindus the military support necessary to impose the Congress party's will upon the Moslems, the Princes and the depressed classes. Churchill felt that any attempt to reopen the Indian constitutional issue in this way at this juncture would serve only to emphasize serious differences between Great Britain and the United States and thus do injury to the common cause. Far from helping the defense of India, it would make the task impossible.

It appears from Hopkins' notes that Churchill said that he personally was quite ready to retire to private life if that would do any good in assuaging American public opinion, but he felt certain that, regardless of whether or not he continued as Prime Minister, the Cabinet and Parliament would continue to assert the policy as he had stated it.

Hopkins, who loved to use the phrase "meeting of minds," was by now convinced that the subcontinent of India was one area where the minds of Roosevelt and Churchill would never meet. He took the position that there was not much sense in burning up the transatlantic cables with more messages on this subject. Since the President's cable had been addressed to him for communication to Churchill, he felt that he should be the one to answer it. Early Sunday morning, he tried to telephone the White House from Chequers but was prevented from getting through by atmospheric conditions. Later he did manage to reach the President and explain that since Cripps had left India the day before, and explanations had been issued by both the British and Indian authorities, nothing more could be done about the matter at the present time. Evidently Hopkins told Roosevelt something about the reception of his cable at Chequers and the hour at which it had arrived for the next day the President cabled this message to General Marshall:

> Please put Hopkins to bed and keep him there under 24-hour guard by Army or Marine Corps. Ask the King [George VI] for additional assistance if required on this job.

Marshall had his troubles obeying these orders. Although aided by Dr. Fulton and by General Robert A. McClure, Military Attaché at the American Embassy in London, he found it impossible to keep Hopkins under control. At the end of a long evening after a longer day, Marshall would send Hopkins to bed and then himself sit up with McClure and Wedemeyer to go over various matters. Later one of them would look into Hopkins' room to check up on him and find that he had disappeared through the separate entrance leading to the corri-

dor; hours might pass before Hopkins returned to the suite. There
were many Americans staying at Claridge's in those days, as always,
and he could usually scare up a gin rummy game at almost any hour.

Dr. Fulton has written me an account of some of his troubles in the
task of keeping Hopkins alive:

> Mr. Hopkins was a man of boundless energy and during the trips
> on which I accompanied him he gave unstintingly of himself, without
> regard for his physical condition. It was extremely important that he
> get as much rest as possible and my instructions from Admiral
> McIntire were to stay as close to him as was practical for me to do
> under the unusual circumstances involved and to see that he received
> the necessary rest, medications, and preparations which had been
> prescribed for him by his consulting physicians.
>
> On several instances I believe my presence at his side, at prescribed
> hours for medication, caused Mr. Hopkins considerable annoyance.
> Frequently while in London he would become solicitous for my wel-
> fare and assure me that I should visit my naval medical colleagues for
> weekends and have outside interests and activities. . . .
>
> One particular prescribed preparation was, to say the least, not very
> palatable, and he preferred to take it in tomato juice. I would endeavor
> at every opportunity to stay with him until he took this preparation
> because several times there was mute evidence that he had disposed
> of it in the bathroom in preference to taking it.
>
> If, as frequently happened, he was to dine out with his British
> colleagues or other diplomatic or military dignitaries, I would be sure
> that he had a small package with his necessary medications to take
> with him. Almost invariably following such an evening out the intact
> package would be found on his dresser, in his bathroom, or in his
> dinner coat the next morning.

After the week end at Chequers, Hopkins read a report from New
York which alarmed him. It was a monitoring by the U.S. Government
of the Paris radio, one of the more important and deceptive units in
the Nazi propaganda machine. It said:

> Hopkins and Marshall have been conferring for nearly ten days in
> the British capital. According to the Anglo-American Information
> Services, Roosevelt's delegates have been entrusted with the commis-
> sion of demanding that the British Government prepare an invasion
> of the continent. Roosevelt is said to have given Hopkins and Marshall
> full power to provide all possible aid that England may need for an
> attempt at a second Narvik which will eventually become a second
> Dunkirk. In view of the reiterated announcements of an invasion of the
> continent, launched for the purpose of aiding the Soviet armies which
> are living in expectation of a Spring offensive, military circles in
> Berlin today made a statement which cannot be surpassed for clear-
> ness. The gist of this statement is that Germany can only once more

confirm Hitler's proclamation inviting the British to come in the greatest possible numbers to Europe to measure themselves with the armed forces of the Reich. It is recalled in Berlin that the Fuehrer had made an offer to Britain to evacuate any part of the European continent to enable her to make an effective landing without difficulty.

There were so many elements of accuracy in this French broadcast, directed by Berlin, that one could jump to the jittery conclusion that the enemy must have had secret agents behind the arras at Chequers or a microphone under the green baize at Downing Street. However, this was only one of the more elementary propaganda tactics: an obvious piece of guesswork broadcast in the hope that it might provoke nervous replies which would reveal some part of the truth. It was as if a neurotically jealous husband were to say to a suspected rival, "Don't think I don't know all about what's going on between you and my wife," on the chance that the rival will blanch and mutter, "But how did you find out?" thereby betraying the sordid secret. It sounds silly, but it was tried time and again in this tough war and even sometimes it worked. Actually, in this particular case, the Hopkins-Marshall visit to London was deliberately advertised—if anything, too much so—as a portent of an invasion. As *Time* magazine said in its first report of the mission, "In the U.S. and Britain anxious millions forthwith believed what they wanted to be told; that their forces were about to take the offensive and open a second front in Europe." Anxious millions in Russia, of course, were even more anxious to believe this. The London *Times*, normally well informed on the prevalent point of view on the upper levels of Whitehall, went pretty far in its editorial comment on the main subject under discussion, saying, "There is mounting eagerness both in this country and in the U.S. to pass from defence to offence and to make 1942, not 1943 or 1944, the turning point of the war."

On Monday, April 13, Hopkins attended a meeting of the War Cabinet and the next day he cabled to Roosevelt:

> The serious naval situation which has been developing in the Indian Ocean requires your most urgent consideration. You will be readily aware of the implications of the fact that the Japanese have moved very powerful forces in that area.
>
> Tonight we will have a final meeting with the Defense Council and the Chiefs of Staff and I am very confident of the outcome. Marshall, who has made a splendid impression here, has presented our case with moderation but with great force. I believe we will achieve not only agreement in principle but a real meeting of minds. Everyone here regrets that Admiral King could not also have been present.

The situation in the Indian Ocean was indeed so serious that, with British sea power virtually inoperative in the Bay of Bengal, the Japanese sank more than thirty ships, including an aircraft carrier and two heavy cruisers, within four days.

Roosevelt cabled Hopkins for the Former Naval Person that he had received a very despondent message from Chiang Kai-shek and he believed it essential that despite the situation in the Indian Ocean there must be no curtailment in the supply of airplanes now on the way to General Stilwell for use in Burma.

He expressed the belief that the Japanese would not attempt to make a landing on Ceylon for several weeks and said he hoped that all shipping would be kept out of the Bay of Bengal and that British warships would remain for the time being "under the umbrella of airplanes land-based in Southern India and Ceylon." At the same time Roosevelt cabled Churchill, "I appreciate quite fully the present lack of naval butter to cover the bread," which referred to the critical problem then facing the British of disposing enough ships for the defense of the Indian Ocean while at the same time maintaining the necessary strength of the Home Fleet for the security of the British Isles. Roosevelt proposed to use the U.S. aircraft carrier *Ranger* as a ferry boat to transport fighter planes for the maintenance of the air umbrella from India and Ceylon and he sent units of the U.S. Navy, headed by the new battleship *Washington* and the aircraft carrier *Wasp*, to Scapa Flow to reinforce the Home Fleet both for the defense of Britain and the protection of the convoys around the North Cape to Russia.

On April 14 Roosevelt cabled Hopkins that Litvinov had called in to ask for fuller information about the import of the President's recent invitation to Stalin to send two personal representatives to Washington. In this cable, Roosevelt added that, although he had not yet received official confirmation from Leahy, it seemed true that Laval had returned to power in the Vichy Government.

That night at 10:00 P.M. Hopkins and Marshall met with the Defense Committee (Operations) of the War Cabinet. Present were Churchill, Attlee, Eden, Lyttelton, A. V. Alexander (First Lord of the Admiralty), Sir James Grigg (Secretary of State for War), Sir Archibald Sinclair (Secretary of State for Air), and the Chiefs of Staff—Pound, Brooke, Portal, Ismay and Mountbatten.

Churchill opened this "memorable meeting," as he called it, with all the grace and courtly flourish of which he was master. Speaking of the "momentous proposal" which had been brought from the President by Mr. Hopkins and General Marshall he gave it his cordial and unhesitant acceptance, stating that it was in accord with the classic principles of war. However, he pointed out there was the problem immediately presented by the ominous possibility of a junction being achieved of the Germans advancing through the Middle East with the Japanese advancing through India. A substantial portion of the resources of Britain and America in men and matériel must be set aside to prevent this junction and the most vital points at which these resources could now be applied were in Burma and Ceylon and on and over the Indian Ocean.

Churchill said that the enormous preparations for the trans-Channel operations that would have to go forward in the United Kingdom would hardly escape the attention of the enemy, particularly in and around the ports of Southern England which were so readily accessible to German reconnaissance planes. However, this problem might well be overcome by obscuring the true objectives of the enterprise in a cloud of rumors. He said, "With the whole coast of Europe from the North Cape to Bayonne [the French-Spanish border] open to us, we should contrive to deceive the enemy as to the weight, timing, method and the direction of our attack." Far from attempting to conceal the preparations for invasion, Churchill felt, some sort of public announcement should be made "that our two nations are resolved to march forward into Europe together in a noble brotherhood of arms, in a great crusade for the liberation of the tormented peoples."

General Marshall then spoke, expressing the great relief that he and Hopkins felt that agreement had been reached on basic principles for a frontal assault on the enemy in Northern France in 1943. In the meantime, he said, much would depend upon the development and intensification of the air offensive against Germany, and he also emphasized the desirability of repeated Commando-type raids all along the coast not only for the purpose of harassing and confusing the enemy but, even more importantly, to give our own troops combat experience. He foresaw no shortage of troops for the major operation, but he did believe there would be difficulty in making available the necessary shipping, naval escorts, landing craft and aircraft. However, these were problems to be faced in the United States and he and Hopkins were confident they would be solved.

Marshall spoke at some length of the possibility that they might be compelled to launch the emergency operation, known as SLEDGEHAMMER, sometime before the autumn of 1942. If this were necessary, he said, the American contribution in troops would necessarily be a modest one since there was not enough shipping to transport a substantial force across the Atlantic within the next five months. He said that the President was opposed to any premature operation, involving such great risks, but that if such an operation were made necessary by developments on the Russian Front, American troops should take part in it to the fullest possible extent.

Marshall said that the Chiefs of Staff in Washington had made very careful calculations as to the measures that were necessary for holding the Alaska-Hawaii-Australia line in the Pacific and full provision for this had been made. He said that the U.S. Navy was now getting into position to attack the Japanese flank in the event of any further moves toward Australia. He spoke of the possibility of a Japanese attack on the Soviet Union, in which case the Americans would hope to make arrangements with the Russians to move the forces now based in Alaska into the Maritime Provinces of Siberia.

The next speaker at the memorable meeting was Sir Alan Brooke, Chief of the Imperial General Staff. He seconded the Prime Minister in welcoming the proposal for an offensive in Europe, but he also emphasized problems presented by the Japanese advances toward India. He pointed out that, if the Japanese were to gain unquestioned control of the Indian Ocean, the southern route to Russia would be cut, Turkey would be isolated, the Allies would lose the Middle Eastern oil supplies—which would go to the Germans—and the Germans would have ready access to the Black Sea and to the Russian rear in the Caucasus. The dreaded junction of the Axis partners would, of course, give both of them opportunity for the exchange of materials which they so greatly needed.

Churchill, Marshall and Admiral Pound then discussed the naval problems in the Indian Ocean. The Prime Minister expressed confidence that these problems could be solved with American co-operation. He suggested that if the new U.S. battleship *North Carolina* were sent to Scapa Flow, the British ship *Duke of York* could be released to move to the Indian Ocean; at least one ship of this power had to be kept at Scapa Flow in case the *Tirpitz*, sister ship of the *Bismarck*, were to come out from Trondheim, Norway. Marshall also expressed confidence that the two nations together could provide what was necessary for the Indian Ocean and other theaters and, at the same time, go right ahead with the main project.

It may be noted that the discussions at this meeting produced the contradictory circumstance of the American representatives constantly sticking to the main topic of the war against Germany while the British representatives were repeatedly bringing up reminders of the war against Japan. As he listened to the exchange of views, Hopkins had been scratching notes and doodling on Downing Street notepaper. When it came his turn to speak, he started off by saying that there was no question of doubt that American public opinion was generally in favor of an all-out effort against Japan. This sentiment had been intensified by the bitter ending of the gallant fight on Bataan Peninsula and it would become more acute when General Wainwright was forced to surrender on Corregidor. However, Hopkins said, the President and the American military leaders and the American people were all agreed on one point: *"Our men must fight!"* Obviously, Western Europe was the one place

Page of Hopkins' notes and doodles, made during meeting at 10 Downing Street on evening of April 14, 1942, when Britain agreed to United States plans for a second front.

where the enemy could be fought most quickly and most decisively on land as well as on sea and in the air. Hopkins said that Americans did not want their men to be sent across oceans merely for purposes of sight-seeing: they wanted to engage the enemy and finish the war.

Hopkins said very positively that once this decision was taken to go ahead with the trans-Channel Operation it could not be reversed, for the United States would consider this its major war effort. He said that of course the United States was fighting in its own interests, and the British were doing the same, but now the interests of the two nations coincided and they must fight together.

Attlee agreed that the time had come to take the initiative away from the enemy, and Eden emphasized the supreme political importance of a European offensive on the peoples of the occupied countries, on the Russians and even on the British people, who had become fed up after spending two and a half years on the defensive.

After further remarks by Air Chief Marshal Portal and Admiral Mountbatten, Churchill gave Hopkins assurance that the British Government and people would make their full and unreserved contribution to the success of this great enterprise.

The next day Hopkins cabled exultantly to Roosevelt that the British Government had agreed to the main American proposal and Marshall cabled confirmation of this to the Secretary of War saying that the Prime Minister "declared in an impressive pronouncement his deep appreciation of the purpose and time of our visit." The British Government, Marshall said, now intended to proceed immediately and energetically with all necessary preparations for the major operation. He added that he and Hopkins had lunched with the King and Queen that day and would dine that night with the King and the Prime Minister at 10 Downing Street.

The meetings with the royal family were of a purely social nature and Hopkins made no notes on them. However, one result was that Hopkins got the signature of King George VI on his short-snorter bill.

Confirmation came from Vichy that Laval was being restored to the position of Premier—an unmistakable evidence of further surrender by Pétain to the Germans. On April 15, all American residents of unoccupied France were asked by the U.S. Government to leave for home at the earliest moment and Admiral Leahy was at last given his orders to report back to Washington "for consultation."

Hopkins cabled Roosevelt, "How about nailing that wood pussy Laval to your barn door?" and Roosevelt replied, "Your suggestion being studied but consensus of opinion is that odor still too strong for family of nations."

The American Embassy in London received from Washington a copy of a cable sent by Leahy:

It is of course difficult at Vichy accurately to gauge the reaction of the French public to the impending return of Laval to the Government of France. This is due to the fact that the great majority of the population of this provincial capital consists of Government officials. There seems, however, little doubt that Laval's return is extremely unpopular both with bourgeois elements and the great masses of the French people. On the other hand, in spite of the unpopularity of Laval there is no evidence, at least in Vichy, that the French people will at this time take positive or violent actions either against Laval or against the Vichy Government to demonstrate their dissatisfaction. While it is felt possible that there may be isolated incidents such as have already occurred in occupied France (where I have been reliably informed there were yesterday four or five attacks against members of the German Army, the most serious occurring at Caen), there appears to be in Vichy at the moment at least and possibly to a lesser extent elsewhere, a feeling that nothing can be done to prevent Laval's return. In Government circles we have heard from a number of people whose thorough dislike of Laval and his ideas cannot be doubted, the observation that while his return is to be deplored, he is at least a clever man who may perhaps obtain some concessions from the Germans and may at some future time be able to deceive them.

One of the arguments most often heard from people who believe Laval's return could not be prevented is that it is still too early for the French people to revolt against the Germans and their "collaborationist" friends. The Russian front, which the majority of French people consider is the key to the future of France, still remains a question-mark. In addition, the reverses of the British in the Indian Ocean and in Burma have created in French minds doubt as to British ability to hold their present position in the Near East. Therefore, runs their argument, any positive action taken against the authorities of occupation and their French collaborationist allies would be premature and would bring on terrible German reprisals. In spite of this apparent feeling of helplessness to prevent the return of Laval, should the Germans meet real reverses and find themselves in serious difficulty I believe there is little doubt that the majority of the people of France would be willing, if there seemed to be a possibility of success, to take action in some form or other against their cordially hated oppressors.

I hear the hope expressed from all quarters that the Allied Nations will be able to create some serious military diversion in Europe or North Africa by the despatch of an expeditionary force. We are given to understand that the majority of the French people in the Occupied Zone are counting on this possibility, and from the Unoccupied Zone we receive a great number of letters and expressions of opinion upholding this view. I believe there is doubt that in the French mind the feeling exists that such a move is absolutely necessary and that it must be undertaken at an early date. Otherwise, they feel, Russia will be unable to hold and it will be too late. If it does not take place there is little doubt that among the anti-Axis elements, who are very considerable, there will be a feeling of profound disillusionment.

On the morning of Hopkins' last day in London he had a final meeting in Churchill's bedroom in the annex to 10 Downing Street; Pound, Portal and Ismay were also present. The Prime Minister, lying in bed, reviewed the whole war situation, urging that action be speeded up all down the line, saying "the longer we wait, the hotter the water will become." He hoped more planes could be rushed to India and the *North Carolina* to Scapa Flow.

Churchill, from his bed—which was usually a mass of pink, including its occupant—gave Hopkins the messages he wanted imparted to the President, and in spite of everything they were largely optimistic. Although, during the discussions of the past ten days, it had been obvious British policy to emphasize the grimmer aspects of the situation, Churchill was constitutionally unable to dwell for long on the possibility or even what appeared to others to be the actuality of defeat. He did not really believe that the Japanese would sweep through India and join up with the Germans. He evidently considered it more likely that they would turn around and concentrate on an attempt to knock China out of the war. He urged Hopkins to come back soon, for his visits always exerted a tonic effect in Westminster. While they were talking, a message came from the Embassy saying that Leahy had just sent a secret report that Goering and his staff were at Serqueux near Forges les Eaux in the Seine Intérieur in France; Portal said the R.A.F. had received similar information and were investigating with a view to bombing the place.

Hopkins said a cheerful good-by and he and Marshall flew to Northern Ireland for a brief visit to the American troops there. They had dinner and spent the night in a country house near Londonderry, since the local commanders felt that one of Hopkins' frail condition should be billeted in luxury; this weird episode has been amusingly described in Mrs. Marshall's delightful book, *Together*. The next morning Hopkins received a cable from Roosevelt relayed by Matthews at the Embassy in London through Army headquarters:

This morning we have received reports indicating that Pétain has resigned and although his place has nominally been taken by Darlan it is probable that Laval is in control. Welles and I both feel that there is some chance that orders from Laval will not be accepted by the French in North Africa. I therefore hope that you and Marshall will discuss this changed situation with Mr. Churchill who undoubtedly has further information. I ask that you discuss this whole subject with him although I do not suggest revival of GYMNAST. I have some reason to believe that Orange battleships are now withdrawing eastward from the Bay of Bengal. We are progressing with the loading of the *Ranger*.

Matthews added to this cable that no confirmation had been received in London of the report of Pétain's resignation but that Washington had officially announced the recall of Leahy.

While Marshall went about his inspection trip in Northern Ireland, Hopkins telephoned Downing Street communicating the contents of this cable and saying that he felt it might be wise for him and Marshall to return to London, instead of flying back to the States, to await further developments of the French situation; it seemed possible that some sort of Allied expedition to North Africa might be launched immediately. Churchill agreed on this and Hopkins so cabled the President.

After lunch at the Army camp near Belfast, Hopkins and Marshall flew to Port Patrick, a little village on the West Coast of Scotland. General McClure had accompanied them from London, and in the small hotel in Port Patrick, Hopkins asked McClure to put through a telephone call to President Roosevelt. Anyone who has ever tried to use the telephone in a Scottish village knows that it is a considerable feat in itself to establish contact with some point as much as a dozen miles away. The effect on the local operator of a call to the White House in Washington is something utterly unimaginable. McClure was told to wait, then was put through to one supervisor after another, each of whom wanted to know who he was and why he desired to be put through to the President of the United States. McClure established his identity to the best of his ability, but he could not mention either Hopkins or Marshall who by now had returned to the characters of Mr. Hones and Mr. Mell. At length, McClure was told to hang up and wait. When he was called back to the telephone, he heard a vaguely familiar voice—but it was no one in the White House; he had been put through to Commander Thompson at 10 Downing Street, and he managed to explain to him that "the two friends who are with me" want to speak to the President. Thompson arranged matters in no time and Hopkins was talking to Roosevelt, who told him to come on home without waiting for further bulletins from North Africa. In the meantime, Scotland Yard had been alerted when McClure first made his remarkable call and its operatives closed in on the Port Patrick Hotel. Unfortunately, they made no arrests.

Hopkins and Marshall and Admiral Pound, who had joined them, took off on the Clipper that night from Stranraer, near Port Patrick, and they were in New York for lunch the next day.

On his last day in London Hopkins had received a letter from an English housewife, a Mrs. Martum of Newmarket, Suffolk, enclosing a cutting from the *Daily Express* which stated that "It will not be long now before American bombs fall on Tokyo." Mrs. Martum expressed the hope that this was right. She said, "Lots of people in this country have the wind up about India. . . . We want no soft stuff with Germans or Japs. . . . Let's give it to them thick. . . . May God bless you all who are working so hard to save our dear countrys, also our boys. . . . Let's have *action*, not words."

Mrs. Martum got her wish in a hurry. While Hopkins and Marshall were flying home the news came from an almost incoherent Japanese broadcast of the Doolittle raid on Tokyo. This was only one, valiant, wildly adventurous shot at the enemy, which may have done negligible tangible damage to his power—but it was the first good news for the United Nations that had come from any non-Russian sector of war in many, awful months. The men who risked and sacrificed their lives on this raid helped to accomplish as much as the winning of a great battle would have done in providing a badly needed lift of the heart for countless millions of discouraged people. It was a classic demonstration of the inestimable morale element in war which can turn fear of defeat into assurance of victory. Three weeks later came the Battle of the Coral Sea which Admiral King has described as "the first major engagement in naval history in which surface ships did not exchange a single shot" (there were more of them to come in the Pacific). This marked the beginning of the turning of the tide of Japanese conquest, although there were very few who could realize this at the time.

The whole atmosphere in Washington was changed. The gratification that Hopkins and Marshall had brought back with them from London was communicated from one department and war agency to another; there was a feeling, unfortunately not justified by the immediate facts, that we had passed from the defensive to the offensive phase of the war.

After Hopkins had made his first report at the White House, Roosevelt cabled Churchill that he was delighted with the agreement that had been reached in London. He said, "Marshall and Hopkins have told me of the unanimity of opinion relative to our proposals [for the opening of a Second Front] and I greatly appreciate the messages you have sent me confirming this. I believe that the results of this decision will be very disheartening to Hitler. It may well be the wedge by which we shall accomplish his downfall." Roosevelt expressed doubts that the dreaded junction of the Germans and Japanese would be accomplished. He said he was very pleased to have received a cordial message from Stalin announcing that Molotov and a Russian general were being sent to London and Washington. He added, "I am frank to say that although we still have many mutual difficulties, I feel better now about the joint war situation than I have at any time in the past two years."

Hopkins wrote to his old friend of relief days, Jacob Baker, "I returned from England greatly encouraged about everything but I think the whole business is going to take a lot of doing. I wish I were 25 years younger."

CHAPTER XXIV

The Molotov Visits

THE main work that now confronted Hopkins was the problem of supplies for the Soviet Union. The Germans were increasing the severity of their attacks against the route to Murmansk by submarine and by aircraft and surface craft based in northern Norway. Here in these Arctic latitudes where there was perpetual daylight in summer there was no such thing as refuge under cover of night.

At the time when Hopkins left England, there were fifteen ships in Iceland that had turned back from the Murmansk run; there were twenty-three more there that were waiting for convoys; there were twenty-one more Russian-bound ships halfway to Iceland that had to be rerouted to Loch Ewe in Scotland because of the congestion at Reykjavik. Thus, there were fifty-nine ships loaded with guns, planes, ammunition, oil, tanks, trucks, machinery, medical supplies, etc., for the Russians which were stalled and useless. In order to free some of these idle ships for some useful service their cargoes were unloaded in Scotland, which led to all manner of acrimonious charges from Moscow that the British were "stealing" Lend-Lease material assigned to them. There was consequently an increasing effort to get the ships through at whatever cost—and the cost was awful. In the months of April, May and June, eighty-four ships carrying 522,000 tons left U.S. ports for Murmansk. Forty-four of these, carrying 300,000 tons, got through. Of the remainder, seventeen discharged their cargoes in Scotland and twenty-three were sunk by the enemy or lost by shipwreck. Later, the losses became even worse; in one convoy, twenty-two out of thirty-three ships were sunk. In addition to all other hazards on this route was the horror of the Arctic Ocean itself; the crews knew the terrible death by freezing that confronted even those who might survive the loss of their ships.

The route across the Pacific to Siberia was kept open after Pearl

Harbor for Russian ships because of the Japanese desire to keep the Soviet Union out of their part of the war, but any bullet sent by that route had to travel halfway around the world before it could be fired at a German. The third route, via the Persian Gulf, became the most favorable after the opening of the Mediterranean in 1943 and the expansion of the port of Basra and the Iranian railroad by the "forgotten men" of the Persian Gulf Command. In the meantime, however, a ship could make only two round trips a year on this route and the extremity of the bottleneck at the Basra end made it necessary to unload many cargoes at Karachi in India, where some goods were still piled up awaiting transshipment when the war ended.

Soon after Hopkins returned to the White House he cabled Churchill about the Murmansk convoy situation. Replies came from both Churchill and Harriman, giving the official British view that, in consideration of the enormous difficulties, a new understanding should be reached with the Russians for reducing the promises of supplies to be delivered.

Roosevelt thereupon cabled the Prime Minister that the British and American Naval Chiefs of Staff, Admirals Pound and King, had been discussing ways and means of breaking the log jam of ships loaded with cargoes for Russia. Roosevelt expressed the belief that any unloading and reloading of these ships in the British Isles would produce a "very disquieting impression in Russia" and said that he hoped that, despite all risks, the proposed convoys with additional escorts would be forced through to Murmansk.

Churchill replied to this: "With very great respect what you suggest is beyond our power to fulfill." He pointed out that the convoy problem east of Iceland was no mere matter of antisubmarine escort craft but involved major naval operations. He reported that two damaged British cruisers were now immobilized at Murmansk and that he had just received word that the new battleship *King George V* had collided with the destroyer *Punjabi* which was sunk and her depth charges exploded damaging the battleship. Churchill added, "I can assure you, Mr. President, we are absolutely extended"—and begged that they be pressed no further.

On May 4, Roosevelt sent the following cable to Stalin:

You will have been informed by Litvinov of the grave complications we are having along the northern convoy route. However, I can assure you that we will spare no effort to get off as many ships as possible.

I look forward to a meeting with Molotov. We shall make preparation to provide immediate transportation for him the moment we know the route he is to follow. I had hoped that he can stay with me at the White House during his visit to Washington but we can make available to him a private house nearby if that is preferable.

I wish to express my appreciation for the cordial reception you have extended to Admiral Standley of which I have been informed.

The reply from Stalin arrived ten days later:

I thank you for the message conveyed through Ambassador Litvinov. I have already requested Prime Minister Churchill to contribute to the speediest overcoming of certain difficulties in connection with the transportation and convoying of ships to the U.S.S.R. Since the delivery of materials in May from the U.S.A. and England is of the utmost urgency, I make a similar request to yourself, Mr. President.

The journey of Mr. Molotov to the U.S.A. and England must be postponed for a few days owing to uncertain weather conditions. It appears that this journey can be made on a Soviet airplane both to England and to the U.S.A. I would at the same time add that the Soviet Government considers that Mr. Molotov's journey should be accomplished without any publicity whatever till the return of Mr. Molotov to Moscow, as was done when Mr. Eden visited Moscow in December last.

In regard to the place of residence of Mr. Molotov during his sojourn in Washington, Mr. Molotov and I thank you for your kind suggestions.

Some indication of the magnitude and complexity of the shipping problem at this time can be found in the following memorandum which Hopkins sent to Lewis Douglas:

I wonder if I could see the statistical material which you get on a monthly basis which shows the efficiency of the turn-around.

Could I have the same thing that shows the relative efficiency of repair?

Incidentally, are our merchant ship repair facilities used on a 24-hour basis? Is there adequate personnel in these facilities? What inducement is there to the companies to finish the job with all possible speed? What are the general terms of contract? Is it on a cost-plus basis? What are the average hours worked by employees in merchant ship repair yards? Are the facilities adequate or do the ships have to remain for a long period of time awaiting their turn?

Are you satisfied with the security of the stevedoring? Do we still permit enemy aliens to work on the docks and, if so, why? How many are there and in what ports? How adequate is the investigation machinery? Are you sure about the complete loyalty of some of the stevedoring managements? You know there have been charges that the Nazis are mixed up in these companies.

Do you think the docks are properly guarded and are these guards all military people or are there still private guards on some of these docks? Who investigates the loyalty of private guards?

Has an inquiry been made as to whether there are any stevedores or guards who were ever members of the Bund or the Christian

Front, or similar organizations, the membership of which we may assume do not want us to win this war?

Douglas, it will be remembered, had resigned as Director of the Budget in 1934 largely because of his violent disagreements with the President over the whole philosophy of spending for relief. He had subsequently been outspoken in opposition to Roosevelt in the campaigns of 1936 and 1940. There was, therefore, every reason on the record why he and Hopkins should have disliked each other intensely. However, after the defeat of Willkie, Douglas had asked for war service of any kind and Hopkins had been largely responsible for bringing him into a position of authority with Admiral Land in the War Shipping Administration. All of the questions in the foregoing memorandum were not answered immediately; but they were answered ultimately.

In the performance of his limitless duties as "Commander in Chief of the United Nations," Roosevelt could not entirely ignore the existence of domestic political affairs, much as he would have preferred to do so. Nineteen forty-two was a Congressional election year and, while that was not a consideration which ranked high on the priorities list in the White House, it was a matter of life or death on Capitol Hill. The Senators and Representatives who faced hard fights for re-election knew that they could keep their records clean insofar as the war was concerned by voting loyally for all the vast appropriations that were required, and they did so; furthermore, an attitude of vigilance over expenditures was maintained through various media of investigation, notably the Truman Committee. However, seriously controversial political issues were created by measures which involved arbitrary interference with the civilian economy. The American people, who were so willing and proud to give whatever was required of them in blood and sweat, were loudly reluctant to cut down on their normal consumption of red meat and gasoline and their use of such essentials as electric toasters and elastic girdles. More than any other people on earth, Americans were addicted to the principle that you can eat your cake and have it; which was entirely understandable, for Americans have been assured from the cradle that "there is always more cake where that came from."

In the frantic weeks and months following Pearl Harbor, Roosevelt paid little attention to the question of controls on the civilian economy. As a convenient means of dodging the necessity of confronting this tough problem, he accepted the advice of those who said that everything could be settled on a purely voluntary basis. As a result of which, the specter of inflation was beginning to haunt the land, and this was something that Roosevelt could clearly recognize with his keen memories of the First World War and its distressing aftermath.

In a Message to Congress on April 27 and a Fireside Chat the following day, he took cognizance of the dangerous situation and called for a seven-point program:

(1) We must tax heavily, and in that process keep personal and corporate profits at a reasonable rate, the word "reasonable" being defined at a low level.

(2) We must fix ceilings on the prices which consumers, retailers, wholesalers, and manufacturers pay for the things they buy; and ceilings on rents for dwellings in all areas affected by war industries.

(3) We must stabilize the remuneration received by individuals for their work.

(4) We must stabilize the prices received by growers for the products of their lands.

(5) We must encourage all citizens to contribute to the cost of winning this war by purchasing war bonds with their earnings instead of using those earnings to buy articles which are not essential.

(6) We must ration all essential commodities of which there is a scarcity, so that they may be distributed fairly among consumers and not merely in accordance with financial ability to pay high prices for them.

(7) We must discourage credit and installment buying, and encourage the paying off of debts, mortgages, and other obligations; for this promotes savings, retards excessive buying, and adds to the amount available to the creditors for the purchase of war bonds.

Before each of these seven points he used the words "To keep the cost of living from spiralling upward. . . ." However, he did not really face up to the necessity of rigid rationing and price control; his generalizations were too broad and the Congressmen who were fearful of their constituents' wrath were able to evade the issue until Roosevelt presented it to them in precise and unmistakable terms four months later.

In his Fireside Chat, Roosevelt did have one passage of importance in indicating the direction of strategic policy:

In the Mediterranean area matters remain, on the surface, much as they were. But the situation there is receiving very careful attention.

Recently we have received news of a change in government in what we used to know as the Republic of France—a name dear to the hearts of all lovers of liberty—a name and an institution which we hope will soon be restored to full dignity.

Throughout the Nazi occupation of France we have hoped for the maintenance of a French government which would strive to regain independence to re-establish the principles of "liberty, equality, and fraternity," and to restore the historic culture of France. Our policy has been consistent from the very beginning. However, we are now concerned lest those who have recently come to power may seek to force the brave French people to submission to Nazi despotism.

The United Nations will take measures, if necessary, to prevent the use of French territory in any part of the world for military purposes by the Axis powers. The good people of France will readily understand that such action is essential for the United Nations to prevent assistance to the armies or navies or air forces of Germany, Italy, and Japan.

The overwhelming majority of the French people understand that the fight of the United Nations is fundamentally their fight, that our victory means the restoration of a free and independent France—and the saving of a France from the slavery which would be imposed upon her by her external enemies and her internal traitors.

We know how the French people really feel. We know that a deep-seated determination to obstruct every step in the Axis plan extends from occupied France through Vichy France to the people of their colonies in every ocean and on every continent.

These words, of course, were aimed directly at the French people— in metropolitan France, North and West Africa and, most specifically at the moment, the island of Madagascar. As Roosevelt spoke in this Fireside Chat about rationing and price control, he knew that a British force was on the way to seize the strategically vital French island off the East Coast of Africa. Madagascar was athwart the sea route from the Cape of Good Hope to Middle Eastern ports, including Basra, and to India. It would have been an enormous prize for the Japanese and, in view of the naval situation in the Indian Ocean at the time, there was too large a possibility that the Japanese might be able to take it. If they had landed forces on the island, the Vichy French authorities would presumably have yielded to them without a struggle as they had done in Indo-China. Therefore, the British move, which had been fully discussed between London and Washington and with Hopkins and Marshall at the recent conferences, was heartily approved by Roosevelt as a demonstration of the ability of the United Nations to get to some important point before the enemy did. On May 1, Churchill cabled Roosevelt the terms to be offered to the local governor, providing the following guarantees: that the territory would remain a part of the French Empire, that those Frenchmen on the island who wished to return to France would be repatriated as opportunity offered, that salaries and pensions of all officials who elected to co-operate would be continued, that trade would be restored and various economic benefits granted, etc. It was hoped that the governor and other authorities would see the light of reason and offer no resistance to the British. The hope was in vain. Roosevelt expressed his approval of the measure in messages to Vichy as soon as news was flashed from the British commander that the forces were moving, but the old men of Vichy asserted the sacred "honor" which impelled them to defend French sovereignty to the death against British, American or Free French forces, though not against Germans or Japanese. Admiral Darlan sent a message to the authorities on Madagascar:

> Do not forget that the British betrayed us in Flanders, that they treacherously attacked us at Mers-el-Kebir, at Dakar and in Syria, that they are assassinating civilians in the home territory [by the bombing] and that they have sought to starve women and children in Djibouti.

As a result, the fighting on Madagascar went on for months.

Some time later highly interesting information was received from S. Pinkney Tuck, Counselor of the American Embassy in Vichy, concerning the attitude of General Weygand, who had been in retirement in Cannes since his dismissal from command in North Africa six months previously. The information was indirect, for Weygand was under such strict surveillance that, as Tuck said, "The General could not even blow his nose without it being heard in Vichy"; but General Strong, head of G-2 in the War Department, believed that the information had the ring of authenticity. These were Weygand's views as reported:

He believed that the Allies should land in *continental* France, preferably in the northern, German-occupied portion, rather than in North Africa. He said that the military and administrative structure which he had built up in North Africa had sadly deteriorated since his retirement —that the morale there was so poor that an American landing would be met with general apathy if not direct hostility. He felt strongly that fighting between Frenchmen and Americans should be avoided at any cost, for there had been already too much fighting between the British and French. Tuck said in his cable:

> On the other hand he [Weygand] believes that practically the whole French army in metropolitan France would not hesitate to give up its allegiance to a tottering government of Vichy and come to the support of an American force landed in France itself. He considers it highly important that French patriots should at once formulate plans for the establishment of a provisional government which would be recognized immediately by the occupying forces and which would provide the necessary legal authority which would be psychologically indispensable at least to the officers of the French army.

In his April 28 speech, Roosevelt said:

> Our planes are helping the defense of French colonies today, and soon American Flying Fortresses will be fighting for the liberation of the darkened continent of Europe.

This referred to a subject over which there was some controversy between London and Washington. The British wanted American heavy bombers to be turned over to the R.A.F. and manned and operated by their own crews. The U.S. Air Force leaders—General Arnold, General Carl Spaatz, General Ira C. Eaker—wanted to get into action themselves, with American bombers manned by American crews under American command operating from bases in the United Kingdom.

Roosevelt cabled Churchill expressing his belief that all reserve American airplanes, except for a reasonable number held in the British Isles, should be removed from a reserve status, which was in effect a status of inactivity, and put into operation to maintain the maximum continuous combat competition with the enemy. He said, "I think that the minimum number of planes consistent with security should be held in reserve and for operational training purposes and the maximum number should be applied in combat, and that United States pilots and crews should be assigned for the manning of American-made aircraft on the various combat fronts to a far greater extent than at present. I am sending General Arnold and Admiral Towers to London for discussion of the very important details of broad policy implied in this message."

Churchill replied to this in characteristic terms:

> We understand and respect the generous impulse which inspires the United States air force to engage American lives in the conflict at the earliest moment. God knows we have no right to claim undue priority in the ranks of honour. Let us each do our utmost. So may it be to the end.

Churchill went on to urge that Arnold and Towers proceed to London at the earliest possible moment. (Admiral John H. Towers was Chief of the Navy's Bureau of Aeronautics.) Despite the warm assurances at the start of Churchill's cable, the R.A.F. still wanted the bombers without the crews and many further difficulties had to be overcome before the U.S. Eighth Air Force could start its historic operations from Britain during the following summer.

The problem of getting aircraft to the Soviet Union was much harder to solve. After the winter interlude of counterattacks, the Russians now faced the spring and summer months of renewed German offensive and their most pressing need was for fighter aircraft rather than bombers. Since there were no pursuit planes at that time with sufficient range to fly the Atlantic at any point, the grievous shipping problems were involved, although they could be reduced to a certain extent by assembling the planes in Africa and flying them into Russia by way of Iran. There was a far easier and more obvious route by way of Alaska to Siberia. Hopkins discussed this with General Eisenhower on May 1 and practical and comparatively simple plans were drawn up in the War Department by which the planes could be flown directly from aircraft factories all over the United States to Soviet fields in Siberia within a few days; yet this was one of the proposals on which the always suspicious Russians proved obdurate and, although they agreed "in principle," it was a painfully long time before they would make the actual necessary arrangements for putting into operation the sensible delivery route by way of Fairbanks, Alaska.

One exchange of correspondence at this time showed how acute was the determination to disarm Russian suspicions of American motives: Hopkins received a suggestion that in view of "the various strategic considerations which make eastern Siberia a region of prime importance" the United States Government might well consider the desirability of introducing "individuals of proven ability and discretion," (i.e., secret agents) into Siberia under the guise of Lend-Lease representatives. Hopkins rejected this suggestion, saying:

> I don't see how the Siberian business can work out by having a Lend-Lease person in that area. The whole question of air routes to Russia has been and is being thoroughly explored and I hesitate because of my relationship with the Russians to explore it in any other than the direct manner.

On May 1, Hitler and Mussolini had another of their meetings, this time near Salzburg, and again the world waited for the next big German offensive to start. It was surprisingly late this year. Churchill said:

> We now wait in what is a stormy lull, but still a lull, before the hurricane bursts again in full fury on the Russian front. We cannot tell when it will begin; we have not so far seen any evidences of those great concentrations of German masses which usually precede their large-scale offensives. They may have been successfully concealed, or may not yet have been launched eastward. But it is now the tenth of May, and the days are passing. We send our salutations to the Russian armies, and we hope that the thousands of tanks and aeroplanes which have been carried to their aid from Britain and America will be a useful contribution to their own magnificently developed and reorganised munitions resources.

The consensus of opinion was that, when the German drive did come, it would move in a southeasterly direction toward the Middle East—either through the Caucasus, or through Turkey, or both. Turkey was one of the most important battlegrounds for economic and political warfare and, among neutral nations, by all odds the most favored object for Lend-Lease aid. Hopkins received reports on the situation from his friend, Ambassador Steinhardt, in Ankara:

> I find no evidence that the Germans intend to attack Turkey in the immediate future. While they have prepared bases in the Balkans for that purpose, there are insufficient German troops at present available in Greece and Bulgaria to launch such an attack. In any event it would

take them at least two weeks to move their troops into position. I think the critical moment for the Turks will be when the coming German offensive in southern Russia either stalls or goes through to the Caucasus. On the happening of either of these two events the Germans will have to decide whether to try and go through the difficult terrain in Turkey or keep hammering at the Russians. It is most unlikely that either of these two conditions will exist before July or August.

I am convinced that in their present frame of mind the Turks will fight if they are attacked. . . .

While I believe the army will give a good account of itself if attacked, you must expect no such resistance as the Russians have offered for the Turks possess no tanks and only a small obsolete air force which probably would not last more than 2 or 3 days against the Germans. Furthermore, they have very limited artillery. On the other hand, if they fall back into the mountains they should be able to make the going very tough for the Germans particularly if by that time the R.A.F. and some British artillery come to their assistance.

As I telegraphed you to London the March shipments of Lend-Lease material and the new Lend-Lease procedure have had a marked effect on Turkish morale. The highest Government officials have gone out of their way during the past 2 weeks to tell me of their keen satisfaction with the increased shipments. The disappointment they felt earlier in the year has been completely dissipated. They are now contrasting the unfulfilled German promises of armament with our steadily increasing deliveries so that I think that phase of the matter is now in good shape. I am very grateful to you for stepping up and speeding up these deliveries which have materially strengthened our position here.

The result of all this is that the Turks fear the Germans and ardently hope for an Anglo-American victory while at the same time they mistrust the Soviets and are doubtful that the United States and Great Britain will be able to restrain a victorious Soviet Union from taking the Straits away from them. It is difficult to predict just how far this situation may develop. I keep hoping that both the Turks and the Russians will have the good sense not to let the matter go any further than the mutual recriminations which have already taken place.

On May 12 Hopkins received a strictly unofficial message indicating that Churchill was considering the possibility of calling Lord Halifax back to London for service in the War Cabinet and as Leader of the House of Lords. His place as British Ambassador would be taken by Lord Beaverbrook. Hopkins discussed this proposal with the President and cabled Churchill that "The idea of Max coming is of course agreeable and it is believed here that he could be extremely useful in the light of the problems which confront our two countries." If this idea was pursued any further, I have seen no record of it, but it was highly interesting and significant to both Roosevelt and Hopkins at the time because

Beaverbrook had established himself publicly as well as privately as a vigorous, uncompromising advocate of the Second Front.

On April 23, he had come out flat-footed on this subject in a speech that he gave in New York. Even though Beaverbrook was no longer in the government, his association with Churchill was known to be so close that his expression of opinion was widely interpreted as a statement of official British policy. However, it is my understanding that Beaverbrook had not cleared this speech with Churchill or anyone else in the British Government but he had discussed it at length with the President and Hopkins in the White House. He thus had official though off-the-record American sanction for it. The naming of Beaverbrook as Britain's Ambassador following his statements would be, in effect, another form of commitment to the Second Front.

With the approach of Molotov's visit to Washington, plans for the great offensive in Europe occupied more and more attention in the White House although Hopkins continued his close associations with Dr. Soong, President Quezon and the Pacific War Council. In all preparations for amphibious warfare, then and for a long time thereafter, the biggest bottleneck was landing craft. Roosevelt discussed this subject at great length with Hopkins and drew two sketches of a landing craft which he had in mind. These sketches were drawn on a memorandum pad that someone had printed and inscribed "From the desk of Franklin D. Roosevelt." The President disliked these pads and rarely if ever used them again. I do not know what kind of craft he was illustrating in these sketches, or whether they provided any guidance to the naval architects. There was a protracted argument at the time over the design of the fifty-foot tank lighters. The production schedule called for the completion of six hundred of these within three months—and this requirement was made with the SLEDGEHAMMER operation in mind—but it took twice that long to do the job. "Responsibility for this production lag," says the official record, "could hardly be charged to industry or to the Government agencies supervising production. The chief difficulty was the failure of top officials responsible for strategic planning to anticipate the need for landing craft in the North African campaign sufficiently far in advance." It was also due to the Navy's reluctance to devote shipbuilding facilities and scarce materials to the construction of vessels to be used for essentially Army operations. In March, 1942, landing craft were tenth on the Navy's Shipbuilding Precedence List. By October, just before the North African landings, they had gone up to second place, preceded only by aircraft carriers, but the next month they dropped to twelfth place. General Marshall wrote that of all the problems of implementation of strategy faced at the Teheran Conference a year later "the greatest by far was the critical shortage of landing craft."

In one of his frequent outbursts of impatience, Hopkins said, "Esti-

Roosevelt's sketches of a landing craft, drawn on eve of Molotov's visit to Washington to press for early opening of a Second Front.

mates can be made and agreed to by all the top experts and then decisions to go ahead are made by the President and the P.M. and all the generals and admirals and air marshals—and then, a few months later, somebody asks, 'Where are all those landing craft?' or 'Whatever became of those medium bombers we promised to China?' and then you start investigating and it takes you weeks to find out that the orders have been deliberately stalled on the desk of some lieutenant commander or lieutenant colonel down on Constitution Avenue."

Allowing for some slight elements of exaggeration, this was all too often the truth, particularly in 1942, when the President's production goals were still referred to derisively in the War and Navy Departments as "the numbers racket." There were many officers, pardonably skeptical concerning the extravagant program that had come from the White House, who believed they could count only on the minimum of production and were consequently determined to fight or to connive, if need be, to keep that minimum for their own services.

In London, Molotov negotiated the treaty of Anglo-Soviet Alliance which was mainly a restatement of the military agreements made on July 12, 1941, and the principles of the Atlantic Charter as applied to the postwar world and particularly to any revival of the German menace.

On May 28, Churchill cabled Roosevelt a report of his talks with Molotov. Both the Prime Minister and Eden had been careful to avoid making any of the positive commitments that the Russians wanted regarding the establishment of a Second Front in 1942; they had limited themselves to discussion of the present state of the elaborate plans for BOLERO, SLEDGEHAMMER and ROUNDUP and had urged Molotov to stop again in London when, they felt sure, it should be possible to talk more definitely about the future. (Meaning, of course, after they had been advised what the President said to him.) In this same cable, Churchill said that Mountbatten was soon to arrive in Washington to inform the President and the Chiefs of Staff concerning certain difficulties that had arisen in the planning and to present a new suggestion (known as JUPITER) for a landing in the north of Norway through which a junction could be effected by land with the Russians, thereby greatly simplifying the task of getting supplies through to the Soviet Union. Churchill added, "We must never let GYMNAST pass from our minds," and said that he and Molotov had made great progress in "intimacy and good will." This cable provided the first danger signal to Roosevelt and Hopkins, Marshall and King, that British thinking was beginning to veer toward diversionary operations far removed from the main point of frontal attack across the Channel.

Molotov arrived at the White House about four o'clock in the afternoon of Friday, May 29. He then met with the President, Hull, Hopkins, Ambassador Litvinov and two interpreters, M. Pavlov and Samuel H.

Cross, the latter Professor of Slavic Languages and Literature at Harvard University. The record of this first meeting, as written by Cross, is as follows:

After the customary introductions and greetings, Mr. Molotov presented Mr. Stalin's good wishes, which the President heartily reciprocated. To the President's inquiry as to Mr. Stalin's health, Mr. Molotov replied that, though his Chief had an exceptionally strong constitution, the events of the winter and spring had put him under heavy strain.

Mr. Molotov described his flight from Moscow to London and thence to Iceland, Labrador, and Washington as not especially unpleasant or wearing. His plane had flown from Moscow to London direct, over the front and Denmark, in about 10 hours, but this was not particularly good time, as the same trip had been made before in 7-½ hrs. He explained that his military adviser had broken his knee-cap in an automobile accident in London, and was, thus, detained in England. Mr. Molotov consequently regretted that he would have to act as both diplomat and soldier. The President remarked that none present were military specialists, but that Mr. Molotov would have an opportunity next day to talk with General Marshall and Admiral King.

Mr. Molotov expressed his intention to discuss the military situation fully. He had covered it in detail with Mr. Churchill, who had not felt able to give any definite answer to the questions Mr. Molotov raised, but had suggested that Mr. Molotov should return through London after his conversations with the President, at which time a more concrete reply could be rendered in the light of the Washington discussions.

The President noted that we had information as to heavy Japanese naval concentrations in the Fuchia and Mariana Islands, but that we could not tell as yet whether they were directed against Australia, Hawaii, Alaska, or perhaps Kamchatka. Mr. Molotov said he was not informed about this, but he had no doubt the Japanese would do anything in their power to intimidate the Soviets.

To Mr. Molotov's remark that Hitler was the chief enemy, the President noted his agreement and mentioned his repeated statements to the Pacific Conference that we should remain on the defensive in the Pacific until the European front was cleared up. It had been difficult, he added, to put this view across, but, in his opinion, it was now accepted.

The President remarked that he had one or two points to raise which had been brought up by the State Department, and could be discussed by Mr. Molotov or between Mr. Litvinov and Secretary Hull, as seemed expedient.

The President then inquired what information Mr. Molotov had as to the Nazi treatment of Soviet prisoners of war. The Commissar replied that, from such data as Moscow received, not only from their own agents, but also from Polish and Czech sources, it was plain that the Russian prisoners were brutally and inhumanely handled. Direct reports to the effect had been received from some 25 Soviet prisoners who had escaped from Norway into Sweden. Mr. Molotov remarked that the Germans felt themselves bound by no rules, though the Soviets (he implied) were acting according to the Hague convention to the best of their ability.

The President expressed the hope that at least some arrangements might be made to exchange lists of names of prisoners of war. Mr. Molotov replied with emphasis that his government was not disposed to negotiate any arrangement with the Germans which would give the latter the slightest pretext for claiming that they (the Germans) were observing any rules whatever, because the fact was, they were not doing so. He showed no interest in the President's original suggestion. The President remarked that we had a similar problem in connection with our own nationals in Japanese captivity. While there was, for the moment, no official confirmation of radio reports of positive maltreatment, these prisoners were being fed on the Japanese army ration, which was starvation fare for any white man.

The President then had a memorandum on the state of Soviet-Turkish relations, which had become considerably less cordial than was previously the case. The memorandum expressed the willingness of our government to cooperate in any way toward the improvement of these relations. Mr. Molotov replied succinctly that he was ready to discuss this matter.

The President also referred to the disturbances among the Kurds in Eastern Iran and expressed his hope that the trustful cooperation now existing between the Soviet and the Iranian authorities would continue and manifest itself hereafter as occasion might arise. Mr. Molotov said he was familiar with the situation and shared the President's hope.

In the course of conversation the President asked Mr. Molotov whether he had noted any intensification of reports on the deterioration of German domestic morale. Mr. Molotov admitted the increased frequency of such reports, but failed to comment on their significance.

The President described his plans for continuing the conversations and for receiving Mr. Molotov's staff and the flyers who brought him over. Mr. Molotov decided to spend Friday night at the White House, and ostensibly withdrew to rest, though between adjournment and dinner he took a walk with Mr. Litvinov, whom it had been decided not to include in the next day's conversations, to the Ambassador's obvious annoyance.

Hopkins' personal record of this same meeting was as follows:

Molotov and the President greeted each other very cordially, Molotov expressing his warm appreciation for the invitation to come to America and extending to the President the warm greetings of Stalin. It was pretty difficult to break the ice, although that did not seem to be due to any lack of cordiality and pleasantness on the part of Molotov.

The President had two or three memoranda on his desk which I had never heard of before, which were obviously given him by the Department of State, in which the Department was offering their good offices in alleged difficulties between the Russians and the Iranians on the one hand and the Russians and Turks on the other. I gathered Molotov was not much impressed. I at any rate so imagined and in front of the President he raised the point that they thought they knew a good deal more about their relations with Iran and Turkey than we did. I confess I did not see in what way our good offices were to be executed.

The State Department also obviously wants Russia either to sign or adhere to the Geneva Convention of 1929 relative to the care and treatment of prisoners of war. This agreement requires that the adhering countries permit a neutral body, such as the International Red Cross, to inspect the prison camps. You don't have to know very much about Russia, or for that matter Germany, to know there isn't a snowball's chance in hell for either Russia or Germany to permit the International Red Cross really to inspect any prison camps. Molotov's final answer was that "Why should we give the Germans the diplomatic advantage of pretending to adhere to international law. Germany might well say that they would agree and then not, of course, do anything about it because you couldn't trust them."

Molotov indicated that it would be a mistake from a propaganda point of view to give Germany the chance to say that they were the people who upheld international law. He said that all the reports that Russia has of the treatment of Russian prisoners indicates that they are getting a very bad deal. Twenty-six prisoners recently escaped from Norwegian prison camps came back telling of starvation and beatings on the part of the Germans. I gather this is going to be a pretty difficult nut to crack for the State Department.

Hull later handed me the attached memorandum indicating the things he wanted taken up with Molotov while he is here. One of the interesting things about this is that none of these things has anything to do with the war on the Russian front, although the first four are matters of considerable importance to us but very little to the Russians unless we really mean business.

The President got into a discussion with Molotov about the Japanese. Molotov said the Japs are going to use every possible measure to prevent the movement of any divisions from Siberia to the German front and he thought they were going to constantly threaten Siberia so that no troops could be moved.

The President told Molotov he thought the Japanese fleet might strike in any one of four directions—either at Australia and New Caledonia, or at Midway, Guam and Hawaii, or at the Aleutian Islands, or, finally, at Kamchatka.

Molotov indicated that Kamchatka, while defended, was only lightly so because they did not have the forces or the guns to spare to protect it adequately.

There was some discussion of the use of poison gas. Molotov said that they had evidence that the Germans were moving large amounts of gas to the Russian front, although up to the present it had not been used.

The conference seemed to be getting nowhere rapidly and I suggested that Molotov might like to rest.

Litvinov acted extremely bored and cynical throughout the conference. He made every effort to get Molotov to stay at the Blair House tonight but Molotov obviously wanted to stay at the White House at least one night, so he is put up in the room across the way.

I went in for a moment to talk to him after the conference and he asked that one of the girls he brought over as secretaries be permitted to come and that has been arranged.

Following is the memorandum handed to Hopkins by Hull:

A. The Establishment of an Airplane Ferrying Service From the United States to the Soviet Union Through Alaska and Siberia.

B. Establishment of a Civil Air Service between the United States and Vladivostok or Some Other Railway Point in Siberia Through Alaska.

C. The Establishment of a Civilian Air Service Between the United States and the Soviet Union Through Africa and the Middle East.

D. The Supply Route Over the Soviet Union to China.

E. Finland.

F. Economic Matters.

G. Iran.

H. Turkey.

I. Prisoners of War Convention—1929 Geneva.

The same group, with the exception of Hull, reassembled in the Oval Study at 7:40 for cocktails and dinner and conversation that lasted until midnight.

During the course of the evening, Roosevelt talked a great deal of his desire to start the process of disarmament after the war, maintaining arms only for the purpose of policing the world, particularly Germany and Japan to make sure that they would not regain powers of aggression. It was his persistent belief that world economy could not recover if all nations, large and small, had to carry the burdens of heavy armament in order to survive. He said to Molotov what he said to many others during these war years: he believed that a peace could be established and guaranteed for at least twenty-five years, or as long as any of his and Stalin's and Churchill's generation could expect to live—which was what Roosevelt meant when he spoke of the "foreseeable future."

Professor Cross later noted:

At the close of the conversation the President asked Mr. Molotov whether there were any Americans he particularly wanted to see, to which Mr. Molotov replied that he would, if possible, like to exchange greetings with ex-Ambassador Davies. Earlier in the evening he had spoken appreciatively of Admiral Standley, of whom the President remarked that he had chosen him because he was direct, frank, and simple. Mr. Molotov agreed that these were among the Admiral's conspicuous qualities.

The whole evening's conversation, on Mr. Molotov's part, was marked by a somewhat unexpected frankness and amiability, which leads, not unnaturally, to the supposition that, since the Soviets want something very seriously, the word had gone out from Mr. Stalin to be somewhat more agreeable than is Mr. Molotov's custom.

Hopkins later told me—but this was not included in his written record—that Roosevelt was unusually uncomfortable and "his style was cramped" in these meetings primarily because of the enormous language difficulty and the inevitable waits while each statement was translated, with additional delays while the two interpreters discussed shadings of meanings with one another. There was also the fact that in all of Roosevelt's manifold dealings with all kinds of people, he had never before encountered anyone like Molotov. His relationship with the Kremlin from 1933 to 1939 had been through Litvinov who, although qualifying as an old Bolshevik, had a Western kind of mind and an understanding of the ways of the world that Roosevelt knew. During the years 1939-1941 of the Nazi-Soviet pact Roosevelt had few personal contacts with Ambassador Oumansky, leaving that tough proposition largely to Hull and Welles. However, Roosevelt was by no means appalled by the new and strange problem in human relations that Molotov presented. It offered a challenge which stimulated him to spare no effort to discover the common ground which, he was sure, must somewhere exist.

The next morning the President and Hopkins met with Molotov, General Marshall and Admiral King, and Pavlov and Cross. Hopkins wrote no personal record of this or of the two further meetings. Professor Cross's record was as follows:

After a brief private conference between the President and Mr. Molotov, conversations were resumed at 11 A.M. The President asked Admiral King whether there was any special news from the Pacific. The Admiral replied that there was nothing of importance save some momentary disagreement between General MacArthur and Admiral Nimitz as to an operation against the Solomon Islands. Admiral King thought this difference was due to a misunderstanding, since Admiral Nimitz had in mind a specific project for destruction of installations rather than anything like a permanent occupation.

Opening the general discussion, the President remarked to Admiral King and General Marshall that he first wished to place them au courant with the questions Mr. Molotov had raised, and he hoped that Mr. Molotov himself would then put the situation before them in detail. Mr. Molotov, the President continued, had just come from London, where he had been discussing with the British authorities the problem of a second (invasion) front in Western Europe. He had, the President added, been politely received, but had as yet obtained no positive commitment from the British. There was no doubt that on the Russian front the Germans had enough superiority in aircraft and mechanized equipment to make the situation precarious. The Soviets wished the Anglo-American combination to land sufficient combat troops on the continent to draw off 40 German divisions from the Soviet front. We appreciated, he continued, the difficulties of the situation and viewed the outlook as serious. We regarded it as our obligation to help the Soviets to the best of our ability, even if the extent of this aid was for the moment doubtful. That brought up the question, what we can do even if the prospects for permanent success might not be especially rosy. Most of our difficulties lay in the realm of ocean transport, and he would in this connection merely remark that getting any one convoy through to Murmansk was already a major naval operation. The President then suggested that Mr. Molotov should treat the subject in such detail as suited his convenience.

Mr. Molotov thereupon remarked that, though the problem of the second front was both military and political, it was predominantly political. There was an essential difference between the situation in 1942 and what it might be in 1943. In 1942 Hitler was the master of all Europe save a few minor countries. He was the chief enemy of everyone. To be sure, as was devoutly to be hoped, the Russians might hold and fight on all through 1942. But it was only right to look at the darker side of the picture. On the basis of his continental dominance, Hitler might throw in such reinforcements in manpower and material that the Red Army might *not* be able to hold out against the Nazis. Such a development would produce a serious situation which we must face. The Soviet front would become secondary, the Red Army would be weakened, and Hitler's strength would be correspondingly greater, since he would have at his disposal not only more troops, but also the foodstuffs and raw materials of the Ukraine and the oil-wells of the Caucasus. In such circumstances the outlook would be much less favorable for all hands, and he would not pretend that such developments were all outside the range of possibility. The war would thus become tougher and longer. The merit of a new front in 1942 depended on the prospects of Hitler's further advantage, hence the establishment of such a front should not be postponed. The decisive element in the whole problem lay in the question, when are the prospects better for the United Nations: in 1942 or in 1943.

Amplifying his remarks, Mr. Molotov observed that the forces on the Soviet front were large, and, objectively speaking, the balance in quantity of men, aviation, and mechanized equipment was slightly in Hitler's favor. Nevertheless, the Russians were reasonably certain they could hold out. This was the most optimistic prospect, and the Soviet morale was as yet unimpaired. But the main danger lay in the probability that Hitler would try to deal the Soviet Union a mighty crushing blow. If, then, Great Britain and the United States, as allies, were to create a new front and to draw off 40 German divisions from the Soviet front, the ratio of strength would be so altered that the Soviets could either beat Hitler this year or insure beyond question his ultimate defeat.

Mr. Molotov therefore put this question frankly: could we undertake such offensive action as would draw off 40 German divisions which would be, to tell the truth, distinctly second-rate outfits? If the answer should be in the affirmative, the war would be decided in 1942. If negative, the Soviets would fight on alone, doing their best, and no man would expect more from them than that. He had not, Mr. Molotov added, received any positive answer in London. Mr. Churchill had proposed that he should return through London on his homeward journey from Washington, and had promised Mr. Molotov a more concrete answer on his second visit. Mr. Molotov admitted he realized that the British would have to bear the brunt of the action if a second front were created, but he also was cognizant of the role the United States plays and what influence this country exerts in questions of major strategy. Without in any way minimizing the risks entailed by a second front action this summer, Mr. Molotov declared his government wanted to know in frank terms what position we take on the question of a second front, and whether we were prepared to establish one. He requested a straight answer.

The difficulties, Mr. Molotov urged, would not be any less in 1943. The chances of success were actually better at present while the Russians still have a solid front. "If you postpone your decision," he said, "you will have eventually to bear the brunt of the war, and if Hitler becomes the undisputed master of the continent, next year will unquestionably be tougher than this one."

The President then put to General Marshall the query whether developments were clear enough so that we could say to Mr. Stalin that we are preparing a second front. "Yes," replied the General. The President then authorized Mr. Molotov to inform Mr. Stalin that we expect the formation of a second front this year.

General Marshall added that we were making every effort to build up a situation in which the creation of a second front would be possible. As an officer, he appreciated how serious present conditions were, and the necessity of quick action. He had been greatly encouraged by the Russian resistance and counter-offensive on the southern front. Frankly speaking, we had the troops, all adequately trained; we had the munitions, the aviation, and the armored divisions. The difficulties lay in transport, but the convoy problem was complicated by the necessity of sending tonnage to Murmansk, and the delivery of aircraft to the British Isles, where the heavier planes could be shipped by air under their own power, was limited by present deliveries to the Soviets.

Strategically the idea was, said General Marshall, to create as quickly as possible a situation on the continent under which the Germans would be forced into an all-out air engagement, but they will not engage on this scale without the pressure of the presence of our troops on the ground. General Marshall added that, while Mr. Molotov based his considerations on the number of German divisions (40) which the Soviets would like to see diverted from their front, what we had to base our own action on was the number of men we could ship across the Channel in order to provoke an all-out battle for the destruction of the German air-force. The essential preliminary to a successful continental operation was to make the German aviation fight; we must therefore have an air-battle.

The President then asked Admiral King to outline his point of view. The President observed that sending each convoy to Murmansk had become a three-dimensional naval engagement on account of providing defense not only against the lurking German major units (Von Tirpitz, Scharnhorst, Gneisenau, Prinz Eugen) but also against enemy submarines and air-craft. Admiral King concurred in the President's estimate of the situation. Getting convoys into Murmansk and Archangel was a major problem because of the heavy German units in Narvik and Trondjem and the German air-bases in Northern Norway. German reconnaissance planes shadowed our convoys from Iceland to Murmansk and, when a convoy approached, they caused it to be attacked by both submarines and surface craft. This complex situation also rendered it necessary for large forces of the British Home Fleet to remain at sea to guard against attacks from heavy German ships which are stationed nearer to the convoy routes. Similarly, the United States Navy has had to reinforce the British fleet with such heavy ships so that the British should have enough such ships on hand in order to maintain their convoying forces on the requisite level. At present we were running two convoys in opposite directions simultaneously, i.e., one would be leaving Murmansk as another left Iceland, so that the necessary cover could be provided in one operation.

Admiral King added it would be helpful if the Soviet air force could make additional efforts toward aiding the convoys, especially by air-attacks on the German air and submarine bases at Narvik and Kirkenes, and remarked that such additional cooperation was justifiable by the importance to the United States and Great Britain of the safe arrival of munitions in Northern Russia. The situation was obviously complicated, the Admiral continued, by the southward drift of the polar ice which limited the range of movement by the convoys. In one convoy due in Murmansk the previous day (Friday, May 29) we had lost 5 ships out of 35, together with one destroyer, and other ships of the convoy had been damaged. To be sure, as the ice withdraws northward during the summer, the convoys would have more room to maneuver in, but this advantage would be pretty well cancelled out by increased visibility during long summer days. The route by which ships could be put into Archangel during the summer was obviously longer, but we might even so gain something by increased freedom of movement.

The President then remarked to Mr. Molotov that we had in Khartum 24 bombers of the finest and heaviest type, and inquired what the Soviet attitude would be to having these bombers fly north to bomb the Rumanian oil-fields and then go on to land at Rostov or somewhere in the neighborhood. The President added that it did not seem expedient to turn these planes over to the Russians, as we do with the 200 pursuit planes supplied them monthly, but only for the reason that it took two months to train a bomber crew. Mr. Molotov said the whole idea was entirely acceptable and, in fact, his government would not mind an arrangement whereby Soviet bombers could shuttle back and forth across Germany to be serviced and rearmed in England.

The President also referred to the advisability of delivering fighter planes to the U.S.S.R. by air from Alaska to Siberia and then across the latter west-ward. Mr. Molotov objected, however, that, while this method would be appropriate for supplying the Soviet Far-Eastern Command, he doubted its efficacy or practicability for the delivery of planes to the Western front because of the long distance involved and the difficulty of arranging for gasoline depots.

The conversation was then adjourned for lunch.

The gathering at lunch in the White House that day—Saturday, May 30—was as follows: The President, Molotov, Litvinov, Vice-President Wallace, Hull, Marshall, King, Forrestal, Senator Connally, Congressman Bloom, the Soviet Military and Naval Attachés, General Burns, the President's Naval Aide, Hopkins, Pavlov and Cross.

Cross has written:

The conversation during lunch was mainly desultory. The President described to Mr. Molotov the acquisition of the new Lincoln portrait, and commented upon the nearness of the Confederate lines to Washington during the early days of the Civil War. When Hitler was brought into the conversation, the President remarked that, after all, Mr. Molotov had seen and talked with Hitler more recently than anyone else present, and perhaps Mr. Molotov would be willing to communicate his impressions of the man. Mr. Molotov thought a moment, then remarked that, after all, in the world, it was possible to arrive at a common understanding with almost anyone. Obviously Hitler had been trying to create a good impression upon him. But he thought he had never met two more disagreeable people to deal with than Hitler and Ribbentrop. To the President's remark that Ribbentrop had formerly been in the champagne business, Mr. Molotov observed drily that he had no doubt Ribbentrop was better in that line than in diplomacy. On being informed of Senator Connally's functions as Chairman of the Senate Foreign Affairs Committee, Mr. Molotov asked the Senator what he considered the most serious diplomatic problem now confronting the United States. When the Senator answered "Vichy," Mr. Molotov remarked that there was nothing genuine about the Vichy Government, and that they were a nuisance.

At the close of lunch, the President secured the general attention and spoke substantially as follows: He was glad to welcome our distinguished guest, whose nation was contributing so signally to the successful prosecution of the war. His conversations with Mr. Molotov had been friendly and frank. The President hoped they would lead to definite and salutary results. There was, however, one Russian whom he looked forward to meeting, and that was Mr. Stalin, whose masterly leadership was carrying his country through so serious a crisis. After a toast to Mr. Stalin, the President emphasized that this luncheon was entirely off the record, since no press announcement of Mr. Molotov's visit would be released until after the Commissar's safe return to Moscow.

When the President had concluded his remarks, Mr. Molotov rose and said he was happy to answer. His visit was unusual, and he had traveled unusual paths across the front and the ocean. His visit was going well and attaining its purpose. The enemy to be met was not only cruel and powerful, but was driven by a limitless appetite. Mr. Molotov wished to remind his hearers that the Soviet, by bitter experience, knew best what Hitler is. Hitler wanted more territory, and was becoming more insatiable day by day. The Red Army was doing its best, but we must reckon fully with all possible dangers. Mr. Molotov thanked the President for his generous toast to the great Soviet leader and general. President Roosevelt, he added, was popular in the Soviet Union because of his clear understanding of the interests of his people and the farsightedness with which he promoted these interests. He proposed the President's health, thanking him for his statesmanlike handling of the grave international problems with which he was confronted in his high office. Mr. Molotov added that his grateful acknowledgments were equally addressed to all members of the United States Government concerned with the prosecution of the war.

The President then asked Mr. Molotov if he would not give the guests a picture of the current military situation. Mr. Molotov then remarked that the present operations were the beginning of the summer offensive period for which Hitler had been preparing. Marshal Timoshenko had begun his Kharkov offensive as an offset to the German drive on the Kerch peninsula. This drive had resulted unfavorably for the Russians. The Soviets had originally possessed superiority of forces in the Eastern Crimea, but had used this superiority ineffectively because of the inefficiency of the local commander, General Kozlov, who had proved weak and had not, as a matter of fact, taken part in previous operations against the invading forces. A concentration of aviation and of armored units, supported by Rumanian troops, had enabled the Germans to achieve a relatively easy success. This was regrettable but there was no use in disguising the facts. The

German drive in the Crimea necessitated speeding up by several days the opening of Marshal Timoshenko's Kharkov offensive. As far as personalities went, the Soviets had found that inexperienced officers and men were the least effective. For example, Marshal Timoshenko was the more dependable because he had had field experience since the beginning of the invasion, while Kozlov was an instance of the opposite state of affairs in both respects.

The Germans' easy success in the Crimea had rather surprised them, and had led to boastful German talk about new and secret weapons which they actually did not possess—a characteristic and usual form of German propaganda. The Soviet tactics used at Kharkov to encircle the city on the north and south had been at first very successful, and in the first three days netted 400 German tanks damaged or destroyed. This reverse had led the Germans to start the Izyum-Barvenkovo movement with 6 armored divisions, infantry, and aviation. Southeast of Kharkov the Soviet troops had opened out a salient which the Germans were now trying to even out, and were thereby seriously endangering the Soviet forces in the salient. Marshal Timoshenko commands the southwestern front, while the southern front (Rostov-Voroshilovgrad) is commanded by General Malinovski under Timoshenko's supervision. Mr. Molotov reminded his audience that he had been away from Moscow two weeks, but he believed the situation was still serious, especially if the Red troops were cut off in the salient just mentioned. He would not undertake to speak positively on the outcome of the present struggle. The Germans might next concentrate on Moscow or Rostov, or even make an effort to penetrate the Caucasus along the line Novorossisk-Maikop-Baku. Success in this last effort would confer vast advantages upon Hitler, particularly with respect to oil. The morale of the Red Army was excellent, and its confidence in ultimate victory unimpaired. To a question by the President regarding guerilla operations, Mr. Molotov replied that the partisans were most active in the Moscow-Smolensk-Mozhaisk (Dorogobuzh) sector. They numbered 19,000 irregulars and parts of 2-3 cavalry divisions under General Belov. They were in absolute control of an egg-shaped area measuring some 60 kilometers east and west by 20-30 kilometers north and south. They were, however, less conspicuous in other areas.

At the close of lunch, the President casually mentioned to Mr. Molotov that we had never got around to declaring war on Rumania, as it seemed something of a waste of effort. Mr. Molotov said that might be the case, but the Rumanians were fighting against the Soviets and causing some trouble by helping the Nazis. The President then turned to Senator Connally and Congressman Bloom with a query as to the probable attitude of their respective Committees toward a formal declaration of war upon Rumania. Their thought was that there would be no objection, whereupon the President suggested that appropriate action might take place during the coming week (of May 31). On taking leave of Mr. Molotov, Senator Connally assured him that the enemies of the U.S.S.R. were our enemies, a sentiment which Congressman Bloom emphatically shared.

After lunch the President returned to his study, where he received the officers and crew of Mr. Molotov's bomber and the members of the Commissar's clerical staff, who were presented by Mr. Litvinov. The President addressed a few words of cordial greeting to the group, congratulated the flyers, and expressed the hope that, now they had found the way, they would return again, bringing the Commissar with them once more.

The President handed Mr. Molotov a list of 8,000,000 tons of Lease-Lend material which we should produce during the year from July 1, 1942, but stated that we could ship only 4,100,000 tons of this total.

The group then broke up about 3:30 P.M.

During his stay in Washington, Molotov bore the code name of "Mr. Brown." His visit imposed a strain on Steve Early and on Byron Price, Director of the Office of Censorship, for, in accordance with Stalin's request, the presence of Mr. Brown in Washington could not be made known to the public. It was utterly impossible to keep the White House correspondents from finding out about it and this was one occasion when Early and Price asked for voluntary censorship and it was observed until the official announcement was released a week after Molotov's departure.

Evidently, the Russian airplane which had brought Molotov blew a tire, for the following note came to Hopkins from Colonel K. M. Walker:

Bolling Field is flying the airplane tire off the Russian ship to Akron, Ohio, this afternoon.

The Chief Engineer of the Akron people will be on the job personally and will work all tonight and tomorrow rebuilding the tire, which they expect to have available to be flown back to Washington Tuesday morning.

Everything else about the ship is o.k. The Russians are well pleased with the service and cooperation they have been receiving.

There were no meetings with Molotov in the White House between Saturday lunch and Monday morning.

There was a meeting with the Chiefs of Staff Sunday afternoon (General Arnold was at that time in London) which Hopkins described:

The President had a conference this afternoon for an hour with General Marshall, Admiral King and myself, in which we discussed the final statement the President would make to Molotov.

The President told General Marshall and Admiral King that he thought the matter was a little vague and the dangerous situation on the Russian front required that he, the President, make a more specific answer to Molotov in regard to a second front.

The President read a draft of a cable which he had prepared to send to Churchill. Marshall thought that the use of the word "August" was unfortunate and would arouse great resistance on the part of the British. I agreed with this.

There was then considerable discussion as to the Russian convoy by the northern route and the effect of the withdrawal of that route or, at any rate, a marked cutting down of the number of ships on the "Bolero" operation.

I expressed the opinion that if the Russians could get those munitions which they could actually use in battle this year, such as tanks, airplanes, spare parts, guns and ammunition, that they probably would be quite satisfied if they had definite assurances of "Bolero" in 1942.

Clearly the revision in our shipping to Archangel would provide more ships for "Bolero." By the same token, according to King, it would very substantially relieve the pressure on the British Home Fleet and make more destroyers available for the Atlantic convoy.

Marshall, I believe, thinks that "Bolero" is inevitable some time in 1942 merely by the force of circumstance.

The President asked me if I would redraft the cable to the Former Naval Person and the final draft is the one that was sent.

(*Note.* In the foregoing Hopkins seems to have made the mistake, which Roosevelt also did in some messages, of referring to BOLERO as the trans-Channel operation itself.)

Following is the cable to Churchill to which Hopkins referred:

I think that Molotov's visit has been a real success. We have got on a personal footing of candour and of friendship as well as can be managed through an interpreter. He will leave here in two or three days.

Molotov has clearly expressed his anxiety concerning the next four or five months. I think that this is sincere and that it is not put forward for the purpose of forcing our hand.

I am, therefore, more anxious than ever that BOLERO shall begin in August and continue as long as the weather permits.

After discussion with the Staffs, I believe that the German air forces cannot be destroyed unless they have been forced to take the air by preliminary or temporary actions by ground forces. If we can start this phase early in August we can produce one of the following results:

1. Divert German air forces from the Russian front and attempt to destroy them.

2. If such air forces are not moved to the west, we can increase our operations with ground forces and determine on the establishment of permanent positions as our objective.

I am especially anxious that Molotov shall carry back some real results of his mission and give a favourable report to Stalin. I am inclined to believe that the Russians are a bit down in the mouth at present. Our Combined Staffs are now working on proposals to increase the shipping for BOLERO use by making large reductions

of materials for Russia which we could not manufacture in any case
before 1943. This should not diminish the supplies which the Russians
could use in combat this summer, such as ammunition, guns, tanks
or planes.

In this same cable, Roosevelt suggested to Churchill that he would
like to have a talk with Field Marshal Smuts, saying, "I think it may
be of help to him in his home problems to get a picture of the general
situation from a fellow Dutchman like me." He also acknowledged
receipt of a set of the complete works of Winston Churchill, saying he
was "thrilled" by them and "shall always cherish them."

At this same meeting with Marshall and King, on May 31, there was
also considerable discussion of the New Russian "Protocol" (program
of Lend-Lease aid) which would go into effect July 1, at the expiration
of the First Protocol, drawn up when Beaverbrook and Harriman were
in Moscow nine months previously. The Staffs in Washington and
London had been working out the details of the Second Protocol and
had arrived at the schedule of 4,100,000 tons of shipments which Roosevelt had handed to Molotov after lunch the previous day. Now, in view
of the critical shipping situation, it seemed that this program must
be cut down if any major transatlantic operation were to be undertaken
in 1942. On this, Hopkins wrote the following note:

> The attached memorandum was written by the President at the
> conference with General Marshall and Admiral King this afternoon.
> The memorandum indicates how the total number of tons of ship-
> ping to Russia might be cut down. The problem is how many ships
> this would release for "Bolero."
> The President is very insistent, however, that all of the tough items
> of supply go through.

The President's memorandum:

Present Plan:

4,100,000	tons made up of
1,800,000	Planes tanks guns
2,300,000	General Supplies

New Plan:

1,800,000	Planes tanks guns
700,000	General Supplies
2,500,000	tons

4,100,000	
2,500,000	
1,600,000	saving

The final meeting of the President, Molotov and Hopkins was held at 10:30 on Monday morning, June 1, with Litvinov, Pavlov and Cross the only others present. This is Cross's record:

The President opened the conversation by remarking that the Washington press representatives knew about Mr. Molotov's visit, but had been very decent about making no reference to it. He suggested that, after Mr. Molotov's safe return to Moscow, the Soviet Government might simultaneously inform Messrs. Maisky and Litvinov of his arrival, and set an hour at which synchronized announcements of his visit might be released in London and Washington. Mr. Molotov accepted this suggestion.

On the basis of State Department memoranda, the President then went on to say he had a few points to mention, mostly for Mr. Litvinov's attention. We had, the President continued, reports from Finland that representative groups in that country wish to make peace with the Soviet Government. They could not, however, mobilize their strength to demonstrate to Finnish public opinion the possibility of peace unless something concrete were done by Moscow or Washington. These groups had asked the United States to ascertain a possible basis for peace, and the United States Government would proffer its good offices for this purpose if the Soviet Government wished to avail itself of them.

In the whole of Monday morning's conversation, Mr. Molotov was much more gruff and assertive than in the previous interviews, perhaps for the purpose of playing the big shot in Mr. Litvinov's presence. In this case, at any rate, he immediately became terse and pressing. "I should like to know," he asked, "whether these Finns are official." "No," replied the President, "they are merely a number of leaders of public opinion, but not the Finnish Government." "Do they want peace?" inquired Mr. Molotov. The President replied in the affirmative. "Have they any special conditions in view?" Mr. Molotov asked. "No," said the President. "They express no desires as to the basis on which peace should be concluded?" "No," answered the President, "what they want is to show the Finnish people that peace is possible with safety to Finland." Mr. Molotov then inquired whether these groups were able to represent Finland. The President replied that our information was confined to the statement that several such representative private groups existed. Mr. Molotov then observed that he would discuss the matter with Mr. Stalin.

The President next observed that postal connections and official travel between Washington and Kuibyshev were slow and difficult. We were running a plane service as far as Basra which we would be disposed to extend as far as Teheran if the Soviets would send down a connecting plane to that point, perhaps once a week. Mr. Molotov replied without hesitation that his government would establish such a Kuibyshev-Teheran service, but at the start only once in two weeks. He directed Mr. Litvinov to carry on with the detailed arrangements.

The President then noted that, for substantially the same purpose we should like to organize a civilian air service from Washington to Nome, and then continue on to some convenient point at the east end of the Trans-Siberian, e.g., Petropavlovsk. The President remarked that it was immaterial whether the American planes flew over to Petropavlovsk, or whether the Soviets sent their own planes over to Nome. He also raised the point of organizing a civilian ferrying service for military planes from Nome to Siberia. Admiral Standley had already talked on this subject to Mr. Stalin, who had said he would study the question. Mr. Molotov observed that both these suggestions were under advisement, but he did not as yet know what decision had been reached.

The President remarked that he wished Mr. Molotov would take up one other matter with Mr. Stalin. We knew, he said, that there would be two kinds of post-war settlements: first, those among the United Nations and, second, arrangements for the reconstruction of the other nations with a view to ensuring a more stable form of peace. The President continued by saying that he had a new thought based on old experience. He believed that, instead of requiring interest on war-time advances, all the United Nations should work out a plan covering a long-term repayment of capital only. He hoped Mr. Molotov would discuss the point with Mr. Stalin for the purpose of exploring it without commitments. Mr. Molotov agreed to do so. The President observed that some such arrangement would facilitate matters for Great Britain, the Soviet Union, and the United States, and also prove helpful for other nations.

(At this point Mr. Hopkins inquired of the President whether the latter cared to discuss his project for setting up a special post-war fund under international trusteeship. This question was not translated to Mr. Molotov and thus did not figure in the discussion.)

On the President's previous suggestion Mr. Molotov commented that he thought Mr. Stalin would be interested, and promised that the proposal would be attentively studied. Both he and Mr. Stalin thoroughly appreciated the role played by the United States in the initiation of such proposals.

The President then recalled that he had already developed his ideas about disarming Germany and Japan, about control and inspection of their munitions industries to preclude surreptitious rearmament, about the future police activities of the four major nations, and about their role as guarantors of eventual peace. He had omitted one other point: viz., that there were, all over the world, many islands and colonial possessions which ought, for our own safety, to be taken away from weak nations. He suggested that Mr. Stalin might profitably consider the establishment of some form of international trusteeship over these islands and possessions.

In reply Mr. Molotov declared that he had considered and reported to Moscow the President's earlier proposals as to post-war organization. He had received an answer from Mr. Stalin, who was in full accord with the President's ideas on disarmament, inspection, and policing with the participation of at least Great Britain, the United States, the Soviet Union, and possibly China. This idea had the full approval of the Soviet Government, which would support it fully. He had no doubt that the President's trusteeship principle would be equally well received in Moscow.

The President then pointed out that the acceptance of this principle would mean the abandonment of the mandate system. For example, after the last war the Japanese had received a mandate over the previously German islands in the Pacific, which they had fortified. These islands were small, but they ought not to be given to any one nation. The Japanese should, of course, be removed, but we did not want these islands, and neither the British nor the French ought to have them either. Perhaps the same procedure should be applied to the islands now held by the British. These islands obviously ought not to belong to any one nation, and their economy was substantially the same everywhere. The easiest and most practical way to handle the problem of these islands over a long period would be to put them under an international committee of 3-5 members.

The President then inquired of Mr. Litvinov whether he was ready to abandon the League of Nations. "Anything for the common cause," the Ambassador replied.

Turning to the question of colonial possessions, the President took as examples Indo-China, Siam, and the Malay States, or even the Dutch East Indies. The last-mentioned would some day be ready for self-government, and the Dutch know it. Each of these areas would require a different lapse of time before achieving readiness for self-government, but a palpable surge toward independence was there just the same, and the white nations thus could not hope to hold these areas as colonies in the long run. Generalissimo Chiang Kai-shek therefore had the idea that some form of interim international trusteeship would be the best mode of administering these territories until they were ready for self-government. They might, the President added, be ready for self-government in 20 years, during which the trustees might endeavor to accomplish what we accomplished in the Philippines in 42 years. The Generalissimo, then, was thinking of the principle of trusteeship looking toward independence. The President hoped Mr. Molotov would discuss this suggestion with Mr. Stalin.

The Commissar expressed the opinion that this problem deserves serious allied attention, and it would certainly receive such attention in the U.S.S.R. For him it was obvious that any decision upon it would depend on the guarantees exercised by Great Britain, the Soviet Union, and the United States (with China, perhaps), coupled with such control functions as would prevent Germany and Japan from arming again to menace other nations with war. Starting from this principle, Mr. Molotov expressed his conviction that the President's proposals could be effectively worked out. The President said he expected no difficulties once peace was achieved.

The President then interjected that he had to entertain the Duke and Duchess of Windsor at lunch at twelve, but that he had one more point to discuss. Mr. Molotov also noted that he had another question to present.

The President then went on to say that on the previous day he had discussed questions of tonnage and shipping with the Chiefs of Staff. Every week we were building up troop and plane concentrations in England with a view to getting at the Germans from there as quickly as possible.

We were also shipping landing craft. But the time-element involved depended on available ships. We hoped and expected to open a second front in 1942, but we could progress more rapidly only with more ships. The Chiefs of Staff had therefore suggested that, in order to speed up the opening of the Second Front, the Soviet Government, with this in mind, should reconsider the Lease-Lend list previously submitted, remembering that, of the 4,100,000 tons which were to be shipped during the year from July 1, 1942, only 1,800,000 tons are materiel ready to be used for military purposes on the Russian front this summer. The rest was mostly raw materials and other items for the production of materiel which would not be ready for use this summer. 2,300,000 tons, in fact, represented items that would not be used for fighting at all. The President therefore proposed that the Soviet Government consider reducing its Lease-Lend requirements from 4,100,000 tons to 2,500,000 tons. This reduction would release a large number of ships that we could divert to shipping to England munitions and equipment for the second front, and thus speed up the establishment of that front. Mr. Hopkins further emphasized that there would be no cut in the volume of tanks and ammunition being shipped. Everything that the Red Army could use in actual fighting would still go forward.

Mr. Molotov replied that, while he would report this suggestion at home, he hoped that such non-military supplies as metals and railroad materiel, which have a direct bearing on the solidity of the present front, would not be cut too much, as they also were in large degree essential. In checking over the Lease-Lend list, his Government would have to reckon with the degree in which any reduction on non-military items would impose restrictions on the Russian rear, e.g., on electric plants, railroads, and machinery production. These were, after all, comparatively vital, and he hoped these needs would not be lost from view. He remarked again that he had a couple of points for discussion.

The President repeated that we expected to set up a second front in 1942, but that every ship we could shift to the English run meant that the second front was so much the closer to being realized. After all, ships could not be in two places at once, and hence, every ton we could save out of the total of 4,100,000 tons would be so much to the good. The Soviets could not eat their cake and have it too.

To this statement Mr. Molotov retorted with some emphasis that the second front would be stronger if the first front still stood fast, and inquired with what seemed deliberate sarcasm what would happen if the Soviets cut down their requirements and then no second front eventuated. Then, becoming still more insistent, he emphasized that he had brought the new treaty out of England. "What answer," he asked, "shall I take back to London and Moscow on the general question that has been raised? What is the President's answer with respect to the second front?"

To this direct question the President answered that Mr. Molotov could say in London that, after all, the British were even now in personal consultation with our staff-officers on questions of landing craft, food, etc. We expected to establish a second front. General Arnold would arrive next day (Tuesday, June 2nd) from London, and with him Lord Mountbatten, Marshal Portal, and General Little, with whom it was planned to arrive at an agreement on the creation of a second front. Mr. Molotov should also say in London that we could proceed toward its creation with the more speed if the Soviet Government would make it possible for us to put more ships into the English service. Mr. Molotov, the President observed, would be back from New York either Tuesday or Wednesday (June 2 or 3). After General Arnold had reported to General Marshall, the President hoped Mr. Molotov would discuss further arrangements with General Marshall.

The conversation thus ended with decreased tension on the Russian side. The President bade Mr. Molotov a cordial farewell, wished him a safe return home, and presented the Commissar with his photograph. The meeting broke up at about 12.10 P.M.

After that meeting, Hopkins went with the President to Hyde Park where they remained for three days. While at Hyde Park, Hopkins received the following memorandum from General Burns:

At a luncheon today at the Soviet Embassy, Mr. Litvinov and his distinguished guest pressed for an answer to the four requests which they said had been submitted to you on June 1st.

They are as follows:

1. Sending of one caravan of ships monthly from the ports of America directly to Archangel under escort by U.S. naval ships.

2. Monthly supplies of 50 bombers B-25 by flight through Africa with their delivery at Basra or Teheran.

3. Delivery of 150 bombers Boston-3 to the ports of the Persian Gulf and their assembly there.

4. Delivery of 3000 trucks monthly to the ports of the Persian Gulf and their assembly there.

The following information is submitted for a basis upon which to make a reply:

Item 1. No suggestion. This is a matter to be decided by the highest level.

Item 2. The proposed Protocol provides for a monthly quota of 12 B-25 bombers to be flown across Africa and to be delivered to the Russians at Basra or Teheran.

Item 3. The proposed Protocol provides for the delivery of 100 A-20's each month through October to the ports of the Persian Gulf and for their assembly there. After October, war developments will determine rate. (The A-20's are the equivalent of the Boston-3.)

Item 4. Our information is to the effect that 3,000 trucks per month could be shipped to the Persian Gulf and be assembled there.

Hopkins noted his reply on this as follows:

I talked to the President about General Burns' memorandum.

I asked Burns if he would not see Molotov this evening and advise him formally, but not in writing, as follows:

In regard to No. 1, that we were acting jointly with the British Admiralty in regard to convoying merchant ships to Murmansk and that independent United States naval convoy could not be established, but that every effort would be made to get the ships through as long as possible. I told Burns to emphasize to Molotov the importance of air support from the Russians, both in attacking the airports from which Germany is operating and to give far more adequate air cover to the convoy coming in.

In regard to No. 2, I told Burns to tell Molotov that the commitment we made relative to bombers was final.

In regard to No. 3, the answer is the same as for No. 2.

In regard to No. 4, to tell Molotov that we could deliver 3000 trucks monthly.

After his subsequent meeting with Molotov, Burns sent this information to Hopkins:

Mr. Molotov made no comment with reference to the rendering of more effective Soviet air support to the northern convoy route.

He seemed to desire a more definite answer to Request No. 1 (monthly U.S. convoy from America to Archangel). I repeated that my understanding is that while the President is most anxious to move the maximum amount of supplies to Russia, he does not feel that more specific commitments as to convoys can be made at this time.

Mr. Molotov asked me to thank the President for his prompt consideration of these four requests and for his decisions thereon. He said that while he had hoped they would be granted in full, he was deeply grateful for the help offered. He stated we could rest assured that all munitions supplied to the U.S.S.R. would be put to work against the Germans as promptly and effectively as possible, and that Russia could be relied upon to continue the war until victory is won. I told him I was sure the President and the country had that same feeling about Russia. He seemed to be very friendly and very appreciative of the efforts being made to assist his country.

Hopkins also noted while at Hyde Park:

> Steve Early called me up at Hyde Park today and said that the President had asked the State Department to prepare a draft of a proposed public statement which would be made concurrently in Moscow and Washington when Molotov arrives in Moscow.
>
> Steve said this was submitted to the Russians, who did not like it and had in turn submitted their own proposed draft, which is attached.
>
> I talked to General Marshall about this and he felt that the sentence about the second front was too strong and urged that there be no reference to 1942. I called this particularly to the President's attention but he, nevertheless, wished to have it included and the only amendment made was the one recommended by Mr. Hull, namely, that his name be excluded from those participating in a military conference and a sentence be added, which I drafted as follows:
>
> "Mr. Cordell Hull, Secretary of State, joined in subsequent conversations on non-military matters."

The reference to the Second Front which Molotov wrote and which appeared in the public statement issued on June 11 was: "In the course of the conversations full understanding was reached with regard to the urgent tasks of creating a Second Front in Europe in 1942."

The exact meaning of those words and all the implications involved in them provoked interminable and often violently acrimonious discussion for a long time thereafter.

Hopkins later was given an Aide Memoire which the British authorities had handed to Molotov on this subject. It said:

> We are making preparations for a landing on the Continent in August or September 1942. As already explained, the main limiting factor to the size of the landing force is the availability of special landing craft. Clearly, however, it would not further either the Russian cause or that of the Allies as a whole if, for the sake of action at any price, we embarked on some operation which ended in disaster and gave the enemy an opportunity for glorification at our discomfiture. It is impossible to say in advance whether the situation will be such as to make this operation feasible when the time comes. We can therefore give no promise in the matter, but, provided that it appears sound and sensible, we shall not hesitate to put our plans into effect.

After Molotov's departure, Hopkins wrote a letter about things in general to Winant:

> Molotov's visit went extremely well. He and the President got along famously and I am sure that we at least bridged one more gap between ourselves and Russia.

There is still a long ways to go but it must be done if there is ever to be any real peace in the world. We simply cannot organize the world between the British and ourselves without bringing the Russians in as equal partners.

For that matter, if things go well with Chiang Kai-shek, I would surely include the Chinese too. The days of the policy of the "white man's burden" are over. Vast masses of people simply are not going to tolerate it and for the life of me I can't see why they should. We have left little in our trail except misery and poverty for the people whom we have exploited.

I think the publicity release gives all I can tell you about the second front. I have a feeling some of the British are holding back a bit but all in all it is moving as well as could be expected.

Our victory at Midway may turn out to have been a great one. So much so that it may change the whole strategy of the Pacific. After all, it is fun to win a victory once in a while. Nothing that I know of quite takes its place.

The new Lend-Lease Agreement with Russia, I think, also helps.

Lyttelton has made a fine impression here and I am sure he is going back greatly encouraged.

The visit of Oliver Lyttelton, who had replaced Beaverbrook as Minister of Production, resulted in the establishment of the Combined Production and Resources Board on June 9. The Combined Food Board also came into being at this time.

The Production Board should undoubtedly have been formed at the Arcadia Conference along with the Combined Chiefs of Staff and the Munitions Assignment Board. It had been considered impossible then because neither the War Production Board in the United States nor the British Ministry of Production had begun to function. Although now launched with Lyttelton and Donald Nelson as its two members, it never exercised adequate co-ordinating authority. The main reasons for its failure have been recorded in "Industrial Mobilization for War":

Despite early efforts, CPRB did not engage in comprehensive production planning or in the long-term strategic planning of economic resources. The American and British production programs for 1943 were not combined into a single integrated program, adjusted to the strategic requirements of the war. CPRB's isolation from the sources of decision regarding production objectives, its failure to develop an effective organization, its deference to other agencies and its tardiness in asserting its jurisdiction, the inadequacy of program planning by the agencies upon whom CPRB relied for forecasts of requirements, the delay of the Combined Chiefs of Staff in formulating strategic objectives for 1943—all these contributed to a result that saw adjustments in the American and British production programs for 1943 made by the appropriate national authorities in each case, rather than through combined machinery.

The trouble was that the "appropriate national authorities" in the United States were not only Nelson and his associates in WPB, but also the procurement officers of the War and Navy Departments with whom the civilians were engaged throughout the war in one of the many running battles of Washington.

After returning to the White House from Hyde Park, Roosevelt cabled Stalin that Molotov's visit had been a very satisfactory one and that he was anxiously awaiting the news of the Foreign Commissar's safe return to Moscow. At the same time he cabled Churchill, "Molotov warmed up far more than I expected and I feel sure that he now has a much better understanding of the situation than he had previously. I must confess that I view the Russian front with great concern. However, our operations in the Pacific are going well and I am certain that we are inflicting some severe losses on the Japanese fleet. Our aircraft are giving a very good account of themselves. I shall keep you informed about the outcome of the present battle [Midway] which is still indecisive but we should know more about it before this day is over."

These two cables from Roosevelt to Churchill and Stalin were sent on June 6, 1942, which was the date of the decisive Battle of Midway in the Pacific and also two years to the day before the real Second Front was at last opened in Northern France.

CHAPTER XXV

The Decision Is Changed

THE Battle of Midway was, in the Pacific, what the Battle of Britain had been in stopping the Germans on the Channel and what Stalingrad was to become in the war on the Russian Front. It was, as Admiral King has written, "the first decisive defeat suffered by the Japanese Navy in 350 years. Furthermore, it put an end to the long period of Japanese offensive action, and restored the balance of naval power in the Pacific."

On that day, Hopkins wrote to Churchill:

This note will, I hope, reach you by the hand of Franklin Roosevelt, Jr., who is leaving today to join his destroyer.

From the last 48 hours we have had our minds on the Jap attack on Midway and Dutch Harbor. Our reports this morning are quite good. Whether the beating they have taken is going to force them to withdraw we do not know, but it rather appears so. When you add this to the Coral Sea business, it will change the relative value of our naval forces in our favor very substantially.

The Japs simply cannot stand the attrition and I am sure we can beat them down gradually in the air and on the sea until finally they must collapse. This does not mean there will not be bad news in the Pacific. I think there will be plenty of it, but I am sure their days of pushing around there with impunity are over.

The Molotov visit went off well. I liked him much better than I did in Moscow. Perhaps it was because he wasn't under the influence of Uncle Joe! At any rate, he and the President had very direct and straightforward conferences.

We are disturbed here about the Russian front and that anxiety is heightened by what appears to be a lack of clear understanding between us as to the precise military move that shall be made in the event the Russians get pushed around badly on their front.

The full implications of Arnold's visit are still being analyzed here and I think probably the President will not come to grips with them for a day or two.

I confess that I am somewhat discouraged about our getting into the war in a manner that I think our military strength deserves, but I have always been an impatient person and I have no doubt that our time will come.

You have no idea of the thrill and encouragement which the Royal Air Force bombing has given to all of us here. Whatever happened to the list of cities marked for inevitable destruction? I imagine the Germans know all too well what they have to look forward to.

I am sure there are certain matters of high policy which you must come to grips with the President on and he is hopeful that you can make a quick trip and I fancy will be cabling you about it at once.

Oliver is here and getting about his business quietly but effectively. He had lunch with the President yesterday and is off to Detroit today. He will get a chance to have some real talks with the President before he goes back.

I saw Mountbatten for a moment yesterday. The President is going to spend the evening with him next Tuesday.

Above all, I am ever so glad to learn of your good spirits and health. The timid souls here and in England, heartily joined, no doubt, by every Nazi-minded person in our two countries, would like to see you laying bricks in the countryside of Kent. I gathered when I was in England that you didn't want to do that for awhile. I think it might be all right just after Laval's funeral.

Give my love to Clemmie and Mary. Why don't you bring Clemmie with you? She would be worth far more than all Brendan's propaganda pills.

On the night of May 30 the R.A.F. had put over its first 1,000-bomber raid on Cologne, a demonstration of power which gave a formidable boost to morale in the United Nations. General Arnold was with Churchill at Chequers that day, urging the case for U.S. bombing operations from Britain. Arnold quoted Churchill as saying, "Your program apparently will provide an aerial striking force equal to, or in some cases larger than, that provided and planned by us. Perhaps your program is too ambitious. You are trying to do, within a few months, what we have been unable to accomplish in two or more years." Churchill stuck to his argument that for the time being the United States should deliver heavy bombers without crews to the R.A.F. until full production could be reached and there would be more than enough for all. In the meantime, Churchill undoubtedly felt—although he was far too polite to say so—that the British were more competent to use the weapons than were their American allies.

Hopkins noted on that night of the Cologne raid:

The Prime Minister called me at 7:00 p.m. today, obviously from Chequers where he was entertaining Winant, Harriman, Arnold, Somervell and Eisenhower for the week end.

The Prime Minister was obviously in good spirits and told me he was sending twice as many bombers that night over Germany as had ever gone before. He indicated the weather was good and he was very hopeful of the outcome. They were apparently planning to stay up all night to learn the results.

He also indicated that the battle in Africa was going well and said to me, "I may see you very soon."

Later Arnold and Harriman called from England.

Arnold indicated he was coming home at once; that he felt his mission had been very successful and he too was very hopeful about the night's bombing operations.

Eisenhower and Somervell were then on a quick trip to London for discussion of problems of planning and supply. They returned to Washington a few days later, Arnold bringing with him Admiral Lord Louis Mountbatten, who conveyed to the U.S. Chiefs of Staff the disturbing impression that there might be some question of revision of the ROUNDUP-SLEDGEHAMMER agreements made by Marshall and Hopkins in London six weeks previously. It was believed in Washington that Mountbatten was expressing the attitude of the British Chiefs of Staff, rather than his own.

Mountbatten had dinner with Roosevelt and Hopkins and then returned to London to report his conversation to the Prime Minister, after which he sent a summary of this report to the President, as follows:

I was so very grateful to you for giving me the opportunity of such a long and interesting talk last Tuesday and I did my best to convey all that you told me to the Prime Minister and the Chiefs of Staff. In order to make sure that I correctly conveyed your points I propose recapitulating here what I told the Prime Minister.

I pointed out that you stressed the great need for American soldiers to be given an opportunity of fighting as soon as possible, and that you wished me to remind the Prime Minister of the agreement reached last time he was in Washington, that in the event of things going very badly for the Russians this summer, a sacrifice landing would be carried out in France to assist them. I pointed out that no landing that we could carry out could draw off any troops since there were some 25 German divisions already in France and Landing Craft shortage prevented our putting ashore an adequate number. The chief German shortage lay in fighter aircraft and all our efforts were being bent towards provoking fighter battles in the west.

I said that you had asked for an assurance that we would be ready to follow up a crack in German morale by landing in France this autumn and that I had given you an assurance that such an operation was being planned and was at present held at two months' notice.

I pointed out that you did not wish to send a million soldiers to England and find, possibly, that a complete collapse of Russia had made a frontal attack on France impossible. I said that you had asked whether we could not get a footing on the Continent some time this year, even as late as December, in which case you would give the highest possible priority to the production and shipping of Landing Craft, equipment and troops. The need for securing a port for supplying the troops under winter weather conditions made it clear that we should have to capture a port such as Cherbourg and hold a suitable line such as the Cherbourg Peninsula possibly expanding across towards St. Nazaire and eventually holding the whole of Brittany.

I made a point that you were sure that, in any case, when the operation came off we should have to secure the Atlantic ports and not go rushing off in the direction of Germany until we were firmly established, unless German morale had really cracked.

I pointed out that you did not like our sending out divisions from England while American troops were still being sent in and that you suggested that we should leave about six divisions in England and that the corresponding six American divisions should be sent straight to fight in North Africa, either round the Cape to fight in Libya or straight into Morocco with a view to joining hands with the Army of the Nile and re-opening the Mediterranean. In the latter connection, I told the P.M. how much you had been struck by his remark in a recent telegram: "Do not lose sight of GYMNAST."

This would mean that Dakar would fall into our hands without having to fight for it and I mentioned that you considered this important because the climate was not suitable for European soldiers to fight in.

As a result of the recent losses inflicted by the U.S. fleet on the Japanese fleet, particularly their aircraft carriers, there was a general desire to take the offensive from Australia using the existing U.S. marine forces and combat shipping. General Marshall had suggested going for Timor and General MacArthur had telegraphed on his own suggesting making for Rabaul. I said that you and General Marshall were anxious that two British aircraft carriers with their destroyer screen should join the American naval forces in Australia to support these operations, and that there had also been a suggestion that the amphibious force which had assaulted Madagascar should be used for operations against the Japanese. . . .

I was so thrilled and heartened by all I saw in America, particularly by the American army which is forging ahead at a quite unbelievable rate.

(The deletions made in the above document before the final paragraph referred primarily to technical matters.)

There was an increasing conviction in Washington that the British were now inclined to dissuade the Americans from entertaining any ideas of engaging the Germans in force on land or in the air in 1942. This is what Hopkins meant when he wrote, "I am somewhat discouraged about our getting into the war in a manner that I think our military strength deserves." (He meant the European war, of course.) When it was made known that Churchill was about to embark on another trip to Washington Marshall determined that the Prime Minister should be given an opportunity to observe for himself the quality of the U.S. Army and the advanced state of its training.

On June 9 Hopkins noted:

> Ambassador Litvinov came to see me last night and told me the Russian Government had agreed to our flying bombers to Russia via Alaska and Siberia.
>
> I told him that I would ask General Arnold to get in touch with him to work out all the plans for the route.
>
> It seems to me this is one of the tangible results of Molotov's visit and I doubt very much if this would have been approved on any other basis.
>
> I imagine the real reason the Russians approved our flying planes through Siberia is that in the event Japan attacks them we will already have organized a quick method of getting bombers to Vladivostok.
>
> I later told General Arnold of Russia's agreement and he has agreed to get in touch with Ambassador Litvinov at once.

At that time, Japanese forces were landing on Kiska and Attu in the Aleutian Islands—the nearest advance they made to the North American continent—and Roosevelt cabled Stalin:

> The situation in the Alaskan and North Pacific area is developing in such a way as to provide tangible evidence of intentions of Japanese preparations to conduct operations against the Siberian maritime provinces. We are prepared to come to your assistance with our air power in the event of such attacks if suitable landing fields in Siberia can be made available to us. The operations of the Soviet Union and the United States must be carefully co-ordinated in order to carry out such operations.
>
> I believe that an immediate exchange of detailed information concerning existing bases in the Alaskan and Siberian areas and the starting of secret staff talks between our joint navy, army and air representatives are essential to our common security in order to meet this new danger from Japan. I am very happy to be told by Litvinov that you have given approval to the movement of our aircraft from Alaska through Siberia to your battlefronts against Germany. I propose that you and I designate representatives to meet in Moscow and Washington at once and that these representatives be empowered to make definite plans and initiate action which I consider to be a matter of great urgency.

A decisive battle was being joined in Libya between the advancing German forces under Rommel and the British under Auchinleck.

Churchill, always interested in this theater and almost always optimistic about it, advised Roosevelt that he expected "considerable results" here, "or even a complete decision." Free French forces under General Joseph-Pierre Koenig covered themselves with glory and suffered heavy losses in the hopeless defense of Bir Hacheim which ended June 10, leaving only the fortress of Tobruk between Rommel and Egypt. On this same day the Germans announced that the village of Lidice in Czechoslovakia was being leveled and its name "extinguished," its men shot, its women put into concentration camps, its children distributed through "appropriate educational institutions" in Germany—all in reprisal for the killing near this quiet village of Reinhardt Heidrich, deputy to Heinrich Himmler of the Gestapo. This act of calculated ferocity, advertised by the Germans themselves with such brazen cynicism, made it unnecessary for the Allies to invent propaganda to arouse the world's indignation and make certain that there would be the will to fight this war to the death. The barbaric fury and suicidal stupidity of the atrocities at Lidice were duplicated by the Germans throughout the conquered territories of the Soviet Union. Hatred was generated which in itself provided the strongest insurance against the possibility of the Russians making a separate peace.

The hopes and fears of the sorely tried Russian people were now concentrated on the beautiful Crimean seaport of Sevastopol which had been cut off and besieged for eight months. The Germans had been pounding it with dive bombers and, on June 7, they launched all-out infantry and tank attacks in a determined effort to end the city's epic resistance before starting their major drive toward the Caucasus. It was evident that Sevastopol could not hold out much longer. The Russians were now more than ever in desperate need of nourishment for their faith in ultimate victory. The Soviet Government's propaganda to their own people had established the term "Second Front" as the veritable talisman of deliverance.

On the evening of June 18, there was an Extraordinary Session of the Supreme Soviet of the U.S.S.R. held in the Kremlin for the purpose of ratifying the Alliance with Britain and welcoming Molotov home. The foreign correspondents in Moscow were invited to attend and to give to the world descriptions of this celebration of Anglo-American-Soviet solidarity. Molotov gave the principal speech, saying:

> I cannot but associate myself with the words Mr. Eden spoke at the time of the signing of the Treaty: "Never in the history of our two countries has our association been so close. Never have our mutual obligations in relation to the future been more perfect." This is unquestionably a happy omen. . . .

Naturally, serious attention was given to the problems of the Second Front during the talks, both in London and Washington. The

... In view of letter of yesterday)
ask Marshall & King the following

"On the assumption that the
Russian army will be hard pressed
and retreating in July; that the
German forces are in August[1]
dangerously threatening Leningrad
and Moscow and[2] have made a
serious break thru on the Southern
front threatening the Caucasus.

And on the further assumption
that American ground forces supported
by air — in a direct attack
on the German forces, with or without

Message to Marshall and King, drafted jointly by Roosevelt and

British or Russian assistance +
can force a withdrawal of German
forces from the Russian front. -
On the above assumptions
- at what point or points can:

A. American (FDR)
ground forces, prior to Sept 15, 1942
on German forces or in German controlled area
plan + execute an attack, which
can withdrawal of German
forces from the Russian front

B. British forces in the same area
or in a different area; aid in
the same objective."

Marshall ...

Hopkins, July 20, 1942, revealing their anxiety about the situation on the Russian Front.

results of these talks can be seen from the identical Anglo-Soviet communiques. This has a great importance for the peoples of the Soviet Union, because the establishment of a Second Front in Europe would create insuperable difficulties for the Hitlerite armies on our front. Let us hope that our common enemy will soon feel on his own back the results of the ever-growing military co-operation of the three great powers.

Two days after this Extraordinary Session—at which Molotov expressed nothing more definite than his *hope* for a Second Front in 1942 —Roosevelt and Hopkins at Hyde Park were discussing the possibility of collapse on the Russian Front and together they drafted a message to Marshall and King as follows:

> On the assumption that the Russian Army will be hard pressed and retreating in July: that the German forces are in August (1) dangerously threatening Leningrad and Moscow and (2) have made a serious break thru on the Southern front threatening the Caucasus—
> On the above assumptions—
> At what point or points can:
> A. American ground forces, prior to September 15, 1942—plan and execute an attack on German forces or in German controlled areas which can compel withdrawal of German forces from the Russian front.
> B. British forces in the same area or in a different area, aid in the same objective.

Roosevelt added a note to this that Marshall was to come to the White House at eleven o'clock the following morning (Sunday) and was to be joined there by Sir Alan Brooke an hour later. The day before this message Churchill had arrived at Hyde Park and the British Chiefs of Staff in Washington. That Saturday night, June 20, the President and Prime Minister and Hopkins took the train to Washington and then spent Sunday morning, afternoon and evening in conference with the Chiefs of Staff. On Monday morning Roosevelt, Churchill and Hopkins met with Secretaries Stimson and Knox, then with Dr. Soong, and then with General Eisenhower and Mark Clark who were about to leave for London and the newly formed European Theater of Operations. After lunch, Hopkins went to New York to give a speech at Madison Square Garden at a Russian war relief rally in observance of the first anniversary of the German attack on the Soviet Union.

He said in this speech:

> And what of our 3,000,000 trained ground troops with their modern mechanized equipment? I want to assure this audience that General Marshall, the great leader of this army, is not training these men to play tiddlywinks.
> A second front? Yes, and if necessary a third and a fourth front, to pen the German Army in a ring of our offensive steel.

He spoke of Roosevelt in a way that may have sounded to some like phony platform sentimentality but which represented Hopkins speaking strictly from the heart:

> The President, as no other American, knows and loves the trees and valleys of our country. He knows its mountains and hills and plains. He knows the factories and farms, the cities and towns and villages. He knows Maine and California, New York and Nebraska and Idaho and Georgia. Above all, he knows the homes—miners' homes, farmers' homes, Negroes' homes, the homes of his friends in Hyde Park. While he loves the trees and hills and the valleys, above all else, he is devoted to the people who make up America.
>
> And tonight as he sits in the White House, talking to Mr. Churchill, planning the strategy of this gigantic struggle for freedom with his military advisers, you can be sure that the one thought above all others that guides him is his devotion to our people. He has confidence in us and knows that we trust in him. Never during these trying days and nights have I known him to falter once in his supreme assurance of victory. If he sleeps well at night, it is because of a deep and abiding faith in the righteousness of our cause. If he laughs it is because he knows that wars are not won by being miserable.

There were a few men in authority—conspicuously Stimson and Marshall—who felt that too much of the strategic planning then going on in the White House was concerned with the third and fourth fronts mentioned by Hopkins and not enough with the second.

Churchill had stated his conception of the problems in writing to the President when they first met at Hyde Park. In this letter he said that all arrangements were proceeding to enable six or eight divisions to be landed on the coast of Northern France in September, 1942. But, though all preparations were being made, the British Government would not be in favor of undertaking a limited operation in 1942 if it were likely to lead to disaster. An unsuccessful operation, he argued, would not help the Russians, would expose the French population to Nazi vengeance and would gravely delay the main operation in 1943. He expressed the view of the British Government that the Allies should not make any substantial landing in France in 1942 unless they were going to stay there. He said that the British military staffs had been unable to devise any plan for a landing in September, 1942, which had any chance of success. Churchill then went on to put a number of pointed questions. Had the American staffs devised such a plan? If so, what was it? What forces would be employed? At what points would they strike? What landing craft and shipping were available? Who was the general who was prepared to command the enterprise? What British forces and assistance would be required? If there were a plan which offered a reasonable prospect of success, the British Government would welcome it and share to the full the risks and sacrifices which it involved. But if there was no plan which commanded the confidence of any responsible authority, and if no substantial landing could be made in France in September, 1942, could the Allies afford to stand idle in the Atlantic theater during the whole of that year? Ought they not to be preparing some other operation, by which they might gain advantage and take some of the weight off Russia? It was in this setting, Churchill concluded, that the operation GYMNAST should be studied.

Here, then, was the argument that the proponents of the Second Front had feared: the revival of GYMNAST, the North African operation, instead of SLEDGEHAMMER, the trans-Channel assault in 1942. Stimson noted that Churchill had "taken up GYMNAST, knowing full well I am sure that it was the President's great secret baby." It may be said that neither Stimson nor Marshall had serious objection to the North African operation in itself; it was considered feasible and there were many strategic points in its favor; but mounting it and maintaining it would involve the diversion of such a vast amount of shipping as well as naval and air forces and troops to the Mediterranean area that the BOLERO build-up could not possibly be continued at a sufficient rate through the summer and autumn of 1942 and even through the following winter. Thus, if GYMNAST were decided on, adequate strength for a full-force invasion of the Continent could not be established in the United Kingdom in time for the spring of 1943.

This was the beginning of the protracted and often bitter dispute over the Second Front. Much has already been written on this extensive subject, and in most of it Churchill appears as the archvillain from the American and Russian points of view. Certainly, in this argument, he demonstrated to the limit his qualities of indomitability, or of pigheadedness, whichever word you prefer. He was accused by some of a cowardly fear of risking British lives—and that accusation was made by Stalin in brutally blunt words to Churchill's face. The charge of cowardice could hardly stand up against Churchill who, in 1940, had deliberately risked the lives of the entire British population, including his own, when the United States was still "neutral" and the Soviet Union was associated with the Germans in the Molotov-Ribbentrop pact; but there was no doubt about his reluctance to sacrifice British lives, and American lives, on the beaches of Northern France. He dramatized the possible cost of invasion in many lurid figures of speech: describing the Channel as a "river of blood"—recalling the carnage of Passchendaele and the Somme in the First World War—describing his emotions as he stood in the House of Commons and looked about him "at the faces that are not there," the faces of the generation that was lost in 1914-1918.

In previous chapters I have underscored Churchill's repeated statements that, in the West, this would never be "a war of vast armies,

firing immense masses of shells at one another." He had a healthy
respect for the German ground forces. He knew that the British could
never equal them numerically on land—and it was a long time before
he developed any confidence in the "battle-worthiness," as he called it,
of the American infantry. He persisted in the belief that Germany
could be defeated by the combination of superior sea and air power
plus superior wits. He said time and again that a disastrous defeat
suffered by the Allies on the French Coast would be "the only way in
which we could possibly lose this war."

It has often been said that Churchill's advocacy of the "soft underbelly"
approach to Europe demonstrated his farsightedness—that he was
motivated by the long-range purpose of keeping the Red Army out of
the Danube Valley and the Balkans. In the opinion of some of the
American authorities who were involved in the strategic discussions,
this claim gave Churchill credit for too much prescience. He may have
had such thoughts in mind in 1944, but certainly not in 1942; and one
may ask, in this connection: if Anglo-American strength had been
concentrated in Southern and Southeastern Europe, what eventually
would have stopped the Russians from marching into the Ruhr and
Saar and even into Normandy? The American Chiefs of Staff believed
that Churchill's strategic concepts were much more easily explained:
he had an incurable predilection for "eccentric operations," which had
guided him in the First as well as the Second World War; he preferred
operations which depended on surprise, deception and speed, in terrain
(for example, the Balkan valleys) where there was not sufficient room
for huge ground forces to be deployed. He shrank from the conception
of a frontal attack; indeed, it might be said that, in certain ways, he
agreed with General MacArthur's (and Willie Keeler's) famous principle of, "Hit 'em where they ain't!"

Right or wrong—for better or worse—Churchill's arguments always
made an appeal to Roosevelt, who was also interested in saving lives.
One can only guess at the extent of the conflicts that went on in Roosevelt's mind and heart and soul when he had to decide whether to follow
the advice of his own most trusted advisers (including Hopkins) or
Churchill's warnings that the Channel would be a "river of blood."

When the discussions of June, 1942, shifted from Hyde Park to the
White House, the situation had undergone a shocking change in Libya.
Rommel had defeated and all but destroyed the British armored forces
in a tremendous tank battle. And on Sunday morning, June 21, the
President handed the Prime Minister a slip of paper with the news that
Tobruk had fallen. The year before Tobruk had withstood siege for
thirty-three weeks. Now it had crumpled within a day before the first
assault. This was a body blow for Churchill. It was another Singapore.
It might well be far worse even than that catastrophe in its total effect—

for, with Tobruk gone, there was little left with which to stop Rommel from pushing on to Alexandria, Cairo—and beyond. The prospect of a German-Japanese junction now loomed larger than ever as a possibility or even probability, and remained so for weeks thereafter. Rommel did break through quickly into Egypt, pausing—only for breath, it seemed—before the precariously held lines at El Alamein.

This sudden turn disrupted the staff talks even before they could be started. The discussions in the White House on that Sunday continued through lunch and dinner and far into the night. Churchill poured out his matchless prose in opposition to the trans-Channel operation in 1942, and in favor of GYMNAST as a means of relieving the crisis in the Mediterranean. He was vigorously opposed by Marshall and Hopkins, and Roosevelt—for all that GYMNAST was "his secret baby"—refused to depart from the previous agreement. Thus, there was no revision then of plans for BOLERO and ROUNDUP—but concentration of attention was forcibly diverted from the northern French Coast to the Valley of the Nile. The situation there and on the southern end of the Russian Front, in General Marshall's words, "threatened a complete collapse in the Middle East, the loss of the Suez Canal and the vital oil supply in the vicinity of Abadan. It was a very black hour." The White House conferees were therefore desperately concerned with radical revisions of the shipping and allocation schedules to rush supplies, principally hundreds of Sherman tanks, around Africa to the Red Sea. Here was one of the occasions when Roosevelt had to make decisions, enormous in their implications and dangers, pretty much on snap judgment. Churchill said later, "Nothing could have exceeded the delicacy and kindness of our American friends and Allies. They had no thought but to help." Also, when he could view this tragic time with his normal humor, he confessed that he had then been the unhappiest Englishman in North America since General Burgoyne.

He read stories from London in the American papers stating that the House of Commons was demanding his immediate return "to face his accusers," that this was his "supreme political crisis as Prime Minister," etc., and his visit was cut to only six days. However, Marshall did not want him to get away without seeing some American infantry. Accordingly, Churchill spent June 24 in the South with Marshall. He later wrote that he was "astonished at the mass production of divisions under General Marshall's organization and inspiration. But of course to make a fine professional Army on a great scale from wartime recruits requires at least two years, and better three." He was most courteous and cordial in his expressions of enthusiasm for the exercises that he saw—but he was profoundly skeptical of the ability of American troops to compete with the Germans in ground warfare on a massive scale.

On his last day in Washington, June 25, Churchill lunched with the

President, Prime Minister Mackenzie King of Canada, Hopkins and the members of the Pacific War Council; Halifax, Soong, Quezon, Nash, Van Kleffens (of the Netherlands), Owen Dixon (Australia) and Leighton McCarthy (Canada). It seems that nothing of any great moment except some group photographs developed from this meeting. For obvious domestic political reasons, Hopkins was careful to keep out of the group photographs.

Later that day, Hopkins noted,

The Prime Minister and the President had not agreed upon any joint statement which the two of them would make upon Churchill's arrival in London.

I went down to the doctor's room where the President was having his nose treated for sinus and he dictated the attached notes to me.

I later redrafted this and gave it to the Prime Minister and the President that night when the three of us had dinner together. The final draft which appeared in the press is attached.

This press release, which was conspicuously lacking in news value, stated that the President and Prime Minister had "covered very fully all of the major problems of the war," that "the transportation of munitions of war and supplies still constitutes the major problem of the United Nations," that "the coming operations . . . will divert German strength from the attack on Russia" and finally that "the over-all picture is more favorable to victory" than it had been in 1941.

One subject that came up during their first talks at Hyde Park was not mentioned in this press release nor in any other public statement until four months after Roosevelt's death: the progress of experiments on the fission of uranium. "This difficult and novel project," as Churchill then called it, was known by the British code name of "Tube Alloys" and the American designation "S-one." Churchill later cabled Hopkins concerning the discussions at this time, "My whole understanding was that everything was on the basis of fully sharing the results as equal partners. I have no record, but I shall be much surprised if the President's recollection does not square with this."

Also during these June meetings Hopkins imparted to Roosevelt and Churchill the news that he was engaged to be married to Mrs. Louise Macy, whom he had met only recently when she applied for some sort of war service (she had been working as a nurse's aid in a New York hospital) and was given an introduction to him by mutual friends. Both the President and Prime Minister were delighted that their friend had found such happiness—and Roosevelt immediately told the prospective bride that she would find it easy to make herself at home in the White House.

On June 25 Churchill had a final dinner with Roosevelt and Hopkins

and then departed to "face his accusers" in London. Hopkins accompanied
him to the airplane in Baltimore. Churchill took with him all the fervent
best wishes of his American associates for strength with which to meet
this trial—but he left behind him a growing sense of alarm that the
Second Front was not going to be established in 1942 or in 1943 either.

The disagreement at this stage gave evidence of becoming so acute
that the U.S. Chiefs of Staff seriously considered radical revision of the
long-determined grand strategy of Germany first. MacArthur in Australia had made his own plans for an offensive in the Southwest Pacific.
These were co-ordinated with Navy plans in Washington into the conception of a major offensive against the Japanese in 1942 and 1943
along the line of eastern New Guinea to the Admiralty Islands and up
through the Celebes Sea to the west of the Philippines to Camranh Bay
in Indo-China and Hong Kong. This would have involved committing
the bulk of American ground forces to fighting the war against Japan
on the mainland of Asia in 1943—which would have meant leaving the
war against Germany in Europe to be fought out as best they might by
the Russians and British. Stimson has said that this drastic plan was a
"bluff"—designed "to bring the British into agreement with BOLERO."
Roosevelt called it "a red herring" and said that using it to force British
agreement was a little like threatening to "take up your dishes and go
home." There is, however, considerable difference of opinion as to this;
the Hopkins papers shed no light on it, but it is my impression that the
plan was far more than a bluff in General Marshall's mind and certainly
in Admiral King's. Indeed, the first step in it—the assault on Guadalcanal—was approved on June 25, the last day of Churchill's short stay
in Washington. One may indulge in some pretty wild speculation as to
the consequences had the plan been followed through—including the
thought that the first atomic bomb might have fallen on Berlin instead of
Hiroshima.

The details of this plan were of course well known to Dill and other
British representatives on the Combined Chiefs of Staff who kept their
own government informed about it. There is no indication that it was
ever formally offered as a serious proposal to the British.

In any case, the situation became so critical on the Russian Front
and in Egypt and in the Battle of the Atlantic early in July that a
showdown was enforced. Churchill had once said—it was in the speech
that Hopkins had seen him prepare at Chequers in February, 1941—that
Hitler "may tear great provinces out of Russia; he may march to the
Caspian; he may march to the gates of India." That prophecy was made
four months before the Germans attacked the Soviet Union. It seemed
at the time to be the veriest oratorical fear mongering. But now it
seemed horribly close to fulfillment.

With the fall of Sevastopol, the storm of German offensive broke at last in full fury and the Wehrmacht swept eastward to Voronezh, Rostov and across the Don in the advance that ended only in the streets of Stalingrad and the mountains of the Caucasus.

The desperateness of the situation in Egypt was set forth in a telegram to General Marshall that Roosevelt and Hopkins drafted on the morning of June 30 in the President's bedroom at Hyde Park. It was as follows:

> Are there any moves that we can make immediately that might favorably affect the situation in the Middle East? What is your personal opinion about the coming course of events there?
>
> On the assumption that the [Nile] Delta will be evacuated within ten days and the Canal blocked, I ask the following questions:
>
> 1. What asurances have we that the Canal will be really blocked? Do we know the specific plan? Could you talk to Dill about this at once? An effective blocking of the Canal is essential.
>
> 2. From what point or points would the British operate from Africa by air, land and sea? Also from what point or points in Asia Minor?
>
> 3. What would Rommel's or Germany's next move be? Do you think it would be Cyprus and Syria? Is the objective the Mosul oil fields?
>
> 4. What British forces could be moved to these areas and what would be the probable strategic defense of the oil fields?
>
> 5. Will you give me your judgment on kind of air and land force in Syria that would tend to hold Turkey in line?
>
> 6. What consideration should be given to strong defense of Basra or Black Sea area?

Marshall's reply came back immediately. He said that the British could block the Suez Canal so effectively that it was estimated that six months would be required to reopen it—that the British would probably have to withdraw to the upper Nile region—that Rommel's primary objective was destruction of the British Army, next the occupation of Cyprus and Syria and eventually the seizure of the Mosul and Basra area—also probable action to cut the American air ferry route across Africa to the Middle East, the Soviet Union and the Far East. Marshall said that the defense of Syria and holding Turkey in line would require "expansion far beyond our capacity" and, considering the defense of Basra, "a major effort in this region would bleed us white."

Marshall further stated that there were no moves that the United States could make immediately that could favorably affect the situation in Egypt. He gave the President the following appraisal of the situation:

> Army G-2 estimates Rommel may reach Cairo in one week; Army Operations say two weeks and a minimum of another week to re-fit before further movement, which will probably be directed towards destruction of the remaining British forces. I feel that we need 48

TELEGRAM

The White House
Washington

June 30, 1942
12 A.M.

On the assumption that, *Alexandria* *the Delta* and Cairo will be evacuated within ten days and *Suez* *the Canal* blocked, I ask the following questions

1. What assurance have we that the canal will be really blocked? do we know the specific plans? Could you talk to Dill about this at once? An effective blocking of the canal is essential.

2. From what point or points would the British operate from *Africa* by air, land and sea? *Also from* "what points in Asia Minor"?

3. What would Rommel's or Germany's next move be? Do you think it would be Cyprus and Syria? Is the objective the Mosul Oil

Roosevelt's and Hopkins' joint draft of a telegram to Marshall, July

TELEGRAM

The White House
Washington

Fields?

4. What British forces could be moved to these areas and what would be probable strategic defense of oilfields

5. Will you give me your judgment on kind of air and land force in Syria that would tend to hold Turkey in line?

6. What consideration should be given to strong defense of the Basra & Black Sea area.

Roosevelt

FOR

30, 1942, dealing with the situation in the Middle East.

hours more to judge the capacity of Auchinleck to meet the situation, as he is now in field command. Rommel is greatly extended and if checked by destruction of his supply bases and interruption of his supply lines, he would be in a difficult position.

Evidently the "48 hours" mentioned by Marshall did not yield any signs of encouragement for on July 2 Marshall sent the following message to Hopkins:

In the event of a disaster in the Middle East it is believed to be important to the future conduct of the war that the United Nations present to the world a solid front. To this end it is suggested that the President guide public comment so as to indicate that the United Nations stand together in adversity as they ultimately will in victory.

Roosevelt had to make some very rapid and difficult decisions concerning diversion to the depleted British forces of Lend-Lease material that was in the Middle East en route to Turkey, Russia and China. The most important items in this were bombers which could be used in hammering Rommel's supply lines and thus hamper the reinforcement of his far-extended army. When some heavy bombers that were destined for China were turned over to the British, Chiang Kai-shek made emphatic protest in Chungking to General Stilwell who reported to the President as follows:

C.K.S. believes the President is sincere and feels these orders were given without his knowledge or consent. Feels that Allies do not regard China as part of allied war effort. China has done her best for five years. Questions whether Allies are doing their best for China. If crisis exists in Libya a crisis also exists in China. He had assurances that Tenth Air Force was to operate in China and expected notification before any part of it was taken away. Now it appears that Allies have no interest in China theatre and he wants an answer yes or no to the question "Do the Allies want the China Theatre maintained?" Madame then added that pro-Japanese activity here was pronounced and the question was whether or not the United States wants China to make peace. Both C.K.S. and Madame were bitter about this matter and they were not mincing words when they asked for an unequivocal answer to the question as to whether or not the Allies were interested in maintaining the China War Theatre.

Believe this matter of such importance that it should be presented by an Officer who knows the background and the issues involved thoroughly. I am returning General W. R. Gruber to the United States at once by air and request confirmation of this action. C.K.S. made an urgent plea that either I go myself or that I send a well qualified officer and was obviously relieved to know that I was planning it. In my opinion the matter has reached a very serious stage.

Roosevelt immediately cabled the Generalissimo from Hyde Park as follows:

I have just received message forwarded to me by General Stilwell.

The rapid advance of the Axis forces in the Middle East, suddenly confronted the United Nations with a most critical situation. This movement, if not stopped, will result in the severance of the air routes to India and China, and seriously interfere with if not interrupt our sea lanes to India. It is imperative that the Middle East be held. All reinforcements possible are being rushed to block the Axis advance.

The urgency of the situation demanded that any and all planes immediately available be despatched to preserve our lines of communication to the China theatre. Accordingly the heavy bombers of the Tenth Air Force were ordered to the Middle East. The diversion of these planes is a temporary measure compelled by this sudden crisis. Upon arrival of sufficient air power to secure our lines of communication, the planes will be returned to the Tenth Air Force.

A decision has not been made as to the theatre in which the squadron of A-Twenty light bombers now departing from the United States will be used. This squadron has been ordered to await instructions at Khartoum. In the meantime the medium bombardment and pursuit echelon of the Tenth Air Force will continue in the support of your forces.

I reassure you that the United States and our Allies do regard China as a vital part of our common war effort and depend upon the maintenance of the China theatre as an urgent necessity for the defeat of our enemies.

On July 4 Churchill cabled mentioning that there were forty A-20 bombers (known as "Bostons") which were then approaching Basra headed for Russia. The Prime Minister asked if the President would feel inclined to suggest to Stalin that these forty bombers were desperately needed by the British. Churchill said, "With Russia in the thick of the battle, this is a hard request and I shall quite understand if you do not feel able to do as I ask."

Roosevelt then cabled Stalin pointing out that the critical situation in Egypt directly affected the supply route through the Middle East to Russia. He mentioned Churchill's urgent request for the forty A-20 bombers for immediate use in the battle of Egypt and said, "since it is not possible for me to express judgment on this, due to the limited information available here, I am asking that you make the decision as to these bombers with the interests of our total war effort in mind." Stalin replied that he had no objection to the transfer of these bombers to the British, whereupon Roosevelt notified Churchill of the transfer and then cabled Stalin an expression of his deep appreciation. He informed Stalin that he had arranged for immediate shipment of 115 additional medium tanks to Russia complete with ammunition and spare parts.

A month later when Churchill was in Moscow, he expressed his thanks to Stalin for the forty Bostons and Stalin said, "Those were American aircraft. It will be time enough to thank us when we give you some of our Russian bombers."

Of the situation in the Battle of the Atlantic, Churchill cabled Roosevelt on July 14 that sinkings in the preceding seven days were close to 400,000 tons, "a rate unexampled in this war or the last." At this rate, even assuming that the President's high production goals for shipping were met (they were eventually surpassed), the sinkings would exceed the building of ships by 2½ to 1.

The day following this grim announcement, Churchill sent Roosevelt for approval a copy of a very long cable that he proposed to send Stalin, setting forth the formidable naval problems encountered in getting convoys past Bear Island (between the North Cape of Norway and Spitzbergen) to Murmansk through the dangers presented by German U-boats, surface vessels and aircraft. Churchill, who addressed Stalin as "my comrade and friend," was offering the painful suggestion that convoys on this route must be suspended during the remaining summer period of perpetual daylight.

Roosevelt replied to this cable that he had consulted with Admiral King and had come to the reluctant conclusion that he must agree on the suspension of convoys to Murmansk for the time being. He said he thought that Churchill's message to Stalin was a good one. He asked the Prime Minister to consider the possibility that American railroad men should take over the operation of the route from the Persian Gulf to the Soviet Union, since all possible efforts must be made to develop this line of supply as an alternative to the Murmansk route.

On that same day, July 15, Roosevelt and Hopkins returned to Washington from Hyde Park and met with Marshall and King. It was on this occasion that Marshall, whose patience had been exhausted by the off-again-on-again status of the Second Front planning, offered most strongly the alternative plan for major American operations in the Southwest Pacific. Out of these talks came Roosevelt's determination to settle the matter, and he cabled Churchill, "Marshall, King and Hopkins leaving for London at once."

This was a very tense day in the White House. The U.S. Chiefs of Staff were in a "fish or cut bait" mood. With the Russian and Chinese situations heavily in mind, it seemed that Allied unity was in immediate peril—and Marshall was a soldier who had an extraordinary appreciation of the strategic necessity of Allied unity. Furthermore, he was responsible for the training of millions of men who could not meet Churchill's test of "battle-worthiness" until they had been in battle. Roosevelt was certainly not in favor of "getting tough" with Churchill, or subjecting him to any arbitrary threats—in fact, this was the occasion when the President

made the remark about "taking up your dishes." He had every reason to
be sympathetic with Churchill in the serious domestic political problems
with which he was then involved. Following the disasters in Libya, there
had been another and much more potent revolt in the House of Commons. Facing a Vote of Censure moved by Sir John Wardlaw-Milne,
Churchill described the demands of his opponents in these scathing
terms:

> The mover of this Vote of Censure has proposed that I should be
> stripped of my responsibilities for Defence in order that some military
> figure or some other unnamed personage should assume the general
> conduct of the war, that he should have complete control of the Armed
> Forces of the Crown, that he should be the Chief of the Chiefs of the
> Staff, that he should nominate or dismiss the generals or the admirals,
> that he should always be ready to resign, that is to say, to match him-
> self against his political colleagues, if colleagues they could be con-
> sidered, if he did not get all he wanted, that he should have under him
> a Royal Duke as Commander-in-Chief of the Army, and finally, I pre-
> sume, though this was not mentioned, that this unnamed personage
> should find an appendage in the Prime Minister to make the necessary
> explanations, excuses and apologies to Parliament when things go
> wrong, as they often do and often will. That is at any rate a policy.
> It is a system very different from the Parliamentary system under
> which we live. It might easily amount to or be converted into a dicta-
> torship. I wish to make it perfectly clear that as far as I am concerned
> I shall take no part in such a system.

Such demands on the Prime Minister had an unpleasantly familiar
ring in the President's ears. The same kind of criticism had been raised
in the United States, although not with the same authority. Arthur
Krock had written in the *New York Times*:

> Advocates of a joint Army-Navy general staff with a single head
> contend that the absence of such an establishment compels, as a sub-
> stitute, the operation of a joint political-military command and lays
> directly upon the President in Washington, or Mr. Hopkins on his
> errand with the Chief of Staff of the Army, the responsibility to decide
> technical points of warfare for which neither has been trained.

Krock likened Hopkins' role to that of the "political commissars" who
accompanied the Russian armies on their invasion of Finland in the Winter War of 1939-1940. However, neither Krock nor anyone else had
been able to tell Roosevelt just how he might evade his own supreme
responsibility as Commander in Chief without amending the Constitution. Thus, the American complaints about the conduct of the war carried
little weight.

When it came to a division in the House of Commons on the Vote of
Censure, Churchill was supported 473 to 25. Hopkins cabled him:

We are delighted by today's action in the House of Commons. The military defeats you suffer are ours also and we will share together the certain victories to come, so I know you will be of good heart. More power to you. We are passing through some of the bad days of this war and no doubt there will be others. The timid and the faint-of-heart who run for cover with every set-back will have no part in the winning of this war. Your own courage and tenacity and strength and everlasting confidence will bring your country through and you know that the President does not quit.

Churchill replied, "Thank you so much, my friend. I knew you and the President would be glad of this domestic victory." Nevertheless, it was evident to both Roosevelt and Hopkins that the victory was not solid enough to satisfy the Prime Minister whose powers of emotional endurance were now being tested to the limit after six months of mortification. This was a highly important consideration in the negotiations of far-reaching consequence which followed. It was further indication of the fact that the political element was always present in the determination of military decisions—a fact which had been foreseen by the framers of the Constitution of the United States.

On the evening of July 15, Hopkins had dinner as usual with Roosevelt and a long conversation afterward. He made careful notes during this conversation, quoting Roosevelt directly:

I cannot agree that if it be impossible to develop BOLERO in 1942 that we should turn our faces away from Germany and toward Japan.

In the first place I am not content with the British Cabinet position. I want to know what our men on the ground—Eisenhower, Spaatz, Clark and Stark—think. Do they agree with the British Cabinet? Can you get a confidential report from them?

Even though we must reluctantly agree to no SLEDGEHAMMER in 1942, I still think we should press forward vigorously for the 1943 enterprise. I see nothing in the message from England to indicate any luke-warmness on their part for the 1943 enterprise. I am somewhat disturbed about this readiness to give up 1942. Will they also give up 1943?

But my main point is that I do not believe we can wait until 1943 to strike at Germany. If we cannot strike at SLEDGEHAMMER, then we must take the second best—and that is not the Pacific. There we are conducting a successful holding war. Troops and air alone will not be decisive at once—it requires the increasing strength of our Navy—which takes time.

If SLEDGEHAMMER cannot be launched then I wish a determination made while you are in London as to a specific and definite theatre where our ground and sea forces can operate against the German ground forces in 1942.

The theatres to be considered are North Africa and the Middle East.

GYMNAST has the great advantage of being a purely American enterprise, it would secure Western Africa and deny the ports to the enemy, it would offer the beginning of what should be the ultimate control of the Mediterranean—it is the shortest route to supply. The other theatre is the Middle East; here we would possibly have no resistance—we can use our forces either in Egypt or from the head of the Persian Gulf. Both Russia and England are sorely pressed in this area.

Either of the above operations will require a substantial reduction in BOLERO for the next three months. I am prepared to accept this.

Under any circumstances I wish BOLERO and ROUNDUP to remain an essential objective even though it must be interrupted.

I am prepared to consider in event SLEDGEHAMMER is not mounted—an appropriate transfer of air and landing craft to the Southwest Pacific.

The conversation summarized in those notes led to the drafting of the final orders which Hopkins, Marshall and King took with them to London, as follows:

July 16, 1942.

MEMORANDUM FOR
    Hon. Harry L. Hopkins
    General Marshall
    Admiral King

SUBJECT: Instructions for London Conference—July, 1942.

1. You will proceed immediately to London as my personal representatives for the purpose of consultation with appropriate British authorities on the conduct of the war.

2. The military and naval strategic changes have been so great since Mr. Churchill's visit to Washington that it became necessary to reach immediate agreement on joint operational plans between the British and ourselves along two lines:

(a) Definite plans for the balance of 1942.

(b) Tentative plans for the year 1943 which, of course, will be subject to change in the light of occurrences in 1942, but which should be initiated at this time in all cases involving preparation in 1942 for operations in 1943.

3. (a) The common aim of the United Nations must be the defeat of the Axis Powers. There cannot be compromise on this point.

(b) We should concentrate our efforts and avoid dispersion.

(c) Absolute coordinated use of British and American forces is essential.

(d) All available U.S. and British forces should be brought into action as quickly as they can be profitably used.

(e) It is of the highest importance that U.S. ground troops be brought into action against the enemy in 1942.

4. British and American materiel promises to Russia must be

carried out in good faith. If the Persian route of delivery is used, preference must be given to combat material. This aid must continue as long as delivery is possible and Russia must be encouraged to continue resistance. Only complete collapse, which seems unthinkable, should alter this determination on our part.

5. In regard to 1942, you will carefully investigate the possibility of executing SLEDGEHAMMER. Such an operation would definitely sustain Russia this year. It might be the turning point which would save Russia this year. SLEDGEHAMMER is of such grave importance that every reason calls for accomplishment of it. You should strongly urge immediate all-out preparations for it, that it be pushed with utmost vigor, and that it be executed whether or not Russian collapse becomes imminent. In the event Russian collapse becomes probable SLEDGEHAMMER becomes not merely advisable but imperative. The principal objective of SLEDGEHAMMER is the positive diversion of German Air Forces from the Russian Front.

6. Only if you are completely convinced that SLEDGEHAMMER is impossible of execution with reasonable chances of serving its intended purpose, inform me.

7. If SLEDGEHAMMER is finally and definitely out of the picture, I want you to consider the world situation as it exists at that time, and determine upon another place for U.S. Troops to fight in 1942.

It is my present view of the world picture that:

(a) If Russia contains a large German force against her, ROUND-UP becomes possible in 1943, and plans for ROUNDUP should be immediately considered and preparations made for it.

(b) If Russia collapses and German air and ground forces are released, ROUNDUP may be impossible of fulfillment in 1943.

8. The Middle East should be held as strongly as possible whether Russia collapses or not. I want you to take into consideration the effect of losing the Middle East. Such loss means in series:

(1) Loss of Egypt and the Suez Canal.

(2) Loss of Syria.

(3) Loss of Mosul oil wells.

(4) Loss of the Persian Gulf through attacks from the north and west, together with access to all Persian Gulf oil.

(5) Joining hands between Germany and Japan and the probable loss of the Indian Ocean.

(6) The very important probability of German occupation of Tunis, Algiers, Morocco, Dakar and the cutting of the ferry route through Freetown and Liberia.

(7) Serious danger to all shipping in the South Atlantic and serious danger to Brazil and the whole of the East Coast of South America. I include in the above possibilities the use by the Germans of Spain, Portugal and their territories.

(8) You will determine the best methods of holding the Middle East. These methods include definitely either or both of the following:

(a) Sending aid and ground forces to the Persian Gulf, to Syria and to Egypt.

(b) A new operation in Morocco and Algiers intended to drive in against the backdoor of Rommel's armies. The attitude of French Colonial troops is still in doubt.

9. I am opposed to an American all-out effort in the Pacific against Japan with the view to her defeat as quickly as possible. It is of the utmost importance that we appreciate that defeat of Japan does not defeat Germany and that American concentration against Japan this year or in 1943 increases the chance of complete German domination of Europe and Africa. On the other hand, it is obvious that defeat of Germany, or the holding of Germany in 1942 or in 1943 means probable, eventual defeat of Germany in the European and African theatres and in the Near East. Defeat of Germany means the defeat of Japan, probably without firing a shot or losing a life.

10. Please remember three cardinal principles—speed of decision on plans, unity of plans, attack combined with defense but not defense alone. This affects the immediate objective of U.S. ground forces fighting against Germans in 1942.

11. I hope for total agreement within one week of your arrival.

(signed) FRANKLIN D. ROOSEVELT
Commander-in-Chief

The seemingly strange statement at the end of Paragraph 9 of the above document was an expression of belief that, after the conquest of Germany, Japan's surrender could be enforced without the need for an invasion of her home islands.

Of all the instructions given by Roosevelt to Hopkins and the Chiefs of Staff, the most important—and, indeed, the ultimate determining factor—was this: *U.S. ground forces must be put into position to fight German ground forces somewhere in 1942.*

In this, Roosevelt was thinking not only of the effect on the Russians if eight autumn and winter months were to pass with no substantial action by Anglo-American forces; he was thinking also of the effect of inaction on the spirit of the American and British people, who might well begin to feel bogged down in the deadly lethargy of another period of "Phony War."

The question of terminology for the various trans-Channel operations was clarified by Roosevelt as follows:

The term "Bolero" shall be used to designate the preparation for and movement of United States Forces into the European Theater, preparations for their reception therein and the production, assembly, transport, reception, and storage of equipment and supplies necessary for support of the United States Forces in operation against the European Continent.

The term "Sledgehammer" shall be used to designate an offensive operation of the British and American troops against the European Continent in 1942 to be carried out in case of German internal collapse or imminent Russian military collapse which necessitates an emergency attack in order to divert German forces from the Russian front.

The term "Roundup," or any other name which the Prime Minister may desire, shall be used to designate an offensive operation against German dominated Europe to be carried out by combined American and British forces in 1943 or later.

Roosevelt and Hopkins also contrived some code names for their own private use in cables—as follows: Marshall was "Plog"; King, "Barrett"; Eisenhower, "Keuren"; Spaatz, "Depew"; Clark, "Robert"; Stark, "Draiss"; Churchill, "Moses Smith"; Cripps, "Mrs. Johansen"; Portal, "Rev. Wilson"; Brooke, "Mr. Bee."

Every one of these code names represented was taken from Hyde Park. Grace Tully has told me that William Plog was Mrs. James Roosevelt's superintendent for many years (he always called the President "Mr. Franklin"), Depew was her chauffeur, Robert McGaughey was her butler and, as this is written, is still at Hyde Park. Moses Smith rented a farm on the place and was the moving spirit of the Franklin D. Roosevelt Home Club. Reverend Wilson was Rector of St. James Church, Christian Bee caretaker of Roosevelt's hilltop cottage, Barrett ran the farm, Van Curan (misspelled by Hopkins) worked with Plog, Draiss worked on roads and trees, Mrs. Johansen was a neighbor who ran a gas station and restaurant near Mrs. Roosevelt's cottage.

Hopkins, Marshall and King flew from Washington in a Stratoliner on July 16. They were accompanied by Steve Early, who was to make a study of the British Information Services but take no part in the strategic discussions. Also in the party were General Walter Bedell Smith (later Chief of Staff to Eisenhower and Ambassador to the Soviet Union), Colonel Hoyt S. Vandenberg, Dr. Fulton and Colonel Frank McCarthy and Commander R. E. Libby, the last two being aides to Marshall and King.

Hopkins usually loved to go on trips. Despite his fear of flying, he was thrilled as any normal person would be by all the trappings of official mystery and high significance—the secret orders, the special passports, the drive (usually at dawn) in a White House car to the airport, the passage through saluting sentries to the carefully guarded olive-drab transport plane with its "Destination Unknown" classification, etc. Then, at the other end, the landing at a blacked-out airfield, the greeting by quietly efficient officers who conducted the Very Important Person to a large Daimler limousine which bore on its windshield that inexpressibly impressive word "PRIORITY"—and finally the welcome from a Prime Minister who considered him one of the half-dozen most

influential individuals on the face of the earth. Few men could have
been impervious to the excitement of all of this, and Hopkins was certainly never one of those few.

This time, however, he hated to go. He wanted to stay home and be
married.

°On arrival at Prestwick in Scotland, it was found that the weather
over England was too bad to permit flying on to London. Churchill had,
therefore, provided a special train and Commander Thompson was on
hand to greet the distinguished visitors. He informed them of the
Prime Minister's wish that the train stop near Chequers so that they
might proceed there directly and spend the week end (it was Saturday,
July 18) with him. However, that did not fit in with Marshall's and
King's plans. Time being short, they wanted to get to London immediately and start their talks with Eisenhower, Clark, Spaatz and Stark,
as Roosevelt had directed, and then with the British Chiefs of Staff. So
the train did not stop at Chequers. Shortly after their arrival at Claridge's,
Churchill had Hopkins on the telephone, and the conversations then and
subsequently must have been hot ones. Hopkins reported to Roosevelt,
"The Prime Minister threw the British Constitution at me with some
vehemence. As you know, it is an unwritten document so no serious
damage was done. Winston is his old self and full of battle." Hopkins
did his best over the telephone to try to persuade the Prime Minister
that no rudeness had been intended, that Marshall and King had been
expressly instructed by the President to meet first with Eisenhower—
but his best was evidently not good enough, and Hopkins finally concluded that he must go to Chequers himself to try to absorb some of the
wrath. He did so and peace was restored. Churchill had too much
respect as well as affection for "Lord Root of the Matter" to subject
him to the protracted, and often calculated, rages which cowed others.

The whole mission of the Chiefs of Staff and Hopkins in London was
a secret one—indeed, no public announcement of it was made until
several weeks later—but it was extremely difficult for any of the
hundreds of people who went about Claridge's to miss the fact that top-
level conferences were in progress. With remarkable speed, sixteen
rooms on the fourth floor of Claridge's were converted into a military
headquarters, complete with message center, scrambler telephones, safes
for documents, and a U.S. sentry posted at every door (the sentry at
Admiral King's room was, of course, a Marine).

On Monday, July 20, Hopkins made his first report to the President—
but the only copy of this cable in his papers is such an awkward paraphrase that I have paraphrased it again, translating the code names:

> Our first conferences on Saturday were exclusively with our own
> people here. Eisenhower, Spaatz and Clark are anxious to go ahead
> with SLEDGEHAMMER. Stark is lukewarm. Marshall and his

Wednesday – 3. P.M
Conference on

10, Downing Street,
Whitehall.

"Sledgehammer"

Church
Portal
Pound
Brooke
King
Ismay
Mountbatten

Britain no
We say yes
copy attached

Hopkins' summary of the British and American positions on Sledgehammer, *as stated during a meeting at 10 Downing Street, July 22, 1942.*

staff worked all Saturday night on details. I spent Sunday and Sunday night at Chequers with Churchill who is pretty restless and quite
unhappy that we did not go to see him in the first place. However, all
of this was cleared up over the weekend and he is now in the best
of spirits. I had a long conference this morning with Marshall and
King and we are going to push for SLEDGEHAMMER. We then
went to the first formal conference at Downing Street. The whole field
was thoroughly outlined but there was no discussion of the merits of
the various operations under consideration. We stayed there for
lunch. This afternoon, Marshall and King are conferring with Brooke,
Portal and others. We meet again at six and then I am invited to dine
with the Prime Minister. I would say that in general satisfactory
progress is being made.

A different SLEDGEHAMMER was now being advanced: the
seizure of the Cotentin Peninsula to be held as a bridgehead on the continent until ROUNDUP could be mounted. This changed it from an
emergency, "sacrifice" operation into a permanent gain. I am not clear

Hopkins' personal reaction to the British position, expressed in a note probably to Marshall.

just when the U.S. Chiefs of Staff decided on this,—it had certainly been under consideration for months—but presumably the final planning was done by Marshall and Eisenhower in London. Also under consideration, but only as a pretty remote possibility, was the sending of American ground forces all the way around Africa either to reinforce the British in Egypt or, if Suez were lost, to oppose the Germans in Syria or the Persian Gulf area; Roosevelt had mentioned this in his orders to Hopkins, Marshall and King.

If Hopkins felt somewhat optimistic on Monday afternoon, before the "merits of the various operations" were discussed, forty-eight hours later he was writing, on a sheet of Downing Street notepaper, "I feel damn depressed." This was written as a note—to whom, I do not know, but probably Marshall—during a formal conference held Wednesday afternoon, July 22. The meeting was opened by Marshall with the statement that the American Chiefs of Staff had now had three meetings with the British Chiefs of Staff and a point had been reached where it was

necessary for the Americans to report to the President. In other words—
the discussions had come to complete stalemate. Roosevelt was consequently informed that the British would not willingly go ahead with
SLEDGEHAMMER. Furthermore, as Hopkins indicated, the U.S.
Navy officers involved had been inclined to respect the British position
from the strictly naval point of view; they considered that the representatives of the Royal Navy knew what they were talking about in pointing
to the perils of weather that would beset a trans-Channel operation late
in September or October when the northern French Coast became a "lee
shore." There was sufficient unanimity on the British side and a large
enough fragment of doubt on the American side to make it impossible
to push through the agreement for SLEDGEHAMMER.

Roosevelt then cabled Hopkins, Marshall and King that he was not
particularly surprised at the disappointing outcome of the London talks
and he agreed that mere acquiescence on the part of the British was not
sufficient for the carrying out of plans of such magnitude. He therefore
repeated the directive that he had given them before they left Washington—that some other operations involving American ground troops
against the Germans in 1942 must be worked out. He suggested the
following in order of priority: (1) a new form of offensive with Algeria
and/or Morocco as targets; (2) the original North African operation
(GYMNAST) carried out by American troops only in the first stages;
(3) the operation into northern Norway; (4) reinforcement of the
British by American troops in Egypt for an offensive there; (5) American operations through Iran into the Caucasus.

Roosevelt added that intelligence had been received from the American
Legation in Berne, Switzerland, indicating that plans were under way
for substantial strengthening of the coast defenses and air bases in
French Morocco, and it was therefore urgent that any contemplated
Allied operations in this area should not be too long delayed. It was
estimated (by the source of this information) that an Allied force of
150,000 could succeed in occupying all the French air bases in North
Africa, those near Tunis being the most important. The French troops
in Morocco would be most likely to join with the Allies, those in Tunis
would be less likely. It was stated that although General Nogues could
not be relied on in the beginning, a quick Allied success would probably
win him over.

Having relayed this information, Roosevelt urged Hopkins, Marshall
and King to reach a decision with "our friends" as quickly as possible.

This was the really conclusive order from the Commander in Chief.
It was based on that one factor which Roosevelt considered so important: U.S. ground forces must be put into position to fight German
ground forces somewhere in 1942.

The next day, Hopkins cabled Roosevelt:

I want you to know that Marshall and King pushed very hard for SLEDGEHAMMER. We are naturally disappointed but good will prevails nevertheless. Now that the decision has been made we are hard at work on the next steps. I believe that our people will finally turn to an expanded GYMNAST, first, because of the difficulty of mixing our troops with the British in Egypt, and secondly because if we go to Syria we may not do any fighting there. Your message has been received but it is important that you express your ideas on these matters by cable today. We are bothered by logistical problems particularly escort vessels but I have hope that it will be worked out today. It is my belief that we can give King some additional air and landing craft in the Pacific. It is also my hope that you will consider putting some of our air squadrons into Russia. We will press for early decisions.

The next day, Roosevelt sent a longer and more detailed cable repeating that he favored the launching of the North African operation in 1942 even though, as he frankly admitted, it involved the abandonment of ROUNDUP as the primary objective for the time being. He said he saw no reason why the transport problem could not be worked out so as to put 80,000 American infantry and air force personnel into the initial operation, using American forces then in the United Kingdom and others sent directly across the Atlantic from the United States. He believed that after the original bridgeheads and ports had been secured, the American forces should drive eastward from Algiers to Tunis, and that British forces should push southward from Morocco toward Dakar so as to secure the bulge of Africa. He again emphasized that "time is of the essence to forestall air concentrations by the Germans" which may affect the proposed operations.

On July 25 Hopkins cabled Roosevelt that there was a tendency in the discussions to postpone a final decision on GYMNAST until September 15. He strongly urged the President to name a date for GYMNAST not later than October 30, 1942, since the situation in Russia was so serious that delay was dangerous. He said, "What I fear most is that if we do not now make a firm decision on GYMNAST and fix a reasonably early date there may be procrastinations and delay. Although I believe that the intention here is to mount the operation aggressively, unless the written language of the orders is precise there may be difficulties when it comes to carrying out the orders by the secondary personnel" (meaning, of course, that the whole project might become bogged down on desks in the Pentagon Building and the War Office in Whitehall).

Roosevelt immediately replied that plans should proceed at once for the GYMNAST landings not later than October 30. He asked Hopkins to tell the Prime Minister that he was delighted that the decision had finally been made and that orders were now "full speed ahead." He emphasized the need for absolute secrecy. He told Hopkins to come home immediately, adding, "Tell Winston that not even he can stop that wedding. Give him my best."

That evening, Hopkins, Marshall and King left for Prestwick, flew to Iceland where they paused to inspect the installations and forces there, and arrived back in Washington on July 27. Three days later Hopkins and Louise Macy were married at noon in the Oval Study, with President Roosevelt acting as best man. The ceremony was performed by the Reverend Russell Clinchy, of Hartford, Connecticut. Present were: Mrs. Roosevelt, Hopkins' three sons and his daughter, members of Mrs. Macy's immediate family, General Marshall, Admiral King, Sam Rosenman and the present biographer.

One might have thought that the hatred that dogged Harry Hopkins would have let up for a spell—but one would have been wrong. After his marriage, it became more virulent in its manifestations than ever. The first of these was the amazing story of the yacht, *My Kay IV*. Two weeks after the wedding, Senator Prentiss M. Brown received the following letter from one of his constituents:

> Five men, all whose employment is contributing to war production, paused today at noon to discuss the discouraging newspaper headlines and expressed their sorrowful opinions of the task ahead. One man interrupted and related the following to us, emphasizing his distrust of administration sincerity and his discouragement.
>
> This is the story. A man by the name of Fruehauf—that name is well-known in truck-trailer manufacturing circles—offered his yacht docked in Detroit to the Government. It was commandeered but conversion for Naval use delayed. On inquiry, it was disclosed that conversion was delayed so that Harry Hopkins could and is reported to be now cruising the Great Lakes with his bride. Presumably, this yacht is being operated at the expense of taxpayers.
>
> That, in my opinion, is another example of "acts" which are damaging morale and its companion, hopeless discouragement.
>
> Of course, Mr. Hopkins' "Honeymoon" is no business of mine but delaying conversion of a requisitioned yacht for his convenience and probable operation at the expense of taxpayers is my business.

Senator Brown referred this to Secretary Knox. Later a similar letter was received by Senator Millard E. Tydings—but this time it was said that Mr. Fruehauf was cruising with his family off New London when the yacht was forcibly seized by the Coast Guard and turned over to Hopkins and bride. (As if anyone were likely to do any pleasure cruising along the Atlantic Coast in those days!) Tydings also referred this to Knox. The rumor got into the New York Stock Exchange, whose members happily spread it far and wide. It became so persistent, despite frequent denials by busy officials, that the F.B.I. investigated it, as they did innumerable other demoralizing rumors in wartime. It seemed that a fifty-five-foot boat, owned by Roy Fruehauf of Detroit, had been purchased by the Coast Guard after some weeks of negotiation. When the actual requisition came through, Fruehauf was on a fishing cruise on Lake Superior with his wife and two friends, but was permitted to finish his cruise and return in his own good time to Detroit, where the boat was turned over to the Coast Guard in an orderly manner. Then a special crew was put aboard and the boat ordered on a "secret mission" to Amherstburg, on the Canadian side of Lake Erie, there to pick up some Canadian officials (one of whom, the rumor said, was Prime Minister Mackenzie King). It was then to proceed to a designated spot on the lake and transfer the officials to the vessel *City of Cleveland*, where they would meet with "a personal representative of the President" (of course, Hopkins).

The F.B.I. learned that the Canadian officials were not of the top echelon—one of them being a fire chief. On board the *City of Cleveland* were members of the Federal Employees Association of Cleveland, on an excursion cruise, the highest ranking official among them being the chairman of their Recreation Committee. The boats did not meet as planned—the weather was too rough—so the Canadians were deposited in Cleveland, two of them seasick. Such were the facts concerning the *My Kay IV*. Just why there was any talk of a "secret mission" was unexplained—but presumably someone had been talking big.

The F.B.I. reported as follows of its interview with Mr. Fruehauf:

He stated that some time after the boat was turned over, perhaps a week to the best of his knowledge, he received a telephone call from the Associated Press advising him that this agency had received a report from a Chicago representative that he had been forced to return to Detroit from his vacation cruise so that Mr. Hopkins could use the boat on his honeymoon. He stated that he emphatically denied this story but apparently was not believed because he continued to receive telephone calls from the Associated Press and from other newspaper agencies. He stated that thereafter for several weeks he was besieged with calls from newspapermen, magazine publishers, and divers individuals in connection with this story which in the meantime had spread rapidly. Mr. Fruehauf advised that one of the most recent inquiries concerning this story came from Fulton Lewis, a news commentator connected with a Washington, D.C., radio broadcasting station. He stated that some of these sources even reported to him that the rumor was prevalent that he and his party had been forcibly ejected from their boat in Georgian Bay and were forced to make their own way back to civilization. He stated that he has since denied the story so many times until he feels that there is no one left who has not inquired about it at least once.

Hopkins and his bride actually spent their honeymoon on a small farm in Connecticut and he was back at work in Washington eleven days after the wedding. But the rumor of the *My Kay IV* continued in circulation for many weeks. In fact, three months later, on the eve of the North African landings, Hopkins was asking for legal advice as to whether there was anything he could do about this malicious lie; the answer was, "probably not." Nor could he do anything about the rumor, given wide publicity, that Mrs. Hopkins had received a wedding present of half a million dollars' worth of emeralds from Lord Beaverbrook as a mark of appreciation for her husband's service in giving Lend Lease to the British. That one even went to the extent of an announcement by Representative Joseph W. Martin that proposals would be introduced for a Congressional investigation of the private and public activities of Harry Hopkins and the whole administration of Lend Lease. Nothing, of course, ever came of this, since the smearers had too much sense to make the mistake of granting Hopkins his day in court.

CHAPTER XXVI

The Turning Point

I T IS evident that even after Hopkins, Marshall and King returned from London on July 27, there were further attempts to change the President's mind about the North African operation, the name of which had been changed for security reasons from GYMNAST to TORCH. Roosevelt, however, insisted that the decision had been made and must be carried through with expedition and vigor. This was one of the very few major military decisions of the war which Roosevelt made entirely on his own and over the protests of his highest-ranking advisers. Admiral Leahy had just been appointed to the unprecedented position of Chief of Staff to the Commander in Chief, and subsequently he became in effect Chairman of the Chiefs of Staff Committee. At this time, however, he had been out of touch with the progress of strategic planning; his return from Vichy was long delayed by the saddening illness and death of his wife.

On July 31 Churchill sent Roosevelt a cable which has considerable significance in the light of developments of the following year and a half. The Prime Minister pressed for a decision concerning the naming of the commanders for the various operations in prospect in the European theater. He said, "It would be agreeable to us if General Marshall were designated for Supreme Command of ROUNDUP and that in the meantime General Eisenhower should act as his deputy here." This nomination of the most vehement proponent of the Second Front would hardly seem to indicate that Churchill was attempting to relegate the plan completely to the Files of Forgotten Things. Churchill suggested that Eisenhower should superintend the planning and organization of TORCH and that General Sir Harold Alexander should be in command of the task force from the British Isles and an American (who turned out later to be General George S. Patton) in command of the task force from the United States. This suggestion was made, of course, shortly before Churchill decided to place Alexander in supreme command of the British forces in Egypt.

Roosevelt was content to leave the question of supreme command of ROUNDUP in abeyance for the time being—and, as will be seen in later chapters, that turned out to be a very long time. He was now concerned primarily with the problem of how to explain to Stalin that there would be no Second Front in Northern France in 1942. Churchill planned a trip to the Middle East and suggested that he proceed on from there via Teheran to Moscow. On July 31, Stalin extended an invitation to the British Prime Minister and the Chief of the Imperial General Staff to come to the U.S.S.R. "to consider jointly urgent questions of war against Hitler as a menace" which has "just now reached a special degree of intensity." Roosevelt cabled Churchill the following thoughts on the handling of the difficult negotiations:

It is essential for us to bear in mind our Ally's personality and the very difficult and dangerous situation that he confronts. I think we should attempt to put ourselves in his place, for no one whose country has been invaded can be expected to approach the war from a world point of view. We should tell Stalin quite specifically, in the first place, that we have decided upon a course of action for 1942. Without advising him of the precise nature of our proposed operations, I think we should tell him without any qualification that they are going to be made.

I agree with you that we should run another northern convoy if there is any chance of success, despite the great risk which is involved. But I think that you should not raise any false hopes in Stalin relative to this.

The Russian need is urgent and immediate. I believe it would mean a great deal to the Russian people and their army if they were to know that units of our air forces were fighting with them in a very direct manner. I am discussing this matter of putting air power directly on the Russian front and I am hopeful that this can be done. I imagine that Stalin is in no mood to engage in strategic discussions of a theoretical nature and I am sure that, except for our major operation, the giving of our direct air support to the Russians on the southern end of their front is the enterprise that would suit Stalin best.

Although it had been planned that Churchill would conduct his talks in Moscow with no American representative present, after he had left London Harriman conceived the idea that it might be a good idea for him to go along and Roosevelt cabled him authority to do so with no special instructions. Accordingly, Harriman caught up with Churchill in the Middle East and flew with him to Moscow where they arrived late in the afternoon of August 12. Despite his extensive traveling, Churchill was ready to plunge immediately into the conference at the Kremlin, scorning all suggestions that he might like to have a few hours' rest.

Harriman cabled to Roosevelt the following day as follows:

Last night the Prime Minister and I had an extended meeting with Stalin. Also present were Molotov, Voroshilov and the British Ambassador. British and American strategic plans for the rest of 1942 and 1943 and their effect on the Russian military situation formed the center of discussion.

It is my belief that, considering all the circumstances, the discussion could not have been better developed nor more satisfactory conclusions reached. Churchill explained the various possibilities of SLEDGE-HAMMER and the reasons for its postponement in full detail and told of the plans for and proposed strength of the major trans-Channel operation.

At every point Stalin took issue with a degree of bluntness almost amounting to insult. He made such remarks as—that you cannot win wars if you are afraid of the Germans and unwilling to take risks. He ended this phase of the discussion by stating abruptly but with dignity that although he did not agree with the arguments he could not force us to action. He showed little interest in ROUNDUP, expressing the opinion that grave difficulties confronted it. Up to now, the atmosphere was tense, no agreement having been reached on any point.

Thereupon, Churchill described the bombing campaign against Germany and expressed the hope that participation by the U.S. Air Force would produce a substantial increase in this bombing. This produced the first agreement between the two men. Stalin took over the argument himself, saying that homes as well as factories should be destroyed. Churchill agreed that civilian morale constituted a military objective but that the destruction of the homes of workers was only a by-product of near misses on factories. Now there began an easing of the tension and an increasing understanding of common purpose. Stalin and Churchill, between them, soon had destroyed most of Germany's important industrial centers.

With great adroitness, Churchill seized the opportunity presented by this friendlier interchange to bring the discussion back to the Second Front. He explained the TORCH decision and the tactics thereof. He emphasized the need for secrecy. He said he wished he had the same power that Stalin exercised over the press, which further relieved the tension. Stalin expressed a great deal of concern over the political repercussions which might result from the TORCH operation.

Churchill drew a picture of a crocodile, pointing out that it was as well to strike the soft underbelly (the Mediterranean) as the snout (Northern France). He then brought the discussion back to the Russian front saying that you and he were exploring the possibility of sending an Allied air force to the southern end of the Russian Front after Rommel had been defeated in Egypt. He asked Stalin how he would receive such a suggestion and Stalin replied, briefly and simply, "I would accept it gratefully."

Thereafter, Stalin summed up the strategic advantages of TORCH, showing a masterful grasp of its implications. He asked specifically that the political angle be handled with the utmost delicacy and that it be launched at the earliest possible moment—earlier even than you have implied. He showed real enthusiasm for the operation.

After the conclusion of the three days of conference, Harriman returned to Washington, bringing with him the full details of all the talks. After the first two hours—which Churchill described as "bleak and sombre"—the TORCH plan for landings at Casablanca, Oran, Algiers and, if possible, Bizerte, was presented, and Stalin made no secret of his intense immediate interest in it. He asked whether a date had been set, saying he would withdraw that question if it were embarrassing, but Churchill told him that it was to be October 1 at the latest. Stalin then asked: would this bring Vichy France into the war on Germany's side—and would it bring in Spain—and where would the operation eventually lead? Churchill assured Stalin that the prime target was still the Continent in the west, and Harriman assured him that Roosevelt was in full agreement with the Prime Minister on the decisions reached.

Suddenly Stalin exclaimed, "May God help this enterprise to succeed!" (The translation of this remark, as given by Churchill to Roosevelt, was: "May God prosper this undertaking!") I have been told that it was by no means unusual for Stalin, who had been educated for a time in a religious seminary, to invoke the aid of the Deity.

Stalin expressed some doubts about the political soundness of the North African operation, but he was remarkably quick to name four outstanding military advantages:

It would take the German enemy in the rear.

It would provoke French and Germans to fight each other.

It would put Italy out of action.

It would make it all the more advisable for Spain to stay neutral.

After this meeting, which had lasted for three hours and forty minutes, Churchill and Harriman felt elated, as Harriman had stated in his cable. Both were enormously impressed at the intelligence of Stalin's instantaneous appreciation of TORCH. Churchill sent a long cable to Roosevelt confirming Harriman's and Roosevelt dictated a cable to the Prime Minister which Hopkins took down:

The cordiality shown by Mr. Stalin and his understanding of our difficult problems make me very happy. Give him my warm regards and keep me advised of progress. I wish I could be with both of you so that the party could be made complete.

On the second day of the meetings in Moscow, August 13, Churchill called on Molotov and had a short talk with him which was evidently less satisfactory—Molotov expressing the view that the North African operation was "ambiguous" and reminding Churchill of the communiqué that had been issued after his visits to London and Washington two months previously.

At eleven o'clock that night there was another large meeting in the Kremlin, with Stalin, Molotov, Churchill, Harriman, Cadogan, General Wavell, General Brooke and Air Chief Marshal Sir Arthur Tedder. Stalin opened this meeting by handing copies of an aide memoire to Churchill and Harriman, as follows:

As the result of an exchange of views in Moscow which took place on the 12th August of this year, I ascertained that the Prime Minister of Great Britain, Mr. Churchill, considered that the organization of the second front in Europe in 1942 to be impossible.

As is well known, the organization of a second front in Europe in 1942 was pre-decided during the sojourn of Molotov in London, and it found expression in the agreed Anglo-Soviet communique published on the 12th June last.

It is also known that the organization of a second front in Europe had as its object the withdrawal of German forces from the Eastern front to the West, and the creation in the West of a serious base of resistance to the German-Fascist forces and the affording of relief by this means to the situation of the Soviet forces on the Soviet-German front in 1942.

It will be easily understood that the Soviet Command built their plan of summer and autumn operations calculating on the creation of a second front in Europe in 1942.

It is easy to grasp that the refusal of the Government of Great Britain to create a second front in 1942 in Europe inflicts a moral blow to the whole of the Soviet public opinion, which calculates on the creation of a second front, and that it complicates the situation of the Red Army at the front and prejudices the plan of the Soviet Command.

I am not referring to the fact that the difficulties arising for the Red Army as the result of the refusal to create a second front in 1942 will undoubtedly have to deteriorate the military situation of England and all the remaining Allies.

It appears to me and my colleagues that the most favourable conditions exist in 1942 for the creation of a second front in Europe, inasmuch as almost all the forces of the German army, and the best forces to boot, have been withdrawn to the Eastern front, leaving in Europe an inconsiderable amount of forces and these of inferior quality. It is unknown whether the year of 1943 will offer conditions for the creation of a second front as favourable as 1942. We are of the opinion, therefore, that it is particularly in 1942 that the creation of a second front in Europe is possible and should be effected. I was, however, unfortunately unsuccessful in convincing Mr. Prime Minister of Great Britain hereof, while Mr. Harriman, the representative of the President of the United States, fully supported Mr. Prime Minister in the negotiations held in Moscow.

(signed) J. STALIN

From that point on, the visitors from the West encountered "very rough sledding," as Harriman put it. The cordial atmosphere of the previous night's meeting had vanished. Stalin made it painfully clear that the Soviet Government took no interest in the TORCH operation. He spoke caustically of the failure of the Western Allies to deliver the promised supplies to the Soviet Union. He spoke of the tremendous sacrifices that were being made to hold 280 German divisions on the Eastern Front. He said that he thought it would not be too difficult for the British and Americans to land six or eight divisions on the Cherbourg Peninsula. Churchill described in great detail the perils of an operation across the English Channel, but Stalin was unimpressed. It was at this point that Stalin made the observation that if the British infantry would only fight the Germans as the Russians had done—and indeed as the R.A.F. had done—it would not be so frightened of them. Churchill said, "I pardon that remark only on account of the bravery of the Russian troops."

At one point, Harriman reported, Churchill became so voluble and so eloquent in his defense of Anglo-American policy, that the British interpreter, spellbound, forgot his own job of taking down every word and put aside his pencil the better to listen to the Prime Minister's oratory. Churchill did not overlook this lapse. He turned on the interpreter, scolding him vigorously, and then started to repeat everything he had said for the unhappy civil servant to write down and translate. During this diversion, Stalin threw back his head and roared with laughter, saying to Churchill, "I do not understand your words but I like your spirit." After that, the tension was reduced, but this meeting never became friendly. At the end, Harriman asked about the plans for ferrying American aircraft across Siberia, and Stalin curtly dismissed this with the statement that "Wars are not won with *plans*."

The next day, Harriman made the following reply to Stalin's aide memoire:

I have had an opportunity to study the memorandum of the 13th August you handed me last night, an identical copy of which you simultaneously gave to the Prime Minister. I have also had an opportunity to read the Prime Minister's aide-memoire of the 14th August replying to your memorandum.

I do not believe that any useful purpose would be served in comments by me additional to what the Prime Minister has said. I feel, however, that I must reaffirm his statement that no promise has been broken regarding the second front.

There was considerable puzzled speculation in the British delegation as to what had produced the dismaying reversal in Stalin's attitude as between the first night's session and the second. It was recalled that there had been a similar change from hot to cold when Eden had visited Moscow the previous year, and Harriman said that much the same technique had been used when he and Beaverbrook were there. The same technique was to be encountered on subsequent occasions and the most usual explanation of it was that when Stalin got really tough he was expressing the attitude of the mysterious Politburo rather than his own personal appraisal of the main issue.

On the evening of August 14, there was the usual state dinner in the Kremlin which Harriman described in the following cable:

Last night we dined in force at the Kremlin with all members of the Soviet General Staff as well as all members of the Defense Committee. Stalin seemed to be entirely oblivious of the unpleasant exchanges of the previous night. He was in the best of spirits and most cordial to the Prime Minister and myself. When Churchill arrived at the dinner, however, he still appeared somewhat annoyed by the rough treatment he had received but he became more and more interested in his talks with Stalin as the evening progressed. The subjects of discussion ranged from theories of military tactics to post-war policies. Churchill talked in some detail about the air squadrons for the Southern Russian front which you and he have in mind.

Churchill left this function at 1:30 A.M. rather than wait to see a lengthy film, and Stalin accompanied him the long distance through corridors and down staircases to the main entrance of the Kremlin where the two oddly met Allies parted with a genial handshake.

At seven o'clock on the evening of August 15, Churchill went to the Kremlin for a final meeting with Stalin and came out of it more surprised than ever—for now the atmosphere of cordiality was completely restored and enthusiasm for the TORCH operation and its beneficial consequences was again running high. At the end of this session (to which Churchill had brought another interpreter), Stalin asked, "Why not come over to my apartment in the Kremlin and have some drinks?" Although Churchill's airplane was to take off at dawn, he, of course, accepted this invitation and remained for seven hours, discussing all manner of subjects including the possibility of a meeting between Stalin and President Roosevelt in Iceland. Churchill expressed the hope that Stalin would have occasion to visit England and assured him of "a magnificent reception." Stalin expressed his appreciation of this invitation but said that, at this particular time, receptions were not very important—all that mattered was victory. After this session, Churchill got home at 3:30 A.M., wrote and dispatched a long cable to Roosevelt, and at 4:30 started off for the nine-and-a-half-hour flight to Teheran.

His stamina was extraordinary for a man of nearly sixty-eight or of any other age over twenty-one that one could mention. He reported to Roosevelt that the meetings had ended in an atmosphere of the greatest good will and that a personal relationship of real importance had been established.

Roosevelt cabled Stalin:

It is a matter of regret to me that I could not have joined with you and Mr. Churchill in the Conferences in Moscow. I am fully cognizant of the urgent requirements of the military situation particularly in relation to your own Eastern Front. We have gained, I believe, a toehold in the Southwest Pacific from which the Japanese will find it very difficult to dislodge us. We have had substantial naval losses there but the advantage gained was worth the sacrifice and we are going to maintain hard pressure on the enemy.

I am very well aware that our real enemy is Germany and that we must bring our forces and our power against Hitler at the earliest possible moment. I can assure you that this will be done just as soon as it is humanly possible to arrange for the shipping. In the meantime, more than a thousand tanks will leave this country for Russia in August and other critical supplies, including aircraft, are being expedited.

Believe me when I tell you that we are coming as quickly and as powerfully as possibly we can. Americans understand that Russia is bearing the brunt of the fighting and the casualties this year and we are filled with admiration for the magnificent resistance you are putting up.

The "toehold in the Southwest Pacific" to which the President referred was on the beaches of Guadalcanal, Tulagi and Florida Islands where the Marines had landed on August 7. The chart of the Solomon Islands, forming a sort of spearhead which pointed northwest toward Japan, was now on the walls of all the map rooms in Washington and it remained up for months and years as one of the greatest battlegrounds of American history. The capture and defense of these islands from Guadalcanal to Bougainville demanded extraordinary heroism and endurance by the ground forces and precariously based air forces, and the narrow channel known as "The Slot" was the scene of recurrent naval actions which were fought in the manner of old-fashioned, bareknuckled slugging. In the Hopkins papers is a message, handwritten by Roosevelt and himself, which was sent to all the Chiefs of Staff when the Japanese counterattacks on Guadalcanal were most severe. It gives a good indication of the intensity of Roosevelt's feeling about this remote but desperately important area:

My anxiety about the Southwest Pacific is to make sure that every possible weapon gets into that area to hold Guadalcanal. And that having held it in this crisis that munitions and planes and crews are on the way to take advantage of our success. We will soon find ourselves engaged in two active fronts and we must have adequate air support in both places even tho it means delay in our other commitments, particularly to England. Our long range plans could be set back for months if we fail to throw our full strength in our immediate and impending conflicts.

I wish therefore you would canvass over the week end every possible temporary division of munitions which you will require for our active fronts and let me know what they are. Please also review the number and use of all combat planes now in the continental United States.

A month after the first landings in the Solomons, MacArthur started to wrest the initiative away from the Japanese on New Guinea. Starting from defensive positions around Port Moresby—and with a hopelessly defensive state of mind prevailing in the troops there—MacArthur started to push back through the jungles and up the slopes and across the ridges of the Owen Stanley Range. Roosevelt was enthusiastic about this phenomenal campaign, in which the Air Force under General George C. Kenney played a brilliant part, acting not only as an attacking force but as almost the sole train of supply and reinforcement for the ground troops. This was the start for MacArthur on the long road back to Manila. But it was far more than that in the war as a whole: the advances on New Guinea and in the Solomons, although relatively small in scale, marked the beginning of the offensive phase for the United Nations. Except for the back-and-forth drives in the Libyan Desert and the Russian winter counterattacks, this was the first time that the arrows indicating advances on the daily newspapers' war maps started to point into enemy territory.

However, it was a long time before those arrows in the Southwest Pacific could give much satisfaction. On September 7, three American heavy cruisers and an Australian cruiser were surprised and sunk in The Slot between Guadalcanal and Savo Island and the position of the land forces was critical and terrible with the Japanese largely in control of the sea communications.

On the Russian Front, the great, final historic test had come in the shattered streets of Stalingrad. Within a week after Churchill's departure from Moscow, the Germans broke through across the Don to the Volga north of Stalingrad, thus cutting off all access to the city except by barges across the river from the east, and this hazardous line of communication was subject to constant attack by the Luftwaffe, which had command of the air, and it was soon also under artillery fire from German positions in the center of the city itself. The southward drive of the German armies reached the foothills of the Caucasus by the eastern shore of the Black Sea before September 1.

On August 19 occurred the attack by Canadian forces supplemented

My anxiety about the S. W. Pac.
is to make sure that every possible
weapon gets into that area to hold Guadalcanal.
and that having held it in this crisis
that munitions and planes and crews are on the
way to take advantage of our success
We will soon find ourselves engaged
in two active fronts and we must
have adequate air support in both
places even tho it means delay
in our other commitments, particularly
to England. Our long range plans

Message (to Joint Chiefs of Staff) drafted jointly by Roosevelt

could be set back for months if
we fail to throw our full strength
in~~~ in our immediate and
impending conflicts

I wish therefore you would answer
over the week end every possible
^{temporary} diversion
of munitions which you will require
for our active fronts and let me
know what they are. Please ^{also} give us
the number and use of all ^{combat} planes
now in the continental United States

Roosevelt

by British Commandos and a few Americans on the French port of Dieppe. It was insisted that this should not be considered a Commando raid—or even a "raid" of any kind—but a "reconnaissance in force." Whatever it may have accomplished in reconnaissance, or in losses inflicted on the Germans in the attendant air battle, it was a deplorable venture from the propaganda viewpoint, for it seemed to confirm all Hitler's boasts about the impregnability of the European Fortress and it put a fearful damper on the Russians' hopes for a Second Front.

During this summer Roosevelt had established his week-end retreat called Shangri-la in the Maryland hills about sixty miles north of Washington. This enabled him to get away from the White House at times when it was dangerous for him to travel even as far from base as Hyde Park. It was a simple woodland lodge with four bedrooms. There was a bathroom for the President and one for the guests with a door that couldn't be locked. There were other camp cottages for the secretaries, the telephone exchange, the Secret Service, etc., and a Marine training camp surrounding the place. There was one living and dining room. The staff consisted of Filipino sailors from the now idle yacht, *Potomac*, and the food was far better than that in the White House.

Roosevelt sat by the hour on the little screened porch with a fine view over the Catoctin Valley. He worked on his stamp collection, he played solitaire and he wrote his name or his initials in books from his library. He had started doing this, he said, because people were always "borrowing" books from the White House and not returning them—and Bennett Cerf, the waggish publisher, once ventured to ask him, "Do you think, Mr. President, that people are *less* likely to steal books that have been autographed by you?" But he persisted in the belief that this was an effective precaution. He gave one of these books to me that August, 1942. (I have the accompanying note to prove I didn't steal it.) It was an old Book of Psalms that someone had sent him—it bore the name of Mrs. Herbert Lloyd Stoddard of Los Angeles, California. He had been through this book and marked certain passages—he wanted me to study them with a view to future speeches—and one that he marked was the last verse of the thirty-ninth psalm:

O spare me, that I may recover strength, before I go hence, and be no more.

On the week ends at Shangri-la the dispatches came in and the President and Hopkins read them in the living-dining room, which was also the only office, or on the porch, and wrote out and sent messages to Marshall and cables to Churchill, Stalin or Chiang Kai-shek. Sometimes generals or admirals drove up from Washington on matters of pressing import, the veins on their temples distended with urgency, and I often thought that they must be annoyed by the calmness with which their

Commander in Chief received them and their reports. On August 30 Harriman arrived there with his descriptions of the meeting of Churchill and Stalin in Moscow two weeks previously.

The situation in Stalingrad by then was so bad that, in the appreciations that came from G-2 in the War Department, the city could be written off as already lost to the Germans. Harriman, however, brought with him a sense of optimism. He thought the Russians could prevent the breakthrough which would have cut them off from the Caucasian oil fields and given the Germans a clear road into Iran and the Middle East. However, nobody could possibly have been optimistic enough to predict the cataclysmic reversal that was to take place at Stalingrad.

Harriman had stopped off at Teheran, which he described as a delightful spot, to study the problems of the supply route from Basra over the Iranian railroad into the Soviet Union. Stalin had emphasized the critical need of the Russians for motor trucks which he put on the same priority level with tanks, and the Iranian route seemed the best for such heavy equipment. Harriman was on familiar ground in considering railroad-building problems and when he rejoined Churchill in Cairo he made the proposal that U.S. Army engineers take over the responsibility of expanding the port facilities at Basra and the communications by rail and road through Iran to Trans-Caucasia. Some of the more conservative of the British officers viewed this with alarm, for it meant putting foreigners (i.e., Americans) in control of an essential line of Empire communications. Churchill asked: "And in what *better* hands could it be?"

It was during this trip that Churchill made the important changes in the British command in Egypt, putting in Generals Alexander and Montgomery.

Harriman also reported Stalin's favorable response to the suggestion of British and American air forces operating in the Caucasus.

Roosevelt cabled Churchill that the United States was prepared to take over the Persian railroad and was developing plans for its operation. He said that he had heard that American Army officers had been encountering difficulties on this with their British opposite numbers. He said that he had received discouraging news that morning about the forthcoming Murmansk convoy and added, "Of course I will do everything I can with Stalin if the decision is against our sending further convoys." He said, of the progressing preparations for the North African landings, "We are in this together and I have great confidence in our success."

There was continued correspondence between London and Washington about the planning of the TORCH operation. The British were dubious about the landings on the Moroccan Coast because of the perils presented by the Atlantic Ocean surf—and there were authorities in Washington, including Secretary Stimson, who agreed with the British estimates of these hazards. On August 30, Roosevelt cabled Churchill:

> I have considered carefully your cables in reference to the Torch operation. It is my earnest desire to start the attack at the earliest possible moment. Time is of the essence and we are speeding up preparations vigorously.
>
> I feel very strongly that the initial attacks must be made by an exclusively American ground force supported by your naval and transport and air units. The operation should be undertaken on the assumption that the French will offer less resistance to us than they will to the British.
>
> I would even go so far as to say I am reasonably sure a simultaneous landing by British and Americans would result in full resistance by all French in Africa whereas an initial American landing without British ground forces offers a real chance that there would be no French resistance or only a token resistance.
>
> Then your force can come in to the eastward. I realize full well that your landing must be made before the enemy can get there. It is our belief that German air and parachute troops cannot get to Algiers or Tunis in any large force for at least two weeks after initial attack. Meanwhile your troops would be ashore we hope without much opposition and would be moving eastward.
>
> As to the place of the landings it seems to me that we must have a sure and permanent base on the Northwest coast of Africa because a single line of communication through the Straits is far too hazardous in the light of our limited joint resources.
>
> I propose therefore that:
>
> (a) American troops land simultaneously near Casablanca and near Oran.
>
> (b) That they seek to establish road and rail communication with each other back of the mountains. The distance is little more than 300 miles. This gives to the enterprise a supply base in Morocco which is outside the Straits and can be used to reinforce and supply the operations in Algiers and Tunis.
>
> The real problem seems to be that there is not enough cover and combat loadings for more than two landings. I realize it would be far better to have three with you handling the one to the eastward a week after we get in. To this end I think we should re-examine our resources and strip everything to the bone to make the third landing possible. We can give up the Russian convoy temporarily at that time and risk or hold up other merchant shipping. It is essential, of course, that all ships now assigned to Eisenhower for his two landings remain intact. Hence the eastward landing must be made on ships not now available to Torch. I will explore this at our end. Can we not get an answer on this within forty-eight hours or less?

I want to emphasize however that under any circumstances one of our landings must be on the Atlantic.

The directive to the Commander-in-Chief of the operation should prescribe that the attack should be launched at the earliest practicable date. The date should be consistent with the preparation necessary for an operation with a fair chance of success and accordingly it should be determined by the Commander-in-Chief, but in no event later than October 30th. I still would hope for October 14th.

Churchill made the following reply:

We could not contest your wish if you so desire it to take upon the United States the whole burden, political and military, of the landings. Like you, I assign immense importance to the political aspect. I do not know what information you have of the mood and temper of Vichy and North Africa, but of course if you can get ashore at the necessary points without fighting or only token resistance, that is best of all. We cannot tell what are the chances of this.

Churchill said that it had always been agreed that this was to be primarily an American enterprise but he made the point that it could not be represented as exclusively so since it was hardly possible to disguise the presence of the British Navy. Churchill persisted in advocating that Algiers should be occupied simultaneously with Casablanca and Oran saying that here was "the most friendly and hopeful spot where the political reaction would be most decisive through North Africa," which proved to be the case.

In all the discussions preceding TORCH it was obvious that the eternally sore subject of de Gaulle and the Fighting French would again manifest itself. Roosevelt was obdurate on this point. He wrote, "I consider it essential that de Gaulle be kept out of the picture and be permitted to have no information whatever, regardless of how irritated and irritating he may become." In the subsequent protests over American policy on this there were further attacks on the State Department—repercussions of the "so-called Free French" blunder; but this policy was attributable directly to Roosevelt himself and not to the State Department, and Churchill did not offer firm opposition to it. As Professor Langer has written,

Both at Dakar and in Syria, the British had employed Frenchmen to fight Frenchmen. These incidents had left a very bad and almost indelible impression. The French in North Africa were determined to oppose any repetition of this situation, and there can be no doubt that the use of Fighting French forces would have led to civil war.

In an effort to avoid bloodshed by making the strongest possible appeal to the minds and hearts of the French in North Africa, it was decided that the military forces on the TORCH operation should be accompanied for the first time by so-called "psychological warfare teams," including civilians, to move in with the troops to disseminate anti-German, pro-Allied propaganda through every means available—the press, radio, movie theaters, posters, etc. This novel phase was planned in London, largely by Robert Bruce Lockhart, for the British, and James P. Warburg and Percy Winner, for the Americans. One instance of it: a radio transmitter was installed on the battleship *Texas*, tuned to the wave length of Radio Maroc at Rabat, then under Vichy control. It broadcast from offshore while the landing craft were moving in on D-Day, and the Moroccans were startled to hear the voice of President Roosevelt and renditions of the "Marseillaise" apparently coming from their own local radio station but actually from phonograph records on the *Texas*. From that time on there was no major Allied landing from Normandy to the Philippines that did not have a Psychological Warfare Division as part of the force.

At a meeting in London on the morning of September 22, Churchill, Eisenhower and their staffs reviewed the whole TORCH prospect. Because of the expansion of the operation and the added shipping required for transport of men and matériel from the United Kingdom and the United States, Eisenhower made the decision that the date must be postponed to November 8. Following this meeting, Churchill informed Roosevelt that these shipping requirements would also probably compel the abandonment for that year of JUPITER, the landings in northern Norway, which were almost constantly under consideration for three years but which never took place. In the same cable, Churchill informed Roosevelt of a new British operation which had then been ordered; this was known as LIGHTFOOT and it was the drive by Generals Alexander and Montgomery from Egypt which was to begin with the memorable victory at El Alamein.

The postponement of the date for TORCH had considerable political significance in the United States; November 3 was election day and it would have been obviously advantageous to Roosevelt to have this exciting news received before the voters went to the polls—but, as Roosevelt said at the time, this was a decision that rested with the responsible officer, Eisenhower, and not with the Democratic National Committee.

Roosevelt had to give a great deal of attention to the domestic political scene in this summer and fall of 1942. He hated it but he couldn't escape it. The Congressional election was approaching and the partisan voices, temporarily stilled during the phase of national unity enforced by Pearl Harbor, were becoming more and more strident. They had plenty of targets for criticisms—more, in fact, than most of them knew about. The progress of production was in some important respects disappointing and in a few respects downright alarming. The war manpower situation was in a dreadful mess. There was even more than the usual bickering and backbiting between departments and agencies. In the battle of Washington, as on most of the real fighting fronts, this was the lowest point of the war. Worst of all was the failure of the Congress to do anything toward meeting the threat of inflation. The President's requests for higher taxes and more rigid controls on the civilian economy had been ignored or evaded by Congressmen afraid to face the voters, especially the farmers. Roosevelt himself was in a weak position politically, for millions of votes were lost by the shifting of manpower into the armed forces or to new centers of industry, while the farm vote largely stayed put.

Roosevelt was urged to take drastic action to stabilize farm prices, for which Congress was willing to provide a floor but no ceiling. The principal force in this urging was Leon Henderson, Director of the Office of Price Administration and currently the center for the storms of criticism and complaint. A public servant of exceptional ability, courage and imperviousness, Henderson had an unfortunate flair for flamboyant publicity: he was often photographed dancing the rhumba and wearing funny hats and that made him all the more unpopular with the conservative elements which as always were strongest in the rural areas.

It was usual for the President to speak to the nation on Labor Day and Roosevelt decided that this was the occasion for decisive action against inflation. The preparation of that speech was ten days' work— at Shangri-la, the White House and Hyde Park—and involved some arguments among Roosevelt's advisers. The President had the power to stabilize prices and wages by Executive Order without reference to Congress and some of us believed that he should do just that immediately and not run the risk of hostile action or no action at all on Capitol Hill. There were unquestionably many Congressmen who fervently hoped that he would do it this way and thereby absolve them from all responsibility for decision on such a controversial issue. (It was an ironic fact that many of the Congressmen who were loudest in accusing Roosevelt of dictatorial ambitions were the most anxious to have him act like a dictator on all measures which might be unpopular with the people but obviously valuable for the winning of the war.) Roosevelt himself was in favor of an arbitrary Executive Order to achieve stabilization, and his speech was at first written as a proclamation and explanation of that; but some of his advisers, notably Hopkins and Henderson, strongly recommended that he put the issue up to Congress in the form of an ultimatum—"you act before October 1st or I will"— and their arguments finally prevailed.

Roosevelt concluded his speech of September 7 with these words:

Battles are not won by soldiers or sailors who think first of their
own personal safety. And wars are not won by people who are concerned primarily with their own comfort, their own convenience, their
own pocketbooks.

We Americans of today bear the gravest of responsibilities. All
of the United Nations share them.

All of us here at home are being tested—for our fortitude, for our
selfless devotion to our country and our cause.

This is the toughest war of all time. We need not leave it to historians of the future to answer the question whether we are tough
enough to meet this unprecedented challenge. We can give that
answer now. The answer is "Yes."

Roosevelt did not have much to say about the military situation in
that speech. There was not much that he could say without informing
the enemy of future plans.

Of the Eastern Front in Europe he said that the Russians "are
fighting not only bravely but brilliantly" and "will hold out." This, of
course, was during the bitterest phase of the Battle of Stalingrad.

Of the Southwest Pacific: "We must not overrate the importance
of our successes in the Solomon Islands, though we may be proud of
the skill with which these local operations were conducted." Roosevelt
spoke thus cautiously of a critical battle because he knew, as the public
did not, of the severe naval losses we had sustained and he was seeking
to prepare the people for possible news that the Japanese had driven the
Marines from the positions so precariously held on Guadalcanal.

Roosevelt said further:

In the Mediterranean and the Middle East Area the British, together with the South Africans, Australians, New Zealanders, Indian
troops and others of the United Nations, including ourselves, are
fighting a desperate battle with the Germans and Italians. The Axis
powers are fighting to gain control of that area, dominate the Mediterranean and Indian Ocean, and gain contact with the Japanese
Navy. The battle is now joined. We are well aware of our danger, but
we are hopeful of the outcome.

The European Area. Here the aim is an offensive against Germany.
There are at least a dozen different points at which attack can be
launched. You, of course, do not expect me to give details of future
plans, but you can rest assured that preparations are being made
here and in Britain toward this purpose. The power of Germany must
be broken on the battlefields of Europe.

After this speech, Roosevelt decided to take a trip around the country
to see the Chrysler plant in Detroit (now making tanks), the Ford
plant at Willow Run (B-24 Liberators), the Kaiser shipyards in Portland, Oregon, and the Higgins yards in New Orleans, the Boeing plant
in Seattle (B-17 Flying Fortresses), and various army training camps,

airfields and naval stations. It was a good chance for the President to see a great deal of production and training progress—and he was one capable of understanding the essentials of what he saw—but the main purpose of the trip was, of course, for political influence on the Congress and on the Congressional elections.

Merriman Smith, of the United Press, has written of this trip in his book, *Thank You, Mr. President*, and emphasized the irritation caused by the secrecy surrounding all of Roosevelt's wartime journeys. It would seem to have been greatly overdone—especially on occasions such as this one when the President was visible and often audible to millions of citizens over a route of some nine thousand miles. There were many stories at the time of workers who came home late for supper, explaining to their wives that "President Roosevelt was at the plant," and, when the wives saw no mention of this important event in the local newspapers, they accused their husbands of lying. Smith described one incident at the Kaiser shipyards:

After his daughter, Mrs. John Boettiger, had launched a ship—on the record and in full view of cameras—the President took over the meeting. There must have been twenty thousand people swarmed around a high ramp on which the President's open automobile was parked.

"You know," he said to the people over the loudspeaker system, "you know I am not supposed to be here today."

The crowd laughed and the President joined in the merriment. Damned if I saw anything to laugh about. Here was the President of the United States making an important public appearance in front of twenty thousand people, yet the newspapers and radio stations had to play like they knew nothing about it.

Although three reporters whose normal duty was to send news to thousands of outlets around the world were standing only a few feet from him, the President went on with his joke:

"You are the possessors of a secret which even the newspapers of the United States don't know," he told the shipworkers.

"I hope you will keep the secret because I am under military and naval orders, and like the ship that we have just seen go overboard, my motions and movements are supposed to be secret."

Roosevelt loved all this air of mystery. It was part of his nature to wear the mantle of military security like a small boy playing "cops and robbers." Furthermore, he loved to irritate the press which had so often irritated him.

He returned to Washington on October 1, the deadline set for Congressional action, and the next day the Stabilization Act was sent to the White House and he signed it, expressing certainty that it would "assist greatly in bringing the war to a successful conclusion" and "will make the transition to peace conditions easier after the war." The same day he sent for James F. Byrnes to leave the Supreme Court and assume the post of Director of Economic Stabilization which made him, in effect, Assistant President in charge of the home front. This relieved Roosevelt of a considerable amount of work and worry and it consequently greatly reduced the accumulation on Hopkins' desk. Hopkins later laughed and said, "Shortly after Jimmy Byrnes moved in I went to talk to him about something and he told me, 'There's just one suggestion I want to make to you, Harry, and that is to keep the hell out of my business.' He smiled very pleasantly when he said it, but by God he meant it and I'm going to keep the hell out." It is improbable that Hopkins was entirely faithful in living up to this resolve.

In the elections on November 3 the Republicans gained forty-seven votes in the House, which was only nine short of a majority. They gained ten votes in the Senate. Roosevelt had only just escaped the overturn inflicted on Wilson in 1918 and he was now down to the narrowest margin of his entire Presidential career.

During September and October Wendell Willkie made the journey to Africa, the Middle East, the Soviet Union and China which he described in his influential book, *One World*. He flew this enormous distance in an Army transport plane with, of course, Roosevelt's hearty approval; he was accompanied by Joseph Barnes, formerly foreign editor of the *New York Herald Tribune*, and Gardner Cowles, publisher of the *Des Moines Register and Tribune* and *Look* magazine. Because both Barnes and Cowles were then working for the government in the Office of War Information, the former as Deputy Director of the Overseas Branch and the latter as Director of the Domestic Branch, there might have seemed to be a propaganda intent in their presence on the trip. But Willkie solicited and needed no official aid in that field. Cowles was a very close friend and ardent supporter of his and Barnes spoke Russian and other languages fluently and had a background of distinguished service as correspondent in Moscow, Europe and the Far East, and Willkie himself selected them as traveling companions.

Willkie's trip did an enormous amount of good and it also stirred up some trouble. In Moscow he heard very direct accusations that the British had "stolen" American Lend-Lease material intended for Russia (this referred to the ships which were diverted from the Murmansk route to Scotland). In Chungking Willkie heard the Generalissimo's expressions of bitterness against the Allies in general and Britain in particular and also against the American Ambassador, Clarence E. Gauss, and General Stilwell. The long feud between Stilwell and Chennault was then much in evidence.

From Moscow Willkie chided the Allies for failure to open a Second Front and from Chungking for failure to make an all-out effort in aid of China—two statements which caused Roosevelt to remark, "You can't have it both ways." (It might have been added that at this stage of the war it couldn't be had either way.) Shortly before Willkie returned to Washington via the Northwest Passage from Siberia on October 14, Roosevelt let fall some remarks about "typewriter strategists" at a press conference, including an impish imitation of Willkie's pronunciation of some words, and Willkie consequently ended his mission of good will in a fury of rage at the President.

It is my belief that Roosevelt really regretted having yielded to the temptation, which so frequently seemed to afflict him at press conferences, to indulge in unworthy wisecracks at Willkie's expense. He was talking off the record, but he had plenty of reason to know that his little quips would be given wide circulation by the correspondents present, many of whom were accurate reporters. There is no doubt in my mind that Roosevelt had far more admiration for Willkie than for any opponent he ever faced; he respected Willkie's enormous courage, if not his political acumen, and was profoundly and eternally grateful for Willkie's persistent battle against the isolationism of the Old Guard in the Republican party. Once I heard Hopkins make some slurring remark about Willkie and Roosevelt slapped him with as sharp a reproof as I ever heard him utter. He said, "Don't ever say anything like that around here again. Don't even *think* it. You of all people ought to know that we might not have had Lend Lease or Selective Service or a lot of other things if it hadn't been for Wendell Willkie. He was a godsend to this country when we needed him most." The skeptical might suspect that Roosevelt's affectionate regard for Willkie was due at least in part to the fact that he had defeated him, but he had none of the same respect or regard for Herbert Hoover or Thomas E. Dewey, whom he also defeated.

When Willkie was in Chungking on his "One World" trip he heard that there had been criticism of his previous statements in Moscow about the Second Front. He exploded to the press that he had been commissioned by Roosevelt to do certain things, but he had not been limited by any instructions to any precise mission. "When I speak for myself," he said, "I am Wendell Willkie, and I say what I damned please." He obviously had not been thoroughly informed concerning the TORCH operation nor the situation in general. This was a circumstance that was incomprehensible to the Russians and the Chinese, and even to the British: that a statesman of the finesse of Roosevelt could authorize a globe-circling jaunt by any compatriot of Willkie's eminence without "briefing" him thoroughly in advance so that he would know which points to emphasize and which to soft-pedal in all his statements, both public and private. But such was the case. Willkie was authorized to go on his own and "say what I damned please," and he did.

Roosevelt was not greatly disturbed by Willkie's statements during his trip or the speeches that he made after his return. But Hopkins was fearful that Willkie was doing serious damage to the cause of Allied unity. He was particularly angered by the reports, which Willkie never made public but which were freely circulated, of the dinner in Moscow when Stalin had accused the British of "stealing" Lend-Lease material. Hopkins knew all about this particular subject and, in fact, shared a considerable part of the responsibility for diverting some ships from the Murmansk route at times when the cost of getting convoys through was prohibitive. During October, Harriman in London cabled Hopkins about three loaded ships then lying idle in Scotland awaiting a convoy to Murmansk. This was the time of the enormous diversion of shipping for the North African operation and the British wanted to unload these ships so that they could be used elsewhere. Hopkins replied to Harriman:

> It is essential in my belief that the three ships that you mention should be unloaded. We need every possible ship that is going through to Russia during the next two months. Although I realize that there may be compelling reasons for you and Stark to decide not to unload these ships—and we must of course accept your judgment on this point—I think you should tell Stark how very urgent are our needs for merchant ships here immediately. Douglas agrees with me on this. We have already advised Moscow about these matters and it seems to me to make no additional difficulty even if Maisky cables his Government. Under any circumstances, I think the ships should be unloaded.

There was a very heavy load of messages between Washington, London and Moscow during these terribly tense and critical weeks of the fighting in Stalingrad and the Solomons, the immeasurably complex preparations for TORCH, and the build-up of British forces in the Middle East preparatory to the battle of El Alamein. Just before Roosevelt left for his swing around the country on September 17, he wrote a note to Admiral Leahy to make sure that Hopkins got all the cables:

> I am anxious to get the cables to me from the Prime Minister and other heads of government in various countries, and my replies to them, coordinated through Harry because so much of them refer to civil things.
> I am asking him to see that all of the military aspects of these cables are referred to you and the Combined Chiefs of Staff and he will co-ordinate them and give them to me for my approval.

When Roosevelt was in Seattle, Churchill sent cables containing a message he proposed to send to Stalin relative to the canceling of another convoy (PQ 19) to Murmansk and the proposal to establish a British-American strategic air force on the Russian flank in the Caucasus.

The latter proposal had been originally discussed by Churchill and Stalin in August and approved by Roosevelt. The argument for the canceling of PQ 19 was a powerful one; the preceding convoy to Murmansk had lost one ship out of three but had required seventy-seven warships for escort duty. In view of the enormous naval requirements of the impending TORCH operation, it would be obviously impossible to assign anywhere near that number of warships for another convoy.

When Hopkins read these messages, he immediately cabled Churchill:

> The President is now at a distant point and your urgent messages are being relayed to him there. I very strongly urge you not to send Stalin the proposed message until you hear how the President feels about it. It seems very clear to me that the turning point in the war may well depend on what is now said to Stalin and what firm commitments we are prepared to make to him. I shall do everything possible to assure prompt answer to your messages.

At the same time Hopkins cabled Harriman that 3,000 trucks were on the way to Russia by the southern route that month, that another 1,000 would undoubtedly be dispatched before the month ended, that he was trying to get the Persian railway problem unscrambled that afternoon, that he was taking up with General Arnold the question of delivering more transport planes to Russia by way of Siberia, etc. Hopkins sent a telegram to Roosevelt in the Northwest as follows:

> I have just talked to Leahy and our Chiefs of Staff are giving consideration to the Former Naval Person's cables to you today. Will meet with Leahy late this afternoon to send draft of reply for your consideration.
>
> I have no doubt there are compelling reasons for discontinuing the northern convoys for the balance of this year.
>
> In replying to the Former Naval Person relative to a wire to Stalin, I hope you will give full consideration to the importance of the proposal for a joint allied air force on the Caucasian front. Churchill's previous proposal to do this only in the event of a victory in the Middle East seems to me to be totally inadequate. I believe the only thing that will do the trick is a firm commitment to put a token force on this winter and a real force on ready to make the fight next spring. Obviously our planes and manpower must come out of the Bolero commitment. Our Chiefs of Staff are inclined to let the British do the Russian job, we reinforcing in the Middle East.
>
> Without having any opinion on the military necessities of this suggestion, I feel very strongly that from every other consideration it is essential that we join with the British rather than have the British carry that responsibility alone.
>
> I realize that any air force in the Caucasus would be almost a token force between now and Christmas but it surely could be built up with British cooperation to an effective fighting unit by next spring. It

seems to me we must assume that Germany can not break through the Caucasus this winter and to make our plans accordingly. There are, of course, logistic problems involved in this of a serious nature. It seems to me they can be overcome in view of the great urgency of the situation.

If we must now tell Stalin that the convoys on the northern route must be discontinued, then it seems to me that it is almost imperative that we make a direct and firm offer to place our armed forces at his side in Russia against Germany. It is clear that the only armed force which we can get there is our air force and that the only place you can get any part of our force is further to cut in on air to England. This does not necessarily mean any reduction in the big bombers.

I do not, of course, suggest a diversion of any planes which are needed for special operations in the Southwest Pacific or anywhere else. Indeed, I have a feeling that Bolero will have to supply them with additional reinforcements before we are through.

I hope you can take this up again with the Chiefs of Staff. I think that the Prime Minister's wire which he is asking you to endorse is going to be a terrible wet blanket at this particular time.

The most important thing that you could say to Stalin now is that England and the United States are going to send a joint air force to help fight Germany on the Caucasian front.

You will hear from us late tonight.

From his train, en route from San Diego, California, to San Antonio, Texas, Roosevelt cabled Churchill that, whereas he was inclined to agree that the realities of the situation required cancellation of PQ 19, he did not feel that Stalin should be notified of this "tough blow" to his hopes any sooner than was absolutely necessary. He spoke of progress being made in plans for the Allied air force in Trans-Caucasia, and said that perhaps it would be as well to wait to notify Stalin about PQ 19 until these plans were complete. Roosevelt added, "I am having a great trip. Our war production is good but it must be better. The morale of our forces is excellent and their training is far advanced."

On October 5, Roosevelt, having returned to Washington, sent a cable to Churchill which indicated he had reconsidered the question of canceling the convoy PQ 19:

Our greatest reliance today is the Russian Front and we simply must find a way to help them directly aside from our diminishing supplies. It is my very strong feeling that we should make a firm commitment to put an air force into the Caucasus and that this operation should not be contingent on any other developments. . . . I feel most strongly that we should not tell Stalin that the PQ 19 convoy will not sail. I have talked with Admiral King about this and I would like to urge that we use a different technique in which the guiding factors are dispersion and evasion. We would thus let a convoy sail in successive groups comprising the fastest ships we have loaded and are now loading for Russia. Each of these groups would consist of two or three ships, to sail at intervals of twenty-four to forty-eight hours, supported by two or three escorts. We would have to take the risk of having them sail without the full naval covering support needed to protect a convoy from the battleship *Tirpitz* or the German heavy cruisers. In so far as air attack is concerned, we know that the longer nights will be of help and that in all probability the weather would not be against us every day.

It is my belief that we would thus stand a good chance of getting through as high a proportion of the ships as we did with PQ 18. I think it is better under any circumstances that we run this risk rather than endanger our whole relations with Russia at this time.

Please advise me when you are sending your message to Stalin and I shall immediately send him a similar message. I am certain however that both our messages should be phrased so as to leave a good taste in his mouth. Our Ambassador in Moscow has asked for permission to come home to deliver a very important message in person and I have some fears as to what that message might be.

General Marshall reported that it would be entirely possible to build up a group of U.S. heavy bombers in the Caucasus by the end of the year. Roosevelt then cabled Churchill suggesting that the United States should provide the heavy bombers for VELVET—the code name given the Caucasian operation—and that the British should provide the medium or light bombers and the fighter escorts.

On October 7, the following message was received by Roosevelt from Stalin:

As it is reported, the difficulties in the deliveries arise in the first place from the shortage of tonnage. In order to relieve the tonnage situation, the Soviet Government would be willing to agree to a certain curtailment of the deliveries of American war materials to the Soviet Union. We are willing to discard for the time being all of the deliveries of tanks, artillery, munitions, pistols, etc. But at the same time we are extremely in need of an increase in the deliveries of pursuit planes of modern type (such as "Aircobra") and of securing to us under all conditions of certain other supplies. It should be borne in mind that the "Kittyhawk" planes do not stand the fight against present German pursuits.

It would be well if the United States would in any case secure the following monthly supplies to us: 500 pursuit planes, from 8,000 to 10,000 trucks, 5,000 tons of aluminum, from 4,000 to 5,000 tons of explosives. In addition, it is essential to secure the delivery within 12 months of 2 million tons of grain (wheat) as well as such quantity as possible of fats, concentrated food and canned meat. We could import a considerable amount of food via Vladivostok by Soviet ships, provided the United States agree to cede to the U.S.S.R. at least 20 to 30 ships to reinforce our merchant marine. All of this I already talked over with Mr. Willkie, confident that he will report it to you.

As to the situation at the front you certainly know that during the recent months our situation in the South and especially in the region of Stalingrad has worsened due to the fact that we are short of planes, first of all pursuit planes. The Germans proved to have a great reserve of planes. The Germans have in the South at least a two to one superiority in the air which deprives us of the possibility to cover our troops. The experience of the war has shown that the bravest armies become helpless if they are not protected from the blows from the air.

Roosevelt replied to Stalin that arrangements for the Allied air force in the Caucasus were being expedited—that he was trying to find additional planes and also additional merchant ships for the Russians to operate across the Pacific supply line to Vladivostok—that he had just ordered that a complete automobile tire plant be made available for setting up in the Soviet Union—and that very substantial reinforcements were being sent to the Persian Gulf area to develop that route into Russia.

The President made no mention of the convoy PQ 19, which never sailed. The "trickle method" was adopted, sending ships singly with no armed escort whatsoever, and this was continued with fair success until the descent of the long Arctic winter night made it possible to resume regular convoys.

While Ambassador Standley was en route from Moscow with the important message which Roosevelt awaited with some apprehension, Hopkins cabled Harriman that "None of us knows exactly why Standley is coming home."

The message carried by Standley, however, proved to be substantially the same as the message dated October 7 quoted above. Roosevelt then cabled Stalin that he had received from the Ambassador a full report on the "fighting qualities and strength of your Army and the urgency of your need for supplies." Stalin's brief acknowledgment of this message was delivered by Litvinov to Hopkins for the President. Hopkins was now more than ever "Roosevelt's own, personal Foreign Office."

On October 24, Churchill cabled Roosevelt that he was baffled and perplexed by the correspondence from Moscow—or, rather, the almost total lack of it. Two weeks previously he and the President had sent long, parallel messages to Stalin detailing the proposals for supplies and for the air force in the Caucasus. The only reply that Churchill had received consisted of two words, "Thank you." Churchill had sought to obtain further information through the British Ambassador in Moscow, Sir Archibald Clark Kerr, who had been able to gain nothing but evasive replies from Molotov's secretary. Churchill wondered what was going on inside the Soviet Union. Roosevelt cabled him:

Having come to the conclusion that the Russians do not use speech for the same purposes that we do, I am not unduly disturbed about the responses or lack of them that we have received from Moscow.

I feel very certain that the Russians are going to hold throughout this winter. We must be able to prove to Stalin that we have carried out obligations one hundred per cent and we must therefore proceed vigorously with our plans for supplying them and for setting up an air force to fight on their front.

Nothing has been heard here about difficulties in arrangements for landing fields on the Caucasus front but I shall explore this immediately from this end.

The mysterious silence out of Moscow at that time was not due, as some alarmed authorities (not including Roosevelt or Churchill) then feared, to the possibility of a separate, negotiated Russo-German peace; it was the direct result of the historic circumstance of improvement in the situation at Stalingrad. The need for immediate help became less desperate day by day and the Russians never did agree to the project for a British-American air force in the Caucasus. Some time later General Burns prepared a memorandum for Hopkins which is printed in full because it was an excellent statement of Hopkins' own views on the subject of relations with the Soviet Union:

1. There is nothing new or original in this paper. It is simply a summary of what is believed to be the consensus of best ideas.

2. We not only need Russia as a powerful fighting ally in order to defeat Germany but eventually we will also need her in a similar role to defeat Japan. And finally, we need her as a real friend and customer in the post-war world.

3. *With reference to the importance of Russia in the defeat of Germany.*

No arguments are necessary. She is as essential as the United Kingdom and the United States.

4. *With reference to the importance of Russia in the defeat of Japan.*

It is generally conceded that the "step-by-step" plan for reaching Tokyo by way of the Pacific Islands must be supplemented by large scale bombing attacks based upon Asia which will have as their target the very heart of the Japanese Empire and the source of its strength.

This will require very substantial ground forces for the defense of bases, and in addition a large air force, together with its personnel, its ground installations, its planes, its gas, its spare parts, its ammunition and all other supplies. An operating force of 1000 bombers requires approximately 200,000 tons of supplies per month. This strength can hardly be placed in Asia without the assistance of Russia.

Even though we captured Burma, the capacity of the Burma Road is relatively negligible—perhaps 25,000 tons per month—and could not be made substantial for many, many months.

We could take into Asia only a negligible quantity of men and supplies by way of the Persian Gulf and the circuitous route to China to the north of the Himalayas—perhaps 10-20,000 tons per month. Of course, its capacity could be gradually increased but its maximum probabilities are not great. Even this route goes through Russia.

We can hardly hope to reach the Chinese coast without the capture of Singapore and other strong points in that region and such capture may be beyond our capabilities for a long while to come.

However, if Russia would join with us, we would not only have her forces to help us but in addition, we could move men and supplies to Russia and through Russia to the eastward by way of the Trans-Siberian Railway to Eastern Asia. Furthermore we could move some supplies—certainly planes and perhaps some ships—by way of Alaska and Siberia.

In other words, with Russia as an active and powerful ally, we should be able to bomb Japan effectively in the not too distant future. Without her, the time factor may be much longer. And we must remember that each month of this war will cost us many lives and billions of treasure.

Even though we cannot obtain the help of Russia as an active ally against Japan, it would be of great importance if she would assist us in getting men and supplies into China.

5. If it is accepted that Russian help is necessary to defeat both Germany and Japan, it is conversely true that the defeat of Russia by one or both of these countries might prevent us from defeating either Germany or Japan.

Such a defeat might occur if we do not help Russia to the limit, for her war with Germany has deprived her of a great part of her population, of her raw materials, of her industries, of her transportation, of her reserves, and of her food lands.

Such a defeat might also occur if Japan should now join Germany in the war on Russia. It seems therefore that it would be much more advantageous to our cause if a Russo-Japanese war could be postponed until Germany is defeated.

6. *With reference to our need for Russia as a real friend and customer in the post-war period.*

If the Allies are victorious, Russia will be one of the three most powerful countries in the world. For the future peace of the world, we should be real friends so that we can help shape world events in such a way as to provide security and prosperity.

Furthermore, Russia's post-war needs for the products of America will be simply overwhelming. She must not only rehabilitate her war losses in homes, industries, raw materials and farms, but she must provide the resources for the inevitable advances in her standards of living that will result from the war.

7. From the above, it seems evident that Soviet relationships are

the most important to us of all countries, excepting only the United Kingdom. It seems also evident that we must be so helpful and friendly to her that she will not only battle through to the defeat of Germany and also give vital assistance in the defeat of Japan, but in addition willingly join with us in establishing a sound peace and mutually beneficial relations in the post-war world.

8. *Suggestions for improving relationships.*

(a) Arrange for a conference between the President and Mr. Stalin at some appropriate time and place.

(b) Establish a better spirit of "Comrades-in-Arms" by sending General Marshall, Admiral King and General Arnold or other appropriate military representatives to confer with corresponding Russian officials in Moscow or some other appropriate location and to discuss freely our plans, our capabilities and our limitations.

(c) Do everything possible in a generous but not lavish way to help Russia by sending supplies to the limit of shipping possibilities and by sending forces to Russia to join with her in the fight against Germany.

(d) If at all feasible, arrange with Britain and Russia for an attack on Narvik and the Northern Norway Coast to open up the Northern Supply Route to Russia and to deprive Germany of Swedish iron ore.

(e) Send to Russia an ambassador of top rank as to national standing, vision, ability and willingness to serve the country first.

(f) In general, treat Russia as one of the three foremost powers in the world.

(g) Establish the general policy throughout all U.S. departments and agencies that Russia must be considered as a real friend and be treated accordingly and that personnel must be assigned to Russian contacts that are loyal to this concept.

(h) Work to the general plan of assisting Russia to defeat Germany, of postponing a war between Japan and Russia until Germany is defeated, and of seeking Russian assistance at the proper time as an ally in the war with Japan. If this last cannot be achieved, then strive to obtain her agreement to assist in the transportation of supplies into China.

(i) Offer Russia very substantial credits on easy terms to finance her post-war rehabilitation and expansion.

(j) Agree to assist, in every proper and friendly way, to formulate a peace that will meet Russia's legitimate aspirations.

On the same day, October 24, that Churchill sent his message to Roosevelt confessing perplexity and bafflement, he sent another short cable that was full of the emotions of one who, having for long stared defeat in the face, now saw the first glimmer of victory. He said that the battle in Egypt had begun that evening at eight o'clock, London time, that the whole force of the Army would be engaged, and that a victory there would be fruitful for the main enterprise in Algeria and Morocco. The Prime Minister told the President, most movingly, that "all the

Sherman tanks you gave me on that dark Tobruk morning will play their part" in the battle now joined.

This was the first word of El Alamein which came to Roosevelt with his breakfast at Shangri-la; it was four months almost to the day after "that dark Tobruk morning." But it was impossible to be exultant, for those were indescribably nerve-wracking days for everyone aware of the fact that great armadas carrying tens of thousands of men had sailed from the United Kingdom and the United States across the submarine-infested seas to North Africa. The TORCH operation was on and the possibilities for leakage in Washington could be (and were) so terrifying that it seemed inevitable the enemy would know all about it and would have ample time to take effective measures for combating it.

The Chinese Foreign Minister, T. V. Soong, had gone from Washington to Chungking in October and, on November 2, he cabled Hopkins asking if an airplane could be placed at the disposal of Madame Chiang Kai-shek who, according to Soong, was seriously ill, and had been urged to go to the United States for treatment. Soong said that the Chinese Government intended to ask Owen Lattimore to accompany Madame in the event that the flight could be arranged and that she should enter a hospital immediately upon her arrival in the United States, deferring any official visits in Washington until after she had undergone treatment. Hopkins immediately cabled Soong that the President was greatly disturbed to hear of Madame's illness and that steps were being taken to make an airplane immediately available for her transportation from Chungking to New York.

The cabled correspondence about this complicated arrangement was carried on during the tense days preceding the TORCH landings.

Hopkins referred the matter to General Marshall who, on November 5, advised him:

A stratoliner will go to Chengtu, China, via Karachi arriving there on or before November 12 to bring Madame Chiang Kai-shek to this country. The plane should arrive in Washington about November 18, weather permitting.

A doctor and nurse will accompany the plane while Madame Chiang Kai-shek is aboard. The plane's capacity will permit a total of eight in the Madame's party. I will keep you advised of any further developments.

Soong thanked Hopkins for the rapid arrangements and said the Madame would be bringing her own doctor and nurse.

The final stages of preparation for TORCH involved a great deal of very careful word choosing for the various messages from the President to Pétain, Franco, General Antonio Carmona (President of Portugal), Yves Chatel (Governor General of Algeria), the Sultan of Morocco and the Bey of Tunis. These messages were to be flashed as the troops hit the beaches—and at the same instant every international radio transmitter in the United States and Britain would start broadcasting the same program which had been in preparation for weeks. Every word of General Eisenhower's proclamations had been cabled back and forth between London and Washington and scrutinized and many words revised, for it was obvious that the slightest political slip could cost lives.

Most interesting of all was the drafting of the message to Pétain. I don't know who drafted this first, but when the text of it was cabled to Churchill he protested that it was "much too kind." The Prime Minister reminded the President that Pétain had "used his reputation to do our cause injuries no lesser man could have done." Roosevelt then took a good look at the message and what he did to it can be observed in an accompanying reproduction. The original draft started out:

My dear old friend:
  I am sending this message to you *not only* as the Chef d'Etat of the United States to the Chef d'Etat of the Republic of France, *but also as one of your friends and comrades of the great days of 1918. May we both live to see France victorious again against the ancient enemy.*
  When your government concluded, *of necessity,* the Armistice Convention in 1940, it was impossible for any of us to foresee the program of systematic plunder which the German Reich would inflict on the French people.

The words that I have italicized were cut out by Roosevelt. At the end of the message he deleted a reference to "the venerated hero of Verdun," and "my warm regards" and the subscript, "your friend."
Pétain replied:

  It is with stupor and sadness that I learned tonight of the aggression of your troops against North Africa.
  I have read your message. You invoke pretexts which nothing justifies . . . France and her honor are at stake. We are attacked; we shall defend ourselves; this is the order I am giving.

Thus, for the "honor" of the Vichy Government, was enacted the sordid spectacle of Frenchmen shooting at and killing Americans and Americans shooting at and killing Frenchmen. It was like a tragic misprint on the pages of history. Intense hostility to Britain had been expected in North Africa—at one time, it had even been planned to have British troops participating disguise their nationality by wearing American uniforms—but fortunately these fears proved to be greatly exaggerated. There was little if any difference in the reception accorded to the British as contrasted with American troops by the local populace. As it happened, by all odds the stiffest resistance was offered in Morocco

TELEGRAM

The White House
Washington

Marechall Petnein

October 15 1942

~~My dear old friend,~~

I am sending this message to you [~~personally~~] as the Chef d'Etat of the United States to the Chef d'Etat of the Republic of France. ~~But also as one of your~~ ~~friends and comrades of the great days of 1918.~~ [May] we ~~both live to~~ see France victorious ~~again against the Boche once.~~

When your government concluded, [~~of necessity~~] the Armistice Convention in 1940, it was impossible for any of us to foresee the program of systematic plunder which the German Reich would inflict on the French people.

That program, implemented by black mail and robbery, has deprived the French population of its means of subsistence, its savings; it has paralyzed French industry and transport; it has looted French factories and French farms -- all for the benefit of a Nazi Reich and a Fascist Italy under whose governments no liberty loving nation could long exist.

As an old friend of France and the people of France, m y anger and sympathy grows with every passing day when I consider the misery, the want, and the absence from their homes of the flower of French manhood. Germany has neglected no opportunity to demoralize and degrade your great nation.

Today, with greedy eyes on that empire which France so laboriously constructed, Germany and Italy are proposing to invade and occupy French north Africa, in order that they may execute their schemes of domination and conquest over the whole of that continent.

I know you will realize that such a conquest of Africa would not stop there but would be the prelude to further attempts by Germany and Italy to threaten the conquest of large portions of the American hemisphere, large dominations over the Near and Middle East, and a joining of hands in the Far East with those military leaders of Japan who seek to dominate the whole of the Pacific.

It is, evident, of course, that an invasion and occupation of French North and West Africa would constitute for the United States and all of the American Republics the gravest kind of menace to their security --just as it would sound the death knell of the French Empire.

Roosevelt's message to Pétain, referred to Churchill for his approval,

TELEGRAM

The White House
Washington

In the light of all the evidence of our enemy's intentions and plans, I have, therefore, decided to dispatch to North Africa powerful American armed forces to cooperate with the governing agencies of Algeria, Tunisia and Morocco in repelling this latest act in the long litany of German and Italian international crime.

These indomitable American forces are equipped with massive and adequate weapons of modern warfare which will be available for your compatriots in North Africa in our mutual fight against the common enemy.

I am making all of this clear to the French authorities in North Africa, and I am calling on them for their cooperation in repelling Axis threats. My clear purpose is to support and aid the French authorities and their administrations. That is the immediate aim of these American armies.

I need not tell you that the ultimate and greater aim is the liberation of France, and its Empire from the Axis yoke. In so doing we provide automatically for the security of the Americas.

I need not again affirm to you, ~~the venerated home~~ that the United States of America seeks no territories and remembers always the historic friendship and mutual aid which we have so greatly given to each other.

I send to you and, through you, to the people of France ~~my deep hope~~ that we are all of us soon to enter into happier days. *and belief*

~~Your~~

Franklin D Roosevelt

(end)

and revised by Roosevelt after Churchill protested that it was "much too kind."

to General Patton's Western Task Force which was entirely American, in naval and air as well as ground forces. This action was the responsibility of General Nogues, one of the most dubious characters in the Vichy hierarchy, and by Admiral Michelier, whom Professor Morison has described as "an honorable man." There is considerable room for speculation as to whether either Nogues or Michelier would have ordered such determined resistance if the secret of the landings had been less well kept and both had been made aware of the strength of the forces that were moving in on Morocco and Algeria. Nogues took it to be merely another Commando raid, and French gunnery officers at Casablanca later testified they had no knowledge for hours of the nationality of the ships at which they were shooting. However, once resistance was offered, "honor" dictated that it must continue until overcome by force. In three days of fighting, the French suffered heavy losses in ships and in men; American losses were not as heavy, but they were deplorable because they were so unnecessary. Furthermore, the delay in landing caused by the resistance gave the U-boats time to assemble and do a considerable amount of damage.

At a White House conference some time later, General T. T. Handy, Chief of the Operations Division of the War Department, expressed the opinion that "TORCH was unquestionably the most complex operation in military history," and perhaps it still retains that distinction even after OVERLORD. General Marshall had firmly opposed it, and so had General Eisenhower, who is quoted as having described the day when the decision was made by Roosevelt as possibly the "blackest day in history." Yet, the decision having been made, it was carried out with extraordinary skill. Counting every mistake that was made in the military operations, it was a brilliant performance. The same could not be said for the concurrent and subsequent political conduct of affairs.

At noon on Sunday, November 8, a few hours after the landings, while there was still fighting at Algiers and Oran as well as on the Atlantic beaches, Secretary Hull suddenly summoned press correspondents to the State Department for one of the most ill-advised conferences of the war. After all the criticism provoked by the St. Pierre-Miquelon episode, and continued off and on after that trivial episode, it was entirely understandable that Hull would wish to indulge in some gloating at the evidence that the Vichy policy had paid off in North Africa. But his public expressions of triumph were premature. The worst in criticism of Washington's policy was yet to come.

There have been all manner of charges brought in connection with "the Darlan deal": it has been said that secret arrangements had been made with him by Robert Murphy three weeks before TORCH and that Darlan's presence in Algiers on the night of November 7 was prearranged and not the surprise and embarrassment to Allied authorities that they pretended. I believe that if such charges were true the fact would have become evident long since no matter how powerful or comprehensive the attempts to suppress it. If there are those who can accuse Roosevelt and Churchill of being capable of such duplicity—and there are those who can and do accuse them both of every form of perfidy—it is still virtually impossible to imagine Generals Eisenhower and Mark Clark and many other soldiers and sailors suddenly developing the exceptional talents as actors that the performance of this fabulous masquerade would have required. There was no previous deal with Darlan, but there was a degree of unaccountable miscalculation and misinformation which caused a subsequent deal with him to seem to be the only solution.

There may be reason to suspect that Darlan himself had at least an inkling of what was afoot and remained deliberately in Algiers where he had gone to visit his critically ill son (there was no masquerade about this son's paralysis). According to Murphy, when the grim-visaged French admiral was awakened to receive the news that the Allied forces were moving in early in the morning of D-Day, Darlan turned purple, paced the floor for fifteen minutes, and exclaimed, "I have known for a long time that the British were stupid, but I always believed the Americans were more intelligent. I begin to believe that you make as many mistakes as they do." However, it is still possible that he was not taken totally by surprise. As soon as he was sure that this was a full-scale operation, he indicated a quick willingness to do business with the "stupid" Allies, which represented a complete turning of his anti-British Vichy coat. The records show that within a few hours of his purpling before Murphy—still on the morning of D-Day—he telephoned Nogues in Morocco and ordered him to cease resistance—and it is most important to note that Nogues refused to obey this order.

Whatever Darlan's reasons for being in Algiers on that tremendous occasion, he *was* there, and the consequences of his presence were almost sufficient to ruin Eisenhower's great career as supreme commander before it had even had time to get started.

When Murphy told Darlan that the Americans had brought the noble, gallant General Henri H. Giraud by submarine out of metropolitan France to be the new leader in North Africa, Darlan said, "He is not your man, for politically he is a child. He is a good divisional commander, nothing more." This must have come as an affront to Murphy who had been responsible for the secret communications with Giraud through General Charles Mast and Jacques Lemaigre-Dubreuil who, according to Langer, "long before the war had been prominent in French fascist movements and might be regarded as a typical example of the French banker and big-business man who was not only ready but eager to play the Nazi game." According to Murphy, Lemaigre-Dubreuil was a "courageous, patriotic Frenchman, who hates the Germans and Italians with an intelligent implacability and favors the Allies."

While Darlan was pacing the floor with Murphy in Algiers, and while Patton off the coast of Morocco was cursing the British and American short-wave radio stations for what seemed to him a premature broadcast of Roosevelt's recorded speech, Eisenhower was having his troubles in a session with Giraud on the Rock of Gibraltar—and the ultimate description of that heated interview can safely be left to Eisenhower himself. A tentative agreement with the proud French soldier was finally reached and on Monday, the day after the landings, Giraud moved on to Algiers to assume political command of French North Africa. Darlan's estimate—"he is not your man"—proved lamentably correct. Eisenhower issued a public statement which he later regretted: "It is expected that his [Giraud's] presence there will bring about a cessation of scattered resistance." All that it did bring about among French colonial authorities was resistance to Giraud. As Roosevelt cabled Churchill, two days later:

> In regard to de Gaulle, I have heretofore enjoyed a quiet satisfaction in leaving him in your hands. Apparently I have now acquired a similar problem in brother Giraud. I wholly agree that we must prevent rivalry between the French emigré factions and I have no objection to a de Gaulle emissary visiting Giraud in Algiers. We must remember there is also a catfight in progress between Giraud and Darlan, each claiming full military command of French forces in North and West Africa. The principal thought to be driven home to all three of these prima donnas is that the situation is today solely in the military field and that any decision by any one of them, or by all of them, is subject to review and approval by Eisenhower.

On the same day that cable was sent, November 11, Nogues in Morocco received another order from Darlan to cease fire and this time he obeyed, having fought for three days in defiance of the first order. Nogues' capitulation now may have been due to the fact that on this day the Germans marched into unoccupied France and the Vichy Government, under Pétain and Laval, no longer could maintain even the pretense of independent authority. (Nogues was also influenced by the fact that his remaining forces were by now completely surrounded and further resistance would only mean more French casualties, civilians as well as soldiers, and destruction of much of Casablanca.) In any case, it now seemed evident that Darlan was the only authority who could command the obedience of the French officers in North Africa—and that included Pierre Boisson, Governor of Dakar, and Admiral Jean Pierre Esteva, Governor of Tunisia. (Boisson, who was far from the Germans, did respect Darlan's authority, and the fortress of Dakar went to the Allies without the firing of a shot; Esteva, who was surrounded by Germans, chose to go on collaborating with them.) Therefore, Eisenhower and Clark, with the powerless Giraud on their hands, with long and tenuous lines of communication behind them and the rapid push into Tunisia ahead of them, made the only arrangement which seemed practical or even possible: the deal with Darlan. Eisenhower took full responsibility for this. Roosevelt quoted him as having said later, when they met in Casablanca, "I believe in a theatre commander doing these things without referring them back to his home Government and then waiting for approval. If a mere General makes a mistake, he can be repudiated and kicked out and disgraced. But a Government cannot repudiate and kick out and disgrace itself—not, at any rate, in wartime."

However, Eisenhower was not the prime target for the barrage of criticism laid down in the American and British press and on the radio. Because Hull had been so importunate in claiming a substantial share of the credit for the success in North Africa, he and the State Department were given a huge and unfair share of the blame for a deal which seemed a sordid nullification of the principles for which the United Nations were supposed to be fighting. The widespread protests could be summed up in the statement: "If we will make a deal with a Darlan in French territory, then presumably we will make one with a Goering in Germany or with a Matsuoka in Japan."

Liberal opinion in the United States and Great Britain was understandably outraged, and Hull indignantly attributed all of it to "ideological"—which meant, "Communist"—propaganda. However, in a message sent a few weeks later to Churchill, Stalin said:

It seems to me that the Americans used Darlan not badly in order to facilitate the occupation of Northern and Western Africa. The military diplomacy must be able to use for military purposes not only Darlan but, "Even the Devil himself and his grandma."

(Ambassador Maisky in translating this said it was an old and strong Russian proverb.)

On November 14, Roosevelt received a long cable from Eisenhower which I heard him read aloud to Hopkins. It was a remarkable statement of Eisenhower's reasons for the Darlan deal. Roosevelt was deeply impressed by it and, as he read it with the same superb distribution of emphasis that he used in his public speeches, he sounded as if he were making an eloquent plea for Eisenhower before the bar of history. While preparing this book, I asked Eisenhower for permission to publish this message in its original form, and he freely granted such permission, but the Security authorities required that it could be published only in paraphrase. No paraphrase can do justice to Eisenhower's actual choice of words, but here is the substance of the message:

Existing French sentiment in North Africa does not even remotely resemble prior calculations and it is of utmost importance that no precipitate action be taken which will upset such equilibrium as we have been able to establish.

The name of Marshal Pétain is something to conjure with in North Africa. From highest to lowest, everyone attempts to create the impression that the shadow of the Marshal's figure dominates all his actions and, in fact, his very life. The military and naval leaders, as well as the civil governors, agree that only one man has the obvious right to assume the mantle of Pétain and that man is Admiral Darlan. Even General Giraud clearly recognizes this overpowering consideration and he has modified his own ambitions and intentions accordingly. . . .

It must be understood that if we repudiate Darlan and attempt from the outside to dictate the personnel of the coalition to run North Africa, the following will be the consequences:

a. French armed forces here will resist us passively and, in certain instances, actively.

b. The hope of securing co-operation in this area will be lost at great cost to us in stagnation of operations and in requirements for additional troops.

c. The opportunity for gaining some assistance from remaining French naval and military units in North Africa will disappear.

d. The last glimmer of hope with respect to the Toulon Fleet will be gone.

e. Admiral Esteva, in Tunis, will not co-operate and our hope of getting Tunisia quickly will not be attainable. Admittedly, Esteva may already be helpless, but there is still a chance of his being able to assist.

Admiral Cunningham and General Clark, together with my full staff, have assisted me in making what we consider to be the only possible workable arrangement designed to secure advantages and avoid disadvantages. No one who is not on the ground can have a clear appreciation of the complex currents of prejudice and feeling that influence the local situation. Also, it should be clear that General Giraud's earnest participation in this arrangement indicates the necessity for the agreements we have made.

In the event the British and U.S. Government, after analysis of this radio, are still dissatisfied with the nature of the agreement made, I suggest that a mission of selected U.S. and British representatives (including the Free French if deemed advisable) be dispatched immediately to Algiers where they can be convinced in short order of the soundness of the moves which have been made.

Roosevelt attached great importance to Eisenhower's confession of astonishment at the situation as he found it in North Africa; it did "not even remotely resemble prior calculations." When the supreme commander of a major military operation makes an admission like that it indicates that there must have been something wrong with his Intelligence Service. This is all the more surprising since North Africa had not been enemy territory, into which secret agents could be introduced only with the utmost difficulty and at their own extreme peril, but was friendly territory with which the U.S. maintained diplomatic relations. Therefore, the headquarters of Robert Murphy in Algiers and all the American consulates in that area and in Spanish Morocco were centers of Intelligence with large staffs which included observers of undoubted competence as well as courage. Yet Eisenhower was astonished when the local French failed to hail Giraud as a conquering hero. This led to a display of political crudity which made the U.S. Government look ridiculously amateurish.

Roosevelt made no bones of his own attitude, publicly as well as privately. Two days after the Eisenhower cable, the storm of criticism of the Darlan deal had reached such proportions that Hopkins, Rosenman and I strongly urged the President to issue a statement to the press. We had a draft of such a statement which had been prepared originally by Elmer Davis and Archibald MacLeish. When Roosevelt read it, he made substantial revisions, all of them calculated to make the language tougher and more uncompromising. The statement as he issued it was as follows:

I have accepted General Eisenhower's political arrangements made for the time being in Northern and Western Africa.

I thoroughly understand and approve the feeling in the United States and Great Britain and among all the other United Nations that in view of the history of the past two years no permanent arrangement should be made with Admiral Darlan. People in the United Nations likewise would never understand the recognition of a reconstituting of the Vichy Government in France or in any French territory.

We are opposed to Frenchmen who support Hitler and the Axis. No one in our Army has any authority to discuss the future Government of France and the French Empire.

The future French Government will be established, not by any individual in Metropolitan France or overseas, but by the French people themselves after they have been set free by the victory of the United Nations.

The present temporary arrangement in North and West Africa is only a temporary expedient, justified solely by the stress of battle.

The present temporary arrangement has accomplished two military objectives. The first was to save American and British lives, and French lives on the other hand.

The second was the vital factor of time. The temporary arrangement has made it possible to avoid a 'mopping-up' period in Algiers and Morocco which might have taken a month or two to consummate. Such a period would have delayed the concentration for the attack from the West on Tunis, and we hope on Tripoli. . . .

Admiral Darlan's proclamation assisted in making a 'mopping-up' period unnecessary. Temporary arrangements made with Admiral Darlan apply, without exception, to the current local situation only.

I have requested the liberation of all persons in North Africa who have been imprisoned because they opposed the efforts of the Nazis to dominate the world, and I have asked for the abrogation of all laws and decrees inspired by Nazi governments or Nazi ideologists. Reports indicate that the French of North Africa are subordinating all political questions to the formation of a common front against the common enemy.

It will be noted how frequently Roosevelt inserted the word "temporary" into that statement. This was a fact which certainly did not escape the attention of Darlan himself. He wrote a rather plaintive letter to Clark saying that Roosevelt's words tended to substantiate the view that "I am only a lemon which the Americans will drop after they have squeezed it dry." He expressed the hope that the U.S. Government would appreciate the difficulties of his position and "not give Frenchmen the impression that the authority of the leader which has brought it [French Africa] back into the struggle is a diminished one."

In addition to his statement to the press, Roosevelt together with Hopkins drafted the following message to Eisenhower:

Marshall has shown me your despatch giving your reasons for placing Darlan in charge of the civil administration of North Africa. I want you to know that I appreciate fully the difficulties of your military situation. I am therefore not disposed to in any way question the action you have taken. Indeed you may be sure of my complete support of this and any other action you are required to take in carrying out your duties. You are on the ground and we here intend to support you fully in your difficult problems.

However I think you should know and have in mind the following policies of this Government:

1. That we do not trust Darlan.

2. That it is impossible to keep a collaborator of Hitler and one whom we believe to be a fascist in civil power any longer than is absolutely necessary.

3. His movements should be watched carefully and his communications supervised.

I have not consulted Churchill in regard to this message but I am sending a copy of it to him at once and I am sure he will approve.

I want to add a personal note to you and Clark to tell you what great confidence we have in both of you and how satisfied we are with the progress of events. This message is not to be made public.

This message was written to make clear on the permanent record just how Roosevelt viewed this malodorous situation.

The whole Darlan deal, and the tremendous repercussions therefrom, provided much material for the de Gaulle propagandists who were broadcasting regularly from London and from Brazzaville in Equatorial Africa. It also inspired plenty of gleeful quips by Goebbels and his satellite broadcasters in Rome and Paris and throughout Europe. It seemed to confirm the impression that, while the Americans talked big about the principles of the Four Freedoms and the Atlantic Charter, they actually knew nothing about Europe and could be hoodwinked by any treacherous gangster who offered them collaboration.

I think I am justified in expressing the opinion that the British Foreign Office derived a certain private satisfaction from the embarrassment of the U.S. Government throughout the Darlan affair and its ridiculously protracted aftermath. The British could assume a very virtuous position of loyally supporting an Ally but taking no direct responsibility for the Ally's political blunders. There was no doubt that, in the first place, Churchill and his colleagues were not happy about Roosevelt's insistence that the North African operation should be proclaimed an entirely American affair, even to the extent of putting American insignia on aircraft of the R.A.F. and American uniforms on British troops. It was obvious that the British, after their long, lonely struggle to keep alight the flame of European liberty, would hardly relish the spectacle of the Americans suddenly becoming the noble liberators of Europe. But the unfortunate developments in North Africa tended to change all that. Churchill made it clear to the House of Commons that "neither militarily nor politically are we directly controlling the course of events." He also made it clear that he gave his vigorous support to the decisions of President Roosevelt and of the generals in whom Roosevelt had reposed confidence. Churchill has subsequently stated in a letter to me that he had no previous knowledge of the negotiations with Admiral Darlan, but he would not have hesitated to deal with him, in the circumstances which befell Generals Eisenhower and Clark. In his messages to the President, however, Churchill urged strongly that the British and American Governments must find a means of reconciling the positions of Giraud and de Gaulle so as to frustrate the taunting accusations of the enemy propagandists that each Ally had its own "pet" Frenchman.

It was a time, indeed, when recriminations between the United Nations were not in order. It was a time when the news from all fronts was incredibly good.

The great British victory at El Alamein had been concluded just before the landings in North Africa, and approximately a week later the Red Army turned to the offensive at Stalingrad. On the night of November 12 the naval battle of Guadalcanal, which lasted twenty-four minutes and which Admiral King described as "one of the most furious sea battles ever fought," shattered the last formidable Japanese attempt to drive American forces from their positions in the Solomons. In that brief but important action, two American admirals were killed—Norman Scott and Daniel Callaghan—the latter Roosevelt's former Naval Aide and great friend.

In a speech to the New York Herald-Tribune Forum on November 17, Roosevelt said: •

> During the past two weeks we have had a great deal of good news and it would seem that the turning point in this war has at last been reached. But this is no time for exultation. There is no time now for anything but fighting and working to win.

We tried to persuade the President to go further than that—to say something like "the tide has definitely turned"—but he insisted on using the cautious subjunctive. I doubt that careful study of all the words that he spoke would reveal any statement about the progress of the war that could be termed even slightly overoptimistic. In this case, however, his caution was of no particular avail. The newspapers featured the one phrase, "TURNING POINT OF WAR REACHED SAYS F.D.R."—and the public took that assurance as final.

Churchill, whose record on hopeful utterances was not quite equal to Roosevelt's, was even more cautious at this time. He summed up the situation in his famous words, "Now, this is not the end. It is not even the beginning of the end. But it is, perhaps, the end of the beginning." In the same speech he made an even more famous statement, "Let me, however, make this clear, in case there should be any mistake about it in any quarter. We mean to hold our own. I have not become the King's First Minister in order to preside over the liquidation of the British Empire." Churchill had waited a long time for an opportunity to say just that. He had suffered and seethed when Roosevelt urged him to establish an independent, federated India, when Roosevelt proclaimed that the principles of the Atlantic Charter extended also to the Pacific and Indian Oceans and everywhere else on earth, when the Australian and New Zealand Governments insisted on withdrawing crack divisions from the Middle East; he had even consented now and then to refer to it as the British *Commonwealth*. But now, with the wine of victory coursing in his veins, he hurled at all and sundry, at friend as well as foe, the defiance that he never for one instant had abandoned: "Here we are and here we stand, a veritable rock of salvation in this drifting world."

On the evening of the day, November 9, that Churchill made this speech, he had a conversation with Winant, Eden, and General

"Beedle" Smith which lasted, according to Smith's report to Marshall, "the greater part of the night." Churchill wanted Marshall, King and Hopkins to return to London for another full-dress conference on future plans. He was reluctantly abandoning the idea of JUPITER, the Norwegian operation, and turning to the thought of getting Turkey into the war with her forty-five divisions of superior fighting men armed and equipped by the Allies for an invasion of the Balkans. According to Smith's report, Churchill appeared to be cooling on the ROUNDUP plan for Northern France, except as an ultimate deathblow against an opponent tottering and reeling from blows struck elsewhere (the soft underbelly).

Nevertheless, two weeks later Churchill was cabling Roosevelt in great concern over what appeared to be American abandonment of ROUNDUP in 1943. This, he said, "would be a most grievous decision." He said that TORCH could be considered no substitute for ROUNDUP. He conceded that it might not be possible to mass the necessary strength for an invasion of Northern France in 1943, but "if so it becomes all the more important to make sure we do not miss 1944." He repeated the hope that Hopkins, Marshall and King would come to London or that he and his staff go to Washington.

Roosevelt replied as follows:

Of course we have no intention of abandoning the plans for ROUNDUP. It is impossible for anyone to say now whether or not we will be given the opportunity to strike across the Channel in 1943. But we must obviously grasp the opportunity if it comes. Determination as to the strength of the forces that we should apply to BOLERO in 1944 is a matter requiring our joint strategic considerations. My present thought is that we should build up our present striking force in the United Kingdom as rapidly as possible, this force to be available immediately in the event of a German collapse. We should build up a very large force for later use in the event of Germany remaining intact and assuming a defensive position.

The mounting of TORCH, according to the conclusions reached at the meeting last summer in London by the Combined Chiefs of Staff, postponed necessarily the assembling of the required forces in the British Isles. . . . The North African operations must naturally take precedence until we have provided adequately against situations which may possibly develop in Spanish Morocco or in Tunisia. We are much more heavily engaged in the Southwest Pacific than I anticipated a few months ago. . . . I believe that we should arrange a military strategic conference between Russia, Great Britain and the United States as soon as we have knocked the Germans out of Tunisia and secured the danger against any real threat from Spain. It is my hope that the military situation in North Africa will be such that we may hold this conference within a month or six weeks. . . . It is my strong feeling that we must sit down with the Russians round a table. My information is that this conference could be held in Cairo or in Moscow—that we could each be represented by a small group meeting in utmost secrecy—that any conclusions reached at this conference would of course be subject to approval by the three of us. I should in all probability send General Marshall to head up our delegation but I presume that all of the three Services would be represented. . . . Please advise me what you think of this proposal as soon as you can.

On November 25, Roosevelt held a conference with Leahy, Marshall, King, Arnold and Hopkins, the record of which was as follows:

The President first discussed the question of what operations should be undertaken as soon as the following have been accomplished in North Africa: first, a secure situation to the south and east of Spanish Morocco; and, second, the complete occupation of Tunisia. He asked General Marshall for his estimate of when Tunisia would be occupied.

General Marshall replied that, unless the Axis forces develop some unforeseen strength, he estimated that the occupation of Tunisia could be accomplished in from two to three weeks, provided that two divisions were sufficient to accomplish the task. He stated that if, on the other hand, General Eisenhower found it necessary to commit four divisions for the purpose, the complete occupation would take somewhat longer because of the delay involved in assembling this number of troops.

The President then asked General Marshall for his estimate as to the time required for driving Axis forces from Tripoli.

General Marshall replied that, if we succeed in taking Tunisia, and barring the breakdown of General Alexander's forces due to over-extension, the Axis powers would find themselves in an impossible situation in Tripoli and would be forced to evacuate that area by what might be termed attrition.

The President then asked if any information had been received about the fortified position which he had been informed of about ten miles inside of the Tunisian border from Tripoli. He was informed that no reports had been received concerning this position. (A message will be sent to General Eisenhower, asking if any information is available on this subject.)

The President and General Marshall then discussed the possibilities of future operations. Action in Turkey was discussed, and it was agreed that there were many diplomatic questions involved, and that probably Turkey would not consider aligning herself with the United Nations until she had been given considerable armament and other munitions of war. In this connection, General Marshall stated that he felt that, if we were to strengthen the Turkish forces, it would be better to give them small arms and ammunition for their infantry units, but to have the heavier artillery and mechanized weapons manned by American troops.

General Marshall said that before any operations were decided on very careful consideration should be given to the cost of actually clearing the Mediterranean for sea traffic. He felt that the occupation of Sicily, Sardinia, and Crete would be necessary for this, and pointed out that a careful determination should be made of whether or not the large air and ground forces required for such a project could be justified, in view of the results to be expected.

The President then asked General Marshall what he considered to be the lines of action open to the Axis powers.

General Marshall replied that he considered that, in order of probability, their lines of action were as follows: first, occupation of Spain; second, a continued drive through the Caucasus; and, third, an attack against the British Isles.

There followed a discussion concerning the production program. The President initiated this discussion by stating that the 82,000 combat airplane program had his approval and must be carried out.

Admiral King and Admiral Leahy advised the President that Mr. Nelson had informed them that, if this air program was carried out, many of the essential features of the naval program could not be accomplished without some delay.

The President was of the opinion that the aircraft program would not conflict with the Navy program in any way.

The rest of this discussion was concerned with problems of production and allocation.

This same day Roosevelt cabled Stalin:

We are going to drive the Germans out of Africa soon, I hope, and then we will give Mussolini's Fascists a taste of some real bombing. I feel quite sure that they will never stand up under that kind of pressure.

We have hit the Japanese very hard in the Solomon Islands. We have probably broken the backbone of the power of their Fleet. They have still too many aircraft carriers to suit me, but soon we may well sink some more of them. . . . We are going to press our advantages in the Southwest Pacific and I am sure that we are destroying far more Japanese airplanes and sinking far more of their ships than they can build. I send you my warmest congratulations on the most encouraging news that we are receiving from the Stalingrad area.

Roosevelt did not include in this cable the information that the U.S. Navy in the Pacific was at that moment down to its last aircraft carrier and, during most of November, this lone survivor, the *Enterprise*, was damaged and out of action; but a tremendous force of new aircraft carriers was on the way.

Evidently Stalin had broken his long and apparently ominous silence to Churchill with a cable of congratulations on the developments in Egypt and in the TORCH area. On November 24 Churchill cabled

Stalin his desire for a tripartite military staff conference—with emphasis on hopes of persuading Turkey to enter the war—and on December 2 Stalin's amiable and even cordial reply was relayed to the White House. Stalin said that he shared Churchill's views on the importance of developing personal relations—that he was grateful for measures taken to resume convoys to Murmansk, despite the difficulties presented by considerable naval operations in the Mediterranean—that he was in full agreement with Churchill and Roosevelt about Turkey and the arrangement of a Moscow conference on future military plans. He hoped that there was no change of mind "in regard to your promise given in Moscow to establish a Second Front in Europe in 1943." He said cautiously that the Russian counteroffensive in Stalingrad was so far successful partly because of weather conditions—fog and snow—which interfered with the operations of the Luftwaffe. He expressed the intention of the Russians to start a new offensive on the central front within the next few days.

In the midst of these cabled negotiations, Madame Chiang Kai-shek approached the United States, and Roosevelt sent Hopkins to New York as his representative to extend greetings. Hopkins wrote of this:

Madame Chiang Kai-shek was to arrive on Thursday, November 26, 1942, at Mitchel Field at 9:00 a.m. I had previously arranged that planes land only at military fields so there would be little probability of her entrance being discovered, because the Chinese were anxious to get her into the hospital before it became known. The plane actually arrived on Friday, November 27, 1942, at 2:00 p.m., and I met Madame Chiang Kai-shek and drove back to the Harkness Pavilion with her where they had arranged for her to occupy all of the twelfth floor.

On the trip in she told me that she wanted to make it clear to the President she was here for no other purpose than medical treatment and rest. However, in the same breath she proceeded to raise many questions relating to China and the United States.

She first told me how greatly disturbed they were in China over negotiations between Japan and the United States immediately prior to Pearl Harbor. Everyone in China was afraid that we were going to sell them down the river and she, at any rate, believes that the intervention of a few of us here prevented that from happening and she expressed great gratitude to those of us in the Administration who urged that a firm line be taken with the Japs and that under no circumstances should the Chinese position be compromised.

She expressed more forcibly than I had heard anyone express it before her belief that the two wars against Germany and Japan can both be won but that the way to do it is to put all our strength into defeating Japan. From what I could gather, she is perfectly willing we should take the pressure off Germany. I did not argue this point unduly with her beyond saying that I thought such a strategy was unfeasible. She seemed strangely uninterested in what our Navy was doing in the Solomon Islands and apparently confined her interest entirely to what we are doing in China proper. She laid great emphasis on keeping the Chinese population in the mood to fight. She felt that they had reached a very low ebb on two occasions; once, prior to Pearl Harbor and once on the collapse of Burma.

She is apparently quite critical of both the British and ourselves in relation to that enterprise, although she did not state so positively. She thinks Stilwell does not understand the Chinese people and that he made a tragic mistake in forcing Chiang Kai-shek to put one of his best divisions in Burma where it was later lost. She said Chiang Kai-shek did this against his best judgment. . . . [Some words were garbled here.]

It is pretty clear she does not like Stilwell and expressed the greatest admiration for Chennault. She spent a good deal of her time in explaining an article in *Life* magazine which attacked the British Government vigorously. She wanted me particularly to read that article as being her point of view.

I told her Mrs. Roosevelt wanted to see her and arranged for an appointment with Mrs. Roosevelt at the hospital the next morning. Inasmuch as the newspapers were bound to get hold of the story, it seemed best to get a news release issued immediately.

After this greeting, Hopkins joined the President at Hyde Park and then returned with him to Washington. For Roosevelt by now was convinced that the major strategic problems of the future could not be settled by the Combined Chiefs of Staff—there must be a face-to-face meeting of the President, the Prime Minister and Stalin themselves. Hopkins influenced Roosevelt strongly along these lines. His own experience in Moscow had convinced him that there could be no really free discussion with the Russians, on a give-and-take basis, on anything less than the topmost level. Hopkins had been the first effective protagonist of a personal meeting of Roosevelt and Churchill; he was now the ardent protagonist of a meeting of the two of them with the great leader of the Soviet Union. Early in December Averell Harriman returned to London with Oliver Lyttelton, who had been in Washington attempting to straighten out the then enormously confused affairs of the Combined Production and Resources Board. (Nobody, it must be noted, ever succeeded fully in straightening them out.) Roosevelt conveyed messages to Churchill through Lyttelton—as he had indicated in a cable on November 25, previously quoted—and he gave Harriman the express assignment of discussing this proposed Big Three conference with Churchill and reporting back thereon, but not through State Department channels.

Churchill, agreeing to the proposal for a conference, wanted to include

Eden in it because of Eden's vital position of authority as member of the War Cabinet as well as Foreign Secretary. But Roosevelt did not want to include Hull at this conference. He realized that, if Eden attended, it would be only proper that Hull should also be there; so he made it a firm condition that Eden be excluded.

On December 7, Harriman cabled Hopkins that he felt he had been "thoroughly beaten up" after three talks with the Prime Minister on the arrangements for the forthcoming conference. However, Harriman said, Churchill had finally come to understand Roosevelt's point of view and had agreed to leave Eden out. He continued to insist that he must have his full secretariat and an adequate staff of cipher men to keep his map room going twenty-four hours a day. Churchill also wanted to bring along Lord Leathers because of the vital importance of the shipping factor in all planning.

In the preparations for this and other conferences, there were often differences of opinion between Roosevelt and Churchill as to the number of aides that each would bring with him. Roosevelt, loving secrecy, and knowing that the more individuals who were made privy to the secret the more chance there was of it becoming public property, liked to travel with the smallest possible staff; Churchill, equally fond of secrecy but more confident of the discretion of responsible officers, preferred to be accompanied at all important meetings by a large staff of experts.

In his cable to Hopkins, Harriman said, "Khartoum appears to be the most practical oasis," this location being considered at that time because of the continuing hope that Stalin would be able to join the conference. There are no records of cables in the Hopkins papers relative to the invitation to Stalin to meet with Roosevelt and Churchill at this time. Presumably messages relating to this were conveyed through Ambassador Litvinov. Notes written by Hopkins en route to Casablanca and included in the next chapter state that Stalin twice refused Roosevelt's "urgent invitation" to a Big Three meeting, the reason for refusal being his constant concern with the immediate military situation on the Russian Front.

During the latter part of December there were very encouraging signs of the settlement of the always difficult French political situation. Following Roosevelt's "temporary expediency" statement about the Darlan deal, de Gaulle had made various proposals to Admiral Stark in London looking toward the establishment of French unity and including the suggestion that he himself might go to Washington to discuss these proposals with the President. This suggestion, forwarded by Stark, was accepted and de Gaulle was to leave for Washington on or about Christmas Day. In the meantime, he sent his deputy, General d'Astier de la Vigerie, to Algiers to confer with Eisenhower and Giraud on plans for a new French National Committee to include both de Gaulle and Giraud, replacing the Darlan administration. Evidently these discussions proceeded satisfactorily and Roosevelt was hopeful that the North African political mess was about to be straightened out and that there was to be a final end to all the distasteful talk about the British and American Governments having their own "pet" Frenchman. However, these hopes were shattered in a sudden, violent manner. On December 24, Darlan was assassinated. Rumors were immediately circulated in Algiers that this was part of a Royalist plot which involved threats of assassination of Eisenhower, Giraud, Murphy and others. Adherents of de Gaulle who had been of great aid to the Allies in the North African landings were accused of participation in this new plot and several of them were arrested and imprisoned. One of them was the brother of d'Astier de la Vigerie. On December 25, de Gaulle had his luggage packed and, I believe, was on his way to the airport when he was informed that, in view of the consequences of Darlan's assassination, Churchill and Roosevelt had decided that the General's proposed visit to Washington should be canceled. The beginnings of the achievement of French unity were thereby delayed for five months, during which some animosities deepened to an almost irreparable extent. It was a deplorable mischance.

On December 28, Marshall sent Hopkins the following letter:

DEAR HARRY:

Following in clear text are messages between General Eisenhower and myself concerning the proposed trip:

To General Eisenhower: December 23rd

Under consideration is plan for U.S. Chiefs of Staff to meet with British Chiefs of Staff in North Africa. Time of meeting will be in near future but depends upon Tunisian and Spanish situation. Journey would be by air. It is desired that the meeting be held on land. Are there facilities for such a meeting in Fedalla or other detached places in Morocco?

It is proposed to keep the party small but exact numbers have not been determined. My idea is that Patton will be charged specifically with insuring the necessary secrecy and protection. This would free you to give your entire attention to the battle in the East and to securing the Straits.

Some of the party, including myself, would visit your headquarters. Please give me your opinion on feasibility and practicability of holding meeting as indicated. Do not discuss any of this with British until clearance is given from here.

The President and Prime Minister will be in or join the party later.

To General Marshall: December 24th

It is feasible and practicable to hold the meeting indicated in your message. The general area as mentioned is probably best suited and there are locations which will be satisfactory. We will have necessary information available for you when you require it.

To General Eisenhower: December 24th
The code word for this project is 'Symbol.' There has been mentioned a hospital being built or prepared in the hills some 60 miles from Oran. Would this be suitable for our purpose? If so, how far is it from airfields? Is the Fedalla hotel, which I previously mentioned, clear of the town? Are there any surrounding buildings?

To General Marshall: December 26th
Fedalla Hotel is not clear of town and there are buildings closely adjoining. It is also quite conspicuous from air and sea. Kitchen has been destroyed by shellfire. Hospital in vicinity of Oran is being investigated; details later. Will make further investigation of sites in vicinity of Fedalla where we are confident a suitable place can be found.

To General Marshall: December 28th
Churchill's secretary arrived here yesterday with detailed information on the trip. Smith has sent him on reconnaissance of Casablanca-Fedalla area accompanied by a selected officer of this headquarters. Casablanca-Fedalla area seems to be the only one considered desirable by British and Smith is familiar with facilities and requirements and is making preliminary arrangements based on information we now have as to Churchill's desires. Reconnaissance of area will be completed in about two days and report will be forwarded to you immediately.
Anticipate that security will be provided by Patton's forces and administrative and secretarial and stenographic personnel mainly from this headquarters where competent people are available. Adequate communications will be installed by anticipated date of trip.

On December 29, Eisenhower reported:

Reconnaissance by Churchill's secretary and Smith's representative have found a very suitable site for operation "Symbol." It consists of a hotel surrounded by a group of excellent villas situated five miles south of Casablanca and one mile inland. Area is detached and lends itself to segregation and can be guarded easily. Airfield is two miles distant which is satisfactory for B-24's except in very rainy weather. If protracted spell of bad weather precedes Symbol, landing field at Marrakech, 120 miles distant, can be used and onward air carriage can be arranged.
Proposal is to set up two independent establishments, one American, one British, in two first-rate villas which have all essentials and are extremely well appointed in every way. That for President might have been made to order so far as lower floor appointments are concerned and will make movement from room to room easy.
Main group of assistants will live in hotel and in certain smaller villas adjacent. Offices and meals in hotel except for two independent establishments which will cater for themselves. Couriers, clerical personnel can be provided from here for American contingent.

Reconnaissance of Fedalla indicates that hotel there is unsuitably located and has suffered from bombardment. Brigadier Jacob, representing General Ismay, who made his side of reconnaissance agrees with scheme which he feels sure will be satisfactory to Churchill.

Please give us earliest possible information as to composition of United States parties and any special advance arrangements required. Smith understands generally what will be needed by American party.

On December 31, there was the usual New Year's Eve party for the family and old friends at the White House. At midnight, as always, the President raised a glass of champagne and proposed a toast to "the United States of America," and this year he added, "and to United Nations victory." During the evening, a movie had been shown and there were very few of those present who had any idea as to the significance of its selection. It was Humphrey Bogart and Ingrid Bergman in "Casablanca."

CHAPTER XXVII

The Casablanca Conference

ON JANUARY 7, 1943, Roosevelt delivered his annual State of the Union Speech to the 78th Congress which had been elected two months previously and in which his usually formidable majority had been all but wiped out. There were expectations that he would seize this opportunity to be tough and quarrelsome with the largely hostile legislators, but this was perhaps the most amiable and conciliatory speech he ever made to the Congress, at any rate, since the end of the New Deal honeymoon. The newspapers reported that, during his forty-seven-minute address, he was interrupted forty-five times by applause and even occasional cheers. Although present on this occasion, I cannot vouch for the accuracy of those figures, but I do remember that at the end of the speech the President was given a loud and warm ovation by Republicans as well as Democrats.

Confidence was promoted by the very fact that Roosevelt devoted a large part of his speech to talking about the postwar world. He said:

> Victory in this war is the first and greatest goal before us. Victory in the peace is the next. That means striving toward the enlargement of the security of man here and throughout the world—and, finally, striving for the Fourth Freedom—Freedom from Fear.
>
> It is of little account for any of us to talk of essential human needs, of attaining security, if we run the risk of another World War in ten or twenty or fifty years. That is just plain common sense. Wars grow in size, in death and destruction, and in the inevitability of engulfing all nations, in inverse ratio to the shrinking size of the world as a result of the conquest of the air. I shudder to think of what will happen to humanity, including ourselves, if this war ends in an inconclusive peace, and another war breaks out when the babies of today have grown to fighting age.

As Roosevelt said those words he knew that one month previously at Stagg Field in Chicago the first self-maintaining nuclear chain reaction had been achieved—"the half way mark on the road to the atomic bomb."

During the long period of preparation of this speech we tried to persuade the President to say something like, "It is within the realm of possibility that this 78th Congress may have the historic privilege of aiding in making of the peace"—which, of course, was a way of saying that the war might end before January 1, 1945. That would undoubtedly have brought the house down, but Roosevelt would not go that far in hopeful prophecy. He crossed out the last words and substituted, "helping greatly to save the world from future fear." In his analysis of the war situation, which was written with the collaboration of General Marshall, Roosevelt said, "great rains and appalling mud and very limited communications have delayed the final battles of Tunisia. The Axis is reinforcing its strong positions." This provided the most important factor in all the military discussions at the Casablanca Conference. Recorded in the preceding chapter was General Marshall's estimate, of November 25, that the occupation of Tunisia would be accomplished in from two to three weeks *unless the Axis forces develop some unforeseen strength.* That development had certainly occurred. Hitler poured such numerous reinforcements by air and by sea across the narrow straits from Sicily that a major campaign was required, and in the end a major victory resulted.

Late in the evening of January 9, Roosevelt and Hopkins left the White House to travel by train to Miami. So complete was the secrecy surrounding this journey that the usual crew of Pullman porters, waiters and cooks was taken off the cars and the service on the train was rendered by the Filipino sailors from Shangri-la. Despite all precautions, the word was quickly passed around Washington that the President had gone off on an important trip; he was said to be heading for various destinations all the way from Siberia to Bagdad. The same rumors attended every one of his journeys during the war, and there were some pompous officials who made it their business to absent themselves from Washington when he did, leaving instructions with their secretaries to say to all telephone calls, "Mr. So-and-So is out of the city at this time," in a tone so mysterious that there would be excited whisperings that "Mr. So-and-So is with the President's party."

On this trip to Casablanca, Hopkins carried with him for the first and, so far as I know, the only time an unusual certificate of identification, as follows:

TO WHOM IT MAY CONCERN   January 9, 1943
      This is to certify that the bearer, Mr. Harry L. Hopkins, whose description appears below, is a member of the party of the President of the United States.

Age: 52
Height: 6 feet
Weight: 165 lbs.
Hair: Brown
Eyes: Brown
                    signed: FRANKLIN D. ROOSEVELT

Register No. 1

The journey from Miami to North Africa was made in a Pan American Boeing clipper, the crew of which, under the command of Captain Howard M. Cone, had been converted from civilian to naval status so that the aircraft operated under Navy orders. During the trip across the South Atlantic and after the arrival at Casablanca, Hopkins wrote some descriptive notes, as follows:

Monday evening, January 11th,—'43
Trinidad.

We left Miami at 6:05 this morning and landed here at 4:45 P.M. all this after two nights and a day on the train from Washington. Eleanor and Louise [Mrs. Roosevelt and Mrs. Hopkins] said good-night at the rear door and I must say that I didn't like the idea of leaving a little bit, only because Louise had been very unhappy all evening because of the political attacks on us.

(*Note.* This referred, of course, to the legends relative to the yacht, *My Kay IV*, and the Beaverbrook emeralds.)

Admiral Leahy—Admiral McIntire, the President's doctor, Captain McCrea, his Naval Aide—and a half dozen Secret Service men, Arthur, his butler, two or three army officers, made up the party. Grace Tully was going along as far as Jacksonville.

To bed early and up late with a long, sleepy Sunday thru the Carolinas and Georgia to Miami. We were called at 4:30 Monday morning. Knowing my airplane capacity, I ate nothing—found the President alone in his car and we laughed over the fact that this unbelievable trip was about to begin. I shall always feel that the reason the President wanted to meet Churchill in Africa was because he wanted to make a trip. He was tired of having other people, particularly myself, speak for him around the world. For political reasons he could not go to England, he wanted to see our troops, he was sick of people telling him that it was dangerous to ride in airplanes. He liked the drama of it. But above all, he wanted to make a trip.

(*Note.* I do not know what Hopkins meant by "political reasons." It seems improbable that, more than a year after Pearl Harbor, and nearly two years before the next election, Roosevelt should have been worrying about the Irish vote. On a later occasion, I believe, Hopkins advised the President against going to England as he would have received a channel was agreed upon. But it dragged - in spite of Marshall, and it was obvious that nothing was going to happen. The result of that trip was the landing in N. Africa in Nov. 1942. On the assumption that we are going to drive the Germans out of Africa, it became clear to me that there was no agreed upon plan as to what to do next. We had to strike somewhere - across the channel, at Sardinia, Sicily or thru Turkey. But where?

Furthermore I told the President that the next major strategic move should not be made without consultation with Stalin. Twice Stalin refused the urgent invitation of the President to meet with himself and Churchill. The Russian front was too urgent. The next best thing was a meeting between Churchill, Roosevelt and their respective staffs. And the President wanted to meet in Africa! Churchill agreed. The army have found a safe place outside of Casablanca. And we are off to

Hopkins' descriptive notes, written during the trip across the South Atlantic en route to Casablanca, giving the genesis of the forthcoming meeting.

tremendous ovation and some Americans might have disapproved of that in wartime.)

The genesis of it was this. Last July, Marshall, King and I went to London. I had told the President that there seemed to be no determination on the part of the Chiefs of Staff of either the U.S. or England to fight in 1942. This in spite of the fact that Marshall and I had gone to England in April '42 when the plan to cross the Channel was agreed upon. But it dragged—in spite of Marshall, and it was obvious that nothing was going to happen. The result of that trip was the landing in N. Africa in November 1942. On the assumption that we are going to drive the Germans out of Africa it became clear to me that there was no agreed-upon plan as to what to do next. We had to strike somewhere—across the Channel, at Sardinia, Sicily or thru Turkey. But where?

Furthermore I told the President that the next major strategic move should not be made without consultation with Stalin. Twice Stalin refused the urgent invitation of the President to meet with himself and Churchill. The Russian Front was too urgent. The next best thing was a meeting between Churchill, Roosevelt and their respective staffs. And the President wanted to meet in Africa. Churchill agreed. The Army had found a safe place outside of Casablanca. And we are off to decide where we shall fight next. King, Marshall and their Aides are ahead of us by two days to iron out all possible differences in advance.

The President was carried on to the plane this morning in the dark —it taxied out of the harbor and long before sunrise took off with few people knowing the President was on his way to Africa. I sat with him, strapped in, as the plane rose from the water—and he acted like a sixteen-year-old, for he has done no flying since he was President. The trip was smooth, the President happy and interested. Dr. McIntire was worried about the President's bad heart—nothing happened—he slept for two hours after lunch. He asked the pilot to go over the Citadel in Haiti. We saw no ships and made a perfect landing at the Naval Base in Trinidad. The Admiral and General met us—took us for cocktails and dinner at a hotel run by the Navy. And at 9 to bed for we are to be called at 4:15 a.m.

The next notes were written by Hopkins during the flight from Belem, Brazil, to Bathurst:

Tuesday evening January 12—

And on the dot of 4:15 I was called after a good healthy sleep. Dr. McIntire told me that Leahy was running a fever and would have to be left behind. This is a tough break for him. I felt that he never had his heart in this trip and was going only because the President wanted him to. He doesn't seem to be unhappy at the idea of remaining in Trinidad till we get back.

We had a leisurely breakfast with Admiral Oldendorf and General Pratt—the President still treats it as a first-class holiday—he told some of his old favorite stories and seemed to be in no hurry to get off tho the Secret Service were having fits. We drove down to the dock in the dark having seen but a handful of soldiers and this visit will be exposed to the public only by a photograph taken by a Navy photographer at dinner.

The ship took to the air beautifully and the ride all the way to Belem—we landed at 3:15 P.M.—was as smooth as glass. We flew tho at about 9,000 feet and McIntire was quite disturbed about the President, who appeared to be very pale at times. We flew over the Citadel in Haiti—the wild, wastelands of Honduras—hit the South American coast and Dutch Guiana. We flew over acres of desolate jungle. Why anyone should want to explore them is beyond me. The Amazon delta is a great sight with the river mouth widening out to a width of one hundred miles—the equator cutting it in two. Belem is now a thriving Brazilian port—about ten merchant ships—a coast-guard cutter—and dozens of small native fishing craft. We have established a Ferry Command post there and 250 American soldiers move all the bombers that go to Africa to the next hop, Natal. The other day they put 52 planes thru in 24 hours.

We drove to the Officers' Quarters—and were given a first-class rum drink—(I wangled two bottles and a cold turkey to take to Africa). Jonas Ingram who commands our operating fleet in the South Atlantic was there—a hearty, ribald, fighting Admiral that suits me. I saw four or five officers that I knew in Washington. We left at six, getting off just at dark.

Bathurst—W. Africa—
Wednesday evening, January 13,—1943

They serve cocktails on this flying boat—everybody was feeling pretty good so we had one before dinner last night. But everyone was dog-tired so we turned in early. The President slept late, his first night on an airplane, and woke up in the best of spirits. McCrea had an earache—the heating system on the stove went out—I taught Ross McIntire gin-rummy—talked to the President about our pending conference—read a detective story—saw three escort vessels hunting something. (I learned later they thot we were out of gas)—and finally got dressed after sighting land. A long, tiresome trip of 18½ hours.

We landed in this big harbor at the mouth of the Gambia River—an old slave post. The cruiser *Memphis* and one of our destroyers are in port. Captain McCown met us—we took a trip around the harbor in a motor whaleboat. The President was hoisted to the deck and one of the men carrying him slipped as he stepped on to the cruiser and the President landed on his rear. We had dinner with the Captain. This boat was built for a flagship—the President has the Admiral's quarters and I have the Captain's next door.

McIntire heard that we had to fly over mountains 13,000 feet to get to our rendezvous with Churchill. Something will have to be done about that in the morning for the President can't stand that height.

The final entry in these handwritten notes (Hopkins never had them typed) was made after the arrival at Casablanca.

Friday morning, January 15,—1943

The sleeping was none too good on the *Memphis* Wednesday night so I finished my detective story only to find on the last page that I had read it before. We breakfasted together—the Secret Service seem to have our destination nicely balled up. McCrea had a good cigar and doesn't care—the President likes it—I think it is very funny that the President of the U.S. doesn't know where he is going to land in N. Africa. The height of the mountains seems to have shrunk during the night.

(*Note.* The flight from Bathurst to Casablanca was made in an Army C-54 transport plane. There·was a deviation from the straight route because Roosevelt wanted to have a look at Dakar, the fortress to which he had given so much attention during the past four years, and at the new French battleship *Richelieu* in the harbor there. After crossing the western rim of the Sahara Desert, the aircraft did fly over the Atlas Mountains but, as Hopkins wrote, they had evidently "shrunk" as the highest altitude attained was 11,500 feet.)

We got in a motor whaleboat to the dock (at Bathurst)—and a 17-mile ride to the airfield. There we have about 250 men who service our bombers moving from Bathurst north or across Africa into Russia and China. There were about one dozen big bombers on the field. The soldiers had built a big ramp for the President and we took off in a Douglas C-54. The destination proved to be Casablanca —we went seven hours over desert that is hardly worth fighting for —we saw an American airfield used to move fighter planes to the battle areas—it is supplied entirely by air. We crossed the Atlas Mountains—great snow-capped peaks seemed incongruous after the desert. Then we suddenly came on the fertile fields of N. Africa— looking like the Garden of Eden should look and probably doesn't— camels—olive groves—oranges—wheat-fields—no cows—rain—miles of black earth. The President missed nothing. We landed at the airport about 15 miles from Casablanca. The President's son Elliott was there to meet him. Much "hush hush" and the President, Elliott and I were hustled into a car blacked-out with mud to drive to our Villa. It is a lovely, modern, California bungalow—part of a hotel— taken over by the Army. The President, Elliott and I are staying here.

Churchill has a house about fifty yards away. I went over to bring him back for a drink before dinner. He was in fine form but looked older. We walked back—and the three of us had a long talk over the military situation. The British Eighth Army is attacking tonight.

(*Note*. This was the attack at Buerat which led to the capture of Tripoli eight days later and the subsequent advance into Tunisia from the east.)

The two staffs are in the big hotel across the street and just before dinner I found them all having a cocktail. The President invited the British and American Chiefs to dine with him and Churchill and Averell. Much good talk of war—and families—and the French. I went to bed at 12 but I understand that the Pres. and Churchill stayed up till two.

There was quite a family gathering in the President's villa, "Dar es Saada," during the eight days at Casablanca. Aside from Lieutenant Colonel Elliott Roosevelt, there were Lieutenant Franklin D. Roosevelt, Jr., U.S.N.R., who was serving on a destroyer with the Atlantic Fleet, Captain Randolph Churchill, of the British Special Service Brigade (Commandos) and Sergeant Robert Hopkins, whom Eisenhower had ordered out of a foxhole in Tunisia. There was some criticism in the American press on the ground that there were many less fortunate soldiers and sailors overseas who did not get special leave and transportation for visits with their fathers, but Roosevelt paid no attention to this; when he traveled to theaters in which any of his sons were serving, he saw them.

As the most obvious immediate objective for consideration at Casablanca, Churchill repeated a paragraph from a message that he had sent to Roosevelt after the successful conclusion of TORCH and the Battle of El Alamein:

The paramount task before us is, first, to conquer the African shores of the Mediterranean and set up there the naval and air installations which are necessary to open an effective passage through it for military traffic; and, secondly, using the bases on the African shore to strike at the under-belly of the Axis in effective strength and in the shortest time.

The Chiefs of Staff had been in session for three days prior to Roosevelt's arrival and had considered the various operations that might be launched after the final defeat of the Germans in Tunisia. The targets for attack which were considered included Sardinia, Sicily, Crete, Rhodes, the Dodecanese Islands and the mainland of Greece. There was considerable argument before Roosevelt and Hopkins joined the Conference, and there was more argument thereafter, with Marshall still urging the invasion of Northern France in 1943. The U.S. Chiefs of Staff appear to have been by no means unanimous at this Conference: King as a sea power man saw the enormous advantage of increased security in the Mediterranean, and Arnold as an air power man could not fail to be tempted by the prospect of obtaining such advanced bases as

Foggia in Italy. By Monday, January 18, four days after Roosevelt's arrival, the Combined Chiefs of Staff had agreed on the decision to attack Sicily, and this proposed operation was given the code name HUSKY. In Marshall's words, this decision was made "because we will have in North Africa a large number of troops available and because it will effect an economy in tonnage which is the major consideration. It is estimated that possession of the North coast of Africa and Sicily will release approximately 225 vessels which will facilitate operations in Burma, the Middle East, and the Pacific." Not only would occupation of Sicily deprive the enemy of the base from which to attack Allied shipping in the Mediterranean at its narrowest point, it would give the Allies a base for the establishment of much broader air coverage for their shipping in the Mediterranean—their only base up to then having been lonely little Malta. Marshall said that another consideration in favor of the operation against Sicily was "the possibility of eliminating Italy from the War."

However, insofar as Hopkins was concerned, he was again disappointed and depressed by the further postponement of ROUNDUP; he was always solidly with Marshall in the conviction that there was no really adequate substitute for the opening of a Second Front in France. Plans were made at Casablanca for a large operation, known as ANAKIM, in Burma—a land offensive in the north for the purpose of reopening the Burma Road and an amphibious operation in the south to recapture the port of Rangoon. Rabaul on the island of New Britain was named as the next main objective in the South Pacific—but this attack was never made and Rabaul was one of the strongpoints that remained isolated in Japanese hands to the end of the war, its effectiveness nullified by surrounding operations.

The purpose of the Casablanca Conference had been almost entirely military but Roosevelt and Churchill immediately became involved in the politics of the inescapable French situation. There had been another and even more violent outburst of criticism in the United States and Britain over the tendency to deal with the discredited men of Vichy. This criticism was all the more bitter because of the emphatic assurances given by Roosevelt in his "temporary expediency" statement. Added to other powerful voices in the United States was that of Wendell Willkie who had been persuaded by Stimson to tone down his protests during the Darlan period but who was now ready to roar.

Before Darlan's assassination, Murphy had sent a message to the State Department saying that Darlan felt that Marcel Peyrouton would be of great help to him in the government of North Africa, since Peyrouton had a reputation as an able administrator in that area, particularly in his knowledge of the many problems of the Arabs in Tunisia. Murphy therefore urged, in Darlan's behalf, that Peyrouton be given authorization and transportation to Algiers from Buenos Aires, where he was living in self-imposed exile. Hull approved this, and arrangements were accordingly made in a routine manner and, as Roosevelt later stated, without his knowledge. Peyrouton went to Rio de Janeiro to await transportation by air to Africa and, early in January, press correspondents discovered his presence there and the probable reasons for it. The newspapers presented the unsavory details of Peyrouton's record as a particularly brutal Minister of the Interior in the Vichy Government. (He had later gone as Ambassador to Argentina, where his activities were also suspect.) Apparently the only good thing to be said for him was that he hated Laval, had been largely responsible for the overthrow of Laval in December, 1940, and had even recommended to Pétain that Laval be shot. When Laval returned to power in 1942, Peyrouton resigned his post as Ambassador, choosing to remain in Buenos Aires for obvious reasons.

When Sumner Welles learned of Peyrouton's presence in Rio he gave orders for the cancellation of his further passage and when Hull learned of Welles's orders he overruled them, taking the position that the State Department should not assume responsibility for denying a request by Murphy which had been transmitted with the authority of General Eisenhower. (All cables out of North Africa were signed with Eisenhower's name.) So Peyrouton went on to Algiers, arriving there about the same time Roosevelt arrived at Casablanca. The outraged protests from the United States and Britain were plainly audible in the villa "Dar es Saada." St. Pierre and Miquelon were alive again.

On the first day of the Casablanca Conference, Roosevelt conferred with Churchill, Hopkins, Eisenhower, Murphy and Harold Macmillan, whom Churchill had sent to Algiers after the TORCH operation to serve with Murphy as political adviser to General Eisenhower. After the first of these meetings, Roosevelt remarked to Hopkins, "Ike seems jittery." Eisenhower had ample reason to seem jittery. He had been suffering from a bad cold pretty steadily since coming to North Africa, and he had been forced to take to his bed with severe grippe just before the assemblage of "Top Brass" was to descend on him at Casablanca. Although the initial operation under his command had been an inspiring success, he had subsequently seen the high hopes for quick victory in Tunisia frustrated; far worse than this for a good soldier was the bewildering political mess in which he found himself involved and for which he was so ill prepared.

As Butcher recorded in his diary, "Eisenhower's neck is in a noose, and he knows it." However, he stated his case to the President and Prime Minister with courage and candor. He made no attempt to disguise his ignorance of European politics, having spent most of the prewar years in the Philippines. He said that when the name of Peyrouton was mentioned to him by Darlan and Murphy he had no idea who the man was and no knowledge of his background except that he had once been a successful official in Algiers, Tunisia and Morocco. Eisenhower felt that this appointment should be checked with the State Department, which first said "Yes" to it and then "No" and finally "Yes." (Eisenhower of course did not know that the "No" was from Welles and the final "Yes" from Hull.) He defended his much-criticized action in imposing political censorship on North Africa on the ground that the de Gaullists were pouring hostile propaganda from their station in Brazzaville, and he did not want to advertise the conflict to the world by permitting the radio stations in Morocco or Algiers to talk back in this verbal war. (Years later, however, Eisenhower said to me that he believed this action had been a mistake—that "Censorship is never the answer.")

It was on this occasion that Eisenhower made the previously quoted remark to Roosevelt that generals could make mistakes and be fired but that governments could not. He was entirely ready to take the rap for whatever went wrong.

For a time there was some doubt whether Eisenhower would remain in supreme command for HUSKY. General Alexander, who outranked him, was now moving into Tunisia from the south with the victorious British forces under the field command of General Montgomery. Here was tough professional competition for Eisenhower at a moment when his own position was most insecure, and I believe he would not have been greatly surprised if he had been put under Alexander or transferred elsewhere. However, he was given the supreme command and a fourth star, which made him equal in rank to his subordinates, Alexander, Cunningham and Tedder. In announcing this later to the House of Commons Churchill said, "I have great confidence in General Eisenhower. I regard him as one of the finest men I have ever met." What weighed most heavily with Churchill and Roosevelt in arriving at this decision, aside from Marshall's persistent faith in Eisenhower, was the tremendous admiration and affection for him of the British officers who had served with him, most importantly Admiral Cunningham, a fighting sailor who was held in very high esteem by the two Naval Persons. Thus, Eisenhower had achieved his first important victory in the merging of officers of two nations and three services into one effective and harmonious command. After Hopkins returned to Washington from Casablanca he told me that Eisenhower had said to Patton, "I don't mind if one officer refers to another as that son of a bitch. He's entitled to his own opinion. But the instant I hear of any American officer referring to a brother officer as that *British* son of a bitch, out he goes." Eisenhower maintained that basic policy with historic success all the way into Berlin where he added the adjective "Russian" to "British."

His phenomenal and painful education of himself in the complex politics of Europe was perhaps the most brilliant of his great achievements.

Eisenhower left Casablanca on the second day of the Conference and flew back to Allied Force Headquarters in the center of the arc of hills that make a beautiful amphitheater of Algiers. He had promised Hopkins that he would promptly see Peyrouton and try to find out about him. The next day, January 17, he sent a letter addressed to Hopkins "somewhere in Africa" as follows:

DEAR HARRY:

I sent you a message today following a conference with Peyrouton, who just called at my office. He recited his past history to me, and one thing that struck me was that the day Laval returned to power, Peyrouton sent in his resignation as French Ambassador to Argentina. This may or may not be true but it could easily be checked. He seems to be a realist, and the general views he expressed were contained in the telegram I sent you.

I cannot tell you how valuable it was to me to have the chance to talk to the President and yourself and to the Combined Chiefs of Staff, particularly General Marshall. There is no doubt that great good will come out of your meeting there, and I often regret that you people who are occupying the top positions cannot get together with greater frequency.

I am enclosing with this letter a short note to the President, which I request that you pass on to him if you think it an appropriate one.

If you can possibly get up here, I assure you of a warm welcome and I will do all in my power to let you see everything that can be arranged within the time you may have.

With warm personal regard,

Cordially,
signed: IKE EISENHOWER

On January 16, Roosevelt sent the following cable to Hull:

General Giraud arrives here tomorrow and Mr. Churchill and I have arranged that General de Gaulle shall be brought here on Monday. I feel sure that the British can be brought around to our point of view and it appears that we must get a civilian into the administrative picture here. Apparently Giraud lacks administrative ability and the French army officers will not recognize de Gaulle's authority. Since there are no French civilians readily available in this area, what would be your opinion of having Jean Monnet come here? It appears he has kept his skirts clear of political entanglements in recent years and my impression of him is very favorable. I believe that Morgenthau knows and trusts Monnet. It had been my hope that we could avoid political discussions at this time, but I found on arrival that American and British newspapers have made such a mountain out of rather a small hill that I should not return to Washington without having achieved settlement of this matter. All well here and I send you affectionate regards. I am particularly anxious that the mention of Monnet be kept completely secret as everything will be spoiled if there is any leak.

The suggestion of the name of Monnet, which was made largely at Hopkins' instigation, did not find favor with Hull who replied that from the information available to him he was not disposed to believe that Jean Monnet was the right man for the job. He said that Monnet had been identified with the banking firm of Lazard Frères which was closely tied in with the de Gaulle organization in London, and Monnet had dealt extensively with Pleven who acted as de Gaulle's adviser on foreign affairs. These associations, according to Hull, "would clearly create doubts in a great many French minds." Hull added that any Frenchman who received British and American endorsement in the North African situation must be of such quality that there could be no question as to "his outstanding integrity and his loyalty to all the best elements of France"—and Hull certainly was not inclined to include the leaders of the Free French Movement among such elements.

Hull suggested as alternative candidates for Peyrouton's job Roger Cambon and Alexis Leger. However, Giraud convinced Roosevelt and Churchill that Peyrouton was the only man with experience enough to handle the immeasurably difficult situation and his appointment as Governor General of Algeria was announced on January 19. When Roosevelt was asked later if he had approved the sending of Peyrouton to North Africa he replied that he had not approved it or even known about it. Churchill also stated that he had known nothing of the transfer of Peyrouton from Argentina, but, in the light of what he learned at Casablanca, he found no fault with the step.

A month later Hopkins persuaded the President to authorize the sending of Monnet to North Africa to work with Giraud on handling the substantial Lend-Lease supplies for the equipping of the French Army. This was one of several occasions when Hopkins was successful in circumventing the State Department.

Roosevelt's statement in his message to Hull that de Gaulle would arrive "Monday" proved overconfident. Anthony Eden was having plenty of trouble in London. On January 17, Eden handed de Gaulle the message from Churchill inviting him to Casablanca. "When he had finished reading it," Eden reported, "he expressed no pleasure." (One might observe that, in this sentence, Eden made a strong bid for the British and therefore world's understatement championship.) De Gaulle was offended because he had not been notified in advance of the impending Conference, as he had not been notified in advance of the landings in North Africa. Eden could hardly explain that both these circumstances had been due to Roosevelt's insistence that previous information to de Gaulle might jeopardize military security. This implied no disrespect for the general as a military man of honor. It reflected Roosevelt's belief that the de Gaulle organization contained a superabundance of press agents.

De Gaulle told Eden and through him Churchill that he had sent Giraud several messages suggesting a meeting but had received no favorable response. He said he would be glad to conduct "simple and direct talks with Giraud" but not in "the atmosphere of an exalted Allied forum." He felt that such an atmosphere would suggest to the world the application of "pressure" on the two French leaders.

Roosevelt became more and more irritated by de Gaulle's refusal to budge. If French political problems had constituted nothing more than "a rather small hill," as he said in his message to Hull, he would have been only too glad to laugh off this situation and forget it, leaving de Gaulle to sulk in his tent on Carlton House Terrace, but Roosevelt knew what the criticism would be if he returned to Washington without having achieved any rapprochement between de Gaulle and Giraud. There were a great many jokes back and forth between the villas about getting the "bridegroom" together with the "bride," but the situation was essentially a serious one and everybody knew it. Roosevelt was uncomfortable and unhappy about the squabbles over French politics because the newspapers and columnists and radio commentators who were loudest in their denunciation of this manifestation of American policy were, for the most part, the most ardent supporters of Roosevelt's liberal policies, both foreign and domestic.

In the Hopkins papers is an unsigned memorandum dated December 24, 1942, the very day of Darlan's assassination, which seems to me an admirable statement of Roosevelt's fundamental point of view in dealing with the French problem:

> The sovereignty of France rests with the French people. Only its expression was suspended by German occupation. The indispensable element for the restoration of France is the assurance of conditions making that expression possible when the time comes.
>
> No French political authority can exist or be allowed to attempt to create itself outside of France. It is the duty of the United States and Great Britain to preserve for the people of France the right and opportunity to determine for themselves what government they will have, and the French people as well as the world must receive that solemn assurance.
>
> The present dissensions are due to the concealed competition for future political power. De Gaulle seeks recognition by England and the United States on the basis of suppressed but assumed endorsement by the French people. Darlan will attempt to build a regime on the basis that he represents Pétain, the regularly constituted regime of France.

The sympathy of the French that expressed itself for de Gaulle, reflects not a choice of de Gaulle as the future head of the French government, but the French anxiety to continue to *fight* Germany alongside of England and the United States. They would, however, certainly resist a government, even if provisional, which would owe its initial authority to foreign recognition. The basis of legitimacy which permitted Darlan to effectively bring North Africa alongside the Allies, is due to the fact that he represented what was then the existing constituted authority of Vichy. He was thus able to give orders which were followed by the local military commanders and the local administration. Indeed, while as it has been proved since, most responsible officials wanted at heart to cooperate with America and Great Britain, their action had to be determined by an order from the regular central authority. Men entrusted with authority in an orderly society are not revolutionaries, and it is to be revolutionary to act contrary to the orders of the central accepted authority. Admiral Darlan gave the order that was wished for—but the order had to be given. He alone could give it, not General Giraud at that time.

But now that this has been done, and that the various local commanders have sided with the Allies, it is important to prevent the use which Darlan made of Pétain's authority from being developed into a legitimacy recognized or fostered by the Allies. Such a development in North Africa would be a denial of those conditions which alone will enable the French people to give free expression to their sovereignty.

In those paragraphs may be found the basic reasons for Roosevelt's refusal to recognize any provisional government of France whether headed by de Gaulle or by anyone else. But the clash of personalities and the deplorable tendency of the State Department to hold and repeatedly to assert old grudges gave to these relationships qualities that were as unnecessary as they were unhappy. Throughout the years of war, Roosevelt fluctuated considerably in his attitude toward de Gaulle, and so did Churchill—but they seldom fluctuated the same way at the same time.

On January 19 Hopkins dictated the following notes to Chief Ship's Clerk Terry who generally traveled with the President as a secretarial aide:

Had breakfast with General Arnold. He feels that the Southern Pacific plans are too vague and that until we get Rabaul it is impossible to make additional plans, and that material should not be tied up on any theoretical assumption that we are going to get to Truk.

Arnold feels that in spite of the plan to open the Burma Road which has been agreed upon here, he is very doubtful that this will be done, and thinks that the only intelligent move immediately is to strengthen Chennault's air force and get at the bombing of Japan as soon as possible. Arnold tells me that he cannot tell exactly how this can be done until he goes to China after this conference is over. He is sure, however, that it can be accomplished. He tells me that General Bissell, the Air Force commander in India, is very antagonistic to Chennault and that that complicates Chennault's supply line. Arnold is very confident, however, that the whole business can be worked out. He tells me that King is asking for airplanes in the Southwest Pacific for which at the moment there are no airfields. On the other hand, he realizes we must be ready for any eventuality out there, and Arnold is sure that we can provide all the airplanes that are needed.

Arnold tells me that after the battle is over in Africa, both the Germans and ourselves are going to be licking our wounds for a couple of months. After that, the air battle will be one between our bombers and the Italian fighters and antiaircraft. Arnold tells me that the going is a little tougher here lately and that our losses have been heavier, but we still have knocked down about 1.8 Germans to 1 American. He tells me that he has worked out a satisfactory arrangement with the Middle East Air Command about the oncoming air battle in Tunisia.

Arnold insists that the targets from England are selected by the British, but he seemed to me to be a bit vague on this point, and I am sure that this needs to be settled definitively, so that the Admirals and the Navy can't continue to say that Arnold is picking out some soft targets and is not making an adequate attack on the submarine bases and factories making submarine supplies.

The Prime Minister told me he wanted to see me this morning. He had not yet heard from London about de Gaulle and seemed to be unhappy about the President's decision to close up the conference with the Chiefs of Staff here on Wednesday afternoon.

Had a call from Count Poniatowski, who is acting as General Giraud's civilian aide, who wanted to see me, but I sent for Harriman because I had learned that at one time he had been Harriman's brother-in-law.

I arranged with the President about the schedule for the rest of the week. The President agreed that we should close this up at a pretty early date and that he should review the troops on Thursday, have dinner with the Sultan on Friday, and get off to the south not later than Saturday morning.

Had a long talk with Count Poniatowski and Harriman. I did not tell him that de Gaulle had refused to come, because the President thinks that is British business and that they should acquaint Giraud of this fact. The Count told me what they proposed to say to de Gaulle in case he came down. It boils down that they are going to tell him that Giraud is going to be top-dog and that they will be glad to play with de Gaulle all around the world in a secondary capacity. He also told me the things he wanted to take up with the President, which included the adequate arming of the French Army, adjustment of exchange rates, the organization of a new French layout with Giraud in charge and de Gaulle No. 2 man, and then some other vague business about French sovereignty. I told him that there would be no trouble with the President about the arming of the French Army and the exchange rates, although I couldn't say what those rates would be, and that I thought the President thought that Giraud should land on top, but as far as sovereignty is concerned, he is treading on very difficult ground because the President stuck by his position that sovereignty rested exclusively with the French people, and that he would recognize no one, not even Giraud, as representing France. I told Harriman to see the President and tell him what had gone on at this conference, and I went over to see Churchill.

I found Churchill in bed and he told me that while the second raid on Berlin looked pretty good, the weather had been bad and he was not sure how much damage had been done. He told me that he was sure his forces attacking Tripolitania were much further along than they had anticipated and that that was very good. I asked him what was bothering him about winding up the business with the Chiefs of Staff on Wednesday and he told me that he didn't have anything specific in mind, that he thought the Chiefs of Staff were going to work out a pretty good agreement. He did tell me, however, that he intended to fly to Cairo as soon as the President left and work out the new Middle East Command with General Wilson in charge, and that he wanted to meet the President of Turkey perhaps in Cyprus, and push him pretty hard on the business of getting Turkey into the war, and giving us some adequate air bases, and to attack Roumanian oil fields. He told me he intended to take the line that Turkey should not wait until the last minute, but that if they were recalcitrant he would not hesitate to tell the Turks that in the event of their remaining out, he could not undertake to control the Russians regarding the Dardanelles and that their position would be intolerable.

I arranged to have dinner with Harriman and Churchill tonight because the President and Elliott are dining with General Patton. The Prime Minister was anxious that the President not tell Giraud that de Gaulle had refused to show up, because he was hoping to get a message from de Gaulle any minute. He said he wanted to come to see the President around five or six o'clock tonight. I went back to the house and told the President that the Prime Minister did not want Giraud told.

I attended the conference between the President, Giraud, Murphy, Captain McCrea, Elliott, and Giraud's Military Aide, Captain Beaufre. The President laid out to Giraud in a masterful fashion, his concept of French resistance, emphasizing the fighting. McCrea has made complete minutes of this meeting. I gained a very favorable impression of Giraud. I know he is a Royalist, and is probably a right-winger in all his economic views, but I have a feeling that he is willing to fight. He is about six feet, two inches and a man of about 63 or 64. He has the appearance of health and vigor. He spoke with a good deal of modesty, but with confidence. Had a feeling that he had made up his mind that he was going to do whatever the President wanted in Africa. Apart from fighting in the war, it is impossible to tell whether or not he has political ambitions. He did not give me that impression except when he stressed later, with great vigor, his determination to head the civil as well as the military areas in Africa.

Giraud speaks no English, but the President's French seemed to me to be better than usual, and Murphy, who did the interpreting, didn't have much to do. It was only when the President wanted to be perfectly sure that Giraud knew what he was saying on an important matter, that he had Murphy interpret. Giraud laid out his problems, which his aide had previously told me, and the President settled them all to Giraud's complete satisfaction, but on the sovereignty point he was adamant, and insisted that Giraud, at the moment, act only as a representative in North Africa, and that he not in any sense speak for France, and that the understanding about all other French possessions should be worked out only when de Gaulle arrived. The President and Giraud then went out on the back porch and a flock of Army Photographers took pictures of them, and later of McCrea, Giraud's aide and me with the President and Giraud. On the whole I thought it was a very satisfactory conference and I am sure that Giraud and the President have mutual confidence in each other.

We had lunch with the President, Averell, Robert and Elliott. I took a nap after lunch and then General Patton arrived to take Elliott and me downtown to do a little shopping. We went by the docks and saw the beaches on which our men landed at Casablanca and saw how the Navy knocked the hell out of the Jean Bart. A great convoy of ours was just steaming into sight. We saw the steel landing fields for airports being loaded on the trains and American soldiers and sailors everywhere in the city. Shopping was pretty fruitless except for some rugs. I got back to the house about six o'clock and found the Prime Minister and his son, Randolph, talking to the President about this and that. I am going off to dinner with the Prime Minister. Averell, Randolph and Robert in a few minutes.

Of the deliberations of the Combined Chiefs of Staff at Casablanca Churchill said, "there never has been, in all of the interallied conferences I have known, anything like the prolonged professional examination of the whole scene of the world war in its military, its armament production and its economic aspects." Although the production situation was, of course, far better than it had been at the first meeting in Washington a year before, there was one item of insufficiency on the gigantic list which seriously affected all the strategic calculations of the time—and that item was escort vessels. There were not enough destroyers and destroyer escorts to defend the convoys to Russia and to all the other far-flung theaters of war, and there were only two transports, the *Queen Mary* and the *Queen Elizabeth*, with sufficient speed to cross oceans without escort. After the war, I asked a group of men who had been engaged in grappling with the production problems whether they could name any outstanding failures, the avoidance of which might have shortened the war; their answer was unanimous—the escort vessel program.

On January 21, Roosevelt, Hopkins, Harriman, Murphy and McIntire drove with Patton to Rabat, eighty-five miles northeast of Casablanca, for a visit to the American troops of the Fifth Army, in training there under General Clark's command. The Commander in Chief had lunch in the open air with some 20,000 soldiers. The menu: boiled ham, sweet potatoes, green string beans, fruit salad, bread, butter, jam and coffee. I am indebted to Captain George Durno, former White House correspondent who accompanied the President on the Casablanca trip, for including in his official report the list of selections played by the 3rd Division Artillery Band during lunch that day: "Chattanooga Choo Choo," "Missouri Waltz," "Naughty Marietta Waltz," "Deep in the Heart of Texas," and "Alexander's Ragtime Band."

On that same day, which should have marked the windup of the Conference, the welcome news was received that Eden had at last prevailed with de Gaulle and that the leader of the Fighting French would arrive in Casablanca on the morrow. After Hopkins returned from the trip to Rabat, he received a note from Churchill suggesting a program for the following day, which included this item:

Dinner. At the White House (Dry, alas!); with the Sultan. After dinner, recovery from the effects of the above.

(Roosevelt's villa was always referred to by Churchill as the White House.)

Hopkins later wrote the following note on the first meeting of Roosevelt and de Gaulle:

The General arrived cold and austere, accompanied by his aide and for the first time met President Roosevelt.

In the middle of the conference I noticed that the whole of the Secret Service detail was behind the curtain and above the gallery in the living room and at all doors leading into the room and I glimpsed a Tommy Gun in the hands of one. I left the conference and went out to talk to the Secret Service to find out what it was all about and found them all armed to the teeth with, perhaps, a dozen Tommy Guns among the group. I asked them what it was all about. They told me they could not take any chances on anything happening to the President. None of this hokus pokus had gone on when Giraud saw the President and it was simply an indication of the atmosphere in which de Gaulle found himself at Casablanca. To me the armed Secret Service was unbelievably funny and nothing in Gilbert and Sullivan could have beaten it. Poor General de Gaulle, who probably did not know it, was covered by guns throughout his whole visit. To the best of my knowledge, the Secret Service put on this little act on their own.

I attended all the meetings of the President and de Gaulle. Robert
Murphy, I think, was always in attendance. There developed out of
these meetings at Casablanca an apocryphal story which I think the
President encouraged. The story was that at the first conference de
Gaulle compared himself to Clemenceau, while at the next conference
he indicated that Joan of Arc was perhaps more his prototype and the
President is alleged to have said to de Gaulle that he should make
up his mind which one of these he was really like because he surely
could not be like both of them. This story is pure fiction . . . altho
I heard the President tell the story, indicating that that was the kind
of impression General de Gaulle made on him during the various
conferences they held. Later, as the President told the story, I have
no doubt it took on more authenticity and finally came to be accepted
as a fact. Naturally, this story must have gotten back to General de
Gaulle as it was printed very widely in the American papers.

General William H. Wilbur, a Regular Army officer who had just
been awarded a Congressional Medal of Honor by the President, wrote
the following penetrating report on his own interview with de Gaulle:

23 January 1943

I called on General de Gaulle at his villa this afternoon at four
o'clock. As we were both in the same class at the Ecole Supérieure
de Guerre, we started on a friendly basis. He seemed inclined to
unburden himself to me, and told me the entire situation.

He told me that before our arrival in Morocco, his forces were the
only French Forces that had been fighting for the liberty of France;
that they were the only elements that represented the true France;
that without question the whole of the France that is willing to fight
for its rights rested with people who were with him. He said that
there had grown up the mystery of the Marshal and the mystery of
La France Combattant, that these had become almost two religions.
He said that the real Marshal Pétain had died in 1925, and that the
present Marshal was weak, was vain, and had the spirit and attitude
of a grandfather.

He said that when Darlan came into power he represented the collaborationists. De Gaulle and his people could have no traffic with
him. Darlan in his opinion had remained too long.

General Giraud did not in his present position, and could not in
his present position represent the government of France because he
held a position by virtue of the vote of Nogues, Boisson, and Chatell,
all of whom were representatives of the Vichy Government.

He said that he had offered General Giraud the command of the
troops, but that General Giraud in his present position could not
represent the true France. His thesis was that General Giraud should
join the France Combattant, rather than that the Gaullists should join
the present government.

He said that it was perfectly possible that the United States might make the decision that he should be deprived of supplies and equipment and that under such circumstances England and the others would have to agree to the United States' decision and that he, de Gaulle, would have to fold up.

He said that even if General Giraud succeeded in reaching France at the present time, he would find that the people would rise against him and that communism would result. I told him that as a friend of France I deplored the present situation, that it was of great importance that the French compose their differences now before the invasion of the continent took place; that they must compose their differences before the peacetable was reached or that the French would find themselves in a very weak and poor position. I told him that I personally, and many Americans, were extremely sorry for the French, that we felt that the French people must be undergoing a very severe winter, that it was only by unity that we would reach them at the earliest possible date.

I stated that it seemed to me that General de Gaulle, who I knew had the real interest of France at heart, must be willing to withdraw from any position if no other way could be found to accomplish the union of those who wished to fight to liberate France. We discussed the situation of his adherents in Morocco. He is very anxious to have those individuals who wish to serve with his forces be permitted to join them. He asked for my address so that he could communicate with me further. I told him that many Gaullists had come to me with their stories. He asked me if any others came to see me, if I would tell them that I had seen him, that he had seen General Giraud, that they had not been able to compose their differences, but that he was sending a liaison officer to join Giraud.

I emphasized the necessity for calm and order in Morocco—and suggested that his adherents not only should not cause trouble but should also do everything they could to help the American effort. He agreed to do that.

Hopkins dictated more notes to Terry on the afternoon of January 22:

Had breakfast with Robert, who told me more of his experiences at the front. The President did not get up until ten, and I went in to talk to him about calling off the Press Conference which was scheduled for twelve. It was perfectly clear that there was no meeting of the minds as to the exact statement that should be released. In view of the fact that de Gaulle was just arriving, it seemed to me that the wisest thing to do was to postpone the Press Conference until we were ready to make a final statement. The President rather reluctantly agreed to this, but I told him that it was essential that we have a meeting of the minds with Churchill. The question of whether any reference to Stalin's having been invited must be decided, and a careful statement relative to the Southwest Pacific ought to be included, and if the de Gaulle thing might be in the bag in another 24 hours, a much better statement on that could be made. The President told me to go over and see Churchill and tell him the conference was called off. I found Churchill in bed in his customary pink robe, and having, of all things, a bottle of wine for breakfast. I asked him what he meant by that and he told me that he had a profound distaste on the one hand for skimmed milk, and no deep rooted prejudice about wine, and that he had reconciled the conflict in favor of the latter. He commended it to me and said he had lived to be 68 years old and was in the best of health, and had found that the advice of doctors, throughout his life, was usually wrong. At any rate, he had no intention of giving up alcoholic drink, mild or strong, now or later.

Churchill seemed to be relieved over the fact that the Press Conference was not going to be held. We discussed the state of the conference for some time and he seemed satisfied with the outcome. I told him it seemed to me like a pretty feeble effort for two great countries in 1943. I told him, however, that I had watched this war develop for a long time now, and realized that the Chiefs of Staff may agree to do nothing today, but tomorrow, when the President puts the heat on, they will suddenly decide they can do a little more than they think they can at this conference. At any rate, everything seems to be settled from a military point of view. The Prime Minister told me that de Gaulle was definitely arriving at noon and that he hoped they would get somewhere.

Churchill said he wished the pictures were going to be taken later in the day, because he didn't look his best at twelve o'clock. He told me he could put on a very warlike look whenever he wanted to.

They set up for pictures in the rear of the President's villa and shot the Chiefs of Staff and aides with the President and the Prime Minister. They had a little difficulty getting a picture of the Prime Minister and the Chiefs of Staff alone, because nobody seems to know who makes up the Chiefs of Staff in the British and the U.S. Government, and I think there were two or three in, that didn't belong there. The President gave a Medal of Honor to General Wilbur, and that was ground out for the benefit of the American people. Incidentally, Wilbur, who is a Regular Army officer, was passed over by the Army, and strange to say, passed over on the recommendation of General Patton. They cordially dislike each other, but Wilbur was the only man who spoke French fluently and who knew something about North Africa, so Patton agreed to bring him along, and since he has done such a magnificent job over here, of course they have had to promote him.

I lunched with Mountbatten and Averell, and Mountbatten told me a fantastic story about a non-sinkable ship made of ice which the British are working on, and he wants our cooperation. Mountbatten also believes very strongly that we should attack Sardinia rather than Sicily, because it can be done three months earlier, and he believes it is very important to keep the Germans on the run, once we can knock them out of Tunisia. Mountbatten claims all the younger officers in the British lay-out agree with this, but the big boys on the Chiefs of Staff have overruled their subordinates. Mountbatten told me that crossing the Channel was a hell of an enterprise. The Germans have armed to the teeth. He is working on a new explosive which he thinks the British have got, which would permit the explosive to be loaded into an antiquated submarine and banged up against a cliff 50 feet high, on the French coast, and the explosive can be so regulated as to permit them to blow a road right into France, which would be followed by his Commandos. He says he gets no more interest in this, however, than he does in his non-sinkable ship made of blocks of ice. Mountbatten always gives you the impression of being a courageous, resourceful, fighting man, but I fancy the British Chiefs of Staff push him around pretty much. At any rate, he cautioned us not to say anything to anybody about his urging the attack on Sardinia instead of Sicily.

The President had been lunching with Marshall and I came in on the tail end of that. Marshall was talking about the difficulties of not having Eisenhower a full General. He said it was difficult to do in view of the fact that Eisenhower's army is mired in the mud, and the President told General Marshall that he would not promote Eisenhower until there was some damn good reason for doing it, that he was going to make it a rule that promotions should go to people who had done some fighting, that while Eisenhower had done a good job, he hasn't knocked the Germans out of Tunisia. Marshall said he was cutting out all unnecessary overhead in Africa and was going to get his troops placed in a position where they could really fight. He thinks we should push the arming of the French as rapidly as we can so that they can take over some of our duties.

Later that afternoon Bob Murphy and Averell came in and discussed gossip about the lunch between de Gaulle and Giraud. Apparently de Gaulle spent the lunch telling Giraud that certain Frenchmen, notably Boisson and Nogues, should be thrown out of their jobs as Governors, and apparently they got down to no real discussion relating to the business of their getting together. De Gaulle, who had arrived at noon, had lunch and spent the afternoon with Giraud and his crowd, and was not going to see the Prime Minister until 6:30, which meant the President could not see de Gaulle until after the President's dinner that night with the Sultan.

The Sultan arrived at 7:40, which caused me to put on my black tie for the first time on this trip. He had expressed a desire to see the President alone prior to Churchill's arrival at eight, and he came loaded with presents—a gold dagger for the President, and some gold bracelets for Mrs. Roosevelt and a gold tiara which looked to me like the kind the gals wear in the circus, riding on white horses. I can just see Mrs. Roosevelt when she takes a look at this. The Sultan wore white silk robes. Apparently the etiquette prevents the drinking of liquor publicly, so we had nothing alcoholic either before, during or after dinner. I fortified myself an hour earlier, however.

Also, no part of a pig could be eaten, and the Sultan didn't smoke. He had a young son there with a red fez on, which he kept on while eating. He was a kid about thirteen and seemed quite bright. At dinner I sat next to General Nogues, the Governor, who is the bird that de Gaulle wants pitched out of here. He has been the Resident Governor here for many years. He obviously likes it, because he lives in a big palace and is the big shot in this part of the world. I wouldn't trust him as far as I could spit. He didn't seem to me to be in a very easy frame of mind, because I imagine that he knows perfectly well that we may throw him out at any minute. Churchill was glum at dinner and seemed to be real bored. A smart British Marine walked in about the middle of the dinner with a despatch, but I have a feeling Churchill cooked that up beforehand, because I saw the despatch later and it certainly wasn't one that required the Prime Minister's attention at the dinner. Took some pictures after dinner. The President gave the Sultan his picture in a handsome silver frame, and a good time seemed to be had by all, except the Prime Minister.

The Prime Minister then told the President about his visit with de Gaulle. He said he had handled de Gaulle pretty roughly and told him that he had to cooperate with us and Giraud, and suggested the President see de Gaulle at 10:30 in the morning. I told the President that would delay the whole business, and if he felt up to it, I hoped he would see de Gaulle tonight. The President agreed, and Bob Murphy went over to get de Gaulle and Churchill went home.

The final full-dress meeting of Roosevelt, Churchill and Hopkins with the Combined Chiefs of Staff—Marshall, King, Arnold, Somervell, Pound, Dill, Brooke, Portal, Mountbatten and Ismay—was held on the afternoon of Saturday, January 23.

The Chiefs presented an eleven-page paper containing their proposals for the conduct of the war in 1943. It is interesting to note that as a result of eleven days of deliberations they gave top priority to "security of sea communications." This meant that they considered the Atlantic Ocean the most important battlefield of the war and that the shortage of escort vessels was the first need to be met.

Second on the priorities list—and closely involved with the first item—was "assistance to Russia in relation to other commitments."

Third on the list was "Operations in the Mediterranean"—the plan for the capture of Sicily giving as the target day "the favorable July moon," naming Eisenhower to be in supreme command with Alexander as his deputy and Cunningham and Tedder as naval and air commanders.

Fourth on the list was "Operations in and from the United Kingdom" —provisions for the continued build-up of American forces (BOLERO) and for operations against the Channel Islands and another against the Cotentin Peninsula on August 1, 1943.

Fifth on the list was "Pacific and Far East Theatre"—operations in the Aleutians, from Midway toward Truk and Guam, advances in the East Indies and the reconquest of Burma (ANAKIM).

The three final items on the list were provisions for a study of the Axis oil positions—for naval and air command in West Africa—and a provision that "all matters connected with Turkey should be handled by the British."

As Hopkins had told Churchill at breakfast he had felt that the results at Casablanca represented "a pretty feeble effort," but when he read this new document prepared by the Combined Chiefs of Staff he scribbled a penciled note to General Sir John Dill as follows:

> JACK:
>   I think this is a *very* good paper and damn good plan—so I am feeling much better.
>
> HARRY

It is not clear to me whether there was any serious contemplation at Casablanca of the extension of the Sicilian operation to the Italian mainland. Certainly, the plan to land at Salerno and take Naples and the Foggia air base was made before HUSKY was launched. General Mark Clark's Fifth Army was kept separate from the rest of the Allied force and trained for this specific purpose, and did not take part in the Sicilian battles.

Hopkins wrote the following notes on the events of the last day in Casablanca:

> Sunday, January 24
>   Up at 7 to get the communiqué—(official announcement of the conference which had been kept a total secret)—the telegram to Stalin —and one to the Generalissimo in final shape. Robert and Averell came in to breakfast—and then Bob Murphy who had just been to see Giraud. Giraud was quite willing to cooperate with de Gaulle but was unwilling to work under him. Bob told me that Macmillan thinks that de Gaulle is going to be difficult and insist on being top dog. Macmillan came in a moment later and told us that de Gaulle's proposition to Giraud is that "he (de Gaulle) is to be Clemenceau and Giraud Foch." I told him that the President would not stand for that but might agree to a joint leadership of the two of them—with Giraud running Africa and de Gaulle the rest of the show.

(*Note*. It was this remark by Macmillan that provided the genesis of the widely circulated Roosevelt anecdote previously mentioned by Hopkins. When Roosevelt heard what Macmillan had said about de Gaulle's proposal, he exclaimed, "Yesterday he wanted to be Joan of Arc—and now he wants to be the somewhat more worldly Clemenceau.")

Giraud to win the war and liberate France.
The secret service called me out to tell me
Churchill was outside. He was talking to Giraud
saying good bye to him. Churchill walked
in and I went after Giraud believing
that if the four of them could get into
a room together we could get an agreement.
This was nearly twelve o'clock and the press
conference was to be at that hour. The President
was surprised at seeing Giraud but took it
in his stride. De Gaulle was a little
bewildered. Churchill grunted. But the
President went to work on them with
Churchill backing him up vigorously. De
Gaulle finally agreed to a joint statement
and before he could catch his breath, the
President suggested a photograph. By
this time the garden was full of
camera men and war correspondents who
had been flown down the day before.
I don't know who was the
most surprised — the photographers or De Gaulle
when the four of them walked out — or rather
the three of them because the President was

A page from Hopkins' notes on the Casablanca Conference, describing how the famous photograph of the Giraud–de Gaulle handshake was set up.

I left them in my room and went to see the President to tell him the news. He was none too happy about it but I urged him not to disavow de Gaulle even tho he was acting badly. Believing as I did and still do that Giraud and de Gaulle want to work together I urged the President to be conciliatory and not beat de Gaulle too hard. If there is any beating to be done let Churchill do it because the whole Free French Movement is financed by them. I told the President I thought we would get an agreement on a joint statement issued by de Gaulle and Giraud—and a picture of the two of them. Bob and I then told Macmillan that Churchill had to bring de Gaulle around.

Churchill had amended the communiqué and General Jacob brought it around and I revised it some more. I got the final draft at 11.15 which the President approved with slight modifications in language.

Giraud arrived at 11.30—de Gaulle was with Churchill by this time. Giraud wanted a confirmation on supplying his army but the President referred him to Eisenhower. The conference went well. Giraud will play ball with de Gaulle. Giraud goes out, de Gaulle and his staff come in, de Gaulle calm and confident—I liked him—but *no* joint communiqué and Giraud must be under him. The President expressed his point of view in pretty powerful terms and made an urgent plea to de Gaulle to come to terms with Giraud to win the war and liberate France. The Secret Service called me up to tell me Churchill was outside. He was talking to Giraud, saying goodbye to him. Churchill walked in and I went after Giraud believing that if the four of them could get into a room together we could get an agreement. This was nearly 12 o'clock and the press conference was to be at that hour. The President was surprised at seeing Giraud but took it in his stride. De Gaulle was a little bewildered. Churchill grunted. But the President went to work on them with Churchill backing him up vigorously. De Gaulle finally agreed to a joint statement and before they could catch their breath, the President suggested a photograph. By this time the garden was full of camera men and war correspondents who had been flown down (from Algiers) the day before.

I don't know who was the most surprised—the photographers or de Gaulle when the four of them walked out—or rather the three of them because the President was carried to his chair. I confess they were a pretty solemn group—the cameras ground out the pictures. The President suggested de Gaulle and Giraud shake hands. They stood up and obliged—some of the camera men missed it and they did it again. Then the Frenchmen and their staffs left and Churchill and the President were left sitting together in the warm African sun —thousands of miles from home—to talk to the correspondents of war and the waging of war. It would be flashed around the world the moment a release date was fixed.

The President gave a background statement—not for quotation— but he chose his words very carefully and talked from notes. The only important addition to the communiqué was the President's statement that he and Churchill were determined to accept nothing less than unconditional surrender of Germany, Japan and Italy. The President talked for about fifteen minutes. He told them of his visit to our troops and later agreed to be quoted on that. Churchill supplemented this with a masterly review of the military situation. He emphasized his personal friendship for the President and said the two of them were going to see the war thru together. They have had no disagreements.

I talked after the conference to a number of newspapermen I had met in Washington, London and Moscow. The fact that Churchill and Roosevelt were in Africa was a complete surprise.

At 1.15 we drove to Marrakesh—picnic lunch on the way. Everyone tired but relaxed. As the British had fixed up the lunch we had plenty of wine and Scotch. We were put up at the villa of the late Moses Taylor—very pleasant. Our host was a young archaeologist named Pendar (Louise had once rented his flat in Paris)—he was one of our secret agents in N. Africa prior to the landings.

Averell, Randolph, Robert and I went to visit a big fair—storytellers—dancers—snake-charmers—and 15,000 natives. Very colorful. The great trading market was near—but nothing much to sell—tho thousands ever milling thru. Dinner was good—army style—company aglow—much banter—Churchill at his best. The President tired.

After dinner we agreed on the draft to Stalin—Averell and I had rewritten it. I made a draft for the Generalissimo. They agreed and both dispatches were put on the cables. At 2 a.m. we retired leaving a call for 7.

Robert roomed with me—he is flying to Algiers with Averell early in the morning.

The cables to Stalin and Chiang Kai-shek were lengthy reports on the results of the Casablanca Conference, the message to Stalin being more specific as to actual plans. In both cables, much emphasis was placed for obvious reasons on the importance of opening up the Mediterranean to Allied shipping and thereby greatly facilitating the delivery of supplies to the Persian Gulf for Russia, and to India for the Burmese operations and for China.

Hopkins' next notes were written on arrival at Bathurst the following afternoon, January 25:

Up early for breakfast—very cold—said goodbye—Churchill was up and we talked a bit. Drove to the field with Robert and saw him fly off to the front again. The big ramp was rolled up again and the President pushed up on his wheel-chair. Churchill had suddenly decided to drive out to the field with us, wearing his ever flaming bathrobe, bed-room slippers and the inevitable cigar. Churchill and I took one last walk together—he is pleased by the conference—expressed great confidence of victory—but warned of the hard road ahead.

We had an uneventful trip of eight hours to Bathurst—we skirted the Atlas Mountains because McIntire did not want the President to fly so high. Incidentally, Churchill has his paints and palette with him and promises to paint the mountains from the tower in the villa. He told me he was going to send it to the President as a remembrance of the conference. The President has a bad cough and looks very worn. When we got to the *Memphis* he had a little fever. Everybody went to bed by 9. I went to sleep reading a history of the Gambia River. The British can have it.

Tuesday January 26

Aboard the *Memphis*. Slept well and long. The President is still running a little fever—but it seems to be nothing very serious. I think the fishing we had planned is off. Ross says that he won't let the President go to Liberia unless the fever clears up. But I don't believe anyone can stop the President from going. Loafed all morning. All lunched together. Lord Swinton, the British High Commissioner, is coming aboard at 4 and—doctor or no doctor—the President is going to get on a tug and go up the Gambia.

That is the end of the Hopkins notes for this trip. Roosevelt did go up the Gambia on *H.M.S. Aimwell,* a seagoing tug that had been built at Bay City, Michigan, and transferred to the Royal Navy under Lend Lease. At 7:10 the following morning the President made the four-hour flight to Liberia for lunch with President Edwin Barclay, then back to Bathurst for dinner, and at 11:30 that night took off on the flight across the South Atlantic to Natal, Brazil, where he met the next day with President Getulio Vargas. (A week later, Brazil entered the war.)

On the day, January 31, that Roosevelt returned to Washington the Battle of Stalingrad ended with the capture of Field Marshal von Paulus and some sixteen of his generals together with all that remained of the surrounded German forces. Now the road to victory appeared to many hopeful people to be a broad, smooth highway on which the traffic signs were all one-way—and the arguments about the phrase, "unconditional surrender," were already beginning and were to continue throughout the war and perhaps far into history.

There were many propaganda experts, both British and American, who believed that the utterance of these words would put the iron of desperate resistance into the Germans, Japanese and Italians and thereby needlessly prolong the war and increase its cost; there are some who still believe that it did so. These critics were not necessarily opposed to the principle of total defeat—but they considered it a disastrous mistake for the President to announce it publicly.

There were others who objected violently to the principle itself, and who, as this is written in 1948, are still attributing the world's postwar troubles to the enforcement of unconditional surrender on Germany. I can make no comment on this theory in this book.

I wrote Winston Churchill asking him if he had discussed the unconditional surrender statement with Roosevelt before the press conference at Casablanca, and his reply was as follows:

> I heard the words "Unconditional Surrender" for the first time from the President's lips at the Conference. It must be remembered that at that moment no one had a right to proclaim that Victory was assured. Therefore, Defiance was the note. I would not myself have used these words, but I immediately stood by the President and have frequently defended the decision. It is false to suggest that it prolonged the war. Negotiation with Hitler was impossible. He was a maniac with supreme power to play his hand out to the end, which he did; and so did we.

Roosevelt himself absolved Churchill from all responsibility for the statement. Indeed, he suggested that it was an unpremeditated one on his own part. He said, "We had so much trouble getting those two French generals together that I thought to myself that this was as difficult as arranging the meeting of Grant and Lee—and then suddenly the press conference was on, and Winston and I had had no time to prepare for it, and the thought popped into my mind that they had called Grant 'Old Unconditional Surrender' and the next thing I knew, I had said it."

Roosevelt, for some reason, often liked to picture himself as a rather frivolous fellow who did not give sufficient attention to the consequences of chance remarks. In this explanation, indicating a spur-of-the-moment slip of the tongue, he certainly did considerably less than justice to himself. For this announcement of unconditional surrender was very deeply deliberated. Whether it was wise or foolish, whether it prolonged the war or shortened it—or even if it had no effect whatsoever on the duration (which seems possible)—it was a true statement of Roosevelt's considered policy and he refused all suggestions that he retract the statement or soften it and continued refusal to the day of his death. In fact, he restated it a great many times.

Although Roosevelt implied that he went into the press conference at Casablanca unprepared, Hopkins wrote in his description of the conference that Roosevelt consulted notes as he talked. The photographs of the conference show him holding several pages which had been carefully prepared in advance. Those pages contained the following paragraph:

> The President and the Prime Minister, after a complete survey of the world war situation, are more than ever determined that peace can come to the world only by a total elimination of German and Japanese war power. This involves the simple formula of placing the objective of this war in terms of an unconditional surrender by Germany, Italy and Japan. Unconditional surrender by them means a reasonable assurance of world peace, for generations. Unconditional surrender means not the destruction of the German populace, nor of

the Italian or Japanese populace, but does mean the destruction of a philosophy in Germany, Italy and Japan which is based on the conquest and subjugation of other peoples.

What Roosevelt was saying was that there would be no negotiated peace, no compromise with Nazism and Fascism, no "escape clauses" provided by another Fourteen Points which could lead to another Hitler. (The ghost of Woodrow Wilson was again at his shoulder.) Roosevelt wanted this uncompromising purpose to be brought home to the American people and the Russians and the Chinese, and to the people of France and other occupied nations, and he wanted it brought home to the Germans—that neither by continuance of force nor by contrivance of a new spirit of sweet reasonableness could their present leaders gain for them a soft peace. He wanted to ensure that when the war was won it would stay won.

Undoubtedly his timing of the statement at Casablanca was attributable to the uproar over Darlan and Peyrouton and the liberal fears that this might indicate a willingness to make similar deals with a Goering in Germany or a Matsuoka in Japan.

It is a matter of record that the Italians and the Japanese were ready to accept unconditional surrender as soon as effective force was applied to their homelands. Whether they might have done so sooner, or whether the Germans might ever have done so, under any circumstances whatsoever, are matters for eternal speculation. One thing about Roosevelt's famous statement is certain, however—he had his eyes wide open when he made it.

CHAPTER XXVIII

The Political Sector

WHEN Hopkins returned to Washington from Casablanca he found a formidable pile of clippings of newspaper attacks upon him and his wife. Added to the fantastic story of the Beaverbrook emeralds was a great deal of sensational material about the dinner for the Hopkinses given at the Hotel Carlton, on December 16, by Bernard M. Baruch. According to the various reports, there were from sixty to eighty guests present and Baruch paid anywhere from $10 to $40 per person. (I was one of the guests and can say that it was a large party but I haven't the faintest idea what it cost.) Whatever the statistics, there was plenty of reason to regret the whole episode. The *American* magazine had just published an article by Hopkins with the title, "You and your Family will be Mobilized," in which he wrote of the extreme toughness of the war, and the need for ever greater sacrifices on the part of the people. He said:

> Rationing and priorities far more widespread than at present will determine the kinds of food . . . we shall have and will affect every detail of our daily lives. Under total war our overall standard of living will be as low as it was at the bottom of the depression in 1932. . . . No family should object to meat rationing when they realise the beef and bacon they don't get is being served to their sons and brothers in the Army.

The newspapers had fun aplenty quoting those words together with the Carlton menu which ran from caviar and *pâté de foie gras* through beef alamode, corned beef in jelly and Virginia ham, to three kinds of ice cream, plus vintage champagne (imported). Naturally enough, the term "Lucullan orgy" managed to creep into many of these accounts. Baruch gave this dinner as his wedding present to Hopkins and his bride. It was a generous, friendly gesture, made with no thought of possible political consequences, for there were comparable (and often far more lavish) parties being given then in Washington and in all other American cities. But this one involved the loathed name of Hopkins.

The enemy propagandists did not overlook the attacks on Hopkins. One Berlin broadcast stepped up the value of the Beaverbrook emeralds to five million dollars, adding, "Although the White House issued sharp denial, various New York newspapers continue to express themselves sharply against such a case of corruption."

Of course, Hopkins was long accustomed to vilification and had learned to disregard it—or, at any rate, to make a successful pretense of doing so. He knew that the really savage attacks came from the Patterson-McCormick-Hearst newspapers and were therefore expressive of their hatred of Roosevelt and their temporarily frustrated isolationism. Ordinarily, he would have muttered "to hell with them," and gone on about his business. But now it was different. These attacks were directed at his wife as much as himself—and, in some scurrilous instances, even more so—and he was embittered and enraged and determined to fight back with suits for libel. He believed that citation of the manner in which all this material had been used by Goebbels would strengthen his case. Roosevelt talked him out of this, saying, "This is a fight in which you would be licked before you could even get started. The whole proceedings would give them a glorious opportunity to pile on the smears—and, after what you would have to take, what earthly good would it do you to win a verdict and receive damages of one dollar?" Hopkins was very reluctant indeed to take this good advice, but he had to do so as there were a great many subjects larger in importance than his own offended sensibilities to occupy his attention.

The completion of the gigantic Russian victory at Stalingrad changed the whole picture of the war and of the foreseeable future. With one battle—which, in duration and in the terrible casualties, had amounted to a major war in itself—Russia assumed the position as a great world power to which she had long been entitled by the character as well as the numbers of her people. Roosevelt knew that he must now look beyond the military campaigns of 1943 to the actual shape of things to come in the postwar world.

First, however, he had to look to some housecleaning in his own Administration. There was more warfare in the War Production Board involving Donald Nelson and Charles E. Wilson, on one side, and Ferdinand Eberstadt, on the other. All three were distinguished businessmen but they were giving a good imitation of traditional bureaucrats battling over jurisdictional frontiers. Eberstadt had the backing of the War and Navy Departments who had come to the conclusion that Nelson must go. The crisis came to a head shortly after Roosevelt's return from Casablanca and he reluctantly decided that he must intervene. He wrote to Bernard M. Baruch asking him to take over the Chairmanship of the War Production Board. Baruch was ill at the time and could not get to Washington for several days, and when he did arrive he learned that Roosevelt had changed his mind and that Nelson was to remain on the job. Nelson, having been informed of what was afoot, had suddenly taken bold, drastic action: he demanded and received Eberstadt's resignation and spread the story of the quarrel in the press. I have heard and read many different versions of this episode. I do not know just what part Hopkins played in it, but it seems evident that he backed Nelson and persuaded the President to give him another chance. He also persuaded Nelson to delegate a very large amount of authority for the direction of W.P.B. to Wilson.

In Nelson's own account of this ruckus, he quoted Roosevelt as saying:

I wish the job could be accomplished without these head-on collisions. I believe that there are ways of maneuvering so that head-on collisions can be avoided. It is my experience with businessmen in government that they always get into these battles, not alone with one another but with the heads of other government agencies. They don't know how to administer the things they must administer as well as the politicians know how.

I am sure that is an accurate quotation. Roosevelt often talked, usually with amusement, of the difficulties of businessmen in adjusting themselves to the weird ways of government. This time he was certainly not amused—and he was even less amused a year and a half later when open strife developed between Nelson and Wilson on the eve of a national election. For the time being, however, peace prevailed in W.P.B. and production went forward at a remarkable rate.

On February 2, Churchill emerged from his talks with President Inonu of Turkey, and reported to Roosevelt that he thought this visit had been a great success. Despite Churchill's cheerfulness about his Turkish visit, Hopkins remarked a short time later that, insofar as he could learn, Inonu had been extremely agreeable and equally noncommittal. Churchill had proposed in his talks with Inonu—as he did in a public speech a few weeks later—that, as part of the United Nations world organization there should be established a Council of Europe and a Council of Asia. The former would come first, after the defeat of Germany and Italy, while Britain and the U.S. (and, Churchill thought, probably Russia) were applying their full, combined forces for the administration of punishment to "the greedy, cruel Empire of Japan." Most of Churchill's conversations with Inonu, however, had been concerned not with long-range prospects, but with the immediate desirability of getting Turkey into the war on the side of the United Nations. He and Roosevelt made further attempts to achieve that end at Cairo ten months later, but they met with no success until after the Yalta Conference, less than three months before Germany's unconditional surrender.

When Stalin received the message from the President and Prime Minister that they had dispatched at the end of the Casablanca Conference, he cabled Roosevelt as follows:

> Thank you for the information in your friendly joint message on the decision made at Casablanca in regard to operations to be carried out during the last nine months of 1943 by British and American armed forces. It is my understanding that by the decisions you have taken you have set yourselves the task of crushing Germany by the opening of a Second Front in Europe in 1943 and I should be very obliged for information concerning the actual operations planned for this purpose and on the time scheduled for carrying them out.
>
> I can give you assurance that the armed forces of the Soviet Union will do everything in their power to carry on offensive operations against Germany and her allies. But our troops are now tired and in need of rest and will be unable to continue the present offensive beyond the middle of February, and we intend, circumstances permitting, to wind up our winter campaign at that time.

This was not easy to answer. The situation in Tunisia was discouraging—and it was soon to become a great deal worse—and Eisenhower sent a long, detailed cable expressing the opinion that it would be dangerous to launch the Sicily operation as planned. If it were to be attempted too early, said Eisenhower, "it is unlikely to succeed."

When Churchill read that message he immediately cabled Hopkins stating his strong belief that the Sicilian operation could be launched in June and he said he considered it would be "an awful thing" that for three months the Americans and British would be killing no German soldiers while the Russians were chasing around one hundred eighty-five divisions. He said "If we had yielded to the fears of the professionals we should not have had any TORCH." Churchill asked Hopkins to convey his felicitations to the President on a speech just delivered and to express his gratitude for certain references to himself.

The Roosevelt speech to which the Prime Minister referred was given on Lincoln's Birthday at the annual dinner of the White House Correspondents' Association. Roosevelt said:

> I spent many hours in Casablanca with this young general [Eisenhower]—a descendant of Kansas pioneers. I know what a fine, tough job he has done and how carefully and skilfully he is directing the soldiers under him. I want to say to you tonight—and to him—that we have every confidence in his leadership. High tribute was paid to his qualities as a soldier when the British Government, through Mr. Churchill, took the lead at Casablanca in proposing him for the supreme command of the great Allied operations which are imminent.

Roosevelt was very careful in choosing his words on the subject of France:

In the years of the American and French Revolutions the fundamental principle guiding our democracies was established. The cornerstone of our whole democratic edifice was the principle that from the people and the people alone flows the authority of government.

It is one of our war aims, as expressed in the Atlantic Charter, that the conquered populations of today be again the masters of their destiny. There must be no doubt anywhere that it is the unalterable purpose of the United Nations to restore to conquered peoples their sacred rights.

French sovereignty rests with the people of France. Its expression has been temporarily suspended by German occupation. Once the triumphant armies of the United Nations have expelled the common foe, Frenchmen will be represented by a Government of their own popular choice.

It will be a free choice in every sense. No nation in all the world that is free to make a choice is going to set itself up under the Fascist form of government, or the Nazi form of government or the Japanese war lord form of government. Such forms are the offspring of seizure of power followed by the abridgement of freedom. Therefore, the United Nations can properly say of these forms of government two simple words: "Never again."

The right of self-determination included in the Atlantic Charter does not carry with it the right of any government to commit wholesale murder or the right to make slaves of its own people or of any other peoples in the world.

And the world can rest assured that this total war—this sacrifice of lives all over the globe—is not being carried on for the purpose or even with the remotest idea of keeping the Quislings or Lavals in power anywhere on this earth.

Of the war in the Pacific, Roosevelt said:

We do not expect to spend the time it would take to bring Japan to final defeat merely by inching our way forward from island to island across the vast expanse of the Pacific.

There are many roads which lead right to Tokyo. We shall neglect none of them.

He said that at Casablanca Churchill had offered to make a formal statement pledging that, after the defeat of Germany, all British Empire resources and manpower would be devoted to the final attack on Japan. "I told him," said Roosevelt, "that no formal statement or agreement along these lines was in the least bit necessary—that the American people accept the word of a great English gentleman."

In case anyone had failed to hear him the first time, Roosevelt told the White House correspondents, and all the rest of the world, that "the only terms on which we shall deal with any Axis government or any Axis factions are the terms proclaimed at Casablanca: 'Unconditional Surrender.'"

It was now decided that Anthony Eden should make a visit to Washington to start the discussions of the postwar organization. He was due to make this trip immediately, but on February 18, Churchill was taken seriously ill. Hopkins immediately cabled him the expression of anxiety that was felt by so many millions of people, and Churchill replied that he might be indisposed for another week but that the situation was well under control. He said that Eden's trip to the United States must be postponed because of this illness.

Churchill's doctors called him "the world's worst patient" and he was described as "restive and cantankerous and constantly calling for the forbidden cigars." It was not until February 24 that it was announced that he was suffering from pneumonia, but on that day he again cabled Hopkins that he was feeling definitely better now and "so is Gandhi." (This was a reference to one of Gandhi's most determined hunger strikes.) He asked Hopkins, as always, to present to the President his warmest regards.

During Churchill's illness he managed to give a great deal of attention to the subject of the atom bomb. There had been discussion of this vast subject at Casablanca, during which the Prime Minister expressed considerable concern because the previous Anglo-American co-operation and full exchange of information on research and experimentation seemed to have been ended. Hopkins promised to look into this matter on his return to Washington. On February 16, Churchill cabled Hopkins, saying: "I should be very grateful for some news about this, as at present the American War Department is asking us to keep them informed of our experiments while refusing altogether any information about theirs."

On February 24, Hopkins cabled Churchill:

I have been making inquiries as a result of your request to me in regard to Tube Alloys. It would be of help to me to have Anderson send me a full memorandum by pouch of what he considers is the basis of the present misunderstanding. Since I gather the impression that our people here feel that no agreement has been breached, I should like particularly to have copies of any recorded conversations or references or memoranda which would reveal the nature of the misunderstanding.

From his sick bed on February 27, Churchill sent Hopkins two long cables, one of them a complete record of all Anglo-American dealings since the first exchanges in 1940. He expressed the conviction that this record proved that, on grounds of fair play, he could justify his request

for restoration of the policy of joint work in developing the joint resources of the two countries. He said, "Urgent decisions about our program both here and in Canada depend on the extent to which full collaboration between us is restored, and I must ask you to let me have a
firm decision on United States policy in this matter very soon."

It will be noted that Churchill was conducting this correspondence
on the atomic project with Hopkins rather than with the President and
he continued to do so for many months thereafter. In a subsequent
cable he said that if the full pooling of information on progress in nuclear
fission were not resumed, then Britain would be compelled to go ahead
separately in this work and that would be "a sombre decision." Hopkins
talked to the President and Stimson about this and also to Vannevar
Bush and Conant. The whole difficulty arose from the fact that, since the
project had passed from the research phase to the actual design and
manufacture of a weapon, control of it had passed from the hands of the
civilian scientists into the War Department. Bush stated in a memorandum to Hopkins on March 31:

> The adopted policy is that information on this subject will be fur-
> nished to individuals, either in this country or Great Britain, who need
> it and can use it now in the furtherance of the war effort, but that,
> in the interests of security, information interchanged will be restricted
> to this definite objective.
> There is nothing new or unusual in such a policy. It is applied
> generally to military matters in this country and elsewhere. To step
> beyond it would mean to furnish information on secret military mat-
> ters to individuals who wish it either because of general interest or
> because of its application to non-war or post-war matters. To do so
> would decrease security without advancing the war effort.

This, of course, was a sound position, but the British objection was
that it gave the United States exclusive possession of all the fruits of
joint research including the possible use of atomic energy for industrial
purposes after the war.

The war news at this time was bad. In their first encounter with
Rommel's forces in Tunisia, in mid-February, American troops were
given a severe mauling at Faid and Kasserine Passes and had to abandon a lot of hard-won ground, including some air fields. Some people
in Algeria were saying, "The Germans will be back here within a week."
These local defeats were not as serious as that, but they were particularly discouraging because they seemed to confirm the impression that
American infantrymen would require another year or more of intensive
training before they could become a match for the Germans; however,
the effects of Kasserine Pass proved salutary for, as "Beedle" Smith
put it, "We needed to be given a bloody nose to knock some of the
cockiness out of us."

Hitler, who had refused to cut his losses by ordering withdrawal at Stalingrad, was now doing the same thing in Tunisia: he was still pouring in reinforcements and building up such strength that, when the campaign ended three months later, the German and Italian losses in killed and captured in Tunisia numbered some 350,000 men.

A few more than that, but probably very few, were successfully evacuated to Sicily. The enemy lost nearly 200,000 tons of matériel on land alone in this campaign in addition to a great deal that was sunk at sea and shot down in the air. It was, in the end, a major victory—but at the time of Kasserine Pass it looked like a lamentable fiasco.

The Russians' offensive had ended, as Stalin predicted it would, by February 15, and the Germans then seized the initiative and recaptured Kharkov.

Stalin sent a message to Churchill, which, as always, was instantly relayed to Roosevelt. There is no copy of this in Hopkins' papers but it evidently raised some embarrassing questions relative to tardiness in Tunisia and the opening of a second front in France. Roosevelt's reply to this, dispatched February 22, was as follows:

> It is a matter of regret to me as it is to you that the Anglo-American campaign in North Africa did not go ahead as planned. The schedule was interrupted by unexpectedly heavy rains that made transportation of our troops and supplies extremely difficult over the roads leading to the front lines from the distant landing ports. . . .
>
> The importance of a major effort on the continent of Europe at the earliest practicable date is fully understood by me. You may be assured that the American war effort will be projected to the European continent, to reduce the Axis forces opposing your heroic army, as soon as possible when transportation facilities can be provided following the successful conclusion of the North African campaign.

There were, however, more and more questions from Moscow and very few indications of cordiality. Among the latter was a comment by Stalin on the successful bombing of Nuremberg, Munich, Stuttgart and Essen, "From the bottom of my heart I welcome British aviation striking hard against German industrial centres."

The prevailing tension was not lessened when, on March 8, Ambassador Standley was quoted as informing American newspaper correspondents in Moscow that Russia was getting American supplies in quantity but was keeping the fact from the people and was leading them to believe that Russia was fighting unaided. In his book, *The Year of Stalingrad*, Alexander Werth has written that the Standley statement "shocked and pained many Russians, who thought it callous and in poor taste." The attitude of the White House toward the statement was somewhat similar, but Harriman reported from London:

Many of my friends here, both British and American, seniors and juniors, are secretly pleased at the way Standley spoke out in Moscow even if this was an indiscretion. The feeling is growing here that we will build trouble for the future if we allow ourselves to be kicked around by the Russians. As an example of this: Maisky has been conducting private talks with American journalists regarding the inadequacy of aid for Russia from the United States in addition to his public statements about the Second Front.

The interests and the enormous needs of China were also given sharp emphasis at this time. In the latter part of February Madame Chiang Kai-shek, now recovered from her illness, was a guest at the White House and made a very powerful speech on behalf of China's cause before a joint session of Congress, where the war in the Far East was always more popular than the war in Europe.

With her extraordinary charm and intellectual vigor she was both winning and persuasive as a propagandist, and the Combined Chiefs of Staff were alarmed that she would bring about a radical change in basic policy. But Roosevelt held to the "Germany first" principle and the developments in Europe were making the logic of this principle appear all the more obvious.

After her departure from the White House, Hopkins wrote the following memorandum:

Mme. Chiang Kai-shek asked me to see her Saturday afternoon and I had a talk of one and a half hours with her. While she said her conversations with the President had gone very well and she believed the conferences she would have with the President tomorrow would satisfactorily complete her talks, I sensed that she was not altogether happy about her visit. She was quite insistent about getting the planes for the new 15th Air Force in there on time and said to me: "We do not want promises that are not fulfilled. The President has told me the planes will get there and he must not let me down with the Generalissimo."

She then outlined her views at great length about the post war world, the first burden of which was that we could be sure China would line up with us at the peace table. This is due to the fact that China has confidence in Roosevelt and his policy and is willing to make a commitment in advance because of that confidence.

She told me she thought some immediate move should be made to get the four great powers talking about the post war affairs and that the President should be Chairman of that group.

She pressed me pretty hard to go to China; said she had a wire from the Generalissimo urging it. I told her that if Mrs. Roosevelt is going soon I could see no purpose in my going; that I did not want to go unless there is a real reason for my doing so; that we knew already exactly what the Generalissimo wanted and that I was in sympathy with his views and would do everything I could to get them accomplished, because I thought they were right. She did not seem to be impressed by this argument. She looked tired and a little dispirited.

Sunday morning I told the President about my talk with Madame and her desire to get everything off her chest to him that day. The President obviously feels they have covered the businesses adequately, but I urged him to listen to her when he saw her later in the day and let her do the talking. I saw him again after his conference with Mme. Chiang which lasted from 4:00 to 5:30 Sunday afternoon and he told me he had learned nothing new but had given her every chance to tell her story and he seemed quite satisfied with the total sum of her visit here.

She is coming down again to spend a night or two before she leaves for China.

Dr. Soong told me privately that the Generalissimo did not want her to go to England and she told me she was going home as soon as her speaking engagements were over.

Anthony Eden arrived in Washington on March 12. According to a memorandum from John G. Winant to the President, Eden's mission was to be "limited to the most effective method of preparing for meetings between the governments of all the United Nations to consider questions arising out of the war." That would seem to be a rather broad limitation and was certainly treated as such, as the conversations with Eden, who was in the U.S. for more than two weeks, covered a vast variety of subjects in the political conduct of the war and in the construction of the hoped-for postwar world.

Shortly before Eden's arrival, Roosevelt met with Welles and Hopkins who made these notes:

We discussed the implications of Eden's visit at some length. The President told Welles he wanted to have his first meeting with Eden very informal and preferred that Welles not be present. He said that he would have dinner with Eden Saturday night alone with me.

I raised the question as to whether or not our government was going to agree to the various setups which must be made within the United Nations to discuss various matters and whether or not the main committee should be made up of four members, representing the British Empire, Russia, The United States and China. The British are going to push for committees of 7 or 8, which will include separate membership for Canada and Australia. I said I believe by this technique we would be constantly outvoted and that I thought we should put our foot down in the very beginning in this Food Conference and insist on the main committee of 4 members only and let the British Government decide whether they want their membership to come from England or Canada. Both Welles and the President agreed to this. I told them I was sure England was going to press this when Eden got here and I believe we should be very firm about it.

The President then discussed at some length his notion of the postwar shipping problem. We are going to have, by all odds, the largest merchant marine in the world after the war. Our position with Great Britain will be reversed.

I told him our control of shipping would be a powerful weapon at the Peace Table and that we should not hesitate to use it. The President said he was anxious to get into a discussion of communications and transportation between the United Nations as soon as this Food Conference could get off the ground.

He got on his old subject of the manhandling of the news by the Press and said he was going to try to work out some international news broadcasts which all of the United Nations would use, giving factual information and not colored in any way, and that they would require the radio stations in Germany, Japan and Italy to use these international releases. He also said under no circumstances should Germany, Italy and Japan be permitted to own or operate any commercial air lines.

I went to see Halifax an hour before dinner tonight and he told me he was a little disturbed about Eden's proposal to go to the West Coast. He thought in view of Mme. Chiang's going there, many people might think it was an attempt at counter-propaganda. He also felt he should not go to the Middle West. I told him all problems of exactly what he would do and where he should go could be left until he gets here, because any arrangements can be made very quickly.

Roosevelt talked a great deal on that subject of a United Nations news service. He believed there should be what he called "Free Ports of Information" established at strategic points around the world so that there would be no area wherein the people could be denied access by totalitarian censorship to the same news that was available to all other people. He also believed in a system of strategic bases—he gave as examples, Dakar, the tip of Tunisia and Formosa—which would be under United Nations control. This idea is mentioned in some of Hopkins' memoranda of the Eden conversations quoted subsequently. Roosevelt believed then, as he had believed when Molotov visited Washington a year previously, that France and other occupied countries in Europe should not have to bear the economic and physical burden of rearmament after the war—that the burden of ensuring postwar security should be borne by the nations that were of necessity already armed for combat purposes.

The first notes that Hopkins wrote after Eden's arrival were dated March 15, 1943, as follows:

The President, Mr. Eden and I dined last night and discussed, in great detail, the post-war geographical problems of Europe.

RUSSIA. Eden stated he thought Russia was our most difficult problem; that she undoubtedly had two different plans up her sleeve—

one based on British-American cooperation with Russia and the other on the assumption that the U.S. would withdraw from all interest in European affairs after the war. Eden said he believed that Russia preferred and hoped for the former because Stalin was not prepared to face the implications of Russia's control over European affairs, and England would probably be too weak to face Russia alone diplomatically. I asked him what he thought Russia's demands at the Peace Table would be. Eden said he thought they first would demand that the Baltic States be absorbed as states in the USSR. He felt Stalin would insist upon this for reasons of security and that he would make out a case that there had been a plebiscite in 1939 which indicated the desire of the Baltic States to join the USSR.

The President stated that he thought that this action on the part of Russia would meet with a good deal of resistance in the United States and England; that he realized that, realistically, the Russian armies would be in the Baltic States at the time of the downfall of Germany and none of us can force them to get out. He, the President, said he thought the United States would urge Russia not to take them into the USSR without a new plebiscite but agreed that they would have very close economic military arrangements with the Soviet pending a plebiscite.

Eden thought Stalin would not agree to this and would be insistent that we agree to the absorption of the Baltic States into the Soviet Union.

The President said he realized that we might have to agree to this, but if we did, then we should use it as a bargaining instrument in getting other concessions from Russia.

POLAND. Eden said he thought that Russia would demand very little territory of Poland, possibly up to the "Curzon Line." This would not affect Poland unduly from an economic point of view. Eden said he believed that Stalin wanted a strong Poland, providing the right kind of people were running it and that (Russian) policy at the Peace Table would depend on this.

The President said it would be difficult to work out geographical boundaries on this basis because, while there might be a liberal government in Poland at the time of the Peace Conference, they might well be thrown out within a year.

FINLAND. Eden thought that Russia would insist on the line which was drawn up at the end of the last war and he even thought this was reasonable and the President shared this point of view. Eden said that Stalin had told him he was going to insist on Hangoe for security reasons. The President said that with the emergence of air power this would not be necessary, but Eden reiterated that he was sure Stalin was going to insist on it. Both agreed that this would be a difficult matter to handle. Eden indicated that he thought there would be no trouble with Russia about the Straits, because, after all, it merely was a way of entrance from one locked sea into another. If Stalin really wanted to find a water route he would go after a new arrangement at the Suez Canal or Gibraltar. Stalin would surely demand Bessarabia. Both the President and Eden agreed that Russia should have Bessarabia because it has been Russian territory during most of its history.

POLAND. Eden said that the Poles are being very difficult about their aspirations. He told a story of how the British Government wanted to turn a cruiser over to the Poles and Sikorsky insisted on naming it "The Lemburg" after the city over whose sovereignty Russia and Poland are bound to have a bitter fight. Eden stated that he told Sikorsky that naming this cruiser "The Lemburg," would merely irritate the Russians and there was no earthly reason for giving it that name because Lemburg is not a seaport. However, Sikorsky insisted and would not take the cruiser when the British refused to permit it to be named "Lemburg." Eden said Sikorsky was forever meeting with the small states of the Balkans promoting Polish ambitions; that all this was known to the Russians and Eden thinks Sikorsky is doing far more harm for Poland than good. Poland has very large ambitions after the war and Eden says that privately they say that Russia will be so weakened and Germany crushed that Poland will emerge as the most powerful state in that part of the world. Eden thinks this is completely unrealistic. Poland wants East Prussia and both the President and Eden agree that Poland should have it. Eden said that the Russians agree privately with this but are not willing to tell this to the Poles because they want to use it as a bargaining instrument at the Peace Table. Poland will want her original boundaries as they existed prior to the war. The President said that, after all, the big powers would have to decide what Poland should have and that he, the President, did not intend to go to the Peace Conference and bargain with Poland or the other small states; as far as Poland is concerned, the important thing is to set it up in a way that will help maintain the peace of the world.

The President said he thought we should make some arrangement to move the Prussians out of East Prussia the same way the Greeks were moved out of Turkey after the last war; while this is a harsh procedure, it is the only way to maintain peace and that, in any circumstances, the Prussians cannot be trusted.

FINLAND. Eden said that the Finns were trying to use both Great Britain and the United States now to approach Russia about peace. He, Eden, thought the Russians would not deal with Finland in that roundabout way and Eden thinks that Stalin will not answer the note from the United States Government and that we should tell the Finns to talk direct to the Russians. Eden thinks Russia wants an independent Finland but is going to insist on a line that will not threaten Leningrad. He, Eden, thinks the Finns must give way here. The President said he thought that probably Russia is not too anxious to make peace with Finland now because they are containing 7 good divisions (German) in Finland which, if peace is declared, would move down on the Russian front. The Russians, the President said, were containing these 7 divisions with 5 inferior divisions at the present time. Both Eden and the President expressed the belief that the Finnish post-war problem would be difficult to arrange.

SERBIA. The President expressed his oft repeated opinion that the Croats and Serbs had nothing in common and that it is ridiculous to try to force two such antagonistic peoples to live together under one government. He, the President, thought that Serbia, itself, should be established by itself and the Croats put under a trusteeship. At this point Eden indicated his first obvious objection to the Trustee method which the President is going to propose for many states. Eden did not push it but it was clear to me that the British Government have made up their minds that they are going to oppose this. Eden thought the President's opinion about the inability of the Croats and the Serbs to live together a little pessimistic and he, Eden, believed it could be done.

CZECHOSLOVAKIA, RUMANIA, BULGARIA, TURKEY, GREECE. Both Eden and the President thought that none of these countries offered real difficulties from a geographical point of view.

AUSTRIA and *HUNGARY*. Both agreed that Austria and Hungary should be established as independent states. Eden said he thought Stalin would want to be pretty arbitrary about Hungary because the Russians do not like the Hungarians, and that Stalin would be unwilling to give them any favors at the Peace Table.

GERMANY. Eden said that the most important thing we had to get a meeting of the minds on in regard to Germany was the question of whether we were going to be able to deal with Germany as a unit after the war, disarming them, etc., and also for the peace, or whether we were going to insist that it be broken up into several independent states. Eden said that from the conferences he had had with the Russians he was sure that Stalin would not trust the Germans; that in his speech the other day when he said the Russian armies were going to stop at the German Border, this was for propaganda purposes inside Germany (Eden believed); that he, Stalin, has a deep-seated distrust of the Germans and that he will insist that Germany be broken up into a number of states. The President said he hoped we would not use the methods discussed at Versailles and also promoted by Clemenceau to arbitrarily divide Germany, but thought that we should encourage the differences and ambitions that will spring up within Germany for a Separatists Movement and, in effect, approve of a division which represents German public opinion.

I asked what they would do if that spontaneous desire did not spring up and both the President and Eden agreed that, under any circumstances, Germany must be divided into several states, one of which must, over all circumstances, be Prussia. The Prussians cannot be permitted to dominate all Germany.

Eden said he believed that one of the reasons Stalin wanted a second front in Europe was political; that if Germany collapsed he had no desire, in Germany, to take the full responsibility for what would happen in Germany or the rest of Europe, and he believed it was a fixed matter of Russian foreign policy to have both British and United States troops heavily in Europe when the collapse comes. Eden expressed this purely as his private opinion and said that he was sure that in Russia a different view was held in some quarters but, nevertheless, he thought he had stated Stalin's position.

We, then, discussed at some length, the political effect of our troops being in Italy as against France at the time of the collapse of Germany and, while both Eden and the President thought it would not be as advantageous, it was far better than not being there (on the Continent) at all.

I told the President it was important that we have the frankest kind of talk with Mr. Eden about potential differences in Europe and that, at the moment, I saw two: 1. The people of Serbia and Croatia and, 2., the problem of what countries, free and otherwise, should be disarmed in Europe. I felt that from what Mr. Eden had said he would not believe in a disarmed Poland or France and I thought it would be very unfortunate if he went back to London without fully understanding the President's position in this, even if he did not fully agree and that he, Eden, should tell the President, frankly, what are his objections to the disarmament of countries like France and Poland. The President reiterated to Eden what he had told Churchill, that after Germany is disarmed what is the reason for France having a big military establishment?

I suggested to Eden, in the light of this evening's conversation, that he articulate in his own mind the potential differences which the British and ourselves might have in Europe and, secondly, the differences which either or both of our countries might have with Russia in Europe and see if we could not come to grips with those, even though they would not be decided definitely at this conference. I suggested that we not explore anything beyond the European situation tonight and that we give two more evenings—one to the problems of the Southwest Pacific and the Far East and a third evening to Africa. I said it was clear that in these latter two areas there were bound to be conflicts of opinion but, nevertheless, I thought that we should exchange, with complete frankness, our points of view about such ticklish subjects, as *HONG KONG, MALAYAN STRAITS, INDIA.*

I said I thought no useful purpose would be served at this stage of the war, and surely no useful purpose at the Peace Table, by Great Britain and ourselves having no knowledge of our differences of opinion. Both the President and Eden agreed to this and plans will be made for these conferences soon.

In the meantime, I suggested that Hull, Eden and the President meet tomorrow for tea and the President asked me to arrange it.

Eden and I left and went to the Carlton for some oysters and reviewed the evening's conference. Eden thought that some real progress was made and he was surprised that he and the President seemed in as much agreement as they were about the European situation. He realized that the rest of the world might not be so easy to get a meeting of the minds on. Eden expressed his amazement at the President's intimate knowledge of the geographical boundaries of Europe and said that this knowledge would be of tremendous advantage in any conference.

On March 16, Hopkins wrote of a meeting with Litvinov:

I called to see the Ambassador this evening and asked him what he believed the Russian demands at the Peace Table would be. He said that they, of course, would want the Baltic States; that Russia considered them now part of the U.S.S.R.; that they had always been historically part of Russia, apart from the fact that they were essential to them for security reasons.

Litvinov said he thought Russia had no desire to occupy all of Finland and, indeed, would like to see a healthy, independent country there, but that Russia would insist on moving the line about to a point where the Russian armies were at the end of the Finnish War.

I asked him what about Hangoe and he said he had no idea how his government would feel about that.

He said he thought Russia would agree to Poland having East Prussia but that Russia would insist on what he called "her territorial rights" on the Polish frontier. Said he did not anticipate any great difficulty with Poland about this although he said Poland would make "outrageous" demands. He felt that Great Britain and the United States should decide what was to be done about Poland and "tell them" rather than ask them.

He said he assumed that everybody would agree that Russia should have Bessarabia.

I asked him about their ambitions in the Far East and he was reluctant to discuss this in any way. He said he was sure Russia would like to see Germany dismembered; certainly Prussia should be cut off from the rest of Germany and probably 2 or 3 other additional states created.

In connection with the above interview, Eden told Hopkins of a talk he had had just before leaving London with Maisky, the Russian Ambassador there. Maisky, making it clear that he spoke for himself alone and not with any specific instructions from his government, expressed the hope that Eden would make no definite commitments for detailed postwar settlements while in Washington. Eden gave assurance that the talks would be "entirely exploratory." Maisky, like Litvinov, expressed Russia's determination to absorb the Baltic states, and he also said that Germany should be broken up, but he did not exclude the possibility that its various parts might be joined in some sort of federal union. He said that Russia would certainly want reparations, not in money but in kind. Maisky evidently expressed much the same views as regards Poland, Finland and Rumania that Litvinov did, but he added that his government desired the use of bases in these countries and would not look with favor on the re-establishment of the same kind of government as that which had existed in Poland before the war or which had the political coloration of the current Polish Government-in-Exile.

Maisky said that the Soviet Government was not enthusiastic about the proposal for a future federation of Europe. He believed that a federation including a number of small countries would have negligible significance, either from the military or the political point of view, although there might be some advantage in an economic federation. Eden disagreed on this, saying the very fact of the smallness of some of the countries made federation all the more desirable, politically and militarily as well as economically. He could point to the tragedies of Holland, Belgium, Luxembourg and France in the spring of 1940, and to Yugoslavia and Greece in the spring of 1941, as instances of the disasters that resulted from a lack of agreement on military and political policy in advance of the German aggressions. Maisky saw the cogency of this argument and thought that his government probably would not oppose a Balkan federation, provided it excluded Rumania, nor a Scandinavian federation which excluded Finland. He described such arrangements as "vegetarian"—meaning, presumably, innocuous. He also spoke of the possibility of a Polish-Czech federation, saying that all such considerations depended on whether or not Poland was to have a government friendly to the Soviet Union. He certainly did not believe that the small European nations should have the same voice as the big ones in the postwar organization—for example, Albania's vote should not be equal to Britain's.

On March 17 Hull, Eden and Hopkins had tea with the President in his study, and Hopkins wrote:

> Hull said he hoped that we could find a way to avoid any long-winded trials of Hitler and his principal associates after the war; that he hoped we could find a way to get the ones that should be shot and do it quietly. He said he thought a public trial would be very bad; that we should settle with Hitler in the same way he would handle us if he were to do it.
>
> We discussed, for some time, the question of precisely what our procedure in Germany during the first 6 months after the collapse of Germany should be.
>
> I said I thought there was no understanding between Great Britain, Russia and ourselves as to which armies would be where and what kind of administration should be developed. I said that unless we acted promptly and surely I believed one of two things would happen—either Germany will go Communist or an out and out anarchic state would set in; that, indeed, the same kind of thing might happen in

any of the countries in Europe and Italy as well. I said I thought it required some kind of formal agreement and that the State Department should work out the plan with the British and the one agreed upon between the two of us should then be discussed with the Russians. The President agreed that this procedure should be followed. It will, obviously, be a much simpler matter if the British and American armies are heavily in France or Germany at the time of the collapse but we should work out a plan in case Germany collapses before we get to France.

Hull expressed his pleasure that Great Britain and the United States seemed to be getting closer together on the French question.

The President discussed the importance of the United Nations holding certain strong points like Bizerte, Dakar and the Harbor of Formosa after the war. These should be held by the United Nations.

The next Hopkins notes are dated March 22, and describe a luncheon in the President's study at which Eden and Hull again were present:

The President stated that he wanted no negotiated armistice after the collapse; that we should insist on total surrender with no commitments to the enemy as to what we would or would not do after this action. The President stated that he doubted if a peace treaty should be signed for some time after the collapse of Germany and Japan.

Eden raised the question, in a delicate way, as to the President's Constitutional powers, during this interim while we are still technically at war with Germany, to agree to forming an independent Austria, as an example. The President replied that he thought he did have the power without reference to the United States Senate—at any rate, enough power to make the independence of Austria stick. It was clear from Eden's reply that he had some doubt about this.

After lunch he told me he thought it a matter of great importance because England, China, Russia and the other United Nations wanted to be sure of the President's power to reach any agreement which would be binding prior to the actual signing of a peace treaty, which treaty, of course, would have to go to the Senate for confirmation.

We discussed the same situation with regard to East Prussia being turned over to Poland and the President's power to agree on a new eastern boundary line for Poland.

The President told Eden again that he did not like the idea of turning the Baltic States over to Russia and that she would lose a great deal of public opinion in this country if she insisted on this action. The President said he thought the old plebiscite was probably a fake and while he had no doubt that the Baltic States would vote to ally themselves with Russia, he thought Russia should take the trouble to go through the motions of getting that done, in the meantime having an agreement with Great Britain and the United States that Russia would control the foreign affairs and their finances until the new plebiscite could be taken. Eden again told the President that he thought Russia was going to be pretty insistent on the Baltic States.

Eden said he hoped the Japanese Mandated Islands would be turned over to us, preferably in outright ownership. The action would be approved by the United Nations. The President has always felt that these islands would be put under some kind of trusteeship, but it becomes clearer all the time that Eden thinks very little of a trusteeship and would rather have the full responsibility in the hands of one country.

Eden stated that in his conference with Hull this morning, Hull had told him he thought Churchill had made a serious mistake in his speech yesterday by not mentioning China amongst the great powers. Both the President and Hull agreed on this point. The President told Eden he thought that China might become a very useful power in the Far East to help police Japan and that he wanted to strengthen China in every possible way. Eden expressed a good deal of doubt about this on the theory that he doubted very much if China could stabilize herself and may well have to go through a revolution after the war. He said he "did not much like the idea of the Chinese running up and down the Pacific." This was not further pursued but from what Eden said it made me think the British are going to be pretty sticky about their former possessions in the Far East.

Eden is coming to the White House to spend the weekend and will be at lunch on Saturday.

I raised the question as to where our armed forces would be expected to be after the fall of Germany and, indeed, during the whole period of our policing the aggressor nations. The President said our armies, of course, would have to be in Germany and Italy and he assumed that the British and Russian troops would be there also. He said that so far as the other strong points of the world that had to be held were concerned, we should split up our troops—the British, for instance, would be in Tunisia or Bizerte and we would be in Dakar and, probably Formosa. Eden seemed to agree to this although he made no comment in regard to it except to say that he was glad to hear the President say our troops would be in Germany.

A large part of Eden's time while he was in Washington was devoted to discussion of the limitless problems of shipping. This subject was hardly within the scope of his department, but it was virtually impossible to consider any phase of the war without coming down to the present need for more and more transport. The American losses of matériel in Tunisia had greatly increased the demand for supplies in that theater, and the shipping requirements for HUSKY were vast. Britain's food supply was so low that more stringent rationing had to be imposed.

On March 29, Hopkins cabled Harriman:

Our shipbuilding program fell behind by some 46 ships in the first two months of this year, but Vickery is still hopeful that, in 1943, we will surpass the goal of 18 million tons. We are now exploring every possible means of getting hold of additional ships but I believe there is no possibility of our being able to assign additional ships for the British import program other than those which have been promised by Douglas. . . . Anthony's trip here has been good. Everyone likes him and we have made a thorough and frank exploration of everything with which the United Nations are concerned. He will return to London fully advised.

Hopkins also cabled Churchill that Eden's visit "has been a great success."

The President directed Hopkins to organize a small committee to study the availability of shipping.

On March 27, there was a meeting of Roosevelt, Eden, Hull, Welles, Halifax and William Strang, Assistant Undersecretary of State in the Foreign Office, which Hopkins described as follows:

Hull raised the question of the 60 or 70 thousand Jews that are in Bulgaria and are threatened with extermination unless we could get them out and, very urgently, pressed Eden for an answer to the problem. Eden replied that the whole problem of the Jews in Europe is very difficult and that we should move very cautiously about offering to take all Jews out of a country like Bulgaria. If we do that, then the Jews of the world will be wanting us to make similar offers in Poland and Germany. Hitler might well take us up on any such offer and there simply are not enough ships and means of transportation in the world to handle them.

Eden said that the British were ready to take about 60 thousand more Jews to Palestine but the problem of transportation, even from Bulgaria to Palestine is extremely difficult. Furthermore, any such mass movement as that would be very dangerous to security because the Germans would be sure to attempt to put a number of their agents in the group. They have been pretty successful with this technique both in getting their agents into North and South America.

Eden said that the forthcoming conferences in Bermuda on the whole refugee problem must come to grips with this difficult situation.

Eden said he hoped that on our side we would not make too expansive promises which could not be delivered because of lack of shipping.

There was a general discussion about the organization of the United Nations after the war. 1. The President and Welles were very emphatic that the United States could not be a member of any independent regional body such as a European Council; they felt that all the United Nations should be members of one body for the purposes of recommending policy; that this body should be world-wide in scope. 2. That there would be under this body regional councils with similar advisory powers made up of the nations geographically located in the regions; but, finally, that the real decisions should be made by the United States, Great Britain, Russia and China, who would be the powers for many years to come that would have to police the world.

The President was very insistent with Eden that China should be a member, although it was clear to me that Eden still was not convinced of the wisdom of the procedure. The President feels that China, in any serious conflict of policy with Russia, would undoubtedly line up on our side.

I said that Churchill's speech in which he advocated a purely European Council of Nations, had a very unfortunate effect over here. Eden said he was sure Churchill had not meant to exclude the United States and that he rather felt that Churchill spoke on the spur of the moment and that he, Eden, agreed that the United Nations should be organized on a global basis.

The whole idea of the trusteeship of mandated islands, etc. was discussed and the President and Eden seemed to be much closer together than they were at the beginning of their conferences on this policy.

The President made it clear that he did not want a commitment made in advance that all those colonies in the Far East should go back to the countries which owned or controlled them prior to the war. He specifically mentioned Timor and Indo-China. He suggested that all the specific problems which Mr. Eden had raised in his visit here be referred to the State Department and they asked to start exploratory discussions with the British or with any other country in regard to all of them.

I said I thought it would have a very bad effect, both in England and the United States, if the world got the impression that the United States and England were, together, planning the future of the world without consulting anyone else. Eden agreed to this and said the British were conducting direct conferences on matters that concerned them and Russia and he assumed we would do the same thing.

That same day Hopkins received a cable from Churchill stating that the Australian Prime Minister was anxious that the Order of Knight Grand Cross of the Bath be conferred on General MacArthur. Churchill said, "I cannot think that General Marshall or Admiral King would take it amiss that a junior like MacArthur should receive the G.C.B., as their position is so far above his, and I have the feeling that our gratitude to them must be expressed at a later date in the war. However, I am also told that Admiral Nimitz would have claims to receive equal decoration with General MacArthur. Is this really so?"

Hopkins replied:

It is felt here that high ranking officers should not be given honors at this time. Decorations for bravery in combat are all right but most people believe that the decorating should stop there. If, however, you decide to give a decoration to MacArthur, neither the world nor the war will come to an end any sooner and I doubt if Marshall, King or Nimitz will lose any sleep because of it. The Tunisian news is great.

(*Note.* The King conferred the GCB on MacArthur and also on Eisenhower on May 26. The good news referred to by Hopkins was the breaking of the Mareth Line by the British Eighth Army and a wide American advance in Central Tunisia. The Allies pushing from east and west in North Africa were at last joining up.)

On March 29, Hopkins wrote his final note on the Eden visit, following a dinner given by Cordell Hull at the Carlton Hotel:

> After dinner Eden and I sat up for a couple of hours reviewing the results of his trip. He, obviously, felt that from his point of view it had been altogether worthwhile, particularly from the point of view of his having had a chance to get well acquainted, first with the President and, second, with Hull. He told me he was going to invite Hull to come to England. While he found Hull a little difficult to talk to and obsessed with the problems of the Free French, nevertheless, he thought that he and Hull did see eye to eye on the major world problems.
>
> Eden said he had learned of the importance of Congress and particularly the Senate in any post-war discussions and he had not fully understood the working arrangement between the President and Congress. He found it pretty difficult to envision the wide separation of the powers of the executive and legislative branches.
>
> The President has once or twice urged the British to give up Hong Kong as a gesture of "good will." In fact, the President had suggested a number of similar gestures on the part of the British and Eden dryly remarked that he had not heard the President suggest any similar gestures on our own part.
>
> Eden, obviously, felt he got on extremely well with the President and I think this is true. The President liked Eden's frankness and admired his wide knowledge of world affairs.

Hopkins told Eden that he had asked Adolf Berle, Assistant Secretary of State, about the questions of the President's constitutional powers that Eden had raised. Berle's opinions were as follows:

> The recognition of a newly created state is a purely executive act and does not depend upon treaty or other executive action. If, after surrender and before a peace treaty, the President determines that a specific territory is so separated as to have become independent, he can recognize its existence by recognizing its government, either provisionally or definitively, and by sending a minister or officer having diplomatic powers to represent the United States interests near its government. No congressional action is needed in the first instance. Conceivably, when the post of minister was formalized, the Senate could decline to confirm a nominee to the post, or the Congress could decline appropriations to maintain it. But neither of these issues need be raised if the President chose to appoint an army officer or civilian representative as, say, High Commissioner, with the rank and powers of a minister or ambassador; or if the State Department agreed to

receive in Washington a delegate or diplomatic representative from that country.

Ultimately, of course, treaties of friendship, commerce, and so forth, would have to be negotiated, and they could be defeated in the Senate; but this is hardly likely, if sufficient time elapsed so that the new state was actually in existence.

The handling of the military forces of the United States could be so managed as to foster, in fact, the setting up of an independent state or states; for the military authorities could accept, deal with, and guide the organization of the local authorities to a point where they could be recognized as the government of the country—assuming that the population of the country was prepared to accept such a government.

In my judgment, the President could not enter into an agreement, in advance, with the government of a third power—say, British—to take any of the foregoing steps, in a fashion which would bind his successors. He could merely make a pledge as to the policy he would carry out. A successor could decline to be bound by such an agreement, and the government, as such, would not be bound. But—

In my judgment the President could, as commander-in-chief and under his war power, enter into military agreements in the nature of staff agreements, with the commander-in-chief of a third power as to military action and policy. Included in this could be an agreement for the handling of the military forces looking toward the creation of an independent state or states, especially if these were part of enemy or quasi-enemy territory. The precise binding quality of staff agreements has never been fully ascertained under our practice; but it is fairly arguable that agreements of this sort, so far as they related to military policy, are binding to a large extent even on a successor, since a commander-in-chief, having the power to lay and carry out campaigns, must be deemed to have the power necessary to make agreements reasonably appropriate to carrying out such campaigns. In this view, the President has the power, by military agreement, to create a situation in which all of the characteristics of an independent state will be created except that of recognition by this government.

During Eden's visit there was a very considerable amount of spadework done on the organization of the United Nations. From this work there resulted the UNRRA organization and the conferences at Moscow, Teheran, Bretton Woods, Dumbarton Oaks, Yalta and finally San Francisco.

At a press conference on March 30 after Eden's departure, Roosevelt spoke of the conversations in a very general way, emphasizing the fact that they were purely "exploratory," and that he hoped there would soon be similar conversations with the Russians. He said, "If you want to be didactic and put it in terms of figures, I would say that so far . . . we are about ninety-five per cent together." I asked Hopkins at the time what the other five per cent consisted of, and he replied, "Mostly France." Eden had stated the British view that they would greatly prefer to deal with one strong French authority, established in Algiers and representing all possible elements of French opinion. Roosevelt and Hull said that they preferred "to keep the position fluid," and to deal with French individuals—for example, they wished to deal separately with the French authorities in the Pacific islands and with those in Martinique. Roosevelt persisted in his belief that no single French authority could be set up by the Allies, and recognized by them, without eventually incurring the bitter resentment of the people of metropolitan France itself. This was the margin of disagreement—but actually, at that time, the French political situation was improving. Jean Monnet had arrived in Algiers and was rendering considerable service to Giraud. Monnet was dedicated to the achievement of unity among the French factions and the eventual French Committee of National Liberation owed much to his efforts. John J. McCloy, Assistant Secretary of War, made a visit to North Africa which was most helpful to Eisenhower and to the situation in general, for McCloy was one who believed that the time had come to put the Vichy policy away in the files as finished business and to concentrate our policy on strengthening the leaders of the French Resistance groups who were largely devoted to de Gaulle. Giraud took an increasingly firm pro-democracy, anti-Pétainist position and, advised by Monnet, publicly expressed his hopes for a union with de Gaulle. Months were to pass before this union was achieved, but progress toward it was being made.

I do not know to what extent Roosevelt and Eden considered the problems that would arise from the establishment of Allied military government in Italy, but this subject was certainly discussed at great length by Roosevelt and Hopkins shortly after Eden left. A long memorandum had been prepared by the State Department outlining its views as to the policy to be followed in Sicily and in any other parts of Italy which the Allies might occupy. Hopkins had a carbon copy of this memorandum and the revisions that he made in pencil and that Roosevelt made in ink on this copy provide eloquent testimony to the breadth of the differences of opinion that existed between the White House and its next-door neighbor to the westward on Pennsylvania Avenue. Following are two paragraphs which give the general idea:

State Department version:

On the basis of unconditional surrender the entire fascist party leadership ("hierarchy") from local party secretaries to the top should be removed from any posts of government.

The services of local technical and professional officials, although nominally party members, may be retained and the lower ranks of the

.10.

inadvisable for the same reasons. A certain
number of officers and men for interpreter
duty, etc., would of course be essential.

8. The prerogatives of the Crown should
be considered as suspended. The royal power *should,*

9. is known among the Italian people and the
army may require special treatment of
this question as the situation develops.

10. *If* there should be due regard, within
the requirements of military security, for
the person of dignitaries and for the institutions of the Church. The special position
of the Vatican will of course be respected.

Insert A.

SECRET

-4-

[at the top] should be removed from any post
of Government authority.

8. The services of local technical and
professional officials *apart from Fascist activities although primarily* —
Party members may be retained *for the lesser posts*
of the existing political administration
(executive, judicial, police, fiscal, public
health, etc.) may be continued in the performance of their normal functions, responsible to
the military administration, after the elimination of all the political agents of the
Fascist Party.

9. *In general,* All prefects (Provincial
governors), although they are primarily administrators, should *in general* be removed, and
military officers of the occupying forces put
in their places. On the other hand, the
municipal authorities (mayors and police chiefs,
local magistrates, etc.) might well be permitted
to carry on their functions provisionally. It

SECRET

Three pages of the State Department memorandum on the policy to be pursued by the Allied military government in Sicily and Italy, showing Roosevelt's and Hopkins' drastic revisions, including addition by them of an Italian Bill of Rights.

existing political administration (executive, judicial, police, fiscal, public health, etc.) may be continued in the performance of their normal functions, responsible to the military administration, after the elimination of all of the political agents of the fascist party.

Same paragraphs in Roosevelt-Hopkins version:

On the basis of unconditional surrender, the entire fascist party membership from the highest to the lowest should be removed from any post of government authority.

The services of local technical and professional officials, free from fascist associations, can be used.

In another paragraph, the State Department said:

The prerogatives of the Crown should be considered as suspended. *The moral power of the Crown among the Italian people and the army may require some special treatment of this question as the situation develops.*

The words that I have italicized in the foregoing were cut out by Roosevelt, and provisions for an Italian Bill of Rights were substituted. Roosevelt wanted the prerogatives suspended—*period*—with no loopholes left for an exercise of the "moral power" of the House of Savoy. Subsequent history, however, records the melancholy fact that he did not have his way on this point. Roosevelt later sent a message to Churchill saying,

I feel that in the initial stages of HUSKY we should avoid all risk of implications that would arise from any possible use of Italians in high positions such as Mayors of large towns and prefectures. I believe that it is highly preferable to remove any Italians from these positions as they are all prominent fascists. We should replace them with army officers for the time being and thus avoid stirring up Italian factions and producing repercussions at home.

Roosevelt certainly wanted to take all possible precautions against a repetition of the North African political blunders, but these precautions proved insufficient.

In considering the problems of military government in Italy, it was inevitable that Roosevelt and Hopkins should think of that brilliant, devoted and tempestuous character, Fiorello LaGuardia.

There were hundreds and thousands of Mayors in the United States and some of them, such as Kelly, Crump, Curley and Hague, were of substantial political importance; but, when you spoke of "The Mayor" in the White House during the Franklin Roosevelt years, you could be referring only to the little Mayor of New York. Although LaGuardia was a singularly shrewd politician, he was a man of high honor and ferocious courage and independence. A sometime Republican, he had been a consistent supporter and champion of Roosevelt's policies throughout the New Deal and the battle against isolationism. When the Office of Civilian Defense was formed before Pearl Harbor, Roosevelt named LaGuardia to direct it. The Mayor was not very happy in that job and certainly not very successful. He did not like the word "defense"—or "civilian" either. He had served with distinction as a fighter pilot in the First World War and he wanted to serve actively and in uniform in this one. He was constantly begging his close friend, Hopkins, to help him to get into service, and the War Department was constantly turning down his applications. Hopkins felt certain that LaGuardia could be of tremendous help to Eisenhower in the Sicilian operation and he urged the President to commission the Mayor and assign him to AFHQ in Algiers. LaGuardia had been broadcasting to Italy regularly over the short-wave transmitters, and it was learned later that these broadcasts were very effective as propaganda with the Italian people. Therefore, as an American general, or even colonel (LaGuardia would have settled for almost any rank), he could have gone to Italian soil as an acknowledged friend.

On March 17, after a talk with Roosevelt, LaGuardia wrote a long-hand note to Hopkins which expressed his intense excitement:

> *Dear Harry*: I saw the Chief yesterday—and I am so happy that I can be of service to my country—besides cleaning the streets of NYC. I expect to get my medical exam next week. The Chief indicated I could be commissioned right after I finish the Executive Budget in early April.
>
> I am to be assigned to General Eisenhower's staff and am confident that I will be able to do a good job and be really useful.
>
> After I am finished with the medicos, I will want to have a talk with you, to bring me up to date in certain matters with which you are familiar.
>
> *Fiorello*
>
> P. S. Writing this by hand as I do not want office to know until last minute.

Subsequently it seemed to Hopkins all the more desirable that La-Guardia be given this assignment. There was considerable argument between London and Washington as to the political aspects of Eisenhower's command once the Allied forces had landed on Italian soil. The British wanted the civilian advisers, Macmillan and Murphy, to go along with the troops. The Americans insisted that military government in Italy should be exclusively military. The British thereupon assigned an experienced diplomat, Lord Rennell, who had been commissioned major general, to head the Civil Affairs Division on Eisenhower's staff. Hopkins wanted LaGuardia to be Rennell's "opposite number." Secretary Stimson, however, again refused to agree to this appointment.

In the middle of April, Roosevelt left for another tour of training camps and production centers and a visit with the President of Mexico. Hopkins sent him a telegram on April 19, begging him to intercede with Stimson in behalf of the "Little Flower." I do not know what Roosevelt did about this thereafter—but LaGuardia, to his infinite disappointment, never got into uniform, and the civil affairs job in Sicily was given to Charles Poletti, a former Lieutenant Governor of New York. Hopkins could not quarrel with this excellent appointment, but he always felt that LaGuardia had been given a raw deal.

While the President was away on his trip, Hopkins was again the co-ordinating point for all cables into the White House—and there were plenty of them, from London, Chungking, Moscow, North Africa and many other places. There was a pressing need for new decisions to be made in respect to Southeast Asia and the Pacific as well as to the European and Mediterranean theaters. (The Middle East had at last faded into the background as a problem.) In the midst of all this, on April 22, Hopkins wrote a memorandum to his two aides, Dr. Lubin and Oscar Cox, as follows:

> I wish you two fellows would put your minds on the terminology to take the place of Social Security and similar words.
> I can remember the time when they changed all the names of the charity societies to Family Welfare Societies and now I understand they are trying to get rid of these names.
> All this makes sense to me as we develop in our concept of the relation of people to government. All terminology that connotes poverty, insecurity, etc. finds little favor with the American people.
> I don't think much of the "Beveridge scheme" for America. I think what we have to provide is real security in terms of full employment. I don't mean to say that sickness insurance and old age should not be in this, but I don't think it can be the cornerstone of any American program.
> Could you give me a digest of what our National Resources Board said in that long-winded tome of theirs. Get out the best things of that.

This was proof that Hopkins had not entirely changed his character; he was getting ready for the day when, the present world conflict having ended in total victory, he would resume his career as a fighter for the extension and amplification of the New Deal.

CHAPTER XXIX

Trident and Quadrant

AFTER the end of the Eden conferences in Washington, Churchill cabled asking Hopkins and General Marshall to join General Brooke and himself for a meeting with Eisenhower in North Africa, which the Prime Minister referred to as "Torch Land." On April 9, Churchill cabled Hopkins that he was greatly pleased to hear of a telephone call to Eden, then in Canada on the way home, indicating that it was agreed that the meeting should be held. The main purpose of the conference was to insure that there would be no undue delays in the launching of the Sicilian operation and to determine the answer to the question, "Where do we go from there?"

Hopkins replied that "Anthony must have misunderstood me" and said that the President felt that the time for another meeting was not propitious until the situation in Tunisia was clarified. Churchill replied that he was greatly disappointed.

It was then decided that Churchill should come to Washington with his Chiefs of Staff for full-dress conferences in May. On May 2, he cabled Hopkins that he was well aware that the President was distracted by domestic affairs, particularly the coal crisis, and he suggested that on this occasion it might be well for him to stay at the British Embassy rather than at the White House. He confessed that he was disturbed by certain differences of opinion relative to future operations which seemed to exist beneath the surface; he did not specify what these differences were, but he did state his determination to bring them out into the open and settle them.

The coal crisis referred to was one of the recurrent eruptions of John L. Lewis. It compelled Roosevelt to issue an order to Harold Ickes, as Secretary of the Interior and Solid Fuels Administrator for War, to take over all the bituminous and anthracite mines and operate them under the U.S. flag and the protection of the U.S. Army. On May 2 Roosevelt made an extraordinary appeal over the radio to the miners to go back to work as a patriotic duty. But just as the President was being wheeled from his study to go down to the Oval Room on the ground floor of the White House where he made his broadcasts, word came that the melodramatic Lewis had just announced that he had concluded an agreement with Ickes for the return of the miners to work in two days. Roosevelt gave the speech anyway.

At 4:15 on the afternoon of Friday, May 7, the U.S. II Corps and French troops broke into Bizerte in Tunisia, and five minutes later the British First Army entered Tunis. This was the real ending of this campaign, although there remained several days of mopping up and of gathering in the huge haul of prisoners, including Col. General Dietloff von Arnim, the German commander, who had taken over when Rommel was recalled to fight again elsewhere.

On May 11, Hopkins went to Staten Island to meet Churchill, Beaverbrook and party of nearly a hundred, who had crossed on the *Queen Mary* together with several thousand German and Italian prisoners of war. Hopkins then accompanied the guests to Washington for the two weeks' conference which bore the name TRIDENT and at which the date—May 1, 1944—for the Normandy invasion was at last definitely set.

Roosevelt would not hear of the suggestion that Churchill stay at the British Embassy throughout the conference, so the Prime Minister went straight to the White House, although he later spent two or three days at the Embassy. The week end of May 15 was spent at Shangri-la. Roosevelt also invited Beaverbrook to Shangri-la, but Churchill and Beaverbrook were at the time having one of their clashes—I believe this one was over the old subject of imperial preference—and Beaverbrook concluded that his presence on the week end might be an embarrassment; so he wrote a letter from the Wardman Park Hotel declining the invitation:

My Dear Mr. President:

The prospect of spending three days with you has been a joyous vision.

But some of the newspapers seek to associate me with the Prime Minister. And that always leads to complications for him in the British Parliament.

So I will reluctantly acknowledge on that account that I must forego the paths of pleasantness.

Later on, I will ask if I may come to see you.

This letter was referred to Hopkins who telephoned Beaverbrook saying, with some indignation, "The President of the United States is not in the habit of selecting his guests in deference to the sentiment of the British press or any other press." Beaverbrook went to Shangri-la.

On the drive from the White House to the Catoctin Hills, the President's car passed as usual through the old town of Frederick, Maryland. Churchill saw the roadside signs advertising Barbara Fritchie candy, and asked about them. Roosevelt explained that Barbara Fritchie was a semilegendary character of our Civil War about whom John Greenleaf Whittier had once written a poem. All the President could remember of it was:

> "Shoot, if you must, this old gray head,
> But spare your country's flag, she said."

Whereupon Churchill proceeded to recite the entire poem, stating afterward that he had not thought of it in at least thirty years. A little further on he saw a road sign pointing to Gettysburg and asked him how far away that was. It was, roughly, forty miles. He said, "Why, this may have been the very road by which Longstreet moved up," and then went on to review the whole battle. A few days later, Churchill was invited to speak again before a joint session of Congress and in that speech he compared the present status of the Second World War—after Stalingrad and Tunisia—to the status of the Civil War after Gettysburg. (This proved to be an amazingly accurate estimate of the time that remained before victory.) Churchill's speech to the Congress was so informative that Congressmen were louder than ever in their complaints that, "The only time we get to find out what's going on in the war is when the British Prime Minister visits Washington and tells us."

This TRIDENT conference represented by far the largest gathering of high-ranking officials and officers that had yet taken place in the war. Here is a list of the forty-eight guests at a luncheon in the White House on May 25:

British	*American*
The Prime Minister	The President
Lord Halifax	Mr. Stimson
Lord Cherwell	Colonel Knox
Admiral Pound	Mr. Harriman
General Brooke	Mr. Hopkins
Air Marshal Portal	Mr. Stettinius
Lt. General Ismay	Admiral Leahy
Field Marshal Dill	Admiral King
Admiral Noble	Admiral Wilson Brown
Air Marshal Welsh	Admiral Edwards
Lt. General Macready	Admiral Cook
Field Marshal Wavell	Admiral Horne
Admiral Somerville	Commander Long
Lord Moran	General Marshall

British	*American*
Brigadier Jacob	General McNarney
Brigadier Redman	General Somervell
Major-General Holmes	General Deane
Captain Lambe	General Wedemeyer
Brigadier Porter	General Street
Air Commodore Elliot	General Watson
Brigadier Kirkman	General Hall
Major-General Kirby	General Stilwell
Commodore Edwards	General Chennault
Major-General Cawthorne	

The most interesting names on this list were those of Wavell, Stilwell and Chennault. This was the first of the major conferences with representation of field commanders from the war in the Far East. Churchill had brought Wavell from India by way of London and Stilwell and Chennault had been summoned from China in an attempt to straighten out the persistent differences between them and between Stilwell and Chiang Kai-shek. After his unhappy observation of high-level goings-on in Washington, Stilwell wrote, "The inevitable conclusion was that Churchill has Roosevelt in his pocket. That they are looking for an easy way, a short-cut for England, and no attention must be diverted from the Continent at any cost. The Limeys are not interested in the war in the Pacific, and with the President hypnotized they are sitting pretty."

The bitterness of Stilwell, as commander of a neglected theater, was understandable. As I have said in a previous chapter, officers of Mac-Arthur's staff liked to say that "Churchill has Roosevelt in his hip pocket," because of the priority given to the defeat of Germany. And once, in July, 1944, I heard a British commander in Italy complain about the neglect of *that* theater because, as he put it, "Churchill is mere putty in Roosevelt's hands." It is probable that, with the exception of Eisenhower and Nimitz, there was no theater commander in the war who did not feel that he was the most neglected, most abused and most basely cheated of them all, and that if it hadn't been for Certain Sinister Influences in High Places *his* theater would have been recognized as the decisive battleground and he would have been given top priority in the allocation of men and matériel. It is also probable that none had as much right to feel this way as did Stilwell. In the cases of Eisenhower and Nimitz, of course, they had no substantial grounds for complaint for they were given top priority and the record indicates that they knew how to use it to win and end the war.

Actually, despite Stilwell's hatred of the "Limeys," there were many occasions in the recurrent disputes when Churchill was heartily on the same side with Stilwell in opposing policies advocated by the Generalissimo. At the time of the TRIDENT conference, the Chinese demands were especially insistent and the problems of morale in the Far East were acute. A message from the Generalissimo to the President strongly supported Chennault's argument that all air transport tonnage into China during the next three months be devoted to aviation gasoline and supplies for a decisive air offensive from Chinese bases. Joseph Alsop, the columnist, who was later to go with Chennault to Chungking and to become his most effective personal propagandist, wrote to Hopkins:

> The Chinese are really frightened about the future for the first time in my experience. . . . You will recall that in my talks and communications with you, I have never to date said a word about the danger of internal collapse in China, but have stuck always to the straight military results to be expected from an air effort in that area. . . . Speaking perfectly cold-bloodedly, I can tell you that T. V. [Soong] and the ablest people around him are downright terrified of what may happen if there is not some sort of immediate, fairly spectacular action to revive the spirits of the Chinese people and troops.

It was obvious that no "spectacular action" could be accomplished immediately or even for many months on the ground in Burma and since the building up of Chennault's Fourteenth Air Force was what the Generalissimo most desired, at the moment, Roosevelt's decision went against Stilwell. Furthermore, Roosevelt needed no urging from Churchill (and if he did need it, he did not get it) to concentrate his primary attention on the major operations on the continent of Europe. Now, at last, he was firm in his insistence on the massive invasion of Northern France which was given its ultimate code name, OVERLORD, and detailed plans for which were ordered to be drawn in London immediately.

Hopkins wrote no extensive notes on this conference such as he had written at Casablanca—at any rate, there are none in his papers—but the specific decisions of the conference were recorded as follows:

An Operation to seize the Azores Islands:

The purpose of this was to provide another base in the Battle of the Atlantic against the U-boats and also to provide a new air base for the ferrying of bombers and for transport planes which would enable the saving of more than one hundred million gallons of high octane gasoline a year by shortening the route from the U.S. to Africa and the United Kingdom and eventually to the European continent. (I have seen no computation of the concomitant saving of ships, aircraft and lives. But, because of this saving, the Azores operation was given the code name LIFEBELT.) The capture of the Azores was to be planned by the British Chiefs of Staff and mounted from the United Kingdom and carried out in midsummer. When the British Cabinet in London were informed of this proposal to seize the Azores they protested that no military attack should be decided upon until efforts had been made to get the concession of bases from the Portuguese Government by diplomatic negotiations. Churchill did not believe that there was the slightest fragment of a chance that the Portuguese Government would agree to permit the establishment of bases and that any request to them would only result in the strengthening of the defenses of the islands. However, as it turned out, the diplomatic negotiations were conducted and by October 12, 1943, Churchill was able to announce that they had succeeded.

Combined Bomber Offensive from the United Kingdom:

The Chiefs of Staff approved the plan for a tremendous increase in the bombing of Germany and German-occupied Europe by the R.A.F. and the U.S. Eighth Air Force. This offensive was planned in four phases, to reach its peak in April 1944. Involved in it was the destruction of German strength in fighter planes.

Cross-Channel Operations:

As has been said, the date was fixed for May 1, 1944. The initial assault was to consist of nine divisions (two of them airborne) with twenty more divisions immediately available for movement into the bridgehead when it was secured. Four American and three British divisions were to be moved from the Mediterranean after November 1 for OVERLORD, and further American divisions were to be moved steadily from the U.S. at the rate of three to five per month.

Operations in the Mediterranean to eliminate Italy from the War:

Eisenhower was instructed to plan operations beyond HUSKY provided HUSKY itself did not bring about Italian surrender, these plans to be reviewed later by the Combined Chiefs of Staff.

Bombing of Ploesti:

This was the attack by two hundred American bombers on the Rumanian oil fields which was carried out on August 1. It caused substantial damage but at very heavy cost.

Operations in the Burma-China Theater:

Although there was provision for "vigorous and aggressive land and air operations at the end of the 1943 monsoon" in Burma, Stilwell did not get the American infantry divisions for which he was begging. Chennault's air operations were to be strengthened, and there were plans for small-scale amphibious operations on the Burmese west coast. Preparations were to continue for the eventual launching of ANAKIM, but these preparations were only "administrative"—which meant they were to be made on paper, not loaded on ships.

Operations in the Pacific:

These included ejection of the Japanese from the Aleutians, seizure of the Marshall and Caroline Islands, seizure of the remaining Japanese positions in the Solomons, the Bismarck Archipelago and New Guinea. There was also to be an intensification of the far-reaching campaign by U.S. submarines and raids against Japanese lines of communication by the aircraft carrier task forces which were now beginning to be built up in great strength.

Most important, the Chiefs of Staff could report that sufficient personnel and matériel were available for all proposed operations. No serious deficiencies were apparent—with the exception of steel for landing-craft construction. But that appeared to be a very large exception when the Teheran Conference assembled six months later.

A confident atmosphere prevailed during these TRIDENT meetings in Washington—it was the first of all the conferences that was held with tabulations of actual victories over Germany on the books—and hopes were high for the achievement of a better world in the future. During these days the first of the United Nations conferences (on food) assembled at Hot Springs, Virginia—the U.S. and British Governments announced the abandonment of "extra-territorial rights" in China, an action of immense importance throughout the Far East—and the Soviet Government announced the dissolution of the Comintern, which was heralded as abandonment by the Russians of any plan they may have had to communize the world. After the end of the conference Churchill and Marshall flew to North Africa where they were joined by Eden. On May 31, de Gaulle and Giraud announced their agreement on the formation of a French executive committee, consisting of themselves, General Georges Catroux, René Massigli, Jean Monnet, General Alphonse Georges and André Philip, for the organization at last of a unified French Provisional Government-in-Exile.

In spite of all these manifestations of encouragement—or, possibly, because of them—British and American relations with the Soviet Union, which had been none too good for months, now became appreciably worse. Following Standley's outburst, it had been obvious that he must be recalled, but the selection of his successor was not an easy one for Roosevelt to make. He tried to persuade Joseph E. Davies to go back to his old job in Moscow, but the state of Davies' health made it impossible for him to accept the post. He strongly urged that Hopkins be made Ambassador to the Soviet Union; Roosevelt flatly rejected this suggestion, for he did not want Hopkins to be away from Washington for any length of time.

Davies agreed to make a brief trip to Moscow in May to convey to Stalin Roosevelt's suggestion that the two of them should meet and straighten matters out. It was Roosevelt's belief that he might be able to break the ice with Stalin more readily if Churchill were not present; with personal relations established a meeting of the Big Three could be held later on. After eleven hours with Stalin, Davies reported that his suggestion had at first evoked a great many suspicious questions concerning the purpose of this meeting, but Stalin became convinced that there was no purpose other than a friendly one and he agreed to meet Roosevelt on July 15, providing for a possible postponement of two weeks if developments on the Eastern Front compelled it. After Davies left Moscow, Stalin received copies of the full plans drawn up at the TRIDENT conference and he was evidently not impressed. In the latter part of June—I do not know the exact date—he sent Churchill a cable in which he reviewed at length all the assurances that had been given during the past thirteen months relative to the opening of a Second Front, and concluded with words which could be interpreted only as charges of deliberate bad faith by the Western Allies.

Churchill usually consulted Roosevelt on the text of any important cable that he was sending to Stalin and there was often a considerable amount of discussion back and forth between London and Washington on the precise choice of words. But now Churchill was evidently so angry that he sent off a scorching cable to which Roosevelt would never have agreed had he been given a chance to read it in advance. During this period of tension, Stalin recalled Litvinov from Washington, and Maisky from London. There was now an atmosphere alarmingly reminiscent of that which had preceded the Molotov-Ribbentrop Pact of August, 1939, and the fears of a separate Russo-German Armistice were revived. The Roosevelt-Stalin meeting was postponed indefinitely. It was fortunate that Hitler did not know how bad the relations were between the Allies at that moment, how close they were to the disruption which was his only hope of survival.

Hopkins had an unusual (for him) experience at this time: he was given some friendly publicity. Harold Ross, the brilliant but indescribable editor of *The New Yorker*, assigned one of his best men, Geoffrey T. Hellman, to do a profile of Hopkins, and Hellman paid several visits to the White House and persuaded Hopkins to talk freely about the old days at Grinnell, the welfare work in New York City, the passions and the hatreds of the New Deal era and the peregrinations during the war. When Hopkins read this profile—which said that he resembled "an animated piece of shredded wheat"—he wrote a note of appreciation to Hellman and remarked, "I seem to turn out a mixture of a Baptist preacher and a race track tout." (He might say the same about this book if he had lived to read it.)

In "Notes and Comment" in the July 3, 1943 issue of *The New Yorker*, E. B. White wrote the following:

We received a letter from the Writer's War Board the other day asking for a statement on "The Meaning of Democracy." It presumably is our duty to comply with such a request, and it is certainly our pleasure.

Surely the Board knows what democracy is. It is the line that forms on the right. It is the don't in don't shove. It is the hole in the stuffed shirt through which the sawdust slowly trickles; it is the dent in the high hat. Democracy is the recurrent suspicion that more than half of the people are right more than half of the time. It is the feeling of privacy in the voting booths, the feeling of communion in the libraries, the feeling of vitality everywhere. Democracy is a letter to the editor. Democracy is the score at the beginning of the ninth. It is an idea which hasn't been disproved yet, a song the words of which have not gone bad. It's the mustard on the hot dog and the cream in the rationed coffee. Democracy is a request from a War Board, in the middle of a morning in the middle of a war, wanting to know what democracy is.

Hopkins showed that to the President who read it and roared—as he always did when somebody told him a story that struck him as funny—"I LOVE it!"—with a sort of rising inflection on the word "love." Roosevelt read White's definition of democracy to various gatherings, adding to it, "Them's my sentiments exactly." He almost used this quotation in the speech that he gave at the end of July, but he was talked out of it on the ground that it might sound too frivolous, particularly to foreigners.

Beaverbrook remained in the U.S. for a month after Churchill had left and, before his return to England, at the end of June, he handed Hopkins a memorandum which bore the title, "Present and Future":

It was a year ago that the Prime Minister came to Washington to make the plans which have now culminated in the fall of all North Africa.

The dominant question then was whether to launch a Second Front. The decision, taken against the sombre background of defeat in Libya and impending retreat in Russia, was that the project was too ambitious, and that a lesser objective should be chosen—the clearance of the southern shore of the Mediterranean. Such a plan involved gambling on Russia's ability to stand, *for one more campaign*, on her own. In the event, Russia did hold fast, and North Africa succeeded. These two achievements have meant, for the British and Americans, that the spectre of defeat has been almost entirely banished.

It is against a new background of established confidence that fresh decisions have now to be taken. The odds have moved heavily in favour of the Allies—the wasting assets of the Luftwaffe, the damage to German industry from the air, the strain on German manpower, the development of American strength, the Russian offensive successes, the opening of the Mediterranean—cumulatively these advantages are impressive.

But for all that, in the West and in the East, the game is still "all to play for." The Russians are only back where they were this time last year. The Anglo-Americans are nowhere on the mainland of Europe.

This year, as last, the dominant question is the Second Front. For this reason: that so long as it is unattempted, there remains for Germany not only the chance, albeit an outside one, to knock out or mortally wound the Russian armies, but also time to prepare the defences of "Festung Europa."

Can *we* afford more time for preparation? The Germans have a most powerful army in the East. The Russians used up men and resources at a heavy rate last winter in an offensive which stopped short of its fullest aims. There is always the risk that Japan will stab in the back. It cannot be said that Moscow, Baku or Leningrad are out of danger. It can still less be said that we and the Americans could in any measurable space of time win without Russian assistance.

Can the Germans ignore the threat of a Second Front? They can and certainly will. To do otherwise would be to allow the initiative to slip finally from their grasp. They are likely to go even further. They will ignore or treat lightly any blow from the West which is not delivered against a vital point. Knowing that the primary object of a Second Front would be to divert troops from the East they will go almost to any lengths to prevent that occurring.

Add to these factors the change in the Anglo-American situation in the last year. Then there were strong grounds for saying that a Second Front would be nothing but a forlorn hope involving the risk of final disaster, and there was much truth in the contention that in a year we should be vastly stronger. Today, of the three major United Nations, we and the Russians are as strong as we shall ever be. Certainly American potential is still developing, and in a year's time the United States will be more powerfully armed. But can we afford the new delay? Even suppose that Germany leaves Russia alone, will she, given a "year of calm" in which to organise for defence, grow much weaker? Can bombing alone make all the difference? We have the weapons now, and the men, and the Germans are uncertain of themselves, their calculations seriously upset. None of these facts can guarantee success for the launching of a major Second Front. They do go far to insuring that its failure will not spell disaster.

Surely the inference is inescapable that the question today must be not whether but where to launch the Second Front. The preliminaries are over, brilliantly performed. If they do not prove to have been the curtain raiser, the conclusion will be hard to escape, in occupied Europe especially, that the main play is never destined for performance.

But the "where" of the Second Front is all-important. To be more than a diversion the attack must come at a spot where success will bring an immediate *mortal* threat to the enemy. The Second Front can, if it is a real one, apparently fail and yet succeed. It can, if it is only a diversion, apparently succeed and yet in reality fail.

The invasion of Italy? It might prove a major psychological blow at the enemy, but it could not guarantee decisive results. It could be parried by redrawing the southern boundary of the Fortress of Europe at the Alps and Dolomites, fighting a delaying action meanwhile.

The invasion of Northern Norway? It would mean a link-up with the Russians, but again the decisive threat to Europe would be lacking.

A landing in Southern Greece? The passes northwards to the Balkans and the Danube valley could be held by small forces.

When any of these objectives had been achieved, the game, so far as the core of German Europe was the goal (and there can be no other) would still be "all to play for."

But two places of attack promise immediate results. A descent, through the Dardanelles, with Turkish connivance or assistance, on the Eastern Balkans, would lay open the whole Danubian plain and jeopardise all the German forces in southern Russia. A landing in Northern France would point straight at Paris, at the Ruhr and at the Rhine. If either plan succeeded the enemy would be exposed to an intolerable strain before he had time to conserve, perfect and organise his defences.

There are factors, such as the exact shipping position, relative to the Second Front, which may be unknown to the layman. There are two factors which the military will ignore at our peril. One is the danger to Russia, the other the danger of stalemate. There seems a real danger that we shall go on indefinitely sewing the last button on the last gaiter, and the risk is increased by the undoubted fact that a real Second Front will always entail big risks, always remain the most difficult operation in military warfare. But if we are not prepared to accept the risks, face the difficulties, suffer the casualties, then let us concentrate at once exclusively on the production of heavy bombers and think in terms of 1950.

Harriman accompanied Beaverbrook on his flight back to London where they arrived June 30. Roosevelt had given Harriman messages to· be delivered orally to Churchill relative to the proposal for an intimate meeting of the President with Stalin previous to any formal conference of the Big Three. Hopkins well knew how unenthusiastic the Prime Minister was about this proposal and laughed as he wished Harriman the best of luck in his mission. A few days later Roosevelt received a report from Harriman:

Max and I arrived late Wednesday afternoon after two nights on the plane with little sleep to find an invitation to dine with the Prime Minister that evening. Max was tired and would have preferred to go to bed. He was not, therefore, in too good a mood. The dinner was argumentative and some of the fundamental disagreements between the two men came out. This type of argument with Max always upsets the Prime Minister.

Max left at midnight. I stayed to give the Prime Minister alone your several messages. The talk, which started with the proposed meeting, developed into a two hour discussion on every subject—from de Gaulle to China to India to Poland, etc., coming back throughout the talk to Russia and the question of the meeting.

I have never had a better opportunity to be direct and frank and, as he has since been more friendly than ever, it is obvious that he accepted the sincerity of my statements even though he did not always agree with them.

He firmly believes a three-cornered meeting is in the interests of the war but he admitted that his viewpoint is colored by considerations of the reaction in Great Britain. My main argument was based on the long view as against the immediate—(1) the value of the intimate understanding that in all probability would result from a tete-a-tete, impossible with three persons, and (2) the great importance of the favorable reaction of the American people to it and to your participation. I explained the difference in the public reaction in the United States to a personal meeting of two as compared with a three-cornered meeting on British soil in which it would appear that he, Churchill, had been the broker in the transaction.

There is no doubt in my mind as to his sincere desire and determination to back you up in anything that you finally decide to do and, although I must emphasize his disappointment if he is not present, I am satisfied he would accept it in good part and that it would in the long run improve rather than adversely affect your relations with him.

If a meeting of three were held reasonably soon after your first meeting alone, he recognizes, I believe, the logic of the historic sequence of the two tete-a-tete meetings culminating in the third with three present.

Whatever Churchill may have said to Harriman on this occasion indicative of sympathetic understanding and acceptance of Roosevelt's proposal, he certainly lost no time in doing everything he could to prevent the "tete-a-tete." It was all very well for Churchill and Stalin to meet without Roosevelt, because it was then generally assumed that the President's infirmity made it impossible for him to travel such great distances. But it was obvious, in view of Churchill's record of readiness to take off for any given point at any given moment, that his non-attendance at a top-level conference in Alaska, Siberia or elsewhere, would be accepted by the British people as proof of the fact that he had not been invited, and the Prime Minister's prestige might suffer. Therefore, hardly had Harriman left 10 Downing Street in the early hours of the morning before Churchill was hard at work drafting a message to Roosevelt with a counterproposal for a preliminary conference of the British, Russian and American Foreign Secretaries (Eden, Molotov and Hull or Welles) to smooth out various controversial points before any meeting of the Big Three, or any part thereof, should be held. Roosevelt was by now none too confident that he could persuade

Stalin to meet with him in any event and he agreed to Churchill's suggestion, which was then taken up with the Russians, who eventually accepted it.

On June 30, Roosevelt also made a proposal for a meeting between himself and Chiang Kai-shek at "some place midway between our two capitals," during the autumn. The palliative decisions taken at the TRI-DENT conference had produced only a temporary calm in Chungking, and there was now more trouble over the question of command in the China-Burma-India theater, and more disputes between the Generalissimo, Stilwell and Chennault which had to be referred to Washington for settlement. Roosevelt told Hopkins to arrange a morning meeting of Leahy, Marshall and Somervell. Of this meeting, which was held in the President's bedroom, Hopkins wrote:

> The President indicated his very strong dissatisfaction with the way our whole show is running in China. He stated that Stilwell obviously hated the Chinese and that his cablegrams are sarcastic about the Chinese and this feeling is undoubtedly known to the Chinese and the Generalissimo. Furthermore, the President said that it is quite clear the Generalissimo does not like Stilwell.
>
> General Marshall told of his difficulties and said he realized that Stilwell was indiscreet but he is the only high ranking officer we have that can speak Chinese and that, while he, obviously, does not like Chinese officialdom, he has great regard for the Chinese people. . . .
>
> What the President wants is to have an independent command from Stilwell but Marshall resists this and on good military grounds primarily, that Chennault knows nothing about logistics, that he was, for many years, a paid employee of the Chinese Government and, hence, under the undue influence of the Generalissimo. Marshall admits that Chennault is probably a tactical genius and, as such, wants to encourage him.

Marshall has told me that his only serious difference of opinion with Hopkins in the entire war was over this issue as between Stilwell and Chennault. I cannot pretend to express any opinion as to the merits of this unpleasant dispute. Hopkins was unquestionably influenced by the eloquent pleadings that flooded in from Chennault and Alsop and also by innumerable communications from and with his friend T. V. Soong, and he was inclined to be critical of Stilwell's violent intransigence and therefore favorable to Chennault. Ideological considerations, which were later to become of so much importance in all arguments of the Chinese problem, did not enter into it at that time. Marshall and King were vehemently on the side of Stilwell who had faith in the Chinese Communists as forming a stronger and more reliable fighting force against the Japanese. Hopkins was on the side of Chennault, who was close to the Fascist-tinted Kuomintang. Churchill favored Stilwell, in so far as he was on any side at all. Stalin apparently was not greatly interested in either faction in China, believing that neither would be a potent fighting factor in this war. Roosevelt had high regard for both Stilwell and Chennault, as fighting men, but his one overriding concern was to keep China in the war and to hold the friendship of the Chinese people for the United States and he had those objectives in mind in every decision that he made. He believed that there was no chance that the Chinese Communists would surrender to the Japanese as long as Russia was in the war against the Axis, whereas there was always the possibility that the Kuomintang might make a separate peace. In any case, Chiang Kai-shek was head of the government with which the U.S. Government must deal and the maintenance of good relations was difficult enough under the circumstances without the frequent disturbances created by Stilwell. Thus, whether or not Stilwell had the right on his side—and he certainly had a great deal of it—he was unquestionably a serious nuisance and there were many times when Roosevelt was on the verge of ordering his recall. Fortunately, in September, 1943, a semblance of harmony was established in Chungking, largely due to the efforts of Madame Chiang Kai-shek and her sister, Madame Kung, in Stilwell's behalf.

Roosevelt also had more domestic troubles during this summer. The "Armistice" negotiated between Lewis and Ickes did not solve the coal crisis and there were further work stoppages. Congress passed the Smith-Connally Anti-Strike Bill. On June 25, Roosevelt vetoed it and immediately both the Senate and the House produced better than the two-thirds majority necessary to override his veto. This was the worst reversal Roosevelt ever had in his dealings with the Congress on social legislation. More than half the votes in the Senate for overriding the veto, and almost half of those in the House, were cast by Democrats, giving clear proof of the fact that on domestic issues of this nature the President could no longer control his own party.

On June 29, as the hazardous Sicilian expedition was about to embark and the tension with Moscow was most acute, Vice-President Wallace delivered his all too blatantly public blast against the Secretary of Commerce, Jesse H. Jones, charging that he had obstructed the efforts of the Board of Economic Warfare to build up stock piles of critical and strategic war materials in 1940, 1941, and even after Pearl Harbor. This was undoubtedly the worst of all the public brawls that marred the record of the Roosevelt Administration and it gave to the American people—not to mention the people of other United Nations—an alarming sense of disunity and blundering incompetence in very high places. Roosevelt was extremely angry at Wallace for this outburst and at Jones for the manner in which he snapped back. On July 15, Roosevelt dissolved the Board of Economic Warfare, of which Wallace was Chairman, and put its functions and various others connected with foreign economic matters, which had been in Jones's department, under the authority of Byrnes, whose title now was Director of the Office of War Mobilization. Those who were around the White House at the time of this disagreeable incident felt there was now no chance that Roosevelt would support Wallace at the Democratic Convention in 1944.

On June 16, Roosevelt and Churchill jointly issued a statement which had been prepared a month before and held until the psychological moment when the success of the Sicilian operation was assured. It was a message to the Italian people, saying:

> The sole hope for Italian survival lies in honorable capitulation to the overwhelming power of the military forces of the United Nations. . . . All your interests and all your traditions have been betrayed by Nazi Germany and your own false and corrupt leaders: it is only by destroying both that a reconstituted Italy can hope to occupy a respected place in the family of European nations.

That statement was broadcast to Italy by all the available British and American radio transmitters, including some new ones that had been installed on the North Coast of Africa, and it was also delivered through millions of airplane leaflets. Three days after this a large force of American bombers made the first air raid on Rome, concentrating their accurate attack on the railroad yards through which the Germans had been sending reinforcements to the south. At the same time, it was announced that Hitler and Mussolini were meeting in Northern Italy; hearing this news, the outside world did not tremble at the thought "Where will the monsters strike next?"—it seeming more probable that they were discussing the best means of booking passage for Argentina. Sunday afternoon, July 25, Rosenman and I were with the President at Shangri-la, Hopkins having left that morning to go on a trip with General Arnold for some salmon fishing on the Restigouche in Canada. We had been working on a speech to be delivered the following Tuesday mainly for the purpose of trying to save the National Resources Planning Board from death at the hands of Congress; the N.R.P.B. was very dear to Roosevelt's heart, but to the conservative majority on Capitol Hill the very word "plan" was considered a Communist invention and any planning board must be part of a plot to disrupt the capitalist system of free enterprise. Roosevelt made the point in this speech that we had *planned* the North African campaign more than a year ago and we had *planned* the Sicilian campaign more than six months ago, and it was none too soon to start planning for postwar reconversion; he presented for the first time the proposal for a G.I. Bill of Rights, the plan for which had been drawn by the N.R.P.B.

The President's speech was in virtually final form late in the afternoon of this quiet, summer Sunday, when Steve Early telephoned from Washington to say he had just heard a news flash over the radio to the effect that Mussolini had resigned. The announcement had been picked up from the Rome radio which, of course, was at that time a highly unreliable source for any kind of news. The President seemed quite surprised but not tremendously excited by this report and said, "I wonder how we could get any confirmation on that." I thereupon telephoned to my associates in the O.W.I. short-wave broadcasting center in New York and asked them what they knew about the story. They had heard it, all right, and had communicated with the B.B.C. authorities in London who were inclined to believe it true; the O.W.I. people had subsequently been trying to get confirmation of it from the White House or any other official source in Washington, while the White House was now trying to get confirmation from *them*. I reported this to the President and he said, "Oh—we'll find out about it later." We then resumed work on the speech, had a leisurely dinner, then drove back to Washington, arriving at the White House late in the evening and the President went to his study to try and reach Churchill on the telephone. It was to me an amazing glimpse into Roosevelt's manner of life: for a matter of more than five hours all that the President of the United States heard of the downfall of the first of the Axis dictators was the chance report on a radio news flash from Steve Early and from what I had learned about the B.B.C. appraisal from my own office. One would have thought that during those hours dispatches would have been flashing constantly from and to all directions, even on the radio-equipped Secret Service cars during the drive back to Washington.

The next day the speech was substantially revised to meet the new developments. In it, Roosevelt said:

> Our terms to Italy are still the same as our terms to Germany and Japan—"Unconditional Surrender."
> We will have no truck with Fascism in any way, shape or manner. We will permit no vestige of Fascism to remain.

By then it became clear that the King of Italy had managed to remain on his throne throughout the palace revolution and had appointed Marshal Badoglio Prime Minister. The question immediately arose as to whether the Allies should treat with the new regime as a legitimate, non-Fascist government, overlooking the fact that the king had accepted if not blessed the Mussolini regime throughout its disgraceful career and that Badoglio had been the Duce's commander in chief in the rape of Ethiopia. Again there were howls of protest from those who had been outraged by the measures of "expediency" in North Africa and who believed that the last vestiges of the Vichy policy should have been buried with Darlan. The merest suggestion of recognition of the Badoglio government brought down more and more opprobrium on the State Department which by now was regarded in liberal circles as the very citadel of reaction and of the policy of "doing business" with the avowed enemy. However, the State Department was by no means the predominant policy-making instrument in consideration of the new situation in Italy. It was a matter of cold, hard military calculation. General Eisenhower and the Combined Chiefs of Staff were conscious of the enormous possible advantage of having any Italian government, regardless of its political coloration, which would have the authority to deliver an immediate surrender. The question of immediacy was all-important, for the Allies wanted to move into Naples, Foggia and Rome itself before the Germans could reinforce these points. Furthermore, and of much greater importance ultimately, was the factor of Winston Churchill's long-established conviction that constitutional monarchy was the strongest and most stable form of government for European states. Churchill was firmly in favor of the retention of the House of Savoy, just as he was later obdurate in his support of the restoration of the Greek King. In this connection, I was interested to read the following about the aftermath of the First World War in *The Gathering Storm*, the first volume of Churchill's tremendous memoirs of the Second World War:

> The prejudice of the Americans against monarchy, which Mr. Lloyd George made no attempt to counteract, had made it clear to the beaten [German] Empire that it would have better treatment from the Allies as a Republic than as a Monarchy. Wise policy would have crowned and fortified the Weimar Republic with a constitutional sovereign in the person of an infant grandson of the Kaiser, under a Council of Regency. Instead, a gaping void was opened in the national life of the German people. All the strong elements, military and feudal, which might have rallied to a constitutional monarchy and for its sake respected and sustained the new democratic and Parliamentary processes, were for the time being unhinged. The Weimar Republic, with all its liberal trappings and blessings, was regarded as an imposition of the enemy.

That passage dispels any mystery as to Churchill's attitude in the settlement of both World Wars: he had been reared under a constitutional monarchy, he had served the Crown throughout his public career, and he had scant respect for the stability of the republican form of government as it had been tried in Europe. Certainly, in all of his subsequent dealings with Roosevelt, he made every attempt to avoid what he considered to be Lloyd George's serious mistake in accepting American opposition to the restoration of dethroned dynasties.

Shortly after the Italian surrender, Hopkins wrote down his own views on this matter:

I have grave misgivings about both the King and Badoglio. Certainly neither of them, by any stretch of the imagination, can be considered to represent a democratic government.

It is very easy to recognise these people, but it is awfully hard to throw them overboard later.

I surely don't like the idea that these former enemies can change their minds when they know that they are going to get licked and come over to our side and get help in maintaining political power.

However, the prospect of removing Italy from the war without serious bloodshed—which meant possession of the air bases on the Italian mainland and elimination of the Italian Fleet as a threat to shipping in the Mediterranean—was so overwhelmingly tempting that long-term considerations of morality were apt to be shoved aside. It seemed a supreme opportunity for the attainment of objectives by political maneuvering rather than force, and the psychological warriors in North Africa who had scored such a resounding success with their propaganda barrage against Mussolini now stepped up their attacks by radio broadcasts and leaflets. They started assuring the Italians that, if they were to surrender "honorably," the Italian prisoners of war in British and American hands would be restored promptly to their homes—a promise that was obviously impossible to fulfill. When Churchill heard of this, he was furious and he cabled Hopkins expressing his views on the "anonymous and unauthoritative low-level propaganda pumped out by the machines."

Churchill certainly did not object to the political maneuvering, but he did object strenuously to the proffering of the olive branch on a silver platter.

In Badoglio's first public statement after the fall of Mussolini, he indicated that Italy would not seek a separate peace with the Allies; he said, "the war goes on," but he did not add *"positively."* There was little doubt in the minds of either Roosevelt or Churchill that peace feelers would soon begin to emerge from Rome, unless the Badoglio regime were to be rapidly overthrown by German power and a puppet, quisling government set up under Mussolini or any available Fascist. This presented a situation the handling of which, on a minute-to-minute basis, was a matter of overwhelming importance in its effect on relations with Russia, on the morale of Germany, the satellite states and even Japan—and, ultimately, on the whole future structure of world peace. It was obvious, therefore, that the time had come for another Roosevelt-Churchill conference, and arrangements were rapidly made for a meeting on the citadel of Quebec. As usual, the Chiefs of Staff assembled first to lay the groundwork for military discussion, arriving in Quebec on August 12. The following day the Prime Minister joined the President at Hyde Park for some preliminary conversations. En route, Churchill went far out of the way to give his daughter, Lieutenant Mary Churchill, a look at Niagara Falls; he told assembled newspapermen that he had seen the Falls some thirty years before and that the principle of the thing still seemed to be about the same. Roosevelt arrived in Quebec for the conference, which bore the name QUADRANT, on August 17. In the President's party were Hopkins, Leahy, Early, Grace Tully, Louise Hackmeister and Admiral Wilson Brown, who had succeeded McCrea as Naval Aide. Churchill was accompanied by Eden, Bracken, Leathers and the usual large staff and during subsequent days Hull, Stimson and Knox arrived in Quebec and so did T. V. Soong, this being the first time that China was represented in these top-level deliberations, apart from the meetings of the Pacific Council.

This gathering came none too soon. Shortly after the conference started, Roosevelt and Churchill sent the following message to Stalin:

> The British Ambassador in Madrid reported to us on August 15th that General Castellano, representing Badoglio, had arrived there bearing a letter of introduction from the British Minister at the Vatican. Castellano declared that he had authorization from Badoglio to state Italy's willingness to surrender unconditionally if she could thereupon join the Allies. This seems a firm offer, the British Minister at the Vatican having confirmed that Badoglio had stated in writing that he had given authorization to Castellano. We do not intend to enter into any bargain with Badoglio's Government for the purpose of inducing Italy to change sides. We recognize, on the other hand, many advantages in the acceleration of the campaign which might result. Our invasion of the mainland of Italy will begin probably before September 1st, and approximately a week later we shall make our full-scale landings at AVALANCHE [the Salerno Beachhead south of Naples]. It would seem likely that Badoglio's Government will not survive that long. There are one or more German armored divisions outside Rome, and once they suspect that Badoglio is playing them false they would be able to overthrow him and set up another Fascist Government under Farinacci, for instance. Or, the Badoglio Government might collapse and plunge all of Italy into anarchy.

Therefore (this message continued), authorization had been sent to Eisenhower to send emissaries to meet with Castellano in Lisbon, which was evidently considered slightly more friendly ground than any point in Franco's Spain. This mission was entrusted to the tough-fibred "Beedle" Smith, accompanied by Brigadier K. W. D. Strong, a British officer, who was G-2 on Eisenhower's staff. Castellano was undoubtedly aware of Roosevelt's statement about "no truck with Fascism" and was at great pains to convince Smith and Strong that the new regime had purged itself of all elements of the old one. Speaking as a soldier, he gave full credit for Mussolini's overthrow to the Italian high command. He said that sentiment against the Duce had increased in strength and determination in the Army throughout the long, humiliating series of Italian reverses in the field, beginning with the beatings administered by the surprising Greeks and continuing through to the loss of the last vestige of the Italian African Empire and of Sicily. The Army did not feel strong enough by itself to get rid of the inflated Duce, so a junta of three was formed to foment discontent within the Fascist machine. Count Grandi was enticed into the plot with the promise that if Mussolini fell he could save Fascism by becoming Mussolini's successor. However, as soon as Mussolini had been defeated in the Grand Council, the Army moved in and threw out Grandi and his accomplices. They regarded Grandi as half traitor and half dupe, and they despised Count Ciano as a man who had stabbed his father-in-law in the back. Castellano told Smith and Strong that the principal Italian desire was, first, for protection against the Germans during their present phase of defenselessness and, then, an opportunity to join with the United Nations in fighting the Germans. Eisenhower's representatives said that all they were authorized to offer were terms for a military capitulation which must be accepted unconditionally, but they said that the Allies were prepared to give assistance and support to any Italian forces or individuals who would fight against the Germans or work to obstruct the German military effort.

Having completed the preliminary conversations with Castellano, Smith and Strong returned to Algiers and the Italian general returned to Rome. Responsibility for decisions as to further steps was then passed back to Quebec. Roosevelt and Churchill kept Stalin informed of every subsequent development so that the Soviet Union would be in full agreement with all the terms of Italian surrender and would, indeed, participate in its acceptance.

Otherwise, on the political side, the principal accomplishments of the Quebec Conference were an Anglo-American agreement on the draft of a Four Power Declaration, to involve the Soviet Union and China, as well as the United Kingdom and the United States, for the establishment of an effective international organization—and an agreement to disagree on extending recognition to the French Committee of National Liberation in Algiers which, by now, was under the domination of de Gaulle.

In the military field, the principal decisions were the reaffirmation of the target date (May 1, 1944) for OVERLORD and the establishment of the Southeast Asia Command under Mountbatten, with Stilwell as Deputy Supreme Allied Commander.

Churchill was by no means reconciled to the Normandy invasion nor to any other major operation in Western Europe. In accordance with the TRIDENT agreement three months previously, an outline plan for invasion had been drawn up in London, and implementation of it had started, but the experiences of 1942 when decisions agreed to in April were reversed in July led the American Chiefs of Staff to fear that Quebec would end up with another reversed decision in favor of a diversionary "eccentric operation" in the Mediterranean area against the soft underbelly. Churchill advanced his usual and always powerful warnings of the appalling casualties that might be suffered. He pointed again and again to the map of France, showing the tremendous logistical advantages enjoyed by the Germans, the quantity of supply lines running east and west, the roads and railroads built by the French in their own defensive plan to supply and reinforce the Belgian frontier and the Maginot Line from the Channel ports. However, the Air Force now had achieved the answer to this: the concentrated, unrelenting bombing of all German lines of communication which would disrupt the system of supply and restrict facility of maneuver. The combined bombing offensive was given the code name "Operation POINTBLANK," and the Italian part of it was called "Operation STRANGLE." The ultimate story of the success of this huge and prolonged application of air power is written in the German records.

At Quebec the decision was made—for the first time, in so far as I know—to supplement the Normandy invasion with landings by American and newly armed French forces in the Toulon-Marseilles area of Southern France. This was an operation—it was known first as ANVIL and later as DRAGOON—against which Churchill fought implacably until within a few days of its accomplishment on August 15, 1944, whereupon he turned up aboard a British destroyer in the Mediterranean and, with apparent exultation, waved the victory sign to the astonished troops as they headed for the Riviera beaches.

As to the war against Japan: aside from the creation of the complicated and largely abortive (through no fault of its own) South East Asia Command, the Quebec Conference appears to have accomplished little except the listing of a considerable number of individual operations most of which never took place.

Quebec was unique among all the conferences up to that time in one vital respect: at last the Chiefs of the Naval Staffs could report that victory was being won in the war against the U-boats. Escort vessel production had been stepped up and the tide had at last turned in the Battle of the Atlantic. The Germans eventually found ways to overcome the Allied advantages in the defense of convoys—but they did not do so, fortunately, until it was too late.

Another piece of extremely favorable news that came out of Quebec was set forth in a message from Churchill and Roosevelt to Stalin:

Following the decisions taken at the TRIDENT Conference, the British Government entered into negotiations with the Government

of Portugal in order to obtain air bases and naval facilities in the
Azores. In accordance with this, the British Ambassador in Lisbon
invoked the alliance between England and Portugal which has lasted
unbroken for 600 years, and invited the Portuguese Government to
grant the desired facilities. Dr. Salazar was oppressed, of course, by
fear of vengeful German bombing and of the possibility of attack on
Portugal by Spanish forces. The British agreed to furnish him with
fighter airplanes and anti-aircraft artillery which are now en route,
and have informed Dr. Salazar that in the event of a Spanish attack,
the Allies will immediately go to war with Spain and render fullest
possible aid. Since neither of these contingencies seems probable, no
precise military convention earmarking particular troops for this purpose has as yet been made. Dr. Salazar has now agreed that the British, with Portuguese collaboration, may start to make use of the
Azores in the early part of October. As soon as the British are established on these Islands and Salazar is relieved of anxieties, pressure
will be brought to extend the use of the facilities by ships and aircraft
of the United States.

The use of the Azores is of great importance in the war in the Atlantic. The German U-boats have now quit the North Atlantic, where
our convoys have been running without loss since mid-May. The
U-boats are concentrating more on the southern route. We shall be
able to attack them with aircraft based in the Azores. In addition to
which, the ferrying of United States heavy bombers to Europe and
Africa will be greatly facilitated.

Hopkins had with him at the Quebec Conference a document headed,
"Russia's Position," which was quoted from "a very high level United
States military strategic estimate" (the source was otherwise unidenti-
fied). It contained the following:

Russia's post-war position in Europe will be a dominant one. With
Germany crushed, there is no power in Europe to oppose her tremendous military forces. It is true that Great Britain is building up a
position in the Mediterranean vis-a-vis Russia that she may find useful in balancing power in Europe. However, even here she may not
be able to oppose Russia unless she is otherwise supported.

The conclusions from the foregoing are obvious. Since Russia is
the decisive factor in the war, she must be given every assistance and
every effort must be made to obtain her friendship. Likewise, since
without question she will dominate Europe on the defeat of the Axis,
it is even more essential to develop and maintain the most friendly
relations with Russia.

*Finally, the most important factor the United States has to consider
in relation to Russia is the prosecution of the war in the Pacific.* With
Russia as an ally in the war against Japan, the war can be terminated
in less time and at less expense in life and resources than if the reverse were the case. Should the war in the Pacific have to be carried

on with an unfriendly or a negative attitude on the part of Russia, the difficulties will be immeasurably increased and operations might become abortive.

This estimate was obviously of great importance as indicating the policy which guided the making of decisions at Teheran and, much later, at Yalta.

Toward the end of the Quebec Conference, word was received from Stalin agreeing to a meeting of the Foreign Secretaries in Moscow and this news was greeted enthusiastically for it meant the beginning of the long desired collaboration of the Big Three, as well as the easing of the dangerous tension that had existed between the Western Allies and the Soviet Union. The Germans had made their final attempt to launch an offensive against the Russians in the middle of July. This, it appeared, was no more than a propaganda demonstration to attempt to persuade the German people and the rest of the world that the Wehrmacht still retained some semblance of its former, fearsome striking power, but it petered out within a week, whereupon the Russians seized the initiative and never relinquished it.

Churchill accompanied Roosevelt back to the White House after the Quebec Conference and remained in Washington off and on for three weeks, during which time the British and Canadian troops landed on the Italian boot, General Clark's Fifth Army landed at Salerno, and Italy surrendered. On September 6, Churchill went to Cambridge, Massachusetts, to receive an honorary degree from Harvard University. This ceremony had been long planned and Roosevelt, a member of the Class of 1904, took a great deal of interest in it. He telephoned various suggestions to President Conant expressing the hope that there would be plenty of pageantry and color in the ceremony. Conant conceived the idea that the Prime Minister should be outfitted with the scarlet academic robe of Oxford, from which he had received the LL.D. degree, rather than the austere American cap and gown. There were none of these robes in Cambridge or in Boston but Conant finally located one at Princeton and borrowed it for the occasion.

In the speech that he gave at Harvard, Churchill made a statement that he would hardly have dared to make at any previous and less propitious moment in the war or, indeed, at any previous time since the Declaration of Independence. He said, "This gift of a common tongue is a priceless inheritance, and it may well some day become the foundation of a common citizenship. I like to think of British and Americans moving about freely over each other's wide estates with hardly a sense of being foreigners to one another." He also said, "The price of greatness is responsibility. If the people of the United States had continued in a mediocre station, struggling with the wilderness, absorbed in their own affairs, and a factor of no consequence in the movement of the world, they might have remained forgotten and undisturbed beyond their protecting oceans: but one cannot rise to be in many ways the leading community in the civilized world without being involved in its problems, without being convulsed by its agonies and inspired by its causes." I doubt that Churchill ever made any important utterance on American soil during the war without the previous knowledge and approval of the President; in fact, he often consulted Roosevelt by telephone or cable before making his reports on the war situation to the House of Commons. He certainly talked to Roosevelt before suggesting even the remote possibility of "common citizenship" and was assured by the President that the United States had advanced so far from its isolationist position that this would not outrage public opinion or provoke another Boston Tea Party.

After the Quebec Conference—and after practically every other conference in the war—Hopkins was in a state of utter depletion and had to go to the Naval Hospital for rest and revival. (His frequent visits to this hospital often impelled the critics of the Administration to ask why the taxpayers' penicillin should be wasted on the restoration of Hopkins.) One of the most interesting pieces of reading matter that now came to his sickbed was a full-page feature from the *Chicago Sunday Tribune* with a huge colored cartoon that showed Hopkins leering, and hovering over his shoulder was the sinister image of Grigoryi Efimovich Rasputin. In the accompanying article, Walter Trohan (who was later to collaborate in the writing of *Jim Farley's Story*) achieved a remarkable effect in juxtaposition. He wrote: "One evening in 1907, a tall, broad-shouldered peasant strode across the highly polished floor of the salon of Count Alexander Pavlovich Ignatiev. . . . He bowed clumsily to an ill assorted circle of nobles, politicians, schemers, charlatans, adventurers, clergy, and dignitaries. . . . The ugly face, with a large pockmarked nose . . . the rough peasant clothes, unkempt brown hair, stringy brown beard gave him a wild appearance. . . . Rasputin went on to sway Russia by the power of his eye. Nicholas, the czar of all the Russias, fell on his knees before this curious mixture of penitent and debauchee and called him a 'Christ'. The czarina believed in him implicitly. For almost nine years this preacher of redemption thru sin virtually ruled Russia. . . . His murder foreshadowed the end of the Romanoff dynasty and the collapse of the Russian empire in the World War.

"On a May day in 1933 a lean, gangly figure with thinning brown hair and dandruff made his way with his face twisted by a sardonic grin thru an ill assorted group of representatives, crackpots, senators, bums, governors, job seekers, political leaders, and toadies . . . in the person of Harry Lloyd Hopkins, son of an Iowa harness maker,

Santa Claus had come to town. He emptied his hands of other people's money. This strange and contradictory figure spent on and on to sway a nation and then the world. The President of the United States brought him into his official family and then into his private family and poured his innermost thoughts into the spender's prominent ears. The wife of the President adopted his small child in all but name."

Trohan quoted Representative Dewey Short of Missouri as having said in "a message of extraordinary importance" to the House of Representatives: "Would the followers of the Rasputin of the White House . . . and there are many in high and important places in our government today . . . use this war as a smoke screen to saddle upon America a type of government and a kind of economy entirely foreign and contrary to those we have ever known?"

Hopkins wrote to Joseph E. Davies saying that he had never yet known a lawyer who would agree that *anything* was libelous, but he asked, "Can't you dig up some bright, young men in your office who will tell me that these bastards can be sued for libel?" The Davies reply expressed the opinion that Hopkins would find it difficult to win a libel suit because he occupied a public position and was, therefore, fair game for any kind of insult—so Hopkins merely pasted the Trohan article in his scrapbook.

This diversion came at the time of the Italian surrender, and two days thereafter Hopkins wrote to his brother-in-law, Captain Donald Duncan, who was then on the aircraft carrier *Essex* in the Pacific:

> The Italian show is fantastic, but none of us know yet just what all the implications are. For myself, I think we are in for some pretty rough fighting in Italy, particularly if the Germans really decide to try to hold the northern half. We have every reason to be hopeful that we are going to get the Italian fleet intact.
>
> Louise and I are hoping to get a house before the first of November and have a place of our own, which will suit me no end.

Hopkins' guess about the prospect of "tough fighting in Italy" proved lamentably correct. The daring plan to take Rome with an American airborne operation, synchronized with the Salerno landings, had been frustrated by German seizure of the Rome air fields—a development which seemed no more than momentarily disappointing at the time but which resulted in the black winter at Cassino and the Anzio beachhead, the record of which has been told in the writings of Ernie Pyle, the drawings of Bill Mauldin and the terrible casualty lists.

On September 20, Hopkins read a copy of the proposed agreement whereby Italy would be permitted to enter the war not as an "ally" but as a "co-belligerent," and he wrote the following memorandum and sent it to the President:

I hope you will not encourage Eisenhower to recognize Italy as a co-belligerent. This will put them in exactly the same status as the rest of our allies. Nor do I think there is enough evidence that Badoglio and the King can be trusted for us to arm any of their divisions. I should think that Eisenhower could quietly look the other way if some of the armistice terms are being violated, such as Italian naval ships being used to transport our troops, or Italian bombers from Sardinia fighting the Germans.

Would it not be better in paragraph 2 to cut out the words "to wage war against Germany" and substitute "to assist us in the war"?

I cannot see that a declaration of war by Badoglio gets us anywhere except a precipitated recognition of two men who have worked very closely with the Fascists in the past. I think we should get every possible advantage out of them, but I don't think we are under any obligation to them.

I don't see why, if Eisenhower wants to use the Italian crews and Italian ships, he does not go ahead and do it, providing he thinks he can trust them. I simply hate to see this business formalized until we have had a much better look at Badoglio and the King. McFarlane, the British general's, report on them was certainly none too good.

I would not throw out Badoglio but recognitions would be an inevitable step. Could you not tell Eisenhower to keep on as he is for the present and make the decision in another week?

The news that Mr. and Mrs. Harry Hopkins had rented a house in Georgetown gave the Washington gossip columnists a welcome topic for their conjectural chatter. Was the controversial couple moving voluntarily or by request? Hopkins had lived in the White House for three and a half years and, since his marriage, there had been more and more protests against his permanent guest status not only in the press but even in the halls of Congress. The merry-andrews of the capital were referring to the White House as "that 2-family flat." There were ugly rumors, none of them carrying the weight of any authority whatsoever (authority, of course, was the last thing that the gossip columnists needed), concerning interfamily clashes upstairs at 1600 Pennsylvania Avenue. For obvious reasons, Hopkins and his wife had cherished the natural desire to have a home of their own where they could live and entertain their friends as they pleased, free from the circumscriptions which were inevitable in the Executive Mansion. Hopkins did not move into the Georgetown house until after his return from the Teheran Conference in December, and he spent very little time in it during the two years that remained of his life.

In its October issue, the *American* magazine printed an article by Hopkins entitled, "We Can Win the War in 1945." Hopkins, in the hospital, received a letter from a lady in Colorado who had two sons in the service. She said:

Mr. Hopkins, many of us feel that God is really the only one who can straighten out this appalling mess; and we are praying daily that he will hasten the end of this war. If God decides to end this war in 1943, no doubt he can and will do so, but it would surely be nice if he could have a little cooperation from you and the President and Winston. When you say, "in 1945," I am sure you don't mean, "by that time the election will be over," but don't you think most of the people will believe that is what you have in mind? . . . Every day this war continues, you and the President will become less popular. . . . I am not trying to tell you and the President what to do. I am only begging of you not to drag your feet; not to hold the boys back, for political or any other infamous reasons.

This was a letter to which Hopkins made immediate reply:

You can be sure that I do not want the war to last an hour longer than necessary and nothing would please me more if we could have victory this year. I merely expressed my opinion that that is highly unlikely. There are friends of mine who believe that we may defeat Germany even by the end of this year. I happen not to share their view.

One thing you can be sure of is that our military leaders want to end the war as soon as possible.

My own feeling is that the war is progressing well and that the Allies are attacking with intelligence and vigor, but I believe that it cannot be done overnight.

I have three boys in the armed forces and I surely understand how anyone feels who has sons in the army or navy. I am glad mine are there. I would not have them anywhere else, but I hope they get home safely.

Considerable annoyance was occasioned at this time by the publication of a photograph that had been taken during a Churchill visit to Hyde Park by a British Army officer, a member of the Prime Minister's official party. This was especially galling to Steve Early who had to take the violent and largely unanswerable protests of the American correspondents whenever British sources released news to which they had not been given access. (No American photographers had been permitted at Hyde Park on this particular occasion.) Hopkins sent a sharp cable to Brendan Bracken:

One hell of a row has been raised here by publication of this picture and the President feels that there must be something done to put an end to this sort of business. It serves to add to the already developing antagonism against Britain since all the newspapers that get beat with a picture like this promptly find some way to take a crack at your country. This publication comes on top of the disclosure prematurely in London of the fact that Italy is determined to declare war on Germany, revealed in a dispatch from Reston to the New York Times passed by British censorship. . . . Altogether too many things of this type are happening in London. I believe you should give your most serious personal attention to this business and don't underrate for a moment the effect that this kind of thing is exerting on relations between our two countries. We are in the midst of fighting a tough war and why in God's world do we have to cope with such leaks? I put it mildly in saying that the highest circles here are irritated with this type of thing.

Bracken replied at length disclaiming all responsibility for the Hyde Park photograph and saying, "We are just as much upset as you are by premature releases," and, "knowing, as I do, that many publishers in the United States are eagerly searching about for any excuse to attack the President, you may rely upon us to do everything in our power to prevent their getting any ammunition from Great Britain."

At this time Beaverbrook returned to the Cabinet as Lord Privy Seal and Hopkins wrote to him, "Needless to say, I am delighted you are back in the Government, although this will probably mean that I will hear none of your unrestrained conversation again."

London papers printed the report that Hopkins would replace Winant as Ambassador—and that Winant would replace Frances Perkins as Secretary of Labor—and the *Chicago Tribune* printed the report from "sources close to the State Department" that Hopkins might be made Ambassador to Russia. Following the previous report, Winant sent a cable to Hopkins which revealed poignantly the difficulties of his position:

During the past six months a situation has developed which has cut down my usefulness. I have had no business delegated to me as Ambassador that could not have been done by an efficient Foreign Service officer. I have been by-passed continuously. I have had no contacts with the Prime Minister except on two occasions when he invited me to meet with him so that he could bring me up to date on Anglo-American relations. Nine-tenths of the information I receive comes from British sources. Matters of serious importance relating to our foreign policy go to Mr. Churchill or Mr. Eden through other channels. Officials of the British Government have been friendly and frank with me but they are quick to appreciate when one in my position has been deprived of his authority.

Formerly, I saw a great deal of Brendan Bracken and usually met with him officially at least one and even three or four times a week. I have not seen him at all in the last six months except to meet him by chance in the street or shake hands with him at some function. I do not think he is any less friendly personally but he happens to be quicker and more sensitive than most in gauging relationships.

There has been a whispering campaign in the past few months that

I was to be relieved of my post and succeeded by Averell, and yester-day I read in the London papers that I am to be succeeded by you. Such reports would do no damage were it not for the fact that you and Averell have done a considerable part of the exchange of com-munications that normally should be done by the Ambassador.

I know that you have enough difficulties at home without worrying about my troubles. But this situation has begun to affect my job and I know you would want to help me. I think the President and Stet-tinius should know that no Ambassador can be an effective representa-tive here in London unless he is given more information and more support than I am receiving.

Hopkins wrote a letter to Winant in which he said:

I know exactly how you feel about it and if I were in your shoes I would feel just the same.

There is, of course, nothing to the story of my becoming Ambas-sador to Great Britain and never any notion that Harriman would become Ambassador there. The President has repeatedly stated to me and others that he wanted you to stay there throughout the war and has always refused to consider replacing you when they had other jobs in mind for you here in America. I know the President not only has absolute confidence in you, but feels you are doing the best job of any Ambassador to England. I am sure the country shares this view. I certainly do.

It looks to me as though the Russian offensive is not going to stop this winter but that they are going to push it further ahead, which, together with our increased bombing of Germany, is going to make it pretty tough on Hitler and I do not see how he can stand it for more than another 8 months.

I do wish I could see you to talk over all the implications of your cable which disturbed me a good deal. I know of no one who has made a greater contribution to the war than you have and that opinion is shared by all of your friends here.

Winant's complaints were based on far more than the awkward situa-tion, referred to in an earlier chapter, which resulted from Harriman's unusual position as Lend-Lease representative in London. Inadequacy of information from Washington to principal American representatives throughout the world was a far more serious matter. The British and the Soviet Foreign Offices, in peacetime as well as in war, were so en-meshed with the whole system of control of both political and military policy that the channels of communication were clearly established from the highest authorities in London and Moscow to every outpost thereof, so that the merest consul in the most remote office knew precisely what policy decisions were being made and what his instructions were for implementing them. The archaic and disjointed machinery of the State Department and the Foreign Service, however, was woefully unable to cope with the requirements of a global war in which the United States had suddenly assumed the position of a pre-eminent world power. There was, for one thing, the essential question of security, since most important policy decisions were linked directly or indirectly with military plans, and the State Department machinery was full of leaks as well as creaks. That is why both Roosevelt and Hopkins sent all of their vital messages through military communications instead of through the regular diplomatic channels which would have kept the State Department and the various embassies and legations informed as to the progress of the correspondence. In view of Winant's reference to the fact that Harriman in London often possessed information which had not been given to him, it should be noted that after Harriman became Ambassador to the Soviet Union in October he himself began to complain in cables to Hopkins that nobody was telling him anything and that he was put in the humiliating position of depending upon the Russian Foreign Office for news as to the latest decisions made by his own government in Washington.

On September 25, Roosevelt announced the resignation of Sumner Welles as Under Secretary of State and the appointment of Edward R. Stettinius, Jr., to that position. This marked the unhappy conclusion of the protracted conflict between Hull and Welles. It had at last reached a point at which even Roosevelt could no longer produce a semblance of pacification with temper-softening words. Roosevelt was very anxious to have Welles go to Moscow for the conference with Molotov and Eden, but the situation was impossible and Welles felt he had no course but to get out of government service altogether. To the best of my knowledge, Hopkins wrote nothing about the Hull-Welles dispute and I never heard him comment on it one way or the other, although he frequently referred to its existence, as did many others in Washington. I know that he had very high respect for Welles and would rather deal with him than with anyone else in the State Department. Furthermore, it must be evident to those who have read this far in this book that Hopkins was frequently in disagreement with Hull, particularly in the interminable insistence on the sanctity of the Vichy policy which by now had been extended into Italy to cover the arrangements of "expediency" with King Victor Emmanuel and Badoglio. However, in his memoirs, Hull has written of Hopkins, "I never had any friction, much less clashes, with him," and this was certainly true of their relations which, while never really warm, were invariably courteous. Hopkins may have wished now and then that the President would accept one of Hull's recurrent threats to resign and be done with it, but he well knew why Roosevelt did not wish to lose a Secretary of State whose prestige was so high and influence so strong with the United States Senate. Here, again, Roosevelt was mindful of the ghost of Woodrow Wilson, who had seen victory won on the battlefields only to be lost on Capitol Hill when a minority of Senators proved able to raise an uproar powerful enough to repudiate the President and the League of Nations.

Roosevelt's concept of his dependence on Hull was justified by the enormous success of the Moscow Conference in October, and its consequent profound effect on Congressional opinion. On November 5, as Hull was returning from Moscow, the Senate approved by a vote of eighty-five to five the Connally Resolution providing for postwar collaboration to secure and maintain peace for the world and for the establishment of a general international organization that might become a new League of Nations. Incidentally, one of the five votes against this Resolution was cast by Hiram Johnson, a member of the vociferous minority that had defeated Wilson in 1919. This new and decisive action by the Senate strengthened Roosevelt's hand immeasurably as he embarked for the first conference of the Big Three at Teheran. It served notice on the other United Nations that in the settlement of the Second World War, as contrasted with the first one, the mortal Roosevelt had the backing of the Legislative branch which Wilson had so disastrously lacked.

Stettinius, at Roosevelt's direction, made a determined effort to reorganize the State Department and bring it up to date. He drew up an enormous and impressive chart with myriad boxes in orderly array. But he found out that this rearrangement could produce no real change in the character of the State Department as long as the occupants of the boxes, particularly on the upper middle level of divisional chiefs, remained the same; and they did remain the same, for these were the permanent career men who knew that they would still be there when the Franklin Roosevelt Administration had been replaced by another one, which might well be reactionary and isolationist in accordance with the inexorable ebb and flow of American politics, and they were determined to keep their records clean of New Deal or One World taints against that highly possible day. It would be unfair to place the blame for this on the career men themselves. They were the neglected, underpaid and often much maligned creatures of circumstance. Their point of view was reflective of that of the nation itself which had lived so long under the illusion of isolationism. The State Department, which should have been the vital instrument of our most important national policy, had been relegated to the status of the querulous maiden aunt whose sole function is to do all the worrying for the prosperous family over the endless importunities of the numerous poor relations living on the other side of the tracks.

CHAPTER XXX

Cairo, Teheran and Overlord

PRIOR to the Quebec Conference, it had been generally assumed that the supreme command for OVERLORD would be British: for one thing, the huge operation was to be mounted in the United Kingdom and, for another, it was Britain's turn to take top rank, since the high command in North Africa, Sicily and the first phases of the campaign on the Italian mainland had been entrusted by common agreement to the American Eisenhower. Churchill had promised the new post to Sir Alan Brooke, the Chief of the Imperial General Staff. However, it had become evident that, whereas in the original force for the securing of the beachhead the British troops would be about equal in strength if not superior to the Americans, in subsequent operations through France and into Germany the American forces would be steadily increased until they outnumbered the British by a ratio of approximately five to one. Therefore, Churchill agreed at Quebec that the supreme command should go to an American and there was no question of doubt in his mind that this American should be General Marshall. Nor was there any doubt in Roosevelt's mind at that time that Marshall was the one man pre-eminently qualified to assume this awful responsibility and to push the tremendous enterprise through to triumph and this opinion was vociferously supported by both Stimson and Hopkins. There were considerations in this that went well beyond awareness of Marshall's capabilities as a great soldier: from Churchill's point of view Marshall's selection was important because of his enormous prestige with the British Cabinet and the British people, who might have had reservations about Eisenhower or any less celebrated American general —and from the point of view of Roosevelt, Stimson and Hopkins, Marshall was the only one who could be trusted thoroughly to stick to the main objective without yielding to the persuasions and the blandishments of Churchill with whom he would be in close and constant touch in his London headquarters. It must be borne in mind that at this time although Eisenhower had proved his ability as a great general there was still plenty of uncertainty as to whether he possessed the qualities of statesmanship required in the performance of this supreme assignment; there were still memories of the Mediterranean political messes.

Marshall was accordingly informed that he was to assume command, at the same time retaining his status as Chief of Staff while Eisenhower would be recalled to Washington as Acting Chief of Staff; as Mrs. Marshall has written, they started surreptitiously to move their belongings out of the Chief of Staff's residence at Fort Myer. But then there started a hullabaloo which assumed fantastic proportions and which resulted, as was so often the case, in vicious newspaper and Congressional attacks on Hopkins. The appointment of Marshall to the supreme command of OVERLORD was vehemently opposed by Admiral King and General Arnold on the ground that Marshall could not be spared from his position as their colleague and, indeed, acknowledged leader in the Joint Chiefs of Staff. Admiral Leahy agreed with them on this and said so when Roosevelt asked for his opinion, but he made no positive attempts to influence the President's decision. King, however, was by no means diffident in stating his opinion. He said, "We have the winning combination here in Washington. Why break it up?" He said that if the proposed appointment went through, Marshall would be wearing "two hats," one as Chief of Staff and the other as supreme commander. This was always productive of confusion and danger; for instance, as King pointed out, Stilwell was at the moment wearing "five hats"—as Chief of Staff to the Generalissimo, as Deputy to Mountbatten, as supreme commander of the C.B.I. theater, as field commander in Northern Burma and as controller of the distribution of Lend Lease to China, this last post being in some ways the most important and by all odds the most controversial of all. King pointed out and so did Arnold that neither Eisenhower nor anyone else who might be appointed Acting Chief of Staff could possibly have Marshall's extraordinary sense of the requirements of global war, his knowledge of land, sea and air logistics, his balanced judgment as to the importance of one theater or one ally or one arm of the service as opposed to another. Furthermore, if Eisenhower were to become Acting Chief of Staff the regrettable but real lack of cordiality which characterized the relationship between him and MacArthur could become a source of major embarrassments. So violent was the sentiment in the Navy and in the Air Force for keeping Marshall in Washington—and, no doubt, in some of the upper echelons of the ground forces as well—that it inevitably erupted into print. An editorial appeared in the *Army and Navy Journal*, which was always described as "unofficial but authoritative." It said that "powerful influences would like to eliminate Marshall as Chief of Staff," adding that this "action would shock the Army, the Congress and the nation at large." The implication was that Marshall was being forcibly removed by the politicians from the high post in which he had performed so faithfully and so brilliantly and was being literally kicked upstairs. General Pershing was impelled to write to Roosevelt expressing his "deep conviction that the suggested transfer of General Marshall would be a fundamental and very grave error in our military policy." Roosevelt replied, "You are absolutely right about George Marshall—and yet, I think you are wrong too! . . . I think it is only a fair thing to give George a chance in the field—and because of the nature of the job we shall still have the benefit of his strategical ability. The best way I can express it is to tell you that I want George to be the Pershing of the Second World War—and he cannot be that if we keep him here." This letter was written on September 20, and showed that Roosevelt had then made his decision on Marshall's appointment to OVERLORD. A few days later, the *Army and Navy Register*, which was also "unofficial but authoritative," came out with an editorial which was less openly indignant but far more subtle than the one in the *Journal*. The *Register* stated that the opinion was held in "some military circles" that "the European Command would not be a promotion from his place as Chief of Staff of our Army, but only removal from Washington, where it is said that some concerned with strategy do not want him." The *Register* did not specify directly who the "some" might be but it stated that Marshall was known "to have had some differences over strategy" with Churchill and added, "It is understood that Harry Hopkins prefers Lt. General Brehon B. Somervell" for the post of Chief of Staff. With that, the uproar really started. Because Somervell was one of the many Army engineers who had been associated with Hopkins in W.P.A., the charge was immediately raised and shouted that this was all part of the New Deal plot to use the war emergency as a means of communizing America. A *Washington Times Herald* headline shouted, "GLOBAL W.P.A. SEEN AIM IN MARSHALL 'PLOT'," and an editorial on the same subject in the *Cheyenne Tribune* bore the heading, "HOPKINS' SLIMY HAND." It was charged in the House that Hopkins, backed by an oft-cited "sinister" clique consisting of Justice Felix Frankfurter, Samuel I. Rosenman and David K. Niles, was planning "to turn the War Department into a global political organization," and that the activities of the men behind this plan were "nothing less than treasonous." It mattered little to any of the embittered isolationists that Frankfurter, Rosenman and Niles had no more influence on the making of military decisions or plans or selections than did Fala, the President's Scottie; it mattered a great deal, however, that all three of them were Jews. Those same three names—and usually

Henry Morgenthau's was added—were invariably linked by the isolationist press with Hopkins (reared in the Methodist Church) as masterminds of the alien conspiracy against the American way of life.

The editorials in the *Army and Navy Journal* and the *Register* which had provoked the subsequently disgraceful uproar had undoubtedly been planted by someone in high authority in the War or Navy Department; I do not know who it was and it makes little difference on the final record but there was then and probably always will be the possibility of terrible dangers in the deliberate and irresponsible use of the malicious "leak" as a political weapon. Hopkins wrote to a friend that it was "amazing" that the story involving him and Somervell should have been cooked up—but it was not so amazing in view of the fact that whoever did the cooking wanted to create the maximum amount of public alarm and was smart enough to know that the best way to do that was to inject the fell name of Hopkins, the White House Rasputin.

Through all the hullabaloo, Marshall himself said not a word, while Mrs. Marshall continued quietly to move the furniture from Fort Myer to the family home in Leesburg, Virginia, in anticipation of her husband's departure for his new post in London. Marshall most scrupulously refrained from making any attempt to influence Roosevelt's decision one way or the other, but those who knew him best have testified that never had he wanted anything so much in his whole career as to end it in the field in command of the decisive trans-Channel invasion which he had been the first to propose and for which he had been fighting with unflagging determination ever since he and Hopkins had traveled together to London in April, 1942, when the United Nations' cause was at its lowest ebb. And Marshall knew that he had no friend more eager than Hopkins to see his wish fulfilled.

A light note in the midst of the unpleasant ruckus was struck by a monitoring of a Nazi propaganda broadcast from Paris which said, "General George C. Marshall, the U.S. Chief of Staff, has been dismissed. President Roosevelt has taken over his command. This occurred two days ago, but has not yet been commented on in Washington."

Marshall passed this on to Hopkins with the note: "Dear Harry: Are you responsible for pulling this fast one on me? G.C.M."

Hopkins showed this to Roosevelt who then wrote in pencil on the same note: "Dear George—Only true in part—I am now Chief of Staff *but* you are President. F.D.R."

Since Marshall was then a four-star general and, therefore, outranked by a British field marshal, there were many suggestions that he be given the latter title which would have made a rather ridiculous combination with his own name—and in addition to that, both he and Roosevelt were opposed to the use of a title which had never existed in the U.S. Army. Stimson wrote a letter to Roosevelt urging that he ask Congress to confer on Marshall the rank of General of the Armies which was then held only by Pershing, this promotion to be made with Pershing's consent. Stimson wrote, "I do not think we can safely postpone the date of his taking command beyond November first. The fatal delays and diversions which may sabotage Overlord will begin in the U.K. this autumn and nothing but his direct presence and influence will save us from them. No one dreads more than I do the loss of his influence in theatres other than the European theatres, but I hope that the rank and title which I have suggested will help to preserve that influence indirectly in those far away theatres even if not directly. I have talked this matter over with Harry and I think on most of these points he is in full sympathy with me."

On September 26, after the "Global W.P.A." scareheads had begun to appear, Churchill cabled Hopkins expressing his concern about all the newspaper talk to the effect that Marshall was to become Supreme Commander-in-Chief of all the forces in Western Europe. Churchill said that it was his understanding of the agreement at Quebec that while Marshall would be in a position to advise with the British Chiefs of Staff and the Combined Chiefs of Staff he would not be empowered to make decisions outside the sphere of OVERLORD. At the end of his cable, the Prime Minister asked Hopkins, "Please let me know whether there is anything wrong with this message." This was an embarrassing question for Roosevelt: in order to meet the trumped-up accusations that Marshall was being "demoted" or "kicked upstairs," the President wished to announce that Marshall's new post would be far more important and comprehensive than that of any mere theater commander, and it was obviously desirable to have unified command for all operations against Germany particularly in the strategic bombing offensive from bases in the United Kingdom, in Italy and even in the Middle East. On September 30, Hopkins wrote the following note:

The Prime Minister telephoned to say that he hoped that he and the President could make a joint statement at an early date relative to any changes in the Command.

He stated that he was under considerable pressure to answer the newspaper reports and he seemed quite disturbed that he had had no reply to his cable to me.

He thought that the statement should be timed after our next good success in Italy. While he did not say so, I imagine he might have preferred that the statement be made at the time of the fall of Rome.

He said he was holding Eden in London until we get word from Stalin about the place of the Conference. He was, obviously, quite irritated that Stalin had delayed his answer for so long.

FCC-L-211

BULLETIN

PARIS IN FRENCH AT 6:00 PM TO FRANCE:

TEXT- "GENERAL GEORGE C. MARSHALL, THE U.S. CHIEF OF STAFF, HAS BEEN DISMISSED. PRESIDENT ROOSEVELT HAS TAKEN OVER HIS COMMAND.

"THIS OCCURRED TWO DAYS AGO, BUT HAS NOT YET BEEN COMMENTED UPON IN WASHINGTON."

EM 10/5-411P

Vichy broadcast reporting Marshall's dismissal, with Marshall's and Roosevelt's comments thereon.

WAR DEPARTMENT
OFFICE CHIEF OF STAFF
WASHINGTON

Dear Harry:

Can you use this personally to squelch this rot
or me on me —

G.C.M.

Dear George — only too sad to have a new chief of staff, but to remain Pres.
F.D.R.

Two days later, Hopkins cabled to Churchill:

> The hullabaloo in the newspapers over here about Marshall is dying
> out. The McCormick-Patterson press inspired it for their own nefari-
> ous purposes. There is no basic change that I know of in the agree-
> ments reached at Quebec relative to Command. Our friend has your
> message on this same subject. He is away now, returning Monday,
> and will reply to you then. I think his feeling is that we should not
> permit the press to stampede us into any premature announcements.
> Give Clemmie my love. See you in Rome.

It was generally assumed at this time, early in October, that the fall
of Rome would rapidly follow that of Naples. Roosevelt, ordinarily so
chary of making optimistic predictions, cabled Stalin on October 4, "It
looks as if American and British armies should be in Rome in another
few weeks." On the same day, Hopkins wrote the following memorandum for the President:

> I feel very strongly that, from the point of view of organization,
> Marshall should have command of all the Allied forces, other than
> the Russian, attacking the Fortress of Germany.
> It is essential that there be one strategic air force and that our
> bombers not be frozen either in England, Italy or Africa. It is only
> human nature for a theatre commander to want to hang on to his
> airplanes. By the same token, the disposition of the ground forces,
> the use of ships and landing craft should be under a single commander.
> I have talked to General Wedemeyer about this—who had previ-
> ously been consulted by General Marshall. Wedemeyer feels that, from
> a military point of view, it is sound organization.
> While we might have to give someone like Montgomery command
> of Overlord in order to satisfy the British, I think it would be wise
> for us to agree to that in order to get our main objective of Marshall's
> command over the whole business.
> It seems to me that, above everything else, we want liquidity in our
> offensive in Europe against Germany and, whether we want it or not,
> the march of events, it seems to me, will undoubtedly require it.
> It is simply impossible for anybody to know at what point or points
> we may need to change our emphasis and the force of our attack.
> If Churchill would agree to such an organization, then I can see no
> difficulty about the early announcement of the change in commanders.
> Indeed, there would be every reason for doing it.
> I believe there is a good chance of getting Churchill to agree to this.

Roosevelt subsequently cabled Churchill in much the same terms. He
also informed Churchill that, although the press had been beating its
drums rather loudly about Marshall's appointment, the story by now
was "pretty much of a dead cat." He said that if decisions were to be
influenced by such press campaigns, "We will find ourselves with the
newspapers running the war." Commenting on the failure of the attempts

to arrange the Foreign Secretaries' meeting at some point more accessible than Moscow, Roosevelt said to Churchill, "The answer we got from Uncle Joe relative to the Moscow meeting was not unexpected so it seems there is nothing to do but take the trip there and we are organizing accordingly." (Stalin was often referred to as "Uncle Joe" or sometimes merely as "U.J." in the Roosevelt-Churchill cables.)

In back of Churchill's objections to the granting of all-inclusive authority to Marshall in the European war was his indefatigable determination to play his own strategic hand in the Eastern Mediterranean, the area that was now dearer to his heart than ever. Indeed, in the latter part of September, Churchill had authorized General Sir Henry Maitland Wilson, commander in the Middle East, to launch expeditions which seized the Dodecanese Islands of Cos, Samos and Leros in the Aegean Sea. The Germans then sent out sea and airborne forces and took these islands back; at Leros the British lost some 5,000 first-class troops, with four cruisers and seven destroyers either sunk or damaged. This surprising setback was shocking and humiliating at a time when the Germans appeared to have lost the power to capture the initiative anywhere. Churchill wanted to arrange an immediate meeting of Marshall, Eisenhower, and himself in Algiers to arrange more diversionary moves in the Mediterranean and it appears from Hopkins' notes that some heated words were exchanged over the transatlantic telephone about the Dodecanese fiasco. Hopkins informed Churchill that there was no chance of Marshall's being sent to another meeting, and that any proposals for new moves could be handled by the Combined Chiefs of Staff. After one conversation, the security authorities in the War Department discreetly asked Hopkins to caution the Prime Minister against making too explicit statements in these telephone talks to which so many people, including the enemy, might be listening.

Churchill had another source of worry in these days, which was of considerably less vital importance. Five United States Senators had made a world tour—through the United Kingdom, North Africa, the Middle East, India, China, Australia, Hawaii—and had come out of it with some very sour observations on the British Empire and the manner in which, according to their version of it, the British were using American Lend Lease to promote their own political interests. Churchill sent Hopkins a very long cable containing a statement that he proposed to make in the House of Commons refuting the Senators' charges point by point. He asked Hopkins to show this statement to Roosevelt and to ascertain his views thereon—this being one of the many occasions when the Prime Minister relied on Hopkins' discretion as though the latter were his own Ambassador in dealing with the President. Hopkins promptly showed the cable to Roosevelt and then cabled Churchill: "The inexorable events of the war are rapidly crowding the statements by the five Senators off the front pages and I therefore question whether you should feel inclined to say anything. Would it not be better to postpone your statement for a week or so, so as not to put yourself in the position of answering this backstage talk by the Senators?"

Churchill then telephoned Hopkins expressing gratitude for the advice from "you and your friend," and when he was asked questions in the House of Commons a few days later about the five Senators he gracefully ducked the issue by saying, "I have come to the conclusion that there would be no advantage in this Government taking part in this wordy warfare, especially at a time when British and United States Armies are engaged shoulder to shoulder in battles taking place or impending on the Italian Front and when the Royal Air Force and the United States Eighth Air Force in a perfect brotherhood of arms are making heavy sacrifices in their attacks on Germany." Following that statement, the "wordy warfare" went with the wind on Capitol Hill and little more was heard of it.

Preparations were now going forward for the meetings with Chiang Kai-shek in Cairo and with Stalin in Teheran. This was no time for trivia. On November 10, Stimson wrote to Hopkins: "I have reflected over our talk of yesterday and am putting on paper in this letter to you my reflections on the chance that they may be useful for you or the President. *In re OVERLORD:* My best estimate of the situation is that preparations are going all right. Provided there are no further diversions or delays, we shall be ready on the scheduled time. . . . The task for our Commander-in-Chief is to hold the situation firmly to the straight road which has been agreed to and which it is now on. He should tolerate no departures from the program. . . . So the one prayer I make for the Commander-in-Chief is steadfastness—a very difficult virtue but one more needed than any other in this particular problem. *The problem of command*: I believe that Marshall's command of Overlord is imperative for its success. To make it effective he should be there very soon. The success of Overlord is so much the most important thing in the world horizon that Marshall should take up that command in spite of all counter reasons which I can envisage. . . . I anticipate that his European command will be extended in future to all auxiliary movements in Western Europe even if that is not now agreed upon. No successor Chief of Staff should be appointed for the present but that post should be carried on by an acting chief. I anticipate that Marshall's presence in London will strongly tend to prevent any interferences with Overlord even if they were attempted, and as to other theaters of operation we shall have to take our chances of carrying on along the present plans which have been pretty well laid out. Certainly they are in far better situation than they were two or three months ago. These are my views. Good luck!"

On November 13, the President sailed from Hampton Roads, Virginia, on the new battleship, *U.S.S. Iowa,* which was commanded by Roosevelt's former Naval Aide and good friend, Captain John McCrea. Also traveling on the ship were Hopkins, Generals Marshall, Arnold, Watson, Somervell and Handy and Admirals Leahy, King, Brown, McIntire and Cooke. There were some highly important discussions among the Chiefs of Staff aboard the *Iowa*; trained to anticipate and prepare for all kinds of trouble, they expected that Churchill would be ready to propose various alternatives to the Second Front in the forthcoming conferences and that his array of arguments and persuasions might again divert Roosevelt from the main objective. It was their experience that, while the Prime Minister invariably gave his most enthusiastic and eloquent approval to OVERLORD in principle, he steadfastly refused to accept it as a scheduled fact, preferring to believe that German power could be worn down by attrition to the point of collapse, whereupon the Anglo-American forces in the United Kingdom could perform a triumphal march from the Channel to Berlin with no more than a few snipers' bullets to annoy them. Whether or not these apprehensions were fully justified, they were so substantial that the U.S. Chiefs of Staff drew up papers looking toward compromise arrangements in the event that their British opposite numbers, dominated by the Prime Minister, should present a solid wall of resistance. They considered—and events proved that they were right—that the principal battle would be over the question of unified command over all European operations from the North Cape to the Golden Horn. In a memorandum to the President, signed by Leahy, the Joint Chiefs said:

> The necessity for unified command, in our opinion, is so urgent and compelling that, in spite of the fact that the bulk of the forces, both ground and air, will ultimately be American, we are willing to accept a British officer as over-all commander for European operations provided the man named is Sir John Dill. This indicates the weight we give to the matter of undivided command and responsibility. Sir John Dill is well known to our officials and to the American public. He has worked on an intimate personal basis with the U.S. Chiefs of Staff since our entry into the war. We have the highest opinion of his integrity of character and singleness of purpose. He understands our organization, our characteristics, our viewpoint on many subjects, and our way of doing business.
>
> If the proposal outlined above is adopted—and it must be—then Eisenhower should remain in command in the Mediterranean. The question as to what individual should immediately command the cross-Channel phase of OVERLORD is a matter which can be discussed further.

In considering the foregoing document, it must be remembered that Leahy, King and Arnold were all hoping that Roosevelt would not appoint Marshall to the field command, and that Marshall himself was taking no part in the discussion, although certainly supporting the naming of Dill.

On the second day out aboard the *Iowa*, there was an extraordinary episode which caused the Navy's most ominous warning, "THIS AIN'T NO DRILL!" to be shouted from the bridge. (The statement is generally entered in the log, if one survives, as, "This is NOT a drill!"— but I believe that few sailors have ever said it that way in the heat of the moment.) Hopkins wrote a description of this episode, as follows:

> This afternoon the Captain arranged for an anti-aircraft drill. Three balloons are released—tied together—and the batteries of forties and twenties let loose when the balloons reach a proper height and distance from the ship. The other method is for the five-inch battery to fire one shell—it explodes at perhaps 20,000 feet—then the other five-inch guns try to hit the ball of smoke left by the original explosion.
>
> The President was wheeled from the luncheon table to the deck just outside his mess—Wilson Brown, Ross McIntire, Pa Watson and I went along. The firing began—it seemed pretty good to me altho the five-inch guns made a whale of a racket in spite of the cotton which all of us put in our ears.
>
> We had just moved to the port side to see the five-inch guns fired the second time. Suddenly an officer from the bridge two decks above leaned over and yelled "It's the real thing! It's the real thing!" The President doesn't hear well anyway and with his ears stuffed with cotton he had a hard time getting the officer's words which I repeated to him several times before he understood. I asked him whether he wanted to go inside—he said, "No—where is it?"
>
> Just as I got to the starboard side to find out—everything fired at once at the wake of a torpedo about six hundred yards away—the firing lasted about thirty seconds. The wake went well astern.
>
> It was a torpedo all right—but *not* from a German submarine. One of our destroyers had let loose a torpedo directly at the Iowa. The first the Iowa heard about it was flash from the destroyer that a torpedo was moving toward the Iowa and it was four or five minutes later that the message came that the torpedo was fired by our own escort.
>
> The commander of the destroyer explained it as follows—the torpedo was in place but with no primer attached—the torpedo must have been unloosed because of the heavy seas in some unaccountable fashion. But Admiral King and Captain McCrea thot this pretty thin. An investigation is afoot.
>
> Can you imagine our own escort torpedoing an American battleship —the newest and biggest—with the President of the United States aboard—along with the Chief of Staff of the Army and the Chief of Naval Operations.
>
> In view of the fact that there were twenty Army officers aboard, I doubt if the Navy will ever hear the last of it.

HARRY L. HOPKINS

WASHINGTON

to see the five inch guns fired the second time. Suddenly an officer from the bridge two decks above leaned over and yelled "Its the real thing"! "Its the real thing"! The President doesn't hear well anyway and with his ears stuffed with cotton he had a hard time getting the officers words which I repeated to him several times before he understood. I asked him whether he wanted to go inside — he said "No — where is it"?

Just as I got to the starboard rail to find out — sure thing fired it was in the wake of a torpedo about six hundred yards away — the firing lasted about thirty seconds — the wake went well astern.

It was a torpedo alright — but *not* from a German submarine. One of our destroyers had let loose a torpedo directly at the Iowa. The first the Iowa

Page from Hopkins' memorandum of an episode which occurred during Roosevelt's trip to Teheran aboard the U.S.S. Iowa.

The records give the identity of the hapless destroyer from which the torpedo was accidentally fired, but I am not going to mention her name in these pages. Her skipper probably did not know who, if any, were the passengers aboard the *Iowa*. It was bad enough for him to know that one of his own torpedoes had been loosed toward the great ship and caused her to maneuver to avoid being hit. It would have been worse, of course, had he been aware that the President of the United States was one of the possible victims. But, had he known that the President's party included Admiral King, he would undoubtedly have attached the anchor to his neck and plunged himself to the bottom of the sea rather than live to face the awful consequences.

The *Iowa* arrived at Oran on November 20, where the President was met by Eisenhower and his staff and the three sons who were in that theater, Elliott, Franklin D., Jr., and Robert Hopkins. Roosevelt then flew to Tunis in the C-54 transport plane which had already been given the unofficial but enduring name, "The Sacred Cow." The next day, Sunday, he went for a tour of the Tunisian battlefields with Eisenhower, who did not realize at the time that he was being subjected to most searching scrutiny and appraisal. Roosevelt showed great interest in the site of ancient Carthage—which had once been subjected to unconditional surrender—and he wondered if any of the battles of the Punic Wars had been fought in the same places as the recent Tunisian campaign. He concluded that the Carthaginian armies had probably avoided these forbidding mountains which provided very bad terrain for elephants. Roosevelt, in his casual, seemingly offhand manner, also talked about the future—particularly OVERLORD. He said to Eisenhower, "Ike, you and I know who was the Chief of Staff during the last years of the Civil War but practically no one else knows, although the names of the field generals—Grant, of course, and Lee, and Jackson, Sherman, Sheridan and the others—every schoolboy knows them. I hate to think that 50 years from now practically nobody will know who George Marshall was. That is one of the reasons why I want George to have the big Command—he is entitled to establish his place in history as a great General." Roosevelt also told Eisenhower of the plan to bring him back to Washington as Acting Chief of Staff. It is probable that Eisenhower expressed to the President his total lack of enthusiasm for a career in the Pentagon Building, but he was a soldier, and he would go where he was sent. Later, Eisenhower was somewhat less certain that these decisions had been finally made, for Admiral King told him of his personal belief that Roosevelt would in the end refuse to move Marshall from his present position. However, King said that in the event he should be proved wrong about this he would certainly welcome Eisenhower to the councils of the Joint Chiefs of Staff.

When the Presidential party took off for the flight to Cairo late Sunday evening, Eisenhower did not know what the future might hold for him and he remained in ignorance for more than two weeks while the memorable conferences were taking place.

On the fourth and last day of the first Cairo Conference some forty-three American and British press correspondents formed themselves into a committee, of which the able Cyrus L. Sulzberger of the *New York Times* was chairman, and signed a round robin letter to Hopkins which began:

> The undersigned correspondents representing all Anglo-American and Dominion newspapers, agencies and radio chains are addressing this to you as an influential friend of the press.
>
> We wish to express the strongest dissatisfaction with the manner in which we are being treated during the present important conferences. We demand that we be taken further into confidence of the authorities on an off-the-record basis and be given some idea of what everything is about in order to prepare our advance material.
>
> We request a conference with yourself wherein we could present some of our problems to a person known to be our friend, of sufficient influence and energy to help us out, and of sufficient experience and understanding to be able to do so.

There followed specific requests, including one for a press conference with the President, Prime Minister and Generalissimo, and for another conference in the event that a Russian delegation might arrive in Cairo after the Chinese had departed. It was suspected that Stalin himself might appear, it not then being known of course that the British and American delegations were going on to Teheran to meet him there. (Andrei Vishinsky, Assistant Commissar for Foreign Affairs, was in Cairo at this time and conferred with Roosevelt and others but took no part in the meetings relative to the war against Japan.)

Had Hopkins met the press, there was not much he could have told them other than the agreements that were subsequently announced in the official communiqué. There was not much more that he could have told them even after V-J Day when the security bars were down. For while this first Cairo Conference had plenty in the way of "color"—the Pyramids, the Sphinx and the extremely chic costumes of Madame Chiang Kai-shek, about which the correspondents could write much more skillfully than Hopkins could—its principal news value was the mere fact that it was held; aside from the declaration assuring the freedom and independence of Korea, the effect of these meetings on the progress of the war or on history was negligible.

The military talks produced a semblance of agreement on an expansion of the ANAKIM plan to drive the Japanese out of Burma and reopen the long-sealed land communications with China: there was to be a determined ground offensive in the north by Chinese, British and

newly assigned American troops under Stilwell's field command, coupled
with large amphibious operations in the south directly under Mountbatten, who would have the benefit of strong units of the Royal Navy,
especially aircraft carriers, which could now be diverted from service
in the Mediterranean because of the surrender of the Italian Fleet.
Chiang Kai-shek was particularly insistent on the necessity for the
amphibious operation. From the records of the few formal meetings
involving the three nations, it would appear that the Generalissimo was
usually reluctant to commit himself on specific details of plans, hedging
each statement with reservations and qualifications; Stilwell, on the
other hand, was not afflicted with any excessive cautiousness in stating
his views as to precisely what was needed to ensure success in Burma.
Of course, the language difficulties presented so many obstacles that
only the larger generalities were sure of getting through. It was quite
clear, however, that Chiang Kai-shek was not interested in the ground
operations in the north, in which his own Chinese divisions would provide the bulk of the manpower, unless the British would agree to
synchronize with them the major moves by land, sea and air in the
south to cut off the Japanese lines of supply and reinforcement, including the railroad that they had constructed from Bangkok to Rangoon.
In one of his few positive statements appearing on the record, the
Generalissimo said, "Burma is the key to the whole campaign in Asia.
After the enemy has been cleared out of Burma, his next stand would
be in North China and, finally, in Manchuria. The loss of Burma would
be a very serious matter to the Japanese and they would fight stubbornly and tenaciously to retain their hold on the country." In all
these discussions, there persisted the question as to just how important
was Burma as a front on which to engage the enemy—as compared with
the various possible battlegrounds in the Pacific Ocean area—and this
always led to the larger question: just how important was China itself
as a front? There is no doubt that Roosevelt and the U.S. Chiefs considered the maintenance of the Chinese Front to be essential, and there
is also no doubt that the Japanese were finally defeated by the attacks
from the Pacific with no decisive battle being fought anywhere on the
mainland of Asia. The huge Japanese forces on the mainland were left
stranded and largely unengaged just as were those in the garrisons at
Rabaul and Truk.

Churchill viewed the proposals for large operations in Burma with
scant enthusiasm; he considered Burma solely as an outpost of the
Empire, rather than as an area of strategic importance. He wanted to
drive the Japanese out of it, not so much for the purpose of gaining
access to China as to avenge a mortal insult to imperial prestige, and he
did not relish the idea that the Americans or, more especially, the
Chinese should have any share in the credit for its liberation. He always

went along with the proposition that the supply route to China must be reopened in order to sustain Chinese morale and to keep this gigantic mass of humanity in the war, but it is apparent that he did this out of deference to Roosevelt's sentiments—or, perhaps, he thought of them as "whims"—and not from any profound convictions of his own.

The most important objectives in Southeast Asia, from Churchill's point of view, involved the re-establishment of British power in Singapore and Hong Kong. This was by no means merely a matter of the advancement of imperial interests. It was based on strategic concepts with which, I believe, Admiral King and Admiral Nimitz were ultimately in agreement; it was the point of view of those who believed in winning the war against Japan primarily by sea power—destroying the Japanese lines of communication and subjecting the home islands to a strangling blockade. Generals Marshall and Arnold and, of course, MacArthur and Stilwell, disagreed with this point of view. They believed that total victory could not be achieved as long as there were substantial Japanese forces on the mainland of Asia, in China, Indo-China, Malaya and Burma (and also the Philippines) which could continue to operate independently for a long time even after their lines of communication with the home islands had been cut.

However, it appears that at Cairo the U.S. Chiefs of Staff were united in approval of the full ANAKIM operation and Roosevelt supported that formula at these first meetings, for he was determined that this conference should be a success from the Chinese point of view. Here was certainly an instance of a sharp division between the British and the Americans on nationalistic lines. It had been intended that Mountbatten's Southeast Asia Command could be organized on the same brotherly, binational basis as Eisenhower's, and this might have been possible if Mountbatten had been completely independent of control by his home government. But that was obviously out of the question, for the decentralization which prevailed in the American military system, giving exceptional authority and freedom of decision to the theater commander, did not obtain with the British. In Eisenhower's command, harmonious and wholehearted co-operation was possible because British and American objectives could be summed up in one word—"Berlin." In Southeast Asia, on the other hand, the British and Americans were fighting two different wars for different purposes, and the Kuomintang Government of China was fighting a third war for purposes largely its own. I believe it may be said, without descending to a low level of chauvinism, that Roosevelt was the only one of the leaders in the entire war against Japan who adhered to the main military objective of destroying the enemy's power and compelling his surrender by the most direct means in the shortest possible time. Hopkins did not set down his views on this subject of Allied disunity in respect to the Far East and the reader will have to take my word for it that I have given a faithful reflection of them. He could not ignore the fact that such disunity existed, nor could Roosevelt, Marshall, King and Arnold, for there were too many emphatic and repeated reminders of it. Hopkins was certainly vehement in his denunciation of any American who by word or deed tended to aggravate it while the war was on, but he was also one who believed that the record is worse than valueless which, like the royal sundial, tells only of the "shining hours" of sweetness and light.

Despite Churchill's obvious reluctance to commit considerable British forces to the proposed campaigns in Burma, Roosevelt at this time went down the line in supporting the view of Chiang Kai-shek, Stilwell, and possibly also of Mountbatten. Therefore, when the Generalissimo and Madame departed for Chungking on November 28, their hopes were high that at last China's demands were to be met with measures that were more than mere words. These hopes, however, were short-lived. The agreement at Cairo did not stick for more than ten days, and it was not until after American forces had started to strangle Japan from the Pacific, in the last six months of the war, that the first trucks started to roll over the Ledo or Stilwell Road from Burma into China. By then it was too late to matter much.

During these days at Cairo, Roosevelt had to spend many hours on the enormous mass of White House papers that had accumulated during his week at sea and been flown from Washington. Included in this were twenty-nine Congressional bills of which he signed twenty-seven and vetoed the other two. It was always necessary for the President to act on these bills within ten days—he could not delegate his authority to anyone in his absence—and this was the consideration which limited the scope of his travel. No previous President could have gone as far from Washington while Congress was in session as Roosevelt did because only the development of the air transport (including the establishment of the intermediate bases) made it possible for documents to be delivered and returned within the ten-day period.

During these days at Cairo, Hopkins formed a friendship with Charles E. Bohlen, a young State Department career man who had been brought along by Harriman from the Embassy in Moscow because of his fluency in the Russian language. Hopkins asked him all manner of questions about the Soviet Union and was surprised and impressed by the objectivity and lack of bias as well as by the considerable scholarship revealed in his answers. Hopkins told Bohlen in characteristic words of the low opinion he had formed of many of the Foreign Service men that he had encountered in his travels, describing them as "cookie-pushers, pansies—and usually isolationists to boot." Bohlen gave so vigorous and intelligent a defense of the State Department, and explanation of the hopeless handicaps under which its personnel often must work, that

Hopkins subsequently persuaded the President to appoint Bohlen to a post in the White House where he would act as a liaison officer with the State Department, thereby filling a really long-felt want. From then on, Bohlen's star was very much in the ascendant, and he later became Counselor of the Department under Secretary Marshall.

On Thursday evening, November 26, Roosevelt was host at a Thanksgiving Dinner at his villa, the residence of Ambassador Alexander C. Kirk, near the Pyramids of Giza some miles west of Cairo. The guests included the Prime Minister, his daughter Sarah, Eden, Winant, Steinhardt and Elliot Roosevelt and Robert Hopkins. Roosevelt proposed Churchill's health, telling of the origin of the American Thanksgiving Day tradition, and of how this old custom was now being spread by American soldiers all over the world, and he expressed his particular delight that this year he could share the Thanksgiving celebration in company with his great friend, the Prime Minister. Evidently, at this point, he seemed to have reached the conclusion of his remarks, and Churchill arose to respond, but Roosevelt told him that he had not yet finished. He then went on to say that Thanksgiving was traditionally a family festival and that this year Britain and America formed one family which was more united than ever before. He was now really finished and, according to the official record, "The Prime Minister responded in his usual masterful and inspiring manner."

There was a meeting at Cairo of Roosevelt, Churchill and the Combined Chiefs of Staff, Hopkins being the only other civilian present, at which a general survey was made of future European operations in anticipation of the forthcoming discussions with Stalin at Teheran. Churchill gave a lengthy résumé of the general situation, reviewing the long series of Allied successes in the Mediterranean which, in recent weeks, had turned into a succession of disappointments on the Italian Front north of Naples and in the Dodecanese Islands. He urged that, despite the heavy German reinforcements that had been sent to the front in Italy, the Allied campaign there should be pushed more vigorously than ever with a view to capturing Rome at the earliest possible date—for "whoever holds Rome holds the title deeds of Italy." He placed particular emphasis on the assurance that he had in no way relaxed his zeal for OVERLORD but he recommended that this major operation should not be such a "tyrant" as to rule out every other activity in the Mediterranean. Among the various activities that he mentioned was the capture of the Island of Rhodes, which had been the ultimate objective of the recent, ill-fated Dodecanese campaign. He said that when the Allies had reached the Pisa-Rimini Line north of Rome, decisions could be taken as to whether the next move should be to the left (toward Southern France) or to the right (into the Balkans). The U.S. Chiefs of Staff had no doubt in their own minds as to just what all this signified. They felt certain that whenever the persistent Prime Minister started talking about Rhodes, or veering toward the "right" from Northern Italy, he was resuming the advocacy of strategic diversions into southeastern Europe and away from Northern France. They prepared themselves for battles at Teheran in which the Americans and the Russians would form a united front.

Roosevelt's party on the trip to Teheran numbered approximately seventy, including the indispensable Filipino mess men from Shangri-la. On the flight from Cairo of 1,310 miles the "Sacred Cow" flew over the Suez Canal, Jerusalem, Baghdad, the Euphrates and Tigris Rivers and the Iranian railroad which by now had become a vital link in the gigantic network of world supply lines.

At Teheran, Roosevelt, Hopkins, Leahy, Brown and Major John Boettiger (the President's son-in-law) at first occupied quarters in the American Legation as guests of the Minister, Louis G. Dreyfus. This Legation was at some distance from the compounds of the Russian and British Embassies which were close together. Harriman told Roosevelt of Stalin's concern over the strong possibility that there were many enemy agents in the city and the distinguished visitors might be subjected to what was described as "an unhappy incident"—a polite way, of course, of saying "assassination"—while driving back and forth between their separated residences.

On the day after his arrival at Teheran—this was Sunday, November 28—Roosevelt agreed to accept Stalin's invitation to move to a villa in the Russian Embassy compound where complete security could be enforced. It certainly was enforced, and the President and his party were never permitted to forget it, for the servants who made their beds and cleaned their rooms were all members of the highly efficient NKVD, the secret police, and expressive bulges were plainly discernible in the hip pockets under their neat, white coats. It was a nervous time for Michael F. Reilly and his own White House secret service men, who were trained to suspect *everybody* and who did not like to admit into the President's presence anyone who was armed with as much as a gold toothpick.

Roosevelt arrived at his new quarters at three o'clock in the afternoon and fifteen minutes later Stalin came to call. This was the first meeting of the wartime leaders of the Soviet Union and the United States. Aside from the President and Marshal Stalin, the only two present at this meeting were the interpreters, Bohlen and Pavlov.

Roosevelt greeted Stalin with the statement, "I am glad to see you. I have tried for a long time to bring this about." Stalin, "after suitable expressions of pleasure at meeting the President, said that he was to blame for the delay in this meeting; that he had been very occupied because of military matters." Roosevelt asked Stalin how things were going on the Russian Front, and Stalin gave a realistic picture of the situation which was somewhat less favorable at the moment than the information then available to the Western Allies had indicated. Roosevelt said that among the main topics for discussion at Teheran were measures which would bring about the removal of thirty or forty German divisions from the Eastern Front and Stalin agreed that such a transfer would be most helpful. Roosevelt then said that, by the end of the war, the American-British merchant fleet would have achieved such proportions that it would be more than the two nations could possibly need and he felt that some of these ships should be made available to the Soviet Union. To this, Stalin replied that an adequate merchant fleet would be of great value, not only to the Soviet Union, but for the development of relations between the Soviet Union and the United States after the war, which he hoped would be greatly expanded. He said that if equipment were sent to the Soviet Union from the United States, a plentiful supply of the raw materials from that country could be made available to the United States.

There was considerable discussion of French affairs during which Stalin surprised the President by expressing the opinion that it was Pétain rather than de Gaulle who represented "the real physical France." There was no doubt in Roosevelt's mind on this and subsequent occasions that Stalin considered the collaborationists more important than the fighters of the resistance movement in expressing French sentiments.

Mention of Indo-China brought the conversation around to the Far East and Roosevelt told Stalin of his conversations with Chiang Kai-shek and the plans for offensive operations in Burma. Stalin expressed a low opinion of the fighting quality of Chinese troops but said that this was the fault of their leaders. Roosevelt referred to one of his favorite topics, which was the education of the peoples of the Far Eastern colonial areas, such as Indo-China, Burma, Malaya and the East Indies, in the arts of self-government; he pointed with pride to the American record in helping the people of the Philippines to prepare themselves for independence. He cautioned Stalin against bringing up the problems of India with Churchill, and Stalin agreed that this was undoubtedly a sore subject. Roosevelt said that reform in India should begin from the bottom and Stalin said that reform from the bottom would mean revolution.

This meeting lasted forty-five minutes but, like all conferences with the Russians, most of the time was taken up in the arduous process of translation. At four o'clock, Churchill and the Combined Chiefs of Staff arrived for the First Plenary Session of the Teheran Conference, which bore the exultant code name, EUREKA. Also present at this first session were Hopkins, Eden and Molotov—and it should be noted that throughout the Teheran Conference Hopkins acted, in effect, as Secretary of State in relationship to the two Foreign Ministers. Stalin's only Chief of Staff was Marshal Voroshilov, and Leahy and King represented the U.S. Joint Chiefs. Marshall and Arnold were not present; they had misunderstood the time of the meeting and had gone off on a sightseeing tour around Teheran.

Stalin and Churchill agreed that the President should take the chair at this first meeting and he opened it by saying that he was glad to welcome the Russians as "new members of the family circle" and to assure them that these conferences were always conducted as gatherings of friends with complete frankness on all sides. He believed that the three nations represented would work together in close co-operation not only for the duration of the war but for generations to come. Churchill said that here was represented the greatest concentration of power that the world had ever seen and that in the hands of those present was the happy future of mankind; he prayed that they might be worthy of this God-given opportunity. Stalin said that this fraternal meeting did indeed represent a great opportunity and it was up to those present to use wisely the power which their respective peoples had given them.

Roosevelt then expressed the American point of view toward the war. He had the impression that Stalin knew very little about the progress of the war against Japan and he therefore dealt with that subject first. He said, according to the record, "that the United States was more directly affected by the war in the Pacific and that the United States forces were bearing the chief burden in that area with, of course, help from Australian and British forces; the greater part of the U.S. naval establishment was in the Pacific and over a million men were being maintained there. He pointed out as evidence of the immense distances in the Pacific that one supply ship operating from the United States could make only three round trips a year. The allied strategy in the Pacific was based on the doctrine of attrition which was proving successful. We were sinking more Japanese tonnage than the Japanese were able to replace. He said that the allies were moving forward through the southern islands and now through the islands to the east of Japan. On the north little more could be done due to the distance between the Aleutian and Kurile Islands. On the west our one great objective was to keep China in the war, and for that purpose an expedition was in preparation to attack through North Burma and from Yunnan province. In this operation Anglo-British forces would operate in North Burma and Chinese forces from Yunnan. The entire operation would be under the command of Lord Louis Mountbatten. In addition, amphibious operations were planned south of Burma to attack the important Japanese bases and lines of communication in the vicinity of Bangkok. The President pointed out that although these operations extended over vast expanses of territory the number of ships and men allocated for the purpose was being held down to a minimum. He summed up the aims of these operations as follows: (1) to open the road to China and supply that country in order to keep it in the war, and (2), by opening the road to China and through increased use of transport planes to put ourselves in position to bomb Japan proper.

"The President then said he would turn to the most important theater of the war in Europe. He said he wished to emphasize that for over one year and a half, in the last two or three conferences which he had had with the Prime Minister, all military plans had revolved around the question of relieving the German pressure on the Soviet front; that largely because of the difficulties of sea transport it had not been possible until Quebec to set a date for the cross-channel operations. He pointed out that the English Channel was a disagreeable body of water and it was unsafe for military operations prior to the month of May, and that the plan adopted at Quebec involved an immense expedition and had been set at that time for May 1, 1944."

At this point, Churchill interposed the remark that the British people had every reason in the past to be thankful that the English Channel was such a disagreeable body of water.

Roosevelt then went on to say that although he was not in favor of any secondary operations which might tend to delay the cross-Channel invasion, OVERLORD, he and the Prime Minister had been discussing possible future operations in Italy, the Adriatic and Aegean Seas, and from Turkey as a base in the event that the Turks might be induced to enter the war. The President also informed the Marshal of the plans for landings in Southern France.

Stalin then spoke of the war in the Pacific, making no bones of the fact that the Soviet Government welcomed all Anglo-American successes against the Japanese. He said that up to now the Russian forces had not been able to join in the war against Japan because of their heavy involvements with Germany. He explained that the Russian forces in Siberia were sufficient for purely defensive purposes but that they would have to be increased threefold before they could be strong enough to engage in offensive ground operations against the Japanese—and he added that when Germany was finally defeated the necessary Russian reinforcements could be sent to Eastern Siberia and then, he said, "We shall be able by our common front to beat Japan." (This was the first assurance given to Roosevelt or Churchill to that important effect.) Stalin gave a detailed analysis of German strength on the Russian Front and described the difficulties encountered by the Red Army in advancing over recaptured terrain where the Germans had systematically destroyed all possible facilities for communication and supply. Referring to the Italian campaign, he said that great benefit had resulted from the freeing of the Mediterranean to Allied shipping but he did not believe that further advances up the Peninsula would be of much avail, for the Alps presented "an almost insuperable barrier, as the famous Russian General Suvorov discovered in his time." He said the entry of Turkey into the war might be helpful in opening the way to the Balkans, but that the Balkans were far from the heart of Germany, and the only direct way of striking at that heart was through France.

Churchill gave assurance that both he and the President had long agreed as to the necessity of the cross-Channel operation and that it was now planned to put one million men on the continent of Europe in May, June and July, 1944. He said that the operations in North Africa and Italy had always been considered as secondary to OVERLORD. Stalin said that he had not meant to convey the impression that he considered these operations as secondary or to belittle their significance since they were of very real value.

Churchill said that the original force for OVERLORD would consist of nineteen American and sixteen British divisions, that being the maximum number that Britain could afford because of its manpower limitations. The additional divisions for the subsequent exploitation of OVERLORD would come in a steady stream from the United States. He said that there might be delays in the launching of OVERLORD—the great bottleneck at the moment being the shortage of landing craft—and that pending such delays the Allied forces should not remain idle. He then reverted to the desirability of getting Turkey into the war, as he did over and over again with a persistence that was both admirable and monotonous.

Roosevelt surprised and disturbed Hopkins by mentioning the possibility of an operation across the Adriatic for a drive, aided by Tito's Partisans, northeastward into Rumania to effect a junction with the Red Army advancing southward from the region of Odessa. Hopkins thereupon scribbled a note to Admiral King: "Who's promoting that Adriatic business that the President continually returns to?" To which King replied, "As far as I know it is his own idea." Certainly nothing could be farther from the plans of the U.S. Chiefs of Staff. Churchill was quick to associate himself with Roosevelt's suggestion, but Stalin asked if the continuation of operations in or from Italy would in any way affect the thirty-five divisions which he understood were earmarked for OVERLORD. Churchill replied at some length that they would not.

Stalin then expressed the opinion that it would be unwise to scatter forces in various operations throughout the Eastern Mediterranean. He said he thought that OVERLORD should be considered the basis for all operations in 1944 and that after the capture of Rome the forces used there should be sent into Southern France to provide a diversionary operation in support of OVERLORD. He even felt that it might be better to abandon the capture of Rome altogether, leaving ten divisions to hold the present line in Italy, and using the rest of the Allied force for the invasion of Southern France. He said it had been the experience of the Red Army that it was best to launch an offensive from two converging directions, forcing the enemy to move his reserves from one front to the other. Therefore, he favored simultaneous operations in Northern and Southern France, rather than the "scattering" of forces in the Eastern Mediterranean. He stated quite plainly, and repeated it several times, his conviction that in any case Turkey would not agree to enter the war.

Churchill said that he could not believe the Turks would be so "mad" as to reject this opportunity to join with the United Nations under the most favorable circumstances, but Stalin observed that there were some people who apparently preferred to remain "mad."

Roosevelt said that if he were to meet with President Inonu of Turkey he would, of course, do everything possible to persuade him to enter the war, but that if he were in Inonu's place he would demand so heavy a price in airplanes, tanks and equipment that the granting of these requests would result in indefinite postponement of OVERLORD.

This first meeting ended at 7:20 P.M.—having lasted three hours and twenty minutes—and thereafter Roosevelt signed four more Congressional bills and a Proclamation and worked on his mail until dinnertime, 8:30, when he was host to Stalin, Molotov, Churchill, Eden, Sir Archibald Clark Kerr (British Ambassador in Moscow), Hopkins, Harriman and the three interpreters. This dinner represented a major achievement by the Filipino sailors who had moved only four hours previously into a strange kitchen, which, because of the haste with which the house had been made available, lacked most of the essential equipment, including a range. These deficiencies had been rapidly supplied and the dinner was served successfully.

Hopkins noted that Stalin was grayer than when he had seen him last in the summer of 1941 and also much dressier, now wearing a uniform with gold epaulettes each bearing a large, white star fastened with a red pin. Stalin doodled and smoked during the meetings. His voice was quiet—barely audible—and he seemed to expend no effort in placing emphasis on anything as he talked to the interpreter. Harriman has said that Stalin in greeting Hopkins at Teheran displayed more open and warm cordiality than he had been known to show to any foreigner; evidently the Marshal saw in Hopkins one who had made promises and done his level best to keep them.

At dinner on the first evening Roosevelt and Stalin discussed Fairbanks, Alaska, as a suitable spot for a later meeting. Stalin again expressed himself on the subject of France whose ruling class, he felt, was rotten to the core; he described the former Vichy Ambassador to Moscow, Bergery, as typical of the majority of French politicians. He did not consider that France could be trusted with any strategic positions outside her own borders in the postwar period. He still seemed to attach little importance to de Gaulle as a real factor in political or other matters.

The conversation turned to the subject of postwar treatment of Germany and the frontiers of Poland. Stalin said that Poland should extend to the Oder and that the Russians would help the Poles to establish their frontier thus far west, but he was not specific about Poland's eastern frontier. According to the record: "The President then said he would be interested in the question of assuring the approaches to the Baltic Sea and had in mind some form of trusteeship with perhaps an international state in the vicinity of the Kiel Canal to insure free navigation in both directions through the approaches. Due to some error of the Soviet translator Marshal Stalin apparently thought that the President was referring to the question of the Baltic States. On the basis of this understanding, he replied categorically that the Baltic States had by an expression of the will of the people voted to join the Soviet Union and that this question was not therefore one for discussion. Following the clearing up of the misapprehension, he, however, expressed himself favorable in regard to the question of insuring free navigation to and from the Baltic Sea."

The following memorandum was written on Stalin's views concerning postwar Germany:

In regard to Germany, Marshal Stalin appeared to regard all measures proposed by either the President or Churchill for the subjugation and for the control of Germany as inadequate. He on various occasions sought to induce the President or the Prime Minister to go further in expressing their views as to the stringency of the measures which should be applied to Germany. He appeared to have no faith in the possibility of the reform of the German people and spoke bitterly of the attitude of the German workers in the war against the Soviet Union. As evidence of the fundamental German devotion to legality he cited the occasion in 1907 when he was in Leipzig when 200 German workers failed to appear at an important mass meeting because there was no controller at the station platform to punch their tickets which would permit them to leave the station. He seemed to think that this mentality of discipline and obedience could not be changed.

He said that Hitler was a very able man but not basically intelligent, lacking in culture and with a primitive approach to political and other problems. He did not share the view of the President that Hitler was mentally unbalanced and emphasized that only a very able man could accomplish what Hitler had done in solidifying the German people whatever we thought of the methods. Although he did not specifically say so, it was apparent from his remarks that he considered that Hitler through his stupidity in attacking the Soviet Union had thrown away all the fruits of his previous victories.

As a war time measure Marshal Stalin questioned the advisability of the unconditional surrender principle with no definition of the exact terms which would be imposed upon Germany. He felt that to leave the principle of unconditional surrender unclarified merely served to unite the German people, whereas to draw up specific terms, no matter how harsh, and tell the German people that this was what they would have to accept, would, in his opinion, hasten the day of German capitulation.

If Roosevelt made any comment on this expression of opinion on the controversial question of unconditional surrender, it was not recorded. But the subsequent record proves that he did not change his mind.

The next morning, Monday, military staff talks were held at which it was determined that it would be feasible to mount an operation against Southern France with a two-division assault and a ten-division follow-up to be launched simultaneously with OVERLORD D-Day or from two to three weeks preceding it. In the study of personnel available in the Mediterranean theater made at this meeting appeared the note, "Eisenhower states that 370,000 Italian troops are now cooperating with Allied Forces," which seemed a remarkable number only ten weeks after Italy's surrender and with two thirds of Italy still in German hands.

During these talks, Voroshilov asked a great many searching questions about innumerable details concerned with the actual preparations for OVERLORD. He was not interested in what the plans were, or the "program" for production; he wanted to know what was actually being *done*. He asked General Brooke point-blank if he attached the same importance to OVERLORD that General Marshall did. Brooke replied in the affirmative but added that he knew how strong the German defenses of Northern France were and that under certain circumstances OVERLORD could fail. Voroshilov said that the British and American forces had clearly demonstrated their superiority over the Germans in the fighting on land in North Africa and more particularly in the air over Europe and that if the U.S. and British staffs really had the will and the desire to go through with OVERLORD it would be successful and would "go down in history as one of our greatest victories." He admitted the difficulties of a trans-Channel operation, as had Stalin, but said that the Russians had encountered comparable difficulties in the crossing of wide rivers and had overcome them because they "had the will to do it."

Marshall, whom both Stalin and Voroshilov obviously recognized as the supreme advocate of OVERLORD and therefore their friend, said that he wished to offer one comment: "The difference between a river crossing, however wide, and a landing from the ocean is that the failure of a river crossing is a reverse while the failure of a landing operation is a catastrophe." Marshall went on to say, "My military education and experience in the First World War has all been based on roads, rivers, and railroads. During the last two years, however, I have been acquiring an education based on oceans and I've had to learn all over again. Prior to the present war I never heard of any landing-craft except a rubber boat. Now I think about little else."

Voroshilov said admiringly to Marshall: "If you think about it, you will do it."

While this meeting was going on, Roosevelt attended to more mail. According to Harriman, Churchill sent over a message suggesting that he and the President have lunch together preparatory to the next Plenary Session that afternoon. But Roosevelt was too conscious of the presence of the NKVD men and did not want the report to be spread that he and the Prime Minister were hatching their own schemes. Harriman conveyed Roosevelt's regrets to Churchill who was not pleased by them and remarked that he could accept rebuffs as well as the next one—but, as Harriman told it, he said, "I shall insist on one thing: that I be host at dinner tomorrow evening. I think I have one or two claims to precedence. To begin with, I come first both in seniority and alphabetically. In the second place, I represent the longest established of the three governments. And, in the third place, tomorrow happens to be my birthday."

Roosevelt lunched quietly with his own household. His son Elliott had arrived that morning from Egypt, his plane having been delayed by engine trouble. After lunch the President had a short session with the Joint Chiefs of Staff, who reported their conclusions on ANVIL, the Southern France operation, and presented memoranda they had prepared for the President to discuss with Stalin for measures to be taken in anticipation of Russia's entry into the war against Japan. At 2:45 Stalin arrived. (The President's log book indicates that Molotov was also present, but the minutes of the meeting make no mention of his being there.) Roosevelt said he wished to lend Stalin a report from a U.S. Army officer who had been with Tito in Yugoslavia and had the highest respect for the work being done there by the Partisan forces. Stalin thanked the President and said he would read the report with interest and return it. Roosevelt then gave Stalin three memoranda:

(1) A request for permission for U.S. bombers from Britain to use Russian air bases for refueling, rearmament and emergency repair in the proposed "shuttle bombing" of Germany.

(2) A request that planning be started at once with a view to establishing bases for upwards of 1,000 U.S. heavy bombers in the Siberian Maritime Provinces for an air offensive against Japan.

(3) Requests for the exchange of information and for further preliminary planning for eventual operations against Japan. In this memorandum Roosevelt said:

Specifically, I have in mind the following items:

a. We would be glad to receive combat intelligence information concerning Japan.

b. Considering that the ports for your Far Eastern submarine and destroyer force might be threatened seriously by land or air attack, do you feel it desirable that the United States should expand base facilities sufficiently to provide for these forces in U.S. bases?

c. What direct or indirect assistance would you be able to give in the event of a U.S. attack against the northern Kuriles?

d. Could you indicate what ports, if any, our forces could use, and could you furnish data on these ports in regard to their naval use as well as port capacities for dispatch of cargo?

Stalin promised to study these documents. (He later agreed to the shuttle bombing not only from bases in the United Kingdom but from Italy as well; he explained that he must defer consideration of the requests relative to the Far East until after his return to Moscow.)

Roosevelt then asked Stalin if he cared to discuss the future peace of the world and Stalin said there was nothing to prevent them from discussing anything they pleased. Whereupon, Roosevelt gave Stalin an outline of his concept of an organization, based on the United Nations, for the preservation of world peace. It was to consist of three main bodies:

First—an Assembly composed of all members of the United Nations which would meet in various places at stated times for the discussion of world problems and the making of recommendations for their solution. Stalin asked if this Assembly was to be world wide in scope, or merely European, and Roosevelt said it should be world wide.

Second—an Executive Committee which would consist of the U.S.S.R., the U.S., the U.K. and China, together with representatives of two European nations, one South American, one Middle Eastern, one Far Eastern and one British Dominion. This Executive Committee would deal with all nonmilitary questions—such as economy, food, health, etc.

Stalin asked whether this committee would have the right to make decisions which would be binding on all the nations. Roosevelt was indecisive in his answer to that one. He did not believe that the Congress would permit the United States to be bound by the decision of such a body. He said that the Committee could make recommendations for settling disputes with the hope that the nations concerned would be guided thereby.

The third body, as set forth by Roosevelt, was what he termed "The Four Policemen"—the U.S.S.R., U.S., U.K. and China. This, as its name implied, would be the enforcing agency—with power to deal immediately with any threat to the peace or any sudden emergency. The President cited the Italian attack on Ethiopia in 1935 as an example of the failure of the League of Nations to deal promptly and forcibly with an act of aggression. He said that had the Four Policemen existed at that time it would have been possible to close the Suez Canal and thereby prevent Mussolini from attacking Ethiopia.

Stalin expressed the opinion that this proposal for the Four Policemen would not be favorably received by the small nations of Europe. For one thing he did not believe that China would be very powerful when the war ended—and, even if it were, European states would resent having China as an enforcement authority for themselves. He therefore suggested, as an alternative, that there be one committee for Europe and one for the Far East—the European committee to consist of Britain, Russia, the United States and possibly one other European nation. The President said that this suggestion was somewhat similar to one made by Churchill for regional committees—one for Europe, one for the Far East, and one for the Americas—and Roosevelt doubted that the Congress would agree to American participation in a purely European committee which might be able to compel the involvement of American troops. He said that only a crisis such as the present one could compel the Congress to agree to such a step—that it would not have been possible to send American troops to Europe in the present war had it not been for the Japanese attack on Pearl Harbor.

Stalin said that if the President's suggestion for a world organization were carried out—particularly the Four Policemen part of it—this might require the sending of American troops overseas. Roosevelt said that he had only foreseen the sending of American naval and air forces to Europe and that any land armies needed in the event of a future threat would have to be provided by Britain and the Soviet Union.

He saw two possible kinds of threat—one minor, and one major—to world peace. The minor threat might arise from a revolution or civil war in a small country, or the kind of Tacna-Arica dispute that sometimes arises between relatively small neighboring states. This could be met by application of the quarantine method, the closing of limited frontiers and the imposition of embargoes.

The major threat would be provided by a gesture of aggression on the part of a large power; in this case the Four Policemen would send an ultimatum to the threatening nation and, if the demands were not immediately met, they would subject that nation to bombardment and, if necessary, invasion. (There seems to be no evidence of any discussion of the possibility that the offending aggressor might be one of the Four Policemen.)

Stalin talked of the immediate problem of the future treatment of Germany. He said that he had discussed the question on the previous day with Churchill and considered that the Prime Minister was too hopeful in assuming that Germany could not rise again. It was Stalin's belief that Germany would be able to recover its power completely within fifteen or twenty years unless forcibly prevented from doing so, and that therefore there must be more certain safeguards than those provided by the type of organization which the President had proposed.

Stalin said that, to provide insurance against another career of aggression by Germany, the United Nations must gain and maintain control of physical strong points not only within Germany and along the borders of Germany, but also at strategic bases outside Germany. He mentioned Dakar specifically as one of such bases. He applied the same rules to the future containment of Japan, naming the islands in the vicinity of Japan as essential bases for the prevention of future aggression.

Stalin said that any organization or committee that might be set up for the preservation of peace must have the power not only to make decisions in times of emergency but to have continued military occupation of the necessary bases against Germany and Japan.

Roosevelt said that his agreement with Marshal Stalin on this was one hundred per cent. He said that although he was fully cognizant of the present weakness of China, he had insisted that the Chinese must participate in the four-power declaration at Moscow because he was thinking far into the future and believed that it was better to have the 400 million people of China as friends rather than as possible enemies.

There was then some discussion of the ability of the Germans to convert apparently peaceable industries secretly to wartime purposes. Stalin said that the Germans had shown great skill in such deception, but Roosevelt expressed confidence that if the world organization were sufficiently strong and effective it could prevent repetition of Germany's secret rearmament.

It was now 3:30, and Stalin and Roosevelt moved over to the large conference room of the Russian Embassy where Churchill, acting on behalf of King George VI, presented to the Marshal the "Sword of Stalingrad." Following this impressive ceremony, the twenty-eight participants in the conference sat down at the large round table and went to work on the Second Plenary Session. It started with a review of the morning staff session by Brooke, Marshall and Voroshilov, and then Stalin fired the big question:

"Who will command OVERLORD?"

Roosevelt replied that this had not yet been decided. Stalin thereupon made it clear that until a supreme commander were named he could not believe in the reality of the operation. Roosevelt must have been sorely tempted at that moment to name General Marshall as supreme commander and have done with it, but he did not do so, for reasons known only to himself. He said that the decisions taken at this Conference would affect the choice of the particular officer, and this probably meant that he would appoint Marshall only if the command involved *all* of Western and Southern Europe instead of OVERLORD alone.

Churchill then launched forth on a lengthy statement along familiar lines. He ranged from the Channel to Southern France to Italy to Yugoslavia to Rhodes and so to Turkey, dwelling for some time on that favorite subject. The record states that the Prime Minister "summed up the tasks before the conference as (1) to survey the whole field of the Mediterranean, and (2) how to relieve Russia, and (3) how to help OVERLORD."

Stalin said, "If we are here in order to discuss military matters, among all the military questions for discussion, we, the U.S.S.R., consider OVERLORD the most important and decisive." He said that, from the Russian point of view, Turkey, Rhodes, Yugoslavia and even the capture of Rome were not important. He recommended that a directive be given to the military staffs as follows:

"(1) In order that Russian help might be given from the East to the execution of OVERLORD, a date should be set and the Operation should not be postponed. (2) If possible the attack in Southern France should precede OVERLORD by two months, but if that is impossible, then it should be launched simultaneously with or even a little after OVERLORD. This would be an operation in direct support of OVERLORD as contrasted with diversionary operations in Italy or the Balkans. (3) The Commander-in-Chief for OVERLORD should be appointed as soon as possible. Until that is done, OVERLORD cannot be considered as really in progress." Stalin added that the appointment of the Commander-in-Chief was the business of the President and Mr. Churchill but that it would be advantageous to have the appointment made here in Teheran.

Churchill made a final and, one must say, gallant attempt in behalf of Rhodes and Turkey as strategic points, but Roosevelt said that it seemed that he and the Prime Minister and the Marshal were agreed on the main directive to the Chiefs of Staff which was to go ahead on the assumption that OVERLORD was the dominating operation and, while the Staffs might make recommendations for subsidiary operations in the Mediterranean area, they must be careful to consider nothing that could possibly cause a delay in OVERLORD.

Stalin thereupon said to Churchill that he would like to ask him a rather indiscreet question: did the British really believe in OVERLORD or were they expressing their approval of it merely as a means of reassuring the Russians? The record is not quite clear at this point but it would seem that Churchill now accepted the inevitable and said that Britain would hurl every ounce of her strength across the Channel at the Germans. Tension still existed, however, so Roosevelt observed that within an hour a very good dinner would be awaiting all of them, with Marshal Stalin as their host, and that he for one would have a large appetite for it. He suggested that the Combined Chiefs of Staff meet again in the morning and settle the matter of OVERLORD once and for all. The meeting then ended.

The official records of these meetings were written with so much circumspection that the inherent drama was largely obscured; but it was far too big to be totally disguised. One cannot read these deliberately dry

Sketch drawn by Roosevelt, at Teheran, showing his conception of the basis of the United Nations Organization.

and guarded accounts without the feeling that here were Titans determining the future course of an entire planet. This was indeed the Big Three. Churchill employed all the debater's arts, the brilliant locutions and circumlocutions, of which he was a master, and Stalin wielded his bludgeon with relentless indifference to all the dodges and feints of his practiced adversary; while Roosevelt sat in the middle, by common consent the moderator, arbitrator and final authority. His contributions to the conversations were infrequent and sometimes annoyingly irrelevant, but it appears time and again—at Teheran and at Yalta—that it was he who spoke the last word.

Sometime during the Teheran Conference Roosevelt drew three circles, which represented his conception of the basis of the United

Nations Organization. The center circle was marked "Executive Committee," the one on the right was marked "4 Policemen" and the one on the left "40 United Nations" (The General Assembly) under which came "I.L.O.-Health-Agriculture-Food." This, so far as I know, was the first crude outline of the U.N. structure put down by Roosevelt who, unlike Hopkins, loved to draw charts.

The dinner on Monday evening was marked by a great deal of "teasing" of Churchill by Stalin; I am not qualified to say whether it was intended or accepted in a spirit of good-humored raillery, but it was evidently unremitting throughout the evening. At one point, when the question of postwar control of strategic bases was being discussed, Churchill stated that Britain did not desire to acquire any new territory but intended to hold on to what she had and to reclaim what had been taken from her—specifically Singapore and Hong Kong—and that while she might eventually release portions of the Empire of her own free will, she could not be compelled to give up anything without a war. Stalin commented on this that Britain had fought well in the war and that he personally favored increases in the British Empire, particularly in the area around Gibraltar which was presently the property of Franco's Spain. When Churchill asked what territorial interests Russia might have in the future, Stalin was quoted as having replied, "There is no need to speak at the present time about any Soviet desires—but when the time comes, we will speak."

During the dinner, Stalin made a surprisingly frank statement of the past quality of the Red Army. According to the record, "He said that in the winter war against Finland the Soviet Army had shown itself to be very poorly organized and had done very badly; that as a result of the Finnish War, the entire Soviet Army had been reorganized; but even so, when the Germans attacked in 1941, it could not be said that the Red Army was a first class fighting force. That during the war with Germany, the Red Army had become steadily better from the point of view of operations, tactics, etc., and now he felt that it was genuinely a good army. He added that the general opinion in regard to the Red Army had been wrong, because it was not believed that the Soviet Army could reorganize and improve itself during time of war."

Stalin had been annoyed that the afternoon conference had ended with reference of the OVERLORD problem to the Combined Chiefs of Staff, for he could not understand why the decision should not be made there and then by Roosevelt, Churchill and himself without interference by a mere "military committee." This was another evidence of the fact, noted by Hopkins on his first trip to Moscow, that there was no real authority in the Soviet Union below the top. However, when the Big Three met again before lunch the next day, Tuesday, Roosevelt asked Churchill to read Stalin the results of the Staff meeting and, when this had been done, Stalin expressed great satisfaction with the decision and promised that the Red Army would undertake offensive operations concurrently with OVERLORD which would demonstrate the importance that the Russians attached to the opening, at last, of the Second Front. But—Stalin again asked—"When will the Commander-in-Chief be named?" Roosevelt said that he would need three or four days to consider the matter and to discuss it with his staff. He said that it had been decided that morning to appoint one commander for OVERLORD, another for the Mediterranean, and probably a third to command the Southern France operation temporarily during the landing phase and the advance up the Rhone Valley to the junction with the main forces in Northern France. Stalin approved this as sound military doctrine—and the military discussions at Teheran were thereby ended; but Churchill had not quit yet.

Perhaps when Churchill's own memoirs of these later years are published there will be revelation of the extent to which he was influenced in his thinking about OVERLORD by the possibility of German collapse before an invasion as a result of some such uprising against Hitler by German generals as that which was actually attempted and bungled after the invasion in July, 1944. There is no doubt that Roosevelt never took this possibility very seriously as a solution to the problems of achieving total victory. Here again he was influenced by grim memories of the results of the Armistice in 1918. Indeed, at the time of the Trident Conference, he decided to issue a statement explaining that the unconditional surrender formula meant that the United Nations would never negotiate an armistice with the Nazi Government, the German high command, or any other organization or group or individual in Germany; this statement was never issued because, Roosevelt said, Churchill persuaded him against it. It seems evident that Stalin would have agreed with Churchill on that point but that he certainly agreed with Roosevelt that Germany could not be defeated by anything less than the application of overwhelming armed force on the continent itself in the west.

It is not a matter of record, but it is the testimony of some who were present at this conference that Stalin was told, unofficially (and not by Roosevelt) that the President would appoint Marshall to the OVERLORD command and that Stalin made evident his conviction that no wiser or more reassuring choice could be made.

Extreme amiability prevailed throughout lunch and a short Plenary Session in the afternoon and at dinner that evening (this was Churchill's sixty-ninth birthday party; Roosevelt's gift to him was a Kashan bowl which he had purchased that day at the local U.S. Army "PX"). During lunch the extremely important question of Russia's need for warm water ports was brought up by Churchill, who said that his government not only recognized the legitimacy of this requirement but also hoped to see Russian fleets, both naval and merchant, on all the seas. Stalin remarked that the British had not felt that way in Lord Curzon's time, and Churchill replied that those were other days. Stalin smiled and said that Russia also was quite different in those days. It was Roosevelt who mentioned the possibility that Russia might have access to the port of Dairen in Manchuria—and he did so for the first time here, at Teheran, and not at Yalta (when, according to legend, he was so enfeebled as to be *non compos mentis*). Stalin immediately expressed the opinion that the Chinese would object to this proposal, but Roosevelt said he thought they would agree to having Dairen made a free port under international guarantee. It is my understanding that Roosevelt was not merely guessing about this—that he had, in fact, discussed this very point with Chiang Kai-shek in Cairo a few days previously.

While Stalin, Churchill and Roosevelt were having lunch that day, Eden, Molotov and Hopkins were meeting for lunch at the British Legation. The main topics of conversation were the future United Nations strategic strongpoints about the world, in which Hopkins took considerable interest, and the question of getting Turkey into the war, about which he appeared to be indifferent. Indeed, in response to a question by Molotov as to whether Turkey's entry would cause a delay in OVERLORD, Hopkins replied that it was the President's impression and that of the U.S. Chiefs of Staff that it would cause such a delay. In that case, said Molotov, Stalin would be opposed to getting Turkey into the war. Eden said it had been proposed that President Inonu be invited to meet the President and Prime Minister in Cairo a few days hence and suggested that a Russian representative be present at these meetings.

On the subject of strategic bases, Hopkins said: "The location of these future strong points and what they will require in the way of land, sea and air forces will have to be worked out with a view as to who would be a potential future enemy. The President feels it essential to world peace that Russia, Great Britain and the United States work out this control question in a manner that will not start each of the three powers arming against the others. The question of building up bases in the Pacific should not be a difficult one. We Americans do not want sovereignty over any of the islands that are freed from the Japanese. The United Nations may exercise some sort of protective influence over them. As regards the Philippines, when they gain their independence we would still consider it advisable to have naval and air bases there under United States rather than United Nations control."

At the dinner that Tuesday evening, Churchill described Roosevelt as one who had devoted his life to the cause of the weak and helpless, one who through his courage and foresighted action in 1933 had indeed prevented a revolution in the United States and had steadily since then "guided his country along the tumultuous stream of party friction and internal politics amidst the violent freedoms of democracy." Proposing a toast to Stalin, Churchill said that the Marshal was worthy to stand with the mightiest figures of Russian history and merited the title of "Stalin the Great."

In reply, according to the record, "Marshal Stalin said that the honors which had been paid to him really belonged to the Russian people; that it was easy to be a hero or a great leader, if one had to do with people such as the Russians. He said that the Red Army had fought heroically but that the Russian people would have tolerated no other quality from their armed forces. He said that even persons of medium courage and even cowards became heroes in Russia. Those who do not, he said, are killed."

It was at this dinner that Stalin made his frequently quoted statement that without American production, the war would have been lost.

Roosevelt expressed the belief that the Teheran Conference had increased the hopes for a better world—and by a better world he meant one in which the ordinary citizen can be assured the opportunity for peaceful toil and the just enjoyment of the fruits of his labors.

Hopkins also made an after-dinner speech at Teheran, telling the Russians that he had made a long and thorough study of the British Constitution, which is unwritten, and of the War Cabinet, whose authority and composition are not specifically defined. He said that as a result of this study he had learned that "The provisions of the British Constitution and the powers of the War Cabinet are just whatever Winston Churchill wants them to be at any given moment." This observation was greeted with loud laughter, particularly from the Prime Minister himself.

At lunch on Wednesday, the final day, there was long discussion of the proposed meeting with the Turkish officials. Hopkins was firm in asserting that before any such meeting there must be detailed agreement as to exactly what form of military assistance should be promised the Turks if they were to enter the war. When Churchill mentioned the requirements for landing craft for an assault on the island of Rhodes in the month of March, Hopkins was so anxious to have the record straight that he wrote out his own version of his comments for inclusion in the minutes, as follows: "Mr. Hopkins again pointed out that the United States Chief of Staff had not given consideration to the detailed requirements of the Turkish Operation. The whole of the Mediterranean was soon to come under the Combined Chiefs of Staff—hence the resources must be examined in the light of that fact. It should be clearly understood that the American side believe that there are no landing craft available for an attack on Rhodes—and more important still that even if the landing craft were available—no decision has been reached as

Mr. Hopkins again pointed
out that the United States Chief
of Staff had not given consideration
to the detailed requirements of the
Turkish operation. The whole of the
Mediterranean was soon to come under
the Combined Chiefs of Staff - hence the
resources must be examined in the
light of that fact.
    It should be clearly understood
that on the American side believe
that there are no landing craft available
for an attack on Rhodes - and more
important still that even if
the landing craft were available -
no decision has been reached as

Hopkins' memorandum for insertion in the minutes of the Teheran to whether or not the landing craft could not be used to better advantage in ~~augmenting~~ some other operation ~~either Crodon or the attack on the~~ South ~~France~~.

Under every circumstance it should be clearly understood that no mention can be made, to President Inonu implied or otherwise that an amphibious landing can be made on Rhodes.

meetings, clarifying the American position on possible military assistance to the Turks.

to whether or not the landing craft could not be used to better advantage in some other operation. Under any circumstances it should be clearly understood that no mention can be made to President Inonu, implied or otherwise, that an amphibious landing can be made on Rhodes."

Here was an instance of Churchill's friend, "Lord Root of the Matter," attempting to nail down an issue so firmly that the Prime Minister would not be able to pick it up and run with it again, particularly in the conferences with the Turks when it might suddenly assume the character of an inescapable commitment.

Following the discussion as to how to get Turkey into the war there was talk about how to get Finland out of it, but no definite conclusions appear to have been reached. During this meeting, Hopkins passed a note to Roosevelt: "Mr. President: What do you think of letting the Russians give dinner tonight—your last chance at Russian food? Harry." To which Roosevelt replied: "O.K. But I have to leave *early* as we sleep at the camp. F.D.R."

During the afternoon, Roosevelt had a private talk with Stalin and Molotov for the purposes of putting them in possession of certain essential facts concerning American politics. It was a cause of wonderment to the President that the Russian leaders appeared to be so inadequately informed as to conditions in the United States or the character of public opinion. They had their full quota of diplomatic representatives and the members of numerous wartime missions to furnish intelligence—in addition to which there was, presumably, the entire membership of the American Communist party. It could only be assumed that, as was so often the case with the most extensive intelligence systems, Moscow believed and trusted those agents who reported what Moscow most wanted to hear—whereas those who sent in objective and sometimes discouraging reports which approximated the truth were suspected of having been contaminated by their capitalistic environment and were transferred to less attractive posts, such as Siberia. The Russians were not the only ones who erred in this respect: American representatives in Moscow whose reports were too favorable were suspected of having gone Communist, and the State Department was traditionally on the alert against any of its Foreign Service officers who displayed the slightest tendency to become pro-British. Thus, it was always safest for those who wrote reports to take an aggressively chauvinist line toward all foreigners.

Roosevelt felt it necessary to explain to Stalin that there were six or seven million Americans of Polish extraction, and others of Lithuanian, Latvian and Estonian origin who had the same rights and the same votes as anyone else and whose opinions must be respected. Stalin said that he understood this, but he subsequently suggested that some "propaganda work" should be done among these people.

Later, Churchill and Eden arrived for the final meeting. There was a discussion of the division of the Italian Fleet on which agreement was immediate, and then one on the frontiers of Poland in which Roosevelt did not take part; it ended with evolvement of a formula much like that which was eventually adopted. There was extensive discussion of

Note from Hopkins to Roosevelt during final meeting at Teheran.

the dismemberment of Germany. Roosevelt submitted a plan for five autonomous states: (1) Prussia (reduced), (2) Hanover and North-west, (3) Saxony and Leipzig area, (4) Hesse-Darmstadt, Hesse-Kassel and the area south of the Rhine, (5) Bavaria, Baden and Wurtemberg—whereas the Kiel Canal and Hamburg, and the Ruhr and the Saar, to be under United Nations control. When Roosevelt offered this suggestion, Churchill exclaimed, "To use an American expression, the President has said a mouthful!" Churchill agreed that Prussia should be separated from the rest; he believed that the southern states should be detached to become part of a Danubian Confederation.

Stalin was not enthusiastic about either proposal, but said that of the two he preferred Roosevelt's. He felt that dismemberment meant dismemberment—that the Prussian officers and staffs should be eliminated but that otherwise he saw little difference between the people of one part of Germany and another. As to putting any parts of Germany in any Confederation, he said that, whatever form it might take, if there were Germans in it they would soon dominate it and the threat of a greater Germany would be revived. He said that there would always be a strong urge on the part of the Germans to unite and that the whole purpose of any international organization must be to neutralize this tendency by applying economic and other measures including, if necessary, force. This discussion ended up nowhere; it was decided that the subject should be considered further by the European Advisory Commission in London.

It had been planned to continue the conference another day, but the weather forecasts indicated that conditions would become unfavorable for flying over the mountains to Cairo and it seemed advisable for the President to leave the following (Thursday) morning. This meant a considerable rush in preparing the official communiqué (which was one of the war's most inspiring statements) and the Declaration on Iran. The latter document was carried by Harriman from Roosevelt to Stalin to Churchill, who all signed it. Then Harriman turned it over to General Patrick J. Hurley who took it to the Shah of Iran, who also signed it. A year later Harriman reported in a memorandum which was confirmed as to factual points by Bohlen that intensive search had failed to reveal the whereabouts of this signed document. Hurley was consulted but he could not remember where he had put it. It finally was located in a White House file.

After dinner Thursday evening Roosevelt said good-by to Stalin. He believed in his heart that the final words of the Teheran Declaration —"We came here with hope and determination. We leave here friends in fact, in spirit, and in purpose"—were more than mere words. He had disagreed with the two men with whom he had been dealing on various important points—he had found Stalin much tougher than he had expected and at times deliberately discourteous, and Churchill's tireless advocacy of his own strategic concepts had been more than ever taxing to patience; but there was one fault in these two men which was gloriously conspicuous by its absence, and that fault was hypocrisy, for all that was great and all that was regrettable in both of them stood out in such unmistakably bold relief that no mask could be thick enough or pliable enough to cover it. Roosevelt now felt sure that, to use his own term,

Stalin was "getatable," despite his bludgeoning tactics and his attitude of cynicism toward such matters as the rights of small nations, and that when Russia could be convinced that her legitimate claims and requirements—such as the right to access to warm water ports—were to be given full recognition, she would prove tractable and co-operative in maintaining the peace of the postwar world.

If there was any supreme peak in Roosevelt's career, I believe it might well be fixed at this moment, at the end of the Teheran Conference. It certainly represented the peak for Harry Hopkins.

Before he could leave this area, Roosevelt had an engagement to fulfill with the American troops of the Persian Gulf Command, and he drove from the Russian Embassy to Camp Amirabad where he spent the night as guest of General Connolly, one of the engineer officers who had been with Hopkins in W.P.A. (The Patterson-McCormick press evidently overlooked the opportunity to find another "plot" in this.) On Thursday morning, Roosevelt took a jeep ride around the camp and made a speech to the isolated, homesick, sun-scorched G.I.'s, who could never even know the stimulus of an air-raid alert or a sounding of GQ. At 9:45 A.M. the President's party took off for Cairo, where a lot more White House mail including nine more Congressional bills and a Proclamation of a "Day of Prayer" had accumulated. On Saturday morning President Inonu and the Turkish delegation arrived, and some mad wag in Cairo circulated the report that all the Turks wore hearing devices so perfectly attuned to one another that they all went out of order at the same instant whenever mention was made of the possibility of Turkey's entering the war.

In the background of this meeting with the Turks were Churchill's talks at Adana following the Casablanca Conference, and a meeting at Cairo between Eden and Numan Menemencioglu, the Turkish Foreign Minister, only three weeks before Teheran. The latter talks had been somewhat less than negative, which accounted for Stalin's lack of confidence in any further attempts. Roosevelt was also skeptical and Hopkins even more so, but Churchill was never discouraged. I believe that the U.S. Chiefs of Staff were actively alarmed that Turkey *might* come into the war and thereby, as General Marshall liked to put it, "burn up our logistics right down the line."

Roosevelt participated with Churchill in two of the meetings with the Turkish President and Foreign Minister. There was another meeting on what was known as "The Foreign Secretaries' level" involving Numan, Eden and Hopkins. (Laurence Steinhardt was present at all these sessions.) And, finally, after the conference appeared to have ended on a basis of "no decision," Churchill held another meeting on his own with Inonu and Numan in an attempt to revive the subject and start all over again.

I see no need to attempt to give a detailed account of these lengthy conversations which ended just about where they began. The record is complete and available for future study by someone who may want to write on "The Failures of the Second World War." Suffice it to say that during the talks Roosevelt frequently betrayed a considerable amount of sympathy for the Turkish point of view and even stated, on one occasion—and this is set forth in the solemn record—that it was quite understandable that these distinguished and amiable gentlemen should "not want to be caught with their pants down."

The Turks were willing to enter the war only when they could be sure they were strong enough to prevent the quick destruction of their country. The strengthening process would inevitably take time, and time was the one thing Churchill did not want to concede, for OVER-LORD was now only six months away and the moment was approaching when its postponement would be impossible.

During the three days—Saturday, Sunday, Monday, December 4-6—that the Turks were in Cairo, conferences of tremendous importance, immediate and permanent, were being held by the President, Prime Minister and the Combined Chiefs of Staff. In an earlier chapter I have expressed my belief that there was only one occasion in the entire war when Roosevelt arbitrarily overruled the unanimous decision of his own Chiefs of Staff; there is, admittedly, some question as to the accuracy of that belief but, if it is true, then this second conference at Cairo was certainly the one occasion. Moreover, Roosevelt felt impelled to renege on his own promise to Chiang Kai-shek, made ten days previously, that the two powerful operations in South East Asia would go forward: the land offensive in North Burma, known as TARZAN, and the amphibious moves, first against the Andaman Islands in the Bay of Bengal, known as BUCCANEER. The British, who would have predominant responsibility for supplying the forces for BUCCA-NEER, were firm in opposition to it. Churchill pointed out that Stalin's sudden and voluntary statement at Teheran of Russia's intention to join in the war against Japan changed the whole strategic picture, removing the need for the establishment of air bases in China since the bases in Eastern Siberia would be more readily accessible by way of Alaska and much more suitable for the bombing of the main industrial centers in Japan. It was undoubtedly the shipping problem, emphasized by Lewis Douglas who was present at Cairo, which influenced Roosevelt's reluctant decision to abandon BUCCANEER altogether, or so to restrict it in scope that it became of inconsequential value. There was plenty of bitterness over this reversal as has been testified by Stilwell's memoirs and the unpublished recollections of the U.S. Chiefs of Staff. But Roosevelt summed up his concept of the basic plan of action as follows:

trip
China

THE WHITE HOUSE
WASHINGTON

Cairo,
December 5, 1943.

MEMORANDUM FOR:

The Prime Minister.

~~The President~~ propose*s* to send over ~~his~~ *my* signature the
following message to the Generalissimo tonight. Do you concur
in this action?

"Conference with Stalin involves us in combined
grand operations on European continent in late spring
giving fair prospect of terminating war with Germany
by end of summer of 1944. These operations impose so
large a requirement of heavy landing craft as to make
it impracticable to devote a sufficient number to the
amphibious operation in Bay of Bengal simultaneously
with launching of Tarzan to insure success of operation.

"This being the case: Would you be prepared go ahead
with Tarzan as now planned, including commitment to
maintain naval control of Bay of Bengal coupled with
naval carrier and commando amphibious raiding operation*s*
simultaneous with launching of Tarzan? Also there is
the prospect of B-29 bombing of railroad and port Bangkok.

"If not, would you prefer to have Tarzan delayed until
November to include heavy amphibious operation. Meanwhile
concentrating all air transport on carrying supplies over
the hump to air and ground forces in China.

"I am influenced in this matter by the tremenduous
advantage to be received by China and the Pacific through
the early termination of the war with Germany.

F D R

I agree.

W
5. XII

"A. Accept OVERLORD and ANVIL [Southern France] as the paramount operations of 1944.

"B. Make every effort to get the additional 18-20 landing craft for operations in the Eastern Mediterranean.

"C. Let Admiral Mountbatten be told that he can keep what he has got, but is going to get nothing else; and that he must do the best he can."

On December 5 Roosevelt and Hopkins prepared and Churchill agreed to the following message to the Generalissimo:

> Conference with Stalin involves us in combined grand operations on European continent in the late spring giving fair prospect of terminating war with Germany by end of summer of 1944. These operations impose so large a requirement of heavy landing craft as to make it impracticable to devote a sufficient number to the amphibious operation in Bay of Bengal simultaneously with launching of Tarzan to insure success of operation.
>
> This being the case: Would you be prepared go ahead with Tarzan as now planned, including commitment to maintain naval control of Bay of Bengal coupled with naval carrier and commando amphibious raiding operations simultaneous with launching of Tarzan? Also there is the prospect of B-29 bombing of railroad and port Bangkok.
>
> If not, would you prefer to have Tarzan delayed until November to include heavy amphibious operation? Meanwhile concentrating all air transport on carrying supplies over the hump to air and ground forces in China.
>
> I am influenced in this matter by the tremendous advantage to be received by China and the Pacific through the early termination of the war with Germany.

No mention was made in this message of the most important factor of all: Stalin's statement relative to Russia's entry into the war against Japan. This was deliberately omitted because of the constant apprehension that no secret was secure in Chungking—and the damage that might result from a leakage on this one was obviously inestimable.

On the same Sunday that Roosevelt made this decision which exerted so considerable an effect on relations with China—and perhaps on the whole course of the war not only in the Far East but in Europe as well—he made the momentous decision concerning the supreme command for OVERLORD. He made it against the almost impassioned advice of Hopkins and Stimson, against the known preference of both Stalin and Churchill, against his own proclaimed inclination to give to George Marshall the historic opportunity which he so greatly desired and so amply deserved.

Marshall has written me of this occasion:

Harry Hopkins came to see me Saturday night [at Cairo] before dinner and told me the President was in some concern of mind over my appointment as Supreme Commander. I could not tell from the Hopkins' statement just what the President's point of view was and in my reply I merely endeavored to make it clear that I would go along wholeheartedly with whatever decision the President made. He need have no fears regarding my personal reaction. I declined to state my opinion.

The next day the President had me call at his Villa, either immediately before or immediately after lunch, I think the latter, where, in response to his questions, I made virtually the same reply I made to Hopkins. I recalled saying that I would not attempt to estimate my capabilities; the President would have to do that; I merely wished to make clear that whatever the decision, I would go along with it wholeheartedly; that the issue was too great for any personal feeling to be considered. I did not discuss the pros and cons of the matter. If I recall, the President stated in completing our conversation, "I feel I could not sleep at night with you out of the country."

Roosevelt thereupon announced his selection of Eisenhower. It was one of the most difficult and one of the loneliest decisions he ever had to make: as events proved, not only in Western Europe but in the whole superb direction of the war, it was surely one of the wisest.

From Cairo, Roosevelt flew back to Tunis and, when he was met there by Eisenhower, said, "Well, Ike—you'd better start packing." Eisenhower at first thought that this meant confirmation of his assignment to Washington as Acting Chief of Staff. On the subsequent flight to Malta and then to Sicily Roosevelt talked at great length to Eisenhower about the prodigious difficulties that he would confront during the next few months at his new headquarters in London, where he would be surrounded by the majesty of the British Government and the powerful personality of Winston Churchill, who still believed, in Roosevelt's opinion, that only through failure of a frontal attack across the Channel into France could the United Nations lose the war. Eisenhower listened attentively to this advice as "The Sacred Cow" droned over the Mediterranean waters where he had made a name for himself.

After Teheran, Hopkins cabled Molotov: "I greatly enjoyed the conferences we held together and I hope that they may be continued. The meetings of Marshal Stalin and the President have, I am sure, done an infinite amount of good in bringing our two countries more closely together for the waging of the war and the peace. I send you my warmest regards."

Molotov replied to this cordial message in kind, saying: "Just like you I cannot but express my satisfaction regarding our work together at the Teheran Conference and the possibility of continuation of this work in the future. The meeting of Premier Stalin with President Roosevelt is of the greatest importance for drawing closer together the peoples of our countries in the interests of the cause of speeding up our common victory and postwar collaboration. Best wishes."

Of utmost significance were the reports from the American Embassy in Moscow on the Russian newspapers which indicated an almost "revolutionary change" in the Soviet attitude toward the United States and Great Britain. It appeared that the whole propaganda machine was turned on to promote enthusiasm for the "Historic Decisions" at Teheran which had solidified Allied unity in the common purpose to shorten the war and to make secure the peace.

On Christmas Eve, Roosevelt made a world-wide broadcast from Hyde Park. He paid tribute to Churchill, saying, "The heartfelt prayers of all of us have been with this great citizen of the world." (Churchill had suffered another severe attack of pneumonia in Africa.) Of Stalin, Roosevelt said, "He is a man who combines a tremendous, relentless determination with a stalwart good humor. I believe he is truly representative of the heart and soul of Russia; and I believe that we are going to get along very well with him and the Russian people—very well indeed."

This was the first Christmas in years that Hopkins had not spent with the Roosevelts. He and his wife and daughter were now moved into their small but cheerful house in Georgetown and Hopkins was very happy with his new surroundings and the prospects for a better world. The President's daughter, Anna Boettiger, had come to visit the family for Christmas and she occupied the Lincoln Study, where Hopkins had lived for three and a half years. She stayed on there, giving invaluable company and comfort and help to her father until he went to Warm Springs to die.

There now must follow a long lapse in this narrative. On New Year's Day, 1944, Hopkins was having a fine time with a gathering of friends, when suddenly he seemed to droop and said that he felt as if he had a cold coming on and had better go upstairs to bed. He was out of commission thereafter for nearly seven months. He went first to the Navy Hospital, then to Miami, and from there to the Mayo Clinic for another severe operation (which was referred to in the letter from Roosevelt that appears in the first chapter). Early in May he went to White Sulphur Springs for a long convalescence.

Some desperate appeals reached him during his illness and a large percentage of them were concerned with China. At one point, T.V. Soong cabled him, "Several years ago when you were in hospital, I recall that against the injunction of your doctor you hurried from hospital when a vital international principle was at stake. Today a fateful decision is again being made . . ." On another message relayed from Soong, Hopkins wrote, "I can't do this sort of thing out here. Tell them I'm *sick*."

On February 2 he knew that an amphibious operation designated FLINTLOCK was on—it was an attack on Kwajalein Atoll in the Marshall Islands—and he knew that his eighteen-year-old son Stephen, a private first class, was there with the Marines. He wrote his son the following letter:

> You can imagine how much my thoughts have been with you during the last few days and I hope that all has gone well. I am sure it has. The Japs can never withstand the force we are throwing at them in the Marshalls.
>
> David is on an aircraft carrier somewhere in that show and it may be you have already seen him.
>
> I heard from Robert a day or two ago and he is being assigned to a new theatre which will get him in the big European push whenever it comes.
>
> Louise and Diana are both well and altogether enjoying the new house.
>
> I have been laid up for the past month in the navy hospital and will probably be here for a couple of weeks more. Then I am going to take a real rest in Miami Beach for another month. It has been nothing serious but I seem to have had more difficulty in bouncing back this time . . .
>
> Do write me if you get a moment, but I presume you will be pretty busy during the next few weeks so I will not expect to hear from you.
>
> At any rate you know that I wish you the best of luck.

That letter was never delivered. While Hopkins was on the train bound for Florida, he received the following telegram: "I am terribly distressed to have to tell you that Stephen was killed in action at Kwajalein. We have no details as yet other than that he was buried at sea. His mother has been notified. I am confident that when we get details we will all be even prouder of him than ever. I am thinking of you much. F.D.R."

When the details did come in, Hopkins was given cause for pride. Stephen had been killed on his first day in combat—the day before his father wrote the above letter. He was carrying ammunition to an isolated machine-gun unit. It was a routine job, of the sort that is done by thousands of soldiers every day in war, and Stephen did it until he fell with the same courage that so many other boys miraculously displayed when it was their duty to do so.

In the hospital, Hopkins was visited by his old Grinnell friends, Robert and Florence Kerr, and he talked to them by the hour about his son, Stephen. He had two messages of sympathy from recent, wartime friends which touched him greatly. One was from Sir John Dill, who himself had only a few months more to live. He wrote: "Harry, this war has hit you very hard. I know of no one who has done more by wise and courageous advice to advance our common cause. And who knows it? Some day it must be known. George Marshall and I have been talking today of the great part which you have played and are playing. So may this sorrow not weight you down too much and may you soon be fit and well to rejoice your friends and continue your great work."

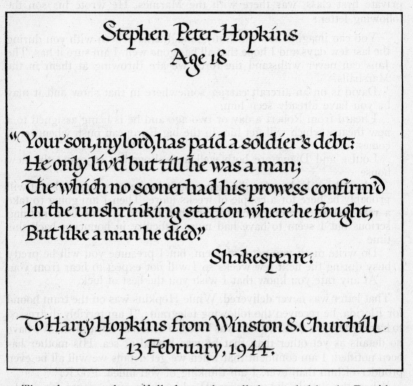

Stephen Peter Hopkins
Age 18

"Your son, my lord, has paid a soldier's debt:
He only liv'd but till he was a man;
The which no sooner had his prowess confirm'd
In the unshrinking station where he fought,
But like a man he died."

Shakespeare.

To Harry Hopkins from Winston S. Churchill
13 February, 1944.

The other was a beautifully lettered scroll, forwarded by the President to Hopkins at the Mayo Clinic. It was inscribed:

> Stephen Peter Hopkins
> Age 18
> "Your son, my lord, has paid a soldier's debt:
> He only liv'd but till he was a man;
> The which no sooner had his prowess confirm'd
> In the unshrinking station where he fought,
> But like a man he died."
>   SHAKESPEARE

To Harry Hopkins from Winston S. Churchill
13th February, 1944

The quotation is from the final scene of *Macbeth*.

When Hopkins moved early in May from Rochester, Minnesota, to the Army's Ashford General Hospital in White Sulphur Springs, there were the usual protests from some of the press. "Who entitles this representative of Rooseveltian squandermania to treatment and nursing in an Army hospital?" was one of the questions. The War Department issued a statement that Hopkins was entitled to this hospitalization as Chairman of the Munitions Assignment Board and that the Secretary of War had authorized his admission.

He was there when the forces went across the Channel into Normandy on D-Day, June 6. He told me a long time later that during the months in hospital he thought endlessly about the various problems that had arisen since 1939, and of how the bottlenecks had been broken and the desperate shortages of strategic materials converted into surpluses, and it all seemed in retrospect as if it had been easy. For production was America's game and the challenge had only to be clearly stated to be met. But, he said, there was one miracle that he could not explain: how did it happen that the United States, an unwarlike and unprepared country if there ever was one, was suddenly able to produce so large and so brilliant a group of military leaders, competent to deal with situations that had never before existed in the history of the world? Where did they come from? And what had they been doing during all those twenty years when our Navy had been used merely to pose for newsreels and our Army had been kicked around like "a mangy, old dog"?

In this connection, I looked into the 1939 edition of *Who's Who in America* and found that although Marshall, King, Arnold, Stark and MacArthur were listed, among those *not* mentioned among the even faintly prominent of that time were: Generals Eisenhower, Bradley, Stilwell, Mark Clark, Patton, Patch, Hodges, Wedemeyer, Spaatz, Kenney, Eaker and Chennault of the Army, or Vandegrift and Howland Smith, of the Marine Corps, or Admirals Nimitz, Halsey, Spruance, Mitscher, Kinkaid, Hewitt, Sherman and Kirk, of the Navy. Considering the list of all the commanders from Pearl Harbor on, it was extraordinary how few failed to meet the tremendous opportunities presented. There was none of the agonizing trial-and-error period through which Lincoln had to pass before he found Grant. This time, with remarkably few exceptions, the right men were assigned in the first place.

Another thought that Hopkins expressed when he had time for reflection was this: "In trying to figure out whether we could have got across the Channel successfully in 1942 or 1943, you've got to answer the unanswerable question as to whether Eisenhower, Bradley, Spaatz, Patton, Beedle Smith, and also Montgomery and Tedder and a lot of others, could have handled the big show as they did if they hadn't had the experience fighting Germans in North Africa and Sicily?"

The debate about the Second Front will probably continue for as long as any of the immediate participants in it shall live, and after that all that will matter is that it actually happened precisely when it did and new world history was made. No one today wastes much time wondering whether William the Conqueror did the right thing in selecting the year 1066.

CHAPTER XXXI

The Fourth Term

ON JULY 4, 1944, Hopkins left the hospital in White Sulphur Springs and flew back to Washington to continue his convalescence in his Georgetown home. During the next three weeks he went to the White House very occasionally to see the President, but he was incapable of doing much work or catching up with the bewildering series of victories that were being achieved all the way from Guam and Saipan in the Marianas Group, within B-29 range of Japan itself, to the Vitebsk-Mogilev line, which represented the last ditch for the Germans on Russian soil. (This huge area of victory, be it said, did not include Burma and China; indeed, the military situation in China was about to become much worse than at any time since the Marco Polo Bridge "incident" in 1937.)

On June 28, the Republicans had nominated Thomas E. Dewey as their candidate for President. On July 11, Roosevelt announced that he would run for a fourth term if nominated by the Democratic National Convention, which was to be held in Chicago during the week of July 19. While the convention was in progress, Roosevelt traveled to San Diego and there embarked for Pearl Harbor to meet with Admiral Nimitz and General MacArthur for the determining of future strategy in the war in the Pacific. The main decision to be made there, as I understand it, was between the Navy plan to devote the ground forces to landings on Formosa, and the MacArthur plan to liberate the Philippines; Roosevelt ultimately decided in favor of the latter, and there were some cynics (especially in the Navy) who remarked in undertones that perhaps the President's choice had been influenced by the thought that the Philippines would provide a more popular victory in an election year.

On July 19, Churchill cabled Hopkins explaining his concern about the forthcoming Southern France operation (ANVIL). There was continuing debate about the wisdom of that move—and Churchill was still arguing doggedly for the application of Anglo-American forces to the Balkans. At this late stage, the Prime Minister may have been concerned by the smashing Russian advances, especially those toward Southeastern Europe. The shattering of the Vitebsk-Mogilev line brought the Red Army well into Poland and Lithuania and close to East Prussia; the Russians had already entered Rumania and reached the eastern tip of Czechoslovakia and there appeared to be nothing that could stop them from pushing on to the Danube and across it into Bulgaria and Yugoslavia to the borders of Greece and Turkey. Churchill emphasized the need for another major conference saying that affairs were getting into a most tangled state for the Three Great Powers—or, he added, for the Four Great Powers, if China were still included. He asked if Hopkins would accompany the President on the Pacific journey, and Hopkins replied:

> I am remaining here in Washington and not going with the President. I am able to work only two or three hours a day. Things seem to be going extremely well in the war and I think that Hitler is now really on the run. The President showed me his message to you suggesting a conference which I imagine will soon come off and I hope to be there. I look forward to Beaverbrook's arrival which will assure a big breeze here in Washington.

Hopkins then wrote to Sir John Dill: "The Prime Minister sounds a little jittery, but maybe he is turning his professional manners loose on me."

On that same day, July 20, occurred the following events: General Tojo resigned as Premier of Japan, being succeeded by General Kuniaki Koiso; a bomb planted in a conference room almost brought the life of Adolf Hitler to a timely end; and F.D.R. was renominated for a fourth term, the Democrats naming Senator Harry S. Truman as his running mate on the following day.

The British Eighth and the American Fifth Armies had been advancing steadily up the Italian Peninsula since the breakthrough at Cassino and from the Anzio beachhead and the taking of Rome on June 4, just two days before OVERLORD D-Day, a juxtaposition of events which appeared to be due to superb co-ordination of Allied planning but which was actually largely fortuitous. The Germans had been driven back to the line from Pisa through the outskirts of Florence to Ancona and it seemed that the Allies would soon reach the Valley of the Po. During the six weeks since the first landings in Normandy, the build-up there had gone ahead at such a phenomenal rate that it approximated a total of one million and a half men, a million and a half tons of matériel, and upwards of half a million vehicles—and all this had been done without benefit of a large port, the harbor at Cherbourg not yet having been cleared. On July 26 came the break through St. Lo, followed by the immortal sweep of the Third Army across the base of the Brittany Peninsula and up the Loire and across the Seine.

Hopkins wrote to the President saying that his talks with Beaverbrook had "indicated to me how difficult it is to hold a formal economic conference with Great Britain on any single subject at this particular time. Max, himself, was quite unhappy, not so much because he did not have his way about the agreement but because he claims he senses a good deal of hostility there. One of our present difficulties is that everybody thinks the war is over. I hope if you decide to speak on the radio from Seattle, that you will scotch this. I think the American people have no idea of the severe tests we have ahead of us, particularly in the complete defeat of Japan."

The "hostility" sensed by Beaverbrook was attributable to the sentiment, widely expressed in Washington at that time, that while the American forces in France were dashing ahead at a devil-may-care rate of speed and with thrilling success, the British under Field Marshal Montgomery on the Allied left flank seemed to be "dragging their feet." It was reported that Eisenhower was so annoyed and worried about this that he had even appealed to the Prime Minister to visit the 21st Army Group Headquarters near Caen in Normandy to try "to persuade Monty to get on his bicycle and start moving." Montgomery had always been a highly controversial figure, and also a conspicuously independent one. After the Teheran Conference, the U.S. Joint Chiefs of Staff were depressed to hear that Montgomery had been named to command the ground forces in OVERLORD; although they had utmost respect for his demonstrated qualities as a superb soldier, they considered him a commander of the "down to the last shoelace" school, and they feared that he would delay and postpone to such an extent that the one opportunity favorable as to weather for this enormous and complex operation would be lost. However, in this respect, they were pleasantly disappointed—for once Montgomery became involved in OVERLORD he was its determined champion and helped greatly in "beefing it up" and in resisting every attempt to sabotage it—and he accepted the date set by Eisenhower and stuck to it. It is not for me to comment on the reasons for or against his subsequent delays, but I may say that I look forward with great interest to reading what the two highest living authorities, Eisenhower and Churchill, have to say about this subject. Much has been written about it already by considerably lesser authorities and the disputes between Bradley and Patton and Montgomery have been underscored and, quite possibly, overemphasized. Although these are represented as Anglo-American disputes which are said to demonstrate the hopeless differences between the two nations, it should be pointed out that at the very same time there were immeasurably more bitter and more irreconcilable feuds between two American generals in China, Stilwell and Chennault, and two other American generals who were commanding adjoining forces in the Marianas campaign and both of whom happened to bear the name of Smith. Hopkins, of course, had been deeply involved in the Stilwell-Chennault fracas, but he was glad to have no part in the distasteful battle of the Smiths in which the adherents of these two honorable generals (one Army and one Marine Corps) hurled charges of extreme ugliness.

The Hopkins papers are very incomplete at this point for, although he was given access to all the cables that passed through the White House to and from the President on the Pacific trip, he no longer had any real responsibility for them. He was now an adviser but not a prime factor. On June 26, he cabled Roosevelt:

Having given considerable thought to the forthcoming conference, I feel that while it would have been advantageous for you to have gone almost anywhere for a meeting with Churchill and Uncle Joe together, it seems to me that in view of Uncle Joe's message you have nothing to gain by going to meet Churchill alone. I believe that the world would construe a conference between you and Churchill somewhere in Europe or in England as a political meeting which had left Russia out in the cold. You may well want to take up various important matters with Churchill soon, in which case, it would be much better to have him come to you instead of you going to him, and the sooner the better. As to Uncle Joe, he obviously wants to postpone his next meeting with you until after Germany collapses.

On August 6, Churchill sent Hopkins a long cable in which he explained his grief, in the midst of victory, that there still should be differences of opinion between the Allies on strategy. This was barely a week before the embarkation of the troops for the landing in Southern France, but Churchill was still attempting to prevent this operation from taking place. He said that the Riviera coast was well fortified, that Toulon and Marseilles were veritable fortresses, and that the enemy in that area was much stronger than the Allies could hope to be. This time, however, he did not urge that the ten divisions for ANVIL should be sent into the Balkans; he recommended strongly that they be dispatched around to the west coast of France to join with the OVERLORD forces in the region of St. Nazaire. He figured that in this way they would be brought into the main campaign far more quickly, for he estimated that even if the landing in Southern France were successful there would be a long, slow, bitter fight up the Valley of the Rhone and that it would take ninety days for these forces to effect a junction with Eisenhower's armies in the north.

Hopkins replied to Churchill that, while he had not heard from the President concerning the proposed change in ANVIL plans, he felt sure that the answer would be in the negative. He expressed his own view that "it would be a great mistake to change the strategy now; it would delay the sure liberation of France rather than aid it. Our tactical position today, it seems to me, is precisely as it was planned and as we anticipated it when ANVIL was laid on. Furthermore, it is my belief that northern advance from Southern France would go much more quickly than you expect. There is not enough enemy strength there to stop us. The French resistance fighters will rise up and abyssiniate large numbers of Germans and also, let us hope, Laval." It was indeed much quicker than Churchill expected. The forces under the brilliant command of General Alexander M. Patch—one of the most widely unrecognized heroes of the war—took Toulon and Marseilles far ahead of schedule, then swept northward and established contact with General Patton's Third Army near Dijon exactly four weeks after they had first hit the Riviera beaches.

It appears that there was some talk about holding the forthcoming Roosevelt-Churchill conference in Scotland, and doubtless the President would have loved that, but he agreed with Hopkins' advice and sent a radiogram naming Bermuda as a possible meeting place. Churchill said that he had received reports of the climate there in September and suggested a return to the Quebec citadel in September, which was agreed on. Various communications passed between Hopkins and Churchill preparatory to this conference. They related largely to what was called "Phase Two"—the period following German surrender when Lend Lease would be continued to Britain, on a somewhat different basis, to aid in the promotion of British economic recovery. There was also the usual discussion concerning the size of the delegations that each nation would send to the conference, and some understandable confusion arose among the Canadian hosts, who had to make all the arrangements for accommodations, when Roosevelt notified Mackenzie King that the American delegation would number not more than fifteen or twenty people and that the British would have a like number, whereas the lists furnished by the Chiefs of Staff showed that there would be some three hundred Americans and two hundred and twenty-five British. (The larger figures were correct.) Through all these communications Hopkins spoke as one who would of course be present at the conference—as he had been present at every major conference thus far in the war, including some at which he was the only American delegate—but on August 28 he sent the following cable: "Dear Winston— Although I am now feeling much better I still must take things easy and I therefore feel that I should not run the risk of a set-back in health by attempting to fight the battle of

Quebec on the Plains of Abraham where better men than I have been killed."

Churchill replied that he was greatly depressed to hear this news.

Hopkins' excuse was hardly convincing, for he had never allowed considerations of his health to stop him from going anywhere at any time when he thought he might accomplish something. If he had ever given any thought to the importance of his own survival, he would probably have spent the entire war in bed, subsisting on liver extract and amino-acid powder. The fact of the matter was—and this was later confirmed by Hopkins to Churchill directly—that a distinct change had come about in the character of his relationship with the President. I do not know just when this was made known to Hopkins, or how it was made known, but Roosevelt's need for Hopkins' counsel and even more for his companionship was no longer so great that the President was willing to defy the criticism which invariably arose in the hostile press whenever Hopkins took Hull's place at an important conference. There was no open breach between them, as there had been irreparably between Wilson and House. There was simply an admission that while the friendship continued and Hopkins would still be useful in various ways, particularly on the domestic political front, he was no longer physically fit to share the burden of responsibility for the big decisions of the war. The trouble was that he had been out of commission too long and Roosevelt had of necessity lost confidence in his ability to stand up under the strain of a job that could never be performed on a part-time or even on a forty-eight-hour-a-week basis.

The fact that this considerable but temporary change in the Roosevelt-Hopkins relationship did not become publicly known proves that very few people were aware of it. If even an intimation of it had been passed about official Washington, there would surely have been a leak here or there, and the hostile columnists would have been overjoyed to advertise it. They might eventually have mourned the loss of Hopkins as an always convenient whipping boy, but they could not possibly have resisted the immediate, glorious opportunity to hold festival rites over his fall from favor.

On September 1, John G. Winant sent the following letter to Hopkins from London:

You do not know how greatly your decision not to go on to the Conference has been regretted by our friend here. His message to the President will have told you of his illness on arrival which is only known to a dozen people here. Tonight his temperature is back to normal and he seems on the way to a quick recovery. But each journey has taken its toll and the interval between illnesses has been constantly shortened. There is no one that I have known here who cares so much about friendly relationships between Great Britain and the United States, and few people anywhere who have been more loyal in their friendship to the President.

The Conference will undoubtedly consider the planning of the war against Japan. No thoughtful person can approach the problem without remembering that Great Britain has been fighting for five years and that they are at the bottom of the barrel as regards manpower. Men from 16 to 65 are conscripted, and women from 18 to 50. The country has been on short rations for this entire period. I live on them and know what this means. The British Army is older than our Army. The British Navy is older than our merchant seamen. Only the Royal Air Force has been able to continue to recruit the youth of the country. In the Battle of Britain it saved Britain. In the intervening years its continuous operation has done much to save life in the other services, but it has taken a frightful toll of the youth of the country.

When the war with Germany is over the war with Japan will begin for Great Britain, in spite of the early defeats at Hong Kong and Singapore, and the fighting in Burma. I have talked about this with many soldiers and sailors and airmen. I knew General Wingate well, and had something to do with his assignment to the Far East. He told me once that out of every 100 men they sent him, sixty had to carry forty. That means that you have to have a selective army if you are to fight the Japanese successfully in tropical areas. I have talked with Admiral Cunningham, and he told me that special arrangements should be made for Navy personnel who move to the Far East. Men should have better wages than at present and both soldiers and sailors' families should be given larger family allowances if the wanted men are to continue in active service. The Royal Air Force is better positioned to move eastward but adjustments would also have to be made in that service.

The careful planning that General Marshall has made to prepare our armies for the transition period as we move from the western theater eastward, by educational films and in other ways, has no counterpart in the present British thinking. The whole field of psychological preparation for what for them will be the second war has been largely neglected.

It has always interested me that the plans for demobilization following the defeat of Germany have been treated with the utmost secrecy for fear of creating misunderstandings in the United States in relation to the serious intentions of Great Britain to fight a war against Japan. And yet there are many people who are now mobilized in the war against Germany who would be utterly useless in fighting a war against Japan. I have never questioned this policy since the President is a friend of Great Britain, and even a sensible demobilization in a presidential campaign might be used against him.

All that is one side of the picture. The really gallant people of Great Britain are as anxious to join us in the fight against Japan as we are ourselves to defeat Japan, and yet for all that there has seeped into this country through military channels a belief that the British Navy is not wanted in the Pacific. I know the practical side that many of our Navy men feel that the British Navy was built for short hauls with available ports that ringed the world, and that conversion would mean clogging our navy yards and strengthening the British Navy in the postwar years. There is some truth to it all, and yet if we allow the British to limit their active participation to recapture areas that are to their selfish interests alone and not participate in smashing the war machine of Japan, if British soldiers don't cross the Atlantic to our ports and entrain for our Pacific ports in order to move against Japan, and if we shuck the British air force in order to prove our own dominance in the air, we will create in the United States a hatred for Great Britain that will make for schisms in the postwar years that will defeat everything that men have died for in this war. Repetition of the tragedy of 1918 will be unforgivable.

I have not found more than a dozen Englishmen interested in this problem, and no one from the United States in any way concerned about it.

What are you doing about it? I hope the President is interested.

Delivery of this letter must have been rapid, for Hopkins replied on September 4:

I hasten to reply to your letter relative to the implications of the British participation in the war against Japan. First of all I want to assure you that a number of us are greatly concerned about it and I am very hopeful that the President will land up on the right side of this problem.

I am well aware of the attitude in certain circles here, but I am convinced that they are not, in any sense, representative of public opinion. The difficulty, in matters of this kind, is that public opinion gets no opportunity to express itself and, indeed, can know nothing about it until the damage is irrevocable.

There, obviously, must be some demobilization of the British Armed Forces after the collapse of Germany, just as I have no doubt there will be some of our own. Ours will be less dramatic and, therefore, will receive far less attention. It will, no doubt, take the form, first, for practical purposes, of stopping of enlistments and inductions in the Armed Forces, but I have no doubt that hundreds of thousands of men will be quietly separated from the Armed Forces for good and sufficient reasons. It is quite easy to accelerate the discharges either simply by raising the standards as to physical fitness or age. The same will not be true in England. There is no possibility of her transferring the whole of her Armed Force either to the occupation of Germany or for the war against Japan. Such a force as England now has under arms will not be required, but I hope the British will continue their policy of playing this down for nothing could be worse than to have any public announcement of British plans for demobilization.

We simply must find a way to have Great Britain take her full and proper place in the war against Japan. This, with the best goodwill in the world, is full of many difficulties—transportation, supply, etc.

You know as well as I that we do not have a chance to get a genuinely good peace unless Russia, Great Britain and the United States can see eye to eye and this means far more than the narrow confines of government in the Foreign Offices. It means, so far as Great Britain and the United States are concerned, that great masses of people must approve our policies. The more I see of the problems and conflicts engendered by the kind of thing that you have written me about, the more I realize how essential it is for us to have men managing our affairs who have a deep and profound conviction not only about world peace and the harnessing of Japan and Germany, but about the bold moves which must be made if a world economy is to be developed which can provide the environment without which our goals can never be attained.

In saying all this, I would say that I hope very much that you, personally, are going to remain close to this thing in some capacity or other for the next few years. Needless to say, I believe the President is essential to it and there is little hope of accomplishing much without his re-election. This, I should tell you, I believe will take place, but I am the world's worst political guesser.

As ever, with this note I send my warmest and most affectionate regards.

Among "the bold moves which must be made," in Hopkins' opinion, were the continuance of some form of Lend Lease by the United States even after the cessation of hostilities, and a relaxing by Britain of the system of imperial preference which was so dear to Beaverbrook's heart and which had been something of a bone of contention ever since the drafting of the Atlantic Charter. The day before Roosevelt left for Quebec, Hopkins wrote him a note saying, "I think it is important, in Quebec, that you tell the Prime Minister how strongly you feel about knocking down some of the trade barriers to get somewhere in terms of world trade. I have a feeling that the Prime Minister thinks that that is a pet hobby of Secretary Hull's and that you may not think it of great importance. I think it is essential to our future bargaining with Great Britain that you disabuse the Prime Minister's mind of this. I rather think that he thinks that the genius of this program in America lies with Secretary Hull, while the truth of the matter is that it is a program that, from the beginning, has been pushed by you."

The physical setting of the second Quebec Conference was familiar but the surrounding atmosphere was utterly new and strange. More than nine months had passed since the last Roosevelt-Churchill meetings at Teheran and Cairo—the longest lapse since the first encounter at Argentia—and in that time the whole aspect of the war and of the world had changed completely. Now the Germans were fighting on both

Eastern and Western Fronts *on their own soil*. Deep in the consciousness of all the Allied leaders, military and civilian, who were old enough to have served in the First World War, was the hope if not the conviction that the Germans would quit, as they had done in 1918, once they were forced back behind their own frontiers. It was true that they now had the Siegfried Line in the West, but these fortifications were broken near Aachen by American troops on September 15 after an assault of only two days; and there was no Siegfried Line in the East. Furthermore, the intelligence reports and estimates of German strength in the West indicated that total collapse might be imminent. There was even consideration of the possibility that the Germans might deliberately permit the Anglo-American forces to break through and surge across Germany in the hope that in this way the Reich would be spared from the awful vengeance that it had earned at the hands of the Russians.

There was, in short, a general belief among the higher authorities assembled at Quebec that German surrender could come within a matter of weeks or even days. (Roosevelt was less optimistic than most about this.) The Allies were well prepared for war to the death in Europe, but they were very ill prepared for the cataclysm of sudden total victory. It will be remembered that when the question of the future treatment of Germany had come up for discussion among the Big Three at Teheran, agreement had not been reached or even nearly approached. It had been decided to refer this explosive subject to the Russian-British-American Advisory Committee in London and there it had remained through many long months of inconclusive conversations and "exchanges of view" on all manner of subjects, beginning with the primary one as to which nation would occupy which zone. It was felt that some specific directive must be issued to General Eisenhower and various proposals were made—the most famous or most notorious of them being "The Morgenthau Plan." The circumstances of the origination of this plan, and of its initialed approval by Roosevelt and Churchill, and of the violent repercussions when news of it was leaked to the press, have been described in detail from various points of view by Cordell Hull, Henry L. Stimson and Henry Morgenthau, Jr., himself—and Winston Churchill will undoubtedly be heard from on this subject in due course. The Hopkins papers, while full of relevant material, tell nothing which has not already been revealed. There is no doubt that Hopkins, as a member of the President's Special Cabinet Committee, joined with Hull and Stimson in opposition to the plan, and I can confirm from my personal knowledge Stimson's statement that Roosevelt subsequently made no secret of his regret that he had ever agreed to initial the proposal. Indeed, on October 20, six weeks after the Quebec Conference, Roosevelt gave demonstration of his reaction to the episode by dismissing *all* specific planning for the treatment of Germany; he said, in a memorandum to Hull, "I dislike making detailed plans for a country which we do not yet occupy," adding that the details were "dependent on what we and the Allies find when we get into Germany—and we are not there yet." (After the first break into Germany near Aachen, the Allied advance had been halted.)

Roosevelt gave evidence of the extent to which Hopkins' position had changed at that time. In a memorandum, also addressed to Hull, on the progress of the Quebec Conference, he wrote: "We have discussed the question of the scope and scale of mutual lend-lease aid between the United States and the British Empire after the defeat of Germany and during the war with Japan. We have agreed that a temporary joint committee shall be set up to consider this question. Among American membership would be Stettinius, Morgenthau and Crowley."

In neglecting to appoint Hopkins even to membership in a committee for consideration of the subject which, for more than three and a half years, had been Hopkins' particular province, Roosevelt was undoubtedly influenced by political considerations. Unpleasant suggestions had reached the President's ears to the effect that Hopkins was too thoroughly under the domination of the British, or of the Russians or the Chinese, to be a reliable representative of American interests in these important negotiations relative to postwar material and economic aid. Of course, similarly dark intimations and even worse ones about Hopkins had been reaching Roosevelt ever since the earliest days of the feud with Harold Ickes in 1933, and Roosevelt had paid no heed to them; but he paid heed to them now.

I had been overseas in the European and Mediterranean theaters since early in February, 1944, so I knew very little directly of what was going on in the White House during OVERLORD and the Democratic Convention and ANVIL and the second Quebec Conference. On September 12, Hopkins sent me a message saying that the President wanted me to come back. I was in liberated Paris at the time but I flew immediately to London, boarded a C-54 (bucket seats) of the Army Transport Command and flew the usual route via Prestwick, Iceland and Newfoundland to Washington. On arrival, I learned from Hopkins, Rosenman, Pa Watson and Steve Early that there was some cause for alarm about the forthcoming political campaign. There appeared to be a considerable amount of lethargy among the voters which could result in a small registration and an even smaller turnout on election day. This had happened in the Congressional election of 1942 and had resulted in substantial Republican gains. It was obvious that if large masses of people, particularly in organized labor, were so sure the President could not lose that they would feel no need to register and vote the President could be defeated. Dewey was traveling up and down the country making carefully planned and generally unexceptionable speeches which were well calculated to mobilize the maximum Republican vote but at the same time to create no particular excitement. He did not attack the conduct of the war. He did not attack Roosevelt's social objectives. He repeatedly described the present administration as a group of "tired old men," and this was not easily refuted, for those in highest authority were unquestionably tired and were getting no younger day by day. Dewey also referred repeatedly to the recurrent wrangles and squabbles and unseemly cat and dog fights that broke into the public prints with disagreeable frequency. Here again he was on sure ground: there had been another final bust-up in the War Production Board which resulted in the resignation of Charles E. Wilson due to a series of press attacks which, he said, had been instigated by Donald Nelson (Roosevelt sent Nelson to China on an apparently meaningless mission and appointed Julius Krug as Acting Chairman of W.P.B.). Later, during October, the long-suppressed enmities between Stilwell and Chiang Kai-shek and Chennault burst out in violent explosion and Roosevelt was compelled to issue orders for the recall of Stilwell who had become, and deservedly, a popular hero to the American people.

However, it was not what Dewey was doing or saying that provided the present cause for worry to Hopkins and the others in the White House; it was the indifferent attitude of Roosevelt himself. He seemed to feel that he had done his duty by allowing his name to be placed before the American people, and if they did not want to re-elect him, that would be perfectly all right with him. As Watson put it, "He just doesn't seem to give a damn." Therefore, the main problem was to persuade the President to descend from his position of dignified eminence as Commander in Chief and get into the dusty political arena where he was still undisputed champion.

There was a great deal of extremely ugly whispering about the state of Roosevelt's health. When he had made his acceptance speech just before his departure for the Pacific tour in July, a photograph had been taken in which he appeared haggard, glassy eyed and querulous—and this photograph had been given very wide advertisement in the press and in the pamphlets with which the Republicans were flooding the country. On his return from the Pacific trip, Roosevelt had made a nation-wide broadcast from the Bremerton Navy Yard at Seattle; when he delivered this speech he wore his leg braces for, I believe, the first time since he had returned from Cairo and Teheran and he was in such pain that he had to support himself by holding on to the lectern with all the tremendous strength of his arms and hands, which made it extremely difficult for him to turn the pages of his reading copy and made the speech sound faltering and uncertain to the listeners who were accustomed to the calm, confident and cheerful assurance that he always conveyed. It was a significant fact that, after this speech, the public opinion polls indicated a sudden and ominous slump for Roosevelt and a consequent rise in Dewey's stock.

When I first went in to see the President after my return from Europe—I had not seen him for eight months previously—I was shocked by his appearance. I had heard that he had lost a lot of weight, but I was unprepared for the almost ravaged appearance of his face. He had his coat off and his shirt collar seemed several sizes too large for his emaciated neck. But I soon began to suspect that the fears expressed by Hopkins, Watson and the others were groundless. He seemed to be more full of good humor and of fight than ever. He asked me if I had listened to any of Dewey's speeches and when I said I had not yet had the pleasure, he said, "You ought to hear him. He plays the part of the heroic racket-buster in one of those gangster movies. He talks to the people as if they were the jury and I were the villain on trial for his life." Then Roosevelt said, "I'm going to give a speech to Dan Tobin's boys next Saturday night and I expect to have a lot of fun with that one." He handed me a sheet of paper, saying it was a paragraph he had dictated to Grace Tully for use in this speech. It read as follows:

The Republican leaders have not been content to make personal attacks upon me—or my wife—or my sons—they now include my little dog, Fala. Unlike the members of my family, Fala resents this. When he learned that the Republican fiction writers had concocted a story that I had left him behind on an Aleutian Island and had sent a destroyer back to find him—at a cost to the taxpayer of two or three or twenty million dollars—his Scotch soul was furious. He has not been the same dog since. I am accustomed to hearing malicious falsehoods about myself but I think I have a right to object to libelous statements about my dog.

When I read that, I knew precisely what kind of speech he proposed to give at the dinner of the Teamster's Union. He was certainly not going to remain on the lofty Commander-in-Chief level.

Whenever the Hearst-Patterson-McCormick press referred to my activity as a "ghost writer," they always spoke of my background as a Broadway playwright and the one play invariably identified with my name was "Idiot's Delight." It was often suggested that my function in the White House was to stud the President's speeches with wisecracks. Therefore, I was generally given credit for the famous reference to Fala—and I should like to be able to claim this credit, but I had never even heard of the rumored episode in the Aleutian Islands until I read the paragraph quoted above. This paragraph may be said to have set the very keynote for the 1944 campaign; in a way, it was comparable to the "Martin, Barton and Fish" line in 1940; as someone observed at the time, "From now on the American people will consider this as a contest of Dewey versus Fala."

In a much earlier chapter I have said that various experts—including Judge Rosenman, who had seventeen years' experience working on Roosevelt's speeches—considered that the address to the International Brotherhood of Teamsters was the greatest campaign speech of his career. It can well be studied as a masterpiece of political strategy and tactics. He started off, "Well, here we are together again—after four years—and what years they have been! I am actually four years older—which seems to annoy some people. In fact, millions of us are more than eleven years older than when we started in to clear up the mess that was dumped in our laps in 1933." In these three sentences, which were greeted with loud laughter and cheers, Roosevelt dealt with the accusation that he was an old man (and a tired and feeble one), he brought the attention right back to the "Hoover depression" and the basic achievements of the New Deal; and, most important, he conveyed assurance to those of the people who loved him that the same F.D.R. was still with them and not floating somewhere out of sight in the stratosphere occupied solely by such mysterious, Olympian figures as Churchill and Stalin.

He said further, "There are enlightened, liberal elements in the Republican party, and they have fought hard and honorably to bring the party up to date and to get it in step with the forward march of American progress. But these liberal elements are not able to drive the Old Guard Republicans from their entrenched positions. . . . Millions of Republicans all over the nation are with us . . . in our unshakable determination to build the solid structure of peace. And they, too, will resent this campaign talk by those who first woke up to the facts of international life a few short months ago—when they began to study the polls of public opinion." This was Roosevelt's bid for the independent Republican vote, for the support of those liberals who resented the repudiation of Wendell Willkie—and Roosevelt never neglected in his subsequent speeches to appeal to these independents who formed, in his opinion, a group large enough to hold the balance of power as between the immovable factions who were committed to vote either Republican or Democratic regardless of what was said or done in this campaign.

Roosevelt said to me at this time that, if there were fifty million people who would actually vote on election day, you could figure roughly that some twenty million of them were determined to vote Democratic and another twenty million were determined to vote Republican (give or take a few million either way) regardless of the issues or the candidates; this left ten million more or less uncommitted independents who were subject to persuasion during the course of the campaign, and it was to these that the strongest appeals must be made. I believe that it was Roosevelt's hope that this independent twenty per cent of the population, which actually held the balance of power, would increase in strength and in political consciousness and he certainly directed his own influence toward that end.

A substantial number of Negroes was included in the independent minority as Roosevelt reckoned it. It was obvious that anyone with his exceptionally positive social views would be implacably opposed to racial discrimination and in favor of the perpetuation of such reforms as the Fair Employment Practices Commission, so that he never had to make any fabricated, hypocritical appeals to win the votes of Negroes in those parts of the country where Negroes enjoyed the same constitutional privileges as other free American citizens. Similarly, the record of his Administration spoke for itself to organized labor and frustrated the ferocious attempts of John L. Lewis to divert any substantial part of the labor vote to the Republicans.

The Teamsters speech—or "that speech about Fala," as it was sometimes known—accomplished its objectives; it put the needed excitement into the campaign, it stimulated the overconfident Democrats with a will to rush forth and register and vote, and above all it disrupted Dewey's carefully cultivated self-assurance and caused him to start swinging wildly against the most artful dodger of them all. More and more Dewey felt impelled to appeal to the prejudices of his immediate audiences in order to get applause. He had been giving a well-rehearsed performance as a liberal crusader, albeit a soundly practical one; but now his speeches began to sound more and more like those of his running mate, John W. Bricker, whom Alice Longworth was said to have summarized as "an honest Harding." Dewey seemed to forget that these audiences were recruited by the local Republican machine and were therefore composed largely of people who would still have been grimly and irrevocably determined to vote against Roosevelt even if the Republican candidate had been named Tommy Manville instead of Tom Dewey. Such audiences greeted in stony silence the advocacy of any policy, such as minimum wages or social security, which smacked of the despised New Deal. In bidding for their cheers, and for their hoots and catcalls whenever Hopkins or Ickes or Frances Perkins was mentioned, Dewey ignored the great mass of undecided voters who were listening over the radio and who, while they might be tired of the Roosevelt Administration and ready to concede that it was "time for a change," did not want that change to involve a recession to the kind of "normalcy" which followed the First World War.

Roosevelt never made this same mistake of addressing himself primarily to the loyal Democrats who were stuffed into the convention hall or the baseball park where he happened to be giving his speech. He knew well enough that it was easy to get roars of approval, or laughs, or shouts of "No! No!" or "Give it to 'em, Frank!" whenever he wanted them. His main arguments were directed into the microphone to those whose minds were not running in narrow partisan channels.

He made no major campaign speech for four weeks, although he gave one radio talk before registration week from the White House. After it became apparent that registration was heavy all over the country, it seemed to me that he never had any doubt as to victory. He mapped out a schedule well in advance:

October 21—A speech on foreign policy at a dinner in the Waldorf-Astoria Hotel in New York.

October 27—(Navy Day) Speech on the war at Shibe Park in Philadelphia.

October 28—Speech on postwar domestic problems at Soldier Field, Chicago.

November 4—General roundup speech at Fenway Park, Boston.

November 7—The usual short, election eve Fireside Chat from Hyde Park.

This was an easy schedule and it was carried out with none of the frantic strain or epidemics of jitters that marked the final stages of the campaign against Willkie in 1940. There was no third term issue now, no accusations of warmongering—indeed, about all that Dewey dared to say about the war was that it was rapidly drawing to a close. He made one costly blunder with a chance remark charging that insufficient supplies were being sent to General MacArthur's theater; the public learned that he did not know what he was talking about when, on October 20, forces under MacArthur landed in the Philippines and, in the subsequent Battle for Leyte Gulf, the Japanese Navy was all but obliterated.

There was, however, one serious question in this campaign: Roosevelt's health. There were innumerable baseless and incredibly malicious rumors, but there was some visible support for them—for he was now truly crippled. The frail muscles in his legs and hips had become flabby through long disuse in the months between Teheran and the Bremerton speech, during which time he had made no public appearances at which he would have to stand up—and he never wore the painful braces except on such necessary public occasions. It was now felt that he would probably never again be able to stand up and walk. Therefore, he had to make all his speeches sitting down, at a dinner table or from his automobile in the midst of some open space.

Actually, during the weeks of this campaign, he did manage to regain the use of his legs sufficiently to be able to stand up and speak from the back platform of his train for as long as half an hour. I do not know what sort of exercises he took to accomplish this, but I believe that it was largely due to the determination of Mrs. Roosevelt who supported him in refusal to accept physical defeat as she had done when he was first stricken in 1921.

As the campaign went along Roosevelt improved visibly in strength and resilience. He had been too long away from the people, and he knew it, and he was unmistakably glad to come home to them. On the evening of October 20, I rode with him to the train and then to New York for his foreign policy speech. Hopkins did not go on any of the campaign trips this year because his wife was ill. When we arrived at the Bush Terminal in Brooklyn on Saturday morning, the weather was terrible, with bitter cold wind and driving, stabbing rain. Roosevelt had a fifty-mile drive ahead of him through four boroughs in an open car—the purpose of course being to enable millions of people to see with their own eyes that he was alive and laughing. It had not been anticipated that his physical condition would be subjected to so rigorous a test as this day imposed. I had planned to go along on this tour in one of the following cars, but when I got off the train and took a look at the weather I decided that I might as well listen to the President's progress over the radio. Roosevelt made the whole trip and ended up in a state of high exhilaration, grateful to the disagreeable elements for giving him such a fine opportunity to prove that he could take it.

An important factor in the preparation of the foreign policy speech was one Republican Senator, Joseph H. Ball, who had been appointed originally by his friend Governor Harold E. Stassen (now serving in the Navy in the Pacific) and had been a leader in the fight against isolationism on Capitol Hill. He was an important spokesman for the independent wing of the Republican party which was generally identified as "the Willkie vote" and to which Roosevelt made repeated, direct appeals. Ball made it known both publicly and in a private talk with Hopkins, that he would give his support to whichever candidate took the firmest, most unequivocal position on the cardinal issues relating to the postwar world organization; the most important and controversial of these was the question as to whether the United Nations would have the authority to commit the United States to the use of armed force in emergencies without waiting for an act of Congress. Dewey ducked this question, evidently discounting Ball's political influence and feeling that he should run no risk of losing isolationist votes. But Roosevelt knew that the isolationists were unalterably opposed to him anyway and that while Ball was personally no major figure on the political scene he happened to be expressing the sentiments of large numbers of open-minded voters who wanted a world organization equipped with teeth and guts as well as with moral principles. In his speech to the Foreign Policy Association, Roosevelt said:

The power which this nation has attained—the moral, the political, the economic and the military power—has brought to us the responsibility, and with it the opportunity, for leadership in the community of nations. In our own best interest, and in the name of peace and humanity, this nation cannot, must not, and will not shirk that responsibility. . . .

Peace, like war, can succeed only where there is a will to enforce it, and where there is available power to enforce it.

The Council of the United Nations must have the power to act quickly and decisively to keep the peace by force, if necessary. A policeman would not be a very effective policeman if, when he saw a felon break into a house, he had to go to the Town Hall and call a town meeting to issue a warrant before the felon could be arrested.

It is clear that, if the world organization is to have any reality at all, our representatives must be endowed in advance by the people themselves, by constitutional means through their representatives in the Congress, with authority to act.

If we do not catch the international felon when we have our hands on him, if we let him get away with his loot because the Town Council has not passed an ordinance authorizing his arrest, then we are not doing our share to prevent another World War. The people of the Nation want their Government to act, and not merely to talk, whenever and wherever there is a threat to world peace.

The references to the Town Council and the local constabulary provided another evidence—like the "garden hose" analogy—of Roosevelt's ability to reduce an enormous and even revolutionary issue to the familiar scope of a small town. The position that he thus took seemed a highly courageous one; actually it was based on cold, hard, common sense and superior knowledge of the true temper of the American people. Senator Ball thereupon announced his support of Roosevelt. The isolationists howled, but the independent voters were effectively impressed.

In this foreign policy speech, Roosevelt went out of his way to speak of the action of the United States Government in granting independence to the Philippines, saying that this was another step in making good the same philosophy which animated the policy of the Good Neighbor. He then repeated a statement he had made in a speech to the Filipinos in the fall of 1942 which had attracted little or no attention at the time but to which the President attached enormous importance: "I like to think that the history of the Philippine Islands in the last forty-four years provides in a very real sense *a pattern for the future of other small nations and peoples of the world. It is a pattern of what men of good will look forward to in the future.*" Those italics are mine but the emphasis was certainly Roosevelt's. In this repeated statement he was underscoring the differences between himself and his respected friend Winston Churchill on the extension of the principles of the Atlantic Charter to such areas as Burma, Malaya, the Netherlands East Indies and Indo-China.

Roosevelt was annoyed by an editorial that appeared in *Life* magazine during this campaign. In an attempt to cleanse Dewey and the Republicans of the taint of isolationism of which Roosevelt constantly reminded the people, *Life* said that isolationism was a completely dead issue—as dead as "locofocoism." Roosevelt said, "Anybody who thinks that isolationism is dead in this country is crazy. As soon as this war is over, it may well be stronger than ever. And as for locofocoism—it isn't dead either. Harry Luce ought to spend more time reading the *Congressional Record*." (In fact, it might be said that Roosevelt was the greatest locofoco since Andrew Jackson.)

During the preparation of the next speech to be given at Philadelphia, I suggested to Roosevelt that he might well use a quotation from Winston Churchill who had said, in a recent House of Commons speech, that "The United States was now at the highest pinnacle of her power and fame." (Churchill, who well knew that his speeches were widely quoted if not always heard in the United States, often made remarks which could be construed as not unhelpful to Roosevelt's campaign for re-election.) When I made that suggestion to the President he said, very seriously, "What Winston says may be true at the moment, but I'd hate to say it. Because we may be heading before very long for the pinnacle of our weakness." I reproduce those words because they were burned into my memory, and my curiosity. There was no time at the moment to ask him to enlarge on that strange statement, and I never found an opportunity again to ask him just what he meant. I've always assumed that he was looking forward to the approaching moment when the reaction might set in, and isolationism again be rampant, and the American people might again tell the rest of the world to stew in its own juice.

During the latter part of October, Hopkins heard from General Marshall the amazing story of how someone, apparently in the armed services, had imparted to Dewey the fact that the United States had broken the Japanese codes before Pearl Harbor, and of Marshall's urgent message to Dewey that the revelation of this fact would be calamitous. Hopkins wrote of this:

Later that day I repeated this conversation to the President. The President was surprised at the action Marshall had taken but expressed no criticism of that action. He merely stated that he felt confident that Governor Dewey would not, for political purposes, give secret and vital information to the enemy. His only other further comments were: "My opponent must be pretty desperate if he is even thinking of using material like this which would be bound to react against him." The President wondered what officer or government official had been so faithless to his country as to give Governor Dewey the information. To the best of my knowledge the government never discovered who gave Governor Dewey this military information.

The Navy Day speech at Philadelphia was an exuberant recitation of the record of the "tired, quarrelsome, old men" of the Roosevelt Administration in the war. It was delivered in the wake of glorious news from MacArthur, Nimitz and Admirals William F. Halsey and Thomas C. Kinkaid, Commanders of the Third and Seventh Fleets in the Pacific, and Roosevelt did not neglect to make capital of certain statements by certain Republican orators (no names mentioned, of course) to the effect that MacArthur's forces had been deliberately starved by presumably envious authorities in Washington. From Philadelphia we traveled to Chicago. In this speech, Roosevelt wanted to mention the number of jobs that the United States would be able to provide for its citizens in the postwar economy. Rosenman had a considerable number of estimates as to this figure from various authoritative sources. As I remember, the highest of these estimates was slightly over fifty-seven million. When we asked Roosevelt which of these figures he wanted to use, he said, "Oh—let's make it a good round number—sixty million." Even Henry Wallace later conceded that he thought the President had gone much too far in setting a goal so impossible of attainment, and it is sad to think that Roosevelt did not live to see his "good round number" exceeded in 1947.

At Soldier Field in Chicago, the President's open car, with the tray of microphones laid across it, was placed in the middle of the football field, with something over a hundred thousand people in the enormous stadium surrounding it. The distances were so great that he would be in the middle of a sentence before the reverberations of the cheers or laughs provoked by the preceding sentence had come back to him. Standing by his car, I had the impression that some remote sections of the gigantic crowd present could not have a very precise idea of just what it was that he was saying; however, that did not bother him as long as his words were getting through clearly over the radio. On the train going back to Washington that night, Roosevelt was strongly urged by advisers, principally Frank Walker, to schedule another speech, preferably in Cleveland, Ohio, during the forthcoming, final week of the campaign. Roosevelt refused to do so. He was in high good humor and it was plainly evident that he had no worries whatsoever as to the outcome of the election. But he was later inclined to regret this decision, for he figured that had he gone to Cleveland he might well have carried Ohio and thereby brought about the defeat of Senator Robert A. Taft who, as it turned out, was re-elected by a very narrow margin.

During the next week Rosenman and I had some talks with various Democratic political leaders, who seemed to be greatly alarmed that Dewey was making dangerous progress in his campaign to hang the Communist label on the Roosevelt Administration. It was said that the hatred and fear of Communism were much greater than any of the emotions inspired by Nazism or Fascism. There were charges that Roosevelt had secretly begun to sell out to Uncle Joe Stalin at Teheran and that after the war he would complete the process of delivering the American free enterprise system over to Communist control. We asked if anybody were taking any part of this seriously—aside from the Polish-Americans who were naturally concerned for the future independence of their homeland—and we were told that the "Red Scare" was having an ominously positive effect in the Middle West, especially in the rural districts. Then we asked what were the farmers' principal causes for complaint at present. The reply was, "Today the farmer for the first time in his life goes down to Main Street on Saturday night with his pockets full of money and he cannot find anything to spend it on." We did not know how to cope with that problem, but when we reported these conversations to the President he did not seem greatly disturbed. He said in his Boston speech: "When any political candidate stands up and says, solemnly, that there is danger that the Government of the United States—your Government—could be sold out to the Communists—then I say that candidate reveals shocking lack of trust in America. He reveals a shocking lack of faith in Democracy—in the spiritual strength of our people."

Roosevelt himself was at his most unsolemn in this speech. He poured his own brand of ridicule on his opponent. He said, "Everybody knows that I was reluctant to run for the Presidency again this year. But since the campaign has developed I tell you frankly that I have become most anxious to win." Merriman Smith, the United Press White House correspondent, has written that Roosevelt's attitude toward Dewey was one of "unvarnished contempt"—and I can only add that Smith is a notoriously accurate reporter.

Hopkins later wrote: "The President told me he meant it when he said that this was the meanest campaign of his life. He said he thought they hit him below the belt several times and that it was done quite deliberately and very viciously. He was particularly resentful about the whispering campaign which he believes was a highly organized affair."

Traveling to Boston on this occasion evoked some painful memories for me of the trip four years previously when Roosevelt was being urged and even tearfully begged to give assurance to the mothers of America that their boys would never be sent into any foreign war. I asked the President if he would please, as a special favor, make reference to that earlier Boston campaign speech, and he did so, in these words: "We got into this war because we were attacked by the Japanese— and because they and their Axis partners, Hitler's Germany and Mussolini's Italy, declared war on us. I am sure that any real American would have chosen, as this Government did, to fight when our own soil was made the object of a sneak attack. As for myself, under the same circumstances, I would choose to do the same thing—*again and again and again.*"

The crowd instantly recognized this allusion, for that phrase had been dinned in their ears for four years, and they roared their approval.

During the final week before election, five of us in the White House put $5.00 each in a pool on the President's electoral vote. The guesses were as follows: Watson—400; Rosenman—431; Hopkins—440; Early—449; Sherwood—484. (I had clear possession of the high field.) The correct figure was 432, so Rosenman, who was holding the stakes, kept them.

Hopkins cabled bulletins to Churchill and Beaverbrook before and during election day. Although describing himself as "the world's worst political forecaster," he did not hesitate to predict that "this will not be merely an election, it will be a census" for Roosevelt. He informed Beaverbrook that if this prediction proved wrong, "I will underwrite the British National Debt and subscribe to the *Chicago Tribune*."

On the afternoon of November 7, he cabled Churchill, saying, "I have no reason for changing my opinion that it will be a Roosevelt landslide. The voting is very heavy in industrial centers. We are not likely to know definitely before 10:00 our time which will make it pretty late even for you." Apparently Churchill remained up most of the night to get the news. Hopkins' final bulletin consisted solely of the words, "It's in the bag."

There were no evidences of tension at Hyde Park on election night that I could discern, for the first reports of the turnout of voters in New York City had given clear enough indication of the outcome. All that the President appeared to worry about was the size of his majority which, naturally, he hoped would be overwhelming. It was not quite that; it was not a "landslide" when judged by previous Roosevelt standards. But it was big enough and it produced a considerable increase in Democratic strength in Congress—which, however, proved of little value to Roosevelt in the few months that remained to him, for the conservative coalition still held the balance of power on Capitol Hill.

During this election campaign, on October 8, there had come the sudden shocking news of the death of Wendell Willkie. He had served a great purpose in times of direst peril, but that purpose was lamentably far from being completed. It was my belief in 1943 and early in 1944 that if Willkie were to win the Republican nomination Roosevelt would not run for a fourth term. I had no tangible basis for this belief, and it was a doubly hypothetical surmise because it was evident for a long time to Roosevelt that Willkie had no chance whatever of being nominated. Greatly as the Old Guard lords of the Republican machine hated Roosevelt, they had come to hate Willkie even more, and, be it said to his eternal credit, Willkie went out of his way to court their hatred by scorning their support.

After returning to Washington, the President, Mrs. Roosevelt and Hopkins had a talk about the future, of which Hopkins wrote:

Mrs. Roosevelt urged the President very strongly to keep in the forefront of his mind the domestic situation because she felt there was a real danger of his losing American public opinion in his foreign policy if he failed to follow through on the domestic implications of his campaign promises. She particularly hoped the President would not go to Great Britain and France and receive great demonstrations abroad for the present, believing that that would not set too well with the American people.

She impressed on both of us that we must not be satisfied with merely making campaign pledges; the President being under moral obligation to see his domestic reforms through, particularly the organizing of our economic life in such a way as to give everybody a job. She emphasized that this was an overwhelming task and she hoped neither the President nor I thought it was settled in any way by making speeches.

It has often been said that Mrs. Roosevelt acted as the President's "eyes and ears," and so she did—but there were many others, particularly Hopkins, who helped in performing that function. There was no question of doubt, however, concerning the uniqueness of Mrs. Roosevelt's position as the keeper of and constant spokesman for her husband's conscience, and she continued to perform these duties after his death.

CHAPTER XXXII

Beginnings of Dissension

I T IS not improbable that one of the factors in restoring Hopkins to his former position with Roosevelt was the Morgenthau Plan episode. Roosevelt admitted that he had yielded to the importunities of an old and loyal friend when he affixed his initials to this document, and this was precisely the kind of thing against which Hopkins—who was no respecter of old friendships—was practiced in protecting him. Hopkins had agreed with Stimson and Hull on the general outline for treatment of Germany and would have been quick to detect the dangerous implications in the Morgenthau Plan, and Roosevelt realized this and was sorry that he had not taken Hopkins with him to Quebec. Of far greater importance, however, was an incident early in October in connection with a cable to Stalin which had consequences of very considerable importance. The background of this incident was as follows:

By October 1, both Finland and Bulgaria had quit the Axis and the Red Army had occupied both countries. The Russians had advanced over most of Estonia, Latvia and Lithuania, and across Poland as far as the Vistula; they had advanced into Hungary and Yugoslavia, and had reached the frontiers of Greece and Turkey. British forces had landed in Greece. The question of control over Southeastern Europe now presented a problem of pressing urgency and Churchill was naturally so concerned about it that he felt that another Big Three conference must be held without a moment's delay. Obviously, it was difficult for Roosevelt to embark on a long journey in the midst of a political campaign, but Churchill took the unassailable position that the advancing Russians were not going to wait until the returns were in from Michigan, South Dakota and Oregon, and he suggested that he and Eden should proceed to Moscow immediately and try to arrive at an understanding with Stalin and Molotov in respect to the delimitation of "spheres of influence" in the Balkan area. This proposal worried Hopkins a great deal, for he believed that, if such a conference were to be held with no

American representative present, it would be generally assumed that
Churchill had been authorized to speak for Roosevelt—and, in fact, that
this was what Churchill would undoubtedly undertake to do. Were
Harriman, the Ambassador, to attend any of the meetings in the negative capacity of "observer," the impression of American commitment to
support any decisions that might be reached would be all the stronger.
On the other hand, as Bohlen pointed out to Hopkins, it might well be
assumed in European countries that American abstention from these
conferences was a confession that the United States had "washed its
hands of European political problems."

While Hopkins well knew that there was nothing Roosevelt could do
to prevent Churchill and Stalin from discussing any subject that they
pleased, whether it related to the Balkans, or all of Europe or the Far
East, he believed it to be of utmost importance that Roosevelt should
make it entirely clear that no decision they might reach would be considered as valid by the United States until these matters could be
discussed and settled by the three nations in conference together. Of
course, Hopkins was by no means sure that the meetings would result
in any agreements, but just as much damage would be done if they
ended up in a serious row between the British and the Russians.

On October 3 Hopkins learned that Roosevelt was dispatching a cable
to Churchill in which he did in effect wash his hands of the whole
matter, with the implication that he was content to let Churchill speak
for the United States as well as for Great Britain. Hopkins immediately
investigated and learned that this cable was already going out over the
wires of the Map Room. He thereupon took one of the quick and arbitrary actions, far beyond the scope of his own authority, which had
gained for him the admiration and the affection of Roosevelt ever since
the beginnings of the New Deal: he gave orders to the officers on duty
in the Map Room that transmission of the President's message to Stalin
was to be stopped. The officers had no way of knowing that there had
been any change in Hopkins' position in the White House and they
complied with his order. Hopkins then went straight to Roosevelt's bedroom—the President was shaving at the time—and told what he had
done and the reasons why he had done it. Roosevelt had been thinking
about other matters when that cable was drafted, and had been persuaded that the safest course for him to take was to avoid all semblance
of American participation or even interest in the Moscow meetings by
sending vague messages to Churchill and to Stalin merely wishing them
good luck. He now listened very attentively to Hopkins and came to the
conclusion that a serious mistake had almost been made. When he had
finished his shaving, he and Hopkins drafted a cable to Harriman,
instructing him to deliver the following message to Marshal Stalin
immediately:

It had been my hope that no important meeting would be held until you and Mr. Churchill and I could get together but I understand the Prime Minister's wish to confer with you now. There is in this global war literally no question, either military or political, in which the United States is not interested. You will naturally understand this. It is my firm conviction that the solution to still unsolved questions can be found only by the three of us together. Therefore, while I appreciate the necessity for the present meeting, I choose to consider your forthcoming talks with Mr. Churchill merely as preliminary to a conference of the three of us which can take place, so far as I am concerned, any time after our national election.

Therefore, I am suggesting that Mr. Harriman be present at your forthcoming meetings with Mr. Churchill as an observer for me, if you and Mr. Churchill approve. Of course Mr. Harriman could not commit this government relative to any important matters which, very naturally, may be discussed by you and the Prime Minister.

I wish to reiterate to you my complete acceptance of the assurances that we have received from you relative to the war against Japan. You will have received by now from General Deane the statement of the position taken by our Combined Chiefs of Staff on this. The war against Germany is being successfully waged by our three great countries and surely we shall have no less success joined together in crushing a nation which, I feel sure in my heart, is as great an enemy of the Soviet Union as she is of the United States.

Roosevelt then informed Harriman that he would very much have preferred to have the next conference between the Big Three. He instructed Harriman to bear in mind the important fact that there could be *"no subjects that I can anticipate that might be discussed between Stalin and the Prime Minister in which I will not be greatly concerned. It is important that I retain complete freedom of action after this conference is over."* (The italics are mine.) Roosevelt further instructed Harriman to keep Hull and himself informed throughout the conversations and to come home immediately after them to make a full report.

Stalin expressed his appreciation of the President's clarifying message, saying that he had previously been under the impression that Churchill would be authorized to speak for Roosevelt as well as for himself.

Here, then, was another occasion when Roosevelt had reason to be grateful for Hopkins' willingness to act first and ask for authority later.

Two days before this cable was sent, Cordell Hull left his office in the State Department for the last time. He had told Roosevelt that he must resign. Roosevelt at first refused to accept it, but Hull was a very sick man and his life depended on the relinquishing of all the responsibilities of his office. At length Roosevelt persuaded him to postpone announcement of his resignation until after election day, for obvious reasons, and Hull did so. The question as to who should succeed him was a matter for long and prayerful consideration and discussion in the White House. James F. Byrnes was an obvious choice for the post, especially because of his high standing with the Senate which, sometime within the fourth term, would be called upon to vote on United States participation in the United Nations. Hopkins opposed Byrnes on the ground that Roosevelt was going to be his own Secretary of State, particularly in direct dealings with Churchill and Stalin, and Byrnes (who had once told Hopkins to "keep the hell out of my business") was not one to conform placidly to the role of a mere mouthpiece. The name of Sumner Welles was also mentioned, and I believe that Roosevelt would have preferred him to all others; but his appointment would have been a direct affront to Hull and provocative of intense resentment on Capitol Hill. When it was finally decided that Stettinius should be promoted from Under Secretary to the senior Cabinet post there was no doubt in anyone's mind that Hopkins was largely responsible. As the well-informed Marquis Childs wrote, "Those of his enemies who took satisfaction in counting Hopkins out at the time of his illness after the Teheran Conference will have to guess again. His influence in the Administration is perhaps greater than it ever was." Childs by the way was one of the few Washington columnists who was on friendly terms with Hopkins and who occasionally received from him some of the "background information" that was constantly being handed out in Washington, usually through the back door and seldom from so authoritative a source. Another of Hopkins' friends in the later years was Walter Lippmann, and so were two of the most powerful of the broadcasters, Raymond Gram Swing and Walter Winchell. (Hopkins never underrated the importance of the radio audience, and neither most certainly did Roosevelt.)

Shortly after the Stettinius appointment, Hopkins noted:

Stimson asked me to have lunch with him today.

At the end of our lunch it was clear that the reason he had asked me to see him was that he wanted to know whether the President wished him to resign. He stated that he realized that he was getting along in years and that he is not as strong as he used to be and that he had been seriously considering the wisdom of resigning.

I told him that I doubted very much that the President wanted him to resign, in fact, was quite sure that he did not. I told him that, from my point of view, he was the most respected member of the Cabinet; that he had the confidence of the American people, the rank and file of the army and of General Marshall. I told him, further, that I was sure he had the President's complete confidence.

Hopkins did not overstate the case. Stimson was seventy-seven years old and his working hours were limited and no doubt his great pride had been injured by the numerous sneering references to "tired old men," but he was then as he had been throughout the past four critical years as firm and reliable a tower of strength as any President had ever been privileged to lean on. He continued to serve with unfaltering ability and distinction until after the war had ended.

Beaverbrook reported from time to time in letters to Hopkins on the situation in England. Following are some of his observations:

Here in Britain we are passing through a strange phase in public life. For the first time, the English are not absolutely sure of themselves. They are anxious about their future. And this in some measure is due to the extent to which they have had to rely on outside assistance in the war. Without your friendship, we would never have got it. We know that you came with a discerning eye. You saw the prospect of defeat and the possibility of resistance and you decided to back the resistance. But having come so far with the assistance for which you were primarily responsible, the British must very soon go forward under their own power. And it is a prospect which causes them some misgivings at present. . . .

Here we are somewhat in the doldrums. The rockets come to us in London at the rate of 6 a day. Last Saturday morning we suffered a disaster when one fell in a suburban district, causing the heaviest death toll of any single bomb incident of the war. I do not know how much injury we shall have to sustain before the winter is over. The slogan of "London can take it" will prevail. But there may be quite a lot to take.

The Prime Minister is fully alive to the situation. He knows very well how much the public can stand before they begin to grumble and knows too how to suppress the grumbles when they come. His method is to set up in the people's minds a feeling of kinship with the men at the battlefront. So far he has never spoken too soon.

Anyway the rocket is to be preferred to the flying-bomb with its two warnings—first the siren and then the noise of the approaching engine. That experience was strange indeed. For while there was noise there was safety. Only when the engine cut off and silence fell did you stand in need of prayer.

The political parties are squaring up for the election. In my view it should not be delayed too long. For the government is now unable to deal with post-war issues, the limit of the capacity to compromise has been reached.

It would seem that with victory in sight—and despite the frequent reminder given by the V-2 rockets that the war was still on—the political coalition which had held together under Churchill since the beginning of Britain's darkest and finest hour was beginning to show signs of cracking. But so was the great world coalition which had been envisaged at the Atlantic Conference by Roosevelt and Churchill and realized by them in the White House within three weeks after Pearl Harbor; and the first evidences of rupture at this time were not between the Soviet Union and the Western Allies, but between Great Britain and the United

States, and the main points at issue, ironically enough, were the very principles of the Atlantic Charter itself.

One of the first public actions taken by Stettinius incurred the furious and vehemently expressed wrath of Winston Churchill. During November there were political crises in three European countries, Belgium, Italy and Greece, in all of which the Allied military forces were predominantly British. It seemed that Britain was backing the more conservative elements in these countries as opposed to the liberals or leftists who had been the most aggressive in resistance to the Germans and Fascists. The situation in Belgium was by no means clear, and perhaps it was actually no more so in Italy and Greece, but in the two latter countries it appeared that Churchill's well-known predilection for constitutional monarchy was dictating policies which were against the people's will. In Italy, King Victor Emmanuel had been dethroned in January, 1944, by unanimous vote of the various party leaders, and a regency had been formed under Crown Prince Umberto. In Greece, from which the Germans had been ejected only within the past few weeks, there had been no time to set up any real government, but some American observers believed that popular enthusiasm for the return of King George was close to nonexistent. The situation in all three countries was complicated by the fact that battlefronts existed in each (in the case of Belgium, they were just beyond her frontiers) so that all were military zones of communications where law and order must be enforced by means of whatever instruments were most conveniently at hand for the purpose; but American liberal opinion had already heard too much of this explanation in connection with the various "temporary expediency" arrangements or deals and was impatient for some proof of the establishment of democracy and application of the Four Freedoms in all liberated areas. This liberal opinion—which was feeling particularly potent after the recent election—was becoming increasingly suspicious of Churchill's apparent determination to restore the unsavory status quo ante in Europe. Moreover, they were suspicious of State Department policy in these matters. When Stettinius announced his first appointments on the Assistant Secretary level, anguished cries were raised that the State Department had been shaken up only to emerge more reactionary than ever. Liberals, both Democratic and Republican, who had voted and actively campaigned for Roosevelt, forgathered in consternation to ask each other, "Who won the election, anyway?" Hopkins was given a large share of responsibility for the new appointments and suddenly found himself in the unaccustomed position of being criticized as a convert to Toryism. (I told him that he could number me among the critics.) Hopkins well knew that these protests could not be dismissed as the mere rantings of Roosevelt haters; he knew that even though the President had just been re-elected he was going to need all the support he could get in the forthcoming battle for the peace.

At this same time, in late November, the crisis became acute in Italy. The coalition Cabinet headed by Premier Ivanoe Bonomi resigned. In the attempt to form a new Cabinet, Count Carlo Sforza was a leading spokesman of the parties to the left. Sforza was well known and greatly respected in the United States, where he had spent many years of exile, as an unflagging enemy of Fascism. He had strongly opposed the retention of the House of Savoy in the new Italy and had criticized State Department policy on numerous occasions. (The State Department's memorandum on the proposed plan for Allied Military Government in Italy, mentioned in Chapter XXVIII, had provided that "Italian political leaders in exile should have no part in the operations or administration. Their long resistance abroad, their lack of intimate contact with the people . . . largely invalidate their claim to act as trustees or spokesmen for the Italian nation." This dictum, which would seem to have applied primarily to Sforza, was amended by Roosevelt and Hopkins to provide that such exiled leaders should have no part in the operation "in its initial stages," with the rest of the remarks struck out.)

The British Embassy in Rome intervened in the Cabinet crisis to the extent of letting it be known that His Majesty's Government would not give its approval to any Italian Cabinet in which Sforza held a prominent post. With this, the American liberal hue and cry became really intense and it was assumed that Churchill and the British Government were making these arbitrary, antidemocratic moves with the blessing of the United States Government. Stettinius was now beginning to realize how Hull had felt under comparable fire. Roosevelt was away in Warm Springs for a rest and was not, I believe, paying a great deal of attention to the situation. On December 5, Stettinius issued a public statement saying:

> The position of this government has consistently been that the composition of the Italian government is purely an Italian affair except in the case of appointments where important military factors are concerned. This government has not in any way intimated to the Italian government that there would be any opposition on its part to Count Sforza. Since Italy is an area of combined responsibility, we have reaffirmed to both the British and Italian governments that we expected the Italians to work out their problems of government along democratic lines without influence from outside.

He added, "This policy would apply in an even more pronounced degree with regard to governments of the United Nations in their liberated territories." This last was sharply aggravating to Churchill, for it applied obviously to Belgium and even more so to Greece, which was by now becoming the hottest spot of all. The embattled Prime

Minister thereupon dispatched a cable to Roosevelt which may well
have been the most violent outburst of rage in all of their historic
correspondence. Churchill said he would undoubtedly have to make a
statement to the House of Commons in view of the Stettinius statement
and he would try to keep his remarks free from the "acerbity" that
the new Secretary of State had displayed in his public language. It is
quite possible that Churchill would have been compelled to discuss
these subjects before the House even if Stettinius had said nothing,
for a debate was precipitated by an amendment regretting British
intervention in Greece and in other parts of liberated Europe. During
this debate, Churchill made several references directly and indirectly
to American opinion. He said: "Poor old England! (Perhaps I ought
to say, 'Poor old Britain!') We have to assume the burden of the most
thankless tasks, and in undertaking them to be scoffed at, criticized
and opposed from every quarter; but at least we know where we are
making for, know the end of the road, know what is our objective. . . .
We have not attempted to put our veto on the appointment of Count
Sforza. If tomorrow the Italians were to make him Prime Minister or
Foreign Secretary, we have no power to stop it, except with the agreement of the Allies. All that we should have to say about it is that we
do not trust the man, we do not think he is a true and trustworthy
man, nor do we put the slightest confidence in any Government of
which he is a dominating member. I think we should have to put a
great deal of responsibility for what might happen on those who called
him to power." (Churchill always preferred to think of his own country
as "England" rather than "Britain," just as he greatly preferred the
word "Empire" to "Commonwealth." The word "Britain" was largely
an American contrivance to avoid giving offense to the Scots, the Welsh
and the Ulstermen, if not to the actual Irish.)

Following this, relations between the White House and Downing
Street were more strained than they had ever been before. Hopkins
received plenty of information to indicate that his honored friend, the
Prime Minister, was in an extremely dangerous and explosive mood
which might make plenty of trouble at the forthcoming Big Three
Conference which was now in prospect for the end of January; and if
Hopkins had lacked such information he had only to read the cables
and the ample space provided between the lines of Churchill's public
utterances.

The vote in the House of Commons supporting the government position was 279 to 30 and Churchill cabled Hopkins that he could have
had a much larger majority if he had chosen to apply the full force of
the government whip. However, Winant wrote to Hopkins: "The
Parliament is definitely to the Right of the country, and did not reflect,
in my opinion, the extent of a troubled public opinion. Protest resolu-

tions passed by big trade union groups were an indication of this fact. The Conservatives in Parliament are also going to make the Polish-Russian debate scheduled for this week difficult. This is the first time that I have felt the Government weakened following a Vote of Confidence by the Parliament. The man most hurt, in my judgment, was the Prime Minister. It is a time here when many people are discouraged by the prolongation of the war and I hope that, without surrender of principle, we can so work out our difficulties as to encourage the continuation of the coalition government here."

The situation in Greece was indeed an ugly one. There had been serious fighting in the streets of Athens involving British forces and members of the resistance groups which bore the initials, "E.A.M." and "E.L.A.S." It was reported that some of the rebels had marched through the streets shouting, "Long Live Roosevelt!" American public opinion was not too well informed as to the merits of this complicated situation or the extent to which the resistance groups might be under Communist domination; all that was apparent on the surface was that British troops, engaged in the task of "liberation," were killing Greek patriots who had been fighting the Germans, and it was even possible that the British were using American Lend-Lease weapons for this purpose.

Although there were no American troops involved in Greece, units of the Mediterranean Fleet of the U.S. Navy had been operating under British command, aiding in the transport service to Greece. This led to an incident which Hopkins described as follows:

On Saturday night, December 9, 1944, at about 7 p.m., the White House operator told me that "John Martin" was calling me on the overseas phone. This is the name the Prime Minister uses in his telephone calls.

The connection was very bad and I could not, therefore, know what the Prime Minister was talking about. He sounded as tho he was very angry and stirred up about something and wanted me to do something about it. I got the words "Greece" and "Halifax." Inasmuch as it was impossible to make him understand what I was saying, I told him I would find out about it in the morning.

I then tried to get Halifax on the phone to see if he knew what it was all about but could not reach him.

On Sunday morning I went to the Map Room and saw in the morning news summary a sentence that Admiral King had ordered Admiral Hewitt, our American Commander of the Mediterranean Fleet, not to permit any American LSTs to be used to transfer supplies to Greece. King's actual cable was not available.

I went to see Admiral Leahy about this and told him that I thought Admiral Hewitt was under the command of General Wilson and that it seemed funny to me that Admiral King would issue an order directly to Hewitt without consultation with the Joint Chiefs of Staff or the Combined Chiefs of Staff. I told Leahy that I thought King was getting into the political arena and that we would undoubtedly hear from the British about it. I told him, furthermore, that I felt that, while we should keep our troops out of Greece, and let the British do the policing, withdrawing the LSTs was like walking out on a member of your family who is in trouble. Under any circumstances, we had told the British that they could use our airplanes to send their paratroopers into Greece and the action of Admiral King did not jibe with that. I told him I thought Admiral King should withdraw his order and, if Admiral King or the Joint Chiefs of Staff thought that such an order should be issued, the recommendation should be made to the President and that he should make the decision because it was in the political sphere. I told Admiral Leahy that irrespective of the merits of Admiral King's action, I thought he had gotten off base from an organization point of view. Leahy agreed with this and told me that when he saw the message he called King and told him he thought King had made a mistake, but he did not tell King to countermand the order.

While I was with Leahy he called Admiral King up and told King he was talking to me and we both felt it was a mistake and Leahy suggested to King that he withdraw the order. King readily agreed and did so. A few minutes later Lord Halifax, the British Ambassador, called me and said he had to see me urgently and then I pasted together what the Prime Minister was talking about and this was undoubtedly it.

I met Halifax at my house at 12:30 and he had a full-blown protest which he was going to make to Stettinius, but Stettinius was out of town and his instructions were to tell it to me, which he did in no uncertain terms.

Halifax said he was sure Churchill was planning to send a very strong protest to the President and that already the British Chiefs of Staff had said they never heard of such an order and had sent instructions to Wilson to go ahead and use the ships.

I told Halifax I hoped Churchill would not send the message; that I was sure the President knew nothing about it; that the matter was all cleared up anyway and that I knew instructions had gone to Admiral Hewitt countermanding the previous order and that I thought it would just make trouble if Churchill submitted a protest. I asked Halifax, in the light of the fact that the matter was now settled, if he would not cable Churchill and tell him I thought that any cable from him on this matter would serve no useful purpose but merely complicate the Greek situation further. I told him that public opinion about the whole Greek business in this country was very bad and that we felt the British Government had messed the whole thing up pretty thoroughly.

Churchill expressed his warm appreciation of Hopkins' timely and effective action and said that he had canceled the message that he had prepared for dispatch to the President. The tension was eased for a few days and Roosevelt sent friendly and soothing messages to Churchill and also to Stalin. But then, as Winant had predicted, the debate on Poland in the House of Commons caused further serious ructions. Speaking of the future Polish frontiers, Churchill said, "All territorial changes must await the conference at the peace table after victory has been won, but to that principle there is one exception, and that exception is, changes mutually agreed." This was an unfortunate misstatement on Churchill's part which was later corrected by Eden, but it conveyed the disturbing suggestion of "secret agreements" among the big powers for the carving up of the small ones, and it revived the ugly accusations against which Roosevelt had been compelled to defend himself time and again ever since the Atlantic Conference. This speech was made on December 15, and the following day Hopkins cabled Churchill,

> Due to the Greek situation and your statement in Parliament about Poland public opinion has rapidly deteriorated here. I must confess I am greatly disturbed by this turn of diplomatic events which gives publicity to our various difficulties at a time when the battle is joined in Europe and in Asia and all of our energy is required for the defeat of the enemy. Although I do not know what the President or Stettinius may be compelled to say publicly it is quite possible that one or both of them will have to proclaim their determination in unequivocal terms to do everything we can to seek a free world and a secure one.

There was plenty of indignation in Whitehall at the somewhat sanctimonious, holier-than-thou attitude which the United States was assuming toward a situation in which it was undoubtedly concerned but for the solution of which it was taking no responsibility whatsoever. It seemed that whenever developments were favorable in any part of the world, the United States was entirely ready to share in the credit—but whenever and wherever things went wrong, the United States was quick to absolve itself of all blame. As one British observer expressed it, "America is like an inverted Micawber, waiting for something to turn down."

It remained for Churchill to take the one dramatic and strenuous and thoroughly characteristic action which could convert criticism into applause. With fine contempt for his advanced age (he had now passed his seventieth birthday) and for the risks both political and physical that were involved, he suddenly boarded an airplane and flew to Athens on Christmas Day, taking Eden with him. He thereby brought an end to hostilities and established a temporary regency under Archbishop Damaskinos, obtaining from King George the assurance that he would not attempt to return to the country "unless summoned by a free and fair expression of the national will." That ended the Greek crisis for the time being, but there were profoundly conflicting forces there which could not be suppressed permanently.

Hopkins cabled Churchill a Christmas greeting in which he said, "No one knows better than I what a gallant role you are playing in the greatest drama in the history of the world. On this fateful Christmas, I want you to know that I am well aware of the heavy burdens that you carry. I am proud to be known and even to be attacked by some of my countrymen as your good friend."

This was certainly a fateful Christmas. The American and British people had been given cause to forget all about political or ideological disputes by the shocking and bewildering news of the German break-through in the Ardennes and the resultant Battle of the Bulge. Three months before it had seemed that Germany might quit at any moment. Now, it seemed that a large part of the triumphant American and British forces in Holland, Belgium and Northern France might be pushed into another Dunkirk. At the same time, the Russians had driven up the Danube Valley past Budapest and were advancing toward Vienna. To those in official Washington and London who knew that the Big Three were soon to meet again in conference to consider the long-deferred problems of the postwar world, it appeared possible for a time that the Western Allies might be in a seriously weakened condition as compared with the Russians. However, such apprehensions were very short-lived for it soon became apparent that Hitler's bold and alarming thrust was to end in a German disaster.

Hopkins wrote the following on the genesis of the Yalta Conference:

As early as the middle of September, 1944, the President was contemplating a second conference with Stalin and Churchill. There were a variety of pressing problems which the President believed warranted such a conference and both Churchill and Stalin were agreeable to the conference. Churchill was, indeed, insistent on it. The reasons were obvious.

By this time we had agreed upon our full-out and final assault on the German citadel and yet there were no firm agreements as to what was to be done with Germany once she was defeated. The machinery of the European Advisory Council moved so slowly that it was quite possible to visualize the collapse of Germany without any plans or agreements having been made.

Altho at Teheran Stalin had made a firm commitment insofar as Soviet participation in the war against Japan was concerned, that needed to be clarified as to precise dates and the extent of Soviet participation.

On the political side there was no agreement as to reparations against Germany; the problem of dismemberment of the Reich was hanging fire; there was no agreement as to zones; nothing as to whether or not we were going to encourage or discourage a central

German Government or, indeed, in what way the Allies were going to utilize German machinery. The policy toward war criminals was stalemated; the earmarks of trouble in Poland were already obvious—neither the eastern frontier nor the western frontier was settled. Our whole policy toward the Far East needed a thorough-going understanding, particularly so far as the Soviet Union was concerned. We knew from Teheran that the Russians wanted certain things as a condition to their declaring war on Japan or, at any rate, they said they wanted them and it was extremely important for the United States in particular, in view of our historic relationship with China, to protect China's interests in these negotiations. Things regarding the Far East had to be settled otherwise we might find the three allies going their separate ways. The place of France in European and world affairs was in an irritating state. France wanted a Zone of Occupation. She had not been given one. France wanted to be on any Control Commission governing Germany. The Allies had given her no assurances on this point. France wanted a clear-cut statement regarding the Allies' ambitions in the French Empire, particularly Indo-China. France had good reason to believe that President Roosevelt was not enthusiastic about returning Indo-China to the Empire, and were thoroughly suspicious of the Allies on this point. France wanted to have a full part in world affairs and the decision on this point, if not made at an early date, would cause endless troubles. Furthermore, there was the hang-over of the Dumbarton Oaks United Nations Conference. The voting procedure had not been settled. There seemed to be no way to settle it except by the three heads of state getting together. Indeed, all of the things I have mentioned would, in my opinion, have been hopelessly delayed without a conference.

The President, as usual, began to play with ideas about places for the conference and suggested a wide variety of locations, none of which included Russia. I told the President, as soon as the discussion started, that there was not a chance of getting Stalin out of Russia at this time in the light of the military situation on Germany's eastern front and that if he did not look out we would wind up with a lot of long-winded, irritating cables back and forth getting exactly nowhere and that we might as well make up our minds first at least to go to some convenient point in Russia—preferably in the Crimea. The President was not opposed to this but in view of the forthcoming elections, considered it to be unwise. About this time, too, it became perfectly clear that the President had to conduct a vigorous campaign for the election which made a conference prior to election out of the question. And, because he felt it to his political disadvantage to indicate Russia as the place of the meeting, he postponed all discussion of the place until after the election was over. As soon as the election had taken place I saw Gromyko, the Russian Ambassador, and told him that we wanted to arrange the conference. Gromyko said that he knew Stalin was prepared for the Conference but that he doubted that he could leave Russia in view of the great Soviet offensive against Germany. I asked Gromyko whether there was any place in the Crimea at which it was fit to hold a conference, and he said he was sure there was but made no further comment. A couple of weeks later the President got a message from Stalin saying he understood the President was willing to go to the Crimea and suggesting Yalta as a desirable place. This was the first indication anyone around the President had that the President would even consider a conference in Russia. All of the President's close advisers were opposed to his going to Russia; most did not like or trust the Russians anyway and could not understand why the President of the United States should cart himself all over the world to meet Stalin. This argument carried no weight with me. The all-important thing was to get the meeting. There was not a chance of getting that meeting outside of the Crimea. The President's advisers gave me a lot of acid criticism when they found out that I was the one who had talked to Gromyko about the possibility of going to the Crimea. When they descended on the President to urge him not to go the President wavered again and cooked up a lot of counter proposals, none of which made any sense. I was sure the President would wind up by going to the Crimea, the primary reason being that it was a part of the world he had never visited and his adventurous spirit was forever leading him to go to unusual places and, on his part, the election being over, he would no longer be disturbed about it for political reasons.

Churchill was none too keen about the Crimea because he prefers a warm climate and more comfort than he thought the Crimea could afford, but he was so anxious to have the meeting that he would have gone to Moscow if necessary.

The holidays were then coming on, the President had to open the Congressional session and negotiations were then entered into and naval officers and embassy officials in Moscow hurried to the Crimea to find out if the physical conditions were such to warrant the President going to Yalta. Harriman's report was in the affirmative.

Roosevelt's State of the Union Message of January 6, 1945, was more than twice as long as usual, running to some eight thousand words; he did not deliver it in person, sending it up to the Capitol for a clerk to read out, and he was therefore not limited as to time. He gave a comprehensive survey of the war—General Marshall participated in preparing the military parts of it—and dwelt at length and in a most reasonable spirit with the subject of Allied unity in general and with such problems as Greece and Poland in particular. At Hopkins' strong instigation, Roosevelt agreed to express his real friendship for France. He spoke of the "heroic efforts of the resistance groups . . . and of all those Frenchmen throughout the world who refused to surrender after the disaster of 1940." He said that the liberation of France "means that her great influence will again be available in meeting the problems of peace. We fully recognize France's vital interest in a lasting solution of the German problem and the contribution which she can make in achieving international security," resuming "her proper position of strength and leadership." When these words were written I thought that the ashes of the Vichy policy had at last been thrown to the winds. However, as Hopkins was soon to find out, the end of the troubles with de Gaulle was not yet.

There were some disturbances in Washington during January over the dropping of Jesse Jones from the Cabinet and the appointment of Henry Wallace to succeed him as Secretary of Commerce, and over the air transport of a dog named "Blaze" which Colonel Elliott Roosevelt had shipped from England to his wife. While the latter episode was providing happiness for some newspaper publishers, a list of officers scheduled to be promoted came to the President's desk and on this list was the name of his son Elliott, who was recommended for brigadier general. The President was urged to drop this name quietly before the list went to Congress for approval, but he flatly and indignantly refused to do so. He said, "Elliott on his record has earned promotion. He did not ask that the dog be put on the plane or given high priority. And I'm not going to have him punished for something he did not do." Roosevelt knew perfectly well what the newspapers would say about this, but he didn't give a damn.

The Fourth Inaugural was held on January 20 on the South Portico of the White House instead of at the Capitol. It was a short, simple ceremony, the brevity being due to the fact that the President was determined to stand up throughout it. (I don't think that he ever wore his braces and stood up again.) It was a bitter cold day but Roosevelt stood there with no hat, no overcoat, wearing a lightweight suit, as he always did, with no waistcoat. His Inaugural Address lasted only about five minutes but he worked over it with more care and more interest than he had shown in the preparation of any speech in two years. I had the feeling that he was summing up his most profound beliefs when he said, "We have learned to be citizens of the world, members of the human community. We have learned the simple truth, as Emerson said, that 'the only way to have a friend is to be one.'"

Frances Perkins has written that she and Mrs. Henry Wallace were frightened by the President's appearance—"he looked so badly." I did not feel this at the time. In fact, I thought he seemed immeasurably better in health and strength and spirits than when I had gone to see him after my return from London four months previously. I had watched him improve steadily throughout the campaign and now, at this Inaugural, I believed he was ready for anything that the next four years might bring.

That night he celebrated his sixty-second birthday. It was ten days ahead of time because of his imminent departure.

On the following day, Sunday, January 21, Hopkins took off for

London in "The Sacred Cow." It had been decided that he should spend two or three days with Churchill in an attempt to promote a more amiable mood prior to the gathering at Yalta, for the tensions created during December had evidently not been entirely relaxed. Bohlen accompanied Hopkins on this trip, which was made via Bermuda and the Azores.

Hopkins wrote no notes during his short stay in London, but he reported later that his host was no less "volcanic" than he had expected. Before leaving he sent a radio message to Roosevelt, who was by now at sea on the *U.S.S. Quincy,* reporting that the visit had been "very satisfactory." He quoted Churchill as saying that from all the reports he had received on present conditions at Yalta, "We could not have found a worse place for a meeting if we had spent ten years on research."

From London Hopkins flew to Paris where he was taken by Ambassador Jefferson Caffery to see Foreign Minister Georges Bidault and then de Gaulle. The meeting with Bidault was most cordial, Hopkins stating that Franco-American relations were at "a pretty low ebb" and it was high time to find out what was the cause and to correct it. Bidault recognized in Hopkins "a devoted, loyal friend and assistant of President Roosevelt" and described himself as equally loyal and devoted to de Gaulle, but he confessed frankly that the General was at times difficult to handle. "General de Gaulle believes that Frenchmen always try to please the man to whom they are talking. The General thinks they overdo it and he adopts a different attitude. He makes no effort to please."

When Hopkins went to see de Gaulle he believed that by making candid admission of past differences and demonstrating a sincere desire to wipe them from the slate he could penetrate the General's austere façade. He was wrong. As Caffery reported, the General was neither "very responsive" nor "very conciliatory." De Gaulle asked, "If you really mean that you believe that relations between the United States and France are not all that they should be, why don't you do something about it?" He mentioned, for example, the failure to extend to him an invitation to attend the Crimea Conference. He conceded that the United States had helped France by arming and equipping her troops and in other material ways—"but you always seem to do it grudgingly and under pressure."

Hopkins gave further assurances of good will but the interview ended in the same conditions of frost with which it had started. However, Hopkins was not discouraged and the next day in the course of a luncheon with Bidault and other Cabinet Ministers he expressed the President's cordial desire to meet de Gaulle at some French point on or near the Mediterranean and even suggested that arrangements might be made for de Gaulle to attend the final stages of the Yalta Conference when European political matters would come under consideration. Bidault promised to discuss these suggestions with de Gaulle and inform Hopkins of the General's reactions. Caffery reported to the State Department: "Mr. Hopkins made an excellent impression and was very sympathetic. His stay here was very useful and timely."

Hopkins then went on to Rome where he was the guest of Ambassador Kirk at whose villa near Cairo he and the President had stayed in 1943. On January 30, he was taken by Myron C. Taylor for an audience with the Pope. Hopkins told His Holiness of the President's high regard for him and appreciation for the Vatican's unfailingly sympathetic attitude toward the United States and her cause in these troubled years. He told of his recent meeting with de Gaulle and expressed his admiration for the valiant French general—an opinion to which Taylor ventured to register his dissent. The twenty-minute audience was in the Pope's library, and Taylor later said that when they left Hopkins was in a glow of exaltation, revealing a surprisingly deep religious feeling. He said that the Pope subsequently stated that he had been greatly impressed by Hopkins as a man of exceptional force of character.

From Rome, Hopkins went to Allied Force Headquarters at Caserta, near Naples, and there he was overwhelmed with hospitality by two old friends, General Ira C. Eaker and General Joseph T. McNarney. (The latter had been on the PBY flight to Archangel in July, 1941.) He was joined in Naples by Stettinius and they flew together to Malta to await the President's arrival. Hopkins by now was quite ill.

The Combined Chiefs of Staff had been meeting at Malta—and had been engaged in the most violent disagreements and disputes of the entire war. (One can read the official minutes of these meetings without suspecting that a single harsh word had been exchanged, but some of those who were present tell a much more colorful story of what went on.) The point at issue was the selection of a strategic plan for the final knockout blow against Germany. One plan was advanced by the British Chiefs, another by Eisenhower; the latter was not present at Malta but he was volubly and vehemently represented by Beedle Smith. The arguments reached such a point that Marshall, ordinarily one of the most restrained and soft-spoken of men, announced that if the British plan were approved by the Prime Minister and President he would recommend to Eisenhower that he had no choice but to ask to be relieved of his command. The issue was settled by the Combined Chiefs in Eisenhower's favor without need for reference to higher authority, and the plan was followed which ended three months later in junction with the Russians and Germany's surrender.

Sick as he was at Malta, Hopkins went into action in behalf of relief and rehabilitation in Europe, a subject on which he had been working for a long time. The U.S. Chiefs of Staff contended, as it was their duty to

do, that American shipping in the Atlantic should be transferred to the
Pacific after V-E Day except that which was required to supply American
forces still remaining in Europe. In putting up a fight for the retention
of enough shipping to supply the needs of the civilian population of Britain
and the Continent, Hopkins was not animated solely by humanitarian
considerations, or the kind of "starry-eyed, dogooder idealism" which
was identified with the Santa Claus philosophy of the New Deal. He
knew that there could be no recovery and no peace and no democracy
in Europe if its people did not have enough to eat and the tools and
materials with which to get back to work. He did not have to argue
this point at any great length with Marshall and King. Their respect
for Hopkins was such that they agreed to leave the arbitration of
matters relating to allocation of shipping in his hands; but, as events
proved, he never had a chance to exercise this authority.

On February 2, Roosevelt arrived in the Grand Harbor of Valetta on
the *Quincy*, and Admiral King has told me that when he went aboard the
cruiser and saw the President he was alarmed for the first time by
the state of his health. King had seen him last at the Inauguration, less
than two weeks before. Since then, Roosevelt had had ten days at sea,
with favorable weather. Normally, no matter how tired and worn he
might appear when he started off on a cruise, he emerged from it
looking healthy and hearty and acting that way. It now seemed to King
that instead of improvement there had been serious deterioration. But
the President was as always buoyant and excited at the prospect of new
adventures as he left the *Quincy* to make the rest of his journey by air.

The night of February 2-3 was a busy one at the Luqa airfield at
Malta, which had been for so many years a prime target for German
and Italian bombs. Transport planes were taking off at ten-minute intervals from 11:30 P.M. to dawn to carry some seven hundred people,
including the President and the Prime Minister, fourteen hundred
miles across the Aegean and Anatolia and the Black Sea to Saki airfield
in the Crimea.

CHAPTER XXXIII

The Yalta Conference

THE accommodations at Yalta were unexceptionable for those on the Very Important Person level and the Russians seemed eager to convince their Anglo-American guests of the warm friendliness of their hospitality. However, this was war-ravaged territory and space was so limited that, according to the records, sixteen U.S. Army colonels had to share one bedroom. Hopkins had a bedroom to himself in the Livadia Palace where Roosevelt was staying, and he spent most of his time in it, leaving his bed only to go down to the Grand Ballroom for the full dress meetings. He was so extremely ill that at one point Dr. McIntire wanted him to be moved to the Navy Communications ship, *U.S.S. Catoctin,* which was moored at Sevastopol eighty miles away. (It was considered unsafe to bring the ship to Yalta because of the danger of lingering German mines, and signal corps men had laid land lines from the Livadia Palace to the ship so that Roosevelt could have his own channels of communication.) Hopkins attended none of the big dinners at Yalta—in fact I believe he was not permitted so much as a taste of vodka—so that his condition at least became no worse and he was able to stick it out to the end. James F. Byrnes has written, "Members of our delegation frequently held meetings there [in Hopkins' bedroom] because Dr. McIntire insisted he remain in bed."

Robert Hopkins was the only son at this conference but there were three daughters, Anna Boettiger, Section Officer Sarah Churchill Oliver (of the W.A.A.F.) and Kathleen Harriman. Roosevelt's party also included James F. Byrnes, Edward J. Flynn and Steve Early, who saw to it that this conference got much better press coverage than had any of its predecessors despite the fact that Roosevelt firmly refused to permit even the wire service men—"the three ghouls"—to go along with him.

The President and Prime Minister arrived at Yalta on Saturday, February 3. Stalin and his party arrived early Sunday morning and he and Molotov came to call on Roosevelt at four o'clock that afternoon. After thanking his hosts for all the arrangements that had been made to promote the comfort and convenience of the guests, Roosevelt said that during the trip across the ocean on the *Quincy* numerous bets had been made as to whether the Americans would get to Manila before the Russians got to Berlin. Stalin laughed and said that those who had bet on Manila would win. Roosevelt remarked on the destruction that he had seen here in the Crimea and Stalin told him that it was nothing as compared with the Ukraine, for in the Crimea the Germans had been outflanked and had been given little time to carry out planned demolition, whereas in the Ukraine they had destroyed everything with sadistic calculation and method. Stalin then asked how things were going on the Western Front; Roosevelt told him that General Marshall would later give a detailed outline of the situation, but he could say now that a limited offensive was due to start on February 8 and another on the twelfth and that the main drive of the Anglo-American forces would begin in about a month's time. Stalin was gratified to hear this and expressed the hope that the Allies would shortly capture the Ruhr and the Saar and thereby deprive the Germans of their only remaining sources of coal, the Russians having already captured the Silesia Basin. Roosevelt said that with the two forces now coming closer together from east and from west, he believed that it would be possible for General Eisenhower to establish direct communication with the Red Army and thereby achieve direct co-ordination of tactical operations.

Roosevelt asked Stalin how he had got along with General de Gaulle, who had visited Moscow in December. Stalin replied that he had found de Gaulle to be an uncomplicated individual and also unrealistic in his estimates of France's contribution to the winning of the war.

Roosevelt said that there had been disagreements between himself and the British over the general policy toward France and also over the question of zones of occupation in Germany. Stalin asked whether the President thought that France should have a zone of occupation and, if so, for what reason. Roosevelt evidently made a somewhat equivocal reply and Stalin and Molotov both said that this was a topic for discussion here at Yalta; they indicated that they did not view the idea with much favor.

This meeting was held in the President's study at Livadia and a few minutes before five, they moved down to the Grand Ballroom for the first formal conference. Stalin was accompanied by Vishinski, Gromyko, Gusev, (the Soviet Ambassador in London) and Maisky as well as Molotov and three Chiefs of Staff. Hopkins felt too ill to come to this meeting—which must have meant that he was very sick indeed—and ill health had prevented General Hap Arnold from coming to Yalta at all, the U.S. Army Air Forces being represented by General Laurence S. Kuter, Assistant Chief of Air Staff for Plans.

At the start of the meeting, Marshal Stalin suggested that President Roosevelt should again preside. The discussion, which lasted for nearly three hours, dealt almost entirely with the military situation. General Antonov read a prepared paper giving a detailed analysis of developments on the Eastern Front and expressed the hope that the Allies would soon advance in the West and would paralyze German communications by bombing in order to prevent the shifting of troops across Germany from west to east and from Norway and Italy. Marshall reviewed the situation in the West, Portal spoke for the Air Force, and Cunningham talked of the new German technical developments which tended to revive the U-boat threat. At one point, the Prime Minister made mention of the possibility that the Allies might aid the Russian campaign on the Eastern Front by an expedition across the Adriatic into the Balkans, but this proposal does not appear to have been pursued any further.

Roosevelt was host at the dinner which followed this meeting. The Filipino mess men were on duty, but the food was strictly Russian: caviar, sturgeon, beef and macaroni, sweet cake, tea, coffee, vodka and five kinds of wine. (In the White House the guests would have had to content themselves with one kind of California sauterne.) In his report, Bohlen stated that "very good humor" prevailed throughout the meal, but he added a bit of conversation on the side between himself and Vishinski which sounded mildly caustic. Vishinski said that the Soviet Union would never agree to the right of the small nations to judge the acts of the Great Powers and, when Bohlen ventured the opinion that the American people were not likely to approve of any denial of the small nations' rights, Vishinski said that the American people "should learn to obey their leaders." Bohlen then suggested that it might be a good idea for Vishinski to visit the United States and try to tell that to the people, and Vishinski remarked that he would be glad to do so.

During the informal conversation at this dinner Churchill remarked that he was constantly being "beaten up" as a reactionary but that he was the only one of the three representatives present who could be thrown out of office at any time by the votes of his own people. He added that personally he gloried in this danger. This led Stalin to observe, jokingly, that evidently the Prime Minister feared the results of the forthcoming elections in Great Britain. Churchill replied that not only did he not fear them but he was proud of the right of the British people to change their government whenever they wished to do so. He went on to speak of the rights of the small nations and quoted a very apt proverb: "The eagle should permit the small birds to sing and care not wherefor they sang."

At breakfast the following morning, a courier delivered to Roosevelt

White House mail which had been dispatched from Washington on January 31. The courier had been five days in transit, which meant that Roosevelt was now at the extreme edge of the distance that he could travel from Washington under the ten day limitation on his power to act on Congressional bills. (Subsequent couriers managed to make the trip in three days.) The foreign secretaries met that day for lunch with Molotov at the Koreis Villa, where Stalin and staff were staying. (Churchill was at Vorontsov Villa, twelve miles away.) At the start of this lunch, Harriman announced the news that Manila had been taken and Molotov "immediately proposed a toast to this victory of the Allied Armies." There followed toasts by Eden and Stettinius to Molotov, by Molotov to Hull and to Clark Kerr, the British Ambassador, more toasts by Stettinius to his Dumbarton Oaks colleagues, Gromyko and Cadogan, by Molotov to Harriman, by Harriman to Vishinski, by Byrnes to the Red Army, by Gromyko to Byrnes and by Maisky to the closest possible unity between the peoples, governments and chiefs of the United Nations. It was decided that these meetings should be officially named "The Crimean Conference"—a futile decision, as it turned out, because the conference always has and undoubtedly always will bear the name of Yalta. There does not appear to have been much more of importance discussed at the luncheon, except that Molotov made it clear that the Soviet Government expected to receive reparations in kind from Germany and hoped that the United States would furnish the Soviet Union with long-term credits. Stettinius said that he was ready to discuss these matters at any time.

The second formal meeting was held at four that afternoon and despite all the luncheon toasts the conference really got down to business. The Chiefs of Staff, with the exception of Leahy, were not present at this meeting, but Hopkins dragged himself out of bed for it and attended all the main meetings thereafter. Hopkins was too ill to write extended memoranda at Yalta as he had done at other conferences, but the precise records of his later conferences in Moscow (Chapter XXXV) throw considerable light on his attitude toward the progress made at Yalta. Byrnes has provided a lucid account of the meetings that he attended in his book, *Speaking Frankly*, and Churchill will write another. (I often wonder when, if ever, Stalin will be heard from.)

None of the momentous conferences of the Second World War has provoked more subsequent controversy than this one; Yalta has been blamed for many of the ills with which the world was afflicted in the years following the total defeat of Nazi Germany and Japan. The belief has grown that Roosevelt made various "surrenders" to the Russians at Yalta, and the more kindly critics attribute these to the fact that he was a dying man. The complete records of the Conference, as they appear in the Hopkins papers, do not seem to substantiate this theory.

Roosevelt appears to have been in full possession of all of his faculties. Only at the end of seven days of long meetings, covering a wide range of tremendous subjects, did he make a concession which, in my belief, he would not have made if he had not been tired out and anxious to end the negotiations relative to Russia's entry into the war with Japan. This will be discussed later in this chapter. Of all the "surrenders" supposed to have been made, those most often cited and emphasized relate to the establishment of the veto power in the Security Council of the United Nations and the granting to the Soviet Union of two additional votes in the General Assembly. These two points have often been linked together under the general term, "the voting formula," but they were entirely separate problems and the first of them was not a subject of contention at Yalta.

The principle of the veto was stated by the United States Government and the British Government in their separate "Tentative Proposals for a General International Organization" as drafted in July, 1944, prior to the Dumbarton Oaks Conference. Throughout that conference, and the five months that followed it before Yalta, there was complete agreement that in matters which might affect world peace the veto could be exercised by any one of the four (or, if France were included, five) major powers. The arguments with the Russians that arose at Dumbarton Oaks and resulted in failure to agree on a voting formula for the Security Council were concerned not with the principle of the veto but with the precise extent to which any power should be denied the right to vote on a dispute in which it was a participant. Various compromise proposals on this were made by Stettinius, for the United States, and Cadogan for Britain, but Gromyko, for the Soviet Union, was unbudgeable. On September 18, 1944, he had said confidently to Stettinius, "The Russian position on voting in the Council will never be departed from." When Stettinius expressed the fear that this unyielding attitude might break up the world organization even before it started, Gromyko said flatly that no world organization would exist in which a major power was denied the right to vote in any dispute, whether it was a participant therein or not.

It was at this same time that the question of more votes than one was raised. Stalin said, in a cable to Roosevelt, "You, of course, know that the Ukraine and Byelorussia, which are constituent parts of the Soviet Union, are greater in population and in political importance than certain other countries which we all agree should belong to the number of initiators of the establishment of the International Organization. Therefore, I hope to have an opportunity to explain to you the political importance of this question which has been brought up by the Soviet Delegation at Dumbarton Oaks."

On December 5, 1944, the United States Government prepared a new compromise proposal on the voting formula which was forwarded to the British and Russian Governments and which was again presented by Stettinius when this general subject first came up for discussion at Yalta. Agreement on it was reached with, it would appear, no argument at all. There certainly was no evidence on the record of opposition by Churchill, a stanch European, who was always at all these meetings a zealous and unflagging champion of the rights of small nations. Indeed, the British had been heartily in favor of the veto as a means of preventing any encroachments on their own imperial interests. The United States had favored it as a form of insurance against the commitment by the United Nations Council of American forces to action in all sorts of possible wars in all parts of the world—and Roosevelt, with the memory of Woodrow Wilson always alive in him, was particularly conscious of the importance of this point when the United Nations Charter would eventually be submitted for ratification by the Senate.

According to the December 5 compromise formula, the main concession to Russia provided that a major power could by its veto prevent the Council from taking action, such as application of sanctions or of war itself, against said power. What Russia yielded in this compromise was this: a major power could not by its veto prevent the Council even from considering and thereby advertising the involvement of said power in any dispute. The British and Americans at Yalta did not consider this a negligible concession, for it represented a considerable relaxing of the rigid position taken by Gromyko (in accordance, of course, with his orders from Moscow) at Dumbarton Oaks. The differences of opinion on this may be indicated by quotation of two American editorials which represented viewpoints dominated by neither Russophilia nor Russophobia. The *Providence Bulletin* said, "It is a sizable concession on the part of the Powers who possess the military force, especially on the part of Russia, that the smaller nations can haul one up to the bar of the organization and make their charges of grievances and injustice against a Great Power." The *Savannah News* said, "If this compromise plan on the Council's voting procedure is allowed to stand at the San Francisco peace conference next month, the people of the United States might as well make up their minds that the new world organization will fail as miserably as did the old League. . . . The time to have a real peace organization—with teeth in it—is NOW, without fear, favor or compromise."

It was at the fourth formal meeting on February 7 at Yalta that the Russians made their request for two or possibly three additional votes in the United Nations Assembly—and Roosevelt wanted it to be absolutely clear that they meant the Assembly and not the Council. Stalin and Molotov wanted final agreement to be reached then and there so that the

Ukraine and Byelorussia could be invited to the San Francisco Conference.

In response to this proposal, Roosevelt embarked on a long speech in which he employed his familiar tactics for attempting to dodge an immediate issue by maneuvering the conversation into the realms of irrelevancy. He mentioned the fact that certain countries are large in area, though small in population, and referred in this connection to Brazil

Mr. President
I think you should
try to g et this referred
to Foreign ministers before
there is trouble.
Harry

Note passed by Hopkins to Roosevelt at the Yalta Conference during the discussion of the Russian request for additional votes in the United Nations Assembly.

which he said was smaller in area than the U.S.S.R. but larger than the United States. On the other hand, there were some countries that were small in area but large in population, such as Honduras and Haiti, etc. Evidently Stalin began to betray signs of impatience and irritability as Roosevelt's vagrant remarks were translated to him, for Hopkins scribbled the following note: "Mr. President—I think you should try to get this referred to Foreign Ministers before there is trouble. Harry."

There is no doubt that Roosevelt had come to Yalta determined to oppose the Russian demand for the two additional votes. In fact, it is my understanding that he had previously told the Cabinet and Congressional leaders in Washington that if the Russians were to insist on this point he would demand forty-eight votes for the United States. Now, at Yalta, Churchill spoke out strongly in favor of the admission of the two republics. I do not know what his reasons were for this, but it seemed evident to the Americans present that he was influenced by British imperial considerations and especially the problem of India.

When the Foreign Secretaries' meeting considered the issue the following day, Eden supported Molotov, and Stettinius reserved his position. It was agreed, however, that only those countries which had signed the United Nations Declaration by the day on which the Yalta Conference should end would be invited to the San Francisco Conference. Subsequently, in view of the British unwillingness to join him in objecting to the two extra votes, Roosevelt decided to agree to support the Russian proposal at San Francisco but insisted that it must be a matter for full discussion and free vote at the later conference and not a *fait accompli* at Yalta.

At the fifth formal meeting, February 8, both Stalin and Molotov expressed confidence that they could obtain the signatures of the Ukraine and Byelorussia to the United Nations Declaration while the Yalta Conference was still in session. (Presumably this involved the dispatch of one brief order to Moscow.) They felt that such signatures would entitle the two republics to invitation to the San Francisco Conference. Again Roosevelt made a bid to change the subject, whereupon Stalin said, "I do not want to embarrass the President, but if he will explain his difficulties we will see what can be done."

Roosevelt then said that this was a technical question, but an important one, which involved the granting to one of the Great Powers of two additional votes in the Assembly. He repeated that this was a matter which must be left for decision by all the United Nations representatives gathered at San Francisco, but he gave assurance that the United States would support the Soviet proposal. Again, Stalin proposed that the problem could be settled then and there by obtaining the signatures of the two republics—and again Roosevelt said that he did not think this would overcome the difficulty. Whereupon Stalin finally withdrew the proposal and the President expressed his appreciation of the Marshal's action in doing so.

Roosevelt proposed what he considered an "insurance clause" for use in the event that there would be howls of protest in the Congress against American support for two additional votes for Russia in the United Nations Assembly: this was a proposal that the Soviet Union would support a demand for two additional votes for the United States in case such a demand were to be made. Stalin agreed to this, apparently without argument.

In the official records of the Yalta Conference is set down a poignant interruption by Roosevelt when Churchill was pointing out that Britain's claims to Hong Kong would be protected by the veto formula and Stalin was asking, "Suppose that Egypt should raise the question of the return of the Suez Canal?" Roosevelt then reminded them that in the Teheran Declaration they had said: "We recognize fully the supreme responsibility resting upon us and all the nations to make a peace which will command good-will from the overwhelming masses of the peoples of the world."

Roosevelt tried to keep the discussion on that basis, and he left Yalta believing he had been largely successful in doing so.

Stalin was at first obdurate on the subject of French participation in the control of Germany, and throughout most of the conference Roosevelt was inclined to agree with him. But, as Hopkins expressed it, "Winston and Anthony [Eden] fought like tigers for France." And Hopkins worked constantly from his sick bed to support them. His failure to generate any warmth in de Gaulle had not altered his conviction that France must be restored to its proper dignity, not only as its just historic due, but because stability in Europe was inconceivable without a strong and influential France.

At the second formal meeting, Stalin said that he would not object to France being given a zone provided it was carved out of the British and American zones and did not affect the Russians, but he added that if this were the case then the Belgians and the Dutch and "other states" (presumably in Eastern Europe) should also participate in the occupation of Germany; he remained adamant in opposition to the inclusion of France in the Allied Control Commission for Germany. Churchill argued stoutly that without French power, Britain alone could not undertake to contain Germany on the Western Front. Roosevelt at this time said that "he favored the acceptance of the French request for a zone, but that he agreed with Marshal Stalin that France should not take part in the control machinery." Eden expressed the conviction that unless France did take such a part she would not accept responsibility for the occupation of a zone. As was usually the case when the Big Three could not come to unanimous agreement on any point, the matter was referred to the Foreign Secretaries "for further study."

At a meeting of the Foreign Secretaries two days later, the same division occurred with Molotov and Stettinius opposed to French participation and Eden in favor of it.

At the fourth formal meeting, Churchill and Stalin again argued the point. Churchill said that "he did not wish France to be included in the present club [the Big Three] which he felt was very exclusive, at least for a while. He added, however, that he felt that the fact of permitting France to join the Control Commission would keep them quiet for a while." Roosevelt said that "he agreed that France should not join this body but he was doubtful whether this would keep them quiet."

Before the seventh formal meeting on February 10 (this was after Byrnes's departure from Yalta), Hopkins finally persuaded Roosevelt to side with Churchill on this controversial point. When at the meeting, Eden brought up the subject of France, the record states that:

The President then said that he had changed his mind in regard to the question of the French participation in the Control Commission. He now agreed with the views of the Prime Minister that it would be

Note from Hopkins to Roosevelt, written during the protracted discussions of France's role in the control of Germany, suggesting that "French participation on Control Commission might be considered later" in the Conference.

impossible to give France an area to administer in Germany unless they were members of the Control Commission. He said he thought it would be easier to deal with the French if they were on the Commission than if they were not.

Marshal Stalin said he had no objections and that he agreed to this.

Reading this record, it would seem that Stalin's concurrence with Roosevelt's reversal of position had come with dramatic suddenness. Such was not the case. Actually Roosevelt had previously informed Stalin privately through Harriman of his long-delayed change of mind and heart on this and Stalin had said that since this was the President's considered decision he would go along with it.

A message had reached Hopkins at Yalta from Bidault via Caffery that it was felt that nothing was to be gained by following through on Hopkins' suggestion that de Gaulle be invited to participate in the final meetings of

Mr. President

The Russians have given
in so much at this conference
that I don't think we should
let them down. Let the British
disagree if they want to – and continue
their disagreement at Moscow. Simply
say it is all referred to the
Reparation Commission with the
minutes to show the British disagree
about any mention of the 10 billion.

Harry

Hopkins' note to Roosevelt, written during the final meeting at Yalta, suggesting a solution to the deadlocked reparations discussion.

the conference, but that de Gaulle had stated that he would be delighted to meet Roosevelt on his trip home from Yalta at any place and at any time that the President designated.

It seemed to Hopkins that the old, festering sore which had developed from the original fleabite at St. Pierre and Miquelon was at last to be healed. However, on February 14, after Roosevelt and Hopkins had left Yalta and were aboard the cruiser *Quincy* on Great Bitter Lake near Suez, a message came from Caffery stating that de Gaulle had again assumed an attitude of frigid haughtiness and announced that it was not convenient for him to go to Algiers to meet Roosevelt. When Caffery heard this he indignantly reminded Bidault of de Gaulle's previous assurance that he would be delighted to meet the President, which assurance had been duly communicated to Roosevelt through Hopkins. Bidault said in effect, "Yes, I know he did. I have been doing everything to make him go but he has changed his mind and you don't know how stubborn he is." Caffery reported that de Gaulle was in a sulky mood because the public statements issued at the end of the Yalta Conference had not paid sufficient attention to him personally. Thus he lost his last chance to establish the cordial relations with President Roosevelt which would have added so much to his own prestige with the French people.

The question of the Russian claim for reparations in kind from Germany was argued back and forth throughout the Yalta Conference. Both Churchill and Roosevelt said that public opinion in their countries was opposed to the whole concept of reparations in view of the unfortunate results of the Treaty of Versailles—and Stalin was later to confess to Hopkins that he became pretty fed up with hearing about American and British public opinion, believing that the President and Prime Minister kept on referring to it merely as a device to justify their own personal opinions and prejudices. The Russians never did succeed in understanding that public opinion could be a determining factor even with the powerful heads of state; Stalin had said to Roosevelt at Teheran that the way to overcome the moral objections of the American people to absorption of the Baltic States in the Soviet Union was to subject them to a propaganda campaign, and Vishinski had expressed precisely the same point of view in his remark to Bohlen that the American people should learn to obey their leaders.

In the final meeting at Yalta, the whole question of reparations seemed to have reached a deadlock. It was decided that the matter should be referred to an Interallied Commission to be set up in Moscow, but it seemed impossible to agree on the terms of the basic directive on which this Commission would proceed. During the argument, Hopkins wrote the following note and passed it to Roosevelt: "The Russians have given in so much at this conference that I don't think we should let them down. Let the British disagree if they want to—and continue their disagreement at Moscow. Simply say it is all referred to the Reparations Commission with the minutes to show the British disagree about any mention of the 10 billion." Roosevelt took that advice, believing he had left the door open for all sorts of deliberations in the future.

Thus, the decision on reparations was deferred as the question of the dismemberment of Germany had been; however, unlike the question of dismemberment, it was not permitted to die of inanition, as Roosevelt undoubtedly hoped it would be. After Roosevelt's death, the Russians were arguing that he had supported their claim. They cited as their authority for this contention his statement, as Byrnes has written, that the Reparation Commission should "take in its initial studies as a basis for discussion, the suggestion of the Soviet Government, that the total sum of reparations should be 20 billions and that 50% should go to the Soviet Union." That was the basis of the ten billion dollars claim, but a reading of the quoted statement plus a knowledge of Roosevelt's oft-proclaimed point of view would certainly suggest that he was carefully making no commitment whatsoever. I believe it can be proved that he made no commitment on any policy concerned with the postwar treatment of Germany except on the matter of Allied military occupation and the principle of trial and punishment for the war criminals.

The record of Roosevelt's pertinent statements and his known character indicates very strongly his conviction that there were too many questions remaining to be answered about Germany before any blueprints could be drawn; for example—was there any fragment of truth in the hopeful reports that there was a formidable anti-Nazi and pro-democratic movement among the German people, or that there were any separatist movements in Bavaria or in any other part of the Reich? Even at this late date in the war—in February, 1945—the German territory aside from East Prussia that had been occupied by Russian, British, American or French forces was still infinitesimal, and the state of mind of the German people that might follow collapse of the Nazi Government remained a gigantic question mark.

At Yalta, Roosevelt was adhering to the basic formula of unconditional surrender; beyond that, he demanded only—to quote one of his favorite phrases—"freedom of action." Therefore, when he said that the Reparations Commission should "in its initial studies" take the Soviet suggestion in regard to reparations "as a basis for discussion," it may be assumed that he meant precisely what he said and no more.

During the fourth formal meeting, Roosevelt first made the proposal for a meeting of all the United Nations to be held in the United States at the earliest possible moment, perhaps even within the next four weeks, for the actual setting up of the world organization. (April 25 was eventually selected as the date and San Francisco as the place.) While

All of the below refer to Churchill's opposition to early calling of conference of United Nations.

I still think the [crossed out]

There is something behind this talk that we do not know — of its basis.

Perhaps we better to wait till later tonight what is on his mind.

All this is [crossed out] ! local politics

I am quite sure now he is thinking about the next election in Britain.

The exchange of comments between Hopkins and Roosevelt during the fourth formal Yalta meeting, as Churchill argued against calling the United Nations Conference in the near future.

he heartily approved this suggestion "in principle," Churchill advanced all sorts of arguments against holding such a conference in the near future. While Churchill was arguing, Hopkins wrote a note to Roosevelt, "There's something behind this talk—we do not know of its basis. Perhaps we better wait till later tonight [to find out] what is on his mind." To which Roosevelt added, "All this is local politics." Whereupon Hopkins wrote, "I'm quite sure now he is thinking about the next election in Britain." This was a consideration with which Roosevelt could readily sympathize.

The outcome on other principal subjects considered at Yalta can be summarized as follows:

Liberated Areas—The communiqué issued on this spoke for itself. It was a heartening reaffirmation of the principles of the Atlantic Charter, all the more welcome after the unpleasant situations that had arisen in Belgium, Italy and Greece. At the sixth formal meeting on February 9, the next to last day of the conference, Molotov offered an amendment to the communiqué: "And in this connection support should be given to the political leaders of these countries who took an active part in the struggle against the German invaders." Stalin pointed out, perhaps with a trace of impishness, that Churchill need have no anxiety that this Molotov amendment was designed to apply to Greece. At a later meeting of the Foreign Secretaries that same evening, Stettinius said that the United States could not accept this amendment since it suggested "too much interference in the affairs of these countries and involved taking decisions on who had collaborated with the enemy, which should be left to the peoples of these countries themselves." Eden expressed full concurrence with these views and the amendment was finally dropped.

Poland—The principles of the Liberated Areas agreement of course applied here, but the discussions of Poland's precise boundaries and the composition of its provisional government seemed to have taken up more time than was devoted to any other subject in the conference. Certainly, the British and Americans left Yalta with the belief that this difficult problem had reached an honorable and equitable solution. They soon learned that they were wrong. Similarly, it was believed that the agreement reached on Yugoslavia guaranteed to that gallant, tortured country the opportunity to achieve a representative government in accordance with truly democratic principles.

The Dardanelles—While Stalin stated his country's desire for a modification of the Montreux Convention, he did not press for an immediate agreement on this. Churchill said that the British certainly felt that the present position of Russia with her "great interests in the Black Sea should not be dependent on the narrow exit." He said that, since this might affect the position of Great Britain in the Mediterranean more than it would that of the United States, he suggested that it should be discussed at a later meeting of the Foreign Secretaries in London. Stalin agreed.

Iran—On this one subject the Western Allies ran into a blank wall of disagreement. Following is the text of the final discussion at the Foreign Secretaries meeting on February 10:

> *Mr. Eden* inquired whether Mr. Molotov had considered the British document on Iran.
>
> *Mr. Molotov* stated that he had nothing to add to what he had said several days ago on the subject.
>
> *Mr. Eden* inquired whether it would not be advisable to issue a communiqué on Iran.
>
> *Mr. Molotov* stated that this would be inadvisable.
>
> *Mr. Stettinius* urged that some reference be made that Iranian problems had been discussed and clarified during the Crimean Conference.
>
> *Mr. Molotov* stated that he opposed this idea.
>
> *Mr. Eden* suggested that it be stated that the declaration on Iran had been reaffirmed and re-examined during the present meeting.
>
> *Mr. Molotov* opposed this suggestion.

In that bit of dialogue appears the Molotov whom future Secretaries of State, Byrnes and Marshall, came to know so well.

Trusteeships—This subject had been discussed in the conferences with Anthony Eden in the White House in March, 1943 (Chapter XXVIII) and Hopkins recorded at the time that it was becoming clear that Eden "thinks very little" of the idea of trusteeships of which Roosevelt always thought so much. When Stettinius brought this subject up at the sixth formal meeting at Yalta, on February 9, it instantly became clear that Churchill thought even less of it. Stettinius reported that at a meeting of the Foreign Ministers it had been agreed that "The five Governments which will have permanent seats on the Security Council should consult each other prior to the United Nations Conference [on] providing machinery in the World Charter for dealing with territorial trusteeship and dependent areas." Thereupon Churchill exploded that he did not agree with one single word of this report. He said that he had not been consulted about this nor had he even heard of it previously, adding that he would never consent under any circumstances to the United Nations thrusting interfering fingers into the very life of the British Empire. He enlarged at some length and with considerable vigor on his historic assurance that as long as he was Prime Minister he would never yield one scrap of Britain's heritage. When Stettinius explained that the trusteeship principle was intended to apply to such areas as the Japanese mandated islands in the Pacific, but not to any part of the British Empire, Churchill accepted the explanation but stated positively that this important distinction must be made quite clear. He said that

Britain had no desire for any territorial aggrandizement, and he had no objection to the trusteeship principle as applied to enemy territory. He asked Stalin how he would feel about a proposal to have the Crimea internationalized for use as a summer resort. Stalin replied that he would be glad to give the Crimea for use as a permanent meeting place for the Three Powers.

Roosevelt told Stalin privately that he thought that Hong Kong should be given back to the Chinese or internationalized as a free port, but I do not know if he ever made that suggestion to Churchill. The decisive discussions (they are all on the record) relative to the Far East and Russia's entry into the war against Japan were conducted between Roosevelt and Stalin with Churchill not present, although he joined in signing the final written agreement which has been the subject of so much controversy since its terms were made public.

In *Where Are We Heading?* Sumner Welles has offered serious criticism of elements in this agreement. Welles saw no valid objection to the return of southern Sakhalin and the Kurile Islands to Russia, since these positions, which the Japanese had seized, were highly important and even essential to Russian security in the Far East; nor was there objection to the internationalization of Dairen (provided it ever were truly "internationalized") nor to the granting of permanent autonomy to Outer Mongolia. "However," Welles wrote, "the restoration to Russia of the right formerly possessed by the Imperial Russian Governments to dominate Manchuria through the control of the Chinese Eastern and South Manchurian railroads, and the lease of Port Arthur as a naval base, necessarily fall into a different category. These concessions, which will make it altogether impossible for a new unified China to exercise full sovereignty within Manchuria, are all the more objectionable in view of China's absence from the conference table where they were decided." Such criticism from Welles could hardly be dismissed as coming from one who did not know what he was talking about or who was embittered by hatred of Roosevelt. But it may be said that in writing them Welles had the considerable advantage of hindsight.

It is quite clear that Roosevelt had been prepared even before the Teheran Conference in 1943 to agree to the legitimacy of most if not all of the Soviet claims in the Far East, for they involved the restoration of possessions and privileges taken by the Japanese from the Russians in the war of 1904. It is also clear that the failure to notify the Chinese immediately of the Yalta discussions was due to fear of the security of secrets in Chungking. Stalin told Roosevelt at Yalta that he intended to start the movement of twenty-five Russian divisions across Siberia to the Far East and this operation must be conducted in utmost secrecy, and Roosevelt said that when this movement of troops had been completed (presumably within three or four months) he would send an American officer to Chungking via Moscow to inform Chiang Kai-shek of the agreements. Stalin insisted that these agreements must be put in writing and must contain the statement: "The Heads of the three Great Powers have agreed that these claims of the Soviet Union shall be unquestionably fulfilled after Japan has been defeated."

This, in my opinion, was the most assailable point in the entire Yalta record, and the most surprising in that it involved Roosevelt in the kind of firm commitment that usually he managed to avoid. It denied him the postwar "freedom of action" which he valued so highly; for, if China had refused to agree to any of the Soviet claims, presumably the U.S. and Britain would have been compelled to join in enforcing them.

It must be said that in all considerations of Far Eastern matters at Yalta Roosevelt's principal concern was based on American war plans against Japan. The immensely costly operations at Iwo Jima and then at Okinawa were about to be launched, and the plans had been made for the major invasion of the Japanese home islands in the fall of 1945. MacArthur's calculations were based on the assumption that the Russians would contain the great bulk of Japanese forces on the Asiatic mainland as they had contained the Germans in Eastern Europe. Obviously, the entry of the Soviet Union forcibly into the Japanese war by midsummer —before the major invasion—could mean the saving of countless American lives, and might even make the final invasion unnecessary. Of course, at the time of Yalta, the perfection of the atomic bomb still seemed to be only a remote possibility for the uncertain future; it was not until three months after Roosevelt's death that assurance came from Los Alamos that the long years of research and experiment on this decisive weapon had achieved success.

In spite of all of which, it is my belief that Roosevelt would not have agreed to that final firm commitment had it not been that the Yalta Conference was almost at an end and he was tired and anxious to avoid further argument. I believe that he was hopeful that, when the time came to notify the Chinese, he would be able to straighten the whole thing out with Chiang Kai-shek—but that hope, of course, was not realized.

During the discussion of the Far Eastern agreements—and there was not much discussion—Stalin said to Roosevelt that if his conditions were not met it would be very difficult to explain to the Russian people why they must go to war against Japan. (Here the Marshal was obviously using the "public opinion" tactic which he complained of when used by Roosevelt or Churchill.) He said that the Russian people had clearly understood that they must fight the Germans to defend the very existence of their homeland, but that they could see no such threat from the Japanese. However, Stalin said, if the required political conditions were met, then it would not be difficult for him to explain to the Supreme Soviet and the people just what was their stake in the Far Eastern war.

Stalin agreed to the establishment of American air bases at Komsomolsk and Nikolaevsk in the near future, and later on Kamchatka, the delay in the latter case being due to the presence there of a Japanese Consul who could not fail to notice the presence of U.S. Air Force personnel. Stalin also agreed to the immediate institution of American-Russian military staff talks for joint planning.

It was agreed that "in two or three months after Germany has surrendered and the war in Europe has terminated the Soviet Union shall enter the war against Japan on the side of the Allies."

Stalin again expressed his lack of confidence in China as a world power. He said that he could not understand why the Kuomintang Government and the Communists should not maintain a united front against the Japanese. He felt that Chiang Kai-shek should assume leadership for this purpose but that there was a need for some new leaders around the Generalissimo. He said there were some good men in the Comintern and he did not understand why they had not been brought forward. (He later restated these views more explicitly in his talks with Hopkins in Moscow.)

Roosevelt said that the new American Ambassador, General Hurley, and General Wedemeyer were much more successful than their predecessors in bringing the Communists in the North together with the Chungking Government. He said that the blame for the breach lay more with the Comintern and the Kuomintang than with the rank and file of the so-called Communists.

Stalin asked Roosevelt whether any foreign troops would be stationed in Korea. Roosevelt replied in the negative, and Stalin expressed his approval of this.

A large dinner was given by Stalin on the evening of February 8 and a smaller one (with only the principals attending) by Churchill on the last evening, February 10. The record of the principal toasts at the former dinner was as follows:

Marshal Stalin proposed a toast to the health of the Prime Minister, whom he characterized as the bravest governmental figure in the world. He said that due in large measure to Mr. Churchill's courage and staunchness, England, when she stood alone, had divided the might of Hitlerite Germany at a time when the rest of Europe was falling flat on its face before Hitler. He said that Great Britain, under Mr. Churchill's leadership, had carried on the fight alone irrespective of existing or potential allies. The Marshal concluded that he knew of few examples in history where the courage of one man had been so important to the future history of the world. He drank a toast to Mr. Churchill, his fighting friend and a brave man.

The Prime Minister, in his reply, toasted Marshal Stalin as the mighty leader of a mighty country, which had taken the full shock of the German war machine, had broken its back and had driven the tyrants from her soil. He said he knew that in peace no less than in war Marshal Stalin would continue to lead his people from success to success.

Marshal Stalin then proposed the health of the President of the United States. He said that he and Mr. Churchill in their respective countries had had relatively simple decisions. They had been fighting for their very existence against Hitlerite Germany but there was a third man whose country had not been seriously threatened with invasion, but who had had perhaps a broader conception of national interest and even though his country was not directly imperilled had been the chief forger of the instruments which had led to the mobilization of the world against Hitler. He mentioned in this connection Lend-Lease as one of the President's most remarkable and vital achievements in the formation of the Anti-Hitler combination and in keeping the allies in the field against Hitler.

The President, in reply to this toast, said he felt the atmosphere at this dinner was as that of a family, and it was in those words that he liked to characterize the relations that existed between our three countries. He said that great changes had occurred in the world during the last three years, and even greater changes were to come. He said that each of the leaders represented here were working in their own way for the interests of their people. He said that fifty years ago there were vast areas of the world where people had little opportunity and no hope, but much had been accomplished, although there were still great areas where people had little opportunity and little hope, and their objectives here were to give to every man, woman and child on this earth the possibility of security and well being.

In a subsequent toast to the alliance between the three great powers, *Marshal Stalin* remarked that it was not so difficult to keep unity in time of war since there was a joint aim to defeat the common enemy which was clear to everyone. He said the difficult task came after the war when diverse interests tended to divide the Allies. He said he was confident that the present alliance would meet this test also and that it was our duty to see that it would, and that our relations in peacetime should be as strong as they had been in war.

The Prime Minister then said he felt we were all standing on the crest of a hill with the glories of future possibilities stretching before us. He said that in the modern world the function of leadership was to lead the people out from the forests into the broad sunlit plains of peace and happiness. He felt this prize was nearer our grasp than anytime before in history and it would be a tragedy for which history would never forgive us if we let this prize slip from our grasp through inertia or carelessness.

The mood of the American delegates, including Roosevelt and Hopkins, could be described as one of supreme exultation as they left Yalta. They were confident that their British colleagues agreed with them that this had been the most encouraging conference of all, and the immediate response of the principal spokesmen for British and American public opinion added immeasurably to their sense of satisfaction with the job that had been done. As soon as Roosevelt came on board the *Quincy* on Great Bitter Lake (so ominously and perhaps so appropriately named) he received floods of messages telling of the enthusiastic response to the publication of the Yalta communiqués in the United States. One of the cables quoted Herbert Hoover as saying, "It will offer a great hope to the world." William L. Shirer called it "a landmark in human history." Raymond Gram Swing said, "No more appropriate news could be conceived to celebrate the birthday of Abraham Lincoln." Senator Barkley cabled, "Accept my sincere felicitations upon the historic Joint Statement released today. I had it read to the Senate immediately upon release and it made a profound impression. Senator White, Minority Leader, joined me in the expressions of commendation and satisfaction on the floor of the Senate. I regard it as one of the most important steps ever taken to promote peace and happiness in the world."

Joseph C. Harsch wrote, in the *Christian Science Monitor,* "The Crimea Conference stands out from previous such conferences because of its mood of decision. The meetings which produced the Atlantic Charter, Casablanca, Teheran, Quebec—all these were dominated, politically, by declarative moods. They were declarations of policy, of aspirations, of intents. But they were not meetings of decision. The meeting at Yalta was plainly dominated by a desire, willingness and determination to reach solid decisions."

Hopkins later said to me, "We really believed in our hearts that this was the dawn of the new day we had all been praying for and talking about for so many years. We were absolutely certain that we had won the first great victory of the peace—and, by 'we,' I mean *all* of us, the whole civilized human race. The Russians had proved that they could be reasonable and farseeing and there wasn't any doubt in the minds of the President or any of us that we could live with them and get along with them peacefully for as far into the future as any of us could imagine. But I have to make one amendment to that—I think we all had in our minds the reservation that we could not foretell what the results would be if anything should happen to Stalin. We felt sure that we could count on him to be reasonable and sensible and understanding —but we never could be sure who or what might be in back of him there in the Kremlin."

CHAPTER XXXIV

The Terrific Headache

SOME time after his return to the United States, Hopkins wrote the following memorandum:

The last night before the Yalta conference broke up the President flabbergasted Churchill by telling him for the first time that he was going to fly to Egypt and had arranged for the King of Egypt, Ibn Saud and Hailie Selassie to hold conferences with him aboard the cruiser in Great Bitter Lake on three successive days. There were a number of people present when the President told Churchill about this and Churchill had no adequate opportunity to ask the President what these visits were all about. Later that night he, Churchill, sought me out, greatly disturbed and wanted to know what were the President's intentions in relation to these three sovereigns. Fortunately I could tell him I did not know because I had asked the President the same thing. I had already made up my mind that it was, in the main, a lot of horseplay and that the President was going to thoroughly enjoy the colorful panoply of the sovereigns of this part of the world who thought that President Roosevelt of the United States could probably cure all their troubles. I did know he intended to talk to Ibn Saud about the Palestine situation. Nothing I said, however, was comforting to Churchill because he thought we had some deep laid plot to undermine the British Empire in these areas.

The next day the Prime Minister told the President that he was also going into Egypt after a brief visit to Greece and see each of these sovereigns himself, and had already sent the messages asking them to remain in Egypt for conferences with him immediately after the President had left.

The public aspects of these conferences have been widely written about and I, therefore, do not intend to repeat those here. The only really important thing was the discussion the President had with Ibn Saud about Palestine and this was short and to the point.

I am sure the President did not realize what kind of man he was going to be entertaining when he invited Ibn Saud to meet him—a man of austere dignity, great power and a born soldier and, above all, an Arabian first, last and all the time. He had spent his life fighting and enjoyed it and his subjects all enjoy fighting and they don't like the Jews. So, when the President asked Ibn Saud to admit some more Jews into Palestine, indicating that it was such a small percentage of the total population of the Arab world, he was greatly shocked when Ibn Saud, without a smile, said "No." Ibn Saud emphasized the fact that the Jews in Palestine were successful in making the countryside bloom only because American and British capital had been poured in in millions of dollars and said if those same millions had been given to the Arabs they could have done quite as well. He also said that there was a Palestine army of Jews all armed to the teeth and he remarked that they did not seem to be fighting the Germans but were aiming at the Arabs. He stated plainly that the Arab world would not permit a further extension beyond the commitment already made for future Jewish settlement in Palestine. He clearly inferred that the Arabs would take up arms before they would consent to that and he, as religious leader of the Arab world, must, naturally, support the Arabs in and about Palestine. The President seemed not to fully comprehend what Ibn Saud was saying to him for he brought the question up two or three times more and each time Ibn Saud was more determined than before. I fancy Ibn Saud was fully prepared for the President's plea to which he, the President, was wholly committed publicly and privately and by conviction.

There is no doubt that Ibn Saud made a great impression on the President that the Arabs meant business. None of this had anything to do with the merits of the case. I know the conference in relation to Palestine never came to grips with the real issues but developed into a monologue by Ibn Saud and I gained the impression that the President was overly impressed by what Ibn Saud said. And I never could reconcile the President's statement at a press conference later that he had learned more from Ibn Saud about Palestine in five minutes than he had learned in a lifetime—because the only thing he learned which all people well acquainted with the Palestine cause know, is that the Arabs don't want any more Jews in Palestine. They have been threatening the British for years with civil war if the lid is opened any farther and Ibn Saud merely told the President what he had undoubtedly told the British, and anybody else who wanted to ask him, many times before.

The *Quincy* remained at Great Bitter Lake from Monday until Wednesday, February 14, and then proceeded through the Suez Canal to Alexandria, where Churchill came aboard for lunch, this being the last meeting of the two Naval Persons. John G. Winant also came aboard and traveled with Roosevelt on the ship from Alexandria to Algiers.

On the first day out, the ship's newspaper, The *U.S.S. Quincy Star,* issued a FLASH! FLASH! bulletin from Guam: "Pacific fleet Commander Admiral Nimitz announces tonight that a powerful American task force is attacking military targets in and around Tokio." This was February 15 and a great day for the United States Navy, for it was the first time that an American fleet had attacked the Japanese home islands and it represented the beginning of the ultimate payoff for Pearl Harbor. Roosevelt well knew what this meant: the attacking fleet, known as Task Force 58, under the command of Admirals Spruance and Mitscher, was in itself the most powerful force that had ever gone to sea; it consisted of twenty aircraft carriers, all of which had been built during the present war, escorted by some ninety battleships, cruisers and destroyers. At this same time, as Roosevelt also knew, another huge United States fleet was moving up from the Marianas for the attack on the island of Iwo Jima which began four days later. If this piece of news from the far Pacific created excitement on the *Quincy,* I can report from the other end of the line that the news of the Yalta Conference was received without any appreciable display of emotion by those involved in Task Force 58, with which I happened to be traveling at the time on board the aircraft carrier, *U.S.S. Bennington.* Most interesting of all to the American sailors who were there within range of the Honshu coast was the statement that the United Nations Conference would be held at San Francisco, for this selection of location inspired the hope that "Maybe now at last the Big Guys will begin to look out our way."

During the three days between Alexandria and Algiers, Hopkins felt desperately ill and was confined to his cabin, which was inaccessible to Roosevelt. Statements were being prepared by the President and Steve Early for release to the press at Algiers. One of these related to the curt and abrupt refusal of General de Gaulle to accept Roosevelt's invitation to a meeting. Bohlen brought Hopkins a draft of the proposed statement in which Roosevelt made no attempt to disguise his anger at de Gaulle; Hopkins sent back messages pleading with the President not to lower himself to such a petulant level, and the statement was revised.

Roosevelt, who was tired out himself, had arranged to appear before the Congress immediately after his return to Washington and deliver a speech on the Yalta Conference. (Churchill was to make his report to the House of Commons on February 27.) Roosevelt's speech must be prepared on the *Quincy* during the trip across the Atlantic and naturally he expected Hopkins to help in its preparation, but Hopkins sent word through Bohlen that he must leave the ship at Algiers and go to Marrakech for a few days' rest and fly from there back to Washington. Although Roosevelt made no particular attempt to persuade Hopkins to change his mind about this, he was disappointed and even displeased. He was sure that Hopkins could get far better care on the *Quincy* than in Marrakech, and he apparently suspected that the desire to leave the ship was due more to boredom than anything else. It was difficult for Roosevelt to imagine anyone feeling miserable on board a ship. But Hopkins dreaded a nine-day voyage across the Atlantic during which he would probably remain confined to his cabin, with seasickness added to his other ills. So he was glad of a chance to escape, but he had cause later to wish that he had stayed with the ship.

Rosenman had been hastily summoned from London, where the President had sent him to work on the problem of relief for Britain and the liberated countries, and he joined the *Quincy* at Algiers to aid in the preparation of the speech, but Rosenman had no knowledge of what had gone on at Yalta, aside from the announcements that he had read in the newspapers, and neither Steve Early nor Anna Boettiger nor anybody else on board knew much about the full, inside story, or just how much of it should be revealed at this time with due regard for the wishes of the Russians and the British. Thus, with Hopkins gone, Roosevelt had to do all of the real work entirely by himself.

When Hopkins left the *Quincy* to go ashore at Algiers, the President's "good-by" to him was not a very amiable one—a circumstance which it is sad to record, for Hopkins never saw his great friend again.

At the same time, the beloved Pa Watson lay ill in his cabin on the *Quincy* and within two days he was dead. This was an awful blow for Roosevelt. As I have said before, he kept his personal sorrows strictly to himself: he had given no evidence to anyone of his emotions when his mother died—he had seemed to wish not even to talk about it to anyone—and it was the same after the deaths of his old friends and loyal associates, Louis Howe, Marvin McIntyre and Missy LeHand. But he made no attempt to hide the grief caused him by the loss of Pa Watson. Indeed, the very extent to which he talked about his sadness gave alarm to those who knew him best for it suggested that he himself was failing. The *Quincy* was not "a happy ship" on this cruise.

Hopkins remained for four days at the beautiful Taylor villa in Marrakech where he and Roosevelt had stayed after the Casablanca Conference. On February 24, he arrived back in Washington and three days later he flew to the Mayo Clinic where he remained until April 13. Roosevelt returned to Washington on February 28 and made his speech to the Congress on March 2. Roosevelt delivered this speech sitting down—explaining at the start, "it makes it a lot easier for me not having to carry about ten pounds of steel around on the bottom of my legs," and so far as I know this was the only time that he ever made public reference to his physical infirmity. He was extremely casual in this speech, ad-libbing a great deal of it. He made no claims to the achievement of perfection at Yalta. He said, "It has been a long journey. I hope you will all agree that it was a fruitful one. Speaking in all frankness, the question of whether it is entirely fruitful or not lies to a great extent in your hands. For unless you here in the halls of the American Congress—with the support of the American people—concur in the decisions reached at Yalta, and give them your active support, the meeting will not have produced lasting results."

After this speech, disillusionment began to set in. Speaking of the voting procedure in the Security Council, Roosevelt said, "It is not yet possible to announce the terms of it publicly, but it will be in a very short time." There was some question as to why this could not have been announced before—and there began to be speculation as to whether there were other secret agreements as yet unrevealed. On March 5 announcement of the voting formula was made by Stettinius from Mexico, where he had gone from Yalta for the Chapultepec Conference. Press opinion on this was very much divided, most of those who criticized the veto provision interpreting it as a "sell-out" to Stalin. The most important criticism came not from the irreconcilable isolationists but from the "perfectionists" who wanted the peace to be pure and unadulterated, and it was this criticism which irritated Roosevelt most acutely—perhaps because he himself was a perfectionist at heart. By the middle of March, a situation had developed in Rumania which indicated that the Russians were determined to set up governments in Eastern Europe in conformance with their own interpretation of the word "friendly" and without regard for the principles of the Atlantic Charter which had just been reaffirmed. There began to be editorial murmurings that Rumania might be providing the first test of the good faith of the Yalta agreements. However, Rumania was a Nazi satellite country and at that stage there were few who could become greatly concerned about its fate. But Poland was another matter. Poland was not only the first European country to have been ravaged in this war—it remained always as a disturbing reminder of the cynical Molotov-Ribbentrop pact. And now it was beginning to appear evident that a complete deadlock had developed among the British, Russian and American conferees in Moscow over the composition of the Provisional Polish Government, and that the Russians were demanding that the Lublin Government, which was entirely under their control and unrepresentative of any other Polish factions, should participate in the San Francisco Conference without further argument. Then it was announced that Molotov would not go to San Francisco, the Russian Delegation there to be headed by Gromyko. Since Eden was to head the British Delegation, and Stettinius the American, Molotov's abstention was generally interpreted as a blunt confession that the Soviet Government did not attach much importance to the conference. This was a very serious blasting of the high hopes which Yalta had inspired that the peoples' representatives would actually build at San Francisco the firm foundation for the permanent structure of world peace; but the structure would obviously lack one of its four cornerstones without Russia. There was now a growing feeling of uneasiness, born of the unknown and the inexplicable, regarding the true relationship between the Soviet Union and the United States, Great Britain and other United Nations. (Hopkins, in the hospital, was "bewildered" by these developments, as he stated very plainly to Stalin in conversations recorded in the next chapter.) It was beginning to be feared that a monstrous fraud had been perpetrated at Yalta, with Roosevelt and Churchill as the unwitting dupes. Then, suddenly, there came a news break which made the whole situation look very much uglier.

Roosevelt had announced that the American delegation at San Francisco would be completely bipartisan—he was not going to make the mistake that Wilson had made in failing to take any Republicans to Versailles; Congress would be represented by Senators Tom Connally and Arthur Vandenberg and by Representatives Sol Bloom and Charles A. Eaton. On March 23 the President summoned members of this delegation to the White House and informed them in strictest confidence of the arrangement made at Yalta whereby the United States and Britain would support the Russian request for three votes, in return for which Russia would support the United States request for three votes if it were put forward. This important piece of information was conveyed either accidentally or through a deliberate "leak" to the *New York Herald Tribune* and was printed on March 29. The White House and the State Department were immediately besieged by newspapermen demanding confirmation or denial of this story and the White House was compelled to issue a statement admitting that it was true. Then the press quite naturally wanted to know why had it been kept a secret—and how many more secrets were left over from Yalta? And if Russia had been granted votes for two of her republics, would she now demand votes for all the others? Roosevelt was in Washington for only a few hours at this time, en route from Hyde Park to Warm Springs—Hopkins was still at the Mayo Clinic—and Stettinius had to bear the brunt of the insistent and vociferous questioning. It was plainly apparent that not even his own Assistant Secretaries in the State Department had heard of the arrangement until the news was broken in the press. Indeed, the State Department had been conducting an "educational" campaign intended to emphasize the absolute equality of the United Nations voting procedure which gave the little fellow exactly the same rights as the big one.

This was one of the worst all-around botches of the war and a seemingly unnecessary one. It is understandable that Roosevelt might have wanted to withhold announcement of this somewhat questionable arrangement from the original Yalta communiqué so that it would not mitigate the effect of the over-all achievement; even so, it would have been far better to have included it in that communiqué and get it over with. By waiting, as Roosevelt did, to figure out a way to release it under the most favorable possible circumstances, he succeeded only in having it burst out under the worst possible circumstances. This was the aspect of it that was inexplicable—obviously it was going to be revealed anyway at San Francisco four weeks later, and Roosevelt, of all people, had reason to know that the moment he made the facts known however confidentially to a group of delegates there was danger of leakage to the press. It can only be said that this time he made a mistake which was thoroughly uncharacteristic of him—he underrated the intelligence of the American people—and that was the mistake that normally he left to his opponents. Actually, the greatest part of the resultant uproar was not concerned with the concession to Russia but with the utter, insulting absurdity of the American claim for three votes. All question of the United States demeaning itself by making such a demand was immediately and happily dropped. As for the Russian request, that was not considered a matter of serious importance or as a cause for any undue alarm. The *Herald Tribune,* which had produced the first eruption, expressed the healthy, intelligent attitude in an editorial: "While an assembly 'packed' by as many as sixteen Russian votes would obviously be inadmissible, a difference of two or three, one way or the other, in an international assembly of sixty or seventy members could have no possible practical significance. Even as matters stand, the United States will be able to count on the sympathetic votes of the Philippines, Cuba and others quite as surely as the United Kingdom will be able to count on those of the dominions and almost as surely as the Soviets will be able to count on White Russia and the Ukraine. To make a tortured issue out of such inconsequentialities would have been to endow them with an altogether fictitious importance." However, substantial damage had been done and from then on the very word "Yalta" came to be associated in the public's mind with secret and somehow shameful agreements. When the Far Eastern discussions were finally disclosed they were viewed with intense suspicion as further evidence of devious dealings, although there had been good and sufficient reason to withhold these until Russia was ready to go into action against Japan.

It was during this last week in March that I saw Roosevelt for the last time. I had just returned from a long trip around the Pacific during which I had gone to Manila at the President's request to talk to General MacArthur in an attempt to learn something about his ideas for the future military government of Japan. It was extremely difficult for any emissary from Washington to get through to MacArthur in those days. It was reported that even generals from the War Department on inspection tours were being refused permission to enter the Philippine theater and those who did were as carefully chaperoned as if they were attempting to visit the Russian Front. I, however, being an obscure and relatively inoffensive civilian, encountered no difficulties and was most hospitably received. General MacArthur talked to me for nearly three hours in the temporary headquarters that he had set up in the awful, heart-rending desolation of Manila, and I came away enormously impressed with the extent of his understanding of the Orient and the breadth of his views.

On March 24 I went to see the President in his office and then walked over with him to the White House proper where we had lunch with Anna Boettiger on the sun porch on the roof above the South Portico. I said that, while I had no idea what decisions were being made as to who would be supreme commander in the Pacific when the forces under MacArthur and those under Nimitz merged for the final assault on Japan, I believed strongly that MacArthur was the ideal choice for Military Governor of Japan after the surrender—and victory in the Pacific appeared a great deal nearer than I had imagined before I made this trip. I told the President what I had heard MacArthur say on this subject, and Roosevelt observed, rather wistfully, "I wish that he would sometimes tell some of these things to *me*." He then asked me to put my observations in the form of a short memorandum, and I did so as follows:

1. General MacArthur's intelligence service on the enemy and enemy-held territory is superb, due largely to the Filipino guerrilla organization which was organized and directed under his command.

2. On the other hand I was shocked by the inaccuracy of the information held by General MacArthur and his immediate entourage about the formulation of high policy in Washington. There are unmistakable evidences of an acute persecution complex at work. To hear some of the staff officers talk, one would think that the War Department, the State Department, the Joint Chiefs of Staff—and, possibly, even the White House itself—are under the domination of "Communists and British Imperialists". This strange misapprehension produces an obviously unhealthy state of mind, and also the most unfortunate public relations policy that I have seen in any theatre of war.

3. From the strictly military point of view, it seems to me that the operations in this theatre have been magnificent. The quality and the morale of the troops in the field are exceptionally high. I could detect no evidences of serious criticism of the co-ordination and cooperation of land, sea and air forces.

Following is a brief summary of General MacArthur's views on the future handling of Japan which he expressed to me at considerable length and with great positiveness and eloquence:

Tracing the history of Japan, particularly in the past century, the General expressed the conviction that the "imperial sanctity" idea is a myth fabricated by the military for their own purposes. Essential to the continuance of this myth, he said, is the legend of invincibility; the Emperor remains a god only as long as the Army and Navy are all-conquering. The total destruction of Japanese military power, therefore, can involve (for the Japanese civil population) destruction of the concept of Hirohito's divinity. This will result in a spiritual vacuum and an opportunity for the introduction of new concepts. The Japanese people will have inevitable respect for as well as fear of the instruments of their own defeat. Believing that might makes right, they will conclude that we of the U.S.A. must be right. Furthermore, the prestige throughout Asia that we have established by our Philippine policy and which will be vastly increased by conquest of Japan will make us the greatest influence on the future development of Asia. If we exert that influence in an imperialistic manner, or for the sole purpose of commercial advantage, then we shall lose our golden opportunity; but if our influence and our strength are expressed in terms of essential liberalism we shall have the friendship and the cooperation of the Asiatic peoples far into the future.

It seemed to be General MacArthur's view that the Japanese civil population if treated with stern justice and strength would be more capable of eventual redemption than are the Germans.

While I was with the President that day, he talked about the speech he was to give on Jefferson Day, about two weeks hence, and his speech for the opening of the San Francisco Conference. He laughed and said, "You know Steve [Early] doesn't think I ought to open that conference —just in case it should fail. He thinks I ought to wait to see how it goes and then, if it is a success, I can go out and make the closing address, taking all the credit for it. But I'm going to be there at the start and at the finish, too. All those people from all over the world are paying this country a great honor by coming here and I want to tell them how much we appreciate it." For the Jefferson Day speech, he asked me to look up some Jefferson quotations on the subject of science. He said, "There aren't many people who realize it, but Jefferson was a scientist as well as a democrat and there were some things he said that need to be repeated now, because science is going to be more important than ever in the working out of the future world."

The Jefferson quotation that I found, and that Roosevelt used in his undelivered speech, referred to "the brotherly spirit of science, which unites into one family all its votaries of whatever grade, and however widely dispersed throughout the different quarters of the globe."

I did not know it at the time but I realized later that when Roosevelt spoke of the importance of science in the future he was undoubtedly thinking of the imminence of the atomic age. He said in this last speech, "Today we are faced with the pre-eminent fact that, if civilization is to survive, we must cultivate the science of human relationships—the ability of all peoples, of all kinds, to live together and work together in the same world, at peace."

I wished him a happy holiday in Warm Springs, then went down to the Cabinet Room—where Hopkins, Rosenman and I had worked so many long hours—and I wrote the memorandum on MacArthur, then walked to the Carlton Hotel and told my wife that the President was in much worse shape than I had ever seen him before. He had seemed unnaturally quiet and even querulous—never before had I found myself in the strange position of carrying on most of the conversation with him; and, while he had perked up a little at lunch under the sparkling influence of his daughter Anna, I had come away from the White House profoundly depressed. I thought it was a blessing that he could get away for a while to Warm Springs, and I was sure the trip across the country to San Francisco would do him a lot of good. The thought never occurred to me that this time he might fail to rally as he always had. I couldn't believe it when somebody told me he was dead. Like everybody else, I listened and listened to the radio, waiting for the announcement—probably in his own gaily reassuring voice—that it had all been a big mistake, that the banking crisis and the war were over and everything was going to be "fine—grand—perfectly bully." But when the realization finally did get through all I could think of was, "It finally crushed him. He couldn't stand up under it any longer." The "it" was the awful responsibility that had been piling up and piling up for so many years. The fears and the hopes of hundreds of millions of human beings throughout the world had been bearing down on the mind of one man, until the pressure was more than mortal tissue could withstand, and then he said, "I have a terrific headache," and then lost consciousness, and died. "A massive cerebral hemorrhage," said the doctors—and "massive" was the right word.

The morning after Roosevelt's death Hopkins telephoned me from St. Mary's Hospital in Rochester, Minnesota. He just wanted to talk to somebody. There was no sadness in his tone; he talked with a kind of exaltation as though he had suddenly experienced the intimations of immortality. He said, "You and I have got something great that we can take with us all the rest of our lives. It's a great realization. Because we know it's *true* what so many people believed about him and what made them love him. The President never let them down. That's what you and I can remember. Oh, we all know he could be exasperating, and he could seem to be temporizing and delaying, and he'd get us all worked up when we thought he was making too many concessions to expediency. But all of that was in the little things, the unimportant things—and he knew exactly how little and how unimportant they really were. But in the big things—all of the things that were of real, permanent importance —he never let the people down."

The next afternoon, Saturday, we went to the funeral service in the East Room of the White House. I was sitting on a little gilt chair at the extreme right of the assemblage when I felt a hand squeeze my shoulder. I looked up and it was Hopkins, who had flown in from Rochester. He himself looked like death, the skin of his face a dreadful cold white with apparently no flesh left under it. I believed that he now had nothing left to live for, that his life had ended with Roosevelt's.

When President Truman came into the East Room nobody stood up, and I'm sure this modest man did not even notice this discourtesy or, if he did, understood that the people present could not yet associate him with his high office; all they could think of was that the President was dead. But everybody stood up when Mrs. Roosevelt came in.

After the service, Hopkins asked my wife and me to come to his house in Georgetown. He went to bed and I sat with him for a long time and listened as he talked. He didn't seem like death now. Fire was shooting out of his sharp eyes in their sunken sockets. I drastically revised my impression of earlier that afternoon that he had nothing left to live for. "God damn it," he said, "now we've got to get to work on our own. This is where we've really got to begin. We've had it too easy all this time, because we knew he was there, and we had the privilege of being able to get to him. Whatever we thought was the matter with the world, whatever we felt ought to be done about it, we could take our ideas to him, and if he thought there was any merit in them, or if anything that we said got him started on a train of thought of his own, then we'd see him go ahead and do it, and no matter how tremendous it might be or how idealistic he wasn't scared of it. Well—he isn't there now, and we've got to find a way to do things by ourselves."

Hopkins talked at length of the new administration. He said, "I'm pretty sure that Jimmy Byrnes and Henry Wallace and Harold Ickes are saying right now that they'd be President of the United States today if it weren't for me. But this time I didn't have anything to do with it. I'm certain that the President had made up his mind on Truman long before I got back to the White House last year. I think he would have preferred Bill Douglas, because he knew him better and he always liked Bill's toughness. But nobody really influential was pushing for Douglas. I think he'd gone off fishing out in Oregon or someplace. And Bob Hannegan was certainly pushing for Harry Truman and the President believed he could put him over at the Convention. So the President told him to go ahead and even put it in writing when Bob asked him to. People seemed to think that Truman was just suddenly pulled out of a hat—but that wasn't true. The President had had his eye on him for a long time. The Truman Committee record was good—he'd got himself known and liked around the country—and above all he was very popular in the Senate. That was the biggest consideration. The President wanted somebody that would help him when he went up there and asked them to ratify the peace."

Hopkins said he was going to turn in his resignation at once and he thought the whole Cabinet should do likewise and get out. He made exceptions of Stimson and Forrestal, who should obviously remain to the end of the war, and he said he guessed Morgenthau ought to stay long enough to see the next bond drive through. But, he said, "Truman has got to have his own people around him, not Roosevelt's. If we were around, we'd always be looking at him and he'd know we were thinking, 'The *President* wouldn't do it that way!'" Hopkins predicted that the last one to quit the Cabinet voluntarily would be Henry Wallace.

That night we boarded the funeral train for Hyde Park. (Hopkins felt too exhausted to make this last, sad trip.) It was the same train with the same crew that we had traveled with on campaign expeditions.

In the rose garden that Sunday morning I was standing behind General Marshall and Admiral King. Across the garden was a detachment of cadets from West Point, and on the other three sides were lines of soldiers, sailors and marines wearing ribbons that meant Cassino, and the Persian Gulf, and the Solomons Slot, and the bocage country, and Leyte, and Medjez El Bab, and Midway and Ploesti and Iwo Jima and the Hump. In a memorial to Roosevelt in the soldiers' magazine, *Yank*, they wrote: "He was the Commander in Chief, not only of our armed forces, but of our generation."

Standing there in the rose garden I could see over the high hedge the top of a lilac bush that was just beginning to bloom and I thought of what Walt Whitman had written eighty years ago almost to the day at the end of another war and of another President's life.

As I said near the beginning of this book, I could never really understand what was going on in Roosevelt's heavily forested interior. But, as a result of my observation of him and the time that I have had to digest that observation and the opinions of others, I am sure of one thing: although crippled physically and prey to various infections, he was spiritually the healthiest man I have ever known. He was gloriously and happily free of the various forms of psychic maladjustment which are called by such names as inhibition, complex, phobia. His mind, if not always orderly, bore no traces of paralysis and neither did his emotional constitution; and his heart was certainly in the right place. Furthermore, he was entirely conscious of these extraordinary advantages that he enjoyed, and this consciousness gave him the power to soar above circumstances which would have held other men earthbound.

CHAPTER XXXV

The Last Mission

IN HIS first talks with President Truman after Roosevelt's death, Hopkins said that he would remain in Washington for a few weeks— he had set the date for his retirement from government service as May 12—and would make available to the new Chief Executive every scrap of knowledge that he possessed concerning Roosevelt's unrecorded plans and hopes and apprehensions for the future—and there was, of course, a considerable amount of knowledge that only he possessed. Truman said that he was genuinely sorry to see Hopkins go, and there is no doubt that he meant just this, for he had great respect for this ardent man with whom he had been associated in the earliest days of the relief program and, as a result of the work of the Truman Committee, he knew better than most the real nature of Hopkins' contribution to the vast organization of the United States for total war and total victory. He told Hopkins that he wanted him to stay on at his side to give the same kind of advice and counsel and assistance that he had given the late President. But Hopkins was obviously at the end of his physical rope. He said that he would require a very long rest before he could be capable of doing any real work, and that then he intended to devote himself to the sedentary occupation of writing his memoirs.

During the days before the San Francisco Conference, Hopkins wrote two short, personal memoranda. The first of them contained the following footnote:

Stalin sent for Ambassador Harriman soon after he learned of President Roosevelt's death and told Harriman that he wanted to give some immediate assurance to the American people to indicate his, Stalin's, desire to continue on a co-operative basis with this country. Harriman promptly told him that the thing the American people would appreciate most would be to send Molotov to the San Francisco Conference. Stalin asked Harriman if he was merely speaking for himself or was he sure that our government would support that request and said that he, Stalin, was prepared to tell Molotov to go.

Molotov was present at the conference and indicated his reluctance to go but Stalin told both Harriman and Molotov that Molotov would go to San Francisco. Harriman cabled this information home and the State Department prepared a cable from Truman to Stalin saying we would be glad to welcome Molotov here.

The other memorandum was inspired by an "inside" story in Drew Pearson's column in the *Washington Post* on April 22. Pearson had written: "Though it may get official denial the real fact is that American advance patrols on Friday, April 13th, one day after President Roosevelt's death, were in Potsdam, which is to Berlin what the Bronx is to New York City," but "the next day withdrew from the Berlin suburbs to the River Elbe about 50 miles south. This withdrawal was ordered largely because of a previous agreement with the Russians that they were to occupy Berlin and because of their insistence that the agreement be kept." Pearson stated that this agreement had been made at Yalta. Hopkins indignantly wrote:

This story by Drew Pearson is absolutely untrue. There was no agreement made at Yalta whatever that the Russians should enter Berlin first. Indeed, there was no discussion of that whatever. The Chiefs of Staff had agreed with the Russian Chiefs of Staff and Stalin on the general strategy which was that both of us were going to push as hard as we could.

It is equally untrue that General Bradley paused on the Elbe River at the request of the Russians so that the Russians could break through to Berlin first. Bradley did get a division well out towards Potsdam but it far outreached itself; supplies were totally inadequate and anyone who knows anything about it knows that we would have taken Berlin had we been able to do so. This would have been a great feather in the army's cap, but for Drew Pearson now to say that the President agreed that the Russians were to take Berlin is utter nonsense.

During those last weeks in Washington, Hopkins remained at home, most of the time in bed. Old friends and associates who came to see him included: T. V. Soong, Leon Henderson, Jean Monnet, Sam Rosenman, Anthony Eden, David Niles, Oliver Lyttelton, Frances (Mrs. Edwin M.) Watson, Morris Ernst, Grace Tully, Dr. Herbert Evatt, Isador Lubin, Colonel James Roosevelt, Laurence Steinhardt, Frank Walker, Lord Halifax, Howard Hunter, Steve Early, Felix Frankfurter, General Marshall, Bernard Baruch, Aubrey Williams, James Forrestal, Walter Lippmann, General Arnold, Edward Stettinius, John J. McCloy, Robert Lovett, Admiral Leahy, Robert E. Hannegan, General Somervell, Donald Nelson, Admiral King, James F. Byrnes, Raymond Gram Swing, Joseph E. Davies, Mrs. Eleanor Roosevelt.

On May 1 the Hamburg radio declared that Adolf Hitler was dead. On May 2 the Russians captured Berlin and hostilities in Italy ended officially following the unconditional surrender of Field Marshal Von Kesselring.

On May 4, all German forces in the Netherlands, Northwest Germany and Denmark surrendered to Field Marshal Montgomery's 21st Army Group, and General Patch's U.S. Seventh Army, having captured Berchtesgaden, drove through the Brenner Pass and joined up with General Clark's Fifth Army.

On that day Hopkins received the following telegram from Eden, Molotov and Stettinius in San Francisco: "At a dinner last night we three drank a special toast to you in sincere recognition of the outstanding part you personally have played in bringing our three countries together in the common cause. We regret that you are not with us at this moment of victory. With our affectionate personal regards."

Hopkins replied somewhat sententiously to this: "Thanks so much for your cordial message. This day of victory over the evil forces of mankind was won by millions of Allied soldiers and sailors. It is the prelude, not only of the complete destruction of the military might of Japan, but also of the building of a sure foundation of peace in which the common people of the earth shall share the fruits of the victory."

On May 8, Hopkins cabled Churchill, "I want you to know that I have been thinking of you very much today," and Churchill replied, "Your message reached me while I was sending one to you. Among all those in the grand alliance, warriors or statesmen who struck deadly blows at the enemy and brought peace nearer, you will ever hold an honored place." With these and other encomiums—including one from General Marshall which has been quoted in an earlier chapter—to cover the scars of the many wounds that he had received, Hopkins felt that he could now retire forever from public life and have some fun. However, less than a week after V-E Day, it seemed that the San Francisco Conference was going on the rocks. Molotov and Eden were both headed for home. Harriman and Bohlen were on an airplane flying eastward across the continent with a sense of despair in their hearts. They asked each other whether there was any conceivable way of saving the situation. With considerable hesitancy, Bohlen suggested the possibility that President Truman might send Hopkins to Moscow to talk things out directly with Stalin and Molotov. Bohlen's hesitancy was due to the thought that Harriman, as American Ambassador in Moscow, might resent the idea of Hopkins invading his own province and taking over his duties in direct negotiation with the Soviet Government; but Harriman was enthusiastic about the suggestion and, on his arrival in Washington, went immediately with Bohlen to see Hopkins in his Georgetown house to present this suggestion to him. Both Bohlen and

Notes made by HLH prior to a conference with Marshal Stalin

HARRY L. HOPKINS
WASHINGTON

Notes made by Hopkins prior to his last conference with Stalin in May, 1945: Public opinion in America is in your hands   No economic interest   No committments relative to Poland   No Cordon Sanitaire No opposition to any govt the Poles want so long as it be one not opposed to Soviet Union

But   1. Want to work out with the three of us   2. A free election 3. A genuinely independent country   4. Not by unilateral action

Harriman have told me that Hopkins' response was wonderful to behold. Although he appeared too ill even to get out of bed and walk across "N" Street, the mere intimation of a flight to Moscow converted him into the traditional old fire horse at the sound of the alarm. But he expressed the despondent conviction that Truman would never agree to send him on this mission.

Harriman then went to the White House and presented the suggestion to the President, who said he was much interested in the idea but would need some time to think it over. Several anxious days followed with Hopkins fearing that it would all come to nothing, but then Truman sent for him and asked him if he felt capable of making the long journey; Hopkins' reply was an immediate, enthusiastic affirmative.

He left Washington on May 23, less than two weeks after his retirement from government service. On this trip, the war in Europe being over, he was accompanied by his wife, and also by Harriman and Bohlen. They flew first to Paris and then straight across Germany. When Hopkins looked down at the ruins of Berlin, he said, "It's another Carthage." They arrived in Moscow on the evening of May 25. The first meeting in the Kremlin was at 8:00 P.M. on May 26. Present were: Stalin, Molotov and Pavlov and Hopkins, Harriman and Bohlen. The full record of this meeting follows:

After an exchange of amenities during which Marshal Stalin expressed his great pleasure on seeing Mr. Hopkins again, there was a brief conversation concerning Mr. Hopkins' flight in over Germany.

Mr. Hopkins asked Mr. Molotov if he had recovered from the battle of San Francisco.

Mr. Molotov replied that he did not recall any battles but merely arguments at San Francisco.

Mr. Hopkins then said before he told Marshal Stalin the reason why President Truman had asked him to come to Moscow, he thought the Marshal would be interested in a brief description of President Roosevelt's state of mind just prior to his death. He said that on the way back from Yalta it had been clear to him that President Roosevelt was very tired and that his energy was on the decline. On the other hand, on the morning of his death he had done a good deal of work and had written a number of important letters relating to domestic and foreign policies. None of his doctors had expected he would have a stroke. In fact his principal doctor, Admiral McIntire, had not even been at Warm Springs. The President never regained consciousness after his stroke and had died without any suffering whatsoever. Many of those who had been closest to him had felt that his quick, easy death was really preferable to his lingering on as a hopeless invalid. Mr. Hopkins said that the President had died fully confident of the victory which was in sight.

Marshal Stalin observed that Lenin had also died of a cerebral hemorrhage following a previous stroke which had left his hand paralyzed.

Mr. Hopkins said that on the trip home from Yalta the President had frequently reviewed with him the results of the Crimea Conference and that he had come away from that Conference with renewed confidence that the United States and the Soviet Union could work together in peace as they had in war. President Roosevelt on the trip home had frequently spoken of the respect and admiration he had for Marshal Stalin and he was looking forward to their next meeting which the President hoped would be in Berlin.

Marshal Stalin remarked that he recalled the toast at the Crimea Conference to their next meeting in Berlin.

Mr. Hopkins said that he recalled his first meeting with the Marshal in July, 1941, during the troubled and anxious days of the German offensive. He said he remembered vividly the frankness with which Marshal Stalin had told him of the Soviet position and of the unalterable determination of the Soviet Union to wage war against Germany until final victory was assured. He had returned to the United States and conveyed to President Roosevelt his own conviction that the Soviet Union would hold fast and President Roosevelt had thereupon initiated the program of assistance to the Soviet Union. At that time most people believed that a Germany victory was inevitable but President Roosevelt, in spite of all such opinions had decided otherwise and through his leadership he had put through a program of aid to Russia.

Marshal Stalin observed that at that time there had been many doubts of the ability of the Soviet Union to keep going.

Mr. Hopkins said that although in 1941 the United States was not in the war, President Roosevelt had already decided that Hitler was just as much an enemy of the United States as he was of Great Britain and the Soviet Union.

Mr. Hopkins then said that a few days ago President Truman had sent for him and had asked him to come to Moscow to have a talk with Marshal Stalin. There were a number of things that he and Mr. Harriman hoped to discuss with Marshal Stalin and Mr. Molotov while he was in Moscow, but before going into those specific questions he wished to tell the Marshal of the real reason why the President had asked him to come, and that was the question of the fundamental relationship between the United States and the Soviet Union. Two months ago there had been overwhelming sympathy among the American people for the Soviet Union and complete support for President Roosevelt's policies which the Marshal knew so well. This sympathy and support came primarily because of the brilliant achievements of the Soviet Union in the war and partly from President Roosevelt's leadership and the magnificent way in which our two countries had worked together to bring about the defeat of Germany. The American people at that time hoped and confidently believed that the two countries could work together in peace as well as they had in war. Mr.

Hopkins said there had always been a small minority, the Hearsts and the McCormicks, who had been against the policy of cooperation with the Soviet Union. These men had also been bitter political enemies of President Roosevelt but had never had any backing from the American people as was shown by the fact that against their bitter opposition President Roosevelt had been four times elected President. He said he did not intend to discuss this small minority but to discuss the general state of American opinion and particularly the present attitude of the millions of Americans who had supported President Roosevelt's policy in regard to the Soviet Union and who believed that despite different political and economic ideology of the two countries, the United States and the Soviet Union could work together after the war in order to bring about a secure peace for humanity. He said he wished to assure the Marshal with all the earnestness at his command that this body of American public opinion who had been the constant support of the Roosevelt policies were seriously disturbed about their relations with Russia. In fact, in the last six weeks deterioration of public opinion had been so serious as to affect adversely the relations between our two countries. He said he wished to emphasize that this change had occurred in the very people who had supported to the hilt Roosevelt's policy of cooperation with the Soviet Union. He said that for the moment he was not going into the reasons why this had occurred, or the merits of the case, but merely wished to emphasize that it was a fact. The friends of Roosevelt's policy and of the Soviet Union were alarmed and worried at the present trend of events and did not quite understand why, but it was obvious to them that if present trends continued unchecked the entire structure of world cooperation and relations with the Soviet Union which President Roosevelt and the Marshal had labored so hard to build would be destroyed. Prior to his departure President Truman had expressed to him his great anxiety at the present situation and also his desire to continue President Roosevelt's policy of working with the Soviet Union and his intention to carry out in fact as well as in spirit all the arrangements, both formal and informal, which President Roosevelt and Marshal Stalin had worked out together. Mr. Hopkins added that as the Marshal knew he had not been well and he would not be in Moscow unless he had felt the situation was serious. He also said he would not have come had he not believed that the present trend could be halted and a common basis found to go forward in the future.

Mr. Hopkins said that it was not simple or easy to put a finger on the precise reasons for this deterioration but he must emphasize that without the support of public opinion and particularly of the supporters of President Roosevelt it would be very difficult for President Truman to carry forward President Roosevelt's policy. He said that, as the Marshal was aware, the cardinal basis of President Roosevelt's policy which the American people had fully supported had been the concept that the interests of the United States were world wide and not confined to North and South America and the Pacific Ocean and it was this concept that had led to the many conferences concerning the peace of the world which President Roosevelt had had with Marshal Stalin. President Roosevelt had believed that the Soviet Union had likewise worldwide interests and that the two countries could work out together any political or economic considerations at issue between them. After the Yalta Conference it looked as though we were well on the way to reaching a basic understanding on all questions of foreign affairs of interest to our respective countries, in regard to the treatment of Germany, Japan and the question of setting up a world security organization, to say nothing of the long term interests between the United States and the U.S.S.R. He said in a country like ours public opinion is affected by specific incidents and in this case the deterioration in public opinion in regard to our relations with the Soviet Union had been centered in our inability to carry into effect the Yalta Agreement on Poland. There were also a train of events, each unimportant in themselves, which had grown up around the Polish question, which contributed to the deterioration in public opinion. President Truman feels, and so does the American public, although they are not familiar with all the details, a sense of bewilderment at our inability to solve the Polish question.

Marshal Stalin replied that the reason for the failure on the Polish question was that the Soviet Union desired to have a friendly Poland, but that Great Britain wanted to revive the system of *cordon sanitaire* on the Soviet borders.

Mr. Hopkins replied that neither the Government nor the people of the United States had any such intention.

Marshal Stalin replied he was speaking only of England and said that the British conservatives did not desire to see a Poland friendly to the Soviet Union.

Mr. Hopkins stated that the United States would desire a Poland friendly to the Soviet Union and in fact desired to see friendly countries all along the Soviet borders.

Marshal Stalin replied if that be so we can easily come to terms in regard to Poland.

Mr. Hopkins said that during his visit here there were a number of specific questions that he and Mr. Harriman hoped to discuss with Marshal Stalin and Mr. Molotov but that the general statement he had just made concerning public opinion in the United States was the principal cause of anxiety at the present time. He said he had wished to state frankly and as forcibly as he knew how to Marshal Stalin the importance that he, personally, attached to the present trend of events and that he felt that the situation would get rapidly worse unless we could clear up the Polish matter. He had therefore been glad to hear the Marshal say that he thought the question could be settled.

Marshal Stalin replied that in his opinion it was best to settle it but not if the British conservatives attempted to revive the *cordon sanitaire*.

Mr. Hopkins said that he had in mind the other following questions to discuss with Marshal Stalin while he was in Moscow: (1) The desire of President Truman to meet Marshal Stalin in order to discuss all of the problems arising out of the end of war in Europe and the time and place of such a meeting.

Marshal Stalin said that he had already replied to President Truman concerning the place of meeting and he had suggested the region of Berlin.

Mr. Hopkins said that that message must have come in after he had left and Marshal Stalin instructed Mr. Molotov to give a copy to Mr. Hopkins and Ambassador Harriman.

Mr. Hopkins said the second question he desired to discuss was the setting up of the Control Council for Germany. General Eisenhower had already been appointed the American Representative on the Control Council and he hoped that at an early date the Soviet Representative would be named so that the Council could meet and get to work.

Marshal Stalin apparently had not heard of the appointment of General Eisenhower and stated that Marshal Zhukov would be appointed the Soviet Representative on the Control Council for Germany. He implied that this appointment would be announced shortly.

Mr. Hopkins said the third question he wished to discuss was that of the Pacific War and the future relations of the United States and Soviet Union to China. He said that although he realized the answer would depend on a good many considerations it would be most useful to the American military authorities if he could take back some idea of the approximate date of the entry of the Soviet Union into the war in the Pacific.

Marshal Stalin said he would discuss that question with his advisors and let Mr. Hopkins know.

Mr. Hopkins concluded that there was of course the Polish question which he hoped to discuss here. He added that if Marshal Stalin for his part had any political questions concerning the United States which were worrying him he would of course be glad to discuss them.

Marshal Stalin replied that they had in fact several disturbing questions on their minds in regard to the United States. He added that he was very glad that the President had sent Mr. Hopkins to Moscow and thus give him this opportunity to explore all these questions.

Mr. Hopkins stated that he would certainly not have gotten out of bed to come to Moscow had he not believed that the future well-being of hundreds of millions of people depended on the relationship of the United States and the Soviet Union, nor would he have come had he not believed that any difficulties could be reconciled.

Marshal Stalin said he hoped that Mr. Hopkins's views would prove to be right.

Mr. Hopkins said he would stay here as long as it was necessary to accomplish what could be accomplished, although naturally he did not wish to be away too long.

Marshal Stalin said he was entirely at Mr. Hopkins's service and now that war in Europe was over he had more time at his disposal than he had, for example, a year ago.

Mr. Hopkins said he hoped the Russians would find the body of Hitler.

Marshal Stalin replied that in his opinion Hitler was not dead but hiding somewhere. He said the Soviet doctors thought they had identified the body of Goebbels and Hitler's chauffeur, but that he, personally, even doubted if Goebbels was dead and said the whole matter was strange and the various talks of funerals and burials struck him as being very dubious. He said he thought that Borman, Goebbels, Hitler and probably Krebs had escaped and were in hiding.

Mr. Hopkins said that he knew the Germans had several very large submarines but that no trace of these had been found. He said he hoped we would track Hitler down wherever he might be.

Marshal Stalin said he also knew of those submarines which had been running back and forth between Germany and Japan, taking gold and negotiable assets from Germany to Japan. He added that this had been done with the connivance of Switzerland. He said he had ordered his intelligence service to look into the matter of these submarines but so far they had failed to discover any trace and therefore he thought it was possible that Hitler and company had gone in them to Japan.

Ambassador Harriman then said he wished to observe that President Truman in selecting Mr. Hopkins had chosen a man who, as the Marshal knew, had not only been very close to President Roosevelt but personally was one of the leading proponents of the policy of cooperation with the Soviet Union. President Truman had sent him to have the kind of frank talk with Marshal Stalin that we all knew Marshal Stalin liked to have. Ambassador Harriman continued that we had, as Marshal Stalin knew, very intimate relations with Great Britain which had been developed since the American Revolution and that the Soviet Union of course had their special relations with Great Britain and that although President Roosevelt had 'always felt that the three powers had a special responsibility, nevertheless it was obviously desirable that the United States and the Soviet Union should talk alone on matters of special interest to them and that that was also one of the reasons for Mr. Hopkins's visit.

Marshal Stalin said he thought the Ambassador's remarks were correct and very much to the point.

Mr. Hopkins then said that at San Francisco Mr. Molotov had scored a neat trick on us by quoting President Roosevelt and Mr. Hull on the Argentine question.

Marshal Stalin and *Mr. Molotov* laughed and *Mr. Hopkins* observed that it was possible that some time in the future we might be quoting Marshal Stalin's own words to him.

Marshal Stalin then said that there was one question he wished to raise and that was the question of a peace conference to settle the

European War. He said the question was ripe and, so to speak, knocking at the door.

Mr. Hopkins replied that he thought the forthcoming meeting between the President, Marshal Stalin and the Prime Minister would be a preliminary step toward such a conference. He said he knew in general President Truman's views on the subject and would be glad while he was in Moscow to convey them to Marshal Stalin along general lines.

Marshal Stalin replied that he felt the uncertainty as to the peace conference was having a bad effect and that it would be wise to select a time and place so that proper preparations could be made. The Versailles Conference had been badly prepared and as a result many mistakes had been made. He repeated that he had already sent a message to President Truman suggesting Berlin as a place for their preliminary meeting.

(In a message received subsequently from Mr. Molotov it was explained that the reference to Berlin as a suggested place of meeting had not been in a message to President Truman but in a reply from Mr. Molotov to Mr. Joseph Davies concerning a meeting between Marshal Stalin and the President alone.)

(*Note*. This completes the record of the first meeting.)

The second meeting, involving the same six participants as the first, was held in the Kremlin at 8:00 P.M. on May 27. Following is the record of this meeting, in full:

Mr. Hopkins said that last night the Marshal had indicated that there were a number of questions concerning the United States which were worrying him. He asked Marshal Stalin if he would perhaps care to begin with these questions.

Marshal Stalin said he would not attempt to use Soviet public opinion as a screen but would speak of the feeling that had been created in Soviet governmental circles as a result of recent moves on the part of the United States Government. He said these circles felt a certain alarm in regard to the attitude of the United States Government. It was their impression that the American attitude towards the Soviet Union had perceptibly cooled once it became obvious that Germany was defeated, and that it was as though the Americans were saying that the Russians were no longer needed. He said he would give the following examples:

(1) The case of Argentina and the invitation to the San Francisco Conference. At Yalta it had been agreed that only those states which had declared war on Germany before the first of March would be invited but at San Francisco this decision had been overturned. He said it was not understood in the Soviet Union why Argentina could not have been asked to wait three months or so before joining the world organization. He added that the action of the Conference and the attitude of the United States had raised the question of the value of agreements between the three major powers if their decisions could

be overturned by the votes of such countries as Honduras and Porto Rico.

(2) The question of the Reparations Commission. At Yalta it had been agreed that the three powers would sit on this Commission in Moscow and subsequently the United States Government had insisted that France should be represented on the same basis as the Soviet Union. This he felt was an insult to the Soviet Union in view of the fact that France had concluded a separate peace with Germany and had opened the frontier to the Germans. It was true that this had been done by Pétain's Government but nevertheless it was an action of France. To attempt to place France on the same footing as the Soviet Union looked like an attempt to humiliate the Russians.

(3) The attitude of the United States Government towards the Polish question. He said that at Yalta it had been agreed that the existing government was to be reconstructed and that anyone with common sense could see that this meant that the present government was to form the basis of the new. He said no other understanding of the Yalta Agreement was possible. Despite the fact that they were simple people the Russians should not be regarded as fools, which was a mistake the West frequently made, nor were they blind and could quite well see what was going on before their eyes. It is true that the Russians are patient in the interests of a common cause but that their patience has its limits.

(4) The manner in which Lend Lease had been curtailed. He said that if the United States was unable to supply the Soviet Union further under Lend Lease that was one thing but that the manner in which it had been done had been unfortunate and even brutal. For example, certain ships had been unloaded and while it was true that this order had been cancelled the whole manner in which it had been done had caused concern to the Soviet Government. If the refusal to continue Lend Lease was designed as pressure on the Russians in order to soften them up then it was a fundamental mistake. He said he must tell Mr. Hopkins frankly that if the Russians were approached frankly on a friendly basis much could be done but that reprisals in any form would bring about the exact opposite effect.

(5) The disposition of the German Navy and merchant fleet which surrendered to the Allies. Stalin said that as we knew certain units of the German Army who had been fighting against the Russians had been anxious to surrender to the western allies but not to the Russians, but under the surrender terms German troops were supposed to surrender to the army against which they had fought. He said, for example General Eisenhower as an honest man had correctly turned over to the Soviet Command in Czechoslovakia some 135,000 German troops who had tried to surrender to the American Army. This was an example of fair and honest behavior. However, as regards to the German fleet which had caused so much damage to Leningrad and other Soviet ports not one had been turned over to the Russians despite the fact the fleet had surrendered. He added that he had sent

a message to the President and Prime Minister suggesting that at least one-third of the German Navy and merchant marine thus surrendered be turned over to the Soviet Union. The rest could be disposed of by Great Britain and the United States as they saw fit. He added that if the Soviet Union had been entitled to a part of the Italian fleet they certainly had more right to their fair share of the German fleet, since they had suffered five million casualties in this war. He said that the Soviet Government had certain information leading it to believe that both the United States and England intended to reject the Soviet request and he must say that if this turned out to be true it would be very unpleasant. The Marshal concluded by saying that he had completed the range of his account.

Mr. Hopkins said he first of all wished to express his appreciation of the frankness with which Marshal Stalin had exposed his worries. He said that insofar as he and Ambassador Harriman were able they would answer equally frankly and if on certain points they did not have full information they would endeavor to obtain it. He said he would take the case of the German fleet first. From conversations he had had with Admiral King he was able to state that the United States had no desire to retain any portion of the German fleet and merely wished to examine the vessels for possible new inventions or technical improvements. After that we were prepared to sink the share turned over to us. He also said that he had always understood that the fleet was to be divided between the United States, the Soviet Union and Great Britain and that insofar as the United States was concerned there was no objection to whatever disposition the Soviet Government wished to make with its share. He added that he thought that this matter could be definitely settled at the forthcoming meeting of the three heads of Government.

Mr. Hopkins then said on the subject of Lend Lease he thought it had been clear to the Soviet Union that the end of the war with Germany would necessitate a reconsideration of the old program of Lend Lease to the Soviet Union.

Marshal Stalin said that was entirely understandable.

Mr. Hopkins continued that the history of Lend Lease showed that although in certain cases we had not always been able to meet every Soviet request we had nonetheless freely accepted commitments which we had done our best to carry out in spirit as well as in fact.

Marshal Stalin said that was undoubtedly true.

Mr. Hopkins stated that even prior to the end of the war in Europe we had made an agreement with the Soviet Union known as Annex 3 to Protocol I, which involved delivery of supplies which might be of use in the Far East. He said that this grew out of recent conferences in which Far Eastern matters had been discussed. He emphasized that this commitment was accepted in full by the United States and we were in the process of carrying it out. In regard to the unloading of the ships he said that that was a technical misunderstanding and did not in any sense represent a decision of policy on the part of

the United States. That it had been the action of one government
agency involved in Lend Lease and that it had been countermanded
promptly within twenty-four hours. He said that no one who was responsible for Lend Lease policy or American Government policy had
had anything to do with that mistaken order. The only question which
had to be reconsidered was the program of deliveries to the Soviet
Union which had been based on the needs of the war against Germany and that it had been made clear that on the basis of this reconsideration we would be glad to reconsider any Soviet requests and
that he thought some were now being considered. He said he wished
to emphasize that he had seen no tendency on the part of those responsible for American policy to handle the question of future Lend
Lease to the Soviet Union in an arbitrary fashion. It was in fact a
question of law, since the basic Lend Lease Act made it clear that
materials could only be delivered which would be useful in the process
of the war. The United States Government, however, had interpreted
this in its broadest sense and had included in addition to munitions
of war foodstuffs and other non-military items.

Marshal Stalin said this was true.

Mr. Hopkins concluded by saying that there had naturally been
considerable confusion in the United States Government as to the
status of Lend Lease towards Russia at the end of the war and that
there had been varying legal interpretations but that he wished to
emphasize that the incident to which Marshal Stalin referred did not
have any fundamental policy significance.

Marshal Stalin said he wished to make it clear that he fully understood the right of the United States to curtail Lend Lease shipments
to the Soviet Union under present conditions since our commitments
in this respect had been freely entered into. Even two months ago it
would have been quite correct for the United States to have begun to
curtail shipments but what he had in mind was the manner and form
in which it was done. He felt that what was after all an agreement
between the two Governments had been ended in a scornful and abrupt
manner. He said that if proper warning had been given to the Soviet
Government there would have been no feeling of the kind he had
spoken of; that this warning was important to them since their economy was based on plans. He added that they had intended to make a
suitable expression of gratitude to the United States for the Lend Lease
assistance during the war but the way in which this program had been
halted now made that impossible to do.

Mr. Hopkins replied that what disturbed him most about the Marshal's statement was the revelation that he believed that the United
States would use Lend Lease as a means of showing our displeasure
with the Soviet Union. He wished to assure the Marshal that however
unfortunate an impression this question had caused in the mind of
the Soviet Government he must believe that there was no attempt or
desire on the part of the United States to use it as a pressure weapon.
He said the United States is a strong power and does not go in for

those methods. Furthermore, we have no conflict of immediate interests with the Soviet Union and would have no reason to adopt such
practices.

Marshal Stalin said he believed Mr. Hopkins and was fully satisfied
with his statement in regard to Lend Lease but said he hoped Mr.
Hopkins would consider how it had looked from their side.

Ambassador Harriman then suggested that he and Mr. Molotov
might go into the details of the whole Lend Lease matter together
with Mr. Mikoyan the following day.

Mr. Hopkins concluded the discussions of Lend Lease by stating
that he thought it would be a great tragedy if the greatest achievement
in cooperation which the Soviet Union and the United States had on
the whole worked out together on the basis of Lend Lease were to
end on an unsatisfactory note. He said he wished to add that we had
never believed that our Lend Lease help had been the chief factor in
the Soviet defeat of Hitler on the eastern front. That this had been
done by the heroism and blood of the Russian Army.

Mr. Hopkins then turned to the question of the Reparations Commission. He said it was true that we had suggested France as an
additional member and that the Soviet Government had indicated that
if France was to be a member there were other countries with equal
or better claims to be represented. He said that he had not been directly involved in this question since the Yalta Conference because
of his illness but so far as he knew our only motive was that France
was to be represented on the Control Council for Germany and it
therefore appeared reasonable and logical that she should participate
in the reparations discussions. He said he realized that the Soviet
Union had reluctantly agreed to the participation of France in the
Control Council at the Crimea Conference. In any event the situation
now was that the three powers were to go ahead and begin discussions
in Moscow without France. He wished to state that he also had in
mind the doubts which Stalin and Molotov had in regard to the subject of reparations and how seriously they regarded this question. He
wished only to say that the United States for its part considered reparations a most important and serious question which must be
thrashed out in the Reparations Commission. He said he did not of
course know, but he felt that we would probably not insist in an unyielding manner on the question of the admission of France.

Marshal Stalin replied that Poland, which had suffered even more
than France should certainly be represented if France was to be, and
that Yugoslavia also deserved a place.

Mr. Hopkins then said in regard to the Argentine question, since
he had not been at San Francisco he would ask Ambassador Harriman to explain that situation. He added that he had been at Yalta
and he must say that the Marshal was right in regard to the decision
there.

Ambassador Harriman said that he hoped that he could speak
frankly on the subject of the Argentine and that Mr. Molotov would

forgive him if he spoke in that fashion. He said he had not been at Mexico City and therefore was not familiar with all of the implications of certain commitments taken there. In brief, however, the situation was that we came to San Francisco with a commitment which President Roosevelt assumed at Yalta to support the admission of the Ukraine and White Russia as original members of the world organization and also with certain commitments with the South American countries in regard to Argentina. At San Francisco, at Mr. Molotov's request, Mr. Stettinius had taken up with the Latin American countries the question of their willingness to support the Crimea Decision in regard to the Ukraine and White Russia. The Latin American countries had immediately tried to connect this question with that of the admission of the Argentine. Mr. Stettinius had made it plain that he would not make any such connection and if Mr. Molotov recalled the Latin American countries had voted solidly in support of the Yalta decision. There was, however, another step to the Ukraine and White Russia question, namely that of inviting them to the Conference, concerning which the United States had taken no commitment at Yalta. Mr. Harriman said that he, personally, felt that if Mr. Molotov had not introduced the question of an invitation to the present Polish Government we might have been successful in persuading the Latin American countries to postpone the question of Argentina, but that once Mr. Molotov had connected the question of Argentina with that of an invitation to the present Polish Government, Mr. Stettinius felt that because of the willingness of the South American countries to support the Crimea Decision and the invitation to the Ukraine and White Russia, he was committed to vote for the admission of Argentina.

Mr. Molotov said that his request for more time had not been granted.

Marshal Stalin said in any event what had been done could not be put right and that the Argentine question belonged to the past.

Mr. Hopkins then said with the Marshal's permission he would like to review the position of the United States in regard to Poland. He said first of all he wished to assure the Marshal that he had no thought or indeed any right to attempt to settle the Polish problem during his visit here in Moscow, nor was he intending to hide behind American public opinion in presenting the position of the United States.

Marshal Stalin said he was afraid that his remark concerning Soviet public opinion had cut Mr. Hopkins to the quick and that he had not meant to imply that Mr. Hopkins was hiding behind the screen of American public opinion. In fact he knew Mr. Hopkins to be an honest and frank man.

Mr. Hopkins said that he wished to state this position as clearly and as forcibly as he knew how. He said the question of Poland *per se* was not so important as the fact that it had become a symbol of our ability to work out problems with the Soviet Union. He said that we had no special interests in Poland and no special desire to see any particular kind of government. That we would accept any government in Poland which was desired by the Polish people and was at the same time friendly to the Soviet Government. He said that the people and Government of the United States felt that this was a problem which should be worked out jointly between the United States, the Soviet Union and Great Britain and that we felt that the Polish people should be given the right to free elections to choose their own government and their own system and that Poland should genuinely be independent. The Government and people of the United States were disturbed because the preliminary steps towards the re-establishment of Poland appeared to have been taken unilaterally by the Soviet Union together with the present Warsaw Government and that in fact the United States was completely excluded. He said he hoped that Stalin would believe him when he said that this feeling was a fact. Mr. Hopkins said he urged that Marshal Stalin would judge American policy by the actions of the United States Government itself and not by the attitudes and public expressions of the Hearst newspapers and the Chicago Tribune. He hoped that the Marshal would put his mind to the task of thinking up what diplomatic methods could be used to settle this question, keeping in mind the feeling of the American people. He said he himself was not prepared to say how it could be done but that he felt it must be done. Poland had become a symbol in the sense that it bore a direct relation to the willingness of the United States to participate in international affairs on a world-wide basis and that our people must believe that they are joining their power with that of the Soviet Union and Great Britain in the promotion of international peace and the well being of humanity. Mr. Hopkins went on to say that he felt the overwhelming majority of the people of the United States felt that the relations between the United States and the USSR could be worked out in a spirit of cooperation despite the differences in ideology and that with all these factors in its favor he wished to appeal to the Marshal to help find a way to the solution of the Polish problem.

Marshal Stalin replied that he wished Mr. Hopkins would take into consideration the following factors: He said it may seem strange although it appeared to be recognized in United States circles and Churchill in his speeches also recognized it, that the Soviet Government should wish for a friendly Poland. In the course of twenty-five years the Germans had twice invaded Russia via Poland. Neither the British nor American people had experienced such German invasions which were a horrible thing to endure and the results of which were not easily forgotten. He said these German invasions were not warfare but were like the incursions of the Huns. He said that Germany had been able to do this because Poland had been regarded as a part of the *cordon sanitaire* around the Soviet Union and that previous European policy had been that Polish Governments must be hostile to Russia. In these circumstances either Poland had been too weak to oppose Germany or had let the Germans come through. Thus Poland had served as a corridor for the German attacks on Russia. He said Poland's weakness and hostility had been a great source of weakness to the Soviet Union and had permitted the Germans to do what they wished in the East and also in the West since the two were mixed together. It is therefore in Russia's vital interest that Poland should be both strong and friendly. He said there was no intention on the part of the Soviet Union to interfere in Poland's internal affairs, that Poland would live under the parliamentary system which is like Czechoslovakia, Belgium and Holland and that any talk of an intention to Sovietize Poland was stupid. He said even the Polish leaders, some of whom were communists, were against the Soviet system since the Polish people did not desire collective farms or other aspects of the Soviet system. In this the Polish leaders were right since the Soviet system was not exportable—it must develop from within on the basis of a set of conditions which were not present in Poland. He said all the Soviet Union wanted was that Poland should not be in a position to open the gates to Germany and in order to prevent this Poland must be strong and democratic. Stalin then said that before he came to his suggestion as to the practical solution of the question he would like to comment on Mr. Hopkins' remarks concerning future United States interests in the world. He said that whether the United States wished it or not it was a world power and would have to accept world-wide interests. Not only this war but the previous war had shown that without United States intervention Germany could not have been defeated and that all the events and developments of the last thirty years had confirmed this. In fact the United States had more reason to be a world power than any other state. For this reason he fully recognized the right of the United States as a world power to participate in the Polish question and that the Soviet interest in Poland does not in any way exclude those of England and the United States. Mr. Hopkins had spoken of Russian unilateral action in Poland and United States public opinion concerning it. It was true that Russia had taken such unilateral action but they had been compelled to. He said the Soviet Government had recognized the Warsaw Government and concluded a treaty with it at a time when their Allies did not recognize this government. These were admittedly unilateral acts which would have been much better left undone but the fact was they had not met with any understanding on the part of their Allies. The need for these actions had arisen out of the presence of Soviet troops in Poland; it would have been impossible to have waited until such time as the Allies had come to an agreement on Poland. The logic of the war against Germany demanded that the Soviet rear be assured and the Lublin Committee had been of great assistance to the Red Army at all times and it was for this reason that these actions had been taken by the Soviet Government. He said it was contrary to the Soviet policy to set up Soviet administration on foreign soil since this would look like occupation and be resented by the local inhab-

itants. It was for this reason that some Polish administration had to
be established in Poland and this could be done only with those who
had helped the Red Army. He said he wished to emphasize that these
steps had not been taken with any desire to eliminate or exclude
Russia's Allies. He must point out however that Soviet action in
Poland had been more successful than British action in Greece and
at no time had they been compelled to undertake the measures which
they had done in Greece. Stalin then turned to his suggestion for the
solution of the Polish problem.

Marshal Stalin said that he felt that we should examine the composition of the future Government of National Unity. He said there
were eighteen or twenty ministries in the present Polish Government
and that four or five of these portfolios could be given representatives
of other Polish groups taken from the list submitted by Great Britain
and the United States (Molotov whispered to Stalin who then said
he meant four and not five posts in the government). He said he
thought the Warsaw Poles would not accept more than four ministers
from other democratic groups. He added that if this appears a suitable
basis we could then proceed to consider what persons should be selected for these posts. He said of course they would have to be friendly
to the USSR and to the Allies. He added that Mikolajczyk had been
suggested and he thought he was acceptable and that the question
was now who else. He inquired of Mr. Hopkins whether possibly
Professor Lange might be willing to join the government.

Mr. Hopkins said he doubted whether Professor Lange, who was
an American citizen, could be induced to give up his American citizenship for this purpose but that of course was only a private opinion.

Marshal Stalin then said it might be wise to ask some of the Warsaw leaders to come to Moscow now and to hear what they had to
say and to learn more of what had been decided. He added that if we
are able to settle the composition of the new government he felt that
no differences remained since we were all agreed on the free and un-
fettered elections and that no one intended to interfere with the Polish
people.

Mr. Hopkins said he would like to have some time to consider the
Marshal's suggestion.

Marshal Stalin then said that there were three other questions they
had not touched on:

(1) Future policy in regard to the occupation of Germany;

(2) Japan; and

(3) Meeting of the three heads of Government.

In reply to Mr. Hopkins' question *Marshal Stalin* said that he was
prepared to meet at any time but had not yet heard from the President and Prime Minister whether the Berlin area was acceptable or
not.

In conclusion *Mr. Hopkins* said he felt it would be most desirable
if Marshal Stalin could announce publicly as soon as possible the appointment of Marshal Zhukov as Soviet Representative on the Con-

trol Council for Germany so that that body could start its work as soon as possible.

Marshal Stalin said he was prepared to announce Marshal Zhukov's appointment either tomorrow or the next day or whenever we wanted.

It was agreed that the next meeting would take place at 6 P.M. tomorrow, May 28th.

(*Note.* This completes the record of the second meeting.)

After each of these meetings, Hopkins reported on them in detail by cable to Truman and the State Department, which kept the British Foreign Office fully informed as to the progress of the conversations. It will be noted that Hopkins was now most scrupulous in keeping to the formal "channels." He had never reported to Roosevelt in the same way—not, at any rate, since his first trip to England in January, 1941. So complete was his knowledge of Roosevelt's state of mind before he departed on each trip that he usually needed only to cable something like "making good progress along lines we discussed" or "having some difficulties on SLEDGEHAMMER but will explain this when I see you." He knew that Roosevelt did not want long reports from him in which the language was necessarily somewhat guarded, preferring to wait until Hopkins could give him a full account in characteristic terms in the privacy of the Oval Study. However, this time, the fate of the San Francisco Conference and perhaps of the whole future of world peace was at stake and the issue could not wait for Hopkins' return to Washington.

Hopkins' cabled report on the third meeting was as follows:

1. By August 8 the Soviet Army will be properly deployed on the Manchurian positions.

2. The Marshal repeated his statement made at Yalta that the Russian people must have a good reason for going to war and that depended on China's willingness to agree to the proposals made at Yalta.

3. For the first time he stated that he was willing to take these proposals up directly with Soong when he comes to Moscow. He wants to see Soong not later than July 1 and expects us to take the matter up at the same time with Chiang Kai-shek. This procedure seems from our point of view most desirable in light of Stalin's statements about the Far East which follow.

4. Stalin left no doubt in our mind that he intends to attack during August. It is therefore important that Soong come here not later than July 1. Stalin is ready to see him any time now.

5. He made categorical statement that he would do everything he could to promote unification of China under the leadership of Chiang Kai-shek. He further stated that this leadership should continue after the war because no one else was strong enough. He specifically stated that no Communist leader was strong enough to unify China. In

spite of the reservations he expressed about him, he proposes to back the Generalissimo.

6. Stalin repeated all of his statements made at Yalta that he wanted a unified and stable China and wanted China to control all of Manchuria as part of a United China. He stated categorically that he had no territorial claims against China and mentioned specifically Manchuria and Sinkiang and that in all areas his troops entered to fight the Japanese he would respect Chinese sovereignty.

7. The Marshal stated that he would welcome representatives of the Generalissimo to be with his troops entering Manchuria in order to facilitate the organization in Manchuria of Chinese administration.

8. He agreed with America's "Open Door" policy and went out of his way to indicate that the United States was the only power with the resources to aid China economically after the war. He observed that for many years to come Russia would have all it could do to provide for the internal economy of the Soviet Union.

9. He agreed that there should be a trusteeship for Korea under the United States, China, Great Britain and the Soviet Union.

10. We were very encouraged by the conference on the Far East.

This was followed by another cable on the same meeting:

1. Japan is doomed and the Japanese know it.

2. Peace feelers are being put out by certain elements in Japan and we should therefore consider together our joint attitude and act in concert about the surrender of Japan. Stalin expressed the fear that the Japanese will try to split the allies. The following are his statements about surrender:

A. The Soviet Union prefers to go through with unconditional surrender and destroy once and for all the military might and forces of Japan. Stalin thinks this is particularly to our interest because the Japanese have a deep seated antipathy to the United States and if the war lords, the industrial leaders and the politicians are permitted to withdraw to Japan with their armies undefeated, their navy not totally destroyed and their industrial machine partially intact, they will start at once to plan a war of revenge. Stalin made it quite clear that the Soviet Union wants to go through with unconditional surrender and all that is implied in it.

B. However, he feels that if we stick to unconditional surrender the Japs will not give up and we will have to destroy them as we did Germany.

C. The Japanese may offer to surrender and seek softer terms. While consideration of this has certain dangers as compared with (A) it nevertheless cannot be ruled out. Should the Allies depart from the announced policy of unconditional surrender and be prepared to accept a modified surrender, Stalin visualizes imposing our will through our occupying forces and thereby gaining substantially the same results as under (A). In other words, it seemed to us that he proposes under this heading to agree to milder peace terms but once we get into Japan to give them the works.

3. The Marshal expects that Russia will share in the actual occupation of Japan and wants an agreement with the British and us as to occupation zones.

4. He also wants an understanding between the Allies as to areas of operation in China and Manchuria.

At this same meeting in which Far Eastern matters were discussed, there was also some talk about the endless problem of postwar treatment of Germany, which was far from settlement even now, three weeks after V-E Day. In his report to Truman, Hopkins said:

On two occasions Stalin has emphasized the importance of planning at once for the organization of the Peace Conference in so far as it related to Europe. Apparently he is thinking about a formal conference and he emphasized that the Allies were not properly prepared at Versailles and that we should not make that mistake again. At your forthcoming meeting he will bring this up.

We reminded Stalin some days ago that he had made a speech in which he said that he did not favor the dismemberment of Germany. This appeared to be contrary to the position he took both at Teheran and Yalta. His explanation of this action on his part was that his recommendation had been turned down at Yalta and more specifically that Eden and Strang on behalf of the British had stated the dismemberment was to be accomplished only as a last resort and that Winant, who was present at the Conference at which this discussion took place in London, interposed no objection, hence Stalin states that it was his understanding that both Great Britain and the United States were opposed to dismemberment. I undertook to tell him that this was not the case; that while you had made no final decision in regard to this, the United States considered this an open question and that you would surely want to thrash it out at your next meeting. I told him that he must not assume that the United States is opposed to dismemberment because he may learn from you that just the opposite was the case. He then said that dismemberment was a matter which the three Allies must settle among themselves and that he would keep an open mind in regard to it.

He went into some detail regarding the definition of the German General Staff and stated that it would be desirable if the members of that Staff could be detained for ten to fifteen years and if a legal way could be found to prosecute and convict the General Staff as a war criminal organization that would be all the better. The Soviets have captured certain members of the General Staff whom they consider to be war criminals and who they propose should be prosecuted as such under any circumstances. Stalin stated that the Soviets permitted no prisoners of war to go to work on farms or in factories. As to exactly what he was doing with prisoners of war he was somewhat noncom-

mittal but he indicated that he was bringing many of them back to
White Russia and the Ukraine to work in mines and on reconstruction.
He said that he did not know just how many prisoners of war they had
but he thought they had about 2,500,000 of which 1,700,000 were
Germans and the balance Rumanians, Italians, Hungarians, etc. He
stated that the officers were not repeat not being required to work. You
can be sure that at your next meeting Stalin will have some pretty
specific proposals to make about prisoners of war, and more particularly, I believe, about war criminals. He did not, as we anticipated,
express any criticism of our handling of war prisoners. Stalin outlined
in some detail his administrative procedure in local German communities, but I shall delay a report on that until I return home. He said
he believed we should do everything to encourage them to get to
work on their farms in order to provide food for themselves, and
indicated that we should cooperate in getting their light consumer
goods industries going. He indicated that Germany should be permitted those heavy industries required for the rehabilitation of their
transportation systems, electric power, water, sewage, etc.

Although he promised that he was going to appoint Zhukov as his
member of the Control Council for Germany, it has not yet been done.
We shall at tonight's meeting again urge him to announce at once
Zhukov's appointment.

On May 30, the fourth day in Moscow, Hopkins and his wife enjoyed
some sightseeing, particularly a visit to the Russian Ballet School. When
he met Stalin at the meeting at six o'clock that evening, he told his host
how greatly he had enjoyed seeing this school which was then as it has
always been the veritable fountainhead of ballet art for the entire world.
Hopkins noted, "Marshal Stalin said that although he had been twenty-
eight years in Moscow, he had never visited the Ballet School"—precisely
like the traditional New Yorker who says, "I've lived here all my life
but I've never yet seen the Statue of Liberty." Hopkins assured the
Marshal that this was something not to be missed.

The topics discussed at this fourth meeting were the disposition of the
German Fleet, arrangements for the forthcoming Potsdam Conference
and Poland. Hopkins stated the basic American attitude toward the
infinitely difficult Polish question in the following conversation:

> Mr. Hopkins said he would like to accent once again the reasons for
> our concern in regard to Poland, and indeed, in regard to other
> countries which were geographically far from our borders. He said
> there were certain fundamental rights which, when impinged upon or
> denied, caused concern in the United States. These were cardinal
> elements which must be present if a parliamentary system is to be
> established and maintained. He said for example:
> 1. There must be the right of freedom of speech so that people
> could say what they wanted to, right of assembly, right of movement
> and the right to worship at any church that they desired;

2. All political parties except the fascist party and fascist elements who represented or could represent democratic governments should be permitted the free use, without distinction, of the press, radio, meetings and other facilities of political expression;

3. All citizens should have the right of public trial, defense by council of their own choosing, and the right of habeas corpus.

He concluded that if we could find a meeting of minds in regard to these general principles which would be the basis for future free elections then he was sure we could find ways and means to agree on procedures to carry them into effect. He then asked the Marshal if he would care to comment in a general sense or more specifically in regard to the general observations he had made concerning the fundamentals of a new Polish state.

Marshal Stalin replied that these principles of democracy are well known and would find no objection on the part of the Soviet Government. He was sure that the Polish Government, which in its declaration had outlined just such principles, would not only not oppose them but would welcome them. He said, however, that in regard to the specific freedoms mentioned by Mr. Hopkins, they could only be applied in full in peace time, and even then with certain limitations. He said for example the fascist party, whose intention it was to overthrow democratic governments, could not be permitted to enjoy to the full extent these freedoms. He said secondly there were the limitations imposed by war. All states when they were threatened by war on their frontiers were not secure and had found it necessary to introduce certain restrictions. This had been done in England, France, the Soviet Union and elsewhere and perhaps to a lesser extent in the United States which was protected by wide oceans. It is for these reasons that only in time of peace could considerations be given to the full application of these freedoms. For example he said that in time of war no state will allow the free unrestricted use of radio transmitters which could be used to convey information to the enemy. With reference to freedom of speech certain restrictions had to be imposed for military security. As to arrest, in England during the war individuals dangerous to the state had been arrested and tried in secret; these restrictions had been somewhat relaxed but not entirely repealed in England since the war in the Pacific was still going on.

He said, therefore, to sum up: (1) during time of war these political freedoms could not be enjoyed to the full extent, and (2) nor could they apply without reservations to fascist parties trying to overthrow the government.

Marshal Stalin continued that he wished to give a few examples from Russian history. He said that at the time of the revolution the Russian communist party had proclaimed the right of freedom of religion as one of the points of their program. The Russian Patriarch and the entire then existing church had declared the Soviet Government an anathema and had called on all church members not to pay taxes nor to obey the call to the Red Army but to resist mobilization, not to work, etc. He said what could the Soviet Government do but to in fact declare war on the church which assumed that attitude. He added that the present war had wiped out this antagonism and that now the freedom of religion, as promised, could be granted to the church.

Mr. Hopkins said he thoroughly understood the Marshal's opinions. He added that when he had left the Crimea Conference President Roosevelt had thought the Polish matter was virtually settled. He had been relaxed and pleased over the situation. Mr. Hopkins said he and all the other American representatives thought the same and felt that in very short time Mr. Molotov, Mr. Harriman and Sir Archibald Clark Kerr would be able to carry out the Crimea Decision. Since that time he had been sick and out of touch with Washington and had only followed events from the press and from personal letters which he had received from time to time. He must confess that he had been bewildered and disturbed that one thing after another seemed to occur to prevent the carrying out of the decision which all had thought was clear and sure. He said that if, with his knowledge, he had been bewildered as to the real reason for this it was easy to imagine how bewildered and concerned the masses of people in the United States were over the situation. Mr. Hopkins said that he must say that rightly or wrongly there was a strong feeling among the American people that the Soviet Union wished to dominate Poland. He added that was not his point of view but it was widely held in the United States and that friends of international collaboration were wondering how it would be possible to work things out with the Soviet Union if we could not agree on the Polish question. Mr. Hopkins added that for himself he felt very strongly that if we could find a meeting of the minds on the substance of what we wished to see in the new Polish state we should be able to overcome the difficulties. He himself had had difficulty in understanding the immediate causes of disagreement, namely interpretation of wording such as the role of the existing government in the future Provisional Government of Poland. He concluded that he felt that the three great powers should in a short time be able to settle this matter.

Marshal Stalin replied that this was true but it was necessary for all three Governments genuinely to wish to settle this matter. If one of them secretly did not wish to see it settled then the difficulties were real.

Mr. Hopkins replied that as far as the United States Government was concerned we had no interest in seeing anyone connected with the present Polish Government in London involved in the new Provisional Government of Poland and he did not personally believe that the British had any such idea.

After this fourth meeting, Hopkins cabled Truman that Stalin had agreed to meet with the President and Churchill in the Berlin area about July 15. In this cable, he added:

I completed the exposition of your position relative to Poland with Stalin. The conference tonight was encouraging. It looks as though Stalin is prepared to return to and implement the Crimea decision and permit a representative group of Poles to come to Moscow to consult with the Commission. We are having what we both emphasized would be an informal exchange of views on possible candidates to come here for consultation with the tri-partite Commission at an early date. Harriman, in preparation for this exchange of views, will go over with the British Ambassador the list of candidates already submitted by us and the British.

The fifth meeting on May 31 involved a detailed discussion of names of various candidates for the Polish Government. In this, Hopkins had to rely on the information he had received from Harriman, Bohlen and the State Department. He recognized such names as Mikolajczyk or Lange, but as names of other men came up he had no direct knowledge of their political background or the precise extent of their reliability. In all of these discussions of Poland, Hopkins repeated many times that it was the desire of his government that the Polish Government should be friendly to the Soviet Union, and Stalin agreed that this was all that he demanded. But, here again, as Roosevelt had said to Churchill, "The Russians do not use words for the same purposes that we do": and there was apparently no way of translating the word "friendly" from one language to the other so that it would end up meaning the same thing.

After the fifth meeting, Mr. and Mrs. Hopkins had a private dinner with Stalin at which were present some twenty of the most important men in the Soviet Union, including several members of the Politburo— Mikoyan, Beriya, Kaganovich and Shvernik and Malenkov and Voznesenski (then alternate members). George Kennan who was identified as the author of the famous "Mr. X" article in the magazine, *Foreign Affairs,* some two years later, was also present at this dinner. After dinner Hopkins had a private conversation with Stalin, nobody else being present except the interpreter, Pavlov. Hopkins wrote the following record of this:

Last night after dinner I saw Stalin alone with Mr. Pavlov, interpreter. I told him that I wanted to impress on him as earnestly as I knew how the unfavorable effect in America caused by the detaining of the fourteen Poles within Poland and, specifically, those that were charged only with having illegal radio transmitters. I made it clear to him that I was not talking about the others charged with more serious crimes. I told him that I believed we would have no great difficulty with getting the list approved of names who might come to Moscow to consult with the Moscow Commission, if this business could be settled. I made it clear that while I did not know anything about the merits of the case, I nevertheless felt that even though the

Marshal thought the offense was far more serious than it appeared to us, it was in the interest of good Russian-American relations that I hoped he would release these prisoners.

I told Marshal Stalin that if the solution of the Polish matter waited until the conference in Berlin on the 15th of July it would stir up endless trouble and probably take most of the time of the Berlin meeting. I outlined at great length the American position in regard to the Soviet Union after the war and told him that we believed the repeated assurances which he had given us that the Soviet Union also wanted to have a firm and friendly understanding with us; that we assumed that that was correct. But if that were to be accomplished I told him it had to be done in an environment that made it possible for President Truman to carry American public opinion with him.

I reminded him again of the many minority groups in America who were not sympathetic to the Soviet Union and told him very forcefully that he must believe me when I told him that our whole relationship was threatened by the impasse of Poland. I made it clear again to Stalin that Poland was only a symbol, that the United States had equal interests in all countries in this part of the world and that if we were going to act or maintain our interests on a tripartite basis, it was hopeless to do so without a strong American public opinion. I told him there was no hope of getting certain minority groups in sympathy with this position for many years and perhaps never, and reminded him again that he should not assume that the Chicago Tribune or the Hearst press had any real influence on American public opinion; that I was speaking for and on behalf of the millions of Americans who support a policy of cooperation with the Soviet Union.

I told Stalin further that I personally felt that our relations were threatened and that I frankly had many misgivings about it and with my intimate knowledge of the situation I was, frankly, bewildered with some of the things that were going on.

Stalin then said that he was unwilling to order those Poles released who were charged only with use of illegal radio sets. He stated that he had information in regard to these prisoners which was not available to us and inferred that all of them were engaged in what he called diversionist activities. He stated that he believed that Churchill had misled the United States in regard to the facts and had made the American Government believe that the statement of the Polish London Government was accurate. Just the opposite was the case.

Marshal Stalin stated that he did not intend to have the British manage the affairs of Poland and that is exactly what they want to do. Nevertheless, he stated that he believed me when I told him it was having an unfavorable effect on public opinion in America and he assumed the same was true in Great Britain, and therefore he was inclined to do everything he could to make it easy for Churchill to get out of a bad situation because if and when all the evidence is published it would look very bad for the British and he does not want to make the situation worse than it is. He stated that the men must be tried but that they would be treated leniently and he clearly inferred that he was going to consider at once what could be done in regard to these prisoners that I was concerned with to clear the matter up.

He did not, however, indicate at any time that he was not going to have them tried. I asked him that if he was determined to go through with the trial, when the trials would be held, reminding him that so long as things were in this kind of a state it was bound to create friction between all of us.

His reply to that was he did not know but that he would find out and let me know tomorrow. He said that we must take into consideration Russian opinion as well as American opinion; that it was the Russian forces that had liberated Poland and said that if they had not gained the victory in Poland, with such a great loss of Russian life, nobody would be talking about a new Poland. He said several times that he blamed the British for conniving with the London Poles, and each time I reminded him that we had no desire to support in any way the Polish Government in London.

He listened very attentively to everything I said in the first part of the conversation and I gained the impression that he is going to consider the move which the Soviet Union will make and that we would hear from him at an early date.

I closed the conversation by telling him that I thought the real solution lay in his releasing these men entirely so that we could clear the atmosphere not only for the immediate discussions about Poland but in preparation for the Berlin Conference.

He repeated that the men should be tried but that he would let me know.

During the next few days, Hopkins took it easy in Moscow waiting for further orders from Truman. Voluminous cables passed back and forth between Washington, London and Moscow containing comments on all the various Polish names mentioned. Churchill cabled Hopkins his congratulations on the splendid job that he was doing and he cabled Truman that a break in the deadlock seemed to be resulting from Hopkins' devoted efforts. In one of these cables, Churchill referred to "The Iron Curtain" which had descended over Europe; this phrase did not come into popular currency until a long time later.

On June 6, Hopkins had his sixth and last meeting with Stalin and Molotov, with Harriman and Bohlen also present. During this, the following conversation took place:

Marshal Stalin said that he wished to thank Mr. Hopkins for his great assistance in moving forward the Polish question.

Mr. Hopkins then said he would like to raise an entirely separate question with Marshal Stalin and that relates to the impasse which had come about at the San Francisco Conference in regard to voting precedure in the security council. He said he had received an urgent message from President Truman to take this up with Marshal Stalin and to indicate the seriousness of this matter. He said it referred to the Soviet insistence that nothing could be discussed by the security council without the unanimous vote of the permanent members exclusive of those involved in a particular situation. He said that the United States Government had agreed with the Marshal that there must be unanimity among the members in regard to all questions involving enforcement action in any of its aspects but that in the consideration of methods for the peaceful settlement of disputes, parties to the dispute, whether permanent members or not would abstain from voting. He added that the United States thought the Yalta formula as agreed on safeguarded the freedom of discussion and the right of any member to bring before the council any situation for discussion. And that this right, which was rightly a question of the agenda, should therefore be decided by the council by simple majority without any power having the right to veto it. He said he earnestly hoped the Marshal would see eye to eye with us and the other sponsoring powers and France who were agreed on this question.

Mr. Molotov said that the Soviet position was based squarely on the Crimea decision and that in matters involving peaceful settlement parties to dispute would not vote and that the full unanimity applied only to enforcement action. The Soviet position was that the same formula for peaceful settlement should apply in deciding whether or not the council should take up and discuss any given question. (Ensued a conversation in Russian between Mr. Molotov and Marshal Stalin from which it was clear that the Marshal had not understood the issues involved and had not had them explained to him. During this conversation Marshal Stalin remarked that he thought it was an insignificant matter and that they should accept the American position.)

Marshal Stalin then stated that he had no objection to a simple majority being applied in discussions relating to pacific settlement but of course not to any matter involving enforcement action. He said he stressed this aspect because he knew these considerations were raised by the small nations. He had most respect for the small nations (but) it must be admitted there was a tendency among them to exploit and even to create differences between the great powers in the hope that they would obtain the backing of one or more of the great powers for their own ends. He said it was a mistake to believe that just because a nation was small it was necessarily innocent. He added that it should not be understood he would only say this in secret since he was quite prepared to tell the little nations this to their faces. He said, after all two world wars had begun over small nations.

Mr. Hopkins said he thought that possibly the difficulties at San Francisco had grown more out of misunderstandings than real differences.

Marshal Stalin continued that certain statesmen were interested in getting hold of the votes of small nations and that this was a dangerous and slippery path since obviously the small nations would like to get great nation support.

Marshal Stalin then stated that he was prepared to accept the American position on the point at issue at San Francisco in regard to voting procedure.

Mr. Hopkins then said he had one more question to raise and he hoped Marshal Stalin would not think he was always raising troublesome questions. He said the American people through the American Red Cross were anxious to show their admiration and respect for the Polish people by sending them relief in the form of medical supplies which, unfortunately, would only be of moderate proportions. He said for this purpose American Red Cross desired to send three representatives headed by Dr. Bowers to handle the distribution of these supplies. He added that these men would, of course, refrain from any political activity and as a member of the Central Committee of the American Red Cross he was prepared to guarantee that.

Marshal Stalin said he had no objection but it was necessary to obtain the opinion of the Polish Provisional Government, which could be done when they came to Moscow.

Mr. Hopkins then told Marshal Stalin of his plan to leave tomorrow, stopping in Berlin and going on to Frankfurt. He said he looked forward to what for him would be a pleasant spectacle, the present state of Berlin and he might even be able to find Hitler's body.

Marshal Stalin replied that he was sure that Hitler was still alive.

Mr. Hopkins then expressed to Marshal Stalin, on the part of Mrs. Hopkins and himself, their great appreciation for the many kindnesses and courtesies they had received during their stay in Moscow. He said it had been a great pleasure for them to have been here and he only wished to repeat what he had said before, that our two countries had so much in common that they could find a way to work out their problems. He added that these meetings here had left him with renewed assurances on that point.

Marshal Stalin said he fully shared Mr. Hopkins' views.

Following this last meeting, Hopkins cabled Truman: "Marshal Stalin agrees to accept the United States position regarding voting procedure in the Council." This was the real news that the San Francisco Conference had been saved.

Hopkins and his wife left Moscow early in the morning of June 7 and arrived in Berlin in time for lunch. The word had been passed along to the Russian military authorities there to show the distinguished travelers every consideration and these orders were obeyed to an almost embarrassing extent. The Hopkinses may have been the first American civilians to be shown into some of the Nazi holy places which were then completely under the control of the Red Army. Yielding to some of the eternal temptations of the souvenir hunter, Hopkins helped himself to several books from Hitler's private office and presented these to friends on his return.

From Berlin they flew to Frankfurt to spend a day at General Eisenhower's new headquarters, and from there to Paris. Hopkins wrote the following personal notes:

One of the difficulties in negotiating the Polish agreement in Moscow was that President Truman had sent me without discussing it in advance with Churchill. Altho, at the time of my departure, he acquainted him with my impending visit to Moscow, no British representative was present at any of my conferences with Stalin and I was in no position to deal directly with Churchill. Fortunately, Clark Kerr, the British Ambassador to Moscow, was an old friend of mine and quite in sympathy with my visit and I am sure he reported very fully to the British Foreign Office and Churchill. And, more than that, he was making recommendations to Churchill urging the British to back us up. I began to hear from Kerr that Churchill was obviously quite disturbed about the whole business but there was not very much he could say because it was probably to his political interest to get agreement on the Polish question before the British elections.

When I reached Frankfurt there was an urgent telephone message from Churchill which I answered and in which he insisted on my going to London. I stalled about this, telling him my health was not too good and that I thought I ought to get right back but would let him know, and that under any circumstances I would not go without the approval of the President. I felt it unwise for me to go to England and see Churchill before reporting to Truman, so I gave Churchill no encouragement. Churchill wired Truman and Truman replied in the negative to Churchill. I was not acquainted with this until I got to Paris when Churchill again called me and told me the answer had come from Truman and expressed great regret at the decision and acted a little petulant about it over the telephone. I told him, however, that there was nothing I could do about it and, under any circumstances, my health was such that I felt I should not do anything but go right home.

I had several long talks with Eisenhower during the 24 hours Mrs. Hopkins and I spent at his country place about 15 miles outside of Frankfurt. Amongst other things, Eisenhower told me that he and his family had always been Republicans and had voted against Roosevelt every time up until 1944; but that he did vote for Roosevelt this last time.

He discussed his future at great length, repeatedly emphasizing that he did not want to go into politics. This seemed to be apropos of nothing in particular that I had said. He told me, however, that a good many people passing through raised the question of his running for President—obviously on the Republican ticket.

He seemed pretty dubious about the Allied Control Commission and was very fearful that the several governments would not give the Allied Control Commission sufficient power. I told him I was sure that the Russian Government intended to control General Zhukov completely and repeated to him the story of Vyshinski being in

Zhukov's ear all during our conversation in Berlin that Thursday afternoon. Eisenhower told me the same thing had happened to him the day before. Zhukov had seemed unwilling to reply to any of his questions without first consulting Vyshinski. When I saw Eisenhower on my way to Moscow he asked me to raise this question with Stalin and I did. Stalin made it very clear that Zhukov would have very little power concerning political affairs in Germany. I also told Eisenhower that I thought the British Foreign Office would write the ticket for Montgomery and that he should look forward to several departments in our government having much to do with his decisions.

As the Representative of the Allied Control Commission, Eisenhower being the good soldier that he is, of course is prepared to go through with the assignment, but he has no misapprehensions about the fact that he is almost certain to be deflated from his present outstanding position in the world.

I told Ike of Stalin's anxiety to have him come to Moscow on the 24th of June and if that was not convenient, any time before the time of the Berlin Conference or immediately after the Berlin Conference. Eisenhower told me he had been invited to Moscow sometime before but that the War Department had refused him permission to go, altho he was very anxious to do so. Eisenhower thought it a mistake that he did not go when he was asked. He agreed that if he was to go to Moscow we should invite Zhukov to come to the United States. I took this matter up later with President Truman when I got back and he was all for the idea.

Ike told me during my visit that he was going to say his piece about universal military training and about a single combined military department in Washington after the war.

Eisenhower lives in a very lovely but modest home, surrounded by a great German forest and you get no impression of his having any side or pretentiousness about him. He talked at great length and freely about the strategy and tactics of the war and is quite satisfied with his whole record. He is anxious to get our troops back to their agreed occupation zones and thinks that any further delay will make trouble in Russia.

He expressed great appreciation of my getting Stalin to appoint Zhukov so promptly to the Allied Control Commission.

He has not many clear-cut views as to what the Allies should do about Germany but treats his impending job with the Allied Control Commission as that of a servant of the people to carry out their overall policies.

While I was there he was mixed up with very serious difficulties with the French who, against his orders, were maintaining soldiers in Italy and had refused to withdraw them. He said the French General had a technical right to refuse but in view of the United States request de Gaulle's position was indefensible. He said that the matter was out of his hands, however, and in the hands of the President. I saw the various dispatches later in Paris in which the French Commander in

Italy had written a very abrupt and threatening note to the American Commander and had refused point-blank to remove his troops and stated that if any effort was made to move the French troops he, the French General, would consider it an unfriendly act. At the Embassy in Paris the question arose as to whether de Gaulle actually knew of this letter and had inspired it. It is unthinkable that the French General would take such high-handed action without some assurance that he would be backed up in Paris, so most of the people in the Paris Embassy seemed to think that de Gaulle knew of the action. The telegram from President Truman, which I read, had been received by de Gaulle the day before and had been answered unsatisfactorily. Truman put it right on the line that unless those troops were moved at once he would stop all Lend Lease to the French troops. In fact, he told de Gaulle that he had ordered them stopped. In view of the fact that de Gaulle already had a public fight on with the British over the Levant, it seemed to me that he was being put in a pretty tight corner if he was going to take on the United States on the issue he had chosen. Later he backed down and the troops were removed.

Caffery, our Ambassador in France, urged Truman not to release the correspondence. There is no doubt in my mind that if the correspondence had been released at that particular moment de Gaulle's position in France would have been untenable and he would have been forced to resign. I learned later that Churchill wanted Truman to release it and so did Admiral Leahy but Truman finally decided that he would not do so.

When I returned to Washington I urged Truman to acquaint Stalin of the French incident.

Eisenhower arranged for us to have his suite at the Raphael Hotel where he always stayed and late Friday afternoon we flew to Paris.

Hopkins' report in the foregoing memorandum on some of Eisenhower's statements on political matters was, I believe, not entirely accurate. Eisenhower once told me (it was in London in March, 1944) that his family had always been Kansas Republicans but that he himself had never voted in his life. He felt that since an Army officer must serve his government with full loyalty and devotion regardless of its political coloration, he should avoid all considerations of political partisanship. He conceded that there were other Army officers who felt differently about this for equally honorable reasons. Einsenhower did say to me, as he evidently said to Hopkins, that he had been opposed to the third term simply because he was naturally conservative and a respecter of tradition, but he was most emphatic in expressing his hope that Roosevelt would run for a fourth term and would be re-elected.

Hopkins arrived back in Washington on June 12 and breakfasted with Truman the next morning. The President congratulated him warmly on the extent of his accomplishment in Moscow and urged him to go to the Potsdam Conference the next month. But Hopkins knew that Byrnes would by then have succeeded Stettinius as Secretary of State, and he felt sure that his presence at Potsdam would create inevitable embarrassment, not because of any differences of opinion or ill will between the two men, but simply because of the obvious fact that both Stalin and Churchill were long accustomed to dealing with Hopkins and might therefore seem to by-pass Byrnes's authority. Truman appreciated the validity of these points and did not urge Hopkins to reconsider.

This was an extraordinary moment in Hopkins' life, for he now found himself in the thoroughly unfamiliar position of enjoying a very good press. He was even, for a few days, something of a national hero. Of all the tributes paid to him, the one that touched him most came from a lady in Paris, Missouri, who was unknown to him—Mrs. Mary P. Blanton, wife of the editor of the *Monroe County Appeal*. She wrote: "When I read the editorial in my husband's weekly paper this morning my impulse was to send it to you. None of us are averse to praise and 'Those who stand in high places' may need a little at times. I hope your health is much improved and that you will soon be well and strong. The Middle West is proud of your work for our country."

The editorial that Mrs. Blanton enclosed was as follows:

PALACE GUARD SAVED THE DAY

Harry Hopkins is receiving much applause from newspapers and politicians who tried so hard to destroy him before Roosevelt's death. Always they sneered at him as "the palace guard." When a recent crisis arose between Russia on one hand and Britain and America on the other, President Truman sent Harry to Moscow to iron things out. Although in wretched health, he made the trip and did the job, thus proving the late president knew what he was doing when he kept this great American around. A lot of those who now applaud him should be apologizing to him for past slanders.

Despite Editor Blanton's admonition, I know of no instances of apologies being made to Hopkins for "past slanders." However, from now on the hate-drooling columnists did not pay much attention to him. They took little further interest in the White House Rasputin, probably because Hopkins' great friend, their real target, was dead. They now had nobody left to slander but the great friend's widow.

CHAPTER XXXVI

Conclusion

ON JULY 2, 1945, Hopkins finally severed his connection with the United States Government. In his letter to President Truman, he said, "I want you to know how, along with millions of other Americans, I applaud your courageous and liberal administration of this government's domestic and foreign policy. The fact that you are surrounding yourself with competent and able men but adds to the confidence this nation has in you." In replying, Truman paid handsome tribute to Hopkins' varied contributions to the war effort and did not overlook his earlier accomplishments as relief administrator. The President's letter ended, "I am sure that you must feel much pride and a deep sense of accomplishment in all your great and patriotic service to our country during the last twelve years."

Later, Hopkins realized that he had other posts—such as Chairman of the Munitions Assignment Board, member of the War Production Board, Chairman of the President's Soviet Protocol Committee, etc.—and he sent letters resigning from these as he remembered them.

Hopkins' old friend, Admiral "Betty" Stark, wrote to him: "Well done, thou good and faithful servant. I could nail that old Navy signal 'Well Done' to every mast. There is much ahead of you, and God grant you health and a position where your splendid self may continue achievement . . . without undue strain on your health. Take care of yourself. My good wishes are ever with you—and my gratitude for all you have done for our country. We all owe you much. Keep cheerful."

Listening to a broadcast about himself by Walter Winchell, Hopkins was so pleased that he was moved to write a letter of appreciation, which was unusual for him, mainly because he was given so few opportunities to express gratitude for kind words uttered in public. He said to Winchell: "I don't know of anyone in semi-public life who stuck by Roosevelt as devotedly as did you. You really fought against Hitler in the days when

THE WHITE HOUSE
WASHINGTON

August 18, 1945

Dear Harry:

Your July tenth letter resigning
as Chairman of The President's Soviet
Protocol Committee reached me in Babelsburg,
just outside of Berlin and Potsdam, where
I was billeted.

The first time you are in Washington
I wish you would come in and see me. There
are several things I want to talk to you
about.

Sincerely yours,

Harry.

Honorable Harry L. Hopkins
Somes Sound
Somesville, Maine

Take care of yourself! Get well.

it was none too popular and I think you deserve all the credit in the world for it. A more timid person would have backed away from that one."

Hopkins gave up his house in Georgetown and moved to New York expecting to spend the rest of his life happily in the surroundings that he loved best. The Mayor, Fiorello LaGuardia, for whom he had tried so hard and so ineffectually to get a commission in the Army, now obtained for him appointment as impartial chairman for the New York clothing industry. This job involved a salary of $25,000 a year and not very onerous duties and Hopkins was glad to get it.

On July 4, he wrote to Winant of his decision not to go to Potsdam:

I am sorry I am not going to see you soon because I was looking forward to another visit with you. I had to stop this running around the earth at some point and this seemed as good a time as I could possibly find. While I am feeling better, I have a long way to go to be in the kind of shape I want to be in and I don't want to have to get started all over again.

I can't tell you how pleasant it has been all these years to work with you. I am sure our paths will cross frequently. At any rate I am anxious to keep in touch with you always and will let you know how things go with me.

The war in the Pacific seems to be moving as satisfactorily as we could hope but there are vital decisions still to be made.

The Germany I saw was a shambles, but I confess I am a little disquieted by suggestions I hear from some quarters that we do little or nothing to prevent the Germans from starting this business all over again. I have no confidence in them whatever but I have a good healthy respect for their ability to hit us again in another 25 years.

It looks as tho, if we all put our minds on it, we could throw Franco out of Spain, which would surely be a good riddance. Perhaps the House of Savoy could go along with him without anybody losing a heartbeat.

Hopkins, who had no particular record of scholarship to his credit, was surprised and delighted to receive an announcement from Oxford University that "the Hebdomadal Council desires, subject to your consent, to submit to the Convocation of the University at an early date a proposal that the Honorary Degree of D.C.L. be conferred upon you, in recognition of your eminent services to the Allied cause." He hastily communicated his consent and planned to go to England to receive the degree on October 25.

When the results of the British general election were announced Hopkins said, in a letter to General Ismay, "The news of the P.M.'s defeat is staggering. I thought the Elections would be close and that Labor might have a chance to win but I never dreamed it would be the landslide it was. I only hope the P.M. did not take it too badly. He has been a gallant fighter and his deeds will go down in Anglo-Saxon history for all time."

Hopkins wrote to Beaverbrook: "I have heard from some of your men about publishing rights on anything I may want to write and I wish very much that you would put your mind on it. Specifically I am going to write at least two books and I think quite possibly three or four more. The first two are going to be a book on the war and the second book on Roosevelt as I knew him. I intend to take my time writing them and, under no circumstances, will the book on the war be published until the war with Japan is over. And I don't want to do any slipshod job on Roosevelt."

Hopkins engaged an assistant, Sidney Hyman, to help in the organization of his voluminous papers preparatory to the writing of all the books that he planned. Hyman, a graduate of the University of Chicago, had been active in Midwestern political affairs before the war, in which he served with honor as an officer in the First Armored Division in the North African and Italian campaigns. (This division was one of the few American units available for the operations known as MAGNET and GYMNAST when they were first planned at the Arcadia Conference in December, 1941.)

Hyman has written, of his first association with Hopkins in August, 1945:

> I felt that HLH was skidding around in his mind in search for a form he could give the book. He began everywhere and nowhere all at once. One day he would start to work on an introduction to the book, and the next day he would jump to the Yalta Conference and ask to see materials related to it. Every time the newspapers carried a story "disclosing" a wartime secret, Hopkins would immediately re-examine his own documents as they bore on that event. It was under the prodding of current news items, for instance, that he wrote the memordandum about the conversation between FDR and Ibn Saud, and between General Marshall and Governor Dewey.

> When I put his papers into some rough order, he made several quick samplings of their contents and often expressed surprise at the presence of some memorandum he had written. He indicated to me that he had not only forgotten the record he made (the memoranda of his first London trip, for instance) but he had also forgotten the incident described in the record. When he went through papers that bore on his private life, he would sometimes snatch out a letter, stare at it, and snort. He made a point of the fact that all of these letters should be kept and none of them destroyed. Incidentally, he had earlier asked that I go through all his files and throw away "irrelevant" materials. But I didn't throw away as much as one paper clip. Referring to the kind of letters he wanted saved, Hopkins said: "This is

the sort of thing I would object to having destroyed in the Roosevelt papers. The whole story of Roosevelt—and my story is part of it—is going to come out anyway in the next fifty years. I feel we will both come out with credit. And I don't see any point in trying to edit my past by destroying papers which showed precisely what I did and how I did it. I want people to know that I played politics; I also want them to know *why* I played politics."

In his random, scattered approach to this book he quickly tired of the sampling process and at the time of his death had not gone through more than one file drawer. In the same way that he would snort at the letters he plucked out, he would pluck books off the shelves and leaf through them. One day I saw him pick up a book put out by the W.P.A. It was an expensive printing job, with many plates and a very substantial-looking binding. He flourished the book and said to me, "This is pure boondoggling. The people who attacked us for things like this were perfectly right. Of course, I would have been a God-damned fool to have agreed with them." At the same time he was very proud of the guidebooks put out by the W.P.A., and while he discarded several hundred novels and books on economics and politics when he moved into his Fifth Avenue house, he gave an honored place on his library shelf to the W.P.A. series.

The paragraphs that Hopkins did get down on paper were hastily dictated and I do not believe that he ever bothered even to reread them and work them into proper form. They were rambling and repetitious, and I have deleted some unimportant passages in the following:

I know no person in his right mind but that he believes if this nation ever had to engage in another war Great Britain would be fighting on our side, and yet, to hear some people talk about the British, you would think the British were our potential enemies. I believe that the British have saved our skins twice—once in 1914 and again in 1940. They, with the French, took the brunt of the attack in the First World War, and the Germans came within a hair's breadth of licking them both before we got into it. This time it was Britain alone that held the fort and they held that fort for us just as much as for themselves, because we would not have had a chance to have licked Hitler had Britain fallen. . . .

Many Britishers do not make it particularly easy for those of us who want to see a close-working relationship with Great Britain. When the Prime Minister said that he was not selected to be the King's Minister to liquidate the Empire, every isolationist in America cheered him. Before that, he had never been very popular with our isolationists in America. There is constant friction between our business interests and we think—and I have no doubt with some good reason—that Great Britain would take an unfair advantage of us in trade around the world. It is footless to ignore the fact that the American people simply do not like the British Colonial policy. . . .

A little old-fashioned frankness on diplomatic levels would help.

The wiping out of our trade barriers—and we have taken the first step in that—including reduction of our tariffs and the abolition of the British Empire preference scheme would go a long way towards accomplishing that end. The American people must realize the plain and simple truth that the British live by trade. We are probably powerful enough, if we want to use that power, to seriously injure that trade, but I do not believe it is to our self-interest to do it. Why should we deliberately set about to make a weak Great Britain in the next hundred years unless we go on the assumption that war will be waged no more?

Two great powers such as the United States and Great Britain can afford to have minor differences. That is bound to be the case, but we cannot afford to indulge in a deliberate program on either side which is going to force our two peoples further and further apart.

If I were to lay down the most cardinal principle of our foreign policy, it would be that we make absolutely sure that now and forever the United States and Great Britain are going to see eye to eye on major matters of world policy. It is easy to say that. It is hard to do, but it can be done and the effort is worth it.

As to our relations with the Soviet Union:

We know that we and Russia are the two most powerful nations in the world in manpower and raw materials. We know that we have been able to fight side by side with the Russians in the greatest war in all history. We know or believe that Russia's interests, so far as we can anticipate them, do not afford an opportunity for a major difference with us in foreign affairs. We believe we are mutually dependent upon each other for economic reasons. We find the Russians as individuals easy to deal with. The Russians undoubtedly like the American people. They like the United States. They trust the United States more than they trust any power in the world. I believe they not only have no wish to fight with us, but are determined to take their place in world affairs in an international organization, and above all, they want to maintain friendly relations with us.

The great enigma about the Soviet Union in the years to come is the policy which new leaders of Russia will have toward the promotion of world-wide Communism. There is every indication that the Soviet Government today is becoming more and more nationalistic. They are going to see to it that their borders are protected from unfriendly states and I, for one, do not blame them for that.

There can be no question that the United States' permanent longtime relations with the Soviet Union are going to be seriously handicapped, not so much by our fundamental differences in ideology as between a capitalist economy and a socialist state, but between our fundamental notions of human liberty—freedom of speech, freedom of the press and freedom of worship. The American people want not only freedom for themselves, but they want freedom throughout the world for other people as well, as they simply do not like the notion that you cannot say what you please when you want to say it.

If Russia wants a socialist state—and incidentally, anyone who thinks that the Soviet Union is moving to the right economically is, in my opinion, greatly mistaken—that is surely their own business. They are absolutely sure it is going to work better for the hundred and eighty million citizens of the Soviet Union than a capitalist economy would work. They do not think much of the way the capitalist economy worked in places like France, Belgium and Holland just before the war. They seem to have a pretty healthy respect for ours, however.

The thing the American people must look out for is that there is a minority in America who, for a variety of reasons, would just as soon have seen Russia defeated in the war and who said publicly before we got into the war that it did not make any difference which one— Russia or Germany—won. That small, vociferous minority can take advantage of every rift between ourselves and Russia to make trouble between our two countries. There are plenty of people in America who would have been perfectly willing to see our armies go right on through Germany and fight with Russia after Germany was defeated. They represent nobody but themselves and no government worth its salt in control of our country would ever permit that group to influence our official actions.

The Soviet Union is made up of a hundred and eighty million hard-working proud people. They are not an uncivilized people. They are a tenacious, determined people who think and act just like you and I do. Our Russian policy must not be dictated by people who have already made up their minds that there is no possibility of working with Russians and that our interests are bound to conflict and ultimately lead to war. From my point of view, that is an untenable position and can but lead to disaster.

France is another country whose strength and power are selfish assets to the United States. In the years to come, the French will be but a few hours from our shores. They have fought by our side ever since our Republic was founded and, indeed, joined with us in our own great Revolution. Our foreign policy towards France should not be governed by the personalities of the people who happen for the moment to be in executive power in either of our countries.

General de Gaulle has done some tremendous things for France. One thing he did was to make her people hold their heads high again and be proud they were Frenchmen, and to forget the humiliation of defeat in planning for the future. It is equally sure that General de Gaulle has not always been the easiest man to get on with in diplomatic affairs. There is no use of now trying to place the blame for the personal differences between President Roosevelt and General de Gaulle, but the important thing to the American people is not the temporary head of the Republic of France, but the forty million Frenchmen who make up that great country. . . .

There are still plenty of people in America who think that old General Pétain was a great patriot and there are some of the old crowd in France who think like them. These people are usually scared to death because France, as, indeed, all of Europe, is moving on economic fronts to the left. It is a plain fact that the great masses of people in Europe are determined to find a new economic basis for a better life for themselves and their children. . . .

France must be sure of our friendship, not doubtful about it. France was betrayed by her military leaders, her industrialists and decadent politicians. We are the only nation in the world that can give France any economic support in this critical hour of her trial and haven't we every interest to do it?

When I speak of France, I might as well be speaking of all of Western Europe and this gets into a fundamental definition of our foreign policy in Europe and that is this: The United States first wants to do everything it can to prevent another war, hence we have an interest in every part of the world where war might break out, but even more than that, the United States' interests are not served by having any countries in Europe become totalitarism states, I don't care what label they give it.

That gets right into the question of the United States engaging in an aggressive, affirmative policy of promoting the democratic processes in Western Europe. . . . It surely is to our interest to see that the countries of Western Europe do not starve or freeze this winter, because as sure as that happens, governments are going to be overthrown and those who believe in the totalitarism system can well come into power and they are not dislodged easily. I do not see for the life of me why we should be diffident and apologetic and unaggressive about promoting the democratic process throughout the world. We do not want anything out of it for ourselves. We have no selfish interests in terms of land, but surely we do not want to see the people of the world enslaved with any more totalitarian governments. I simply think the Western world is not big enough for the kind of democracy we have and, for instance, Mr. Franco in Spain. . . .

I might say in passing here that I do not belong to the school that believes that a country like the Argentine can do as they please at our back door. I do not see why we should play ball in any way with that Fascist-dominated country.

I have had people all over the world ask me what the American interest is in places like Iraq, Iran, Poland, Greece and so on. I give them two answers that I think are controlling in the United States. The first is world security and the second is our interest in human freedom and justice throughout the world. I do not mean to say we do not have a proper economic interest and that we should not insist on our rights in all areas in the world for freedom of trade, but the American people in terms of a long-range foreign policy are never going to carry that as a major banner in our foreign affairs.

Nor do I see why this nation should not state unequivocally its belief in the political and economic freedom of all people throughout the world. Now, you can say that that spells the doom of all the Colonial Empires. Well, it probably does. A lot of those great Colonial

States whenever they want freedom badly enough are going to get it, because none of these Colonial powers have enough soldiers to prevent them from having freedom when they really want it. You cannot dilute this business of freedom. Either you believe in it, or you don't. You can think of a hundred and one reasons why this and that Colonial country—or, for that matter, Puerto Rico—should not be free, but none of those reasons has ever made sense to me.

I am not recommending that we stir up revolutions all over the world, but I do say that the United States should not cooperate in any international enterprise that will tend to solidify for all time a political relationship which does not give actual and complete freedom to the people who want it.

If I were to indicate a country in which the United States, for the next hundred years, had the greatest interest from political and economic points of view, I would name the Republic of China. With the defeat of Japan, China will become one of the greatest land powers on earth. I do not say that she will be one of the most powerful for many years to come, but she will have regained her heritage in Manchuria and we hope that there will arise out of the welter of war a unified China.

(*Note.* This was written on August 1, 1945; Hopkins still believed that a settlement fair to China had been achieved at Yalta.)

It is ridiculous to assume China is not going to have great problems —internal political and economic problems—after this war is over. There are a great many things that need to be done in terms of human freedom in China, and I have no doubt that those things will be done. The United States, through the espousal of the "Open Door Policy," has an absolutely clean record in China over the years. We must keep it so. China is going to depend upon us. There is no other country in the world that they can look to for economic support after this war is over. The Soviet Union is going to have all it can do to develop its own internal economy and Great Britain does not have the resources to help China to the road to anything that resembles prosperity. True, it will be a slow and painful process and their standards of living for years to come will not resemble ours, but in many ways, with the end of this war, China will almost be our nearest neighbor. . . .

There are appalling economic differences between the masses of people in China and those who rule it. The great land reform is long overdue, but these things the Chinese people themselves will insist upon because there will be great revolutionary force at work in China to reform their economic system and I think some of the new leaders in China, notably T. V. Soong, understand that thoroughly and are quite prepared for the kind of economic reform that must come to China.

When the results of the Potsdam Conference were announced, Hopkins was asked what he thought of them. He said, "I don't know. It looks as if President Truman and Jimmy Byrnes did a good job—but you can't tell what the real problems are unless you're *there* and intimately involved in them and understanding all the background circumstances and the implications of what is said and what isn't said. The way the situation changes from day to day—or minute to minute—if you lose touch with it for as long as I have [one month] you're just about as ignorant of it as anybody else." Certainly, at that time (about August 1) Hopkins had no idea that the Japanese war would end so soon, even though he did know that the Russians were about to come into it. He was eager to see Bohlen to hear his account of what went on at Potsdam.

Hopkins wrote down a few paragraphs of his views on the question of domestic policy. He said that it had been five years since he had been actively engaged in matters relating to the domestic scene, but he had talked to a great many soldiers and sailors and "the one great question-mark in their minds is how are they going to earn a living?" He went on to say:

> We can and should have our schemes of social insurance for the old and the sick, but it would be a terrible day for America if the rest of us did not want to earn our living by work, or could not earn our living by work.
>
> These soldiers coming home simply are not going to understand our boasting about our capitalist economy if it can't deliver the goods in terms of the opportunity for work.
>
> I sense in some quarters a defeatist attitude towards this business of providing jobs for sixty million people. They think it is quixotic, or that it is radical. I can't for the life of me understand what they propose to do for the people that can't get work, but I think the other side of the picture is this: That this business of providing full employment has captured the imagination of the vast majority of the American people. They do not know just how it is going to be done, but they do not want any hesitancy on the part of their political leaders or their industrial leaders or labor leaders to assume that it is possible.
>
> Fortunately, in all probability for a few years after the war, apart from the adjustments that will have to be made in closing down the war plants, there will be a tremendous demand for goods and hence, a large over-all employment, but the time is coming, and the planning must be made now, when the government, industry, agriculture and labor will have to sit down together and find the way and means to assure that these opportunities shall be available.
>
> I believe that during the war many thousands of business men have gained a healthy respect for government and do not look at public institutions as something they wish to have no part of. After all, they know the tax structure is controlled by government. The government very largely controls credit. It is the biggest single business in the country. What the farmer and laborer do not want is to see

government running their affairs, but it is axiomatic that their affairs cannot be run without having a relationship to government.

I would hate to see the backbone of full employment ever be public works for the sake of providing employment. It is a proper instrument to use when industrial employment slides off, but it surely is the line of least resistance.

On September 4, Hopkins made his last trip to Washington to receive the Distinguished Service Medal from President Truman. Secretary Stimson wrote to him: "Your Distinguished Service Medal represented a service that was not only most distinguished and successful in crises of most far-reaching importance but was rendered by you with a courage which was as great as it was modest. I have rejoiced in the recognition of your work which it symbolized. I share your exultation in our former trials. In the words of Virgil, *haec olim meminisse juvabit.*"

After the award of the medal which was made in the White House garden in the presence of the Chiefs of Staff and many of Hopkins' other friends and associates, he had a private talk with Truman in which he told the President all that he knew of the negotiations with the British relative to the development of the atomic bomb. As has been recorded in earlier chapters, Hopkins had been associated with this development since the very inception of the National Defense Research Council. But he was completely out of touch with it in the final months preceding the Los Alamos test and he did not know that the bomb had become a reality until he read the dread name of Hiroshima in the headlines.

Early in October, he received a letter from General Eisenhower in Berlin: "I do not need to tell you that this job is an unholy mixture of irritations, frustrations and bewildering conflicts. Nevertheless I try to keep my sense of humor and keep swinging with both hands. We have really made progress both toward the allied and the strictly national objectives, but there is much to do and in a job such as this we are particularly vulnerable to day by day criticism. An administrative blunder, even if local and temporary, is news; constructive progress is not dramatic."

Eisenhower confessed in this letter that he had been thinking "about the possibility of writing a book." He said, "I have even, from time to time, tried to draft a bit of narrative just to satisfy myself that I had something to say that was worth hearing. Actually I have not convinced myself of this at all and regardless of attractiveness of offers, it is the one thing on which I will have to be quite sure before I would ever consent to undertake such a job." By this time—October—Hopkins was unable to do any real work of any kind. His health was deteriorating steadily—and, as usual, he said it was "a touch of flu." He was restless and unhappy and casting about for new things in which to become interested. Hyman has written:

It is my impression that on moving into his Fifth Avenue house, Hopkins seemed torn between a desire to hang on to everything he had done in the past, and at the same time to strip himself free of everything, as though he meant to get down to his own bare-bones. (He commented on the fact that he was returning to New York to work among the same sort of people he had first met in New York thirty years before.) One day he asked me to contact art dealers and find out what they would be willing to pay for a great number of etchings he had had since the days of his marriage to Barbara Duncan Hopkins. An art auctioneer came over to the house one day to look at the collection and told me that their only value arose from the fact that Hopkins owned them—and that if the art concern was to make any money out of the deal, the sale would have to be advertised as "A Harry Hopkins Auction." I passed this information on to Hopkins, who balked at the idea of any such deal. But he asked to see the dealer. This man showed up on a day during which Hopkins had received and turned down four telephone calls from various important people. While he had earlier declared himself in no way fit to handle those calls, it was surprising to see him come down out of his bedroom to spend the whole afternoon cross-examining the art dealer on the nature of the auction business. In the first five minutes, the dealer told Hopkins that the whole lot of etchings wouldn't bring more than $200. Hopkins lost interest in the sale but he kept the dealer from two until five-thirty in the afternoon. The dealer seemed a little thinner when he left Hopkins' house. Hopkins had gouged out everything this man knew about the art auction business.

Hopkins spent less and less time at the Garment Union office—which was little enough to begin with—though he did arbitrate one case. I heard him talk of his work there and say that he found it of great interest. He was not merely content to be an impartial arbitrator, but proposed to bring about considerable changes in the structure of the garment industry.

At about this time, there were two crippling strikes in the City of New York. One was an elevator strike, and the second one was a strike among coal-barge operators. He had been in bed during both strikes. But then, he received word that both the elevator operators and representatives of the real estate interests were considering calling on him to arbitrate their difficulties. In watching the effect of this on Hopkins, I had a sense of a man being brought back from the dead. The dreaminess and irascibility that settled over him when he was sick were sloughed off. He got dressed, came downstairs and spent some time on the phone barking out orders and directions. I may be quite wrong about this—but I felt that he wanted very badly to be back on active duty again. But the strike was settled without him, and Hopkins returned to his bed. A short while thereafter, the same thing happened in the case of the tugboat strike, and once again he seemed to be sparked with new life when he was approached to mediate that strike.

Hopkins spent a lot of time studying catalogues and advertisements from the larger New York department stores, for he had contemplated the possibility of getting into this business ever since his association with Jesse Straus, of R. H. Macy and Company, during the days of the first Relief Program in New York State. He also made a considerable study of modern paintings because of his wife's interest in this subject. With the advice and instruction of Monroe Wheeler, Director at the Museum of Modern Art in New York, Hopkins attacked this unfamiliar subject with the same penetrating curiosity and quick understanding that he had applied to silicosis and flood relief and grand strategy and other problems that he had been compelled to cope with in the course of his strange career. When he went to Memorial Hospital he had in his room a small Renoir, lent to him by a friend, Mrs. Barbara Wescott, and originals or reproductions of paintings by Utrillo, Picasso, Yves Tanguy, Serge Ferat, Marsden Hartley and others, loaned by Wheeler.

By the middle of October, Hopkins was confined to his own house and largely to his bedroom. He read the newspapers and listened to the radio and often felt the urge to express himself officially, as though he were still drafting cables for the President to send. On October 24, having read the results of elections in France, he wrote to de Gaulle:

I hasten to congratulate you on the implications of the French election. Irrespective of the merits of the various political parties concerned, the election showed to the world the great vitality of French democracy and I think that much of the credit of this orderly outpouring of the French people to express their convictions at the polls is due to your patient and determined handling of your nation's affairs during the past dark and trying years.

France and the French people are emerging now into their own heritage, and, while I have no doubt the path ahead is going to be trying and difficult, I am as completely confident of the outcome as you have always been.

While I am no longer in the government, I keep in close touch with affairs in Washington and I am following the fortunes of France with an ever growing interest.

De Gaulle thanked him for his sympathy and his vision and said, "I am happy to see that you have not lost contact with Washington so that your country may still profit by the counsels of your great experience."

On November 2, Hopkins wrote to the War Department in behalf of a private soldier in California, whose wife and child had been stricken with infantile paralysis. He suggested that the Department might explore the possibility of releasing this man from the Army, but he said he wished to emphasize that "I am not requesting that anything be done for him that would not be done for any other soldier in similar circumstances."

A few days after writing that letter Hopkins was ordered to the hospital and he remained there to die.

The Pearl Harbor Investigation had started in the Congress and Hopkins worried about it a great deal, for he knew that the main purpose of some of the Republicans and all the isolationists of both parties was to affix the blame for the Japanese attack entirely on Roosevelt. Weak and helpless as he was, Hopkins was obsessed with fears and suspicions that some of the high-ranking witnesses before the Congressional Committee would distort their testimony in order to absolve themselves from any possible share of the responsibility. His fears were groundless. He read the records of the hearings as they piled up day after day and he expressed to Hyman his particular admiration and high praise for the manner in which Admiral Stark had conducted himself before the Committee. He knew that Stark was one officer who might have grounds for resentment against Roosevelt, and who himself was one of the principal targets for criticism, but the former Chief of Naval Operations revealed his devoted loyalty and his unassailable honor under fire. There were many times when Hopkins asked the doctors to let him get out of bed and go down to Washington to give his own testimony, but he was utterly unable to do so.

He also worried a great deal about financial matters. With the arrival of the New Year, 1946, he had been in the hospital for two months and it was becoming more and more evident that his condition was not improving and it would be a long time before he could perform even his light duties as Chairman of the clothing industry. Furthermore, he did not know when he would be able to get to work on his book, for which he had already received (and spent) advance royalties. His expenses were heavy and he was going into debt, borrowing money from friends, including Bernard Baruch.

On January 22, 1946, Hopkins wrote what I believe was the last letter of his life. It was to Winston Churchill, who was then on holiday in Miami Beach. He said:

> Only being laid up in the hospital prevented me from meeting you at the boat the other day and I do hope you will find it possible to get to New York because it appears altogether unlikely that I could possibly be in Florida during the next month.
>
> All I can say about myself at the moment is that I am getting excellent care, while the doctors are struggling over a very bad case of cirrhosis of the liver—not due, I regret to say, from taking too much alcohol. But I must say that I dislike having the effect of a long life of congenial and useful drinking and neither deserve the reputation nor enjoy its pleasures.
>
> The newspapers indicate you and Clemmie are having a quiet and delightful time and I hope you won't let any Congressional Committee of ours bore you.

Do give my love to Clemmie and Sarah, all of whom I shall hope to see before you go back, but I want to have a good talk with you over the state of world affairs, to say nothing of our private lives.

A week later Hopkins was dead. The post-mortem revealed no cirrhosis of the liver, and no cancer. He was killed by a disease known as hemochromatosis, the result of his inadequate digestive equipment.

Hopkins had spent so much time at death's door during the past nine years, that the final act of passing through it must have been for him pretty much of a routine matter. He was generally unconscious for days before he died, but I am sure that if he had any moment of awareness of the imminence of death he did not accept it calmly, in a spirit of resignation, but did his best to fight against it, for he certainly wanted to live on with his family, whom he loved, and to know how everything was going to come out.

The day after Hopkins' death, I read an editorial in the *Los Angeles Times* which recited the familiar complaint that he was "never elected by the people to a public office" and that his activities as Presidential adviser were "out of bounds by any constitutional concept," and ·it added, "Americans need not concern themselves now whether Harry Hopkins was great or little or good or bad; their care should be that the phenomenon of a Harry Hopkins in the White House does not recur."

The editorial did not state just what measures should be taken to prevent such a recurrence—possibly a law providing that the President's personal friends and advisers, and even his guests at the White House, must be elected by popular vote or at least be made subject to approval by the Senate. However, I suspect that what the *Los Angeles Times* was really expressing was the hope that a phenomenon like Franklin D. Roosevelt would not recur. I believe that Roosevelt's closest friends join in that particular hope, not for the sake of his memory, which will take care of itself, but in the interests of the nation and indeed of the entire world which must never again be in the position in time of peril of placing so much reliance on the imagination and the courage and the durability of one mortal man.

I came out of my own experience of five years of government service in wartime with alarmed awareness of the risks that we run of disastrous fallibility at the very top of our Constitutional structure. There is far too great a gap between the President and the Congress, particularly if he is, as every President should be, endowed with exceptional qualities. It is all very well to say that this gap might be closed by more efficient, businesslike methods in the White House; but the extraordinary and solitary Constitutional powers of the President remain and, in times of crises, they are going to be asserted for better or for worse.

To go back to the beginning, it may be that George Washington was too great a man for the nation's eventual good. For the Founding Fathers established the office of President with the knowledge that Washington was there to fill it. They fitted the office to his tremendous measurements. They established the triheaded system of checks and balances to ensure that no President would ever become king. But, having taken this precaution, they gave the President the supreme authority of a Commander in Chief in peacetime as well as in war.

In the Lincoln Memorial in Washington are the words, IN THIS TEMPLE AS IN THE HEARTS OF THE PEOPLE FOR WHOM HE SAVED THE UNION THE MEMORY OF ABRAHAM LINCOLN IS ENSHRINED FOREVER. Those are beautiful words, but they are very ominous ones. They perpetuate admission that had not this one man been born and miraculously elected, the Union would have been destroyed.

The remarkable luck that we have had in meeting major emergencies in the past should not prevent us now from giving most serious consideration to the question: where is the guarantee that this luck will hold? Presumably it lies in the genius of the American people, but one does not need to have access to any secret documents to know how difficult it is for this genius to express itself or even to realize itself. In the fateful years of 1933 and 1940 the people needed and demanded leadership which could be given to them only by the President, the one officer of government who is elected by all the people and whose duty it is to represent the interests of the nation as a whole rather than the purely local or special interests which are too often the predominant concerns of the Congress. There is no factor in our national life more dangerous than the people's lack of confidence in the Congress to rise above the level of picayune parochialism; the threats of Communism or Fascism are trivial as compared with this. Some Americans have looked enviously at the British parliamentary system, particularly as it demonstrated itself when, in the face of approaching disaster, the hapless, anachronistic government of Neville Chamberlain was superseded by the vigorous and truly representative government of Winston Churchill —a historical change which was achieved in an orderly manner, within a matter of hours, and entirely within the House of Commons whose authority and dignity continued unimpaired. However, I doubt that there are many thoughtful Americans who believe that this venerable British system or anything like it could be made to work with us. Our own problems, and they are very large ones, will be worked out in accordance with our own Constitutional system, with the President remaining in the White House and the Congress on Capitol Hill; but surely a way can be found to diminish the distance between these two points.

Roosevelt has often been blamed for widening the gap between the Executive and Legislative branches. I think he only revealed it. He brought the essential problems out into the open and gave them a much needed airing. He was more successful than any previous President in dramatizing and personalizing the processes of government for the people. One obvious result of his influence was the enormously healthy increase in the number of votes cast in national elections. Of course, previous Presidents had not enjoyed the peculiar advantages afforded by the mechanical development of the radio, but future Presidents will have ever greater access to this means of direct communication, plus television, plus God knows how many other contrivances. This tends greatly to increase the solitary power of the President and to make him all the more indispensable in emergencies when he happens to enjoy popularity and prestige comparable to Roosevelt's.

That word "indispensable" was flung at Roosevelt time and again in tones of wrathful scorn by his domestic enemies, and they could always sting him with it, since he could make no effective retort. There are few documents recorded in this book which interested me more than the memorandum written by Hopkins on May 28, 1939 (it appears in Chapter IV) describing a long talk with Eleanor Roosevelt: "She thinks that the causes for which he fought are far greater than any individual person, but that if the New Deal is entirely dependent upon him, it indicates that it hasn't as strong a foundation as she believes it has with the great masses of the people." I believe that there Mrs. Roosevelt was expressing her husband's point of view as well as her own, and events proved that the survival of the New Deal reforms was not dependent on Roosevelt or on any other individual. Nevertheless, history must record the unalterable fact that in 1940 Roosevelt *was* indispensable—not because there were no other able and far-seeing and courageous statesmen in the United States—but simply because he was the only one whom most of the American people re-elected, regardless of the third term tradition, and chose to follow through the gathering shadows of the Second World War.

This was a fundamental circumstance, and we may all pray that it will never recur; but as we look ahead into the dread prospects of the atomic age we can be none too sure that it will not. Our need for great men in the Presidency will continue, and our need for great men in the Congress will increase.

When I was coming to the end of the long work on this book, I went to London for final checking of some of the material included and I attended the unveiling by Mrs. Roosevelt of the statue of her husband in Grosvenor Square. That evening—April 12, 1948—The Pilgrims Society gave a dinner for Mrs. Roosevelt at which Winston Churchill expressed his solemn conviction "that in Roosevelt's life and by his actions he changed, he altered decisively and permanently, the social axis, the moral axis, of mankind by involving the New World inexorably and irrevocably in the fortunes of the Old. His life must therefore be regarded as one of the commanding events in human destiny." The Former Naval Person also said of his old friend, "The longer his life and times are studied, the more unchallengeable these affirmations which I have made to you tonight will become." These were the words of a great student of history who knew whereof he spoke. I believed at the time of Roosevelt's death—and this belief has been fortified by all I have learned subsequently—that as more and more of the record is revealed, the greater his stature will become. But the story of his life is by no means ended, nor is the task to which he set himself anywhere near complete. As Hopkins said to me after the funeral service in the White House, "Now we've got to get to work on our own. This is where we've really got to begin."

Hopkins was able to do one job on his own—his last trip to Moscow— and after that there was too little life left in him. I believe that he went to his death with grave misgivings for the immediate future. I do not believe that he had any apprehensions as to the imminence of another war, for he could not conceive the possibility of anything so suicidal or so unnecessary. What he did fear was that there would be innumerable attempts to foul the record for partisan or for vindictive or selfish personal reasons, and that such attempts might be temporarily successful, and the people might become mired in another age of decadent disillusionment such as that which followed the First World War, or another age of unbridled rapacity such as that which followed the Civil War. These were the real fears that Hopkins took with him into death, and it would seem that so far they have not been justified. He also took with him the knowledge that there were very few men who ever lived who were as fortunate as he in the possession of such enemies and such friends.

OPERATION CODE NAMES

ABC-1—first American-British outline of grand strategy for the war (March, 1941).

ANAKIM—code name for land offensive in North Burma to drive out Japanese and reopen Burma Road and an amphibious operation in the south to recapture port of Rangoon.

ANVIL—original code name for landing of American and French forces in the Toulon-Marseilles area of Southern France. Later changed for security reasons to DRAGOON.

AVALANCHE—code name for landings at the Salerno beachhead south of Naples.

BOLERO—code name given to process of building up required U.S. forces and supplies in the British Isles.

BUCCANEER—code name for briefly projected amphibious offensive against the Andaman Islands in Bay of Bengal.

DRAGOON—final code name of French-American landings in Southern France.

FLINTLOCK—code name of attack on Kwajalein Atoll in the Marshall Islands.

GYMNAST, SUPER-GYMNAST—early code names for landings in Algiers and French Morocco.

HUSKY—code name for invasion of Sicily.

JUPITER—code name for suggested landing in Norway.

LIFEBELT—code name for projected operation to seize Azores for use as a base in Battle of the Atlantic and as an airbase for ferrying bombers and transport planes. Aim of operation finally achieved by diplomatic negotiations.

LIGHTFOOT—code name for drive by Generals Alexander and Montgomery from Egypt in October, 1942. Battle of El Alamein marked the beginning of this operation.

MAGNET—code name for movement of first American forces to Northern Ireland.

OVERLORD—final code name for the cross-Channel invasion.

POINTBLANK—code name of combined British-American bombing offensive of German communication and supply lines.

ROUNDUP—code name for major combined cross-Channel offensive against German-dominated Europe, to be mounted in 1943 or later. Later changed to OVERLORD.

SLEDGEHAMMER—1) originally code name for a limited trans-Channel assault in 1942, planned originally as emergency operation in case of imminent collapse of Russian Front or internal German collapse.

2) later used as code name for operation to seize the Cotentin Peninsula to be held as a European bridgehead until ROUNDUP could be mounted.

STRANGLE—code name of combined bombing of German communication and supply lines in Italy.

TORCH—final code name for the North African landings.

VELVET—code name of plan for building up a British-American air force in the Caucasus by end of 1942.

NOTES

CHAPTER I

2. The quotation of the statement made by Roosevelt to Wendell Willkie on January 19, 1941, was told many times by Willkie and this version of it has been checked with Mrs. Willkie.

4. The analogy between Hopkins' position and that of Colonel House has often been made and there were, of course, some resemblances. However, the personalities of Wilson and House, on the one hand, and of Roosevelt and Hopkins, on the other, were widely different and so consequently was the quality of the relationships.

 In connection with the quotation from Roosevelt, "Harry is the perfect Ambassador," etc., when Roosevelt used a relatively modern slang expression such as "Oh, yeah?!" he would usually add "as my boy Johnny says." I do not know just why John Roosevelt was credited with the origination of these expressions but presumably, since he was the youngest, he was the most fecund source during the later years when I was around the White House. Near the end of his life Roosevelt picked up the expression, "So what?" from his son John and he loved to use it.

5. The quotation from Winston Churchill, "I have been present," etc., was in a public statement made immediately after Hopkins' death. The subsequent anecdote about "Lord Root of the Matter" was told me by Churchill himself.

9. Quotations are made from *The Roosevelt I Knew*, by Frances Perkins (The Viking Press); "The Morgenthau Diaries," published in *Collier's*, September, 1947; *On Active Service in Peace and War*, by Henry L. Stimson and McGeorge Bundy (Harper & Brothers).

CHAPTER II

14. The best biographical sketches of Hopkins that I have read appeared in *Fortune* magazine (July, 1935) and *The New Yorker* (August 7 and 14, 1943), the latter a profile by Geoffrey Hellman.

CHAPTER III

40. The comment by Hopkins on Roosevelt's First Inaugural Address was quoted from a preface that he wrote for *Nothing to Fear* (Houghton Mifflin), edited by B. D. Zevin.

 Quotations from the First Inaugural and from all other speeches and official writings by Roosevelt, and from his press conferences, in this chapter are quoted from *The Public Papers and Addresses of Franklin D. Roosevelt*, edited by Samuel I. Rosenman. This same great source has been used for similar quotations up to Chapter XII.

Quotations of Ernie Pyle were from the *Washington News*, of Walter Lippmann from the *New York Herald Tribune*, of Gerald W. Johnson from his book, *Roosevelt—Dictator or Democrat?* (Harper & Brothers); of Ernest K. Lindley from his book, *The Roosevelt Revolution* (The Viking Press).

55. The issue of *Time* magazine which featured Hopkins on its cover and which is quoted at various points in this chapter was dated February 19, 1934.

56. The survey of the whole relief program from which quotations on the work of C.W.A. are made appeared in *Fortune* magazine, October, 1934.

57. The Gutzon Borglum letter to Aubrey Williams was dated December 20, 1933.

59. Hopkins' press conference from which quotations are made was held on April 4, 1935. (Incidentally, as these notes are being written, I read that orators at the Republican Convention of 1948 are still quoting Hopkins as having said, "The people are too damned dumb to understand." It will be seen from the transcript of his remarks that this particular statement was directed not at the people but at the critical orators.)

72. Harold Smith, Director of the Budget during the war years, whose remarks to me are quoted in this chapter and in later chapters, kept very careful records of his many talks with President Roosevelt which will be of inestimable value to students of this era.

Chapter IV

78. The Hopkins notes on the Ohio situation were made in a diary which he kept spasmodically at that time. Most of his notes in this and subsequent chapters were written not in diary form but as strictly personal memoranda for his future reference; some of these were dictated, and many more were written in longhand and never even entrusted to a secretary for copying. Once Jerome Beatty visited Hopkins in the White House and expressed the hope that he was keeping a careful diary. Hopkins replied, "No one who keeps a diary would last long around here." And when I first went to work in the White House, General Watson asked me if I were keeping a diary and, when I told him that I had formerly done so but had abandoned it, he advised me to keep right on abandoning it.

80. Quotations from Hugh Johnson in this and subsequent chapters are from his column syndicated by the Scripps-Howard newspapers; so was the Talbert cartoon referred to.

89. The memorandum by Hopkins quoting Thomas J. Corcoran on the Supreme Court fight was one of those written in longhand and never typed until incorporated in this book. Hopkins wrote it in April, 1939, while on a visit to Warm Springs with the President.

92. The extent to which Roosevelt fostered the Hopkins candidacy for the Presidential nomination must remain among the more controversial points in this book. I can make no claims to personal knowledge on this subject. I merely present the story as I found it in the Hopkins papers supplemented by numerous interviews with various persons involved with Roosevelt and Hopkins at that time. Of course, the recollections of individuals on such matters of secret political maneuvering are apt to be colored and confused by

page

bias of one form or another, and I have been inevitably influenced by my own estimates of the reliability of information that I have received. Grace Tully, who has been immeasurably helpful to me in checking the accuracy of much of the material in this book, has expressed emphatic disbelief that Roosevelt ever made any attempt to "build up" Hopkins as a Presidential candidate. She has said, "F.D.R. and Harry both were too smart to imagine that Harry, politically unpopular and *divorced*, could possibly be nominated." I must say that I should consider that an extremely sensible statement were it not for the very substantial mass of evidence that I have found to the contrary. Miss Tully also questions the statement that Senator Robert M. La Follette could have been considered for the post of Secretary of State. She has said, "Harry was devoted to Bob La Follette but knowing him as well as he did how could he have thought for one moment that he was not an isolationist considering his background and devotion to his father?" Here again I can only quote the statement as Hopkins wrote it in the spring of 1938 when, it must be added, the isolationist-interventionist issue had not been joined.

107. Like many other government officials, Hopkins obtained the originals of cartoons of himself and had them framed and hung on the walls of his home (when he had one). One cartoon of which he was particularly proud—and I have never been able to identify the source of it—appeared at the time of his departure from W.P.A. and appointment as Secretary of Commerce; it showed him as the man who had spent nine billion dollars of public funds without a penny of it sticking to his fingers.

114-115. The memorandum by Hopkins describing his visit to Warm Springs was like the previously noted memorandum quoting Corcoran on the Supreme Court fight, written in longhand and never typed. In this memorandum, Hopkins mentioned Roosevelt's tendency to repeat the same anecdotes and reminiscences many times to the same listeners. On this, Grace Tully has written me, "I must say he never deviated in his stories, which Missy and I heard one dozen times a year—all of them—but we loved them, provided they were spaced a bit." Roosevelt was never one to say, "Stop me if you've heard this." I always felt sure that he was perfectly well aware that he had told the same story to the same audience but he went right ahead with it, regardless. It was for him a superb exercise in relaxation.

117. In reference to Hopkins' memorandum of May 28, 1939, describing a luncheon and talk with Mrs. Roosevelt at the White House: I have not questioned Mrs. Roosevelt about this or, as I have said in the Introduction, on any other points connected with the preparation of this book. My reluctance to consult so great and in many respects so final an authority on much of this material was due to my feeling that it would be embarrassing to Mrs. Roosevelt to assume any degree of responsibility, even indirectly, for any of this material.

Raymond Swing, having read proofs of this chapter, wrote to question me about my "distaste for Harry having had political ambitions." He said, "I cannot as yet share your prejudice against his aspiring to be President, although I do not believe he would have made a good one, but as you wrote the passages on this question you left the impression that you knew things worse than you have included in the book. Is this so?" The answer to that is "No." Certainly the desire to become President of the United States is not an unworthy one, but it seemed to me that some of Hopkins' tactics were discreditable (and, indeed, so were some of those employed by Abraham Lincoln in his quest of the nomination in 1860), and I believe that Hopkins himself later regretted them. He certainly intended to make no secret of them had he lived to write his autobiography. Evidence of this is provided by remarks he made near the end of his life to Sidney Hyman, quoted in Chapter XXXVI.

CHAPTER V

127. The Elmo Roper Public Opinion Polls cited in this and other chapters appeared originally in *Fortune* magazine; the George Gallup Polls were clipped for the most part by Hopkins from the *Washington Post*.

Although it is correct to say that the Rome-Berlin-Tokyo Axis had not been formed at this time (September, 1939) and did not come into being until the Tripartite Pact of a year later, there was association of Germany, Italy and Japan in the anti-Comintern Agreement. However, the Roper Poll quoted limited its questionnaire to "The present European war."

130. Sir Robert Bruce-Lockhart's book, *Comes the Reckoning*, has been published in Great Britain by Putnam's, but has not at this writing appeared in the United States.

133. The famous meeting in the President's study of Roosevelt, Hull, Garner, Borah, and others in the summer of 1939 was first described by Joseph Alsop and Robert Kintner in *The American White Paper* (Simon and Schuster) and again in *The Memoirs of Cordell Hull* (Macmillan).

137. The quotations from Sumner Welles on his trip to Europe in the winter of 1940 are from his book, *Time for Decision* (Harper & Brothers).

139. The first quotation from Winston Churchill at the end of this chapter was from his book, *Into Battle* (Cassell & Co.); the second quotation was from reports made by W. Averell Harriman of conferences in Moscow in August, 1942, at which he was present. (The speeches included in *Into Battle* were published in this country by G. P. Putnam's Sons under the title, *Blood, Sweat and Tears*.)

The Churchill war speeches appeared in *Into Battle*, covering May, 1938 to November, 1940; *Unrelenting Struggle* (Little, Brown & Company), covering 1941; *The End of the Beginning* (Little, Brown & Company), covering 1942; *Onwards to Victory* (Little, Brown & Company), covering 1943; *Dawn of Liberation* (Little, Brown & Company), covering 1944; *Victory* (Little, Brown & Company), covering 1945; and *The Secret Session Speeches of Winston Churchill* (Simon and Schuster).

CHAPTER VI

Although, as I have stated in this chapter, none of the secret cables quoted in part or summarized was included in the Hopkins papers, I have seen the full text of all those that I have mentioned and can assure the reader that I have not suppressed or glossed over any points of importance.

142. Reference is made to Edmond Taylor's book, *The Strategy of Terror* (Houghton Mifflin), which deserves to be studied as a profound discussion of psychological warfare, or "political warfare," as it was called in England.

CHAPTER VII

Published works on which some of the material in this chapter was based included: *The Arsenal of Democracy* (Harcourt, Brace & Company), by

Donald Nelson; *On Active Service in Peace and War* (Harper & Brothers), by Henry Stimson and McGeorge Bundy; *Together* (Tupper and Love, Inc.), by Katherine Tupper Marshall; *The Battle against Isolation* (University of Chicago Press), by Walter Johnson; *Scientists against Time* (Little, Brown & Company), by James Phinney Baxter; *Atomic Energy for Military Purposes* (Princeton University Press), by Henry De Wolf Smyth.

160. The Hopkins press conference from which quotations are made was held on May 23, 1940.

Chapter VIII

Quotations are made in this chapter from *Jim Farley's Story* (McGraw-Hill [Whittlesey House]) and from *You're the Boss* (The Viking Press), by Edward J. Flynn.

173. Missy LeHand's joke about "The man who came to dinner" was not, of course, to be taken literally, since George S. Kaufman and Moss Hart had written this highly successful comedy a year before Hopkins went to dine at the White House and remained for three and a half years.

174. My authority for the statement that "Roosevelt considered Willkie the most formidable opponent for himself that the Republicans could have named" was Roosevelt himself. He remarked on this to me when the campaign was in its final stages that fall. I made no note of his exact words but they were, in effect, "all the Isolationists would vote against me no matter whom the Republicans nominated. Willkie was the only one of the likely candidates who could have a good chance of cutting in on the Independent vote."

199. In mentioning a Republican broadcast on election eve I have said that the rumors that American troops might be sent to seize the island of Martinique were "not entirely baseless." Special detachments had already been in training in amphibious operations for the capture of Martinique in the event of any likelihood that Germany might seek to exploit this strategic possession of the Vichy Government in the Western Hemisphere. Such American action, of course, was never taken, but it was most seriously contemplated. I doubt that Roosevelt would have hesitated to send U.S. forces to Martinique if he had considered this necessary to prevent it from falling into the hands of Hitler.

Chapter IX

203. The quotation from Marquis W. Childs was in his article, "The President's Best Friend," in the *Saturday Evening Post*, April 19, 1941.

206. The original members of the Cuff Links Gang, aside from Howe, Early, and Marvin McIntyre, included Charles H. McCarthy, Thomas Lynch, Kirke L. Simpson, Stanley Prenosil and James P. Sullivan. Samuel I. Rosenman became a member during later years, and so did such old friends as Henry Morgenthau, Basil O'Connor and Henry Hooker. Added during the White House years were Hopkins, Watson, Ross McIntire and myself. The annual meeting of this Gang was at dinner on Roosevelt's birthday and a poker game followed. The ladies who joined these gatherings (but certainly not the poker game) were Mrs. Roosevelt, Mrs. Morgenthau, Miss LeHand, Miss Tully, Marion Dickerman, Nancy Cook, Margaret Durand and Malvina C. Thompson. It was Roosevelt's pleasant practice to give a present to each of the guests at these birthday parties. These presents required a great deal of

page

preparatory imagination and work on his part and many of them possessed historical as well as sentimental value. We generally chipped in to buy a joint gift for him in the form of old prints or rare books that we believed would add to his collections.

210. The reorganization plan, proposed originally in 1938, which in 1939 caused the Bureau of the Budget to be put into the Executive Offices, was the result of recommendations made by a committee of which Louis Brownlow was chairman and Charles E. Merriam and Luther Gulick members.

211. Many observers referred, as Harold Smith did, to Hopkins' position as that of a sort of Chief of Staff to the President. The position held after July, 1942, by Admiral William D. Leahy was that of Chief of Staff to the President in his capacity as Commander in Chief of the Armed Forces of the United States, but not as the political head of the United States Government.

218. The paragraphs quoted from Carl Sandburg were dictated by him in the White House on October 27, 1940.

219. The quotation from Hopkins on Roosevelt's speeches was in the preface that he wrote for *Nothing to Fear*, previously noted.

CHAPTER X

223. Most of the material on Roosevelt's cruise in December, 1940, was taken from the log of the *U.S.S. Tuscaloosa.*

Reference is made here to the motion pictures seen on shipboard. Roosevelt was very fond of movies in general, and so were both Churchill and Stalin. Roosevelt had no particular favorites, although he was greatly pleased with Darryl F. Zanuck's production; "Wilson," in 1944. There was no question of doubt as to what was Churchill's favorite: it was "Lady Hamilton," starring Laurence Olivier and Vivien Leigh, and produced by Alexander Korda who was rewarded with a Knighthood for this dramatic tribute to British sea power. Churchill saw this picture over and over again and members of his staff, though enjoying and admiring it greatly the first two or three times, eventually wished that the Prime Minister would develop an enthusiasm for some other film. I have been told that Stalin's favorite non-Russian film was "The Great Waltz," the Metro-Goldwyn-Mayer production based on the life and works of Johann Strauss.

The remarkable letter from Churchill to Roosevelt, dated December 7, 1940, has been quoted in part in the *Morgenthau Diaries* and the *Hull Memoirs*. I asked for Churchill's permission to quote it in full and such permission was withheld; I believe that Churchill will publish it in the second volume of his memoirs.

226-227. The quotation from Hopkins on the inception of Lend Lease was a personal recollection. So was the quotation from Roosevelt on the State Department deletion in his "Arsenal of Democracy" speech.

CHAPTER XI

230. Miss LeHand was present at the conversation between Roosevelt and Hopkins mentioned at the start of this chapter and made some notes on it.

235. The American Embassy in London kept a complete record of Hopkins' appointments and travels during his visit to Great Britain at this time.

237. Hopkins' letters to Roosevelt on Claridge's stationery, dated January 10 and 13, 1941, were largely notes for the refreshment of his own memory when he should return to Washington and report directly to the President. He made no attempt at literary style. Miss LeHand gave these notes back to him when he returned to the White House and he never had them typed out.

241. In reference to Roosevelt's habit of going to bed at a reasonable hour: Grace Tully points out that frequently when his baskets were piled up with letters, memoranda, reports, etc., he would sit up until well after midnight with her and perhaps a relay of secretaries to get through this tiresome work. It was always amazing to me to watch him at work with these baskets: his patience seemed infinite.

250. In Hopkins' report of his lunch at Buckingham Palace is mention of "the firing of the U.P. gun." This was a demonstration of some sort of device; the missile became caught in the rigging of the battleship on which Churchill and Hopkins were standing and it exploded, almost ending their careers.

259. The "note written later," in which Hopkins revealed more of Anthony Eden's views on the Far Eastern situation, was part of a memorandum written after Pearl Harbor; it is published in full in Chapter XIX.

CHAPTER XII

265. The "bread-and-butter letter" from Hopkins to Churchill was dated March 19, 1941.

267. The quotations from the Roosevelt speech following the passage of Lend Lease were taken from mimeographed copies as issued to the press. The same applies to all subsequent quotations of Roosevelt's speeches. *The Public Papers and Addresses of Franklin D. Roosevelt*, as edited by Samuel I. Rosenman, ended with the start of the third term in January, 1941. As this is written, Judge Rosenman is editing the final volumes for the years 1941-1945 and these will be published by Harper & Brothers. It should be noted that the mimeographed copies of the speeches were not always ultimately accurate, for they obviously did not include Roosevelt's sometimes extensive ad-libbing; I believe that the *New York Times* was the only newspaper which invariably transcribed the Roosevelt speeches and printed them in full exactly as delivered.

272. The memorandum by Admiral Yarnell was dated January 9, 1941.

273. Although, in the plan known as A.B.C.—1, "Subversive Activities and Propaganda" were listed as item number three in the primary measures to be taken against Germany, the United States Government had no plans for any propaganda organization or, indeed, any idea where such an organization would be put in the Administration. In July, 1941, Roosevelt authorized Colonel William J. Donovan to organize the Office of Coordinator of Information, but the word "Information" applied to intelligence rather than propaganda. As part of the Donovan organization, I organized the Foreign Information Service which began to study and then carried on the operations of psychological warfare in many parts of the world outside the Western Hemisphere. In June, 1942, the Foreign Information Service became the Overseas Branch of the Office of War Information.

274. The quotation of Charles A. Beard is from his book, *President Roosevelt and the Coming of the War 1941* (Yale University Press).

276. The memorandum from Admiral Turner to the Chief of Naval Operations was dated April 12, 1941.

The letter from Harriman to Hopkins on "living in a nightmare" was dated May 6.

277. Material on the President's cruise of March 19-April 1 is taken largely from the log of the *U.S.S. Potomac.*

282-287. All of the letters, memoranda, etc. from which bits are quoted in this chapter were dated between the latter part of March and the early part of July.

290. Admiral Stark's letter to Hopkins relative to the Iceland Expedition was dated June 17.

CHAPTER XIV

301. The appreciation shown to Hopkins by Ambassador Winant was written by General Raymond E. Lee and dated May 27, 1941.

303-308. The letter from Stimson to Roosevelt was written June 23. The British estimate subsequently quoted was written July 1. The Davies memorandum was July 8. The Swope letter to Hopkins was also dated June 23.

313. The message from Churchill to Wavell concerning Harriman was dated June 3, and the Harriman memorandum, July 16.

318. One of the most peculiar blanks that I encountered in the Hopkins papers concerned the genesis of his first trip to Moscow. It had been my understanding that there was no mention of this between him and Roosevelt before he left Washington. His papers contained no evidence as to when or how it was decided that he would make the trip, or what instructions he received from the President. The only relevant document prior to his departure was the cable containing Roosevelt's message to Stalin, which was signed by Sumner Welles. I talked to Welles, Churchill, Ismay, Harriman, and others about this but there was no clear recollection by any of them as to how the subject had come up. It seemed to be the general impression that Hopkins had arranged it by telephone to the President from London or Chequers. Winant, however, remembered very clearly the drafting of a cable by Hopkins to the President on July 25, and a brief reply from the President telling him to go ahead. Winant had no record of these cables; in fact, he spent a long time searching for them for use in his own book, *A Letter from Grosvenor Square.* After a year and a half of search, I abandoned the hope of finding these cables, although I assumed they would turn up eventually in the Roosevelt files. In October, 1947, I suddenly learned, through John E. Masten, that both cables had been included in the millions of words of the Pearl Harbor Investigation; they had been brought out by Grace Tully from the Roosevelt files because they happened to have bearing on the Far Eastern situation. When I learned this, I communicated the news to Winant at his home in Concord, New Hampshire. He was greatly interested and told me he would be in New York shortly and would like to look at the copies I had obtained. A few days thereafter I learned of his sudden, shocking death.

319. Concerning Churchill's week ends: Commander Thompson has pointed out to me that, although there were usually many guests at Dytchley, there were very few at Chequers who were not connected in one way or another with Churchill's official business. However, that covered a very wide range.

Chapter XV

323. Much of the description of Hopkins' flight to Moscow and return was given me in London in August, 1941, by Wing-Commander D. C. McKinley and Squadron-Leader C. M. Owen with whom I got in touch through the courtesy of Marshal of the Royal Air Force Lord Tedder.

326. The description of the dinner given for Hopkins in Archangel on his arrival there was from an article by him in the *American* magazine for December, 1941, entitled "The Inside Story of My Meeting with Stalin." There is a later quotation from this same article in this chapter: Hopkins' remarks on Stalin, "Not once did he repeat himself, etc."

Chapter XVI

350. In this chapter is the statement that Churchill, informing the Dominion Prime Ministers of the forthcoming Atlantic Conference, had said that he had never met Roosevelt. Long after I had written this—and, indeed, when this chapter was already in type—I read the following in *The Gathering Storm*, the first volume of Churchill's tremendous work on the Second World War: "I had met him [President Roosevelt] only once in the previous war. It was at a dinner at Gray's Inn, and I had been struck by his magnificent presence in all his health and strength." Evidently Churchill, before he wrote this, had conducted further searches through the voluminous files of his memory.

358. In connection with the military staff talks at the Atlantic Conference mention is made of the British plan for ROUNDUP, the invasion of Normandy. I am not entirely sure if the American Chiefs of Staff had been aware of this and other long-range and extremely remote plans before they arrived at Argentia, but it is my belief that they had already been acquainted with all of them and had participated in the making of some of them.

362. When portions of this chapter were published in *Collier's* (in the United States) and in the *Sunday Express* (in Great Britain) the statement that, to the officers of the British Government, the Atlantic Charter was "not much more than a publicity hand-out" produced a certain amount of protesting correspondence in the *London Times*. Even so, I must let my statement stand. Of course, on January 1, 1942, the terms of the Atlantic Charter were incorporated in the first Declaration of the United Nations to which His Majesty's Government solemnly subscribed, and then the Charter for the first time achieved the status of a formal State Paper.

364. The American destroyers which accompanied the *Prince of Wales* from Newfoundland to Iceland were of course part of the regular, routine U.S. Navy escort which was by then guarding the convoy routes in the Western Atlantic.

CHAPTER XVII

367. The quotations of General Marshall on the extension of Selective Service debate, and many other quotations of him, Admiral King and General Arnold, are from *The War Reports* (J. B. Lippincott Co.) of the three Chiefs of Staff which have been published in one volume.

The *New York Times* editorial quoted was from the issue of August 13, 1941, and so also was the quotation of Senator Wheeler.

369. The Churchill cable referring to "Mr. Sherwood" was dated September 25.

369-372. The Hopkins description of the Labor Day speech was dated September 2 and his memorandum on the "Shoot on Sight" speech was dated September 13.

373. The message from Churchill to Hopkins described as "one of the gloomiest" was dated August 29, and the Hopkins memorandum thereon was dated September 6.

374. The first request from Churchill to Roosevelt for help in transporting two divisions to the Middle East was dated September 1.

374-375. Roosevelt's cable to Churchill reopening the question of the transports was dated October 7. Churchill's reply was dated October 9.

375. The conversation between Hopkins and Stettinius is quoted from the latter's book, *Lend-Lease—Weapon for Victory* (Macmillan).

376. The memoranda from Hopkins to Roosevelt complaining about statements by an admiral and a general were dated November 7 and November 12.

377-378. The first note from Roosevelt to Hopkins concerning Channel Key was dated October 21, and the Hopkins note thereon, October 22. The letter from Julius F. Stone, Jr., was dated November 5, and the Roosevelt note thereon, November 15.

379. The memorandum from Admiral Stark to Secretary Hull was dated October 8.

380. The news story quoted from the *Washington Times-Herald* was in its issue of November 8. There would appear to be some confusion in this as to the identity of the destroyer mentioned. Although the name given is the *Kearny*, the mention of "loss of most of her officers and crew" would indicate that the *Reuben James* was meant.

CHAPTER XVIII

386. The message from Beaverbrook to Hopkins on the eve of his departure for Russia was delivered from the British Embassy on September 22.

393. The memorandum written by Beaverbrook following his return from Russia was dated October 19.

394. Hopkins' letter to Churchill about increase of production was dated September 29.

Roosevelt's cable to Harriman congratulating him on the Moscow results was dated October 9.

395, 396. The memorandum from Marshall to Hopkins on Faymonville was dated October 10, and Hopkins' letter to Secretary Stimson was dated October 14.

398. In connection with the proposal to use an aircraft carrier to ferry planes to the Persian Gulf for the Russians: I have certainly done insufficient justice in this book to the part played by Captain Granville Conway, USN, in the solution of all manner of shipping problems during the war. I believe it was he more than anyone else who worked out the system for employing tankers as transports for aircraft, which produced an enormous saving in time and in shipping, particularly on the long route round the Cape of Good Hope. Harry Hopkins had enormous respect for Conway and gratitude to him for invaluable services rendered.

400. Myron Taylor's report of his interview with Salazar was undated.

The meeting of the President's Soviet Protocol Committee, from the minutes of which quotation is made, was held on November 25, 1942.

CHAPTER XIX

404. Owen Lattimore's cable to Currie was dated August 12, 1941.

The Arnstein Report, entitled "The Present Trucking Operations as conducted on the Burma Road and Recommendations for their Improvement," was, I believe, undated, but was received by Hopkins some time in August.

405. The message from Major McHugh was dated August 9.

406. The message from Madame Chiang Kai-shek to Currie was received September 4.

406-408. The letter from T. V. Soong to Donovan was dated August 16; that from Soong to Roosevelt, October 24; and Soong to Hopkins, November 13.

428. The memorandum by Hopkins describing his conversation with Roosevelt following the issuance of the Roberts Report was dated January 24, 1942. It is my understanding, but I have not verified it, that Justice Roberts himself delivered the text of this Report to the President in his office in the White House. He intended to make the request to the President that the Report be made public, at least in part. Roosevelt asked the Justice to sit down while he read the entire document. When he had finished, he said that the Report must be given to the public in full and, indeed, called in Steve Early and told him to release it to the press immediately and without change.

434. Competent authority, reviewing my manuscript, has informed me that, at the time of Pearl Harbor, General Marshall did not have facilities for communication with Honolulu by scrambler telephone. Therefore the Committee's Report, which I have quoted, must have been in error.

435. The letter from Secretary Knox to a member of Congress disclaiming responsibility for any catastrophe in any Shore Establishment was dated August 23, 1941. The Hopkins note thereon was in a letter to Archibald MacLeish, March 6, 1942.

CHAPTER XX

444. On the evening of the day—I believe it was New Year's Day, 1942—when Churchill returned to Washington from Ottawa, I happened to go with

Hopkins into the Prime Minister's bedroom at the White House. There were quantities of New York and Washington newspapers containing the reports of the Canadian speech and the editorial comments thereon (including one in the *New York Herald Tribune* which is quoted in the next chapter). Churchill was obviously and quite naturally pleased with the favorable response and he observed that he was greatly impressed by the loyalty and patriotism of the American press and was not accustomed to such wholehearted enthusiasm at home. Hopkins emitted one of his short, sharp, derisive laughs and said, "Just wait! We are still young in this war and the newspapers haven't had time to get back to normal. In a few weeks' time you'll find they will be criticizing everything." However, Churchill continued to have a very good press in the United States throughout the war.

445. The British suggestions for the agenda of the Arcadia Conference and the bases of grand strategies had been in a radio message from *H.M.S. Duke of York* on December 18 when Churchill and his staff were in mid-Atlantic.

445-446. Relative to the principle of "Germany first": the German potential "in productive power and scientific genius" was certainly demonstrated in the last year of the war in Europe with the development of the V-1 flying bombs, the V-2 rockets, jet propulsion for aircraft and the tremendously important and dangerous technical improvements in submarines. All of these came, fortunately, after the successful establishment of a Second Front in the West, and at a time when German production was being subjected to severe bombardment by the superior Allied air forces. Had Germany been given more time, the story of the war in Europe would have been a very different one.

446. My statement that "There were not more than two occasions in the entire war" when Roosevelt overruled his Chiefs of Staff is a debatable one. The one occasion about which there can be no question of doubt was at the second Cairo Conference in December, 1943 (Chapter XXX), and the other possible occasion was the making of the TORCH decision (Chapter XXV). Captain T. B. Kittredge of the Historical Section of the Joint Chiefs of Staff has pointed out to me, "It may be true that the President formally overruled them on very few occasions but this was only because informal discussions of the President with Leahy, Marshall, King and Arnold usually led them to know in advance the President's views. They, no doubt, frequently recognized the advantages of accepting the President's suggestions with their own interpretations, rather than of risking an overruling by presenting formally proposals they knew would not be accepted."

The basis of the United Nations Declaration: the conditions for an association or alliance of the anti-Axis powers had been under consideration in the State, War and Navy Departments at least since January, 1941. Before the Arcadia Conference, the Secretary of State together with his staff and officers of the staffs of General Marshall and Admiral Stark had prepared drafts of two documents which were submitted to the President shortly before Churchill's arrival. One of these became, with some modifications, the Declaration of the United Nations. The other was a plan for an inter-Allied war organization under a Supreme War Council; this was rejected by Roosevelt as too complicated and generally impracticable.

454. Roosevelt's message to the Filipino people was printed in the form of a leaflet in English and Tagalog and delivered somehow or other to the Philippines. This was the first American propaganda leaflet in the war against Japan.

Three years later the U.S. Navy was dropping quantities of leaflets on Tokyo from carrier-based aircraft. During the Arcadia Conference, the R.A.F. dropped the first American propaganda leaflets on France: these featured, of course, a picture of the Statue of Liberty and the assurance, "To you who gave us Liberty we will restore Liberty." The preparation and production of leaflets for Europe became a joint Anglo-American operation in London and, in 1944, reached the considerable total of eleven million leaflets a day.

460. I have never been entirely clear as to the difference between GYMNAST and SUPER-GYMNAST. It is my impression that the latter included the landings in French Morocco, which were favored by the Americans, in addition to those at Algiers.

476. Roosevelt's conversation with Knudsen (described in the Hopkins memorandum of January 16, 1942) must have been a particularly disagreeable one for the President who had real admiration and warm affection for Knudsen. Roosevelt loved to tell a story of how, in the spring of 1941, Knudsen had sent him a list of some twenty names of prominent businessmen for appointment to executive positions in the Office of Production Management. Needless to say, most of the important men in this agency were Republicans. Having inspected this new list, Roosevelt said to Knudsen, "There must be some mistake here, Bill. One of the men on this list is a Democrat." Knudsen laughed and said, "It's all right, Mr. President—I have checked on this man and found out that last year he voted for Willkie."

Chapter XXI

479. The quotation at the start of this chapter was from *The Memoirs of Cordell Hull* (Macmillan).

480. The quotations of Foreign Office cables were from memoranda prepared by the British Embassy.

481. The fact that Ira Wolfert was the sole American press correspondent on the scene at the landings on St. Pierre and Miquelon was viewed with some suspicion in Washington, it being assumed that he had been taken into the secret purposefully by an emissary of de Gaulle's. Such was not the case. Wolfert, representing the North American Newspaper Alliance, had gone to Canada on a tip which was actually several weeks out of date. Learning that Admiral Muselier had suddenly left Ottawa for Halifax, Wolfert went there to seek him out. Muselier and his staff were living in a Halifax hotel under assumed names, but Wolfert was smart enough to find them and then to bluff them into the belief that he knew all about their projected enterprise when, actually, he knew nothing. Muselier thereupon put him under arrest, which was completely illegal but effective, and took him along under guard on the expedition in order to keep him quiet. Thus, Wolfert's exclusive story was the result of his exceptional enterprise and skill as a newspaperman plus pure accident.

486-488. The quotations of Professor William L. Langer were from his book *Our Vichy Gamble* (Knopf). This book traced the history of the Vichy policy and relations with de Gaulle and other French leaders up to the time of Darlan's assassination—which, it may be said, marked the point when the final justification for the policy ended.

CHAPTER XXII

494. Hopkins' cable to Churchill congratulating him on the vote in the House of Commons was dated January 29, 1942, Roosevelt's was dated January 31, and the cables from Beaverbrook to Hopkins and from Churchill to Roosevelt on this same subject were dated February 1.

495. The cable from Roosevelt to Churchill referring to Hopkins' health was dated February 11.

The quotation of an Anglo-American intelligence appraisal of the Russian prospects was from a memorandum to the Chief of Staff by General Raymond E. Lee on February 13. The summary of General Mason Macfarlane's report on his talks in Moscow was transmitted to Hopkins by Field Marshal Sir John Dill on February 11.

496. Roosevelt's cable to Stalin about the January-February shipments was dated February 9, and Stalin's reply, February 19.

498. The quotations of Professor Samuel Eliot Morison were from his book, *The Battle of the Atlantic, 1939-43* (Little, Brown & Co.).

504. Roosevelt's Washington's Birthday speech of 1942 had been announced at least three weeks in advance, giving the Japanese plenty of time to get the submarine to the California coast. It had always been Steve Early's practice to build up the radio audience for the President's speeches with plenty of advance publicity and he did this extraordinarily well. Now, however, the practice had to be abandoned.

505. Roosevelt's letter to the War Department about air-raid alarms was dated February 26.

505-506. The cable from Van Mook to Hopkins about the desperate situation in Java was dated February 23, and Hopkins' reply was sent the following day.

The letter from Soong to Hopkins, referring to Roosevelt as "the one hope of mankind," was dated April 24.

508. Roosevelt's cable to Curtin in Australia was dated February 20; his cable to Churchill about the Casey appointment was dated March 22.

509-510. The cable to Churchill prepared by the Chiefs of Staff and signed by Roosevelt was dated March 7, and Roosevelt's personal message on the subject of global strategy was dated March 9. Churchill's reply was dated March 13.

It should have been stated in this chapter that, following Roosevelt's personal message to Churchill of March 9, some confusion prevailed over the question of command in the Pacific, and General MacArthur may have been led to believe that he was to have supreme command of the entire war in the Pacific. This was straightened out early in April in accordance with the proposals made by the United States Chiefs of Staff: MacArthur's command was limited to the Southwest Pacific area, and Admiral Nimitz was given command of the remainder of the Pacific, both acting under the directions and supervision of the U.S. Joint Chiefs.

512. The quotation of Sumner Welles on the proposal to the Indian leaders was from his book, *Where Are We Heading?* (Harper & Brothers).

Chiang Kai-shek's quotation of Gandhi was included in a cable sent by the Generalissimo to Soong on April 19.

513. Harriman's message to the President about the alternate land route to China was dated January 31. Roosevelt's cable to Chiang Kai-shek about the ferry service was dated February 9.

514. Chiang Kai-shek's cable to Roosevelt about his observations in Burma was dated April 13.

516. Hopkins' letter to Roosevelt about Quezon was dated June 9 and Quezon's letter to Hopkins, June 19.

CHAPTER XXIII

519. The War Plans Division had considered the possibility of seizing a bridgehead in the Cherbourg or Brittany peninsulas with the SLEDGEHAMMER operation in 1942. However, the plan which Hopkins carried with him to London was, as stated, for a trans-Channel assault east of the mouth of the Seine.

I do not know the date of Marshall's memorandum to the President concerning the selection of Western Europe as the theater for the first great Allied offensive, but this was presumably about April 1, 1942.

521. Roosevelt's cable to Churchill about the Hopkins-Marshall trip was dated April 1.

The quotation of the *Richmond News Leader* was dated April 9.

522. Hopkins' note to Lovett about the New York Giants was dated March 4 and his cable to Harriman about Aunt Bessie's lumbago, May 18.

523-524. Hopkins' notes on the first session at No. 10, Downing Street, were dated April 8. His cable to Roosevelt and his notes on the following session were dated April 9.

528. Hopkins' cable to Roosevelt about shipping losses was dated April 14.

529. The cable from Soong which reached Hopkins in London was delivered April 11.

530, 531. Roosevelt's cable to Hopkins containing a message for Churchill about the Indian problem was dated April 11. His cable to Marshall about putting Hopkins to bed was dated April 13.

532. The monitoring of the Paris radio was cabled from Washington April 13.

534. The cables from Roosevelt to Hopkins and Churchill relative to supplies for the Far East were dated April 15.

538. Hopkins' cable to Roosevelt concerning Laval, and Roosevelt's reply, were both dated April 15. The reference to "wood pussy" revived a White House joke of the 1940 campaign. Talking of misrepresentations and falsehoods made by certain Republican orators, Roosevelt wanted to say something like, "I am now going to nail these to the barn door, just as, when I was a boy, we used

to nail to the barn door the skins of small, predatory animals such as rats, weasels and wood pussies." After considerable debate, Roosevelt decided not to use that analogy.

539-540. Leahy's report from Vichy to Washington reached Hopkins in London on April 17. Roosevelt's cable to Hopkins asking him to discuss the new French situation with Churchill was sent late that same day and reached Hopkins in Northern Ireland on the morning of April 18.

542. The letter to Hopkins from Mrs. Martum was dated April 16.

542-543. Roosevelt's cable to Churchill after Hopkins' return was dated April 22, and so was Hopkins' letter to Jacob Baker.

CHAPTER XXIV

545. Roosevelt's cable to Churchill about the Murmansk convoys was dated April 29 and Churchill's reply to it, May 1.

546. The memorandum from Hopkins to Lewis Douglas was dated June 12.

550. The report from S. Pinkney Tuck on the attitude of Weygand was dated June 5.

551. Roosevelt's cable to Churchill about American bombers in Britain was dated
. May 19. Churchill's reply was the following day.

552. The letter to Hopkins from Steinhardt was dated April 24.

553. Hopkins' cable to Churchill concerning the appointment of Lord Beaverbrook as Ambassador was dated May 16.

554. The quotation concerning the production lag on landing craft was from *Industrial Mobilization for War* (U.S. Government Printing Office).

568-569. The note from Colonel Walker to Hopkins was dated May 31, as were the notes written by Hopkins about the meeting of the President with Marshall and King and Roosevelt's cable to Churchill about the Molotov visit.

575-576. The note from General Burns on his meeting with Molotov was dated June 3, as was Hopkins' note on his reply to this. The subsequent message from Burns was dated June 4.

577. Hopkins' letter to Winant about the Molotov visit was dated June 12.

CHAPTER XXV

581. The quotation of Churchill by General Arnold appeared in the latter's report on his conversations in London. There were protracted arguments between the R.A.F. and the U.S.A.A.F. over heavy bombing tactics, the Americans favoring daylight "precision" bombing and the British adhering to night-time, "saturation" bombing. In pursuance of their policy, the Americans suffered heavy losses, but the ratio was reduced as the strength of American fighter escorts (which had considerably longer range than the Spitfires and Hurricanes) was increased at United Kingdom bases. Later in the war, of course, the combined air forces with their different tactics maintained a

round-the-clock bombardment of Germany. At dawn, as the last Lancasters were returning from their missions, the first Flying Fortresses were taking off.

582. Hopkins' note on the telephone calls from Churchill, Arnold and Harriman was dated May 30, 1942. The reference in this to "the battle in Africa going well" is interesting in view of subsequent developments.

The letter from Mountbatten to Roosevelt was dated June 15.

584. The cable from Roosevelt to Stalin relative to the situation in the North Pacific was dated June 17.

585. Churchill's cable to Roosevelt speaking of "a complete decision" in Libya was dated June 1.

The quotation of Molotov's speech at an Extraordinary Session of the Supreme Soviet was from *The Year of Stalingrad* (Knopf), by Alexander Werth.

588. The Roosevelt message to Marshall and King relative to a possible German breakthrough in Russia was dated June 20.

590. The quotation of Stimson in this and the following chapter was from his book, *On Active Service in Peace and War* (Harper & Brothers).

592. The quotation of Churchill about General Marshall's "mass production of divisions" was from a letter to me in response to the questionnaire mentioned in the Introduction.

593. Hopkins' note on the last day of Churchill's visit was dated June 25.

The Churchill cable to Hopkins referring to "Tube Alloys" was dated February 27, 1943.

598-599. The Stilwell cable reporting his conversation with Chiang Kai-shek relative to the diverted bombers was dated June 27, and Roosevelt's cable to the Generalissimo was sent the same day.

599. Roosevelt's cable to Stalin thanking him for authorizing the transfer of bombers was dated July 9.

600. Roosevelt's cable to Churchill reluctantly agreeing on the Murmansk convoys was dated July 15, as was his cable announcing the imminent departure of Marshall, King and Hopkins for London.

601. The quotation of Arthur Krock was in the *New York Times*, April 17, while Hopkins and Marshall were in London discussing the plans for ROUNDUP.

602. Hopkins' cable to Churchill expressing delight at the vote in the House of Commons was dated July 2, as was Churchill's reply.

607. Hopkins' cable to Roosevelt about Churchill throwing the British Constitution at him was dated July 20.

610, 611, 612. Roosevelt's cable to Hopkins, Marshall and King giving his views on various alternative operations was dated July 23. His next cable on this subject was dated July 24. His final cable referring to Hopkins' wedding was dated July 25.

612. At the end of July, after Hopkins had left Washington for his honeymoon, the Joint Chiefs of Staff unanimously recommended against the North African landings, but the President summoned them to the White House to inform them that the decision to undertake the TORCH operation as early as possible must be carried out. He insisted that preparations for the landings must be pushed forward rapidly and vigorously.

612-613. The material on the yacht, *My Kay IV*, was taken from a report made on this strange episode by the F.B.I.

CHAPTER XXVI

616. Roosevelt's cable to Churchill before the latter's departure for Moscow was dated July 29, 1942.

618. Roosevelt's cable to Churchill in Moscow was dated August 14.

620. Harriman's reply to Stalin's aide memoire was dated August 15.

622. Roosevelt's cable to Stalin after the meetings had been concluded was dated August 18.

Roosevelt's message to the Chiefs of Staff expressing anxiety about the Southwest Pacific was dated October 24. At this time there was considerable controversy between General Arnold, on the one hand, and Admiral King and General MacArthur on the other as to the allocation of air forces. Arnold was arguing for concentration of air power in the United Kingdom for the air offensive against Germany. King argued that there was risk of disaster in the Pacific unless adequate forces were sent there.

627. Roosevelt's cable to Churchill relative to the Persian railway was dated September 15.

629. Churchill's reply to Roosevelt about "the whole burden" of TORCH was dated September 1.

630. The operation known as LIGHTFOOT—the British drive from Egypt toward Tripoli and Tunisia—had been in process of planning since the meetings in London in July. Therefore, Churchill's reference to it in his September 22 cable to Roosevelt was merely confirmation of the fact that it was going forward and that it had been given its code name.

636. Hopkins' reply to Harriman relative to unloading ships in Scotland was dated October 27.

637. Hopkins' cable to Churchill stating that messages had been forwarded to the President was dated September 22, as was his telegram to Roosevelt reporting on a conversation with the Chiefs of Staff.

638. Roosevelt's cable to Churchill from the train between California and Texas was dated September 26.

640. Roosevelt's cable to Stalin relative to the air force in the Caucasus and other measures for aid was dated October 8.

641. Roosevelt's cable to Churchill about the Russians not using "speech for the same purposes that we do" was dated October 27.

General Burns's memorandum to Hopkins on Russia was dated December 1.

page

645. Churchill's cable to Roosevelt about the message to Pétain was dated November 2.

648. The quotation of Eisenhower relative to the day of the TORCH decision was from *My Three Years with Eisenhower* (Simon and Schuster), by Harry Butcher.

649. The quotations of Murphy's report on his meeting with Darlan early in the morning of November 8 were from Professor Langer's book, *Our Vichy Gamble*.

650. Roosevelt's cable to Churchill about his troubles with Giraud was dated November 11.

651. Stalin's message to Churchill relative to the Darlan deal was received in Washington December 2.

654. Roosevelt's message to Eisenhower relative to Darlan was dated November 16.

655. There was no question of doubt that Churchill was fully informed of all stages of the negotiations with Darlan by Admiral Sir Andrew Cunningham who participated in these with General Mark Clark and, indeed, strongly urged to Clark and Eisenhower the importance of reaching agreement with Darlan, not only to stop resistance to the landings near Oran and Casablanca, but also to get the support of Boisson in West Africa, of Esteva in Tunis, and possibly also to get the French fleet to leave Toulon and join the Allies. Churchill in turn urged Roosevelt to approve these arrangements. However, the British Foreign Office subsequently made few efforts to prevent all the blame from being placed on the Americans.

657. Churchill's cable to Roosevelt about the possible abandonment of ROUNDUP was dated November 24 and Roosevelt's reply was dated November 25.

659. Roosevelt's message to Stalin about the Solomons was dated November 25.

660. Hopkins' memorandum on the arrival of Madame Chiang Kai-shek was dated November 30.

CHAPTER XXVII

679. Despite the cancellation of de Gaulle's projected visit to Washington, an exchange of messages continued between de Gaulle and Giraud (through Admiral Stark and General Eisenhower) in an effort to find means of achieving unification and co-ordination of the anti-Vichy French factions. It was agreed that General Georges Catroux, representing de Gaulle, should proceed at once to Algiers, with the possibility that he would take over the Governorship and civil administration of North Africa. Then came news of the imprisonment of de Gaulle adherents in Algeria following the assassination of Darlan, and after that the revelation that Peyrouton was being imported from South America. De Gaulle was understandably angered by these developments and his negotiations with Giraud were broken off a few days before the start of the Casablanca Conference. These factors should be borne in mind in considering de Gaulle's resentment when he was suddenly, arbitrarily summoned to proceed to a conference of which he had not previously been informed. He could hardly be blamed for expressing "no pleasure" when Eden handed him the message from Churchill on January 17, 1943.

page

681. Captain T. B. Kittredge, USN, who has been so helpful to me in so many ways in the preparation of this book, has furnished me with a footnote on the de Gaulle relationship. He is particularly expert on this subject since he was Admiral Stark's principal aide in London in the handling of the extremely delicate liaison with de Gaulle and his associates. He has written me the following record:

On 16 December, 1942, Stark spent the evening with de Gaulle as he (Stark) was leaving the next day for Washington and expected de Gaulle to be arriving there a week later. In a long and friendly conversation, de Gaulle pointed out that (a) nothing in his past experience qualified him to act as political and military leader of the French in continuing the war against Germany after defeatist sentiments had led nearly all French leaders to expect a quick German victory in 1940. (b) He had been unable to persuade French leaders whom he wanted to serve on the French national committee (Reynaud, Herriot, Jeanneney, Louis Marin—even Leon Blum) to leave France by underground channels to go to London. Hence de Gaulle was surrounded by Frenchmen who happened to be available in London, whom he had not known before, and of whose trustworthiness he was not certain. (c) He was convinced that French representation in Allied higher political and military councils was essential, in conducting the war against Germany, in liberating the Allied countries, and in reestablishing national governments and a new international order in Europe. (d) He was also convinced that French culture, intelligence and capacities of leadership were so widely diffused in France that when any elite or governing class failed France, through decadence or defeatism, new individuals were always projected upward out of the French masses, to give enlightened and inspired leadership to "eternal France"; that this had been true through the centuries, from the time of Charlemagne to that of Hitler. (e) Thus de Gaulle referred to the rise of the Capetian royal house, to Joan of Arc, to Henri IV, to the revolutionary leaders (1789-93), to Napoleon, finally to Poincaré and Clemenceau; de Gaulle added—"perhaps this time I am one of those thrust into leadership by circumstances, and by the failure of the other leaders."

Admiral Stark was much impressed by this historical and philosophical analysis and suggested that de Gaulle, on meeting Roosevelt (a great student of French history and politics) should attempt to make the President understand his concepts.

This de Gaulle attempted at Casablanca; but later told Admiral Stark that he had hardly ever been permitted to finish a sentence. The President was determined to make de Gaulle understand and accept the attitude of the Roosevelt administration toward France; and did not seem interested in, or to have any patience with, de Gaulle's views, perhaps expressed in his usual cold, standoffish and brusque manner.

According to Kittredge, de Gaulle was later informed that Roosevelt had told the Joan of Arc and Clemenceau story to General Vargas in Brazil, and de Gaulle was so deeply offended "he never wanted again to meet the President."

684. References to the *Queen Elizabeth* and *Queen Mary*: early in 1941 it was considered that each of these ships could carry a maximum of 4,000 troops; early in 1942 this capacity had been increased to 7,000; by 1944 each of them was carrying nearly 16,000 troops on every eastbound voyage from New York to the Clyde.

691. Although there was no record of it in the Hopkins papers, I believe that at Casablanca General Marshall and Admiral King again proposed that, if the British were not prepared to undertake the cross-Channel operation in 1943, United States forces should be diverted to the war against Japan, rather than

444

page

to the Mediterranean for "eccentric operations," or to the United Kingdom where they might remain out of combat for a year or more.

696. Expressions of views by Stalin on the subject of unconditional surrender will be found in Chapters XXX and XXXV.

Chapter XXVIII

698. Hopkins' article in the *American* magazine, "You and Your Family Will Be Mobilized," appeared in the November, 1942, issue.

700. The quotation of Roosevelt by Donald Nelson appeared in the latter's book, *Arsenal of Democracy*.

701. Stalin's cable to Roosevelt and Churchill acknowledging their message from Casablanca was dated January 30, 1943.

Churchill's cable to Hopkins referring to Eisenhower's message about postponement of HUSKY was dated February 13. The cable from Eisenhower to the Combined Chiefs of Staff had been sent February 11.

703. Hopkins' first cable to Churchill about the latter's illness was dated February 18 and Churchill's reply was the following day.

705. Stalin's message to Churchill about the bombing of Germany was received in Washington March 18.

706. Harriman's cable to Hopkins about Admiral Standley's statement was dated March 14.

Hopkins' memorandum on Madame Chiang Kai-shek at the White House was dated February 27.

707. Hopkins' memorandum on the meeting with Roosevelt and Welles before Eden's arrival was dated March 10, as was the memorandum from Winant to the President on the forthcoming visit.

718. Hopkins' cable to Churchill on the proposed award for General MacArthur was dated March 29.

719. Adolf Berle's memorandum on the President's constitutional powers was dated March 25.

724. Hopkins' copy of Roosevelt's cable to Churchill on the removal of Fascists in Italy bore no date.

Chapter XXIX

727. Churchill's cable suggesting another meeting with Marshall and Hopkins, and Hopkins' reply to it, were both dated April 9.

729. In reference to Churchill's statement that the Second World War had just passed the Gettysburg phase: the Battle of Gettysburg was fought some twenty-one months before the end of the Civil War, and Churchill's speech to the Congress was a little less than two years before the end of the war in Europe.

During the lunch in the White House at which there were forty-eight guests, whose names are listed in the text of this chapter, Army or Navy photographers took several feet of motion picture film of the hats that were piled on the shelves outside of General Watson's office and this "shot" was used most effectively in "The True Glory," the great motion picture record of victory in Europe which was directed by Carol Reed, for the British, and Captain Garson Kanin, for the U.S. Army.

730. The quotations from General Stilwell are from his book *The Stilwell Papers* (Wm. Sloane Associates). Churchill wrote me, in response to my questionnaire, that he had "a great respect and liking for General Stilwell and was very sorry when he was recalled."

734. The profile of Hopkins by Geoffrey T. Hellman was published in *The New Yorker* in the issues of August 7 and 14, 1943.

737. Harriman's letter to Roosevelt describing his session with Churchill was dated July 5.

739. Hopkins' memorandum on the meeting in the President's bedroom concerning China was dated July 15.

744. The Hopkins memorandum on the new regime in Italy was dated September 22.

Churchill's cable about the propaganda to Italy was dated August 2.

745. The Roosevelt-Churchill cable to Stalin from Quebec was dated August 16.

The reports by General Smith and Brigadier Strong on their first encounters with Castellano were cabled from AFHQ in Algiers to the War Department on August 20.

747. The Roosevelt-Churchill cable to Stalin relative to the Azores was dated August 16.

748. The War Department document entitled "Russia's Position" was dated August 10.

750. The article by Walter Trohan likening Hopkins to Rasputin appeared in the *Chicago Sunday Tribune*, August 29.

751. The Hopkins letter to Captain Donald Duncan was dated September 10.

753. The letter to Hopkins from the lady in Colorado was dated September 2 and Hopkins' reply, September 7.

753-754. Hopkins' cable to Brendan Bracken (through Winant) was dated October 15. Bracken's reply was dated October 21.

Hopkins' letter to Beaverbrook about the latter's return to the government was dated September 27.

754-755. Winant's cable to Hopkins about the difficulties of his position was dated October 16, and Hopkins' letter in reply was dated October 25.

CHAPTER XXX

761. The letter in which Hopkins described as "amazing" the story involving him in a "plot" against General Marshall was dated October 2.

762. The Stimson letter to Roosevelt about postponing the date when Marshall should take over command was dated September 16.

Churchill's cable to Hopkins expressing concern about all the newspaper talk was dated September 26.

page

764. Hopkins' cable to Churchill about the newspaper hullabaloo was dated October 2. Roosevelt's cable to Churchill on the same subject was dated October 4.

765. Hopkins' notes on a telephone conversation with Churchill relative to the Dodecanese were dated October 7. On October 12, General Marshall's aide, Colonel Frank McCarthy, wrote to Hopkins about cautioning the Prime Minister relative to statements over the telephone.

765-766. Churchill's cable to Hopkins about the five Senators was dated October 14. Hopkins' replies were dated October 14 and 15. Churchill's statement in the House of Commons was reported in the *New York Times*, October 19.

767. The memorandum from the Joint Chiefs to the President on board the *U.S.S. Iowa* was dated November 17.

768. Hopkins' memorandum on the torpedo episode was undated, but the episode was confirmed in the ship's log.

771. The letter to Hopkins signed by forty-three press correspondents at Cairo was dated November 26.

782. The memorandum on Stalin's views concerning postwar Germany was written presumably by Bohlen and dated November 28.

793. In reference to Hopkins' after-dinner speech about the British Constitution: Hopkins said to me in the fall of 1944 that it was his observation that Churchill was able to exercise considerably more authority than he actually possessed as Prime Minister because of the dominant force of his tremendous personality.

Chapter XXXI

810. Hopkins' cable to Churchill stating that he was not accompanying Roosevelt on the Pacific trip was dated July 20, 1944.

811. Hopkins' letter to Roosevelt about his talks with Beaverbrook was dated August 5.

813. Hopkins' cable to Churchill concerning proposed changes in ANVIL was dated August 7.

The ANVIL forces were under the over-all command of General Jacob L. Devers and included the American Seventh Army, under General Patch, and the French First Army, under General Jean de Lattre de Tassigny. Devers was then serving under Field Marshal Sir Henry Maitland Wilson as Deputy Supreme Allied Commander in the Mediterranean theater. After General Patch's Seventh Army had joined up with the forces under Eisenhower in Northern France, Devers went to that theater to take command of the Sixth U.S. Army Group.

Roosevelt's message naming Bermuda was received at the White House August 8, and Churchill's cable naming Quebec, August 10.

Hopkins' cable to Churchill saying that he was not going to Quebec was dated August 28.

817. Hopkins' memorandum to Roosevelt about trade barriers just before the Quebec Conference was dated September 8.

819. Roosevelt's memorandum to Hull on progress at Quebec was dated September 16.

827. The Hopkins memorandum on the Marshall-Dewey incident was written some time in October, 1945. Reference is made to this in a quotation from Sidney Hyman which appears in Chapter XXXVI.

828. When Roosevelt gave his speech at Shibe Park in Philadelphia on October 27, Postmaster General Frank C. Walker was sitting next to him. Walker has told me that, at one point, he saw the President ruffling back through the pages of his reading copy, while going right on talking. Now and then, Roosevelt would glance down at one of these earlier pages but proceed with the delivery of text that he was not even looking at. After the speech, Walker asked Roosevelt what he had been doing, and the President explained that there was some point he had made early in the speech that had gone over so well he thought he would like to make it again. This was another demonstration of Roosevelt's amazing assurance and command of the situation when delivering a speech.

   While we were on the train en route to Chicago on October 28, 1944, Sam Rosenman and I were discussing with Roosevelt various industrial improvements which would follow the war and help to achieve the goal of sixty million jobs. One of them was "streamlined railroad trains capable of greatly increased speed," but Roosevelt refused to include that in his speech, saying, "Trains go too fast as it is." I have read several times that Roosevelt loved speed, and it would have been in his nature to do so; but it was my observation that he liked to travel at a moderate pace in all vehicles except his own wheelchair.

830. Hopkins' pre-election cable to Beaverbrook was dated November 6.

831. Hopkins' memorandum on his talk with the President and Mrs. Roosevelt after the election was dated November 10.

Chapter XXXII

834. Roosevelt's cable to Harriman containing a message for Stalin was dated October 4, 1944.

835. The quotation of Marquis Childs was from the *Washington Post*, December 4. Hopkins' memorandum on his lunch with Stimson was dated December 12.

836. Beaverbrook's letter to Hopkins on the situation in England was dated October 23.

839. Winant's letter to Hopkins about the vote in the House of Commons was dated December 11.

840. Hopkins' memorandum on the telephone call from "John Martin" and subsequent developments was dated December 12.

843. Hopkins' memorandum on the genesis of the Yalta Conference was written some time in October, 1945. It represented his final attempt to get to work on the writing of his own memoirs of the war years.

CHAPTER XXXIII

853. The quotations of James F. Byrnes on the Yalta Conference were from his book *Speaking Frankly* (Harper & Brothers).

854. Stalin's cable to Roosevelt mentioning (I believe for the first time) the additional votes for the Ukraine and Byelorussia was dated September 7, 1944.

870. In reference to the quotation of Hopkins made by me at the end of this chapter on the subject of relations with the Soviet Union: further expression of his views on this may be found in Chapter XXXVI.

CHAPTER XXXIV

871. Hopkins' memorandum on the meetings of Roosevelt with the three kings was written by him at the same time in October, 1945, when he wrote of the genesis of the Yalta Conference.

CHAPTER XXXV

883-884. Hopkins' memorandum on Harriman's conversation with Stalin after Roosevelt's death was dated April 23, 1945, as was the memorandum on the Drew Pearson column.

902-903, 907. Hopkins' cable to Truman reporting on his third meeting with Stalin was dated May 29. The subsequent cable on the same meeting was dated May 30. His reports on the fourth meeting were also dated May 30.

908. Hopkins' memorandum on his after-dinner conversation with Stalin was dated June 1.

910. Churchill's cable of congratulations to Hopkins in Moscow was dated June 2.

912. Hopkins' final cable to Truman from Moscow was dated June 6.

913. Hopkins' memorandum on his meeting with Eisenhower was dated June 13.

916. The letter to Hopkins from Mrs. Mary P. Blanton was dated June 21.

CHAPTER XXXVI

917. President Truman's letter to Hopkins was dated July 3, 1945.

Admiral Stark's letter to Hopkins was dated July 5, 1945.

Hopkins' letter to Winchell was dated June 18, 1945.

919. The letter stating that Oxford University wished to confer the Honorary Degree of D.C.L. on Hopkins came from Douglas Veale and was dated June 19, 1945.

Hopkins' letter to General Ismay was dated July 28, 1945.

920. Hopkins' letter to Beaverbrook was dated July 6, 1945.

927. Stimson's letter to Hopkins was dated September 14, 1945.

General Eisenhower's letter to Hopkins was dated October 3, 1945.

Following is the full text of the War Department citation of Hopkins for the Distinguished Service Medal which was read aloud by President Truman in the Rose Garden of the White House on September 4, 1945:

Mr. Harry L. Hopkins performed services of outstanding value to the United States of America from December, 1941, to July, 1945. As Special Adviser to the President during critical months of World War II, he assumed tasks of utmost urgency and far-reaching consequences, lightening the burden of the Commander-in-Chief. He gave great assistance to the armed forces in their relationships with the Chief Executive, attacking with piercing understanding the tremendous problems incident to the vast military operations throughout the world. As Chairman of the Munitions Assignment Board, he channeled matériel to all Allied forces with a skill measurable in terms of the steady successes which have been achieved in crushing Germany and closing with Japan in the final struggle. As Chairman of the President's Soviet Protocol Committee, he determined supply quotas to be dispatched to Russia, accomplishing this mission with statesmanshiplike skill. At major conferences of world powers he threw his every effort toward the speedy solution of weighty problems. With deep appreciation of the armed forces' needs and broad understanding of the Commander-in-Chief's over-all policy, with exceptional ability to weld our Allies to the common purpose of victory over aggression, Mr. Hopkins made a selfless, courageous and objective contribution to the war effort.

Index

Set in Linotype Old Style #1
Format by A. W. Rushmore
Manufactured by The Haddon Craftsmen
Published by HARPER & BROTHERS, *New York*